ROGET'S SUPER THESAURUS

THIRD EDITION

Marc McCutcheon

WRITER'S DIGEST BOOKS
CINCINNATI, OHIO
www.writersdigestbooks.com

DEDICATION

To my wonderful parents,
Mary and Errol McCutcheon

ABOUT THE AUTHOR

Marc McCutcheon is a writer and lexicographer who lives in South Portland, Maine, with his wife, Deanna, and two children, Kara and Matthew. His most recent books include *Damn, Why Didn't I Write That; The Girl Named Pluto; Descriptionary; Writer's Guide to Everyday Life in the 1800s;* and *The Compass in Your Nose & Other Astonishing Facts About Humans.*

Visit our Web site at www.writersdigest.com for information on more resources for writers.

To receive a free weekly e-mail newsletter delivering tips and updates about writing and about Writer's Digest products, register directly at our Web site at http://newsletters.fwpublications.com.

07 06 05 04 03   5 4 3 2 1

Library of Congress Cataloging-in-Publication Data

McCutcheon, Marc
   Roget's superthesaurus / by Marc McCutcheon.—3d ed.
      p.   cm.
   ISBN 1-58297-253-2 (alk. paper)   ISBN 1-58297-254-0 (pbk. : alk. paper)
      1. English language—Synonyms and antonyms. 2. English language—Terms and phrases. I. Title.

PE1591.M416   2003
423'.12—dc22
                                                                    2003057647
                                                                    CIP

Edited by Kelly Nickell and Michelle Ruberg
Designed by Angela Wilcox
Cover by Brian Roeth
Production coordinated by Robin Richie

INTRODUCTION

Welcome to the updated and expanded edition of
Roget's Superthesaurus.

You now hold in your hands what we feel is the most
innovative and useful thesaurus on the market. It has
been carefully crafted to provide:

. . . a **comprehensive bank of synonyms** to help you avoid repeti-
tiveness and improve word accuracy. For example, did the
man *walk*, *squelch*, or *slog* through the mud? As every professional writer knows, the right synonym choice is crucial in
adding power, depth, and pizzaz to compositions.

. . . a **reverse dictionary component (WORD FIND)** to show
you the *exact* word when you know what a thing is but not
what the thing is called.

Beyond the need to locate synonyms for, say, CAT (kitty,
feline, tabby, etc.) you'll sometimes need to know words used
to accurately *describe* a cat. For instance, what do you call
that white patch under a cat's neck? (Locket.) The white
patches on the feet? (Mittens, gloves.) The reflective eye
layer that glows in the dark? (Tapetum.) A mating cry? (Caterwaul.) One who loves cats? (Ailurophile.) This exclusive
reverse dictionary component will, once and for all, stop you
from calling something a "doohickey" or a "thingamajig."
Astonishingly, it's the one extremely useful component that
other thesauri have overlooked over the years, and only *Superthesaurus* has it. Just look under a main subject word
(CAT) to find listed underneath in WORD FIND all related
or descriptive terms (caterwaul, mittens, queen, ruff, etc.)

. . . a **built-in vocabulary book.** Throughout the thesaurus, vocabulary words are CAPITALIZED, given a pronunciation
key, and sampled in a sentence. No need to buy a separate
vocabulary builder. *Superthesaurus* highlights hundreds of
sharp words to help you bushwack your way out of the wilderness of Tarzan-like communication and into the vernacular
of the world's greatest wordsmiths. Once again, no other thesaurus has this component. It's a *Superthesaurus* exclusive.

. . . **quotations that double as synonyms**. Many entries throughout *Superthesaurus* have them. For example, you may want to call MOUNTAINS hills or peaks, but if you really want to impress, why not quote Lord Byron and call them the "Palaces of Nature"? You'll find such quotes immediately following the normal list of synonyms.

. . . **antonyms**. For when you need the opposite of a synonym. For example, an antonym of ATTRACTIVE would be *Repulsive*. Antonyms are always listed at the very end of an entry.

Superthesaurus is arranged alphabetically. It has no space-wasting index to make itself look bigger than it really is. To find the word you want, simply turn to its order in the alphabet. Typically, you'll make just *one* reference stop instead of two or three, as is necessary in indexed formats.

Unlike most other thesauri, *Superthesaurus* includes many "minor" words as head entries. That way annoying cross references are greatly reduced. When you encounter a "minor" word, at least two or three synonyms are given in the hope that one of those words will be the one you need. That way you again sidestep the need for a time-consuming cross-reference.

Usages are divided by separate entries for adjective [*a*.], adverb [*adv*.], noun [*n*.], pronoun [*pron*.], verb [*v*.], and preposition [*prep*.] Separate senses within each part of speech are clearly delineated by number, by brief definition or definitive word, or, occasionally, when meanings are closely-related, by a simple semi-colon between word lists. Slang or informal words are delineated by a simple [*] asterisk.

Use *Superthesaurus* to sharpen your writing in letters, reports, articles, novels, and poetry. Use it to beef up your vocabulary, locate a quotation, or help you fill out that challenging crossword puzzle. The longer you use *Superthesaurus* the more you'll appreciate its extra features.

If you need synonyms, any old thesaurus will do. If you want to become a word master, turn to the one source that puts it all together: *Superthesaurus*.

A

aback (taken) *adv*. startled, taken unawares, surprised, confused, *thrown off guard.

abaft *a*. aft, astern, rearward, behind, back.

abandon *n*. unrestraint, carelessness, free-spiritedness, spontaneity, wildness, wantonness, intemperance, impulsiveness, devil-may-care attitude. ANT. *restraint, reserve, restriction, self-consciousness.*

abandon *v*. leave, desert, discard, forsake, quit, dump, *turn one's back on, cast off, reject, relinquish, discontinue, renounce, lay aside, *leave in the lurch, *cut one's losses, *throw in the towel, strand, drop, give up, *wash one's hands of, *deep six, ditch. ANT. *stick with, take up, continue, adopt.*

abandoned *a*. **1.** DESERTED given up, forgotten, left behind, rejected, stranded, forsaken, cast off, cast aside, discarded, destitute, forgotten, scorned, desolate, friendless. **2.** UN-RESTRAINED unreserved, uncontrolled, dissolute, wild, loose, immoral, wicked, shameless, licentious, lewd, wanton. ANT. *1. used, adopted, taken up, befriended. 2. restrained, reserved, moral, seemly.*

abase *v*. humble, humiliate, degrade, *prostrate oneself, deflate, *put down, debase, vitiate, devalue. ANT. *honor, *puff up.*

ABASHED *a*. [uh BASHED] embarrassed, ill at ease. *Mary spoke unabashedly about contraceptives.* SYN. embarrassed, ashamed, humiliated, red-faced, disconcerted, discomfitted, mortified, chagrined, disgraced. ANT. *reassured, relaxed, cool.*

ABATE *v*. [uh BATE] to subside, lessen, reduce. *The pain from a stubbed toe will gradually abate.* SYN. subside, lessen, reduce, weaken, slacken, diminish, decrease, wane, dwindle, decline, let up, taper off. ANT. *grow, expand, intensify, surge.*

abattoir *n*. slaughterhouse, butchery.

abbey *n*. monastery, cloister, friary, convent, nunnery, ministry.

WORD FIND
area restricted to members: cloister
governed by prior or prioress: priory
orders: Benedictine, Dominican, Franciscan, Jesuit, Paulist, Trappist
resident: monk, friar, nun
superior or head: abbot, abbess

abbreviate *v*. shorten, abridge, condense, cut, reduce, contract, curtail, clip, compress, synopsize. ANT. *expand, broaden, enlarge.*

abbreviation *n*. shortening, condensation, abridgement, contraction, reduction, summary, synopsis, brief, abstract, short version, short form.

WORD FIND
ABCs: fundamentals, rudiments, basics, simple elements
AC: alternating current; air conditioning
A.D.: anno Domini; in the year of the Lord
a.k.a: also known as
anon: anonymous
ASAP: as soon as possible
aux.: auxiliary
AWOL: absent without leave
B.A.: Bachelor of Arts
B.C.: before Christ
blvd.: boulevard
B.S.: Bachelor of Science
BTU: British thermal unit
BYOB: bring your own booze
CB: Citizens Band
C: Celsius, centigrade
c: copyright
Cdr.: Commander
CEO: chief executive officer
chm.: chairman
cl.: centiliter
cm.: centimeter
c/o: care of
co.: company
COD: cash on delivery
Col.: Colonel
corp.: corporation
CPA: certified public accountant
CPR: cardiopulmonary resuscitation
cu.: cubic
DA: district attorney
DC: direct current
D.D.: Doctor of Divinity
D.D.S.: Doctor of Dental Science
DOA: dead on arrival
Dr.: Doctor
DST: daylight-saving time
d.t.'s: delirium tremens
EEG: electroencephalogram
e.g.: exempli gratia; for example
EKG: electrocardiogram
ERA: earned run average
ESP: extrasensory perception
Esq.: Esquire
et al: et alia; and others
etc.: etcetera; and so forth

F: Fahrenheit
FM: frequency modulation
f.o.b.: freight on board
FYI: for your information
g: gram
GIGO: garbage in, garbage out
GOP: Grand Old Party
HMS: His/Her Majesty's Ship
Hon.: Honorable
hq.: headquarters
ibid: ibidem; in the same place
i.e.: id est; that is
IQ: intelligence quotient
ISBN: International Standard Book Number
kg: kilogram
km: kilometer
l: liter
lb.: pound
L.P.N.: licensed practical nurse
Ltd.: limited
M.A.: Master of Arts
MC: master of ceremonies
M.D.: Doctor of Medicine
mg: milligram
ml: milliliter
mm: millimeter
MO: modus operandi; method of operation
MP: Military Police
mph: miles per hour
ms.: manuscript
M.S.: Master of Science
M.S.W.: Master of Social Work
N/A: not applicable
oz.: ounce
PA: public address (system)
PC: personal computer
Ph.D.: Doctor of Philosophy
p.m.: post meridiem; afternoon
pp.: pages
pro tem: pro tempore, for the time being
P.S.: postscript
PX: post exchange
RBI: runs batted in
RFD: Rural Free Delivery
RIP: rest in peace
R.N.: registered nurse
rpm: revolutions per minute
RSVP: respondez s'il vous plait, please answer
Rx: pharmaceutical prescription
SASE: self-addressed stamped envelope
SOS: save our ship/souls
TBA: to be announced
TGIF: thank God it's Friday

TKO: technical knockout
UFO: unidentified flying object
VIP: very important person
viz.: videlicet, that is to say, namely
VP: vice president

ABDICATE v. [AB duh KATE] to relinquish, surrender or give up one's power, office or responsibilities. *The king abdicated in 1452.* SYN. relinquish, step down, retire, resign, renounce, yield, surrender, quit, abandon, repudiate, give up, withdraw. ANT. *usurp, assume power, take charge.*

abdomen n. stomach, belly, gut, midsection, paunch, tummy, *breadbasket, *spare tire, *middle-aged spread.

abdominal a. intestinal, visceral, duodenal.

abduct v. kidnap, steal away, make off with, seize, grab, spirit away, snatch, *shanghai.

aberrant a. abnormal, deviant, deviating, unusual, anomolous, irregular, atypical, unconventional, odd, freakish, weird, errant, peculiar, *off the beaten track. ANT. *normal, usual, typical, *par for the course.*

ABERRATION n. [AB uh RAY shun] something atypical, unusual or unexpected; a deviation from the norm. *A blizzard in Texas is an aberration of local weather patterns.* SYN. deviation, abnormality, irregularity, quirk, freak, nonconformity, departure, oddity, anomaly, peculiarity, eccentricity, *oddball. ANT. *norm, average, mean.*

ABET v. [uh BET] to incite, encourage or support, especially in the performance of a wrongdoing. *She was arrested for aiding and abetting a drug smuggler.* SYN. incite, encourage, support, sanction, conspire, goad, spur, egg on, endorse, promote, help, inflame. ANT. *discourage, prevent, prohibit, undermine.*

abettor n. assistant, co-conspirator, inciter, instigator, confederate, accomplice, accessory, *partner in crime.

abeyance n. suspension, cessation, inaction, intermission, pause, latency, remission, dormancy, quiescence. ANT. *continuance, continuation, prolongation.*

ABHOR v. [ab HOR] to hate, detest or be disgusted by. *We abhor bigots.* SYN. hate, detest, loathe, despise, view with horror, scorn, shrink from, be sickened by, feel disgust for. ANT. *love, cherish, embrace.*

abhorrent a. loathsome, detestable, despicable, disgusting, abominable, horrible, sickening, nauseating, hateful, repulsive, offensive, repugnant, heinous. ANT. *nice, attractive, good, commendable, admirable.*

abide v. **1.** TO WAIT FOR await, stand fast, stay, remain, bide. **2.** TOLERATE put up with, withstand, *hang in there, bear, accept, submit to, stomach. **3.** RESIDE dwell, stay, live, lodge.

abide by v. comply, obey, observe, respect, conform to, adhere to.

abiding a. enduring, lasting, everlasting, eternal, unchanging, permanent, indestructible, durable. ANT. *short-lived, impermanent, transient.*

ability n. capability, faculty, facility, power, skill, talent, prowess, flair, competence, aptitude, capacity, knack, know-how, expertise, dexterity, proficiency, finesse, mind for, eye for, native ability, eye-hand coordination. ANT. *inability, incompetence, ineptitude, inadequacy.*

ABJECT a. [AB ject] the absolute worst or most miserable. *They live in abject poverty.* SYN. miserable, wretched, stark, hopeless, pitiful, pathetic, degrading, squalid, humbling, destitute.

abjure v. give up, renounce, forswear, recant, retract, disclaim, take back, renege, disavow, withdraw. ANT. *uphold, swear by, maintain.*

ablate v. erode, wear away, melt, vaporize, evaporate, remove.

ablaze a. blazing, flaming, on fire, aflame, burning, *going up in smoke, consumed by flames, roaring, crackling. ANT. *extinguished.*

able a. capable, habile, skillful, talented, competent, qualified, practiced, expert, deft, adroit, masterful. ANT. *incompetent, ineffectual, weak, unskilled, unable.*

able-bodied a. healthy, fit, strong, robust, capable, sound, in fine fettle, strapping. ANT. *infirm.*

abloom a. flowering, in flower, blooming.

ablution n. washing, cleansing, bath, scrubbing, purification, decontamination, showering.

ably adv. capably, competently, deftly, expertly, adroitly.

abnegate v. give up, forgo, abstain, renounce, abdicate, refrain, forbear. ANT. *indulge, binge, imbibe.*

abnegation n. self-denial, renunciation, abstinence, abdication, relinquishment.

abnormal a. atypical, irregular, odd, unusual, aberrant, deviant, unnatural, unexpected, unconventional, weird, eccentric, queer, offbeat, extraordinary, anomalous, strange, mutant. "Not conforming to standard. In matters of thought and conduct, to be independent is to be abnormal."—Ambrose Bierce. ANT. *normal, usual, standard.* SEE ECCENTRIC, NEUROTIC, PSYCHOTIC

abnormality n. aberration, anomaly, deviation, peculiarity, oddity, freak, deformity, malformation, irregularity, eccentricity, mutant, singularity.

aboard a. on board, on deck, topside, in, boarded, consigned.

abode n. residence, home, living quarters, habitation, habitat, dwelling, domicile, lodging, roof over one's head, *pad, *digs, nest.

WORD FIND

animal: den, lair, hutch, warren, sty, burrow, diggings.

bird: nest, roost, aerie, aviary, cote.

abolish v. end, destroy, eliminate, eradicate, stop, annul, quash, extinguish, defeat, terminate, repeal, stamp out, uproot, do away with, abrogate. ANT. *institute, establish, adopt.*

abolition n. ending, annulment, moratorium, abrogation, repeal, elimination, eradication, termination, dissolution.

abolitionist n. opponent, subversive, activist, advocate, propagator.

A-bomb n. atomic bomb, thermonuclear bomb, *physics package. SEE NUCLEAR BOMB

ABOMINABLE a. [uh BOM un uh bul] loathsome, nasty. *The crossbow was an abominable invention.* SYN. nasty, vile, loathsome, abhorrent, heinous, despicable, atrocious, hateful, execrable, awful, horrible, deplorable, repulsive, disgusting. ANT. *admirable, nice, commendable.*

Abominable Snowman n. yeti, beast, creature. SEE MONSTER

abominate v. loathe, despise, hate.

abomination n. **1.** SOURCE OF LOATHING anathema, bête noir. **2.** LOATHING aversion, abhorrence, hatred, disgust, repugnance, detestation.

aboriginal a. indigenous, native, endemic, first, original, primitive.

aborigine n. native, first inhabitant, indigene, primitive, settler, original, *bushman.

WORD FIND

AUSTRALIAN ABORIGINE

weapon: boomerang, waddy, nulla, woomera, blowpipe.

wilderness: outback

abort v. **1.** MISCARRY expel. **2.** FAIL fall short, miss, go awry. **3.** CANCEL cut short, terminate, *scrub, *axe, *ditch, *can, *deep-six.

abortion n. 1. MISCARRIAGE feticide, termination, aborticide, dilation and evacuation, expulsion, infanticide. "The direct murder of the innocent."—Pope Pius XI. "If men could get pregnant, abortion would be a sacrament."—Florynce R. Kennedy. 2. FAILURE incompletion, defeat, disaster, blunder, monstrosity.

abortive a. unsuccessful, fruitless, futile, useless, vain, unproductive, ineffectual, failing. ANT. successful, fruitful, effective.

abound v. teem, overflow, flood, *be knee-deep in, jam with, pack with, be abundant with, proliferate, swell, swarm.

about prep. 1. ENCIRCLING on every side, all around, enveloping, encompassing, surrounding. 2. APPROXIMATELY almost, nearly, close to, more or less, roughly. 3. REFERRING TO concerning, in reference to, regarding, relative to, as respects, dealing with, touching on.

about adv. 1. IN THE REVERSE DIRECTION backwards, around, opposite direction. 2. HERE AND THERE hither and thither, helter-skelter, far and wide.

about-face n. reversal, turnaround, volte-face, change of heart, *flip-flop, *backpedaling, *a 180, recantation.

above adv. 1. OVERHEAD up, skyward, higher up, over, atop, heavenward. 2. GREATER more, larger, over and above. 3. SUPERIOR higher, greater, outranking, surpassing.

aboveboard a. open, forthright, honest, in plain view, *on the table, straightforward, frank, candid, plain, direct, square, *on the up and up. ANT. underhand, under the table, dishonest, sneaky.

above suspicion a. irreproachable, inculpable, scrupulous, chaste, *having clean hands, innocent, pure.

abracadabra n. hocus-pocus, spell, incantation, charm, chant, invocation, mumbo jumbo, gibberish.

abrade v. scrape, chafe, grate, rub, erode, scuff, grind, scour, wear.

abrasion n. 1. SCRATCH scrape, chafe, excoriation. 2. FRICTION scratching, scraping, wearing away, erosion, chafing.

abrasive a. 1. ANNOYING irritating, cutting, nasty, saber-tongued, acid-tongued, galling, hurtful, biting, sarcastic. 2. SCRAPING scratching, chafing, grating, eroding, grinding, grating, scouring, wearing, rough, coarse, rasping. ANT. 1. conciliatory, soothing. 2. smooth.

abrasive n. abradent, scourer, scraper, polisher, burnisher, buffer.

WORD FIND
course corundum: emery
dark, granular mineral used in grinding, polishing: aluminum oxide, corundum
jewelry and metal polisher made of ferric oxide: rouge
knife-sharpening stone: whetstone
manicuring stick: emery board
metal-polishing limestone: rottenstone
polishing powder made of chert or limestone: tripoli
rough carpenter's paper: sandpaper
rough file used on wood: rasp
volcanic rock used for scouring, smoothing: pumice

abreast a./adv. beside, side by side, aside, *cheek to jowel. ANT. single file.

ABRIDGE v. [uh BRIJ] to shorten, reduce or lessen. *To bring down costs, the new dictionary will be abridged and printed in paperback.* SYN. contract, shorten, condense, decrease, reduce, cut, abbreviate, diminish, *boil down, curtail. ANT. expand, broaden, enlarge.

abridgement n. condensation, reduction, summary, digest, abstract, brief, synopsis, outline. ANT. enlargement, expansion.

abroach a. opened, broached, let out.

abroad a./adv. overseas, out of the country, away, traveling, touring. ANT. at home.

ABROGATE v. [AB roh gayt] to abolish or annul. *The board decided to abrogate the old rule.* SYN. abolish, cancel, repeal, annul, revoke, rescind, terminate, eliminate, quash, do away with, *scrub.

abrupt a. 1. SUDDEN unexpected, surprising, unforeseen, swift, precipitate, unanticipated. 2. CURT gruff, brusque, brisk, discourteous, rude. 3. STEEP sheer, precipitous. ANT. 1. anticipated, expected. 2. courteous, polite, gracious.

abscess n. swelling, fester, boil, pimple, carbuncle, ulcer, pustule.

abscission n. cutting, separation, removal. SEE OPERATION, SURGERY

ABSCOND v. [ab SKOND] to flee secretly and go into hiding. *His plan was to abscond with the smuggled goods as quickly as possible.* SYN. flee, take flight, depart, withdraw, decamp, retreat, escape, go into hiding, *vamoose, *skedaddle, clear out, skip town, *make tracks, *scram, *fly the coop, *cut and run, *split, *beat feet, *duck out, *make oneself scarce, *give the slip.

absence n. **1.** NONATTENDANCE AWOL, nonappearance, truancy. **2.** LACKING dearth, need, want, privation, void, vacuum. ANT. *1. attendance, presence. 2. fulfillment, abundance.*

absent a. **1.** AWAY elsewhere, gone, out, truant, AWOL, on leave, *playing hooky. **2.** PREOCCUPIED absent-minded, *out to lunch, abstracted, daydreaming, *off in space, *out of it. ANT. *1. present, here, attending. 2. attentive, alert, on one's toes.*

absentee n. *no-show, truant, malingerer.

absenteeism n. absence, truancy, desertion, malingering, shirking, *skipping, *calling in sick.

absently adv. inattentively, absent-mindedly.

absent without leave a. AWOL, truant.

absent-minded a. inattentive, scatterbrained, *out to lunch, dreamy, oblivious, daydreaming, lost, forgetful, abstracted, preoccupied, absorbed, remote, *spacey, *head in the clouds, distrait. ANT. *attentive, alert, sharp, focused.*

absolute a. **1.** TOTAL utter, complete, perfect, pure, unadulterated, consummate, outright, entire, undiluted, unmitigated. **2.** DEFINITE positive, unquestionable, certain, actual, exact, undeniable, unequivocal, indisputable. **3.** AUTHORITARIAN dictatorial, tyrannical, despotic, autocratic, totalitarian, iron-handed. ANT. *1. incomplete, imperfect. 2. indefinite, questionable, uncertain. 3. democratic.*

absolutely adv. **1.** TOTALLY utterly, completely, perfectly, entirely. **2.** DEFINITELY positively, unquestionably, certainly, undeniably, *no ifs, ands or buts, *no two ways about it, surely, precisely, conclusively.

absolution n. forgiveness, remission, pardon, clearance, acquittal, amnesty.

ABSOLVE v. [ab ZOLV] to free from blame, guilt or responsibility. *They have been absolved of their sins.* SYN. acquit, exonerate, forgive, pardon, vindicate, remit, free, clear, exculpate, excuse. ANT. *charge, accuse, blame, condemn.*

absorb v. **1.** DRINK UP suck, assimilate, blot, sop up, sponge, osmose, consume. **2.** ENGROSS fascinate, interest, mesmerize, grip, rivet, enthrall, spellbind, comprehend, assimilate, understand. ANT. *1. spit out, spew, discharge, repel. 2. bore, confuse, tire.*

absorbed a. **1.** ASSIMILATED blotted, consumed, taken in, *sucked up. **2.** ENGROSSED interested, fascinated, riveted, mesmerized, captivated, spellbound, immersed, involved, focused, rapt. ANT. *bored, restless, unfocused.*

absorbent a. bibulous, pervious, permeable, porous, spongelike, retentive, *thirsty.

absorbing a. engrossing, arresting, enthralling, riveting, spellbinding, fascinating, interesting, mesmerizing. ANT. *tedious, dull.*

absorption n. **1.** ASSIMILATION consumption, osmosis, retention, digestion, soaking up. **2.** ENGROSSMENT fascination, interest, captivation, riveting, enthrallment, spellbinding.

ABSTAIN v. [ub STANE] to voluntarily hold back, to refrain from or go without. *Everyone is trying to abstain from smoking.* SYN. refrain, desist, eschew, go without, forebear, *swear off, shun, spurn, *stay on the wagon, deny oneself. ANT. *indulge, imbibe.*

abstainer n. teetotaler, *health nut, ascetic. "A weak person who yields to the temptation of denying himself a pleasure."—Ambrose Bierce.

ABSTEMIOUS a. [ab STEEM ee us] eating and drinking in moderation, abstaining from drink, practicing restraint. *Sylvester Graham of graham cracker fame was noted for his clean-living, abstemious lifestyle.* SYN. temperate, moderate, self-restraining, teetotaling, sober, abstinent, ascetic, self-denying.

abstention n. abstaining, abstinence, refraining.

ABSTINENCE n. [AB stuh nunce] abstaining, voluntary self-denial, the swearing off of unhealthy food and drink. *Longevity and abstinence often go hand in hand.* SYN. abstaining, self-restraint, teetotalism, sobriety, chastity, temperance, forbearing, self-denial, self-abnegation, asceticism, celibacy, moderation. "The beginning of saintliness."—Moses Luzzato. ANT. *indulgence, extravagance, *pigging out.*

ABSTRACT a. [AB STRACT] not easily identified or defined, not based on the concrete, abstruse, theoretical, nonrepresentational. *His notions of the universe were wildly abstract and difficult to envision.* SYN. nonrepresentational, theoretical, conceptual, abstruse, indefinite, incomprehensible, general, nonspecific, amorphous, symbolic, recondite. ANT. *specific, clear, concrete.*

abstract n. **1.** CONDENSATION brief, abridgement, synopsis, summary. **2.** ART nonrepresentational art form, amorphous art form, geometrical art form. "A product of the untalented, sold by the unprincipled to the utterly bewildered."—Al Capp. SEE ART

abstract v. **1.** TAKE AWAY remove, extract, detach, separate. **2.** SUMMARIZE synopsize, abbreviate, condense, abridge.

abstracted *a.* lost in thought, lost in reverie, preoccupied, daydreaming, brooding, absent-minded, withdrawn, in a trance, *off in space, remote, inattentive, *out to lunch. ANT. *alert, attentive, sharp.*

abstraction *n.* absent-mindedness, preoccupation, reverie, daydreaming, withdrawal, brooding, reflecting, mulling.

ABSTRUSE *a.* [ab STROOS] difficult to understand. *Einstein's abstruse theories confound all but the brightest scholars.* SYN. recondite, deep, incomprehensible, complex, inscrutable, undecipherable, profound, unfathomable, *clear as mud, arcane, esoteric, cerebral. ANT. *clear, simple, obvious, *child's play.*

absurd *a.* ridiculous, ludicrous, laughable, silly, preposterous, foolish, outrageous, asinine, idiotic, loony, stupid, crazy, nonsense. ANT. *serious, weighty.*

absurdity *n.* joke, foolishness, nonsense, idiocy, *bullshit, *bunk, *fiddle faddle, *hogwash, piffle, *rubbish, *tripe, drivel, twiddle-twaddle.

abundance *n.* lots, plenty, loads, piles, slew, hoard, *scads, *tons, *oodles, plethora, surplus, bounty, *miser's hoard, profusion, enough, bountiful, overflowing, wealth. ANT. *scarcity, dearth, paucity.*

abundant *a.* plentiful, bountiful, copious, profuse, abounding, more than enough, immeasurable, inexhaustible, teeming, overflowing. ANT. *scarce, scant, rare, sparse.*

abuse *n.* **1.** MISTREATMENT maltreatment, ill-treatment, injury, harm, assault, cruelty, torment, brutality, molestation, exploitation, terrorizing, *stepping on, torturing, beating, thrashing, battery. **2.** INSULTING OR HARSH LANGUAGE belittlement, degradation, denigration, deprecation, tongue-lashing, defamation, maligning, invective, criticism, upbraiding, dressing-down, ridicule, vilification, put-downs, verbal abuse. ANT. *1. care, kindness. 2. sweet talk, compliments, flattery.*

abuse *v.* **1.** MISTREAT maltreat, ill-treat, injure, exploit, harm, assault, disrespect, terrorize, molest, brutalize, manhandle, *step on, strong-arm, torture, beat, thrash, rape. **2.** VERBALLY ABUSE OR USE HARSH LANGUAGE belittle, degrade, denigrate, deprecate, tongue-lash, defame, malign, criticize, upbraid, dress down, ridicule, vilify, put down, insult, *dis, *dig, *dump on, *bad-mouth, *trash. ANT. *1. coddle, respect, nurture, pamper, dote on. 2. sweet talk, flatter, compliment.*

abusive *a.* **1.** HARMFUL injurious, cruel, brutal, hurtful, exploitive, dominating, ruthless, rough, disrespectful. **2.** VERBALLY ABUSIVE offensive, insulting, vile, nasty, denigrating, gross, obscene, disparaging, critical, ridiculing, maligning, upbraiding, cutting. ANT. *1. helpful, kind, nurturing. 2. sweet, *honey-tongued, flattering.*

abut *v.* border on, lean on, adjoin, end on, conjoin, juxtapose.

abutment *n.* junction, juxtaposition, connection, conjunction.

abutter *n.* neighbor.

abuzz *a.* buzzing, chattering, babbling, busy, jumping, hopping, active, animated, spirited, astir, kinetic, restless, bustling. ANT. *silent, lifeless.*

abysmal *a.* **1.** UNFATHOMABLE immeasurable, deep, bottomless, vast, abyssal, immense. **2.** DESPAIRINGLY BAD wretched, awful, pitiful, the lowest, depressing, miserable. ANT. *1. finite, measurable. 2. impressive, commendable, favorable.*

abyss *n.* depth, chasm, void, fissure, the deep, gulf, hole, bottomless pit.

abyssal *a.* unfathomable, abysmal, deep, immeasurable, bottomless. ANT. *shallow.*

AC *n.* **1.** AIR CONDITIONING. **2.** ALTERNATING CURRENT.

academia *n.* academe, scholarly world, school, college, groves of academe, ivy halls, academic community. SEE COLLEGE, EDUCATION, UNIVERSITY

academic *a.* **1.** SCHOLARLY scholastic, collegiate, university, professorial, studious, bookish, erudite, learned, cultured. **2.** THEORETICAL hypothetical, conjectural, speculative, suppositional, immaterial, moot. ANT. *1. real world, rough-and-tumble, practical. 2. accessible, understandable, meaningful.* SEE COLLEGE, SCHOOL, TEACHER

academic *n.* scholar, student, teacher, professor, pupil, educator, tutor, doctor.

academics *n.* studies, courses, school work.

academy *n.* **1.** SCHOOL private school, institute, institution, secondary school, prep school, finishing school. **2.** ASSOCIATION fellowship, institution, atheneum, club.

Academy Award *n.* Oscar.

a capella *a./adv.* choral, voices only, without instruments.

ACCEDE *v.* [ak SEED] to agree or consent to. *Peer pressure forced the last holdout to accede.* SYN. **1.** CONSENT agree, concede, submit to, give in, give assent, yield, acquiesce, *cave in. **2.** ATTAIN assume, enter upon, inherit.

accelerant n. catalyst.

accelerate v. speed up, race, hasten, step up, *put the pedal to the metal, *floor it, *gun it, *squeal out, *burn rubber, *red line, *peel out. ANT. *decelerate, slow down, wind down, brake, stop.*

acceleration n. speeding up, increasing velocity, *stepping on it, quickening. ANT. *decelerating, slowing, braking.*

accelerator n. throttle, gas pedal.

accent n. **1.** EMPHASIS stress, significance. **2.** EMPHASIS OF PRONUNCIATION stress, accentuation, delivery, attack, inflection, articulation, enunciation, rhythm, tone. **3.** REGIONAL SPEAKING MANNER brogue, burr, drawl, twang, dialect. **4.** EMBELLISHMENT ornament, dressing, touch.

accent v. accentuate, highlight, underscore, underline, spotlight, emphasize, point up, punctuate. ANT. *downplay, ignore, hide.*

accentuate v. SEE ACCENT

accept v. **1.** TAKE receive, get, welcome, acquire, obtain. **2.** SUBMIT TO allow, tolerate, take in stride, endure, capitulate, stand for. **3.** BELIEVE IN adopt, acknowledge, agree, concur, confirm, *swallow, *buy, recognize, affirm, *take as gospel. ANT. *1. reject, give, refuse. 2. reject, refuse, oppose. 3. disbelieve, reject.*

acceptable a. adequate, good enough, worthy, satisfactory, suitable, respectable, fair, passable, tolerable, okay, *up to snuff, *passes muster. ANT. *unacceptable, subpar, objectionable, poor.*

acceptance n. acknowledgement, approval, adoption, assent, recognition, agreement, *the okay, *the green light, *the go-ahead. ANT. *rejection, refusal, disagreement.*

accepted a. **1.** RECEIVED taken, acquired, welcomed. **2.** AGREED UPON acknowledged, approved, recognized, endorsed, believed in, affirmed, sanctioned, upheld, authorized, accredited, conventional, normal, standard. ANT. *2. rejected, refused, unconventional.*

access n. entry, entree, admission, passage, pathway, approach, ingress, admittance, doorway. SEE ENTRANCE

accessible a. **1.** OBTAINABLE reachable, attainable, available, at hand, handy, approachable. **2.** FRIENDLY AND OPEN approachable, available, obliging, familiar, sociable, genial, gracious, *having an open door policy. **3.** EASY TO UNDERSTAND comprehensible, simple, lucid, uncomplicated, unsophisticated.

ANT. *1. unobtainable, out of reach, unavailable. 2. closed, unfriendly, unapproachable. 3. abstruse, cerebral, complex, difficult.*

accession n. succession, assumption, inauguration, attaining, assuming office, ascending the throne, coming to power.

accessorize v. supplement, add on, ornament, adorn, attach, equip, trim, accent.

accessory n. **1.** EXTRA add-on, attachment, adornment, peripheral, accent, supplement, trimming, equipment, gear, appendage, trapping. **2.** ACCOMPLICE confederate, confidante, cohort, associate, *partner in crime, co-conspirator, helper, assistant.

accident n. **1.** CHANCE fluke, serendipity, luck, fortuity, circumstance, happenstance, twist of fate. "An inevitable occurrence due to the action of immutable natural laws."—Ambrose Bierce. **2.** MISHAP mistake, blunder, misfortune, calamity, casualty, misadventure, disaster, catastrophe, wreck, *crack-up, *pile-up, *fender-bender, collision, *rear-ender, *T-bone, *sideswiping, crash, rollover. "A condition in which presence of mind is good, but absence of body better."—Foolish Dictionary.

accidental a. chance, fortuitous, serendipitous, random, freak, unforeseen, unintentional, haphazard, unwitting, *flukey, inadvertent, unpremeditated. ANT. *planned, intended, premeditated.*

accidentally a. fortuitously, randomly, unwittingly, haphazardly, by chance, unintentionally, by some fluke. ANT. *intentionally, planned, by design.*

accident-prone a. clumsy, *klutzy, inept, *two left feet, bungling, bumbling, attention-seeking, neurotic, having a death wish, *all thumbs. ANT. *coordinated, nimble.*

acclaim n. applause, acclamation, ovation, cheers, praise, bravos, kudos, approval, adulation, honor, plaudits. ANT. *boos, hisses, jeers, heckles, catcalls, *razzing, *Bronx cheers.*

acclaim v. applaud, cheer, approve, *give thumbs up to, extol, praise, *sing the praises of, laud, hail, shout, bravo. ANT. *razz, *give a Bronx cheer, boo, hiss, reject, disapprove.*

acclaimed a. applauded, cheered, praised, approved, extolled, hailed, lauded. ANT. *rejected, jeered, booed, *razzed.*

acclamation n. applause, ovation, cheers, whistles, plaudits, bravos. SEE ACCLAIM

ACCLIMATE v. [ACK luh mate] to adapt, adjust or accustom (oneself) to a different environment or situation. *Lowlanders have a difficult time acclimating themselves to the thinner air supply found at high altitudes.* SYN. accustom, adapt, adjust, habituate, get used to, inure, naturalize, familiarize, fit in, condition, harden.

acclimatize *v.* SEE ACCLIMATE

ACCOLADE *n.* [AK uh LADE] an award or honor. *The dance troupe is winning accolades from critics nationwide.* SYN. honor, recognition, tribute, praise, acclaim, applause, exaltation, kudos, credit, award, prize.

accommodate *v.* **1.** OBLIGE aid, assist, help, perform a kindness, serve, furnish, do a favor, grant, indulge, lend a hand. **2.** HOUSE lodge, quarter, put up, board, furnish a room, shelter, entertain, take in. **3.** ADAPT accustom, adjust, bend, conform, acclimate, reconcile, modify, fit, tailor.

accommodating *a.* obliging, helpful, pleasing, gracious, considerate, hospitable, benevolent, charitable, cooperative, sympathetic. ANT. *disobliging, unsympathetic, cold-hearted, ungracious.*

accommodation *n.* **1.** ASSISTANCE aid, favor, service, grant, kindness, nicety, courtesy, help. **2.** LODGING room, quarters, housing, *digs, bed and breakfast, boarding, furnishing, suite, berth, bed, shelter, flat, arrangements. **3.** ADAPTATION adjustment, habituation, acclimatization, modification, change, fitting, conformation, reconciliation. ANT. *1. rejection, turning away, hindrance. 3. maladjustment, rigidity.*

accompanied *a.* escorted, paired, tended, chaperoned, shown around, guarded, protected.

accompaniment *n.* backup, harmony, background, instrument, rhythm player, *sidekick.

accompany *v.* go with, escort, pair, tend, chaperone, show around, protect, guide, usher, be one's sidekick, *hang out with, consort, keep company, *shadow, *tag along, join.

ACCOMPLICE *n.* [uh COM pliss] one who accompanies or assists another in a wrongful act; a partner in crime. *Machine Gun Willy and two accomplices robbed the bank.* SYN. associate, colleague, ally, cohort, collaborator, confederate, accessory, abettor, co-conspirator, henchman, partner in crime, right-hand man, consort, *gun moll. "One associated with another in crime, having guilty knowledge and complicity, as an attorney who defends a criminal, knowing him guilty."— Ambrose Bierce. SEE CRIME, CRIMINAL

accomplish *v.* achieve, effect, bring to fruition, fulfill, complete, consummate, attain, bring about, perform, *pull it off, effectuate, produce, execute, score, realize, engineer, make happen, *cut the mustard, *nail it. ANT. *fail, fall short, *blow, *choke.

accomplished *a.* **1.** ACHIEVED completed, fulfilled, consummated, attained, brought about, finished, performed, executed, realized, *pulled off, *nailed, brought to fruition, produced. **2.** SKILLED proficient, talented, expert, practiced, adept, perfected, masterly, *crack, *crackerjack, deft, experienced, learned, polished. ANT. *1. uncompleted, unfulfilled, failed, *blown, fallen short. 2. unskilled, unseasoned, amateur, *green, *rough around the edges.*

accomplishment *n.* achievement, fulfillment, realization, deed, fait accompli, execution, attainment, completion, consummation, feat, coup, effort, performance, success. ANT. *failure, defeat, *flop, *washout, debacle.*

ACCORD *n.* [uh CORD] harmony, mutual understanding. *They ended their hostilities and reached accord.* SYN. harmony, agreement, concurrence, concert, unison, unity, accordance, rapport, mutual understanding, concordance, *a meeting of the minds, consensus. ANT. *discord, friction, disagreement, dissidence.*

accord *v.* **1.** CONCEDE grant, bestow, accede, allow, give, acquiesce. **2.** HARMONIZE concur, correspond, match up, *see eye to eye, *sing from the same hymnal, jibe.

accordant *a.* in agreement, agreeing, congruous, harmonious, matching. ANT. *opposing, divergent.*

accordingly *adv.* **1.** FITTINGLY properly, correspondingly. **2.** THEREFORE hence, consequently, thus, so, subsequently, whereupon, as a result.

according to *prep.* **1.** IN ACCORDANCE WITH in line with. **2.** PER à la, as stated by, on the authority of, as reported by.

ACCORDING TO HOYLE *Sl.* according to the ultimate authority, according to the guy who wrote the rule book, an idiom derived from card game expert Edmond Hoyle. *We are proceeding correctly, according to Hoyle.* SYN. according to rule, *by the book, *by the numbers, correct, indisputable, according to the highest authority, gospel.

accordion *n.* concertina, *squeezebox, melodeon, *groanbox, *windbox, *stomach Steinway.

ACCOST v. [uh COST] approach or greet aggressively. *Sally was accosted by an ambitious salesman.* SYN. assail, greet, approach, *hit on, confront, assault, annoy, hail, intrude, address, call, buttonhole, solicit.

account n. **1.** CHRONICLE explanation, report, story, description, narrative, statement, detailing, *blow-by-blow, *play-by-play, rundown, version. **2.** FINANCIAL RECORD balance, ledger, books, credits and debits, computation, reckoning, accrual, profit and loss statement, register, invoice, tab, calculation. SEE BANK **3.** WORTH importance, value, weight, consequence, significance, merit.

account v. **1.** RECKON add up, calculate, balance the books. **2.** ANSWER FOR explain, give a reason for, justify, rationalize. **3.** CONSIDER hold, regard, deem, estimate, judge, believe, rate, view.

account of, on prep. because of, since, for the sake of, by virtue of.

account, on no prep. under no circumstances, for no reason, never.

account, take into prep. consider, allow for, think about.

accountability n. responsibility. SEE ACCOUNTABLE

accountable a. responsible, liable, beholden, answerable, obligated, duty-bound, culpable, held to blame. ANT. *excused, exempt, *let off the hook.*

accountant n. bookkeeper, auditor, CPA, certified public accountant, controller, comptroller, bank examiner, clerk, *number cruncher, *bean counter, *pencil pusher, *desk jockey, actuary. SEE ACCOUNTING, BANK, MONEY

accounting n. **1.** RECORDING AND INTERPRETING FINANCIAL ACCOUNTS bookkeeping, balancing the books, reckoning, crediting and debiting, auditing, computing, calculating, recording. **2.** FINANCIAL STATEMENT account, balance sheet, ledger, spreadsheet, accrual, budget, invoice.

WORD FIND

account book: ledger, daybook, journal

annual accounting period: calendar year, fiscal year

cheating on records to hide profits: cooking the books

collection of assets after business closes: liquidation

computer program organizing financial data into rows and columns: spreadsheet

decreasing value of asset over time: depreciation

discrepancy corrections: reconciling

ease of converting assets to cash: liquidity

employee pay: payroll

enter a transaction: log

entry of earnings not yet received or of expenses not yet paid: accrual

examination of accounts: audit

examiner of accounts: auditor

expenses greater than income: negative cash flow

expenses less than income: positive cash flow

head accountant of business or government: controller, comptroller

increasing value of asset over time: appreciation

items and property of value: assets

losing money: in the red

making money or realizing net profit: in the black

money owed to creditors: accounts payable, liabilities, outstanding accounts

money to be received: accounts receivable

month by month budget: rolling budget

net profit or loss: bottom line

payout: disbursement

profit and loss statement: P & L

project income and expenses for the year: annualize

pure profit: net

record-keeping method having equal credit for each debit: double-entry accounting

records: books

revenues before costs are deducted: gross

state-licensed accountant: CPA, certified public accountant

total assets minus liabilities: net worth

uncollectable debt: write-off

value of assets beyond what is owed on them: equity

withdrawal of funds by business owner: draw

accoutre v. dress, equip, outfit, gear up.

accoutrement n. trappings, outfit, clothes, dress, equipment, gear, attire, habiliment.

accredit v. **1.** AUTHORIZE certify, sanction, recognize, license, qualify, approve, legitimize, endorse, validate, warrant, vouch for. **2.** ATTRIBUTE credit, ascribe, assign, charge.

accretion n. growth, accumulation, augmentation, addition, enlargement, expansion, increase. ANT. *shrinkage, dispersement, scattering.*

accrual n. growth, accumulation, amassing, increase.

accrue v. accumulate, add up, grow, amass, increase, collect, expand, pile up, compound.

acculturation n. naturalization, assimilation, nationalization, culture shock.

accumulate v. heap, collect, pile up, gather, accrete, expand, aggregate, stack up, grow, accrue, swell, amass, assemble. ANT. *throw off, shed, shuck, disperse, scatter.*

accumulation n. collection, heap, pile, gathering, accretion, assembly, aggregation, agglomeration, conglomeration, mass, growth, accrual, swelling, hoard, stockpile. ANT. *dispersal, disbursement, shedding, scattering.*

accuracy n. precision, correctness, exactness, fidelity, factualness, veracity, truth, meticulousness, perfection. ANT. *inaccuracy, imprecision, slackness.*

accurate a. correct, precise, right, error-free, unerring, perfect, exact, actual, factual, *on the button, *on target, *on the money, *on the mark, flawless, veracious, faultless, meticulous, faithful. ANT. *incorrect, wrong, flawed, imperfect, inaccurate.*

accurately adv. correctly, precisely, rightly, perfectly, flawlessly, exactly, actually, factually, meticulously. ANT. *inaccurately, incorrectly, wrongly.*

accursed a. cursed, condemned, damned, ill-fated, doomed, bedeviled, hexed, ruined, undone, stricken, *done for. ANT. *blessed.*

accusation n. charge, *rap, blame, implication, indictment, insinuation, allegation, complaint, citation, smear, inculpation, recrimination.

accusatory a. accusing, finger-pointing, blaming. ANT. *recriminatory.*

accuse v. charge, blame, indict, implicate, cite, finger-point, prosecute, inculpate, impeach, recriminate, impute, *hang on, *finger for, *pin on.

accused n. defendant, suspect, alleged perpetrator. SEE COURT, CRIME, LAW

accuser n. incriminator, prosecutor, *fink, *stool pigeon, *tattletale, *rat, informer, plaintiff, adversary.

accustom v. familiarize, habituate, acquaint, adapt, get used to.

accustomed a. **1.** USUAL customary, characteristic, conventional, established, familiar, fixed, set, everyday, general, routine, traditional. **2.** USED TO habituated, familiarized, acclimated, acquainted with, naturalized, adapted, in the habit of, toughened, seasoned. ANT. *1. unusual, uncharacteristic, unconventional. 2. unaccustomed to, unfamiliar with, unseasoned, green.*

ace n. expert, champion, master, star, hero, *crack hand, *crackerjack, *hotshot, *pistol, *whiz, *whiz kid. ANT. *loser, benchwarmer, second-stringer.*

ace v. hit it, nail it, score, execute, succeed, hit the bullseye, defeat, *smoke the competition. ANT. *blow it, *choke, lose.*

acedia n. apathy, ennui, indifference, despair.

ace in the hole n. hold out, card up one's sleeve, secret weapon, reserve.

acephalous a. **1.** HEADLESS. **2.** LEADERLESS.

acerbate v. **1.** EMBITTER sour, poison, gall. **2.** EXASPERATE aggravate, ruffle, annoy, disturb, *rattle one's cage, perturb, provoke.

ACERBIC a. [uh SUR bick] anything sour, bitter or sharp. *She was an insulting, acerbic-tongued witch.* SYN. sour, bitter, harsh, sharp, astringent, acidic, acrid, tart, caustic. ANT. *sweet, honeyed, nectarous, saccharine.*

acerbity a. **1.** SOURNESS bitterness, astringency, sharpness, harshness, tartness, acidity, acridity, pungency. **2.** NASTINESS irritability, annoyance, sharpness, sourness, bitterness, brusqueness, rancor, sarcasm, venom, acrimony, ill humor, grouchiness. ANT. *1. sweetness, nectarous. 2. sweetness, friendliness, good humor.*

aces a. great, excellent, wonderful, top-notch, fabulous. ANT. *horrible, inferior, dreadful.*

ache n. pain, twinge, pang, soreness, stitch, spasm, throb, discomfort, hurt, pounding, stabbing, smarting, burning, pinching.

ache v. **1.** HURT throb, pound, pang, twinge, pain, spasm, stab, sear, smart, suffer, agonize. **2.** SYMPATHIZE pity. **3.** YEARN FOR long for, hunger, crave, need, pine for.

achievable a. doable, attainable, reachable, obtainable, feasible. ANT. *impossible, unthinkable.*

achieve v. accomplish, realize, do, attain, complete, bring about, effect, produce, carry off, succeed, consummate, actualize, follow through, engineer, *pull off, *swing, score, win one. ANT. *fail, fall short, *blow it, *choke, quit.*

achievement n. accomplishment, attainment, production, success, score, exploit, feat, fulfillment, realization, acquirement, consummation, *master stroke, coup, masterpiece, creation, triumph, conquest, *feather in one's cap.

ACHILLES' HEEL n. [uh KILL eez HEEL] a metaphor used to illustrate a vulnerability or a mortal weakness, from the myth of Achilles, whose body was immunized from harm everywhere but on his heel. *Nobody is all-powerful; even dictators have at least one Achilles' heel.* SYN. weakness, vulnerability, *soft underbelly, susceptibility, frailty, fragility, chink in the armor, deficiency, failing, handicap. ANT. *omnipotence, strength, immortality.*

acid n. corrosive, astringent, chemical. ANT. *alkali.*

WORD FIND

ant irritant: formic acid

aspirin: acetylsalicylic acid

corrosive used in explosives: sulfuric acid, oil of vitriol

mild antiseptic: boric acid

milk-derived: lactic acid

odoriferous corrosive poison used in explosives, antiseptics: phenol

protein-forming: amino acids

stomach acid: hydrochloric acid

urine-derived: uric acid

vinegar ingredient: acetic acid

vitamin C: ascorbic acid

white poison in insecticides: arsenic acid

acid n. Sl. LSD, *blotter, *blue cheer, *blue heaven, *California sunshine, *D, *dot, *electric Kool Aid, *flash, *green dragon, *orange sunshine, *purple haze, *travel agent, *wedding bells, *yellows. SEE DRUG, NARCOTIC

acid a. 1. OF TASTE sour, bitter, tart, astringent, harsh, sharp, biting, acerbic, vinegary. 2. ILL-TEMPERED OR SHARP-TONGUED sarcastic, caustic, *saber-tongued, venomous, nasty, cutting, vitriolic, biting, stinging, snide, sardonic, acerbic, scathing. ANT. *1. sweet, sugary, honey. 2. good-humored, sweet, kind, warm, flattering.*

acidhead n. Sl. *junkie. SEE ADDICT

acidity n. sourness, bitterness, acerbity, sharpness, harshness, astringency, causticity.

ACID TEST n. [ASS id test] a test of value, quality or genuineness, a metaphor evolved from the jeweler's nitric acid test to determine the authenticity of gold. *The voluntary adoption of expensive, double-hulled tankers has long served as an acid test of the oil industry's sincerity concerning environmentalism.* SYN. trial, proving ground, analysis, proof, verification, substantion.

acidulous a. sour, tart, harsh, citric. SEE ACID

acknowledge v. 1. ADMIT recognize, own up to, accept, grant, concede, acquiesce, declare, profess. 2. THANK recompense, reward, repay, requite. 3. RESPOND TO notice, address,

nod at, recognize, greet, salute, hail. ANT. *1. deny, refuse, refute. 3. ignore, overlook, pass over, snub.*

acknowledgement n. 1. ADMISSION avowal, recognition, acceptance, granting, concession, acquiescence, declaration, profession, confession. 2. THANK YOU recompense, reward, repayment, remittance, expression of gratitude. 3. RESPONSE notice, address, nod, recognition, greeting, salute, hailing, bow, curtsy, reply. ANT. *1. denial, refusal, refutation. 3. ignoring, oversight, snub.*

ACME n. [ACK me] the very highest; the peak. *The award was the acme of his career.* SYN. summit, pinnacle, peak, high point, zenith, crown, apex, top, apogee, greatest, best, supremacy. ANT. *lowest, valley, pit, bottom.*

acne n. pimples, *zits, blackheads, pustules, facial eruption, skin inflammation, blemishes, pockmarks, *pizza-face, rosacea.

acolyte n. altar boy, assistant, attendant, helper, aid.

acorn n. oak nut, fruit.

acoustic a. sound, sound properties, hearing, auditory, phonic, audio, aural.

acoustics n. sound qualities, echoes, noise properties, sound transmission, sound frequencies.

WORD FIND

absorbs all sound, produces no echoes: anechoic

boom produced by object moving faster than sound: sonic boom

harmonious sound: consonance

hearing tester: audiometer

high frequency sound above human hearing: ultrasound

inharmonious sound: dissonance

less than speed of sound: subsonic

lowest sound audible to ear: threshold frequency

noise made from blend of all audible frequencies: white noise

prolonged sound caused by vibration or reflection: resonance

quality of sound: timbre

rebounding sound wave: echo

speed of sound: sonic, 741 mph

unit of noise intensity level: decibel

acquaint v. 1. MAKE AWARE inform, advise, enlighten, familiarize, let know, notify, apprise, divulge, clue in. 2. MEET introduce, make conversant, familiarize.

acquaintance n. **1.** ACQUIRED KNOWLEDGE familiarity, understanding, experience, awareness, conversance, enlightenment, cognizance. **2.** ASSOCIATE colleague, neighbor, peer, co-worker. "A person whom we know well enough to borrow from, but not well enough to lend to."—Ambrose Bierce. ANT. *1. ignorance, inexperience. 2. complete stranger.*

acquainted a. **1.** AWARE informed, advised, enlightened, familiarized, apprised of, familiar with, aware of, *clued in, versed in. ANT. *unaware, *clueless.*

ACQUIESCE v. [AK we ESS] to yield, give in or assent without enthusiasm. *The dictator acquiesced only after the Bush administration rattled its saber.* SYN. consent, defer, yield, assent, comply, accede, accept, *buckle under, *cave in, give in, agree, capitulate, concur, abide by, come around, submit, *fall in line. ANT. *resist, fight, challenge, rebuff, make a stand.*

acquiescence n. yielding, compliance, acceptance, consenting, *buckling under, capitulation, submission, concurring, *caving in, deferring, assenting, subservience, servility. ANT. *resistance, making a stand, rebellion.*

acquire v. get, obtain, gain, procure, buy, purchase, earn, catch, *get one's hands on, *get hold of, *land, net, *snag, *scare up, secure. ANT. *give away, sell, lose, relinquish.*

acquired immune deficiency syndrome n. AIDS, sexually transmitted disease (STD), HIV. SEE DISEASE, MEDICINE

acquirement n. skill, ability, education, capability, knowledge, accomplishment.

acquisition n. attainment, procurement, acquirement, securing, purchase, gain, takeover, gift, proceed, grant, obtainment.

acquisitive a. greedy, materialistic, grasping, avaricious, grabby, hoarding, rapacious, *gold-digging. ANT. *generous, unselfish.*

ACQUIT v. [uh KWIT] to release, free or clear one from a responsibility or charge. *Lizzie Borden was acquitted of murder charges against her father and stepmother, but a cloud of suspicion continues to hang over her name.* SYN. **1.** RELEASE, clear, free, excuse, exonerate, absolve, pardon, forgive, relieve, exempt, let off, exculpate. **2.** BEHAVE conduct, act, comport, bear. ANT. *1. convict, condemn, damn.*

acquittal n. discharge, release, clearance, exoneration, pardon, reprieve, exculpation, absolution, liberation.

acre n. 160 square rods, 43,560 square feet, 405 hectare, acreage, parcel, plot, real estate.

acreage n. parcel, plot, holding, land, real estate, property, expanse.

ACRID a. [AK rid] sharp or bitter in taste or smell, or in one's speech. *We opened the jar and immediately smelled something acrid.* SYN. **1.** TASTE OR SMELL bitter, sharp, irritating, harsh, pungent, sour, acid, acerbic, stinging, caustic, stinking, foul-smelling, biting. **2.** SPEECH sarcastic, sardonic, caustic, biting, acid, saber-tongued, venomous, cutting, snide. ANT. *1. sweet, mild. 2. sweet, flattering, good-humored.*

ACRIMONIOUS a. [AK ri MO nee us] bitter, nasty, spiteful. *The divorcing couple survived an acrimonious session in court.* SYN. bitter, biting, caustic, nasty, spiteful, sarcastic, sardonic, sharp, vitriolic, venomous, acerbic, snarling, snide. ANT. *sweet, kind, civil.*

acrimony n. bitterness, nastiness, causticity, vitriol, spite, sarcasm, asperity, harshness. ANT. *sweetness, civility, kindness.*

acrobat n. gymnast, tumbler, aerialist, tightrope walker, stuntman, stuntwoman, circus performer, trapeze artist, contortionist.

acrobatics n. gymnastics, tumbling, somersaulting, flipping, balancing.

acronym n. abbreviation.

acrophobia n. fear of heights. SEE PHOBIA

acropolis n. high city, elevated city, citadel.
WORD FIND
famous Greek temple of: Parthenon

across a. crosswise, crossways, transversely, crisscross, astride.

across prep. **1.** OVER opposite to, to the other side, beyond, in front of. **2.** INTO CONTACT WITH upon, into.

across-the-board a. **1.** WIN, PLACE AND SHOW **2.** ALL everything, comprehensive, sweeping, all-inclusive, blanket, total, complete. ANT. *limited, partial.*

acrostic n. word puzzle, wordplay, word game.

act n. **1.** DEED action, execution, performance, task, turn, endeavor, undertaking, measure, accomplishment, step, exploit, feat. **2.** DECREE enactment, ruling, bill, edict, measure, law, ordinance, amendment, mandate, proclamation, judgment, resolution. **3.** FALSE BEHAVIOR affectation, pose, *false front, pretense, make-believe, put-on, posturing, sham, performance, *Oscar performance, airs, feigning. **4.** STAGE ROUTINE bit, *schtick, sketch. **5.** PART OF A PLAY scene, act one, act two, epilogue, prologue.

act *v.* **1.** DO perform, execute, get involved, spring into action, carry out, achieve, begin, *jump in, undertake, function, move, proceed. "Genius is the ability to act wisely without precedent—the power to do the right thing the first time."—Elbert Hubbard. **2.** BEHAVE conduct oneself, comport, deport, carry oneself, perform, be like. **3.** PERFORM IN AN ENTERTAINMENT portray, personify, impersonate, mimic, role-play, characterize, enact, *ham it up, play a part, star, burlesque.

acting *n.* PERFORMANCE IN AN ENTERTAINMENT depiction, method acting, characterization, impersonation, mimicry, dramatization, portrayal, rendition, *hamming it up, mime, pantomime, theatrics. "Acting is honesty. If you can fake that, you've got it made."—George Burns. "To seem natural rather than to be natural."—Alan Milne.

acting *v.* PRETENDING bluffing, faking, feigning, putting up a false front, playing make-believe, posing, putting up a facade, affecting.

acting *a.* SUBSTITUTING surrogate, functioning, operating, alternate, temporary, deputy, interim, provisional, pro tem, adjutant. ANT. *permanent.*

action *n.* **1.** ACTIVITY motion, movement, functioning, performance, working, energy, commotion. **2.** ACT deed, move, effort, enterprise, exercise, exploit. "Deeds are better things than words are, Actions mightier than boastings."—Longfellow. "Well done is better than well said."—Ben Franklin. **3.** EFFECT influence. **4.** LEGAL ACTION lawsuit, suit, claim, case. **5.** COMBAT battle, hostilities, gunfire, enemy fire, fighting. **6.** EXCITEMENT movement, slam-bang entertainment.

activate *v.* start, begin, initiate, stimulate, spark, actuate, prompt, goad, prod, set in motion, ignite, impel, *flip the switch, energize, motivate. ANT. *stop, turn off, extinguish, paralyze.*

active *a.* **1.** BUSY moving, functioning, working, industrious, on the go, commotive, kinetic, stirring, astir, restless, bustling. **2.** ENERGETIC lively, agile, quick, spry, vital, spirited, hearty, nimble, vigorous, sprightly, alert, frisky, animated. **3.** PARTICIPATING functional, acting, operative. ANT. *1. inactive, static, stationary. 2. dead, slow, tired, paralyzed. 3. inactive.*

ACTIVISM *n.* [AKT uh vizm] taking direct action to bring about political or social change. *Voting is activism in its simplest form.*

SYN. involvement, action, acting, commitment, militancy, advocacy, picketing, striking, boycotting, taking responsibility, influencing, effecting change. ANT. *apathy, passivity, ignoring, indifference.*

activist *n.* doer, *a mover and shaker, *lightning rod, *spark, champion, advocate, *influence peddler, logroller, enthusiast, militant, man of deeds, *catalyst for change.

activity *n.* **1.** ACTION movement, commotion, motion, bustle, hustle. **2.** LIVELINESS energy, vivacity, vigor, alertness, briskness. **3.** PASTIME pursuit, recreation, venture, game, hobby. ANT. *1. inactivity, stillness, inertia. 2. sloth, tiredness, exhaustion.*

act of God *n.* natural disaster, unforeseen event, accident, freak accident.

actor *n.* **1.** DOER perpetrator, participant, activist, executor, mover, agent, operative. **2.** THESPIAN performer, player, actress, star, character, entertainer, mimic, mime, movie idol, matinee idol, impersonator, artist, leading man, leading lady. "A musician who plays on a homemade instrument—himself."—Helen Hayes.

WORD FIND
group: cast, company (stock company), ensemble, repertory, troupe
improvisation: ad lib
main role: lead
minor role: bit player, cameo, extra, spear carrier, walk on
monologue performer: monologist
natural, realistic: method actor
negotiates contracts, finds work: agent
overacting or bad acting: ham, mugger
publicizes: press agent, publicist
secondary role: supporting actor
silent performer: mime, pantomime
substitute: stand-in, understudy
traveling: barnstormer
typecast: character actor
veteran: trouper
SEE ACTRESS, MOVIE, TELEVISION, THEATER

actress *n.* leading lady, starlet, diva, prima donna, ingenue. SEE ACTOR, MOVIE, TELEVISION, THEATER

actual *a.* real, authentic, factual, true, bona fide, existing, concrete, genuine, tangible, certain, veritable, de facto. ANT. *false, imaginary, fictitious, unreal, nonexistent.*

actuality *n.* reality, fact, truth, verity, materiality.

actualize *v.* make real, bring about, realize, effectualize, produce, engineer, accomplish, reach.

actually *adv.* really, in fact, in reality, truthfully, truly, genuinely, literally, in actuality, de facto, as a matter of fact.

actuary *n.* statistician, accountant, insurance professional.

actuate *v.* put into motion, activate, start, ignite, effectuate, motivate, impel, goad, prompt, stimulate, initiate, *put into gear, *get rolling, spur, rouse. ANT. *stop, extinguish, deter, *throw a wrench in the works.*

act up *v.* misbehave, act out, raise hell, *sow one's wild oats, rebel, *kick, *throw a tantrum, carry on.

acuity *n.* acuteness, sharpness, keenness, shrewdness.

ACUMEN *n.* [AK yuh mun] mental sharpness, accurate and quick judgment. *Frank lacks the acumen needed to succeed in the stock market.* SYN. sharpness, shrewdness, quickness, intelligence, perceptiveness, keenness, insight, judgment, astuteness, discernment, acuity, smarts, sagacity, wisdom. ANT. *ignorance, dullness, stupidity, naivete.*

acute *a.* **1.** SHARP pointed, needle-like. **2.** KEEN sharp, shrewd, quick, smart, astute, perceptive, bright, discerning. **3.** SENSITIVE receptive, responsive, perceptive. **4.** SEVERE serious, critical, crucial, vital, important, grave, momentous, urgent, dangerous, intense. **5.** SHRILL high, piercing. ANT. *1. dull, blunt. 2. dull, obtuse, slow, stupid. 3. insensitive, imperceptive. 4. mild, unimportant, insignificant. 5. low, bass.*

A.D. *adv.* anno Domini, in the year of the Lord.

ADAGE *n.* [ADD ij] an old saying illustrating some universal truth. *"Charity begins at home" and "Honesty is the best policy" are popular adages.* SYN. saying, proverb, aphorism, axiom, folk wisdom, motto, maxim, platitude, precept, truism, cliche.

ADAMANT *a.* [AD uh mant] not giving in or yielding, stubborn. *LBJ was adamant about not being typed as a Southerner, because that meant political handicaps.* SYN. unyielding, unrelenting, stubborn, inflexible, unbending, rigid, intractable, obdurate, immovable, firm, resolute, fixed, uncompromising, determined. ANT. *flexible, yielding, acquiescing.*

adapt *v.* adjust, modify, assimilate, conform, suit, reform, acculturate, fit, alter, change, accommodate, orient, bend, acclimate, attune, convert, harden, temper, habituate, evolve, reinvent, retrofit, *change one's spots.

adaptable *a.* adjustable, modifiable, convertible, alterable, changeable, transformable, variable, flexible, pliable. ANT. *invariable, rigid, unbending.*

adaptation *n.* adjustment, modification, alteration, change, transformation, variation, assimilation, conformation, accommodation, hardening, retrofit, tempering, acclimation, evolution, metamorphosis.

adapter *n.* connector, plug, fitting.

adaptive *a.* adjusting, modifying, altering, flexible, hearty, robust.

add *v.* **1.** ADD ON affix, attach, append, tack on, adjoin, suffix, annex. **2.** INCREASE augment, supplement, enlarge, lengthen, amplify, boost, raise, heighten, *beef up, build on. **3.** TOTAL sum up, calculate, compute, figure, tally, reckon, enumerate, count. ANT. *1. subtract, remove. 2. subtract, decrease, reduce.*

addendum *n.* addition, appendix, supplement, attachment, adjunct, codicil, extension, augmentation.

addict *n.* *junkie, *fiend, *dopehead, *head, *freak, *acidhead, *meth head, *cokehead, user, *mainliner, *speed freak, *pothead, *space cadet, enthusiast, devotee, nut, adherent, buff, hound, zealot. SEE DRUG

addicted *a.* hooked, dependent, devoted, attached, obsessed, disposed to, in the habit, *stuck on, zealous about, *nuts about.

addiction *n.* habit, dependency, *monkey, *monkey on one's back, craving, enslavement, obsession, habituation, alcoholism.

addictive *a.* habit-forming, enslaving, hooking.

add insult to injury *v.* aggravate, exacerbate, worsen, *add fuel to the fire, heighten, provoke.

addition *n.* **1.** TALLYING summation, calculation, tabulation, reckoning, computation, counting. **2.** AUGMENTATION addendum, add-on, attachment, extension, increase, supplement, adjunct, annex.

additional *a.* more, extra, added, supplementary, further, over and above, increased. ANT. *fewer, scant, none.*

additive *n.* agent, enhancing agent, preservative.

addled *a.* muddled, befuddled, confused, *numb, mixed up, *out to lunch, *foggy, *dim, *out of it, bewildered, disoriented. ANT. *perceptive, clear-headed.*

add-on *n.* supplement, accessory, peripheral, augmentation.

address *n.* **1.** SPEECH oration, lecture, talk, salutation, letter. **2.** MAILING ADDRESS R.F.D.,

route, street number, P.O. box, destination.
3. LOCATION residence, place, home, quarters, domicile.
address *v.* **1.** DIRECT speak to, greet, approach, salute, acknowledge, write to. **2.** HANDLE consider, deal with, confront, undertake, focus on, take up, engage in.
adduce *v.* cite, prove, provide, illustrate, point out, show, affirm, name.
ADEPT *a.* [a DEPT] highly skilled or proficient. *The project was finished quickly in her adept hands.* SYN. skilled, deft, adroit, expert, masterful, proficient, capable, practiced, dexterous, sharp, competent, *crack, *crackerjack, savvy, talented. ANT. *unskilled, incompetent, fumbling, bumbling.*
adequacy *n.* enough, sufficiency, capability, competence.
adequate *a.* sufficient, enough, suitable, acceptable, satisfactory, respectable, ample, tolerable, okay, admissible, not bad, fair, able. ANT. *inadequate, unsatisfactory, intolerable, insufficient, lacking.*
adequately *adv.* sufficiently, acceptably, satisfactorily, suitably, capably, amply. ANT. *inadequately, insufficiently.*
adhere *v.* **1.** STICK affix, cling, stay, attach, hold fast, cement, fasten, cleave, cohere. **2.** STAY WITH OR BE DEVOTED TO support, observe, follow, abide by, respect, maintain, practice, be attached, keep to, be faithful. ANT. *1. separate, come unglued, repel. 2. stray, condemn, ignore, detract.*
ADHERENT *n.* [ad HEER ent] a supporter or follower of a cause or belief. *The speaker has been an adherent of conservative politics for years.* SYN. follower, supporter, disciple, believer, advocate, backer, fan, devotee, observer, ally, *card-carrying member. ANT. *detractor, opponent, enemy of, critic of.*
adhesion *n.* sticking, stickiness, adherence, attachment, cling, holding fast, hold.
adhesive *n.* glue, tape, velcro, cement, paste, *stickum, binder, gum, mortar, resin, plaster.
AD HOC *a.* [ADD HOK] for a specific purpose, as a committee, impromptu. *An emergency ad hoc committee was formed.* SYN. specified, specific, provisional, special, impromptu.
adieu *interj.* goodbye, farewell, au revoir, adios, sayonara, arrivederci, auf Wiedersehen, *see ya, *toodleloo, *toodles. SEE GOODBYE
AD INFINITUM *adv.* [add in fuh NITE um] forever, endlessly. *The Congressman said*

taxes would continue to rise ad infinitum. SYN. forever, endlessly, continuously, on and on, neverending, perpetually, relentlessly, unlimitedly.
adios *interj.* farewell, adieu, au revoir. SEE GOODBYE
adipose *n.* fat.
adjacent *a.* abutting, juxtaposed, near, close, adjoining, next to, aside, beside, neighboring, contiguous, alongside, bordering, proximate, meeting. ANT. *distant, remote.*
adjective *n.* modifier, qualifier.
adjoin *v.* **1.** ABUT touch, be contiguous to, unite, contact, connect, impinge on, border, verge. **2.** JOIN affix, unite, connect, link.
adjoining *a.* abutting, adjacent, touching, contacting, neighboring, connecting, bordering, contiguous, verging. ANT. *separate, apart.*
adjourn *v.* **1.** RECESS rest, pause, close, delay, suspend, put off, hold. **2.** MOVE transfer.
adjournment *n.* recess, rest, pause, break, delay, intermission, suspension, postponement.
ADJUDICATE *v.* [uh JOO di KATE] to judge and settle a case. *A "kangaroo court" is a court in which a case is adjudicated dishonestly or incompetently.* SYN. judge, adjudge, try, hear, decide, process, arbitrate, mediate, determine, settle, sit in judgment, referee.
adjudication *n.* judgment, decision, determination, settlement.
adjunct *n.* supplement, auxiliary, subordinate, addition, extra, associate, aid, assistant.
adjure *v.* command, charge, entreat, order, require, obligate.
adjust *v.* conform, fit, alter, change, accommodate, bend, suit, accustom, *doctor, adapt, modify, straighten, tune, fine-tune, *fiddle with, calibrate, square, rectify, tweak, service, balance.
adjustable *a.* adaptable, alterable, pliable, conformable, accommodating, modifiable, changeable, serviceable, flexible, tractable.
adjustment *n.* **1.** CONFORMATION fitting, alteration, change, accommodation, adaption, bending, retrofit, *doctoring, modification, calibration, tune up, sizing, rectification, squaring. **2.** SETTLEMENT claim, liability, compensation, reimbursement, remuneration.
adjutant *n.* assistant, aid, helper, administrative assistant, staff officer.
ad lib *n.* improvisation, extemporization, invention, *offhand remark, impulse.
ad lib *v.* improvise, extemporize, *wing it, *fake

it, invent, *play it by ear, speak impromptu, speak off the top of one's head, fabricate, vamp.

AD LIB *a.* [ADD LIB] improvised, unrehearsed. *The act was performed completely ad lib.* SYN. improvisational, unrehearsed, *off the cuff, *on the spur of the moment, extemporaneously, impulsively. ANT. *rehearsed, studied.*

ad man *n.* copywriter, huckster, *BS artist.

admeasure *v.* apportion.

administer *v.* **1.** GOVERN manage, administrate, head, direct, oversee, officiate, superintend, supervise, conduct, regulate, rule, operate, control. **2.** GIVE OUT dispense, mete out, deliver, apply, distribute, provide, give. **3.** HELP serve, lend a hand.

administration *n.* **1.** GOVERNING overseeing, commanding, policy-making, application, execution, legislation, regulation, superintendence, supervision, management. **2.** MANAGEMENT leadership, government, bureaucracy, bureau, cabinet, headquarters, governing body, executive branch, board, command, *front office, legislature, establishment, ministry, board of directors, department, *brass, *the powers that be. **3.** DISPENSATION delivery, application, giving. **4.** TERM OF POWER reign, dynasty, *run, incumbency, tenure.

administrator *n.* manager, supervisor, superintendent, executive, executor, CEO (chief executive officer), bureaucrat, official, director, overseer, governor, head, chair, leader, *paper shuffler.

admirable *a.* model, praiseworthy, enviable, excellent, honorable, respectable, commendable, wonderful, ideal, great, exceptional, revered, laudable, superior. ANT. *despicable, low, rotten.*

admiral *n.* commander. "That part of the warship which does the talking while the figurehead does the thinking."—Ambrose Bierce. SEE NAVAL OFFICER

admiration *n.* esteem, adoration, reverence, approval, regard, idolizing, applause, praise, awe, respect, veneration, glorification, fondness, *foot-kissing, worship. "A very shortlived passion, that immediately decays upon growing familiar with its object."—Joseph Addison. "The daughter of ignorance."—Benjamin Franklin. ANT. *disgust, despising, loathing, disrespect.*

admire *v.* regard, esteem, look up to, respect, revere, idolize, praise, worship, model after,

honor, put on a pedestal, hail. ANT. *loathe, despise, look down on, disrespect.*

admirer *n.* fan, devotee, follower, disciple, supporter.

admissible *a.* acceptable, permissible, allowed, passable, legitimate, legal, lawful, okay, tolerable, proper, suitable. ANT. *inadmissible, illegal, intolerable.*

admission *n.* **1.** ENTRANCE entry, passage, access. **2.** DOOR CHARGE cover charge, ticket, entrance fee, gate. **3.** ACKNOWLEDGEMENT OR CONFESSION admitting, granting, profession, *owning up, *fessing up, revelation, affirmation, disclosure, divulgence, testimony, deposition. ANT. *1. blockage, barring, impediment. 2. concealment, cover-up, secret, confidentiality.*

admit *v.* **1.** LET IN accept, let pass, grant access, check, grant, okay, permit, *give the nod to. **2.** CONFESS acknowledge, concede, grant, *own up, *fess up, *come clean, reveal, disclose, divulge, confide, *sing, *spill the beans, *bare one's soul, testify. ANT. *1. block, bar, refuse. 2. withhold, keep secret, hide, deny.*

admittance *n.* entrance, entry, permission, pass, passage.

admittedly *adv.* confessedly, honestly, truthfully, frankly.

admix *v.* intermix, blend, combine, mingle.

admixture *n.* blend, combination, mixture, compound, melange.

ADMONISH *v.* [ad MON ish] to caution or advise, often scoldingly. *He was admonished for drinking and driving.* SYN. **1.** CAUTION warn, forewarn, advise, exhort. **2.** REPROVE rebuke, berate, scold, *tell off, *come down on, *call on the carpet, *take to task, chastise, reproach. **3.** REMIND apprise, inform, warn. ANT. *2. commend, compliment, reward.*

admonition *n.* **1.** CAUTION warning, forewarning, advice, apprisal, counsel. **2.** REPROVAL scolding, *dressing down, *talking to, reprimand, upbraiding, *slap on the wrist, remonstrance, rebuke, reproach. ANT. *2. commendation, reward, compliment.*

AD NAUSEAM *adv.* [AD NAWZ e um] to the point of illness or disgust. *He went on about his accomplishments ad nauseum.* SYN. to a sickening degree, to nauseating extremes, to the point of queasiness, too much, more than one can stomach.

ado *n.* trouble, fuss, excitement, running around, *to-do, bother, travail, hubbub, confusion.

adobe n. clay, brick.

adolescence n. puberty, pubescence, youth, teen years, *awkward years, minor, immaturity, junior high years, high school age. "A kind of emotional seasickness. Both are funny, but only in retrospect."—Arthur Koestler.

adolescent n. teenager, teen, *teenybopper, youth, sophomore, junior, minor, youngster, *bobbysoxer, *sweet sixteen, juvenile. "One who has reached the age of dissent."—Harold Leslie.

Adonis n. *hunk, *beefcake, *dreamboat, *stud, Greek god, *God's gift to women, *heartbreaker, *lady-killer.

adopt v. 1. TAKE IN ANOTHER'S CHILD take under one's wing, take in, foster, surrogate, mother, father, raise. 2. SELECT OR TAKE UP choose, appropriate, employ, take, espouse, assume, take on, opt, use. 3. VOTE IN select, approve, back, support, sanction, ratify. ANT. 1. orphan, disown, shun. 2. reject, shun, refuse.

adorable a. charming, cunning, cute, appealing, captivating, cuddly, lovely, lovable, sweet, precious, darling, irresistible, *huggable. ANT. gross, disgusting, repulsive, monstrous.

adoration n. love, praise, devotion, worship, veneration, affection, exaltation, reverence, hero worship, idolization, adulation, admiration, infatuation. ANT. revulsion, repulsion, despising, disgust.

adore v. admire, love, worship, hero-worship, idolize, respect, venerate, honor, look up to, praise, revere, glorify, esteem, *carry a torch for, be taken with, deify, *put on a pedestal, *dig, *groove on, adulate, cherish. ANT. loathe, disrespect, despise, *spit on.

adorn v. ornament, don, bedeck, dress, decorate, embellish, beautify, trim, festoon, garnish, spruce up, emblazon.

adornment n. ornament, decoration, dressing, embellishment, bauble, trinket, trimming, spangle, garnish, trapping, frills, finery, frippery, doodad.

adrenalin n. epinephrine, stress hormone, *fight or flight hormone.

adrift a. drifting, free-floating, directionless, wandering, unanchored, at the wind's will, astray, aimless, afloat, derelict, loose. ANT. anchored, grounded, stable.

ADROIT a. [uh DROYT] mentally or physically skilled. Donatello was an adroit sculptor. SYN. skillful, deft, dexterous, expert, clever, *crack, sharp, talented, experienced, masterful, practiced, proficient, nimble, astute. ANT. maladroit, bumbling, fumbling, *dim.

adulate v. flatter, *apple polish, gush, admire, praise, worship, *kiss feet, *brown-nose, fawn, *fall all over. ANT. disrespect, ignore, insult.

adulation n. flattery, *feet-kissing, *apple-polishing, *brown-nosing, worshipping, fawning, exaltation, sycophancy, blarney, toadying, blandishment, slavishness, adoration.

adult a. 1. GROWN-UP, mature, aged, seasoned, of age, developed, ripe, at the age of consent, of legal age. 2. (Pertaining to explicitly sexual material) PORNOGRAPHIC x-rated, graphic, dirty, blue, obscene. ANT. childlike, immature, juvenile, youthful.

adult n. grown-up, mature person, *big person, man, woman, lady, gentleman, elder, authority figure. "An obsolete child."—Theodore Geisel.

ADULTERATE v. [uh DULL tuh RATE] to make impure, to spoil or contaminate. The once pristine waters off Alaska have been adulterated with spilled oil. SYN. spoil, debase, corrupt, defile, contaminate, ruin, devalue, poison, denature, pollute, degrade, taint, water down, depreciate. ANT. purify, concentrate.

adulterer n. adulteress, *cheat, philanderer, fornicator, *Casanova, *skirt-chaser, *wolf, *womanizer.

adultery n. infidelity, unfaithfulness, sex, *sleeping around, promiscuity, affair, fornication, *cheating, *stepping out, *swinging, *fooling around, *playing around, *hanky-panky. "The application of democracy to love."—H.L. Mencken.

advance n. 1. FORWARD MOVEMENT progression, progress, headway. 2. PROGRESSION progress, improvement, innovation, breakthrough, development, discovery. 3. FLIRTATION overture, *move, offer, proposal, invitation. 4. PAYMENT loan, wages, prepayment, front, retainer, deposit.

advance v. 1. BRING FORWARD progress, move ahead, propel, push, come, go, make headway, proceed, forge ahead, continue, gain ground, promote. 2. ASCEND IN RANK promote, step up, *climb up the corporate ladder, move up. 3. HELP hasten, quicken, aid, assist, further, forward, facilitate, back. 4. PROPOSE suggest, put forward, submit, proffer, recommend. 5. PREPAY deposit, retain, loan, front. ANT. 1. stop, reverse, go back. 2. demote, step down. 3. impede, detract, block.

advanced a. 1. AHEAD, SUPERIOR forward, beyond, higher, cutting edge, leading edge, progressive, ahead of the times, liberal, avant-garde, precocious, *light years ahead, developed. 2. GETTING ON IN YEARS aged, venerable, seasoned, experienced. SEE OLD ANT. 1. *behind, backwards, slow, obsolete. 2. young, green.*

advance man n. publicist, press agent.

advancement n. 1. PROMOTION move up, graduation, rise. 2. PROGRESS breakthrough, innovation, development.

advantage n. 1. SUPERIORITY edge, *leg up, *upper hand, head start, help, assistance, aid, favor, leverage, *ace in the hole, odds. 2. BENEFIT gain, profit, blessing, boon, asset. ANT. 1. *disadvantage, liability, handicap, weakness.*

advantage, take v. use, impose upon, *step on.

advantageous a. favorable, opportune, profitable, beneficial, auspicious, expedient, propitious, fortunate, for the best. ANT. *unfavorable, inopportune, harmful.*

advection n. transference.

ADVENT n. [ADD vent] the coming or arrival of. *The advent of television in the 1920s was met with skepticism, even by its inventor.* SYN. 1. COMING arrival, appearance, forthcoming, onset, beginning. 2. THE COMING OF CHRIST Second Coming, Incarnation. ANT. *end, demise, death.* SEE CHURCH, RELIGION

adventure n. thrill-seeking, venture, escapade, expedition, quest, enterprise, geste, dare, risk, danger, hazard, peril, exploration, outing, exploit, undertaking, mission, safari, trek, hunt, odyssey, voyage, *armchair adventure, *cliffhanger. "Something you seek for pleasure, or even for profit, like a gold rush or invading a country . . . the thing you will to occur."—Katherine Anne Porter.

adventurer n. 1. THRILL-SEEKER explorer, soldier of fortune, hero, heroine, risk-taker, *hired gun, daredevil, voyager, wanderer, swashbuckler, pioneer, knight, trailblazer, pirate, Don Quixote, romantic, *armchair adventurer. "An outlaw . . . Adventure must start with running away from home."—William Bolitho. 2. SPECULATOR gold-digger, investor, opportunist, fortune hunter, gambler, entrepreneur, *wide-eyed dreamer. ANT. 1. *homebody, stick-in-the-mud, *killjoy, milquetoast, Nervous Nellie.*

adventuresome a. venturesome, risk-taking, thrill-seeking, adventurous, daring, foolhardy, opportunistic, bold, enterprising. ANT. *cautious, prudent.*

adverb n. modifier.

ADVERSARY n. [ADD ver ser ee] an opponent or enemy. *The two adversaries squared off in the ring.* SYN. opponent, enemy, foe, rival, protagonist, contestant, antagonist, competitor. ANT. *friend, partner, ally.*

ADVERSE a. [ad VURS] unfavorable or harmful. *The game was cancelled due to adverse weather conditions.* SYN. unfavorable, harmful, bad, negative, unpropitious, opposing, unfortunate, hostile, injurious, conflicting, detrimental. ANT. *favorable, positive, propitious, beneficial.*

ADVERSITY n. [ad VUR sit ee] hardship, unfavorable conditions. *He overcame great adversity to succeed in his profession.* SYN. hardship, misfortune, trouble, ill-fortune, bad luck, calamity, difficulty, distress, suffering, setbacks, disaster, hard times. ANT. *good fortune, ease.*

advertise v. publicize, promote, sell, pitch, plug, ballyhoo, hype, tout, push, puff, herald, proclaim, publish, broadcast.

advertisement n. ad, advert, commercial, plug, blurb, spot, broadside, notice, flyer, handbill, classified ad, display ad, placard, circular. "Legalized lying."—H.G. Wells. "The rattling of a stick inside a swill bucket."—George Orwell.

advertising n. promotion, publicity, pitching, ballyhoo, selling, heralding, puffery, touting, drumming up, hyping, pushing, proclaiming. "The science of arresting the human intelligence long enough to get money from it."—Stephen Leacock. "The art of making whole lies out of half truths."—Edgar Shoaff.

WORD FIND

accounts, handles advertising: account executive

ad company: agency

addresses of potential customers: mailing list

ad run in selected locale: spot ad

aggressive style of selling: hard sell

ambitious presentation: dog and pony show

award for radio and TV advertising excellence: Clio

catchy phrase or lyric: hook, jingle, slogan

consumer group serving as guinea pigs: test market

editorial-like newspaper ad: advertorial

dishonest touting of high-priced item after advertising low-priced item: bait and switch

expansion of ad campaign beyond test market: rollout
free item, inducement to buy: premium
good word in: plug
graphic design, art head: art director
hand-distributed ad: handbill
hidden "buy" messages in advertising: subliminal advertising
hinged ad boards worn over shoulders: sandwich board
hyperbole: hype, puffery, ballyhoo
illustrated ad in paper or magazine: display ad
mail advertising: direct mail
multimedia sales effort: campaign
New York cluster of large ad agencies: Madison Avenue
plant in audiences to help sell: shill
pre-ad that arouses interest in upcoming product: teaser
posting ads on public structures without permission: sniping
presentation: pitch
print publicity: ink
promotional material given to media: press kit
public relations: PR
recommendation, affirmation of product's quality by consumer: testimonial
royalty paid to performer each time ad runs: residual
telephone advertising: telemarketing
trademark design: logo
writer of ads: copywriter
SEE RADIO, TELEVISION

advice *n.* counsel, tip, direction, opinion, word to the wise, schooling, guidance, admonition, recommendation, suggestion, hint. "Like snow; the softer it falls, the longer it dwells upon, and the deeper it sinks into, the mind."—Coleridge. "Always a confession."—Emile Herzog.

advisable *a.* recommended, wise, good advice, good counsel.

advise *v.* **1.** COUNSEL recommend, tip, direct, guide, admonish, suggest, hint, give a word to the wise, exhort, point out, forewarn, advocate. **2.** NOTIFY inform, let know, educate, fill in, clue in.

advisement *n.* consideration.

advisory *n.* report, warning, notice, forewarning, caution.

ADVOCATE *n.* [ADD vuh ket] one who speaks for or supports a cause or another person. *The senator was an advocate for senior*

citizens' welfare. SYN. supporter, proponent, pleader, defender, abettor, espouser, champion, activist, propagator, backer, ally, activist, lawyer. ANT. *detractor, opponent, critic.*

ADVOCATE *v.* [ADD vuh kate] To support a cause or a person. *She advocates equal rights.* SYN. support, propagate, defend, back, plead for, promote, champion, espouse, speak for, uphold, endorse, stand up for. ANT. *fight against, criticize, oppose.*

adz *n.* tool, ax, implement.

AEGIS *n.* [EE jis] sponsorship or protection. *The new emission regulations were presented under the aegis of city authorities.* SYN. sponsorship, auspices, protection, patronage.

aerial *a.* **1.** AIRBORNE airy, atmospheric, by air, by aircraft, skyward, heavenward, aloft, up, up and away, supernal. **2.** UNREAL imaginary, ethereal, intangible, fanciful, visionary. **3.** *n.* ANTENNA. ANT. **1.** *grounded, by land.* **2.** *down-to-earth.*

aerie *n.* [AIR ee] nest, perch, lookout, home.

aerobics *n.* cardiovascular exercise, wind exercises, conditioning, calisthenics, *dancercize, gymnastics, *workout.

aeronautics *n.* aircraft design, aircraft construction, aircraft navigation.

aesthete *n.* dilettante, connoisseur, art lover.

AESTHETIC *a.* [es THET ik] pertaining to beauty and that which is pleasing to the eye. *Mark made an aesthetic appraisal of the architecture.* SYN. beauty, beautiful, artistic, pleasing to the eye, gorgeous. ANT. *ugly, unattractive.*

AFFABLE *a.* [AF uh bul] easy going and nice to talk to. *She was an affable woman who fit in well with any social group.* SYN. friendly, easy-going, nice, amiable, sociable, good-natured, warm, approachable, *chummy, *buddy-buddy, congenial, benign. ANT. *cold, stand-offish, nasty.*

affair *n.* **1.** MATTER happening, activity, doing, business, thing, operation, concern, occurrence, event, incident. **2.** SOCIAL FUNCTION *to-do, gala, black-tie affair, function, party, dinner, celebration, get-together, soiree. **3.** LOVE AFFAIR affaire d' amour, affaire de coeur, liaison, tryst, *fling, romance, rendezvous, intimacy, sexual relationship, *thing, adultery.

affect *v.* **1.** INFLUENCE sway, change, act on, evoke, impress, stir, impact upon. **2.** TOUCH THE EMOTIONS move, melt one's heart, warm one's heart, pluck at the heartstrings, disturb, perturb, touch a nerve, stir, *cut to the quick, *hit home. **3.** ASSUME make a pretense, feign, fake, put on, *B.S., adopt, *sham, pose, posture.

AFFECTATION n. [AF ek TAY shun] phony or unnatural behavior, often displayed in an attempt to impress. *His cultured speech was only an affectation.* SYN. pretense, pretentiousness, fraud, airs, show, performance, display, *going Hollywood, act, pose, posture, mannerism, studied manner, *Oscar performance.

affected a. **1.** INFLUENCED impressed, swayed, changed, acted upon, stirred, impacted upon. **2.** TOUCHED perturbed, moved, stirred, impressed, distressed, heartened, warmed, agitated. **3.** ARTIFICIAL phony, fake, assumed, contrived, show-off, counterfeit, pretentious, studied, unnatural, feigned, precious, mannered, *full of it, *Hollywood. ANT. *1. unchanged, untouched. 2. unmoved, unaffected. 3. real, authentic, true, down to earth, sincere.*

affection n. love, warmth, tenderness, friendship, feeling, devotion, *soft spot, solicitude, fondness, regard, attachment, close feelings. ANT. *hatred, loathing, disgust, coldness.*

affectionate a. warm, loving, tender, giving, solicitous, devoted, friendly, *touchy-feely, *lovey-dovey, sensuous, doting, fond, feeling, demonstrative. ANT. *cold, cool, undemonstrative, aloof.*

AFFIDAVIT n. [af uh DAY vit] a written statement made under oath. *His statements to the media contradicted his affidavit.* SYN. sworn statement, testimony, written testimony, sworn report, declaration, deposition.

affiliate n. member, associate, relation, ally, fellow, peer, brother, sister, counterpart, subsidiary, subdivision, branch, part.

affiliate v. associate, connect, network, join, unite, incorporate, connect, band, *team up with. ANT. *disband, break up, scatter.*

affiliation n. association, connection, alliance, network, membership, relationship, union, incorporation, partnership.

AFFINITY n. [uh FIN uh tee] attraction, liking. Also, a close relationship or similarity between things. *Children have a natural affinity for junk food. There was a peculiar affinity between Adolph Hitler and Eva Braun.* SYN. **1.** RELATIONSHIP connection, resemblance, likeness, kinship, compatibility, similarity. **2.** LIKING, ATTRACTION fondness, inclination,

bent, predilection, affection, leaning, partiality, fancy, penchant. ANT. *1. dissimilarity. 2. repulsion, aversion.*

affirm v. assert, declare, firm up, confirm, validate, uphold, proclaim, attest, profess, insist, *swear to, vouch.

affirmation n. assertion, declaration, confirmation, validation, avowal, word, swearing, oath, profession.

AFFIRMATIVE ACTION n. a policy which attempts to prevent discrimination of minorities, as in employment, through hiring quotas or other means. *Affirmative action has opened the employment door for many African Americans.* SYN. fair treatment, balanced treatment, quota system, fair hiring practices, anti-discrimination program, equal opportunity, reverse discrimination. SEE GOVERNMENT, POLITICS

affix v. **1.** ATTACH stick, fasten, bind, fix, connect, staple. **2.** ADD append, annex, tack on. ANT. *1. detach, unfasten, remove. 2. subtract.*

afflict v. plague, distress, trouble, bother, prey on, hurt, harm, pester, beset, burden, molest, agitate, torment, torture, injure, weaken. ANT. *relieve.*

affliction n. hardship, pain, trouble, illness, suffering, burden, plague, curse, handicap, scourge, *cross to bear, torment, torture, misfortune, adversity, calamity. ANT. *blessing, godsend, gift.*

affluence n. riches, abundance, wealth, opulence, plenty, prosperity, luxury, fortune. ANT. *poverty, destitution, lack.*

AFFLUENT a. [AFF loo unt] wealthy, opulent. *The affluent residents of Beverly Hills are rich in material belongings.* SYN. rich, wealthy, prosperous, opulent, well-to-do, well-off, moneyed, *loaded, *well-heeled, *flush, *fat, *filthy rich, *rolling in dough, abundant, plentiful, bountiful. ANT. *impoverished, destitute, *poor as Job's turkey.*

affront n. insult, offense, slight, put-down, dig, disrespect, *crack, *shot, *swipe, injury, denigration, barb, slur. ANT. *compliment, flattery.*

AFFRONT v. [uh FRUNT] to insult or offend. *He was sorely affronted.* SYN. insult, offend, injure, hurt, irritate, annoy, gall, rile, displease, provoke, pique, slight. ANT. *compliment, flatter, adulate.*

aficionado n. devotee, connoisseur, follower, fanatic, enthusiast, *nut. SEE FAN

afield adv. off the beaten track, out of bounds, away, astray.

afloat *adv.* floating, adrift, offshore, at sea, on the water.

afoot *a./adv.* about, up and about, astir.

afraid *a.* scared, frightened, fearful, terrified, panic-stricken, alarmed, apprehensive, anxious, shocked, frozen, rattled, startled, leery, jumpy, *wide-eyed with fear, shaky, quivering, *chicken, *sweating bullets, *spooked, *scared stiff, faint-hearted, paralyzed, *saucer-eyed, horrified. ANT. *courageous, cool, calm, fearless.* SEE FEAR

afresh *adv.* anew, again, once more.

African *a.* Negro, Negroid, black, Nigerian, Egyptian, Algerian, Libyan, Sudanese, Ethiopian, Ugandan, Kenyan, Tanzanian, Angolan, Zambian, Botswanian, South African, Namibian, Bantu, Gabunese, Moroccan, Tunisian, Senegalese, Ghanaian, Bushman, Pygmy, Masai, Zulu.

WORD FIND

bushman: Qung

dance: juba

desert: Sahara, Kalahari, Libyan

garment: tobe, kaross, haik

gold region: Rand

grassland: veldt

house: tembe

hut: kraal, tembe

language: Bantu, Hamite, Swahili, Hausa

tableland: karoo

tree: cola, baobab, baku, sassy, moli, kola, bumbo, gamdeboo

village: dorp, stad, kraal

wind: simoom, simoon

wood: ebony, teak

aft *a.* astern, abaft, back. ANT. *fore, front.*

after *a.* **1.** LATER afterward, thereafter, following, subsequent. **2.** BEHIND preceded by, in back of, following.

after *prep.* in pursuit of, looking for, in search of.

afterbirth *n.* placenta, membranes.

afterlife *n.* heaven, hereafter, eternity, bliss, *the great beyond, immortality. SEE HEAVEN

aftermath *n.* consequence, aftereffect, result, outcome, effect, fallout, repercussions, *ripples, wake, by-product.

again *adv.* once more, repeatedly, anew.

against *prep.* opposite to, contrary to.

agape *a.* or *adv.* **1.** OPEN gaping, wide open. **2.** STATE OF AMAZEMENT dumbstruck, flabbergasted, astonished, saucer-eyed, goggle-eyed, bug-eyed, wonderstruck.

age *n.* **1.** PERIOD OF TIME generation, duration, lifetime, era, epoch, period, century, millenium, cycle, span. **2.** STAGE season, phase, point, year, maturity, majority, minority, adulthood, declining years, youth, adolescence, infancy, middle age. "It takes about ten years to get used to how old you are."—Unknown. "[Something that] doesn't matter unless you're a cheese."—Billie Burke. SEE TIME

age *v.* mature, ripen, develop, grow older, season, weather, mellow, slow down, waste away. "To take in sail."—Emerson. SEE OLD, OLD AGE, OLD-FACED

aged *a.* elderly, old, venerable, advanced, matured, past one's prime, vintage, seasoned, weathered, ripened, ageless, *long in the tooth, *one foot in the grave, old as Methuselah, worn, decrepit, decayed, deteriorated. ANT. *fresh, green, unseasoned.* SEE ANTIQUE, OLD, OLD-FACED

ageless *a.* eternal, infinite, perpetual, timeless.

agency *n.* **1.** ORGANIZATION department, office, bureau, company, corporation, firm, concern, operation. **2.** POWER auspices, action, operation, means, influence, work, activity, medium.

AGENDA *n.* [uh JEN da] a list of things to be done. *What's on your agenda today?* SYN. schedule, list, program, itinerary, calendar, docket, planning, lineup.

agent *n.* **1.** DOER actor, executor, functionary, mover. **2.** REPRESENTATIVE assignee, delegate, deputy, advocate, proxy, middleman, broker, go-between, proctor, salesman, envoy, handler. **3.** FORCE power, instrument, cause, mechanism, means.

AGENT PROVOCATEUR *n.* [a zahn pro vok uh TUR] an agitator or instigator; one who tries to provoke others into action and get them in trouble. SYN. agitator, instigator, goad, troublemaker, rabble-rouser, spark, incendiary. ANT. *peacemeaker.*

agglomeration *n.* heap, jumble, mass, pile, gathering, collection, cluster.

agglutinate *v.* join, attach, adhere, glue, stick.

aggrandize *v.* enlarge, extend, expand, blow up, exaggerate, increase, inflate, puff up. ANT. *minimalize, shrink, deflate.*

aggravate *v.* **1.** MAKE WORSE worsen, exacerbate, intensify, heighten, deepen, *add fuel to the fire, *fan the flames, *rub it in. **2.** ANNOY irritate, *bug, exasperate, vex, provoke, inflame, rile, irk, ruffle, *rub the wrong way, *miff, *yank one's chain, *rattle one's cage, *piss off. ANT. *1. lessen, relieve, mitigate.* 2. *calm, humor, pacify.*

aggravation n. **1.** WORSENING exacerbation, intensification, deepening, inflammation, magnifying, deepening. **2.** ANNOYANCE irritation, vexation, exasperation, inflammation, *pain, *pain in the ass, hassle, nuisance, *headache, *thorn in one's side, bother. ANT. *1. improvement, lessening, relieving. 2. pleasure, delight.*

aggregate n. composite, total, mass, cluster, mix, blend, assembly, sum total, whole.

aggress v. attack, *jump on, initiate.

aggression n. **1.** ASSAULT attack, offensive, raid, invasion, blitzkrieg. **2.** HOSTILITY offensiveness, violence, belligerence, combativeness, pugnaciousness, fight. "An innate, independent, instinctual disposition in man . . . it constitutes the most powerful obstacle to culture."—Sigmund Freud.

aggressive a. **1.** HOSTILE belligerent, combative, offensive, violent, pugnacious, nasty, quarrelsome, militant. **2.** BOLD OR COMPETITIVE enterprising, *go-getting, *high octane, ambitious, assertive, persistent, pushy, vigorous, obnoxious, domineering, forceful, *ballsy. ANT. *1. passive, peaceful, mild. 2. passive, lazy, ineffectual, laid-back, timid.*

aggressor n. attacker, initiator, invader, raider, trespasser, assailant, provoker, offender, instigator.

aggrieve v. distress, wrong, disturb, hurt, injure, offend, slight, trouble, wound.

aggrieved a. wronged, offended, distressed, disturbed, injured, hurt, afflicted, wounded, depressed, troubled. ANT. *comforted, assisted, relieved.*

aghast a. terrified, horrified, horror-struck, dismayed, appalled, stunned, shocked, agape. ANT. *unperturbed, undisturbed.*

AGILE a. [AJ il] nimble and quick. *The agile basketball player darted past the defense to score the winning basket.* SYN. nimble, quick, spry, deft, keen, brisk, light-footed, dexterous, sprightly, active, lithe, lively, supple. ANT. *clumsy, ponderous, oafish.*

agility n. nimbleness, quickness, keenness, sharpness, light-footedness, dexterity, sprightliness, suppleness, liveliness, adroitness. ANT. *clumsiness, slowness, oafishness.*

aging n. maturing, growing, seasoning, senescent, declining, mellowing, getting old, wearing out, wilting. SEE AGE

agitate v. **1.** SHAKE OR MIX stir, move, churn, make turbulent, bounce, disturb, toss. **2.** DISTURB EMOTIONALLY shake up, stir, arouse, inflame, ignite, wind up, jolt, fluster, excite, incite. ANT. *2. becalm, quiet, pacify.*

agitation n. **1.** SHAKING OR MIXING stirring, churning, turbulence, bouncing, disturbance, tossing, turning. **2.** EMOTIONAL DISTURBANCE arousal, excitement, inflammation, stirring, jolt, turmoil, upheaval, commotion, provocation, rabble-rousing. ANT. *2. becalming, quieting, pacifying.*

agitator n. rabble-rouser, firebrand, *mover and shaker, rebel, provocateur, incendiary, anarchist, inciter, troublemaker, instigator, spark.

aglow a. radiant, shining. ANT. *dull, pale.*

agnate a. akin. SEE RELATED

agnomen n. SEE NICKNAME

AGNOSTIC n. [ag NOS tik] one who believes that it is impossible to know whether or not God exists. *Agnostics believe nothing beyond the material world can be known by the human mind.* SYN. disbeliever, freethinker, skeptic, cynic, doubter, doubting Thomas, philosopher, thinker, atheist. "One who doesn't know whether God exists, but is afraid to say so loudly in case God might hear him."— Eugene Brussell. ANT. *believer, faithful one.* SEE RELIGION, ATHEIST

agnosticism n. freethinking, disbelief, faithlessness, doubting, closed-mindedness, skepticism, atheism. "Simply means that a man shall not say he knows or believes that for which he has no grounds for professing to believe."—Thomas Huxley. ANT. *faith, belief, devoutness.* SEE RELIGION

agog a. eager, excited, anxious, enthusiastic, expectant. ANT. *apathetic, indifferent.*

agonize v. suffer, bleed, struggle, worry, fret, torture oneself, stew, lose sleep over, brood over, *sweat bullets, writhe, stay awake nights, grapple.

agony n. suffering, pain, torture, distress, torment, misery, struggle, affliction, sorrow, discomfort, dolor. ANT. *bliss, euphoria, pleasure.*

agrarian a. agricultural, pastoral, rural, rustic. ANT. *urban, citified.* SEE AGRICULTURE, FARM, FARMING

agree v. concur, accord, accede, be of one mind, come to terms, consent, grant, fall in line, side with, *see eye to eye, *square with, harmonize, correspond, coincide, jibe. ANT. *disagree, differ, oppose.*

agreeable a. **1.** CONSENTING conforming, complying, amenable, in accord, accepting. **2.** PLEASING acceptable, good, likable, to one's liking, unobjectionable, appealing, felicitous, pleasurable. ANT. *1. dissenting. 2. disagreeable, unacceptable.*

agreement *n.* **1.** WRITTEN OR ORAL CONTRACT understanding, contract, bargain, deal, covenant, pact, arrangement. **2.** HARMONY, ACCORD conformity, compromise, correspondence, accordance, consensus, accession, understanding, compatibility, uniformity, *meeting of the minds.

agriculture *n.* farming, crop-raising, husbandry, cultivation, agronomy, agribusiness. SEE FARM, FARMING

aground *a.* ashore, beached, stuck fast, stranded.

ahead *a.* in front, foremost, before, forward, advanced, leading, fronting, preceding, outdistancing. ANT. *behind, rearward, back.*

aid *n.* assistance, help, service, support, benefit, helping hand, contribution, benevolence, kindness, welfare.

aid *v.* assist, help, serve, support, benefit, contribute, pitch in, lend a hand, oblige, abet.

aide *n.* assistant, adjutant, *right-hand man, aide-de-camp.

aide-de-camp *n.* assistant, officer, secretary, *right-hand man, aide.

AIDS acquired immune deficiency syndrome, disease, disorder, immunological disorder, immune failure, sickness, illness, sexually transmitted disease, STD.

WORD FIND

virus causing: HIV, human immunodeficiency virus; HTLV, human T-cell lymphocytotropic virus. SEE MEDICINE, DISEASE

ail *v.* trouble, pain, distress, bother, upset, afflict, hurt.

ailing *a.* ill, aching, afflicted. SEE SICK

ailment *n.* illness, malady, affliction. SEE SICKNESS

aim *n.* intention, target, goal, object, purpose.

aim *v.* **1.** POINT direct, draw a bead on, level, train, zero in on, measure, eye. **2.** DIRECT ONE'S EFFORTS shoot for, go for, try for, plan, intend, aspire.

aimless *a.* purposeless, pointless, drifting, straying, wandering, desultory, haphazard. ANT. *focused, directed.*

air *n.* **1.** gas, atmosphere, oxygen, nitrogen, ozone, sky, aerospace. **2.** BEARING manner, attitude, deportment, appearance, aura. **3.** AFFECTATION pose, posture, pretense, manner, haughtiness. SEE ATMOSPHERE, WIND

air *v.* **1.** AERATE ventilate, let out, expose, dry, cool, freshen. **2.** ANNOUNCE PUBLICLY publicize, confess, profess. **3.** BROADCAST transmit, televise.

airborne *a.* aloft, in flight, flying, in the clouds, *in the wild blue yonder. ANT. *grounded.*

air conditioner *n.* AC, air, cooler, fan, blower.

aircraft *n.* airplane, jet, balloon, helicopter, dirigible, blimp, lighter-than-air craft, airship, airliner, zeppelin, *chopper, *egg beater, flying machine, *whirlibird, flying saucer, UFO, ultralight, Learjet, Cessna Citation, Rockwell Sabreliner, Grumman Gulfstream, Concorde, SST, Airbus, Boeing 707-757, Douglas DC-10.

WORD FIND

air hole causing sudden drop: air pocket
air traffic jam: stack
air washed behind: backwash, prop wash, slipstream
altitude measuring device: altimeter
approach to airport: approach, glidepath
automatic flying system: autopilot
boom after exceeding speed of sound: sonic boom
broadside wind hazard: crosswind
cargo, baggage and passengers: payload
climbing stunt turn of 180 degrees: chandelle
cockpit: cabin
course: flight path
cover over motor: cowling
crash-land in water: ditch
dangerous wind condition: wind shear
detracted landing gear and flaps: flying clean
distance required for safe landing: rollout
disturbed air: turbulence
double-winged craft: biplane
drive on ground: taxi
exhaust trail in sky: contrail
falling out of sky due to low air speed: stall
faster than speed of sound: supersonic, hypersonic
flap on trailing edge of wing: aileron, airfoil
flap that slows aircraft or increases rate of descent: spoiler
flashing white lights on wingtips: strobes
flight data recorder: black box
fluid-based controls: hydraulics
green identification light on right side: starboard light
high-speed wind stream: jet stream
ice accumulation: icing
international flight route: corridor
late-night flight: redeye
light, single-seat aircraft: ultralight
long body portion: fuselage
loss of engine combustion during flight: flameout

lowest possible speed before stalling: critical speed

maximum altitude according to weather conditions: ceiling

motorless plane: glider

navigation computer system: inertial navigation system, loran

nose forced up or down by wind: pitching

opposing wind during flight: headwind

oxygen deprivation over 12,500 feet: hypoxia

perfect landing: three-point landing

physics behind flight: aerodynamics

pitch and roll display: artificial horizon

radio landing aid: microwave landing system

raise air pressure: pressurize

rapid, uncontrolled descent: dive, spin

red light on left side of craft: port light

roll and yaw caused by wind gust: Dutch roll

rollover stunt: barrel roll

sideways motion caused by wind: crabbing

speedometer: air speed indicator

stunt flying exhibition: barnstorming

tail flap controlling up and down movement of craft: elevator

tail flap that turns craft: rudder

triangular wing: delta wing

turn: bank

UFO: bogey

unmanned, radio-controlled craft: drone

vertical stabilizer at tail: fin

workshop, shelter: hangar

SEE AIR FORCE, AIRPORT, BALLOON, DIRIGIBLE, ROCKET, SATELLITE, SPACESHIP

Air Force *n.* air defense, air power, strategic air command; A-4 Skyhawk, A-6 Intruder, A-7 Corsair, A-10 Thunderbolt, AC-130 Hercules, B-52 Stratofortress, C-5A Galaxy, C-141 Starlifter, F-4 Phantom, F-14 Tomcat, F-15 Eagle, F-16 air combat fighter, F-101 Voodoo, F-105 Thunderchief, KC-135 Stratotanker, B-2 Stealth Bomber, F-117A Stealth Fighter, P-3 Orion, Harrier.

WORD FIND

air attack: air strike, bombing run, dog fight, strafing

airborne early warning system: AWACS

altitude code for thousands of feet: angels

bombing over large area: carpet bombing

bombs: eggs

distress call: mayday

electronic jamming: music

emergency takeoff: scramble

enemy shot down, code: splashed

fire upon enemy aircraft: engage

gravity suit: anti-g suit

group: echelon, escadrille, squadron, wing

information gathering: reconnaissance

landing, wish to land, code: pancake

missile fired, code: fox away

one aircraft flight: sortie

over land, code: feet dry

over water, code: feet wet

radar confusers comprised of metal foil, strips dropped from air: chaff

reduced visibility, code: popeye

suspected carrier of nuclear weapons, code: purple

target position in relation to aircraft: clock code position

UFO assumed to be enemy: bogey

unmanned reconnaissance craft: drone

SEE AIRCRAFT, AIRPORT, ROCKET, MISSILE, NAVY

airhead *n. Sl.* idiot, dolt. SEE MORON

airplane SEE AIRCRAFT

airport *n.* airfield, airstrip, jetport, air base, aerodrome, landing strip, runway.

WORD FIND

ascent area beyond runway: clearway

baggage conveyor: baggage carousel

barrier, wall that shields passengers from jet exhaust: blast fence

centerline landing, takeoff strip: runway

control center: control tower

driveway leading on or off runway: taxiway

glassed-in enclosure in control tower: cab

ground traffic directors: marshallers

guide lights leading to airport: approach lights, sequence flashers; barrette

loading and refueling area: apron

luggage carrier, assistant: skycap

maintenance and aircraft shelter: hangar

maintenance crew: ground crew

off-runway waiting area: holding bay

overseeing agency: FAA, Federal Aviation Administration

pilot's weather and route info center: flight service center

radio-guided landing system: microwave landing system

tower personnel: air traffic controller

turnoff lanes off runway: rollout lanes

wind direction indicator: wind sock

SEE AIRCRAFT, AIR FORCE, DIRIGIBLE

airs SEE AIR

air sickness *n.* motion sickness, nausea, dizziness, vertigo.

air strike *n.* bombing, bombing run, strafing, carpet bombing, air assault.

airtight *a.* **1.** SEALED TIGHT hermetic, impermeable. **2.** INVULNERABLE, impregnable, flawless, sound.

airy *a.* **1.** BREEZY windy, ventilated, open. **2.** AT HIGH ALTITUDE lofty. **3.** LIGHT delicate, gossamer, diaphanous, thin, ethereal, vaporous, sheer. ANT. *1. stifling. 2. sturdy, solid.*

aisle *n.* walkway, lane, corridor, passageway, nave.

ajar *a.* open, unlatched. ANT. *shut, sealed.*

a.k.a. also known as, alias.

akin *a.* **1.** RELATED kin, kindred, agnate. **2.** SIMILAR like, resembling, analogous, identical, germane.

a la mode *a.* fashionable, in fashion, in style, stylish, chic, *hip, in vogue, *in. SEE FASHION, STYLE

ALACRITY *n.* [uh LAK ri tee] eager willingness. *He accepted his nomination for beauty contest judge with great alacrity.* SYN. eagerness, willingness, enthusiasm, readiness, fervor, quickness. ANT. *hesitance, reservation, reluctance.*

alarm *n.* **1.** FEAR shock, terror, horror, astonishment, anxiety, panic, trepidation, fight or flight response, apprehension, distress. **2.** ALERT siren, bell, horn, whistle, tocsin, call to arms, alarum, blast. ANT. *1. calm, nonchalance, reassurance.*

alarm *v.* **1.** FRIGHTEN shock, scare, terrify, horrify, astonish, panic, distress, startle. **2.** ALERT warn, arouse, caution, signal. ANT. *calm, reassure, soothe.*

ALARMIST *n.* [uh LARM ist] one who overreacts to a situation and spreads alarm needlessly. *Those who believe the world will end soon are generally brushed off as alarmists.* SYN. prophet/voice of doom, scaremonger, Chicken Little, Cassandra.

ALBATROSS (around one's neck) *n.* [AL ba tross] used metaphorically to symbolize a burden of guilt or disgrace; from the albatross that brought bad luck after it was shot and hung around the Mariner's neck in "The Rime of the Ancient Mariner." *Watergate was Richard Nixon's albatross.* SYN. burden, disgrace, cross to bear, millstone, misery, woe, load.

albeit *conj.* even though, although.

album *n.* anthology, folder, scrapbook, notebook, miscellany.

alchemist *n.* pseudo scientist, magician.

ALCHEMY *n.* [AL kem ee] the medieval pseudo sciences involving the transmutation of ordinary metal into gold, the search

for a cure-all medicine and an elixir to increase lifespan. Any seemingly magical process. *The investors quickly bailed out when they learned the company was something on a par with alchemy.* SYN. pseudo science, psuedo chemistry, magic, transmutation, sorcery, wizardry, black magic, black arts, witchcraft.

alcohol *n.* liquor, spirits, *booze, *firewater, *joy juice, *the sauce, *John Barleycorn, *hard stuff, intoxicant, solvent. SEE BEER, COCKTAIL, DRINK, MOONSHINE, WINE

alcoholic *a.* fermented, intoxicating, spiritous, distilled, inebriative, hard. ANT. *non-alcoholic, soft.*

alcoholic *n.* *lush, drunk, *boozer, *rummy, *souse, *sot, *wino, problem drinker, *rum hound, *bar fly, substance abuser.

alcoholism *n.* alcohol dependence, addiction, problem drinking, drunkenness, alcohol habit, substance abuse.

alcove *n.* recess, nook, niche, bower, bay.

ale *n.* beer, lager, stout.

alert *a.* on guard, watchful, ready, vigilant, on one's toes, keen, wide-awake, wary, attentive, *on the ball, *with it, sharp, active, lively. ANT. *asleep, *out to lunch, comatose.*

alert *n.* alarm, signal, warning, tocsin.

alert *v.* warn, signal, inform, notify.

alfresco *a.* outdoors, in fresh air.

algebra *n.* math, mathematics, equations, arithmetic. SEE MATHEMATICS

alias *n.* a.k.a. (also known as), assumed name. SEE PEN NAME

alibi *n.* explanation, defense, plea, excuse, *cover story, pretext.

alien *a.* **1.** FOREIGN strange, odd, unfamiliar, exotic, outlandish. ANT. *ordinary, familiar.*

alien *n.* **1.** FOREIGNER immigrant, illegal alien, outsider, refugee, stranger, noncitizen. **2.** EXTRATERRESTRIAL spaceman, space creature, *little green man, otherworldy creature. ANT. *native, citizen, local.*

ALIENATE *v.* [AY lee uh NAYT] to estrange; to cause another to withdraw; to turn one off. *His crude fat jokes would always alienate the overweight people in the audience.* SYN. estrange, distance, separate, come between, *turn off, turn away, disengage, shut out, ignore. ANT. *unite.*

alienation *n.* estrangement, distance, remoteness, withdrawal, disaffection, separation, dissociation, isolation.

alight *v.* settle, land, light.

align *v.* true, aline, line up, level, make flush.

alignment *n.* positioning, straightening, lining

up, adjustment, evening, sighting, calibration, fine-tuning.

alike *a.* like, similar, identical, comparable, kindred, corresponding, mirror images. ANT. *unlike, disparate, contrasting.*

alimony *n.* support payment, child support, allowance. "Disinterest, compounded annually."—Walter McDonald. "Buying oats for a dead horse."—Arthur Baer.

alive *a.* **1.** LIVING vital, animate, existing, *alive and kicking, organic. **2.** LIVELY alert, vigorous, vivacious, animated, spirited, bubbly, energetic, vibrant, bustling. ANT. *1. dead, inanimate, nonfunctioning. 2. sluggish, lethargic, slothlike.*

all *n.* total, totality, whole, entirety, everything, *bag and baggage.

all *a.* whole, entire, complete, every, each, each and every. ANT. *some, none, incomplete.*

all-around *a.* versatile, multifaceted, complete, diverse, inclusive, comprehensive. ANT. *exclusive, incomplete.*

ALLAY *v.* [uh LAY] to quiet, lessen or relieve. *The babysitter hoped a bedtime story would allay the child's fear of the dark.* SYN. reduce, quiet, lessen, abate, alleviate, mitigate, ease, slake, put to rest, sooth, assuage. ANT. *magnify, intensify, heighten.*

allegation *n.* assertion, accusation, charge, incrimination, claim, statement, complaint, indictment, insinuation.

ALLEGE *v.* [uh LEJ] to make an assertion, particularly without proof. *We allege that Ralph took the last cookie.* SYN. assert, accuse, charge, incriminate, claim, state, complain, indict, declare, insinuate, affirm, attest, purport.

allegiance *n.* loyalty, devotion, support, obedience, fidelity. ANT. *disloyalty, disobedience, betrayal.*

allegory *n.* parable, fable, moral, myth, story, tale.

allergen *n.* irritant, immune trigger, antigen, foreign substance, pollen, dust mite, dander, ragweed.

allergic *a.* immune sensitive, sensitive, susceptible, hypersensitive, averse to.

allergy *n.* sensitivity, susceptibility, hypersensitivity, immune defense, hay fever, aversion. SEE MEDICINE

WORD FIND
extreme alergic reation: anaphylaxis
red blotches: hives

alleviate *v.* lighten, lessen, reduce, relieve, ease,

mitigate, allay, soften, diminish, slake, assuage. ANT. *exacerbate, intensify, aggravate.*

alley *n.* passage, lane, cul-de-sac, deadend, walkway.

alliance *n.* **1.** UNION joining, association, affiliation, partnership, coalition, confederacy, league, federation, consortium. **2.** AGREEMENT pact, friendship, treaty, covenant, understanding, deal, contract.

allied *a.* joined, associated, affiliated, federated, confederate, cooperative, unionized, united, amalgamated. ANT. *independent, sole.*

alligator *n.* *gator, reptile, beast, el lagarto (Spanish), crocodilian.

WORD FIND
related: crocodile, caiman

all-nighter *n.* *redeye, *graveyard shift/duty.

ALLOCATE *v.* [AL uh KATE] to allot or distribute. *The board will allocate funds to help us meet the budget.* SYN. allot, distribute, mete, dole out, assign, designate, earmark, ration, appropriate, set aside.

allocation *n.* distribution, ration, allotment.

all-or-nothing *a.* uncompromising, unyielding. ANT. *accomodating.*

allot *v.* assign, apportion, mete. SEE ALLOCATE

allotment *n.* portion, distribution, share, part, cut, parcel, measure, allocation, ration.

all-out *a.* total, maximum, complete, no holds barred. ANT. *half-hearted.* SEE THOROUGH

allow *v.* **1.** PERMIT let, tolerate, put up with, grant, approve of, *give the green light to, authorize, *give the go-ahead. **2.** ADMIT acknowledge, concede, acquiesce. **3.** ALLOT allocate, give, set aside, plan for. ANT. *1. forbid, prohibit, refuse. 2. deny, reject.*

alloy *n.* mixture, blend, amalgam, amalgamation, compound, union.

WORD FIND
carbon and iron: steel
copper and tin: bronze, pewter
copper and zinc: brass
lead and tin: pewter

allowance *n.* share, allotment, pay, support, ration, appropriation, subsidy, stipend, recompense, contribution, percentage, earnings.

all-purpose *a.* multitalented, multifaceted. ANT. *limited, specialized.* SEE VERSATILE

all right *a.* **1.** SEE OKAY **2.** SEE INTACT, WELL

allude *v.* refer to, hint, suggest, imply, mention in a roundabout way, make an allusion to, *dance around.

allure *n.* attraction, magnetism, charm, appeal, sex appeal, fascination, temptation.

allure *v.* attract, entice, fascinate, bait, charm,

seduce, tempt, captivate, beguile, lure, tantalize.

alluring *a.* attractive, charming, seductive, enticing, fascinating, tempting, bewitching, captivating, beguiling, irresistible, tantalizing, magnetic. ANT. *repulsive, repelling, nauseating.*

ALLUSION *n.* [a LOO zhun] an indirect reference, an implication. *He made an allusion to Dickens when he said, "It was the best of times, it was the worst of times."* SYN. reference, mention, implication, hint, suggestion, casual remark, inference.

ally *n.* associate, partner, confederate, helper, collaborator, colleague, affiliate, friend. ANT. *enemy, foe, adversary.*

almanac *n.* publication, annual, forecaster, calendar, yearbook.

Almighty, the *n.* the Supreme Being, Creator, the all-powerful. SEE GOD

almighty *a.* omnipotent, invincible, invulnerable, all-powerful, supreme. ANT. *powerless, ineffectual.*

almond *n.* nut, kernel.

almost *adv.* nearly, just about, approaching, close to, well-nigh, virtually, verging, practically.

alms *n.* charity, handout, assistance, contribution, donation, benefaction, welfare, dole, aid. SEE CHARITY

aloft *a.* airborne, flying, skyward, high.

alone *a.* **1.** LONE solitary, isolated, friendless, separate, unaccompanied, abandoned, alienated, solo, desolate, lonesome, *solitary as an oyster.* SEE SOLITUDE **2.** PEERLESS unique, without equal, unparalleled, unsurpassed, incomparable, singular. ANT. *1. mobbed, crowded, grouped. 2. ordinary, common, *dime a dozen.*

along *prep.* beside, over the length of, alongside, parallel with.

ALOOF *a.* [uh LOOF] distant or remote. *He was strangely quiet and aloof, like a lone wolf.* SYN. distant, remote, reserved, *at arm's length, cool, standoffish, chilly, *stuck up, unapproachable, closed, unfriendly, unsociable, cold, frosty, detached. ANT. *friendly, warm, open.*

aloud *adv.* audible, loudly, intelligibly, distinctly. ANT. *inaudibly, silently.*

alpine *a.* lofty, alpestrine, high. SEE MOUNTAINOUS

already *adv.* by now, before now, previously, beforehand.

also *adv.* in addition, and, furthermore, plus, as well, *to boot, moreover.

altar *n.* platform, table, shrine.

altar boy *n.* attendant, acolyte.

alter *v.* change, modify, fit, adjust, reform, shift, adapt, revise, correct, amend. ANT. *maintain, keep.*

alteration *n.* change, modification, fitting, adjustment, shift, adaptation, revision, correction, amendment.

altercation *n.* quarrel, fight, argument, dispute, wrangle, *row, bickering, *tiff, squabble, *run-in, *words, falling out. ANT. *peace, harmony.* SEE FIGHT

ALTER EGO *n.* [ALL ter EE go] another side of one's personality. Also, a close friend or companion. *Everyone has an alter ego; Hitler liked dogs.* SYN. **1.** DARK SIDE, private side, id, counterpart, doppelgänger. **2.** SIDEKICK, *buddy, pal, companion, comrade, chum, confidante, soul mate.

alternate *n.* backup, second, stand-in, double, substitute, surrogate.

alternate *v.* take turns, rotate, switch off, change, reciprocate, vacillate.

alternative *n.* choice, option, backup, pick, selection, replacement, substitute.

alternator *n.* generator.

although *conj.* albeit, in spite of, notwithstanding, granting that, even though, regardless of.

altitude *n.* height. SEE ELEVATION

altogether *adv.* completely, wholly, totally, all told, in toto, utterly, entirely, absolutely.

ALTRUISM *n.* [AL troo IZ um] unselfish concern for others, humanitarianism without selfish gain. *Anonymous donation is a rare form of altruism.* SYN. selflessness, humanitarianism, benevolence, kindness, philanthropy, charity, big-heartedness, magnanimity, humaneness. "Disregarding one's own cause."—Eugene Brussell. ANT. *selfishness, greediness, piggishness.*

altruistic *a.* selfless, unselfish, humanitarian, benevolent, kind, giving, philanthropic, charitable, big-hearted, magnanimous, humane. ANT. *selfish, self-centered, greedy, coldhearted.*

always *adv.* forever, everlasting, perpetually, relentlessly, unremittingly, infinitely, eternally, unceasingly, constantly. ANT. *never, temporarily.*

amalgam *n.* mixture, blend, combination, amalgamation, alloy, compound.

amalgamate v. mix, blend, combine, compound, consolidate, fuse, merge, integrate, unite. ANT. *separate, divide, diffuse, disperse.*

amalgamation n. SEE AMALGAM

amass v. lump, pile, heap, accumulate, gather, assemble, collect, compile, save, acquire, *squirrel away, stockpile, hoard. ANT. *disperse, scatter.*

amateur n. nonprofessional, dabbler, dilettante, neophyte, tyro, novice, rookie, layman, *bush-leaguer, *lightweight. "A public nuisance who confounds his ambition with his ability."—Ambrose Bierce. ANT. *professional, master, virtuoso.*

amateurish a. unprofessional, unskilled, inexperienced, bumbling, fumbling, incompetent, inept, unpolished, rough, *bushleague, second-rate, insipid, hackneyed. ANT. *professional, skilled, polished.*

amatory a. sexual, loving, passionate, lustful, amorous, erotic, romantic, sensual, ardent, rapturous. ANT. *indifferent, cool, turned off.*

amaze v. astonish, stun, fascinate, flabbergast, dumbfound, shock, *blow one away, jolt, electrify, *curl one's hair, surprise, *bowl one over, *wow.

amazement n. astonishment, fascination, shock, wonder, surprise, bewilderment, disbelief, awe, wide-eyed wonderment.

amazing a. astonishing, fascinating, stunning, shocking, wonderful, surprising, bewildering, prodigious, awesome, unbelievable, astounding, incredible, marvelous. ANT. *hohum, boring, nothing special.*

ambassador n. diplomat, representative, emissary, delegate, consul, goodwill ambassador, envoy, agent. SEE POLITICS, GOVERNMENT

amber a. gold. SEE YELLOW

ambidextrous a. two-handed, switch hitting; adroit, skillful.

ambience n. atmosphere, air, milieu, environment, climate, setting, surroundings, aura, mood.

ambient a. surrounding, encircling, enveloping, encompassing.

AMBIGUOUS a. [am BIG yoo us] having two or more meanings or interpretations, unclear, confusing. *Politicians often make ambiguous statements in order not to offend anyone.* SYN. unclear, vague, equivocal, hazy, *clear as mud, indefinite, uncertain, obscure, duplicitous, dubious, questionable, lefthanded, muddled. ANT. *clear, unequivocal, certain.*

ambition n. 1. DRIVE determination, striving, spirit, initiative, enterprise, will, motivation, *get up and go, hunger. "The wings of great actions."—Johann Goethe. "Nets to catch the wind."—John Webster. 2. GOAL aspiration, aim, target, dream, desire, wish. ANT. *laziness, apathy, sloth.*

ambitious a. 1. ENTERPRISING aspiring, determined, hard-driving, *go-getting, aggressive, hungry, motivated, hard-working, striving, eager, avid, zealous, emulous, goaloriented, *high octane, industrious. 2. DEMANDING formidable, difficult, lofty, taxing, prodigious. ANT. 1. *lazy, slothful, inert.* 2. *undemanding, simple, humble.*

AMBIVALENT a. [am BIV uh lent] having mixed or contrasting attitudes. *Many people have ambivalent feelings about abortion.* SYN. mixed, conflicting, contradictory, wavering, vacillating, undecided, confused, of two minds, indecisive. ANT. *certain, concrete, *no two ways about it, settled.*

amble v. stroll, saunter, shuffle, ramble, *mosey, *sashay. SEE WALK

ambrosia n. food of the gods, food fit for a king, epicurean delight, delicacy, heavenly spread, gastronomical delight, pièce de résistance.

ambrosial a. fit for the gods, delectable, mouthwatering, heavenly, savory, delicious, tasty, toothsome, divine, sweet-smelling, fragrant, aromatic. ANT. *distasteful, disgusting.*

ambulance n. rescue vehicle, emergency vehicle, medical transport, *meat wagon.

ambulate v. move about, walk, get about, step, *hoof, range, amble.

ambush n. ambuscade, surprise attack, *booby trap, assault, mugging, hiding place, cover, blind.

ambush v. attack, jump, assault, surprise, *bushwack, waylay.

AMELIORATE v. [uh MEEL yuh RATE] to make better. *We could ameliorate environmental degradation by limiting population.* SYN. improve, make better, mend, amend, correct, upgrade, fix, rectify, relieve. ANT. *exacerbate, aggravate, worsen.*

AMENABLE a. [uh MEN uh bul] willing, responsive or agreeable. *He was amenable to change.* SYN. open, acquiescent, cooperative, obedient, tractable, pliable. ANT. *unwilling, closed-minded, disagreeable.*

amend v. 1. IMPROVE better, correct, fix, mend, ameliorate. 2. CHANGE revise, correct, edit, alter, revise, transform. ANT. *worsen, damage, corrupt.*

amendment n. **1.** IMPROVEMENT betterment, amelioration, upgrade, correction, reform, revision. **2.** ADDITION modification, attachment, addendum, supplement, adjunct, rider.

amends n. apology, redress, recompense, atonement, restitution, reparation.

amenity n. **1.** PLEASANTNESS agreeableness, civility, courtesy, geniality, politeness, manners. **2.** COMFORT nicety, extra, frill, luxury, convenience, pleasantry, refinement, creature comfort, facility. ANT. *1. unpleasantness, rudeness, nastiness. 2. discomfort, bare necessity.*

America n. United States, U.S., land of opportunity, New World, country, nation, land mass.

AMIABLE a. [AY mee uh bul] friendly, good-natured. *The dolphin has always been seen as a fun-loving, amiable sort.* SYN. friendly, good-natured, congenial, sociable, agreeable, outgoing, amicable, affable, approachable, good-humored, likable, cordial, warm. ANT. *cold, unfriendly, antisocial.*

AMICABLE a. [AM i kuh buhl] characterized by goodwill. *They came to an amicable agreement.* SYN. friendly, peaceable, affable, easygoing, gracious, congenial, neighborly, benign, amiable, harmonious. ANT. *unfriendly, nasty, aggressive.*

amid prep. amidst, among.

amigo n. friend, *pal, *buddy, chum, sidekick, companion, alter ego, soul mate, crony, *bosom buddy. SEE FRIEND

Amish n. Anabaptist sect, people, group.

amiss a. wrong, improper, awry, incorrect, mistaken, out of place, *screwy, faulty, askew, inappropriate. ANT. *right, correct, okay.*

amity n. friendship, goodwill, peace, harmony, accord, brotherhood, fellowship, understanding, concord. ANT. *hostility, antagonism, discord.*

ammunition n. *ammo, ordnance, shot, bullets, shells, munitions, arms, materiel, explosives, grenades, canisters.

WORD FIND

bullet-holding belt worn over shoulder: bandolier, cartridge belt

cartridge with no projectile: blank

case of projectiles fired from cannon: canister

cast-iron balls: grapeshot

dangerous fragments of: shrapnel

glowing trail across sky, produces: tracer

gun's bullet-storage receptacle: clip, magazine

one shot: round

stockpile of ammo: munitions dump

wagon that carries ammunition: caisson

SEE BOMB, BULLET, GUN, MISSILE, NUCLEAR BOMB, WAR, WEAPON

amnesia n. memory loss, fugue, forgetfulness.

AMNESTY n. [AM nes tee] a pardon, often of a political nature. *The war resistors were granted amnesty.* SYN. pardon, forgiveness, absolution, exemption, excusing, clemency, lenience, immunity. "The state's magnanimity to those offenders whom it would be too expensive to punish."—Ambrose Bierce. ANT. *damnation, sentencing, condemnation.*

among prep. amidst, amid, in, between, in the middle of.

AMOROUS a. [AM uh rus] loving, especially in a physical or sexual way. *Feeling amorous, the couple retired to the bedroom.* SYN. loving, sexual, romantic, seductive, passionate, *turned on, *in the mood, *horny, *hot, lustful, erotic, carnal, affectionate, *touchy-feely, demonstrative, sensuous, tender. ANT. *turned off, repulsed.*

AMORPHOUS a. [uh MOR fus] shapeless, without form. *Abstract art is sometimes completely amorphous.* SYN. shapeless, vague, formless, undefined, nondescript, characterless, nebulous. ANT. *defined, outlined, specific, distinct.*

amount n. **1.** AGGREGATE total, sum, bottom line, *whole shebang. **2.** QUANTITY number, total, count, mass, volume, measure.

amour n. affair, fling, tryst, relationship, dalliance, romance, liaison.

amphetamine n. drug, stimulant, analeptic, *bennies, *crank, crystal, *dexies, *pep pills, *speed, *STP, *tabs, *truck drivers, *uppers. SEE DRUG

amphitheater n. theater, coliseum, gallery. SEE ARENA

ample a. **1.** LARGE spacious, capacious, commodious, huge, immense, extensive, roomy. **2.** ABUNDANT sufficient, plenty, enough, copious, lavish, bountiful, more than adequate. ANT. *1. tiny, cramped, restricted. 2. inadequate, insufficient, small.*

amplify v. increase, heighten, intensify, enlarge, magnify, strengthen, augment, *crank, *beef up, turn up, boost. ANT. *decrease, diminish, turn down.*

amputate *v.* cut off, remove, sever, dismember, excise, lop off. SEE OPERATION

amuck *adv.* berserk, wild, violent.

amulet *n.* charm, talisman, good luck piece, fetish.

amuse *v.* occupy, entertain, interest, divert, beguile, distract, regale, engross, tickle, cheer. ANT. *bore, put to sleep, weary, cloy, depress.*

amusement *n.* entertainment, diversion, pleasure, pastime, distraction, enjoyment, fun, sport, game, play, merriment, *laughs, *jollies. "A metaphysical trick to deceive our anguish."—Jean De Menasce.

amusing *a.* **1.** OCCUPYING absorbing, engrossing, entertaining, diverting, distracting, beguiling, cheering. **2.** FUNNY hilarious, tickling, comical, silly, foolish, ludicrous, zany, side-splitting, whimsical, droll, jocular, *a scream. ANT. *1. boring, somnolent, dull. 2. depressing, grim, sad.*

ANACHRONISM *n.* [a NAK ruh niz em] a person, idea or thing placed in the wrong historical period, as a telephone in the 1700s. Also any thing or person considered outdated. *A television appearing in a Victorian novel would be an obvious anachronism.* SYN. misfit, incongruity, *square peg in a round hole, *fish out of water, oversight, mistake, goof.

analgesic *n.* pain reliever, anesthetic, numbing agent, painkiller, opiate.

analogous *a.* comparable, similar, corresponding, like, congruous, equivalent, akin, cognate, homologous. ANT. *dissimilar, different, opposite.*

ANALOGY *n.* [uh NAL uh jee] A comparison between two similar or dissimilar things. *There is an analogy between self-confidence and speaking ability.* SYN. comparison, similarity, resemblance, semblance, likeness, relationship, kinship, correlation, correspondence. ANT. *difference, dissimilarity.*

analysis *n.* examination, dissection, investigation, study, breakdown, test, assay, evaluation, review, interpretation.

analytical *a.* investigative, inquisitive, evaluative, critical.

analyze *v.* examine, dissect, investigate, study, break down, test, assay, evaluate, review, interpret.

anarchist *n.* rebel, revolutionary, radical, rabble-rouser, nihilist, insurrectionist, terrorist, agitator, "[One who] may want his neighbor to be governed, but he himself doesn't want to be governed."—George Bernard Shaw.

ANARCHY *n.* [AN ar kee] chaos, disorder; absence of government. *The riots brought widespread looting and anarchy.* SYN. chaos, disorder, confusion, lawlessness, rioting, turmoil, mayhem, bedlam, revolution, violence, collapse of authority. ANT. *order, law and order, organization.*

anathema *n.* **1.** THE DAMNED the accursed, the condemned, pariah, outcast, heretic, villain. **2.** CURSE ban, excommunication, denunciation, proscription, imprecation, damnation, condemnation. ANT. *1. the blessed. 2. blessing.*

anatomy *n.* structure, skeleton, framework, composition.

ancestor *n.* **1.** FOREBEAR forefather, father, progenitor, elder, procreator. **2.** PREDECESSOR precursor, forerunner, originator, prototype, antecedent, ascendant. ANT. *1. offspring, descendant, progeny. 2. successor.*

ancestry *n.* lineage, heredity, background, family tree, stock, pedigree, parentage, heritage, history, blood, roots, progenitors, forefathers. "A lamp to posterity."—Sallust.

anchor *n.* mooring, grapnel, hook, support, security, stability, hold, safeguard.

WORD FIND
heaviest, released from the bow: bower
hoist: cat, weigh
hoisting rig: capstan, windlass
light anchor used to free ship run aground: kedge
prongs: flukes
round, flukeless type: mushroom anchor
small: kedge, grapnel, killick
stone: killick
SEE SHIP

anchor *v.* moor, secure, fix, cat. ANT. *weigh anchor, release.*

anchorage *n.* mooring, landing, pier, dock, port, wharf, harbor.

anchorman *n.* anchorwoman, anchor person, newscaster, broadcaster, news coordinator. SEE TELEVISION

ancient *a.* old, aged, venerable, primitive, primordial, antiquated, prehistoric, antediluvian, primeval, timeworn, immemorial, outmoded, fossilized, archaic, *old as the hills, early. ANT. *new, fresh, young, contemporary.* SEE AGE, OLD, OLD AGE

ancillary *a.* subordinate, auxiliary, helper, servant, adjunct, accessory, supplementary. ANT. *principal, main, prime.*

androgen *n.* hormone, steroid, testosterone, androsterone, masculinizing hormone. SEE MEDICINE

ANDROGYNOUS a. [an DRAW juh nus] having male and female characteristics. *Many rock stars dress in an androgynous manner.* SYN. unisexual, bisexual, hermaphrodite, epicene, cross-sexual. ANT. *female, or male.*
WORD FIND
person with these qualities: androgyne
android n. robot, automaton.
anecdotal a. illustrative, characterizing, incidental, limited in scope.
anecdote n. vignette, story, tale, character sketch, narrative, illustration, account, incident.
anemia n. iron deficiency, chlorosis, iron-poor blood, listlessness, weakness, feebleness, fatigue, languor.
anemic a. weak, pale, pallid, wan, colorless, feeble, listless, fatigued, run-down, weary, iron-deficient. ANT. *robust.*
anesthesia n. numbness, insentience, analgesia, loss of feeling.
anesthetic n. analgesic, painkiller, opiate, ether, Procaine, soporific.
anew adv. again, once more, afresh.
angel n. **1.** HEAVENLY BEING cherub, guardian angel, spirit, archangel, seraph, divine messenger, fallen angel, spiritual being, immortal; Gabriel, Raphael. "The dispensers and administrators of the Divine beneficence toward us. . . ."—John Calvin. **2.** WONDERFUL PERSON sweetheart, saint, dear, darling, honey, doll. **3.** FINANCIER backer, supporter, *sugar daddy, underwriter, *meal ticket, benefactor, patron. ANT. *1. devil, demon. 2. jerk, devil, bastard.*
angel dust n. Sl. phencyclidine, PCP, drug, hallucinogen, anesthetic, narcotic, *crystal, *magic dust, *star dust, *angel hair, *cadillac, *monkey dust, *ozone, *purple rain. SEE DRUG
angelic a. saintly, heavenly, spiritual, righteous, seraphic, cherubic, virtuous, chaste, divine, beautiful, lovely, holy, ethereal, radiant. ANT. *devilish, demonic, dark.*
anger n. rage, fury, irritation, annoyance, outrage, indignation, ire, wrath, resentment, temper, venom, *dander, huff, petulance, vexation, passion, animosity, rankling, spitting rage, murderous rage, *slow burn, pique, snarling rage, bitterness, gall, spleen, virulence, ill feelings, infuriation, *piss and vinegar, *burning, *stew, *conniption fit, soreness, umbrage. "[Anger] boils at different degrees."—Ralph Waldo Emerson.

"Momentary insanity."—Horace. "A wind which blows out the lamp of the mind."—Robert Ingersoll. ANT. *glee, calm, affection, goodwill.* SEE ANGRY
anger v. enrage, infuriate, irritate, annoy, outrage, incense, *get one's dander up, rankle, *rattle one's cage, *yank one's chain, embitter, chafe, *burn one up, rile, bristle, antagonize, *raise one's hackles, blow up, *stir up, gall, *piss off, *bend out of shape, *get a rise out of, madden, *make blood boil, inflame, *make one hot under the collar, *miff, *steam, *tee off, *tick off, displease, irk, *get on one's nerves, nettle, provoke. ANT. *please, tickle, pacify, placate.*
angina n. angina pectoris, pain, suffocating pain, crushing pain. SEE HEART
angioplasty n. artery-widening procedure, catheterization, procedure, surgical repair. SEE OPERATION
angle n. **1.** BEND curve, crook, knee, vertex, elbow, acute angle, obtuse angle, right angle, reflex angle. **2.** POINT OF VIEW perspective, viewpoint, position, standpoint, slant.
angler n. SEE FISHERMAN
angry a. mad, enraged, infuriated, *pissed, irritated, annoyed, incensed, *spitting mad, bitter, *boiling, *stewing, burning, bristling, *gone ballistic, raging, *bent out of shape, enflamed, *hot under the collar, *miffed, *steamed, *teed off, *ticked off, displeased, provoked, *hot, irked, indignant, irate, galled, nettled, cross, vexed, wrathful, fuming, *mad as a hornet, *mad as a wet hen, *having a fit, *having a hissy fit, *having a conniption fit, *having a hemorrhage, livid, *blowing a gasket, *blowing a fuse, *in a snit, *having a cow, *spitting tacks, *seeing red, *popping one's cork, rabid, venomous, volcanic, fiery, explosive, peeved, *hot and bothered, *huffy, *in a lather, *sore, *in a tizzy, *bellowing fire and brimstone, *full of piss and vinegar, berserk, frenzied, snarling mad, *throwing a nutty. ANT. *pleased, gleeful, euphoric, placated.*
WORD FIND
Facial expressions and body language: scorching look; piercing look; keep-your-mouth-shut look; eyes narrowed with contempt; level stare; glower; scowl; withering glare; warning look; eyes blazing murderously; eyes sharpening; sneer; frown; snarl; smouldering eyes; lips curling with disgust; spasm of irritation crossing one's face; stony expression; face flushing with indignation; eyes bulging from

their sockets; face turning red, then purple; veins in neck standing out in livid ridges; crazed look; unyielding jaw; sticking out chin defiantly; looking about wildly; eyes raking the room; predatory expression; lips contorted grotesquely; smiling maliciously; face lit with bitter triumph; teeth gritted; lips pursed with suppressed fury; face pinched, tight; arrogantly impassive; rolling one's eyes; knitted brow; gesticulating furiously; nostrils flaring; vein throbbing at temple; veins in neck swelling dangerously; stomach knotting; throwing up hands with disgusted resignation; bunch fists; stalk out; storm out.

Speech, voice tone: grind out the words between clenched teeth; stammer with rage; spit out the words with contempt; spew out the words with malicious glee; mutter peevishly under one's breath; speak with grave deliberation; speak with brutal detachment; speak with bitter resentment; taunt; sputter; splutter; scream in exasperation; mock in a sniveling singsong; sibilate; sniff; snort; speak in ragged bursts; speak in strangled tones; gibber; croak; clip one's words; maunder into one's shirt; speak in stentorian bellows; jeer; hoot; speak in grudging tones; voice rising hysterically; voice thick with insinuation; voice tinged with menace; voice rising an octave; voice degenerating to a guttural rasp; voice ascending to a murderous falsetto; voice growing husky/hoarse; voice dripping with spite; snap, hiss, fume, bark, boom, cry, growl, grumble, huff, pant, roar, shriek, thunder, wail, yammer, blurt.

ANGST n. [ANGKST] a feeling of anxiety, especially that accompanied by unhappiness. *Fortieth birthdays often fill people with angst.* SYN. anxiety, apprehension, nervousness, uneasiness, dread, misgiving, foreboding, free-floating anxiety, blues, depression, sadness. ANT. *tranquility, peace, calm.*

anguish n. distress, suffering, agony, pain, grief, misery, torment, woe, dolor, sorrow. ANT. *joy, euphoria, pleasure.*

angular a. 1. BENT crooked, bending, elbowed, doglegged, cornered. 2. RAWBONED gaunt, bony, lean, spindly, lanky, spare, scrawny, anorexic, skeletonlike. ANT. *1. straight, flat. 2. fat, fleshy, beefy, plump.*

animal n. 1. LIVING ORGANISM beast, creature, mammal, critter, varmint, pet, beast of burden, game, stock, denizen of the forest, vertebrate, invertebrate, quadruped, herbivore, carnivore, ungulate, vermin, scavenger. "Agreeable friends—they ask no questions, they pass no criticisms."—George Eliot. "Man in a stage of arrested development."—Christian Morgenstern. SEE INDIVIDUAL ANIMALS 2. BRUTISH HUMAN pig, *Neanderthal, hoodlum, beast. See chart, page 33.

animal magnetism n. charisma, presence, aura, hypnotic attraction, charm, sex appeal. SEE SEX

animate a. 1. ALIVE living, breathing, vital. 2. ACTIVE animated, dynamic, vigorous, lively. ANT. *1. dead, lifeless. 2. sluggish, dispirited.*

animate v. enliven, breathe life into, vitalize, activate, invigorate, stimulate, quicken.

ANIMATED a. [AN uh may tid] full of life; lively. *After breaking the ice, the party-goers quickly became animated and then drunk.* SYN. lively, full of life, vigorous, lifelike, gay, energetic, spirited, active, vivacious, energized, dynamic, uninhibited. ANT. *stiff, lifeless, wooden, dead.*

animation SEE SPIRIT, MOTION PICTURE

ANIMOSITY n. [AN uh MOSS ih tee] feelings of hatred or hostility. *It's normal to feel a certain amount of animosity toward the tax collector.* SYN. hatred, hostility, enmity, antagonism, bitterness, ill will, dislike, hard feelings, animus, resentment. ANT. *love, affection.*

animus n. hatred, ill will. SEE ANIMOSITY

annals n. chronicles, history, accounts, annuals, history, records, archives, registers.

annex n. addition, new wing, addendum, attachment.

annex v. add, attach, append, join, incorporate, connect, merge, unite. ANT. *detach, disconnect.*

ANNIHILATE v. [uh NIY uh layt] to destroy utterly. *The dictator threatened to annihilate the rebellious town.* SYN. destroy, demolish, obliterate, crush, kill, wipe out, decimate, exterminate, liquidate, nullify *wipe off the map. SEE WAR

annihilation n. demolition. SEE DESTRUCTION

anniversary n. commemoration. SEE HOLIDAY

ANNOTATE v. [AN o tayt] to add notes or comments. *Authors sometimes annotate editions of their books to add clarity.* SYN. commentate, notate, intepret, footnote, expound, elucidate, gloss.

animal (continued)
WORD FIND

Animal	Group	Male	Female	Young
antelope	herd	buck	doe	kid
ass	herd/drove	jack	jenny	colt/foal
badger	cete	boar	sow	cub
bear	sloth	boar	sow	cub
bee	swarm/hive	drone	queen	
buffalo	herd	bull	cow	calf
camel	herd/flock	bull	cow	foal/calf
cattle	herd/drove	bull	cow	calf/heifer
deer	herd	buck/stag	doe	fawn
dog	pack	hound	bitch	puppy/whelp
elephant	herd	bull	cow	calf
elk	gang	bull	cow	calf
ferret	business	dog	bitch	
fish	school/shoal			
fox	skulk	vix	vixen	cub
frog	army/colony			tadpole
goat	herd/tribe	billy	nanny	kid
goose	gaggle/skein	gander	goose	gosling
horse	herd/stable	stallion	mare	colt/foal/filly
kangaroo	troop			joey
leopard	leap	leopard	leopardess	cub
lion	pride	lion	lioness	cub
monkey	troop/tribe			
moose		bull	cow	calf
mouse	nest			
mule	span/barren/rake			
otter		dog	bitch	
ox	herd/drove/yoke			
pheasant	bouquet/covey			
pig	litter/herd	boar	sow	piglet/farrow/shote
rabbit	nest	buck	doe	bunny
rhino	crash			
seal	herd/pod			cub
sheep	drove/flock	ram	ewe	lamb
sparrow	host			
squirrel	dray			
tiger		tiger	tigress	cub
toad	knot			
turtle	bale			
whale	gam/pod	bull	cow	calf
wolf	pack/rout	dog	bitch	cub/pup/whelp

annotation n. note, footnote, commentary, explanation, elucidation.

announce v. proclaim, declare, broadcast, herald, voice, trumpet, state, publish, notify, annunciate.

announcement n. proclamation, declaration, broadcast, heralding, voicing, trumpeting, statement, notification.

announcer n. emcee, broadcaster, reporter, *deejay, newscaster, anchor man/woman, *voice-over, herald, trumpeter, crier.

annoy v. irritate, pester, bother, disturb, *bug,

*get under one's skin, *get on one's nerves, vex, chafe, nettle, ruffle, gall, irk.

annual *a.* yearly, perennial.

annuity *n.* payment, allowance.

ANNUL *v.* [uh NUL] to nullifty, withdraw or invalidate. *The board voted to annul several outdated regulations.* SYN. nullify, withdraw, invalidate, abolish, cancel, eliminate, void, rescind, declare null and void, repeal. ANT. *ratify.*

annulment *n.* invalidation, nullification, cancellation, voiding, elimination, abolishment, repeal.

anoint *v.* consecrate, bless, make holy, rub oil on, smear with oil.

ANOMALOUS *a.* [uh NOM uh lus] strange, out of place. *An anomalous July snowstorm surprised us all.* SYN. deviating, abnormal, irregular, inconsistent, strange, odd, out of place, unexpected, atypical, quirky. ANT. *normal, typical, usual.*

ANOMALY *n.* [uh NOM uh lee] an abnormality or irregularity. *A snowstorm in Florida is an anomaly.* SYN. abnormality, irregularity, exception to the rule, quirk, oddity, deviation, rarity, departure from the norm. ANT. *the norm, regularity, same old thing.*

anonymous *a.* nameless, unknown, unsigned, unidentified, incognito, secret, pseudonymous, uncredited. ANT. *named, showcased, spotlighted.*

anorexia nervosa *n.* eating disorder, dieting disorder, loss of appetite, neurosis, sickness, food aversion. SEE BULIMIA

anorexic *a.* malnourished, emaciated, thin.

answer *n.* 1. REPLY acknowledgement, response, counter, rejoinder, *comeback, retort, reaction, feedback. 2. SOLUTION explanation, resolution.

answer *v.* 1. REPLY acknowledge, respond, counter, rejoin, *come back, retort, react, give feedback. 2. SOLVE explain, resolve. 3. BE ACCOUNTABLE own up to, be held responsible, pay for, atone for, rectify. 4. SERVE measure up, suffice, qualify, satisfy, pass muster.

answerable *a.* liable, responsible, accountable. ANT. *unaccountable.*

antagonism *n.* hostility, enmity, opposition, friction, animosity, discord, rancor, clashing, ill will, rivalry. ANT. *friendliness, agreement, harmony.*

antagonist *n.* opponent, adversary, foe, enemy, rival, disputant. ANT. *friend, colleague, advocate.*

ANTAGONIZE *v.* [an TAG uh niyz] to rile another; to offend or make angry. *Husbands and wives who antagonize one another often end up in divorce court.* SYN. offend, rile, repel, alienate, *piss off, oppose, rankle, *rattle one's cage, *yank one's chain, irritate, fill with hostility, anger, estrange. ANT. *befriend, smooth things over, soothe.*

ante *n.* wager, stake, bet.

antebellum *a.* pre-Civil War, pre-war, before the war, early nineteenth century, historical.

ANTECEDENT *n.* [AN ti SEED unt] what came before or previously. *The buckboard was an antecedent of the Model T.* SYN. forerunner, precursor, predecessor, ancestor. ANT. *descendant, successor.*

antecedent *a.* previous, prior, precursory, preceding, former, first. ANT. *posterior, subsequent, later.*

antechamber *n.* hall, foyer, lobby.

antedate *v.* precede, predate, antecede.

ANTEDILUVIAN *a.* [an ti duh LOO ve un] very old or antiquated; predating the biblical flood. *Few were interested in the politician's antediluvian ideas.* SYN. old, ancient, preflood, B.C., prehistoric, antiquated, early, primordial, primitive, Paleolithic, archaic, outdated, outmoded, passé. ANT. *modern, late.*

antenna *n.* 1. INSECT APPENDAGE feeler, sense organ. 2. SIGNAL RECEIVER aerial, *rabbit ears.

anterior *a.* 1. FORE front, forward. 2. PREVIOUS before, prior, antecedent. ANT. *1. back, aft. 2. after, following.*

anthem *n.* hymn, psalm composition, song, song of praise.

anthology *n.* collection, treasury, compilation, miscellany, omnibus, compendium, album, digest.

antibiotic *n.* medicine, cure, treatment, medication, remedy, preparation, drug, wonder drug, pill; amoxicillin, ampicillin, erythromycin, penicillin, streptomycin, sulfa drug, sulfonamide, tetracycline. SEE DRUG, MEDICINE

antic(s) *n.* foolishness, tricks, pranks, jokes, shenanigans, stunts, tomfoolery, romps.

anticipate *v.* expect, look forward to, foresee, predict, forecast, envision, apprehend.

anticipation *n.* expectation, apprehension, preconception, foresight, dread, prospect, contemplation, foreknowledge.

anticlimax *n.* letdown, disappointment, much

ado about nothing, *dud, *bomb, disillusionment, bathos, *comedown, fizzle.

antidepressant *n.* psychoactive medication, drug, mood enhancer, psychotropic medicine, therapeutic drug, *happy pill; amitriptyline, imipramine, Prozac.

antidote *n.* **1.** ANTIVENIN antitoxin, neutralizer, counteracting agent. **2.** CURE remedy, neutralizer, medicine, vaccine, curative, corrective.

antipasto *n.* appetizer.

ANTIPATHY *n.* [an TIP uh thee] an acute dislike, aversion. *He feels a certain antipathy toward telephone solicitors.* SYN. aversion, dislike, hatred, antagonism, animosity, revulsion, loathing, distaste, abhorrence, enmity, repugnance. ANT. *liking, attraction, appeal, affection.*

ANTIQUATED *a.* [ANT i kwayt ed] obsolete, out of date. *With the introduction of the automobile, the horse and buggy became antiquated.* SYN. obsolete, out of date, outmoded, old-fashioned, demode, dated, archaic, passé, bygone, fossilized, venerable, old-world, seasoned, primordial, antediluvian. ANT. *new, modern, *cutting edge, fresh.* SEE OLD

antique *n.* relic, curio, collectible, heirloom, artifact, antiquity, *hand-me-down, museum piece. "Remnants of history which have casually escaped the shipwrecks of time."— Francis Bacon. "Glorified scrap."—Max Gralnick.

antique *a.* SEE ANTIQUATED

antiquity *n.* **1.** PREHISTORY yore, olden days, dark ages. **2.** SEE ANTIQUE

anti-Semite *n.* Jew-hater, bigot, chauvinist, Nazi.

ANTI-SEMITISM *n.* [an te SEM i tiz um] hatred toward or prejudice against Jews or Judaism. *The Nazis in World War II strongly advocated anti-Semitism, with horrifying results.* SYN. fascism, Nazism, Jew-hating, anti-Jewish sentiment, chauvinism, bigotry, prejudice. "A noxious weed."—William Howard Taft. "The swollen envy of pigmy minds."—Mark Twain.

antiseptic *n.* germicide, disinfectant, sterilizing agent, alcohol, iodine, chlorine.

antiseptic *a.* sterile, disinfected, clean, sanitary. ANT. *septic, contaminated, infected.*

antisocial *a.* **1.** UNSOCIABLE aloof, misanthropic, unfriendly, reclusive, withdrawn, uncommunicative, hermitic, solitary. **2.** HOSTILE

antagonistic, depraved, indifferent, rebellious, destructive, troublesome, cruel. ANT. *1. friendly, warm, gregarious, outgoing. 2. friendly, kind, caring, benevolent.*

ANTITHESIS *n.* [an TITH uh sis] opposite, in contrast. *Love is the antithesis of hate.* SYN. opposite, contrast, reverse, converse, inverse, contradiction, contrary.

antithetical *a.* reverse, converse. ANT. *alike.* SEE OPPOSITE

antitoxin *n.* antivenin, remedy. SEE ANTIDOTE

antsy *a.* *Sl.* fidgety, restless, nervous, impatient, apprehensive, anxious, edgy, ill at ease, *on pins and needles. ANT. *calm, composed.*

anus *n.* rectum, *butthole, *where the sun don't shine.

anxiety *n.* nervousness, tension, angst, apprehension, jitters, *shakes, *pins and needles, uneasiness, *butterflies, foreboding, misgiving, worry, concern, uncertainty, *heebiejeebies, free-floating anxiety. "The essence of conscience."—Freud. ANT. *calm, relaxation, tranquility, ease.* SEE FEAR

anxious *a.* **1.** NERVOUS tense, apprehensive, jittery, shaky, *on pins and needles, uneasy, *sweating bullets, disquieted, fearful, edgy, *uptight, jumpy, *strung out, overwrought, *unglued, *wired, *worked up, ill at ease.

WORD FIND

Facial expressions and body language: wide-eyed, blinking nervously, smiling spastically, forcing a smile, lip-twitching, pacing, throat-clearing, gulping, swallowing a lump in the throat, face paling, nails dug into palms, palms sweating, stomach knotting, stomach clenching and fluttering, fidgeting, finger-drumming, sweating, hyperventilating, spasms crossing the face, swallowing dryly, teeth-grinding/gnashing/clamping, toes curling tightly in one's shoes, hand-wringing, clasping and unclasping hands, struggling to control one's voice, voice strained/constricted/quavering/strangled/rising an octave, adrenalin coursing through arteries, butterflies in stomach, nausea, jitters, heart palpitations.

SEE FRIGHTENED

2. EAGER *itching, impatient, *raring to go, intent, fervent, desirous. ANT. *1. relaxed, calm, cool, at ease. 2. apathetic, indifferent.*

anyhow *adv.* anyway, nonetheless, in any case, regardless.

anyone *pron.* anybody, one, everybody.

apace *adv.* swiftly, quickly, rapidly. SEE FAST

apart *a.* **1.** IN PIECES OR TO PIECES disassembled, dismantled, piecemeal, asunder, disassociated, scattered. **2.** SEPARATE by itself, alone, independent, individual, singly, isolated. **3.** APART FROM besides, with the exception of, save for, excluding. ANT. *1. together. 2. among, amidst, together.*

APARTHEID *n.* [uh PART hiyt] any practice of racial segregation, but especially that in South Africa. *A policy of apartheid separates blacks from whites.* SYN. segregation, separation, discrimination, racism, division. ANT. *integration.*

apartment *n.* flat, room, duplex, rental unit, walk-up, efficiency apartment, place, *pad, *digs, tenement, suite.

apathetic *a.* uninterested, indifferent, uncaring, unmoved, listless, unconcerned, impassive, cool, dispassionate, phlegmatic, unsympathetic, removed. ANT. *passionate, caring, interested.*

APATHY *n.* [AP uh thee] disinterest, indifference. *To bring about change in government is to first overcome voter apathy.* SYN. indifference, disinterest, uninvolvement, dispassion, impassivity, languor, unconcern, detachment, coolness. "The worst sin toward our fellow creatures. . . ."—George Bernard Shaw. ANT. *passion, interest, concern, involvement.*

ape *n.* primate, simian, gorilla, chimpanzee, orangutan, gibbon, monkey. "What an ugly beast . . . and how like us."—Cicero. SEE ANIMAL

ape *v.* mimic, imitate, mock, parody, copy.

aperture *n.* opening, hole, gap, slot, orifice, stoma, crack.

apex *n.* top, peak, tip, zenith, summit, pinnacle, vertex, acme, crown, height. ANT. *bottom, trough, rock-bottom, depth, nadir.*

aphorism *n.* saying, proverb, maxim, axiom, adage, epigram, dictum. "Portable wisdom."—William Alger.

aphrodisiac *a.* seductive, titillating, arousing, erotic, sexy. ANT. *repulsive.*

aphrodisiac *n.* *love potion, eyringo, *Spanish fly, oysters.

APLOMB *n.* [uh PLOM] confidence, poise. *She addressed the audience with great aplomb.* SYN. confidence, poise, self-assurance, composure, savoir faire, equanimity, sangfroid, air. ANT. *anxiety, self-consciousness, insecurity.*

APOCALYPSE *n.* [uh POK uh lips] destruction on a mass scale, as a holocaust; the prophecy of such. *Many await the apocalypse foretold by the Bible.* SYN. mass destruction, devastation, holocaust, end of the world, Armageddon, catastrophe, annihilation, decimation, disaster, *act of God, cataclysm.

apocalyptic *a.* prophetic, revelatory, oracular, prescient.

APOCRYPHAL *a.* [uh POK ruh ful] questionable, unsubstantiated, or suspected to be untrue or inauthentic. *Of the mass of UFO data gathered, much is apocryphal.* SYN. questionable, unsubstantiated, inauthentic, counterfeit, fictitious, doubtful, dubious, spurious, untrue, unproved, erroneous. ANT. *true, substantiated, authentic.*

apologetic *a.* sorry, regretful, remorseful, contrite, *on one's knees, conciliatory, prostrate, penitent, sheepish. ANT. *stubborn, self-righteous, defensive.*

apologize *v.* beg one's pardon, express regrets, retract, make amends, *crawl back on one's hands and knees, atone, beg for forgiveness, *eat crow, *eat humble pie, humble oneself.

apology *n.* regrets, remorse, plea, prostration, retraction, amends, atonement, *eating crow, *eating humble pie, repentance, acknowledgement, defense. "[T]he foundation for a future offense."—Ambrose Bierce.

apostate *n.* renegade, defector, deserter, heretic.

apostle *n.* missionary, advocate, champion, evangelist, proponent, preacher, witness, messenger, follower, disciple.

apothecary *n. Brit.* druggist, pharmacist, chemist.

apotheosis *n.* glorification, deification, immortalization.

apotheosize *v.* glorify.

appall *v.* dismay, horrify, shock, stun, disconcert, astound, frighten, take aback, harrow, disgust, sicken.

appalling *a.* dismaying, horrifying, shocking, stunning, disconcerting, astounding, frightening, ghastly, dreadful, harrowing, disgusting, sickening, upsetting. ANT. *wonderful, pleasing, agreeable.*

apparatus *n.* device, equipment, appliance, machine, tackle, mechanism, gadget, contraption, tool, *doohickey, *gizmo, outfit, instruments, contrivance, *thingamajig, *whatsis.

apparel n. clothing, attire, garments, dress, outfit, garb, costume, accoutrement, raiment, *duds, *threads, *getup. SEE CLOTHING

apparent a. **1.** EVIDENT visible, manifest, clear, obvious, plain, conspicuous, out front, open, unconcealed. **2.** SEEMING ostensible, probable, evident, possible, presumable, outward. ANT. **1.** unclear, vague, hidden. **2.** doubtful, uncertain.

apparition n. ghost, specter, spirit, phantom, spook, manifestation, poltergeist, wraith, presence, hallucination, mirage. SEE GHOST

appeal n. **1.** PETITION entreaty, plea, request, imploration, supplication, application, call. **2.** ATTRACTION charm, allure, charisma, sex appeal, glamour, *je ne sais quoi, *it.

appeal v. **1.** REQUEST plead, entreat, implore, ask, beseech, request, solicit, beg, petition. **2.** ATTRACT interest, tempt, entice, fascinate. ANT. **2.** repel, repulse, disgust.

appear v. **1.** COME INTO VIEW show, emerge, loom, materialize, issue, surface, present, arrive, turn up, *meet the light of day. **2.** SEEM look, be obvious. ANT. **1.** disappear, vanish.

appearance n. **1.** SHOWING presentation, emerging, arrival, materialization, manifestation, coming. **2.** OUTWARD APPEARANCE facade, image, impression, illusion, semblance, exterior, guise. **3.** LOOK form, shape, demeanor, countenance, air, character, mien, features, bearing, aspect.

APPEASE v. [uh PEEZ] to pacify or placate. We tried to appease the angry bear with a bucket of blueberries. SYN. pacify, placate, quiet, satisfy, assuage, relieve, alleviate, soothe, mollify, subdue, smooth over, defuse, conciliate. ANT. aggravate, exacerbate, antagonize.

appellation n. name, title, designation, label, *moniker, *handle.

append v. add, affix, attach, adjoin, annex, tack on. ANT. subtract, remove.

appendage n. adjunct, attachment, limb, member, extremity, offshoot, branch, tail, arm, tentacle.

appendix n. addition, supplement, addendum, appendage, codicil, postscript, epilogue, index, outgrowth.

appertain v. belong. SEE PERTAIN

appetite n. hunger, craving, desire, taste, ravenousness, sweet tooth, thirst, hankering, penchant, yen, passion, yearning. ANT. revulsion, repulsion, distaste.

appetizer n. tidbit, snack, starter, hors d'oeuvre, finger food, dip, cold cuts, kickshaw, olives, anchovies.

WORD FIND
bread, toast or cracker with spread: canape
dough casing filled with minced meat or vegetables: dim sum
drink, alcoholic: aperitif
herring fillet rolled up on pickle or onion: rollmops
Italian marinated vegetables, sliced meats: antipasto
raw vegetables served with dip: crudités.
SEE FOOD

appetizing a. appealing, mouth-watering, delectable, savory, delicious, palatable, inviting, tantalizing, toothsome, luscious, tempting, ambrosian. ANT. nauseating, sickening, repulsive.

applaud v. **1.** CLAP cheer, give a hand, give a standing ovation, hurrah, whistle. **2.** ACCLAIM laud, hail, praise, sing the praises of, commend, cheer, extol, compliment, give a pat on the back. ANT. **1.** boo, hiss, *give a Bronx cheer. **2.** pan, *give thumbs down, knock.

applause n. clapping, ovation, cheers, hurrahs, bravos, whistles, encores, praise, acclaim, plaudits, kudos, tribute, approval. "Often less a blessing than a snare."—Edward Young. ANT. boos, hisses, rejection, denigration, disapproval.

apple n. pome, pippin, fruit, codling.

WORD FIND
apple of one's eye: sweetheart, angel, honey, love, cherished one.
apple-pie order: shipshape, neat, good, orderly, just so.
bright green and crisp: Granny Smith
dark red winter apple: Winesap
late fall variety: Jonathan
red: McIntosh, Red Delicious, Rome (Beauty)
red winter: Baldwin
rough-skinned and mottled winter apple: russet
Russian: Astrachan
wild: crab
yellowish red winter variety: Northern Spy
yellow, large, with red streaks: Gravenstein

apple-polisher n. Sl. *brownnose, toady. SEE FLATTERER

applesauce n. Sl. hokum, baloney. SEE NONSENSE

appliance n. mechanism, apparatus, machine, instrument, contrivance, gadget, *gizmo, modern convenience, contraption.

applicable a. pertinent, relevant, germane, fitting, suited, apposite, appropriate, usable. ANT. inapplicable, irrelevant, impertinent.

applicant *n.* candidate, job seeker.

application *n.* **1.** UTILIZATION employment, use. **2.** REMEDY dressing, ointment, poultice, salve, balm, lotion, medication. **3.** REQUEST solicitation, inquiry, petition, appeal, form, resume. **4.** DILIGENCE attention, *stick-to-itiveness, zeal, devotion. **5.** RELEVANCE pertinence, aptness, suitability.

apply *v.* **1.** UTILIZE use, employ, implement. **2.** DRESS spread on, put on, administer, smear. **3.** DEVOTE dedicate, concentrate, *buckle down, *put one's nose to the grindstone, persevere, *give one's all, be diligent, *focus one's energies. **4.** REQUEST petition, appeal, solicit, requisition. **5.** PERTAIN fit, suit, relate, refer.

appoint *v.* **1.** DESIGNATE name, nominate, select, choose, assign, install, commission, fix, set. **2.** FURNISH equip, accoutre, outfit, arrange.

appointment *n.* **1.** DESIGNATION naming, nomination, selection, assignment, installation, placement, job, office, position, *gig. **2.** ENGAGEMENT assignment, rendezvous, meeting, date, tryst. **3.** FURNISHING equipment, accoutrement, outfit, accessory, fitting, trapping.

apportion *v.* allot, divide, distribute, dole out, allocate, mete.

apposite *a.* relevant, apt, fitting, appropriate, apropos, befitting, proper, suited. ANT. *inappropriate, irrelevant.*

appraisal *n.* evaluation, valuation, assessment, rating, estimate.

appraise *v.* evaluate, valuate, assess, rate, estimate, measure, judge, put a value on.

appreciable *a.* perceptible, significant, substantial, measurable, discernible. ANT. *negligible, insignificant.*

appreciate *v.* **1.** ENJOY esteem, value, prize, regard, respect, like, cherish. **2.** BE THANKFUL FOR be obliged, be grateful, give thanks, acknowledge, credit. **3.** GROW IN VALUE increase, gain, compound, enhance, inflate. ANT. *1. overlook, disregard, ignore. 2. depreciate, decrease, deflate, lose.*

appreciation *n.* **1.** ENJOYMENT esteem, regard, respect, liking, prizing, cherishing, affection. **2.** THANKS gratefulness, gratitude, acknowledgement, thankfulness, credit. **3.** GROWTH IN VALUE increase, compounding, inflation, escalation. ANT. *1. disrespect, disregard. 2. ungratefulness. 3. depreciation, loss, deflation.*

apprehend *v.* **1.** ARREST catch, capture, *nab, *collar, take into custody, seize, incarcerate,

jail. **2.** UNDERSTAND perceive, comprehend, see, *get the picture, recognize, know, grasp.

apprehensible *a.* understandable, comprehensible.

apprehension *n.* **1.** ARREST capture, seizure, incarceration, jailing, *collaring, *nabbing. **2.** UNDERSTANDING perception, comprehension, recognition, grasping. **3.** ANXIETY foreboding, dread, angst, fear, uneasiness, misgiving. ANT. *3. confidence, tranquility, reassurance.*

APPREHENSIVE *a.* [AP ri HEN siv] anxious about the future. *He was apprehensive about his final exams.* SYN. anxious, uneasy, nervous, *edgy, dreading, fearful, full of misgiving, filled with foreboding, distressed, *uptight. ANT. *confident, cocksure, assured, worry-free.*

apprentice *n.* trainee, learner, beginner, novice, *rookie, *greenhorn, student, amateur, neophyte, pupil. ANT. *teacher, mentor, master, guru.*

apprise *v.* notify, inform, fill in, brief, tell, advise.

approach *n.* **1.** METHOD procedure, modus operandi, way, course. **2.** COMING NEAR advance, drawing near. **3.** ACCESS way, entry, passage, course, drive, route, road, pathway.

approach *v.* **1.** NEAR come, draw near, close in, advance, loom, gain on, converge. **2.** APPROXIMATE compare, come close, near, resemble, match up to, be like, equal. **3.** PROPOSE recommend, make overtures to, offer, bring up, suggest, present. **4.** SET ABOUT start, begin, get the ball rolling, tackle. ANT. *1. withdraw, depart. 4. finish up, conclude, close.*

approachable *a.* open, accessible, friendly, warm. ANT. *reserved, uncommunicative, distant.*

approbation *n.* approval, sanction, commendation. SEE APPROVAL

appropriate *v.* take, confiscate, seize, steal, expropriate, impound, claim, assume, commandeer, *pirate, pilfer, pocket.

appropriate *a.* proper, fitting, suitable, correct, apt, befitting, becoming, seemly, right, apropos, *politically correct. ANT. *inappropriate, improper, incorrect.*

appropriation *n.* **1.** ALLOTMENT allocation, funds, stipend, allowance. **2.** SEIZURE capture, confiscation, impounding, stealing, *pirating, commandeering.

approval *n.* **1.** ESTEEM regard, favor, liking, respect, acceptance, good opinion, blessing, honor. **2.** SANCTION consent, support, endorsement, imprimatur, approbation, *the okay, *the nod, *the green light, permission, authorization. ANT. *1. disapproval, rejection, disrespect. 2. denial, refusal, rejection.*

approve *v.* **1.** ESTEEM regard, favor, like, respect, accept, bless, honor. **2.** SANCTION consent, support, endorse, authorize, permit, allow, ratify. ANT. *1. disapprove, disrespect. 2. deny, refuse, reject.*

approximate *v.* approach, come close, near, equal, match, parallel, resemble.

approximate *a.* about, near, close, around, rough, estimated, in the neighborhood, in round numbers, well-nigh. ANT. *exact, precise.*

approximately *adv.* about, close to, nearly, approaching, roughly, estimated, *guestimated, virtually, in round numbers, wellnigh, more or less, around. ANT. *exactly, precisely.*

appurtenance *n.* adjunct, accessory.

April *n.* "Love's spring."—Shakespeare.

apron *n.* pinafore, garment, bib, smock, coverall.

APROPOS *adv.* [AP ruh PO] timely; also, fitting or appropriate. *His speech was particularly apropos for the occasion.* SYN. timely, opportune, fitting, befitting, appropriate, relevant, apt, suitable, germane, pertinent. ANT. *untimely, inopportune, irrelevant.*

apt *a.* **1.** SUITED appropriate, fitting, relevant, germane, apropos. **2.** LIKELY inclined, prone, quick, liable, disposed. **3.** CLEVER quick, bright, adept. SEE INTELLIGENT ANT. *1. inappropriate, irrelevant. 2. unlikely. 3. slow, dull.*

aptitude *n.* ability, talent, flair, knack, gift, skill, capability, faculty, intelligence, proficiency.

aqua *n.* water, liquid, solution.

aquamarine *n.* bluish green.

aquarium *n.* tank, fishbowl.

aquatic *a.* marine, lacustrine, fluvial.

aqueduct *n.* conduit, pipe, channel, trough, watercourse, race.

aqueous *a.* watery. ANT. *dry.*

arable *a.* plowable, tillable, fertile. ANT. *barren, desolate, sterile.*

ARBITER *n.* [AR bi tur] one who judges or mediates. *The arbiter negotiated a settlement between the two conflicting parties.* SYN. judge, mediator, arbitrator, umpire, referee, intermediary, go-between, negotiator, authority, expert, specialist.

ARBITRARY *a.* [AR bi trer ee] random, discretionary, capricious. *He didn't go by any set rules; his decision was arbitrary.* SYN. random, discretionary, capricious, dictatorial, whimsical, fanciful, unscientific, autocratic, personal. ANT. *objective, by set rules, scientific.*

ARBITRATE *v.* [AR bi TRATE] to decide or settle. *An authority will be brought in to arbitrate the dispute.* SYN. decide, settle, mediate, reconcile, negotiate, judge, moderate, adjudicate, referee, umpire.

arbitrator *n.* judge, middleman. SEE ARBITER

arbor *n.* bower, pergola, trellis.

arboreal *a.* treelike, arborescent.

arboretum *n.* conservatory, greenhouse, hothouse, nursery, vinery.

arc *n.* semicircle, curve, arch.

arcade *n.* gallery, cloister, walkway, passageway, piazza, archway.

ARCANE *a.* [ar KANE] mysterious, secret. *Much of the universe remains arcane.* SYN. mysterious, secret, hidden, esoteric, enigmatic, incomprehensible, occult, recondite, abstruse. ANT. *known, knowable, comprehensible.*

arch *n.* **1.** VAULT ogive, dome. **2.** CURVATURE arc, bow, parabola, bend, crescent.

arch *v.* bend, curve, bow, flex, round.

arch *a.* main, chief, principal, top, primary, highest, greatest, foremost. ANT. *least, smallest, minor.*

ARCHAIC *a.* [ar KAY ik] ancient, antiquated. *The crossbow is an archaic weapon.* SYN. ancient, antiquated, obsolete, from an earlier time, outmoded, old-fashioned, passé, old-world, antediluvian. ANT. *modern, fresh, *cutting edge, new.*

archbishop *n.* chief bishop.

archenemy *n.* **1.** Satan, the Devil. **2.** CHIEF ENEMY adversary, nemesis, bête noire.

archeologist *n.* historian, anthropologist.

archeology *n.* history, anthropology. "Frozen history."—Gregory Mason.

archer *n.* bowman.

archetype *n.* model, prototype, original, template, example, exemplar, precursor, mold, classic.

archipelago *n.* chain of islands.

architect *n.* draftsman, designer, builder, creator, engineer, planner.

architecture *n.* drafting, designing, building design. "The flowering of geometry."—Ralph Waldo Emerson. "Frozen music."—Johann Goethe.

WORD FIND

borrowed style of motherland: colonial British and American highly ornamental style of nineteenth century: Victorian

classical Greek and Roman forms revived: Greek Revival, neoclassical, Renaissance

classical orders of Hellenic Greece and Imperial Rome: Corinthian, Doric, Ionic, Tuscan, Composite

domes, round arches and columns of early Greece: Byzantine

eighteenth-century style derived from classical, Renaissance and Baroque: Georgian

elaborately decorative European style from 1550-1700s: baroque

exposed beams style of sixteenth century Britain: Tudor

florid ornamentation, eighteenth-century France: rococo

French Gothic form with flaming tracery, fifteenth century: flamboyant style

futuristic chevron and zigzag style of the 1930s: art deco

Gothic revived: Gothic Revival

Italian, classically derived, fourteenth through sixteenth centuries: Renaissance

Mediterranean style characterized by horseshoe arches, domes, tunnel vaults, geometrical ornaments: Islamic style

pointed arches, rib vaulting, flying buttresses, twelfth through fifteenth centuries: Gothic style

retro style: revival

Spanish, eleventh-fourteenth centuries' style featuring elaborate stucco work and Arabesque designs: Moorish

SEE BRIDGE, BUILDING, CASTLE, CATHEDRAL, CHURCH, HOUSE

archives n. records, chronicles, annals, historical documents, memorabilia.

archivist n. librarian, curator, record-keeper.

arctic a. frigid, cold, freezing, polar, boreal. ANT. *warm, temperate, tropical.*

ARDENT a. [AR dent] passionate, highly enthusiastic. *Bill is an ardent fan of the Celtics.* SYN. passionate, enthusiastic, devoted, intense, zealous, fervent, feverish, torrid, vehement. ANT. *apathetic, cool, dispassionate.*

ardor n. 1. PASSION warmth, love, sensuality, desire. 2. EAGERNESS zeal, enthusiasm, devotion, fervor, intensity. ANT. *coldness, indifference, apathy.*

ARDUOUS a. [AR joo us] extremely difficult. *Mowing a golf course is an arduous task.* SYN. difficult, hard, taxing, demanding, laborious, burdensome, grueling, back-breaking, trying, strenuous, Herculean, exhausting. ANT. *easy, simple, *a snap.*

area n. 1. EXPANSE stretch, range, breadth, space. 2. REGION territory, district, section, locality, tract, stretch, ward, division, lot, sector, belt, quarter, zone. 3. REALM sphere, dominion, province, field.

arena n. 1. stadium, coliseum, amphitheater, stage, ring, hippodrome. 2. DOMINION field, area, realm, province.

argot n. jargon, lingo, cant, idiom, vocabulary, vernacular, parlance, slang.

argue v. 1. PLEAD contend, maintain, hold, assert, expostulate, evince, insist. 2. QUARREL fight, bicker, debate, haggle, quibble, *hash out, *lock horns, altercate, squabble, *have a row, *mix it up, wrangle. ANT. *agree, concur, assent.* SEE ANGRY, WORD FIND

argument n. 1. CONTENTION plea, assertion, proof, pros and cons, evidence, support, reasoning, defense, line of reasoning, grounds, case. 2. QUARRELING disagreement, fight, dispute, debate, altercation, *row, *tiff, *spat, uproar, squabble, imbroglio. "The longest distance between two points of view."— Dan Bennett. ANT. *agreement, accord, concord.* SEE FIGHT

argumentative a. quarrelsome, combative, cranky, contentious, polemical, scrappy, agonistic, eristic, belligerent, pugnacious, touchy, irritable, opinionated. ANT. *agreeable, passive, conciliatory.*

aria n. song, air, melody, solo, vocal piece. SEE OPERA

arid a. 1. DRY dried-up, parched, barren, dusty, sterile, bone-dry, desertlike, desiccated. 2. DULL boring, lifeless, tedious, drab, lackluster, uninteresting. ANT. *1. wet, fertile, humid. 2. lively, colorful, interesting.*

arise v. 1. STAND UP get up, rise. 2. ASCEND move upward, climb, rise. 3. EMANATE originate, spring, issue, well up, occur, stem from, crop up. ANT. *1. recline, lie down. 2. descend, drop.*

aristocracy n. nobility, noblesse, peerage, gentility, privileged class, gentry, elite, *upper crust. "The rich, the beautiful and well born."—John Quincy Adams. ANT. *peasantry, bourgeoisie, commoners.*

aristocrat n. nobleman, high-born, noblewoman, peer, patrician, blue blood, lord, duke, snob. "Fellows that wear downy hats and clean shirts—guilty of education and suspected of bank accounts."—Ambrose Bierce. ANT. *peasant, commoner, bourgeois*.

ARISTOCRATIC *a*. [uh RIS tuh KRAT ik] high-born. *He claimed aristocratic lineage, an assertion at odds with his rough appearance.* SYN. of noble birth, blue-blooded, well-born, genteel, pedigreed, mannerly, civil, worldly, sophisticated, gracious, gentlemanly, courtly, chivalrous, gallant, cultivated, refined, classy, snobbish, haughty, *snotty, hoity-toity, affected, pretentious. ANT. *bourgeois, lower-class, common*.

arithmetic *n*. math, mathematics, addition, subtraction, multiplication, division, figures, calculation.

ark *n*. boat; refuge, shelter.

arm *n*. **1.** LIMB extremity, forearm. **2.** BRANCH extension, offshoot, appendage, projection.

arm *v*. equip, furnish, issue, outfit, accoutre, provide, fit out, load. ANT. *disarm*.

armada *n*. fleet, squadron, argosy, flotilla, navy, convoy, flight.

Armageddon *n*. end of the world, final battle, final battleground, apocalypse, holocaust, war, conflict, showdown between good and evil, struggle, confrontation, devastion, catasrophe.

armaments SEE ARMS

armchair *n*. easy chair, rocking chair, recliner. SEE CHAIR

armed *a*. outfitted, equipped, accoutred, fitted out, *armed to the teeth, *bristling with arms, loaded, fortified, supplied, *packing a rod. ANT. *disarmed, unarmed*.

armistice *n*. truce, cease-fire, peace.

armoire *n*. cabinet, wardrobe.

armor *n*. protective covering, shield, sheathing, mail.

WORD FIND
SUIT OF ARMOR
arm, from elbow to shoulder: brassard
armpit plate: pallette
back and breast plate: cuirass
bearer: armiger, squire
chain: mail
foot: solleret
hand: gauntlet
head: basinet, beaver, visor, armet, sconce, helmet
jacket or tunic: jupon
joint: gusset
leg, knee to ankle: greave
neck: gorget

shoulder: ailette, pauldron
thigh: cuisse, tasset
trunk: tasset
SEE AMMUNITION, BOMB, BULLET, GUN, MISSILE, NUCLEAR BOMB, WAR, WEAPON

armory *n*. arsenal, depot, drill hall.

arms *n*. weapons, armaments, ordnance, munitions, armor, ammunition. SEE AMMUNITION, BOMB, BULLET, GUN, MISSILE, NUCLEAR BOMB, WAR, WEAPON

arm's length, at *adv*. at a distance, aloof, unfriendly.

arms, up in *a*. in an uproar, hostile, prepared for war.

army *n*. **1.** HORDE legion, mass, multitude, throng, swarm. **2.** ARMED FORCES troops, infantry, soldiers, division, battalion, ground forces. "A body of men assembled to rectify the mistakes of the diplomats."—Josephus Daniels.

WORD FIND
absent without leave: AWOL
bursts from antiaircraft guns: flak
clandestine movement: ratline
collective term for ammo, guns, explosives: ordnance
combat fatigue: shell shock
discharge for physical or mental problem: section eight
drab camp uniform: fatigues
eating facility: mess
emergency call-up troops: reserves
enemy ground to be won: bridgehead
enemy role during NATO exercise: orange forces
finishing off defeated enemy: mopping up
form up and come to attention: fall in
fortification, small, of concrete or sandbags: pillbox
friendly role during NATO exercise: blue forces
hiding material: camouflage
i.d. piece on chain: dogtag
infantryman, slang: grunt
items: materiel
jeep: hum-vee
kilometer, slang: click
largest unit: army group
liberty that ends at midnight: Cinderella liberty
lowest grade soldier: buck private
medal for wounds received: Purple Heart
mess hall duty: K.P. (kitchen police)
military store: PX, post exchange
missing in action: MIA

movement of troops: deployment

multilanguage message to return captured soldier, with reward: blood chit

negotiator sent behind enemy lines: parlimentaire

passing safely through minefield: breaching

phonetic alphabet: Alpha, Bravo, Charlie, Delta, Echo, Foxtrot, Golf, Hotel, India, Juliet, Kilo, Lima, Mike, November, Oscar, Papa, Quebec, Romeo, Sierra, Tango, Uniform, Victor, Whiskey, X-ray, Yankee, Zulu.

ranks, in ascending order: (enlisted men) Private E-1, Private E-2, Private First-Class E-3; (noncommissioned officers) Corporal E-4, Sergeant E-5, Staff Sergeant E-6, Platoon Sergeant E-7, Master Sergeant E-8, First Sergeant E-8, Sergeant Major E-9, Command Major Sergeant E-9, Sergeant Major of the Army E-9; (warrant officers) Warrant Officer, grade one; Chief Warrant Officer, grade two; Chief Warrant Officer, grade three; Chief Warrant Officer, grade four; (commissioned officers) Second Lieutenant, First Lieutenant, Captain, Major, Lieutenant Colonel, Colonel, Brigadier General, Major General, Lieutenant General, Four Star General, Five Star General of the Army

recruit training facility: boot camp

request for fire: call for fire, all available

shelter, lodging: billet, barracks

shield from enemy: defilade

shore foothold: beachhead

simultaneous fire at target from multiple guns: salvo

subdivision of a unit: echelon

sweeping line of gunfire: enfilade

tank, armored group: armored division

temporary ammo storage: munitions dump

trial for crime: court-martial

unit separated from larger group: detachment

units, in ascending order of size: unit (at least two soldiers), squad (10), platoon (4 squads), company (2 platoons), battalion (2 companies), group (2 battalions), brigade (2 groups), division (3 brigades), corps (2 divisions), field army (2 corps)

vulnerable troops at high risk: cannon fodder

SEE AIR FORCE, AMMUNITION, BOMB, BULLET, GUN, MARINES, NAVY, NUCLEAR BOMB, WAR, WEAPON

aroma n. scent, odor, smell, fragrance, bouquet, savor. SEE ODOR

aromatic a. fragrant, odoriferous, redolent, pungent, savory, scented, spicy. ANT. *unscented, stinky.*

around prep. about, close to, near, approximately.

arouse v. rouse, enliven, stimulate, awaken, stir, inflame, excite, fire up, shake up, disturb, incite, provoke. ANT. *put to sleep, lull, pacify.*

ARRAIGN v. [uh RANE] to bring before a court and accuse one of a crime. *The court will arraign the suspected murderer today.* SYN. accuse, call to account, charge, indict, incriminate, serve a summons, blame, *point the finger at. ANT. exonerate, absolve, acquit.*

arrange v. **1.** PUT IN ORDER organize, straighten, position, rearrange, sort, classify, alphabetize, systematize. **2.** PLAN devise, scheme, design, make preparations, map out, draw up. **3.** SETTLE resolve, straighten out, determine, come to terms. ANT. *1. mix up, jumble, mess up, disorder.*

arrangement n. **1.** ORDER organization, system, positioning, classification, lineup, configuration, design. **2.** PLAN scheme, design, preparation, provision, *game plan. **3.** MUSICAL COMPOSITION score, chart.

arrant a. notorious, flagrant, out-and-out, glaring, unmitigated. ANT. *inconspicuous.*

array n. **1.** GROUPING arrangement, alignment, lineup, order, muster, marshaling, congregation, collection. **2.** FINERY clothing, attire, dress, garments, *getup, *threads. ANT. *1. disarray, disorder, mess.*

arrest n. apprehension, capture, taking into custody, *collar, *bust.

WORD FIND

book in which arrests are recorded at police station: blotter

photo taken of suspect: mug shot

reading of rights, rule: Miranda rule

record of a criminal's arrests and convictions: rap sheet

SEE DETECTIVE, POLICE, COURT, CRIME, LAW

arrest v. **1.** TAKE INTO CUSTODY apprehend, capture, seize, *collar, *bust. **2.** HALT stop, check, obstruct, delay, slow. **3.** FIX hold, seize, absorb, engross.

arrival n. **1.** COMING landing, entrance, appearance, homecoming, advent. **2.** NEWCOMER visitor, traveler, tourist. ANT. *1. departure, exit. 2. native, local.*

arrive *v.* **1.** COME appear, show up, enter, disembark, land, take place, occur, happen. **2.** SUCCEED attain, reach the top, *make good. ANT. *1. depart, leave, exit. 2. fail, *blow it, lose.*

arrogance *n.* conceit, imperiousness, haughtiness, overconfidence, snobbery, hauteur, hubris, airs, cockiness, insolence, swaggering pomposity, egotism, presumption, condescension. ANT. *modesty, humility.*

arrogant *a.* conceited, imperious, cocky, insolent, superior, pompous, swaggering, egotistical, haughty, presumptuous, condescending, overbearing, hoity-toity, self-important, supercilious, *high and mighty. ANT. *modest, self-effacing, humble.*

arrow *n.* shaft, bolt, dart, projectile, missile.

WORD FIND
barb: fluke
bowstring notch: nock
case: quiver
crossbow: bolt
feather, put on: fletch
feather: vane
like an arrow: sagittal
maker: fletcher
user: archer, bowman

arroyo *n.* gully, gulch, stream bed, creek bed, trench.

arsenal *n.* armory, stockpile, munitions dump, depot, magazine, cache. SEE AMMUNITION, WAR, WEAPON

arson *n.* fire-setting, *torching, pyromania.

art *n.* **1.** CREATIVITY craft, artistry, craftsmanship, handiwork, workmanship, finesse, knack, flair. **2.** CUNNING slyness, artfulness, artifice, craftiness. **3.** WORKS OF ART painting, sculpture, depiction, abstract, simulation, representation, illustration. "By means of appearances . . . the illusion of a loftier reality."—Ralph Waldo Emerson. "An instant arrested in eternity."—James Huneker. "[T]he shadow of humanity."—Henry James. "[A] sublime excrement."—George Moore.

WORD FIND
SCHOOLS AND STYLES
absurd: dada
aggressive painting method: action painting
cubed and other geometrically distorted forms: cubism
cursive, flowing lines, swirling motifs style, late nineteenth century: art nouveau

dark realism, early twentieth century: ashcan school
emotion and color, focus on: expressionism
experimental or unorthodox: avant-garde
geometrical and curvilinear style of the 1920-1930s: art deco
graphic, optical effects: op art
hallucinatory, dreamlike, subconscious imagery: surrealism
idyllic nature scenes, France, nineteenth century: Barbizon School
modern, minimalist style, graffiti, cartoons: new wave
Monet's vague outline style: impressionism
nonrepresentational: abstract
nonrepresentational style that focuses on emotion and the act of painting itself: abstract expressionism
nonschooled: folk art
points or tiny dots creating a whole: pointillism
realistic, photographic: photorealism, hyperealism, tromp l'oeil, magic realism, representational
rich ornamentation, curved lines, sixteenth through eighteenth century: baroque
traditional forms: academic art
Warhol's (Andy) bigger-than-life depictions of everyday objects: pop art
SEE DRAWING, PAINTING, SCULPTURE

artery *n.* channel, vein, blood vessel, canal.

artful *a.* **1.** CLEVER adroit, skillful, ingenious. **2.** CUNNING sly, crafty, shrewd, wily. ANT. *1. unskilled, inept. 2. artless, naive.*

article *n.* **1.** STORY piece, news release, report, write-up, feature. **2.** ITEM object, thing, bit, piece, *thingamajig.

articulate *v.* express, enunciate, voice, pronounce, utter, make clear, elucidate.

ARTICULATE *a.* [ar TIK yuh lut] expressive, eloquent, well-spoken. *The talk show host was an articulate woman.* SYN. expressive, eloquent, well-spoken, intelligible, lucid, smooth-talking, fluent, facile. ANT. *inarticulate, tongue-tied, stammering, mumbled.*

ARTIFICE *n.* [ART uh fis] ingenuity or cleverness; also, cunning, trickery. *He succeeded in fooling us through artifice.* SYN. ingenuity, cleverness, inventiveness, skillfulness, wile, ruse, trickery, contrivance, cunning, craftiness, duplicity, machination, guile, artfulness, deceit, finesse. ANT. *honesty, artlessness, naivete.*

artificial *a.* **1.** UNNATURAL man-made, synthetic, fake, ersatz, counterfeit, imitation, manufactured, *bogus. **2.** AFFECTED mannered, forced, phony, unnatural, theatrical, feigned, *put on, pretentious, contrived. ANT. *1. natural, organic, authentic. 2. sincere, genuine, real.*

artillery n. gunnery, cannons, howitzer. SEE WEAPONS

artisan n. SEE ARTIST

artist n. **1.** EXPERT master, *pro, virtuoso, talent. **2.** ARTISAN craftsman, painter, portraitist, sculptor, technician, designer. "An exhibitionist by profession."—Vincent van Gogh. ANT. *1. amateur, tyro.* SEE ART, DRAWING, PAINTING, SCULPTURE

artistic a. aesthetic, artful, tasteful, graceful, ornamental, decorative, stylish, pleasing to the eye, brilliant, masterful. ANT. *crude, gross, unattractive, tasteless.*

artistry n. quality, skill, talent, virtuosity, creativity, flair, style, finesse, touch, feel, genius.

ARTLESS a. [ART less] unskilled, uncultured, simple, naive. *The man was as artless as a child.* SYN. **1.** UNSKILLED untalented, unschooled, inartistic. **2.** CRUDE plain, simple, primitive, natural. **3.** NAIVE simple, ingenuous, innocent, guileless, unsophisticated, childlike, genuine, direct, natural. ANT. *1. artful, skilled, talented, schooled. 2. artful, sophisticated, worldly. 3. sophisticated, self-conscious, insincere, unnatural.*

arty a. pretentious, *artsy-fartsy, highbrow, affected, assuming. ANT. *down-to-earth, unaffected.*

ascend v. rise, arise, climb, surmount, scale, levitate, soar, escalate. ANT. *descend, drop, fall.*

ascendancy n. supremacy, control, domination, power, preeminence.

ascension n. scaling. SEE ASCENT

ascent n. **1.** CLIMB rise, ascension, progression. **2.** UPWARD SLOPE acclivity, upgrade, elevation, incline, gradient. ANT. *1. descent, fall, drop. 2. declivity, descent.*

ascertain v. learn, verify, find out, determine, certify, *pin down, establish, uncover, discover.

ascetic n. abstainer, celibate, religious fanatic, monk, anchorite.

ascetic a. austere, abstinent, abstemious, self-denying, strict, puritanical. ANT. *hedonistic, self-gratifying, indulgent.*

ascribe v. attribute, credit, assign, charge, connect, associate, link.

ashamed a. embarrassed, humiliated, mortified,

chagrined, humbled, *red-faced, guilty, conscious-stricken, sheepish, abashed, disgraced, flustered, shamefaced. ANT. *proud, high and mighty, arrogant.*

ashen a. pale, pallid, gray, wan, white, sallow, cadaverous. ANT. *rosy, ruddy.*

ashes n. cinders, soot, embers.

asinine a. stupid, moronic, idiotic, sophomoric, silly, absurd, foolish. ANT. *brilliant, wise.*

ask v. **1.** QUESTION query, pose a question, interrogate, quiz. **2.** REQUEST appeal, solicit, express a desire for. **3.** INVITE summon, request, call upon.

askance adv. **1.** SIDEWAYS obliquely, sidelong, askew. **2.** SUSPICIOUSLY OR DISAPPROVINGLY disdainfully, dubiously, skeptically. ANT. *1. straight-on, directly. 2. respectfully, confidently.*

askew a. awry, aslant, sidelong, crooked. ANT. *straight.*

asleep a. slumbering, *snoozing, *catching some ZZZs, *catching forty winks, napping, dozing, *comatose, hibernating, dormant. ANT. *awake, alert.*

aspect n. **1.** LOOK air, mien, bearing, manner. **2.** FEATURE facet, side, angle, point, element, view.

aspen n. poplar tree.

asperity n. harshness, roughness, sharpness, nastiness, ill temper, venom, irritability, crossness, hostility, acrimony, surliness, irascibility. ANT. *mildness, softness, good cheer.*

aspersion n. disparagement, slander, abuse, defamation, innuendo, smear, slur, vilification, blot, denigration, mud-slinging, calumny.

asphalt n. bitumen, tar, pavement.

asphyxiate v. suffocate, smother, choke, strangle, throttle.

aspirant n. contender, applicant. SEE CANDIDATE

ASPIRATION n. [as puh RAY shun] a drive for or goal of some achievement; an ambition. *He had an aspiration of being a professional baseball player.* SYN. ambition, goal, drive, want, desire, dream, hope, longing, hunger, wish, aim, scheme. "The desire of the moth for the star."—Shelley.

aspire v. strive for, desire, try for, wish for, hope for, hunger for, thirst for, shoot for, aim for.

ass n. **1.** DONKEY burro, jackass, jenny, jack, beast of burden. SEE ANIMAL **2.** BUTTOCKS rear, rump, *buns, *butt. **3.** FOOL idiot, *boob, jerk, clown, *nincompoop, *dolt.

assail v. attack, assault, accost, jump on, lay

into, set upon, *rip into, *light into, impugn.

assailant n. attacker, assaulter, accoster, molester, mugger, aggressor, adversary, enemy, foe.

assassin n. killer, slayer, executioner, *hit man, *liquidator, sniper, gunman, *trigger man. SEE MURDERER

assassinate v. kill, slay, execute, gun down, *hit, *liquidate. SEE MURDER

assassination n. killing, slaying, execution, *hit, *liquidation. "The extreme form of censorship."—George Bernard Shaw. SEE MURDER

assault n. 1. PHYSICAL OR VERBAL ATTACK offense, affront, insult, beating, pounding, pummeling, mugging, molestation, rape, battery, violence. 2. RAID siege, blitz, storming, foray, offensive, invasion.

assualt v. attack, charge, storm, strike, beat, hit, abuse, pound, pummel, mug, molest, rape, commit battery, jump, punch, strongarm, assail, insult, offend, verbally attack.

assay n. examination, test, analysis, probe, investigation, assessment.

assay v. examine, test, analyze, probe, investigate, assess.

assemblage n. group, assembly, collection, cluster, aggregation, congregation.

assemble v. 1. PUT TOGETHER fit, piece, connect, construct, compile, puzzle out, compose, throw together. 2. GATHER amass, congregate, muster, band, convene, meet. ANT. 1. disassemble, disconnect, dismantle. 2. scatter, disband, disperse.

assembly n. 1. FITTING TOGETHER connection, construction, compilation, piecing together. 2. GATHERING mass, congregation, mustering, band, meeting, convention, crowd, multitude, mob. ANT. 1. disassembly, disconnection. 2. scattering, disbanding, dispersal.

assent n. agreement, concurrence, consent, acceptance, accord, approval. ANT. disagreement, dissent.

assent v. agree, concur, accept, consent, concede, approve, grant, acquiesce, go along. ANT. dissent, disagree.

assert v. state, declare, affirm, announce, aver, pronounce, claim, profess, attest, say. ANT. deny, controvert.

assertion n. statement, declaration, affirmation, pronouncement, profession, proclamation, averment, claim, avowal. ANT. denial, disavowal.

assertive a. outspoken, direct, forthright, forward, unreserved, uninhibited, blunt, brash, confident, assured, aggressive. ANT. shy, reserved, inhibited.

assess v. 1. IMPOSE levy, tax, dun, fine, charge. 2. EVALUATE appraise, measure, estimate, judge, consider, weigh.

assessment n. 1. DUNNAGE charge, tax. 2. EVALUATION appraisal, estimate.

asset n. 1. VALUABLE resource, possession, property, cash, inventory. 2. QUALITY strength, gift, blessing, advantage. ANT. 1. liability. 2. liability, handicap, disadvantage.

ASSIDUOUS a. [uh SID yoo us] hard-working, diligent, devoted. The governor has always had an assiduous striving for success. SYN. hard-working, diligent, devoted, persistent, constant, persevering, tenacious, unremitting, tireless, attentive, earnest. ANT. casual, lax, lazy, laid-back.

assign v. 1. DESIGNATE appoint, name, choose, commission, nominate, charge, entrust, cast. 2. ALLOCATE allot, distribute, consign, give, dispense, dole out. 3. ATTRIBUTE ascribe, credit, charge with.

assignment n. task, duty, job, lesson, homework.

ASSIMILATE v. [uh SIM uh LATE] to absorb, digest. Also, to adjust, integrate. The new math is difficult to assimilate. It takes time to assimilate in another country. SYN. 1. ABSORB digest, metabolize, incorporate, master, comprehend, take in. 2. ADJUST integrate, adapt, acclimatize, fit in, homogenize, *do as the natives do, *go native, naturalize. ANT. 1. regurgitate, reject. 2. reject, maladapt, separate.

assist v. help, aid, support, lend a hand, accommodate, attend, serve, contribute, collaborate. ANT. hinder, hamper.

assistance n. help, aid, support, a hand, accommodation, service, contribution, collaboration. ANT. hindrance, obstruction.

assistant n. helper, aide, deputy, attendant, supporter, collaborator, contributor, adjunct, aide-de-camp, gal Friday, right-hand man, *gopher.

associate n. colleague, co-worker, peer, partner, teammate, affiliate, ally, companion, confederate, consort, accomplice, friend, fellow.

associate v. 1. THINK OF TOGETHER link, identify, correlate, group, affiliate, relate, pair. 2. MINGLE WITH hang out, hobnob, befriend, fraternize, consort, run with. ANT. 1. disassociate, separate. 2. shun, estrange, alienate.

association n. 1. GROUP society, club, organization, fraternity, corporation, confederation, league, alliance, union, partnership. 2. FRIENDSHIP fellowship, relationship, affiliation, fraternization, companionship, alliance. 3. LINKING TOGETHER correlation, pairing, lumping together, relationship, connection, juxtaposition.

assorted a. diverse, varied, different, miscellaneous, sundry, mixed. ANT. *same, matching, identical, uniform.*

assortment n. miscellany, mixture, diversity, variety, potpourri, melange, jumble, mixed bag.

ASSUAGE v. [uh SWAY]] to relieve or soothe. *To assuage his appetite, he ate some popcorn.* SYN. relieve, soothe, ease, alleviate, mitigate, allay, pacify, calm, mollify, lessen, lull, *take the edge off. ANT. *aggravate, exacerbate, intensify.*

assume v. 1. TAKE ON take up, adopt, acquire, undertake, tackle, take upon one's shoulders, commit to. 2. SEIZE take, appropriate, usurp, commandeer. 3. FEIGN pretend, simulate, affect, put on, sham, *fake. 4. PRESUME suppose, take for granted, believe, hypothesize, imagine, think, guess, speculate, infer, suspect. ANT. *1. throw off, abandon, renounce 2. return, defer. 3. know, be certain.*

assumed a. 1. FICTITIOUS pretend, make-believe, sham, false, bogus, feigned, fake, phony. 2. SUPPOSED presumed, tacit, inferred, hypothesized. ANT. *1. real, true. 2. known.*

assuming a. presumptuous, arrogant, overconfident, self-important, imperious, egotistic, conceited, *nervy, vain.

assumption n. supposition, presumption, inference, hypothesis, guess, theory, belief, given, hunch, suspicion.

assurance n. 1. CONFIDENCE security, sureness, courage, boldness, self-assurance, conviction, *guts, pluck. 2. PROMISE OR PLEDGE guarantee, vow, oath, word, warranty. ANT. *1. insecurity, doubt, uncertainty.*

assure v. convince, reassure, guarantee, affirm, encourage, certify, pledge, secure, insure, ensure.

assured a. 1. GUARANTEED sure, certain, secure. 2. CONFIDENT self-assured, self-possessed, bold, assertive, poised, unflinching, unhesitating, cocksure, brassy. ANT. *1. uncertain, unsure, gamble. 2. insecure, timid, self-doubting.*

astern a. aft, abaft, rearward. ANT. *fore, front.*

asteroid n. celestial body, planetoid, moonlet, cosmic debris, meteor.

asthma n. respiratory disease, chronic wheeze, chronic cough, obstructive pulmonary disease.

astonish v. amaze, surprise, astound, shock, flabbergast, dumbfound, startle, take aback, *bowl over, stupefy.

astonishing a. amazing, astounding, surprising, shocking, breathtaking, dumbfounding, awesome, *eye-popping, startling, dazzling, bewildering, extraordinary. ANT. *humdrum, expected.*

astonishment n. amazement, surprise, shock, awe, bewilderment, wonder, stupefaction, marvel.

astound v. astonish, amaze, bewilder, shock, surprise, flabbergast, dumbfound, startle, take aback, *bowl over, stupefy, boggle, render speechless, electrify, stagger, confound, *blow one's mind.

astounding a. astonishing, amazing, bewildering, shocking, surprising, startling, *eye-popping, stupefying, mind-boggling, electrifying, staggering, confounding, *mind-blowing, wondrous. ANT. *ho-hum, boring, ordinary.*

astray a. adrift, off course, lost, afield, wrong, *off the mark, *off in left field. ANT. *right-on, accurate, *on the mark.*

astringent a. biting, harsh, sharp, cutting, acerbic, severe, rough, acrid. ANT. *mild, soft.*

astrology n. horoscopy, reading of the stars, divination. "The excellent foppery of the world."—Shakespeare.

WORD FIND

birth, zodiacal sign rising in the east at time of one's: ascent

chart of positions of planets, stars, relationship to birth: horoscope

constellations and signs: Aries (The Ram); Taurus (The Bull); Gemini (The Twins); Cancer (The Crab); Leo (The Lion); Virgo (The Virgin); Libra (The Balance); Scorpio (The Scorpion); Sagittarius (The Archer); Capricorn (The Goat); Aquarius (The Water Bearer); Pisces (The Fishes)

diagram: scheme

legendary astrologer: Merlin

one of twelve sectors in celestial sphere: house

pathway of planets, divided into twelve astrological signs: zodiac

table of positions of stars and planets at specific times: ephemeris
transitional period from one zodiac sign to another: cusp

astronaut *n.* spaceman, cosmonaut, sailor of the stars.

astronomer *n.* stargazer, cosmologist, astrophysicist.

astronomy *n.* stargazing, cosmology, astrophysics.

WORD FIND
eclipse, or passage of one celestial body in front of another: occultation
great circle spanning horizons: meridian
location of celestial object in sky: azimuth, declination, right ascension
path of sun on celestial sphere: ecliptic
point of sky directly overhead: zenith
star motion unrelated to earth's rotation: proper motion
table showing future positions of celestial objects: ephemeris
unit of distance, by speed of light: light year, 5,880,000,000,000 miles; parsec, 3.26 light years
unit of distance, equal to that from the earth to the sun: astronomical unit, 92,900,000 miles
SEE COMET, CONSTELLATION, METEOR, MOON, PLANET, SPACE, STAR

ASTUTE *a.* [uh STOOT] clever, sharp or cunning. *The successful businessman must have an astute mind.* SYN. clever, sharp, cunning, crafty, shrewd, wily, quick, keen, intelligent, sagacious, brilliant, bright, *on the ball. ANT. *dumb, naive, retarded, slow, obtuse.*

asunder *a.* apart, separate, in pieces.

asylum *n.* 1. SANCTUARY refuge, shelter, haven, safe harbor, hospice. 2. HOSPITAL psychiatric hospital, sanitarium, mental institution, insane asylum, *nut house, *booby hatch, *laughing academy, *loony bin, *madhouse.

ASYMMETRICAL *a.* [a si MET ri kul] uneven, unbalanced, or lacking correspondence between two sides. *He described the shape as asymmetrical, that is, a little different on each side.* SYN. uneven, unbalanced, lacking correspondence, lacking coordination, contrasting, not proportionate, not uniform, disproportional, unequal. ANT. *symmetrical, corresponding, matching.*

ATHEISM *n.* [A thee iz um] disbelief in God. *Atheism is the disbelief or denial of the existence of a higher power.* SYN. disbelief, denial, skepticism, rejection of God, impiety, rationalism, freethinking, agnosticism, nihilism, irreverence. "The vice of a few intelligent people."—Voltaire.

atheist *n.* nonbeliever, agnostic, skeptic, free thinker, infidel, *doubting Thomas, heathen. "A man who has no invisible means of support."—John Buchan. "A man who believes himself an accident."—Francis Thompson. "An orphaned heart."—Jean Paul Richter. ANT. *believer, the faithful.* SEE AGNOSTIC

athlete *n.* *jock, competitor, sportsman, champion. SEE SPORT

athletic *a.* strong, fit, skilled, muscular, mesomorphic, sthenic, strapping, vigorous, robust, hardy, staunch, brawny, stout, wiry, supple, coordinated. ANT. *weak, feeble, sedentary, asthenic.*

WORD FIND
competition combo of five track and field events: pentathlon
competition combo of skiing and rifle-dshooting: biathlon
competition combo of swimming, biking and long-distance running: triathalon, *iron man contest
competition combo of ten track and field events: decathlon

atmosphere *n.* 1. AMBIENCE aura, surroundings, air, *vibes, feeling, environment. 2. SKY air, heavens, smog, biosphere.

WORD FIND
ion-rich layer, reflects radio waves, in thermosphere: ionosphere
layer of oxygen in stratosphere, protects earth from ultraviolet radiation: ozone layer
rising column of warm air: thermal
stratum from 0-10 miles up: troposphere
stratum from 10-30 miles up: stratosphere
stratum from 30-50 miles up: mesosphere
stratum from 50-300 miles up: thermosphere
stratum from 300 miles to space: exosphere
trapping of solar radiation and heat by carbon dioxide buildup: greenhouse effect
SEE AIR, RAIN, SNOW, WEATHER, WIND

atoll *n.* coral island.

atom *n.* particle, jot, bit, iota, scintilla, shred, bit. "A specter threatening us with annihilation."—Max Born. SEE SCIENCE

atomic *a.* SEE NUCLEAR

atomic bomb *n.* SEE NUCLEAR BOMB

atomize *v.* separate, disintegrate, vaporize, spray, pulverize.

ATONE *v.* [uh TONE] to make up for a bad deed; to make amends. *Atone for your sins.* SYN. amend, make amends, redeem, do penance, repent, confess, expiate, make reparations, shrive.

atonement *n.* amends, reparations, redemption, expiation, penance, restitution, compensation, redress. "The blood of Jesus Christ . . ."—Bible, John 1:7.

atrium *n.* court.

atrocious *a.* evil, brutal, appalling, cruel, bad, monstrous, unspeakable, vicious, despicable, horrible, abominable, heinous, outrageous. ANT. *good, pleasant, lovely, benevolent.*

ATROCITY *n.* [uh TRAW suh tee] a cruelty, brutality or outrageous thing or act. *The drive-by shooting is an atrocity that originated during prohibition.* SYN. cruelty, brutality, outrage, monstrosity, unspeakable act, horror, savagery, barbarity, crime, abomination. ANT. *kindness, good deed.*

atrophy *n.* degeneration, wasting, deterioration, withering, emaciation, decline, weakening.

atrophy *v.* degenerate, waste, deteriorate, wither, emaciate, decline, weaken.

attaché *v.* 1. FASTEN tie, stick, secure, bind, link, hook, affix, connect, tack, pin. 2. AFFILIATE join, associate, enlist. 3. ASCRIBE attribute, assign, accredit, apply, place. ANT. *1. detach, loosen, free. 2. drop out, quit, dissociate. 3. take, deflect.*

attaché *n.* consul, envoy, aide. SEE DIPLOMAT

attachment *n.* 1. FASTENING tying, connection, joining. 2. DEVOTION regard, affection, crush, affinity, bond, esteem, fondness, love. 3. ACCESSORY appendage, appurtenance, fixture, addition, extension, supplement. ANT. *1. detachment, separation. 2. repulsion, aversion.*

attack *n.* 1. ASSAULT offensive, raid, invasion, siege, ambush, blitz, aggression, strike, incursion, onslaught. 2. ONSET OR RECURRENCE OF AN ILLNESS bout, relapse, throe, seizure, convulsion, spell, turn for the worse.

attack *v.* 1. ASSAULT strike, jump on, raid, besiege, invade, ambush, assail, pounce on, molest, set upon, take the offensive, aggress, mug. 2. VERBALLY ASSAULT *rip into, *tear apart, criticize, abuse, malign, bash, defame, scold, *rake over the coals, damn, censure, *dis, *jump down one's throat, impugn, *bad-mouth, denounce, revile. 3. TO BEGIN WORK ON tackle, dive into, undertake, *jump into with both feet. ANT. *1. retreat, defend,*

lay low. *2. flatter, compliment, praise. 3. procrastinate, avoid.*

attacker *n.* assailant, aggressor, offender.

attain *v.* achieve, accomplish, get, procure, secure, acquire, obtain, realize, fulfill, *make it, win. ANT. *fail, lose, fall short.*

attainment *n.* achievement, accomplishment, getting, procurement, securing, acquirement, obtaining, realization, fulfillment, winning, success, coup, skill.

attempt *n.* try, endeavor, shot, *crack, undertaking, *stab, *the old college try, venture, bid.

attempt *v.* try, endeavor, make an effort, undertake, take a shot at it, *take a crack at it, *take a stab at it, *give it the old college try, venture, make a bid for it, strive.

attend *v.* 1. LOOK AFTER minister to, serve, tend, take care of, nurse, assist, doctor. 2. TO BE PRESENT appear, show up, go to, turn up. 3. ACCOMPANY come with, go hand in hand, escort, be associated with.

attendance *n.* 1. PRESENCE appearance. 2. TURNOUT crowd, house, audience.

attendant *n.* servant, aide, assistant, orderly, steward, valet, consort, escort.

attention *n.* 1. CONCENTRATION mindfulness, consciousness, awareness, heed, notice, thoughtfulness, regard. 2. OBSERVATION notice, recognition, regard, consideration, scrutiny. ANT. *1. absent-mindedness, abstraction, inattention. 2. oversight, disregard.*

attention deficit disorder *n.* ADD, learning disorder, short attention span, hyperactivity.

attentions *n.* consideration, courtesy, devotion, civility, care, respect, service.

attentive *a.* 1. MINDFUL observant, alert, conscious, aware, sharp, thoughtful, noticing, keen, heedful, watchful. 2. CONSIDERATE thoughtful, gracious, courteous, solicitous, accommodating, gallant. ANT. *1. neglectful, unobservant, heedless. 2. inconsiderate, rude, negligent.*

attenuate *v.* thin, dilute, weaken, rarefy, dilute, lessen, decrease, water down, diminish. ANT. *fortify, strengthen, intensify.*

attest *v.* bear witness, certify, verify, confirm, substantiate, support, bear out, testify, warrant, vouch for, pledge, affirm, swear, authenticate. ANT. *refute, deny, belie.*

attic *n.* garret, loft, dormer, clerestory, storage room.

attire *n.* dress, clothing, apparel, garb, costume, raiment, *duds, *togs, outfit, garments, *threads.

attire v. dress, clothe, garb, deck out, fit out, outfit, *doll up, costume, accoutre.

attitude n. **1.** OUTLOOK mind, disposition, frame of mind, temperament, feeling, view, perspective, *mindset, demeanor, bias. **2.** POSTURE stance, manner, bearing, pose, mien, carriage, air.

attitude problem n. *hair across the ass, *chip on one's shoulder.

attorney n. counselor, legal representative, DA, barrister, solicitor, *ambulance chaser. SEE LAWYER, LAW, COURT

attract v. **1.** DRAW pull, magnetize. **2.** ALLURE lure, invite, tempt, interest, charm, captivate, fascinate, beguile, bewitch, *turn on, *spellbind. ANT. *1*. *repel, repulse*. *2*. *repel, repulse, turn off*.

attraction n. appeal, temptation, magnetism, affinity, pull, charm, interest, allure, bewitchment, fascination, enticement, *chemistry, charisma. ANT. *repellant, repulsion, aversion*.

attractive a. appealing, charming, enticing, *nice, beautiful, handsome, winning, fascinating, magnetic, charismatic, tempting, alluring, bewitching, fetching, cute, adorable, pretty, stunning, sexy, comely, *easy on the eyes. ANT. *repulsive, repellant, ugly*.

attribute n. quality, characteristic, trait, feature, distinction, quirk, facet, virtue.

attribute v. assign, ascribe, credit, charge with, blame, impute, account for.

ATTRITION n. [uh TRISH un] a wearing away or reduction, loss by natural means. *The company lost more employees by attrition than by forced layoffs.* SYN. weakening, erosion, reduction, decimation, disintegration, diminution, dwindling, decline. ANT. *buildup, reinforcement, fortification*.

attune v. adapt, adjust, harmonize, acclimate, assimilate.

atypical a. unusual, uncommon, untypical, odd, irregular, abnormal. ANT. *typical, usual*.

AU COURANT a. [o koo RAHN] well-informed, up-to-date. *On the latest fashion, she was always au courant.* SYN. informed, up-to-date, current, *hip, enlightened, aware, *up to speed. ANT. *behind the times*.

auction n. sale, vendue, sell-off.

auburn a. reddish-brown, golden-brown, nut brown, chestnut brown, henna.

AUDACIOUS a. [aw DAY shus] brave, bold. Also, not affected by shame or a sense of propriety. *The soldiers made an audacious foray into enemy territory.* SYN. **1.** BRAVE,

bold, daring, plucky, *ballsy, courageous, dauntless, stalwart, unflinching, *gutsy, adventurous, intrepid. **2.** SHAMELESS, brazen, outrageous, cheeky, brassy, impertinent, rude, forward, insolent, saucy, *ballsy. ANT. *1*. *cowardly, fearful, timid*. *2*. *deferential, polite*.

audacity n. **1.** COURAGE bravery, daring, nerve, pluck, backbone, *guts, *spine, grit, derring-do, mettle, boldness. **2.** SHAMELESSNESS brashness, impudence, effrontery, *gall, *nerve, *cheek, arrogance, impertinence, brass, presumption. ANT. *1*. *cowardice, fear, spinelessness*. *2*. *courtesy, decorum, propriety*.

audible a. perceptible, hearable, discernible, intelligible, clear. ANT. *inaudible, silent, unintelligible*.

audience n. spectators, crowd, onlookers, viewers, house, fans, patrons, turnout, market.

audit n. examination, accounting, review, investigation.

audition n. tryout, trial, hearing, *open mike.

auditor n. accountant, inspector, analyst, bookkeeper.

auditorium n. assembly room, hall, concert hall, gallery, theater, ampitheater, playhouse, lecture hall.

auger n. bore, tool. SEE TOOL

augment v. enlarge, add, increase, extend, enhance, broaden, thicken, maximize, build up, amplify, strengthen, boost. ANT. *decrease, reduce, attenuate*.

augur n. prophet, seer, oracle, prognosticator, diviner, fortune-teller, psychic.

augur v. predict, prophesy, divine, forecast, bode, portend, herald, presage, forewarn.

augury n. **1.** PREDICTION prophesy, divination, forecast, forewarning, soothsaying, forecasting. **2.** OMEN portent, sign, harbinger, herald, forewarning.

AUGUST a. [aw GUST] awe-inspiring, magnificent, worthy of great respect. *Visitors grew silent as they entered the august cathedral.* SYN. grand, magnificent, glorious, imposing, sublime, noble, stately, dignified, regal, supreme, eminent, lofty, distinguished. ANT. *lowly, pedestrian, humble*.

au naturel a. nude, naked, undressed, unclothed, unadorned, natural. ANT. *clothed*.

au pair n. domestic servant, nanny, housekeeper, baby-sitter.

aura n. ambience, atmosphere, mood, feeling, *vibes, air, spirit, nimbus, emanation.

aurora n. aurora australis (southern lights), aurora borealis (northern lights).

auspices *n.* sponsorship, patronage, aegis, sanction, assistance, authority, guidance, protection, supervision.

AUSPICIOUS *a.* [aw SPISH us] favorable, of positive conditions or character. *The economy is improving; it is an auspicious time for opening a new business.* SYN. favorable, propitious, positive, felicitous, fortunate, timely, opportune, promising, good, lucky, rosy, golden. ANT. *unfavorable, untimely, unfortunate, ominous.*

AUSTERE *a.* [aw STEER] severe, stern or plain in appearance, character, etc. Also, self-denying, strict. *The prison's austere facade was chillingly bleak.* SYN. **1.** SEVERE, stern, harsh, grim, stiff, cold, forbidding, rigid, serious, sober, solemn, plain, unadorned. **2.** ASCETIC, self-denying, strict, abstemious, stark. ANT. *1. bright, cheery, sunny, warm, frivolous, ornate. 2. indulgent, extravagant.*

authentic *a.* genuine, real, bona fide, true, actual, simon-pure, *kosher, certified, *the real McCoy, *honest-to-goodness, legitimate. ANT. *bogus, phony, fake, spurious.*

authenticate *v.* validate, certify, confirm, warrant, guarantee, attest, vouch, affirm, substantiate, corroborate, document. ANT. *invalidate, falsify, discredit.*

author *n.* **1.** WRITER novelist, playwright, storyteller, screenwriter, poet, bard, historian, chronicler, biographer, dramatist, journalist, *hack, wordsmith. "A person who you can silence by shutting his book."—Max Gralnik. SEE BOOK, NOVELIST **2.** ORIGINATOR creator, architect, designer, father, founder.

WORD FIND

best-selling author with staying power: brand-name author

multiple books, author of: polygraph

pen name: pseudonym, nom de plume, allonym, ananym, anonym

publicizes author and books: publicist

sells author's books, handles contracts: literary agent

writes a book for someone else who may or may not take credit: ghost writer

authoritarian *n.* dictator, tyrant, despot, disciplinarian, martinet.

authoritarian *a.* dictatorial, tyrannical, repressive, totalitarian, strict, dogmatic, rigid, despotic, imperious, autocratic, domineering. ANT. *libertarian, permissive, liberal, democratic.*

authoritative *a.* official, validated, authentic, true, genuine, documented, sound, certified, reliable, trustworthy, scholarly. ANT. *questionable, frivolous, unsubstantiated.*

authorities *n.* the powers that be, City Hall, officials, government, officialdom, *the law.

authority *n.* **1.** POWER jurisdiction, rule, license, charge, control, command, dominion, administration, influence. "A halter."—Adelard of Bath. "Tyranny unless tempered by freedom."—Stefan Zweig. **2.** EXPERT specialist, professional, scholar, connoisseur, *walking encyclopedia, trusted source.

authorize *v.* permit, give the okay, empower, entitle, license, allow, sanction, *give the green light, warrant, commission.

autobahn *n.* expressway, highway, superhighway, road, drive.

autocracy *n.* dictatorship, despotism, totalitarianism.

autocrat *n.* dictator, tyrant, despot, authoritarian, overlord, *iron-fisted ruler.

autograph *n.* signature, name, inscription, *John Hancock, *John Henry, X.

automated *a.* servo-mechanized, mechanized, computerized, programmed, automatic, motorized, self propelled, robotic.

automatic *a.* **1.** SELF-OPERATING mechanical, self-propelling, self regulating, self-programmed, servo-mechanized, automated. **2.** INVOLUNTARY unconscious, reflex, unpremeditated, spontaneous. ANT. *1. manual, labor-intensive. 2. voluntary, conscious.*

automaton SEE ROBOT

automobile *n.* car, vehicle, sedan, *wheels, station wagon, hatchback, compact, subcompact, *bucket of bolts, *clunker, *junker, *lemon, *gas-guzzler, transport, fastback, *flivver, convertible, *lowrider, *horseless carriage, roadster, town car, *crate, coupe, *hot rod, *jalopy, van, minivan, SUV (sport utility vehicle).

WORD FIND

book listing prices of used cars: blue book

brake components: brake drum, brake shoes, brake lining

brakes, non-skid: anti-lock brakes

bump absorbers: shock absorbers, suspension system, leaf springs, springs, torsion bars

cables used to recharge dead battery: jumper cables

chauffeur-driven: limousine

convertible: *ragtop

cutting tool used in a car accident: Jaws of Life

dashboard warning lights: idiot lights, hazard lights

divider between engine and passenger compartment: firewall
DUI: driving under the influence
DWI: driving while intoxicated
electrochemical power unit: battery
engages and disengages engine from transmission: clutch
engine speed gauge: tachometer
explosion of fuel in exhaust system: backfire
frame: chassis
funeral car: hearse
gearbox: transmission
gears shifted manually: manual transmission
inflatable impact bag: air bag
license plate customized with owner's name or pet word: vanity plate
lifter used to raise car to change tire: jack
mechanic's rolling board used for underbody work: creeper
mileage meter: odometer
OUI: operating under the influence
pedal for manual transmission: clutch
police: squad car, cruiser, patrol car, prowl car
radar detector: *fuzzbuster
shifting to low gear to help slow car: downshift
skidding over sheet of water: hydroplaning
speed automator: cruise control
starting car without key: *hotwiring
sway reducer: sway bar
tailpipe afterburner, burns harmful gases: catalytic converter
tire rotation for proper wear: balancing
used car in perfect condition: cherry
wheel-locking clamp used to stop parking scofflaws: Denver boot
wheel shaft: axle
SEE ACCIDENT, DRIVE, MOTOR, ROAD, TRUCK

AUTONOMOUS a. [aw TON uh mus] acting independently. *It was an autonomous island government, free of the mainland's dictates.* SYN. independent, self-governing, self-ruling, self-reliant, sovereign. ANT. *dependent, subject, overruled, occupied.*

autonomy n. independence, sovereignty, self-rule, self-reliance, home rule, freedom. ANT. *dependence, subjugation.*

autumn n. fall, harvest time, Indian summer. "A second spring when every leaf's a flower."—Albert Camus.

auxiliary a. 1. SUPPORTING assisting, aiding, adjuvant, helping, contributing. 2. SUBSIDIARY subordinate, supplementary, accessory, additional, secondary, reserve. ANT. 2. *main, primary.*

avail n. use, usefulness, benefit, help, aid, advantage, profit.
avail v. utilize, help, assist, aid, serve.
available a. handy, ready, accessible, on hand, at hand, obtainable, on tap, free, at one's disposal. ANT. *unavailable, out.*
avalanche n. 1. SNOWSLIDE landslide. 2. INUNDATION cataclysm, deluge, flood, torrent, barrage.
WORD FIND
air current produced by: avalanche wind
overhang of ice and snow, known for starting avalanches: cornice
SEE MOUNTAIN, MOUNTAIN CLIMBING
AVANTE-GARDE n. [uh vahnt GARD] those involved in innovation or new techniques, especially in the arts. *They were on the cutting edge of a new science; they were the avant garde.* SYN. vanguard, *cutting edge, groundbreakers, innovators, pioneers, trailblazers, experimenters, inventors, new school.
AVARICE n. [AV ur is] unhealthy desire for wealth, greed. *Her avarice compelled her to hobnob with wealthy bachelors.* SYN. greed, cupidity, acquisitiveness, covetousness, rapacity, gluttony, miserliness, "A mere madness, to live like a wretch, and die rich."—Robert Burton. "The spur of industry."—David Hume. ANT. *generosity, benevolence, charity.*
AVARICIOUS a. [AV ur ISH us] greedy. *He was after her money; he was avaricious.* SYN. greedy, covetous, acquisitive, rapacious, piggish, hoarding, predatory, *tight, selfish, *gold-digging, gluttonous. ANT. *generous, giving, beneficent.*
avenge v. revenge, retaliate, take vengeance, *pay back, *get even, punish, vindicate, wreak vengeance. ANT. *forgive, excuse, overlook.*
avenue n. 1. ROAD roadway, drive, lane, boulevard, highway, thoroughfare, promenade, street, parkway, artery, expressway. 2. WAY means, route, path, course.
average n. norm, par, standard, mean.
average a. ordinary, typical, usual, common, standard, *garden variety, middling, intermediate, fair, moderate, median, run-of-the-mill, so-so, everyday. ANT. *exceptional, above par, extraordinary.*
averse a. loath, ill-disposed, opposed, hostile, unfavorable, disinclined, hesitant, unwilling, against. ANT. *agreeable, willing, eager.*
AVERSION n. [uh VUR zhun] an intense dislike or repugnance. *I have an aversion to pickled beets.* SYN. dislike, repugnance, loathing,

antipathy, revulsion, disgust, hostility, hatred, detestation. ANT. *liking, attraction, fondness.*

avert *v.* **1.** TURN AWAY shift, turn aside. **2.** PREVENT ward off, avoid, thwart, deter, preclude, forestall, nip in the bud. ANT. *1. invite. 2. cause, exacerbate.*

aviator *n.* pilot, flyer, airman, ace, aviatrix.

avid *a.* **1.** EAGER enthusiastic, fervent, ardent, flaming, rabid, fanatical, burning, zealous. **2.** DESIROUS greedy, avaricious, rapacious, covetous, voracious. ANT. *1. lukewarm, blasé, bored. 2. indifferent, uninterested.*

avocation *n.* hobby, pastime, interest, pursuit, sideline, work; profession.

avoid *v.* evade, dodge, steer clear of, bypass, elude, sidestep, hedge, duck, shirk, avert, eschew, shun, *give the slip, refrain. ANT. *embrace, meet head on, confront, invite.*

avoidance *n.* evasion, dodging, bypassing, sidestepping, hedging, shirking, ducking out, averting, eschewing, shunning, refraining.

avow *v.* declare, admit, acknowledge, avouch, aver, confess, profess, announce, swear. ANT. *disavow, deny.*

avowal *n.* declaration, admission, acknowledgement, confession, profession, announcement, assertion, affirmation. ANT. *disavowal, denial.*

await *v.* wait for, anticipate.

awake *a.* **1.** CONSCIOUS active, alert, wakeful, astir, wide-eyed, *bright-eyed and bushy-tailed, up. **2.** ALERT watchful, attentive, sharp, circumspect, vigilant, observant. ANT. *1. asleep, unconscious, comatose. 2. inattentive, dull, off guard.*

awaken *v.* wake, rouse, get up, stimulate, activate.

awakening *n.* revival, rousing, invigoration, stimulation, realization, consciousness, rebirth.

award *n.* prize, citation, medal, trophy, honor, reward, decoration, compensation.

award *v.* bestow, present, grant, confer, endow, compensate.

aware *a.* conscious, cognizant, in touch, knowing, mindful, *wise to, wary, sharp, apprised, awake, enlightened, *know the score, versed, *hip, *with it, *plugged in, grounded, au courant. ANT. *unaware, ignorant, *out to lunch, unconscious.*

away *a.* gone, removed, off, absent, out, abroad, remote.

awe *n.* wonder, fear, reverence, astonishment, amazement, stupefaction, veneration, respect, worship, admiration, shock. ANT. *disrespect, disregard, apathy, indifference.*

awesome *a.* impressive, overwhelming, intimidating, moving, formidable, astonishing, amazing, *eye-popping, breathtaking, wonderful, wondrous, stunning, *mind-blowing, stupefying, excellent, *bad, *cool, *dynamite, *gnarly, *gone, immense, super, *ripping, *out of this world, *unreal. ANT. *unimpressive, *ho-hum, *lame, *lightweight, *bush league, trivial.*

awful *a.* horrible, bad, ugly, dreadful, terrible, atrocious, unpleasant, horrendous, ghastly, despicable, inferior, contemptible, rotten, *crappy, appalling, frightful, terrifying. ANT. *good, nice, pleasing.*

awkward *a.* **1.** CLUMSY bumbling, oafish, ungraceful, bungling, ungainly, maladroit, inept, *klutzy, blundering. **2.** UNWIELDY cumbersome, bulky, ponderous. **3.** UNCOMFORTABLE embarrassing, inappropriate, untimely, thorny, delicate, trying, ticklish. ANT. *1. coordinated, graceful. 2. handy, convenient. 3. appropriate, relaxing, smooth.*

awning *n.* canopy, canvas, shelter, sunshade, marquee.

awry *a.* **1.** CROOKED askew, oblique, aslant. **2.** AMISS wrong, off course, astray, askew. ANT. *1. straight, even. 2. right, good, correct.*

ax *n.* broadax, hatchet, pickax, maul, tomahawk.

axiom *n.* maxim, truth, truism, principle, dictum, precept.

axiomatic *a.* self-evident, unquestionable, certain, understood, acknowledged, known, absolute, fundamental. ANT. *questionable, dubious, in question.*

axis *n.* **1.** PIVOT spindle, shaft, hinge. **2.** ALIGNMENT alliance, coalition, league, union.

axle *n.* spindle, rod, bar, shaft, axis, arbor.

ax to grind (having an) wanting or going after something for self-serving reasons, not for the unselfish reasons sometimes presented; a hidden motive. *His support of the project appeard to be civil-minded; in reality he had an ax to grind.* SYN. motive, hidden motive, motivation, agenda, hidden agenda, score to settle, purpose, reason, incentive, driving force.

B

babble *n.* prattle, babel, gibberish, spluttering, mumbling, blabbing, jabber, burble, blubbering, drivel.

babble *v.* prattle, blab, gibber, *yak, jabber, burble, blather, murmur, sputter, mutter, gush, splutter, blat, prate, gurgle.

babe in the woods *n.* easy mark, sucker, dupe, innocent.

babel *n.* confusion, tumult, clamor.

baby *n.* **1.** INFANT newborn, babe, neonate, *bambino, papoose, tot, nursling, nipper, toddler. "It is all gut and squall."—Charles Brown. "An inestimable blessing and bother."—Mark Twain. **2.** SNIVELER whiner, crybaby, *wimp.

WORD FIND

abandoned and found: foundling
ailment: croup
bathtub: bathinette
bed: cradle, bassinet
bounce on one's knee or swing up and down
  in one's arms: dandle
breastfeeder, hired: wet nurse
carriage: buggy, pram, stroller, perambulator
chewy toy: teething ring, pacifier
contented, happy cry: crow
cry loudly: squall
cry weakly: whimper, mewl
dead at birth: stillborn
diaper irritation: diaper rash
embryo implant: test-tube baby
foreskin removal from male: circumcision
illegitimate: love child, bastard
multiple: twins, triplets, quadruplets, quintuplets, sextuplets
murder of: infanticide
outfit: layette
premature infant: preemie
rubber soother: pacifier
soft spot on head: fontanelle
song: lullaby
talk: babble, coo, gurgle
tooth eruption: teething
walking: toddling
whine and whimper: pule
SEE BIRTH, CHILD, CHILDREN, PREGNANCY

baby *v.* spoil, indulge, dote on, pamper, coddle, mollycoddle, overprotect, shelter, smother.

baby *a.* small, wee, miniature, tiny, young, teensy, pocket-sized. ANT. *large, mature.*

baby boom *n.* population explosion, birth spurt, birthrate bulge.

babyish *a.* childish, infantile, juvenile, immature. ANT. *mature.*

baby-sit *v.* tend, watch, sit, care for, *keep an eye on, mind, look after, act as guardian.

baby-sitter *n.* sitter, nanny, governess, guardian.

bacchanal *n.* SEE ORGY, PARTY

bachelor *n.* single, stag, playboy, man about town. "A man who is footloose and fiancé free."—F.G. Kernan.

back *n.* backside, posterior, spine, tail end, hind, rear, stern, rump. SEE ASS

back *v.* **1.** SUPPORT assist, sponsor, *go to bat for, abet, boost, stand behind, promote, endorse. **2.** REVERSE go backwards, backtrack, return, turn tail, rebound, regress, recoil. ANT. *1. undermine, reject, denounce. 2. progress, advance.*

back *a.* **1.** REAR hind, end, posterior. **2.** DISTANT remote, faraway, outermost, rural, secluded. **3.** PAST earlier, previous, dated, bygone. ANT. *1. front, anterior, head. 3. future, upcoming.*

back and forth *adv.* to and fro, from side to side, vacillating.

backbite *v.* slander, malign, *backstab, defame, vilify, gossip, smear, *badmouth, *dump on, *tell tales out of school.

backbone *n.* **1.** SPINE spinal column, vertebrae. **2.** FOUNDATION mainstay, basis. **3.** COURAGE strength, character, mettle, *guts, grit, spunk, fortitude, pluck, resolve. ANT. *3. timidity, cowardice, spinelessness.*

backbreaking *a.* strenuous, arduous, taxing, laborious, crippling, crushing, bankrupting, exhausting. ANT. *light, easy, *child's play.*

back down *v.* give in, cave in, concede, submit, *wimp out, acquiesce, surrender. ANT. *hold one's ground, stand firm.*

backer *n.* supporter, sponsor, promoter, booster, underwriter, angel, financer, advocate, benefactor, patron, investor.

backfire *v.* explode, report, discharge, boom, bang, pop, misfire, go awry, flop, reverse, blow up in one's face, boomerang, miscarry, *bomb. ANT. *go off without a hitch, work.*

background *n.* **1.** DISTANCE backdrop, horizon, offing. **2.** EXPERIENCE upbringing, environment, grounding, family, past, education, circumstances. ANT. *1. foreground.*

backhanded *a.* equivocal, ambiguous, left-handed, underhanded, sarcastic. ANT. *straightforward, clear, definite.*

backhoe n. excavator, *digger, earth mover, heavy machinery.

backing n. support, sponsorship, help, aid, assistance, boost, advocacy, patronage, encouragement, endorsement. ANT. detraction, undermining.

BACKLASH n. [BAK lash] a negative reaction to a previous action. *Ignoring the needs of one's constituency always results in voter backlash.* SYN. repercussion, reaction, backfire, retaliation, response, recoil, impact, effect, consequence, wake, backwash.

backlog n. accumulation, reserve, excess, stock, hoard.

backpedal v. retract, take back, recant, retreat, renege, back down.

backslide v. slip, slide, sin, relapse, deviate, go astray, lapse, leave the straight and narrow, leave the path of righteousness.

backstab v. backbite, attack, smear, slander, *sell down the river, betray, *play Judas, *doublecross.

back talk n. lip, sass, mouth, guff, insolence.

backup n. auxiliary, extra, substitute, alternate.

backward a. 1. TOWARD THE REAR rearward, in reverse, behind. 2. IN REVERSE upside-down, inside-out, wrong, *bassackwards. 3. SHY hesitant, reticent, bashful, reserved, timid, demure. 4. RETARDED slow, behind, simple, inept, stupid, rustic, impeded, laggard, dull. ANT. 3. confident, bold, forward. 4. advanced, quick, brilliant.

backwoodsman n. rustic, yokel, *hillbilly, *hick, *hayseed.

bacteria n. microorganisms, germs, microbes, pathogens, *bugs, bacilli, virus, microscopic agents, streptococci, streptobacilli.

bad a. 1. BELOW STANDARD inadequate, poor, *lousy, *crappy, substandard, unacceptable, awful, faulty, unsatisfactory, *cheesy, slipshod, deficient, inferior, below par, worthless, shoddy. 2. WICKED immoral, evil, corrupt, vile, sinful, demonic, satanic, diabolical, mischievous, mean. "All that proceeds from weakness."—Friedrich Nietzsche. 3. SPOILED rotten, putrid, decayed, tainted, moldy. 4. UNPLEASANT unfavorable, unfortunate, terrible, revolting, awful, dreadful, disagreeable, horrible, distressing, dire, tragic, negative. 5. SEVERE powerful, destructive, serious, dangerous, grave, horrible. 6. INCORRECT erroneous, inaccurate. 7. SORRY low, down, distressed, troubled, gloomy, melancholy, depressed, remorseful. ANT. 1. excellent, good, superior. 2. moral,

good, virtuous. 3. fresh, preserved. 4. pleasant, favorable, good. 5. harmless, trivial, light. 6. correct, accurate. 7. good, proud, glorious.

bad blood n. hard feelings, enmity, hostility, bitterness, resentment, ill will, malevolence, hatred, venom, unfriendliness. ANT. friendliness, good will, amity.

bad breath n. halitosis, *dragon breath.

badge n. 1. emblem, shield, medal, medallion, insignia, symbol, sign.

badger v. bother, nag, harass, pester, bug, needle, hassle, plague, hound, annoy, provoke, peeve, *ride.

badlands n. wasteland, eroded land, desert, *devil's backyard, *devil's sandbox, barren land.

badly adv. inadequately, poorly, unacceptably, abominably, awfully, unsatisfactorily, deficiently, slipshod, below par, wrong, ineptly, terribly. ANT. excellently, perfectly, superbly.

baffle v. 1. CONFUSE perplex, muddle, stump, confound, throw, befuddle, daze, delude, mix up, puzzle. 2. THWART hinder, check, foil, obstruct, impede, bar, frustrate.

baffling a. inscrutable, perplexing. ANT. explainable, decipherable.

bag n. sack, pouch, pack, satchel, tote, carryall, haversack, gunny-bag, duffel, valise, suitcase, portmanteau, briefcase.

bag v. snare, capture, catch, take, trap, kill, seize.

bagatelle n. trifle.

baggage n. luggage, bags, suitcases, valises, trunks, things, paraphernalia, effects, gear.

baggy a. sagging, droopy, puffy, limp, unpressed, loose, slack, fat, billowing. ANT. smooth, tight, pressed, tailored.

bagpipe n. SEE MUSICAL INSTRUMENT

bail n. bond, security, deposit, surety, guarantee, warranty; release. SEE COURT, LAW

bailiff n. court attendant, court official, officer. SEE COURT, LAW

BAILIWICK n. [BAL i wik] one's area of special interest or expertise. *My personal bailiwick is paleontology.* SYN. interest, authority, field, sphere, jurisdiction, realm, domain, territory, area of expertise, department, beat.

bait n. lure, allurement, attraction, bribe, enticement, *come-on, inducement.

bait v. 1. LURE attract, entice, bribe, induce, seduce, tantalize, tempt, draw, interest. 2. GOAD tease, pick on, harass, rile, provoke, annoy, irk, hector, badger, *ride. ANT. 1. repel, repulse. 2. pacify, please, mollify.

bake v. roast, cook, broil, heat.

bakery n. bread shop, cake shop, pastry shop, bagel shop.

balance n. **1.** EQUILIBRIUM parity, equity, equalization, symmetry, correspondence, equipoise, equality. **2.** MENTAL STABILITY composure, self-control, poise, *cool head, stability. ANT. *1. imbalance, inequality. 2. instability, irrationality.*

balance v. **1.** TO MAKE EQUAL equalize, counterpoise, stabilize, level, counteract, equilibrate, steady, match, offset, *walk a fine line, *level the playing field. **2.** COMPARE consider, differentiate, weigh, contrast, evaluate. **3.** ACCOUNT square, debit, credit, tally, audit, compute, calculate, sum up.

balcony n. **1.** PORCH platform, terrace, deck, overhang, veranda, portico. **2.** GALLERY loge, upper deck, mezzanine, *peanut gallery, cheap seats.

bald a. **1.** HAIRLESS bare, glabrous, shaven, *head like a cueball, *skinheaded, *chromedomed. **2.** UNADORNED plain, stark, austere, bare, barren. **3.** FRANK blunt, outright, direct, overt, out-and-out, baldfaced, flagrant, glaring. ANT. *1. hairy, furry, woolly, hirsute. 2. ornate, decorated, embellished. 3. indirect, disguised, subtle.*

balderdash n. bunk, rot, poppycock. SEE NONSENSE

bale n. bundle, packet, bunch, parcel.

baleful a. harmful, sinister, threatening, evil, ominous, deadly, injurious, pernicious, wicked, hazardous, malignant. ANT. *harmless, innocuous, benign.*

balk v. **1.** FRUSTRATE thwart, foil, hinder, impede, prevent, check, retard. **2.** HESITATE recoil, refuse, object, demur, draw back, shy away from, flinch, stop short. ANT. *1. facilitate, clear, help. 2. proceed, progress, *jump in.*

balky a. stubborn, contrary, resisting, resistant, obstinate, mulish, intractable, ornery, unruly. ANT. *cooperative, tractable.*

ball n. **1.** ORB sphere, globe, spheroid, apple, round, bullet. **2.** DANCE prom, masque, shindig, hoedown, *hop.

ballad n. song, love song, folk song. SEE SONG

ballerina n. SEE BALLET

ballet n. dance, toe dancing, choreography, adagio.

WORD FIND

admirer of: balletomane
attire: tutu, tights, leotard
director: impresario
female dancer: ballerina, prima ballerina
jump and land in same position: saute
jump straight in the air with quick changes of leg position: entrechat
jump with legs clung together: soubresaut
knee-bend: plié
leap from one foot to the other: jeté
male dancer: danseur
mincing steps on tiptoes: pas de bourrée
posturing on one leg: arabesque
practice: barre work
practice room bar: barre
running steps: pas couru
secondary, non-principal dancer: coryphee
shoes: toe shoes, ballet shoes
sliding on soles of feet: glissading
solo: pas seul
spin in which head is held still, then turned after body: spotting
split performed in midair: pas ciseaux, grand écart
step: pas
steps performed on tiptoes: temps de point, en pointe
whirlaround: pirouette

balloon n. aerostat, lighter-than-air craft.

WORD FIND

altitude-measuring device: altimeter
anchor line: tether, dragrope, mooring line
ascent/descent speed-measuring device: variometer
basket: gondola
bottom sleeve, where hot air is blown in: appendix, mouth
broadest portion: equator
burner's lighter: sparker
gas: hot air, helium, hydrogen
ground crew: chase crew
ground director of balloon activity: balloonmeister
high-speed launch used in windy conditions: blastoff
interior of bag: envelope
pilot, passenger: aeronaut
propane gas heater: burner
rate of descent: sink
weights, sandbags, used to control altitude: ballast
SEE BLIMP

balloon v. inflate, swell, expand, bloat, puff out, dilate, billow. ANT. *deflate, contract, shrink.*

ballot n. ticket, slate, vote, poll. "The rightful and peaceful successors of bullets."—Abraham Lincoln.

ballpark n. stadium.

ballyhoo *n.* uproar, talk, hype, *hot air, puffery, promotion, *spiel, babble, pitch, *BS, hoopla.

balm *n.* salve, remedy, cure, comfort, soothing agent, curative. ANT. *irritant, abrasive.*

balmy *a.* **1.** MILD fair, gentle, pleasant, temperate, tranquil, calm, soothing. **2.** CRAZY insane, foolish, *nuts, *cuckoo, daft, *crackers, eccentric, weird. ANT. *1. stormy, blustery, inclement. 2. sane, normal, stable.*

baloney *n.* *crap, rot, bunk. SEE NONSENSE

bamboo *n.* cane, grass, reed.

bamboozle *v.* trick, cheat, hoodwink, deceive, dupe, confuse, buffalo, swindle, take, defraud, pull the wool over one's eyes, con.

ban *n.* prohibition, embargo, proscription, interdiction, boycott, taboo, restriction, *blacklisting, stoppage, injunction. ANT. *approval, sanction, allowance.*

ban *v.* prohibit, restrict, stop, banish, boycott, forbid, disallow, bar, exclude, outlaw, close, *blackball. ANT. *allow, sanction, approve, legalize.*

BANAL *a.* [buh NAL; BANE ul] dull, overused, common. *The dialogue was too predictable and tired; it was banal.* SYN. dull, overused, common, tired, trite, hackneyed, insipid, stale, vapid, lackluster, hum-drum, clichéd, platitudinous, flat, inane, unoriginal. ANT. *original, rich, deep, fresh, provocative.*

banality *n.* cliché, platitude, triteness, commonplace, bromide.

band *n.* **1.** GROUP gang, association, company, assembly, mob, crush, throng, bunch, troop, posse, tribe, pack. **2.** MUSICAL GROUP ensemble, combo, trio, quartet, quintet, pentad, sextet, septet, octet, nonet, orchestra.

WORD FIND
advisor: manager
amateur band: garage band
bandstand, concave: band shell
books shows: agent, booking agent
circuit of shows: tour
confidence on stage: stage presence
effects, amplifier: echo, reverb, tremolo
fan of: *groupie
hit song or nonoriginal song performed by: cover
improvisational session: jam session
improvise or make up song on spot: jam
main act: headliner
mistake or muffed note: clam
nightclub entrance fee to pay for: cover charge

passage, individual instrumental: lick, riff
performing exceptionally well or in a groove: *cooking
playdate or job: gig
publicizes, promotes: publicist, promoter
road, set-up crew-member: *roadie
seating, unreserved audience: festival seating
session followed by break: set
singer, lead: frontman
skills, slang for musician's: *chops
speakers: amplifiers, amps, PA system
subgroup of instruments: section
unrehearsed, impromptu performance: jam
SEE MUSIC, MUSICIAN, RECORDING
3. STRIP swath, strap, tie, ribbon, sash, cord, fillet, thong.

bandage *n.* gauze, swath, dressing, compress, *Bandaid.

bandanna *n.* handkerchief, neckerchief, kerchief.

bandit *n.* thief, robber, crook, desperado, outlaw, brigand, *mugger, hoodlum, thug, burglar, highwayman, hold-up man.

bandleader *n.* conductor, *frontman, bandmaster.

bandy *v.* exchange, give-and-take, pass back and forth, *ping pong, circulate, pass along.

BANE *n.* [BANE] harm, destruction. *A wolfpack is the bane of the deer yard.* SYN. death, ruin, evil, downfall, scourge, plague, destruction, curse, undoing, poison. ANT. *blessing, good.*

bang *n.* **1.** NOISE boom, thump, crack, report, eruption, clang, crash, burst, explosion, pop, thud, peal, salvo, slam, clap, shot. **2.** BLOW hit, whack, slam, thwack, rap, smack, belt, punch, clout. **3.** THRILL *Sl.* *kick, *jollies, *charge.

bang *v.* **1.** MAKE NOISE boom, peal, explode, thump, crack, clang, slam, thud, sound, pop, clap. **2.** STRIKE hit, whack, slam, pop, shoot, clap, punch, clout, smack, rap, beat, pummel.

banish *v.* exile, expel, eject, remove, ban, proscribe, excommunicate, deport, outlaw, dismiss, oust, relegate, drum out. ANT. *adopt, invite, embrace.*

banister *n.* handrail, railing, balustrade.

banjo *n.* SEE MUSICAL INSTRUMENTS

bank *n.* **1.** financial institution, savings and loan, S&L, lending institution, thrift, trust company, treasury, credit union, Federal Reserve Bank, mortgage company. "A place where they lend you an umbrella in fair weather and ask for it back when it begins to rain."—Robert Frost.

WORD FIND

assets pledged as security for a loan: collateral

ATM: automated teller machine

ATM access code: pin (personal identification) number

bad check-writing: kiting

CD: certficate of deposit

check guaranteed by bank to be covered: certified check

checking account that earns interest on unused funds: NOW (negotiable order of withdrawal) account

check returned due to insufficient funds: bounced check

clerk: teller

conceal large sums of illegally gained money by depositing in several small accounts: launder

deposit of third party made to assure fulfillment of contract: escrow

document such as draft, deed or bond: instrument

fail to pay off a loan: default

failure to pay loan on time: delinquency

FDIC: Federal Deposit Insurance Corporation

federal banking system and clearinghouse: Federal Reserve System

interest rate charged on loans to member banks by Federal Reserve Bank: discount rate

loan payment, large initial: down payment

loan payment that is larger than all the others: balloon payment

lowest interest rate at a given time: prime rate

messenger/*gopher: runner

office or central bank where bankers meet to settle balances: clearinghouse

one percent of loan paid up front: point

order to bank to refuse payment on a check drawn: stop payment

panicked withdrawals on fear of bank closure: bank run

payment, order for: draft, money order

payment for use of credit or funds: interest

pay off loan in one large installment instead of many smaller ones: commute

record book of deposits and withdrawals: passbook, bankbook

seriousness, payment establishing borrower's: earnest money

signature authorizing payment of check: endorsement

storage space for customer's valuables: safe deposit box

teller's small window: wicket

value of business, home or other investment after all debts are subtracted: equity

vault, personal: safe deposit box

withdrawal in excess of funds in account: overdraft

SEE MONEY, SECURITIES

2. EMBANKMENT slope, hill, ledge, mound, levee. **3.** ROW tier, course, string, line, array, series.

bankrupt *a.* insolvent, *gone belly up, ruined, wiped out, broke, *busted, penniless, in the red. ANT. *solvent, profiting, flourishing, in the black.*

WORD FIND

bankruptcy procedure/code section: Chapter Eleven

bankruptcy *n.* insolvency. SEE BANKRUPT

banner *n.* flag, pennant, ensign, streamer, standard, pennon, bunting, colors.

banner *a.* successful, outstanding, leading, exceptional, foremost, record, red-letter. ANT. *unsuccessful, mediocre.*

banquet *n.* feast, dinner, meal, roast, *spread, repast.

bantam *n.* feisty runt, little spitfire, little scrapper, whippersnapper, swaggerer, *strutting half-pint, *cock of the walk.

banter *n.* teasing, ribbing, jesting, joking, joshing, repartee, badinage, ridicule, kidding, persiflage, raillery.

banter *v.* tease, rib, jest, joke, josh, ridicule, kid, *ride.

baptism *n.* initiation, purification, sacrament, ritual, rite, christening, sprinkling, annointing, immersion, consecration. "The vehicle to heaven, the public agent of the Kingdom, the gift of adoption."—Saint Basil.

WORD FIND

basin: baptistery, font, laver

cloth: chrisom

immersion, by: holobaptism

robe: chrisom

water: laver

BAPTISM OF FIRE *n.* a first or initial experience that proves to be an ordeal. *The new recruits were sent immediately to the front, where they survived a baptism of fire.* SYN. ordeal, trying experience, trial by fire, nightmare, initiation, rite of passage, hell, hardship, test of courage, introduction, entrance, hazing, rude introduction.

baptize v. initiate, purify, annoint, cleanse, immerse, christen, indoctrinate, consecrate, sanctify, sprinkle. SEE CHURCH, RELIGION

bar n. **1.** RAIL OR ROD stick, strip, stake, pole, shaft, crosspiece, boom, spar, paling. **2.** IMPEDIMENT barrier, obstruction, obstacle, constraint, block, snag, restraint, barricade, restriction, stumbling block. **3.** PUB saloon, tavern, gin mill, cocktail lounge, *watering hole, lounge, beer garden, dramshop. **4.** LEGAL SYSTEM lawyers, attorneys, counselors, bar association, solicitors, barristers, judiciary, legal fraternity. **5.** BAND stripe, strip, striation, ribbon, score, line.

bar v. **1.** STOP impede, obstruct, prohibit, hinder, block, barricade, restrict, restrain, prevent, constrain, interdict. **2.** BOLT secure, lock, seal, close, latch. **3.** EXCLUDE prohibit, ostracize, ban, banish, blackball, blacklist, segregate, spurn, boycott, shut out, freeze out. ANT. *1. facilitate, aid, abet. 2. unlock, open, free. 3. include, welcome, embrace.*

barb n. insult, dig, cutting remark, putdown, affront, criticism.

barbarian n. savage, *animal, clod, ignoramus, Neanderthal, philistine, lout, primitive, caveman, lowbrow, redneck, *pig, brute, ruffian, hooligan, dolt, Hun.

barbaric a. savage, animalistic, ignorant, cloddish, primitive, brutish, cruel, lowbrow, rough, doltish, uncultured, vulgar, wild, ill-mannered. ANT. *civilized, cultured, refined.*

barbarity n. barbarism, savagery, ignorance, cloddishness, brutality, cruelty, roughness, vulgarity, wildness, ruthlessness, brutishness. ANT. *civility, nicety, refinement.*

barbarous a. savage, animalistic, coarse, ignorant, inhuman, primitive, uncivilized, brutish, uncouth, rude, wild, rough, doltish, uncultured, vulgar, ill-mannered, vicious, philistine. ANT. *civilized, refined, humane, cultured.*

barbecue v. flame broil, roast, rotisserie, grill, sear, cook out, dry, smoke.

barber n. hair stylist, hairdresser, beautician, haircutter, coiffeur.

barbiturate n. drug, sedative, depressant, *downer.

bare a. **1.** UNCLOTHED naked, nude, stripped, in the buff, exposed, *in one's birthday suit, disrobed. **2.** PLAIN barren, stark, spare, austere, Spartan, unfinished, unadorned, empty. **3.** UNDISGUISED bald, plain, stark, unvarnished, glaring, straightforward, flagrant. ANT. *1. clothed, dressed. 2. ornate, elaborate,* decorated. *3. hidden, covered up, camouflaged.*

bare bones a. basic, essential, unadorned, core, simple, no-frills.

barefaced a. shameless, brazen, bold, frank, audacious, rude, bumptious, outspoken, insolent, impudent. ANT. *reserved, polite, respectful.*

barely adv. hardly, scarcely, just, slightly, merely.

bargain n. **1.** AGREEMENT understanding, pledge, contract, deal, arrangement, promise, covenant. "A transaction in which each participant thinks he has cheated the other."—Anon. **2.** GOOD DEAL steal, good value, a bon marche. "Something you can't use at a price you can't resist."—Franklin Jones.

bargain v. negotiate, dicker, haggle, come to terms, deal, higgle, promise, contract, trade, barter.

barge n. flatboat, scow, freight carrier.

bark n. **1.** WOOF yip, yelp, howl, yawp, bowwow, bay, arf, growl. **2.** COVERING skin, husk, peeling, hide, shell, pod.

bark v. **1.** WOOF yip, yelp, howl, yawp, yap, bowwow, bay, arf, growl. **2.** SHOUT bellow, holler, yell, snap, growl, bluster, roar, snarl, thunder.

BAR MITZVAH n. [bar MITZ vuh] a ceremony recognizing the entrance of a 13-year-old Jewish boy into the adult world of moral responsibilities. *The bar mitzvah is the Jewish boy's great rite of passage into adulthood.* SYN. ceremony, initiation, rite of passage, confirmation, coming of age, celebration, service, SEE BAT MITZVAH, RELIGION

barmy a. eccentric, odd, peculiar, daft, *batty. ANT. *normal, conventional, sane.*

barn n. byre, cowbarn, stables, stalls, shed.

WORD FIND
barn and other farm buildings, collectively: farmstead
erection of: barnraising
fodder storage building next to: silo
grain storage building: granary
upper portion where hay is stored: hayloft
SEE FARM, ANIMAL

barnacle n. crustacean, parasite, limpet, marine creature, shell.

barnstorm v. tour.

barometer n. instrument, gauge, indicator, manometer.

baron n. nobleman, aristocrat, lord.

baroque a. ornate, elaborate, florid, embellished, busy, overworked, rococo, ostentatious, fanciful. ANT. *plain, stark, austere.*

barracks *n.* quarters, housing, building.
barrage *n.* **1.** SUSTAINED ATTACK bombardment, shelling, salvo, battery, volley, assault, enfilade, onslaught, hail, fusillade, wall of fire, rain of fire. **2.** PROFUSION deluge, inundation, rain, mass, plethora, torrent.
barrel *n.* cask, keg, hogshead, drum, firkin, vessel, butt, container, cylinder.
WORD FIND
maker: cooper
part: stave
stopper: bung
barren *a.* **1.** DESOLATE sterile, empty, bare, depleted, void, unproductive, arid, stark. **2.** CHILDLESS infertile, sterile, infecund, unbearing. **3.** DULL boring, uninteresting, stale, uninspiring. ANT. *1. fertile, lush, rich, fruitful. 2. fertile, fecund. 3. interesting, inspiring.*
barricade *n.* barrier, roadblock, blockade, bar, impediment, rampart, bulwark, obstruction.
barricade *v.* bar, block, clog, impede, shut off, fortify, obstruct, secure, defend.
barrier *n.* **1.** PHYSICAL OBSTRUCTION bar, obstacle, barricade, impediment, check, roadblock, wall, rampart, bulwark, fortification, boom, palisade. **2.** HANDICAP limitation, impediment, hindrance, difficulty, obstacle, stumbling block, hurdle, obstacle.
barrio *n.* Spanish quarter, Spanish district, urban district, community, neighborhood, section.
barrister *n.* (primarily British) attorney, counselor. SEE LAWYER
barrow *n.* handcart, pushcart, wheelbarrow, handbarrow.
bartender *n.* barkeep, barmaid, *mixmaster.
barter *v.* trade, exchange, swap, deal, do business.
base *n.* **1.** FOUNDATION support, bottom, stand, pedestal, bed, foot, ground structure. **2.** BASIS essence, core, foundation, source, backbone, root, fundamental, heart, principle. **3.** HEADQUARTERS center, station, home, post, camp.
base *v.* ground, derive, build, establish, rest, construct.
base *a.* **1.** INFERIOR lowly, cheap, impure, debased. **2.** CONTEMPTIBLE low, mean, ignoble, dishonorable, indecent, disgraceful, despicable, sordid, degenerate, unprincipled, incorrigible, disreputable, slavish, wretched, servile, menial, cringing. ANT. *1. superior, pure. 2. noble, virtuous, principled.*
baseball *n.* ball, sport, game, national pastime,

athletic competition. "The greatest conversation piece ever invented in America."— Bruce Catton. "An island of surety in a changing world."—William Veek.
WORD FIND
(common abbreviations)
AAA: the minor league from which big league players are drawn
AA: the second-tier minor league. Also known as a bush league
A: the third-tier minor league. Also known as a bush league
AB: at bat
AL: American League
BA: batting average
BB: base on balls/walks
DP: double play
DH: designated hitter
E: error
ERA: earned run average
FP: fielding percentage
G: game
H: hit
HR: homerun
IP: innings pitched
K: strikeout
MVP: most valuable player
NL: National League
R: run
RBI: runs batted in
SB: stolen base
SHO: shutout
SO: strikeout
SS: shortstop
2B: double
3B: triple
TP: triple play
WP: winning pitcher
ambidextrous hitter: switch hitter
base: bag
baseball, slang for: apple, horsehide
bat, illegal: corked bat
bat's heavy warmup weight: donut
batting fourth in the lineup: batting cleanup
bench area for players, enclosed: dugout
batter's grip, improves: pine tar
batter's spot: batter's box
British game: rounders
catch, spectacular: circus catch, shoestring catch
championship, league: pennant; World Series
dirt track skirting outfield wall: warning track
double play started by the shortstop (6) who

throws to the second baseman (4), who completes the play to the first baseman (3): 6-4-3 double play

drawing of players from schools and minor leagues: draft

fantasy baseball based on statistics: Rotisserie League

fastball, slang: *fireball, *hummer, *smoke

fan's fanciful game of: Rotisserie League Baseball

first-year player: rookie

flyball, high infield: pop up

flyball, short: blooper

fly balls, practice catching: shag flies

grounder, bouncing: chopper

hit ball that bounces into stands: ground rule double

hit often used as sacrifice to move runner on, very short infield: bunt

hit that causes an out but moves an on-base runner along: sacrifice

hitter who can be counted on in critical situations: clutch hitter

hitter who substitute hits for pitcher: designated hitter

hit, weak: nubber, squibber, Texas Leaguer

homerun driving in a total of four runs: grand slam

homerun: four-bagger

homerun, to hit a: go downtown; air it out

illegally alter ball or bat: doctor

locker room, office, etc.: clubhouse

minor leagues: AAA AA, A, farm system, bush leagues

mishandled ball: bobbled; error

out-of-play ball: foul

partial swing of bat not counting as strike: check swing

perform badly, especially in a tense situation: choke

pitch a fastball: *blow it by, *blow smoke, *throw a fireball, *put some mustard on it

pitch, curving or altering trajectory: breaking ball, curveball, forkball, knuckleball, screwball, sinker, slider, spitball, split-fingered fastball

pitch, deceptively slow: off-speed pitch

pitch hitting batter, intentionally wild: beanball

pitch intentionally thrown for a ball outside: pitchout

pitch nearly hitting batter intentionally: brushback pitch

pitch, slow and easy to hit: lollipop

pitch thrown deceptively slow: change-up

pitcher, closing: closer, reliever, stopper

pitcher, illegal motion made by: balk

pitcher, lefthanded: southpaw

pitcher, team's best: ace

pitcher who uses clever pitches instead of speed: finesse pitcher

pitcher's warmup area: bullpen

player making game-losing error: goat

player not currently under contract and free to change teams: free agent

players' nickname: boys of summer

rectangles batter stands in at bat: batter's box

screen, protective: backstop

signal, secret: sign

sign, no pepper: stenciled sign warning players not to play games of pepper, the infield batting and fielding drill that sometimes damages the playing field

statistical rundown in newspaper: boxscore

strike criteria, full swing: break the wrists

strikeout, to: fan, *whiff

strikes, to be called out on: go down looking

substitute runner: pinch runner

throwing arm, powerful: *bazooka, *shotgun SEE ATHLETE, SPORT(S)

baseless *a.* unsubstantiated, unfounded, groundless, unwarranted, flimsy.

bash *n. Sl.* celebration, *wing-ding, spree. SEE PARTY

bash *v.* smash, whack, hit, strike, slam, punch, *clobber, crush, *bop.

bashful *a.* shy, timid, shrinking, embarrassed, blushing, modest, backward, demure, self-conscious, withdrawn, sheepish, retiring, coy. ANT. *brash, confident, swaggering, loud.*

basic *n.* fundamental, rudiment, essential, nuts and bolts.

basic *a.* fundamental, rudimentary, essential, primary, vital, elementary, key, necessary. ANT. *nonessential, superfluous, extra.*

basin *n.* washbowl, sink, vessel, tub, font.

basis *n.* base, foundation, support, root, grounding, nucleus, source, center.

bask *v.* **1.** WARM ONESELF IN THE SUN *catch some rays, sunbathe. **2.** LUXURIATE revel, delight in, wallow, eat up.

basket *n.* container, receptacle, hamper, wickerwork, creel, pannier, scuttle.

basketball *n.* *hoops, *brownball, *B-ball, ball, sport, game, athletic competition.
WORD FIND
blocked shot, illegally: goaltending

block out opponent to get a better angle at a rebound: box out

boundary line at end of court: baseline
defense, player-to-player: man-to-man defense
defense, area: zone defense
defense, slang: D
fiberglass stop: backboard, glass
failure to move ball out of backcourt within ten seconds: backcourt violation
fake a shot: pump fake
fall-away shot: fade away jumper
footrace to basket: fast break
forecourt of the defense: backcourt
free throw lane for a close shot, dribble down the: drive the lane
free throw granted at free throw line for a foul: foul shot, free throw
guarding opponents aggressively from the moment the ball is inbounded: full court press, trapping
hitting shots consistently: *having a hot hand, * in a zone, *on fire, *heating up, *in a groove
leaping ability, measure of: hang time
long range shot: *Hail Mary, *prayer, *from downtown, *bomb, three-pointer
mid-air catch followed by a slam-dunk: alley-oop
missing a lot of shots: cold, ice cold
net shot, nothing but: swish
pass resulting in a score: assist
player, large and powerful and adept at rebounding: power forward
player, largest, plays the posts and rebounds: center
players covering the corner areas: forwards
players, usually smaller, who play the perimeter and bring up the ball and feed to teammates: guards, point guard
possession, head-to-head leap for ball that determines: jump shot
post near basket: low post
post near foul line: high post
ratio of shots taken and scored: field goal percentage
rebounding, aggressive: *crashing the boards
screen or legal block: pick
screen play: pick and roll
shot, close, off-the-backboard: layup
shot, jumping: jump shot, *J
shot, one-handed arc: hook shot
shot, poor: *air ball, *brick
shot, roll-in from very close range: finger-roll
shot that misses everything including rim and backboard: *air ball

slamming the ball through the hoop: dunk, slam-dunk
two-on-one defensive strategy: double team
violation in which player hits opponent's arm: *hack
violation, offensive player standing too long in free throw lane: three-second violation
violation: foul
violation, dribbling: double-dribble, traveling, *walking
violation, running into a stationary opponent while dribbling: charging, offensive foul
violation in which ball is turned over in dribbler's hand: palming
SEE ATHLETE, SPORT(S)

bastard n. 1. ILLEGITIMATE CHILD *love child, misbegot. 2. SCOUNDREL, jerk, son of a bitch, cad, rascal.

bastardize v. debase, defile, degrade, adulterate, corrupt, ruin, spoil.

baste v. moisten, moisturize, soak, wet, saturate, bathe.

BASTION n. [BAS chun] a stronghold or fortified place. *Harvard, a bastion of higher education. The marksmen took refuge behind the bastion.* SYN. stronghold, fortification, fortress, citadel, rampart, bulwark, refuge, garrison, facilities.

bat n. club, stick, staff, racket, cudgel, bludgeon, baton, shillelagh, *lumber, truncheon.

bat v. 1. hit, smack, whack, swing at. 2. wink, blink, flutter.

BAT MITZVAH n. [baht MITZ vuh] ceremony that recognizes the entrance of a twelve- or thirteen-year-old Jewish girl into adulthood. *Her family gathered together to celebrate her bat mitzvah.* SYN. ceremony, rite of passage, confirmation, service, initiation, coming of age, celebration. SEE BAR MITZVAH, RELIGION

batch n. lot, bunch, cluster, assortment, group, pack, aggregate, collection, quantity.

bath n. wash, soak, cleansing, ablution, rinse, sponge bath, tub, shower, wash-up, steep, sauna.

bathe v. wash, soak, cleanse, clean, rinse, sponge off, freshen up, scrub, douche, lave, shower, steep.

bathing suit n. swimming trunks, shorts, swimsuit, bikini, *cutoffs, T-strap, maillot, *jams, one-piece, leotard, string bikini.

bathos n. sentimentality, triteness, insipidness,

mush, *schmaltz, mawkishness, melodrama, bleeding heart, wishy-washyness.

bathroom *n.* restroom, toilet, men's room, ladies' room, *john, *head, latrine, washroom, commode, necessary, water closet, *can, outhouse, privy, *loo, lavatory, powder room.

baton *n.* stick, bat, staff, rod, club, wand, scepter, truncheon, mace.

battalion *n.* unit, body, subdivision, massing, assembly, battle group.

batter *v.* beat, pound, strike, pummel, *sock, thrash, smash, wallop, dash, demolish, mangle, break, shatter, crush.

battery *n.* **1.** ELECTRICAL STORAGE UNIT dry cell, storage cell. **2.** ASSAULT beating, mugging, thrashing. **3.** SERIES array, line, string. **4.** GUNNERY artillery.

battle *n.* war, skirmish, conflict, clash, scuffle, engagement, combat, fray, encounter, assault, fight, *run-in, tussle, confrontation, squabble. SEE WAR, AMMUNITION

battle *v.* fight, clash, skirmish, war, engage, confront, squabble.

battlement *n.* SEE CASTLE

battleship *n.* warship, naval vessel, battlewagon, fighting ship, *tin can, cruiser, destroyer.

bauble *n.* trinket, trifle, knickknack, gewgaw, ornament, bagatelle.

bawdy *a.* indecent, lewd, coarse, improper, obscene, raunchy, dirty, indelicate, lascivious, licentious, ribald. ANT. *clean, proper, chaste*.

bawl *v.* **1.** SHOUT yell, bellow, holler, bark, thunder, cry, howl. **2.** CRY wail, weep, blubber, sob, snivel, whimper, squall.

bawl out *v. Sl.* SEE SCOLD

bay *n.* **1.** bight, cove, inlet, gulf, estuary, strait, lagoon, harbor. **2.** alcove, niche, nook.

bay *v.* bark, howl, yelp, bellow.

bayou *n.* tributary, stream, body of water, creek, river, branch, waterway.

bazaar *n.* marketplace, shop, fair, flea market, rummage sale, street market.

beach *n.* shore, strand, coast, seaside, littoral.

WORD FIND

arm of land connecting two land masses: isthmus, tombolo

channel, small: rill

cross-current swimming hazard: riptide

debris, cargo washed ashore from lost ship: flotsam and jetsam

embankment or headland: bluff, promontory

harbor-protecting structure extending into water: jetty

ledge or shelf of sand deposited by sea over time: berm

marine vegetation washed ashore: wrack

mineral in beach sand: garnet, feldspar, quartz

narrow arm of land extending into water: spit

pillowlike object, egg-casing of skate: mermaid's purse

receding tide: ebb tide

ridge of coral or rock skirting shore: barrier reef

ripples in sand left by swash: swashmarks

sand bar connecting two land masses: tombolo

sea spray: spindrift

shells: abalone, baby bonnet, clam, cockle, conch, cone, cowrie, horn, limpet, mussel, nautilus, oyster, periwinkle, razor, scallop, triton, wentletrap

shelter/bathhouse: cabana

small beach between two cliffs: pocket beach

small rock island at head of promontory: stack

waves: plunger, spiller, comber, train, graybeards, eagre, tidal bore

wave's shallow sweep up beach: swash

SEE OCEAN, WAVE

BEACHHEAD *n.* [BEECH hed] shoreline captured in enemy territory, used as a base for a larger attack. The term is frequently used as a metaphor for any initial establishment or opening base of operations. *The company quickly established a beachhead overseas and has been gaining customers rapidly.* SYN. territory, enemy territory, base, base of operations, staging area, position, footing, ground, foothold, post, entrance, threshold.

beacon *n.* signal light, warning light, smoke signal, guide, lighthouse, bonfire.

bead *n.* droplet, drop, pearl, spheroid, pellet, pill.

beak *n.* bill. SEE NOSE

beam *n.* **1.** SUPPORT girder, brace, rafter, boom, crosspiece, joist, stud, board, two-by-four. **2.** LIGHT ray, shaft, stream, swath, streak.

beam *v.* **1.** TRANSMIT emit, flash, broadcast. **2.** RADIATE glow, shine, glisten. **3.** SMILE BROADLY grin, take on a cheerful glow, radiate. SEE SMILE

bear *n.* **1.** BRUIN ursus, grizzly, mammal, brown bear, black bear, polar bear. **2.** PESSIMIST conservative, *gloomy gus, prophet of doom, Cassandra, naysayer, *killjoy, *worrywart, realist. ANT. 2. *bull, optimist*.

bear v. **1.** HOLD UP support, brace, buttress, uphold, sustain, shoulder. **2.** CARRY convey, bring, lug, tote, haul, move. **3.** TOLERATE endure, suffer, stomach, stand, withstand, put up with, abide. **4.** PRODUCE YOUNG give birth to, produce, beget, yield, reproduce, bring forth.

bearable a. tolerable, endurable. ANT. *unbearable.*

beard n. whiskers, stubble, five o'clock shadow, bristles, *rat's nest.

WORD FIND

anchorlike, short, pointy fringe extending up to bottom lip: anchor

curly, thick, square-cut: Trojan beard

ducktail-like: ducktail beard

forked: swallowtail beard

goatlike chin tuft: goatee, satyric tuft

long tuft extending beneath lower lip, worn by Napoleon III: Imperial

medium, no mustache: Lincolnesque

pointed, short, no sideburns: Van Dyke

rounded: aureole

sideburns, bushy, shaped: muttonchops

slender, pointed: stiletto

spade shaped: spade beard, Shenandoah

Spanish style, pointed, medium length: Cádiz

square-cut, long: tile

tuft of hair under bottom lip: barbiche

twisted or twined: screw beard

SEE MUSTACHE

bearing n. manner, carriage, air, posture, mien, attitude, demeanor, presence, comportment.

bearings n. orientation, location.

BEARISH a. [BAIR ish] pessimistic, particularly when concerning the stock market. *He sold off his stocks because he was feeling particularly bearish.* SYN. pessimistic, cautious, conservative, gloomy, skeptical, uneasy, negative, doubtful, lacking confidence. ANT. *bullish.*

beast n. animal, creature, savage, brute, swine. SEE BARBARIAN, MONSTER

beastly a. savage, brutish, barbaric, heathen, wild, uncivilized, primitive, fiendish, monstrous, vile, boorish, feral, coarse, disagreeable, nasty. ANT. *humane, civilized, cultured, refined.*

beat n. **1.** CADENCE rhythm, pulse, pulsation, meter. **2.** CIRCUIT walk, rounds, route, precinct.

beat v. **1.** BATTER pound, strike, hammer, bang, pummel, thrash, *thump, hit, smack, flog,

cuff, *whomp, *slug, *belt, box, *whale on, punch. **2.** MOLD fashion, forge, shape. **3.** DEFEAT win over, vanquish, rout, best, subdue, *kick butt, outstrip, outdistance, prevail over, *smoke the competition, *leave the competition in one's wake, lick, top. **4.** PULSATE throb, palpitate, vibrate, thump. **5.** WHIP stir, mix.

beat a. tired, exhausted, enervated. ANT. *energized, invigorated.*

beaten a. licked, vanquished, discouraged, demoralized. ANT. *encouraged, heartened.*

beatific a. blissful, serene, angelic, heavenly. ANT. *fiendish, villainous, diabolical.*

beatitude n. blessedness, happiness, bliss, serenity, saintliness, peace.

beatnik n. free spirit, nonconformist, Bohemian, *a stray from the herd, *hippie, *flower child, deviant.

beau n. boyfriend, lover, suitor, swain, sweetheart, fiancé.

beaut n. Sl. *lulu.

beautician n. hairdresser, manicurist, coiffurist.

beautiful a. **1.** ATTRACTIVE pretty, handsome, becoming, comely, fair, lovely, good-looking, *nice, gorgeous, captivating. **2.** EXCELLENT great, fantastic, superb, splendid. ANT. *1. ugly, unattractive, homely, repulsive. 2. awful, terrible, rotten.*

beautiful people n. society people, upper crust, the well-to-do, the wealthy class, the upper class, high society, fashionable society, *the in crowd.

beautify v. dress up, decorate, fix up, adorn, primp, make up, *gussie up, enhance, glamorize. ANT. *deface, spoil.*

beauty n. **1.** ATTRACTIVENESS prettiness, comeliness, fairness, loveliness, good looks, appeal, pulchritude, allure, charm. "A fading flower."—Bible. "Silent eloquence."—French proverb. "God's handwriting."—Emerson. "The power by which a woman charms a lover and terrifies a husband."—Ambrose Bierce. **2.** BELLE goddess, *babe, *fox, *looker, *knockout, sex symbol, enchantress, siren, *vision, *dreamboat, *doll, Venus. ANT. *1. ugliness, repulsiveness, plainness. 2. hag, Quasimodo, dog, eyesore.*

beckon v. summon, call, signal, wave, hail, invite, motion.

becloud v. confuse, muddle, obfuscate, darken, veil, obscure, shroud, mask, bewilder, make unclear. ANT. *clear up, clarify.*

becoming a. **1.** SUITABLE appropriate, proper, fitting, befitting, seemly, comme il faut, right, correct. **2.** ATTRACTIVE comely, flattering, pretty, beautiful. ANT. *1. unsuitable, inappropriate, unbefitting. 2. unflattering, unattractive.*

bed *n.* **1.** BUNK mattress, *sack, cot, berth, hammock, pallet. "The heaven upon earth to the weary head."—Thomas Hood. **2.** LAYER stratum, seam, deposit.

bed and breakfast *n.* inn, B&B, guest house, lodging, accomodations.

bedazzle *v.* bewilder, confuse, daze, dazzle, overwhelm, blind.

bedding *n.* bedclothes, blankets, sheets, covers, quilts, coverlets.

bedevil *v.* plague, torment, frustrate, annoy, torture, *bug, irritate.

bedlam *n.* confusion, uproar, pandemonium, turmoil, noise, chaos, hubbub, madness, madhouse, hullabaloo.

bed of roses *n.* comfort, luxury, paradise.

bedraggled *a.* wet, dirty, limp, sopping, filthy, soggy, disheveled, drenched, unkempt, soiled, sodden, muddy. ANT. *dry, clean, neat.*

bedridden *a.* laid up, infirm, disabled, prostrate, incapacitated, invalid, ill, sick, crippled, ailing, *flat on one's back.

bedroom *n.* chamber, bedchamber, boudoir, bed-sitter.

bed-wetting *n.* enuresis, incontinence.

bee *n.* bumblebee, honey bee, killer bee, drone, worker, Queen bee. "Nature's confectioner."—John Cleveland.

beef *n. Sl.* complaint, gripe, grouse.

beefy *a.* brawny, fleshy, burly, strong, powerful, strapping, Herculian, robust, solid, hulklike, husky. ANT. *skinny, anorexic.*

beehive *n.* hive, beegum, skep, colony, apiary.

beer *n.* ale, lager, malt, bitter, *suds, *stout, *cold one, *brew, *brewski, pilsner, pint. "That which drowns all care."—Robert Herrick.

WORD FIND

cask: keg, puncheon, tun
cup/glass: mug, stein, toby, schooner
foam: head, froth, bead
ingredients: hops, malt (mash), yeast
manufacturer: brewery
mixed with ginger ale: shandygaff
spiced: flip
SEE ALCOHOL, DRINK, MOONSHINE, WINE

befall *v.* happen, occur, come to pass.

befitting *a.* appropriate, suitable, seemly, right. ANT. *inappropriate, improper.*

before *prep.* previous to, preceding, prior to, ahead of.

beforehand *adv.* earlier, previously, sooner, prior to.

befriend *v.* make friends, *get chummy with, get acquainted, get to know, help, stand up for, take under one's wing. ANT. *reject, shun.*

befuddle *v.* confuse, muddle, mix up, confound, perplex, fluster, stupefy, boggle, rattle. ANT. *clear one's mind, sober.*

beg *v.* **1.** PANHANDLE scrounge, *cadge, *bum off from, solicit, *sponge off. **2.** ASK FOR beseech, implore, plead, petition, solicit, entreat.

beget *v.* bear, father, create, generate, engender, propagate, reproduce, sire, bring forth, effect, give rise to.

beggar *n.* panhandler, *moocher, *bum, mendicant, tramp, parasite, *sponger, leech, pauper, derelict, loafer, scamp, fakir. "The only free man in the universe."—Charles Lamb.

begin *v.* **1.** START commence, set in motion, launch, initiate, arise, happen, go ahead, embark, open, get the ball rolling. **2.** COME INTO BEING start, commence, arise, flower, crop up, issue, sprout, originate, inaugurate, spring, get under way, found. ANT. *end, conclude, stop.*

beginner *n.* novice, tyro, virgin, neophyte, *greenhorn, *rookie, *tenderfoot, amateur, trainee, apprentice. ANT. *veteran, old hand, expert.*

beginning *n.* **1.** INITIATION onset, start, commencement, opening, launching, debut, outset, genesis, inception. "A quarter of the journey."—Henry Bohn. **2.** ORIGIN source, root, fountain, seed, germ. ANT. *1. ending, closing, conclusion, finale.*

begrudge *v.* resent, envy, hold against, be jealous, stint.

beguile *v.* **1.** TRICK mislead, cheat, bamboozle, dupe, *burn, *rope in, deceive, delude. **2.** CHARM enchant, bewitch, captivate, delight, amuse, divert. distract. ANT. *2. bore.*

behave *v.* **1.** ACT conduct, deport, comport, perform, function. **2.** MIND shape up, *mind one's manners, *mind one's Ps and Qs, *keep one's nose clean, smarten up, be good.

behavior *n.* **1.** CONDUCT deportment, comportment, demeanor, manner, bearing, ways, etiquette. "The finest of the fine arts."—Emerson. "No truer index to intelligence."—Ibn Gabirol. **2.** ACTION performance, functioning, operation, reaction, response.

behavior modification *n.* therapy, retraining,

psychotherapy, conditioning, reinforcement, reward system, aversion therapy, change, desensitization.

behead v. decapitate, decollate, guillotine, execute.

BEHEMOTH n. [bi HEE muth] anything gigantic. *We saw whales and other behemoths of the sea.* SYN. giant, monster, colossus, mammoth, leviathan, titan, Goliath, whale, hippopotamus.

behest n. order, command, bidding, request, word, edict, demand, urging, decree, say-so, desire.

behind n. buttocks, backside, *ass, rump, *tush, bottom, stern.

behind adv. back, in back of, rearward, trailing, aft.

behold v. look at, regard, observe, notice, view, watch, *feast your eyes on, consider, scrutinize, examine, gaze upon. ANT. *ignore, overlook, disregard.*

beholden a. obligated, indebted, owing. ANT. *freed, unbound.*

behoove v. benefit, befit, be worthwhile, suit, be incumbent upon.

being n. 1. ENTITY creature, organism, person, soul, spirit. 2. EXISTENCE reality, life. ANT. 2. *nonexistence.*

belabor v. dwell on, go on about, *beat a dead horse, pound, hammer home, rehash, repeat, overwork.

belated a. tardy, overdue, late, delayed, past due. ANT. *timely, prompt.*

belch v. 1. BURP eruct. 2. EMIT spew, discharge, spout, erupt, disgorge, expel.

BELEAGUER v. [be LEE gur] to besiege or harass. *He will beleaguer her until she finally gives in.* SYN. besiege, harass, beset, plague, pester, annoy, badger, bother, hound, hector, persecute, victimize, close in on.

belfry n. bell tower.

belie v. misrepresent, disguise, falsify, defy, negate, contradict, twist, conceal.

belief n. conviction, certainty, faith, trust, assumption, presumption, acceptance, confidence, credence, hope, feeling, guess, understanding, notion, judgment, position, hypothesis, credo, dogma. "The most complete of all distinctions between man and the lower animals."—Charles Darwin.

believable a. convincing, plausible, credible, reliable, acceptable. ANT. *unbelievable, farfetched.*

believe v. accept, hold, maintain, presume, know, have faith, swear by, give credence to, trust, suspect, *take as gospel, suppose, assume, guess, surmise. ANT. *disbelieve, doubt.*

believer n. adherent, devotee, follower, apostle, disciple, zealot.

belittle v. disparage, depreciate, put down, diminish, degrade, deride, malign, *take down a peg, *knock, discredit. ANT. *build up, aggrandize, put on a pedestal.*

bell n. campana, carillon, chimes, dinger. "The publicity of God."—R.L. Bruckberger. "The music bordering nearest heaven."—Charles Lamb.

WORD FIND
clapper: tongue
ring by striking with hammer: chime
ringer: sexton
sound: clang, dong, ting, tinkle, tintinabulation, ring, knell, peal, toll, reverberation
tower: belfry

BELLICOSE a. [BEL i KOSE] belligerent, quarrelsome, warlike. *He was eager to fight; he was a notoriously bellicose man.* SYN. belligerent, quarrelsome, warlike, hostile, pugnacious, aggressive, combative, volatile, contentious, peppery. ANT. *peaceful, passive.*

BELLIGERENT a. [buh LIJ ur unt] quarrelsome, hostile, quick to fight. *Belligerent inner city gangs started the riot.* SYN. bellicose, pugnacious, quarrelsome, militant, war-mongering, warlike, hostile, aggressive, combative, volatile, contentious, peppery. ANT. *peaceful, passive, pacific.*

bellow v. roar, shout, holler, thunder, squall, boom, bark, bawl, howl, bluster.

BELLWETHER n. [BEL WETH er] a leader, any thing or person used as an indicator. *IBM has long reigned as a bellwether among computer companies.* SYN. leader, pacesetter, pilot, standard-bearer, guide, *the one to watch, model, role model, indicator, *barometer.

belly n. abdomen, stomach, tummy, *gut, *spare tire, paunch, *middle-age spread, potbelly, *breadbasket.

bellybutton n. navel, umbilicus.

belonging n. relationship, camaraderie, community, kinship, familiarity. ANT. *alienation, anomie, rejection.*

belongings n. things, possessions, stuff, personal effects, worldly goods, chattel.

beloved a. loved, dearest, cherished, adored, darling, precious, worshipped, revered, treasured, esteemed. ANT. *hated, detested, distained.*

below *adv.* beneath, down, under, low, underneath.

belt *n.* band, sash, girdle, strap, cord, thong, cinch, cummerbund.

belt *v.* hit, smack, wallop, thrash, beat, whip. SEE BEAT

bemoan *v.* grieve, lament, mourn, bewail, deplore, rue, cry over.

bemuse *v.* confuse, puzzle, bewilder, befuddle, disconcert, addle, confound, daze, mix up, muddle, stupefy.

bench *n.* **1.** SEAT settee, pew, bleacher. **2.** COURT judiciary, bar, tribunal.

BENCHMARK *n.* [BENCH mark] that which becomes a standard to measure against. *Their new computer quickly became the benchmark for the industry.* SYN. standard, model, gauge, measure, yardstick, bellwether, touchstone, exemplar, high water mark.

bend *v.* **1.** CURVE crook, twist, arc, flex, bow, curl, coil, snake. **2.** GIVE IN yield, acquiesce, *cave in, bow down, capitulate, surrender.

beneath *prep.* under, below, underneath.

BENEDICT ARNOLD *n.* any traitorous person, so named after the famous American Revolution general. *He became a Benedict Arnold, switching sides at the last minute.* SYN. traitor, double-crosser, betrayer, Judas, snake in the grass, quisling, Brutus, turncoat, backstabber.

benediction *n.* blessing, invocation, prayer, grace, benison, consecration. ANT. *curse, damning, malediction.*

benefactor *n.* patron, supporter, financier, underwriter, donor, angel, philanthropist, contributor.

beneficial *a.* helpful, advantageous, rewarding, valuable, good, favorable, propitious, useful, gainful. ANT. *harmful, useless.*

beneficiary *n.* recipient, heir, heiress.

benefit *n.* gain, good, profit, help, favor, service, reward, worth, avail, *perk. ANT. *loss, harm.*

benefit *v.* gain, profit, help, favor, serve, reward, advance, do good. ANT. *harm, disfavor, impair.*

benevolence *n.* kindness, goodwill, charity, humanitarianism, goodness, altruism, generosity, compassion, sympathy. "One of the distinguishing characteristics of man. It is the path of duty."—Mencius. ANT. *meanness, ill will, cold-heartedness, misanthropy.*

BENEVOLENT *a.* [buh NEV uh lunt] kindly, doing good, charitable. *The United Way is a*

benevolent organization. SYN. kind, charitable, generous, humane, good, altruistic, compassionate, sympathetic, philanthropic, benign, giving, beneficent. ANT. *mean, selfish, cold-hearted, malicious, misanthropic.*

BENIGN *a.* [bi NINE] **1.** kindly **2.** advantageous **3.** harmless. **1.** *Uncle Harry's bark is worse than his bite; he's really quite benign.* **2.** *The weather turned out to be rather benign for the tournament.* **3.** *John's tumor was found to be benign.* SYN. **1.** kindly, benevolent, merciful, sympathetic, genial, gracious, goodhearted, altruistic, compassionate. **2.** beneficial, favorable, propitious, auspicious, healthful, helpful, fortunate. **3.** harmless, slight, curable, superficial, innocuous, inconsequential. ANT. **1.** *mean, selfish, malicious, misanthropic.* **2.** *harmful, inopportune, unfortunate.* **3.** *malignant, severe.*

bent *n.* propensity, penchant, inclination, leaning, proclivity, liking, predilection, ability, flair, fondness, aptitude.

bent *a.* crooked, curved, twisted, bowed, contorted, warped, hooked, doubled over. ANT. *straight.*

bent on *a.* determined, bound, intent, fixed.

bequeath *v.* leave, will, consign, hand over, bestow, impart, endow, give.

BEQUEST *n.* [bi KWEST] something given to someone in a will. *She received a bequest of $1000.* SYN. inheritance, gift, endowment, bequeathal, legacy, estate, dower.

berate *v.* scold, upbraid, rebuke, dress down, reproach, tongue-lash, *bawl out, *give one hell, *jump down one's throat, vituperate, *rake over the coals.

bereavement *n.* loss, deprivation, grief, sorrow, heartache, mourning.

bereft *a.* bereaved, left desolate, deprived, lorn, lonely, destitute, wanting, lacking. ANT. *fulfilled, satisfied, consoled.*

berry *n.* fruit, crop.

WORD FIND

amber, apricot-flavored: cloudberry
aphrodisiac, alleged: myrtle
blueberry-like: bilberry, Juneberry
bears, scarlet berries eaten by: bearberries
blackish: huckleberry (whortleberry), blackberry, black raspberry
blackish or dark red: boysenberry
blue: blueberry
bog: cranberries
candles, gray, aromatic berries used for: bayberry
large pink, red, white or yellow: gooseberry

minty breath freshener: wintergreen
orange, red or black: barberry
poisonous: pokeweed berry
purplish-black: elderberry
purplish, red, black or white: mulberry
raspberry-like: boysenberry, blackberry, mulberry
red: boysenberry
red and sweet: strawberry
red, tart: cranberry, currant
tart, black: currant

berserk *a.* deranged, violent, crazed, mad, amuck, insane, maniacal, frenzied, murderous. ANT. *serene, calm, rational.*

beseech *v.* implore, plead, beg, solicit, pray, entreat, urge, press, supplicate.

beset *v.* plague, harass, hound, torment, badger, bother, surround, *bug, hassle, besiege, victimize, vex, beleaguer.

beside *prep.* next to, close to, adjacent to, alongside, abreast of, bordering, by.

besides *adv.* in addition, as well, moreover, plus, also.

besiege *v.* **1.** SURROUND hem in, encircle, enclose, close in on, crowd, lay siege to. **2.** HARASS beleaguer, badger, plague, torment, beset, overwhelm, hound, pressure.

besmirch *v.* soil, sully, dishonor, taint, tarnish, smear, muddy, disgrace. ANT. *glorify, honor.*

best *n.* winner, *cream of the crop, creme de la creme, the finest, *top dog, *blue ribbon winner, *the tops, paragon, the champion. ANT. *the worst, also-ran, loser.*

best *v.* beat, outdo, defeat, outdistance, outclass, conquer, win over, dominate, *wipe the floor with, prevail, *thrash. ANT. *lose,* *choke.

best *a.* finest, utmost, *topflight, *top drawer, unsurpassed, superior, greatest, select, first-rate, choice, preeminent, peerless, unequaled, nonpareil, supreme, tops. ANT. *worst, lowest.*

bestial *a.* animalistic, wild, untamed, savage, fierce, primitive, unrefined, feral, base, barbaric, brutish, inhumane, monstrous. ANT. *humane, civilized, civil.*

bestow *v.* present, give, endow, bequeath, confer, award, consign, donate.

best-seller *n.* hit, hot seller, favorite, *mover, *hot item, a top ten, #1, winner, success, chart-buster, record-breaker. "A book which somehow sold well simply because it was selling well." Daniel Boorstin. SEE BOOK, NOVEL

bet *n.* wager, stake, gamble, parlay, *long shot, risk, proposition, chance.

WORD FIND
bet one's winnings from a previous race on another: parlay
horseracing bet choosing first and second place finishers, not necessarily in correct order: quiniela
horseracing bet choosing first and second place finishers: perfecta
horseracing bet choosing first, second and third-place finishers: trifecta
horseracing bet choosing winners in two races: daily double
horseracing bet in which winnings are shared: pari-mutuel

bête noire *n.* enemy, trouble, *bad news, adversary, devil, black beast, antagonist, Typhoid Mary, Mary Mallon, plague, curse, bane.

betray *v.* **1.** BREAK FAITH turn traitor, deceive, *pull a Judas, sell out, stab in the back, *sell down the river, *two-time, *double-cross, *fink, *rat on. **2.** REVEAL give away, show, disclose, tell on, unmask, divulge, expose. ANT. **1.** *be loyal, be faithful.* **2.** *hide, cover up.*

betrayal *n.* treachery, disloyalty, breech of faith, double-crossing, duplicity, treason, *Judas kiss, perfidy. ANT. *faithfulness, loyalty.*

betrayer *n.* traitor, Judas, conspirator.

betrothal *n.* engagement, vow, pledge to marry.

better *v.* improve, enrich, advance, promote, upgrade.

better *a.* finer, superior, surpassing, topping, first-rate, preeminent, peerless, supreme, excelling. ANT. *worse, inferior, lower.*

betterment *n.* improvement, enrichment, advancement, promotion, upgrading.

between *prep.* amidst, among, within, in the thick, intermediate.

beverage *n.* drink, refreshment, pop, liquid, ale, cooler, liquor, draft.

bevy *n.* group, flock, bunch, band, knot, gaggle, covey, pack, crowd, clique, party, throng.

bewail *v.* bemoan, lament, mourn, wail, cry, deplore, grieve, weep, rue, pine for. ANT. *shriek with joy, celebrate, rejoice.*

beware *v.* be wary, be careful, watch, stay on guard, heed, be on the lookout, stay on one's toes.

bewilder *v.* confuse, puzzle, befuddle, confound, perplex, mystify, baffle, befog, strike dumb, set adrift, disorient, disconcert. ANT. *inform, clarify.*

bewilderment *n.* confusion, puzzlement, befuddlement, perplexity, mystification, bafflement, *discombobulation. ANT. *understanding, clear-headedness, lucidity.*

bewitching *a.* enchanting, charming, beguiling, spellbinding, mesmerizing, captivating, fascinating, seductive, enticing, hypnotizing, alluring. ANT. *repulsive, dull.*

beyond *prep.* past, yonder, inaccessible, unattainable.

bias *n.* partiality, inclination, preference, prejudice, bent, predilection, leaning, proclivity, one-sidedness, *mind-set, favoritism, bigotry. ANT. *impartiality, fairness, objectivity.*

bias *v.* influence, sway, prejudice, indoctrinate, brainwash, twist, slant.

BIBLE *n.* **1.** HOLY SCRIPTURES the Good Book, Word of God, Gospel, Old Testament, New Testament. "That great medicine chest of humanity."—Heinrich Heine. "The book of books, the storehouse and magazine of life and comfort."—George Herbert. "A window in this prison world, through which we may look into eternity."—Timothy Dwight. "God's chart for you to steer by."—Henry Ward Beecher. "Obscene stories . . . voluptuous debaucheries . . . cruel and torturous executions . . . unrelenting vindictiveness with which more than half of is filled . . . it would be more consistent that we call it the word of a demon than the word of God. It is a history of wickedness that has served to corrupt and brutalize mankind."—Thomas Paine. **2.** GUIDEBOOK manual, text, handbook, vade mecum, authority. SEE CHURCH, RELIGION, GOD

WORD FIND

(Books of the Bible)

Apocrypha: Tobit, Judith, 1 Maccabees, 2 Maccabees, Wisdom of Solomon, Ecclesiasticus, Baruch, 1 Esdras, 2 Esdras, Additions to Esther, Prayer of Azariah, Susanna, Bel and the Dragon, Prayer of Manassess

Torah: Genesis, Exodus, Leviticus, Numbers, Deuteronomy

Prophets: Joshua, Judges, 1 Samuel, 2 Samuel, 1 Kings, 2 Kings, Isaiah, Jeremiah, Ezekiel, Hosea, Joel, Amos, Obadiah, Jonah, Micah, Nahum, Habakkuk, Zephaniah, Haggai, Zechariah, Malachi

Writings: Psalms, Proverbs, Job, Song of Songs, Ruth, Lamentations, Ecclesiastes, Esther, Daniel, Ezra, Nehemiah, 1 Chronicles, 2 Chronicles

Old Testament: Genesis, Exodus, Leviticus, Numbers, Deuteronomy, Joshua, Judges, Ruth, 1 Samuel, 2 Samuel, 1 Kings, 2 Kings, 1 Chronicles, 2 Chronicles, Ezra, Nehemiah, Tobit, Judith, Esther, 1 Maccabees, 2 Maccabees, Job, Psalms, Proverbs, Ecclesiastes, Song of Songs, Wisdom of Solomon, Ecclesiasticus, Isaiah, Jeremiah, Lamentations, Baruch, Ezekiel, Daniel, Hosea, Joel, Amos, Obadiah, Jonah, Micah, Nahum, Habakkuk, Zephaniah, Haggai, Zechariah, Malachi

New Testament: Matthew, Mark, Luke, John, Acts of the Apostles, Romans, 1 Corinthians, 2 Corinthians, Galatians, Ephesians, Philippians, Colossians, 1 Thessalonians, 2 Thessalonians, 1 Timothy, 2 Timothy, Titus, Philemon, Hebrews, James, 1 Peter, 2 Peter, 1 John, 2 John, 3 John, Jude, Revelation

bicker *v.* squabble, fight, quarrel, wrangle, spar, debate, haggle, argue. ANT. *agree, concur.*

bicycle *n.* bike, two-wheeler, *wheels, velocipede.

WORD FIND

forerunner with giant front wheel, small rear wheel: ordinary

four-wheeler: quadricycle

one-wheeler: unicycle

reclining position, ridden in: recumbent bicycle

rugged, off-road: mountain bike

safety bar: *sissy bar

seat: saddle

three-wheel passenger vehicle: pedicab, trishaw

two-seater: tandem, bicycle built for two

bid *n.* **1.** OFFER proffer, tender, proposition, submission, proposal. **2.** ATTEMPT try, effort, endeavor, crack.

bid *v.* **1.** OFFER proffer, tender, proposition, propose, submit. **2.** COMMAND call, order, request, instruct, ask, charge.

bidding *n.* command, request, order, charge, direction, behest, mandate, dictate, demand, injunction, invitation.

bide *v.* wait, stay, continue, remain, linger, dwell, *sit tight.

big *a.* **1.** LARGE huge, sizable, immense, gigantic, prodigious, ample, substantial, vast, *heavy-duty, colossal, *Brobdingnagian, massive, voluminous, hulking, gargantuan. **2.** IMPORTANT weighty, consequential, powerful, prominent, eminent, significant, *major league, momentous, *big-time, paramount, major. ANT. *1. small, tiny, pint-sized. 2. insignificant, trivial, *small potatoes.*

bigamy *n.* polygamy, group marriage.

big-hearted *a.* kind, generous, giving, benevolent, noble, compassionate, gracious, forgiving, altruistic, magnanimous, sweet. ANT. *cold-hearted, mean, malevolent, selfish.*

BIGOT *n.* [BIG ut] one who has little or no tolerance for people outside his or her race, religion, political party, sexual orientation, etc. *He was a narrow-minded bigot.* SYN. racist, sexist, chauvinist, *Archie Bunker, zealot, fanatic, Nazi, anti-Semite. "He who will not reason."—William Drummond. "A blind man with sight."—Max Gralnik.

BIGOTRY *n.* [BIG uh tree] intolerance for those who are different or have different ideas, narrow-mindedness. *Archie Bunker was famous for his numerous racist and sexist remarks; he represented the epitome of bigotry.* SYN. intolerance, narrow-mindedness, prejudice, closed-mindedness, unfairness, bias, racism, sexism, chauvinism, provincialism, discrimination. "The disease of ignorance, of morbid minds."—Thomas Jefferson. ANT. *tolerance, open-mindedness, fairness.*

big shot *n.* *big wheel, *big cheese, *VIP, *bigwig, *big gun, high muck-a-muck, somebody, *heavy-hitter, *biggest toad in the puddle. ANT. *nobody*, *bush-leaguer, *second banana, *lightweight.*

bigwig *n.* SEE BIG SHOT

bike *n.* bicycle, *wheels, *ten-speed, tandem, velocipede, dandy, mountain bike. SEE BICYCLE, MOTORCYCLE

bikini *n.* thong, two-piece. SEE BATHING SUIT

bilateral *a.* reciprocal, mutual, two-sided. ANT. *unilateral.*

bilge *n. Sl.* hogwash, rubbish, rot. SEE NONSENSE

bilk *v.* swindle, cheat, defraud, *fleece, *rip-off, rook, *gyp, *take.

bill *n.* **1.** CHARGE invoice, debt, account, tab, *score, *bad news, check, statement. **2.** PROGRAM list, schedule, roster, docket, agenda. **3.** ANNOUNCEMENT handbill, circular, advertisement, bulletin. **4.** PIECE OF LEGISLATION act, draft, measure, proposal. SEE GOVERNMENT, POLITICS **5.** BEAK neb.

bill *v.* charge, tally, invoice, debit, put on one's tab.

billboard *n.* ad, advertisement, panel ad, notice.

billet *n.* quarters, lodging, barracks.

billiards *n.* pool.

WORD FIND
ball's recoil after impact: draw
miss: scratch

shot in which ball first strikes cushion: bricole
shot in which cue ball is bounced off cushion or strikes two balls in succession: carom
shot in which cue is held perpendicularly: massé
stick: cue
white ball: cue ball

billow *v.* swell, surge, undulate, wave, roll, puff up, balloon. ANT. *flatten, collapse, deflate.*

bind *n.* *fix, quandary, predicament, dilemma, *pickle.

bind *v.* **1.** TIE fasten, secure, wrap, rope, gird, lash, strap, truss, bundle, join. **2.** OBLIGATE require, restrict, confine, prescribe, compel, force. ANT. *1. untie, unbind, unravel, loose.*

binge *n.* spree, bender, fling, tear, orgy.

binoculars *n.* field glasses, magnification, magnifying lenses.

biodegrade *v.* degrade, break down, decompose, disintegrate, dilute.

biography *n.* life story, bio, autobiography, memoirs, profile, life experiences. "Dramatic constructions."—Katherine Anthony. "A heroic poem."—Thomas Carlyle. "A region bounded on the north by history, on the south by fiction, on the east by obituary, and on the west by tedium,"—Philip Guedalla. SEE BOOK

biologist *n.* life scientist, ecologist, cytologist, biochemist, geneticist, botanist. SEE SCIENTIST

biology *n.* life science, life processes. SEE SCIENCE

biopsy *n.* tissue sampling, excision, tissue removal. SEE OPERATION, SURGERY

bird *n.* fowl, feathered friend, Anseriformes, Charadriiformes, Columbiformes, Falconiformes, Galliformes, Passeriformes, Psittaciformes. "Dame Nature's minstrels."—Gavin Douglas. "The merry minstrels of the morn."—James Thomson.

WORD FIND
bare spots on underbelly used to warm eggs: brood spots
beak that curves or hooks: aquiline
bird of prey: raptor
cage/enclosure: aviary
calls/songs: trill; cheep; chirp; pipe; warble; coo; whistle; caw; chirrup; chip; chatter; chitter; squawk; twitter; mewl; cluck; croak; peep; honk; quack; cackle; trumpet; ululate; sweet, plaintive call; mournful note; high, lisping note; rasping note;

cheery, lilting melody; discordant screams of jays; forlorn hooting of an owl; liquid ululation of a loon; shrill fluting; piccolo note; caroling notes; exuberant song; wheedling voice; discordant rasp of a starling
claw: talon
collar of hair or feathers: ruff
crest on fowl: comb
domination order: pecking order
earliest known: Archaeopteryx
eggs, group of: clutch
eggs, to sit on: brood
expert on: ornithologist
eyelike spot in peacock tail: ocellus
falcons used as hunters, sport: falconry
feathers, shedding: molting
fleshy neck component on turkey: wattle
flying: flitting, darting, soaring, swooping, banking, diving, spiraling, wheeling, wheeling in intricate chandelles, rising on a thermal
grooming: preening
group of: flock; bevy (quail), charm (finches), chattering (starlings), colony (gulls), convocation (eagles), covey (grouse), exaltation (larks), fall (woodcock), flight (doves or swallows), gaggle (geese), herd (swans), host (sparrows), murder (crows), murmuration (starlings), muster (peacocks), nye (pheasants), parliament (owls), rookery (sea birds), siege (herons), skein (flying geese), team (ducks)
migratory route: flyway
mythical: phoenix, roc
nest: aerie
plumage that is soft and fluffy: down
referring to: avian
reservation: sanctuary
second stomach: gizzard, craw, crop
throat patch: gorget
wingless: apterous
young bird: chick, fledgling, nestling
birth *n.* **1.** CHILDBIRTH delivery, bearing, parturition, labor, childbearing, blessed event, whelping, emergence. "The sudden opening of a window through which you look out upon a stupendous prospect. . . ." —William Dixon. **2.** INCEPTION genesis, beginning, start, debut, emergence, onset, origin, development.
WORD FIND
anesthesia used locally to ease mother's pain: epidural

breathing/relaxation technique: Lamaze method
contractions: labor
dead, infant delivered: stillbirth
delivery assistant: midwife
delivery through mother's abdominal wall: Caesarian section, C-section
feet or buttocks-first presentation: breech presentation
membranes covering head during delivery: caul
peaceful, low-key delivery method: Leboyer delivery
profession: obstetrics
spontaneous abortion: miscarriage
uterine muscular action: contractions
vaginal incision, creates more room for passage of baby's head: episiotomy
SEE BABY, PREGNANCY
birth control *n.* contraception, planned parenthood, abortion. "Copulation without population."—Anon. "Sin against nature."—Pope Pius XI. "Premature murder." —Tertullian.
WORD FIND
Catholic-approved: rhythm method, abstinence
prophylactic: contraceptive, condom, diaphragm, sponge, IUD (intrauterine device), *the pill, *Norplant, spermicide.
sterilization, female: tubal ligation
sterilization, male: vasectomy
SEE CONTRACEPTIVE.
birth defect *n.* congenital defect, congenital malformation, deformity, abnormality, congenital deficiency, disability, mutation.
birthmark *n.* nevus, mole, blemish, spot, port wine stain, beauty mark.
birthright *n.* right, privilege.
biscuit *n.* bread, roll, muffin, scone, cracker, popover.
bisexual *a.* *swinging both ways, *AC-DC, androgynous, hermaphroditic.
bishop *n.* cleric, priest, high priest, clergyman, deacon. SEE CHURCH, CLERGY, RELIGION
bison *n.* buffalo, bovine mammal, quadruped, herbivore, animal.
bistro *n.* bar, tavern, nightclub, saloon, lounge, drinking establishment.
bit *n.* **1.** PIECE fragment, fraction, portion, particle, section, snippet, segment. **2.** MOMENT second, minute, jiffy, flash, *quick as a wink, time, spell, instant.
bitch *n.* *Sl.* complainer, *witch, nag, *rotten egg, *stinker, grumbler, nit-picker, whiner, critic, shrew, spitfire.

bitch v. Sl. complain, nag, *beef, *bellyache, *crab, gripe, grouch, *kick up a fuss, *raise a big stink.

bitchy a. Sl. complaining, fault-finding, nagging, catty, back-stabbing, malicious, vindictive, critical, crabby, negative, *whiny, fussy, picky, grouchy. ANT. sweet, kind, warm.

bite n. mouthful, morsel, spoonful, chunk, snack, nosh.

bite v. nip, chew, champ, chomp, gnaw, munch, nibble, snap, sink one's teeth into, hold, clamp.

biting a. 1. CAUSTIC bitter, cutting, penetrating, piercing, stinging. 2. SARCASTIC cutting, caustic, nasty, bitter, stinging, acerbic, scathing, sharp. ANT. 1. gentle, balmy, soothing.

bitter a. 1. ACRID tart, sour, harsh, acidic, vinegary, acerbic. 2. GRIEVOUS distressing, heartbreaking, wretched, sorrowful, painful, sad, disturbing, cruel. 3. SEVERE piercing, harsh, cutting, penetrating, stinging, sharp. 4. RESENTFUL hostile, sarcastic, nasty, begrudging, spiteful, contemptuous, cynical, peevish, malevolent. ANT. 1. sweet, honeyed. 2. happy, joyous. 3. mild, gentle. 4. friendly, warm, charitable, forgiving.

bivouac n. encampment, stopover, camp, campsite.

bizarre a. weird, strange, odd, outlandish, unusual, peculiar, freaky, wild, unconventional, extraordinary, *way out, *off the wall, fantastic, grotesque, nightmarish, surreal. ANT. ordinary, normal, everyday.

blab v. 1. TELL A SECRET *spill the beans, *let the cat out of the bag, divulge, let slip, blurt out, *squeal, *open one's mouth, *let one's tongue flap, reveal, disclose, tell all, tattle. 2. CHATTER prattle, *yak, gab, talk.

blabbermouth n. *bigmouth, tattletale, informer, *snitch, *squealer, *whistleblower, *fink, *rat.

black a. 1. COLOR ink, jet, raven, carbon, gunmetal, pitch, sable, ebony, tar, soot, coal, coffee, pepper. 2. DARK inky, unlit, shadowy, murky, dusky, gloomy. 3. AFRICAN AMERICAN, negro, colored, African, Afro-American, Negroid. 4. BLEAK gloomy, dismal, grim, dreary, somber, forlorn, mournful, funereal. 5. THREATENING ominous, foreboding, forbidding, menacing. 6. EVIL wicked, diabolical, satanic, nefarious. ANT. 1. white, snowy. 2. sunny, bright, illuminated. 4. cheerful,

bright, hopeful. 5. auspicious, favorable. 6. good, angelic, saintly.

blackball v. ostracize, ban, exclude, blacklist, bar, snub, reject, proscribe. ANT. enlist, welcome, embrace.

blacken v. 1. DARKEN smudge, black, begrime. 2. DEFAME slander, smear, tarnish, drag through the mud, *knock, libel, *badmouth. ANT. 1. lighten, brighten. 2. glorify, honor, respect.

black eye n. bad name, bad reputation, dishonor, brand, smear, stigma.

blackguard n. villain, scoundrel, rogue.

blacklist v. boycott, shut out, penalize, banish, reject, ban, ostracize, blackball, snub.

black magic n. necromancy, sorcery, witchcraft, demon worship, devil worship, Satanism.

blackmail n. extortion, hush money, *the squeeze, milking, bleeding.

blackmail v. extort, *put the squeeze on, *milk, *bleed, *shake down.

BLACK MARKET n. any market where goods or services are bought and sold illegally. They bought them illegally through the black market. SYN. underground, underground market, bootleg market, underworld market.

black out v. lose consciousness, swoon, pass out. SEE FAINT

bladder n. sac, bag, pouch, pocket.

blade n. cutting edge, knife, cutter, razor, scalpel. SEE KNIFE

blah a. Sl. bland, *humdrum, dull, *dull as dishwater, stale, insipid, tedious, flat, monotonous. ANT. electrifying, original, colorful, spirited.

blame n. 1. CONDEMNATION accusation, attribution, incrimination, imputation, impeachment, complaint, recrimination. 2. RESPONSIBILITY onus, liability, fault, guilt, culpability, accountability.

blame v. accuse, condemn, *point the finger at, fault, charge, hold responsible, *pin on, attribute, indict, impute, censure, rap.

blameless a. innocent, *clean, inculpable, above suspicion, above reproach, virtuous, unimpeachable, faultless, spotless. ANT. guilty, at fault, culpable.

blanch v. whiten, bleach, fade, wash out, pale.

bland a. dull, lackluster, uninteresting, insipid, flat, *blah, mediocre, vapid, unstimulating, plain. ANT. stimulating, exciting, rich.

blank n. nothing, zero, void, nil, emptiness, space.

blank *a.* **1.** CLEAR empty, vacant, white, unmarked, untouched, clean, barren, unused. **2.** EXPRESSIONLESS lifeless, dull, vacuous, vacant, dead, glassy, indifferent, deadpan, apathetic. ANT. *1. filled, marked, used. 2. lively, thoughtful.*

blanket *n.* cover, coverlet, quilt, comforter, afghan, spread, bedding.

blanket *v.* cover, bury, carpet, envelope, enclose, overlay.

blare *v.* blast, roar, blow, trumpet, peal, clamor, bellow, resound.

blarney *n.* **1.** FLATTERY apple-polishing, wheedling, fawning, cajolery, *sweet talk, *snow job. **2.** *BUNK *balderdash. SEE NONSENSE

blasé *a.* nonchalant, unmoved, apathetic, jaded, bored, sophisticated, lukewarm, unfazed, cloyed, weary, sated, casual. ANT. *enthusiastic, eager.*

blasphemous *a.* irreverent, irreligious, sacrilegious, impious, profane, disrespectful, ungodly. ANT. *reverent, religious, pious.*

BLASPHEMY *n.* [BLAS fuh mee] any show of disrespect toward the divine, irreverence. *Cursing God for your misfortune is blasphemy.* SYN. irreverence, sacrilege, profanity, disrespect, impiety, desecration, cursing, denouncing. "Denying the being or providence of God. . . ."—William Blackstone. ANT. *reverence, piety, respect.*

blast *n.* boom, surge, roar, explosion, burst, crack, blowup, bang, detonation, eruption, gust, shock wave. SEE WIND

blast *v.* explode, blowup, raze, detonate, level, annihilate, demolish, boom, burst, roar, blare.

blastoff *n.* launch, liftoff, ignition, firing.

BLATANT *a.* [BLAYT unt] loud, glaring or conspicuous. *Wearing Bermuda shorts to the board meeting shows a blatant disregard for dress codes.* SYN. loud, glaring, conspicuous, obvious, obnoxious, brazen, flagrant, showy, flashy, prominent, plain, boisterous, overt, naked, baldfaced. ANT. *subtle, quiet, unobtrusive.*

blather *n.* drivel, foolishness, claptrap, twaddle, *bull. SEE NONSENSE

blaze *n.* fire, flames, conflagration. SEE FIRE

blaze *v.* flame, flash, flare, flicker, radiate. SEE BURN

bleach *v.* whiten, blanch, lighten, fade, wash out, insolate.

bleak *a.* **1.** DESOLATE bare, barren, unsheltered, treeless, desert, stark, raw. **2.** DEPRESSING grim, dreary, gloomy, dismal, mournful, disheartening, cheerless, black, somber. ANT. *1. lush, overgrown. 2. cheery, sunny, bright, hopeful.*

bleed *v.* hemorrhage, ooze, gush, trickle, run, spurt, flow.

BLEEDING HEART *n.* one who is given to excessive sympathy and may be over-eager to help. *The bleeding hearts in Washington wanted to start a new welfare program.* SYN. sentimental fool, liberal, *softy, sympathizer, sucker for a sob story, soft touch.

blemish *n.* flaw, fault, mark, defect, stain, spot, blotch, mole, disfigurement, imperfection, deformity, freckle, speckle, birthmark.

blend *n.* mixture, combination, compound, composite, amalgam, concoction, fusion.

blend *v.* mix, combine, compound, amalgamate, mingle, stir in, merge, meld, alloy, scramble. ANT. *separate, divide.*

blender *n.* food processor, mixer, chopping machine, liquefier, labor-saving device, appliance.

bless *v.* hallow, consecrate, sanctify, ordain, anoint, exalt, glorify, canonize, declare holy. ANT. *curse, damn.*

blessed *a.* **1.** SACRED holy, consecrated, redeemed, sacrosanct, hallowed, sainted, saved, beatified. **2.** FAVORED gifted, fortunate, lucky. ANT. *1. unholy, cursed, condemned.*

blessing *n.* **1.** SANCTIFICATION invocation, benediction, prayer, grace, dedication. **2.** FAVOR good fortune, luck, godsend, benefit, gift, boon, good. ANT. *1. curse, condemnation. 2. misfortune, adversity, bad luck.*

blight *n.* affliction, plague, curse, scourge, infliction, calamity, bane, curse.

blight *v.* ruin, damage, destroy, afflict, devastate, cripple, kill, wither, frustrate, inflict.

blimp *n.* airship, dirigible, zeppelin.

WORD FIND
balloon portion: gas bag
gas: helium
ground crew: riggers
inner airbags inflated or deflated as a ballast control: ballonets
mooring post on ground: mast
passenger/crew compartment: car, gondola
rigid, cigar-shaped dirigible: zeppelin
weights hung from car: ballast bags
SEE BALLOON, AIRCRAFT

blind *a.* **1.** SIGHTLESS unsighted, *blind as a mole, *blind as a bat, *blind as a post, stoneblind, groping. **2.** IGNORANT dense, stupid, unaware, heedless, unseeing, *thick, obtuse, myopic, shortsighted, unperceptive. ANT. *1. seeing, sighted. 2. sharp, understanding, perceptive.*

blinding *a.* dazzling, bright, glaring, brilliant. ANT. *gloomy, dark.*

blindness *n.* sightlessness, impaired vision, glaucoma, color blindness, astigmatism, cataracts, myopia, tunnel vision, typhlosis. SEE EYE

blink *v.* **1.** WINK bat, flutter. **2.** TWINKLE glimmer, sparkle, scintillate, shimmer.

blip *n.* **1.** OBJECT SEEN ON RADAR signal, spot, trace, reflection. **2.** ANOMALY departure, abnormality, oddity.

bliss *n.* rapture, joy, contentment, happiness, elation, euphoria, ecstasy, delight, heaven, nirvana. SEE HAPPINESS

blister *n.* swelling, patch, bubble, bleb, pimple, boil, canker, ulcer.

BLITHE *a.* [BLĪTHE] cheerful and carefree. *She was frequently in blithe spirits on Sunday.* SYN. cheerful, carefree, sunny, lighthearted, buoyant, airy, jovial, merry, cheery, gleeful, playful. ANT. *miserable, depressed, black, downhearted.* SEE HAPPY

blitz *n.* attack, onslaught, blitzkrieg, charge, raid, strike, offensive, bombardment.

blizzard *n.* snowstorm, northeaster, blow, gale, snow squall, blast, whiteout.

bloat *v.* balloon, swell, dilate, billow, inflate, expand, puff. ANT. *contract, deflate, shrivel.*

blob *n.* mass, daub, glov, lump, globule, ball, clump.

bloc *n.* alliance, group, affiliation, faction, cabal, ring, coalition, partnership.

block *n.* **1.** MASS chunk, hunk, brick, lump, bar, cube, square, cake. **2.** OBSTRUCTION obstacle, impediment, bar, snag, stop, barrier, hindrance.

block *v.* obstruct, impede, bar, stop, hinder, close off, occlude, interfere with, intercept, stymie, thwart, barricade, arrest, dam. ANT. *open, free, clear, facilitate.*

blockade *n.* barricade, barrier, obstruction, stop, bar, closure, hindrance, roadblock.

blockhead *n.* idiot, ignoramus, *Charlie Brown, *chowderhead. SEE MORON

blond *a.* golden-haired, flaxen-haired, sandy-haired, platinum, peroxide-blond, *towheaded, strawberry-blond. SEE HAIR

blood *n.* **1.** LIFE-FLUID hemoglobin, gore, plasma. "A very special kind of sap."—Johann Goethe. **2.** KINSHIP kindred, ancestry, pedigree, extraction, lineage, relatives.

bloodbath *n.* massacre, holocaust, murder, slaughter, carnage.

blood, in cold *a.* cruelly, intentionally, indifferently, unfeelingly.

bloodcurdling *a.* terrifying, horrifying, frightening, bone-chilling, spine-chilling, hair-raising. ANT. *reassuring, emboldening.*

bloodless *a.* pallid, wan, pale, colorless, dead, anemic. ANT. *florid, robust, lively.*

bloodline *n.* pedigree, line of descent, ancestry.

bloodshed *n.* bloodletting, slaughter, massacre, carnage, gore, bloodbath, murder, butchery.

bloodthirsty *a.* homicidal, murderous, savage, barbaric, brutal, ruthless, sadistic, cruel, inhuman, *psycho. SEE INSANE, VIOLENT

blood vessel *n.* vein, artery, capillary, arteriole.

bloom *n.* blossom, flower, floret, efflorescence. SEE FLOWER

bloom *v.* blossom, flower, flourish, flare, develop, thrive, come of age, germinate, bear fruit. ANT. *wither, die.*

blooper *n. Sl.* mistake, *goof, blunder, *boo-boo, gaffe, *muff, slip, *boner, *screwup.

blossom *n.* bloom, flower, floret, posy, bud. SEE FLOWER

blossom *v.* bloom, flower, effloresce, flourish, flare, develop, come of age, germinate, bear fruit.

blot *n.* spot, smudge, stain, smear, streak, blemish.

blot *v.* splotch, spot, smudge, stain, soil, smear, streak, blemish.

blotch *n.* spot, splotch, blot.

blouse *n.* pullover, slipover, garment. SEE SHIRT

blow *n.* **1.** WIND gale, tempest, blast, gust, squall, whirlwind. **2.** HIT punch, smack, slug, shot, bash, knock, rap, swat, slap, jolt, clout. **3.** MISFORTUNE reversal, shock, tragedy, upset, calamity, catastrophe. ANT. *2. caress. 3. blessing.*

blow *v.* **1.** MOVE AIR bluster, puff, gust, squall, huff, whiffle, rush, swirl, flow, waft, exhale, breathe. **2.** SOUND toot, trumpet, pipe, honk, whistle. **3.** FAIL *choke, lose, miss, *goof, *screw up, muff, bungle.

blow away *v.* **1.** kill, gun down. SEE MURDER **2.** STUN *throw for a loop, impress, fill with awe.

blow up *v.* **1.** INFLATE fill, expand, pump up, swell. **2.** EXPLODE burst, detonate, rupture, erupt, pop, demolish. ANT. *1. deflate.*

blue *a.* COLOR sky-blue, cobalt, azure, ultramarine, indigo, slate, navy, aquamarine, turquoise, lapis lazuli, royal, powder, electric, robin's egg. **2.** MOOD down, melancholy, depressed, sad, despondent, downhearted, down in the dumps.

blueblooded *a.* aristocratic, noble, upper class, classy. ANT. *common.*

blue collar *n.* *working stiff, *nine-to-fiver, laborer.

blue collar *a.* wage-earning, working class, clock-punching, laboring, proletariat, hardworking, factory-working, assembly-line, unskilled, common, lower class, middle class. ANT. *white collar, upper class.*

blueprint *n.* **1.** ARCHITECTURAL PLAN architectural rendering, draft, plan, design, layout, scheme. **2.** GENERAL PLAN plan, scheme, design, masterplan, game plan, schedule, timetable.

blue ribbon *n.* first prize, first place, award, decoration, recognition, honor.

blues *n.* depression, sadness, downheartedness, discouragement, low spirits, *blahs, *blue funk, doldrums, heavy-heartedness, *dumps, dejection, unhappiness, bad mood, black mood. ANT. *happiness, glee, joy, euphoria.*

bluff *n.* bank, cliff, promontory, headland, ridge, hill, precipice, palisade, scarp. **2.** SHAM *four-flushing, *bull, deception, *humbug.

bluff *v.* **1.** MISLEAD deceive, delude, *bamboozle, dupe, fake, *bullshit, shuck and jive.

bluff *a.* frank, blunt, rough, coarse, gruff, straightforward, abrupt. ANT. *subtle, roundabout, mealy-mouthed.*

blunder *n.* mistake, *goof, fumble, *boo-boo, *muff, gaffe, *flubup.

blunder *v.* *goof, fumble, botch, *muff, *flub, *drop the ball, err, *screw up, bungle, misstep, miscalculate.

blunt *v.* make dull, deaden, flatten, soften.

blunt *a.* **1.** DULL rounded, unpointed. **2.** FRANK candid, upfront, plainspoken, point-blank, straightforward, abrupt, brusque, gruff, curt, terse, direct, bluff. ANT. *1. sharp, pointed. 2. soft-pedaling, mealy-mouthed, subtle, gentle, euphemistic.*

blur *n.* stain, blot, haze, blotch, smear.

blur *v.* **1.** SMUDGE smear, stain, splotch. **2.** DIM cloud, obfuscate, obscure, shadow, veil, shroud. ANT. *2. clarify, sharpen, define.*

blurt *v.* blab, tattle, blabber, gush, spout, let slip.

blush *v.* flush, redden, color, glow, turn scarlet, bloom. "Virtue's color."—English proverb.

"Notice to be careful."—Edgar Howe. ANT. *blanch, pale.*

bluster *n.* boasting, bluff, bragging, braggadocio, swaggering, bullying, bravado, crowing, strutting, ranting, gasconade.

bluster *v.* boast, bluff, brag, swagger, strut, bully, crow, rant, show off, intimidate, storm.

blustery *a.* windy, gusty. ANT. *still, calm.*

board *n.* **1.** PLANK two-by-four, beam, slat, stick, lumber, timber, clapboard, slat, panel. **2.** COMMITTEE directors, council, trustees, advisers, cabinet. **3.** ROOM AND BOARD keep, provisions, meals.

board *v.* **1.** GO ABOARD get on, enter, embark. **2.** ACCOMMODATE feed, lodge, house, quarter. **3.** COVER WITH WOOD sheathe, panel, enclose. ANT. *1. disembark, deplane, detrain, leave.*

boardroom *n.* meeting room, conference room.

boardwalk *n.* walkway, promenade, sidewalk.

boast *n.* bragging, bluster, vainglory, bravado, gasconade, braggadocio, *hot air, vaunt.

boast *v.* brag, *toot one's own horn, crow, bluster, show off, puff, *pat oneself on the back, swagger, strut, gasconade, gloat, flaunt, *blow. ANT. *eat humble pie, downplay.*

boastful *a.* bragging, blustering, vaunting, pompous, vain, arrogant, conceited, *full of hot air, vainglorious, strutting, swaggering. ANT. *humble, modest, self-effacing.*

boat *n.* vessel, watercraft, tub, ship, motorboat, sailboat, jet ski.

WORD FIND

air-propelled: airboat

double-hulled sailboat: catamaran

emergency vessel: lifeboat

fishing: trawler, dragger, longliner, dogger, smack, whaler, sportfisherman

flat-bottomed carrier: barge, scow

flat-bottomed, pole-propelled: punt, ark

flat-bottomed vessel used in construction on water: pontoon

gondolier's song: barcarole

house on water: houseboat

Italian: gondola, vaporetto

log, hollowed out: dugout, pirogue

motorboat, small: runabout

narrow-hulled racing boat rowed by as many as eight: shell

narrow, racing boat rowed by one, two or four rowers: scull

old: hulk

Oriental, flat-bottomed river and coast boat: sampan, junk

pleasure cruiser: cabin cruiser, yacht
race/event: regatta
racing boat: cigarette boat, hydrofoil
rowboat: canoe, kayak, dinghy, shell, dory,
gig, skiff, umiak (eskimo)
service craft: tender
shuttle of passengers, freight: ferry
steam-propelled: paddle steamer, steamboat
triple-hulled sailboat: trimaran
SEE NAVY, SAIL, SHIP, SUBMARINE
bob v. wobble, bounce, waver, quiver.
bodacious a. prodigious, big, bold, audacious.
body n. **1.** PHYSIQUE figure, frame, build, form,
flesh and bones, *bag of bones, anatomy,
torso, trunk. "A pair of pincers set over a
bellows and a stewpan, the whole fixed upon
stilts."—Samuel Butler. "A machine which
winds its own springs."—Julien Mettrie. "A
cell state in which every cell is a citizen."—
Rudolf Virchow. **2.** CORPSE cadaver, carcass,
corpus delecti, mummy, skeleton, *dead
meat, *stiff, remains, carrion. **3.** MASS group,
collection, union, bulk, bunch, majority,
crowd, throng. **4.** MAIN PIECE chassis, fuselage, frame, assembly.
bodybuilding n. weight training, resistance
training, body sculpting, working out, bulk-
ing up, toning up, *pumping iron.
bodyguard n. escort, guardian, security guard,
protector, *muscle.
body language n. nonverbal communication,
nonverbal signaling.
boffo n. Sl. successful, great, blockbusting, rec-
ord-breaking. ANT. lackluster.
bog n. marsh, quag, mire, fen, swamp, quagmire,
slough, morass.
bog down v. mire, get stuck, sink, impede, slow,
stall.
bogeyman n. boogeyman, boogieman, ghost,
specter, hob-goblin, goblin. SEE MONSTER
boggle the mind v. flabbergast, astonish, stagger, amaze, stun, stupefy, *blow one away,
*blow one's mind, dumbfound, *knock
one's socks off, frighten.
bogus a. fake, counterfeit, phony, *sham, artificial, imitation, fraudulent, ersatz, spurious,
pseudo. ANT. genuine, real, authentic.
BOHEMIAN n. [bo HEEM ee un] a nonconformist who is involved in writing or art; a
writer or artist who lives unconventionally.
We lived like bohemians, with no permanent
home and no source of income outside of our
art. SYN. gypsy, artist, dilettante, poet,
writer, dropout, *hippie, *beatnik, *flower
child, panhandler, nonconformist, *free

spirit, vagabond. "A person who works to
live but does not live to work."—Heathcote
Williams.
boil n. blister, swelling, furuncle, pustule, bleb,
abscess, carbuncle, pimple, fester, sore.
boil v. **1.** COOK steam, parboil, seethe, churn,
bubble, simmer, stew, steep, heat, brew. **2.**
RAGE fume, seethe, rave, burn, storm.
boisterous a. rough, rambunctious, rowdy,
loud, raucous, wild, obstreperous, vociferous, turbulent, uproarious, unrestrained, unruly. ANT. quiet, laid-back, calm, restrained.
bold a. **1.** DARING brave, fearless, courageous,
undaunted, adventurous, audacious, confident, plucky, intrepid, lionhearted, *ballsy.
2. BRAZEN insolent, *saucy, *brassy,
*cheeky, fresh, forward, impudent, brash,
rude, *gutsy, *ballsy. **3.** PRONOUNCED striking, loud, bright, flashy, conspicuous, prominent, vivid, colorful, eye-catching. ANT. 1.
cowardly, meek, timid. 2. courteous, polite,
shy, deferential. 3. understated, subtle, weak,
pale.
bolster v. prop up, reinforce, support,
strengthen, fortify, buttress, shoulder, brace,
shore up. ANT. undermine, weaken.
bolt n. **1.** FASTENER bar, lock, latch, rod, catch,
pin, peg, screw, spike, coupling. SEE NAIL,
SCREW **2.** LIGHTNING flash, stroke, thunderbolt, shaft, chain. SEE LIGHTNING, STORM,
THUNDER
bolt v. dart, spring, dash out, rush, flee, make
a break for it, jump, leap, scoot, *hotfoot,
*skedaddle.
bomb n. **1.** EXPLOSIVE charge, shell, missile,
mine, grenade, projectile, depth charge,
atom bomb, hydrogen bomb, *physics package, torpedo, incendiary, blockbuster, warhead, dud, *egg.
WORD FIND
15,000-pound bomb: BLU-82; [daisy cutter]
21,500-pound behomoth, [mother of all
bombs]: MOAB (Massive Ordnance Air
Blast bomb)
antipersonnel mine with fanning fragmentation: claymore mine
boom: report
caves and tunnels, high pressure bombs used
to flush out: thermobaric bomb
explosive chemical used in bombs: TNT,
trinitrotoluene, nitroglycerin
explosive portion of bomb, missile, etc.:
warhead
fire-starting bomb: incendiary bomb
fragmenting, shrapnel-producing bomb:

fragmentation bomb, antipersonnel bomb
fuel detonated in midair: fuel-air bomb
gasoline-filled bottle stuffed with rag: Molotov cocktail
guided bomb: smart bomb
hole: crater
intense bombing: saturation bombing, carpet bombing
jelled gas incendiary: napalm
lead pipe containing home-made charge: pipe bomb
multiple bombs released from canister: cluster bomb
penetrate earth and concrete, designed to: bunker buster, GBU-28 Penetrator
puttylike substance holding charge: plastic explosive
smoke-producing: smoke bomb
stink-producing: stink bomb
timed charge: time bomb
unguided: dumb bomb
SEE AIR FORCE, ARMY, MISSILE, NUCLEAR BOMB, WAR, WEAPON **2.** FLOP failure, fiasco, disaster, *turkey, *dog, loser, *washout. ANT. *2. success, triumph, hit.*

bomb v. **1.** Sl. FAIL flop, fizzle, wash out, *die. **2.** BOMBARD shell, blow up, assault, blitz, pepper, barrage, strafe, *drop the big one, *blow to smithereens, *blow to kingdom come, *bomb back to the stone age, level, blast.

bombast n. grandiloquence, rodomontade, bluster, hot air, pomposity, pretentiousness.

BOMBASTIC a. [bom BAS tik] pompous, high-sounding speech or writing. *He tried too hard to make an impression; his speech was wordy and bombastic.* SYN. pompous, high-sounding, grandiloquent, grandiose, flaunting, pretentious, turgid, euphuistic, inflated, fustian, windy, flamboyant, flowery. ANT. *understated, restrained, subtle.*

bomber n. terrorist, revolutionary, demolition expert, bombardier, subversive, radical, arsonist, extortionist.

bona fide a. genuine, authentic, legitimate, real. ANT. *counterfeit.*

bonanza n. windfall, gold mine, *cash cow, treasure trove, rich vein.

bond n. **1.** ALLEGIANCE tie, relationship, loyalty, connection, attachment, affinity. **2.** GUARANTEE warranty, contract, security, pledge, covenant, agreement.

bond v. attach, tie, bind, connect, fasten, stick, join, fuse, weld.

bondage n. servitude, slavery, serfdom, subjection, subjugation, enslavement, captivity, bonds, shackles. ANT. *freedom, liberty, emancipation.*

bonds n. ties, shackles, fetters, manacles, chains, reins, yoke, handcuffs, bindings.

bone n. ossicle, marrow, cartilage, skull, mandible, vertebrae, rib, humerus, femur, tibia, sternum, clavicle. SEE SKELETON

boner n. Sl. mistake, goof, error, blunder.

bones, feel in one's v. Sl. sense, perceive, expect, have a gut feeling.

bones, make no v. Sl. admit, confess, own up, level.

bone up n. Sl. study, brush up, read up, cram.

bonus n. extra, premium, reward, gift, fringe benefit, *perk, tip, *gravy, recompense, dividend.

BON VIVANT n. [BON vee VAHN] one who has cultured tastes and enjoys the finer things in life, especially good food, drink, etc. *He was a bon vivant who loved fine wines.* SYN. gourmet, connoisseur, epicure, gourmand, cognoscente, aficionado, enthusiast, dilettante.

bony a. skinny, scrawny, anorexic, malnourished, rawboned, lean, gaunt, emaciated, angular. ANT. *fat, brawny, blubbery.*

boob n. Sl. idiot, dolt, moron, imbecile, fool, *dumb-dumb, clown, buffoon, laughingstock.

boo boo n. Sl. **1.** MISTAKE error, blunder, *screw-up, *boner, *goof, oversight, gaffe, slip, misstep. **2.** INJURY, scratch, cut, laceration, sore, bruise, black and blue mark.

booby trap n. pitfall, deadfall, ambush, blind, mousetrap, trip wire, trigger.

book n. volume, hardcover, softcover, paperback, novel, work, opus, tome, publication, best-seller, booklet, pamphlet, treatise, manual, manuscript, log, record, diary, journal, register, ledger, classic, text. "A garden carried in the pocket."—Arabian proverb. "For company the best friends. . . ."—Richard Whitlock. ". . . Portable pieces of thought."—Susan Sontag. "The true university."—Thomas Carlyle. "The compasses and telescopes and sextants and charts which other men have prepared to help us navigate the dangerous seas of human life."—Jesse L. Bennet.

WORD FIND
alphabetical/page-number guide to words and terms: index
avoider of: bibliophobe

back list of sources, related works: bibliography
back: spine
blank page: flyleaf
book published at author's expense: vanity book
burner or destroyer of: biblioclast
burning or destruction of: biblioclasm
category: genre
collecting passion: bibliomania
compilation of various works: anthology
condensed or shortened: abridged
end comment: epilogue
hardcover republished in paperback: reprint
inscription, front: dedication
introduction: foreword
ISBN: International Standard Book Number
jacket description: flap copy, blurbs
large, illustrated book: coffee table book
large paperback: trade paperback
literary works: belles lettres
logo of publisher: colophon
lover of: bibliophile
overstocked book: remainder
printed before 1500 A.D.: incunabula
review or recommendation on jacket: blurb
stealer of books: biblioklept
strange (subject matter): curiosa
title page: frontispiece
vocabulary list: glossary
voracious reader of: bookworm, bibliobibuli
SEE AUTHOR, NOVEL, NOVELIST, WRITER

book v. **1.** MAKE RESERVATION reserve, book passage, arrange for, assign, register. **2.** PROCESS FOR A CRIME, charge, press charges.

booking n. **1.** PLAY DATE gig, engagement, performance date, tour date. **2.** RESERVATION registration, arrangement, retainer.

bookish a. studious, academic, scholarly, well-read, introverted, book-loving, owlish, learned, intellectual, pedantic, *bookwormish. ANT. illiterate, oafish.

bookkeeping n. record-keeping, accounting, auditing, entering.

booklet n. pamphlet, brochure, folder, circular.

bookworm n. reader, book lover, bibliophile, bibliomaniac, bibliobibuli, bibliolater.

boom n. **1.** THUD thunder, report, crack, roar, rumble, crash, bang, shot, fulmination, cannonade, peal, burst, explosion, detonation. **2.** INCREASE growth, expansion, upturn, prosperity, growth, spurt, bull market. ANT. 2. recession, depression, decline.

boom v. **1.** THUD thunder, report, crack, roar, rumble, crash, bang, blow up, backfire, pop, explode. **2.** INCREASE grow, expand, prosper, thrive, spurt, mushroom, *go great guns, grow exponentially, flourish. ANT. 2. recede, decline.

boom box n. Sl. radio, tape player, CD player, audio system, stereo, *ghetto blaster, *ghetto box.

booming a. thriving, growing, profiting, prospering, flourishing, *going great guns, increasing, increasing exponentially, exploding, shooting up, mushrooming. ANT. declining.

boon n. blessing, windfall, benefit, god-send, gift, manna from heaven.

boondocks n. *boonies, *sticks, *North Overshoe, *East Jesus, backwater, bush country, tall timbers, *the rhubarbs, outback, backwoods, hinterland, wilderness, nowhere, unorganized territory, jungle.

boondoggle n. waste, *golden fleece, pork, government pork, frivolity, extravagance, *money down a rathole, white elephant, reckless spending, conspicuous consumption.

boor n. clod, lout, oaf, churl, clodhopper, *yahoo, yokel, bumpkin, rustic.

boorish a. ill-mannered, rude, awkward, uncouth, unrefined, uncultured, churlish, cloddish, vulgar, rustic, coarse, insensitive, tactless, offensive. ANT. refined, sophisticated, cultured.

boost n. **1.** PUSH UP lift, elevation, hand up. **2.** INCREASE raise, hike, expansion, upgrade, gain. **3.** PROMOTION support, encouragement, assistance, backing, fostering, advancement, plug. ANT. 2. decrease, cutback. 3. disparagement, undermining, knock.

boost v. **1.** RAISE push up, hoist, lift, elevate. **2.** INCREASE heighten, raise, hike, jack up, enlarge, inflate. **3.** PROMOTE support, advance, further, plug, foster, advocate. ANT. 1. lower, drop. 2. decrease, lower. 3. undermine, disparage, knock.

booster shot n. SEE IMMUNIZATION

boot n. shoe, overshoe, footwear, clodhopper, *boondockers, *stompers.

WORD FIND

ankle-high boot worn horseback-riding: jodhpur

Eskimo boot made from hide: mukluk

hiking boot with ridged sole: wafflestomper

leather, above the knee in front, below the knee in back: Wellington

military: combat boot, jackboot

old fashioned woman's boot laced up the front: granny

rubber/waterproof: galosh

tooled leather, square or pointed toes: cowboy boot

wading boot: hip boot, wader

western tooled leather: cowboy boot

white, calf-high, worn with mini skirt in the 1960s: go-go boot

work shoe, heavy: brogan

SEE SHOE

booth n. stall, stand, kiosk, shed, enclosure, cubicle, compartment.

bootlegger n. runner, *rum runner, smuggler, illegal distiller, black marketer, pirate, moonshiner, dealer.

bootlicker n. *kiss-up, *brownnose, sycophant, toady, *apple polisher, *yes-man, *foot-kisser, *back-patter, stooge.

booty n. loot, spoils, plunder, prize, winnings, *haul, goods, property, gain.

booze n. Sl. liquor, alcohol, spirits, drink, *firewater, *hard stuff. SEE ALCOHOL, BEER, DRINK, MOONSHINE, WINE

bordello n. brothel, house of prostitution, *whorehouse, *cathouse, *house of ill repute, bagnio.

border n. margin, edge, side, line, verge, fringe, rim, brink, boundary, outer limit, perimeter, periphery, borderland.

borderline a. indefinite, doubtful, marginal, unclear, vague, halfway, ambiguous, equivocal, unclassifiable, one way or the other. ANT. *absolute, decisive.*

bore n. *drag, *yawn, tiresome person, *pill, *wet blanket, *stick in the mud, soporific. "A fellow talking who can change the subject back to his topic . . . faster than you can change it back to yours."—Lawrence Peter.

bore v. 1. DRILL tunnel, burrow, tap, punch, drive, sink, gouge out, auger, mine, ream. 2. TIRE weary, put to sleep, fatigue, tax, cloy, annoy. ANT. *2. excite, stimulate.*

boredom n. tedium, ennui, monotony, apathy, dullness, doldrums, jadedness, indifference, weariness, humdrum, flatness. "What happens when we lose contact with the universe."—John Ciardi. ANT. *excitement, stimulation.*

boring a. tedious, tiresome, *dull as dishwater, *dull as paint drying, soporific, somnolent, wearisome, dull, monotonous, humdrum, unstimulating, uninteresting, prosaic, mundane, *ho-hum, stale, routine. ANT. *exciting, stimulating.*

born v. delivered, brought into the world, brought into existence, cast, hatched, created.

born a. inherent, natural, innate. ANT. *learned, acquired.*

born-again a. reborn, renewed, restored, converted, saved. ANT. *damned.*

borough n. town, community, municipality, burg, township, village, quarter.

borrow v. 1. TAKE TEMPORARILY use, take a loan, obtain, scrounge, *mooch, *hit up, *bum, *sponge. 2. ADOPT FOR ONE'S OWN USE appropriate, imitate, steal, plagiarize, copy, pirate, use. ANT. *1. lend, give, return. 2. originate, invent.*

bosom n. 1. BREAST chest, bust. 2. HEART emotions, soul, spirit, core, depths, inside.

boss n. leader, chief, head, master, headmaster, supervisor, foreman, superintendent, overseer, CEO (chief executive officer), taskmaster, *head honcho, *big cheese, *whip, employer, director, executive, manager, administrator, lord and master, *big enchilada, *chief cook and bottle washer, governor, mayor, vice president, president, prince, princess, king, queen, drill sergeant, sarge, commander, captain, general, first in command, dean, chancellor, godfather, highest authority, ruler, despot, dictator, tyrant, bully, dominator, dominatrix, *pit bull, *alpha male, slave-driver, faultfinder, nag, *biggest toad in the puddle. "[One who] exists to make sensible exceptions to general rules."—Elting Morrison. ANT. *employee, subordinate, underling.* SEE WORK, JOB

boss v. command, control, direct, manage, administrate, supervise, lead, run, press, lord over, domineer, dictate, throw one's weight around, tyrannize. ANT. *submit, follow, jump on command.*

bossy a. domineering, dictatorial, tyrannical, pushy, commanding, authoritarian, iron-handed, high-handed, strict, controlling, overpowering, bitchy, despotic, imperious. ANT. *subordinate, subservient, servile.*

botch v. bungle, *screw up, spoil, ruin, *goof, muff, foul up, fumble, flub, louse up.

bother n. annoyance, irritation, burden, trouble, aggravation, inconvenience, pother, *pain, *headache, *pain in the ass, difficulty, nuisance.

bother v. 1. ANNOY harass, trouble, pester, disturb, irritate, agitate, burden, vex, aggravate, distress, put out, irk, harry. 2. TAKE THE

TROUBLE inconvenience oneself, take pains, *go out of one's way, worry about.

bothersome *a.* annoying, troublesome, irksome, disturbing, aggravating, burdensome, inconvenient, difficult, vexatious, irritating. ANT. *welcome, agreeable, desirable.*

bottle *n.* container, decanter, jug, glass, vessel, vial, carafe, flask, flagon, jar, phial.

bottleneck *n.* obstacle, blockage, jam, hindrance, snag, congestion, obstruction, *tight squeeze, barrier, clog, impediment.

bottom *n.* **1.** BASE foundation, bed, seat, footing, floor, ground, nadir. **2.** ROOT basis, core, essence, gist, source, origin. **3.** REAR buttocks, *fanny, butt, rump, seat, derriere, *tush, *buns, *stern.

bottomless *a.* unfathomable, immeasureable, abysmal, infinite, limitless, vast. ANT. *finite.*

botulism *n.* food poisoning, contamination, illness.

boudoir *n.* sitting room, dressing room, bedroom, private room.

bough *n.* limb, branch.

bouillon *n.* broth, flavoring, soup base, stock, consommé.

boulder *n.* rock, rock mass, stone, glacial erratic.

boulevard *n.* avenue, parkway, concourse. SEE STREET

bounce *v.* **1.** SPRING BACK rebound, bob, bound, recoil, jump, hop, carom, ricochet. **2.** JOUNCE jolt, shake.

bouncer *n. Sl.* security personnel, guard, *muscle, *enforcer, ejector.

bound *v.* **1.** JUMP leap, bounce, spring, vault, gambol, bounce, hop. **2.** RESTRICT restrain, limit, confine, enclose, circumscribe, demarcate.

bound *a.* **1.** TIED fastened, wrapped, secured, trussed. **2.** DESTINED certain, doomed, fated, headed, sure, ordained, assured, determined. **3.** OBLIGATED pledged, required, liable, compelled. ANT. *1. unsecured, unfastened. 2. unsure, indefinite, unconfirmed. 3. released, freed from obligation.*

boundary *n.* border, borderline, line, frontier, verge, periphery, edge, rim, margin, brink, hem, limit, confines, outer limit, bounds, perimeter, demarcation.

boundless *a.* limitless, endless, infinite, immeasurable, vast, inexaustable, unbounded, perpetual, innumerable, everlasting. ANT. *limited, finite.*

bounteous SEE BOUNTIFUL

bountiful *a.* generous, plentiful, abundant, ample, copious, prolific, lavish, bounteous, fat, teeming, *jam-packed, *dime a dozen, luxuriant. ANT. *spare, scant, sparse, lean.*

bounty *n.* gift, reward, present, bonus, benefit, largess, premium, allowance.

bounty hunter *n.* fugitive hunter, criminal hunter.

bouquet *n.* **1.** BUNCH cluster, posy, spray, garland, nosegay. **2.** SCENT aroma, fragrance, essence, perfume, trace, breath, smell. SEE FLOWER

BOURGEOIS *a.* [boor ZHWAW] of the middle-class, boring, conventional and materialistic. *He described himself as a Bohemian; he abhorred our bourgeois ways.* SYN. middle-class, working-class, proletarian, conventional, capitalistic, common, rigid, boring, *square, *politically correct, materialistic, conservative, traditional, respectable, uncultured, philistine. ANT. *Bohemian, unconventional, nonconforming.*

bout *n.* **1.** MATCH contest, battle, struggle, round, go, competition. **2.** PERIOD spell, course, round, turn, shift, term, stint.

boutique *n.* shop, gift store, department, booth, concession, franchise, business.

bow *n.* **1.** BEND curtsy, genuflection, nod. **2.** PROW.

bow *v.* **1.** BEND stoop, curtsy, genuflect, nod, salaam, kneel. **2.** SUBMIT yield, give in, *cave in, *knuckle under, concede, defer, *kowtow, acquiesce, surrender, lay down. ANT. *2. fight, dominate, resist.*

bowel movement *n.* defecation, b.m., discharge, excretion, evacuation, *number two, diarrhea, *crap.

bowels *n.* **1.** INTESTINES guts, entrails, viscera, innards, insides. **2.** INTERIOR depth, core, insides, heart, innermost part.

bowl *n.* dish, receptacle, saucer, basin, vessel, tureen, boat, urn.

bowling *n.* tenpins, candlepins, duckpins, kegling, skittles, bocci.

WORD FIND

area most likely to yield strike: pocket
body movement of bowler after shot: body English
bowler: kegler
central pin: kingpin, headpin
curving shot: hook
gutter, in the: gutter ball
knock down ten with one shot: strike, mark
knock down ten with two shots: spare, mark
one game: string
pin-setting machine: pinsetter

shot that leaves a gap between pins: split
spin imparted on the ball: English
unit of game, 1/10th: frame
wide split: goalposts, mule ears, bedposts

box n. carton, container, crate, receptacle, case, package, bin, chest, trunk, canister, coffer.

box v. fight, spar, fisticuff, tussle, punch, cuff, jab, sock, hit, strike, slug, deliver blows, pound, clout, pummel, *whale, beat, *mix it up.

boxer n. fighter, prizefighter, pugilist.

boxing n. pugilism, fighting, sparring, fisticuffs.

WORD FIND

black eye: mouse
crossover punch: cross
dazed: punch drunk
ear deformation: cauliflower ear
exchange punches: mix it up
hold, embrace: clinch
illegal blow: rabbit punch, below the belt, low blow, kidney punch, head butt
inning: round
jab and cross: one-two punch
movement: bob and weave, dance, footwork, on one's bicycle
powerful punch: haymaker, Sunday punch
practice partner: sparring partner
practice with partner: spar
practice with self: shadow box
punching bag: speedbag, heavy bag, crazy bag
punch with less than full strength: pull a punch
quick, straight punch: jab
ring floor: canvas, apron
stamina program: roadwork
sweeping hook: roundhouse
tie: draw
trainer, assistant: cornerman, cut man, handler
upswinging punch: uppercut, bolo punch
varied punches delivered quickly: combination, flurry
wait of eight seconds after knockdown: mandatory eight-count, standing eight-count
weight and measurements of opponents: tale of the tape
weight division, lightest to heaviest: flyweight, bantamweight, featherweight, lightweight, welterweight, middleweight, light heavyweight, heavyweight, cruiserweight
win by injuring, disabling opponent: knockout, technical knockout, TKO

win by points: decision
win not agreed on by all officials: split decision

boy n. lad, youth, youngster, sprig, junior, sprout, *little shaver, *nipper. "One who has a wolf in his stomach."—German proverb. "Of all the wild beasts, the most unmanageable."—Plato.

BOYCOTT v. [BOY kot] to refuse, usually as a group, to buy a product or deal with a person or company, as a protest against some action. *They agreed to boycott the tuna company until dolphin-safe nets were used.* SYN. *blackball, blacklist, shun, reject, refuse, ban, ostracize, shut out, spurn, proscribe, strike, eschew, avoid, embargo.

boyfriend n. sweetheart, *honey, beau, *steady, suitor, lover, date, *boy toy, swain, flame, *main squeeze.

bra n. brassiere, support cups, lingerie, underwear, padded bra, *peek-a-boo bra, *falsies.

brace n. support, prop, reinforcement, strut, stay, buttress, truss, stanchion.

brace v. reinforce, strengthen, support, prop, bolster, tighten, shore up, fortify.

bracelet n. band, chain, bangle, armlet, jewelry, ornament.

bracing a. invigorating, stimulating, exhilarating, refreshing, energizing, restorative. ANT. *tiring, soporific, draining.*

brackish a. salty, saline, briny.

brag v. boast, gloat, *blow one's own horn, crow, vaunt, swagger, strut, flaunt, puff, *talk big, *shovel it, *blowhard. ANT. *downplay, *hide one's light under a bushel basket, be modest.*

braggart n. bragger, boaster, *blowhard, *windbag, *gasbag, *bag of wind, show-off, egotist, blusterer, braggadocio, peacock, trumpeter.

braid v. plait, weave, twine, interlace, knot.

brain n. **1.** SMART PERSON genius, intellectual, scholar, savant, wizard, prodigy, thinker, mastermind, Einstein, *egghead, sage, wit, mental giant. **2.** MIND *gray matter, *thinking cap, *bean, encephalon, *noodle, *upper story. "An apparatus with which we think that we think."—Ambrose Bierce. "An invention of the universe in order to study itself."—Anon.

WORD FIND

abnormally small brain: microencephalon
ancient portion, regulates hunger, thirst, fighting, sex: limbic system, reptilian brain

base, regulates breathing and circulation: medulla oblongata
body temperature and blood pressure regulator: hypothalamus
connector of right and left hemispheres: corpus callosum
egg-shaped patch controlling speech muscles: Broca's area
exam of brain waves: electroenchephalogram (EEG).
heat, cold, pain, pressure sensor: thalamus
inflammation: encephalitis, meningitis
left or right side: hemisphere
muscular coordinator in back of skull: cerebellum
nerve cell: neuron
outer brain area controlling perception, reasoning, memory: cerebrum
outer layer: cortex, dura mater
seizure disease caused by electrical disturbances: epilepsy
superhuman right-brain functioning: idiot savant syndrome
ANT. 1. *idiot, moron, imbecile.* SEE INTELLIGENCE, THOUGHT

brainstorm *v.* problem-solve, *put heads together, think, create, invent, plan, share ideas, analyze, deliberate, focus on, *rack brains, ponder, conceive, conceptualize, dream, conjure up.

brain trust *n.* advisors, experts, authorities, advisory board, *best and the brighest, panel, council, scholars, cabinet.

brainwash *v.* indoctrinate, program, convert, influence, persuade, condition, train.

brainy *a.* brilliant. SEE CLEVER, INTELLIGENT, SMART

braise *v.* cook, brown.

brake *n.* restraint, curb, constraint, check, control.

brake *v.* stop, slow, decelerate, halt, curb.

bramble *n.* shrub, bush, brush, thorn bush, prickles, nettles, blackberry, raspberry.

bran *n.* husk, fiber.

branch *n.* **1.** LIMB bough, arm, twig, offshoot. **2.** UNIT division, subdivision, department, bureau, wing, affiliate, arm, chapter, office. **3.** TRIBUTARY channel, feeder, stream.

branch *v.* fork, spread, divide, bifurcate, diverge, grow.

brand *n.* make, trade name, line, variety, trademark.

brand *v.* **1.** MARK sear, burn in, label. **2.** STIGMATIZE mark, disgrace, taint, *give a black eye.

brandish *v.* wave, exhibit, shake, show, flourish, hold menacingly, flaunt, wield, swing.

brash *a.* **1.** RECKLESS rash, impetuous, hasty, mindless, incautious, headlong, foolhardy, unwary, impulsive. **2.** PUSHY bold, cocky, impudent, nervy, rude, cheeky, forward, flip, brazen. ANT. 1. *thoughtful, cautious, wary.* 2. *courteous, reserved, respectful, kind.*

brass tacks *n.* essentials, basics, *nitty gritty.

brassy *a.* bold, brazen, loud, impudent, insolent, arrogant, cheeky, nervy, cocky, brash, forward, shameless, bullish, loudmouthed. ANT. *shy, retiring, respectful, timid.*

brat *n.* imp, *holy terror, spoiled child, *enfant terrible, *punk.

bravado *a.* bluff, bluster, swaggering, strutting, cockiness, *show, *crowing, bombast, muscle-flexing, macho posturing. ANT. *timidity, mousiness, cowering.*

brave *v.* face, defy, dare, confront, challenge, *stand up to.

brave *a.* courageous, bold, fearless, valiant, lionhearted, dauntless, heroic, plucky, *gutsy, *ballsy, intrepid, daring, spunky, manly, foolhardy, macho. ANT. *timid, mousy, cowardly, fainthearted, *chicken.*

bravery *n.* courage, fearlessness, boldness, *guts, *balls, daring, spunk, valor, pluck, heroism, intrepidness, manliness, mettle. "Falling but not yielding."—Latin proverb. "Fear sneering at itself."—Maxwell Bodenheim. ANT. *timidity, cowardice, mousiness, fearfulness.*

brawl *n.* fight, tussle, *scrap, donnybrook, *rumble, *slugfest, imbroglio, uproar, row, fracas, quarrel, altercation, melee, riot, *free-for-all.

brawn *n.* muscles, strength, huskiness, *beefiness, robustness, power, might.

brawny *a.* muscular, herculean, beefy, burly, sinewy, powerful, strapping, rugged, husky, solid, stout. ANT. *frail, powerless, weak.*

BRAZEN *a.* [BRAY zun] nervy, especially in a disrespectful way; impudent. *A brazen heckler ruined the show with his rude comments.* SYN. bold, brassy, impudent, nervy, shameless, audacious, cheeky, brash, cocky, loudmouthed, frank, forward, *ballsy. ANT. *quiet, shy, reserved.*

breach *n.* **1.** OPENING hole, break, crack, fissure, gap, cleft. **2.** VIOLATION nonobservance, transgression, infringement, noncompliance, infraction, contravention. **3.** ALIENATION split, separation, falling-out, schism, friction, estrangement, parting of the ways.

breadth *n.* **1.** WIDTH broadness, span. **2.** RANGE extent, scope, span, area.

breadwinner n. wage earner, *one who brings home the bacon, *clockpuncher, income producer.

break n. **1.** FRACTURE crack, rupture, tear, split, fissure, collapse, rift, breach, rent. **2.** PAUSE recess, breather, intermission, lull, letup, rest, hiatus, respite. GOOD FORTUNE opportunity, shot, opening, stroke of luck, chance.

break v. **1.** FRACTURE crack, rupture, tear, split, shatter, collapse, breach, fall apart, bust, burst, snap, pop, smash, pulverize, splinter, demolish, total, disintegrate, mangle. **2.** WEAKEN impair, undermine, diminish, degrade, incapacitate, cripple. **3.** PAUSE rest, recess, take a breather, suspend, stop. ANT. *1. repair, mend, fix. 2. strengthen, fortify. 3. resume, begin.*

breakable a. fragile, delicate, flimsy, brittle. ANT. *sturdy.*

breakdown n. **1.** FAILURE malfunction, collapse, short circuit, disruption, mishap. **2.** ITEMIZATION analysis, list, categorization.

breakthrough n. progress, advance, discovery, innovation, invention, leap forward, finding.

breakup n. separation, disintegration, rift, split, disbanding, dissolution.

breast n. **1.** CHEST bosom, bust, mammary gland, *tit, *boob, teat, udder. **2.** HEART soul, core, inner self, spirit, psyche.

breath n. whiff, puff, air, respiration, sigh, wheeze, whisper, gasp, inhalation, exhalation, aspiration.

breathe v. inhale, exhale, respire, draw a breath, gasp, pant, wheeze, huff, blow, heave, suck, snore, snort, sniff, hyperventilate.

breather n. break, recess, pause, rest, respite, time out.

breathless a. short of breath, out of breath, shortwinded, winded, asthmatic, gasping, wheezing, choking, panting, puffing, suffering from apnea, suffering from dyspnea.

breathtaking a. electrifying, awe-inspiring, shocking, exciting, stunning, astounding, heart-stopping, thrilling, hair-raising, moving. ANT. *boring, anticipated, run-of-the-mill, ho-hum.*

breed n. strain, variety, type, class, genus, race, kind, line, species.

breed v. **1.** REPRODUCE procreate, propagate, bear young, beget, generate, hatch, produce, engender. **2.** TO CAUSE bring about, lead to, produce, foster, create, effect, spawn.

breeding n. cultivation, training, upbringing, development, schooling, rearing, conditioning, manners, refinement. "Concealing how much we think of ourselves and how little we think of the other person."—Mark Twain.

breeze n. **1.** GENTLE WIND zephyr, breath, whiff, sough, draft, waft. SEE WIND **2.** *CINCH *snap, *nothing, *duck soup.

breezy a. **1.** WINDY blustery, drafty, gusty, airy, windswept, fresh. **2.** LIGHTHEARTED easygoing, casual, sprightly, lively, playful, spirited, brisk, animated, vivacious, effervescent. ANT. *1. still, dead calm, becalmed. 2. depressed, morose, spiritless.*

BREVITY n. [BREV i tee] briefness, conciseness. *The speech was too long; the audience begged for brevity.* SYN. briefness, shortness, conciseness, succinctness, terseness, compactness, pithiness, economy, pointedness. ANT. *long-windedness, wordiness, lengthiness.*

brew v. **1.** STEEP boil, ferment, cook, stew, seethe. **2.** DEVISE concoct, invent, cook up, contrive, hatch, formulate, engineer.

brewery n. distillery. SEE ALCOHOL, BEER, DRINK

bribe n. payoff, *hush money, graft, *kickback, *boodle, sop, baksheesh, *grease, inducement, incentive. SEE MONEY

bribe v. pay off, buy off, *grease the palm, suborn, corrupt, entice.

bric-a-brac n. knickknacks, trinkets, baubles, gewgaws, bibelots, virtu.

brick n. block, stone, *soldier, clinker.

bridge n. span, overpass, arch, viaduct, footbridge, catwalk, connector, link, connection, tie, bond.

WORD FIND

arched roadway over a valley: viaduct

cable and girder-supported: bridle-chord bridge, suspension bridge

dual beams or trusses that project beyond their supports, are connected: cantilever bridge

enclosure used in water for repair of: cofferdam

fear of: gephyrophobia

float-supported: pontoon bridge

opens and closes for boat traffic: drawbridge, bascule, swing bridge, lift bridge

protective railing or wall: balustrade, parapet

railroad bridge framework: trestle

support: pier, pile, abutment

bridge v. span, cross, traverse, connect, link, join, unite.

bridle n. restraint, rein, halter, bit, leash, harness, muzzle, check, curb.

bridle *v.* restrain, check, hold back, curb, harness, arrest, inhibit, muzzle.

brief *n.* summary, synopsis, condensation, outline, sketch, precis, abridgement.

brief *v.* inform, fill in, summarize, outline.

brief *a.* **1.** SHORT-LIVED short, fleeting, quick, fast, short-term, instantaneous, momentary, swift, transitory. **2.** SHORT, CONCISE *short and sweet, succinct, abbreviated, to the point, condensed, summarized, compressed, pithy. ANT. *1.* long, prolonged, time-consuming. *2.* long-winded, wordy, time-consuming.

briefing *n.* rundown, outlining, summary, *lowdown, instruction, orientation.

brigade *n.* troop, unit, group, outfit, company, battalion, contingent, legion. SEE MILITARY

brigand *n.* bandit, outlaw, robber, desperado, pirate.

bright *a.* **1.** LIGHT shining, brilliant, blinding, glowing, luminous, radiant, dazzling, blazing, glaring, intense, incandescent, vivid, sparkling, resplendent, effulgent. **2.** SMART intelligent, clever, sharp, quick, witty, brainy, brilliant, astute. **3.** HOPEFUL promising, cheering, golden, rosy, encouraging, auspicious, sunny. **4.** CHEERFUL lively, vivacious, happy, sprightly, merry, lighthearted, joyous, blithe. ANT. *1.* dark, dim, gloomy, black. *2.* stupid, moronic, retarded, bovine, dull. *3.* dark, black, grim, hopeless. *4.* grim, morose, depressed.

brighten *v.* **1.** LIGHTEN illuminate, intensify, furbish, shine, polish, perk up. **2.** CHEER UP lift spirits, perk up, enliven, hearten, buoy, uplift, gladden. ANT. *1.* darken, blacken, tone down. *2.* depress, sadden, make glum.

brilliant *a.* **1.** BRIGHT shining, incandescent, blinding, radiant, glowing, dazzling, blazing, intense, resplendent, scintillating, sparkling, vivid. **2.** SMART intelligent, clever, sharp, quick, witty, brainy, astute, ingenious, wise, scholarly. ANT. *1.* dull, dark, tarnished, grimy. *2.* dull, slow, *bovine, stupid, dim-witted.

brim *n.* rim, edge, verge, lip, margin, brink.

brine *n.* salt water, sea water, saline solution, souse.

bring *v.* **1.** CONVEY carry, bear, transport, take, retrieve, fetch, deliver. **2.** EFFECT cause, make, produce, prompt, start, institute, induce, force, compel.

brink *n.* verge, edge, borderline, threshold, limit, brim, line.

brisk *a.* **1.** QUICK swift, energetic, lively, sprightly, vigorous, bustling, hustling,

*peppy. **2.** BRACING invigorating, cool, chilly, nippy, biting, exhilarating, stimulating. ANT. *1.* slow, torpid, lethargic, dull. *2.* somnolent, sleepy, tiring.

bristle *v.* get angry, seethe, *see red, *raise one's hackles, *get one's dander up, flare, *boil, get indignant, *snap.

brittle *a.* fragile, crisp, delicate, breakable, frail, crumbly. ANT. *solid, rock-hard, unbreakable.*

BROACH *v.* [BROACH] to introduce a topic or start a discussion. *It is time to broach the subject with Ken.* SYN. introduce, start, begin, open, bring up, launch, put forth.

broad *a.* **1.** WIDE vast, voluminous, capacious, deep, fat, expansive, ample, commodious, sweeping, large, immense. **2.** EXTENSIVE comprehensive, blanket, sweeping, universal, general, far-reaching, compendious, catholic, widespread. **3.** OBVIOUS apparent, clear, plain, explicit, straightforward. ANT. *1.* narrow, tight. *2.* limited, specific, confined. *3.* unapparent, veiled.

broadcast *v.* transmit, *beam, put on the air, *air, televise, telecast, relay, radio, cable, spread, disseminate, scatter, announce, report.

broaden *v.* widen, enlarge, expand, deepen, extend, increase, augment, supplement. ANT. *narrow, reduce.*

broad-minded *a.* liberal-minded, open-minded, tolerant, fair, impartial, unprejudiced, unbiased, undogmatic, catholic, free-thinking, accepting, open. ANT. *close-minded, narrow-minded, bigoted, dogmatic.*

brochure *n.* pamphlet, booklet, folder, circular, leaflet, flier, throwaway.

brogue *n.* accent, twang, drawl.

broil *v.* flame-broil, sear, grill, barbecue, heat, cook, roast, burn, singe.

broke *a.* penniless, poor, impoverished, bankrupt, insolvent, destitute, ruined. ANT. *wealthy, affluent, rich, *rolling in dough.*

broken *a.* **1.** BUSTED fractured, ruptured, shattered, splintered, torn apart, pulverized, damaged, smashed, mangled. **2.** NOT WORKING nonfunctioning, broken down, in disrepair, out of order, *on the blink, *on the fritz, *busted, *kaput, *dead. **3.** DEFEATED beaten, crushed, vanquished, disheartened, humbled, fallen. ANT. *1.* whole, intact. *2.* functioning, running, *humming. *3.* invincible, indomitable, triumphant.

broken-hearted *a.* heartbroken, grief-stricken, mournful, forlorn, despairing, dejected, inconsolable, desolate, crushed. ANT. *euphoric, elated, joyous.*

broker n. agent, dealer, intermediary, negotiator, go-between, middle-man.

bromide n. platitude, trite saying, cliché.

brooch n. pin, clip, ornament, breastpin, clasp.

brood n. offspring, young, hatchlings, clutch, litter, spawn, children.

brood v. worry, agonize, fret, ruminate, deliberate, *stew over, mope, muse, meditate, think over.

brook n. stream, creek, *crick, rill, runnel, tributary, branch.

brook v. take, stand for, tolerate, abide, bear, put up with, condone.

broom n. sweeper.

broth n. stock, bouillon, flavoring, soup.

brothel n. bordello, *whorehouse, *cathouse, house of ill repute, *crib, *joy house, massage parlor, house of prostitution, bagnio, bawdyhouse, *sporting house.

brotherhood n. fellowship, fraternity, comradeship, kinship. "All for one and one for all."—Alexandre Dumas.

BROUHAHA n. [BROO ha ha] an uproar. *The scandalous findings caused a brouhaha at city hall.* SYN. uproar, hubbub, commotion, wrangle, stir, clamor, *to-do, ruckus, upset, disturbance, hullabaloo, rumpus, sensation.

browbeat v. intimidate, bully, cow, badger, terrorize, harass, threaten, domineer, *bulldoze, tyrannize, hector.

brown a. auburn, chestnut, chocolate, sorrel, coffee, brunette, fawn, ochre, umber, mahogany, cocoa, dun, tan, beige, cinnamon, ginger, rust, nutbrown, bister, sepia, henna, earth, fox.

brown-nose v. Sl. *kiss up, *suck up, bootlick, toady, fawn, flatter, kowtow, truckle, curry favor with.

browse v. glance, skim, scan, flip through, peruse, skip over.

bruise n. contusion, black and blue mark, ecchymosis, discoloration, blemish, wound, *hickey.

bruise v. contuse, jam, wound, bump, discolor, injure, mark, mar.

bruiser n. bully, fighter, boxer, hulk.

brunette a. dark-haired, brown-haired, black-haired.

brunt n. blow, impact, shock, force, full force.

brush n. 1. BROOM whisk, besom, duster. 2. TOUCH sweep, stroke, scrape. 3. CONFRONTATION clash, encounter, run-in, skirmish, tussle. 4. BUSH scrub, thicket, undergrowth, shrubs, coppice, brake, bramble, brier, bracken.

brush v. 1. SWEEP scrub, whisk, wash, wipe, buff, paint, scuff, dust off. 2. TOUCH sweep, stroke, scrape, glance, graze, caress, tickle.

brush-off n. *cold shoulder, *kiss-off, snub, rejection, slight, rebuff, dismissal.

brush up v. study, bone up, *cram.

BRUSQUE a. [BRUSK] blunt or rough in manner. *The clerk was always discourteous and brusque.* SYN. blunt, rough, abrupt, curt, gruff, short, bluff, terse, discourteous, snippy, sharp, rude. ANT. *courteous, considerate, gracious.*

brutal a. 1. VICIOUS savage, cruel, cold, barbaric, inhuman, ferocious, heartless, bloodthirsty, brutish, ruthless, harsh, hellish, pitiless. 2. HARSH rigorous, tortuous, trying, merciless, hard, painful. ANT. *kind, caring, humane, gentle.*

brutality n. viciousness, savagery, cruelty, coldness, barbarism, ferocity, inhumanity, heartlessness, brutishness, harshness. ANT. *kindness, caring, humaneness, gentility.*

brute n. beast, savage, barbarian, monster, animal, fiend, *Neanderthal, caveman, ogre, swine, devil.

bubble n. globule, droplet, sphere, burble, spheroid, orb, bead, bleb.

bubble v. boil, percolate, simmer, seethe, effervesce, burble, froth, foam, fizz, popple.

buccaneer n. pirate, corsair, privateer.

buck n. stag, deer.

bucket n. pail, vessel, cask, can, scuttle, pot, pitcher, container, holder.

buckle n. clasp, clip, fastener, snap, hitch, hasp.

buckle v. 1. CLASP clip, fasten, snap on, hitch. 2. BEND contort, warp, crimp, bulge, break, collapse, cave in, crumple, give way. ANT. *1. unbuckle, unfasten, release. 2. straighten.*

buckle down v. apply oneself, get serious, *put one's nose to the grindstone.

BUCOLIC a. [byoo KOL ik] of rural or pastoral life; rustic. *We admired a bucolic panorama of rolling hills, grazing cows and old stone walls.* SYN. rustic, rural, countrified, pastoral, agrarian, Arcadian. ANT. *urban, citified, metropolitan.*

bud v. sprout, open, bloom, flower, blossom, shoot. SEE FLOWER

buddy n. pal, chum, friend, comrade, companion, sidekick, crony, alter ego, *bro.

budge v. 1. MOVE inch, shift, stir, roll, dislodge, push, propel, nudge. 2. BEND give in, acquiesce, yield.

budget n. financial plan, appropriation, estimate, overhead, expenses. "A mathematical confirmation of your suspicions."—A.A. Latimer. SEE MONEY, BANK

budget v. apportion, allocate, estimate, ration, allow.

buff n. devotee, enthusiast, fanatic, expert, connoisseur, *bug, *freak, nut.

buff v. clean, shine, polish, rub, burnish, smooth.

buffalo n. bison, animal, mammal, quadriped, herbivore.

buffer n. cushion, pad, shock absorber, guard.

buffet n. sideboard, counter, credenza, shelf, salad bar, cold table, smorgasbord.

buffet v. pummel, beat, cuff, strike, slug, slap, drub, knock, punch, smack, wallop, pound, *hit up-side the head.

buffoon n. clown, fool, jester, joker, prankster, comedian, harlequin, *boob, bozo, zany, merry-andrew.

bug n. 1. INSECT vermin, pest. 2. FLAW defect, fault, imperfection.

bug v. 1. BOTHER annoy, irritate, irk, pester, vex, nettle, badger, plague, disturb. 2. WIRE-TAP eavesdrop, spy.

build n. physique, shape, figure, body.

build v. 1. CONSTRUCT erect, put together, assemble, raise, fabricate, *knock together, engineer, contrive, *throw up. 2. ESTABLISH start, set up, initiate, institute, found, create. 3. FORM shape, mold, model, fashion, create. 4. INTENSIFY compound, escalate, mount, amplify, magnify, grow, swell. ANT. *1. disassemble, demolish, raze. 4. decrease, decrescendo.*

building n. structure, edifice, construction, erection, high rise, *skyscraper, superstructure, framework.

WORD FIND

arches, series of: arcade

brickwork laid in checkered pattern: checkerwork, basketweave

brickwork with alternating courses of bricks laid sideways (stretchers) and head-ways (headers): English bond

brickwork with every other brick laid head-ways (header): Flemish bond

concrete embedded with steel mesh, bars: reinforced concrete

face: facade

gallery between two main stories: mezzanine

inscribed stone: cornerstone

inscription on: epigraph

material: brick, mortar, concrete, reinforced concrete, stone, wood, adobe

monstrous ornament: gargoyle, grotesque

nonopening window: deadlight

outside corner: quoin

rooftop safety wall: parapet

round, domed: rotunda

shelflike projection: cornice

support: joist, beam, girder, pier, buttress, flying buttress

window design, arrangement: fenestration

wing: annex, ell, bay

SEE ARCHITECTURE, CASTLE, CATHEDRAL, HOUSE

bulge n. bump, swelling, protuberance, lump, hump, prominence, outgrowth. ANT. *hollow, hole.*

bulge v. swell, protrude, distend, puff, balloon, stick out. ANT. *contract, shrivel.*

bulimia n. eating disorder, bulimarexia, bulimia nervosa, compulsive eating. SEE ANOREXIA

bulk n. 1. SIZE mass, volume, amount, magnitude, body, extent. 2. BIGGEST PART main, majority, most, lion's share, preponderance, better part.

bulky a. massive, unwieldy, cumbersome, huge, ponderous, prodigious, mammoth, sizable, unmanageable, hulking, voluminous. ANT. *small, wieldy, manageable, pocket-sized.*

bull n. 1. ANIMAL Taurus, bullock, male, steer, ox. 2. Sl. UNTRUTH *bilge, *blarney, *baloney, bushwa, *BS, *hogwash, lies, bunk, *hokum, *horsefeathers, *malarkey, *rot, *rubbish, nonsense.

bull v. charge, drive, thrust, press, bulldoze, *muscle.

bulldozer n. earthmover, grader, plow, heavy machinery.

bullet n. shot, ball, shell, cartridge, trajectile, slug, *lead, pellet, missile.

WORD FIND

bulletproof garment: bulletproof vest

bulletproof shield: mantelet

cartridge with no projectile: blank

container: cartridge

covering: jacket

diameter: caliber

glowing, military: tracer

pointed: spitzer

receptacle: clip, magazine

shotgun pellets: birdshot, buckshot

shotgun projectiles used in riots to stun, not kill: baton rounds

soft, expands when it hits, causing severe damage: dumdum

trajectory deviation: drift

SEE AMMUNITION, GUN

bulletin n. report, flash, statement, announcement, notification, communication, dispatch, publication.

bullfight n. corrida, spectacle.

WORD FIND

assistant on horseback, lances bull's neck: picador

assisting team: cuadrilla

barbed dart: banderilla

cheer: olé

fighter: matador, torero

matador's emergency shelter: burladero

picador's lance: pic

red cape waved: capa

wave of red cloth: capeador

bullheaded a. headstrong, stubborn, mulish, obstinate. ANT. *compromising, yielding, irresolute.*

bullion n. ingot, bar, plate; gold, silver.

bullish a. optimistic, confident, believing, hopeful, sure, assured, steady, unflinching, cocksure, rising, gowing, escalating, climbing, ascending, surging, increasing, gaining, inflating, trending upward. ANT. *bearish, pessimistic, falling.*

bully n. tyrant, thug, tormentor, terrorizer, bruiser, ruffian, rowdy, *browbeater, *dink, swaggerer, oppressor, aggressor, intimidator, *human T-Rex, dictator, *biggest toad in the puddle. SEE BOSS

bully v. domineer, tyrannize, torment, *lord over, threaten, oppress, dictate, *call the shots, intimidate, hector, browbeat.

bulwark n. fortification, rampart, earthwork, bank, wall, reinforcement, barrier, defense, stronghold, bastion, protection.

bum n. loafer, idler, derelict, panhandler, drunk, hobo, vagrant, ne'er-do-well, beggar, tramp, transient.

bumbling a. blundering, stumbling, bungling, clumsy, uncoordinated. ANT. *coordinated, ordered, graceful.*

bummer n. Sl. *downer, bad experience, disappointment, disaster, *pain in the ass, misfortune, *drag.

bump n. 1. COLLISION crash, thud, thump, scrape, tap, jolt, blow, jostle, knock, sideswiping, *fenderbender, impact, crack, nudge. 2. SWELLING lump, bulge, welt, knob, gnarl, nodule, protuberance, dent, *ding.

bump v. 1. HIT thump, collide with, run into, butt, scrape, tap, jar, bang, graze, sideswipe, jostle, smash into, bang. 2. DISPLACE depose, replace, remove, dislodge.

bumpkin n. hick, *hayseed, yokel, rustic,

*goat-roper, clodhopper, yahoo, *cider squeezer, farmer.

bumptious a. arrogant, conceited, pushy, forward, overbearing, cocky, haughty, presumptuous. ANT. *bashful, diffident, retiring.*

bumpy a. rough, jolting, lumpy, jerky, jarring, rugged, *washboard, corrugated, *spine-shattering, *kidney-crushing, choppy, *chuckholed, *potholed. ANT. *smooth, silky, graded.*

bunch n. group, cluster, collection, lot, mass, clump, quantity, assortment, bundle, host, multitude, heap, batch, throng, swarm, number, galaxy, *mess, *oodles.

bundle n. 1. MASS bunch, lot, cluster, heap, group, pile, batch, collection. 2. PACKAGE parcel, packet, box, carton, sheaf, bale, stack, roll.

bungalow n. cottage. SEE HOUSE

bungle v. botch, *screw up, *muff, *blow it, *goof, mess up, blunder, fumble, misstep, miscalculate, *drop the ball. ANT. *succeed, *pull it off, *score.*

bungling a. inept, incompetent, clumsy, blundering, maladroit. ANT. *adroit, nimble, able.*

bunk n. 1. BED cot, berth. 2. Sl. NONSENSE *malarky, *baloney, *hokum, *rubbish, twaddle. SEE BULL, NONSENSE

buoy n. float, marker, beacon, bell.

WORD FIND

mooring: dolphin

type: can, nun, bell, whistle

buoy v. uplift, boost, raise, lift, hearten.

buoyant a. cheerful, lighthearted, resilient, blithe, optimistic, sprightly, mirthful, sanguine, carefree, jaunty. ANT. *depressed, somber, down.*

burden n. load, weight, cross to bear, obligation, stress, millstone, albatross, onus, strain, hardship, responsibility, encumbrance, affliction, workload, incubus.

burden v. load, weigh down, saddle with, encumber, strain, obligate, bog down, hamper, oppress, tax, yoke. ANT. *unburden, lighten, free.*

bureau n. 1. DRESSER chest of drawers, chest, chiffonier, highboy. 2. DEPARTMENT division, branch, agency, office, commission.

BUREAUCRACY n. [byoo ROK ruh see] any form of government administration, especially that which is inefficient and bound by its own red tape. *A bureaucracy requires a contract submitted in quadruplicate when a handshake would do.* SYN. government administration, civil service, officialdom, *the

Establishment, *powers that be, city hall, the system, the authorities, *Big Brother. "A giant mechanism operated by pygmies."—Honore de Balzac. "The anonymous 'they,' the enigmatic 'they' who are in charge."—Joseph Heller.

bureaucrat *n.* government official, civil servant, administrator, politician, clerk, public servant, pencil-pusher, *desk-jockey, *red tape dispenser.

BURGEON *v.* [BUR jun] grow, proliferate. *The deficit is burgeoning out of control.* SYN. grow, proliferate, flourish, develop, sprout, thrive, mushroom, bud, spread, multiply, expand. ANT. *dwindle, diminish.*

burglar *n.* thief, cat burglar, crook, mugger, prowler, *picklock, robber, housebreaker.

burial *n.* interment, inhumation, funeral, entombment, last rites, *deep six. SEE CEMETERY

burlesque *n.* parody, satire, caricature, farce, lampoon, travesty, *send-up, spoof, vaudeville, comedy, *schtick, skits, striptease.

burly *a.* big, heavy, muscular, strong, beefy, brawny, stout, hefty, hulking, rugged, thickset. ANT. *skinny, anorexic, slight.*

burn *v.* **1.** BE ON FIRE OR SET FIRE incinerate, ignite, torch, blaze, flame, light, smolder, kindle, reduce to ashes, rage, go up in smoke, consume, cremate, deflagrate, combust, singe, sear, broil, char, scorch, brand, cauterize. **2.** CONSUME use up, expend, squander. **3.** CHEAT swindle, bilk, take, *rip off. ANT. *1. extinguish, quench. 2. conserve, save.*

burning *a.* **1.** FLAMING blazing, on fire, raging, aflame, fiery, ignited, smouldering, smoking. **2.** SERIOUS dire, crucial, compelling, important, critical, crucial, vital, urgent, pressing. **3.** FERVENT feverish, passionate, frenzied, ardent, enthusiastic. ANT. *1. extinguished, out, quenched. 2. insignificant, trivial. 3. apathetic, cool, unconcerned.*

burnish *v.* polish, smooth, brighten, furbish, buff, shine, gloss, rub.

burnout *n.* exhaustion, dissipation, weariness, combat fatigue, defeat, sapping, *running out of steam, expiration, disillusionment, disenchantment, breakdown.

burn out *v.* tire, fatigue, *run out of steam, become drained, *stress out, become jaded, *get sick of.

burp *v.* belch.

burrow *n.* hole, tunnel, warren, dugout, diggings, den, lair.

burrow *v.* dig, excavate, tunnel, hollow out, furrow.

burst *n.* explosion, outburst, blowout, eruption, discharge, outpouring, spurt.

burst *v.* pop, explode, crack open, rupture, fly apart, blow up, shatter, rip, bust, split, erupt, disintegrate.

bury *v.* **1.** INTER entomb, inhume, sepulcher, lay to rest. **2.** EMBED sink, submerge, implant, engulf. **3.** COVER conceal, hide, cache, stash, secrete. ANT. *1. exhume, dig up. 3. expose, air.*

bus *n.* transport, public transportation, motor vehicle, passenger vehicle, motor coach, jitney, mass transit vehicle.

bush *n.* **1.** SHRUB hedge, plant, thicket, brier, bramble, undergrowth, scrub. **2.** BACKCOUNTRY woods, jungle, the wild, outback.

bushed *a.* exhausted, spent, *pooped. ANT. *energetic, peppy.* SEE TIRED

bush-league *a.* second-rate, *minor league, *small potatoes. ANT. *first-rate, big league, big time.* SEE INFERIOR

business *n.* **1.** OCCUPATION profession, trade, job, career, vocation, calling, work, livelihood, *racket, pursuit. **2.** COMMERCE industry, trade, enterprise, manufacturing, merchandising, buying and selling, mercantilism, marketing. "The art of extracting money from another man's pocket without resorting to violence."—Max Amsterdam. "Riding a bicycle. Either you keep moving or you fall down."—John Wright. **3.** RESPONSIBILITY concern, department, province, affair, duty, interest, subject, matter. **4.** FIRM company, corporation, concern, enterprise, market, store, factory, office, organization, conglomerate, mill.

businesslike *a.* methodical, efficient, organized, orderly, systematic, professional, industrious. ANT. *disorganized, slipshod, unprofessional.*

businessman/woman *n.* merchant, trader, industrialist, entrepreneur, tycoon, capitalist, investor, employer.

bust *n.* chest, bosom, breast.

bustle *n.* activity, commotion, hubbub, hurly-burly, uproar, tumult, flurry, stir, *comings and goings, to-do, pother. ANT. *stillness, calm, peace.*

busy *a.* **1.** ACTIVE bustling, full, *buzzing, *humming, *popping, *hopping, jumping, *on the go, lively. **2.** ENGAGED preoccupied, employed, unavailable, working, active, involved, tied down, tied up. ANT. *1. idle, still, quiet. 2. free, at leisure, lazing around.*

busybody n. meddler, pry, gossip, snoop, blabbermouth, *buttinski.

butcher v. **1.** SLAUGHTER dress, clean, cure, pack, smoke. **2.** KILL slaughter, murder, massacre, slay. **3.** BUNGLE botch, make a mess of, *screw up, ruin.

butter n. servant, *help, food server, staff.

butt/buttocks n. bottom, seat, rump, *tush, *ass, derriere, *fanny, *stern, backside, gluteus maximus.

butt n. subject, target, victim, scapegoat.

butt v. ram, horn, thrust, strike, drive, batter, collide, jab, jam.

butterflies n. anxiety, tension, nerves, jitters, unease, nervousness, nausea, *shakes, *cold sweat, nervous anticipation.

button n. **1.** FASTENER clasp, stud. **2.** PUSHBUTTON switch, toggle, on/off, power switch, tuner, adjustor, knob, dial.

buttress n. support, prop, brace, reinforcement, abutment, stanchion, shore, beam, pier, arch.

buttress v. reinforce, strengthen, fortify, bolster, shore up, prop up.

buxom a. full-figured, *busty, shapely, plump, voluptuous. ANT. *skinny, bony, *flat.*

buy v. **1.** PURCHASE acquire, bargain for, pay for, procure, make a deal, bid, corner, shop, market. **2.** BRIBE corrupt, *pay off.

buzz n. hum, drone, whir, hiss, whizz.

bygone a. former, past, previous, gone by, olden, erstwhile, defunct, forgotten, lost. ANT. *present, current, in the here and now.*

bypass v. go around, avoid, detour around, sidestep, circumvent.

byproduct n. outgrowth, offshoot, spin-off, side effect.

bystander n. observer, onlooker, witness, eyewitness, spectator, passerby.

byte n. eight bits, sixteen bits, unit.

byword n. proverb, adage, motto, maxim, slogan, saying, catchword, watchword, dictum, truth, principle.

C

cab *n.* taxi, cabriolet, hack, hansom.
cabal *n.* **1.** FACTION junta, camarilla, clique, ring, band. **2.** CONSPIRACY plot, intrigue, scheme.
cabalistic *a.* occult, secret, hidden, clandestine, esoteric, mystic, mysterious, conspiratorial, underground. ANT. *overt, open.*
cabana *n.* shelter, bathhouse.
cabaret *n.* nightclub, boite, dinner theater, cafe, supper club, honky-tonk, disco.
cabin *n.* **1.** COTTAGE shack, loghouse, camp, hovel, hut, lodge, chalet, shanty, bungalow. **2.** COMPARTMENT quarters, stateroom, room, chamber.
cabinet *n.* **1.** CUPBOARD commode, bureau, chest, chiffonier, chifforobe, box, case, file, etagere, console. **2.** ADMINISTRATION advisers, council, ministry, board, *brain trust.
cabinetmaker *n.* craftsman, woodworker, artisan, furniture maker, carpenter.
cabin fever *n.* claustrophobia, winter blues, SAD (seasonal affective disorder), restlessness, distress, *climbing the walls, temporary insanity, neurosis, *going psycho.
cable *n.* **1.** WIRE cord, line, rope, chain. **2.** OVERSEAS TELEGRAM wire, cablegram.
cache *n.* stockpile, hoard, stash, supply, store, *nest egg, respository, reserve, hiding place provisions.
cackle *v.* chuckle, chortle. SEE LAUGH
CACOPHONOUS *a.* [kuh KOF uh nus] harsh-sounding, jarring, especially designating incongruent sounds heard over one another. *No one could tell whether the cacophonous heavy-metal band was in tune or not.* SYN. harsh-sounding, jarring, dissonant, discordant, strident, inharmonious, unmelodious, grating, raucous, noisy. ANT. *euphonic, harmonious, melodious.*
cactus *n.* desert plant, saguaro, cholla, prickly pear, cereus, mescal. SEE DESERT
cad *n.* scoundrel, bounder, heel, rogue, rat, rascal, lout, scamp, knave, bastard, *dink.
cadaver *n.* corpse, body, *stiff, carcass, remains, mummy.
cadaverous *a.* pale, ghastly, gaunt, haggard, pallid, ashen, deathly, emaciated, chalky, ghostly, bloodless, having the pallor of death. ANT. *rosy, ruddy, glowing.*
cadence *n.* modulation, meter, rhythm, beat, measure, pulse, tempo, flow, swing.

cadre *n.* nucleus, core, infrastructure, framework.
cafe *n.* coffeehouse, bar, bistro. SEE RESTAURANT
cafeteria *n.* lunchroom, lunch counter, commissary. SEE RESTAURANT
cage *n.* enclosure, jail, pound, lockup, pen, coop, confinement, prison, trap.
cage *v.* confine, trap, enclose, pen, imprison, impound, coop up, shut up, lock up. ANT. *free, release.*
CAGEY *a.* [KAY jee] tricky, not easily caught or fooled. *A fox is a cagey animal.* SYN. tricky, sly, cunning, wary, leery, shrewd, wily, cautious, crafty, careful. ANT. *unwary, trusting, naive.*
cahoots *n. Sl.* partnership, league, collusion, alliance, conspiracy.
CAJOLE *v.* [kuh JOHL] to persuade with flattery, coax. *She cajoled him for hours; he finally gave in.* SYN. persuade, coax, wheedle, *sweet talk, blandish, pander to, *butter up, flatter, stroke, *kiss up, beguile, inveigle.
cajolery *n.* palaver, persuasion, coaxing. SEE FLATTERY
cake *n.* **1.** BAR block, lump, brick, slab, cube. **2.** LOAF batter cake, layer cake, torte, pastry, flan, madeleine, cupcake.
cakewalk *n.* *a snap, *breeze, *child's play, *cinch, *no-brainer, *piece of cake.
calamitous *a.* disastrous, catastrophic, ruinous, devastating, cataclysmic, grievous, fatal, tragic, dire. ANT. *blessed, beneficial, favorable.*
calamity *n.* disaster, catastrophe, devastation, cataclysm, fatality, misery, blow, adversity, ruination, misfortune. "A mighty leveler."—Edmund Burke. "The test of integrity."—Samuel Richardson. ANT. *blessing, good fortune, boon.*
calculate *v.* compute, figure, reckon, add up, sum up, count, evaluate, surmise, judge, forecast.
calculating *a.* shrewd, scheming, crafty, designing, manipulative, plotting, artful, wily, sharp. ANT. *artless, naive.*
calculation *n.* computation, figuring, counting, reckoning, summation, evaluation, estimation, mathematics, arithmetic.
calculator *n.* computer, adding machine, *number cruncher.
caldron *n.* boiler. SEE KETTLE
caliber *n.* **1.** QUALITY value, worth, character,

ability, virtue, distinction. **2.** DIAMETER bore, gauge.

CALIBRATE *v.* [KAL uh brayt] to adjust; to check for accuracy. *The inspector came to calibrate the meat scales.* SYN. adjust, check, correct, fix, test, regulate, measure, align, tune, fine-tune, balance, synchronize.

calisthenics *n.* exercises, workout, aerobics.

call *n.* **1.** SHOUT exclamation, yell, whoop, announcement, outcry. **2.** SUMMONS request, convocation, appeal, draft. **3.** INVITATION solicitation, bidding. **3.** ANIMAL CRY hoot, shriek, bleat, low, bellow, trumpet, ululation. SEE BIRD, SHOUT

call *v.* **1.** SHOUT exclaim, announce, yell, cry, holler, hail, whoop. **2.** SUMMON request, convoke, muster, convene, direct. **3.** NAME designate, label, title, term, christen, dub. **4.** VISIT drop in, ring.

call girl *n.* *hooker, *streetwalker. SEE PROSTITUTE

calling *n.* vocation, metier, occupation, profession, trade, job, business, pursuit, line, forte, passion, *thing, *bag, *racket.

call off *v.* cancel, postpone, *scrub, abort, *kill.

CALLOUS *a.* [KAL us] unfeeling, having no pity. *The callous rioters looted neighborhood stores.* SYN. unfeeling, pitiless, merciless, cold, uncaring, heartless, insensitive, hardboiled, indifferent, cruel, cold-blooded. ANT. *sympathetic, caring, thoughtful.*

CALLOW *a.* [KAL oh] inexperienced, immature. *Some sixteen-year-olds are too callow to be trusted behind the wheel.* SYN. inexperienced, immature, unseasoned, naive, unsophisticated, childish, juvenile, sophomoric, uninitiated, green, unfledged. ANT. *mature, experienced, worldly.*

calm *a.* **1.** STILL motionless, tranquil, quiet, undisturbed, halcyon, windless, smooth, placid, serene. **2.** RELAXED unperturbed, cool, collected, unruffled, unexcited, sedate, tranquil, dispassionate, composed, staid, unflappable, placid. ANT. *1. turbulent, rough, disturbed. 2. nervous, anxious, frenzied, panicky.*

calumny *n.* slander, defamation, malicious statement, libel, smear, mud-slinging, smirch, false accusation, aspersion, slur. ANT. *praise, compliment, acclaim.*

CAMARADERIE *n.* [kah muh RAH duh ree] friendliness and rapport. *The camaraderie between the team's players was obvious.* SYN. fellowship, rapport, friendliness, companionship, bonhomie, brotherhood, friendship, comradeship, conviviality, esprit de corps, fraternization, loyalty, *buddy-buddy atmosphere. ANT. *hostility, antagonism, coldness.* SEE FRIENDSHIP

camcorder *n.* videocassette recorder, camera.

camel *n.* dromedary, beast of burden, quadruped, ruminant.

camera *n.* 35mm, *Polaroid, video camera, camcorder, *Brownie, *Kodak, *Nikon.

WORD FIND
flash receptacle: hot shoe
focusing system: range finder, viewfinder
lens for shooting tiny objects: macro lens
lens producing haze or color effect: filter
lightmeasuring device: light meter, exposure meter, photometer
light producer: flash
long-distance lens: telephoto lens, zoom lens
opening, amount of: aperture
opens and closes when shot is taken: shutter
stand: tripod, highhat
wide field of view lens: wide-angle lens, fisheye, bugeye
SEE PHOTOGRAPHY

camisole *n.* negligee, undergarment. SEE LINGERIE

camouflage *n.* disguise, concealment, facade, cover-up, cryptic coloration, blind, dissimulation, front, masquerade, veil, shroud, mimicry.

camouflage *v.* disguise, conceal, cover up, masquerade, obscure, obfuscate, shroud, veil, hide, simulate, mimic. ANT. *expose, reveal, display.*

camp *n.* **1.** ENCAMPMENT bivouac, cantonment, shelter. **2.** GROUP faction, clique, sect, party, circle.

camp *v.* bivouac, encamp, pitch a tent, rough it, lodge, sleep out.

campaign *n.* **1.** OPERATIONS offensive, strategy, battle plan. **2.** DRIVE crusade, movement, project, push.

campaign *v.* electioneer, run, solicit votes, canvass, crusade, lobby, barnstorm.

camper *n.* recreational vehicle, RV, *tin can, mobile home, *Winnebago.

campus *n.* grounds, yard, quad, dorm, alma mater. SEE SCHOOL, COLLEGE, UNIVERSITY

campy *a.* affected, effeminate, artificial, ostentatious, garish, posturing, flaunting, outlandish, theatrical, *faggy. ANT. *straightlaced, understated, serious.*

can *n.* container, receptacle, vessel, tin.

canal *n.* waterway, conduit, channel, race, aqueduct, passage, trench, culvert, duct, tube.

cancel v. 1. CALL OFF stop, revoke, *kill, break off, void, annul, discontinue, rescind, countermand, abort. 2. OFFSET counter, neutralize, counterbalance, make up for, nullify.

cancer n. carcinoma, tumor, malignancy, sarcoma, malignant neoplasm, growth.

WORD FIND
blood/marrow: leukemia
breast removal: mastectomy
cause, substance: carcinogen
deadly form: malignant
harmless form: benign
mass: tumor, neoplasm, growth
medical branch: oncology
removable: resectable
skin: melanoma, basal cell tumor
spread of: metastasis
treatment: chemotherapy, radiation
tumor removal: lumpectomy
SEE OPERATION, DISEASE

candid a. open, honest, frank, up-front, straightforward, blunt, direct, sincere, foursquare, heart-to-heart. ANT. mealy-mouthed, insincere, indirect.

candidate n. nominee, aspirant, contender, office-seeker, party favorite, hopeful, entrant, *dark horse. SEE GOVERNMENT, POLITICS, ELECTION

candle n. taper, rush, torch, glim.

WORD FIND
burning center: wick
holder: sconce, candelabra, chandelier, girandole, menorah
lighter: taper
maker: chandler
material: wax, carnauba, tallow
wick's end: snuff

CANDOR n. [KAN dur] truthfulness, frankness. In all candor, Mary, you have dragon breath. SYN. truthfulness, frankness, honesty, straightforwardness, bluntness, outspokenness, openness, directness, forthrightness, plain-speaking. ANT. deception, indirectness, duplicity, *doublespeak.

candy n. sweet, confection, bonbon, kiss, lozenge, taffy, caramel, toffee, jellybean, jawbreaker, fudge, drop, wafer, lollipop, nougat, praline, sweetmeat, brittle, cotton candy, peanut brittle, mint, sucker, gumball, chocolate bar, penny candy.

cane n. stick, walking stick, staff, crook, rod.

canker n. lesion, sore, ulcer, blister, cold sore.

cannibal n. man-eater, headhunter, savage, barbarian, carnivore.

cannon n. gun, howitzer, mortar, heavy artillery, ordnance, *Big Bertha, *Long Tom.

WORD FIND
case of projectiles: canister
cast iron balls: grapeshot
continuous firing: cannonade, barrage, salvo
gunner: cannoneer
kick: recoil
shipboard antiaircraft guns: pompom
SEE ARMY, GUN, WEAPON

canny a. shrewd, clever, cautious, careful, cagey, wiley, sly, smart, streetwise, worldly, wary, crafty, sagacious. ANT. naive, careless, unsophisticated, dim-witted.

canoe n. boat, dugout, pirogue, bongo, kayak.

WORD FIND
air chambers: sponsons
angled stroke used to avoid fatigue on long excursions: Canadian stroke
apparel and equipment of canoeist: duffle
braking stroke: jam stroke
carrying canoe over land between water bodies: portaging
deviate from course or float sideways: yaw
distance above water line to gunwales: freeboard, draw, draft
left side facing forward: port
line used to tie or tow: painter
right side facing forward: starboard
side edges, upper: gunwales (pronounced "gunnels")
underside strip: keel
SEE BOAT, RIVER, SHIP

CAN OF WORMS n. a complex or troublesome problem. He opened up a can of worms when he made the "no new taxes" pledge. SYN. problem, difficulty, complexity, Pandora's box, complication, trouble, Gordian knot, entanglement, snarl, knot, predicament, quandary, quagmire, hot water.

canon n. law, decree, doctrine, principle, dogma, edict, statute. SEE LAW

canopy n. awning, cover, sunshade, baldachin, tilt, tarp.

cant n. 1. INSINCERITY piety, *lip service, hypocrisy, pretense, sanctimony. 2. JARGON argot, lingo, dialect, slang, vernacular, patter.

cant v. tilt, angle, overturn, slant, lean, tip, incline.

cantankerous a. bad-tempered, ornery, crabby, touchy, surly, grouchy, irritable, contentious, grumpy, crotchety, testy, cranky, bearish. ANT. cheerful, easygoing, good-humored.

canteen n. flask, bottle, jug.

canter v. lope, saunter, amble, trot, gallop.

canvas n. duck, tent cloth, sailcloth, coarse cloth, fabric, cotton, hemp, flax.

canvass v. analyze, poll, examine, solicit, survey, study, investigate, discuss, electioneer.

canyon n. valley, gorge, gulch, ravine, gully, box canyon, chasm, pass.

cap n. hat, headgear, beret, beanie, tam-o'-shanter. SEE HAT

cap v. top, crown, surpass, beat, transcend, eclipse, defeat.

capability a. ability, know-how, capacity, proficiency, wherewithal, aptitude, *the right stuff, means, power, skill, mind, talent.

capable a. able, competent, skilled, trained, apt, adept, learned, proficient, deft, adept, equal to, expert, masterly, adroit, talented, *having the right stuff. ANT. incapable, incompetent, inept.

capacious a. spacious, roomy, commodious, voluminous, big, ample. ANT. tiny, cramped.

capacity n. **1.** VOLUME proportions, size, dimensions, magnitude, range, contents, space, limit, room. **2.** ABILITY capability, means, power, competence, faculty, aptitude, *the right stuff, mind, talent, skill, proficiency. **3.** POSITION role, responsibility, function.

cape n. **1.** MANTLE cloak, wrap, poncho, shawl, capote, pelisse. **2.** PENINSULA headland, point, promontory.

caper n. prank, escapade, *high jinx, *shenanigans.

caper v. jump, skip, gambol, prance, romp, frisk, hop, leap about.

capital n. **1.** SEAT OF GOVERNMENT principal city. **2.** WEALTH funds, moneys, stock, savings, assets, resources, venture capital, investment capital. "That part of wealth which is devoted to obtaining further wealth."—Alfred Marshall. **1.** SEE GOVERNMENT, POLITICS, LAW **2.** SEE MONEY, BANK

CAPITALISM n. [KAP i tuh LIZ um] free enterprise, business and the pursuit of wealth by private citizens for private gain. *Capitalism is the economic engine that drives America.* SYN. free enterprise, free market, commercialism, mercantilism, *dog eat dog, laissez-faire, private ownership, market economy, private investment. "The unequal sharing of blessings. . . . "—Winston Churchill. ANT. socialism, communism. SEE GOVERNMENT

capitalist n. investor, entrepreneur, financier, tycoon, businessman.

capitalize on v. take advantage of, cash in on, exploit, profit by, utilize.

CAPITULATE v. [kuh PICH yoo LATE] to give up, give in, yield. *The opposing side agreed to capitulate on several points.* SYN. give

up, give in, yield, surrender, acquiesce, accede, come to terms, submit, bow, cave in, knuckle under. ANT. *stand firm, stand one's ground, fight.*

caprice n. whim, impulse, notion, vagary, whimsy, eccentricity, fancy, fickleness.

CAPRICIOUS a. [kuh PRISH us] subject to change on a whim, unpredictable. *Fred is always changing his mind; he is as capricious as the wind.* SYN. fickle, whimsical, unpredictable, unstable, frivolous, impulsive, inconsistent, indecisive, wayward, flighty, crotchety, quirky, *any way the wind blows. ANT. constant, stable, predictable.*

capsize v. overturn, tip, upset, *turn turtle, roll over, keel over.

capsule n. pill, tablet, pellet, ampule, wafer.

captain n. cap'n, master, skipper, boss, chief, manager, head, commanding officer, leader, *old man.

caption n. heading, title, subtitle, legend, inscription.

captivate v. attract, charm, fascinate, spellbind, enamor, enchant, enthrall, bewitch, mesmerize, hypnotize, *knock/sweep off one's feet. ANT. *repel, repulse, turn off.*

captive n. prisoner, internee, convict, hostage.

captive a. imprisoned, confined, held, bound, obliged. ANT. *liberated, emancipated, free.*

captivity n. imprisonment, incarceration, restraint, bondage, custody, detention.

capture n. apprehension, seizure, landing, *bagging, catch, taking, acquisition, netting, recovery, taking into custody, trapping, cornering. ANT. *release, liberation.*

capture v. catch, apprehend, seize, *bag, *nab, *collar, land, snare, net, corner, trap, *round up. ANT. *release, liberate.*

car n. sedan, coupe, roadster, *clunker. SEE AUTOMOBILE, TRUCK

caravan n. train, cavalcade, procession, company, motorcade, column.

carbuncle n. boil, infection, furuncle, canker, sore.

carcass n. corpse, cadaver, body, remains, carrion, *roadkill, *dead meat.

carcinogen n. cancer-causing agent, cancer-causing substance, tumor-forming agent, mutagen, toxin, health hazard, poison, killer, deadly chemical.

CARCINOGENIC a. [kar sin uh JEN ik] pertaining to any substance or source that causes cancer. *Radiation is highly carcinogenic.*

SYN. cancer-causing, tumor-forming, muta-genic, malignant, deadly, unhealthy, haz-ardous, toxic, pernicious. ANT. *benign, harm-less, healthly.*

cardiac arrest *n.* heart failure, heart attack, heart stoppage, coronary thrombosis, myo-cardial infarction.

cardinal *a.* principal, main, chief, utmost, cen-tral, prime, foremost, fundamental. ANT. *in-significant, unimportant.*

cards *n.* playing cards, tarot cards. "The Devil's books."—English proverb.

WORD FIND

authority: Hoyle

card pile remaining after deal: talon, stock

card with value determined before game: wild card

cheat: sharper, card shark, blackleg

game: bridge, baccarat, monte, whist, black-jack, crazy eights, concentration, war, three-card monte, old maid, poker, pi-nochle, canasta, solitaire, gin, rummy, gin rummy, hearts, cribbage, slapjack, ca-sino, euchre

jack, queen or king: face card

outranking suit, card: trump card

same suit group: flush

tie-breaking game: rubber match

care *n.* **1.** CAREFULNESS caution, regard, consid-eration, thought, diligence, pains, prudence, conscientiousness, mindfulness, exactitude, vigilance. **2.** CONCERN worry, anxiety, bother, trouble, burden, problem, tribula-tion, distress. **3.** CUSTODY charge, protec-tion, supervision, safekeeping, administra-tion, guidance, tutelage, keep. ANT. *1. carelessness, negligence.*

care *v.* **1.** BE CONCERNED mind, worry, fret, take pains. **2.** REGARD love, hold dear, prize, cher-ish.

careen *v.* tip, tilt, lurch, totter, pitch, swerve, sway, lean.

career *n.* profession, occupation, vocation, life-work, job, pursuit, work, livelihood, metier, business, field, *thing.

carefree *a.* happy-go-lucky, insouciant, foot-loose, lighthearted, untroubled, breezy, *laid-back, blasé, blithe, devil-may-care, cheerful. ANT. *troubled, careworn, burdened.*

careful *a.* **1.** CAUTIOUS wary, circumspect, heedful, vigilant, leery, guarded, prudent, alert, attentive. **2.** METICULOUS painstaking, thorough, fussy, scrupulous, demanding, conscientious, rigorous, fastidious, punctili-ous, attentive. ANT. *1. careless, reckless, negli-gent. 2. careless, slipshod, sloppy.*

caregiver *n.* attendant, custodian, parent, mother, father, nurse, babysitter, sister, caretaker, nanny, au pair.

careless *a.* unattentive, heedless, reckless, lax, unwary, slipshod, sloppy, slapdash, indis-creet, remiss, neglectful, absentminded, hasty, thoughtless, imprudent, casual, off-hand, rash, unconcerned, lackadaisical. ANT. *careful, attentive, cautious, meticulous, rigor-ous.*

caress *v.* stroke, touch, fondle, pet, pat, brush, graze, rub, snuggle, cuddle.

caretaker *n.* custodian, superintendent, super-visor, janitor, curator, warden, conservator, maintenance man.

careworn *a.* haggard, tired, exhausted, worried, anxious, troubled, heavy-hearted. ANT. *fresh, carefree, light-hearted.*

cargo *n.* freight, load, shipment, payload, con-signment, lading.

CARICATURE *n.* [KAR uh kuh chur] an ex-aggerated portrait or depiction of someone or something, usually for satirical effect. *Gross caricatures of politicians frequently ap-pear in editorial cartoons.* SYN. cartoon, por-trait, sketch, depiction, exaggeration, par-ody, satire, spoof, farce, takeoff, send-up, lampoon, travesty, mockery, imitation, *ap-ing, humorous distortion. "The most pene-trating of criticisms."—Aldous Huxley. "Exaggeration of a fact."—Robert Zwickey.

CARNAGE *n.* [KAR nij] bloody slaughter. *The young soldiers were appalled by the carnage of war.* SYN. slaughter, bloodshed, massacre, bloodbath, butchery, holocaust, decimation, gore, mass murder, annihilation.

CARNAL *a.* [KAR nul] of bodily, not spiritual, pleasure, sensual. *He fought his carnal desires.* SYN. sensual, sexual, of the flesh, bodily, ani-mal, voluptuous, lustful, corporal, lascivious, prurient, erotic, wanton. ANT. *spiritual, moral, godly.*

carnival *n.* festival, fair, gala, celebration, jam-boree, fiesta, jubilee, Mardis Gras, *carny.

carnivore *n.* meat-eater, flesh-eater, predator, carrion-feeder.

carnivorous *a.* flesh-eating, meat-eating, pred-atory. ANT. *herbivorous.*

carol *n.* melody, tune. SEE SONG

carom *v.* rebound, glance, bounce, ricochet.

carouse *v.* drink, party, frolic, wassail, make merry, cut loose, revel, *tie one on. ANT. *sober up, *swear off.*

carp *v.* complain, find-fault, nag, *bitch, scold,

nitpick, *moan and groan, knock, belittle, cavil, criticize. ANT. *praise, compliment.*

carpal tunnel syndrome *n.* sensorimotor disorder, repetitive motion disorder/injury.

carpenter *n.* woodwright, cabinetmaker, woodworker, builder, joiner, contractor, subcontractor.

carpentry *n.* woodworking, construction, building.

WORD FIND

aligned, fitted perfectly: true, plumb

cutting and sizing of lumber before use: millwork

drive nails at an angle: toenail

frame supporter for worker: scaffold

grooves, cut: dado, rabbet

joint: miter, mortise

nail length, designation: penny

out of vertical alignment: out-of-plumb

sawing stand: sawhorse

tools: saw, plane, miter box, chisel, bevel, level, adze, sander

SEE HOUSE, TOOL

carpet *n.* rug, mat, Oriental, Persian, area rug, bearskin, moquette, runner, shag, Wilton.

carriage *n.* **1.** VEHICLE coach, rig, buggy, wagon, cabriolet, brougham, surrey, hansom, landau, phaeton, stagecoach, calash, buckboard. **2.** POSTURE bearing, demeanor, pose, posture, comportment, mien, cast, attitude.

carrier *n.* disease host, Typhoid Mary, vector.

carry *v.* **1.** CONVEY transport, lug, haul, tote, bear, bring, transfer, *schlep. **2.** SUPPORT hold up, shoulder, bear, sustain, buttress.

car sickness *n.* motion sickness.

cart *n.* wagon, truck, handcart, dray, wheelbarrow.

cart *v.* haul, carry, lug, transport, convey, truck.

CARTE BLANCHE *n.* [KART BLANSH] a granting of power, freedom or authority to do as one wishes. *His bosses gave him carte blanche to run the department as he saw fit.* SYN. free rein, license, freedom, authority, power, blank check, sanction, free hand, permission, discretion.

CARTEL *n.* [kar TEL] an association of businesses that works together to control production and pricing of products. Also, an association of nations working toward a common goal. *The oil cartel cut production and caused oil prices to rise worldwide.* SYN. association, trust, monopoly, syndicate, bloc, partnership, coalition, group, board, affiliation, consortium.

cartography *n.* map-making, chart-making, mapping, topography.

carton *n.* box, package, crate, container, case.

cartoon *n.* caricature, drawing, sketch, line drawing, animated feature, funny, comic strip, parody, joke. SEE CARICATURE

cartwheel *n.* handspring. SEE GYMNASTICS

carve *v.* cut, slice, hew, incise, chisel, sculpt, form, fashion, whittle, chip.

Casanova *n.* *womanizer, Don Juan, *ladykiller, *heartbreaker, *Romeo, *skirtchaser, *stud, Lothario, wolf, sex addict.

cascade *n.* waterfall, shower, cataract, falls, deluge, watercourse, torrent, *stairstep. SEE RIVER

cascade *v.* fall, tumble, plummet, plunge, spill, flood, rush, gush, descend, spew, *stairstep.

case *n.* **1.** EXAMPLE instance, sample, occurrence, affair, matter, event, illustration, situation, circumstance. **2.** SUBJECT client, patient, illness. **3.** LAWSUIT suit, action, claim, litigation. **4.** BOX holder, receptacle, container, package, carton, casing, covering, sheathing, jacket.

cash *n.* money, currency, coins, change, legal tender, *dough, *scratch, *bread, liquid assets. SEE MONEY, WEALTH

cashier *n.* teller, counter person, bursar, clerk.

casing *n.* covering, wrapper, sheath, jacket, skin, hull.

casino *n.* gambling hall, gaming house.

cask *n.* barrel, keg, hogshead, firkin, vat, kilderkin, vessel, tun, butt.

casket *n.* coffin, sarcophagus, box, pall. SEE CEMETERY

CASSANDRA *n.* [kuh SAN druh] one who foretells doom or spreads alarm but is disregarded, after the mythological character of the same name. *The economist warned of a stock market crash but was regarded as just another Cassandra.* SYN. alarmist, *Chicken Little, voice of doom, prophet of doom, scaremonger, seer, prognosticator, fortuneteller. "One who is always building dungeons in the air."—John Galsworthy.

casserole *n.* dish, terrine, concoction, mix, mélange, medley, potpourri, stew, ragout, mishmash.

cassette *n.* tape, recording medium, cartridge.

cast *n.* **1.** THROW pitch, toss, shot, fling, heave, sling, hurl. **2.** MOLD form, model, impression, shape. **3.** PERSONAE company, troupe, dramatis personae, actors, actresses, players, performers, repertory, characters. **4.** APPEARANCE complexion, aspect, look, shade, air, semblance.

cast *v.* **1.** THROW fling, hurl, pitch, heave,

*chuck, toss, sling, launch, let fly. **2.** SPREAD scatter, shed, broadcast, disperse, strew, sprinkle. **3.** EMIT radiate, project, send out. **4.** CHOOSE pick, assign, select, *typecast. **5.** MOLD form, shape, set.

castaway n. outcast, pariah, *reject, waif, stray, derelict, exile, vagabond, leper.

caste n. class, group, position, station, rank, status, place, clan, grade, social order.

CASTIGATE v. [KAS tuh GATE] to criticize harshly or punish. *The dictator liked to castigate his underlings in public.* SYN. punish, criticize, chastise, scold, rebuke, discipline, reproach, admonish, *take to task, reprimand, berate, bawl out, blister, *rake over the coals, lambaste, tongue-lash. ANT. *praise, compliment, laud.*

castle n. fortress, citadel, stronghold, keep, manor, chateau, mansion, alcazar.

WORD FIND
attack on: siege
bottlery: buttery
bridge spanning moat: drawbridge
candle storeroom: chandlery
castle used as a prison: bastille
circular turret with a conical roof: pepperbox turret
crossbow storage room: ballistraria
domestic official in charge of supplies: chamberlain, seneschal, steward
door, huge, grated: portcullis
doorman: usher
fort surrounded by fortified village: castellum
gateway, minor: postern
governor of: castellan
holes or slits through which archers shoot: archeria, arrow loops, loopholes, balistraria, murder holes
knight's practice yard: tiltyard
lady of: chatelaine
lights: rushlights
main inner tower, keep: donjon
mass of earth: bastion, rampart
mobile tower used by attackers to reach castle defenders: belfry
notched parapet: battlement
notches, solid area between: merlon
notch in parapet: crenel
outer wall ringing castle: curtain wall
owner: lord
privy: garderobe
roof wall: parapet
seating platform of lord: dais
siege engine used against: catapult, mangon, trebuchet

small tower above main structure: turret
sunny family room: solar
timber tower: brattice
tower/structure protecting a drawbridge: barbican, gatehouse
trench around: moat
turret that overhangs: bartizan
underground prison: dungeon
waste receptacle: cess pit
yard area within outer walls: ward, bailey, courtyard

CASTLE IN THE AIR/CASTLE IN SPAIN n. something unrealistic; a fantasy; a daydream. *Ned had big dreams and was frequently accused of building castles in Spain.* SYN. fantasy, dream, daydream, unrealistic goal, chimera, flight of fancy, lofty aspiration, *pipe dream, wish, wishful thinking.

castrate v. emasculate, geld, neuter, *fix, sterilize, effeminize, eunuchize, debilitate, weaken.

casual a. **1.** CHANCE accidental, random, serendipitous, fortuitous, *flukey, unexpected. **2.** RELAXED nonchalant, cool, blasé, unconcerned, carefree, apathetic, devil-may-care, *laid-back, indifferent. **3.** NONDRESSY informal, sporty, for-play. ANT. *1. planned, predetermined, arranged. 2. intense, serious, *meaning business. 3. formal, dressy.*

casualty n. victim, fatality, dead, loss.

cat n. feline, kitty, kitten, tomcat, pussy, grimalkin, carnivore, pet, quadruped, ratter, alley cat, tabby, mouser, Abyssinian, American Bobtail, American Curl, American Wirehair, Balinese, Bengal, Birman, Bombay, Chartreux, Cornish Rex, Devon Rex, Egyptian Mau, Exotic, Havana Brown, Himalayan, Korat, LaPerm, Maine Coon, Norwegian Forest Cat, Oceicat, Oriental, Ragdoll, Russian Blue, Scottish Fold, Selkirk Rex, Siamese, Siberian, Somali, Sphynx, Tonkinese, Turkish Angora, Turkish Van. "A pygmy lion."—Oliver Herford.

WORD FIND
black and white: piebald
blue gray to slate gray coloring: blue
bred from long line of its own kind: purebred
breeding female: queen
castrated male: gib
domesticated cat living in the wild: feral
father: sire
frill around head in longhaired breed: ruff
hairball: furball
intoxicant: catnip
"kneading" of paws on human's stomach: milk treading

long-bodied, long-limbed: rangy
lover of: ailurophile
mating cry: caterwaul
mixed breed: mongrel, moggie
mother: dam
neutering of female: spaying
newborn kitten group: litter
patches of white on feet: mittens, gloves
paw soles: pads
phobic: ailurophobe
pinkish gray coloring: lilac, lavender
sexually receptive period of female: heat
short-legged: cobby
sneer of male as it smells urine of sexually
  receptive female: flehmen response
striped: tabby, tiger
thin, long tail: whip
tortoiseshell and white coloring: calico
trace colorings: ghost markings
whiskers: vibrissae
white marking from forehead to nose: blaze
white or colored patch under neck: locket
white undercoat with dark tips: chinchilla
cataclysm n. upheaval, disaster, eruption, catastrophe, calamity, devastation, debacle.
catalog n. list, file, inventory, directory, index.
catalog v. list, classify, index, inventory, file.
CATALYST n. [KAT uh list] one that makes
something happen, gets something started
or hastens a process. *Martin Luther King was
a catalyst for change.* SYN. stimulus, motiva-
tor, *spark, *sparkplug, spur, *mover and
shaker, activist, agitator, *whip.
catapult n. launcher, siege engine, slingshot,
sling, trebuchet.
catastrophe n. disaster, misfortune, calamity,
cataclysm, ruin, debacle, devastation, tragedy, mishap, blow, hardship, misadventure.
CATBIRD SEAT (IN THE) n. a high, commanding position; a position of power. *The
author was enjoying his position in the catbird
seat as his third book hit the bestseller lists.* SYN.
high perch, lofty perch, position of power,
throne, commanding position, high place,
position of influence, seat of power, height.
catcall n. shout, whistle, hiss, boo, *Bronx
cheer, *raspberry, jeer, heckle, hoot.
catch n. 1. CAPTURE snatch, seizure, trap, grab,
snare, grasp. 2. CLASP latch, clip, fastener,
lock, hook and eye. 3. TAKE haul, prize,
plunder, booty, spoils. 4. DRAWBACK hitch,
trick, gimmick, snag.
catch v. 1. APPREHEND capture, seize, snatch,
grasp, grip, nab, net, snare, clutch, trap, bag.
2. DISCOVER surprise, *nail, expose, detect,

come upon. 3. COME DOWN WITH AN ILLNESS
contract, get, develop, break out with, be
infected by, fall ill with. 4. UNDERSTAND
comprehend, see, grasp, get, follow, perceive.
catching a. contagious, infectious, communicable, spreading, epidemic, pandemic. ANT.
noncommunicable.
CATCH-22 n. [KACH twen tee TOO] a no-
win situation. *The government's contradictory
regulations frequently put people in Catch-22
situations.* SYN. no-win situation, lose-lose
situation, paradox, contradiction, quagmire,
quandary, dilemma, Gordion knot, horns of
a dilemma.
catchword n. byword, watchword, buzz word,
motto, slogan, shiboleth.
categorical a. absolute, direct, unequivocal,
positive, unqualified, explicit, express, total,
unconditional, without exceptions. ANT.
conditional, qualified.
categorize v. classify, designate, sort, group, label, assign, name, catalog.
category n. class, classification, division, variety, type, kind, sort, order, grade, denomination, genre.
cater v. 1. PROVIDE furnish, serve, provision,
feed. 2. INDULGE humor, gratify, serve, wait
on, pamper, spoil, baby, pander.
caterwaul v. howl, yowl, mewl, screech, wail,
meow, squall, cry, whine.
CATHARSIS n. [kuh THAR sis] a purification or cleansing of the soul; release from
mental turmoil. *Venting tensions in a self-help
group provided Ellen with the catharsis she
longed for.* SYN. purification, cleansing, release, relief, renewal, expurgation, replenishment of spirit, rebirth, fresh start, wiping
clean.
cathedral n. basilica, chapel. SEE CHURCH
CATHOLIC a. [KATH uh lik] universal, general. *His tastes were catholic; in other words,
his tastes were broad.* SYN. universal, general,
broad, all-inclusive, comprehensive, liberal,
all-encompassing, ecumenical, global. ANT.
limited, narrow, sectarian.
CAT scan n. computerized axial tomogrpahy
scan, image, cross-sectional view, body scan,
brain scan, diagnostic procedure.
cattle n. livestock, cows, bulls, steers, farm animals, ruminants, herbivores, herd.
catty a. malicious, spiteful, mean, vicious,
nasty, malevolent, back-biting, back-stabbing, *bitchy, malignant, venomous. ANT.
kind, warm, friendly.

catwalk *n.* walkway, platform, bridge.

Caucasian *n.* Caucasoid, Indo-European, white race, white man, white woman

caucus *n.* meeting, assembly, convention, conference, gathering, session, conclave.

cauldron *n.* caldron, vessel, pot, boiler. SEE KETTLE

caulk *v.* seal, stop up, putty, weatherstrip.

cause *n.* **1.** DETERMINANT agent, reason, root, antecedent, motive, source, origin, mover, occasion, stimulus, mainspring. **2.** IDEAL principle, end, objective, enterprise, goal, purpose.

cause *v.* effect, induce, bring about, produce, incite, provoke, generate, breed, motivate, give rise to, precipitate.

CAUSE CÉLÈBRE *n.* [KOHZ say LEB ruh] a controversial or widely discussed issue. *The O.J. Simpson murder trial was the cause célèbre of the twentieth century.* SYN. controversy, controversial issue, celebrated case, affair, bone of contention, debate, moot point, war of words, uproar, fuss, *hot potato, scandal, political football, outrage, shocker, grist for the gossip mill.

CAUSTIC *a.* [KAW stik] biting, burning or corrosive, as acid. *Wear gloves when handling caustic substances. She was a caustic-tongued witch.* SYN. corrosive, burning, biting, acid, astringent, erosive, sharp, stinging, sarcastic, sardonic, bitter, scathing, cutting, vitriolic, excoriating, acid-tongued, saber-tongued. ANT. *soothing, sweet, honey-tongued, smooth.*

cauterize *v.* burn, sear, char, singe.

caution *n.* **1.** WARINESS care, prudence, heed, vigilance, discretion, guardedness, circumspection, alertness. "The eldest child of wisdom."—Victor Hugo. "What we call cowardice in others."—Oscar Wilde. **2.** WARNING admonition, caveat, advisement, *red flag, *word to the wise, advisory. ANT. *1. rashness, recklessness.*

caution *v.* warn, admonish, advise, alert, forewarn, *raise a red flag, counsel, *better safe than sorry, *stay on one's toes, *watch one's step, *look before one leaps, *sleep with one eye open.

CAUTIONARY TALE *n.* [KAW shun air ee tayl] an event, occurence or story that is used to illustrate a particular hazard; a warning. *The shipping industry offers many cautionary tales about single-hulled oil tankers and shallow waters.* SYN. warning, admonition, caution, caution light, red flag, advisory, *word to the wise, caveat, sign of things to come, *wake-up call, forewarning, portent, omen, illustration, message.

cautious *a.* wary, careful, heedful, circumspect, prudent, discreet, guarded, on guard, alert, on one's toes, vigilant, chary. ANT. *rash, reckless, imprudent.*

cavalcade *n.* procession, parade, column, train, line, caravan.

CAVALIER *a.* [kav uh LEER] arrogant; indifferent to important matters. *The coach took a cavalier attitude toward the rules of good sportsmanship.* SYN. arrogant, haughty, indifferent, casual, supercilious, devil-may-care, lofty, curt, cocky, disdainful. ANT. *obliging, caring, conscientious.*

cavalry *n.* combat troops, armored division, mounted troops.

cave *n.* cavern, grotto, tunnel, hole, *yawning chasm, hollow, cavity, underground chamber, subterranean passage, catacomb.

WORD FIND

carved out from this rock: limestone

crawl space: crawl, crouchway

dripping water and mineral formation: dripstone

entrance area exposed to daylight: twilight zone

explorer: spelunker

exploring: spelunking

geological area with many caves, sinkholes: karst

high, narrow passage: canyon

iciclelike formation hanging from roof: stalactite

iciclelike formation on floor: stalagmite

inhabitant: troglodyte, troglobite, troglophile

joined stalactite and stalagmite: column

large chamber: gallery

pool of water edged with calcite: gour

study of: speleology

tiny, thin stalactite: soda straw

underwater passage: sump, syphon

vertical shaft: chimney, pitch

CAVEAT *n.* [KAV ee at] warning. *The accountant gave us a strong caveat about filing our taxes accurately.* SYN. warning, caution, notice, forewarning, admonition, advisory, advisement, *word to the wise.

cave-in *n.* collapse, toppling, breakdown, rupture, burst, avalanche, landslide.

caveman *n.* cavewoman, primitive human, Stone Age man, prehistoric man, cave dweller, human, hominid, Cro-Magnon man, Neanderthal, troglodyte, anthropoid, hominoid, Homo Erectus, *missing link.

WORD FIND

earliest to latest pre-human: Ardipithecus ramidus, Australopithecus anamensis, Australopithecus afarensis, Australopithecus africanus, Australopithecus robustus, Australopithecus boisei, Homo rudolfensis, Homo habilis, Homo ergaster, Homo erectus, Homo heidelbergensis, Archaic Homo sapiens, Homo neanderthalensis, Cro-Magnon, Homo sapiens.

famous afarensis skeleton, nickname: Lucy

SEE HUMAN

cavernous *a.* hollow, yawning, deep-set, sunken, abysmal, enormous, huge, gaping, roomy, commodious, chambered. ANT. *cramped, claustrophobic, tiny, confined.*

cavil *v.* quibble, object, find-fault, *nitpick, carp, criticize, pick.

cavity *n.* hole, hollow, pit, cleft, chamber, crevice, fissue, pocket, niche.

cavort *v.* frolic, prance, romp, *carry on, *cut up, act up, leap about, horseplay, gambol, frisk, caper.

cay *n.* island, sandbank, coral reef.

cease *v.* end, stop, discontinue, desist, halt, refrain, finish, conclude, quit.

cease-fire *n.* truce, armistice, suspension of hostilities.

ceaseless *a.* unending, relentless, incessant, neverending, perpetual, constant, nonstop, continuous, unremitting. ANT. *ending, fleeting, finite, limited.*

cede *v.* surrender, give up, yield, abdicate, *hand over, grant, relinquish, transfer, resign.

ceiling *n.* **1.** TOPSIDE roof, plafond, rafters. **2.** MAXIMUM limit, restriction, highest point.

celebrate *v.* **1.** COMMEMORATE observe, honor, memorialize, remember, ceremonialize, solemnize. **2.** *PARTY *paint the town red, *whoop it up, *raise the roof, *go out on the town, *go out with a bang, *have a blowout, splurge, revel, carouse, *live it up. **3.** PRAISE honor, extol, laud, pay homage to, acclaim, worship, hail, pay tribute to, exalt.

celebrated *a.* famous, renowned, eminent, prominent, noted, illustrious, acclaimed, popular, lionized, great. ANT. *obscure, little-known, unknown.*

celebration *n.* **1.** COMMEMORATION observance, ceremony, honoring, memorial, remembrance, anniversary. **2.** PARTY *blowout, fiesta, gala, jubilee, *bash, *wingding, festival, spree, frolic, *blast, *rumpus, revelry.

celebrity *n.* **1.** FAMOUS PERSON star, superstar, *somebody, *bigwig, notable, idol, *celeb, *big name, personage, personality, VIP, sex symbol. "Someone who is known for being known."—Studs Terkel. "A person who works hard all his life to become well known, then wears dark glasses to avoid being recognized."—Fred Allen. **2.** FAME renown, notoriety, stardom, eminence, prominence, distinction, note. ANT. *1. nobody, *bush leaguer, unknown. 2. oblivion, obscurity.*

celerity *n.* speed, quickness, alacrity, haste, dispatch, expedition, swiftness. ANT. *slowness, *snail's pace, leisureliness.*

celestial *a.* **1.** HEAVENLY divine, sublime, supernal, angelic, ethereal, blessed, eternal, supernatural. **2.** ASTRAL astronomical, universal, heavenly, extraterrestrial, stellar, sky, planetary, galactic. ANT. *1. earthy, mundane, secular. 2. terrestrial.*

CELIBATE *a.* [SELL uh but] abstaining from sex. *With sexually transmitted diseases running rampant, many singles choose to remain celibate.* SYN. abstinent, continent, upright, virtuous, pure, untouched, virginal, maiden, single, unwed, chaste. ANT. *promiscuous, wanton, sexual.*

cell *n.* **1.** UNIT germ, microorganism, bacterium. **2.** SMALL ROOM compartment, chamber, vault, keep, cloister, coop, booth, lockup.

cellar *n.* basement, downstairs, vault.

cement *v.* join, unite, bond, glue, mortar, bind, seal, fix.

cemetery *n.* graveyard, necropolis, memorial grounds, burial ground, churchyard, golgotha, *bone yard, *city of the dead. "The last resort."—Anon. "The country home I need."—Mark Twain.

WORD FIND

ashes of cremated body: cremains
burial place, vault: tomb
burial site, unit: plot
empty tomb, marker for one whose remains are elsewhere: cenotaph
grave robber: ghoul
gunfighter's, American West: Boot Hill
incinerator: crematory
inscription on gravestone: epitaph
large cemetery: necropolis
memorial building, place: shrine
mound of earth over grave: barrow
mourning statues: weepers
pauper's: Potter's field
preparation facility for the dead: mortuary

RIP: rest in peace

sarcophagus, elaborately carved: solium

sculpted representation of the dead on a monument: effigy

sculptural depiction of the crucifixion: Calvary

stone: headstone, tombstone, gravestone, monument, memorial

tomb housing: mausoleum

underground vaults: catacombs, crypt, cubiculum

urn or vault for bones: ossuary

urn vault: cinerarium

vault: sepulcher

SEE COFFIN, FUNERAL, MONUMENT

censor n. bowdlerizer, arbiter of good taste, expurgator, inspector, Mrs. Grundy, guardian of morals, prude. "A man who knows more than he thinks you ought to."—Laurence J. Peter.

censor v. prohibit, squelch, cut, edit out, abridge, clean up, delete, sanitize, bowdlerize, restrict, inspect, expurgate, review, purge.

censorship n. expurgation, *cleaning up, purification, suppression, removal, editing, purging, sanitizing, deletion.

censure n. disapproval, condemnation, reprehension, rebuke, admonition, criticism, objection, remonstrance, reproof. ANT. approval, blessing, praise.

censure v. disapprove, condemn, rebuke, admonish, criticize, object, remonstrate, denounce, reproach, reprimand. ANT. approve, bless, praise.

census n. head count, population tally, enumeration, demographics, statistics, stats, demography, poll.

center n. middle point, middle, median, focal point, dead center, bull's-eye, midst, hub, pivot, core, heart, nucleus, inside, pith.

center v. concentrate, focus, converge, direct, join, unify, fix.

central a. 1. INNERMOST middle, interior, median, inner, nuclear. 2. VITAL key, indispensable, main, prime, dominant, chief, ruling, fundamental. ANT. 1. outermost, peripheral. 2. peripheral, incidental, marginal.

centralize v. concentrate, converge, focus, consolidate, unify, amalgamate, join. ANT. decentralize, disperse.

centrist n. moderate, middle-of-the-road, in-between, compromising.

cereal n. breakfast food, grain, wheat, oats,

corn, rye, rice, bran, Corn Flakes, Rice Krispies, bran flakes, Cocoa Puffs, oatmeal, farina, Fruit Loops, Apple Jacks, Cocoa Krispies, Cheerios, Life, Grapenuts, Alpha Bits, Fruity Pebbles, Cocoa Pebbles, Boo-Berry, Corn Pops, Raisin Bran, Oat Bran, Total, Special K, Chex, Cream of Wheat, Frosted Flakes, mush, porridge, Wheaties, Trix, Shredded Wheat.

CEREBRAL a. [suh REE brul] of or appealing to the intellect. *His philosophy reveals some advanced thinking; it's very cerebral.* SYN. intellectual, intelligent, brainy, erudite, scholarly, smart, analytical, thoughtful, deep, recondite, abstruse.

ceremonial a. ritual, formal, ceremonious. ANT. informal, unstructured. SEE CEREMONIOUS

ceremonious a. ceremonial, polite, proper, formal, solemn, stately, punctilious, rigid, prim, courtly, starchy, dignified, decorous. ANT. informal, casual, *laid-back.

ceremony n. 1. RITUAL observation, rite, service, function, formality, solemnity, custom, observance. "The wine of human experience."—Morris Cohen. 2. ETIQUETTE protocol, punctilio, formality, decorum, propriety, prescription. ANT. 2. informality.

certain a. 1. SURE positive, cocksure, convinced, undoubting, assured, satisfied. 2. UNQUESTIONABLE doubtless, *beyond a shadow of a doubt, indubitable, definite, indisputable, incontestable, unequivocal, incontrovertible, firm, unambiguous. ANT. 1. uncertain, unsure, doubting. 2. questionable, doubtful, *up in the air.

certainty n. 1. CONVICTION authority, certitude, confidence, assurance, infallibility. 2. FACT truth, reality, *sure thing, *sure bet, actuality, *lock. ANT. 1. doubt, skepticism. 2. uncertainty, fantasy, unknown.

certificate n. document, documentation, instrument, voucher, warrant, license, permit, certification, testimonial, credential, diploma.

certify v. vouch, verify, notarize, attest, assure, guarantee, validate, accredit, authenticate, confirm, depose.

cesarean section n. C-section, surgical birth, surgical delivery, incision.

cessation n. stop, termination, ending, stoppage, letup, ceasing, halt, pause, suspension, discontinuance, close. ANT. continuation, persistence.

cesspool n. sewer, cesspit, sump, cloaca, septic tank.

C'EST LA VIÉ [say lah VEE] that's life, such is life. *Our team lost again; oh well, c'est la vié* SYN. that's life, such is life, oh well, that's how the cookie crumbles, what can you do?, that's reality.

chafe *v.* 1. RUB wear, erode, scrape, abrade, rasp, scour, shred. 2. IRRITATE *rub the wrong way, annoy, irk, rankle, vex, gall, harass, nag, aggravate.

chaff *n.* waste, garbage, refuse, rubbish, trash, discards, remains, wastrel, dross.

CHAGRIN *n.* [shuh GRIN] annoyed embarrassment. *To my chagrin, I discovered that I had left my wallet at home.* SYN. embarrassment, mortification, humiliation, shame, distress, disgruntlement, dismay, annoyance, unease, discomfiture, discomposure, frustration. ANT. *pride, satisfaction.*

chain *n.* 1. LINKS cable, fetter, shackle, irons, manacle, mail. 2. SERIES course, string, train, line, succession, sequence.

chain *v.* tie, shackle, fetter, secure, tether, hitch.

chain reaction *n.* domino effect, ripples in a pond, cause and effect.

chair *n.* 1. SEAT stool, bench, rocker, easy chair, straight-backed chair.

WORD FIND

armless, leather-made, with steel frame: Barcelona chair

bench: settee, settle

folding canvas chair: director's chair

high-backed with side wings: wing chair

king's: throne

reclining: recliner

sling, canvas: butterfly chair, sling chair

spindle-backed, wooden: Windsor chair

suspended on poles and carried: sedan

tabletopped arm for writing, chair with: tablet chair

wicker, with rounded back: basket chair

SEE COUCH

2. SEAT OF AUTHORITY office, appointment, fellowship.

chairman *n.* chairperson, director, principal, leader, chair, speaker, presiding officer, president, moderator, chief, master of ceremonies.

chalice *n.* goblet, vessel. SEE CUP

chalkboard *n.* blackboard, board, slate, panel.

challenge *n.* 1. DIFFICULTY obstacle, trial, test, *hurdle, problem. 2. PROVOCATION dare, ultimatum, *throwing down the gauntlet, threat, summons, bid.

challenge *v.* 1. PRODUCE DIFFICULTY test, try,

make demands, tax. 2. PROVOKE dare, give an ultimatum, *throw down the gauntlet, threaten, gage, defy, summon, beard, make a stand, face off, cross, stare down. 3. QUESTION contest, dispute, object, take exception, disagree.

chamber *n.* room, bedroom, boudoir, parlor, sitting room.

chambermaid *n.* domestic, cleaning lady, maid.

champagne *n.* *bubbly. SEE WINE

champion *n.* 1. VICTOR winner, titleholder, *champ, *top dog, conqueror, vanquisher, *number one, medalist. 2. SUPPORTER backer, advocate, upholder, friend, abettor, defender. ANT. 1. *loser, *also-ran, *poor sport. 2. opponent, detractor.*

champion *v.* support, defend, fight for, stand up for, advocate, back, uphold, espouse, take up the cause. ANT. *oppose, counter, reject.*

championship *n.* competition, playoffs, contest, showdown, meet, title match, crown, *winner takes all, tournament, sporting event, elimination, crowning achievement.

WORD FIND

auto: Indianapolis 500

baseball: World Series; pennant

basketball: championship; Final Four

boxing: title fight

football: Super Bowl

golf: Masters

hockey: Stanley Cup

horse racing: Triple Crown; Kentucky Derby, Belmont Stakes, Preakness, Breeder's Cup

soccer: World Cup

tennis: Wimbledon

chance *n.* 1. LUCK fortuity, fortune, serendipity, fate, destiny, *wheel of fortune, providence, *toss of the dice. "A nickname for Providence."—Nicolas Chamfort. "The instrument of Providence."—Horace Walpole. 2. POSSIBILITY odds, likelihood, probability, prospect, *long shot. 3. RISK gamble, *toss of the dice, *crap shoot, jeopardy, hazard. 4. OPPORTUNITY shot, try, opening, occasion, turn.

chance *v.* 1. RISK gamble, *roll the dice, take a shot, wager, *go out on a limb, *tempt fate, hazard, speculate, try one's luck. 2. HAPPEN occur, transpire, come to pass, befall.

chance *a.* fortuitous, accidental, casual, random, lucky, inadvertent, unplanned. ANT. *planned, designed, arranged.*

chancy *a.* risky, uncertain, *iffy, dicey, speculative, *a roll of the dice, dangerous. ANT. *certain, guaranteed, assured.*

change *n.* 1. ALTERATION modification, transformation, variation, conversion, metamorphosis, shift, remodeling, reformation, adaption, mutation, *about-face, *chameleon, transmutation, refinement, flux, vicissitude. "What people fear most."—Fyodor Dostoyevski. "The unknown."—Eleanor Roosevelt. "Truths being in and out of favor."—Robert Frost. 2. SOMETHING DIFFERENT novelty, variation, switch, change of pace.

change *v.* 1. ALTER modify, transform, vary, convert, metamorphose, shift, remodel, reinvent, reform, adapt, mutate, transmogrify, *do an about-face. 2. SUBSTITUTE transfer, exchange, switch, alternate, swap, trade, replace, interchange.

changeable *a.* variable, alternating, erratic, irregular, chameleon, protean, capricious, fickle, labile, mercurial, inconsistent, mutable, transformable, shifting, volatile, *blows hot and cold. ANT. *steady, invariable, regular, stable.*

channel *n.* conduit, course, strait, waterway, groove, runnel, culvert, trough, run, canal, chase, furrow, rut, trench, sluiceway, flume.

channel *v.* route, direct, guide, send, funnel, lead, siphon.

chant *n.* song, plainsong, recitation, psalm, canticle, hymn, Gregorian chant. SEE SONG

chant *v.* singsong, intone, vocalize, speak in a monotone, utter, recite.

chaos *n.* disorder, confusion, upheaval, turmoil, disarray, anarchy, jumble, unrest, mess, commotion, pandemonium, disorganization, bedlam, turbulence. ANT. *order, organization, regularity, tranquility.*

chaotic *a.* disordered, confused, in disarray, jumbled, messy, turbulent, out of control, topsy-turvy, tumultuous, anarchic, disorganized, random, stormy. ANT. *ordered, organized, systematic.*

chaperone *n.* escort, overseer, guardian, protector, babysitter.

chaperone *v.* escort, accompany, attend, protect, babysit, supervise, safeguard, keep an eye on.

chaplain *n.* clergyman, minister, priest, rabbi, reverend, parson, padre.

chapter *n.* division, section, episode, part, portion, phase, period.

char *v.* scorch, sear. SEE BURN

character *n.* 1. PERSONALITY nature, makeup, individuality, temperament, constitution, appearance, type, sort, kind, qualities. "[W]hat (a man) would do if he knew he would never be found out."—Thomas Macaulay. 2. INTEGRITY reputation, standing, position, repute, distinction, honor, status. "Moral order seen through the medium of an individual nature."—Ralph Waldo Emerson. "Mastery over your thoughts and actions."—Mohandas Gandhi. "What God and the angels know of us."—Horace Mann. 3. ODD PERSON eccentric, oddball, nut, *odd duck, personality, *weirdo, *fruitcake, *original. 4. ROLE impersonation, portrayal, part. 5. WRITTEN SYMBOL cipher, mark, figure, letter.

characteristic *n.* attribute, trait, feature, quality, peculiarity, aspect, mark, distinction, individuality, earmark, idiosyncrasy.

characteristic *a.* typical, representative, indicative, distinguishing, illustrative, idiosyncratic, marked, peculiar, individual. ANT. *atypical, anomalous.*

characterize *v.* 1. PORTRAY describe, represent, depict, sketch. 2. DISTINGUISH specify, define, style, brand, stamp.

charade *n.* pretense, fiction, lie, travesty, act.

charge *n.* 1. FEE debit, *damage, bill, cost, amount, price. 2. CARE custody, burden, duty, trust, onus, obligation, ward. 3. ACCUSATION allegation, indictment, citation. 4. ATTACK offensive, *blitz, assault, raid. 5. ORDER command, directive, demand, instruction, mandate, behest, bidding.

charge *v.* 1. BILL levy, debit, *ring up, demand payment. 2. DEBIT ONE'S CREDIT ACCOUNT take on account, put on one's tab, incur a debt, buy on credit. 3. BURDEN load, weigh, tax, saddle, entrust. 4. ACCUSE allege, indict, impute, blame, incriminate, *point the finger at, impeach. 5. ATTACK raid, blitz, assault, storm, rush, assail. 6. ORDER command, direct, demand, instruct, mandate, bid.

CHARISMA *n.* [kuh RIZ muh] personal magnetism or charm that inspires others to follow one's lead. *John F. Kennedy had great charisma.* SYN. charm, magnetism, appeal, confidence, *star power, presence, dominance, *it, *pizzazz, sex appeal, power, voice of authority, poise, *je na sais quoi, an indescribable something, allure, *the lure of a Svengali.

charismatic *a.* charming, powerful, magnetic, hypnotic, mesmerizing, dominant, appealing, *larger than life, authoritative, confident, poised.

charitable *a.* 1. GENEROUS giving, benevolent, philanthropic, freehanded, humanitarian, magnanimous, bighearted. **2.** KIND forgiving, lenient, humane, benevolent, sympathetic, bighearted, soft, merciful, easy. ANT. *1. cheap, stingy, tightfisted, selfish. 2. mean, cruel, thoughtless, intolerant.*

charity n. **1.** GENEROSITY benevolence, philanthropy, freehandedness, humanitarianism, magnanimity, altruism, softheartedness. **2.** ALMS contribution, welfare, donation, assistance, aid, benefaction, dole, endowment. "The spice of riches."—Hebrew proverb. "A debt of honor."—Immanuel Kant. "Doing good for good-for-nothing people."—Elizabeth Barrett Browning. **3.** KINDNESS forgiveness, tolerance, lenience, benevolence, sympathy, mercy, softheartedness, compassion. ANT. *1. cheapness, stinginess, miserliness. 3. meanness, cruelty, intolerance.*

charlatan n. quack, fake, mountebank, *rip-off artist, imposter, con artist, fraud, swindler.

charm n. **1.** APPEAL attractiveness, allure, grace, magnetism, charisma, enchantment, fascination, *it, *je ne sais quoi, *pizzazz. "A glow within . . . that casts a most becoming light on others."—John Mason Brown. "A way of getting the answer 'yes' without asking any clear question."—Albert Camus **2.** SPELL OR LUCKY PIECE incantation, magic, sorcery, amulet, talisman, good-luck piece, fetish.

charm v. enchant, enamor, fascinate, attract, allure, please, bewitch, captivate, mesmerize, hypnotize, win over, beguile, *sweep off one's feet, spellbind. ANT. *repel, repulse, turn off, disgust.*

charming a. attractive, appealing, alluring, magnetic, charismatic, enchanting, beguiling, bewitching, fascinating, winsome, captivating, smooth, irresistible. ANT. *repellant, repulsive, disgusting, gross.*

charred a. scorched, seared, burned, blackened, singed, carbonized.

chart n. map, graph, diagram, outline, blueprint, layout, plot, table, scheme.

chart v. map, outline, plot, diagram, draft, plan, draw up, design, graph, scheme.

charter n. agreement, contract, franchise, treaty, covenant, sanction, authority, license, permit.

charter v. hire, lease, rent, reserve, commission, employ.

chary a. **1.** CAREFUL cautious, wary, guarded, mindful, circumspect, suspicious, leery. **2.** SPARING cheap, tight, miserly, niggardly, frugal, stingy. ANT. *1. imprudent, rash, reckless. 2. generous, freehanded.*

chase v. **1.** PURSUE follow, track, trail, go after, shadow, *bird-dog. **2.** CHASE OFF oust, drive away, shoo, evict, throw out.

chasm n. abyss, gorge, canyon, void, crevasse, gap, gulch, fissure, ravine, rift, bottomless pit, crater. SEE CANYON, CAVE, HOLE

CHASTE a. [CHAYST] virtuous, pure or moral. *She was a somewhat puritanical woman and chose to remain chaste.* SYN. virtuous, pure, moral, untouched, clean, *squeaky-clean, decent, abstinent, celibate, modest, righteous, immaculate, uncorrupted, virginal. ANT. *immoral, dirty, lewd, wanton, sleazy, promiscuous.*

chasten v. **1.** PUNISH chastise, castigate, correct, admonish, discipline, scold, penalize. **2.** REFINE purify, cleanse, purge.

CHASTISE v. [chas TIZE] to punish or discipline. *He was chastised for being foulmouthed.* SYN. punish, discipline, scold, condemn, castigate, admonish, beat, chasten *rake over the coals, *jump down one's throat, *lay into, thrash, ream, spank, whip, *call on the carpet. ANT. *reward, bless.*

chastity n. virtue, morality, purity, decency, abstinence, celibacy, righteousness, modesty, virginity, innocence. "A monkish and evangelical superstition."—Percy Bysshe Shelley. ANT. *promiscuity, nymphomania, adultery, lewdness.* SEE VIRGINITY

chat v. talk, converse, gab, jaw, *chew the fat, gossip, *shoot the breeze, *rap, palaver, chitchat, prattle, *schmooze.

chateau n. manor, palace, stronghold. SEE CASTLE

chattels n. belongings, personal possessions, *things, *stuff, personal effects.

chatter v. prattle, *gibber-jabber, jabber, babble, blab, chitchat, cackle, palaver, prate. SEE TALK

chatterbox n. talker, *windbag, gossip, blabbermouth, *motor mouth.

CHAUVINISM a. [SHO vin izm] blind loyalty to one's own kind, race, sex, etc., with disdain for those who are different. *The sexes earn unequal pay partly due to male chauvinism.* SYN. jingoism, supremacy, male dominance, female dominance, blind patriotism, provincialism, racism, sexism, narrow-mindedness, ethnocentrism, prejudice, bias, bigotry, intolerance, homophobia, nationalism. ANT. *liberality, broad-mindedness.*

chauvinist n. jingoist, supremacist, blind patriot, provincialist, racist, sexist, nationalist, bigot, *male chauvinist pig, ethnocentrist.

cheap *a.* **1.** LOW-PRICED inexpensive, bargain-priced, reasonable, marked-down, cut-rate, economical, *rock-bottom, *dirt-cheap, dime-a-dozen. **2.** POOR QUALITY worthless, inferior, shoddy, *chintzy, *cheesy, tacky, *two-bit, *crappy, *schlock, shabby, common. **3.** STINGY tight, penny-pinching, miserly, niggardly, stinting, grudging. **4.** CONTEMPTIBLE despicable, low, sordid, vulgar, base. ANT. *1. expensive, priceless, steep, exorbitant 2. superior, select, sterling quality. 3. generous, giving. 4. admirable, noble.*

cheapen *v.* depreciate, degrade, lower, downgrade, diminish.

cheapskate *n. Sl.* penny-pincher, tightwad, miser, niggard, *nickel-squeezer.

cheat *n.* **1.** SWINDLE *rip-off, con, fleecing, sham, deception, *fast shuffle, fraud, flimflam, *dirty pool, trick. **2.** SWINDLER *rip-off artist, con, sham artist, chiseler, sharper, flimflam man, crook, rogue, imposter, fraud.

cheat *v.* defraud, swindle, *rip off, con, burn, bilk, sucker, *rook, screw, fleece, *bamboozle, gouge, *soak, snooker, finagle, double-cross.

check *n.* **1.** RESTRAINT stop, block, obstacle, limitation, control, damper, curb. **2.** EXAMINATION inspection, review, inquiry, investigation, *look-see.

check *v.* **1.** RESTRAIN stop, block, obstruct, limit, control, dampen, curb, constrain, foil, harness. **2.** EXAMINE inspect, review, inquire, investigate, look into, *eyeball, scrutinize. **3.** AGREE correspond, conform.

checkered *a.* **1.** PLAID tattersall, tartan. **2.** VARIED diversified, irregular, patchwork, motley. ANT. *2. consistent.*

check out *v.* investigate, look into, probe, scrutinize, inspect, *eyeball.

cheek *n.* jowl, chop, jaw.

WORD FIND

descriptive: high cheek bones, rawboned, apple cheeks, sunken, pouchy.

cheek by jowl *a.* close, crowded, intimate, side-by-side, familiar.

cheeky *a.* impudent, insolent, saucy, impertinent, brazen, bold, brash, audacious, *nervy, *ballsy, forward. ANT. *timid, shy, mousy.*

cheer *n.* **1.** HURRAH acclamation, shout of approval, *yay, rah, applause, bravo. **2.** CHEERFULNESS high spirits, gladness, gayness, happiness, joyfulness, optimism, joviality, jubilance, buoyancy. "A kind of daylight in the mind."—Joseph Addison. ANT. *1. boo,*

raspberry, hiss. *2. depression, downheartedness.*

cheerful *a.* lighthearted, happy, joyful, blithe, buoyant, sunny, optimistic, sanguine, jocund, roseate, gay, carefree, debonair. ANT. *depressed, gloomy, downhearted, glum.*

cheerless *a.* gloomy, glum, depressed, dark, black, grim, melancholy, funereal, bleak, dismal, dreary, somber, forlorn, despairing. ANT. *cheerful, sunny, lighthearted.*

cheese *n.* pressed curds, American, Swiss, Brie, Edam, Gouda, Limburger, Jack, Parmesan, Gruyere, cream, mysost, cottage, cheddar. "Milk's leap toward immortality."—Clifton Fadiman.

chef *n.* cook, culinary artist, *chief cook and bottle washer, cuisinier.

chemise *n.* shift. SEE DRESS, LINGERIE

cherish *v.* love, adore, hold dear, care for, revere, fancy, hold in high esteem, admire, like, worship, prize, idolize, foster, protect, treasure. ANT. *despise, reject, hate.*

chest *n.* **1.** THORAX breast, bosom, pectorals. **2.** BOX trunk, crate, casket, cabinet.

chew *v.* masticate, chomp, champ, grind, crunch, munch, nibble, gnaw.

chew out *v. Sl.* reprimand, berate. SEE SCOLD

chic *a.* stylish, elegant, fashionable, smart, *snazzy, current, swank, dapper, chichi, *in, sophisticated. ANT. *dowdy, unstylish.*

CHICANERY *n.* [shi KAY nuh ree] deception, trickery. *A con artist uses all manner of chicanery to separate you from your money.* SYN. deception, trickery, deceit, fraud, subterfuge, double-dealing, underhandedness, dishonesty, cheating, duping, sophistry.

chichi *a.* ostentatious. SEE CHIC

chicken *n.* **1.** FOWL hen, biddy, rooster. **2.** *SCAREDY CAT *wimp, *wuss, sissy.

chide *v.* reprove, scold, *dress down, upbraid, rebuke, reproach, admonish, tell off, give a good talking to, criticize, take to task.

chief *n.* head, boss, leader, *top dog, *big cheese, president, director, supervisor, master, ringleader, captain, commander, *biggest toad in the puddle, honcho, *cock of the walk. ANT. *subordinate, underling.*

chief *a.* main, principal, leading, prime, greatest, biggest, supreme, paramount, ruling, cardinal. ANT. *least, smallest.*

chiefly *adv.* mainly, principally, primarily, first and foremost, above all, largely, mostly. ANT. *lastly.*

child *n.* **1.** YOUNGSTER juvenile, kid, youth, toddler, tyke, nipper, *little shaver, lad, lass, tadpole, adolescent, *teenybopper, moppet, brat, *rug rat, *munchkin. "An ever-bubbling fountain in the world of humanity."— Friedrich Froebel. **2.** INNOCENT naif, babe in the woods.

childbirth SEE BABY, BIRTH, PREGNANCY

childhood *n.* youth, boyhood, girlhood, school days, puberty, adolescence. "A garden of god . . . each day a festival radiant with laughter and play."—Micah Lebensohn. "That wonderful time when all you need to lose weight is to bathe."—Anon.

childish *a.* immature, sophomoric, babyish, adolescent, infantile, juvenile, naive, callow, unsophisticated. ANT. *mature, adult, grown-up.*

chill *n.* cold, frigidity, iciness, rawness, briskness, frostiness, nip, shivers.

chilly *a.* **1.** COLD freezing, frigid, raw, biting, icy, brisk, frosty, shivery, anesthetizing, wintry, nippy, arctic. **2.** UNFRIENDLY cold, icy, aloof, cool, hostile, frigid, unsociable. ANT. *1. hot, *roasting, muggy. 2. friendly, warm, congenial.*

chime *v.* ring, peal, toll, knell, sound, tinkle, jingle, tintinnabulate. SEE BELL

CHIMERA *n.* [kye MEER uh] something impossible or fanciful, after the monster of Greek mythology. *Hank's desire to be president was just a chimera.* SYN. fancy, dream, impossibility, daydream, whim, *castle in the air, *pie in the sky, *fool's paradise, *pipe dream, fantasy, illusion, delusion.

chimney *n.* smokestack, flue.

china *n.* dishes, tableware, porcelain, crockery.

chink *n.* opening, slit, fissure, crack, crevice, cleft, hole, gap, rift.

chintzy *a.* **1.** SHABBY tacky, cheap, sleazy, frowzy, *schlock. **2.** STINGY cheap, miserly, tight, stinting. ANT. *1. elegant, classy, stylish. 2. generous.*

chip *n.* fragment, piece, bit, shard, scrap, sliver, shred, flake, dent, mark, nick, scratch, break, crack, flaw, fault.

chip *v.* fragment, nick, crack, crumble, break off, sliver, fracture, splinter, scratch, flake.

chipper *a.* cheerful, buoyant, high-spirited, cheery, sunny, bright, vivacious, zippy, lively, sprightly, gay, jaunty. ANT. *grim, glum, slothful, melancholy.*

chirp *v.* tweet, chip, peep, trill, warble, twitter. SEE BIRD

chisel *v.* cut, gouge, carve, engrave, sculpt, tool, incise.

chivalrous *a.* honorable, courageous, noble, gallant, valiant, brave, courteous, courtly, heroic, lionhearted, quixotic, gentlemanly. ANT. *dishonorable, cowardly, brutish, barbaric.*

chivalry *n.* honor, courage, nobility, gallantry, valor, knight-errantry, bravery, courtesy, courtliness, heroism, lionheartedness. ANT. *cowardice, dishonor, rudeness, discourtesy.*

chock-full *a.* packed, chock-a-block, overflowing, brimming, stuffed, crammed, bursting, filled to capacity, *jam-packed. ANT. *empty, barren, devoid.*

choice *n.* selection, preference, choosing, election, determination, vote, decision, druthers, volition, option, desire, pick, wish.

choice *a.* best, superior, excellent, select, first-rate, cream-of-the-crop, vintage, prime. ANT. *poor, fair, ordinary, inferior.*

choke *v.* **1.** STRANGLE throttle, garrote, asphyxiate, suffocate, smother, stifle, wring. **2.** CLOG obstruct, block, close off, occlude, dam, seal, shut, constrict, restrict. ANT. *2. unclog, free, open.*

choleric *a.* quick-tempered, irritable, angry, hotheaded, irascible, touchy, grouchy, *short-fused, testy. ANT. *easy-going, mild-mannered, imperturbable.*

chomp *v.* bite, chew, crunch.

choose *v.* select, pick, elect, wish for, desire, opt for, decide on, determine, prefer, want, single out, call for, fancy, appoint.

choosy *a.* picky, fussy, finicky, particular, selective, persnickety, fastidious, exacting, overparticular, discriminating. ANT. *undiscriminating, *easy.*

chop *n.* blow, whack, swipe, knock, *wallop, *plug, smack, hit.

chop *v.* cut, hew, lop, hack, fell, split, cleave, slash, slice, dice, mince, rend, sever.

choppy *a.* rough, stormy, wavy, violent, bumpy, turbulent, frothy, wild. ANT. *calm, serene, glassy.*

chore *n.* task, job, duty, burden, work, responsibility, charge, bother, *drag, *pain. ANT. *pleasure, recreation, entertainment.*

chortle *v.* chuckle, snort, snicker, snigger, crow, laugh with glee, guffaw, crackle, giggle. SEE LAUGH

chorus *n.* **1.** CHOIR chorale group, glee club, ensemble, choristers. SEE MUSIC **2.** AGREEMENT unison, harmony, concert.

christen *v.* baptize, name, designate, dub, title.

chronic *a.* long-term, recurrent, perpetual, constant, habitual, prolonged, protracted, lingering, persistent, stubborn, unabating, continual. ANT. *short-term, temporary.*

chronicle n. history, narrative, accounting, record, annals, archive, chronology, register, log, calendar, journal, diary. SEE BOOK

chronological a. in order, ordered, sequential, consecutive, successive, serial, dated. ANT. *random, unorganized, haphazard.*

chubby a. plump, rotund, portly, pudgy, stout, fleshy, *roly-poly, round, *zaftig, tubby, flabby, full-figured, *porky. ANT. *skinny, anorexic, bony.* SEE FAT

chuck v. throw, toss, hurl, heave, pitch, fling, discard, *eighty-six, dump, junk, abandon, get rid of.

chuckle v. chortle, laugh, snicker, snigger, giggle, smile, cluck. SEE LAUGH

chum n. friend, buddy, pal, *bro, companion, comrade, crony, *sidekick, alter ego, *homeboy, *main man, *pardner.

chummy a. friendly, companionable, *palsy-walsy, affectionate, *buddy-buddy, intimate, inseparable, thick, *kissy-huggy, familiar. ANT. *hostile, distant, alienated, estranged.*

chump n. fool, dupe, idiot, *sucker, dope, patsy.

chunk n. hunk, piece, lump, clump, mass, portion, wad, slab, wedge.

chunky a. thick, stocky, thickset, *built like a fireplug, stubby, squat, stout, chubby, pudgy. ANT. *skinny, anorexic, *built like linguine, *like a beanpole, willowy.* SEE FAT

church n. chapel, cathedral, house of worship, temple, synagogue, basilica, meeting house, mosque, tabernacle, the Lord's house, bethel, abbey, sanctuary, denomination, sect, faith, affiliation. "God between four walls."—Victor Hugo. "A hospital for sinners."—L.L. Nash. "Wherever one hand meets another helpfully."—John Ruskin.

WORD FIND

altar area reserved for clergy: chancel, sanctuary, presbytery
balcony for choir: choir loft
baptism basin: font
baptism room/section: baptistery
bell ringer: sexton
bell tower: belfry
bench: pew
bishop's church: cathedral
Buddhist: pagoda
central portion/ main area for congregation: nave
collection/revenue: tithe, benefice
confession booth in the Catholic church: confessional
council of bishops: synod
crucifixion sculptures: Calvary
cup: chalice
district: parish
division, difference of opinion: schism
faith/denomination: (Christian) Roman Catholic, Protestant, Methodist, Presbyterian, Lutheran, Mormon, Episcopalian, Unitarian, Baptist, Eastern Orthodox, Pentecostal, Church of the Nazarene, Seventh Day Adventists, Unification Church; Orthodox Judaism; Islam; Hindu; Buddhist
gallery above side aisle: triforium
governing body: classis
grave digger: sexton
high-ranking clergy: prelate
house of clergyman: parsonage, rectory
Italian cathedral: duomo
Jewish house of worship: synagogue
jurisdiction of archbishop: archdiocese
jurisdiction of bishop: diocese
land/property: glebe
laws of: canon
lay authority: elder
light-admitting upper wall: clerestory
members: congregation, fold, flock, Ecclesia
Moslem: mosque
mosque tower: minaret
nunnery: convent
office, endowed: benefice
outreach church supported by larger church: mission
preaching platform: pulpit
reading stand: lectern, ambo
repository for sacraments: ambry
rite: baptism, benediction, communion, mass
semicircular projection and vaulted roof area at east end behind altar: apse
storage room for altar vessels: sacristy
storage room for clergy and choir's robes: vestry
study of architecture, decoration: ecclesiology
table or raised platform: altar
tower: steeple, spire, belfry
underground vault/burial place: crypt
vestibule: narthex, galilee porch
west-side chapel: galilee
window, arched: lancet window
window, large, round, stained glass: catherine wheel, rose window, marigold window
yard, enclosed: parvis
SEE CLERGY, MONASTERY, RELIGION

churchman n. SEE CLERGY

churlish *a.* surly, mean, grouchy, boorish, loutish, crude, cantankerous, thorny, cranky, cross, huffy, grumpy, dour, sullen, ill-tempered. ANT. *nice, pleasant, civil.*

churn *v.* stir, agitate, shake, seethe, whip, heave, swirl, whisk, beat.

chute *n.* waterfall, rapids, trough, passage, slide, channel, gutter, runway, flume.

CHUTZPAH *n.* [HOOTS puh] nerve, brass, fearlessness. *It takes a lot of chutzpah to cut in line.* SYN. nerve, brass, gall, *balls, audacity, boldness, backbone, spine, cheek, brazenness, arrogance. ANT. *cowardice, mousiness, spinelessness.*

cider *n.* juice, *squeezings, beverage, drink, refreshment.

cigar *n.* stogie, toby, Havana, *smoke, corona, cheroot, panatella, *weed, perfecto.

cigarette *n.* *smoke, *coffin nail, *butt, *cancer stick, *gasper, *fag, *Kent, *Pall Mall, *Salem, *Kool, *Winston, *Camel, *Marlboro, *Chesterfield. "Killers that travel in packs."—Mary S. Ott.

cinch *n. Sl.* breeze, snap, *walk on the beach, *child's play, *piece of cake, *duck soup, no sweat. ANT. *killer, *ballbuster, Herculean task.

cinders *n.* embers, coals, clinkers, slag, ashes.

cinema *n.* film theater, the movies. SEE MOVIE

cipher *n.* 1. ZERO nothing, naught, nil, *zip, *goose egg. 2. CODE cryptography, puzzle, mystery, problem. ANT. *1. infinity*

circa *a.* about, approximately, roughly. ANT. *precisely, exactly.*

circadian rhythm *n.* biorhythm, cycles, body clock.

circle *n.* 1. RING loop, oval, disc, orb, round, compass, hoop, halo, wheel, orbit, sphere, globe, circuit, coil, circlet, crown. 2. CYCLE revolution, series, period, progression, round. 3. ASSOCIATES group, coterie, crowd, clique, fraternity, sorority, gang, assembly. 4. SPHERE OF INTEREST domain, realm, range, field, province, dominion, bailiwick.

circle *v.* go around, circumnavigate, encircle, surround, ring, encompass, circumscribe, wheel, roll, loop, pivot, reel.

circuit *n.* 1. COURSE path, route, cycle, lap, pass, round, tour, run. 2. CIRCLING revolution, orbit. 3. BOUNDARY periphery, border, perimeter, margin, fringe, confines, brink.

CIRCUITOUS *a.* [sur KYOO i tus] roundabout or indirect. *Much to my irritation, the cabbie took a circuitous route to the airport.*

SYN. roundabout, indirect, circular, meandering, rambling, *long way, *far afield, labyrinthine, devious, *off the beaten path. ANT. *direct, straight.*

circular *n.* advertisement, flier, handbill, insert, brochure, leaflet, announcement, letter.

circular *a.* 1. ROUND spherical, spheroid, disklike, globular, oval. 2. CIRCUITOUS roundabout.

circulate *v.* 1. CIRCLE revolve, mill, move around, wander, tour, course, make the rounds. 2. DISTRIBUTE spread, pass out, disperse, disseminate, publicize, announce.

circulation *n.* 1. FLOW movement, coursing, circling, rotation, round, tour, revolution. 2. DISTRIBUTION dissemination, transmission, spread.

circumcise *v.* excise, remove, cut.

circumference *n.* girth, perimeter, periphery, ambit, outline, compass, circuit.

CIRCUMLOCUTION *n.* [SUR kum loh KYOO shun] an overly wordy or indirect way of saying something. *Circumlocution is the tendency to use ten words when one would do.* SYN. periphrasis, long-windedness, prolixity, rambling, verbosity, redundancy, wordiness, repetition, roundaboutness, *beating around the bush, digression. ANT. *directness, brevity, conciseness.*

CIRCUMSCRIBE *v.* [SUR kum SKRIBE] to draw a line around, to set limits. *Points of interest on the map were circumscribed.* SYN. 1. ENCLOSE circle, encircle, surround, outline, encompass. 2. BIND confine, limit, restrict, restrain, prohibit, check, hem in, curb, impede, demarcate.

CIRCUMSPECT *a.* [SUR kum SPEKT] cautious, careful. *John is always circumspect around skunks.* SYN. cautious, careful, wary, mindful, chary, leery, apprehensive, guarded, prudent, vigilant, heedful, scrupulous, judicious. ANT. *careless, reckless, rash.*

circumstance *n.* situation, case, instance, occasion, incidence, occurrence, matter, episode, condition, contingency, concern, place, time.

circumstances *n.* course of events, turn of events, situation, predicament, attending factors, condition, state of affairs.

CIRCUMSTANTIAL *a.* [ser kum STAN shul] incidental; largely insignificant. Also, referring to evidence that may be used in a court case only to infer, not prove, guilt. *The evidence against the accused was weak and mostly circumstantial*. SYN. incidental, indirect, secondary, insignificant, unimportant, trivial, inconclusive, open to interpretation, conjectural, speculative, extraneous, presumed. ANT. *conclusive*.

CIRCUMVENT *v*. [SER kum vent] to get around or avoid. *The thief was able to circumvent punishment through legal loopholes*. SYN. get around, dodge, bypass, avoid, elude, shun, skirt, sidestep, thwart, stymie, outflank, foil, contravene, outwit.

circus *n*. *big top, hippodrome, spectacle, tent show, exhibition, performance, extravaganza.

WORD FIND

arena: ring
procession: caravan, cavalcade
subordinate show: sideshow
swing: trapeze
worker/laborer: rouster, roustabout

cistern *n*. tank, reservoir, vat.

citadel *n*. fortress, fort, stronghold, safehold, bastion, tower, refuge. SEE CASTLE

citation *n*. **1.** SUMMONS subpoena, warrant, charge, call. **2.** CITING quoting, quotation, quote, reference, passage, excerpt, source, extract, text. **3.** HONORABLE MENTION accolade, recognition, commendation, award, reward, kudos.

cite *v*. **1.** SUMMON subpoena, put out a warrant, charge, call. **2.** QUOTE reference, note, excerpt, extract, refer to, provide a source.

citizen *n*. inhabitant, native, resident, subject, national, denizen, freeman, taxpayer, burgher, cosmopolite, *just another brick in the wall, *John/Jane Q. Public. "The most important office."—Louis Brandeis.

city *n*. metropolis, municipality, megalopolis, town, *burg, downtown, suburb, urban complex, boomtown, community, asphalt jungle, urban sprawl, capital, borough. "A herding region."—Elbert Hubbard. "A human zoo."—Desmond Morris. "A stone forest."—John Priestly. "The centre of a thousand trades."—William Cowper. "Millions of people being lonesome together."—Henry Thoreau.

WORD FIND

districts: ward, business district, residential district, ghetto, slums, tenement district, inner city, *skid row, *red light district, tenderloin, hell's kitchen, Chinatown, Little Italy, barrio, greenbelt
official: alderman, councilor, mayor
SEE NEW YORK

city hall *n*. municipal building, town hall, municipal government, city center, municipal center, administrative building, courthouse.

civic *a*. municipal, civil, metropolitan, urban, community, communal, public.

civil *a*. **1.** CIVIC municipal, community, communal, public, urban, metropolitan, civilian. **2.** POLITE courteous, well-mannered, proper, civilized, obliging, gracious, urbane, genteel, refined, diplomatic. ANT. *2. rude, unrefined, barbaric, beastly*.

civilization *n*. **1.** SOCIAL ORGANIZATION culture, refinement, sophistication, education, civility, acculturation, polish, breeding, taming, socialization. "Restrictions, standards, courtesy, indirect methods, justice, reason."—Jose Ortega y Gasset. "To convert a man, a beast of prey, into a tame and civilized animal, a domestic animal."—Friedrich Nietzsche. "A concerted effort to remedy the blunders and check the practical joking of God."—Henry Louis Mencken. "A series of victories over nature."—William Harvey. "The lamb's skin in which barbarism masquerades."—Thomas Bailey Aldrich. **2.** HUMANITY society. ANT. *1. wildness, wilderness, savagery, barbarism, laws of the jungle*. SEE SOCIETY

civilized *a*. cultured, refined, sophisticated, educated, civil, acculturated, polished, bred, tamed, humane, socialized, socially organized, urbane. "To have some quality of consideration for all who cross our path."—Agnes Repplier. ANT. *wild, raw, crude, savage, barbaric*.

civil liberties *n*. rights, freedoms, God-given rights, freedom of speech, freedom of religion.

civil rights *n*. freedoms, civil liberties, constitutional rights.

clad *a*. dressed, clothed, attired.

claim *v*. **1.** DEMAND take, seek, petition, *have dibs on, exact, expropriate, attach. **2.** ASSERT maintain, insist, allege, proclaim, declare, hold, profess, defend, contend.

clairvoyant *a*. psychic, perceptive, telepathic, extrasensory, prescient, prophetic, second-sighted. ANT. *insensitive, unreceptive*.

clam *n*. mollusk, quahog, cherrystone, littleneck, steamer.

clamber *v*. climb, scale, *crab, climb with all fours, scrabble, ascend, crawl, shinny. SEE MOUNTAIN CLIMBING

clammy *a*. damp, moist, dank, cold, slimy, mucous, sticky, pasty, sweaty. ANT. *dry, arid*.

clamor *n.* **1.** uproar, outcry, racket, hullabaloo, ballyhoo, hue and cry, babel, shouting, din, noise, hubbub, tumult, chaos, bedlam, commotion, pandemonium, upheaval, brouhaha, disruption. ANT. *silence, tranquility, serenity, peace.*

clamor *v.* cry out, demand, *put up a fuss, call out, shout, *raise the roof, bellow, howl, yell, insist.

clamorous *a.* noisy, loud, confused, uproarious, tumultuous, chaotic, disruptive, deafening, ear-piercing, vociferous. ANT. *quiet, silent, peaceful.*

clamp *n.* vise, hold, grip, clasp, bracket, clip.

clan *n.* tribe, family, dynasty, group, clique, circle, coterie, band, fraternity, society, gang, ring. SEE FAMILY

CLANDESTINE *a.* [klan DES tin] secret or undercover, an activity associated with illicit activities. *The clandestine meeting took place in an abandoned shipyard.* SYN. secret, undercover, hidden, concealed, surreptitious, *cloak and dagger, *hush-hush, covert, underground, furtive, underhanded, sneaky, conspiratory, back room. ANT. *public, aboveboard, open.*

clang *v.* ring, clank, reverberate, resound, peal, bong, toll, gong, chime.

clannish *a.* cliquish, insular, provincial, snobbish, selective, sectarian, parochial, narrow, tribal, exclusive, class conscious, caste conscious. ANT. *friendly, open, broad-minded, accepting, worldly.*

clap *n.* explosion, crack, thunder, peal, bang, shot, burst, report.

clap *v.* applaud, give a hand, cheer, slap, strike, rap, whack, slam.

CLAPTRAP *n.* [KLAP TRAP] pretentious writing or talk designed to win attention. *That all men are unfeeling Neanderthals is feminist claptrap.* SYN. bombast, hogwash, grandstanding, fustian, pretentiousness, insincerity, speciousness, sensationalism, platitude, inflation, sophistry, *bunk, *bilge, twaddle.

clarify *v.* elucidate, clear up, make plain, explain, show, define, illuminate, simplify, *shed light on, interpret. ANT. *confuse, muddle, obfuscate, *make clear as mud.*

clarity *n.* clearness, lucidity, plainness, intelligibility, comprehensibility, explicitness, legibility, simplicity, transparency, purity. ANT. *obscurity, haze, fog, fuzziness, distortion.*

clash *v.* **1.** CONFLICT disagree, argue, fight, quarrel, *butt heads, wrangle, feud, scuffle, *lock horns, tussle. **2.** CRASH clatter, clang, rattle,

jangle, bang. **3.** MISMATCH contrast, don't go with, are ill-suited together. ANT. *1. agree, harmonize, correspond.*

clasp *n.* catch, hook, snap, fastener, clip, buckle, hasp, pin.

clasp *v.* grasp, grip, embrace, hold, clutch, clench, squeeze.

class *n.* **1.** SORT kind, category, type, group, caste, genus, grade, species, stripe, variety, breed, division, ilk, order. **2.** SOCIAL RANK position, stratum, status, sect, birth, lineage, extraction, place, echelon, hierarchy, pedigree, caste, station, rank, standing. **3.** BODY OF STUDENTS study group. **4.** COURSE subject, period, lesson, curriculum. **5.** *Sl.* HIGH STYLE elegance, excellence, quality, flair, polish, distinction, fineness, refinement.

class *v.* SEE CLASSIFY

classic *n.* model, standard, example, masterpiece, paragon, exemplar, chef-d'oeuvre, ideal, paradigm, archetype, magnum opus.

classic *a.* **1.** EXCELLENT first-class, model, exemplary, superior, extraordinary, quintessential, finest, best, vintage, standard, ideal. **2.** TRADITIONAL established, conventional, tried-and-true, regular, standard, prototypical. ANT. *1. inferior, second-rate, poor. 2. radical, *new wave, avant-garde.*

classical *a.* SEE CLASSIC

classification *n.* **1.** ARRANGEMENT division, grouping, categorization, cataloging, ordering, grading, sorting, *pigeonholing, typing, labeling, assignment. **2.** CATEGORY division, group, class, variety, order, grade, type.

classified *a.* confidential, secret, top secret, private, restricted. ANT. *overt, public, open.*

classify *v.* categorize, arrange, group, catalog, order, grade, sort, *pigeonhole, type, label, assign, organize, rank, systemize.

classy *a.* first-class, fine, elegant, superior, excellent, high-class, polished, smart, stylish, chic, swanky, fashionable. ANT. *low-class, cheap, chintzy, *slummy.*

clatter *v.* rattle, crack, smash, clank, clang, jangle.

clause *n.* article, provision, term, specification, condition, part, section, paragraph, sentence, passage, *catch.

claw *n.* talon, nail, pincer, hook, spur, nipper.

claw *v.* scratch, rip, tear, pierce, lacerate, hook, slash, dig, puncture, gouge, gash.

clay *n.* earth, dirt, loam, mud, soil, sod.

clean *v.* wash, cleanse, launder, scrub, bathe, freshen up, scour, purify, disinfect, sterilize, deterge, swab, spruce up, shampoo, dust, sanitize, decontaminate. ANT. *soil, dirty, be-grime, pollute, mess.*

clean *a.* **1.** NOT DIRTY spotless, washed, fresh, *spic and span, unsoiled, immaculate, *clean as a whistle, laundered, *squeaky clean, scrubbed, antiseptic, scoured, sanitary, bright, sparkling, pure, disinfected, sterile, clear, unpolluted. **2.** VIRTUOUS upright, moral, pure, chaste, sinless, innocent, decent, wholesome, respectable, lily-white. **3.** FAIR sportsmanlike, honest, aboveboard, respectable, by the rules. **4.** TRIM plain, uncluttered, simple, sharp. **5.** COMPLETE thorough, entire, whole, clear-cut. ANT. *1. dirty, filthy, grubby, unsanitary, grimy. 2. immoral, filthy, indecent. 3. unfair, unsportsmanlike, *below-the-belt. 4. busy, ornate, cluttered. 5. incomplete, uncertain.*

clean-cut *a.* neat, trim, groomed, tidy, clean-shaven, conservative, military, Ivy-League, *preppy, old-fashioned, *square, button-down, traditional, *dressed for success. ANT. *sloppy, unkempt.*

cleanse *v.* SEE CLEAN

clear *v.* **1.** CLEAN wipe, tidy, sweep, free, empty, open, rid, remove, liberate, disentangle. **2.** EXONERATE liberate, free, *let off the hook, release, find innocent, absolve, exculpate, acquit, vindicate, *restore one's good name. **3.** PASS OVER miss, *make, steer clear of, hurdle, vault. **4.** CLEAR UP clarify, illuminate, explain, elucidate. ANT. *1. mess up, soil, tangle. 2. find guilty, incriminate. 3. hit, catch. 4. obfuscate, confuse, muddle.*

clear *a.* **1.** APPARENT understandable, clear-cut, obvious, perspicuous, crystal-clear, plain, lucid, transparent, incontrovertible, evident, comprehensible, explicit, unmistakable. **2.** UNOBSTRUCTED open, free, unblocked, unclogged, unhindered, unobstructed, empty. **3.** TRANSPARENT crystal, glassy, see-through, diaphanous, pellucid, translucent, limpid. ANT. *1. unclear, hazy, foggy, fuzzy, incomprehensible. 2. obstructed, blocked, hindered, jammed. 3. opaque, cloudy, fuzzy.*

clearance *n.* authorization, sanction, *okay, *go, *green light, go-ahead.

clear-cut *a.* clear, definite, distinct, unquestionable, unmistakable, explicit, obvious, express.

clearheaded *a.* rational, of sound mind, lucid, alert, sharp, sober, keen, wide-awake, sane, level-headed, sensible, composed. ANT. *muddled, confused, hazy, irrational.*

clearly *adv.* obviously, plainly, apparently, unquestionably, unmistakably, incontrovertibly, conspicuously, undoubtedly, transparently, positively, overtly, indubitably. ANT. *questionably, doubtfully, unclearly, debatably.*

cleavage *n.* cleft, fissure, gap, chasm, rift, valley.

cleave *v.* **1.** STICK adhere, cling, cohere, hold fast, be faithful, be true. **2.** SPLIT divide, chop, carve, sever, slice, part, rend, rip, cut.

cleft *n.* opening, crack, crevice, break, gap, chink, fissure, slit, schism, split, rift.

CLEMENCY *n.* [KLEM un see] forgiveness, lenience, mercy. *The crook was granted clemency in exchange for information.* SYN. forgiveness, lenience, mercy, mildness, compassion, charity, amnesty, sympathy, softening, quarter, mitigation, easing, softheartedness. ANT. *vindictiveness, cruel and unusual punishment, strictness, harshness, heavy-handedness.*

clench *v.* grip, grasp, hold firm, clutch, clasp, hold, constrict, close. ANT. *loosen, release.*

clergy *n.* ecclesiastics, men of the cloth, ministry, priesthood, churchmen, holy order, prelacy, pastorate, presbytery, rabbinate. SEE CLERGYMAN

clergyman *n.* ecclesiastic, minister, priest, rabbi, preacher, canon, cleric, *dominie, reverend, curate, father, pastor, parson, prelate, chaplain, bishop, cardinal, rector, vicar, man of the cloth, deacon, evangelist, theologian, shepherd, pontiff, man/woman of God. "Ambassadors for Christ."—Bible. "A human Sunday."—Samuel Butler.

WORD FIND

abbey's superior female: abbess
abbey's superior male: abbot
assists priest or minister with candles, offerings: acolyte, altar boy
bishop-assisting priest who oversees a territory: archdeacon
bishop, highest ranking: archbishop
cape, short, worn by pope, cardinal and bishop: mozzetta
cathedral superior: dean
collar worn by priest: clerical collar
council of: synod
deacon's wide-sleeved tunic worn over alb: dalmatic
England, parish priest in: vicar
garment, general term: vestment
hat, squarish, with three or four projections, Roman Catholic: biretta
hat worn by bishop: miter
high-ranking minister who oversees a diocese: bishop

Hindu's spiritual teacher: guru
house of: rectory, parsonage, manse
Jewish minister: rabbi
long open cloak worn by bishop: cope
Lutheran, Baptist or Pentecostal minister: pastor
monk/friar's robe: frock
mosque official who calls faithful to prayer from minaret: muezzin
mosque's prayer leader: imam
Muslim authority: ayatollah
pope: pontiff
pope's assistant, second-highest in Catholic hierarchy: cardinal
pope's office: papacy
pope's palace home: Vatican
robe, long and white, worn by priest for Mass: alb
Roman Catholic's highest-ranking: pope
salary: prebend
school for: seminary
sleeveless mantle worn by priest at communion: chasuble
square cloth worn by priest over shoulders: amice
strip one of power due to unethical behavior: defrock
synagogue's prayer leader/singer: cantor
vestment, full-length, usually black, worn by priest: cassock
waist cord of alb: cincture
white, wide-sleeved, knee or hip-length garment: surplice
SEE CHURCH, RELIGION

clerical *a.* ecclesiastical, churchly, ministerial, priestly, pastoral, religious. ANT. *secular, lay.*

clerk *n.* salesman/woman, cashier, teller, office worker, bookkeeper, *desk jockey. SEE OFFICE WORKER

clever *a.* intelligent, adroit, bright, ingenious, smart, dexterous, shrewd, quick, witty, facile, *brainy, versatile, sharp, savvy, inventive, capable, handy, resourceful, imaginative. ANT. *stupid, bovine, dull, moronic.*

cliché *n.* banality, trite remark, bromide, *chestnut, old saw, *old line, *tired line, hackneyed expression, platitude, *old story, stereotype. "Only something well said in the first place."—William Granger.

clichéd *a.* trite, hackneyed, tired, worn out, stereotyped. ANT. *fresh, new, imaginative.*

click *v.* **1.** TICK clack, snap, clink, chink, rattle. **2.** WORK TOGETHER SUCCESSFULLY come together, fit, fall into place.

client *n.* customer, patron, consumer, buyer, *regular.

clientele *n.* clients, customers, patrons, following, trade, business, regulars, market.

cliff *n.* precipice, bluff, scarp, escarpment, overlook, overhang, ledge, headland, promontory, peak, summit, palisade, crag. SEE MOUNTAIN

cliffhanger *n.* serial, *nail-biter, melodrama, episode, thriller.

climate *n.* **1.** WEATHER clime, temperature, meteorological conditions. **2.** ATMOSPHERE air, ambience, feel, tone, undertone, sense, aura, spirit, character, mood, disposition.

climax *n.* culmination, highest point, peak, acme, pinnacle, crest, zenith, maximum, summit, critical mass, apex, turning point, climacteric. ANT. *anticlimax, low, nadir.* SEE ORGASM

climb *v.* ascend, scale, mount, clamber, shinny, *climb hand over hand, rise, swarm, escalade, scramble up, descend. SEE MOUNTAIN CLIMBING

clime *n.* SEE CLIMATE

clinch *v.* **1.** FASTEN secure, fix, make fast, set, attach, bolt. **2.** WIN CONCLUSIVELY OR SETTLE finish off, close, culminate, confirm, decide, put all doubts to rest, sew up, cap, *put on ice.

clincher *n.* crowning blow, finisher, closer, deathblow, culmination, capper, *coup de grace, settler, finishing touch.

cling *v.* stick, adhere, hold, clasp, cleave to, cohere, embrace, be attached to, cherish. ANT. *release, let go, repel.*

clinic *n.* dispensary, infirmary, sick bay, hospital, outpatient ward. SEE MEDICINE, HOSPITAL

clinical *a.* scientific, analytic, objective, detached, impersonal, dispassionate, unemotional. ANT. *personal, subjective, involved.*

clink *v.* jingle, jangle, tinkle, ring, tink.

clip *n.* fastener, clasp, holder, pin, hasp.

clip *v.* **1.** ATTACH fasten, pin, couple, hook, grip. **2.** CUT snip, crop, trim, bob, shorten, shave, shear, scissor, *buzz, prune, mow. **3.** REDUCE shorten, curtail, abridge. ANT. **3.** *lengthen, increase.*

CLIQUE *n.* [KLIK] an exclusive group or circle of people, sometimes of a snobbish nature. *High school is notorious for its cliques.* SYN. coterie, group, crowd, in crowd, circle, band, clan, set, gang, faction, bunch, crew, pack.

cloak *n.* **1.** CAPE mantle, wrap, dolman, overcoat, robe, pelisse, capote. **2.** DISGUISE cover, mask, masquerade, guise, concealment, front, pretext.

cloak v. cover, conceal, hide, mask, disguise, veil. ANT. *uncover, reveal, unmask.*

cloak and dagger a. intrguing, mysterious, melodramatic, dealing in espionage.

clobber v. punch, pound, beat, wallop, pummel, hit, strike, belt, drub, thrash, *slug, *sock.

clock n. timepiece, chronometer, timer, watch, hourglass.

clod n. dolt, moron, idiot, simpleton, dunce, halfwit, ignoramus, oaf, nitwit, blockhead, *chowderhead.

clodhopper n. hick, yokel, bumpkin, hayseed, rustic, farmer, hillbilly, *cider squeezer.

clog n. blockage, obstacle, jam, congestion, stoppage, barrier, occlusion, encumbrance, clot, bottleneck.

clog v. block, obstruct, jam, congest, stop, bar, occlude, encumber, clot, close, choke, fill, impede, stuff, cram, gum up. ANT. *open, free, clear.*

cloister n. 1. SECLUDED REFUGE asylum, retreat, sanctuary, haven, monastery, abbey, convent. 2. COVERED WALKWAY colonnade, arcade, courtyard, ambulatory, promenade, archway, gallery.

CLOISTERED a. [KLOIS terd] secluded, sheltered. *Monks enjoy a cloistered lifestyle.* SYN. secluded, sheltered, reclusive, solitary, sequestered, hidden, shielded, remote, aloof, segregated, hermitic, insular. ANT. *public, conspicuous.*

clone n. double, match, twin, copy, replica, duplicate.

close n. ending, finale, finish, completion, windup, culmination.

close v. 1. SHUT seal, lock, secure, bolt, bar, shutter. 2. COMPLETE finish, *wind down, *call it a day, end, cease, finalize, *put to bed, fold up, terminate, stop, discontinue, shut down. 3. JOIN unite, merge, fuse, couple, connect. ANT. *1. open, broach. 2. begin, start, open. 3. separate, divide.*

close a. 1. NEAR proximate, at hand, handy, next to, immediate, *under one's nose, *within shouting distance, bordering, nigh, in close proximity, approaching, contiguous, neighboring. 2. DENSE cramped, thick, compact, packed, congested, crowded, solid, confined, narrow, stuffed. 3. INTIMATE friendly, familiar, chummy, inseparable, *buddy-buddy, attached, *thick with, *cosy with. 4. SIMILAR comparable, alike, like, much the same, analogous, near, akin. 5. OPPRESSIVE humid, stuffy, airless, muggy, unventilated, heavy, stifling, suffocating,

thick. 6. STINGY tight, miserly, tight-fisted, niggardly, *penny-pinching, penurious. ANT. *1. far, distant, remote. 2. loose, roomy, commodious. 3. unfamiliar, distant, cool. 4. dissimilar, opposite, contrasting. 5. airy, breezy, fresh. 6. generous, free-spending, extravagant.*

close call n. narrow escape, near miss, *close shave, *squeaker, photofinish, *heart stopper, *white-knuckler, cliffhanger.

closefisted a. tightfisted, tight, cheap, stingy, miserly, niggardly, penny-pinching, parsimonious, penurious. ANT. *generous, giving, openhanded.*

close-minded a. narrow-minded, intolerant, blind, unreceptive. ANT. *broad-minded.*

closemouthed a. uncommunicative, taciturn, quiet, reserved, laconic, tight-lipped, reticent, retiring, secretive, mute. ANT. *talkative, loquacious.*

closet n. storeroom, cupboard, locker, compartment, wardrobe, cubbyhole.

close shave n. SEE CLOSE CALL

closure n. conclusion, capping, ending, tying up loose ends, finality, completion, finishing.

clot n. grume, embolism, lump, mass, coagulation, occlusion.

clot v. coagulate, congeal, set, thicken, clog, coalesce, solidify. ANT. *thin, liquefy, flow.*

cloth n. fabric, textile, material, weave, dry goods.

clothe v. dress, attire, fit out, garb, don, vest, put on, outfit, deck out, doll up, tog, costume, caparison, adorn. ANT. *strip, undress.*

clothes n. pl. SEE CLOTHING

clothing n. apparel, dress, attire, garb, wear, garments, habiliments, wardrobe, getup, duds, *threads, *rags, costume, finery, outfit, vestment, tog, *civvies. "Two-thirds of beauty."—Welsh proverb. SEE BOOT, COAT, DRESS, HAT, JACKET, PANTS, SHIRT, SHOE, SKIRT, SWEATER

cloud n. vapor, mist, fog, haze, steam, puff, veil, billow, overcast, gloom, nebula. "The only birds that never sleep."—Victor Hugo.

WORD FIND
aircraft trail: contrail
boiling, billowing or breastlike, severe thunderstorm: mammatocumulus
bulging: billowing
cauliflowerlike, fair-weather cloud: cumulus, stratocumulus
circle around sun or moon: halo
continuous, layered, low: stratus

descriptive: buttermilk sky
feathery tuft: cirrus, mare's tail
fleecy cumulus cloud: woolpack, sheep, alto-cumulus
gray, thick and shapeless rain cloud: nimbo-stratus
horsetail-like cirrus cloud: mare's tail
mass broken off by wind: rack
rain-producing: nimbus
referring to: nubilous
ripples or bands: cirrocumulus, mackeral sky
study of: nephology
swift-moving, dark storm patch: scud
thunder and lightning: thunderhead
thunderhead's anvil-shaped top: incus
veils, thin and white, covering most of sky: cirrostratus
wisp trailing from rain cloud: virga
SEE FOG, RAIN

cloud *v.* befog, darken, obscure, veil, dim, cloak, blind, muddle. ANT. *clear, illuminate.*

cloudy *a.* **1.** OVERCAST gray, dreary, dismal, hazy, murky, partly sunny, nubulous, lowery, lowering, turbid, leaden, misty, foggy, murky. **2.** OBSCURE vague, indistinct, blurry, nebulous, fuzzy, unclear, hazy, confused, muddled, mysterious. ANT. *1. clear, sunny, bright, radiant. 2. clear, distinct, certain.*

clout *n.* **1.** BLOW rap, hit, whack, clip, *sock. **2.** INFLUENCE power, weight, *pull.

cloverleaf *n.* interchange, overpass, on-off ramp. "Our national flower . . . the concrete cloverleaf."—Lewis Mumford. SEE STREET

clown *n.* buffoon, jester, joker, merry-andrew, comic, *cutup, prankster, zany, mime, harlequin, card, wit. SEE CIRCUS

CLOY *v.* [KLOY] to make sick of something from having too much. *Try to eat a pound of chocolate and it will soon cloy.* SYN. sicken, satiate, surfeit, displease, nauseate, glut, sate, overdo, gag, weary, pall. ANT. *entice, tantalize.*

club *n.* **1.** STICK bat, cudgel, billy, mace, truncheon, blackjack, bludgeon, shillelagh. **2.** ASSOCIATION organization, society, fraternity, sorority, clique, affiliation, coterie, alliance, lodge, order.

club *v.* hit, strike, bat, batter, cudgel, baste, beat, clout, blackjack, slug.

clue *n.* hint, tip, tipoff, *lead, sign, telltale, inkling, inference, pointer, implication, *dead giveaway, evidence, suggestion, trace, mark.

clump *n.* **1.** CLUSTER aggregation, bunch, group, lump, mass, clod, thicket, bushes. **2.** THUMP clomp, stomp, bump, bang, thud, *thunk.

clumsy *a.* **1.** KLUTZY oafish, inept, ungainly, bumbling, maladroit, awkward, gauche, graceless, fumbling, *all thumbs, *having two left feet, cloddish, butterfingered, blundering, lumbering, uncoordinated. **2.** UNWIELDY awkward, cumbersome, bulky, unmanageable, ponderous. ANT. *1. coordinated, graceful, nimble, adroit. 2. handy.*

cluster *n.* bunch, clump, mass, group, body, crowd, assembly, knot, collection, congregation.

clutch *v.* grasp, snatch, seize, grip, grab, catch, nab, snare, clench, hold, squeeze. ANT. *release, drop.*

clutches *n.* power, control, grip, hands, rule, possession, custody.

clutter *n.* mess, disorder, jumble, litter, trash, disarray, hodgepodge, chaos. ANT. *order, neatness, tidiness.*

clutter *v.* mess, disorder, jumble, litter, *trash, strew about, scatter. ANT. *neaten, order, arrange, clean.*

coach *n.* **1.** TRAINER teacher, tutor, instructor, mentor, *whip, taskmaster, drillmaster, athletic director. **2.** CARRIAGE stage, brougham, landau, phaeton, coupe, buggy.

coach *v.* train, teach, tutor, instruct, *whip into shape, drill, direct, guide, school, cram.

coachman *n.* driver, jehu, hack, whip.

coagulate *v.* clot, curdle, mass, lump, congeal, gel, thicken, set, condense, cake. ANT. *thin, liquefy.*

COALESCE *v.* [KOH uh LES] to come together or merge as one, fuse. *The two factions will coalesce in order to fight a common enemy.* SYN. come together, merge, unite, fuse, weld, consolidate, blend, cohere, integrate, incorporate, combine, mingle. ANT. *divide, fragment, split, separate.*

COALITION *n.* [KOH uh LISH un] an alliance or union. *The coalition of environmentalists will be lobbying for cleaner air.* SYN. alliance, union, association, confederacy, faction, league, bloc, partnership, cartel, consolidation, cooperative, merger.

coarse *a.* **1.** ROUGH gritty, scratchy, grainy, harsh, unpolished, bumpy, bristly, unrefined. **2.** INFERIOR poor, second-rate, shoddy, common, mediocre. **3.** VULGAR unrefined, crude, rough-hewn, crass, uncouth, offensive, uncultured, earthy, foulmouthed, ill-mannered, churlish, impolite. ANT. *1. smooth, polished, refined. 2. superior, first-rate, high quality. 3. refined, cultured, polite, gentlemanly, well-mannered.*

coast n. shore, beach, strand, seaboard, seaside, littoral. SEE BEACH

coast v. glide, slide, skim, glissade, drift, roll.

coast guard n. marine patrol, marine rescue.

coat n. 1. FUR pelt, fleece, wool, hide, pelage, fell. 2. COATING covering, finish, layer, lamination. 3. OVERCOAT jacket, wrap, tog, topcoat, windbreaker.

WORD FIND

classic with black velvet collar: chesterfield

formal: tails, tuxedo

full-length: maxi

large overcoat: greatcoat

long, loose with wide sleeves cut in one piece with shoulders: raglan

long raincoat or overcoat with several pockets, belt: trenchcoat

midlength: midi

raincoat: slicker, trenchcoat

sportcoat: blazer

toggle-buttoning: toggle coat, duffel coat

waterproof coat with drawstring hood: stadium coat

woman's long coat with large pockets: duster

woolen, plaid and short: mackinaw

SEE JACKET

coax v. cajole, wheedle, persuade, talk into, lure, press, *rope in, beg, *butter up, beguile, blandish, play up to, con, sweet talk, inveigle.

cocaine n. narcotic, drug, *coke, *snow, *crack, *Bernice, *blow, *Doctor White, *freebase, controlled substance, *snort, *crystal, local anesthetic, *ice, *nose candy, *poison, *speedball, *stuff, *sugar, *white lady, *wings, *Bolivian marching powder, *foo-foo dust, *happy dust, *joy powder, *Peruvian, *paradise, *stardust, *white horse, *witch, *mojo, *gift of the sun god.

WORD FIND

cigarette laced with cocaine: *coolie, *woola

cocaine and heroin: *Belushi

dose: line

high: *buzz, *rush

inhale burning fumes of: freebase

inhale through nostrils: snort, blow, toke, toot

injectable cocaine: *soda

intravenous mix of cocaine and heroin or amphetamine: *speedball

marijuana and cocaine inside a cigar: *blunt

numbness caused by: *freeze

pipe: crack pipe

purify: freebase

rock cocaine: *crack

rocks of crack rolled into a marijuana cigarette: *woolie

transporting or smuggling: trafficking

under the influence: *chalked up

utensil: coke spoon

SEE DRUG, NARCOTIC

cock n. rooster, cockerel.

cock v. prick, raise, stick up.

cockeyed a. 1. CROOKED askance, askew, lopsided, cross-eyed, awry, off-center. 2. RIDICULOUS silly, foolish, preposterous, stupid, absurd, whacky, *cockamamie, insane, *nuts. ANT. 1. straight, centered. 2. sane, rational.

cockpit n. cabin, flight deck.

cocksure a. confident, self-assured, unblinking, unflinching, sure, positive, certain, cocky, arrogant, overconfident, full of oneself, egotistical, bloated, swaggering, strutting, overbearing, smug, brash. ANT. unsure, uncertain, timid, mousy, shy, tentative.

cocktail n. mixed drink, beverage, aperitif. SEE ALCOHOL, DRINK, GLASS, LIQUEUR, WINE

WORD FIND

bourbon, bitters, soda, sugar: old-fashioned

bourbon, boiling water, sugar, cloves, cinnamon: hot toddy

bourbon, mint leaves, syrup: mint julep

gin, cherry brandy, lemon, club soda, powdered sugar: Singapore sling

gin, club soda, lime and ice: gin rickey

gin, cream, crème de cacao, nutmeg garnish: Alexander

gin, grenadine, cream: pink lady

gin, rum, tequila, vodka: Long Island iced tea

gin, rum, scotch, white crème de cacao, light cream: Barbary Coast

gin, vermouth, olive: martini

glass: cocktail glass, cooler, delmonico, highball, shot glass, snifter, wine glass

Irish whiskey, hot coffee, whipped cream: Irish coffee

Kahlúa, cream: sombrero

peach schnapps, vodka, pineapple juice, cranberry juice: sex on the beach

red wine, fruit juice and brandy: sangria

rum, orange juice, sour mix, grenadine: shark bite

rum, pineapple juice, coconut cream: pina colada

rum, sweet and sour: Daiquiri

rum, vodka, brandy, bourbon, lime: tidal wave

Scotch, drambuie: rusty nail

Scotch, vermouth, cherry garnish: Rob Roy
sloe gin, Southern Comfort, orange juice: slow comfortable screw
sloe gin, sweet and sour, soda, cherry garnish: sloe gin fizz
tequila, orange juice, grenadine: tequila sunrise
tequila, sweet and sour, rim of glass frosted with salt: Margarita
vodka, beef bouillon: bull shot
vodka, Kahlúa: black Russian
vodka, orange juice, Galliano: Harvey Wallbanger
vodka, orange juice: screwdriver
vodka, triple sec, cranberry juice, lime juice: cosmopolitan
vodka, triple sec curacao, lime juice: Kamikaze
vodka, worcestershire sauce, tomato juice: Bloody Mary
whiskey, ginger ale: highball
whiskey, sweet and sour, cherry: whiskey sour
whiskey, vermouth with cherry: Manhattan

cocky *a.* SEE COCKSURE

coddle *v.* pamper, mollycoddle, baby, indulge, spoil, cater to, cosset, dote on.

code *n.* **1.** SECRET WRITING cipher, cryptograph, cryptogram. **2.** LAWS regulations, standards, rules, canon, ethics, system, charter.

codicil *n.* appendix, addendum, rider.

codify *v.* classify, order, group, catalog, file, organize, arrange.

COERCE *v.* [koh URS] to force one to do something by intimidation or threats. *Your peers can coerce you to do things you know are wrong.* SYN. force, compel, persuade, bully, impel, strong-arm, pressure, railroad, constrain, impel, scare, make, cow, intimidate, *twist one's arm.

coercion *n.* force, pressure, duress, bullying, persuasion, strong-arm tactics, railroading, constraint, scare tactics, intimidation, threats, menacing, *heat, *arm-twisting.

coffee *n.* espresso, cafe au lait, cafe noir, cappuccino, *mud, *machine oil, brew, *battery acid, *joe, *java, *pick-me-up, *decaf, mocha, *crude, *blackstrap, *paint remover. "Break fluid."—R.R. Anderson.

coffer *n.* chest, strongbox, safe, vault.

coffers *n.* treasury, funds, finances, capital, means, assets, reserves. SEE MONEY, BANK

coffin *n.* casket, pine box, catafalque, sarcophagus, pall, *wooden overcoat. "An ornamental . . . box which no one cares to open."—

Elbert Hubbard. SEE CEMETERY, FUNERAL, DEATH

COGENT *a.* [KOH junt] strongly convincing. *His argument was cogent.* SYN. convincing, compelling, persuasive, effective, forceful, powerful, meaningful, conclusive, sound, potent, weighty. ANT. *unconvincing, ineffective, weak.*

cogitate *v.* ponder, consider, meditate, weigh, think over, contemplate, deliberate.

cognate *a.* alike, akin, associated, related, kindred, common, generic, affiliated, connected. ANT. *unlike, unrelated, different.*

COGNIZANT *a.* [KOG ni zunt] aware; conscious. *Are you cognizant of the deteriorating environment?* SYN. aware, conscious, informed, familiar, knowing, acquainted with, enlightened, mindful, apprised, in the know, understanding. ANT. *ignorant, unaware, oblivious.*

cohere *v.* **1.** STICK adhere, cling, attach, bind, hold, unite, join. **2.** AGREE harmonize, correspond, concur, coincide.

coherence *a.* agreement, consistency, harmony, correspondence, concurrence, congruity, unity, cohesion, accord. ANT. *incoherence, inconsistency.*

COHERENT *a.* [ko HEER unt] intelligible; making sense. *He'd had a few drinks but he was still coherent.* SYN. intelligible, rational, logical, lucid, articulate, understandable, comprehensible. ANT. *incoherent, unintelligible, confusing, nonsensical.*

cohort *n.* associate, colleague, companion, sidekick, supporter, buddy, pal, chum, accomplice, ally, comrade.

coiffure *n.* hairdo, *do, cut, permanent, trim. SEE HAIR

coil *n.* ring, helix, circle, spiral, vortex, loop, convolution, corkscrew, curlicue, braid.

coil *v.* wind, spiral, twist, turn, loop, twirl, corkscrew, snake, twine, convolute, sinuate.

coin *n.* piece, specie, copper, change, money, legal tender, coinage, *pin money. SEE MONEY

coin *v.* devise, invent, make up, create, conceive, originate, think up, dream up, fabricate, compose, mint, neologize.

coincide *v.* agree, equal, synchronize, square, accord, dovetail, fit, correspond, harmonize, jibe, match, be synonymous, be concurrent. ANT. *disagree, differ.*

coincidence *n.* happenstance, chance, fluke, fortuity, accident, serendipity, synchronicity, *fickle finger of fate.

coincidental *a.* chance, accidental, fortuitous, fluky, serendipitous, lucky, casual, circumstantial. ANT. *deliberate, planned.*

coitus *n.* sexual intercourse, copulation, fornication, mating, consummation, congress, *nookie, heterosexual union, *roll in the hay. "Making the beast with two backs."— Shakespeare. SEE SEX

cold *n.* virus, *bug, cough, runny nose, *sniffles, fever, coryza, nasal congestion. "An ailment cured in two weeks with a doctor's care, and in fourteen days without it."—C.C. Furnas.

cold *a.* **1.** CHILLY frigid, wintry, icy, freezing, arctic, nippy, cool, raw, biting, brisk, bitter, numbing, *anesthetizing, below zero, frosty, piercing, stinging, algid, hyperboreal, gelid, drafty, Siberian, bone-chilling, *teeth-chattering cold. **2.** UNFRIENDLY OR ALOOF icy, distant, frosty, stony, apathetic, unsociable, unfeeling, remote, unapproachable, closed. **3.** COLD-BLOODED uncaring, unfeeling, cruel, mean, icy, cool, stony, insensitive, heartless, distant, soulless, brutal, callous, ruthless, merciless. ANT. *1. hot, sweltering. 2. warm, friendly, open. 3. sympathetic, humane, merciful.*

cold-blooded *a.* SEE COLD

cold feet *n. Sl.* fear, anxiety, second thoughts, reservations, timidity.

cold shoulder *n.* coldness, snub, brush-off, a frosting, dismisssal, disregard, aloofness.

cold sore *n.* blister, herpes, canker sore, ulceration.

cold war *n.* *war of words, hostilities, rivalry, one upsmanship, idle threats, tension, macho posturing, antagonism.

coldhearted *a.* SEE COLD

coliseum *n.* arena, stadium, ampitheater, bowl, theater.

collaborate *v.* work together, cooperate, team up, conspire, collude, join forces, coauthor.

collaborator *n.* contributor, partner, coworker, colleague, *partner in crime, coauthor, confederate, quisling.

collage *n.* composition, assemblage.

collapse *n.* **1.** CAVE-IN fall, cataclysm, toppling, breakdown, failure, foundering, buckling, crash, undoing, downfall, disintegration. **2.** FALLING ILL breakdown, fainting, succumbing, seizure, prostration, loss of consciousness.

collapse *v.* **1.** CAVE IN fall, crumple, crumble, topple, break, give way, give out, fail, founder, buckle, slump, fold up, *collapse like a house of cards. **2.** FALL ILL keel over, break down, succumb, wilt, be stricken, lose consciousness, slump over, swoon.

collar *v.* nab, seize, catch, capture, nail, apprehend, bring into custody. SEE ARREST

collate *v.* sort, order, group, arrange, juxtapose.

collateral *n.* security, insurance, warranty, surety, pledge, guarantee, bond.

collateral *a.* secondary, ancillary, subordinate, indirect, supporting, corroborating, parallel, incidental, supplementary. ANT. *primary, fundamental.*

colleague *n.* associate, co-worker, confederate, cohort, collaborator, partner, confrere, *partner in crime, compatriot, peer, teammate.

collect *v.* **1.** ACCUMULATE OR ASSEMBLE gather, harvest, reap, amass, hoard, save, round up, pile up, squirrel away, compile, congregate, flock, group, muster, convene, meet, cluster. **2.** OBTAIN acquire, solicit, raise, *pass the hat, get. **3.** PICK UP get, fetch, gather, take away. **4.** PULL ONESELF TOGETHER gather one's wits, calm down, *get it together, regain one's composure, relax.

collected *a.* composed, calm, cool, levelheaded, unruffled, unperturbed, self-possessed, poised, unflappable, placid, at ease, nonchalant. ANT. *agitated, nervous, flustered, perturbed, ill-at-ease.*

collection *n.* **1.** ACCUMULATION cumulation, mass, group, assortment, assembly, pile, gathering, stockpile, store, hoard, cluster, congregation, aggregation, compilation, anthology, hodgepodge. **2.** OFFERING tithe, offertory, contribution, alms.

collective *n.* cooperative, co-op, company.

collective *a.* combined, composite, aggregate, mutual, corporate, common, cumulative, compound, joint, unified. ANT. *individual, separate.*

college *n.* university, school, academy, institution, institute of higher learning, seminary, alma mater, *halls of ivy, vocational school, polytechnic, graduate school, campus. "[Where one] may learn the 'principles' of salesmanship from a Ph.D. who has never sold anything, or the 'principles' of marketing from a Ph.D. who has never marketed anything."—Abraham Flexner. "A place where pebbles are polished and diamonds are dimmed."—Robert Ingersoll.
WORD FIND
advanced degree: postgraduate degree, master's, doctorate

advanced studies after graduation: postgraduate work
agricultural college: cow college
brotherhood: fraternity
charge for instruction: tuition
course: major, minor, elective
dining hall: refectory
exams: midterms, finals
general knowledge studies: liberal arts
girl: coed
graduate: alumnus
graduates: alumni
graduate "with great praise" or honors: magna cum laude
graduate "with highest praise" or highest honors: summa cum laude
graduation ceremony: commencement
grounds: campus, quad, quadrangle
half year: semester
housing: dorm, dormitory
leave of absence, professor's: sabbatical
official: dean, regent, provost, registrar
permanence of position granted to professor: tenure
president: chancellor, prexy
relating to: collegiate
sisterhood: sorority
student: freshman, *frosh; sophomore; junior; senior
teacher: professor
treasurer: bursar
SEE DEGREE, SCHOOL, UNIVERSITY

collegiate *a.* collegial, academic, scholarly, learned, bookish, university.

collide *v.* **1.** CRASH INTO bump, meet head-on, smash, plow into, bang, hit, sideswipe, *t-bone. **2.** DISAGREE clash, conflict, oppose.

collision *n.* crash, *smashup, *fenderbender, impact, bump, accident, *crack-up, blow, jolt, pileup, wreck.

cologne *n.* perfume, fragrance, scent, toilet water.

COLLOQUIAL *a.* [kuh LOH kwee ul] designating informal or conversational speech, writing, etc. *A relaxed, colloquial form of writing is often best.* SYN. conversational, informal, everyday, *street, chatty, casual, familiar, vernacular, folksy, homey, simple, unaffected, unstudied. ANT. *formal, literary, pedantic.*

colloquy *n.* talk, conversation, dialogue, discussion, chat, discourse, council, conference.

COLLUSION *n.* [kuh LOO zhun] a conspiracy. *Fred worked in collusion with the drug cartel to smuggle narcotics.* SYN. conspiracy, secret agreement, intrigue, *dirty dealings, complicity, *cahoots, deceit, racket, scheme, fraud.

colony *n.* **1.** SETTLEMENT community, outpost, dependency, province, possession, territory. **2.** GROUP community, band, flock.

color *n.* **1.** HUE tint, shade, tinge, cast, tone, coloring, pigment, dye, paint, stain. **2.** COMPLEXION color, tone, bloom, blush, flush, ruddiness, rosiness, glow.

color *v.* **1.** PAINT dye, tint, tinge, stain, suffuse, cast, daub, wash, blazon, imbue. **2.** BLUSH redden, glow, flush, bloom, brighten, burn, flame, turn crimson.

colored *a.* distorted, influenced, biased, partial, exaggerated, jaundiced, prejudiced, misrepresented, affected. ANT. *unbiased, objective.*

colorful *a.* **1.** BRIGHTLY OR VARIOUSLY COLORED vivid, vibrant, multihued, chromatic, striking, showy, gaudy, pavonine, iridescent, rainbowlike, florid, loud, kaleidoscopic, screaming, variegated, graphic, eye-catching, picturesque, psychedelic. **2.** INTERESTING unusual, dynamic, eccentric, distinctive, unique, offbeat, glamorous, extravagant. ANT. *1. achromatic, pallid, lackluster. 2. dull, drab, nondescript, *ho-hum, *as distinctive as a plain brown wrapper, *as distinctive as a brick in the wall.*

colorless *a.* **1.** ACHROMATIC blanched, pale, pallid, lackluster, bleached, washed-out, neutral, faded, dull, gray, transparent. **2.** UNINTERESTING dull, drab, nondescript, *ho-hum, *as distinctive as a plain brown wrapper, lifeless, vapid, *as eye-catching as a brick in the wall. ANT. *1. chromatic, vivid, vibrant, pavonine. 2. colorful, distinctive, glamorous.*

colors *n.* flag, banner, standard, insignia, badge.

colossal *a.* huge, gigantic, gargantuan, massive, titanic, monstrous, towering, immense, monumental, Brobdingnagian, enormous, *humongus, awe-inspiring, mammoth, herculian, prodigious, staggering, mighty, commanding. ANT. *microscopic, tiny, pocket-sized, pint-sized, insignificant, Lilliputian.*

colossus *n.* giant, titan, monster, leviathan, behemoth, mammoth, mountain, Gargantua, Goliath, Cyclops, Hercules, Samson, Godzilla. ANT. *midget, dwarf, *shrimp, *pipsqueak.* SEE MONSTER, STATUE, WHALE

colt *n.* foal, yearling. SEE HORSE, ROOKIE

coltish *a.* frisky, frolicsome, playful, gamboling, spirited, romping, perky. ANT. *lethargic, slothful.*

column *n.* **1.** PILLAR support, pilaster, post, pier, upright, shaft, pylon.

WORD FIND
base: plinth, pedestal
classical orders: Ionic, Doric, Corinthian,
  Composite, Tuscan
eight columns, having: octastyle
five columns, having: pentastyle
four columns, having: tetrastyle
man-figure column: atlas
porch, columned: portico
series of: colonnade
six columns, having: hexastyle
ten columns, having: decastyle
top: capital
two columns, having: distyle
woman-figure column: caryatid
SEE ARCHITECTURE, BUILDING
2. LINE row, file, formation, string, procession, train.

coma *n.* unconsciousness, stupor, catalepsy, oblivion, deep sleep. SEE SLEEP

comatose *a.* unconscious, cataleptic, stuporous, insensate, *out of it, lifeless, unresponsive, inert, sluggish. ANT. *conscious, alert, cognizant.*

comb *v.* **1.** SEARCH seek, look over thoroughly, rake, scour, *beat the bushes, **2.** DRESS HAIR fix, arrange, brush, style, smooth, unsnarl.

combat *v.* fight, struggle, contend, battle, oppose, contest, war, clash, skirmish. ANT. *make peace, pacify, surrender, cooperate.*

combatant *n.* fighter, warrior, soldier, contender, battler, assailant, enemy, foe, antagonist. ANT. *peacemaker, dove.*

combative *a.* contentious, antagonistic, pugnacious, belligerent, aggressive, quarrelsome, militant, hawkish, hostile. ANT. *peaceful, passive, deferential.*

combination *n.* **1.** MIXTURE mix, amalgam, amalgamation, blending, aggregation, conglomeration, assemblage, joining, union, compound, composite, consolidation. **2.** ASSOCIATION alliance, union, affiliation, coalition, league, faction, federation, partnership, bloc.

combine *v.* **1.** MIX join, unite, amalgamate, blend, aggregate, conglomerate, assemble, compound, consolidate, merge, wed, mingle. ANT. *separate, divide.*

combustible *a.* flammable, inflammable, ignitable, burnable, explosive, incendiary. ANT. *safe, calming, diffusing.*

combustion *n.* burning, ignition, flame, kindling, incineration, blazing, oxidation.

come *v.* **1.** APPROACH near, draw near, close in, move toward, advance. **2.** SHOW UP show,

appear, make an appearance, arrive, pop in, roll in, turn up, *blow in, drop in, materialize, check in. **3.** TAKE PLACE occur, arrive, happen, fall, arise, ensue, transpire, come to pass. ANT. *1. go, leave, depart.*

comeback *n.* **1.** REVIVAL resurgence, rebirth, return, recovery, rally. **2.** SNAPPY REPLY retort, rejoinder, riposte, repartee, witticism, esprit de l'escalier, answer.

comedian *n.* comic, comedienne, joker, clown, humorist, funnyman, wit, entertainer, buffoon, jester, *zany, cutup, *card, *top banana. ANT. *straight man.*

comedy *n.* **1.** FARCE burlesque, vaudeville, slapstick, parody, satire, lampoon, travesty, comedy of errors, comedy of manners, sendup, takeoff, sitcom, *schtick, *bit, skit, *stand-up. **2.** HUMOR joking, jesting, silliness, hilarity, gags, buffoonery, cutting up, parody, satire, drollery, *poking fun, slapstick, physical comedy, black comedy, *one-liners. "A funny way of being serious."— Peter Ustinov. "The very last alternative to despair."—Franklin Marcus. ANT. *1. tragedy. 2. solemnity, seriousness, gloom.*

comely *a.* attractive, beautiful, fair, lovely, pretty, handsome, pleasing, *nice, good-looking, cute, bonny, winsome, fine. ANT. *ugly, repulsive, plain, homely.*

come-on *n.* *Sl.* inducement, enticement. SEE LURE

comet *n.* celestial body, *iceball, orbital debris, *cosmic wanderer, *stellar nomad, *ethereal snowball.

WORD FIND
icy center: nucleus
mistaken for a: meteor, fireball
nucleus and coma: head
orbital point farthest from sun: aphelion
orbital point nearest to sun: perihelion
surrounding gas and particles, envelope:
  coma
trailing particles: tail
vast repository of: Oort Cloud
SEE ASTRONOMY, SPACE

come upon *vi.* meet, encounter, chance, come across, bump into.

comeuppance *n.* punishment, retribution, just deserts, discipline.

come up with *vi.* invent, create, think up, originate, produce, propose, suggest, put forth.

comfort *n.* **1.** WELL-BEING ease, peace, tranquility, happiness, coziness, creature comforts, satisfaction, luxury, contentment. "That stealthy thing that enters the house as a guest, and then becomes a host, and then a master."—Kahlil Gibran. **2.** SOLACE consolation, relief, reassurance, sympathy, commiseration, cheer, support, succor, lift, alleviation, help. ANT. *1. discomfort, agony, pain. 2. aggravation.*

comfort *v.* console, soothe, reassure, unburden, support, uphold, alleviate, hearten, bolster, cheer, mitigate, solace, relieve, salve, gladden, assuage. ANT. *aggravate, trouble, burden.*

comfortable *a.* **1.** FEELING GOOD at ease, at peace, tranquil, cozy, satisfied, content, carefree, untroubled, serene, *in a bed of roses, *in clover, satisfactory, agreeable, relaxed, pleasant. **2.** WELL-OFF FINANCIALLY prosperous, well-to-do, wealthy, sufficient, ample. ANT. *1. uncomfortable, miserable, troubled. 2. broke, poor, destitute, squalid.*

comforter *n.* quilt, bedcover.

comic *n.* SEE COMEDIAN

comical *a.* funny, hilarious, laughable, humorous, whimsical, jocular, zany, amusing, slapstick, farcical, loony, droll, rich, side-splitting, wacky, witty, ludicrous. ANT. *tragic, solemn, serious, grave.*

coming *n.* advent, arrival, emergence, nearing, approach, forthcoming.

coming *a.* approaching, advancing, forthcoming, nearing, impending, imminent, next, at hand, anticipated, on the horizon, in the offing. ANT. *distant, retreating, far-off.*

command *n.* **1.** ORDER imperative, charge, dictate, directive, prescription, ultimatum, fiat, injunction, behest, word. **2.** CONTROL rule, power, authority, leadership, government, dominion, influence, supremacy, say-so, direction, upper hand. SEE LAW

command *v.* **1.** ORDER demand, charge, dictate, direct, make, prescribe, decree, require, bid, enjoin, summon, *give the word, exact, compel, warrant, give an ultimatum. **2.** CONTROL rule, govern, oversee, direct, supervise, lead, direct, dominate, dictate, run, head, master, reign.

commandeer *v.* appropriate, expropriate, confiscate, usurp, hijack, seize, take.

commander *n.* leader, captain, chief, boss, head, *head honcho, commanding officer, *CO, *brass, skipper, superior, *biggest toad in the puddle, *Sir, *Ma'am. ANT. *subordinate, underling, follower, toady, *kiss-up.*

commanding *a.* **1.** AUTHORITATIVE powerful, in charge, dictatorial, dominating, ruling, controlling, supervisory, governing, imposing, impressive, imperious. **2.** OVERLOOKING

wide, expansive, dominating, prominent, far-reaching, towering.

commandment *n.* edict, law. SEE COMMAND

commemorate *v.* honor, memorialize, remember, observe, salute, pay tribute, immortalize, solemnize, celebrate. ANT. *dishonor, neglect, ignore.*

commence *v.* begin, start, initiate, launch, open. ANT. *end, terminate.*

commencement *n.* **1.** BEGINNING start, outset, onset, opening, genesis, dawn, inauguration. **2.** GRADUATION CEREMONIES graduation. ANT. *1. ending, termination.*
WORD FIND
address: valedictory
square, flat hat: mortarboard
SEE GRADUATION

commend *v.* **1.** RECOMMEND extol, laud, praise, acclaim, endorse, acclaim, applaud, compliment. **2.** ENTRUST turn over, assign, relegate, consign, confer, confide, transfer. ANT. *1. disparage, smear, criticize.*

commendable *a.* praiseworthy, laudable, meritorious, admirable, exemplary, noble, estimable, excellent. ANT. *contemptible, despicable, rotten.*

commendation *n.* recommendation, praise, acclaim, approval, kudos, rave, *pat on the back, *good word, plaudit, *points, tribute, award, *thumbs up. ANT. *criticism, disparagement, demotion.*

COMMENSURATE *a.* [kuh MEN sur it] equal; proportionate. *The pay scale is commensurate with experience.* SYN. equal, proportionate, coextensive, corresponding, parallel, coinciding, to scale, appropriate, relative, in accord, fitting, compatible. ANT. *disproportionate, divergent, inconsistent.*

comment *n.* remark, commentary, observation, statement, utterance, mention, *crack, criticism, word, opinion.

comment *v.* remark, observe, state, utter, mention, *make a crack, criticize, critique, say a word or two, opine, touch on, make note, expound, mention, point out.

commentary *n.* comment, analysis, remark, observation, exposition, criticism, critique, interpretation, review, opinion.

commentator *n.* reporter, analyst, reviewer, critic, pundit, interpreter, observer, editorialist.

commerce *n.* business, trade, marketing, exchange, buying and selling, merchandising, *wheeling and dealing, industry, mercantilism, traffic. "The great civilizer."—Robert Ingersoll. SEE BUSINESS

commercial n. advertisement, ad. SEE ADVERTISEMENT, ADVERTISING

commercial a. **1.** MERCANTILE business, trade, marketing, exchanging, profit-making, merchandising, industrial, entrepreneurial, retail, wholesale. **2.** MARKETABLE salable, in demand, *hot.

commingle v. mingle, blend. SEE MIX

COMMISERATE v. [kuh MIZ uh RATE] to pity or feel sorry for. *Twins turning forty commiserate together.* SYN. pity, feel sorry for, sympathize, condole, share one's sorrow, grieve with, console, ache for, bleed for, comfort.

commission n. **1.** AUTHORIZATION relegation, entrusting, power, authority, charge, trust, vesting. **2.** BOARD committee, delegation, council, agency. **3.** COMPENSATION fee, share, cut, remuneration, royalty, payment, allowance, stipend.

commission v. appoint, assign, delegate, authorize, order, enlist, consign, charge, engage, invest, hire, contract for.

commit v. **1.** PERPETRATE do, effect, execute, perform, *pull off, enact, transact, carry out. **2.** ENTRUST charge, vest, appoint, delegate, relegate, engage, consign. **3.** INCARCERATE imprison, place in custody, confine, institutionalize, hospitalize. **4.** PLEDGE devote, obligate, bind, swear, give one's word, dedicate, engage.

commitment n. pledge, promise, dedication, vow, promise, undertaking, charge, obligation, responsibility, liability.

committee n. board, council, panel, commission, task force, cabinet, steering committee, ad hoc committee. "A thing which takes a week to do what one good man can do in an hour."—Elbert Hubbard. "An arrangement enabling one to share the blame with others."—Franklin P. Jones.

commode n. potty, *john. SEE TOILET

commodious a. spacious, roomy, capacious, large, ample, vast, extensive. ANT. *cramped, tight, small.*

commodity n. product, article, goods, item, thing, merchandise, property, object, ware.

common a. **1.** ORDINARY commonplace, average, everyday, usual, typical, standard, routine, regular, general, stock, *run-of-the-mill, universal, familiar, prevailing, widespread. **2.** COMMUNITY communal, collective, shared, public, mutual. **3.** BASIC simple, rudimentary. **4.** LOW sleazy, base, vile, mean, cheap, inferior, coarse, second-rate, vulgar.

ANT. *1. extraordinary, uncommon, rare. 2. private, individual. 3. advanced, complex. 4. superior, refined, high-class.*

commonly adv. usually, as a rule, generally, regularly, routinely, normally, ordinarily, on average, habitually. ANT. *rarely, seldom, *once in a blue moon.*

commonplace a. SEE COMMON

common sense n. good sense, savvy, sound judgment, native intelligence, *horse sense, prudence, acumen, levelheadedness, instinct, wisdom, experience. "The shortest line between two points."—Ralph Waldo Emerson "Genius dressed in its working clothes."—Ralph Waldo Emerson. ANT. *stupidity, ignorance, rashness.*

commotion n. turmoil, hubbub, stir, uproar, agitation, to-do, bustle, flurry, excitement, hurly-burly, turbulence, ruckus, disquiet, rumpus, chaos. ANT. *peace, tranquility, serenity, stillness.*

communal a. common, shared, mutual, community, collective, joint, public, shared, cooperative. ANT. *private, individual.*

commune n. cooperative, collective, *kibbutz, community.

commune v. **1.** TALK converse, confide, confer with, discuss, communicate, speak intimately with. **2.** PONDER think, meditate, reflect, contemplate, muse.

communicable a. contagious, infectious, catching, transmittable, spreadable. ANT. *nontransmittable, incommunicable.*

communicate v. convey, transmit, disclose, impart, pass on, interface, reveal, touch base, tell, report, announce, proclaim, converse, express, correspond, inform, broadcast, enlighten, inform, relate.

communication n. **1.** CONVEYANCE correspondence, contact, interchange, disclosure, exchange, transmission, intercourse, expression, interface, interplay, interaction. **2.** CORRESPONDENCE communique, report, dispatch, news, message, bulletin.

communicative a. talkative, open, forthright, expressive, loquacious, expansive, unreserved, candid, *gabby, voluble. ANT. *closed, taciturn, reserved.*

communion n. **1.** INTIMACY sharing, rapport, exchange, give and take, disclosure, closeness, communication, harmony, fellowship, union, oneness. **2.** SACRAMENT Holy Communion, Mass, Eucharist, breaking of bread. ANT. *1. alienation, distance.*

communiqué *n.* report, bulletin, announcement, communication, message, dispatch.

communism *n.* collectivism, Bolshevism, Marxism, Leninism, socialism. "What is thine is mine, and all of mine is thine."—Plautus. "Abolition of private property."—Communist Manifesto. ANT. *capitalism.* SEE GOVERNMENT, POLITICS

community *n.* neighborhood, borough, suburb, bedroom community, hamlet, district, public, people, residents, citizenry, population, group.

commute *v.* **1.** CHARGE substitute, alter, modify, reverse, adjust, mitigate, soften. **2.** TRAVEL shuttle, drive, carpool, bus.

compact *n.* agreement, contract, treaty, bond, bargain, deal, understanding, arrangement, pact, covenant.

compact *v.* pack, condense, compress, concentrate, consolidate, squeeze together, contract, cram. ANT. *loosen, expand, blow up.*

compact *a.* **1.** DENSE solid, compressed, pressed, thick, close, firm, tight-knit, impermeable. **2.** SMALL portable, tiny, handy. **3.** SHORT concise, brief, succinct, pithy, condensed, abridged. ANT. *1. loose. 2. large, ponderous. 3. elongated, prolonged, expanded.*

companion *n.* friend, partner, sidekick, comrade, confederate, colleague, fellow, alter ego, chum, buddy, associate, escort, mate, counterpart, double. SEE FRIEND

companionable *a.* friendly, warm, easy-going, congenial, sociable, good-natured, *buddy-buddy, outgoing, gregarious, agreeable, clubby, jolly. ANT. *nasty, aloof, cold, antagonistic, unfriendly.*

company *n.* **1.** COMPANIONSHIP friendship, fellowship, *chumminess, society, presence. **2.** VISITOR guest, caller, friends over. **3.** GROUP band, party, troupe, throng, gathering, assembly, entourage. **4.** FIRM corporation, business, concern, establishment, partnership, enterprise, outfit.

comparable *a.* similar, alike, akin, near, corresponding, approaching, analogous, cognate, parallel, close, equal, on a par with. ANT. *dissimilar, different, *like apples and oranges.*

compare *v.* **1.** EXAMINE FOR DIFFERENCES OR SIMILARITIES contrast, weigh, inspect, size up, correlate, match, relate, stack up against, scrutinize, differentiate. **2.** RESEMBLE correspond, take after, approximate, equal, *hold a candle to. **3.** LIKEN equate, identify with, match, tie.

comparison *n.* **1.** EXAMINATION OF DIFFERENCES OR SIMILARITIES contrasting, inspection, sizing up, correlation, differentiation, matching, weighing, measurement, scrutiny, study. **2.** RESEMBLANCE correspondence, approximation, relation, similarity, likeness, connection, affinity. **3.** LIKENING equating, identification with, matching, parallel, analogy.

compartment *n.* cell, unit, cubicle, room, capsule, bay, stall, booth, nook, cubbyhole, pigeonhole, niche, receptacle, slot, section, division, category.

compassion *n.* sympathy, empathy, feeling, heart, pity, mercy, love, charity, ruth, grace, commiseration, concern, kindness. ANT. *indifference, cold-bloodedness, disregard.*

compassionate *a.* sympathetic, feeling, kindhearted, merciful, loving, charitable, concerned, magnanimous, humane, tender, soft, clement. ANT. *indifferent, cold-blooded, unfeeling.*

compatible *a.* congruous, harmonious, sympathetic, agreeable, simpatico, congenial, accordant, *in sync with, *on the same wavelength, in rapport, consistent. ANT. *incompatible, incongruous.*

COMPEL *v.* [kum PEL] to force. *Conscience compels one to file a tax return honestly.* SYN. force, make, drive, oblige, insist, coerce, constrain, press, require, command, necessitate, bully.

COMPENDIUM *n.* [kum PEN dee um] a summary. *We were provided with a compendium of the most salient points.* SYN. summary, abstract, abridgement, synopsis, brief, digest, precis, syllabus, condensation.

compensate *v.* **1.** REMUNERATE reimburse, recompense, pay, repay, make restitution, refund, *make good. **2.** OFFSET neutralize, counterbalance, counteract, countervail, balance, equalize, cancel out.

compensation *n.* remuneration, reimbursement, recompense, pay, repayment, restitution, refund, allowance, recoupment, stipend, *take, consideration, benefit, settlement, reward, wages, salary.

compete *v.* vie, contend, contest, go up against, rival, take on, combat, tussle, spar, *lock horns, face off, *match wits, grapple, battle, *go head to head.

competence *n.* adequacy, ability, capability, proficiency, skill, *know-how, *the right stuff, *what it takes, expertise, mastery, adroitness, finesse, fitness. ANT. *incompetence, inadequacy, inability.*

competent *a.* adequate, able, capable, proficient, skillful, expert, masterly, adroit, fit, qualified, sufficient, equal, *on the ball, sharp, *up to snuff. ANT. *incompetent, inadequate, unable, lacking.*

competition *n.* **1.** CONTEST match, bout, rivalry, contention, championship, clash, encounter, engagement, meet, tournament, trial, one-on-one, emulation, struggle, *dog-eat-dog, battle, conflict, dogfight, tug-of-war, battle royal, free-for-all, fight to the death, *one-upmanship, fight for supremacy, *jockeying for position. **2.** OPPOSITION rival, competitor, challenger, opponent, contender, adversary.

competitive *a.* rivaling, aggressive, striving, *high-octane, ambitious, combative, feisty, *cutthroat, *dog-eat-dog, *go-getting, *tough as nails, grueling, Olympian, adversarial.

competitor *n.* contender, rival, opposition, adversary, challenger, competition, opponent, contestant.

compilation *n.* **1.** COLLECTION assembly, assemblage, accumulation, assortment, anthology. **2.** COMPILING gathering, collecting, assembling, accumulating, consolidating.

compile *v.* gather, accumulate, assemble, amass, consolidate, congregate, group, organize, anthologize, order.

COMPLACENT *a.* [kum PLAY sunt] to be satisfied with oneself to the point of smugness. *The former Olympian had grown so complacent that he neglected to practice.* SYN. satisfied, self-satisfied, smug, contented, at ease, pleased with oneself, self-assured, unconcerned, untroubled, *full of oneself, secure. ANT. *insecure, troubled, uneasy, unsatisfied.*

complain *v.* gripe, grumble, *bitch, protest, crab, *kick, *piss and moan, *raise a fuss, gripe, *beef, *bellyache, nag, carp, find fault, pick, grouse, whine, *squawk. ANT. *praise, compliment, laud.*

complaint *n.* **1.** GRIEVANCE *beef, criticism, gripe, protest, stink, cavil, grumble, problem, grouse, charge, objection. **2.** MALADY illness, disorder, ailment, affliction, disease, pain.

complaisant *a.* agreeable, obliging, pleasing, solicitous, gracious, accommodating, deferential, conciliatory, compliant. ANT. *disagreeable, contrary, difficult.*

complement *n.* **1.** *ROUNDING-OFF crown, finishing touch, consummation, completion, clincher, balance, supplement, rest, remainder. **2.** TOTAL aggregate, the entirety, sum, *the works, *the whole shooting match.

complement *v.* round out, complete, crown, consummate, supplement, clinch, perfect.

complementary *a.* completing, crowning, finishing, filling, consummating, perfecting, fulfilling, corresponding, reciprocal, parallel. ANT. *contradictory.*

complete *v.* finish, conclude, fulfill, end, realize, *wrap up, accomplish, actualize, close, *wind up, *call it a day, finalize, crown, *put to bed. ANT. *start, begin, break ground.*

complete *a.* **1.** WHOLE entire, full, total, all, intact, plenary, uncut, unabridged, undivided, integral. **2.** THOROUGH absolute, total, perfect, dyed-in-the-wool, utter, outright, unqualified, full-fledged, unmitigated. **3.** FINISHED done, concluded, fulfilled, ended, realized, *wrapped up, *polished off, accomplished.

completion *n.* finish, conclusion, fulfillment, end, realization, *wrapping up, accomplishment, closing, *winding up, finalization, crowning, consummation. ANT. *start, beginning.*

complex *a.* complicated, intricate, difficult, knotty, convoluted, tangled, unfathomable, inscrutable, manifold, perplexing, Gordian, labyrinthine, undecipherable, cryptic, abstruse, involved. ANT. *simple, easy, clear.*

complexion *n.* **1.** SKIN COLORING tone, cast, hue, tinge, tint, pigmentation.

WORD FIND

aged: leathery, lined like an old boot, parchmentlike, like scalded milk, liver-spotted, age-spotted, cadaverous, gaunt, craggy, furrowed, mottled, withered, pendulous, rosaceous, moled, weatherbeaten, raw-boned

brown/black: ebony, pitch, brown as the Congo/Mississippi/Rio Grande, honey, golden brown, leathery, lentil, mahogany, dark as a mill pond, molasses, russet, mottled, nutbrown, obsidian, olive, raven, raisin, tawny, tarnished penny, weathered acorn, tanned

healthy: peaches and cream, apple-cheeked, scrubbed, rosy, glowing, ruddy, pink, blushing

pink/red: scarlet, crimson, burned, rosy, lobster

sickly: cadaverous, leaden, ashen, ghastly, pale, pallid, wan, blanched, pasty,

chalky, jaundiced, sallow, flushed, clammy
white: alabaster, lily-white, ivory, milky, creamy, beige, fair
2. CHARACTER aspect, appearance, quality, look, bearing, cast.

complexity n. complication, intricacy, involvement, entanglement, knot, Gordian knot, perplexity, maze, labyrinth, convolution. ANT. *simplicity, clarity.*

compliance n. yielding, assent, conforming, obedience, observation, acquiescence, deference, complaisance. ANT. *noncompliance, disobedience.*

complicate v. entangle, *mess up, convolute, confuse, make complex, snarl, bedevil, *add fuel to the fire, confound, involve, embrangle. ANT. *simplify, clarify.*

complicated a. complex, intricate, involved, entangled, knotty, difficult, convoluted, perplexing, elaborate, manifold, labyrinthine, abstruse, problematic, recondite, deep, incomprehensible. ANT. *simple, easy, straightforward.*

complication n. problem, difficulty, complexity, knot, hitch, snag, entanglement, obstacle, stumbling block, *fly in the ointment.

COMPLICITY n. [kum PLIS i tee] participation as an accomplice in a wrongdoing. *There was apparent complicity between the unhampered drug runners and town officials.* SYN. conspiracy, collusion, collaboration, partnership, confederacy, abetment, machination, intrigue, *backdoor arrangement.

compliment n. praise, tribute, *good word, *pat on the back, commendation, flattery, acclaim, kudos, *posy, homage, blandishment. ANT. *insult, disparagement.*

compliment v. praise, pay tribute to, *pat on the back, commend, flatter, puff up, *give a posy, *take one's hat off to, cheer, laud, salute, *stroke, *slather, *kiss up. SEE FLATTER

complimentary a. **1.** FLATTERING laudatory, commendatory, congratulatory, favorable, approving, cajoling, *apple polishing. **2.** FREE gratis, on the house, gratuitous. ANT. *1. insulting, critical, disparaging.*

comply v. yield, assent, conform, obey, observe, acquiesce, defer, respect, abide by, adhere, follow. ANT. *disobey, disregard.*

component n. part, element, ingredient, constituent, fundamental, unit, factor.

component a. constituent, fundamental, basic, essential, composing, integral. ANT. *unnecessary, superfluous.*

comport v. behave, conduct, act, carry, bear, acquit, deport.

compose v. **1.** CONSTITUTE make up, comprise, form, be part of. **2.** CREATE write, invent, author, formulate, devise, fashion, make, produce. **3.** CALM tranquilize, collect, simmer down, cool down, *chill, *get it together, contain, allay. ANT. *3. *lose it, break down.*

composed a. tranquil, calm, collected, cool, *together, levelheaded, nonchalant, self-possessed, unruffled, unperturbed, serene. ANT. *nervous, distraught, catatonic, tense.*

composite n. combination, mixture, consolidation, blend, amalgam, compound, synthesis, fusion.

composite a. combined, consolidated, mingled, blended, melded. ANT. *separated, segregated.*

composition n. **1.** CREATION synthesis, invention, fabrication, formulation, devising, making. **2.** WRITING opus, essay, paper, work, creation, piece, draft, exposition, dissertation, thesis, arrangement. **3.** STRUCTURE arrangement, organization, formulation, constitution, form, makeup, content, fabric.

compost n. organic matter, humus, decayed matter, fertilizer.

composure n. tranquility, calm, cool, self-possession, serenity, equanimity, poise, *head, aplomb, presence of mind, equilibrium. ANT. *nervousness, anxiety, panic.*

compound n. composite, blend, mixture, combination, amalgam, consolidation, concoction, synthesis.

compound v. combine, consolidate, blend, mix, amalgamate, concoct, synthesize, fuse.

compound a. combined, composite, complex, manifold, synthesized, conglomerate, multiform. ANT. *simple, pure, elemental.*

comprehend v. understand, get, grasp, realize, see, fathom, apprehend, catch, recognize, appreciate, *get the picture, discern.

comprehension n. understanding, grasp, realization, apprehension, recognition, perception, cognizance, discernment.

comprehensive a. all-inclusive, extensive, exhaustive, thorough, complete, encyclopedic, sweeping, *across the board, in depth, umbrella. ANT. *limited, narrow, exclusive.*

compress v. compact, pack, condense, press, contract, constrict, squeeze, shrink, wring, squash, shorten, reduce. ANT. *expand, stretch, enlarge.*

comprise v. include, contain, consist of, make

up, form, compose, constitute, incorporate, embody.

compromise *n*. concession, *give-and-take, agreement, conciliation, deal, *happy medium, trade-off, *middle ground, balance, accommodation, golden mean. "Simply changing the question to fit the answer."—Merrit Malloy.

compromise *v*. **1.** GIVE AND TAKE strike a deal, trade off, bargain, find the middle ground, strike a balance, accommodate, find a happy medium, make concessions, agree, *give your shirt but keep your pants, *split the difference. **2.** ENDANGER jeopardize, imperil, expose, implicate, discredit.

COMPULSION *n*. [kum PUL shun] a strong drive or force, a compelling impulse. *He had a strange compulsion to giggle at the funeral.* SYN. drive, force, pressure, constraint, coercion, need, urge, urgency, obsession, desire, impulse.

compulsive *a*. compelling, obsessive, uncontrollable, irresistible, urgent, crazed.

COMPULSORY *a*. [kum PUL suh ree] mandatory, required. *The tests are compulsory; no one can skip them.* SYN. mandatory, required, obligatory, requisite, imperative, forced, nonelective. ANT. *voluntary, elective, optional.*

COMPUNCTION *n*. [kum PUNK shun] the uncomfortable feeling caused by guilt, conscience. *He felt no compunction over his crimes; he had no conscience.* SYN. guilt, conscience, qualm, uneasiness, misgiving, regret, self-reproach, shame, pangs of guilt, contrition, remorse, penitence, twinge.

computation *n*. calculation, reckoning, estimation, figuring, tallying, account.

compute *v*. calculate, reckon, figure, tally, account, count, add, subtract, sum, determine, work out, measure, total.

computer *n*. calculator, data processor, microprocessor, PC, laptop, *number cruncher, adding machine, *micro, supercomputer, mainframe, workstation, PDA, notebook, Apple™, Macintosh™, *Mac, IBM™, Compaq™.

WORD FIND

AI: artificial intelligence
auxiliary device: peripheral
aversion: cyberphobia
blinking symbol showing where next character will appear on screen: cursor
bps: bits per second
byte: eight bits of memory space

calculating, rows and columns program: spreadsheet
California manufacturing mecca: Silicon Valley
CD, write data or music on to: burn
CD-Rom tray: caddy
chip: microprocessor, integrated circuit
Clarke's mad computer in 2001, Arthur C.: Hal
clean up hard drive: defrag (defragmentation)
clicker, hand: mouse
communication between, means of: protocol
compaction, data: compression
copies of files to safeguard from accidental loss, make multiple: back up
CPU: Central Processing Unit
device enabling communication with other computers over phone lines: modem (MOdulator, DEModulator)
device enabling computer to read, write info on disks: disk drive
devices, physical: hardware
disrupting prank or criminal program that infects other computers: virus, worm
document-creating programs: word processor; desktop publishing
drafting and blueprint creation system: CAD (Computer Aided Design)
easy to use: user-friendly
engineering process of deciphering how something works by taking it apart: reverse engineering
enthusiast: hacker, *chiphead, *geek
EPROM: erasable memory chip
execute program: run
failure and freeze-up: crashed; down
flaw in software or hardware: bug
giant computer serving multiple users: mainframe
GIGO: garbage in, garbage out
handheld computer, battery-powered: PDA (Personal Digital Assistant), Palm Pilot™, organizer
injury from repetitive keyboard work: carpal tunnel syndrome
instructions: program
Internet, connected to the: online
keyboard and monitor portion: terminal
language/program: AGOL, BASIC, C, COBOL, FORTRAN, JAVA, PASCAL, PROLOG
linkage of several computers: network
logic that recognizes partial truths, computer: fuzzy logic

mail sent from one computer user to another: e-mail

main circuit board: motherboard

MP3 format, digitize CDs to: rip

MS-DOS: Microsoft Disk Operating System

multiple things at once, doing: multitasking

network, company: intranet

network, international: the Internet, World Wide Web

operating systems: Linux; Windows; Macintosh, MS-Dos, Unix

options to choose on screen: menu

paper printout: hard copy

paper propelling device: tractor feed

plugged in, where on the computer devices are: port

portable computer, small: laptop, notebook, PDA (Personal Digital Assistant), organizer

printout, long paper: *wallpaper

programs: software

RAM, memory chip group or: random access memory

read-only memory chip: ROM

restart computer: reboot

science fiction involving computer culture: cyberpunk

screen, TV-like: monitor

screen imagery designed to protect monitor from permanently burned-in images, moving: screen saver

secret opening designed into program to allow access at later date: trap door

software designed to boost performance of an application: plug-in

software shared free by all: freeware

software supplied free with one's computer: bundled software

software not ready for general sale, test: beta test software

speech recognition technology: voice recognition, speech recognition

start up computer: boot up

stick-like controller used with games in place of mouse: joystick

storage area, data: memory, cache, hard disk

storage area, temporary data: clipboard

storage medium, data: disk, diskette, floppy disk, cartridge, CD-ROM, Zip disk

superimposed screen within a screen: window

transfer data from your computer to another's: upload

transfer data from another computer to yours: download

transfer data to memory: store

virus protection program: anti-virus; vaccine; antidote; *DDT

virus type: strain

SEE INTERNET, ONLINE

comrade *n.* friend, companion, partner, pal, buddy, associate, sidekick, confederate, chum, colleague, co-worker, confrere. ANT. *stranger, enemy.*

con *v. Sl.* *rip off, cheat, swindle, defraud, trick, deceive, bamboozle.

conceal *v.* hide, cover, secrete, cloak, obscure, disguise, stash, lie low, camouflage, shield. ANT. *display, show, spotlight.*

concealment *n.* covering, hiding, cover-up, disguising, shielding, camouflaging, front, secretion, hiding place, hideaway, blind, shield, cover, refuge.

concede *v.* admit, grant, yield, acknowledge, acquiesce, avow, confess, yield, *cave in, fold, come around, give up. ANT. *fight, deny, reject, refute.*

CONCEIT *a.* [kun SEET] an overblown sense of one's positive attributes, egotism. *His swaggering conceit was sickening.* SYN. egotism, pride, vanity, bigheadedness, arrogance, vainglory, self-love, immodesty, narcissism, swagger, self-worship, self-importance. ANT. *modesty, self-effacement, humility.* "God's gift to little men."—Bruce Barton. "The quicksand of success." —Arnold Glasow.

conceited *a.* egotistical, proud, vain, bigheaded, arrogant, vainglorious, *full of oneself, *in love with oneself, puffed up, immodest, narcissistic, swaggering, strutting, self-worshipping, self-important. ANT. *modest, self-effacing, humble.*

conceivable *a.* imaginable, possible, thinkable, comprehensible, credible, believable. ANT. *inconceivable, impossible.*

conceive *v.* **1.** FORM develop, create, think up, invent, concoct, dream up, devise, originate, fabricate, hatch, *cook up, imagine. **2.** UNDERSTAND comprehend, apprehend, see, imagine, grasp, realize, follow.

concentrate *v.* **1.** THINK center, focus, *rack one's brains, study, fix one's attention toward, consider, absorb oneself in, engross oneself in, ponder, scrutinze, *zero in on. **2.** COLLECT, GATHER assemble, amass, intensify, focus, converge, consolidate, congregate, center, cluster. ANT. *2. spread out, scatter.*

concentration *n.* **1.** THINKING centering, focus, study, fixation, consideration, absorption, engrossment, pondering, scrutiny, attention, single-mindedness. **2.** COLLECTION, GATHERING assemblage, mass, intensification, focus, converging, consolidation, congregation, centralization, cluster, agglomerate. ANT. *1. diversion, absentmindedness, mind-wandering. 2. spread, scattering, dispersal.*

concept *n.* idea, thought, notion, conceptualization, *brainchild, conviction, view, image, impression, theory, hypothesis.

conception *n.* **1.** BEGINNING origination, birth, genesis, inception, start, formation, germination, dawn. **2.** IDEA thought, notion, conceptualization, conviction, view, image, impression, theory, hypothesis.

concern *n.* **1.** AFFAIR care, business, matter, interest, department, job, worry, responsibility. **2.** WORRY trouble, anxiety, unease, disquiet, apprehension, distress. **3.** BUSINESS ESTABLISHMENT company, firm, outfit, house.

concern *v.* **1.** BEAR ON deal with, regard, involve, pertain to, touch, relate to, affect, interest. **2.** WORRY trouble, make anxious, put ill-at-ease, disquiet, distress, disturb, bother, pain.

concerned *a.* **1.** INVOLVED WITH interested, active, caring, attentive, solicitous, connected, mixed up in. **2.** WORRIED anxious, troubled, ill-at-ease, disquieted, distressed, disturbed, bothered, pained, uneasy. ANT. *1. disinterested, detached, removed. 2. indifferent, nonchalant, untroubled.*

concerning *prep.* regarding, about, with reference to.

concert *n.* **1.** AGREEMENT harmony, concord, accord, union, unison, league, cooperation, collaboration. **2.** SHOW recital, *jam, gig, performance, symphony, philharmonic. ANT. *1. disunity, disagreement, discord.*

concerted *a.* united, joined, joint, cooperative, collaborative, interactive, combined, mutual. ANT. *individual.*

concession *n.* yielding, granting, giving-in, conceding, capitulation, compromise, assent, acknowledgement, trade-off, allowance, permit, right.

CONCILIATORY *a.* [kun SIL ee uh tor ee] willing to make peace, placatory. *The warring gangs were largely conciliatory after the riots.* SYN. placatory, placative, appeasing, pacific, peacemaking, reconciling, mollifying, yielding, amicable, accommodating, deferential. ANT. *bellicose, aggressive, belligerent.*

CONCISE *a.* [kun SISE] brief and to the point.

A concise letter to the editor is always best. SYN. brief, to the point, succinct, short, pithy, pointed, terse, compact, summary, *boiled down, *in a nutshell, crisp, laconic. ANT. *long-winded, wordy, verbose, rambling.*

conclave *n.* secret meeting, council, synod, meeting, session, congress, assembly, *pow-wow.

conclude *v.* **1.** END close, finish, terminate, complete, wind up, *wrap up, stop, consummate, *knock off, *call it a day, break off. **2.** INFER deduce, reason, decide, assume, surmise, presume, suppose, reckon, figure. **3.** SETTLE resolve, come to terms, work out, decide. ANT. *1. start, open, commence.*

conclusion *n.* **1.** ENDING closing, finish, termination, completion, winding up, *wrap up, stopping, consummation, finale, denouement. **2.** INFERENCE deduction, reckoning, supposition, figuring, presumption, assumption, judgment. **3.** SETTLEMENT resolution, coming to terms, agreement, understanding. ANT. *1. start, opening, commencement.*

conclusive *a.* decisive, final, settled, determining, convincing, definitive, incontestable, clinching, unmistakable, undeniable, absolute, resolving, irrefutable, *litmus test. ANT. *inconclusive, *iffy, questionable, uncertain.*

concoct *v.* compound, invent, devise, create, *whip up, formulate, hatch, fabricate, *slap together, prepare, think up, dream up.

concoction *n.* compound, mixture, invention, creation, formulation, fabrication, brew, preparation, contrivance, medley, synthesis.

concomitant *a.* attendant, accompanying, associative, accessory, supplementary, auxiliary.

CONCORD *n.* [KON kawrd] harmony, peaceful relations. *The former enemies have now lived in concord for thirty years.* SYN. harmony, peace, agreement, accord, friendship, unity, goodwill, understanding, rapport. ANT. *discord, disagreement, conflict.*

concourse *n.* **1.** CONGREGATION throng, confluence, convergence, mob, gathering, flock, assemblage, multitude, crush. **2.** PASSAGE mall, walkway, promenade, boulevard, esplanade, path.

concrete *a.* **1.** REAL actual, material, definite, solid, substantial, factual, physical, tangible. **2.** SPECIFIC distinct, explicit, particular, precise, express. ANT. *1. abstract, theoretical. 2. general, vague.*

concubine *n.* mistress, *live-in lover, kept woman, odalisque.

CONCUR *v.* [kun KUR] to agree; to arrive at

a mutual understanding. *The opposition made such perfect sense that Ben had no choice but to concur.* SYN. agree, assent, go along, accord, correspond, see eye to eye, echo, coincide, cooperate, synchronize, be in step with, consent, harmonize, accede. ANT. *disagree, differ.*

concurrent *a.* **1.** HAPPENING TOGETHER coinciding, parallel, synchronized, coincident, simultaneous. **2.** IN AGREEMENT in accordance, harmonizing, consistent, corresponding, in rapport, compatible. ANT. *2. in disagreement, differing, contradictory.*

concussion *n.* shaking, agitation, jolt, blow, shock, jarring, impact, bang, bump, pounding, buffeting.

condemn *v.* **1.** CRITICIZE censure, denounce, decry, reprove, deprecate, vilify, rebuke, disapprove, disparage, pass judgment on. **2.** DOOM sentence, damn, convict, adjudge, punish, *send up the river. ANT. 1. praise, commend, laud. 2. liberate, absolve.*

condemnation *n.* criticism, censure, disapproval, remonstration, deprecation, rebuke, reproach, denunciation, judgment, sentencing, damning, punishment. ANT. *praise, approval, absolution.*

condensation *n.* **1.** ABRIDGEMENT reduction, compression, consolidation, summary, brief, synopsis, outline, digest. **2.** LIQUEFACTION dew, moisture, precipitation, *sweating.

condense *v.* abridge, reduce, compress, shorten, consolidate, summarize, synopsize, outline, contract, boil down, concentrate, curtail, encapsulate. ANT. *expand, lengthen, enlarge.*

CONDESCEND *v.* [KON di send] to lower oneself to the level of another with lesser status. Also, to talk down to someone. *Our teacher was willing to condescend and take the advice of students. He fancied himself a big shot and spoke condescendingly to everyone.* SYN. **1.** descend, humble oneself, bend, *come down off one's high horse, vouchsafe, deign, stoop, lower oneself, yield. **2.** talk down to, patronize, talk down one's nose, regard with hauteur.

condescending *a.* superior, arrogant, *high and mighty, patronizing, lofty, snobbish, disdainful, lordly, pretentious, *snooty, haughty, imperious. ANT. *down-to-earth, unpretentious, unassuming.*

condiment *n.* seasoning, flavoring, spice, sauce, relish, mustard, catsup, ketchup, horseradish, salsa.

condition *n.* **1.** PROVISION stipulation, qualification, proviso, consideration, requirement. **2.**

STATE situation, order, circumstance, stage, predicament, position, *lay of the land. **3.** HEALTH fitness, shape, constitution, state. **4.** AILMENT malady, illness. SEE DISEASE

condition *v.* get fit, train, prepare, get in shape, build up, work out.

conditional *a.* subject to, dependent, contingent, limited, relative, provisional, qualified, *with strings attached, tentative. ANT. *unconditional, unrestricted.*

condolence *n.* sympathy, commiseration, consolation, compassion, pity, comfort, support, solace.

condom *n.* contraceptive, prophylactic, *rubber, *protection, *raincoat.

CONDONE *v.* [kun DOHN] to overlook or forgive a negative action. *The church does not condone infidelity.* SYN. overlook, forgive, pardon, *look the other way, ignore, excuse, let go, make allowances for, wink at. ANT. *condemn, damn, denounce.*

CONDUCIVE *a.* [kun DOO siv] leading to or promoting. *Rain pattering on the roof is conducive to good sleep.* SYN. leading to, promoting, contributing, instrumental, helpful, ancillary, tending, favorable. ANT. *adverse, counter, deleterious.*

conduct *n.* **1.** BEHAVIOR manner, comportment, bearing, demeanor, ways. **2.** MANAGEMENT administration, direction, supervision, rule, organization, regulation, leadership.

conduct *v.* **1.** BEHAVE deport, demean, act, bear, acquit. **2.** MANAGE administer, direct, supervise, rule, organize, regulate, execute, handle. **3.** LEAD guide, escort, show the way, usher, marshal.

conductor *n.* leader, director, guide, manager, marshal, supervisor, usher, maestro.

conduit *n.* pipe, tube, channel, duct, drain, sewer, canal, course, passage, trough, race.

confection *n.* sweet, candy, comfit, dainty.

confederacy *n.* alliance, league, union, federation, coalition, bloc.

confederate *n.* ally, associate, accomplice, colleague, abettor, collaborator, partner, co-conspirator, cohort. ANT. *adversary, foe.*

confederation *n.* SEE CONFEDERACY

confer *v.* **1.** GIVE bestow, grant, present, award. **2.** HAVE A CONFERENCE talk, discuss, speak, parley, consult, deliberate, *powwow.

conference *n.* talk, discussion, meeting, consultation, seminar, dialogue, *powwow, convention, *bull session, symposium. "A gathering of important people who singly can do nothing, but together can decide that nothing can be done."—Fred Allen.

confess *v.* admit, acknowledge, reveal, disclose, allow, *own up, *come clean, *fess up, level, divulge, *open up, *spill it. ANT. *deny, cover up, keep secret.*

confession *n.* admission, acknowledgement, revelation, disclosure, allowance, leveling, declaration, profession, avowal. "A medicine to the erring."—Cicero.

confidant *n.* confidante, friend, intimate, bosom buddy, companion, lover, alter ego, counselor, therapist. SEE FRIEND

confide *v.* **1.** SHARE INTIMATE INFORMATION confess, disclose, divulge, share feelings, reveal, *unload, intimate, *get off one's chest. **2.** ENTRUST charge, consign, relegate, trust, commit, assign.

confidence *n.* **1.** BELIEF trust, reliance, sureness, faith, dependence, assurance. **2.** SELF-CONFIDENCE self-esteem, self-assurance, courage, self-reliance, heart, faith in oneself, mental toughness, pluck, backbone, spine, nerve. ANT. *1. uncertainty, doubt. 2. insecurity, diffidence, self-doubt.*

confidence game *n.* con game, swindle, *rip-off, trick.

confident *a.* self-confident, self-assured, cocky, plucky, bold, dauntless, faithful, sure, secure, certain, positive, convinced, presumptuous. ANT. *insecure, unsure, diffident.*

confidential *a.* secret, private, privy, classified, *off the record, *between you, me and the bedpost, personal, restricted. ANT. *public, open.*

configuration *n.* arrangement, outline, contour, form, conformation, structure, figure, build, shape.

confine *v.* enclose, restrict, shut in, imprison, restrain, limit, keep, jail, coop up, incarcerate, intern, hold, detain, bound, quarantine. ANT. *free, liberate, release.*

confinement *n.* restriction, shutting in, imprisonment, enclosure, keeping, incarceration, holding, detainment, bounding, quarantine, detention, captivity. ANT. *freedom, liberation, release.*

confirm *v.* **1.** STRENGTHEN firm up, establish, buttress, reinforce. **2.** VALIDATE ratify, prove, establish, attest, substantiate, vouch, sanction, authenticate, affirm. ANT. *1. weaken, contradict. 2. disprove, question, contradict.*

confirmation *n.* validation, ratification, proof, verification, authentication, substantiation,

affirmation, corroboration, support, sanction, nod, okay. ANT. *question, contradiction, repudiation.*

confirmed *a.* **1.** SUBSTANTIATED validated, proven, verified, authenticated, corroborated. **2.** ESTABLISHED deep-rooted, *dyed-in-the-wool, deep-seated, habitual, chronic, inveterate, ingrained. ANT. *1. unconfirmed, unsupported, questionable. 2. new, sometimes.*

confiscate *v.* seize, appropriate, take, impound, expropriate, preempt, sequester, commandeer, usurp.

conflagration *n.* fire, blaze, inferno, firestorm, holocaust, wildfire, hellfire.

conflict *n.* **1.** FIGHT battle, war, clash, combat, struggle, contest, tussle. **2.** DISAGREEMENT clash, contention, discord, dissension, hostility, argument, opposition, dispute, confrontation. ANT. *1. peace, amity. 2. agreement, accord.*

conflict *v.* **1.** FIGHT battle, wage war, clash, combat, struggle, contest, tussle. **2.** DISAGREE clash, contend, oppose, differ, *lock horns, square off, be at odds with, spar. ANT. *1. settle, conciliate. 2. agree, harmonize.*

conflicting *a.* contradictory, contrary, inconsistent, incompatible, discrepant. ANT. *corresponding, congruous.*

confluence *n.* **1.** CONVERGENCE juncture, meeting, union. **2.** CROWD throng, gathering, assembly.

conform *v.* **1.** MAKE THE SAME correspond, match, be like, harmonize, fit, jibe, assimilate. **2.** ADAPT adjust, accommodate, integrate, suit, follow, fall into line, *go with the flow, comply, *do as the Romans do, *swim with the stream. ANT. *2. deviate, *march to the beat of a different drummer, differ.*

conformation *n.* shape, build, form, structure, figure, configuration.

conformist *n.* follower, *yes man, *sheep, *one of the herd, *brick in a wall, emulator. ANT. *nonconformist, rebel, free spirit.*

conformity *n.* **1.** AGREEMENT correspondence, harmony, affinity, congruity, accord, likeness, similarity. "The herd-fear."—E. Stanley Jones. **2.** COMPLIANCE obedience, observance, assent, yielding, acquiescence, submission. ANT. *1. disagreement, incongruity, difference. 2. noncompliance, disobedience, rebellion.*

confound *v.* confuse, puzzle, mix up, bewilder, perplex, mystify, flabbergast, nonplus, daze, muddle, dumbfound. ANT. *clarify.*

confront v. face, oppose, stand up to, challenge, cross, encounter, *go up against, meet, dare, defy, beard, brave. ANT. avoid, back away from, retreat from, dodge.

confrontation n. meeting, challenge, encounter, crossing of paths, showdown, face-off, set-to, contest, dare, defiance, fight. ANT. avoidance.

confuse v. 1. BEWILDER mix up, perplex, throw off, baffle, mystify, muddle, bemuse, puzzle, confound. 2. DISORDER jumble, mix up, mess up, disarrange, discombobulate, disarray, *foul up, mingle, blend. ANT. 1. clarify, explain. 2. straighten, order.

confusion n. 1. BEWILDERMENT perplexity, bafflement, mystification, puzzlement, disorientation, fog, daze, befuddlement. 2. DISORDER jumble, mess, disarray, disorganization, tangle, upheaval, labyrinth, muddle, *snafu, anarchy, chaos, bedlam, pandemonium. ANT. 1. lucidity, clarity. 2. order, organization, tidiness.

confute v. disprove, refute, invalidate, *shoot full of holes, negate, contradict, rebut, discredit.

congeal v. solidify, thicken, jell, set, stiffen, coagulate, clot, curdle.

CONGENIAL a. [kun JEEN yul] friendly, compatible, having similar tastes. The party atmosphere was low-key but congenial. SYN. friendly, compatible, agreeable, suitable, pleasant, cordial, kindred, companionable, convivial, sociable, like-minded, sympathetic, affable, harmonious, *en rapport. ANT. hostile, incompatible, disagreeable.

CONGENITAL a. [kun JEN i tul] existing at birth. The baby had a congenital heart defect. SYN. inborn, natal, natural, connate, inherent, innate, intrinsic, hereditary, in the blood, genetic. ANT. acquired.

congested a. overcrowded, clogged, blocked, overfilled, stuffed up, plugged, occluded, jammed, glutted, packed, choked. ANT. clear.

congestion n. overcrowding, clogging, blockage, stuffiness, plug, cramming, jam, occlusion, repletion, fullness, bottleneck.

conglomerate n. composite, aggregate, hodgepodge, chain, multinational, partnership, company, trust, firm.

conglomerate a. clustered, massed, amassed, combined, aggregate, mixed, composite. ANT. divided, separate.

congratulate v. felicitate, hail, commend, salute, applaud, toast.

congregate v. gather, mass, cluster, collect, flock, group, crowd together, muster, convene, throng, concentrate. ANT. scatter, disperse.

congregation n. assembly, group, mass, cluster, collection, flock, crowd, throng, gathering, parishioners.

congress n. assembly, council, association, conference, delegation, legislature, legislative body, government, committee, caucus, session, Parliament, Senate, House of Representatives, Capitol Hill. "The great commanding theatre . . ."—Thomas Jefferson.

WORD FIND

assistant party leader in House or Senate: whip

break: recess

committee that sets rules for debate on bills: Rules Committee

debate's time-limiting process: cloture

influencing of member by special interest group: lobbying

House of Commons: lower legislative house of British Parliament

House of Lords: upper legislative house of British Parliament

House: U.S. House of Representatives

kill or remove a bill from consideration: table a bill

legislative house: chamber

meeting of House and Senate: joint session

member: congressman, senator, representative, legislator, statesman

messenger/*gofer of: page

minimum member attendance necessary to transact business: quorum

newly elected member: freshman

official controlling access, maintaining order: sergeant at arms

presides in House of Representatives: Speaker of the House

presides in Senate after Vice President: president pro tempore

proposed legislation: bill

Senate: upper legislative body of U.S. Congress

speaking and work area of: floor

speech, long-winded: filibuster

transcript of daily debates, votes, House and Senate: Congressional Record

SEE ELECTION, GOVERNMENT, POLITICS

congressman n. senator, representative, legislator, statesman, politician. "[One] who votes for all appropriations and against all taxes."—Henry Ashurst.

congruent a. corresponding, in agreement, harmonious, parallel, consonant. ANT. *incongruent, disagreeing.*

conifer n. evergreen, coniferous tree, pine, spruce, fir.

CONJECTURE n. [kun JEK chur] a guess or inference made from incomplete information. *The evidence was comprised of little more than conjecture.* SYN. guess, guesswork, inference, deduction, supposition, surmise, assumption, speculation, theory, hypothesis, inkling, *shot in the dark. ANT. *fact, certainty.*

conjecture v. guess, infer, deduce, assume, suppose, surmise, speculate, theorize, hypothesize, gather.

conjugal a. matrimonial, connubial, nuptial, marital, wedded. ANT. *unmarried, single.*

conjunction n. combination, union, alliance, juxtaposition, connection, meeting, merger, joining.

conjure v. summon, call upon, beckon, raise, invoke, make magic, cast a spell, bewitch.

conjurer n. sorcerer, illusionist, sorceress. SEE MAGICIAN

connect v. join, link, unite, tie, bind, couple, attach, wed, merge, hitch, cohere, yoke. ANT. *disconnect, detach, separate.*

connection n. 1. LINK tie, coupling, bond, juncture, union, association, relationship, marriage, network, attachment. 2. ASSOCIATE friend, relative, kin, sibling, acquaintance, contact, go-between, agent.

CONNIVE v. [kuh NIVE] to conspire in a wrongdoing or at least look the other way. *They connive to get what they want.* SYN. conspire, scheme, collude, plot, *be in cahoots with, look the other way, intrigue, finagle, have a hand in, cabal, cooperate.

CONNOISSEUR n. [KON uh SUR] an expert, especially on the fine arts or in matters of taste. *The expert wine taster is truly a connoisseur.* SYN. expert, authority, cognoscente, aesthete, afficianado, buff, dilettante, virtuoso, judge, specialist, devotee, epicure, gourmet, critic, maven, *nut, freak.

connotation n. inference, allusion, implication, suggestion, sense, undercurrent, meaning, reference, nuance, hint.

connote v. suggest, convey, denote, imply, infer, hint at, mean, indicate, designate, signify, allude to.

connubial a. conjugal, marital, matrimonial, nuptial, wedded, married, spousal. ANT. *unwedded, single.*

conquer v. vanquish, defeat, overcome, overpower, overthrow, subdue, master, beat, dominate, win, triumph. ANT. *surrender, lose, fall, bow.*

conqueror n. victor, winner, champion, master, vanquisher, subduer, conquistador. ANT. *loser, victim, the defeated.*

conquest n. victory, triumph, win, defeat, domination, overthrow, coup, subjugation, subjection, occupation, spoils, plunder, booty, winnings. SEE WAR

conscience n. moral judgment, principles, *little voice, scruples, ethics, standards, integrity, sense of right and wrong, superego. "That inner tribunal."—Anton Boisen. "One's soul companion."—Evelyn Brenzel. "The muzzle of the will."—Elbert Hubbard. "A thousand witnesses."—Richard Taverner. ANT. *indifference, cold-bloodedness.*

conscientious a. 1. MORAL principled, ethical, virtuous, upright, honest, scrupulous, good, upstanding, honorable. 2. CAREFUL thorough, painstaking, particular, responsible, attentive, exacting, thoughtful, diligent, meticulous. ANT. *1. immoral, unprincipled, unscrupulous. 2. slack, slipshod, careless.*

conscious a. 1. AWAKE AND AWARE alert, perceiving, sentient, cognizant, responsive, recognizing, apprehending, mindful, knowing, apprised, *on the ball. 2. DELIBERATE intended, intentional, calculated, willful, premeditated, designed, on purpose. ANT. *1. unconscious, dead, oblivious. 2. accidental, unplanned, inadvertent.*

consciousness n. awareness, alertness, thoughts, cognizance, familiarity, recognition, knowledge, perception, mind, mindfulness, concern, heed. ANT. *unconsciousness, oblivion, ignorance.*

conscript n. draftee, recruit, enrollee, soldier.

CONSECRATE v. [KON suh KRATE] to make or declare sacred or holy. *Fans gathered to consecrate the shrine of Elvis Presley.* SYN. sanctify, exalt, honor, hallow, bless, devote, dedicate, annoint. ANT. *desecrate, defile, revile.*

consecutive a. successive, sequential, serial, progressive, orderly, in order, in turn, following, succeeding. ANT. *random, irregular.*

CONSENSUS n. [kun SEN sus] an opinion held in common, agreement. *The committee finally reached a consensus.* SYN. agreement, unanimity, concord, accord, unison, harmony, concordance, single-mindedness. ANT. *disagreement, dissension, discord.*

consent *n.* permission, approval, assent, okay, nod, *go-ahead, acceptance, agreement, *say-so, sanction, allowance. ANT. *dissent, refusal, veto.*

consent *v.* agree, permit, approve, allow, grant, accept, sanction, *give the green light, *give the nod, okay, assent, acquiesce. ANT. *refuse, veto, object.*

consequence *n.* **1.** RESULT outcome, effect, upshot, aftermath, fallout, repercussion, reaction, reverberation, wake. **2.** DISTINCTION status, influence, stature, standing, eminence, rank, prestige, notability, power. ANT. *1. cause, source. 2. insignificance, unimportance.*

consequential *a.* important, significant, weighty, notable, substantial, momentous, serious, far-reaching, considerable, *heavy. ANT. *inconsequential, insignificant, trivial.*

consequently *adv.* therefore, hence, thus, so, accordingly, ergo.

conservancy *n.* conservation, preservation, land trust.

conservation *n.* preservation, protection, safeguarding, management, saving, supervision, maintenance, husbandry, environmentalism, reservation, safe-keeping, care. ANT. *squandering, waste.*

conservationist *n.* environmentalist, preservationist, activist, *green, *tree hugger.

conservative *n.* traditionalist, right-winger, diehard, champion of the status quo, moderate, obstructionist, *stick-in-the-mud. "A man who believes nothing should be done for the first time."—Alfred Wiggam.

CONSERVATIVE *a.* [kun SURV uh tiv] favoring traditional, nonprogressive ways; moderate. *He doesn't like change; his politics are conservative.* SYN. **1.** TRADITIONAL right-wing, rightist, conventional, die-hard, unchanging, stable, old line, hidebound, opposed to change, unprogressive. **2.** CAUTIOUS moderate, safe, middle-of-the-road, careful. ANT. *1. radical, liberal, progressive.*

conservator *n.* curator, caretaker, custodian, restorer, guardian, keeper.

conservatory *n.* **1.** GREENHOUSE botanical garden, arboretum, nursery, hothouse. **2.** SCHOOL institute, academy, school of fine arts.

conserve *v.* preserve, save, protect, keep, guard, safeguard, maintain, husband, sustain. ANT. *squander, exhaust, denude.*

consider *v.* ponder, heed, regard, study, think about, deliberate, contemplate, mull over,

inspect, ruminate, note. ANT. *ignore, forget, nevermind.*

considerable *a.* **1.** LARGE sizable, big, substantial, appreciable, respectable, tidy, extensive, great. **2.** IMPORTANT significant, noteworthy, momentous, weighty, distinguished, consequential, substantial, respectable. ANT. *1. small. 2. insignificant, trivial.*

considerate *a.* thoughtful, kind, benevolent, conscientious, respectful, accommodating, polite, solicitous, magnanimous, gracious, tactful. ANT. *inconsiderate, rude, thoughtless.*

consideration *n.* **1.** THOUGHT study, regard, attention, reflection, contemplation, analysis, review, examination. **2.** THOUGHTFULNESS kindness, benevolence, respect, accommodation, courtesy, solicitude, tact. **3.** FACTOR concern, issue, extent, problem, point. **4.** COMPENSATION recompense, fee, payment, remuneration, reward. ANT. *2. thoughtlessness, rudeness, carelessness.*

consign *v.* hand over, deliver, entrust, commit, convey, transfer, remit, deposit, assign.

consignment *n.* assignment, entrusting, delivery, transferal, trust, conveyance, remittance, deposit.

consistency *n.* agreement, harmony, correspondence, coherence, compatibility, consonance, similarity, uniformity, congruity. ANT. *inconsistence, incongruity, disagreement.*

consistent *a.* **1.** IN AGREEMENT harmonious, corresponding, coherent, compatible, similar, uniform, homogenous, accordant. **2.** UNCHANGING steady, constant, regular, undeviating. ANT. *1. inconsistent, incompatible. 2. changing, inconsistent.*

consist of *vi.* comprise, include.

consolation *n.* solace, comfort, sympathy, compassion, condolence, succor, relief, support, pity, alleviation. ANT. *grief, discouragement.*

console *v.* comfort, solace, sympathize, condole, soothe, relieve, support, pity, alleviate, cheer, commiserate. ANT. *grieve, distress, dishearten, depress.*

consolidate *v.* combine, merge, unite, amalgamate, strengthen, band, concentrate, unify, league, mass, firm up. ANT. *separate, disband, weaken.*

consonant *a.* in agreement, harmonious, accordant, corresponding, consistent, congruent, parallel, coherent. ANT. *disagreeing, discordant, incongruent.*

consort *n.* partner, companion, husband, wife, spouse, mate, associate, friend.

consort *v.* associate, fraternize, keep company

with, *hang out with, mingle, mix with, *run with, *chum with.

consortium n. partnership, association, alliance, league.

CONSPICUOUS a. [kun SPIK yoo us] attention-grabbing, striking. *A stretch limousine is conspicuous in rural America.* SYN. attention-grabbing, striking, noticeable, obvious, outstanding, prominent, unusual, overt, arresting, distinguished, glaring, flagrant, loud, *sticking out like a sore thumb. ANT. *inconspicuous, hidden, indistinct.*

CONSPIRACY n. [kun SPEER uh see] a working together in secret to commit a wrongdoing, a plotting. *Some believe the assassination of John F. Kennedy was a conspiracy to remove the president from power.* SYN. plotting, plot, scheme, intrigue, connivance, collusion, cabal, treachery, machination, foul play, web, *wire-pulling.

conspirator n. schemer, plotter, accomplice, engineer, collaborator, colluder, *wire-puller, subversive, traitor, *backstabber, betrayer.

conspire v. plot, scheme, intrigue, connive, collude, machinate, engineer, collaborate.

constable n. police officer, officer of the law, peace officer, *cop, sheriff. SEE POLICE

constant a. **1.** UNCHANGING steady, regular, invariable, firm, permanent, solid, fixed, stable. **2.** PERPETUAL endless, never ending, relentless, continual, nonstop, unremitting, sustained, incessant, persistent. **3.** FAITHFUL loyal, steadfast, devoted, tried-and-true. ANT. *1. variable, unstable. 2. intermittent, occasional, sporadic. 3. disloyal, unfaithful, fickle.*

constellation n. **1.** GATHERING cluster, collection, array, assemblage, group, body. **2.** A FORMATION OF STARS configuration, asterism.

WORD FIND

NORTHERN HEMISPHERE
Andromeda: Andromeda
arrow: Sagitta
bear, great: Ursa Major, Big Dipper
bear, little: Ursa Minor, Little Dipper
Berenice's Hair: Coma Berenices
Cassiopeia: Cassiopeia
Cepheus: Cepheus
charioteer: Auriga
dolphin: Delphinius
dragon: Draco
filly: Equuleus
fox: Vulpecula
giraffe: Camelopardallis

Hercules: Hercules
herdsmen: Bootes
hunting dogs: Canes Venacti
lion, little: Leo Minor
lizard: Lacerta
lynx: Lynx
lyre: Lyra
northern crown: Corona Borealis
Pegasus: Pegasus
Perseus: Perseus
sea serpent: Hydra
serpent bearer: Ophiuchus
serpent: Serpens
shield: Scutum
swan: Cygnus
triangle: Triangulum
SOUTHERN HEMISPHERE
air pump: Antlia
altar: Ara
bird of paradise: Apus
centaur: Centaurus
chameleon: Chameleon
clock: Horologium
compasses: Circinus
crane: Grus
crow: Corvus
cup: Crater
dog, greater: Canis Major
dog, lesser: Canis Minor
dove: Columba
flying fish: Volans
furnace: Fornax
hare: Lepus
hunter: Orion
Indian: Indus
keel: Carina
mariner's compass: Pyxis
microscope: Microscopium
net: Reticulum
octant: Octans
painter: Pictor
peacock: Pavo
Phoenix: Phoenix
poop deck: Puppis
river: Eridanus
sail: Vela
sculptor: Sculptor
sculptor's tool: Caelum
sextant: Sextans
southern cross: Crux
southern crown: Corona Australis
southern fish: Piscis Austrinus
southern fly: Musca
southern triangle: Triangulum Australe
square: Norma

swordfish: Dorado
table: Mensa
telescope: Telescopium
toucan: Tucana
unicorn: Monoceros
water snake: Hydrus
whale: Cetus
wolf: Lupus
ZODIAC
archer: Sagittarius
bull: Taurus
crab: Cancer
fishes: Pisces
goat: Capricornus
lion: Leo
ram: Aries
scales: Libra
scorpion: Scorpius
twins: Gemini
virgin: Virgo
water bearer: Aquarius

CONSTERNATION n. [kon stur NA shun] dismay or shock that leaves one feeling helpless or confused. *The sudden collision filled him with consternation.* SYN. dismay, shock, fear, anxiety, panic, bewilderment, confusion, alarm, stupefaction, horror, terror. ANT. *composure, calm, presence of mind.*

constipation n. irregularity, sluggish bowels, straining at stool.

constituency n. electorate, voting body, residents, voters, district. SEE POLITICS, ELECTION, GOVERNMENT

constituent n. **1.** COMPONENT part, element, unit, ingredient, rudiment. **2.** VOTER elector, balloter, citizen.

constitute v. **1.** COMPRISE form, make up, consist of, incorporate, integrate, compose. **2.** APPOINT name, empower, authorize, install, nominate, deputize. **3.** ESTABLISH create, institute, develop, set up, originate, found.

constitution n. charter, code, law, rules, canon, Bill of Rights. "A means of assuring that depositories of power cannot misemploy it."— John Stuart Mill.

constitutional a. lawful, legal, statutory, chartered, prescribed. ANT. *unconstitutional, improper, illegal.*

constrain v. **1.** FORCE compel, drive, press, coerce, oblige, make, impel, pressure, prevail upon. **2.** RESTRAIN confine, curb, restrict, check, limit, shut in, bar, hold down, incarcerate, imprison.

constraint n. **1.** FORCE pressure, obligation, compulsion, coercion, duress, necessity. **2.**

RESTRICTION limitation, restraint, check, curb, control, repression, inhibition, confinement. **3.** UNEASE inhibition, reticence, reserve, shyness, diffidence, bashfulness, self-consciousness, restraint.

constrict v. **1.** NARROW squeeze, bind, tighten, shrink, contract, clamp, cramp, compress, pinch, strangle, choke. **2.** LIMIT restrict, hold in, impede, arrest, block, curb. ANT. *1. expand, widen, loosen. 2. free, liberate.*

constriction n. narrowing, contraction, squeezing, strangulation, compression, stricture, clamping, cramping, pinching, clenching, choking, stenosis, bottleneck. ANT. *opening, loosening.*

construct v. build, assemble, put together, erect, *throw up, *slap together, fabricate, engineer, raise, frame, fashion, form. ANT. *raze, demolish, tear down.*

construction n. **1.** CONSTRUCTION building, erection, assembling, fabrication, raising, framing, putting up, fashioning, manufacturing, formation. **2.** BUILDING structure, framework, assembly. **3.** EXPLANATION interpretation, rendition, translation, reading.

constructive a. helpful, useful, beneficial, practical, valuable, positive, effective. ANT. *hurtful, negative.*

construe v. explain, interpret, translate, spell out, infer, define, read, understand.

consultant n. expert, authority, professional, *pro, advisor, counsel, mentor, guide, specialist, master, maven, veteran.

consulate n. embassy.

consult v. refer to, check with, confer, inquire, seek advice, discuss, talk, deliberate, ask, *pick one's brains, compare notes.

consultation n. conference, meeting, discussion, talk, conversation, deliberation, council, *powwow, parley, hearing, session.

consume v. **1.** INGEST eat, drink, swallow, devour, guzzle, absorb, down, *gobble, *wolf, *scarf, *polish off. **2.** EXPEND use up, deplete, exhaust, spend, waste, squander, drain, fritter away, finish. **3.** DESTROY level, raze, demolish, annihilate, wreck, ruin, devastate, lay to waste. **4.** ENGROSS absorb, engage, arrest, preoccupy, fix, fascinate, rivet. ANT. *2. save, collect, hoard.*

consumer n. buyer, customer, purchaser, enduser, patron, shopper.

consummate v. complete, perfect, fulfill, achieve, finish, crown, effectuate, *put the finishing touch on, cap, clinch, realize.

CONSUMMATE a. [kun SUM it] supremely

accomplished, complete. *He is at the top of his field, a consummate violinist.* SYN. accomplished, skilled, supreme, superior, best, ultimate, unsurpassed, superlative, masterful, excellent, complete, thorough, inimitable, peerless. ANT. *run-of-the-mill, mediocre, amateurish.*

consummation *n.* completion, perfecting, fulfillment, finishing, crowning, *finishing touch, cap, realization, attainment.

consumption *n.* use, expenditure, utilization, depletion, loss, devouring, exhaustion, reduction, exploitation. ANT. *conservation, preservation.*

contact *n.* **1.** TOUCHING meeting, connection, union, contingence, proximity, junction, collision. **2.** CONNECTION acquaintance.

contact *v.* **1.** TOUCH meet, graze, impinge, strike, brush. **2.** COMMUNICATE WITH get in touch with, call, seek, reach, look up, find, approach.

contagious *a.* communicable, catching, transmittable, transmissible, spreading, infectious, epidemic, endemic. ANT. *noninfectious.*

contain *v.* **1.** HOLD accommodate, carry, receive, have a capacity for. **2.** COMPRISE include, consist of, involve, embody, incorporate. **3.** KEEP IN CHECK hold in, restrain, control, suppress, repress, stifle.

contaminate *v.* pollute, adulterate, spoil, taint, sully, corrupt, defile, poison, degrade, befoul. ANT. *purify, cleanse, sterilize.*

contamination *n.* pollution, adulteration, spoilage, corruption, defilement, degradation, poisoning, fouling, taint, impurity.

contemplate *v.* **1.** LOOK AT watch, gaze at, behold, survey, eye, consider, regard, scrutinize. **2.** THINK ABOUT ponder, mull over, brood over, meditate, reflect, ruminate, dwell on, *chew on, consider, *turn over in one's mind.

contemplative *a.* thoughtful, intent, introspective, absorbed, pensive, meditative, reflective, ruminative, musing, rapt. ANT. *thoughtless, blank, vacuous.*

contemporary *a.* **1.** MODERN present-day, up-to-date, here and now, current, late, *hot, new, *cutting edge, recent, now, *fresh as today, extant. **2.** COEXISTING coincident, attending, simultaneous, synchronous, concurrent, of the same time. ANT. *1. old, yesterday, historical, past, ancient.*

contempt *n.* **1.** DISDAIN scorn, repugnance, disgust, disrespect, disregard, derision, revulsion, abhorrence. **2.** DISGRACE shame, dishonor, humiliation, disrepute. ANT. *respect, esteem, honor.*

contemptible *a.* despicable, shameful, low, detestable, wretched, abhorrent, wicked, mean, loathsome, disgusting, ignominious, shabby, cheap, repugnant. ANT. *honorable, respectable, admirable.*

contemptuous *a.* disdainful, scornful, disrespectful, arrogant, sneering, insolent, insulting, derisive, *high and mighty, supercilious, condescending, haughty. ANT. *complimentary, deferential, respectful.*

contend *v.* **1.** MAINTAIN assert, claim, hold, state, declare, argue, insist, prescribe. **2.** VIE struggle, strive, contest, battle, wrestle, tussle, fight, scuffle, clash.

contender *n.* contestant, competitor, rival.

content *n.* **1.** MEANING intent, essence, significance, idea. **2.** SATISFACTION happiness, pleasure, comfort, fulfillment, gratification, delight, contentment.

content *v.* satisfy, please, comfort, delight, gratify, gladden, cheer. ANT. *discontent, trouble, upset.*

content *a.* satisfied, happy, pleased, comfortable, at ease, carefree, fulfilled, complacent, serene. ANT. *discontented, miserable, troubled.*

contention *n.* **1.** DISPUTE argument, disagreement, debate, controversy, squabble, altercation, fight, wrangling, *beef, *bone to pick, quarrel. **2.** STRIVING struggle, contest, battle, fight. **3.** ASSERTION point, stand, claim, opinion, belief, view, plea. ANT. *1. agreement, accord, harmony.*

CONTENTIOUS *a.* [kun TEN shus] quarrelsome. *He couldn't get along with anyone; he was contentious.* SYN. quarrelsome, belligerent, testy, disputatious, argumentative, combative, nasty, disagreeable, *shortfused, petulant, antagonistic. ANT. *easygoing, accommodating, placatory, peaceable.*

contentment *n.* satisfaction, happiness, pleasure, comfort, ease, fulfillment, complacency, serenity, tranquility. "The only riches, the only quietness . . . "—George Pettie. "Natural wealth."—Plato. ANT. *discontent, dissatisfaction, misery.*

contest *n.* competition, match, struggle, rivalry, battle, challenge, meet, round, duel, trial, war, marathon, tourney.

contest *v.* argue, debate, dispute, challenge, oppose, call into question, object to, conflict, contend, vie, fight, scrap, square off, battle. ANT. *acquiesce, cave in, give in, surrender.*

contestant *n.* contender, competitor, combatant, opponent, rival, adversary, challenger.

context *n.* frame of reference, framework, relationship, connection, substance, circumstances, meaning.

contiguous *a.* touching, meeting, contacting, connecting, next to, abutting, adjoining, nearby, proximate, adjacent, close. ANT. *distant, removed, remote.*

continence *n.* self-restraint, moderation, self-control, forbearance, refraining, abstinence, virtue, chastity. ANT. *incontinence, indulgence, excess.*

contingency *n.* possibility, emergency, eventuality, chance occurrence, accident, fortuity, uncertainty, happening, probability.

CONTINGENT *a.* [kun TIN junt] dependent, subject to. *When we schedule the outing is contingent upon the weather.* SYN. dependent, subject to, conditional, hinging on, controlled by, incidental to, provisory.

continual *a.* never ending, perpetual, unending, incessant, relentless, unceasing, constant, nonstop, eternal, unremitting, around-the-clock. ANT. *finite, ending, sporadic, intermittent.*

continuance *n.* persistence, prolongation, protraction, perpetuation, duration.

continue *v.* **1.** KEEP ON persist, carry on, persevere, extend, maintain, sustain, press on, prolong, progress, remain, abide. **2.** RESUME carry on, restart, begin again, pick up where one left off, proceed, renew. ANT. *stop, end, cease.*

continuity *n.* continuance, continuation, persistence, prolongation, protraction, perpetuation, endurance, constancy, extension. ANT. *interruption, stoppage, intermittence.*

continuous *a.* constant, never ending, perpetual, unbroken, connected, uninterrupted, unremitting, incessant, nonstop, infinite, protracted. ANT. *intermittent, broken.*

contort *v.* twist, turn, wrench, distort, screw up, warp, knot, convolute, gnarl, torture, misshape. ANT. *straighten, smooth.*

contorted *a.* twisted, turned, wrenched, distorted, bent, warped, convoluted, knotted, gnarled, misshapen, tortured. ANT. *straight.*

contour *n.* outline, profile, shape, form, figure, lines, curves, silhouette.

contraband *a.* illegal, black-market, bootleg, unlawful, illicit, *hot, forbidden, prohibited, smuggled, taboo, trafficked. ANT. *legal, allowed, lawful.*

contraceptive *n.* birth control device, condom, diaphragm, IUD, Norplant, *the pill, prophylactic, sponge, shield, spermicide, *rubber, *protection. SEE CONDOM

contract *n.* agreement, arrangement, understanding, deal, covenant, pact, transaction, compact, bond, gentleman's agreement, obligation, pledge, legal document.

contract *v.* **1.** COMPRESS reduce, narrow, squeeze, shorten, tighten, condense, recede, constrict, cramp, wither. **2.** MAKE AN AGREEMENT agree, bargain, come to terms, bound, *hammer out a deal, put in writing, pledge, promise, guarantee, covenant. ANT. *1. expand, swell. 2. renege, back out.*

contraction *n.* compression, reduction, narrowing, squeezing, shortening, tightening, condensing, recession, cramping, withering, shrinkage. ANT. *expansion, swelling, enlargement.*

contradict *v.* differ, deny, controvert, refute, counter, *fly in the face of, negate, gainsay, repudiate, belie, cancel out. ANT. *agree, corroborate, correspond.*

contradiction *n.* differing, denial, refutation, disagreement, negation, confliction, discrepancy, gainsay, inconsistency. ANT. *agreement, corroboration, correspondence.*

contradictory *a.* differing, conflicting, inconsistent, contrary, discrepant, disagreeing, incongruous, antithetical, at variance. ANT. *consistent, agreeing, corresponding.*

contraption *n.* device, machine, contrivance, gadget, rig, mechanism, appliance, widget, *doohickey, *thingamajig, *Rube Goldberg device.

contrary *a.* **1.** OPPOSITE contradictory, antithetical, reverse, different, counter, incompatible, incongruous, inimical, conflicting. **2.** DISAGREEABLE cantankerous, antagonistic, hostile, inimical, averse, antipathetic, at odds. ANT. *1. identical, consistent. 2. agreeable, accommodating.*

contrast *n.* difference, dissimilarity, opposition, variation, differentiation, disparity, antithesis, polarity, distinction, divergence. ANT. *likeness, similarity, mirror image.*

contrast *v.* **1.** COMPARE differentiate, discriminate, set off, distinguish, weigh. **2.** DIFFER vary, oppose, diverge, contradict, mismatch, conflict.

contravene *v.* **1.** OPPOSE go against, contradict,

reject, repudiate, disagree, gainsay. **2.** VIO-LATE cross, disobey, infract, transgress.

contribute *v.* give, provide, donate, bestow, furnish, supply, grant, dispense, help, hand out, *chip in, *pitch in.

contribution *n.* donation, gift, handout, helping hand, offering, present, charity, input, benefaction, bestowal.

CONTRITE *a.* [kun TRITE] feeling or showing remorse, guilt. *He was obviously contrite; he apologized ten times.* SYN. remorseful, guilty, repentant, regretful, penitent, sorry, apologetic, compunctious, rueful, troubled, ashamed, conscience-stricken. ANT. *indifferent, unrepentant, proud.*

contrition *n.* remorse, repentance, regret, guilt, sorrow, compunction, shame, penitence, self-reproach, ruth, qualms. ANT. *indifference, apathy, pride.*

contrivance *n.* **1.** DEVICE gadget, creation, appliance, mechanism, machine, contraption, implement, invention, *Rube Goldberg device. **2.** DESIGN scheme, invention, artifice, fabrication, machination, ingenuity, trick.

contrive *v.* **1.** DEVISE invent, create, improvise, *rig, design, construct, fabricate, *throw together. **2.** DESIGN plan, plot, scheme, connive, engineer, swing, conspire, machinate, finagle, formulate.

CONTRIVED *a.* [kun TRIVED] overly planned or designed, with a forced or unnatural effect. *The unlikely coincidences in the plot made the story seem contrived.* SYN. forced, unnatural, unspontaneous, labored, phony, manipulated, fake, affected, artificial, strained. ANT. *natural, spontaneous, artless.*

control *n.* command, power, rule, order, direction, mastery, management, supervision, regulation, government, *upper hand, *the whip, influence, jurisdiction, dominion.

control *v.* command, rule, order, direct, master, manage, supervise, run, regulate, govern, influence, dominate, guide, *hold sway over, lead, quarterback, reign, call the shots, dictate, preside over, *be in the driver's seat, *rule with an iron hand, manipulate.

controversial *a.* debatable, moot, arguable, polemical, contestable, questionable, suspect, controvertible, disputable, at issue, unsettled. ANT. *unquestionable, indisputable, unequivocal.*

controversy *n.* debate, argument, dispute, issue, disagreement, moot point, war of words, brouhaha, fuss, flak, quarrel, wrangling, polemics, embattlement. "A battle in which

spittle or ink replace the . . . cannon ball."—Ambrose Bierce.

controvert *v.* oppose, argue, dispute, deny, gainsay, refute, rebut, challenge, contest, debate. ANT. *agree, affirm, go along.*

contusion *n.* bruise, black-and-blue mark, discoloration, injury, bump, *mulberry patch.

CONUNDRUM *n.* [kuh NUN drum] a problem without an apparent solution; a puzzle; a mystery. *Solving the world's population problem is a political conundrum.* SYN. problem, puzzle, mystery, enigma, riddle, brainteaser, *mind-boggler, *hard nut to crack, *stumper, question mark, mystery.

convalesce *v.* recuperate, recover, rehabilitate, restore, revive, get better.

convalescence *n.* recuperation, recovery, rehabilitation, restoration, revival, rejuvenation, cure, return to health, strengthening. "That part that makes the illness worth while."—George Bernard Shaw.

convene *v.* convoke, summon, round up, call up, assemble, gather, congregate, meet, muster, rally, get together.

convenience *n.* **1.** SERVICE usefulness, utility, suitability, benefit, expedience, handiness. **2.** APPLIANCE OR SERVICE time-saver, accessory, comfort, luxury, amenity, facility, help, *life-saver. **3.** SPARE TIME free moment, leisure, chance, opportunity. ANT. *2. inconvenience, trouble, bother, *a pain.*

convenient *a.* **1.** SERVICEABLE handy, accommodating, useful, advantageous, beneficial, conducive, helpful, timesaving. **2.** NEARBY at hand, accessible, central, adjacent, handy, next-door, close, proximate. ANT. *1. inconvenient, troublesome, unsuitable. 2. remote, distant, inaccessible.*

convent *n.* nunnery, abbey, cloister. SEE CHURCH, RELIGION

convention *n.* **1.** MEETING assembly, gathering, caucus, council, *powwow, congress, convocation. **2.** CUSTOM practice, code, habit, tradition, orthodoxy, etiquette, law.

conventional *a.* **1.** CUSTOMARY usual, traditional, normal, accepted, regular, standard, orthodox, routine, prevailing. **2.** COMMON unoriginal, everyday, run-of-the-mill, conforming, pedestrian, trite, prosaic, undistinguished, humdrum. ANT. *unconventional, unorthodox, radical, avant-garde, original.*

converge *v.* meet, come together, join, intersect, merge, unite, mingle, connect. ANT. *separate, divide.*

conversant *a.* familiar, knowledgeable, acquainted with, au courant, informed, up-to-date, versed, learned, experienced, au fait, abreast. *hip. ANT. *unfamiliar, unacquainted with, ignorant, oblivious.*

conversation *n.* talk, dialogue, discourse, discussion, exchange, communication, chat, colloquy, interlocution, conference, intercourse, gab, *rap, palaver, tête-à-tête, give-and-take, *small talk. "The image of the mind. As the man is, so is his talk."—Publius Syrus. "Our account of ourselves."—Ralph Waldo Emerson.

conversationalist *n.* talker, *blabbermouth, communicator, *bag of wind, *bigmouth, *blowhard, *motormouth, *windbag, *yakker.

converse *n.* opposite, reverse, antithesis, obverse.

converse *v.* talk, discuss, communicate, chat, hold a dialogue, confer, discourse, gab, *chew the fat, *rap, *shoot the breeze, confabulate, commune, *schmooze, *flap one's chops, *jibber-jabber, *yack.

conversion *n.* change, changeover, transformation, transmutation, switch, metamorphosis, reversal, remodeling, modification, *about-face, *turnaround, adaptation.

convert *n.* proselyte, novitiate, neophyte, catechumen.

convert *v.* change, transform, transmutate, switch, metamorphose, reverse, remodel, modify, *do an about-face, *do a turnaround, adapt.

convertible *n.* *ragtop, *breezer, SEE AUTOMOBILE

convey *v.* **1.** TRANSPORT carry, conduct, transfer, bring, send, move, transmit, forward, deliver, bear, haul. **2.** COMMUNICATE tell, relate, pass along, disclose, reveal, send.

conveyance *n.* transport, transfer, carrying, transmission, movement, carriage, communication, vehicle.

convict *n.* criminal, outlaw, prisoner, malefactor, felon, *jailbird, lawbreaker, *con, inmate.

convict *v.* find guilty, imprison, *send up the river, sentence, damn, condemn.

conviction *n.* **1.** BELIEF faith, opinion, sentiment, tenet, dogma, view, principle, persuasion, doctrine. **2.** ASSURANCE certainty, confidence, surety, fervor, earnestness. ANT. **2.** *uncertainty, doubt.*

convince *v.* prove, sway, persuade, satisfy, *talk into, prevail upon, *sell, *make one see the light, *bring around.

convincing *a.* persuasive, incontrovertible, solid, satisfying, plausible, powerful, credible, conclusive, sound. ANT. *unconvincing, questionable, dubious.*

CONVIVIAL *a.* [kun VIV ee ul] fond of the party life, festive. *A convivial mob poured into the bar.* SYN. festive, jovial, sociable, fun-loving, merry-making, gregarious, jolly, cheerful, *back-slapping, lively, genial. ANT. *grim, sober, solemn, reserved, antisocial.*

convocation *n.* assembly, gathering, convention, congregation, get-together, conference, meeting, council.

convoke *v.* summon, call together, muster, assemble, gather.

convolution *n.* coil, loop, twisting, whorl, roll, spiral, helix, curlicue.

convoy *n.* escort, guard, attendant, accompaniment, protection, defense, contingent, security.

convoy *v.* escort, guard, accompany, attend, protect, defend, shield, secure, guide, shepherd, chaperon.

convulsion *n.* spasm, seizure, fit, throe, paroxysm, tremor, twitch, tic, *spaz, *the shakes.

cook *n.* chef, baker, chef de cuisine, short-order cook, sous-chef.

cook *v.* bake, broil, roast, fry, stir fry, deep fry, braise, boil, steam, simmer, fricasee, frizzle, heat, barbecue, grill, sear, blacken, stew, brown, fold, microwave, *nuke, poach, coddle, parboil, sauté. "[Cooking] An art; a noble science."—Robert Burton. SEE FOOD

cookie *n.* wafer, gingerbread man, confection, sugar cookie, snickerdoodle, pinwheel, peanut butter cookie, molasses cookie, truffle, biscotti, snap, macaroon, fig bar, chocolate chip cookie, *Oreo, sugar cookie.

cool *v.* **1.** CHILL refrigerate, freeze, frost. **2.** COOL IT *Sl.* simmer down, calm down, moderate, dampen, soften, temper, *chill, *take it easy, *don't sweat it. ANT. **1.** *heat, warm.* **2.** *go crazy, *have a nutty, *throw a fit, rage.*

cool *a.* **1.** CHILLY cold, nippy, wintry, brisk, frosty. **2.** CALM collected, composed, relaxed, self-possessed, sedate, tranquil, nonchalant, unflappable, laid-back. **3.** UNFRIENDLY aloof, distant, icy, frigid, remote, standoffish, unapproachable, frosty, superior. **4.** *Sl.* EXCELLENT great, *neat, *nifty, *groovy, *rad, *funky, awesome, *bad, *bitchen, *boss, *def, *fresh, *hot. ANT. **1.** *hot, *roasting.* **2.** *agitated, ruffled, *bent out* of shape, *unglued. 3. warm, friendly. 4. *uncool, no good, bad.

coop n. pen, cage, fold, enclosure, hutch.

cooperate v. comply with, go along, work with, accommodate, aid, collaborate, pull together, *play ball, pool resources, help, contribute, further. ANT. oppose, undermine.

cooperation n. collaboration, assistance, help, give-and-take, concert, complicity, compliance, participation, *playing ball, pooling of resources, accommodation. ANT. opposition, undermining, autonomy.

coordinate v. organize, arrange, order, group, systematize, integrate, mesh, synchronize, classify, sort, regulate.

cop n. Sl. police officer, peace officer, officer of the law, policeman, policewoman, lawman, *John Law, *flatfoot, patrolman, patrolwoman, sheriff, deputy, *the man, *fuzz. SEE POLICE, COURT

cope v. manage, weather, endure, contend, suffer, get by, face, *cut it, *hack it, deal with, handle.

COPIOUS a. [KOH pee us] abundant, abounding, plentiful. We prepared a copious spread of food for Thanksgiving. SYN. abundant, plentiful, plenty, ample, bounteous, overflowing, lavish, replete, generous, liberal, fat. ANT. scant, sparse, meager.

copout v. Sl. quit, back down, withdraw, *blow off, *worm out, renege, skip, *chicken out, *tap dance.

copse n. thicket, grove, wood, scrub, coppice, boscage.

copulate v. have sexual intercourse, make love, mate, fornicate, *fool around, sleep together, breed, *go all the way. SEE SEX

copy n. duplicate, reproduction, replica, imitation, facsimile, *carbon copy, likeness, representation, counterfeit. ANT. original, model.

copy v. 1. DUPLICATE reproduce, replicate, imitate, clone, simulate, represent. 2. IMITATE ape, emulate, pattern, model, mimic, simulate, act like, mirror, impersonate, embody, mock.

copycat n. imitator, mimic, impersonator.

coquet v. flirt, tease, toy with, wink at, strut, vamp, titillate, dally, philander.

coquette n. flirt, tease, vamp, hussy, heartbreaker. "A woman without any heart, who makes a fool out of a man that hasn't got any head."—Madame Deluzy.

cord n. line, rope, twine, string, cordage, cable, wire, binding.

cordial a. warm, friendly, hearty, sociable, genial, affable, amiable, gracious, hearty, heartfelt. ANT. cold, distant, unsociable.

core n. center, nucleus, heart, kernel, root, *meat, crux, essence, bottom line, *nitty-gritty, gist.

cork n. plug, stopper.

corner n. 1. BEND crook, angle, convergence, intersection, junction, juncture. 2. PREDICAMENT *pickle, *jam, *squeeze, tight spot, impasse.

CORNERSTONE n. [KORN ur stohn] a crucial or vital element. Freedom of choice is the cornerstone of democracy. SYN. keystone, linchpin, anchor, mainspring, base, key element, mainstay, pillar, main ingredient, foundation, essential, upholder, main support, indispensable component, strength.

cornucopia n. abundance, riches, wealth.

corner v. trap, back into, catch, bring to bay.

corny a. trite, banal, stupid, stereotyped, hackneyed, sentimental, sappy, insipid, mushy, unsophisticated, *hokey. ANT. sophisticated, original, powerful.

corollary n. deduction, inference, result, outcome, consequence, end, aftereffect, upshot, precipitate.

coroner n. medical examiner, investigator, public officer, doctor, physician.

corporal a. bodily, physical, material, carnal.

corporate a. united, combined, joint, allied, collective, incorporated, common, associated. ANT. individual, single.

corps n. unit, crew, team, force, band, division, troupe, regiment, battalion, company, squadron, outfit.

corpse n. body, cadaver, *stiff, carcass, remains, corpus delecti, bones, the deceased. "A human been."—Kay Goodman. "[L]ike the cover of an old book, its contents torn out, and stript of its lettering and gilding . . . yet the work itself shall not be lost, for it will appear once more in a new and more beautiful edition."—Ben Franklin.

corpulent a. fat, obese, plump, chubby, fleshy, beefy, rotund, tubby, stout, portly, roly-poly, blubbery. ANT. skinny, anorexic, bony.

corral n. pen, enclosure.

correct v. 1. RECTIFY set right, redress, amend, fix, adjust, better, mend, revise, improve, reform, doctor. 2. CHASTISE reprimand, scold, reprove, admonish, dress down, censure, rebuke, discipline. ANT. 1. hurt, complicate. 2. praise, compliment, approve.

correct *a.* **1.** ACCURATE exact, *right, true, precise, *on the button, *on the nose, *on the money, unmistaken, flawless. **2.** PROPER suitable, fitting, appropriate, befitting, seemly, *politically correct, *kosher, acceptable. ANT. *1. incorrect, wrong, inaccurate. 2. improper, inappropriate.*

correction *n.* rectification, modification, adjustment, amendment, improvement, righting, reparation, change.

corrective *a.* remedial, rectifying, counter, reparative, curative, healing, therapeutic. ANT. *hurtful, imparing, damaging.*

correlate *v.* equate, relate, compare, contrast, parallel, correspond, connect.

correspond *v.* **1.** AGREE harmonize, conform, be consistent, be compatible, match, go together, coincide, concur, jibe, fit. **2.** COMMUNICATE BY LETTER write, *drop a line, keep in touch. ANT. *1. clash, disagree, differ.*

correspondence *n.* **1.** AGREEMENT harmony, conformity, consistency, compatibility, match, coinciding, accordance, congruity. **2.** COMMUNICATION letters, *faxes, messages, mail, dispatches. ANT. *1. disagreement, incongruity.*

correspondent *n.* reporter, newsman, newswoman, journalist, broadcaster, stringer, foreign correspondent.

corresponding *a.* equivalent, parallel, analogous, correlative, reciprocal, alike, matching, synonymous, complementary, conforming, consistent. ANT. *counter, against, unlike, opposite.*

corridor *n.* hall, passageway, walkway, gallery, aisle.

CORROBORATE *v.* [kuh ROB uh RATE] to confirm or support the information given by another. *Several witnesses came forward to corroborate the defendant's alibi.* SYN. confirm, support, attest to, verify, certify, authenticate, prove, substantiate, validate, strengthen. ANT. *contradict, refute.*

corrode *v.* dissolve, wear, deteriorate, waste, rust, gnaw away, eat away, erode, oxidize.

corrosion *n.* wear, oxidation, rust, deterioration, decay, erosion, disintegration, fragmentation, degeneration, decomposition.

corrosive *a.* erosive, caustic, acidic, biting, mordant, scathing, cutting, acerbic, wasting, consuming.

corrugated *a.* ridged, crinkled, wrinkled, creased, ribbed, furrowed, pleated, fluted, rough. ANT. *smooth, flat.*

corrupt *v.* demoralize, pervert, debase, spoil, pollute, taint, abase, adulterate, infect, ruin, defile, degrade, debauch, taint.

corrupt *a.* **1.** DISHONEST deceitful, unethical, unprincipled, unscrupulous, crooked, untrustworthy, shady, underhanded, venal, deceptive. **2.** IMMORAL depraved, perverted, degenerate, low, evil, rotten, debased, warped, unprincipled. **3.** IMPURE contaminated, adulterated, unclean, tainted, defiled, polluted, infected. ANT. *1. honest, honorable, scrupulous. 2. moral, virtuous, upright. 3. pure, clean, unaltered.*

corruption *n.* **1.** DISHONESTY deceit, deception, underhandedness, deception, crookedness, *shadiness, fraud, unscrupulousness. **2.** IMMORALITY depravity, perversion, evil, degeneration, baseness, decadence, wickedness, impurity, turpitude, iniquity. **3.** CONTAMINATION adulteration, tainting, defilement, pollution, infection. ANT. *1. honesty, scruples. 2. morality, virtue. 3. purity.*

cosign *v.* endorse, pledge.

cortege *n.* train, retinue, entourage, escort, attendants, procession, court.

cosmetic *a.* beautifying, enhancing, corrective, superficial.

cosmetics *n.* makeup, beautifiers, preparations, *war paint, lip gloss, lipstick, eye shadow, rouge, blusher, mascara, eyebrow pencil, face powder, *face. "Crease paint."—Raymond Cvikota.

cosmic *a.* **1.** OF SPACE interstellar, universal, interplanetary, galactic. **2.** LIMITLESS infinite, vast, neverending, immense, grandiose, measureless. ANT. *2. microscopic, finite, limited, infinitesimal.* SEE SPACE, UNIVERSE

cosmopolitan *a.* worldly, international, global, universal, metropolitan, sophisticated, cultured, cultivated, urbane, unprovincial. ANT. *provincial, small-town, insular.*

cosmos *n.* universe, space, *great beyond, macrocosm, all creation, arc of heaven, creation. "Something for every age to investigate."—Seneca. "All that is or ever was or ever will be."—Carl Sagan. SEE CONSTELLATION, MOON, PLANET, SPACE, STAR, UNIVERSE

cosset *v.* pamper, fondle, coddle, pet.

cost *n.* **1.** EXPENSE charge, price, value, worth, amount, expenditure, payment, outlay, bill. SEE MONEY **2.** LOSS injury, harm, forfeit, expense, detriment, damage, sacrifice, price.

cost-effective *a.* economical, practical, worthwhile, profitable. ANT. *excessive, worthless.*

costly *a.* **1.** EXPENSIVE high-priced, steep, exorbitant, dear, pricey, excessive, *stiff. **2.** SACRIFICING painful, injurious, harmful, ruinous.

3. VALUABLE precious, priceless, luxurious, sumptuous, opulent, exquisite, grand, lavish. ANT. *1. cheap, bargain-priced, economical. 2. painless, harmless. 3. worthless, cheap.*

costume n. outfit, clothing, apparel, garb, attire, dress, ensemble, *getup, raiment, vestments, guise.

coterie n. group, circle, clique, set, club, association, crew, band.

cotillion n. ball, dance.

cottage n. house, cabin, shanty, bungalow, shack, chalet, camp. SEE HOUSE

couch n. sofa, divan, davenport, lounge.

couch v. express, voice, phrase, frame.

couch potato n. *Sl.* slug, sloth, drone, *goof-off, lie-abed, *lazy-bones, shirker, piker, slacker, *sofa spud.

cougar n. mountain lion, puma, panther.

cough v. hack, *bark, gasp, rasp, wheeze, hem, hawk, whoop, clear throat.

council n. meeting, assembly, conference, *powwow, convention, gathering, convocation, session, caucus, congress.

counsel n. **1.** ADVICE guidance, instruction, direction, consultation, recommendation, *word to the wise, suggestion, opinion, warning. **2.** ATTORNEY lawyer, legal representative, counselor, advocate, barrister, solicitor.

counsel v. advise, guide, instruct, direct, recommend, *give a word to the wise, suggest, warn, steer, prompt, advocate.

counselor n. advisor, attorney, lawyer, advocate, guide, instructor, teacher, mentor, confidant.

count n. total, sum, tally, number, outcome, calculation, score, *bottom line.

count v. **1.** ENUMERATE tally, number, total, add up, tick off, sum, calculate, compute. **2.** CONSIDER regard, deem, esteem, rate. **3.** INCLUDE take into account, number among. **4.** MATTER carry weight, rate, *cut ice.

countenance n. **1.** APPEARANCE aspect, face, expression, features, look, mien, visage, cast, air, semblance. **2.** APPROVAL support, acceptance, sanction, encouragement, blessing, backing.

countenance v. approve, condone, allow, permit, put up with, stand for, tolerate, support, back, sanction. ANT. *disapprove, reject, prohibit.*

counter n. stand, table, shelf, display case, *checkout counter.

counter v. counteract, answer, respond, retaliate, return, come back, oppose, check, neutralize, offset.

counter a. contrary, opposite, contrasting, antithetical, inverse. ANT. *corresponding, alike, analogous, consistent.*

counteract v. neutralize, offset, negate, annul, oppose, check, cancel.

counterfeit n. imitation, copy, reproduction, forgery, fake, sham, fraud, phony, replica. ANT. *original, model, *real McCoy, genuine article.*

counterfeit a. *bogus, fake, phony, imitation, sham, fraudulent, *fishy, not genuine, *not kosher, forged, spurious, pseudo. ANT. *real, actual, authentic, genuine.*

countermand n. cancel, override, revoke, repeal, recall, rescind, retract, reverse, overrule.

counterpart n. equivalent, match, correspondent, twin, correlate, duplicate, copy, parallel, mate, analogue, peer.

countless a. innumerable, infinite, multitudinous, untold, *umpteen, limitless, legion, incalculable, many. ANT. *few, finite.*

countrified a. rural, rustic, agrarian, pastoral, *down-home, simple. ANT. *citified, urban, metropolitan.*

country n. **1.** NATION motherland, fatherland, land, commonwealth, state, union, realm, republic. **2.** RURAL AREA backwoods, *boonies, *the sticks, woodlands, wilds, farmland, *cow country, outback, bush.

COUP n. [KOO] a brilliant maneuver or victory, a masterstroke. Also, a coup d'etat. *The chess match ended with an unexpected coup by the challenger.* SYN. masterstroke, maneuver, achievement, accomplishment, stroke, exploit, coup d'etat, action, move, stunt, feat.

COUP DE GRACE n. [KOO de GRAHS] a deathblow, a finishing blow. *A resounding slam dunk was the coup de grace.* SYN. deathblow, finishing blow, finishing stroke, mortal blow, the clincher, knockout punch.

COUP D'ETAT n. [koo day TAH] a violent overthrow of a government or ruler. *The unrest was followed by a coup d'etat and the assassination of the dictator.* SYN. overthrow, change of government, coup, power grab, revolution, uprising, takeover, power play.

couple n. pair, duo, twosome, brace.

couple v. joint, link, unite, pair, attach, connect, yoke, hitch. ANT. *uncouple, detach, disconnect.*

coupon n. refund, rebate, certificate, scrip, discount slip.

courage n. bravery, fearlessness, valor, lionheartedness, *guts, nerve, *balls, boldness, dauntlessness, derring-do, self-assurance, daring, pluck, backbone, *spine. "[L]ies halfway between rashness and cowardice."—Cervantes. "Being scared to death—and saddling up anyway."—John Wayne. "Grace under pressure."—Ernest Hemingway. "Fear holding on a minute longer."—George Patton. ANT. *cowardice, mousiness, *wimpiness, faintheartedness.*

courageous a. brave, fearless, valorous, valiant, lionhearted, *gutsy, nervy, *ballsy, dauntless, bold, daring, plucky, stout, manly, *macho, gallant, intrepid, *gritty, hardy, stouthearted. ANT. *cowardly, spineless, fearful, *wimpy.*

courier n. messenger, carrier, emissary, runner, envoy, *gofer.

course n. **1.** PROGRESSION way, advance, proceeding, passage, flow. **2.** ROUTE path, trail, way, channel, run, track. **3.** PROCEDURE mode, plan, scheme, policy. **4.** CLASS curriculum, subject, program, lessons.

course v. run, flow, traverse, race, rush, surge, speed, tumble.

court n. **1.** COURTYARD enclosure, quadrangle, plaza, square, patio, atrium. **2.** ATTENDANTS entourage, staff, retinue, cortege. **3.** COURT OF LAW court of justice, judiciary, bench, bar, forum, tribunal, municipal building, hall of justice.

WORD FIND

action: suit

appearance before judge without formal trial: hearing

arrest order for failure to appear: bench warrant

blatant show of disrespect for court rules: contempt of court

bond forfeited if accused fails to show up for court: bail

calendar of cases: docket

court order: injunction

court system: judiciary

DA: district attorney, prosecutor

damages awarded beyond plaintiff's loss to punish defendant: punitive damages, exemplary damages, double damages

decision: judgment

decision won without proceedings, for failure of one party to show: default judgment

defendant's suit against plaintiff: countersuit, counterclaim

defending party in a court action: defendant

disposition of case by negotiating guilty plea for lesser charge: plea bargaining

fail to appear after posting bail: jump bail

faulty trial that is voided: mistrial

filer of court action: plaintiff, petitioner

general jurisdiction court: superior court

hearing of charges, entering of plea by accused: arraignment

hears appeals from lower court decisions: court of appeals

higher court that reviews lower court decisions: appellate court

highest: Supreme Court

inquiry, judicial: inquest

intermediary who settles cases out of court: mediator

judge's private room: chambers

jury, citizen's obligation to serve on: jury duty

jury member: juror

jury member's verdict, surveying each: polling the jury

jury's decision: verdict

jury selection process: impaneling

jury spokesman: foreman

jury, trial without: bench trial

jury, twelve-member: petit jury, jury

jury, 12-23 members, evaluates accusations, returns indictments: grand jury

jury unable to reach consensus: hung jury

jury, unethical contact with by lawyer: jury tampering

lawyer: counsel, attorney, barrister (BRIT.), solicitor (BRIT.), advocate

lawyer provided by government for the poor: public defender

lawyer's assistant: paralegal

local criminal and civil court: municipal court

location/jurisdiction: venue

loss claimed by plaintiff: damages

lowest court, holds sessions at different places: circuit court

lying while under oath: perjury

military court proceedings: court-martial

minor claims court: small claims court

officer/guard who maintains order in courtroom: bailiff

order to appear in court: subpoena, summons

order to arrest someone: warrant

order to restrict comments about case outside court: gag order

order to search a location for evidence: search warrant

party to a lawsuit: litigant
pledge to tell nothing but the truth: oath
present or argue a case in court: plead
private suit: civil action
punishment handed down by judge: sentence
questioning of opposing party witness by lawyer: cross examination
retrial from lower court to higher: appeal
ruling, plea for: motion
seat of judge: bench
seat of witness while testifying: witness stand, witness box
similar earlier case used as model in later case: precedent
simulated trial by law students: moot court
suit filed on behalf of a group: class action suit
suspend proceedings: adjourn, recess
suspension of sentencing: stay
sworn statement: affidavit
transcribes court proceedings word-for-word: court reporter, stenographer
unsanctioned court that ignores appropriate legal procedures: kangaroo court
will and estate processing court: probate court, surrogate court
witness who is absolutely vital: material witness
witness who is biased against opponent: hostile witness
witness's pretrial statement given while under oath: deposition
written statement charging one with crime: indictment
SEE LAW

court v. woo, pursue, keep company with, date, take out, curry favor with, pander to, flatter, blandish, cajole, fawn over, *brown-nose, *kiss up to. ANT. reject, shun, avoid.

courteous a. polite, well-mannered, civil, mannerly, respectful, considerate, gracious, refined, gentlemanly, cultivated, formal, ladylike. ANT. rude, impolite, ill-mannered.

courtesan n. prostitute, mistress, harlot, kept woman, concubine.

courtesy n. politeness, good manners, civility, respect, consideration, graciousness, refinement, gentleness, formality, tact. "The art of choosing among one's real thoughts."—Abel Stevens. ANT. rudeness, discourtesy, informality.

courtly a. dignified, refined, polite, mannerly, stately, cultivated, gentlemanly, polished, well-bred, proper, elegant, respectful, suave. ANT. rude, unrefined, rough, ill-mannered.

court-martial n. military court, military trial, military tribunal.

courtship n. dating, wining and dining, wooing, engagement, pair bonding.

cove n. bay, inlet, harbor, anchorage, bight, estuary, lagoon.

COVENANT n. [KUV uh nunt] a contract or binding agreement. They made a covenant to perform their duties on time. SYN. agreement, contract, compact, pact, pledge, promise, trust, commitment, arrangement, concordat.

cover n. 1. COVERING coverup, wrapping, sheet, blanket, tarpaulin, canopy, sheath, folder, spread, canvas, binding. 2. SHELTER refuge, retreat, haven, sanctuary, hiding place, protection.

cover v. 1. WRAP encase, enshroud, overspread, overlay, envelop, cloak, dress, coat. 2. HIDE conceal, shield, veil, screen, cloak, bury, camouflage, secrete, disguise. 3. INCLUDE encompass, incorporate, contain, deal with, comprise, embrace, embody. 4. TRAVERSE cross, pass through, range over. 5. REPORT detail, recount, chronicle, tell. ANT. 1. uncover, unwrap, expose. 2. expose, reveal, show.

COVERT a. [KOH vurt] secret, covered up. No one was permitted to discuss the covert military action. SYN. covered, covered up, secret, hidden, undercover, clandestine, underground, concealed, cloaked, camouflaged, *under wraps, *hush-hush, surreptitious. ANT. open, overt, up-front.

cover-up n. concealment, disguising, masking, camouflage, placing under wraps, burial, evasion, closeting, smoothing-over.

COVET v. [KUH vit] to wish for or desire, especially that of another's. Do not covet thy neighbor's wife. SYN. desire, wish for, want, long for, hunger for, crave, yearn for, lust after, itch for, fancy. ANT. reject, ignore, spurn.

covetous a. desirous, avaricious, greedy, acquisitive, lustful, rapacious, yearning, longing, grasping, grabby, envious. ANT. generous, sharing, benevolent.

covey n. flock, party, band, bevy, group, cluster, clique.

cow n. bovine, ruminant, bull, heifer, calf, *bossy.

WORD FIND
barn: byre, stable
beef breeds: Angus, Beefalo, Belted Galloway, Brahman, Charbray, Hereford, Texas Longhorn

chew cud: ruminate
cornstalks, hay, straw food: fodder
dairy breeds: Brown Swiss, Guernsey, Holstein, Jersey
dehorned animal: pollard
diseases: hoof-and-mouth disease, mastitis, scours
hairy portion of tail: switch
milk gland: udder
moo: low
neck fold on some breeds: dewlap
regurgitated food that is rechewed: cud
stomachs: abomasum, omasum, reticulum, rumen

cow *v.* intimidate, bully, unnerve, frighten, daunt, threaten, buffalo, bully, terrorize, browbeat. ANT. *fortify, embolden, puff up.*

coward *n.* *gutless wonder, *scaredy-cat, *baby, *chicken, *wimp, *wuss, milquetoast, poltroon, dastard, *invertebrate, *sissy, *mouse. "One who in a perilous emergency thinks with his legs."—Ambrose Bierce. "A man in whom the instinct of self-preservation acts normally."—Sultana Zoraya. ANT. *daredevil, hero, *macho man.*

cowardice *n.* timidity, fearfulness, faintheartedness, *wimpiness, *mousiness, pusillanimity, timorousness, *chicken-heartedness, *cold feet. "To know what is right and not do it."—Confucius ANT. *bravery, fearlessness, *guts, *balls, daring.*

cowardly *a.* fearful, timid, frightened, fainthearted, *babyish, *chicken, *wimpy, *mousy, dastardly, craven, *gutless, spineless, timorous, shrinking, *yellow. ANT. *brave, courageous, *gutsy, daring.*

cowboy *n.* cowpuncher, bronco, cowpoke, rancher, *buckaroo, drover, *vaquero, cattle herder, *gaucho.

WORD FIND
breaker of wild horses: bronc buster
calf: dogie
capture of wandering cattle: roundup
cattle identification mark: brand
competition: rodeo
food wagon on the range: chuck wagon
foreman: trail boss
hat: Stetson
herd horses: wrangle
horse herder: wrangler
leather breeches: chaps, chaparejos, leggins
pistol: Colt 45
ranch company: outfit
rides alongside herd: flank rider, swing rider
rides at front of herd: point rider

rides behind herd: drag rider
rides wide of herd and rounds up wandering cattle: outrider
rifle: Winchester
rope: lariat, lasso
sack for personal belongings: war bag
staple: frijoles, beans, jerky
steal cattle: rustle
string of horses assigned to rider: mount
unbranded cow: maverick
unbroken horse: bronco
SEE COW, HORSE

cower *v.* cringe, shrink, flinch, quail, blench, wince, tremble, kowtow, grovel, skulk. ANT. *strut, swagger, tower over.*

cowrite *v.* collaborate, coauthor.

COY *a.* [KOY] shy or affectedly shy, demure. *With men, she was always coy.* SYN. shy, demure, modest, retiring, bashful, shrinking, diffident, blushing, sheepish, self-conscious, *playing hard-to-get, coquettish. ANT. *bold, aggressive, forward, cheeky.*

coyote *n.* canine, carnivore, scavenger, animal, mammal, quadruped, ominvore, coy dog.

cozy *a.* snug, comfy, cushy, warm, snuggled, secure, safe, intimate. ANT. *uncomfortable, insecure.*

crabby *a.* *bitchy, surly, irritable, *cranky, snappish, cross, petulant, grouchy, testy, moody, *touchy. ANT. *sweet, pleasant, good-humored.*

crack *n.* 1. SNAP clap, crackle, pop, slap, bang, thunder, boom, report. 2. FRACTURE break, split, cut, fragment, splinter, tear, rent, cleft, fissure, rupture. 3. HIT blow, clout, clip, whack, pound, bang. 4. REMARK comment, observation, wisecrack, witticism, quip, *zinger, bon mot, *dig.

crack *n. Sl.* rock cocaine. SEE COCAINE

crack *v.* 1. SNAP clap, crackle, pop, slap, bang, thunder, boom. 2. FRACTURE break, split, cut, fragment, splinter, shatter, smash, tear, cleave. 3. HIT strike, clip, whack, clout. 4. LOSE COMPOSURE *lose it, go crazy, *bug out, have a nervous breakdown, *go to pieces. 5. SOLVE OR BREAK, AS A CODE decipher, decode, work out, figure out.

crack *a.* *crackerjack, first-rate, superior, ace, expert, proficient, master. ANT. *inferior, mediocre, seocnd-rate.*

crackdown *n.* attack, assault, stop, restraint, storming, strike.

cracked *a.* fissured, broken, shattered, split.

cracker *n. Sl.* hacker. SEE COMPUTER

crackerjack *a.* SEE CRACK

crackle *n.* snap, pop, sizzle, crepitation.

crackpot *n.* eccentric, *nut, *birdbrain, crackbrain, crank, *screwball.

crack-up *n.* collision, accident, wreck. SEE ACCIDENT

cradle *n.* birthplace, origin, source, fountain, beginning, wellspring.

craft *n.* **1.** SKILL expertise, artistry, facility, mastery, dexterity, ability, knack, knowhow. **2.** CUNNING artfulness, deceit, craftiness, shrewdness, slyness, artifice, guile, trickery, ruse. **3.** TRADE handiwork, job, line, business, vocation. ANT. *1. incompetency, clumsiness, inability. 2. honesty, naiveté.*

craftsman *n.* artisan, artist, artificer, technician, smith, talent, *wiz.

craftsmanship *n.* artistry, handiwork, detail work.

crafty *a.* cunning, shrewd, sly, *foxy, wily, artful, deceitful, underhanded, sharp, designing, scheming, *slippery. ANT. *honest, naive, artless.*

craggy *a.* steep, rugged, rocky, jagged, stony, precipitous, scraggy.

cram *v.* **1.** STUFF fill, crowd, press, compress, ram, squeeze, pack, load, choke, condense. **2.** STUDY *burn the midnight oil, read up, *bone up, *hit the books.

cramp *n.* contraction, spasm, *charlie horse, kink, crick, twinge, stitch, knot.

cramp *v.* restrict, restrain, confine, hinder, hamper, constrict, check, limit, impede, clamp, stymie, inhibit.

crane *n.* hoist, lift, boom, davit, heavy machinery, derrick.

cranium *n.* skull, braincase.

crank *n.* eccentric, *crackpot, character, *nut.

cranky *a.* irritable, ill-tempered, grouchy, surly, moody, ugly, *ornery, grumpy, grouchy, *like a bear, testy, ill-humored, choleric. ANT. *sweet, pleasant, good-humored.*

cranny *n.* opening, crevice, fissure, cavity, gap, chink, cleft, furrow.

crap *n. Sl.* **1.** EXCREMENT feces, dropping, stool, BM, dung, poop, manure, fertilizer, cow chip, guano. **2.** JUNK trash, garbage, refuse, schlock. **3.** NONSENSE *bull, applesauce, absurdity, bunk, *horsefeathers, *hogwash, *poppycock, *bilge, *claptrap.

crappy *a. Sl.* POOR lousy, worthless, sub-par, inferior, junk, trashy, terrible, useless, cheap, shoddy.

crapshoot *n.* risk, risky business, *shot in the dark, iffy proposition, *spin of the roulette wheel.

crash *n.* **1.** BANG clatter, clangor, racket, din, blast, crack, thunder, boom. **2.** COLLISION smashup, wreck, impact, crack-up, pileup, accident, *wipeout, crunch, bump, *fenderbender, *rear-ending, *T-bone, *sideswipe. **3.** BANKRUPTCY financial collapse, failure, ruination.

crash *v.* **1.** BANG clatter, clang, explode, blast, crack, thunder, boom. **2.** SMASH impact, wreck, shatter, total, crack up, disintegrate, collide, bump, jolt, blindside, tumble, *go end over end, *go ass over teakettle, *plow into, ditch, *go down in flames. **3.** GO BANKRUPT fail, collapse, *go belly up.

CRASS *a.* [KRASS] ignorant and insensitive, indelicate. *We were mortified by his crass jokes.* SYN. ignorant, stupid, insensitive, unfeeling, coarse, vulgar, boorish, uncouth, rough, lowbrow, gross, unrefined, philistine, crude. ANT. *sensitive, refined, delicate.*

crate *n.* box, case, carton, container, receptacle.

crater *n.* pit, craterlet, hole, caldera, cavity, depression, impact center, meteorite impression.

crave *v.* **1.** DESIRE long for, yearn for, hunger for, want, covet, thirst for, lust after, ache for, need, require. **2.** BEG implore, beseech, plead for, entreat, solicit, supplicate, pray for. ANT. *1. detest, loathe, spurn, reject.*

craven *a.* cowardly, fearful, dastardly, timid, timorous, yellow, fainthearted, *chicken, *wimpy, gutless, spineless, pusillanimous. ANT. *brave, courageous, fearless, daring.*

craving *n.* desire, longing, yearning, want, need, hunger, thirst, hankering, *yen, lust.

crawl *v.* creep, go on all fours, *belly, worm, inch, wriggle, drag, *go at a snail's pace, writhe, grovel.

craze *n.* fad, mania, rage, *latest thing, fashion, trend, passion.

crazed *a.* SEE CRAZY

crazy *a.* **1.** MENTALLY UNSTABLE insane, deranged, *off one's hinges, *one hinge short of a nuthouse door, demented, psychotic, *nuts, cracked, *out of one's mind, daft, *touched, *out to lunch, *moonstruck, maniacal, mad, *flipped out, flaky, wacky, loco, *potty, *psycho, *loony, buggy, *mad as a March hare, *off the wall, *mental, berserk, hysterical, *gone around the bend, *off one's trolley. SEE NEUROSIS, NEUROTIC, PSYCHOSIS **2.** NOT SENSIBLE impractical, *goofy, *out of one's gourd, unrealistic, ludicrous, *cockamamie, *harebrained, fantastical, absurd, ridiculous, foolish, silly, unsound, irrational. **3.** ARDENT fond, mad, devoted, wild, zealous, enthusiastic, passionate. ANT. *1. sane, stable, levelheaded, lucid, rational. 2. sensible, realistic, practical. 3. cool, indifferent, apathetic.*

creak *v.* squeak, grate, rasp, groan, squeal, screech, squawk.

creampuff *n.* weakling, *wimp, mouse, sissy, *woos, *woosy, *fairy, *wus, *wussy.

crease *n.* fold, ridge, pleat, wrinkle, crimp, crinkle, rumple.

crease *v.* fold, pleat, wrinkle, crimp, crinkle, rumple, pucker.

create *v.* originate, make, think up, develop, invent, design, author, compose, produce, spawn, give rise to, found, formulate, dream up, establish, innovate, fabricate, coin, *hatch, launch, start, conceive.

creation *n.* **1.** CONCEPTION birth, genesis, inception, origination, nativity, generation, establishment, formation. **2.** INVENTION work, handiwork, brainchild, production, piece, innovation. **3.** HEAVEN AND EARTH universe, life, cosmos, world, nature. "The shaping of an indifferent matter into a world of value."—J.E. Boodin.

creative *a.* inventive, artistic, imaginative, resourceful, clever, ingenious, original, innovative, gifted, visionary, inspired, Promethean. ANT. *unoriginal, mindless, sterile, stale, unimaginative.*

creativity *n.* inventiveness, originality, resourcefulness, cleverness, inspiration, vision, ingenuity, genius, fertility, fecundity, talent. "Discontent translated into art."—Eric Hoffer. ANT. *sterility, barrenness, mindlessness, infertility.*

creator *n.* inventor, maker, architect, God, father, originator, mastermind, founder, designer.

creature *n.* beast, animal, *critter, *varmint, living being, mammal, vertebrate, man. SEE ANIMAL, MONSTER

credence *n.* acceptance, belief, trust, credibility, reliance, faith, confidence, assurance, credit, stock. ANT. *disbelief, doubt, distrust.*

credentials *n.* references, qualifications, documents, authorization, testimonial, certificate, license, letter of reference, diploma, title, papers.

credenza *n.* sideboard, buffet, case, shelf, cupboard, bookcase.

credibility *n.* believability, reliability, trustworthiness, soundness, integrity, plausibility, dependability. ANT. *implausibility, questionability.*

credibility gap *n.* discrepancy, disparity, 2 plus 2 not adding up to 4, inconsistency, question.

credible *a.* believable, reliable, trustworthy, sound, plausible, dependable, honest, solid, conceivable, likely. ANT. *incredible, unbelievable, doubtful.*

credit *n.* **1.** BELIEF trust, faith, honesty, credibility. **2.** RECOGNITION acclaim, praise, tribute, notice, commendation, pat on the back, *Brownie points, acknowledgement. **3.** DEBT on account, deferred payment, charge, time, installment plan. "Imaginary riches."—Thomas Peacock. ANT. *1. disbelief, mistrust. 2. blame, disapproval. 3. cash.*

credit *v.* **1.** BELIEVE trust, accept, *buy, have faith in, trust, *take stock in. **2.** ASSIGN TO recognize, accredit, attribute, ascribe, acknowledge. ANT. *1. disbelieve, distrust.*

creditable *a.* commendable, laudatory, meritorious, praiseworthy, worthy, respectable, exemplary, honorable. ANT. *unworthy, disgraceful, despicable.*

credit union *n.* thrift institution, lending institution, cooperative.

credo *n.* belief, creed, tenet, principles, code.

credulous *a.* gullible, naive, trusting, believing, *born yesterday, unsuspecting, unsophisticated, *thick, green. ANT. *incredulous, suspicious, disbelieving, wary, cynical.*

creed *n.* faith, religion, belief, ideology, principles, persuasion, tenet, doctrine, conviction, dogma.

creek *n.* stream, brook, crik, rill, run, rivulet, runnel, spring.

creep *n.* Sl. jerk, *dink, *geek, *goon, *sleazebag, *scumbag, weirdo, *slimeball, pervert.

creep *v.* crawl, worm, snake, writhe, move stealthily, *belly, wriggle, *crab, grovel, slink, skulk, steal, sneak.

creeps, the *n.* Sl. *heebie-jeebies, fear, repugnance, *the willies, *the horrors, *the jumps.

creepy *a.* scary, gruesome, spine-tingling, hair-raising, horrible, disturbing, nightmarish, eerie, revolting, sinister, weird, macabre, chilling, *skin-crawling. ANT. *normal, reassuring.*

cremate *v.* incinerate, burn, reduce to ashes.

cremation *n.* incineration, burning, reducing to ashes.

WORD FIND
remains: cremains

CRÈME DE LA CRÈME *n.* [KREM deh la KREM] literally, cream of the cream; the best of the best. Also, people of high society. *The benefit dinner attrracted the crème de la crème of Washington society.* SYN. best of the best, cream of the crop, the best and brightest, the finest, the elite, pick of the litter, upper class, *upper crust, aristocracy. ANT. *the dregs, refuse.*

CRESCENDO *n.* [kruh SHEN doh] an increase in intensity, or the climax of such an increase. *The music warmed to a fever pitch and ended with a powerful crescendo.* SYN. increase, escalation, surge, upsurge, intensification, broadening, building, rise, ascension, progression, climb, elevation, climax, culmination, peak, pinnacle, crest, summit, apex, zenith, boiling point, critical mass, explosion. ANT. *decrescendo, dissipation, decrease, softening.*

crescent *n.* half-moon, demilune, meniscus, sickle. SEE MOON

crest *n.* **1.** COMB tuft, cockscomb, topknot, plume, mane. **2.** TOP summit, crown, ridge, peak, pinnacle, head, apex.

crestfallen *a.* disappointed, dejected, down, depressed, discouraged, downhearted, dispirited, sad, melancholy, low. ANT. *joyful, euphoric, *up.*

cretin *n.* idiot, imbecile, moron, *retard.

crevasse *n.* fissure, chasm, opening, cleavage, cleft, crevice.

crevice *n.* fissure, crack, gap, cleft, cranny, rent, split, groove, fracture, slit, gash, crevasse, chasm, opening.

crew *n.* group, band, team, company, squad, troupe, mob, gang, party, set, bunch, posse, clique.

crew cut *n.* *buzz cut, *buzzer, *skinner, military haircut, butch cut, *flattop.

crib *v. Sl.* cheat, copy, plagiarize, lift.

crib death *n.* sudden infant death syndrome (SIDS).

crime *n.* lawlessness, wrongdoing, offense, malfeasance, malefaction, antisocial behavior, transgression, corruption, felony, misdemeanor. SEE COURT, LAW

criminal *n.* lawbreaker, outlaw, felon, convict, crook, *hood, larcenist, culprit, desperado, mafioso, scofflaw, recidivist. "A person with predatory instincts who has not sufficient capital to form a corporation."—Howard Scott.

criminal *a.* **1.** ILLEGAL unlawful, illicit, felonious, illegitimate, *shady, crooked, larcenous, homicidal. SEE COURT, LAW **2.** VILLAINOUS wicked, evil, nefarious, degenerate, corrupt, errant. ANT. *1. legal, legitimate. 2. pure, unblemished.*

crimp *n.* fold, pinch, press, crease, pleat, wrinkle.

cringe *v.* shrink, flinch, cower, wince, quail, blench, recoil, grovel, quiver, crouch, bow and scrape. ANT. *stand tall, strut, swagger.*

crinkle *v.* wrinkle, crumple, crimple, pucker, crease, crimp, fold, twist, crackle, rustle. ANT. *smooth, straighten, press.*

crinoline *n.* hoop skirt, petticoat.

cripple *v.* disable, handicap, incapacitate, paralyze, maim, debilitate, immobilize, hamstring, *sideline, *bench, impair, weaken. ANT. *invigorate, strengthen, fortify.*

crisis *n.* turning point, emergency, trouble, *moment of truth, *point of no return, crossroad, catastrophe, disaster, *zero hour, predicament, exigency, *crunch, *pickle, strait, *critical mass. "God's call to us to reach a new level of humanity."—Samuel Miller.

crisp *a.* **1.** BRITTLE crunchy, crumbly, friable, firm, fresh. **2.** CHILLY invigorating, bracing, brisk, refreshing, nippy. **3.** SHORT pithy, succinct, brief, terse, sharp, blunt, pointed. **4.** NEAT tidy, trim, clean, smart, *snappy, spruce. ANT. *1. soft, withered. 2. hot. 3. dull, wordy, verbose. 4. sloppy, slovenly.*

crisscross *v.* intersect, overlap, cross.

CRITERION *n.* [kri TEER ee un] something on which a judgment can be based, a test or standard. *When hiring an employee, our most important criterion is sales ability.* SYN. standard, test, rule, measure, guideline, barometer, gauge, scale, yardstick, guidepost, touchstone.

critic *n.* **1.** REVIEWER analyst, judge, expositor, connoisseur, authority, expert, arbiter, commentator. "A legless man who teaches running."—Channing Pollack. "Brushers of noblemen's clothes."—George Herbert **2.** FAULTFINDER complainer, *nitpicker, *nagger, carper, censor, detractor, quibbler, belittler, attacker.

critical *a.* **1.** FAULTFINDING cutting, censorious, carping, *nitpicking, derogatory, disparaging, captious, unflattering, severe, quibbling, disapproving. **2.** EXACTING particular, judicial, discerning, discriminating, fussy, precise, finicky, demanding, hairsplitting. **3.**

CRUCIAL decisive, serious, grave, important, momentous, significant, pivotal, dire, climacteric, vital, urgent. ANT. 1. *approving, accepting, complimentary. 2. undiscerning, unparticular, *easy. 3. trivial, insignificant.*

CRITICAL MASS n. [KRIT uh kuhl MASS] a critical stage; a crisis point; the point at which something momentous will happen. So named after the minimum mass of fissionable material needed to sustain a nuclear reaction. *Some believe that worldwide environmental damage is approaching critical mass.* SYN. critical point, moment of truth, irreversible momentum, point of collapse, crisis, point of no return, moment of truth, climax, turning point, high noon, explosion.

criticism n. 1. ANALYSIS critique, assessment, review, judgment, evaluation, examination, appraisal, commentary. "The avocation of assessing the failures of better men."—Nelson Algren. "A disinterested endeavor to learn and propagate the best that is known and thought in the world."—Mathew Arnold. "Growing important and formidable at very small expense."—Samuel Johnson. 2. DISAPPROVAL faultfinding, disparagement, belittling, censure, carping, diatribe, *nitpicking, quibbling, *knock, *slam, pan, *swipe, *Bronx cheer, brickbats. ANT. 2. *approval, compliment, praise, raves.*

criticize v. 1. ANALYZE critique, assess, review, judge, evaluate, examine, appraise, dissect, comment on. 2. FINDFAULT disapprove, censure, disparage, belittle, *nitpick, quibble, *knock, *slam, *pan, *swipe, bash, blast, *trash, scathe, *roast, attack, *let have it with both barrels, ridicule, scarify. ANT. 2. *approve, laud, praise, applaud, cheer.*

critique n. analysis, review, assessment, commentary, write-up, report, *pan, *slam, *trashing, rave.

critter n. creature, animal, beast.

croak n. utterance, hoarse tone.

crochet n. needlework, weaving.

crock n. vessel, pot.

crocodile tears n. false show of emotion, put-on, Academy Award performance, Hollywood performance.

croissant n. roll, puff, pastry.

Cro-Magnon n. Homo Sapien, human, hominid, caveman, cavewoman, Paleolithic man.

crony n. friend, companion, comrade, ally, pal, *chum, *buddy, *sidekick, colleague, accomplice.

crook n. 1. BEND curve, hook, bow, angle, turn.

2. CRIMINAL felon, thief, swindler, robber, embezzler, burglar, *con.

crooked a. 1. BENT curved, hooked, bowed, angled, twisted, awry, tortuous, warped, misshapen, skewed, serpentine, lopsided, deviating, zigzag. 2. DISHONEST corrupt, deceitful, shady, fraudulent, shifty, underhanded, tricky, designing, crafty. ANT. 1. *straight, level, aligned. 2. honest, honorable, aboveboard, trustworthy.*

crop n. harvest, yield, production, produce.

crop v. cut, trim, clip, chop, snip, shear, shorten, pare, lop, prune, mow.

cross n. 1. CRUCIFIX crux, rood. "Ladders that lead to heaven."—Samuel Smiles.

WORD FIND

cross-bearer: crucifer

cross-shaped: cruciate, cruciform

cross with circle behind crossbeam: Celtic cross

cross with v-shaped ends: Maltese cross

Egyptian cross with loop on top: ankh, ansate cross

horizontal beam: transom

2. CROSS TO BEAR, BURDEN weight, suffering, adversity, load, albatross, affliction, misfortune, pain.

cross v. 1. TRAVERSE span, pass over, extend, go across, bridge, ply, ford. 2. INTERSECT converge, meet, join, bisect, crisscross, entwine. 3. MIX mingle, blend, crossbreed, hybridize, fuse. 4. HINDER oppose, thwart, frustrate, foil, check, deny, impede, stymie, interfere with. ANT. 4. *help, aid, assist.*

cross a. angry, irritable, crabby, testy, touchy, annoyed, surly, snappy, *pissed, *put out, peeved, ill-tempered, mad, *full of piss and vinegar, waspish, choleric. ANT. *happy, cheerful, good-humored.*

crossbreed n. hybrid, mongrel, mixed breed.

cross-examine v. question, interrogate, *pump, *give the third degree, *put on the hotseat, *grill, *go over with a fine-tooth comb, scrutinize.

cross-eye n. strabismus, walleye, exotropia.

crossing n. crossway, passage, bridge, crossroad, junction.

crossroads n. 1. INTERSECTION crossing. 2. TURNING POINT critical point, climax, high noon, moment of truth, the Rubicon.

CROSS THE RUBICON v. to make an important or life-changing decision; to take a consequential action that will forever change things for better or worse; Julius Caesar's decision to lead his troops across the Rubicon in 49 B.C. was considered an act of war. *The company crossed the Rubicon after deciding to abandon its personal computer line and make toasters instead.* SYN. *jump in with both feet, leave a crossroads, commit, affect change, resolve, take a stand, choose one's fate, seal one's fate, bind oneself.

crotch n. **1.** junction, fork. **2.** groin.

crotchety a. grouchy, irritable, cross, touchy, cantankerous, surly, *ornery, testy, peevish, cranky, eccentric. ANT. *pleasant, good-humored, sweet.*

crouch v. bend, stoop, bow, hunker down, *scooch down, hunch, cower, cringe.

crow n. raven, rook, jackdaw.

crow v. brag, boast, bluster, strut, *toot one's own horn, exult, gloat, vaunt. ANT. *minimize, be humble, *eat crow.*

crowbar n. wrecking bar, pinch bar, lever, pry bar, tire iron.

crowd n. **1.** THRONG crush, flood, multitude, horde, mass, confluence, pack, press, *everybody and his brother, mob, gathering. "The collective wisdom of individual ignorance."—Thomas Carlyle. **2.** GROUP circle, set, clique, clan, coterie, bunch, gang, faction, crew.

crowd v. throng, press, congest, cluster, mass, surge, swarm, pile, squeeze, jam, crush, huddle, squash, *squish, *stand cheek by jowl, jostle, elbow, mob. ANT. *disperse, scatter, thin out.*

crowded a. thronged, congested, massed, swarming, squeezed together, jammed, crushed, huddled, squashed, *squished, mobbed, standing room only, *wall to wall, *sardined, teeming, *standing cheek by jowl, *breathing down each other's necks. ANT. *empty, deserted.*

crown n. **1.** TOP crest, head, pinnacle, zenith, summit, apex, culmination, tip, vertex. **2.** TIARA coronet, diadem, circlet. **3.** ROYALTY sovereignty, monarchy, the throne. ANT. *1. bottom, base.*

crown v. cap, complete, perfect, finish, complete, fulfill, climax, top off.

crucial a. critical, vital, essential, decisive, pivotal, central, dire, pressing, climactic, momentous, life-threatening, important. ANT. *unimportant, insignificant, trivial, incidental.*

crucify v. torture, torment, hang, nail to a cross, rack, excruciate, persecute, brutalize, harrow.

crud n. *crap, filth, muck, matter, rot, decay, incrustation.

crude a. **1.** ROUGH OR UNREFINED IN MANNER coarse, earthy, *gross, tactless, unpolished, uncouth, crass, vulgar, ignorant, churlish. **2.** RAW OR UNFINISHED rough, natural, green, unrefined, ungraded, unpolished, rough-hewn, primitive, unprocessed. ANT. *1. refined, cultured, polished, civilized. 2. refined, finished, polished.*

cruel a. vicious, ferocious, inhuman, inhumane, mean, savage, brutal, merciless, barbarous, sadistic, cold-blooded, heartless, bestial, bloodthirsty, ruthless. ANT. *kind, benevolent, compassionate.*

cruelty n. viciousness, ferocity, inhumanity, meanness, savagery, brutality, barbarity, sadism, cold-bloodedness, heartlessness, bestiality, ruthlessness. ANT. *kindness, compassion, benevolence.*

cruet n. vessel, decanter. SEE BOTTLE

cruise v. sail, navigate, travel, voyage, rove, wander, journey, drift.

cruiser n. patrol car, squad car, prowl car. SEE POLICE

crumb n. fragment, bit, tidbit, morsel, sliver, scrap, shred, speck, splinter.

crumble v. break apart, fall to pieces, disintegrate, fragment, crack, fritter, powder, shred, decay.

crumbly a. friable, brittle, insubstantial, fragile. ANT. *solid.*

crummy a. lousy, poor, cheap, shabby, *crappy, subpar, inferior. ANT. *quality.*

crumple v. **1.** RUMPLE wrinkle, pucker, crinkle, crease. **2.** FALL APART collapse, give way, buckle, topple, fall to pieces, cave in.

crunch v. grind, munch, chew, chomp, masticate, gnaw, champ.

crunch-time n. showdown, critical moment, critical mass, high noon, *do or die time, *sink or swim time.

crunchy a. crisp, crackling, chewy, brittle.

crusade n. campaign, movement, cause, drive, mission, expedition, march, push, battle.

crusader n. champion, campaigner, reformer, visionary, *mover and shaker, fighter, *voice for change.

crush n. infatuation, *puppy love, fancy, passion, fondness, liking, *the hots.

crush v. **1.** MASH squash, press, compress, squeeze, pulverize, crunch, powder, *squish, grind, granulate, trample. **2.** DEFEAT overpower, overwhelm, vanquish, obliterate, humiliate, *blow away, subdue, conquer, squelch, beat down. ANT. *2. surrender, lose, bow down.*

crust n. coating, shell, skin, hull, rind, layer, border, caking, encrustation.

crustacean n. arthropod, sea creature, marine animal, lobster, crab, prawn, shrimp.

crusty a. surly, sour, testy, cranky, crabby, gruff, peevish, irascible, ill-tempered, bearish, grouchy. ANT. *easygoing, good-natured, pleasant.*

crutch n. prop, support, staff, walking aid.

crux n. core, essence, heart, meat, *meat and potatoes, nitty-gritty, gist, root, nub, basis.

cry n. **1.** WEEPING bawling, wailing, whimpering, sobbing, sniveling, blubbering, howling, bewailing, lament. **2.** SHOUT yell, exclamation, call, holler, outcry, utterance, scream, squawk, shriek, yelp, bellow. **3.** PLEADING appeal, entreaty, supplication, imploration, plea, *cri de coeur, request, prayer.

cry v. weep, bawl, wail, whimper, sob, snivel, squall, blubber, howl, burst into tears, break down, mewl, pule, *boohoo, moan, dissolve into tears, convulse with tears, choke up, shed tears, blink back tears.

WORD FIND

body language: curls into a fetal position; clenching-lurching-knotting stomach; throat closing spastically; throat raw; swallows lump in throat; nostrils dilate; chest grows heavy; gulps air spastically; chokes; splutters; screws knuckles into eye sockets

face: snarl of agony, grimace, scarlet, swollen, puffy, contorts grotesquely, twists in anguish, pouts, tremulous, bottom lip curls, eyes take on wounded look, features stricken, eyes transfixed with shock and grief, eyes brim with tears

voice: quavers, cracks, shrill, constricts, rises hysterically, rises an octave, strangled, takes on a hitch, raw with agony, speaks in ragged bursts

SEE GRIEVE, MOURN, SCREAM, TEARS
2. SHOUT yell, exclaim, holler, call, utter, sing out, bellow, hail, crow, scream, yelp, vociferate, squawk

crybaby n. whiner, bellyacher, *wimp, *wuss, complainer, moaner, *bitcher, grumbler, malcontent, griper.

crypt n. tomb, vault, chamber, mausoleum, grave, catacomb, sepulcher, burial place, ossuary. SEE CEMETERY

CRYPTIC a. [KRIP tic] mysterious, hidden. *The customer was dissatisfied with the cryptic message from the psychic.* SYN. mysterious, hidden, enigmatic, secret, mystic, occult, vague, obscure, ambiguous, arcane, esoteric, veiled. ANT. *clear, open, straightforward.*

crystal a. clear, transparent, limpid, pellucid. ANT. *murky, cloudy.*

cub n. baby, youth, young.

cubby hole n. compartment, niche, pigeon hole, nook.

cubicle n. compartment, chamber, stall, box, cell, booth, bay, cabin, room, berth.

cuckoo a. crazy, stupid, out of one's mind, nutty, *flaky. ANT. *sane.*

cuddle v. snuggle, hug, embrace, nestle, nuzzle, curl up, clasp, pet, caress, fondle, squeeze.

cuddy n. cabin, galley, room, closet, cupboard.

cudgel n. club, bat, bludgeon, stick, shillelagh.

cue n. signal, sign, intimation, tip, tip-off, hint, prompt, indication, nod, wink.

cuff v. slap, buffet, hit, strike, box, clout.

cuisine n. food, fare, cookery, cooking, dishes, menu, *grub, *eats, table style.

cul-de-sac n. deadend, alley, impasse, blind alley, trap.

culinary a. cooking, kitchen.

cull v. choose, select, pick, single out, glean, opt for, winnow, garner, collect, sift, sort out.

culminate v. [KULL muh NATE] to come to the conclusion or peak, to climax. *The derby will culminate with the awarding of prizes.* SYN. peak, climax, conclude, finish, end, complete, perfect, crown, cap, top off, *come to a head. ANT. *open, begin, commence, *get the ball rolling.*

culmination n. conclusion, peak, climax, finish, end, completion, crowning, cap, consummation, apex, height, zenith, pinnacle. ANT. *beginning, opening, commencement.*

CULPABLE a. [KUL puh bul] responsible for a wrongdoing, to blame. *She was culpable in the car accident.* SYN. responsible, blameworthy, to blame, accountable, guilty, at fault, liable, amiss, in the wrong, sinful. ANT. *innocent, blameless.*

culprit n. offender, guilty party, wrongdoer, malefactor, miscreant, evildoer, criminal, felon, rascal, sinner, *bad guy.

cult n. followers, following, believers, school, affiliation, clique, band, sect, faction, faith, idolization, devotees, disciples, *underground.

cultivate v. **1.** PREPARE GROUND FOR GROWING plow, till, fertilize, dress, hoe, rake, manure, tend, sow, nurture, foster, plant, farm. **2.** DEVELOP enrich, educate, train, improve, school, enlighten, discipline, refine, civilize. **3.** SEEK THE FRIENDSHIP OF befriend, court, ingratiate, *get on one's good side, *suck up to, *kiss up to, *brownnose, *get cozy with, *play up to, promote, foster. ANT. *1. sterilize, pollute. 2. retard, stunt. 3. alienate, distance, slight.*

cultivation n. **1.** FARMING agriculture, crop-raising, agronomy, gardening, husbandry, tillage. **2.** DEVELOPMENT education, training, schooling, enlightenment, discipline, refinement, scholarship, erudition, culture.

culture n. **1.** EDUCATION AND SOCIAL GROWTH advancement, development, refinement, elevation, improvement, training, accomplishment, erudition, enlightenment, gentility, urbanity, manners, polish, civility. "The best that has been said and thought in the world."—Mathew Arnold. "The developing of an avid hunger for knowledge and beauty."—Jesse Bennet. **2.** INSTITUTIONS AND BELIEFS civilization, the arts, customs, folkways, mores, convention, lifestyle. ANT. *1. regression, degeneration, decline.*

cultured a. cultivated, refined, polished, learned, educated, civilized, enlightened, accomplished, well-bred, erudite, genteel, high-class. ANT. *regressive, primitive, uncultured, illiterate.*

culture shock n. alienation, anxiety, confusion, *stranger in a strange land. ANT. *assimilation.*

culvert n. sewer, drain, conduit, channel, pipe, waterway, gutter, gully, ditch.

cumbersome a. heavy, clumsy, awkward, bulky, unmanageable, unwieldy, hefty, ponderous, massive, incommodious. ANT. *light, compact.*

cummerbund n. sash, band.

cunnilingus n. oral sex, *head, foreplay, *69. SEE SEX

cunning n. "A sinister or crooked wisdom."—Frances Bacon.

cunning a. **1.** CRAFTY shrewd, wily, artful, cagey, sharp, deceptive, guileful, foxy, sly, slick, *streetwise. **2.** INGENIOUS imaginative, clever, skillful, inventive, dexterous, intelligent, masterly, resourceful. ANT. *1. artless, naive, honest. 2. stupid, unimaginative, moronic.*

cup n. glass, goblet, mug, tumbler, chalice, demitasse, stein, vessel.

cupboard n. cabinet, shelf, closet.

cupidity a. greed, avarice, acquisitiveness, rapaciousness, graspingness, covetousness, want, hunger. ANT. *unselfishness, generosity.*

cupola n. dome, belfry.

cur n. scoundrel, knave, cad, villain, blackguard, *dog, *scumbag, wretch, rogue, *snake, *weasel.

curator n. custodian, keeper, conservator, caretaker, steward, manager, administrative director, guardian.

curb n. restriction, check, restraint, control, bar, hindrance, stop, brake, bridle, damper.

curb v. restrict, check, restrain, control, bar, hinder, stop, brake, bridle, dampen, slow, limit, inhibit. ANT. *push, facilitate, help.*

curdle v. congeal, coagulate, clot, clabber, thicken, solidify, spoil, ferment, sour. ANT. *thin, liquefy.*

cure n. remedy, antidote, corrective, medicine, cure-all, panacea, treatment, regimen, *quick fix, elixir, prescription, nostrum. SEE MEDICINE

cure v. remedy, correct, treat, medicate, fix, heal, restore, alleviate, relieve, repair, doctor, rehabilitate.

cure-all n. panacea, elixir, catholicon, nostrum, patent medicine.

curfew n. *lights out, prohibition, ban, restriction.

curiosity n. **1.** INQUISITIVENESS interest, concern, *nosiness, questioning, prying, *thirst for knowledge. "To eat of the forbidden fruit."—Robert Burton. "The lust of the mind."—Thomas Hobbes. "The mother of science."—Charles Singer. "A peep-hole in the brain."—Elbert Hubbard. **2.** CURIO novelty, oddity, rarity, conversation piece, objet d'art, bibelot, wonder, marvel. ANT. *indifference, apathy.*

curious a. **1.** INQUISITIVE interested, concerned, *nosy, questioning, prying, *thirsty for knowledge, inquiring, snooping, wondering, inquisitorial. **2.** ODD strange, rare, novel, peculiar, exotic, quaint, weird, unique, marvelous, queer, unusual. ANT. *1. indifferent, apathetic, unconcerned. 2. common, ordinary, usual, everyday.*

curl n. curve, loop, coil, wave, turn, roll, twist, swirl, whorl, convolution, spiral, corkscrew, ringlet, curlicue.

curl v. curve, coil, twist, bend, loop, wind, turn, snake, meander.

CURMUDGEON n. [kur MUJ un] a grouchy or ill-tempered person. *The prickly, old curmudgeon wouldn't let us walk through his yard* *without yelling at us.* SYN. grouch, *grump, *bear, *grizzly bear, crab, malcontent, *grumbler, *miserable bastard, *sorehead, *grouser.

currency n. money, cash, legal tender, medium of exchange, coins, bills. SEE MONEY

current n. flow, course, stream, rush, run, tide, river, flux, draft.

current a. contemporary, present, now, present-day, modern, up-to-date, in vogue, prevalent, in progress, fashionable, *cutting edge, *leading edge. ANT. *past, bygone, historical, old, dated.*

curriculum n. study program, studies, courses, classes, lessons, subjects.

CURRY FAVOR v. to try to win someone over through flattery. *I was sickened by his attempts to curry favor with the governor.* SYN. flatter, fawn over, stroke, *kiss up to, *brownnose, *bootlick, praise, *fall all over, toady to, *butter up, court, *sweet-talk, blarney, pander to, cajole, win over, *suck up to.

curse n. **1.** JINX spell, *evil eye, evil, *whammy, voodoo, charm, incantation, execration, anathema, damnation, malediction. **2.** SWEARING oath, profanity, expletive, *gutter word, *cuss word, *dirty word, *four-letter word, obscenity. ANT. *1. blessing, benediction.*

cursed a. **1.** JINXED doomed, star-crossed, bedeviled, ill-fated, plagued, damned, stricken, blighted. **2.** HATEFUL detestable, loathsome, damnable, execrable, wicked, evil, abominable, fiendish. ANT. *1. blessed, favored. 2. commendable, honorable.*

cursor n. indicator, marker, pointer, positioner.

CURSORY a. [KUR suh ree] quick and superficial; unthorough. *She made a cursory inspection and moved on.* SYN. quick, hasty, superficial, casual, perfunctory, hurried, slight, desultory, unmethodical, fleeting, shallow. ANT. *thorough, comprehensive, in-depth.*

CURT a. [KURT] brief to the point of rudeness; brusque. *He gave a curt introduction and left.* SYN. abrupt, terse, rude, snappy, short, short and sweet, gruff, unceremonious, sharp, laconic, impolite. ANT. *courteous, polite, loquacious, long-winded, fawning.*

curtail v. shorten, cut, abbreviate, abridge, downsize, boil down, trim, reduce, diminish. ANT. *lengthen, draw out, expand.*

curtain n. drape, shade, blind, valance, portiere, veil, cover, backdrop.

curvaceous a. shapely, voluptuous, *built, statuesque, full-figured, zaftig, buxom. ANT. *anorexic, *built like linguine, bony.*

curve v. bend, arc, bow, turn, veer, twist, hook, loop, spiral, coil, swerve, curl, crook.

cushion n. pillow, pad, bolster, mat, buffer, fender.

cushion v. absorb, dampen, soften, check, protect, muffle, deaden, pillow, stifle.

cushy a. Sl. easy, *comfy, pleasant, agreeable. ANT. *difficult, rough, disagreeable.*

cuspidor n. spittoon, receptacle, vessel.

cuss v. swear, curse.

custodian n. caretaker, guardian, conservator, janitor, keeper, maintenance man, steward, *super, watchman, curator.

custody n. **1.** GUARDIANSHIP keeping, safekeeping, care, protection, wardship, holding, watch, supervision. **2.** CONFINEMENT incarceration, imprisonment, detention, jail, arrest, restraint.

custom n. **1.** PRACTICE habit, convention, rule, fashion, mode, routine, way, law, *right thing to do. "The plague of wise men and the idol of fools."—Thomas Fuller. "The great guide to human life."—David Hume. **2.** TAX levy, toll, tariff.

customary a. usual, conventional, accustomed, established, set, routine, regular, accepted, habitual, fashionable, normal, traditional, orthodox. ANT. *unusual, offbeat, unfamiliar, untried.*

customer n. patron, shopper, buyer, consumer, browser, prospect, client.

cut n. **1.** INCISION gash, laceration, slash, slit, nick, tear, slice, wound, opening, kerf. **2.** REDUCTION decrease, diminution, cutback, decrement, excision, lowering. **3.** SHARE percentage, *piece of the pie, slice, allowance, allotment, quota, kickback. **3.** INSULT *putdown, offense, *dig.

cut v. **1.** INCISE gash, lacerate, slash, slit, nick, tear, slice, wound, open, sever, carve, split, shear, rip, hack, dice, section, lay open, lance, pierce, scotch. **2.** CUT DOWN OR TRIM fell, crop, mow, lop off, truncate, harvest, prune, clip, chop. **3.** REDUCE decrease, diminish, cut back, downsize, excise, lower, lessen, crop, pare, trim, shave. **4.** INSULT slight, snub, affront, spurn, *give the cold shoulder, shun.

cut and dried a. **1.** SETTLED fixed, set, prepared. **2.** ROUTINE unoriginal, ordinary.

cutback n. decrease, belt-tightening, reversal, curtailment, decline, reduction, lowering, abatement.

cute a. adorable, attractive, cunning, pretty,

darling, cherubic, charming, sweet, *cute as a bug's ear, *dollfaced.

cutlery n. knives, cutting tools, utensils, carving set, table instruments, tableware.

cutlet n. chop, slice, cut, patty.

CUT THE GORDIAN KNOT v. to find a quick solution to a deeply entangled problem. *Somebody had to find a way to cut the Gordian knot of Congressional gridlock.* SYN. solve, untangle, *cut through red tape, extricate, free, clear, unsnarl, unravel, crack, work out, resolve, straighten out, *get to the bottom of.

cutthroat a. ruthless, *dog-eat-dog, merciless, *every man for himself, pitiless, *hard as nails. ANT. *compassionate, merciful, benevolent.*

cutting a. insulting, biting, sarcastic, scathing, sharp, sardonic, nasty, mean, caustic, venomous, acerbic, vicious, malevolent. ANT. *complimentary, flattering, kind.*

CUTTING EDGE n. the forefront; the most advanced. *The technology was on the cutting edge.* SYN. forefront, vanguard, avant-garde, leading edge, point, fore, front line, new wave, incoming tide of innovation.

CYBERSPACE n. [SY bur SPAYS] the collective data and communication network of interconnected computers. *More and more people are turning to cyberspace for research purposes.* SYN. computer network, communication network, communication web, Internet, World Wide Web (WWW), *information superhighway, electronic highway, *infobahn, virtual community, data bank, virtual library, global village, online communication medium. SEE INTERNET

cyborg n. android, cybernetic organism, *six-million-dollar man.

cycle n. progression, sequence, succession, rotation, round, series.

cyclone n. tornado, twister, hurricane, windstorm, whirlwind, monsoon.

cylinder n. chamber, drum, tube, pipe, barrel.

cylindrical a. round, tubular, circular, terete.

cynic n. skeptic, nonbeliever, *doubting Thomas, scoffer, realist, pessimist, naysayer, killjoy, misanthrope. "A man who tells you the truth about your own motives."—Russel Green. "A man who, when he smells flowers, looks around for a coffin."—H.L. Mencken. ANT. *optimist, *Pollyanna, believer.*

CYNICAL a. [SIN ik ul] mistrusting and looking for hidden motives in others. *Frank said he wanted to raise money for charity, but Mary was cynical.* SYN. skeptical, unbelieving, doubting, questioning, scoffing, pessimistic, negative, naysaying, misanthropic, sneering, sardonic, mocking, distrustful, suspicious. ANT. *trusting, optimistic, positive.*

cynicism n. "A euphemism for realism. Seeing things as they really are, instead of the way we'd like them to be."—Harry Ruby. "Idealism gone sour."—Will Herberg. SEE CYNICAL

cynosure n. focal point, center of attention.

cyst n. vesicle, sac, blister, bleb.

czar n. autocrat, tsar, ruler, emperor, monarch, overlord, king.

D

dab n. bit, touch, drop, pat, smidgen, speck, dollop, pinch, soupcon.

dab v. daub, touch, smear, smudge, pat, tap.

dabble v. *play around, *mess around, toy with, *fiddle with, putter, tinker, dillydally, trifle.

dabbler n. amateur, hobbyist, tinkerer, dilettante, novice, putterer, layman, nonprofessional. ANT. *master, expert, professional.

dad n. *daddy, father, *pop, *papa, *old man, parent, governor, protector.

daffy a. *nutty, crazy, foolish, silly, *loony, clownish, *goofy, daft, *nuttier than a fruitcake. ANT. rational, sane.

daft a. *nutty, *loony, idiotic. SEE CRAZY

dagger n. knife, dirk, bodkin, stiletto, poniard, Bowie knife, switchblade, bayonet.

WORD FIND
Arabian, double-edged, curved blade: jambiya
handle: hilt, haft, grip, dudgeon
Irish/Scottish, double-edged: skean
knob at butt end: pommel
Medieval: anlace, bodkin, misericord, rondel, swordbreaker
slide projections at the hilt: quillons

daily a. or adv. everyday, day in and day out, quotidian, circadian, per diem.

dainty a. 1. DELICATE exquisite, charming, fine, fragile, precious, lovely, elegant, refined, graceful. 2. DISCRIMINATING fussy, finicky, particular, fastidious, *persnickety, choosy, refined, overrefined. ANT. 1. rough, ugly, ponderous, *built like a brick shithouse, junky. 2. unparticular, easy to please.

dais n. podium, platform, rostrum, stage.

dale n. dell, glen. SEE VALLEY

dalliance n. flirtation, coquetry, *cow eyes, *making eyes at, love affair, affair, *fling, *fooling around, relationship, *hanky-panky.

dally v. dawdle, waste time, *drag feet, lag, put off, idle, delay, procrastinate, *fiddle and diddle, dillydally, shilly-shally. ANT. hurry, rush, *get a move on.

dam n. bank, dike, levee, wall, barrage, obstruction, check, barrier.

dam v. block, obstruct, check, close, bar, impede, stop, slow, restrict. ANT. release, free.

damage n. destruction, injury, loss, harm, breakage, hurt, depreciation, deterioration, wreckage, spoilage, impairment, disfigurement.

damage v. injure, harm, destroy, break, hurt, depreciate, wreck, ruin, impair, cripple, deface, weaken, incapacitate, mar, mutilate, ravage, vandalize.

damages n. cost, expenses, compensation, penalty, reimbursement, amends.

damn v. condemn, criticize, doom, slam, denounce, attack, curse, disparage, censure, excoriate, pan, swear at, objurgate, blast. ANT. praise, commend, give one's blessings.

damnation n. "Everlasting fire."—Bible. "Everlasting torments."—John Sergieff.

damned a. detestable, cursed, infernal, *darned, loathsome, *dang, confounded, *blasted, rotten, revolting. ANT. blessed, fortunate, favored.

damp a. wet, moist, dank, humid, clammy, misty, drizzly, soggy. ANT. dry, arid.

dampen v. 1. MOISTEN wet, sprinkle, spray, rinse, humidify. 2. DEPRESS deaden, muffle, lower, lessen, check, cool, diminish, moderate, chill, mute. ANT. 1. dry, dehydrate. 2. enliven, intensify, increase.

damsel n. maiden, girl, woman, lass.

dance n. ballroom dance, capering, ballet, waltz, polka, square dance, *shindig, hop, prom. "Poetry of the foot."—John Dryden.

WORD FIND
bend backwards under pole: limbo
Bohemian, lively: polka
Brazilian, dips, leaps: samba
Brazilian, like samba: bossa nova
Brazilian, sensual coupling: lambada
Caribbean, like rhumba: beguine
classical ballroom: waltz
country and western swinging two-step: Texas two-step
Cuban: rhumba, conga, mambo
death dance: danse macrabre
French, high-kicking, skirt-lifting: cancan
glissade backwards: moonwalk
group single file procession, three steps and kick: conga
Hawaiian: hula
Italian, whirling folk dance: tarantella
Latin American quickstep and shuffle: cha-cha
Latin American, with stylized posturing: tango
legs scissoring in opposite directions: split
lively folk dance: jig
lively French dance, eighteenth century: cotillion

Middle Eastern female solo, stomach undulations: belly dance
modern jazz: jazz dance
Negro, nineteenth century: Juba
1920s: Charleston
1930s-1940s, hopping: shag
1930s, jitterbuglike: Lindy hop
1940s, acrobatic somersaults, splits: jitterbug
1960s, Chubby Checker: twist
1970s, hip-touching: bump
1980s, prostrate movements: breakdance
1990s, running in position: running man
Oriental head motions: sundari
Polish: polonaise
Russian dance, squatting, arms folded: cossack
sailor's: hornpipe
Scottish, lively folk dance: reel
secret, all-night dance party: *rave
sexually explicit: 1. freak dancing, booty dancing, dirty dancing, grinding, jacking, freaking, the nasty. 2. sexually explicit dance moves, line of dancers performing: freak train SEE RAP
shaking of body part: shimmy
solo male dance around Sombrero: Mexican hat dance
Spanish: flamenco, fandango, bolero, tango
spin: pirouette
square dance: quadrille, hoedown
square dance steps: California twirl, cloverleaf, Dixie chain, do-si-do, promenade, sashay.
stately eighteenth-century dance: minuet
steps: choreography
tap steps: soft shoe, falling off the log, dig, brush, chug, coffee grinder
two-step, ballroom: fox-trot
wooden shoes dance: clog
SEE BALLET
dance *v.* caper, step, *trip the light fantastic, *boogie, *cut a rug, swing, step, prance, *disco, *beat feet, twist, shimmy, strut, prance, sway, hop, *get down, *shake your booty, rock, wiggle one's hips, jig, skip, leap, gambol, romp, *slink, contort, flex, undulate, careen, shuffle, *hoof, clomp, *jockey, *pose, *posture, thrust, quiver, dip, gyrate, convulse, glissade.
dancer *n.* danseuse, ballerina, danseur, *hoofer, terpsichorean.
dandle *v.* bounce on knee, toss up and down.
dandruff *n.* scurf, flakes.
dandy *a.* great, excellent, wonderful, swell, terrific. ANT. *terrible, awful, ghastly.*

danger *n.* peril, threat, hazard, menace, endangerment, *thin ice, jeopardy, vulnerability, *storm clouds on the horizon, pitfall, ticking bomb, *powder keg, *critical mass, *between Scylla and Charybdis, *sword of Damocles. "The spur of all great minds."— George Chapman. ANT. *safety, security.*
dangerous *a.* perilous, threatening, hazardous, unsafe, menacing, jeopardous, risky, precarious, chancy, *touch and go, *ticklish, unhealthy, dire, *hanging over one's head like the sword of Damocles, reaching critical mass, *between Scylla and Charybdis. ANT. *safe, secure, protected.*
dangle *v.* hang, drag, droop, flap, depend, swing, wave, flutter.
dank *a.* damp, wet, chilly, clammy, moist, slimy, dewy, muggy, humid. ANT. *dry, arid, parched.*
dapper *a.* neat, trim, smart, dashing, swank, stylish, well-groomed, spruce, natty, *spiffy. ANT. *sloppy, unkempt, disheveled.*
dappled *a.* mottled, spotted, speckled, stippled, flecked, piebald, variegated, parti-colored. ANT. *uniform, solid.*
dare *v.* **1.** VENTURE gamble, risk, brave, hazard, face, brook, adventure, *run the gauntlet, have the nerve. **2.** DEFY challenge, beard, face, oppose, square off, mock, throw down the gauntlet, look in the eye, provoke, confront, taunt. ANT. *1. pass, beg off, retreat. 2. run away, retreat, knuckle under, *blink.*
daredevil *n.* thrill-seeker, adventurer, show-off, *hotdog, swashbuckler, stuntman, ace, fool.
daring *a.* adventurous, brave, bold, venturesome, plucky, *gutsy, *ballsy, nervy, courageous, fearless, intrepid, reckless, rash, *having icewater in one's veins. ANT. *fearful, afraid, *chicken, *mousy, timid, cautious, *wimpy.*
dark *n.* nightfall, evening, dusk, twilight, midnight.
dark *a.* **1.** BLACK aphotic, dim, dusky, gloomy, unlit, nebulous, inky, shadowy, somber, gauzy, murky. **2.** COMPLEXION swarthy, ebony, black. **3.** DREARY dismal, bleak, gloomy, stygian, depressing, somber, grim, morbid. **4.** WICKED evil, satanic, sinister, hellish, infernal. ANT. *light, bright, sunny.* SEE BLACK, COMPLEXION
DARK HORSE *n.* a relative unknown who is deemed unlikely to win; an underdog. *The dark horse candidate staged a surprising victory.* SYN. sleeper, unknown, underdog, longshot, poor bet, outside shot, upsetter, also-ran,

write-in, unexpected winner, *David (Goliath), giant slayer. ANT. *favorite, frontrunner.*

darling *n.* sweetheart, *honey, *honeybunch, love, beloved, *pet, *sweetie, precious, dear, *apple of one's eye.

darn *interj.* damn, damnation, *dang, *darnation.

dart *v.* flit, dash, rush, bolt, scurry, shoot, spurt, scoot, bound, run, race, fly, tear, speed.

dash *n.* **1.** RACE run, sprint. **2.** A LITTLE trace, bit, smidgen, sprinkle, hint, pinch, taste, drop.

dash *v.* **1.** RUN sprint, race, bolt, speed, zip, rush, dart, bound, charge, shoot, scoot, scamper, tear. **2.** SMASH break, hit, strike, shatter, throw, hurl, slam, fling, sling, splash. **3.** FRUSTRATE confound, discourage, dampen, thwart, circumvent, foil, ruin, spoil, dishearten. ANT. **3.** *encourage, aid.*

dashboard *n.* instrument panel, control panel, indicator panel.

dashing *a.* elegant, debonair, splendid, jaunty, stylish, dapper, swank, chic, fashionable, sharp, flamboyant, rakish. ANT. *awkward, dull, bumbling.*

dastardly *a.* cowardly, fainthearted, timid, craven, mean, base, low, rotten. ANT. *courageous, brave, noble.*

data *n.* information, report, facts, figures, evidence, measurements, statistics, numbers, document, *readout.

data bank *n.* data base.

data processor *n.* computer, calculator, *number cruncher, word processor. SEE COMPUTER

date *n.* **1.** APPOINTMENT engagement, tryst, meeting. **2.** ESCORT companion, partner, lover, *pickup.

dated *a.* out-of-date, obsolete, antiquated, passé, old-fashioned, outmoded, old hat, antediluvian, prehistoric. ANT. *current, *cutting edge, *leading edge, modern, contemporary.*

daub *v.* coat, cover, smear, smudge, plaster, dab, paint, splatter, spot, stain.

daughter *n.* girl, offspring, young, child, *chip off the old block. "The object of a pleasure something like the love between the angels to her father."— Richard Steele. "An embarrassing and ticklish possession." —Meander.

daunt *v.* intimidate, scare, frighten, unnerve, threaten, faze, discourage, dismay, cow, dispirit, overawe. ANT. *encourage, embolden.*

DAUNTLESS *a.* [DAWNT less] fearless; bold. *Although his troops were outnumbered,*

the dauntless captain ordered a raid on the enemy camp. SYN. fearless, bold, brave, unafraid, courageous, intrepid, valorous, stouthearted, unflinching, resolute. ANT. *fearful, afraid, timid, irresolute.*

davenport *n.* sofa, couch, convertible.

dawdle *v.* delay, procrastinate, waste time, dally, *drag one's feet, *fiddle and diddle, loiter, *poke, piddle, shilly-shally, fritter. ANT. *hurry, rush, *beat feet, *get a move on.*

dawn *n.* **1.** DAYBREAK sunrise, sunup, morning, aurora, cockcrow, first light, wee hours, *holy light of dawn. "The time when men of reason go to bed."—Ambrose Bierce. "That single hour of the twenty-four, when crime ceases, debauchery is exhausted, and even desolation finds a shelter."—Benjamin Disraeli. **2.** BEGINNING start, rise, advent, opening, coming, emergence, birth, onset. ANT. *1. sunset, dusk, twilight. 2. close, end, dusk.*

day *n.* light of day, sunup to sundown, twenty-four hours. "Each day is a little life."—Arthur Schopenhauer. "A miniature Eternity."—Ralph Waldo Emerson. **2.** PERIOD time, heyday, age, epoch.

daybook *n.* journal, diary, log, record.

daybreak *n.* dawn, sunrise, morning, first light, sun-up, *crack of dawn, daylight, *first scimitar of light, cock's crowing.

daycare *n.* babysitter, nursery school, preschool, supervision, child care center, tot watch center, kindergarten.

daydream *n.* fantasy, reverie, *castle in the air, figment of the imagination, musing, visualization, fancy, imagining, pipe dream, *woolgathering.

daze *n.* stupor, bewilderment, shock, trance, confusion, *lala land, befuddlement.

daze *v.* confuse, bewilder, shock, befuddle, stupefy, stun, perplex, addle, numb, confound, muddle, dumbfound.

dazzle *v.* amaze, blind, overwhelm, astonish, bewilder, confuse, awe, *bowl over, daze, *blow away, dumbfound.

dazzling *a.* brilliant, blinding, sparkling, glittering, flashy, shining, radiant, resplendent, ablaze, prismatic, meteoric. ANT. *muted, dark, gloomy, dull.*

deacon *n.* cleric, clergyman, deaconess, assistant.

deactivate *v.* shut off, shut down, stop, disconnect, decommission, remove.

dead *a.* **1.** LIFELESS deceased, expired, passed away, departed, perished, extinct, still, defunct, resting in peace, *pushing up daisies, late, stiff, *gone to meet one's maker, *out of one's misery, *kaput, *gone belly up, *down for the count, *crowbait, *buzzard bait, *stone cold, *worm food, *dead as a coffin nail, *carrion, lost, *on ice. **2.** UNRESPONSIVE flat, apathetic, wooden, paralyzed, numb, emotionless, frigid, unfeeling, insensible, insensate, cool, lukewarm. **3.** INOPERATIVE not working, out of order, *on the blink. **4.** ENDED extinguished, snuffed out, terminated, squelched, quenched, smothered, finished. **5.** UNPRODUCTIVE exhausted, unprofitable, sterile, stagnant, useless, barren, spent, worn out. **6.** TOTAL complete, utter, entire, out-and-out, absolute, sure, downright. **7.** BORING dull, tiresome, tedious, stale, bland, *blah, vapid. ANT. *1. alive, lively, animate. 2. lively, spirited, responsive. 3. operating, working. 4. growing. 5. productive, fruitful, fertile. 6. partial, uncertain. 7. lively, interesting, engrossing, riveting.* SEE DEATH, DIE

deadbeat n. debtor, loafer, *bum, freeloader, parasite, sloth, slug, layabout.

deaden v. dampen, dull, numb, muffle, mute, blunt, check, moderate, diminish, suppress, dim, tone down, stifle. ANT. *amplify, enliven, turn up.*

dead end n. cul de sac, impasse.

deadline n. time limit, zero hour, due date, term, cutoff.

deadlock n. stalemate, impasse, *Catch 22, standstill, gridlock, standoff, *Gordian knot, *logjam, *hung jury.

deadly a. fatal, lethal, deathly, mortal, malignant, toxic, killing, dangerous, virulent, death-dealing, pernicious, baneful. ANT. *harmless, benign, innocuous.*

dead-on a. accurate, precise, exact, on the mark, *hitting the bullseye, to the point. ANT. *off the mark, imprecise.*

deadpan a. expressionless, blank, *poker-faced, stony, wooden, unreadable.

deaf a. hearing-impaired, hard of hearing, unhearing, *deaf as a post, *stone deaf.

deafening a. ear-splitting, noisy. SEE LOUD

deal n. arrangement, understanding, contract, transaction, compact, bargain.

deal v. **1.** DISTRIBUTE dole out, allocate, allot, mete out, hand out, dispense, apportion. **2.** DEAL WITH attend to, reckon with, concern, take care of, cope, face, treat, manage, handle. **3.** BARGAIN dicker, negotiate, trade, buy and sell, do business, barter, give and take.

dealer n. salesman, salesperson, broker, buyer, seller, marketer, wholesaler, retailer, merchant, trader, monger, vendor, jobber, peddler, trafficker; (drugs) *pusher, *bagman, *candy man, connection, holder.

dealership n. franchise, outlet, store, shop, market, concession, chain store.

dealings n. relations, transactions, business, arrangements, trade, commerce, exchange.

dean n. senior, elder statesman, ranking member, elder, veteran, headmaster, preceptor, administrator.

dear n. darling, sweetheart, angel, saint.

dear a. **1.** BELOVED precious, loved, treasured, cherished, favored, darling, prized, admired, *near to one's heart. **2.** EXPENSIVE costly, *pricey, *steep, exorbitant, extravagant. ANT. *1. loathed, despised. 2. cheap, reasonable.*

DEARTH n. [DURTH] scarcity, lack. *A dearth of funds has kept me from vacationing in Hawaii.* SYN. scarcity, lack, deficiency, insufficiency, want, shortage, paucity, inadequacy, scantiness, stint, need. ANT. *sufficiency, abundance, plenty.*

death n. demise, end, dying, decease, passing, expiration, parting, termination, release, rest, extinction, mortality, in extremis, *curtains, *lights out, *last roundup, *finis, *grim reaper, *show stopper, afterlife, fatality, oblivion, repose. "When the soul shall emerge from its sheath."—Marcus Aurelius. "A black camel, which kneels at the gates of all."—Abd-El-Kader. "An eternal night."—Algernon Swinburne. "The undiscovered country."—Shakespeare. "The grand perhaps."—Robert Browning. "A pale horse."—Bible. "The port where all may refuge find."—William Alexander.

WORD FIND

after death, occurring: posthumous
DOA: dead on arrival
fear of: necrophobia, thanatophobia
gurgle at last breath: death rattle
herald of: banshee
investigation of: inquest, autopsy, postmortem
march: dirge
mercy killing: euthanasia
notice: obituary, necrology
omen: knell
reminder or symbol of: memento mori, death's head
study of: thanatology
watch: vigil

SEE AFTERLIFE, CEMETERY, CORPSE, DEAD, DIE, FUNERAL, HEAVEN, IMMORTALITY

deathless *a.* eternal. SEE IMMORTAL

deathly *a.* horrible, dreadful, terrible, appalling, macabre, ghastly.

DEBACLE *n.* [di BAH kul] a disaster or sudden collapse. *Thousands lost money in the stock market debacle.* SYN. disaster, collapse, overthrow, catastrophe, ruin, breakdown, rout, washout, downfall, bankruptcy, devastation. ANT. *success.*

debase *v.* degrade, lower, devalue, adulterate, pollute, corrupt, cheapen, depreciate, defile, demean, disgrace. ANT. *elevate, raise.*

debatable *a.* undecided, questionable, moot, controversial, dubious, disputable, doubtful, unsettled, contestable, *the jury's out. ANT. *settled, certain, decided.*

debate *n.* argument, dispute, war of words, contention, wrangle, controversy, contest, deliberation, disagreement, forensic. "Feud for thought."—Cynthia Scott. "The shortest cut between two minds."—Kahlil Gibran.

debate *v.* argue, dispute, *wage a war of words, contend, wrangle, controvert, contest, disagree, deliberate, bicker, *hash out, *lock horns, rebut.

DEBAUCHERY *n.* [di BAW chuh ree] excess, wild living, indulgence. *The rowdiness and debauchery of the party earned the fraternity a suspension from campus.* SYN. indulgence, excess, profligacy, over-indulgence, whoring, immoderation, womanizing, carousal, dissipation, intemperance, *fast living, revelry. ANT. *chastity, clean-living, moderation, abstinence, celibacy.*

debenture *n.* certificate of debt, voucher, bond, I.O.U.

DEBILITATE *v.* [di BIL i TATE] to weaken or handicap. *The illness will debilitate her to the point that she can no longer work.* SYN. weaken, handicap, enervate, enfeeble, cripple, fatigue, exhaust, disable, prostrate, devitalize. ANT. *strengthen, invigorate.*

debility *n.* weakness, infirmity, enfeeblement, handicap, enervation, prostration, languor, frailty, asthenia. ANT. *strength, power, vigor.*

DEBONAIR *a.* [deb uh NARE] friendly, gracious and suave. *The prince was charming and debonair.* SYN. friendly, gracious, suave, charming, jaunty, genial, pleasant, urbane, nonchalant, refined, genteel, gentlemanly. ANT. *coarse, crude, rude, unrefined, unfriendly.*

debrief *v.* 1. QUESTION interrogate, gather intelligence, query, probe, quiz, examine, inquire. 2. SILENCE censor, hush up, still, muzzle, restrain, mute.

debris *n.* rubble, trash, ruins, rubbish, scraps, fragments, remains, junk, litter, waste, *crap, wreckage, flotsam and jetsam, shards.

debt *n.* obligation, liability, bill, debit, arrears, deficit, pledge, due, burden, *red ink. "The slavery of the free."—Publilius Syrus. "A trap which a man sets and baits himself, and then deliberately gets into."—Josh Billings.

debug *v.* troubleshoot, fix, work the bugs out of.

debunk *v.* disprove, expose, refute, unmask, ridicule, deflate.

debut *n.* premiere, *coming out, first time out, introduction, launch, entrance, open, opener, inauguration. ANT. *farewell, swan song.*

debutante *n.* young lady, young woman, ingenue, maiden, deb.

decadence *n.* deterioration, decay, debasement, corruption, decline, regression, degeneration, downfall, degradation, fall. ANT. *growth, progression, revitalization.*

DECADENT *a.* [DEK uh dunt] decaying or deteriorating, in morals, art or other institution. *A decadent lifestyle led to their downfall.* SYN. decaying, deteriorating, declining, corrupt, degraded, *gone to hell, *gone to the dogs, degenerating, on the wane, *on the way out, *circling the drain, debauched. ANT. *growing, progressing, vital, vigorous.*

decal *n.* sticker, picture, design, emblem.

decamp *v.* bolt, flee, escape, *head for the hills, depart, break camp, *make tracks, *hightail it.

decanter *n.* vessel, bottle, pitcher, carafe, flask, container, glass, cruet.

decapitate *v.* behead, decollate, guillotine, ax.

decay *n.* rot, spoilage, decomposition, decline, disintegration, putrefaction, deterioration, degeneration, decrepitude. ANT. *growth, vigor.*

decay *v.* decline, deteriorate, degenerate, atrophy, waste away, wane, rot, decompose, putrefy, wither, disintegrate. ANT. *grow, thrive.*

deceased *a.* passed on, departed, *pushing up daisies. SEE DEAD

deceit *n.* dishonesty, deception, fraud, trickery, cheating, double-dealing, *BS, craft, *funny business, underhandedness, chicanery. "The smiler with the knife under the cloak."—Geoffrey Chaucer. "That glib and oily art."—Shakespeare. ANT. *honesty, truthfulness, fairness.*

deceitful *a.* dishonest, deceptive, fraudulent,

double-dealing, *full of it, crafty, under-handed, treacherous, duplicitous, insincere, artful, shifty. ANT. *honest, truthful, straightforward.*

deceive v. mislead, delude, trick, hoodwink, *pull the wool over one's eyes, dupe, defraud, *buffalo, *con, burn, *screw, beguile, *BS.

decency n. propriety, respectability, righteousness, seemliness, modesty, appropriateness, goodness, good manners, decorum. ANT. *indecency, impropriety.*

decent a. **1.** RESPECTABLE righteous, seemly, proper, moral, correct, modest, appropriate, good, fitting, virtuous, prudent. **2.** ADEQUATE sufficient, passable, tolerable, enough, satisfactory, ample, standard, reasonable. **3.** KIND generous, obliging, thoughtful, gracious, accommodating. ANT. *1. improper, inappropriate. 2. inadequate, insufficient, poor. 3. selfish, coldhearted, inconsiderate.*

deception n. lie, fraud, trick, chicane, deceit, hoax, sham, subterfuge, artifice, treachery, ruse, imposture, sleight of hand, con.

deceptive a. dishonest, misleading, fraudulent, tricky, deceitful, treacherous, bogus, spurious, fallacious, shifty. ANT. *honest, truthful, straightforward.*

decide v. settle, determine, choose, opt, judge, commit oneself, elect, guess, rule, make up one's mind, *fish or cut bait, resolve. ANT. *vacillate, waver, *ride the fence, hem and haw, waffle.*

decided a. definite, certain, absolute, unequivocal, clear, express, sure, unmistakable, settled, undeniable, positive, emphatic. ANT. *dubious, doubtful, uncertain.*

decimate v. slaughter, massacre, destroy, obliterate, wipe out, annihilate.

decipher v. figure out, read, decode, make out, solve, interpret, work out, understand, crack, unravel, puzzle out.

decision n. **1.** SETTLING determination, choice, judgment, election, guess, conclusion, resolution, preference, *roll of the dice. **2.** VERDICT judgment, ruling, finding, decree, sentence. ANT. *vacillation, wavering, waffling, indecision.*

decisive a. conclusive, certain, firm, absolute, unqualified, unmistakable, convincing, undeniable, final, clinching, crucial, critical. ANT. *inconclusive, questionable, inconsequential.*

deck v. outfit, adorn, decorate, clothe, trim, ornament, festoon, array, embellish, beautify.

declassify v. open, publicize.

declaration n. statement, assertion, announcement, communication, utterance, affirmation, proclamation, attestation, testimony.

declare v. state, assert, announce, communicate, utter, affirm, proclaim, attest, testify, profess, avow.

decline v. **1.** REFUSE turn down, reject, forgo, spurn, pass on, demur, *turn thumbs down. **2.** WANE degenerate, deteriorate, lessen, weaken, diminish, ebb, peter out, die out, slump, decay, sink, backslide. **3.** SLOPE slant, incline, pitch. ANT. *1. accept, take. 2. grow, wax, rise.*

decode v. decipher, translate, solve, interpret, figure out, work out, puzzle out, decrypt, read, employ cryptography. ANT. *encrypt.*

decommission v. withdraw, *mothball, deactivate, retire, drydock.

decompose v. rot, putrefy, biodegrade. SEE DECAY

decontaminate v. clean, purify, sterilize, disinfect, autoclave, sanitize, wash, purge, flush, distill.

decor n. decoration, scheme, style, layout, design, embellishment, furnishings.

decorate v. adorn, ornament, beautify, embellish, festoon, dress, trim, deck, garnish, *do up, *jazz up.

decoration n. **1.** ADORNMENT ornament, embellishment, festoon, dressing, trim, garnish, frill, embroidery. **2.** MEDAL award, honor, citation, emblem, badge, purple heart, ribbon.

decorative a. ornamental, beautifying, embellishing, *dressy, garnishing. ANT. *plain.*

decorous a. proper, appropriate, fitting, mannerly, conventional, correct, refined, dignified, comme il faut, suitable, civilized. ANT. *misbehaving, rowdy, improper.*

DECORUM n. [di KOR um] proper manners, propriety. *The children were told to behave with decorum.* SYN. propriety, respectability, conformity, civility, etiquette, good manners, good taste, dignity, grace, protocol. ANT. *bad manners, impropriety, incivility.*

decoy n. lure, bait, enticement, *plant, *shill, magnet, seduction, pitfall, phony, trap, fake, facade.

decrease n. lessening, lowering, shrinkage, reduction, decline, weakening, lightening, contraction, depreciation, drop. ANT. *increase, growth, expansion.*

decrease v. lessen, diminish, lower, shrink, reduce, decline, weaken, lighten, contract, depreciate, dwindle, plummet, drop, sink. ANT. *increase, grow, expand, burgeon.*

decree n. order, act, mandate, command, ruling, edict, ordinance, injunction, fiat, statute, command, dictum.

decree v. order, mandate, command, rule, ordain, enact, proclaim, dictate, prescribe, require.

decrepit a. broken down, weakened, deteriorated, old, worn, dilapidated, antiquated, rickety, withered, enfeebled. ANT. *strong, robust, powerful.*

decriminalize v. legalize, legitimize, sanction.

decry v. disparage, belittle, deflate, detract, deprecate, criticize, *slam, rap, condemn, censure, denounce. ANT. *praise, compliment.*

dedicated a. committed, devoted, determined, wholehearted, staunch, goal-oriented. ANT. *disloyal, indifferent, halfhearted.*

dedication n. commitment, devotion, determination, wholeheartedness, single-mindedness, earnestness, resolve, tenacity, goal-orientation.

deduce v. infer, gather, figure, conclude, reason, assume, judge, presume, *have a hunch, reckon, surmise.

deduct v. subtract, take off, decrease, remove, withdraw, reduce, cut, write off. ANT. *add, increase.*

deduction n. **1.** INFERENCE conclusion, line of reasoning, assumption, judgment, presumption, hunch, reckoning, finding, understanding. **2.** WRITE-OFF expense, subtraction, exemption, allowance, discount, reduction.

deed n. ACT feat, exploit, enterprise, work, achievement, accomplishment, turn, stunt. "Something attempted, something done."—Longfellow. **2.** CONTRACT legal document, conveyance, proof of ownership, certificate, title.

deem v. judge, consider, believe, think, hold, suppose, daresay, regard, understand, imagine, fancy.

deep a. **1.** OF GREAT DEPTH far-reaching, bottomless, cavernous, low, abysmal, unfathomable, immeasurable, subterranean. **2.** PROFOUND abstruse, mysterious, unfathomable, philosophical, complicated, abstract, arcane, intense. **3.** ENGROSSED absorbed, preoccupied, wrapped up, concentrated, immersed, lost. **4.** STRONG intense, dark, rich, heavy, full, powerful. **5.** BASS low, guttural,

booming, rumbling, resonant. ANT. *1. shallow, superficial. 2. trivial, simple, shallow. 3. distracted. 4. light, weak, diluted. 5. high, shrill.*

deep-seated a. deep-rooted, ingrained, *dyed in the wool, inherent. ANT. *learned, acquired, extrinsic.*

deer n. ruminant, whitetail, elk, caribou, buck, doe, roe, quadruped.

WORD FIND
bellowing cry: bell
branch of antler: point
feeding area: yard
female: doe, hind
like a: cervine
male adult: stag, buck, hart
meat: venison
odiferous secretion: musk
pair of antlers: rack
sexual period: rut
soft covering of antler: velvet
tail: flag
track or trail of: slot
young: fawn

deface v. mar, deform, sully, blemish, disfigure, spoil, damage, soil, mutilate, vandalize, scratch.

de facto a. actual, real, in fact, in reality.

defamation n. slander, denigration, smear, slur, mud-slinging, blot, innuendo, libel, disparagement, character assassination, calumny.

defamatory a. slanderous, libelous, denigrating, derogatory, disparaging, scandalous, insulting, calumnious, smearing, injurious. ANT. *flattering, complimentary, honoring.*

DEFAME v. [di FAME] to put down, especially in a libelous or slanderous way. *He proceeded to defame every politician in office.* SYN. slander, libel, smear, put down, mud-sling, blacken, scandalize, malign, disgrace, disparage, insult, smirch, denigrate. ANT. *flatter, compliment, honor.*

defang v. *take the teeth out of, *take the bite out of, emasculate, weaken, undermine, castrate, defuse, disarm.

default v. shirk, *welsh, fail, *stiff, *skip out, *run out on, dodge. ANT. *pay in full, satisfy.*

defeat n. loss, beating, rout, slaughter, debacle, blow, whipping, thrashing, *skunking, humiliation, knockout, licking, *Waterloo, reversal, *drubbing, fall, upset, downfall. ANT. *win, victory, triumph.*

defeat v. vanquish, beat, conquer, subdue, win over, overthrow, best, lick, whip, rout, slaughter, unseat, trounce, *smoke, prevail over, triumph over, *shellac, *skunk, *mop the floor with, humiliate, prostrate, dominate, eclipse, overshadow, tower over, *take the wind out of one's sails. ANT. *lose, knuckle under, concede.*

defeatism *n.* resignation, passive acceptance, giving up, pessimism.

defect *n.* imperfection, flaw, failing, mistake, deficiency, drawback, *bug, irregularity, error, shortcoming, weakness, chink. ANT. *strength.*

defect *v.* leave, desert, change allegiance, turn traitor, abandon, renounce, reject, forsake. ANT. *embrace, uphold, remain.*

defective *a.* imperfect, flawed, irregular, deficient, faulty, lacking, marred, unsound, inoperative, *out of commission. ANT. *perfect, sound, intact.*

defend *v.* **1.** PROTECT fight for, guard, fend off, withstand, hold at bay, shield, secure, ward off, preserve. **2.** SUPPORT advocate, back, uphold, stick up for, stand behind, *go to bat for, plead, justify. ANT. *offend, attack, let down one's guard.*

defendant *n.* accused, suspect, prisoner, party, litigant.

defense *n.* **1.** PROTECTION guard, shield, fortification, shelter, screen, bulwark, stronghold, armament. **2.** JUSTIFICATION explanation, excuse, stand, argument, plea, story, apologia, support. ANT. *1. offense, aggression.*

defenseless *a.* powerless, vulnerable, unprotected, unguarded, unarmed, helpless, weak, impotent, exposed, open to attack. ANT. *guarded, fortified, defended.*

defer *v.* **1.** DELAY postpone, put off, hold off, suspend, *put on the back burner, procrastinate, stall, table. **2.** COMPLY submit, yield, acquiesce, accede, capitulate, give in, assent, agree. ANT. *1. expedite, rush. 2. disagree, stand one's ground.*

DEFERENCE *n.* [DEF ur uns] yielding to another's will, usually out of respect or courtesy. *In deference to her mother's wishes, the teenager was home by midnight.* SYN. submission, regard, consideration, respect, thoughtfulness, yielding, compliance, courtesy, obeisance. ANT. *opposition, rebellion, disrespect.*

deferential *a.* respectful, submissive, compliant, courteous, considerate, obedient, obeisant, acquiescent, regardful, reverential. ANT. *disrespectful, disobedient, rude.*

defiance *n.* rebellion, disobedience, resistance, opposition, challenge, insolence, revolt,

*throwing down the gauntlet, disregard, contempt. ANT. *conformance, acquiescence, deference.*

defiant *a.* rebellious, disobedient, resistant, opposing, challenging, insolent, revolting, *throwing down the gauntlet, fractious, unruly. ANT. *conforming, obedient, acquiescent.*

deficiency *n.* imperfection, lack, shortcoming, insufficiency, inadequacy, failing, flaw, defect, weakness, drawback. ANT. *sufficiency, adequacy, perfection.*

deficient *a.* imperfect, lacking, insufficient, inadequate, failing, flawed, defective, weak, substandard, wanting, *below par, incomplete, faulty. ANT. *sufficient, flawless, perfect.*

deficit *n.* shortage, shortfall, lack, loss, red ink.

defile *v.* dirty, befoul, tarnish, pollute, taint, sully, corrupt, smear, besmirch, soil, contaminate, degrade. ANT. *purify, cleanse.*

define *v.* explain, spell out, describe, outline, delineate, map out, detail, characterize, label, illustrate, construe.

definite *a.* **1.** CERTAIN positive, sure, absolute, fixed, assured, guaranteed, settled, decided. **2.** EXACT clear, unambiguous, explicit, specific, precise, unmistakable, express, concrete. ANT. *1. uncertain, iffy, indefinite. 2. unclear, ambiguous, vague.*

definitely *adv.* absolutely, positively, surely, certainly, doubtless, without question, indubitably, categorically, *no ifs, ands or buts. ANT. *maybe, possibly, uncertainly.*

definition *n.* meaning, elucidation, explanation, characterization, description. "The enclosing of a wilderness of ideas within a wall of words."—Samuel Butler.

DEFINITIVE *a.* [di FIN uh tiv] defining absolutely, conclusive. *The definitive Hall of Famer is Babe Ruth.* SYN. absolute, precise, actual, decisive, thorough, consummate, conclusive, complete, exact, clear-cut, perfect. ANT. *questionable, debatable, inexact.*

deflate *v.* **1.** COLLAPSE contract, deplete, shrink, empty, exhaust, flatten, puncture. **2.** HUMBLE *take the wind out of one's sails, put down, *take down a peg, humiliate, *puncture one's aura of invincibility, mortify. ANT. *1. inflate, fill, swell. 2. puff up, hearten, flatter.*

deflect *v.* turn aside, swerve, bounce off, diverge, divert, veer, twist, hook, ricochet, deviate.

deforestation *n.* clearcutting, denuding, desertification.

deformed *a.* misshapen, malformed, disfigured, grotesque, distorted, misproportioned, bent out of shape, twisted, warped, contorted, unnatural, hunchbacked, gnarled. ANT. *well-formed, flawless.*

deformity n. malformation, disfigurement, distortion, contortion, abnormality, birth defect, hunchback, club foot, hump, harelip.

defraud v. cheat, swindle, dupe, *rip off, fleece, bamboozle, bilk, rook, *con, take for a ride, *sucker.

defray v. cover cost, pay.

defrost v. thaw, warm, de-ice.

DEFT a. [DEFT] skillful. *The deft carpenter made a built-in cabinet for my bathroom.* SYN. dexterous, handy, adroit, adept, clever, proficient, *crackerjack, ingenious, facile. ANT. *unskilled, inept, bumbling.*

DEFUNCT a. [di FUNGKT] no longer in existence. *The company that made horse-drawn carriages is defunct.* SYN. nonexistent, dead, extinct, deceased, obsolete, no more, gone, bygone, *kaput, out of business. ANT. *existing, thriving, living, operating.*

defuse v. disarm, take the teeth out of, mollify, calm, quiet, defang.

defy v. rebel, resist, challenge, flout, disregard, oppose, brave, frustrate, ignore, fly in the face of, dare, *thumb one's nose at. ANT. *obey, comply, acquiesce.*

degenerate n. deviant, pervert, wretch, *pig, deviate, *lowlife, fiend, psychopath, *psycho, *sleazebag.

degenerate v. deteriorate, degrade, rot, decay, fail, sink, regress, decline, fall, backslide, slip, *go to the dogs.

degenerate a. deteriorated, degraded, debauched, dissolute, corrupt, debased, decadent, failing, sinking, regressive. ANT. *upright, honorable.*

degrade v. lower, debase, corrupt, diminish, demean, abase, humiliate, disgrace, shame, dishonor, downgrade, discredit. ANT. *honor, put on a pedestal, worship.*

degrading a. debasing, lowering, corrupting, diminishing, downgrading, humiliating, disgraceful, shameful, cheapening, demeaning. ANT. *uplifting, honorable, dignifying.*

degree n. 1. STEP notch, grade, point, rung, tier, stage, rank, peg. 2. LEVEL intensity, extent, magnitude, capacity. 3. ACADEMIC TITLE diploma, certificate, sheepskin, credentials, shingle, testimonial.

WORD FIND

approved to confer degrees: accredited
B.A.: Bachelor of Arts
baccalaureate: bachelor's degree
bachelor's: undergraduate degree
between bachelor's and doctorate: master's degree
B.S.: Bachelor of Science
ceremonies surrounding handing out of: commencement
C.E.: Civil Engineer
D.D.S.: Doctor of Dental Science
D.Th.: Doctor of Theology
graduating with great honor or praise: magna cum laude
graduating with highest praise: summa cum laude
graduating with honors: cum laude
highest degree: doctorate, Ph.D.
LL.D.: Doctor of Laws
M.A.: Master of Arts
M.B.A.: Master of Business Administration
master's and doctorate: postgraduate degree
M.D.: Doctor of Medicine
Ph.D.: Doctor of Philosophy
recognition of achievement, not schooling: honorary degree
Sc.D.: Doctor of Science
S.J.D.: Doctor of Judicial Science
SEE COLLEGE, EDUCATION, UNIVERSITY

dehydrate v. dry, desiccate.

deify v. worship, revere, exalt, put on a pedestal, idealize, idolize, lionize, elevate.

deign v. deem worthy, see fit, stoop, condescend.

deity n. god, goddess, supreme being, idol. SEE GOD

déjà vu n. familiarity, past-life experience, recognition, acquaintence, knowledge, *past life echo, memory, recall, remembrance.

dejected a. depressed, disheartened, saddened, low, dispirited, *bummed, melancholy, downhearted, heavyhearted, blue, disconsolate, *down in the mouth. ANT. *cheerful, happy, euphoric.*

delay n. postponement, deferment, detention, stall, hindrance, impediment, procrastination, suspension, prolongation, hold, stop. ANT. *rush.*

delay v. postpone, put off, defer, detain, stall, hinder, impede, procrastinate, suspend, prolong, hold, stop, wait. ANT. *expedite, rush, hurry.*

delectable a. delightful, pleasing, pleasurable, enjoyable, satisfying, delicious, tasty, *scrumptious, heavenly, luscious, savory, ambrosial, toothsome. ANT. *disgusting, nauseating.*

delegate *n.* representative, deputy, spokesperson, agent, appointee, proxy, envoy, intermediary.

delegate *v.* appoint, commission, deputize, authorize, charge, commission, empower, nominate, assign, give.

delete *v.* strike out, omit, cancel, erase, scratch, remove, eliminate, exclude, expunge, drop. ANT. *include, insert, add.*

DELETERIOUS *a.* [DEL i TEER ee us] harmful, destructive. *Rock salt is deleterious to a car's paint.* SYN. harmful, injurious, hurtful, pernicious, bad, noxious, detrimental, destructive, damaging, malignant. ANT. *beneficial, helpful, advantageous.*

deliberate *v.* think about, reflect, ponder, consider, weigh, muse, cogitate, turn over, ruminate, mull, contemplate.

deliberate *a.* intentional, willful, designed, on purpose, premeditated, meant, calculated, planned, conscious, knowing. ANT. *accidental, unintentional, rash, impulsive.*

deliberation *n.* thought, contemplation, consideration, circumspection, study, debate, reflection, forethought, pondering, weighing. ANT. *thoughtlessness, carelessness, impulsiveness.*

delicatessan *n.* deli, shop, *takeout.

delicacy *n.* **1.** FRAILTY OR FINENESS fragility, tenderness, lightness, daintiness, airiness, exquisiteness. **2.** GOURMET FOOD tidbit, dainty, appetizer, morsel, goody, rarity, treat, bonne bouche, caviar. **3.** SENSITIVITY consideration, tact, grace, subtlety, finesse, diplomacy. ANT. *1. toughness, durability, sturdiness. 3. insensitivity, thoughtlessness, roughness.*

delicate *a.* **1.** FRAIL fragile, fine, tender, light, dainty, airy, exquisite, diaphanous, slight. **2.** SENSITIVE considerate, tactful, graceful, subtle, diplomatic, discreet, careful. **3.** DIFFICULT *sticky, *ticklish, precarious, critical, sensitive, tenuous. ANT. *1. tough, durable, sturdy. 2. insensitive, inconsiderate, rude.*

delicious *a.* tasty, delightful, *lip-smacking good, appetizing, delectable, luscious, scrumptious, ambrosial, mouth-watering, heavenly, *fit for a king, *yummy, toothsome. ANT. *nauseating, gross, unappetizing.*

delight *n.* pleasure, joy, happiness, gratification, enjoyment, thrill, glee, felicity. ANT. *misery, disgust.*

delight *v.* please, make happy, gratify, thrill, gladden, charm, *tickle, enchant, fill with joy, cheer. ANT. *depress, *piss off, anger.*

delightful *a.* pleasing, gratifying, thrilling, gladdening, charming, joyful, enjoyable, happy, agreeable, delectable, thrilling, enchanting. ANT. *miserable, depressing, unpleasant.*

delineate *v.* **1.** OUTLINE sketch, draft, draw, diagram, rough out. **2.** PORTRAY depict, describe, define, characterize, limn, detail.

delinquency *n.* offense, misdeed, wrongdoing, infraction, transgression, violation, misconduct, dereliction, negligence. SEE LAW, COURT

delinquent *n.* criminal, lawbreaker, outlaw, malefactor, offender, miscreant, culprit, scamp, rascal, *hood.

delinquent *a.* lawbreaking, criminal, irresponsible, derelict, remiss, neglectful, faulty, slack, negligent. ANT. *responsible, trustworthy, law-abiding.*

delirious *a.* confused, incoherent, disordered, muddled, hallucinating, irrational, raving, *out of it, bewildered, deranged, babbling. ANT. *rational, lucid, clearheaded.*

delirium *n.* confusion, incoherence, bewilderment, hallucinations, ranting and raving, derangement, temporary insanity, muddled mind, delirium tremens.

deliver *v.* **1.** TRANSFER carry, convey, transport, bring, send, transmit, forward, surrender. **2.** FREE liberate, save, rescue, emancipate, release. **3.** THROW send, discharge, pitch, shoot, toss, launch, fire. ANT. *2. enslave, shackle.*

deliverance *n.* rescue, emancipation, liberation, freeing, saving, salvation, release.

delivery *n.* transfer, transport, transmittal, transmission, forwarding, consignment, distribution, shipment.

delivery room *n.* birthing room.

dell *n.* vale. SEE VALLEY

delta *n.* deposit, accumulation, sediment, formation, mass, heap, pile, build-up, wash.

DELUDE *v.* [du LOOD] to deceive or fool. *She liked to delude herself into thinking she could sing for a living.* SYN. deceive, mislead, fool, *lead down the garden path, *hoodwink, dupe, misrepresent, beguile, *sucker, brainwash, kid.

deluge *n.* flood, inundation, torrent, downpour, cloudburst, spate, cataract, ocean, sea, *rain of biblical proportion, avalanche.

deluge *v.* flood, inundate, drench, drown, swamp, flush, overflow, submerge, immerse, overwhelm, overrun, engulf, *snow under.

DELUSION *n.* [di LOO zshun] a belief that is unsupported by the facts. *Mary was suffering* *from the delusion that Mike was in love with her.* SYN. fancy, illusion, mirage, vision, self-deception, misconception, fantasy, *pipe dream, *fool's paradise, figment of the imagination, paranoia, megalomania, delusions of grandeur, folie à deux.

delve v. search, dig, unearth, investigate, explore, fish around for.

deluxe a. superior, luxurious, first-rate, first-class, select, sumptuous, choice, elegant, grand, rich, elite, *posh. ANT. *cheap, *cut-rate, run of the mill.*

DEMAGOGUE n. [DEM uh GAWG] a leader who panders to the emotions of the masses in order to win them over. *He knew how to push the voters' buttons; he was a rabble-rouser and a demagogue.* SYN. rabble-rouser, *grandstander, agitator, inciter, opportunist, troublemaker, instigator, *firebrand, mountebank. "[One who] appeals to passions and prejudices rather than to reason."—James Fenimore Cooper. "One who tells you what you want to hear. A statesman tells you what you need to hear."—Max Rafferty.

demand n. requirement, bid, call, order, charge, request, command, petition, ultimatum, injunction, appeal.

demand v. order, insist on, press, ask, bid, compel, requisition, exact, command, necessitate, require, urge, summon, implore.

demanding a. laborious, consuming, time-consuming, hard, back-breaking, difficult, painstaking, arduous, rough, burdensome. ANT. *easy, effortless.*

demean v. lower, debase, humble, degrade, depreciate, *take down a peg, disgrace, humiliate, demote, shame. ANT. *elevate, *put on a pedestal, idolize, honor.*

demeanor n. behavior, manner, deportment, conduct, comportment, bearing, disposition, attitude, air, actions.

demented a. insane, crazy, psychotic, deranged, maniacal, unstable, *flipped out, hysterical, mad, schizophrenic, irrational, *nuts. ANT. *sane, rational, stable.* SEE CRAZY, NEUROTIC

demise n. death, passing, end, expiration, downfall, termination, *lights out, fall. ANT. *birth, beginning.* SEE DEATH

dementia n. senility, Alzheimer's Disease, compromised intellect, failing intellect, failing congnitive abilities, mental disturbance, mental deterioration, insanity, madness, psychosis.

DEMOCRACY n. [de MOK ru see] a government by and for the people. Also, a system of equal opportunity for all. *A democracy attempts to assure fair treatment for all.* SYN. government by and for the people, republic, representative government, constitutional government, commonwealth. "Government by amateurs."—Maxwell Anderson. "Gives every man the right to be his own oppressor."—James Lowell. ". . . mob rule."—Polybius. SEE GOVERNMENT, POLITICS

DEMOCRATIC a. [dem uh KRAT ik] representing the common people, especially with issues of equality. *A democratic government is a fair and just government.* SYN. equal, common, populist, popular, self-governing, constitutional, egalitarian, libertarian, representative, of and for the people, tolerant, fair-minded. ANT. *dictatorial, authoritarian, despotic, autocratic, intolerant.*

demography n. population studies, census-taking, consumer studies.

demolish v. destroy, wreck, raze, level, annihilate, ruin, *trash, obliterate, tear down, fell, wipe out, smash. ANT. *build, create.*

demolition n. destruction, wreckage, razing, leveling, *trashing, annihilation, obliteration, smashing, tearing down.

demon n. devil, fiend, satan, imp, monster, ogre, savage, evil spirit, ghoul, goblin, puck, supernatural being, *fallen angel. SEE MONSTER

demonic a. demoniac, fiendish, possessed, hellish, frenzied, bedeviled, bewitched, devilish, diabolical, satanic, monstrous. ANT. *angelic, saintly.*

demonize v. blacken.

demonstrate v. 1. SHOW illustrate, exhibit, explain, describe, *walk one through, set forth. 2. MAKE EVIDENT prove, establish, substantiate, corroborate, evince, authenticate, validate, verify, document. 3. PROTEST picket, rally, strike, march, parade.

demonstration n. 1. SHOW illustration, exhibition, explanation, description, *walk through, presentation. 2. EVIDENCE proof, substantiation, corroboration, authentication, validation, verification, documentation. 3. PROTEST picketing, rally, strike, march, parade, *sit-in.

demonstrative a. affectionate, *touchy-feely, expressive, outpouring, emotional, gushing, expansive, warm, unrestrained, open. ANT. *reserved, restrained, distant, cold, uptight.*

demonstrator n. protester, striker, objector, conscientious objector, marcher, dissenter, voice of dissent, boycotter, malcontent, rioter.

DEMORALIZE v. [di MOR uh lize] to sap one's morale or confidence. *It will utterly demoralize the team if they suffer one more loss.* SYN. deflate, dishearten, discourage, sap, *take the wind out of one's sails, *take the fight out of, *take the starch out of, crush, undermine, shake one's confidence, dispirit. ANT. *encourage, hearten, puff up.*

demote v. lower, degrade, downgrade, *bust, *bench.

demur v. object, take exception, disagree, dissent, protest, remonstrate, refute. ANT. *agree, concur, acquiesce.*

DEMURE a. [di MYOOR] quiet, reserved or shy. Also, affecting shyness. *She was demure in church but boisterous among friends.* SYN. quiet, reserved, sedate, shy, low-keyed, modest, coy, bashful, blushing, unassuming, self-effacing, timid, retiring. ANT. *loudmouthed, bold, brash, aggressive.*

demystify v. clarify, clear up, explain, make plain.

den n. 1. LAIR hole, cave, burrow, diggings, tunnel, retreat, nest. 2. STUDY library, sanctuary, cloister, retreat.

denial n. rejection, refusal, dismissal, negation, veto, no, turndown, refutation, repudiation, prohibition, declination, contradiction, disallowance. ANT. *acceptance, affirmation, approval.*

denigrate v. belittle, defame, calumniate, *bad-mouth, vilify, malign, put down, slander, assail, criticize, *give a black eye. ANT. *honor, flatter, compliment.*

DENIZEN n. [DEN i zun] an inhabitant. *The denizens of Alaska know how to stay warm.* SYN. inhabitant, resident, native, dweller, citizen, occupant.

denomination n. 1. NAME designation, title, appellation, label, moniker, *handle, class, group, classification, category, type, heading. 2. SECT faith, church, school, persuasion, affiliation.

denote v. mean, designate, signify, indicate, symbolize, tag, represent, connote, stand for, suggest.

denouement n. resolution, end, close.

denounce v. condemn, censure, criticize, attack, proscribe, disparage, impugn, castigate, decry, vilify, damn, stigmatize. ANT. *honor, praise, laud.*

dense a. 1. THICK compressed, compact, solid, firm, tight, concentrated, crowded, packed, impenetrable. 2. STUPID dumb, bovine, dull, *lamebrained, *brain-drained, *slow on the uptake, thick, *dense as a post. ANT. *1. porous, sparse, thin. 2. smart, sharp, quick.* SEE MORONIC, STUPID

density n. thickness, solidity, mass, volume, porousness, inpenetrability.

dent n. indentation, hollow, concavity, dint, *ding, dimple, depression, furrow, notch, scratch.

dentures n. false teeth, *choppers, partial.

denude v. expose, lay bare. SEE STRIP

denunciation n. condemnation, censure, criticism, fulmination, disapproval, castigation, indictment, vilification, reprobration, harangue. ANT. *praise, compliment, advocation.*

deny v. 1. REFUSE turn down, reject, veto, say no, turn thumbs down, prohibit, disallow. 2. CONTROVERT dispute, gainsay, contradict, disclaim, forswear, refute, repudiate. ANT. *1. allow, *give the green light, okay, pass. 2. concede, affirm.*

deodorant n. antiperspirant, *roll on, *b.o. stick, body spray, deodorizer.

depart v. 1. LEAVE go, set out, be off, run along, *hit the road, *split, exit, embark, *shove off, *scram, *beat it, pull out, evacuate. 2. DIVERGE digress, deviate, veer, stray, wander, swerve. ANT. *1. come, arrive. 2. *stay on the straight and narrow, abide.*

departed a. gone, passed, bygone, dead, deceased, former. ANT. *present, living.*

department n. division, section, office, branch, unit, subdivision, bureau, sector, district, precinct.

department store n. retail store, mart, emporium. SEE STORE

departure n. 1. LEAVING going, setting out, running along, exit, leavetaking, withdrawal, exodus, embarkation, parting, adieu, withdrawal. 2. DIVERGENCE digression, deviation, veering, straying, wandering. ANT. *1. coming, arrival.*

depend v. 1. RELY ON bank on, trust, count, bet on, *pin one's faith on, turn to. 2. BE DETERMINED BY hinge on, be subject to, hang on, be contingent on.

dependable a. reliable, bankable, trustworthy, steady, unfailing, responsible, tried-and-true, *good as one's word, loyal, staunch, steadfast. ANT. *unreliable, irresponsible.*

dependence n. reliance, faith, confidence, belief, stock, trust, expectation, need, addiction, dependency.

dependent a. 1. RELIANT helpless, defenseless,

vulnerable, clinging, *tied to mother's apron strings, needful, addicted. **2.** DETERMINED BY hinging on, subject to, hanging on, contingent on. ANT. *1. autonomous, self-reliant, independent.*

depict v. describe, portray, detail, outline, sketch, characterize, limn, represent, paint, show, delineate, narrate, tell.

deplete v. use up, exhaust, run out, consume, empty, drain, spend, bleed, bankrupt, finish, expend. ANT. *restock, replenish, fill.*

DEPLORABLE a. [di PLOR uh bul] bad, wretched or grievous. *The boy's bedroom was in a deplorable state.* SYN. bad, wretched, grievous, disgraceful, shameful, abominable, lamentable, despicable, pitiable, reprehensible, depressing, scandalous. ANT. *agreeable, pleasing, acceptable.*

deplore v. **1.** EXPRESS OR FEEL SORROW lament, grieve, weep, mourn, sorrow, bemoan, rue, bewail. **2.** DISAPPROVE OF censure, condemn, criticize, abhor, hate, object to, reject, decry.

deploy v. spread, distribute, station, position, spread out, arrange, use, utilize.

deport v. expel, banish, exile, extradite, cast out, expatriate, *kick out, *give the boot, ostracize.

deportment n. behavior, conduct, carriage, demeanor, actions, manner, mien, bearing, air, posture.

DEPOSE v. [di POZ] to remove from a position of power. *They are planning to have the president deposed.* SYN. remove, oust, *kick out, dismiss, impeach, unseat, *unhorse, eject, *can, drum out, dethrone, overthrow, *send packing, *ride out on a rail. ANT. *install, seat, empower.*

deposit n. installment, down payment, security, pledge, warranty, collateral.

deposition n. testimony, written statement, sworn statement, affidavit.

depot n. **1.** STATION terminal. **2.** WAREHOUSE storehouse, repository, station, armory, magazine, storage installation.

depraved a. corrupt, debased, immoral, wicked, bad, perverted, vile, shameless, *dirty, warped, evil, low, lecherous, sinful, nasty, iniquitous, debauched. ANT. *virtuous, chaste, moral, clean-living.*

depravity n. corruption, wickedness, perversion, immorality, vileness, shamelessness, evil, lechery, sin, nastiness, debauchery, debasement, vice, degeneracy. ANT. *virtue, morality, clean-living, holiness.*

DEPRECATE v. [DEP ruh KATE] to express one's disapproval toward; to speak out against. *The radio host liked to deprecate environmental extremists.* SYN. put down, belittle, condemn, *slam, disparage, mudsling, disapprove, frown on, reproach, censure, rail against. ANT. *approve of, praise, extol, laud.*

depreciate v. **1.** LOSE VALUE cheapen, downgrade, drop, deflate, diminish, shrink, soften, depress, devalue, decay, wane, fall, ebb. **2.** BELITTLE diminish, put down, disparage, denigrate, deprecate, ridicule, underestimate, minimize, find fault, slight. ANT. *1. appreciate, increase, grow, boom. 2. value, esteem, appreciate.*

depreciation n. devaluation, downgrade, drop, fall, deflation, shrinkage, depression, *bear market, decay, waning, slump, loss, reduction.

depress v. **1.** SADDEN dishearten, distress, *bum out, burden, deject, lower spirits, discourage, *suck the wind from one's sails, dispirit, weigh down, demoralize, weary, enervate. **2.** DEVALUE cheapen, degrade, diminish, weaken, depreciate, lower, lessen. **3.** PUSH DOWN press down, level, lower, step on. ANT. *1. cheer, hearten, buoy. 2. appreciate, heighten. 3. pull.*

depressant n. drug, *downer, tranquilizer, sedative, soporific, mood altering medication.

depressed a. **1.** DOWNHEARTED melancholy, *blue, *bummed out, *down in the dumps, disconsolate, dejected, unhappy, low, woebegone, dispirited, down, sad, glum, suicidal, sullen, *down in the mouth, in the doldrums, despondent, miserable, heavy-hearted, hopeless, in a black mood, carrying the weight of the world, gloomy, empty. **2.** IMPOVERISHED poor, suffering hard times, in a recession. ANT. *1. happy, euphoric, elated. 2. booming, prospering.*

depressing a. disheartening, discouraging, sad, dispiriting, hopeless, dismal, black, gloomy, cheerless, dreary, bleak, disappointing. ANT. *uplifting, cheering.*

depression n. **1.** DOWNHEARTEDNESS melancholia, blues, dejection, unhappiness, sadness, doldrums, *blahs, *blue funk, sorrow, heavyheartedness, despair, gloom, affective disorder, mood disorder, depressive neurosis, depressive psychosis, manic-depression, malaise, hopelessness, postpartum depression, seasonal affective disorder (SAD), withdrawal. **2.** ECONOMIC DECLINE recession, slowdown, downturn. **3.** HOLLOW dent, impression, indentation, recess, concavity. ANT. *1. euphoria, happiness, joy, bliss. 3. boom, good times.*

WORD FIND
childbirth, following: postpartum depression
medication: antidepressants
radical treatment: electroshock therapy
winter blues treated with light therapy: seasonal affective disorder (SAD)

deprivation *n.* loss, privation, need, want, hardship, withholding, dispossession.

deprive *v.* keep from, take away, divest, strip, withhold, deny, shut out, remove, dispossess, cut off, confiscate.

depth *n.* **1.** LOWNESS deepness, bottom, draft, drop, pitch. **2.** PROFOUNDNESS wisdom, insight, perception, astuteness. ANT. *1. height, shallowness. 2. shallowness, superficiality.*

deputy *n.* assistant, representative, agent, delegate, appointee, aide, surrogate, proxy, substitute, *second-in-command, emissary, envoy.

deranged *a.* irrational, insane, crazy, unstable, *off the wall, *nuts, demented, psychotic, berserk, mad, lunatic, *out of one's mind, *flipped, *schizo. ANT. *rational, sane, lucid, stable.* SEE CRAZY, NEUROTIC

derelict *n.* vagrant, outcast, *bum, hobo, tramp, beggar, *ne'er-do-well, *good-for-nothing, pariah.

derelict *a.* neglectful, delinquent, remiss, irresponsible, lazy, slack, careless, lax, shiftless, laggard. ANT. *responsible, conscientious, dutiful.*

DERIDE *v.* [di RIDE] to laugh at; ridicule. *Citizens of the nineteenth century would often deride the automobile.* SYN. laugh at, ridicule, scoff, jeer, mock, taunt, make fun of, heckle, kid, *rib, *razz, *roast. ANT. *take seriously, respect, esteem.*

DE RIGUEUR *a.* [de ree GUHR] necessary or proper; required by the rules of etiquette. *Hats were de rigueur for the first half of the century.* SYN. necessary, called for, fashionable, compulsory, a must, proper, right, correct, required, fitting, comme il faut. ANT. *unnecessary, demode.*

DERISION *n.* [duh RI zhun] contemptuous ridicule. *Her radical ideas were met by widespread derision.* SYN. ridicule, scoffing, disrespect, *dig, insult, mockery, sneering, scorn, satire, contempt, jeer, lampoon, laughingstock, *Bronx cheer. ANT. *respect, esteem.*

derisive *a.* ridiculing, sarcastic, disdainful, mocking, taunting, *smart-alecky, jeering, insulting, *razzing, disrespectful. ANT. *respectful.*

derivation *n.* origin, source, root, beginning, inception, wellspring, ancestry.

derivative *a.* borrowed, copied, unoriginal, imitative, derived, rehashed, uninventive, secondary, warmed-over, *lifted. ANT. *original, new, inventive.*

derive *v.* draw, gain, obtain, extract, get, gather, reap, receive.

derive from *vi.* come from, descend, originate, stem from, arise, emanate, spring from.

DERNIER CRI *n.* [DAIR nee ay CREE] the latest thing, the last word, hip. *In the 90s, a ponytail worn by a man was dernier cri.* SYN. the latest cry, the latest thing, the latest fashion, the last word, the in thing, all the rage, mode, fad, look, in vogue. ANT. *out, passé, outmoded.*

DEROGATORY *a.* [di ROG uh TOHR ee] disparaging or disapproving. *Her derogatory comments robbed me of my self esteem.* SYN. disparaging, disapproving, belittling, deprecatory, censorious, critical, perjorative, unflattering, detracting, disdainful, contemptuous. ANT. *flattering, complimentary, approving.*

derriere *n.* seat, backside, rear, *tush, rump, posterior, bottom haunches, *fanny, *ass, *bum, *can, *keister, *stern. SEE BUTTOCKS

derring-do *n.* valor, daring, courage. SEE BRAVERY

descend *v.* go down, drop, fall, decline, lower, plunge, plummet, submerge, dip, sink, slope, rappel. ANT. *ascend, go up, rise.*

descendant *n.* offspring, progeny, child, seed, offshoot, scion, son, daughter, grandchild, heir. ANT. *ancestor, forebear, parent.*

descent *n.* **1.** MOVING DOWN fall, drop, lowering, sinking, tumble, plunge, plummet, dive, decline. **2.** SLOPE grade, incline, declivity, gradient, slant. **3.** LINEAGE ancestry, forefathers, pedigree, family tree, roots, parentage, genealogy. ANT. *1. ascent, rise.*

describe *v.* illustrate, portray, paint a mental picture, show, detail, explain, depict, chronicle, illuminate, relate, sketch, specify, limn.

description *n.* portrayal, depiction, detailing, chronicle, sketch, explanation, illumination, specification, characterization, elaboration, report, *blow by blow, rundown.

DESECRATE *v.* [DES uh krate] to abuse or disrespect that which is sacred. *The hoodlums* descrated the shrine by covering it with grafitti. SYN. profane, defile, abuse, violate, commit sacrilege, pervert, dishonor, debase, degrade, blaspheme, contaminate. ANT. *worship, honor, consecrate.*

desegregate v. integrate, open, bring together, give equal access, unite, commingle, combine, unify, join hands, associate.

desensitize v. numb, anesthetize, deaden, dull, enervate.

desert n. wasteland, barrens, *parched Eden, *Devil's backyard, badlands, flats, dunes, *desiccated landscape, *neglected plot in God's garden, no man's land, dustbowl, *Euclidian plane, *scorched plain, *thirsty terrain, wilderness, Sahara, Gobi, Kalahari, Mojave. "The sea-like, pathless, limitless waste."—Longfellow. "An old man in a dry season."—T.S. Eliot. "A wild of sand."—Addison.

WORD FIND

ancient desert mountain reduced to eroded nubbin: inselberg

characterized by mesas, gulleys, channels, erosion: badlands

dried-up river bed: arroyo

dune, crescent-shaped: barchan

dune, huge, whalelike: whaleback

dune, long or elongated: seif dune, sword dune

dune, pyramidlike: pyramid

dune, ridged or wavy: transverse dune

dune, starlike: star

dusty whirlwind of small size and duration: dust devil

fertile area, fed by spring: oasis

mosaic-like ground of colorful, polished pebbles: desert pavement, gibber plain, reg

mountain that is eroded and flattened on top: mesa, butte

nomadic Arab: Bedouin

optical illusion: mirage

pertaining to: eremic

plain that becomes temporary lake after rain: playa

plants: barrel cactus, century plant, cereus, cholla, creosote bush, ironwood, Joshua tree, mesquite, ocotillo, prickly pear cactus, sagebrush, saguaro

rain that evaporates before hitting ground: phantom rain

salty plain left by evaporation of lake: salt flat

sandy area of the Sahara: erg

semidesert plain: steppe

valley that is flat and arid: bolson

desert v. abandon, leave behind, forsake, leave, give up, *walk, *leave high and dry, strand, quit, maroon, vacate, jilt, defect, renounce, *bail out, *leave in the lurch. ANT. *remain, stay, stick with.*

deserted a. empty, abandoned, desolate, solitary, barren, derelict, lonely, uninhabited, *godforsaken, vacant, forlorn. ANT. *crowded, mobbed, inhabited.*

deserter n. traitor, defector, fugitive, truant, renegade, runaway, refugee, escapee, derelict, turncoat, *AWOL.

desertion n. abandonment, flight, defection, turning one's back on, forsaking, *washing hands of, resignation.

deserts n. retribution, payback, punishment, reward, comeuppance, revenge, penalty, recompense, due.

deserve v. earn, merit, be entitled to, due, *get what is coming, warrant, expect to get, should be given.

deserving a. meritorious, worthy, due, commendable, laudable, praiseworthy.

DESHABILLE n. ALSO, **DISHABILLE** [DAYS ab ee yay] in a state of undress or partial undress; also, in one's night clothes. *She lounged around the breakfast table in deshabille.* SYN. undress, partial dress, in a state of sloppiness, informal dress, partially covered.

desiccate v. dry, dehydrate, drain, deplete, shrivel.

design n. **1.** COMPOSITION draft, arrangement, motif, plan, pattern, scheme, depiction, idea, sketch, outline, conception, blueprint, diagram, model. **2.** INTENTION purpose, objective, aim, goal, plan, *game plan, target, project. **3.** SCHEME plot, intrigue, machination, plan.

design v. **1.** COMPOSE draft, arrange, plan, pattern, invent, contrive, create, sketch, outline, conceive, blueprint, diagram, model, *cook up, fashion. **2.** INTEND purpose, aim, plan, aspire to, mean.

designate v. **1.** INDICATE specify, signify, point out, denote, assign, connote, mark, name. **2.** NAME entitle, christen, dub, label, denominate, nickname, baptize. **3.** APPOINT elect, name, nominate, choose, select, assign.

designation n. **1.** NAME title, label, appellation, moniker, tag, nickname, honorific. **2.** APPOINTMENT delegation, nomination, selection, assignment.

designing *a.* conniving, plotting, crafty, conspiring, tricky, scheming, double-dealing, artful, calculating, foxy, Machiavellian. ANT. *innocent, artless, open.*

desirable *a.* **1.** AROUSING DESIRE attractive, seductive, fetching, enticing, alluring, tantalizing, sexy, tempting, *hot. **2.** WORTHWHILE beneficial, good, pleasing, agreeable, preferable, profitable, advantageous. ANT. *1. repulsive, repellant. 2. undesirable, worthless, useless.*

desire *n.* want, longing, hunger, thirst, need, *hankering, ache, wish, appetite, passion, lust, libido, fervor, urge, yearning, mania, itch. "The warm beast . . . that lies curled up in our loins and stretches itself with a fierce gentleness."—Albert Camus. "A perpetual rack."—Robert Burton. ANT. *aversion, revulsion.*

desire *v.* want, long for, hunger for, thirst after, crave, need, *hanker for, ache for, covet, wish for, lust after, yearn for.

desist *v.* stop, cease, discontinue, refrain, halt, end, conclude, quit, suspend, hold, arrest. ANT. *go, continue, persist.*

desk *n.* table, workspace, rolltop, ambo, escritoire, lectern, secretary, tambour desk.

desolate *a.* **1.** BARREN abandoned, forsaken, deserted, lonely, uninhabited, isolated, solitary, empty, bleak, remote, *godforsaken, stark. **2.** FORLORN wretched, bereft, abandoned, friendless, forsaken, lonesome, alone, isolated, estranged, despondent, miserable, downhearted. ANT. *1. crowded, inhabited, mobbed. 2. happy, cheerful, befriended.*

despair *n.* hopelessness, depression, dejection, despondency, desperation, discouragement, melancholy, gloom, resignation, anguish, misery. ANT. *hope, euphoria, happiness.*

despair *v.* lose hope, to feel defeat, resign, lose faith, lose heart, despond. "An epitome of hell."—Robert Burton. "The worst poison."—Heinrich Heine. ANT. *hope, look up, think positive.*

desperado *n.* outlaw, criminal, thug, bandit, gunman, lawbreaker, highwayman.

desperate *a.* **1.** RECKLESS careless, dangerous, frantic, headlong, foolhardy, rash, out of control, *on a crash course, frenzied, death-defying. **2.** DESPAIRING hopeless, beyond help, *at the end of one's rope, *back to the wall, incurable, irretrievable, futile, *sunk, lost, critical, grave. **3.** EXTREME critical, grave, serious, crucial, urgent, acute, drastic,

compelling. ANT. *1. careful, cautious, prudent, rational. 2. hopeful, optimistic. 3. trivial, minor, casual.*

desperation *n.* **1.** DESPAIR hopelessness, futility, despondency, depression, melancholy, dejection, discouragement, gloom. **2.** RECKLESSNESS carelessness, frenzy, foolhardiness, rashness, impetuosity, daring, imprudence. ANT. *1. hope, optimism. 2. caution, wariness, prudence.*

despicable *a.* contemptible, vile, loathsome, shameful, disgraceful, awful, beastly, sickening, base, abhorrent, cheap, rotten, unforgivable, detestable. ANT. *honorable, praiseworthy, laudable.*

despise *v.* disdain, hate, loathe, abhor, scorn, spurn, look down on, revile, execrate, detest, *can't stand. ANT. *admire, respect, like.*

despite *prep.* in spite of, regardless of, notwithstanding.

DESPONDENT *a.* [di SPON dunt] deeply depressed, filled with despair. *Alice was despondent after her mother died.* SYN. depressed, despairing, miserable, downhearted, inconsolable, melancholy, forlorn, sorrowful, disheartened, glum, *bummed out, heartbroken, *down in the dumps, suicidal. ANT. *euphoric, joyful, optimistic, buoyant, cheerful.*

DESPOT *n.* [DES put] an absolute ruler, an autocrat. *The despot completely oppressed the citizenry.* SYN. autocrat, tyrant, dictator, *strong man, *Hitler, oppressor, lord, master, authoritarian.

desposition *n.* absolute power, autocracy, tyranny, dictatorship, oppression, authoritarianism, rule with an iron fist.

destination *n.* goal, stop, journey's end, objective, station, terminal, end of the line, port of call.

destiny *n.* fate, lot, destination, future, design, doom, predestination, serendipity, fortune, karma, *wheel of fortune. "A tyrant's authority for crime and a fool's excuse for failure."—Ambrose Bierce. "Not a thing to be waited for, it is a thing to be achieved."—William Jennings Bryan. "An invention of the cowardly and the resigned."—Ignazio Silone.

DESTITUTE *a.* [DES ti TOOT] profoundly poor, impoverished. *The destitute man had lived on the street.* SYN. poor, penniless, indigent, impoverished, broke, *down and out, *dirt poor, lacking, bankrupt, homeless, ruined, *wiped out. ANT. *rich, wealthy, *rolling in dough.*

destroy v. demolish, annihilate, wreck, devastate, wipe out, *total, raze, extirpate, ruin, ravage, obliterate, eradicate, *cream, level, waste, quash, *gut, *nuke, crush. ANT. create, build, preserve.

destruction n. wreckage, demolition, annihilation, ruins, devastation, ravaging, liquidation, havoc, extinction, eradication, slaughter, decimation. ANT. building, creation, preservation.

destructive a. injurious, pernicious, harmful, ravaging, ruinous, catastrophic, fatal, damaging, deleterious, disastrous, malevolent, noxious. ANT. creative, constructive, preserving.

DESULTORY a. [DES ul TOHR ee] moving from one thing to another randomly or haphazardly. She examined the shoes in a desultory fashion. SYN. random, haphazard, unmethodical, disconnected, rambling, aimless, irregular, chaotic, unsystematic, erratic. ANT. methodical, planned.

detach v. disconnect, separate, sever, loose, unhitch, uncouple, divide, free, remove. ANT. attach, fasten.

detached a. 1. DISCONNECTED separated, removed, severed, unfastened, unconnected, unhitched, loose, apart. 2. DISINTERESTED removed, remote, objective, impartial, aloof, dispassionate, neutral, unbiased. ANT. 1. attached, fastened, connected. 2. interested, biased, partial.

detachment a. objectivity, aloofness, unconcern, impartiality, indifference, remoteness, neutrality, isolation. ANT. interest, partiality, bias.

detail n. particular, item, point, fact, feature, specific, component, part, *nuts and bolts, aspect, element, minutiae.

detain v. hold, stop, slow, arrest, restrain, delay, impede, confine, keep, retard. ANT. free, liberate, speed.

detect v. notice, spot, find, discover, uncover, sense, catch, espy, sleuth, *sniff out, ferret out, discern, unmask, *stumble on. ANT. miss, overlook, ignore.

detection n. discovery, spotting, notice, finding, uncovering, sensing, revelation, exposure, espial, ferreting out, *sniffing out.

detective n. sleuth, private investigator (P.I.), *private eye, *dick, operative, *gumshoe, hawkshaw, undercover agent, secret agent, shadow, *tail, *G-man, *snoop. SEE POLICE

DETENTE n. [day TAHNT] an easing of hostilities between nations. Following the treaty was an extended period of detente. SYN. relaxation, cooling off, easing, peace, quietude, relief, tranquility, harmony, softening, suspension of hostilities, quiescence, accord, truce, amity. ANT. hostility, cold war, war, animosity.

detention n. holding, retention, restraint, arrest, confinement, duress, delaying, incarceration, custody, internment. ANT. freedom, liberation.

deter v. prevent, stop, scare off, inhibit, check, dissuade, curb, hinder, bar, stall, cool, daunt, dampen, preclude, discourage. ANT. encourage, speed, facilitate.

detergent n. soap, cleaner, cleanser, scouring powder, solvent, degreaser.

deteriorate v. decay, degenerate, fall apart, crumble, degrade, decline, *go downhill, *go to the dogs, corrode, rot, decompose, depreciate. ANT. improve, grow, strengthen.

determination n. 1. RESOLUTENESS perseverance, steadfastness, fortitude, resolve, tenacity, *backbone, drive, willpower, grit, *stiff upper lip, persistence, single-mindedness, mettle, stick-to-itiveness, indomitability. 2. DECISION conclusion, ascertainment, finding, judgment, settlement, resolution, verdict, opinion.

determine v. 1. DECIDE conclude, ascertain, find, judge, settle, resolve, confirm, verify, *nail down, *sew up, establish. 2. AFFECT THE COURSE OF decide, influence, control, direct, govern, regulate, shape.

determined a. resolute, steadfast, purposeful, firm, *hell-bent, fixed, intent, tenacious, driven, single-minded, settled, stalwart, dogged. ANT. waffling, wavering, lukewarm.

DETERRENT n. [de TUR unt] something that blocks or hinders. A neighborhood watch program proved a useful deterrent to crime. SYN. check, curb, obstacle, stumbling block, bar, defense, impediment, hindrance, discouragement, restraint.

detest v. hate, loathe, despise, abhor, dislike, execrate, *feel sick at the sight of, reject. ANT. like, admire, love.

detestable a. hateful, despicable, loathsome, abhorrent, abominable, sickening, execrable, revolting, obnoxious, beastly, disgusting, contemptible. ANT. admirable, likable.

dethrone v. remove from power, depose, unseat, oust, kick out, impeach, disbar, unhorse, expel.

detonate v. explode, set off, discharge, blow up, fire, touch off.

detonation *n.* explosion, discharge, blow-up, firing, boom, pop, roar.

detour *n.* bypass, *go-around, alternate route, deviation.

detract *v.* lessen, diminish, take away from, undermine, minimize, devaluate, depreciate. ANT. *enhance, increase, add to.*

DETRIMENTAL *a.* [det ruh MEN tul] causing harm. *Neglecting to wax your car is detrimental to its finish.* SYN. harmful, injurious, damaging, deleterious, bad, disadvantageous, inimical, destructive, pernicious. ANT. *beneficial, advantageous.*

detritus *n.* fragments, bits and pieces, grains, debris.

DEUS EX MACHINA *n.* [DEE us eks MAK i nuh] literally, god from a machine. Divine intervention as a means to solve a difficult problem. So named after the unsatisfying practice of bringing in a deity to intervene in some Roman and Greek dramas, now regarded as a hallmark of lazy writing. *The author helped his hero win the battle by creating an unlikely tornado, an obvious deus ex machina.* SYN. god in the machine, divine intervention, contrivance, happy coincidence, device.

devalue *v.* lower, degrade, lessen, cheapen, reduce.

devastate *v.* lay waste, ruin, destroy, demolish, wipe out, *total, level, desolate, ravage, raze, gut, *trash, *blow away, ransack, pillage.

devastation *n.* waste, ruin, destruction, havoc, desolation, ravaging, demolition, wreckage, annihilation, *trashing.

develop *v.* **1.** EXPAND grow, enlarge, elaborate, evolve, advance, mature, flourish, progress, fill out, blossom, bear fruit, enrich, broaden, flesh out, amplify. **2.** GENERATE begin, start, commence, originate, establish, arise, break, transpire, unfold. **3.** CONTRACT acquire. ANT. *1. die, shrivel, regress, shrink, degrade.*

development *n.* **1.** GROWTH expansion, enlargement, elaboration, evolution, advancement, maturation, progress, filling out, flowering, blossoming, enrichment, broadening, fleshing out, amplification. **2.** HAPPENING event, occurrence, circumstance, change, issue, result, advance. ANT. *1. decline, regression, shriveling, withering, death.*

developer *n.* real estate developer, builder, real estate investor, enterpriser, businessman, businesswoman, magnate, land baron, tycoon.

deviant *n.* nonconformist, rebel, original, weirdo, one-of-a-kind, oddball, deviate, radical, pervert.

deviate *v.* diverge, turn aside, veer, depart, stray, drift, wander, swerve, part, meander, err, detour, digress. ANT. *follow the straight and narrow, stay on course.*

device *n.* **1.** INSTRUMENT apparatus, contrivance, tool, appliance, mechanism, rig, machine, gadget, *contraption, outfit, gear, *thingamajig. **2.** SCHEME plan, contrivance, design, ploy, ruse, trick, artifice, gimmick, deus ex machina, stunt, machination.

devil *n.* **1.** SATAN Lucifer, Prince of Darkness, Beelzebub, Mephistopheles, archfiend, el diablo, Lord of the Flies, the Serpent, *Old Harry, *Old Scratch, *the Deuce, *the Dickens, the Adversary, fallen angel. "A liar, and the father of it."—Bible. "The most diligent preacher of all others; he is never out of his diocese."—Hugh Latimer. **2.** BAD PERSON, SPIRIT OR CREATURE demon, fiend, imp, ogre, savage, brute, rogue, hellion, evildoer, beast, villain, scoundrel, brat. SEE RELIGION

devil and the deep blue sea, between the between a rock and a hard place, no choice, *Catch-22, Hobson's choice.

devilish *a.* fiendish, villainous, beastly, hellish, evil, diabolical, brutish, mischievous, demonic, impish, troublemaking, naughty, wicked, infernal, cruel, sinister. ANT. *angelic, saintly, good, virtuous.*

devil-may-care *a.* careless, reckless, happy-go-lucky, foolhardy, rash, nonchalant, cavalier, heedless, casual. ANT. *cautious, careful.*

DEVIL'S ADVOCATE *n.* one who argues for but doesn't necessarily agree with the unpopular side of an issue in order to illustrate all perspectives. *Talk show hosts often play the devil's advocate for argument's sake.* SYN. pleader, apologist, mediator, medium, devil's counsel, defender, devil's champion, devil's surrogate, polemicist.

devious *a.* deceptive, roundabout, crafty, tricky, wily, guileful, sly, treacherous, crooked, dishonest, evasive, underhanded, scheming, shifty. ANT. *honest, aboveboard, straightforward.*

devise *v.* invent, conceive, form, contrive, formulate, *cook up, create, *whip up, plot, scheme, concoct, construct, shape.

devoid *a.* empty, lacking, destitute, vacuous, depleted, denuded, stripped, vacant, bare, wanting, barren. ANT. *full, replete.*

devote *v.* dedicate, give, pledge, commit, vow, consign, apply, direct.

devoted *a.* dedicated, faithful, true, committed, loyal, staunch, zealous, dutiful, devout, constant, earnest, steadfast. ANT. *indifferent, disloyal.*

devotee *n.* fan, fanatic, enthusiast, aficionado, buff, lover, supporter, addict, *nut, adherent, *hound, *fiend.

devotion *n.* dedication, commitment, adherence, allegiance, devoutness, faithfulness, loyalty, fidelity, steadfastness, piety, zeal, reverence. ANT. *indifference, apathy, disloyalty.*

devour *v.* swallow up, eat, consume, gobble up, wolf, gulp, stuff, gorge, bolt, *polish off, guzzle, gormandize, dispatch.

devout *a.* pious, religious, believing, faithful, reverent, worshipping, earnest, holy, orthodox, zealous, ardent, heartfelt, sincere. ANT. *atheistic, agnostic, unbelieving.*

dew *n.* moisture, condensation, water droplets.

WORD FIND

frozen: rime, frost

dewy-eyed *a.* innocent, childlike, naive. ANT. *worldly, experienced.*

dexterity *n.* skill, adroitness, deftness, cleverness, expertise, know-how, knack, touch, aptitude, facility, nimbleness, finesse. ANT. *ineptitude, clumsiness.*

dexterous *a.* skillful, adroit, deft, clever, expert, handy, adept, nimble, proficient, savvy, clever, facile. ANT. *clumsy, inept, uncoordinated.*

diabetes *n.* metabolic disorder, illness, disease, insulin insufficiency. SEE DISEASE, MEDICINE

diabolic *a.* satanic, hellish, devilish, infernal, fiendish, evil, demonic, wicked, villainous, Mephistophelean, malevolent, vicious, cruel, beastly. ANT. *heavenly, saintly, benevolent, angelic.*

diagnosis *n.* identification, conclusion, determination, hunch, opinion, analysis, educated guess. "One of the commonest diseases."—Karl Kraus.

diagram *n.* drawing, chart, illustration, outline, graphic, draft, representation, graph, figure.

dialect *n.* speech, local tongue, provincialism, vernacular, patois, idiom, lingo, argot, slang, cant, colloquialism, accent, pidgin.

dialogue *n.* talk, discussion, conversation, verbal exchange, interlocution, confabulation, communication, conference, tête-à-tête, *rap session, discourse, *powwow, *heart-to-heart.

diameter *n.* breadth, width, caliber.

diametrical *a.* opposite, contrary, conflicting, converse, reverse, antithetical, different. ANT. *alike, similar, matching.*

diaphanous *a.* transparent, sheer, *see-through, translucent, thin, flimsy, gauzy, delicate, chiffon. ANT. *opaque, thick.*

diarrhea *n.* loose stool, *Montezuma's revenge, dysentery, trots, flux, *Aztec two-step, runs, gastrointestinal distress.

diary *n.* journal, chronicle, account, log, record, daybook. "The lavatory of literature."—Elbert Hubbard.

DIATRIBE *n.* [DI uh tribe] a bitter denunciation or criticism. *The talk show host launched into a scathing diatribe.* SYN. invective, criticism, denunciation, harangue, castigation, tirade, abuse, vituperation, *tongue-lashing, rebuke.

dibs *n.* rights, claim.

dice *n.* *bones, *rollers, die, cube.

dicey *a.* risky, chancy, hazardous, a gamble, ticklish, *iffy.

DICHOTOMY *n.* [di KOT uh me] a division of two distinctly different or opposite parts, groups, opinions, etc. *There was a dichotomy of opinions between the races.* SYN. division, split, subdivision, disagreement, difference of opinion, opposition, break, separation, rift, splintering, segmentation.

dicker *v.* haggle, bargain, negotiate, *hash out a deal, higgle, quibble, *talk down, barter.

dictate *n.* directive, rule, order, direction, command, mandate, law, ordinance, decree, bidding, dictum, requirement.

dictate *v.* **1.** PRESCRIBE order, command, direct, rule, charge, lay down the law, demand, enjoin, *call the shots, impose, ordain. **2.** READ ALOUD compose, utter, draft, record.

dictator *n.* tyrant, despot, autocrat, authoritarian, *Hitler, totalitarian, oppressor, overlord, *lord and master, strongman, czar, taskmaster. "Jealous gods monopolizing power, destroying all rivals, compelling exclusive loyalty."—Walter Lippmann. "Rulers who always look good until the last ten minutes."—Jan Masaryk. SEE GOVERNMENT

dictatorial *a.* tyrannical, despotic, autocratic, authoritarian, *Hitleresque, totalitarian, oppressive, overbearing, ironhanded, lordly, high-handed, absolute, *whip-cracking, imperious, domineering. ANT. *democratic, liberal, tolerant.*

diction *n.* vocabulary, wording, articulation, enunciation, expression, eloquence, usage, pronunciation, phraseology, language, inflection, elocution.

dictionary n. lexicon, glossary, word book, reference book, vocabulary. "The most interesting book in our language."—Albert Nock.

dictum n. **1.** PRONOUNCEMENT dictate, declaration, assertion, decree, command, edict, order. **2.** SAYING maxim, adage, proverb, truism, axiom, aphorism.

DIDACTIC a. [dye DAK tik] instructional or educational, especially involving morals. Also, overly preachy or instructional; pedantic. *The audience was asleep after the senator's didactic speech.* SYN. instructional, educational, informative, enlightening, expository, edifying, moralizing, pedantic, preachy, homiletic, pedagogic, sermonizing.

die v. **1.** PERISH expire, pass away, decease, succumb, depart, drop dead, *croak, *kick the bucket, *buy the farm, *cash in one's chips, *bite the dust, *kick off, *give up the ghost, *go belly up, *slip one's cable, *permanently change one's address, *meet one's Maker, meet one's fate, meet one's end, *bow out. "Go the way of all earth."—Bible. SEE DEAD, DEATH **2.** DWINDLE wane, ebb, fade, weaken, abate, decline, subside, slacken, *fizzle out, *peter out, recede, diminish.

diehard n. *bitter-ender, zealot, fanatic, ultraconservative, reactionary, stick-in-the-mud.

die-hard a. tough, tenacious, resistant, stubborn, strong, clinging, defiant, recalcitrant, headstrong, immovable, firm, rigid, unchanging. ANT. *weak-willed.*

diet n. **1.** DAILY FOOD INTAKE food and drink, sustenance, nourishment, nutrition, victuals, foodstuffs, provisions, fare. **2.** FOOD ABSTINENCE abstinence, fasting, regimen, regime, *weight-watching, calorie counting. "A system of starving yourself to death so you can live a little longer."—Jan Murray.

differ v. **1.** CONTRAST vary, stand apart, clash, diverge, be distinguished from, deviate from. **2.** DISAGREE clash, oppose, dispute, conflict, be at variance, take issue, contend, contradict, *lock horns. ANT. 1. *resemble, correspond, match.* 2. *agree, concur, accede, *see eye to eye.*

difference n. **1.** DISSIMILARITY contrast, antithesis, variance, opposition, distinction, asymmetry, differentiation, inconformity, unlikeness, deviation. **2.** DISAGREEMENT argument,

dispute, contention, clash, controversy, dissension, conflict, debate, quarrel, opposition, contradiction. ANT. *1. similarity, likeness, correspondence, mirror image. 2. agreement, concurrence, accord.*

different a. **1.** DISSIMILAR distinct, contrasting, antithetical, opposite, asymmetrical, unlike, variant, *like night and day, divergent, clashing, disparate, incompatible. **2.** SEPARATE distinct, delineated, differentiated, singular, individual, another, exclusive. **3.** VARIOUS several, sundry, assorted, diverse, numerous, miscellaneous, mixed. ANT. *1. the same, alike, resembling, matching. 2. together, whole.*

differentiate v. distinguish, set apart, make a distinction, contrast, separate, characterize.

difficult a. **1.** HARD laborious, arduous, demanding, strenuous, tough, *Herculean, back-breaking, wearisome, burdensome, *Sisyphean, formidable. **2.** COMPLICATED abstruse, intricate, perplexing, recondite, hard, *brain-draining, complex, knotty, enigmatic, unfathomable, problematic. **3.** UNMANAGEABLE intractable, obstinate, unaccommodating, hard to please, unruly, refractory, trying, stubborn, *a pain, fussy. ANT. *1. easy, simple, *a snap, *child's play. 2. simple, uncomplicated, obvious. 3. easy to please, easygoing, accommodating.*

difficulty n. problem, complication, pain, struggle, trouble, bother, trial, *hard row to hoe, dilemma, hardship, obstacle, *fix, snag, impasse, quagmire, hassle, *tough sledding, plight, mess, *hot water, *deep water, straits, *hornet's nest, *Gordian knot, *can of worms, deadlock, gridlock, *pickle. "God's errands and trainers, and only through them can one come to the fullness of manhood."—Henry Ward Beecher. "A harsh nurse who roughly rocks her foster-children into strength and athletic proportion."—William Jennings Bryan.

DIFFIDENT a. [DIF i dunt] lacking confidence, timid. *She became diffident with people in authority.* SYN. timid, shy, bashful, hesitant, unassertive, unsure of oneself, shrinking, timorous, modest, unassuming, insecure, reluctant, fainthearted. ANT. *self-confident, bold, assertive.*

diffuse a. **1.** SPREAD OUT dispersed, scattered, strewn, disseminated, extensive, prevalent, distributed, circulated. **2.** WORDY long-winded, verbose, profuse, rambling, prolix, loquacious, discursive. ANT. *1. concentrated, focused. 2. brief, terse, pithy.*

diffusion *n.* spreading, dispersal, scattering, dissemination, distribution, circulation, propagation.

dig *n.* insult, crack, knock, cutting remark, wisecrack, *slap in the face, taunt, jeer, *low blow, barb. ANT. *compliment, praise.*

dig *v.* excavate, hollow out, shovel, spade, delve, hoe, scoop out, till, unearth, dredge, quarry, sift, root out, mine, exhume, *backhoe.

digest *n.* summary, synopsis, abridgement, abstract, condensation, pre cis.

digest *v.* **1.** ABSORB FOOD assimilate, break down, consume, eat, dissolve. **2.** UNDERSTAND comprehend, absorb, take in, get, grasp, mull over, reflect, ponder, assimilate.

dignified *a.* self-respecting, poised, distinguished, stately, noble, regal, lofty, classy, refined, solemn, formal, imperious, *distingué, decorous. ANT. *undignified, goofy, foolish, sophomoric.*

dignify *v.* elevate, exalt, honor, uplift, aggrandize, ennoble, raise, solemnize, add a bit of class. ANT. *demean, degrade, lower.*

dignitary *n.* *VIP, official, *bigwig, *bigshot, personage, *name, somebody, celebrity, *high muck-a-muck, star, lion. ANT. *nobody, *lightweight, *Joe Blow.*

dignity *n.* self-respect, poise, nobility, stateliness, courtliness, honor, stature, loftiness, solemnity, class, formality, pride, presence. "The quality that enables a man who says nothing, does nothing and knows nothing to command . . . respect."—John W. Raper. ANT. *sheepishness, goofiness, cringing servitude.*

DIGRESS *v.* [di GRESS] to depart or stray from the main subject at hand. *The speech was long-winded; the speaker liked to digress.* SYN. stray, depart, ramble, drift, wander, divagate, deviate, *go off on a tangent, get sidetracked, rove, *beat around the bush.

digression *n.* straying, departure, rambling, drifting, wandering, divagation, deviation, roving, aside, detour.

DILAPIDATED *a.* [di LAP i dayt ud] falling apart; decaying. *The dilapidated building was nearly 200 years old.* SYN. falling apart, broken down, in disrepair, crumbling, tumbledown, decaying, falling down, *on its last legs, in ruins, worn out, run-down, rickety, deteriorated, *shot. ANT. *sound, solid, intact, *good as new.*

DILATE *v.* [DI layt] to widen or make wider. *The pupils of the eyes dilate when viewing an attractive member of the opposite sex.* SYN. widen, expand, enlarge, broaden, extend, swell, grow, distend. ANT. *contract, shrink, constrict.*

dilatory *a.* procrastinating, delaying, putting off, dallying, tardy, postponing, lagging, behind, shilly-shallying. ANT. *on time, prompt, timely.*

dilemma *n.* difficulty, predicament, bind, quandary, plight, impasse, *pickle, *box, *fix, *Catch-22, puzzle, hard choice, problem, Hobson's choice.

DILETTANTE *n.* [DIL i TAHNT] one who dabbles in or has an amateur's knowledge of the arts. *She painted only as a hobby; she was a dilettante.* SYN. dabbler, amateur, hobbyist, layman, nonprofessional, trifler, putterer, tyro, *lightweight. ANT. *professional, master, expert.*

diligence *n.* perseverance, persistence, relentlessness, hard work, industry, care, plugging, assiduity, effort, application, doggedness, pains, earnestness, discipline. ANT. *laziness, slackness.*

DILIGENT *a.* [DIL uh junt] hard-working or industrious, careful and meticulous. *A diligent work force will make our company thrive.* SYN. hard-working, industrious, careful, meticulous, painstaking, sedulous, assiduous, dogged, persistent, busy, unrelenting, steadfast, plugging, tireless, active, toiling. ANT. *lazy, laggard, sluggish, slack.*

dillydally *v.* waste time, procrastinate, vacillate, dawdle, trifle, lag, loiter.

dilute *v.* thin, water down, reduce, weaken, diminish, rarefy, attenuate, *cut, adulterate, moderate. ANT. *concentrate, enrich, strengthen.*

dim *a.* **1.** POORLY LIT faint, dusky, gauzy, gloomy, shadowy, gray, blurry, indistinct, vague, murky, fuzzy, subdued. **2.** DIM-WITTED stupid, bovine, slow, dense, *thick, *dumb as a post. ANT. *1. bright, blinding, brilliant. 2. smart, intelligent, bright.*

dimension *n.* size, extent, range, scope, magnitude, proportion, scale, measure, measurement, span.

diminish *v.* lessen, reduce, decrease, lower, shrink, dwindle, wane, ebb, weaken, fade, depreciate, slacken, abate. ANT. *grow, enlarge, expand.*

diminution *n.* lessening, reduction, decrease, lowering, shrinkage, decline, weakening, depreciation, slackening, abatement. ANT. *growth, expansion, enlargement.*

diminutive *a.* tiny, small, little, miniature, pint-sized, minute, petite, *teeny, Lilliputian, *baby, microscopic, puny. ANT. *huge, gigantic, enormous.*

dimple *n.* indentation, depression.

dimwit *n.* idiot, simpleton, dunce. SEE MORON

din *n.* noise, uproar, cacophony, racket, clamor, commotion, tumult, *hubbub, *hurly-burly, babel, bedlam, clangor. ANT. *silence, peace, stillness.*

dine *v.* eat, sup, lunch, feast, break bread, banquet, feed, *pig out. ANT. *fast.*

diner *n.* cafe, eatery, lunch counter. SEE RESTAURANT

dinghy *n.* rowboat. SEE BOAT

dingy *a.* grimy, dirty, sooty, smoky, soiled, drab, smudgy, shabby, tarnished, dim, faded, smeared. ANT. *sparkling, brilliant, clean, bright.*

dinky *a.* small, tiny, wee, insignificant, trivial. ANT. *gargantuan.*

dinner *n.* meal, supper, repast, feast, banquet.

dinosaur *n.* **1.** SAURIAN sauropod, *terrible lizard, prehistoric creature, theropod.

WORD FIND

aquatic: mosasaur

armored, spiked: ankylosaurus

bony fringe found on heads of some species: frill

death: extinction

duck-billed: hadrosaur, trachodon

era: Mesozoic

evidence of, geological: fossil

giraffe-like giant: brachiosaurus

large herbivore: brontosaurus, apatosaurus, diplodocus, iguanodon

longest herbivore: supersaurus, seismosaurus

meat-eating, ferocious: tyrannosaurus rex, allosaurus

period: Triassic, Jurassic, Cretaceous

plate-backed: stegosaurus

sickle-like claw used for slahing, swift and small and famous for: velociraptor

skull crest, known for long: parasaurolophus

slashing: utahraptor

tallest herbivore: ultrasaurus

three-horned, beaklike mouth: triceratops

winged: pterodactyl

2. RELIC antique, artifact, fossil, outmoded article.

diorama *n.* scene, display, three-dimensional representation, exhibit.

dip *v.* **1.** DUNK immerse, duck, lower, submerge, wet, plunge, sink. **2.** DECLINE decrease, slip, drop off, descend, droop, plummet, plunge.

diploma *n.* certificate, sheepskin, degree, parchment, document.

DIPLOMACY *n.* [di PLOH muh see] the forming and maintaining of good relationships and the skills it requires. *The ambassador used a subtle form of diplomacy to smooth things over with the dictator.* SYN. people skills, tact, tactfulness, statesmanship, politics, *glad-handing, judiciousness, grace, sensitivity, prudence, charm, mediation. "The art of saying 'Nice Doggie' till you can find a rock."—Wynn Catlin. SEE DIPLOMATIC, POLITICS

diplomat *n.* ambassador, statesman, envoy, consul, representative, politician, negotiator, mediator, go-between, minister, emissary, attaché. "A man who says 'perhaps' when he means no."—Elbert Hubbard. "A person who can tell you to go to hell in such a way that you actually look forward to the trip."—Caskie Stinnett. "An honest man sent abroad to lie for his country."—Henry Wooton.

diplomatic *a.* tactful, discreet, gracious, smooth, conciliatory, sensitive, prudent, politic, suave, subtle, artful. "The art of letting someone have your way."—Daniele Vare. ANT. *rude, tactless, uncivil, indelicate, blunt.*

dipstick *n.* rod, measuring stick.

dire *a.* **1.** TERRIBLE disastrous, horrible, calamitous, dreadful, fearful, appalling, grievous, distressing, shocking, catastrophic. **2.** URGENT critical, pressing, crucial, exigent. ANT. *1. wonderful, fortuitous. 2. trivial, unimportant.*

direct *v.* **1.** CONDUCT manage, orchestrate, guide, control, *head up, oversee, supervise, *quarterback, *call the shots, *be in the driver's seat, boss. **2.** AIM point, guide, train, indicate, target, steer, orient, show, usher. **3.** ADDRESS focus, devote, fix, funnel, aim. ANT. *1. follow, obey.*

direct *a.* **1.** STRAIGHTFORWARD frank, honest, explicit, forthright, point-blank, blunt, open, unequivocal, candid. **2.** UNDEVIATING straight, unswerving, true, *as the crow flies, *in a beeline. **3.** IMMEDIATE unimpeded, firsthand, face-to-face. ANT. *1. indirect, mealy-mouthed, roundabout. 2. roundabout, deviating, circuitous. 3. second-hand, indirect.*

direction *n.* **1.** MANAGEMENT orchestration, guidance, control, supervision, leadership, administration, care, command. **2.** POINT OF THE COMPASS course, way, orientation, bearing, heading, route, tack, trajectory. **3.** INSTRUCTION guidance, advice, specifications, prescription, guidelines, recipe. **4.** ORDER command, charge, instruction.

directive *n.* order, command, mandate, instruction, direction, charge, ruling, injunction, ordinance.

directly *adv.* **1.** STRAIGHT *as the crow flies, *in a beeline, undeviatingly, *spang. **2.** IMMEDIATELY without delay, promptly, at once, *first thing, pronto, speedily, straightaway. ANT. *1. indirectly, roundabout, circuitously. 2. eventually, later.*

director *n.* leader, orchestrator, manager, overseer, administrator, supervisor, head, *whip, *kingpin, executive, foreman, overlord, *biggest toad in the puddle, general, quarterback, captain, boss.

directorate *n.* board, staff.

direful *a.* SEE DIRE

dirge *n.* funeral hymn, epicedium, threnody, lament, elegy, death march, mass.

dirigible *n.* balloon, zeppelin. SEE BLIMP

dirt *n.* **1.** SOIL filth, grime, mud, muck, dust, dung, mire, ooze, loam, earth, residue, *crap, *crud, *gunk, *gook, clay. **2.** OBSCENITY pornography, filth, smut, indecency. **3.** GOSSIP rumor, scandal, scoop, talk, exposé, muck, *keyhole journalism.

dirty *v.* soil, stain, muddy, besmirch, mess, spot, begrime, foul, pollute, smudge, smatter, defile.

dirty *a.* **1.** SOILED filthy, unclean, grimy, *grungy, stained, spotted, begrimed, unsightly, squalid, messy, foul, greasy, grubby, polluted, muddy, smudged, *scuzzy, *gross, unsanitary. **2.** OBSCENE pornographic, X-rated, filthy, smutty, indecent, prurient, blue, risqué, off-color, ribald, *raunchy, *raw, explicit, scatological. **3.** UNFAIR unsportsmanlike, dishonorable, dishonest, low, *cheap, rotten, mean, below-the-belt. ANT. *1. clean, sanitary, spotless, sparkling. 2. wholesome, clean, G-rated. 3. fair, sportsmanlike, clean.*

dirty old man *n.* lecher, *sleazebag, *dirty old goat, satyr, pedophile.

disability *n.* handicap, incapacity, infirmity, defect, weakness, restriction, malady, injury, impairment, paralysis, affliction.

disable *v.* cripple, impair, incapacitate, lame, hamstring, damage, weaken, debilitate, *put out of action, handicap, prostrate, paralyze, disarm. ANT. *enable, strengthen.*

disabled *a.* crippled, impaired, incapacitated, lame, injured, weakened, *out of action, handicapped, prostrate, paralyzed, bedridden, confined to a wheelchair, paraplegic, quadraplegic. ANT. *sound, strong, fit, conditioned, powerful.*

disadvantage *n.* drawback, liability, handicap, weakness, impediment, detriment, hurdle, stumbling block, limitation, failing, minus, burden. ANT. *advantage, plus, benefit.*

disadvantaged *a.* underprivileged, handicapped, deprived, unequal, impoverished, poor. ANT. *advantaged, lucky, privileged.*

disadvantageous *a.* unfavorable, detrimental, injurious, deleterious, inopportune, adverse, harmful, detracting, unlucky. ANT. *favorable, opportune.*

DISAFFECTED *a.* [dis uh FEK tid] no longer feeling loyalty or affection for someone or something; alienated. *Government betrayed him and he became disaffected.* SYN. alienated, estranged, discontented, disloyal, unfriendly, separated, hostile, dissatisfied, disgruntled. ANT. *affectionate, loyal, contented.*

disagree *v.* differ, be at odds, dissent, conflict, contradict, contest, contend, argue, clash, oppose, take issue, dispute, see things differently. ANT. *agree, concur, correspond.*

disagreeable *a.* **1.** UNPLEASANT offensive, repugnant, objectionable, repellant, distasteful, disgusting, repulsive, obnoxious, odious, negative, unwanted. **2.** QUARRELSOME grouchy, bad-tempered, contentious, contrary, petulant, standoffish, cross, peevish, surly, irritable, nasty, churlish. ANT. *1. pleasant, welcome, nice. 2. easygoing, pleasant, good-humored.*

disagreement *n.* dispute, difference of opinion, dissent, contention, argument, quarrel, controversy, division, squabble, discord, opposition, spat, falling-out. ANT. *agreement, accord, harmony.*

disallow *v.* reject, veto, prohibit, deny, proscribe.

disappear *v.* vanish, fade, go away, dissolve, recede, evaporate, *vamoose, *go south, evanesce, leave no trace, *fade into the woodwork, dematerialize, vaporize, wane, cease, pass, escape, depart, hide. ANT. *appear, materialize, show.*

disappoint *v.* let down, sadden, deflate, *dash one's hopes, *burst one's bubble, fall short, fail, disillusion, displease, disenchant, frustrate, dishearten. ANT. *live up to expectations, hearten, encourage, fulfill, satisfy.*

disappointed *a.* let down, saddened, deflated, disillusioned, disenchanted, displeased, unfulfilled, unsatisfied, frustrated, disheartened. ANT. *satisfied, fulfilled, happy.*

disappointment *n.* letdown, disillusionment, disenchantment, displeasure, unfulfillment, frustration, dissatisfaction, dud, *bitter pill to swallow, *bust, *drag, *bummer, setback, failure, rude awakening, washout, blow. "The bankruptcy of a soul that expends too much in hope and expectation."—Eric Hoffer. "The nurse of wisdom."—Boyle Roche. ANT. *satisfaction, fulfillment, happiness.*

disapproval *n.* rejection, disfavor, censure, dislike, disparagement, detraction, displeasure, deprecation, dissatisfaction, *thumbs down, animadversion, *boo, *hiss, *Bronx cheer, *raspberry. ANT. *approval, favor, acceptance.*

disapprove *v.* reject, frown on, disfavor, censure, dislike, disparage, condemn, criticize, take a dim view of, object to, *nix, *give thumbs down, dismiss, deprecate, denounce. ANT. *approve, accept, embrace, praise.*

disarm *v.* disable, weaken, take the teeth out of, *defang, neutralize, mollify, charm, conciliate, pacify, win over.

DISARMING *a.* [dis ARM ing] winning one over by charm or removing hostility. *A disarming smile mollified his ire.* SYN. winning, charming, winsome, appealing, irresistible, appeasing, ingratiating, likable, pleasing, agreeable, conciliatory. ANT. *offensive, obnoxious, irritating.*

disarrange *v.* mix up, disorder, scramble, muss, mess, jumble, ruffle.

disarray *n.* disorder, disarrangement, mess, jumble, confusion, tangle, *shambles, chaos, dishevelment, hodgepodge, clutter.

disaster *n.* catastrophe, misfortune, calamity, accident, tragedy, debacle, adversity, *act of God, cataclysm, ruin, blow, hardship, reverse, holocaust.

disaster area *n.* area of devastation, storm center, crisis zone, war zone, flood zone, desolation, path of destruction.

disastrous *a.* catastrophic, calamitous, unfortunate, tragic, cataclysmic, ruinous, dire, devastating, desolating, adverse. ANT. *fortuitous, wonderous, lucky.*

disavow *v.* abjure, disown, repudiate, deny, disclaim, reject, gainsay, contradict, *weasel

out of, *wash one's hands of, recant, retract. ANT. *admit, own up.*

disband *v.* break up, dissolve, fold, separate.

disbelief *n.* doubt, incredulity, questioning, skepticism, rejection, distrust, dissent. ANT. *belief, faith, credulity.*

disburse *v.* pay out, expend, outlay, spend, *shell out, dole out, allocate, mete out.

discard *v.* throw out, reject, toss, dismiss, *can, scrap, dump, eject, junk, jettison, *eighty-six, *scratch, shed. ANT. *keep, retain.*

discern *v.* perceive, detect, apprehend, sense, see, notice, ascertain, observe, make out, spot, distinguish. ANT. *miss, overlook.*

DISCERNING *a.* [di SUR ning] perceptive and sharp. *She was discerning with her fashion choices.* SYN. perceptive, sharp, sagacious, discriminating, astute, hawk-eyed, critical, shrewd, judicious, intelligent, wise, mindful. ANT. *unperceptive, unobservant, mindless.*

discharge *n.* 1. RELEASE liberation, pardon, acquittal, setting free. 2. DISMISSAL *the axe, *the boot, *sack, *walking papers, *pink slip, ejection, ouster, *the gate, firing, layoff. 3. DETONATION firing, shot, explosion. 4. EMMISION expulsion, ejection, exudation, excretion, flow, seepage, oozing. ANT. *1. capture, holding, incarceration.*

discharge *v.* 1. RELEASE set free, liberate, let go, emancipate, dismiss, acquit, pardon. 2. DISMISS fire, lay off, *sack, *give the boot, *give walking papers, *give the axe, *give pink slip, *show the gate/door, eject, oust, *can, relieve of duties, excuse. 3. DETONATE fire, shoot, explode, set off. 4. EMIT eject, exude, excrete, flow, gush, seep, ooze, spew. ANT. *1. capture, hold, incarcerate.*

disciple *n.* follower, believer, devotee, supporter, apostle, adherent, proselyte, pupil.

disciplinarian *n.* authoritarian, tyrant, martinet, taskmaster, *whipcracker, drill sergeant, bully.

discipline *n.* 1. FORTITUDE training, drilling, willpower, self-control, mental toughness, regimen, practice, self-regulation, firmness, diligence, mettle, earnestness, iron will, *grit, *moxie, commitment. 2. PUNISHMENT penalty, consequence, correction, castigation, reprimand. 3. BRANCH OF STUDY specialty, field, subject, curriculum, course. ANT. *1. laziness, sloth. 2. reward.*

discipline *v.* 1. TRAIN drill, harden, self-regulate, test one's mettle, commit, *bite the bullet, toughen, control, exercise, *whip into shape, practice. **2.** PUNISH penalize, correct, castigate, reprimand, *call on the carpet. ANT. *1. let oneself go, slip, neglect. 2. reward.*

disc jockey n. dj, deejay, announcer, radio personality.

disclaim v. deny, repudiate, denounce, disown, disavow, abjure, forswear, reject, renounce. ANT. *admit, acknowledge, own up.*

DISCLAIMER n. [dis KLAYM ur] a denial of responsibility or refusal to accept responsibility. *To protect itself from lawsuits stemming from falls, the company placed a disclaimer on every ladder it made.* SYN. disavowal, denial, retraction, repudiation.

disclose v. reveal, tell, divulge, let slip, make known, *spill the beans, confess, impart, expose, *bare one's soul. ANT. *hide, cover up, withhold.*

disclosure n. revelation, confession, exposé, admission, divulgence, declaration, publication.

disco n. discotheque, club, nightclub, dance hall, cabaret.

discolor v. stain, bleach, fade, spot, wash, tinge, weather.

discomfit v. thwart, foil, frustrate, defeat, disconcert, fluster, distress, perplex, faze, unsettle, discompose, ruffle.

discomfort n. uneasiness, distress, pain, anxiety, irritation, soreness, ache, suffering, malaise, annoyance. ANT. *ease, pleasure.*

DISCONCERTED a. [DIS kun SERT ed] perturbed, disturbed, ruffled. *He saw the policeman and was disconcerted.* SYN. perturbed, disturbed, ruffled, uncomfortable, uneasy, flabbergasted, anxious, upset, taken aback, confused, rattled, shaken up, flustered. ANT. *calm, composed, at ease.*

disconnect v. detach, unhook, uncouple, separate, disengage, undo, unlink, loose, sever, break off. ANT. *connect, attach, engage.*

disconsolate a. inconsolable, depressed, dejected, suicidal, cheerless, downhearted, heartbroken, forlorn, desolate, melancholy, gloomy, hopeless, crushed. ANT. *euphoric, joyous, happy.*

discontent n. dissatisfaction, unhappiness, uneasiness, displeasure, disquiet, unfulfillment, vexation, wanting, dysphoria, restlessness. "The first step of progress."—Thomas Edison. "A perverse and fretful disposition."—Cicero. ANT. *contentment, satisfaction, ease.*

discontinue v. stop, end, cease, terminate,

*knock off, finish, quit, *call it quits, desist, suspend, hold off. ANT. *resume, start.*

DISCORD n. [DIS kord] disagreement; conflict. *The new proposal was met with discord.* SYN. disagreement, dissension, conflict, variance, disunity, disharmony, contention, clashing, difference of opinion, dissonance. "A sleepless hag who never dies."—John Wolcott. ANT. *accord, harmony, agreement.*

discordant a. conflicting, dissonant, unharmonious, incongruous, contrary, inimical, harsh, jarring, sour, strident, incompatible. ANT. *harmonious, euphonious, compatible.*

discourage v. **1.** DISHEARTEN dispirit, demoralize, dampen one's spirits, unnerve, *throw cold water on, daunt, intimidate, cow, *dash one's hopes, *take the wind out of one's sails. **2.** DETER dissuade, hinder, impede, restrain, curb. ANT. *1. encourage, hearten, embolden.*

discouraging a. demoralizing, disheartening, hopeless, daunting, dismaying, dissuasive, dispiriting, deflating, intimidating. ANT. *encouraging, heartening, uplifting.*

discourse n. dialogue, speech, conversation, talk, discussion, communication, chat, lecture, colloquy, *confab, address.

discourteous a. rude, inconsiderate, impolite, ill-mannered, uncivil, brusque, ungracious, indelicate, cavalier, fresh, boorish. ANT. *polite, courteous, civil.*

discover v. find, uncover, discern, detect, learn, espy, unearth, notice, come across, realize, bring to light, spot, descry. ANT. *miss, overlook, pass over.*

discovery n. finding, uncovering, detection, unearthing, strike, espial, breakthrough.

discredit v. **1.** DAMAGE ONE'S REPUTATION disgrace, dishonor, detract, defame, disparage, censure, degrade, tear down, depreciate, demean. **2.** CAST DOUBT ON refute, disprove, discount, disbelieve, question, challenge, reject, scoff. ANT. *1. praise, honor, laud. 2. credit, verify, support.*

DISCREET a. [dis KREET] unobtrusive and tactful, properly reserved. *If you must burp, please be discreet.* SYN. tactful, unobtrusive, reserved, proper, judicious, diplomatic, restrained, prudent, modest, quiet, low-profiled, circumspect, careful, sensitive. ANT. *indiscreet, insensitive, tactless, obtrusive, conspicuous.*

discrepancy n. inconsistency, variance, difference, incongruity, conflict, error, divergence, disparity. ANT. *consistency, agreement.*

discrete *a.* distinct, individual, separate, different, independent, detached. ANT. *indistinct, ambiguous, combined.*

discretion *n.* **1.** PRUDENCE judgment, diplomacy, sagacity, tact, common sense, circumspection, caution, consideration, maturity, wisdom. "That honorable stop."—Shakespeare. "Leaving a few things unsaid."—Elbert Hubbard. **2.** FREEDOM OF CHOICE volition, will, liberty, choice, inclination, preference.

discriminate *v.* **1.** SHOW PREJUDICE favor, show bias, treat unfairly. **2.** DISTINGUISH differentiate, separate, contrast, compare, tell the difference, judge, draw a distinction, discern, segregate.

discriminating *a.* selective, choosy, picky, fussy, judicious, critical, particular, finicky, astute, discerning. ANT. *undiscriminating, unparticular.*

discrimination *n.* prejudice, bias, favoritism, bigotry, inequity, racism, sexism, chauvinism.

discursive *a.* rambling, digressive, excursive, wandering, roving, circumlocutory, rhapsodic, prolix. ANT. *succinct, direct, to the point.*

discuss *v.* talk over, deliberate, converse, confabulate, *hash over, *kick around, argue, dissert, debate, confer, review.

discussion *n.* talk, deliberation, conversation, confabulation, conference, debate, argument, consultation, *powwow, parley, *rap session, *bull session, seminar, symposium.

DISDAIN *n.* [dis DANE] scorn or contempt. *I felt nothing but disdain for the man.* SYN. scorn, contempt, hatred, disgust, dislike, detestation, loathing, abhorrence, haughtiness, *snottiness, snobbishness. ANT. *admiration, respect.*

disdain *v.* despise, loathe, hate, hold in contempt, abhor, sicken at the sight of, spurn, reject, look down one's nose at. ANT. *admire, respect.*

disease *n.* sickness, illness, affliction, ailment, malady, disorder, ill health, condition, syndrome, *bug, debility, infection, virus, infirmity, pathology, plague. "The taxes laid upon this wretched life."—Lord Chesterfield. "Death's servant."—Francis Rous. "Fear made manifest on the body."—Mary Baker Eddy.

WORD FIND

blood: anemia, hemophilia, leukemia, pernicious anemia, sickle-cell anemia

bone: osteoporosis, osteoarthritis, rickets

brain and nervous system: Alzheimer's, aphasia, apoplexy (stroke), encephalitis, epilepsy, Huntington's chorea, hydrocephalus, meningitis, multiple sclerosis (MS), Parkinson's disease, wet brain

bubonic plague: Black Death

cat: FAIDS, Feline Acquired Immune Deficiency Syndrome

cause of: virus, germ, contagion, microbe, bacillus, pathogen

circulatory: aneurysm, arteriosclerosis, atherosclerosis, hypertension, ischemia, peripheral vascular disease, phlebitis, thrombosis

contagious: chicken pox, diptheria, measles, tuberculosis, plague, whooping cough

deficiency: scurvy, beriberi, pellagra, rickets

digestive: appendicitis, cirrhosis of the liver, colitis, Crohn's disease, diabetes, diverticulitis, dysentery, gastroenteritis, gallstones, hepatitis, hiatal hernia, jaundice, pancreatitis, peptic ulcer, typhoid fever

dog: distemper, heartworm, mange, rabies

ear: tinnitus, vertigo

eye: cataract, conjunctivitis, detached retina, glaucoma, lazy eye, pinkeye, retinitis pigmentosa, strabismus, stye, trachoma

flu: influenza, grippe

food poisoning: botulism, salmonella, trichinosis

German measles: rubella

germ destroyer: antibiotic, antibody

gums: gingivitis, periodontal disease, pyorrhea

heart: angina pectoris, arrhythmia, athletic heart syndrome, cardiac arrest, congestive heart failure, coronary artery disease, heart attack, heart murmur, ischemic heart disease, mitral valve prolapse, myocardial infarction, pericarditis, rheumatic heart disease, tachycardia

identification: diagnosis

imagined: hypochondriasis

immune dysfunction: AIDS, Acquired Immune Deficiency Syndrome

joints: arthritis, gout, rheumatism

kissing disease: mononucleosis

livestock: anthrax, foot-and-mouth disease, listeriosis, mange, mastitis

lockjaw: tetanus

lungs, breathing: apnea, asthma, black lung disease, bronchitis, cystic fibrosis, dyspnea, emphysema, pleurisy, pneumonia, tuberculosis

mononucleosis, form of: Epstein-Barr syndrome
muscles: muscular dystrophy, myasthenia gravis, tendinitis, myopathy
nose: rhinitis, sinusitis
origin: etiology
peculiar to or found in only one region: endemic
predicted outcome: prognosis
recurring: chronic
sexually transmitted: venereal disease, herpes, AIDS, gonorrhea (*clap), genital warts, chlamydia, syphilis.
skin: carbuncle, dermatitis, eczema, hives, impetigo, lupus, psoriasis, rosacea, scabies, vitiligo
spine, curvature of: scoliosis
spreading: contagious
spreading rapidly: epidemic
strep throat, related to: rheumatic fever, scarlet fever
swollen salivary glands: mumps
tick, transmitted by: Lyme disease, Rocky Mountain spotted fever
tropical: malaria, sprue, dengue fever, leprosy, yellow fever
warning symptom: prodrome
widespread: pandemic
SEE BRAIN, CANCER, HEART, NEUROSIS

disembowel v. eviscerate, gut, draw.

disenchanted a. disillusioned, undeceived, seeing the real world, disabused, cynical, worldly-wise. ANT. *spellbound, naive, enchanted.*

disengage v. detach, release, free, unfasten, extricate, remove, loose, disconnect.

disfigure v. deface, mar, scar, deform, mutilate, blemish, maim, distort.

disgorge v. vomit, discharge, spew, empty. SEE VOMIT

disgrace n. dishonor, shame, blot, degradation, odium, humiliation, *black eye, discredit, obloquy, defamation, scandal, opprobrium, ignominy, disrepute. "To stumble twice against the same stone."—Cicero. ANT. *honor, credit, grace.*

disgrace v. dishonor, shame, blot, degrade, humiliate, *give a black eye, discredit, spoil, defame, scandalize, smear, taint, embarrass. ANT. *honor, credit, glorify.*

disgraceful a. dishonorable, shameful, degrading, humiliating, discrediting, defaming, scandalizing, embarrassing, ignominious, odious. ANT. *honorable, reputable, admirable.*

disgruntled a. angry, cross, unhappy, peeved,

annoyed, put out, discontented, grouchy, irritable, dissatisfied, disappointed, sulky. ANT. *contented, satisfied, happy.*

disguise n. cover-up, costume, mask, charade, camouflage, facade, guise, getup, pretense, masquerade, cloak, veil, incognito.

disguise v. cover up, mask, camouflage, put up a facade, masquerade, cloak, veil, counterfeit, dissemble, put on a false front, feign. ANT. *expose, reveal, unmask.*

disgust n. revulsion, repulsion, distaste, loathing, abhorrence, aversion, dislike, nausea, repugnance, detestation. ANT. *liking, delight.*

disgust v. revolt, repel, sicken, nauseate, *make one sick, offend, repulse, *turn one's stomach, *turn off, *gross out, appall. ANT. *delight, attract, charm.*

disgusting a. repugnant, loathsome, revolting, repellant, sickening, nauseating, *stomach-turning, repulsive, *gross, offensive, distasteful, noisome, nasty, vulgar, vile, foul. ANT. *delightful, attractive, charming, appetizing.*

dish n. plate, platter, bowl, vessel, saucer, utensil.

dishearten v. discourage, dispirit, dampen, *take the wind out of one's sails, *shake up, daunt, unnerve, *take the starch out of, crush, *put a wet blanket on, *pour cold water on, dash, deject. ANT. *encourage, hearten, embolden.*

disheveled a. in disarray, unkempt, sloppy, messy, slovenly, rumpled, wrinkled, bedraggled, *grubby, mussed, blowzy, uncombed. ANT. *neat, *put together, sharp, groomed.*

dishonest a. untruthful, deceitful, insincere, fraudulent, shady, corrupt, untrustworthy, false, misleading, shifty, treacherous, disingenuous, crooked, two-faced. ANT. *honest, trustworthy, straightforward.*

dishonesty n. lies, improbability, untruthfulness, deceit, deception, lying, fraud, prevarication, insincerity, duplicity, mendacity, falsehoods, disingenuousness.

dishonor n. disgrace, shame, embarrassment, humiliation, discredit, degradation, ignominy, opprobrium, obloquy, scandal, odium, *fall from grace, smear, blot, *black eye. ANT. *honor, esteem, admiration.*

dishonor v. disgrace, shame, discredit, degrade, scandalize, smear, blot, *give a black eye, besmirch, tarnish, *drag through the mud.

DISILLUSION v. [dis i LOO zhun] to remove faulty perceptions and see things as they really are. *Children eventually become disillusioned with Santa Claus.* SYN. disenchant, disabuse, disappoint, enlighten, *bring down to earth, *burst one's bubble, open one's eyes, *clue in, shatter illusions. ANT. *enchant, spellbind, deceive.*

disinclined *a.* unwilling, reluctant, loath, averse, indisposed, opposed, resistant, hesitant. ANT. *willing, eager.*

disinfect *v.* sterilize, sanitize, purify, cleanse, decontaminate, antisepticize, *zap.

disingenuous *a.* insincere, deceitful, lying, artful, false, uncandid, dishonest, crooked, underhanded, two-faced. ANT. *sincere, honest, *real.*

disintegrate *v.* fall apart, crumble, shatter, break up, atomize, pulverize, turn to dust, decompose, decay, erode.

disinterested *a.* indifferent, apathetic, unconcerned, dispassionate, uninvolved, impartial, unprejudiced, unbiased, neutral. ANT. *concerned, biased, prejudiced, involved, riveted.*

disjointed *a.* disconnected, loose, displaced, incoherent, disordered, disorganized, discontinuous, broken, separated, rambling, choppy. ANT. *connected, coherent.*

disk *n.* 1. plate. 2. diskette, floppy disk, magnetic disk, CD.

dislike *n.* hatred, abhorrence, loathing, scorn, detestation, distaste, disapproval, aversion, antipathy, repugnance, repulsion. ANT. *approval, acceptance, love.*

dislike *v.* hate, abhor, loathe, *get turned off by, despise, deplore, scorn, *turn up one's nose at, disapprove, *look down on, frown upon, detest. ANT. *like, fancy, love.*

dislocate *v.* pull out of alignment, displace, dislodge.

disloyal *a.* unfaithful, traitorous, treacherous, back-stabbing, two-faced, treasonous, perfidious, double-crossing, *like a snake in the grass. ANT. *faithful, true, loyal.*

dismal *a.* dreary, gloomy, bleak, depressing, cheerless, grim, black, desolate, melancholy, forlorn, miserable, somber. ANT. *cheerful, sunny, uplifting, bright.*

dismantle *v.* disassemble, take apart, strip, break apart, break down, tear down, demolish, level.

dismay *n.* consternation, horror, discomposure, fright, apprehension, terror, discouragement, trepidation, *cold feet, alarm, dread.

dismay *v.* daunt, dishearten, trouble, frighten, disconcert, appall, intimidate, horrify, cow,

discompose, unnerve, shake, fluster, rattle, consternate.

dismember *v.* amputate, cut up, mutilate, chop up, cut into pieces, mangle.

dismiss *v.* 1. LET GO send away, discharge, release, turn out, expel, rid, excuse, dispense with, free, banish, clear, oust, evict. 2. FIRE lay off, *give the axe, *give the boot, *give walking papers, *send packing, *show the door, *give pink slip, terminate, *can, *sack, set adrift, *bounce. 3. PUT OUT OF ONE'S MIND dispel, disregard, banish, *poohpooh.

dismissal *n.* discharge, release, expulsion, ousting, eviction, *walking papers, layoff, *sack, *pink slip, removal.

disobedience *n.* rebellion, noncompliance, defiance, insubordination, transgression, revolt, recalcitrance, contumacy, insubmission. "The rarest and the most courageous of the virtues, is seldom distinguished from neglect, the laziest and most common of the vices."—George Bernard Shaw.

disobedient *v.* rebellious, noncompliant, defiant, insubordinate, unruly, recalcitrant, insubmissive, fractious, contrary, stubborn, mischievous. ANT. *obedient, compliant, dutiful.*

disobey *v.* defy, rebel, revolt, reject, transgress, oppose, flout, contradict, *thumb one's nose at, disregard, overstep, resist. ANT. *obey, comply, *knuckle under, abide by.*

disorder *n.* 1. DISARRAY jumble, confusion, mess, disarrangement, clutter, disorganization, untidiness, chaos, muddle. 2. DISTURBANCE commotion, upset, agitation, unrest, chaos, turbulence, imbroglio, clamor, rumpus, *hullabaloo, fracas, anarchy, ferment, discord. 3. AFFLICTION ailment, malady, infirmity, sickness, illness, disease, syndrome. ANT. *1. order, organization, arrangement. 2. peace, calm, tranquility.*

disorder *v.* mix up, mess, disarrange, jumble, confuse, shuffle, clutter, disorganize, muddle, disturb, scatter, muss up. ANT. *order, arrange, neaten.*

disorderly *a.* 1. IRREGULAR messy, disarranged, jumbled, confused, shuffled, cluttered, mixed up, disorganized, muddled, scrambled, scattered. 2. UNRULY disruptive, unmanageable, riotous, *out-of-line, unlawful, rowdy, uncontrollable, wayward, obstreperous. ANT. *1. orderly, arranged, organized. 2. orderly, well-behaved, peaceful.*

disoriented *a.* lost, confused, mixed-up, dazed, muddled, bewildered.

disown *v.* repudiate, reject, renounce, disclaim, forsake, disavow, cast off, divorce oneself from, disinherit. ANT. *claim, accept, admit, adopt.*

DISPARAGE *v.* [di SPAIR ij] to belittle, put down. *The coach disparaged the team after yet another loss.* SYN. belittle, put down, criticize, deprecate, denigrate, depreciate, deflate, defame, malign, *dump on, ridicule, discredit. ANT. *praise, commend, laud.*

disparate *a.* different, dissimilar, distinct, contrasting, unequal, uneven, inconsistent. ANT. *comparable.*

DISPARITY *n.* [dis PAIR uh tee] a gap or state of inequality, difference. *There is often a disparity between thoughts and deeds.* SYN. gap, inequality, difference, incongruity, discrepancy, imbalance, disproportion, inconsistency. ANT. *equality, correspondence, consistency.*

dispassionate *a.* unfeeling, unemotional, calm, detached, indifferent, neutral, disinterested, unprejudiced, unbiased, objective, judicial, impartial. ANT. *passionate, involved, interested, biased.*

dispatch *n.* **1.** MESSAGE communication, communique, news, report, bulletin, flash, note. **2.** SPEED promptness, swiftness, alacrity, celerity, quickness, haste, expedition. ANT. **2.** *sloth, sluggishness.*

dispatch *v.* **1.** SEND OFF consign, forward, issue, transmit, speed, express, post. **2.** EXPEDITE hurry, dash off, quicken, push, dispose of, *zip off. **3.** KILL slay, execute, murder, assassinate, put to death, *waste. SEE KILL, MURDER

dispel *v.* dispense with, rid, scatter, drive away, dismiss, banish, oust, eject, rout, disperse, remove, dispose of.

dispensable *a.* unnecessary, disposable, nonessential, inessential, expendable, superfluous. ANT. *indispensable.*

dispensary *n.* medical supply office, infirmary, clinic.

dispensation *n.* **1.** DISTRIBUTION apportionment, allocation, disbursement, allotment, assignment, consignment. **2.** SHARE allotment, quota, portion, consignment, allocation. **3.** ADMINISTRATION management, regulation, direction, operation, supervision.

dispense *v.* give out, distribute, allocate, apportion, dole out, assign, mete out, supply, disperse, parcel out.

dispense with *v.* **1.** dispose of, get rid of, do without, relinquish. **2.** forgo, waive, forswear.

disperse *v.* scatter, distribute, strew, disseminate, spread, broadcast, sow, circulate, diffuse, disband, dissipate.

dispirited *a.* dejected, depressed, downhearted, melancholy, blue, glum, discouraged, *down in the dumps, disheartened, despondent, disconsolate. ANT. *cheerful, euphoric, happy.*

displace *v.* **1.** MOVE dislocate, shift, dislodge, unsettle, transfer, dispossess, relocate, disturb, force out, uproot. **2.** SUPPLANT replace, supersede, succeed, crowd out, take over, usurp.

display *n.* exhibit, exhibition, presentation, advertisement, exposition, layout, spread, staging, panorama.

display *v.* exhibit, show, present, showcase, advertise, lay out, stage, flaunt, demonstrate, parade, spotlight. ANT. *hide, conceal, camouflage.*

displease *v.* annoy, offend, anger, irritate, disturb, irk, disappoint, bother, upset, dissatisfy, disgruntle, *piss off, repulse, pall, insult. ANT. *delight, satisfy, *tickle.*

displeasure *n.* annoyance, dissatisfaction, anger, irritation, disappointment, disgruntlement, dislike, distaste, unhappiness. ANT. *delight, satisfaction, happiness.*

disposal *n.* **1.** THROWING OUT discarding, dumping, junking, dispatching, scrapping, removal. **2.** ORDER placement, distribution, array, arrangement, disposition, grouping. **3.** SETTLEMENT conclusion, dispensation, determination, transfer, end. **4.** POWER liberty, authority, control, direction.

dispose *v.* **1.** THROW OUT discard, dump, toss, scrap, junk, *can, *chuck, *eighty-six. **2.** SETTLE determine, decide, end, finish up.

disposed *a.* inclined, apt, willing, prone, liable, predisposed, likely. ANT. *indisposed, unlikely.*

disposition *n.* **1.** TEMPERAMENT temper, nature, mood, humor, frame of mind, outlook, character, *mind-set, tendency, proclivity, bent. **2.** ORDER placement, distribution, arrangement, grouping, array.

dispossess *v.* divest, deprive, expropriate, strip, confiscate, oust, expel, eject.

disproportionate *a.* unequal, unbalanced, lopsided, inordinate, uneven. ANT. *equal, proportionate.*

disprove *v.* debunk, invalidate, refute, confute, negate, expose, controvert, belie, *shoot holes in, discredit. ANT. *prove, validate.*

disputable *a.* debatable, arguable, dubious,

moot, questionable, controversial, open to argument, unsettled. ANT. *indisputable, settled, unquestionable.*

dispute *n.* argument, debate, controversy, disagreement, conflict, altercation, difference of opinion, contest, *beef, wrangle, dissension, *fuss, *bone of contention, row, imbroglio. ANT. *agreement.*

dispute *v.* argue, debate, disagree, conflict, contest, contend, controvert, *lock horns, wrangle, quarrel, doubt, controvert, bicker, quibble. ANT. *agree, concur, *find common ground.*

disqualify *v.* turn down, shut out, reject, debar, eliminate, remove, declare ineligible.

disquiet *n.* restlessness, anxiety, worry, trouble, distress, unrest, unease, angst, fretfulness. ANT. *serenity, tranquility, calm.*

disquiet *v.* trouble, disturb, bother, disrupt, distress, worry, fret, shake up, fluster, discompose, rattle. ANT. *calm, compose, relax.*

disregard *v.* ignore, nevermind, skip, overlook, forget, omit, *pay no mind, *turn a deaf ear, slight. ANT. *heed, notice, consider.*

disrepair *n.* deterioration, decay, dilapidation, ruin, wreckage.

disreputable *a.* dishonorable, disgraceful, low, shady, cheap, unprincipled, shameful, scandalous, sordid, ignominious, ignoble, unsavory. ANT. *respectable, honorable, classy, noble.*

disrespect *n.* irreverence, incivility, disregard, discourtesy, impoliteness, rudeness, impertinence, insolence, impudence, flippancy, lèse-majesté. ANT. *respect, reverence, civility, deference.*

disrespect *v.* disregard, insult, offend, look down on, disparage, *walk on, take advantage of, *dis, *dump on, slight, *badmouth, *ride, *trash, regard superciliously, regard with hauteur, ignore, dismiss, *turn up one's nose at, snub, rebuff, minimize, underestimate, regard with disdain. ANT. *respect, *kiss up to, honor.*

disrespectful *a.* irreverent, uncivil, discourteous, impolite, rude, impertinent, insolent, impudent, flippant, contemptuous, insulting, *smart-alecky, *out of line, ill-mannered. ANT. *respectful, civil, reverent, deferential.*

disrobe *v.* undress, strip, bare, *peel, slip out of, *shuck, uncover, shed, *drop one's drawers.

disrupt *v.* interrupt, upset, disturb, disorder, unsettle, agitate, *discombobulate, interfere with, break up, disorganize, disconcert.

disruptive *a.* interrupting, upsetting, disturbing, unsettling, agitating, disconcerting, distracting, *discombobulating, trouble-making. ANT. *calming, quieting.*

dissatisfactory *a.* unsatisfactory.

dissatisfied *a.* displeased, unfulfilled, unhappy, discontented, disappointed, critical, disgruntled, malcontented, frustrated, disaffected. ANT. *satisfied, pleased, content.*

dissect *v.* cut up, separate, examine, analyze, inspect, scrutinize, explore, study, *go over with fine-tooth comb.

dissemble *v.* disguise, hide, cover up, mask, dissimulate, conceal, feign, *put on a front, cloak, camouflage. ANT. *reveal, show, expose.*

DISSEMINATE *v.* [di SEM uh NATE] to distribute, spread or scatter. *The head office will disseminate the new information.* SYN. distribute, spread, scatter, disperse, broadcast, propagate, promulgate, circulate, sow, diffuse.

DISSENSION *n.* [di SEN shun] disagreement, difference of opinion. *There was dissension over the issue.* SYN. discord, disagreement, difference of opinion, contention, conflict, strife, dissent, argument, variance, friction, *flak. ANT. *accord, agreement, harmony.*

dissent *n.* disagreement, difference of opinion, contention, conflict, dissension, argument, dispute, discord, schism, nonconformity, opposition. ANT. *agreement, accord, concurrence.*

dissent *v.* disagree, contradict, differ, argue, dispute, oppose, vary, reject, contend, protest. ANT. *agree, concur, assent.*

DISSERTATION *n.* [DIS ur TAY shun] a long report or treatise on a subject, based on one's own research, often a requirement of a doctorate. *She gave her dissertation on the mating practices of turtles.* SYN. thesis, treatise, report, paper, discourse, study, composition, disquisition, essay, exposition.

disservice *n.* wrong, harm, injustice, injury, disfavor, damage.

DISSIDENT *n.* [DIS uh dent] one who disagrees; a dissenter. *A number of dissidents protested the action wih a demonstration.* SYN. dissenter, protestor, nonconformist, objector, separatist, rebel, opposition.

dissident *a.* disagreeing, differing, dissenting. ANT. *assenting, agreeing, concurring*

dissimilar *a.* unlike, different, distinct, divergent, opposite, contrasting, antithetical, disparate, *like night and day. ANT. *like, similar, matched.*

dissimulate v. hide, conceal. SEE DISSEMBLE

DISSIPATE v. [DIS uh PATE] to scatter, thin out, dispel, disappear, exhaust. *The snow finally began to dissipate.* SYN. scatter, thin out, disperse, dispel, disappear, dissolve, exhaust, ebb, deplete, disintegrate, vanish. ANT. *conserve, save, concentrate.*

dissociate v. separate, part, disconnect, detach, segregate, break off, divorce, estrange, distance.

dissolute a. abandoned, immoral, debauched, unrestrained, intemperate, depraved, unbridled, perverted, lecherous, licentious, wanton. ANT. *virtuous, moral, restrained, abstinent.*

dissolution n. dissolving, disintegration, decay, decomposition, death, end, passing, termination, demise, extinction, collapse, disappearance.

dissolve v. 1. MELT diffuse, liquefy, deliquesce, thaw. 2. END terminate, close, finish, break up, discontinue, disband, disperse, evaporate. 3. ANNUL void, cancel, invalidate, nullify, rescind, repeal. 4. VANISH fade, disappear, blur, dematerialize. ANT. *1. thicken, congeal, harden. 2. begin, start, open. 3. validate. 4. materialize, appear.*

dissonant a. 1. INHARMONIOUS harsh, discordant, cacophonous, jarring, grating, raucous, sour, strident. 2. DISAGREEING incompatible, discordant, incongruous, clashing, divergent, opposing, at variance. ANT. *1. harmonious, euphonious, melodious. 2. agreeing, compatible, consonant.*

DISSUADE v. [dis WADE] to discourage or talk out of. *I would dissuade any family member from bungee-jumping.* SYN. discourage, talk out of, deter, advise against, disincline, *throw cold water on, persuade not to, stop. ANT. talk into, persuade to, encourage.*

distance n. 1. SPACE span, length, remoteness, range, area, expanse, interval, stretch, sweep, spread, width, remove, horizon, far reaches, extent. 2. COLDNESS reserve, aloofness, unfriendliness, stiffness. ANT. *2. warmth, closeness, intimacy.*

distant a. 1. FAR far off, remote, removed, afar, away, yonder, far-flung, outlying, out of range, outback, isolated. 2. COLD reserved, aloof, unfriendly, *at arm's length, stiff, cool, frigid, formal, withdrawn. ANT. 1. close, near, at hand. 2. warm, close, intimate, friendly.*

distaste n. dislike, aversion, repulsion, revulsion, abhorrence, disgust, repugnance, disinclination, displeasure. ANT. *liking, attraction.*

distasteful a. disgusting, repulsive, revolting, abhorrent, repellent, offensive, unsavory, unappetizing, obnoxious, unpalatable, disagreeable, tasteless, *gross, nauseating. ANT. *appealing, savory, attractive, pleasing.*

distended a. bloated, swollen, inflated, enlarged, turgid, expanded, bulging, puffed out, ballooned, blown up. ANT. *shriveled, sunken, deflated.*

distill v. extract, purify, boil down, decoct, refine, ferment, concentrate, separate, condense, press out, brew, vaporize.

distillation n. essence, distillate, concentrate.

distinct a. 1. CLEAR obvious, plain, clear-cut, unambiguous, defined, unmistakable, specific, explicit, manifest. 2. SEPARATE individual, unlike, different, unassociated, detached, sole, disparate, discrete. ANT. *1. unclear, vague, fuzzy. 2. associated, joined, linked.*

distinction n. 1. DIFFERENTIATION discrimination, distinguishment, difference, peculiarity, feature, mark, characteristic, earmark. 2. RECOGNITION honor, eminence, achievement, credit, prominence, repute, merit, prestige, renown, consequence.

distinctive a. unique, distinguishing, characteristic, singular, different, peculiar, individual, special, idiosyncratic, unusual. ANT. *common, ordinary, nondescript.*

distinguish v. 1. SEE THE DIFFERENCE differentiate, discriminate, separate, judge, tell apart, ascertain, characterize, classify. 2. DISCERN make out, perceive, see, notice, detect, observe, apprehend, catch, spot, recognize.

distinguished a. 1. EMINENT renowned, famous, prominent, acclaimed, notable, illustrious, celebrated, excellent. 2. DIGNIFIED stately, elegant, grand, magnificent, august, princely, lordly, imposing, *distingue. ANT. *1. unknown, ordinary, pedestrian. 2. undignified, undistinguished, lowly.*

distort v. 1. MISSHAPE contort, deform, twist, warp, gnarl, wrench, screw, knot, disfigure. 2. MISREPRESENT misconstrue, falsify, lie, misinterpret, alter, twist, slant, pervert, stretch, varnish, embellish.

distortion n. misrepresentation, lie, misinterpretation, alteration, stretch, embellishment, falsification, exaggeration, perversion, *BS, fabrication, embroidery. ANT. *truth, accuracy.*

distract v. 1. DIVERT sidetrack, draw away, catch one's attention, entertain. 2. BEWILDER confuse, perplex, befuddle, fluster, discompose, confound, trouble, unsettle.

distraction n. diversion, amusement, entertainment, beguilement, interruption, divertissement, interference, annoyance.

distraught a. anxious, upset, worried, agitated, disturbed, troubled, perturbed, overwrought, crazed, frantic, *out of one's mind, harassed. ANT. *calm, composed, relaxed, tranquil.*

distress n. pain, suffering, anxiety, anguish, difficulty, strain, unhappiness, sorrow, discomfort, agony, angst, torture.

distress v. upset, worry, trouble, strain, disturb, bother, burden, aggrieve, pain, plague, hurt, tax, torment, harass. ANT. *comfort, console, soothe, relieve.*

distress signal n. SOS, Mayday, flare.

distribute v. **1.** APPORTION allot, parcel out, allocate, prorate, issue, ration, deliver, mete, divide, *dole out, disseminate, *divvy, dispense, spread. **2.** CLASSIFY arrange, group, order. ANT. *1. collect, gather, concentrate.*

distribution n. **1.** APPORTIONMENT allotment, allocation, parcel, division, rationing, spreading, delivery, propagation, scattering. **2.** CLASSIFICATION arrangement, grouping, order.

distributor n. dealer, wholesaler, merchandiser, trader, jobber, merchant, outlet, warehouse, salesman, franchise.

district n. area, region, precinct, section, quarter, zone, locale, community, parish, ward.

district attorney n. DA, prosecution officer, lawyer, SEE LAW

distrust n. mistrust, disbelief, doubt, suspicion, wariness, leeriness, incredulity, misgiving, skepticism. ANT. *trust, belief, faith.*

distrust v. mistrust, disbelieve, question, doubt, suspect, be wary of, be leery of, have reservations about. ANT. *trust, believe, have faith in.*

distrustful a. doubting, questioning, skeptical, cynical, suspicious, disbelieving, leery, wary, incredulous. ANT. *trusting, gullible.*

disturb v. **1.** BOTHER trouble, disquiet, disrupt, distress, ruffle, interrupt, annoy, plague, irritate, discommode, perturb, *hassle, *bug, intrude upon. **2.** DISARRANGE disorder, disorganize, jumble, mix up, upset, unsettle.

disturbance n. disruption, commotion, interruption, interference, upset, tumult, annoyance, agitation, perturbation, bother, uproar, rumpus.

ditch n. trench, channel, gully, excavation, trough, gutter, cut, waterway, dike, moat.

ditch v. Sl. dump, junk, discard, abandon, unload, get rid of, desert.

ditsy a. *bubbleheaded, foolish, scatterbrained,

absent-minded, empty-headed, dotty, eccentric, silly. ANT. *sensible.*

ditto n. the same, likewise, the above, the aforementioned.

ditty n. song, tune, composition, number.

diva n. prima donna, lead singer, vocalist. SEE OPERA

dive n. **1.** PLUNGE drop, vault, *header, nosedive, descent, swoop, leap, submergence, immersion, bellyflop, cannonball, half twist, full twist, jackknife, gainer, half gainer, swan dive, backflip. **2.** Sl. *DUMP hole, bar, honky-tonk, tavern.

dive v. plunge, drop, plummet, vault, *do a header, nosedive, pitch, descend, submerge.

diver n. scuba diver, skin diver, *frogman.

diverge v. **1.** SEPARATE come apart, spread, depart, deviate, divide, split, branch off. **2.** DIFFER disagree, vary, conflict, oppose, be at odds. ANT. *1. converge. 2. agree.*

divergence n. **1.** SEPARATION split, fork, branching, parting, deviation, division, digression. **2.** DIFFERENCE disagreement, conflict, variance, odds, incongruity. ANT. *1. convergence. 2. agreement.*

diverse a. **1.** DIFFERENT unlike, disparate, distinct, dissimilar, varied, discrete. **2.** MULTIFORM diversified, sundry, varied, manifold, multifarious, assorted. ANT. *1. similar, like, identical.*

diversify v. vary, branch out, expand, variegate, assort, modify.

diversion n. entertainment, amusement, distraction, pastime, divertissement, fun, pleasure, frolic, sport.

diversity n. variety, difference, assortment, multiplicity, heterogeneity, miscellany, medley. ANT. *sameness, homogeneity.*

divert v. **1.** TURN ASIDE change course, deflect, sidetrack, avert, swerve. **2.** DISTRACT OR AMUSE entertain, draw, absorb, regale, beguile.

diverting a. distracting, amusing, entertaining, absorbing, beguiling, engrossing, magnetic. ANT. *unstimulating, boring, tedious, tiresome.*

divest v. strip, dispossess, deprive, confiscate, relieve of, seize, remove, bare, denude.

divide v. **1.** SEPARATE sever, cleave, part, split, cut, rend, halve, quarter, bisect, sunder, disjoin, disconnect, segregate, section. **2.** APPORTION distribute, share, allocate, mete out, dole, dispense, *divvy up, portion, ration, deal. **3.** CLASSIFY group, categorize, label, sort, arrange. ANT. *1. join, unite, fuse.*

divination n. prophecy, soothsaying, augury,

prognostication, fortune-telling, foretelling, premonition, forecast, presentiment.
WORD FIND
by animal droppings: scatomancy
by bird actions: auspice
by celestial positions: astrology
by choosing random passage in book, especially the Bible: bibliomancy
by communication with the dead: necromancy
by dirt figures: geomancy
by divining rod: rhabdomancy
by dreams: oneiromancy
by entrails of animals: haruspicy
by flight patterns of birds: ornithomancy
by lots: sortilege
by numbers: numerology
by shapes of melting wax: ceromancy
by water: hydromancy

divine v. foretell, predict, prophesy, forecast, foresee, prognosticate, surmise, guess, infer, portend. SEE PROPHECY

divine a. godlike, holy, sacred, omnipotent, omnipresent, omniscient, heavenly, deified, supreme, sanctified, perfect, celestial, angelic, superhuman. ANT. *earthly, mortal.*

divinity n. god, God, deity, goddess. SEE GOD

division n. **1.** PART section, segment, unit, department, branch, sector, subdivision, component, piece, cut, chunk. **2.** DISAGREEMENT difference of opinion, variance, discord, dissension, dissent, rift, feud, argument. ANT. *2. agreement, unity, accord.*

divisive a. [di VIY siv] causing disgreement or discord. *The meeting was tense and divisive.* SYN. negative, fault-finding, dissenting, sowing the seeds of dissension, at odds, alienating, disaffecting, discordant, hostile, nasty, disrupting, segregating. ANT. *uniting.*

divorce n. disunion, separation, *split, breakup, dissolution, annulment, parting. "A hash made of domestic scraps."—Ed Wynn. "Holy deadlock."—A.P. Herbert.

divorce v. **1.** SEPARATE dissociate, split, sever, part, detach. **2.** END MARRIAGE dissolve, annul, split up, break up.

divulge v. reveal, disclose, make known, confess, confide, tell, let slip, impart, expose, *spill the beans, *spill one's guts, blab, leak. ANT. *keep secret, conceal, hide.*

divvy up vt. apportion. SEE DIVIDE

dizzy a. **1.** UNSTEADY light-headed, vertiginous, off balance, reeling, wobbly, *punch-drunk,

whirling, giddy, groggy, bewildered, confused. **2.** SCATTERBRAINED silly, flighty, frivolous, harebrained, foolish, giddy. ANT. *1. sober, balanced, steady. 2. poised, intelligent, thoughtful, rational.*

DNA n. deoxyribonucleic acid. The two-stranded chain component in the nuclei of cells that makes up genes and chromosomes. *The detective traced the accused to the crime scene with DNA fingerprinting.* SYN. nucleic acid, nucleotide chains, double helix, code of life, genetic code. SEE SCIENCE

do v. **1.** PERFORM execute, carry out, complete, undertake, see to it, make, cause, bring about, produce, fulfill, engineer, *swing, effect. **2.** COMPLETE fulfill, accomplish, dispatch, clinch, consummate, dispose of. **3.** SUFFICE serve, pass muster, be adequate, measure up, suit, meet one's needs. **4.** ACT behave, conduct, comport, deport, operate. **5.** TRAVEL THROUGH visit, cover, tour, pass through, explore, experience.

DOCILE a. [DOS ul] easy to train and handle, tractable. *The poodle is considerably more docile than the coyote.* SYN. tractable, malleable, trainable, pliant, manageable, obedient, gentle, accommodating, submissive, compliant, obliging, meek. ANT. *defiant, stubborn, vicious, untrainable, *unbreakable.*

dock n. pier, wharf, landing, quay, marina, slip, berth.

docket n. agenda, calendar, program, schedule, ticket.

doctor n. physician, medical practitioner, M.D., general practitioner, osteopath, homeopath, medic, intern, specialist, resident, medicine man, healer, *doc, *pill pusher, *bones, *sawbones, *quack, witch doctor. "An angel when he comes to cure, a devil when he asks for pay."—English proverb. "Death's pilot-fish."—G.D. Prentice. "The flower of our civilization."—Robert Louis Stevenson.
WORD FIND
ambulance attendant: paramedic, emergency medical technician (EMT)
anesthesia administrator: anesthetist, anesthesiologist
animals: veterinarian
association: American Medical Association, AMA
bone, joint and muscle specialist: orthopedist
children's: pediatrician
digestive system: gastroenterologist

disease authority: pathologist
drug authority: pharmacologist
ear, nose and throat specialist: otolaryngologist
epidemic authority: epidemiologist
eye: ophthalmologist
feeling patient's body with hands to aid diagnosis: palpation
foot: podiatrist
heart: cardiologist
hormone specialist: endocrinologist
knee hammer: percussor
listening for body sounds through stethoscope: auscultation
manipulator of bones and spine: chiropractor
medical examiner: coroner
mental disorders: psychiatrist
national health chief: Surgeon General
nervous system: neurologist
newborns: neonatologist
oath of: Hippocratic oath
prayer, cures by: faith healer
pregnancy and birth: obstetrician
radiology: radiologist
rectum, anus: proctologist
skin: dermatologist
tapping chest, back, abdomen, aid in diagnosis: percussion
trainee: intern
tumor specialist: oncologist
urinary tract, kidneys, prostate: urologist
women's reproductive system: gynecologist
SEE DISEASE, HOSPITAL, MEDICINE, NURSE, OPERATION, SURGERY

doctor *v.* **1.** MEND fix, treat, repair, attend, nurse, medicate, *patch up. **2.** ALTER tamper with, falsify, change, distort, adulterate.

doctrinaire *a.* obstinate, dogmatic, impractical, unrealistic, rigid, speculative, authoritarian, inflexible. ANT. *practical, flexible, open-minded.*

doctrine *n.* principle, belief, conviction, precept, opinion, convention, tenet, dictum, dogma, creed, gospel.

document *n.* paper, record, certificate, form, report, instrument, testimony, contract, writ.

document *v.* support, verify, authenticate, substantiate, prove.

documentary *n.* film, docudrama, investigative report, travelogue, account, cinema verité, narrative, newsreel, short subject. SEE MOVIE

dodder *v.* shake, tremble, totter, falter, shuffle, quiver, potter.

doddering *a.* feebleminded, senile, faltering,

weak, infirm, decrepit, shaky, tottering, shuffling, quivering, *dotty. ANT. *hale, robust, fit.*

dodge *n.* stratagem, subterfuge, sidestep, evasion, escape, ruse, feint, trick, maneuver, ploy.

dodge *v.* avoid, evade, sidestep, elude, escape, *give the slip, duck, get around, *weasel out of, swerve, parry, skirt, bob and weave. ANT. *encounter, meet, confront.*

doer *n.* *go-getter, *mover and shaker, activist, risk-taker, enterpriser.

doff *v.* remove, take off, shed, strip, shuck, disrobe, undress.

dog *n.* canine, hound, *mutt, mongrel, cur, *pooch, puppy, bitch, *flea bag, tyke, *man's best friend. "The one absolutely unselfish friend."—George Vest. "A liberal. He wants to please everyone."—William Kunstler. "The god of frolic."—Henry Ward Beecher.
WORD FIND
Australian wild dog: dingo
back portion between shoulder blades: withers
bark: bay, howl, yelp
breeds: Afghan, Airedale, Alaskan malamute, Alsatian, basset hound, beagle, Belgian sheep dog, bloodhound, border terrier, borzoi, Boston terrier, boxer, bulldog, bull mastiff, bull terrier, Chesapeake Bay retriever, Chihuahua, chow, cocker spaniel, collie, dachshund, Dalmatian, deerhound, Doberman pinscher, elkhound, English setter, English springer spaniel, English toy spaniel, foxhound, fox terrier, German shepherd, golden retriever, Great Dane, Great Pyrenees, greyhound, griffon, harrier, hound dog, husky, Irish setter, Irish wolfhound, Labrador retriever, Lhasa apso, Maltese, mastiff, Mexican hairless, miniature poodle, Newfoundland, Norwegian elkhound, Old English sheepdog, Pekingese, pointer, Pomeranian, poodle, pug, rat terrier, retriever, Rottweiler, Russian wolfhound, Saint Bernard, Saluki, Samoyed, schnauzer, Scottish terrier, setter, Shih tzu, Skye terrier, spaniel, spitz, springer spaniel, staghound, Sussex spaniel, terrier, toy poodle, toy spaniel, water spaniel, Welsh collie, Welsh corgi, whippet, wirehaired terrier, wolfhound, Yorkshire terrier
bristling neck and back hairs: hackles

cheeks, lower: chops
chest hairs or coloration: apron
chest, lower: brisket
chin hairs: beard
claw, vestigial: dewclaw
coat, black or dark brown: sable
coat, glossiness of: bloom
coat, gray or black on white: badger-marked
coat, gray or streaked with gray: grizzle
coat, multicolored: parti-colored
coat, patchy or spotted with two or more colors: pied
coat, reddish brown or purplish brown: liver
coat, streaked or spotted: brindle
coat, white with black spots: harlequin
coat, yellowish blond
coat, yellowish-brown: fawn
disease: distemper, rabies, mange
domed or rounded skull: apple head
ears that are loose and dangling: lop ears
father: sire
fear of: cynophobia
female: bitch
foot cushions: pads
fringe around neck: frill, ruff
fringe on tail, back of legs: feather
hell's guardian: Cerberus
history: cynology
house: kennel
light-colored streak on head: blaze
lineage, especially from same breed: pedigree
long-legged, slight: racy
lover of: philocynic
low to the ground, thickset: cloddy
mating period, female: heat
mixed breed: mongrel
mother: dam
mouth, nose and jaws: muzzle
muzzle that is dark on some breeds: mask
muzzle that is sharply pointed: snipy
nose of more than one color: butterfly nose
ovaries, remove: spay
puppies, unweaned: whelps
range over field looking for game: quarter
sagging back: swayback
sculpted tufts left on sheared dog, esp. poodle: pompon
short-bodied: cobby
shoulders, highest part of: withers
tail, bushy: brush
tail, curled: ringtail
tail, cut short: bobtail, docked tail
tail, feathery: plume
tail, straight, stiff: whip

tail, twisted: screwtail
top dog: alpha
worm parasite: heartworm

dog-eat-dog *a.* vicious, voracious, brutal, aggressive, competitive, cutthroat, ruthless, brother against brother. ANT. *merciful, compassionate.*

DOGGED *a.* [DOG id] tenacious and stubborn, unwilling to give up. *In spite of overwhelming odds, she continued on doggedly.* SYN. stubborn, tenacious, willful, persistent, obstinate, mulish, determined intent, steadfast, resolute, plodding, unflagging, persevering. ANT. *yielding, compromising, irresolute.*

dogleg *n.* bend, turn.

DOGMA *n.* [DAWG muh] beliefs and principles. *My own religious dogma is not unlike others.* SYN. beliefs, principles, doctrine, conviction, creed, gospel, teachings, credo, tenet, article of faith, view, opinion. "A hard substance which forms in a soft brain."—Elbert Hubbard.

DOGMATIC *a.* [dawg MAT ik] stubbornly clinging to one's own beliefs and refusing to consider those of others; overpositive. *Our minister is too dogmatic to consider other views.* SYN. overpositive, closed-minded, opinionated, doctrinaire, biased, authoritarian, narrow-minded, emphatic, prejudiced, fanatical, imperious, dictatorial. ANT. *liberal-minded, open-minded, tolerant, receptive.*

do-gooder *n.* idealist, bleeding heart, philanthropist, humanitarian, *Dudley Do-right, boy scout, good Samaritan, altruist.

doings *n.* actions, deeds, acts, exploits, affairs, events, *goings-on, happenings, transactions.

doldrums *n.* listlessness, depression, *blahs, malaise, boredom, *blues, *dumps, *blue funk, slump, torpor, tedium, stagnation, slump.

dole *n.* welfare, charity, handouts, gift, alms, subsidy, food stamps, relief.

doleful *a.* mournful, melancholy, grief-stricken, downhearted, depressed, melancholy, sorrowful, dejected, disconsolate, sad, *down in the dumps, forlorn, woebegone. ANT. *cheerful, euphoric, happy.*

dole out *v.* distribute, hand out, allocate, dispense, mete, allot, parcel, divide, share.

dollar *n.* buck, bill, one, currency, note, greenback, *simoleon. SEE CURRENCY, MONEY

dollop *n.* lump, mass, blob, portion, modicum, quantity.

dolly *n.* handtruck, car, cart, carrier, transport.

dolorous *a.* sad, sorrowful, painful, grievous, heartrending, miserable, woebegone, wretched, anguished, lamentable, pitiable. ANT. *cheerful, happy, upbeat.*

dolphin *n.* cetacean, marine mammal, bottlenose, sea creature.

WORD FIND
look-alike: porpoise

dolt *n.* dullard, simpleton, blockhead, dunce, *airhead, idiot, *dimwit, *chowderhead, ignoramus, *nitwit, *lunkhead, numskull, moron. ANT. *genius, *Rhodes scholar, *rocket scientist.*

domain *n.* territory, realm, sphere, area, terrain, bailiwick, province, dominion, estate, empire, concern, kingdom, turf.

dome *n.* roof, cupola, hemisphere, vault, rotunda, onion dome, stupa, geodesic dome.

domestic *n.* servant, maid, butler, cook, *live-in.

domestic *a.* 1. HOUSEHOLD home, residential, family, private. 2. NATIVE indigenous, homegrown, homemade. ANT. *1. public. 2. foreign.*

domesticate *v.* tame, break, train, housebreak, gentle, *bust, master, subdue, civilize.

domesticity *n.* home life, homemaking, family life.

domicile *n.* home, residence, house, abode, dwelling, habitation, castle, *roof over one's head, *pad, living quarters, apartment, condo.

dominance *n.* leadership, rule, control, overpowering, power, top dog position, top of the pecking order, high rank, supremacy, upper hand, preeminence, superiority, leg up, command. ANT. *submission.*

dominant *a.* ruling, controlling, supreme, *having the upper hand, reigning, prevailing, preeminent, *in the driver's seat, authoritative, domineering, presiding, lordly, overruling, superior, ascendant, uppermost, proponderant, predominant, paramount, foremost. ANT. *subordinate, inferior, submissive, deferential.*

dominate *v.* rule, control, *have the upper hand, reign, prevail, preside, lord over, govern, master, tyrannize, overshadow, command, overrule, predominate, eclipse, *rule the roost, *run the show, *call the shots, dictate, subdue, overpower, bully, cow, loom over, dwarf, rule with an iron hand, *stand head and shoulders above. ANT. *submit, cringe, defer.*

domination *n.* leadership, rule, control, power, top position, supremacy, mastery, upper hand, preeminence, superiority, command, alpha position, tyrrany. ANT. *submission, subservience.*

domineer *v.* SEE DOMINATE

domineering *a.* overbearing, oppressive, highhanded, *ironhanded, bossy, controlling, lordly, high and mighty, tyrannical, imperious, pushy, authoritarian, bullying, *whipcracking. ANT. *submissive, deferential, cringing.*

dominion *n.* rule, realm, domain, sovereignty, authority, jurisdiction, command, reign, control, supremacy.

donate *v.* give, contribute, pledge, *chip in, grant, confer, bestow, bequeath, make a gift of.

donation *n.* contribution, gift, pledge, present, alms, aid, relief, handout, grant, offering, benefaction.

done *a.* finished, completed, accomplished, fulfilled, concluded, realized, terminated, executed, consummated, ended. ANT. *unfinished, unfulfilled, *up in the air.*

done for *a.* doomed, *had it, beaten, defeated, ruined, finished, *sunk, *washed up, exhausted, tired, dead. ANT. *saved, rescued, revived.*

donkey *n.* ass, mule, burro, jackass, jenny, beast of burden, jack, cuddy, dickey, quadruped.

WORD FIND
cry: bray, hee haw

Don Juan *n.* *ladies' man, Lothario, Casanova, *lady-killer, Romeo, *make-out artist, *wolf, stud, *skirt-chaser, *smooth operator, playboy.

donnybrook *n.* brawl, free-for-all, fight, fray, fracas, melee, fisticuffs, riot, *rumble.

donor *n.* contributor, benefactor, supporter, giver, backer, patron, grantor, subscriber, *angel.

do-nothing *n.* *bum, idler, loafer, sloth, malingerer, moocher, lazybones, *goof-off, laggard, shirker, *couch potato, goldbricker, slacker. ANT. *go-getter.*

donut *n.* SEE DOUGHNUT

doodad *n.* thingamajig, doohickey, whatzit, thingamabob, *goofus, whatchamacallit, gizmo, widget, doomajigger, gadget, *whangdoodle, widget.

doohickey *n.* SEE DOODAD

doom *n.* disaster, ruin, condemnation, death, extinction, Last Judgment, downfall, destruction, tragedy, damnation, annihilation, bane.

doom v. condemn, damn, consign to death, destine to ruin, sentence.

doomed a. condemned, damned, sentenced to death, consigned to ruin, destined for destruction, done for, kaput, *had it, *washed up. ANT. *saved, revived, rescued.*

doomsayer n. Cassandra, *Chicken Little, gloomy Gus, alarmist, voice of doom, prophet of doom, pessimist.

door n. entrance, passage, exit, opening, hatch, gate, portal, access.

doorbell n. chime, ringer, buzzer.

doozy n. Sl. *dilly, *humdinger, exception, *beaut, *corker, *dandy, *killer, *lollapalooza, *lulu, *ripsnorter, *something.

dope n. Sl. **1.** DRUG narcotic, *fairy powder, opiate, *weed, *pot, *reefer, *mojo, *hokus, *stuff, *junk, heroin, cocaine, *happy dust, hash, *smoke. SEE COCAINE, DRUG, MARIJUANA **2.** IDIOT dolt, *dummy, *nitwit, *birdbrain, moron, *retard, dunce, blithering idiot, *chowderhead, *numbskull, *a regular Einstein. **3.** FACTUAL INFORMATION scoop, skinny, news, *score, *poop, *lowdown, inside information.

dope v. drug, dose, sedate, knock out, *spike, anesthetize, *slip a Mickey Finn.

dopey a. stupid, idiotic, moronic, retarded, silly, mindless. ANT. *brilliant, intelligent, thoughtful.*

DORMANT a. [DOOR munt] inactive, asleep. *The dormant volcano had not erupted for 1,000 years.* SYN. inactive, asleep, quiet, resting, still, becalmed, latent, inert, passive, hibernating, quiescent, torpid. ANT. *active, alive, awake.*

dormer n. window, lucarne, gable, projection.

dormitory n. dorm room, hall, quarters, house, living quarters, sleeping quarters.

dose n. measure, portion, amount, quantity, allotment, *shot.

dossier n. file, record, profile, report, history.

dot n. point, spot, speck, period, mark, mote, iota.

dotage n. second childhood, senility, decrepitude, old age, feeblemindedness.

dote on v. lavish attention on, indulge, spoil, wait on, coddle, make of, fuss over, treasure, prize, hold dear. ANT. *neglect, ignore, abuse.*

doting a. lavish, indulgent, spoiling, coddling, demonstrative, devoted, adoring, lovesick, pampering. ANT. *neglectful, abusive.*

dotty a. crazy, *loony, *nuts, mentally unbalanced, eccentric, *goofy, *touched in the head, demented. ANT. *sane.*

double n. duplicate, twin, replica, look-alike, *dead ringer, *spitting image, clone, counterpart, match, mate, stand-in.

double a. paired, twin, two-sided, dual, twofold, binary, duplex, duple. ANT. *single, lone, only.*

double back v. backtrack, retrace steps, return, backpedal.

DOUBLE-BLIND n. [dub ul BLIYND] a medical study or test in which neither the researchers nor the subjects know who is receiving placebos and who is receiving real medicine, employed to assure objectivity. *To attain maximum credibility, most medical researchers must use double-blinds.* SYN. trial, clinical trial, test, study, assay, examination, acid test, double-check, confirmation, check.

double-cross v. betray, stab in the back, double deal, two-time, cheat, be duplicitous, *sell down the river.

double-dealing n. treachery, duplicity, betrayal, disloyalty, two-timing, double-crossing, deceit, infidelity, perfidy, backstabbing, cheating.

DOUBLE ENTENDRE n. [DUB ul on TON druh] a word or statement having two meanings, a risqué ambiguity. *The comedian couldn't be as frank as he wanted, so he used a lot of double entendres.* SYN. ambiguity, double meaning, play on words, innuendo, equivocation, equivoque, tergiversation, pun.

DOUBLE-STANDARD n. [dub ul STAN duhd] a social code or rule that is followed unfairily or without equal measure between sexes, races, groups, etc. *It's okay for a woman to wear a man's suit at work; it is not okay for a man to wear a dress a double standard.* SYN. contrasting principles, social code, two sets of rules, *a rule for Jack but not for Jill, contradictory standard.

doubt n. uncertainty, question, hesitation, mistrust, indecision, misgiving, skepticism, suspicion, lack of faith, lack of conviction, qualm, apprehension, irresolution, dubiety, question mark. ANT. *certainty, faith, confidence, trust.*

doubt v. question, be uncertain, hesitate, mistrust, suspect, lack faith, lack conviction, misgive, waver, *smell a rat, be dubious, harbor suspicion, be skeptical, disbelieve. "The beacon of the wise."—Shakespeare. ANT. *believe, trust, accept.*

doubter n. skeptic, disbeliever, doubting Thomas, questioner, cynic, scoffer, freethinker, iconoclast.

doubtful *a.* **1.** QUESTIONABLE dubious, unclear, hazy, uncertain, unsure, debatable, inconclusive, ambiguous, clouded, undetermined, problematic. **2.** UNLIKELY improbable, farfetched. **3.** DISBELIEVING suspicious, distrustful, hesitant, unsure, uncertain, questioning, skeptical, wavering, irresolute. ANT. *1. certain, sure, clear. 2. likely, probable. 3. believing, convinced.*

doubting Thomas *n.* skeptic, cynic, questioner, *one from Missouri, scoffer, disbeliever.

doughnut *n.* donut, *sinker, cruller, cake, olicook (oil cake).

DOUR *a.* [DOUR] sullen, gloomy. *The unsmiling, dour clerk was terribly unhelpful.* SYN. sullen, gloomy, morose, surly, glum, sour, stern, hard, grim, severe, forbidding, harsh, ill-humored. ANT. *cheerful, good-humored, beaming.*

douse *v.* **1.** IMMERSE wet, drench, submerge, sink, plunge, splash, soak, duck, dunk, sprinkle, saturate, slosh, rinse. **2.** EXTINGUISH put out.

dove *n.* pacifist, peacemaker, lamb.

dovetail *v.* fit, join, mortise, intersect, interlock, correspond, jibe.

dowdy *a.* shabby, sloppy, frumpy, bedraggled, slovenly, wrinkled, frowzy, unkempt, messy, unstylish, unfashionable, disheveled, *dressed in a potato sack. ANT. *chic, smart, put together, *dressed to the nines, sharp.*

down *a.* **1.** DEPRESSED unhappy, melancholy, miserable, downhearted, blue, dejected, disconsolate, low, disheartened, dispirited. **2.** BELOW earthward, groundward, floor level, to the bottom, under, underneath, nether, at the foot of, sub. ANT. *1. up, cheerful, euphoric, high. 2. up, skyward, above.*

down-and-out *a.* broke, penniless, bankrupt, destitute, impoverished, *in the poorhouse, *on the streets, *on the skids, derelict. ANT. *on the rise, rich, successful, *on top.*

downbeat *a.* pessimistic, negative, depressive, cheerless, unhappy, dispirited. ANT. *upbeat, optimistic.*

downcast *a.* dejected, sad, unhappy, miserable, depressed, melancholy, blue, *down in the mouth, *down in the dumps, disheartened, discouraged. ANT. *up, cheerful, happy.*

downer *n.* *bummer, depressing experience, *drag, *bad scene.

downfall *n.* **1.** RUIN collapse, crash, debacle, breakdown, undoing, overthrow, destruction, comeuppance, defeat. **2.** DOWNPOUR cloudburst, rain shower, torrent, deluge,

thunderstorm. ANT. *1. *rise to the top, ascension.*

downgrade *v.* devalue, minimize, reduce, demote, bring down a notch, degrade, make light of, downplay.

downhearted *a.* sad, unhappy, dejected, miserable, depressed, melancholy, blue, *down in the mouth, *down in the dumps, hopeless, disheartened, discouraged. ANT. *up, cheerful, euphoric, hopeful, optimistic.*

downhill *a.* descending, sloping. ANT. *ascending.*

downplay *v.* minimize, play down, make light of, downgrade, devalue, lessen.

downpour *n.* rain storm, rainfall, deluge, cloudburst, gullywasher, torrent, *cats and dogs, preciptation, *rain of biblical proportion.

downright *a.* total, complete, absolute, out and out, thorough, categorical, outright, unqualified, utter, unmitigated, sheer. ANT. *partial, qualified, semi.*

downsize *v.* reduce, cut, pare, shrink, decrease, *cut the fat, trim, lay off.

down to earth *a.* realistic, sensible, no-nonsense, reasonable, practical, sober, plainspoken, pragmatic, earthy, levelheaded, matter-of-fact, *real, natural, true. ANT. *unrealistic, fantastic, impractical, pretentious.*

downtrodden *a.* oppressed, subjugated, dominated, tyrannized, abused, cowed, trampled upon, mistreated, afflicted, *jackbooted, helpless, persecuted. ANT. *uplifted, aided, well-treated.*

downturn *n.* decline, drop, dip, slide, slump, depression, reversal, *bear market.

downy *a.* fluffy, soft, feathery, velvety, fleecy, silky, fuzzy. ANT. *rough, coarse, hard.*

doze *v.* nap, sleep, snooze, *nod off, slumber, drowse, *catch forty winks, catnap.

drab *a.* dull, lackluster, *blah, colorless, boring, dreary, faded, somber, dingy. ANT. *colorful, bright, vivid.*

DRACONIAN *a.* [dray KO nee un] harsh or severe, especially concerning a law or code; named after the code of Draco, from 621 B.C. *Some favor taking Draconian measures to fight crime.* SYN. harsh, severe, strict, cruel, extreme, rough, brutal, serious, dire, ironhanded, drastic, punitive. ANT. *slight, light, inconsequential, petty.*

draft *n.* **1.** WIND breeze, current, puff, whiff, breath, waft, sigh, sough. **2.** MILITARY CONSCRIPTION induction, selection, lottery, recruitment, registration, call of duty. **3.** OUTLINE OR PICTURE rough, blueprint, sketch, overview, formulation, skeleton, drawing.

draft v. **1.** CONSCRIPT induct, recruit, register, select, call up, enlist. **2.** ROUGH IN sketch, outline, delineate, formulate, compose, fashion, shape.

drag v. **1.** HAUL pull, lug, tow, hale, trail. **2.** PROGRESS SLOWLY *go at a snail's pace, crawl, lag, plod, poke along, inch along. **3.** PROTRACT extend, prolong, draw out. ANT. *1. push, shove. 2. rush, fly, speed. 3. shorten.*

dragnet n. search, manhunt, all points bulletin, tracking, chase, pursuit.

dragon n. monster, firedrake, serpent. SEE MONSTER

dragonfly n. insect, bug, *darning needle, *devil's darning needle, *mosquito hawk.

drag queen n. cross-dresser, female impersonator.

drain n. outlet, conduit, channel, pipe, sewer, watercourse, plumbing.

drain v. **1.** DRAW empty, bleed, pump out, withdraw, remove, siphon, tap, broach, milk, release, discharge, filter, flush. **2.** USE UP exhaust, expend, suck dry, consume, deplete, tax, sap, bleed dry. ANT. *fill, replenish.*

drama n. play, show, screenplay, production, melodrama, dramatic arts, tragedy, story, narrative, *tearjerker, dramatization, stagecraft, theatrics. "A slice of life artistically put on the boards."—Jean Jullien.

dramatic a. intense, exciting, emotional, striking, vivid, melodramatic, climactic, moving, tense, histrionic, suspenseful, electrifying, gripping, riveting. ANT. *blah, *ho-hum, prosaic.*

dramatization n. drama, larger than life presentation, show, entertainment, melodrama, adaptation.

dramatize v. play up, emphasize, exaggerate, sensationalize, embellish, *lay it on thick, amplify, intensify, *ham it up. ANT. *play down, understate.*

drape n. curtain, window dressing, hanging, tapestry, valance, shade, blind, drapery.

drastic a. extreme, severe, dire, strong, harsh, exorbitant, radical, intensive, extensive, extravagant, draconian. ANT. *slight, petty, modest.*

draw n. **1.** TIE stalemate, *photo finish. **2.** ATTRACTION pull, magnetism.

draw v. **1.** PULL TOWARD attract, haul, tow, drag, lug, hale, trail, attract. **2.** SKETCH depict, portray, outline, trace, delineate, compose, paint, caricature, draft, fashion, rough out. **3.** DISPLACE **4.** ATTRACT allure, entice, lure,

tempt, seduce, captivate, mesmerize, pull in, bring forth. **5.** ELICIT induce. **6.** DEDUCE extract, formulate, derive, infer, conclude, gather. ANT. *1. push, shove. 4. repel, repulse.*

drawback n. disadvantage, weakness, snag, hitch, hindrance, liability, flaw, handicap, impediment, failing, shortcoming. ANT. *advantage, bonus.*

drawbridge n. bascule bridge. SEE BRIDGE

drawing n. **1.** PICTURE illustration, sketch, diagram, design, outline, pen and ink, depiction, portrayal, study, work of art, figure, caricature, draft. **2.** LOTTERY selection.

drawl n. accent, twang.

drawn a. haggard, gaunt, worn, exhausted, fatigued, unhealthy, pale, taut, tense. ANT. *rested, refreshed, glowing.*

dread n. fear, trepidation, horror, apprehension, qualm, misgiving, dismay, angst, anxiety, *the creeps, awe, *the willies, *heebie-jeebies.

dread v. fear, shudder at the thought of, anticipate with horror, shrink, worry, apprehend, *have cold feet, blanch at the thought of. ANT. *look forward to.*

dreadful a. terrible, unpleasant, horrible, frightful, appalling, distressing, grievous, awful, ghastly, hideous, shocking. ANT. *wonderful, marvelous, fantastic.*

dreadlocks n. braids, locks, dreads, Rastafarian, haircut. SEE HAIR

dream n. **1.** SLEEP VISIONS OR REVERIE daydream, hallucination, *REM sleep, hypnogogic imagery, nightmare, night terrors, incubus, fantasy, figment of the imagination, vision. "The ghost of a shadow."—Joseph Devlin. "Children of an idle brain."—Shakespeare. "The imaginary gratification of unconscious wishes."—Sigmund Freud. "You eat, in dreams, the custard of the day."—Alexander Pope. SEE SLEEP **2.** ASPIRATION goal, ambition, *pipe dream, flight of fancy, aim, wish, desire, *castle in the air, *castle in Spain, fantasy. **3.** PLEASURE delight.

dream v. fantasize, daydream, imagine, muse, fancy, envisage, visualize, conjure up, hallucinate, conceive, lose oneself in reverie.

dreamer n. visionary, fantast, daydreamer, castle-builder. "One who can only find his way by moonlight, and his punishment is that he sees the dawn before the rest of the world."—Oscar Wilde.

dream up vt. think up, concoct, *cook up, devise, invent, hatch, imagine.

dreary a. gloomy, dismal, bleak, gray, cheerless,

depressing, drab, colorless, somber, mournful, funereal. ANT. *sunny, bright, cheerful.*

dredge *v.* clean, deepen, widen, dig up, unearth.

dregs *n.* **1.** SEDIMENT residue, grounds, dross, deposits, settlings, lees. **2.** RIFFRAFF scum, refuse, losers, *bums.

drench *v.* wet, soak, saturate, sop, drown, immerse, submerge, wash, slosh, flood.

dress *n.* **1.** CLOTHING outfit, garb, attire, apparel, costume, habit, habiliment, ensemble, raiment, vestments, *togs, *duds. "The soul of a man."—Shakespeare. **2.** WOMAN'S GARMENT frock, gown, evening dress, skirt, shift, ensemble, formal, wraparound.

WORD FIND

African chemise with bell-shaped sleeves: dashiki

African, long, flowing: seloso

African shift: Ethiopian shirtdress

ankle-length dress popular in late 1960s: maxi

bell-shaped dress with tight bodice: dirndl

black ankle-length dress with high neckline, ruffled sleeves: granny dress

bloused-top dress: blouson

bubble-shaped dress of the 1950s: bubble dress

calf-length dress introduced in the 1960s: midi

chemise: shift

child's sleeveless dress with bib-top apron: pinafore

full, puffed: bouffant

full, triangular: tent dress

glittery, beaded, sequined: diamante

Hawaiian: muumuu

Hindu, wrapped and draped: sari

Indian fringed and beaded: buckskin

Japanese wraparound with sash: yukata, kimono

kiltlike dress with wrap skirt: kiltie

knitted: sweater dress

loose-fitting gown: peignoir

1920s dress with short skirt and long torso: flapper

poor European dress with puffed sleeves, drawstring neckline: peasant dress

pregnant, for women who are: maternity dress

robelike, full-length, embroidered around neck: caftan

Roman-inspired, one shoulder bare: toga

rump protrusion of the nineteenth century: bustle

sack: chemise

shapeless, long: Mother Hubbard

shirtlike, buttoned top, with full or straight skirt: shirtwaist dress

short evening dress: cocktail dress

short-skirted dress of 1960s, 1980s: minidress

snug and narrow with slashed back: sheath

straight-cut, no waistline: chemise, sack

strapless or halter-style: sundress

wraparound: wrap

SEE SKIRT

dress *v.* **1.** CLOTHE garb, attire, vest, deck out, outfit, slip into, wear, clad, don, costume. **2.** DECORATE trim, embellish, adorn, garnish, beautify, festoon, deck. ANT. *1. strip, undress, disrobe.*

dresser *n.* **1.** CHEST OF DRAWERS bureau, chiffonier. **2.** PERSON fashion plate, *clotheshorse, dandy.

dressing-down *n.* scolding, reprimand, upbraiding, *tongue-lashing, castigation, censure, *bawling-out, reproach, talking to.

dressy *a.* fashionable, chic, stylish, formal, *dressed to the nines, smart, sharp, classy, elegant, flashy, *dressed to kill, *hot. ANT. *informal, casual, simple.*

dribble *v.* trickle, weep, run, drip, leak, ooze, drizzle, seep, drivel, slobber, drool.

drift *n.* **1.** HEAP pile, mound, hill, mass, deposit, bank, dune, accumulation. **2.** FLOW current, course, movement, bearing, direction, trend. **3.** MEANING gist, intention, purport, tenor, essence, sense.

drift *v.* **1.** HEAP pile up, mound, mass, deposit, bank, accumulate. **2.** WANDER float, waft, meander, stray, rove, ramble, be borne along by the current/tide/wind.

drifter *n.* wanderer, vagabond, transient, vagrant, nomad, hobo, tramp, derelict.

drill *n.* practice, exercise, training, discipline, regimen, repetition, dry run, warm up.

drill *v.* practice, exercise, train, discipline, test, warm up, ground.

drink *n.* liquid, beverage, refreshment, thirst quencher, soda, soft drink, *pop, punch, nectar of the gods, swallow, sip, swig, taste, *hit, *booze, liquor, shot, nip, *slug, potation, *hard stuff, *rot gut, firewater, draft, quaff, jigger, *snort, *pull. "The social lubricant."—Edward Strecker. SEE COCKTAIL, LIQUEUR, LIQUOR, MOONSHINE

drink *v.* swallow, sip, down, guzzle, *chug-a-lug, swig, quaff, *take a hit, *take a shot, have a taste, quench one's thirst, gulp, imbibe, drain, swill, *wet one's whistle, wash down, tipple, *bend the elbow, *gargle, *have a nip.

drinkable *a.* potable, palatable. ANT. *undrinkable.*

drip *v.* dribble, trickle, leak, drop, weep, seep, sprinkle, splash, run.

drive *n.* **1.** RIDE spin, *cruise, tour, whirl, joyride, outing, jaunt, *Sunday drive, road trip, journey, excursion. **2.** CRUSADE campaign, cause, push, appeal. **3.** DETERMINATION getup-and-go, aggressiveness, ambition, momentum, vigor, energy, hustle, enterprise, *head of steam, self-motivation.

drive *v.* **1.** OPERATE A VEHICLE steer, control, pilot, ride, *cruise, tour, *take a spin, take a road trip, tool down the highway, motor, wheel, speed, travel, *burn up the highway. **2.** PUSH propel, urge, force, press, goad, spur, move, shove, induce, pressure, compel, prod. **3.** HIT throw, strike, ram, shoot, hurl, thrust.

drivel *n.* nonsense, *hogwash, twaddle, foolishness, falderal, gibberish, babble, *rot, *humbug, balderdash, bull, blather.

drivel *v.* slobber, drool, dribble, slaver, salivate.

driver *n.* motorist, commuter, jehu, whip, coachman, chauffeur, operator.

driving *a.* forceful, powerful, pounding, intense.

drizzle *n.* mist, sprinkle, fog, rain, spray, moisture.

drizzle *v.* rain, mist, sprinkle, wet, moisten.

DROLL *a.* [DROLE] amusing in an odd way. *His droll sense of humor tickled us.* SYN. amusing, comical, entertaining, whimsical, quaint, humorous, eccentric, queer, peculiar, jocular.

drone *v.* buzz, hum, purr, whirr, murmur, hiss, bombilate, thrum, intone.

drool *v.* dribble, slobber, drivel, slaver, salivate, foam at the mouth.

drool *n.* saliva, spittle, spit, slaver, slobber, drivel, expectoration, sputum, *loogie.

droop *v.* sag, hang down, slouch, loll, slump, bend, dangle, wither, wilt, languish, bow, settle, stoop, flag.

drop *n.* **1.** DROPLET globule, bead, teardrop, pearl, speck, pinch, splash, dewdrop, drip, blob, driblet, smidgen, trace, dab. **2.** FALL pitch, descent, slope, precipice, plunge, chasm, hole. **3.** DECLINE decrease, fall, downswing, lowering, tumble, slump, reduction, fall-off, depreciation. ANT. *2. ascent, rise. 3. increase, rise, elevation.*

drop *v.* **1.** FALL dive, plunge, descend, plummet, pitch, tumble, *nose-dive, go down, topple,

slump, *keel over, collapse. **2.** ABANDON give up, let go, dismiss, discontinue, cease, end, quit, desert, *write off, forsake, *scrub, leave. **3.** DECREASE decline, fall, lower, reduce, depreciate, tumble, slump, diminish, slacken. ANT. *1. rise, ascend, elevate. 2. take up, adopt. 3. increase, appreciate, rise.*

drop in the bucket *n.* *spit in the sea, pittance, trivial amount, miniscule amount, mite, *small change, *small potatoes, speck.

drop off *v.* deliver, deposit, unload, leave.

drop off *n.* descent, precipice, cliff, slope, hole, decrease, fall.

drop out *vi.* quit, abandon, *turn one's back on, abandon, withdraw, forsake, leave.

droppings *n.* dung, excrement, manure, guano, *crap.

drought *n.* dry spell, dehydration, aridity, dearth, shortage, scarcity, want, insufficiency.

drove *n.* flock, herd, mass, body.

drown *v.* **1.** GO UNDER AND PERISH submerge, asphyxiate, suffocate, sink, flood, inundate, engulf, swamp. **2.** OVERWHELM overpower, overcome, stifle, smother, suppress.

drowsy *a.* sleepy, tired, dozy, half asleep, *out of it, lethargic, drifting off, groggy, somnolent, listless, sluggish. ANT. *alert, awake, energetic, wide-eyed.*

drub *v.* thrash, hit, beat, whip, wallop, pound, club, cane, lash, switch.

drudge *v.* work hard, toil, labor, *break one's back, *do the dirty work, slave away, *keep nose to the grindstone, plod, grind, sweat.

drudgery *n.* menial labor, chore, slave labor, toil, backbreaking work, manual labor, *daily grind, taskwork.

drug *n.* medicine, narcotic, remedy, cure, opiate, dope, pharmaceutical, prescription, pill, substance, chemical, treatment, panacea, physic, preparation, controlled substance.

WORD FIND

addict: *junkie, *hophead, *dope fiend, *druggie, *space cadet, *burnout

addict's alternative to heroin: methadone *angel dust: PCP

cocaine that is smoked: crack *crank: methamphetamine

crack mixed with heroin: *eightball

dance party favorite: ecstasy (methylenedioxymethamphetamine; MDMA)

depressant, muscle-relaxer: barbituate, *downer

ether-purified cocaine: *freebase

hallucinogen: LSD, DMT (Dimethyltrypta-mine), *ecstasy, mescaline, peyote, *psychedelic, *STP
*ice: methamphetamine in smokable form
inject a drug, to: mainline
laughing gas: nitrous oxide
LSD: lysergic acid diethylamide, *California sunshine, *acid
mix of cocaine, amphetamine and heroin: *speedball
mood-altering: psychotropic drug
muscle-building hormone: anabolic steroid
narcotic: heroin
opium-derived: opiate
painkiller: analgesic, codeine, Demerol, morphine, Percodan
painkiller, abused: Oxycontin; oxycodone hydrochloride
poppy-plant, derived from: opium
rape drug rendering unconscious: GHB (Gamma hydroxybutrate)
sex drive arouser: aphrodisiac
sleep-inducing: hypnotic, soporific, tranquilizer, sedative, Quaalude, Seconal
*smack: heroin
stimulant: amphetamine, Dexedrine, *speed, *upper
tranquilizer: sedative, Valium
vomiting, causes: emetic
SEE COCAINE, CURE, HEROIN, OPIUM, MARIJUANA, MEDICINE, NARCOTIC

druggist n. pharmacist, apothecary, chemist. BRIT.

drum n. SEE MUSICAL INSTRUMENT

drunk a. intoxicated, inebriated, under the influence, *three sheets to the wind, *stiff, *crocked, *polluted, *tipsy, *loaded, *loaded for bear, *plastered, *lit up like a Christmas tree, *feeling no pain, *anesthetized, *sloshed, *hammered, *high, *buzzed, besotted, soused, *pickled, *lit, *tanked, *stewed to the gills, *bombed, *blitzed, *smashed, *blotto, *drunk as a lord. ANT. sober, clearheaded.

drunk(ard) n. alcoholic, *lush, problem drinker, *boozer, inebriate, *wino, *rummy, barfly, *sot, dipsomaniac, *alchy, *boozehound. "Like a whiskey bottle, all neck and belly and no head."—Austin O'Malley. "A person who tries to pull himself out of trouble with a corkscrew."—Edward Baldwin.

dry a. 1. DEHYDRATED dessicated, waterless, arid, parched, thirsty, droughty, evaporated, anhydrous, withered. 2. DULL boring, uninteresting, prosaic, tedious, flat, blah,

*ho hum, wearisome, *dull as dishwater, insipid, monotonous, sterile. 3. DROLL humorous, sarcastic, satirical, deadpan. ANT. 1. wet, moist, saturated. 2. interesting, fascinating.

dual a. double, twofold, twin, duplex, binary, matched. ANT. single, lone.

dub v. name, christen, label, title, designate, term, nickname, tag, style, confer, denominate, baptize, knight.

DUBIOUS a. [DOO bee us] doubtful or causing doubt, questionable, uncertain. I was dubious about her chances of winning the lottery. SYN. doubtful, questionable, uncertain, equivocal, indefinite, unclear, unsure, disputable, suspect, debatable, moot. ANT. certain, sure, indisputable.

duck v. 1. LOWER bow, crouch, stoop, dip, double over, drop, bob, bend, hunker down. 2. EVADE dodge, sidestep, elude, avoid, parry, swerve, shun, steer clear. 3. IMMERSE submerge, dunk, dip, plunge, sink. ANT. 1. rise, straighten. 2. meet, confront.

duck soup n. Sl. child's play, *a snap, *a breeze, cakewalk, *piece of cake, *turkey shoot, *walkover.

duct n. conduit, pipe, channel, passage, tube, airway, chimney, smokestack, funnel.

dud n. failure, bomb, lemon, bust, loser, *dog, washout, fizzle, *flop, disappointment. ANT. success, *cocker, winner.

dude n. Sl. 1. GUY man, *buddy, friend, *bro'. 2. AN OVERDRESSED MAN dandy, fop, Beau Brummel, coxcomb, fashion plate, *peacock, clotheshorse.

duds n. SEE CLOTHING

due n. compensation, payment, recompense, *what is coming, rightful claim, reward, *comeuppance, *just deserts.

due a. 1. OWED in arrears, payable, unpaid, outstanding, unsatisfied, not met, mature. 2. APPOINTED TO ARRIVE expected, scheduled, anticipated, slated, booked. 3. FITTING appropriate, deserved, merited, justified, entitled, warranted. ANT. 1. paid, satisfied. 2. unscheduled, unexpected. 3. undue, inappropriate.

due to prep. attributable, because of, accountable.

duel n. combat, contest, fight to the death, clash, engagement, shootout, challenge, joust.

dues n. membership fee, charge, obligation, levy, toll, assessment, payment, tax.

duff n. rump, rear. SEE BUTTOCKS

dulcet *a.* melodious, pleasing, pleasant, sweet, agreeable. ANT. *discordant.*

dull *a.* **1.** STUPID slow, unintelligent, *thick, dense, bovine, retarded, obtuse, doltish, *dumb as a post, dim-witted, half-witted, ignorant. **2.** BORING tedious, *ho-hum, blah, uninteresting, prosaic, dry, tiresome, bland, vapid, *dull as dishwater, humdrum, stale, lackluster, soporific. **3.** SUBDUED quiet, muted, deadened, faded, softened, muffled. **4.** UNSHARPENED blunt, unhoned, edgeless. ANT. *1. sharp, intelligent, quick-witted, bright. 2. exciting, stimulating, colorful, dramatic. 3. overstated, overdone, flashy, loud. 4. sharp, honed.*

dullard *n.* dolt, dunce, *retard, idiot, *dope, *blockhead, *chowderhead, *meathead, *nitwit, imbecile, *half-wit. ANT. *genius, *brain, *Rhodes scholar.*

dumb *a.* **1.** STUPID unintelligent, slow, *thick, dense, bovine, moronic, retarded, obtuse, doltish, dim-witted, *dumb as a post, ignorant, uneducated, unenlightened, dull, *having the IQ of a woodchuck, *having the IQ of a pork rind, brainless, cretinoid, *dead from the neck up, *down a quart, *half-baked, *pea-brained, *three bricks shy of a load, illiterate, vacuous, *not exactly a Rhodes scholar, *not exactly Einstein. **2.** UNABLE TO SPEAK mute, speechless, still, mum, silent, voiceless, tongue-tied. ANT. *1. smart, intelligent, bright, brilliant. 2. loquacious, verbose, *motor-mouthed, talkative.*

dumbbell *n.* moron, imbecile, idiot, *retard, dullard, ignoramus, harebrain, halfwit, nitwit, *pinhead, *airhead, *bubblehead.

dumbfound *v.* stun, nonplus, strike dumb, flabbergast, astound, take aback, stagger, paralyze, render speechless, stupefy.

dumbstruck *a.* shocked, stunned, nonplused, flabbergasted, astonished, astounded, rendered speechless, *blown away. ANT. *taking it in stride.*

dummy *n.* **1.** FIGURE mannequin, straw man, scarecrow, model, puppet, muppet, doll, figure. **2.** MOCK-UP model, imitation, substitute, copy, representation. **3.** IDIOT *lamebrain, *airhead, simpleton, dolt, *nitwit, *dimwit, ignoramus, dunce, moron, *chowderhead, numskull. ANT. *3. genius, *brain, *Rhodes scholar, *rocket scientist.*

dump *n.* **1.** REFUSE YARD junkyard, landfill, dumpsite, hazardous waste site, scrap heap, rubbish heap. **2.** RUNDOWN, MESSY PLACE hole, *pigpen, *pigsty, slum, *rathole, *toilet, *sewer hole.

dump *v.* throw out, drop, get rid of, cast off, empty, *deep six, chuck, scrap, unload, junk, ditch, discard. ANT. *load, fill.*

dumpling *n.* doughball.

WORD FIND

Chinese: wonton, dim sum
Italian: gnocchi
Yiddish: matzo ball

dumps *n. Sl.* blues, depression, blahs, doldrums.

dumpy *a.* stout, *built like a fireplug, short, thickset.

dunce *n.* idiot, moron, dolt, *nitwit, *half-wit, *lamebrain, *airhead, simpleton, ignoramus, *retard, *chowderhead, numskull.

dune *n.* hill, ridge, sand pile, sand drift, hillock, mound, barrow, knoll, hummock. SEE DESERT

dung *n.* excrement, droppings, feces, scat, manure, muck, guano, *cow chips, *cow pies, *crap, *poop.

WORD FIND

dunghill: midden
study of: scatology

dungarees *n.* pants, trousers, jeans, overalls, denims.

dungeon *n.* prison, keep, hold, donjon, enclosure, chamber, confine, oubliette, stronghold. SEE CASTLE

dunk *v.* dip, sink, immerse, submerge, duck, soak, souse, sop.

duo *n.* duet, pair, team.

dupe *n.* victim, *easy mark, *chump, gull, *sucker, *patsy, *pushover, dummy, fall guy, *sap, pawn, *babe in the woods. ANT. *nobody's fool, quick study.*

dupe *v.* *put one over on, trick, fool, take in, delude, *pull the wool over one's eyes, *rope in, deceive, cheat, *snooker, *buffalo, *snow.

duplex *a.* two, double, twofold, paired, dual, twin, coupled, duple.

duplicate *n.* copy, reproduction, carbon copy, match, counterpart, mate, mirror image, facsimile, clone, twin, dead ringer. ANT. *original.*

duplicate *v.* copy, reproduce, replicate, clone, *run off, match, double, counterfeit, parallel, ditto.

duplicitous *a.* deceptive, deceitful, shady, double-dealing, treacherous, two-faced, two-timing, back-stabbing, dishonest.

DUPLICITY *n.* [doo PLIS i tee] deceptiveness, the act of double-dealing or being two-faced. *Shady politicians are skilled in the art* *of duplicity.* SYN. deceptiveness, deception, double-dealing, being two-faced, guile, treachery, backstabbing, *two-timing, deceit, disloyalty, artifice, hypocrisy, dishonesty, *Judas kiss. ANT. *honesty, loyalty, artlessness, straightforwardness.*

durable *a.* lasting, tough, rugged, sturdy, enduring, strong, permanent, sound, stout, stable, solid. ANT. *fragile, flimsy, cheap, shoddy.*

duration *n.* period, time, age, span, term, run, stretch, era, lifetime extent, continuation, course.

duress *n.* coercion, constraint, threat, pressure, force, arm-twisting, compulsion. ANT. *free will.*

dusk *n.* twilight, sundown, sunset, gloom, nightfall, gloaming, evening, moonrise.

dusky *a.* dark, dim, gauzy, murky, gloomy, veiled, twilight, swarthy, gray, shadowy, unlit, somber. ANT. *sunny, bright, radiant.*

dust *n.* particles, lint, grit, ashes, powder, soot, particulate, scales, fragments.

dusty *a.* dirty, sandy, granular, *linty, sooty, powdery, undusted. ANT. *dusted, clean, polished.*

dutiful *a.* conscientious, diligent, obedient, devoted, regardful, accommodating, obliging, faithful. ANT. *lazy, slack, negligent.*

duty *n.* **1.** RESPONSIBILITY charge, task, commission, obligation, trust, requirement, function, assignment, job, burden. **2.** TAX customs, excise, levy, tariff, toll, impost, assessment.

DVD *n.* compact disk, digital video disk, video storage medium.

dwarf *n.* midget, runt, pygmy, gnome, *shrimp, Lilliputian, *squirt, bantam, elf, *peewee, *half-pint, *micro. ANT. *giant, colossus.*

dwarf *v.* eclipse, overshadow, outshine, stand head and shoulders above, tower above, excel, dominate, stunt.

dwell *v.* **1.** LIVE reside, inhabit, stay, abide, *crash, keep house, quarter, lodge, *roost, *bunk, take shelter, domicile. **2.** LINGER OVER think about, pause, harp on, ponder.

dwelling *n.* home, house, residence, domicile, habitation, lodging, abode, homestead, quarters, diggings, castle, *pad, den. SEE HOUSE

dwindle *v.* diminish, decline, decrease, lessen, fade, wane, shrink, ebb, waste away, slacken, die down, drop, decay. ANT. *increase, grow, expand.*

dye *n.* color, tint, pigment, tinge, stain.

DYED-IN-THE-WOOL *a.* through and through, to the very core, deep-down. *The senator had consistently shown himself to be a dyed-in-the-wool conservative.* SYN. through and through, to the core, deep-down, out and out, complete, utter, absolute, true, genuine, full-fledged. ANT. *partial, superficial.*

dying *a.* **1.** EXPIRING perishing, fading, declining, *going downhill, *circling the drain, *at death's door, moribund, doomed, slipping away, not long for this world, *one foot in the grave. "The last gasp."—Bible. "A great leap in the dark."—Thomas Hobbes. "That dreadful season."—Joseph Addison. "A natural appointment from which there is no hope of escape."—Jonathan Miller. **2.** DISAPPEARING passing, declining, becoming extinct, receding, going out. ANT. **2.** *thriving, flourishing, rejuvenating.*

dynamic *a.* active, energetic, vital, vigorous, forceful, aggressive, alive, powerful, spirited, effective, potent, driving, compelling. ANT. *lifeless, dead, ineffectual, weak.*

dynamite *n.* explosive, TNT, nitroglycerin, blasting material.

dynamo *n.* generator, *go-getter, *bundle of energy, *live wire, *spark plug, work horse, *ball of fire, hard worker, mover and shaker.

dynasty *n.* lineage, ascendancy, regency, rule, house, command, crown, regime, empire, succession.

dysfunctional *a.* nonfunctioning, malfunctioning, impaired, abnormal, unhealthy, aberrant. ANT. *well adjusted, *together.*

dyslexia *n.* learning disorder, reading disorder, learning impairment, comprehension disorder.

dyslexic *a.* learning-impaired.

E

each *a.* every, all, respective, any, individual. ANT. *none.*

each *adv.* apiece, per, individually, a person, *a head, *a shot.

eager *a.* enthusiastic, anxious, *champing at the bit, desirous, itching, *gung ho, agog, impatient, *rarin' to go, fervent, ardent, hungry, intent, zealous. ANT. *apathetic, indifferent, lukewarm.*

eagle *n.* raptor, bird of prey, Falconiforme.

WORD FIND
group of: convocation
hooked beak, describing: aquiline
nest: aerie
SEE BIRD

eagle-eyed *a.* sharp-eyed, hawk-eyed, keen-eyed, perceptive, observant. ANT. *dull-eyed, unobservant.*

ear *n.* hearing organ, auditory organ. "The road to the heart."—Voltaire. "The gates to the mind."—Moses Ibn Ezra.

WORD FIND
balance, inner organ of: labyrinth
bones of: anvil (incus), hammer (malleus), stirrup (stapes); ossicles
deformity: cauliflower ear
doctor: otologist
earache: otalgia
eardrum: tympanic membrane
external portion: auricle, pinna
hereditary disorder causing progressive deafness: otosclerosis
instrument: otoscope
nerve: auditory nerve
nerve deafness: sensorineural deafness
ringing in: tinnitus
spiral inner cavity: cochlea
study of: otology
swimmer's ear: otitis externa
vestigial point: Darwin's tubercle
wax: cerumen
whirling, dizzy sensation due to inner ear impairment: vertigo

early *a.* **1.** NEAR THE BEGINNING preceding, prior, initial, young, aboriginal, primal, primeval, primitive, antediluvian, maiden, original, starting, ancient. **2.** TOO SOON premature, ahead of time, beforehand, preceding, advanced, immature, precocious. ANT. *1. recent, modern, latter. 2. late, tardy.*

earmark *n.* characteristic, feature, mark, hallmark, trait, quality, signature, peculiarity, trademark, stamp.

earmark *v.* set aside, reserve, designate, slot, allocate, assign, hold, tag, label.

earn *v.* **1.** MAKE MONEY net, *clear, gross, profit, take in, take home, pull in, gain, realize, collect, get, draw. **2.** DESERVE merit, be entitled to, warrant, achieve, be worthy of.

EARNEST *a.* [UR nist] serious, sincere, no-nonsense, determined. *The team made an earnest attempt at the prize.* SYN. serious, sincere, no-nonsense, determined, heartfelt, wholehearted, devoted, resolute, intent, *meaning business, ardent, fervent, diligent. ANT. *halfhearted, frivolous, insincere, apathetic.*

earnings *n.* pay, wages, salary, net, gross, *take-home, income, profit, compensation, proceeds, gain, return, receipts.

earring *n.* earbob, ornament, jewelry, bauble, jewel, ear clasp, girandole, *fishing lure (sarcastic).

earsplitting *a.* deafening, loud, shrill. ANT. *muted, quiet.*

earth *n.* **1.** GROUND soil, land, dirt, clay, loam, humus, turf, mud, terra firma. **2.** PLANET world, globe, sphere, biosphere, Gaea, terrene, orb, terra, terra firma, *spaceship Earth, vale. "One voice in the cosmic fugue."—Carl Sagan. "The frozen echo of the silent voice of God."—S.M. Hageman. "Footstool of our God" Isaac Watts. "A spot, a grain, an atom."—John Milton.

WORD FIND
center of, pertaining to: geocentric
green earth color: terre verte
inhabitant: earthling, tellurian
outermost shell: crust, lithosphere
personification of: Gaea
pertaining to: terrene
shape: oblate spheroid
study of its shape, size: geodesy
study of its structure: tectonics, geology
subsurface: asthenosphere, mantle, core

earthling *n.* tellurian, inhabitant of earth, human being, terra, man, woman, child of earth.

earthly *a.* terrestrial, terrene, worldly, *down to earth, physical, mundane, global, physical, corporeal, mortal, temporal. ANT. *spiritual, ethereal, otherworldly, divine, heavenly.*

earthquake *n.* tremor, temblor, quake, seism, *earthshake, shock, convulsion, upheaval, cataclysm, *wake-up call.

WORD FIND

center of: epicenter

continental dynamics causing: plate tectonics

following tremor: aftershock

fracture in rock strata, origination of quake: fault

ground waves causing initial roar: primary waves, compressional waves

ground waves causing side-to-side shaking: Love waves

magnitude scale: Richter scale, Mercalli intensity scale

pertaining to: seismic

preceding tremor: foreshock

recorder of earth's vibrations: seismograph

sea wave caused by: tsunami

study of: seismology

SEE VOLCANO

earthmover *n.* bulldozer, grader, backhoe, steam shovel, excavator, heavy machinery.

earthy *a.* folksy, uninhibited, down-home, unsophisticated, coarse, *down to earth, *real, crude, *hard-boiled, unrefined, lusty, ribald, rough, gross. ANT. *sophisticated, refined, dainty, prissy.*

ease *n.* **1.** COMFORT well-being, peace, rest, contentment, *peace of mind, relaxation, tranquility, relief, serenity, leisure. **2.** EASINESS facility, readiness, effortlessness, freedom, *a snap, *child's play, *duck soup, *a walk on the beach, a breeze, *a cinch. ANT. *1. discomfort, pain, difficulty. 2. difficulty, hardship.*

ease *v.* alleviate, lessen, relieve, moderate, comfort, mitigate, diminish, assuage, lighten, simplify, mollify, quiet, smooth. ANT. *aggravate, worsen.*

easel *n.* stand, support, tripod, frame.

easement *n.* right of way, access right.

easily *adv.* **1.** EFFORTLESSLY with ease, readily, handily, without difficulty, trouble free, swimmingly, facilely, dexterously. **2.** BY FAR *hands down, far and away, decidedly, unquestionably, clearly. ANT. *1. arduously, laboriously, with difficulty. 2. barely, hardly.*

easy *a.* **1.** NOT HARD effortless, simple, slight, light, uncomplicated, painless, *cinchy, *child's play, *a snap, *piece of cake, *nothing to it, *duck soup. **2.** FREE FROM TROUBLE OR PAIN relaxed, carefree, untroubled, tranquil, peaceful, serene, comfortable, luxurious, undemanding, secure, pleasant. **3.** EASYGOING relaxed, lenient, gentle, tolerant, soft, mild, permissive, moderate, lax, informal, benign. ANT. *1. difficult, arduous, laborious.*

2. burdensome, hard, troubled. 3. strict, harsh, stern.

easygoing *a.* placid, careless, undemanding, relaxed, lenient, gentle, tolerant, permissive, lax, informal, *happy-go-lucky, *devil-may-care, laid-back. ANT. *uptight, intense, stern, severe, harsh.*

eat *v.* **1.** INGEST FOOD consume, dine, feast, devour, lunch, break bread, sup, *chow down, gorge, scoff, *put on a feedbag, gobble, wolf, nibble, nosh, bolt. **2.** CORRODE erode, dissolve, wear away, rot, decay, disintegrate, waste.

eating disorder *n.* dieting disorder, anorexia nervosa, bulimia, binging and purging, neurosis, sickness, mental illness. SEE ANOREXIA, BULIMIA

eavesdrop *v.* listen in, pry, spy, wiretap, *bug, *snoop, bend an ear.

ebb *v.* recede, decline, fall back, diminish, subside, decrease, wane, retreat, fade, flag, abate, withdraw. ANT. *grow, increase, build, wax.*

EBULLIENT *a.* [i BUL yunt] boiling or bubbling over with excitement. *The crowd was absolutely ebullient with the hometown's victory.* SYN. exuberant, bubbling over with excitement, exhilarated, high-spirited, electrified, effervescent, elated, enthusiastic, irrepressible, *going nuts, zestful, wild. ANT. *subdued, sedate, apathetic, somber.*

eccentric *n.* *nut, character, queer duck, original, oddball, *weirdo, nonconformist, *ding-a-ling, crank, loner, individual, free spirit, one-of-a-kind, *flake.

eccentric *a.* odd, peculiar, weird, *nutty, queer, off-center, flaky, unconventional, idiosyncratic, *off the wall, deviant, *kinky, different, *daft, *potty, irregular, nonconforming. ANT. *normal, conventional, ordinary.* SEE CRAZY

eccentricity *n.* quirk, peculiarity, oddity, idiosyncrasy, abnormality, foible, idiocrasy, curiosity, irregularity, singularity, *kink.

ecclesiastical *a.* churchly, religious, ministerial, parochial, pastoral, clerical. ANT. *lay, secular, mundane.*

ECHELON *n.* [ESH uh lon] any one level in a multi-level group. *It was the upper echelon's responsibility to devise new strategies.* SYN. level, hierarchy, rank, class, position, place, tier, order.

echo *n.* answer, reverberation, rebound, reflection, reply, replication, repercussion, repetition, parroting. "Something that always has the last word."—German proverb. "The shadow of a sound."—Horace Smith.

ECLECTIC *a.* [i KLEK tik] selecting the best from various sources, that which has been selected from diverse sources. *Fran's taste in music is eclectic.* SYN. selective, comprehensive, wide-ranging, assorted, broad, diverse, liberal, multifaceted, catholic, heterogeneous. ANT. *limited, narrow, specialized.*

eclipse *n.* occultation, shadowing, obliteration, obscuring, darkening, penumbra. SEE ASTRONOMY

eclipse *v.* **1.** BLOCK obscure, cover, darken, hide, conceal, dim, veil, overshadow. **2.** OUTSHINE exceed, surpass, overpower, overshadow, outdo, transcend, stand head and shoulders above, dwarf.

ecology *n.* environemental science, study of flora and fauna, habitat science, life science.

economical *a.* **1.** FRUGAL conservative, thrifty, economizing, efficient, *penny-wise, tight, prudent, saving, scrimping. **2.** INEXPENSIVE cheap, *dirt cheap, cost-effective, reasonable, budget, low-priced. ANT. *1. wasteful, extravagant. 2. expensive, costly, dear.*

economize *v.* save, be frugal, *tighten one's belt, pinch pennies, conserve, scrimp, cut corners, stint, cut back. ANT. *waste, squander.*

economy *n.* **1.** THRIFT saving, frugality, conserving, austerity, prudence, skimping, penny-pinching. "To pitch your scale of living one degree below your means."—Henry Taylor. "The art of making the most of life."—George Benard Shaw. **2.** NATIONAL, STATE OR REGIONAL INCOME MANAGEMENT finances, production, GNP, gross national product, spending, distribution of wealth. ANT. *1. extravagance, wastefulness, spending.*

WORD FIND

ban of import or export product: embargo, sanction

buying for want and status instead of need: conspicuous consumption

collective annual value of all goods, services, etc, of nation: GNP, gross national product

debt owed by federal government: national debt

decline, sharp and prolonged economic: depression

demand exceeding supply: seller's market

drop in prices due to a reduction of the money supply: deflation

expansion, economic: boom

exports and imports, difference in worth between: balance of trade

gauge of fluctuating prices of common consumer goods: consumer price index

GNP: gross national product

government incentives to big business resulting in benefit to all: trickle-down theory

group working together to control production and prices, common: cartel

inability to pay one's debts: insolvency

inflation causing shortages, runaway: hyperinflation

imports exceeding exports, condition of: trade deficit

luxuries, money left over for: discretionary income

manufacturing industry, heavy: smokestack industry

medieval economic system of lords and vassals: feudalism

money to work with: capital

monopolies, laws preventing formation of: antitrust laws

price supports, government: subsidies

reducing taxes to spur production, investment and growth, theory of: supply-side economics

selling goods below cost to drive competition out of business: dumping

services than production of goods, economy based more on: service economy

supplies exceeding demand: buyer's market

system of collectively-owned or state-owned production facilities controlling distribution, economic: communism

system of privately-owned businesses designed for profit-making, economic: capitalism, free enterprise system

tariffs and regulations used by nation to limit imports: trade barriers

ups and downs of some businesses, expected: business cycle

zero growth and rising unemployment, period of: recession, slump

ecosystem *n.* habitat, environment, ecological community.

ecstasy *n.* rapture, euphoria, bliss, elation, transport, exaltation, ebullience, heaven, joy, exhilaration, seventh heaven. ANT. *misery, depression, gloom.*

ecstatic *a.* rapturous, euphoric, elated, blissful, transported, exalted, ebullient, in heaven, in seventh heaven, overjoyed, thrilled. ANT. *miserable, depressed, down.*

eddy n. current, vortex, countercurrent, whirlpool, swirl.

edema n. fluid, swelling, accumulation, water retention.

Eden n. garden, paradise, utopia, heaven on earth, garden of Adam and Eve.

edge n. **1.** MARGIN border, boundary, verge, outline, perimeter, skirt, rim, fringe, periphery, limit, brink. **2.** ADVANTAGE leg up, handicap, head start, upper hand.

edgy a. nervous, on edge, tense, uptight, anxious, *wired, jumpy, jittery, *keyed up, restless, ill at ease, *a bundle of nerves. ANT. *calm, tranquil, relaxed.*

edible a. palatable, consumable, fit to eat, comestible, digestible, esculent. ANT. *inedible, disgusting, rotten, *not fit for human consumption.*

edict n. decree, command, proclamation, law, fiat, manifesto, enactment, ruling, act, regulation, ordinance. SEE LAW

edification n. enlightenment, education, improvement, betterment, learning, uplifting, instruction, guidance, teaching.

edifice n. building, structure, skyscraper, tower, construction, highrise. SEE BUILDING

edit v. revise, correct, *blue pencil, refine, check, rewrite, polish, proofread, redact, doctor, cut, delete, condense, *clean up.

editor n. reviser, redactor, rewriter, copy editor. "A bit of sandpaper applied to all forms of originality."—Elbert Hubbard.

edition n. issue, copy, number, printing, volume.

editorial n. essay, opinion piece, think piece, article, commentary.

educate v. teach, instruct, train, enlighten, school, edify, tutor, coach, cultivate, *show the ropes, inform, *drum into.

educated a. trained, enlightened, schooled, learned, literate, cultivated, erudite, scholarly, refined, well-read, well-grounded, knowledgeable. ANT. *ignorant, naive, illiterate.*

education n. training, enlightenment, schooling, learning, edification, erudition, scholarship, literacy, book-learning, instruction, study, grounding, cultivation. "A companion which no misfortune can depress."—Joseph Addison. "A better safeguard of liberty than a standing army."—Edward Everett. "Character development."—William O'-Shea. "A chest of tools."—Herbert Kaufman. "All the minds of past ages."—Bernard de Fontenelle.

educational a. informative, instructional, enlightening, academic, edifying, illuminating, scholastic, didactic.

educator n. teacher, instructor, tutor, mentor, trainer, coach, professor.

educe v. evoke, bring out, draw forth, elicit.

eerie a. weird, unsettling, creepy, macabre, unnatural, spooky, bizarre, strange, unearthly, uncanny, frightening, mysterious.

efface v. erase, obliterate, rub out, cancel, wipe out, fade, expunge, eradicate.

effect n. **1.** RESULT consequence, upshot, reaction, response, aftermath, end, fallout, wake, repercussion. **2.** INFLUENCE impact, force, weight, power, clout, efficacy.

effect v. bring about, cause, actualize, produce, achieve, make, create, generate, accomplish.

effective a. **1.** PRODUCTIVE successful, compelling, sufficient, forceful, efficacious, useful, powerful, persuasive. **2.** OPERATIVE functional, serviceable, in effect, active. ANT. *ineffectual, ineffective, impotent, inadequate.*

effects n. belongings, possessions, goods, things, property, stuff, chattels.

effeminate a. feminine, unmanly, soft, ladylike, womanish, emasculate, *limp-wristed, delicate, *queer, sissyish. ANT. *masculine, virile, macho, manly.*

effervescence n. **1.** FIZZ bubbles, foam, froth, carbonation. **2.** VIVACITY high spirits, exuberance, vitality, liveliness, *zip, spirit, buoyancy, animation, ebullience. ANT. *1. flatness. 2. lifelessness, listlessness, torpor.*

effervescent a. **1.** FIZZY bubbly, foaming, frothy, carbonated. **2.** VIVACIOUS spirited, exuberant, vital, lively, *zippy, buoyant, animated, ebullient. ANT. *1. flat. 2. dead, lifeless, listless.*

effete a. **1.** BARREN unproductive, fruitless, sterile. **2.** SPENT worn out, exhausted, used up, *burned out, enervated, weak. ANT. *fertile, vital, vigorous.*

EFFICACY n. [EF uh kuh see] the capacity to bring about the desired end, effectiveness. *The efficacy of the space agency will be tested with the new mission.* SYN. effectiveness, power, productiveness, capacity, competency, potency, vigor, proficiency, capability, efficiency.

efficient a. effective, effectual, potent, productive, capable, causative, proficient, dynamic, economical, workmanlike, able. ANT. *inefficient, ineffectual, wasteful.*

effigy n. likeness, dummy, figure, representation, image, mock-up.

effort *n.* **1.** EXERTION strain, output, work, trouble, application, muscle, toil, pain, *elbow grease, stress, sweat. **2.** ATTEMPT try, endeavor, venture, *go. **3.** ACHIEVEMENT feat, creation, accomplishment.

effortless *a.* easy, simple, *no sweat, *piece of cake, *child's play, facile, *a snap, cinchy, no problem, *duck soup. ANT. *arduous, laborious, backbreaking.*

EFFRONTERY *n.* [i FRUN tuh ree] audacity, insulting gall. *I can't believe he had the effrontery to cut in line.* SYN. audacity, impudence, boldness, nerve, gall, cheek, insolence, presumption, arrogance, brass, impertinence, rudeness, *chutzpah. ANT. *deference, timidity, respect.*

effulgent *a.* radiant, glowing, luminous, brilliant, resplendent, shining, dazzling, bright. ANT. *dim, dull, dark.*

EFFUSIVE *a.* [i FYOO siv] gushing or highly demonstrative of one's emotions. *It made me uncomfortable to see him so effusive.* SYN. gushing, demonstrative, unrestrained, profuse, expansive, lavish, extravagant, overflowing, unreserved. ANT. *reserved, restrained, taciturn.*

EGALITARIAN *a.* [i GAL uh TARE ee un] believing in equality for everyone. *The constitution ensures an egalitarian government.* SYN. equal, liberal, fair-minded, democratic, just, unbiased, unprejudiced, equitable. ANT. *unfair, inequitable, prejudiced, biased.*

egg *n.* ovum, embryo, roe, spawn.

WORD FIND

crumbed and buttered: shirred eggs
laid at same time: clutch
shape: ovoid, ovate, oval
tester: candler
white: albumen
yolk: vitellus

egghead *n. Sl.* intellectual, *brain, genius, *walking encyclopedia, *know-it-all. ANT. *ignoramus, moron.*

egg on *v.* urge, incite, prod, encourage, spur, push, prompt, goad, rally. ANT. *discourage.*

ego *n.* self, psyche, self-esteem, self-image, self-respect.

egocentric *a.* self-centered, selfish, egotistic, self-absorbed, wrapped up in oneself, narcissistic, vainglorious, conceited. ANT. *giving, other-directed, self-effacing.*

egotism *n.* self-centeredness, selfishness, egoism, self-absorption, conceit, narcissism, vainglory, arrogance, self-worship, vanity, overconfidence. "The anesthetic given by a kindly nature to relieve the pain of being a damned fool."—Bellamy Brooks. "A case of mistaken nonentity."—Barbara Stanwyck.

egotist *n.* egoist, boaster, selfish pig, narcissist, braggart, peacock, *swellhead, egomaniac. "A self-made man who worships his creator."—John Bright.

egotistic *a.* self-centered, selfish, self-absorbed, conceited, narcissistic, arrogant, vainglorious, self-worshipping, vain, smug, overconfident, *puffed up, *swellheaded. ANT. *modest, humble, unpretentious.*

EGREGIOUS *a.* [i GREE jus] extremely bad or outrageous. *Murder is an egregious sin.* SYN. bad, outrageous, flagrant, blatant, extreme, atrocious, monstrous, shocking, grievous, glaring, striking, baldfaced, appalling. ANT. *minor, trivial, petty.*

egress *n.* doorway, outlet. SEE EXIT

ejaculate *v.* discharge, climax, have an orgasm, *come.

ejaculation *n.* release, emission.

eject *v.* throw out, expel, oust, *kick out, *give the boot, evict, ditch, banish, *send packing, *show the door, *bounce, *give walking papers.

ejection *n.* expulsion, ouster, removal, dismissal, exile, *the boot, discharge, banishment, eviction, ostracism.

elaborate *v.* develop, work out, detail, flesh out, fashion, add to, enlarge, amplify, refine, explain.

elaborate *a.* complicated, complex, intricate, detailed, comprehensive, painstaking, thorough, involved, sophisticated, multifaceted, ornate, busy, showy, extravagant. ANT. *simple, plain, unadorned, stark.*

élan *n.* enthusiasm, spirit, vigor, dash, ardor, verve, vivacity, panache, flair, zest.

elapse *v.* go by, pass, transpire, expire, intervene, slip by, lapse.

elastic *a.* flexible, resilient, supple, adaptable, springy, pliant, accommodating, yielding, buoyant. ANT. *inflexible, rigid, stiff.*

elated *a.* happy, ecstatic, euphoric, delighted, excited, in high spirits, *in seventh heaven, exultant, *flying, exhilarated, gleeful, joyful, *tickled. ANT. *miserable, down, depressed, *bummed.*

elation *n.* happiness, joy, euphoria, delight, excitement, high spirits, glee, exhilaration, exaltation, rapture, *cloud nine, ecstasy. ANT. *misery, depression, blues.*

elbow *v.* push, shove, jostle, shoulder, bump, bulldoze, nudge, crowd.

elbow grease *n.* effort, muscle, *oomph, strain, sweat, stress, toil, back, strength.

elder *n.* senior, old-timer, veteran, superior, forefather, ancestor, matriarch, patriarch, *old fogey, *geezer, retiree, graybeard, dowager.

WORD FIND

sixty, or between sixty and seventy: sexagenarian

seventy, or between seventy and eighty: septuagenarian

eighty, or between eighty and ninety: octogenarian

ninety, or between ninety and one hundred: nonagenarian

one hundred-year-old: centenarian

elder *a.* older, senior, superior, higher ranking. ANT. *younger, junior.*

elderly *a.* aged, venerable, seasoned, ancient, *long in the tooth, mature, *over the hill, experienced, senescent, advanced in years, weathered, vintage. ANT. *youthful, young, immature, *green.* SEE OLD, OLD AGE, OLD-FACED

elect *v.* select, choose, pick, opt for, appoint, vote for, settle on, nominate, single out, cast one's ballot.

election *n.* selection, choosing, choice, voting, vote-casting, determination, preference, appointment, designation, nomination, referendum.

WORD FIND

ELECTIONS AND CAMPAIGNING

aid to candidate, solicits votes: electioneer

assembly every four years to elect presidential candidate: national convention

attack on opposing candidate: mudslinging, smear campaign

candidate list: ballot, ticket

convention representatives from one state: delegation

cross-party vote: crossover vote

desires and dictates of voters expressed through vote: mandate

district of voters: constituency

district, smallest voting unit: precinct

fund-raising, fund-distributing committee: political action committee (PAC)

mail-in vote: absentee ballot

majority (large) of votes, victory: landslide

meeting of party to choose candidate: caucus

meeting to generate enthusiasm for candidate: rally

person not on ballot, but written in by voter: write-in

poll public opinion or solicit votes: canvass

popular candidate's trickle-down benefit to weaker party member: coattail effect

preliminary, nominating election: primary

principles of candidate or party: platform

proposal of action, to be voted on: proposition, referendum

random vote poll: straw poll

report of voting trends: poll, returns, exit poll

shake hands and smile: glad-hand

speak from town to town: barnstorm, stump

state representatives chosen to elect president and vice president: electoral college

voting enrollment: registration

SEE CONGRESS, ELECTIONEERING, POLITICS

electioneering *n.* campaigning, canvassing, soliciting votes, *stumping, *barnstorming, promoting. "A war in which everybody shoots from the lip."—Raymond Moley.

elective *a.* chosen, optional, electoral, discretionary, voluntary. ANT. *required.*

electricity *n.* current, power, AC, DC, voltage, spark, charge, *juice.

WORD FIND

atom: electron

cell that converts light to electricity: photovoltaic cell

current regulator: rheostat

drop in voltage through power line: brownout

earth or other large body to which circuit is connected to prevent noise interference: ground

generator: dynamo

material capable of carrying current with little resistance: conductor

particle, electrified: ion

poor conductor and a poor insulator: semiconductor

restrictor of current's flow: insulator

stores electrical charge: capacitor

unit of: amp, ampere, ohm, volt, watt, joule

zero resistance of current: superconductivity

SEE ELECTRONICS, EXCITEMENT

electrify *v.* thrill, shock, startle, stun, excite, dazzle, stir, daze, jolt, *give one a charge, stagger, *take one's breath away. ANT. *bore.*

electronics *n.* integrated circuitry, transistors, chips, solid state components. SEE COMPUTER, ELECTRICITY

elegance *n.* fineness, refinement, grace, opulence, luxuriousness, high style, beauty, grandeur, class, tastefulness, sophistication, poshness, polish.

elegant *a.* fine, refined, graceful, opulent, luxurious, high-styled, stylish, beautiful, grand, classy, tasteful, sophisticated, posh, cultured, fashionable, polished. ANT. *coarse, crude, unrefined, tacky.*

elegiac *a.* sad, sorrowful, mournful, plaintive. ANT. *uplifting, inspiring, happy.*

elegy *n.* dirge, lamentation, lament, funeral song, requiem.

element *n.* component, ingredient, constituent, unit, facet, bit, feature, piece, portion, section, item, factor.

elementary *a.* basic, simple, fundamental, rudimentary, easy, *child's play, uncomplicated, primary, introductory, plain, abecedarian. ANT. *complicated, advanced, difficult.*

elephant *n.* pachyderm, herbivore, quadruped, mammal. "A mouse built to government specifications."—Robert Heinlein.

WORD FIND

call: trumpet, bellow

driver/keeper: mahout

extinct: mammoth, mastadon

female: cow

male: bull

male's violent and sexual frenzy: musth, rut

nose: trunk, snout

rider's seat: howdah

run towards: charge

solitary, vicious outcast: rogue

tooth: tusk

tusk: ivory

young: calf

elephantine *a.* mammoth, gargantuan, jumbo. ANT. *tiny, puny, wee.* SEE HUGE

elevate *v.* 1. RAISE lift, uplift, hoist, escalate, hike up, jack up, heighten. 2. PROMOTE advance, raise, enhance, improve, upgrade, boost, heighten, aggrandize, exalt. ANT. *lower, drop, degrade.*

elevated *a.* lofty, exalted, noble, grand, eminent, high, upstanding, distinguished, admirable, *put on a pedestal. ANT. *lowly, inferior, humble.*

elevation *n.* height, altitude, eminence, high ground, prominence, rise, hill, mountain, lift.

elevator *n.* lift, hoist.

elf *n.* gnome, fairy, hob, pixy, imp, brownie, sprite, dwarf, leprechaun.

elfin *a.* mischievous, prankish, impish, playful, sprightly, small, fleeting.

ELICIT *v.* [i LIS it] to bring out or draw forth. *He tried to elicit a response from the speaker.* SYN. draw, bring out, evoke, extract, wrest, cause, exact, call forth, wring, *arm-twist, *pump, extort.

eligible *a.* qualified, worthy, suitable, appropriate, desirable, fitting, acceptable. ANT. *ineligible, disqualified.*

eliminate *v.* get rid of, remove, discard, cut, reject, omit, drop, kill, eject, oust, shut out, expel, exclude. ANT. *include, get.*

elimination *n.* removal, discard, cut, rejection, omission, dropping, killing, ejection, ouster, expulsion, exclusion. ANT. *inclusion.*

elite *n.* the best, the greatest, *upper crust, aristocracy, *crème de la crème, high society, gentry, blue bloods, nobility, clique, *haut monde, pick. ANT. *the dregs, working class, lower class.*

elitist *n.* snob, highbrow, oligarch, social climber, *snoot, *stuffed shirt, egotist.

elixir *n.* potion, curative, mixture, compound, panacea, cure-all, miracle drug, nostrum, catholicon, solution, substance.

elliptical *a.* oval, egg-shaped, ovoid.

elocution *n.* public speaking, speech, oratory, articulation, recitation, declamation, rhetoric, delivery, eloquence, enunciation, diction. SEE ELOQUENCE, SPEECH

elongate *v.* lengthen, extend, stretch, protract, let out, prolong. ANT. *shorten, shrink, curtail.*

elongated *a.* lengthened, extended, stretched, protracted, let out, prolonged, prolate, oblong. ANT. *shortened, contracted, curtailed.*

elope *v.* run off, abscond, run away with, slip off.

eloquence *n.* persuasiveness, fluency, forcefulness, expressiveness, rhetoric, command of language, way with words, elocution, oratory, articulation. "A gift of the mind, which makes us master of the heart and spirit of others."—Jean de La Bruyère. "What one thinks he has after a cocktail."—Warren Goldberg. "The gift of making any color appear white."—Ambrose Bierce.

ELOQUENT *a.* [EL uh KWUNT] persuasive by means of one's speech, having a way with words, articulate. *There are many eloquent speakers in Washington.* SYN. persuasive, articulate, fluent, forceful, having a way with words, expressive, having a command of the language, silver-tongued, smooth, stirring, cogent, vivid, pointed. ANT. *inarticulate, tongue-tied, stumbling.*

elucidate v. clarify, make clear, explain, illustrate, illuminate, *shed light on, simplify, spell out, interpret. ANT. *obfuscate, confuse, muddy.*

elude v. avoid, evade, escape, *give the slip, dodge, *lose, *throw off the scent, get away, circumvent, baffle, thwart, foil. ANT. *confront, meet, face.*

elusive a. evasive, slippery, shifty, hard to catch, fleeting, eely, baffling, cagey, puzzling, wily. ANT. *comprehensible, easy to grasp, within reach.*

EMACIATED a. [i MAY shee ay ted] lean and scrawny, as from starvation. *Many deer become emaciated through the winter.* SYN. lean, thin, scrawny, wasted, malnourished, anorexic, bony, skinny, skeletal, gaunt, rawboned, drawn, wizened, hollow-eyed. ANT. *beefy, plump, fat, obese.*

e-mail n. electronic mail, online mail, online correspondence, E-message, instant message. SEE COMPUTER, INTERNET

emanate v. issue, proceed, spring, arise, appear, exude, come forth, originate, flow, discharge.

emanation n. emission, discharge, issue, emerging, emergence, effusion.

EMANCIPATE v. [i MAN suh pate] to free. *Lincoln wished to emancipate the slaves.* SYN. free, liberate, release, deliver, loose, unchain, unburden, enfranchise, manumit, save, rescue. ANT. *enslave, fetter, subjugate.*

emancipation n. freedom, liberation, release, delivery, manumission, enfranchisement. ANT. *enslavement, subjugation.*

EMASCULATE v. [i MASS kyuh late] to castrate or weaken; to take away a man's strength. *Kryptonite had the power to emasculate Superman.* SYN. castrate, weaken, effeminate, debilitate, enervate, render ineffectual, soften, *take the teeth out of. ANT. *strengthen, invigorate.*

EMBARGO n. [em BAR go] a government-imposed prohibition on the shipment or receipt of foreign commercial freight. *The president imposed an embargo on French wine.* SYN. prohibition, restriction, ban, blockage, proscription, stoppage, restaint, check, interdiction.

embark v. **1.** BOARD get on. **2.** COMMENCE set out, start, venture, undertake, take up, broach, launch, enter, initiate.

embarrass v. disconcert, make ill-at-ease, make self-conscious, abash, shame, mortify, chagrin, fluster, discompose, fluster, faze.

embarrassing a. disconcerting, humiliating, awkward, mortifying, uncomfortable, discomfiting, shaming, discomposing, ticklish, touchy, undignifying.

embarrassment n. humiliation, shame, chagrin, discomposure, mortification, discomfort, self-consciousness, *egg on one's face, uneasiness, pudency.

WORD FIND

descriptive: cheeks burn; color deeply; toes curl in one's shoes; feel hot and foolish; feel the blood rush to one's face; squirm/wriggle with embarrassment; eyes range the floor, searching desperately for a hole to crawl into; eyelids bat self-consciously; cringe inwardly; smile sheepishly; splutter with embarrassment; stammer self-consciously; ears flush scarlet

embarrassed smiling: dry grins

embarrassing occurrence: contretemps

embassy n. ambassador's office, diplomatic mission, foreign office, consulate, chancellery, chancellory, diplomatic corps.

embattle v. equip, arm, prepare for battle.

embed v. fix, place, insert, bury, enclose, implant, surround, root, plant, deposit.

embellish v. enhance, adorn, ornament, decorate, garnish, elaborate, beautify, touch up, fix up, embroider, play up, exaggerate, overstate.

EMBELLISHMENT n. [em BEL ish ment] something added to increase interest or beauty, as an ornament, musical passage, etc. Also, an exaggeration or bit of fiction, sometimes used to make one's experiences more interesting to others. *His stories were always full of questionable embellishments.* SYN. enhancement, ornamentation, adornment, decoration, beautification, embroidery, exaggeration, enrichment.

embers n. ashes, coals, cinders, clinkers, sparks. SEE FIRE

EMBEZZLE v. [em BEZ ul] to steal, especially when in a position of trust, to commit fraud. *To embezzle company funds and get caught means certain jail time.* SYN. steal, defraud, misappropriate, cheat, defalcate, purloin, *have one's hand in the till, filch, swindle, peculate, *cook the books.

embittered a. bitter, resentful, hostile, disaffected, sour, disillusioned, spiteful, cynical, irritated, sore, rankled.

emblazon v. ornament, color, paint, decorate, embellish.

emblem *n.* symbol, badge, design, representation, crest, trademark, coat of arms, colors, insignia, mark, attribute, image.

emblematic *a.* symbolic, representative.

embodiment *n.* representation, personification, incarnation, materialization, manifestation, realization, incorporation, exemplification.

embody *v.* represent, personify, incarnate, manifest, realize, stand for, incorporate, materialize, substantiate, symbolize.

embolden *v.* encourage, hearten, buoy, reassure, puff up, invigorate, boost, psych up, *give pep talk. ANT. *frighten, cow, unnerve.*

emboss *v.* mold, carve, set in relief, raise, impress, imprint.

embrace *v.* **1.** HUG squeeze, hold, clasp, enfold, clinch, grab, envelop, cuddle, snuggle, *bear hug. **2.** ENCOMPASS take in, include, cover, embody, comprehend, incorporate. **3.** ADOPT take up, espouse, welcome, accept, seize. ANT. *2. exclude, omit. 3. reject, spurn, shun.*

EMBROIDER *v.* [em BROY dur] to exaggerate or embellish by stretching the truth, to add untruthful details. *Some tabloids embroider the truth.* SYN. exaggerate, embellish, stretch the truth, fib, varnish, aggrandize, puff up, overstate, *hype, *blow out of proportion, *make a mountain out of a molehill, fabricate, invent.

embroil *v.* disturb, entangle, trouble, mix up, involve, snarl, muddle, set at odds, rouse, *fan the flames.

embryonic *a.* rudimentary, elementary, beginning, immature, undeveloped, initial, fetal. ANT. *advanced, mature, latter.*

emend *v.* improve, correct, right, fix, edit, redact, revise.

emerge *v.* appear, arise, issue, come forth, surface, materialize, crop up, come out, spring, originate, emanate.

emergency *n.* crisis, exigency, trouble, urgency, plight, contingency, pinch, *pickle, bind, difficulty, clutch.

emergency room *n.* ER, trauma center, critical care facility, triage room, medical crisis unit, intensive care unit (ICU). SEE HOSPITAL, MEDICINE

emergent *a.* new, developing, on the horizon, hatching, coming into view, rising, emerging. ANT. *declining, *yesterday's news.*

emigre *n.* emigrant, defector, expatriate, fugitive.

eminence *n.* **1.** POSITION rank, fame, standing, importance, prominency, distinction, greatness, repute, celebrity, station, loftiness. **2.** HILL rise, elevation, height, prominence, peak, summit, ridge, high ground.

EMINENT *a.* [EM uh nunt] high-ranking and distinguished, noteworthy. *An eminent authority on economics predicted a downturn.* SYN. high-ranking, distinguished, noteworthy, famous, renowned, exalted, excellent, esteemed, celebrated, prominent, illustrious, outstanding, great, dominant. ANT. *little-known, obscure, undistinguished.*

emir *n.* prince, governor, leader, chieftain, commander.

emissary *n.* representative, messenger, agent, ambassador, envoy, go-between, courier, deputy, attaché.

emission *n.* discharge, emanation, expulsion, ejection, issuance, diffusion, transmission, outpouring, leaking.

emit *v.* discharge, emanate, expel, eject, issue, diffuse, outpour, leak, exhale, secrete, exude, excrete, leak.

emollient *n.* balm, salve, lotion, ointment, lenitive.

emollient *a.* soothing, softening, relieving, assuasive, healing, palliative. ANT. *abrasive, hurtful.*

emote *v.* act, overact, dramatize, express, *ham it up.

emotion *n.* feeling, state of mind, sentiment, passion, gut reaction, sensation, heart, drive.

emotional *a.* **1.** FEELING sensitive, passionate, reactive, sentimental, sympathetic, ardent, susceptible, excitable, fervent, fiery, histrionic, temperamental. **2.** MOVING soul-stirring, touching, poignant, heartrending, heartfelt, disturbing. ANT. *1. apathetic, unfeeling, impassive.*

emotionless *a.* apathetic, cold, numb, unfeeling, indifferent, stony, stoical, insensate, dispassionate, heartless, matter-of-fact.

empathize *v.* identify with, relate to, understand, comprehend, sympathize, stand in one's shoes, *be on the same wavelength.

EMPATHY *n.* [EM puh thee] understanding or sharing of another's feelings, thoughts, etc. *As a basketball official, I have a certain amount of empathy for baseball umpires.* SYN. understanding, sympathy, accord, comprehension, rapport, communion, affinity, fellow feeling.

emperor *n.* ruler, sovereign, monarch, czar, dictator, empress.

emphasis *n.* stress, accent, underscoring, importance, force, weight, significance, prominence, highlight, attention.

emphasize *v.* stress, accent, underscore, highlight, accentuate, play up, spotlight, punctuate, italicize, bring to the fore. ANT. *downplay, play down, soften.*

EMPHATIC *a.* [em FAT ik] done with emphasis. *He gave an emphatic denial of any wrongdoing.* SYN. insistent, forceful, impassioned, passionate, vigorous, pointed, stressed, strong, earnest, compelling, striking, vehement. ANT. *vague, halfhearted.*

empire *n.* dominion, realm, rule, kingdom, domain, sovereignty, territory.

EMPIRICAL *a.* [em PIR i kul] based on observation or experience, not theory. *The empirical evidence backed the scientists' claims.* SYN. experiential, experimental, observed, practical, pragmatic, firsthand, factual, verifiable, provable.

emplacement *n.* position, mounting, site, placement.

employ *v.* **1.** MAKE USE OF use, practice, utilize, apply, put to use. **2.** ENGAGE THE SERVICES OF contract for, retain, hire.

employee *n.* worker, personnel, staffer, hired hand, jobholder, wage earner, *company man/woman, *working stiff, *slave.

employer *n.* boss, manager, owner, proprietor, chief executive officer (CEO), director, contractor, *big cheese, overseer, *front office, corporation, company, firm.

employment *n.* **1.** USE utilization, application, operation, usage, exercise. **2.** WORK job, position, occupation, employ, business, trade, field, profession, vocation, situation.

WORD FIND

employing more workers than is necessary: featherbedding

favoritism in which family members and friends are hired first: nepotism

emporium *n.* marketplace, store, trade center, mart, bazaar, mall.

EMPOWER *v.* [em POW ur] to give or invest with power, legal or otherwise, to enable. *Giving children a good education will empower them to succeed.* SYN. enable, authorize, vest, permit, warrant, allow, entrust, validate, commission, accredit.

empress *n.* ruler, queen, regina.

emptiness *n.* void, vacuity, vacuum, nothingness, space, vacancy, desolation, blankness, hole.

empty *a.* **1.** VACANT void, hollow, bare, vacuous, barren, desolate, blank, deserted, abandoned, devoid, stark, evacuated. **2.** MEANINGLESS purposeless, hollow, futile, ineffective, idle, worthless, cheap, insubstantial, vapid, vain. ANT. *1. full, crowded, replete. 2. meaningful, fruitful, effective.*

empty-headed *a.* brainless, witless, *brain-drained, ignorant. ANT. *bright, sharp.* SEE STUPID

EMULATE *v.* [EM yoo layt] to imitate, especially in order to do as well as or better than another. *All the rookie basketball players tended to emulate the top scorer.* SYN. imitate, copy, *take after, use as a role model, model after, ape, mimic; challenge, contend, compete with, vie, match.

emulsion *n.* suspension.

enable *v.* empower, capacitate, allow, endow, authorize, invest, qualify, warrant, sanction, permit, license. ANT. *hinder, block, prevent.*

enabler *n.* facilitator, helper, aid, assistant, contributor, cooperator, accomplice, abettor, partner in crime.

enact *v.* legislate, pass, ratify, sanction, decree, effectuate, institute, establish, order, ordain. ANT. *veto, repeal, reject, table.*

enamel *n.* coating, finish, protective layer, paint, lacquer, varnish, glaze.

ENAMORED *a.* [i NAM urd] in love, charmed. *She is enamored with Hawaii.* SYN. in love, charmed, captivated, infatuated, enthralled, bewitched, entranced, taken, smitten, fascinated, *stuck on. ANT. *repelled, adverse to.*

encampment *n.* camp, campsite, bivouac, stopover, rest area, base.

encapsulate *v.* **1.** summarize, epitomize, condense. **2.** encase, enclose, wrap, box, pack, envelop.

enchant *v.* mesmerize, bewitch, spellbind, charm, captivate, cast a spell on, *sweep off feet, allure, entrance, hypnotize, beguile.

enchanting *a.* mesmerizing, bewitching, spellbinding, charming, captivating, alluring, entrancing, hypnotic, beguiling, enthralling.

enchantress *n.* seductress, sorceress, witch, charmer, siren, *femme fatale, *Circe.

encircle *v.* encompass, surround, circle, circumscribe, band, ring, girdle, envelop, hoop, wreath.

enclose *v.* **1.** SHUT IN surround, *hem in, pen, confine, imprison, encompass, fence off, circumscribe, corral. **2.** INSERT enter, put in, include, add.

encode v. encrypt, cryptograph, cipher, cypher, make secret.

encore n. reprise, return, curtain call, standing ovation, command performance, recall.

encompass v. 1. SURROUND circle, encircle, circumscribe, ring, envelop. 2. INCLUDE contain, comprehend, embody, comprise, take in, cover, embrace. ANT. 2. exclude, omit.

encounter n. meeting, confrontation, conjunction, brush.

encounter v. meet, confront, come face to face, happen upon, chance upon, cross paths, see, accost, face, bump into.

encourage v. hearten, embolden, spur, inspire, rally, reassure, root for, *buck up, *psyche up, foster, steel, fortify, support, cheer, buoy, *give a shot in the arm. ANT. discourage, dishearten, *take the wind out of one's sails, deflate.

encouragement n. support, assurance, help, buoying, heartening, *bucking up, boost, reassurance, *shot in the arm, *pep talk, stimulus, lift, inspiration, cheer, fortitude, *psyching up, backing. ANT. discouragement, disheartening, deflation.

ENCROACH v. [en KROCH] to intrude or trespass, to move into another's domain. Humans continue to encroach upon wildlife habitat. SYN. intrude, trespass, invade, infringe, *horn in, usurp, *make inroads, interlope, impose upon, overstep the bounds, infiltrate.

encumber v. burden, weigh down, hinder, impede, obstruct, hold up, cramp, saddle, oppress, hamper, handicap. ANT. free, facilitate, lighten.

encumbrance n. burden, weight, hindrance, impediment, obstruction, saddle, handicap, millstone, cross.

encyclopedia n. reference work, tome, cyclopedia, lexicon, glossary, fact book, book of knowledge, education book, volume.

encyclopedic a. broad, extensive, comprehensive, complete, diverse, wide-ranging, catholic, general, exhaustive, thorough. ANT. limited, specific, narrow.

end n. 1. LIMIT terminus, borderline, extremity, boundary, edge, extent, tip, point, pale. 2. FINISH completion, conclusion, close, stop, cessation, finale, finis, termination, expiration, windup, consummation. 3. PURPOSE aim, intention, object, reason, point, objective, motivation. 4. RESULT outcome, consequence, effect, upshot. ANT. 2. start, beginning, opening. SEE DEATH

end v. stop, finish, cease, wrap up, conclude, close, terminate, wind down, consummate, expire, discontinue, desist, drop. ANT. start, begin, open.

endanger v. imperil, jeopardize, expose, tempt fate, put at risk, compromise, hazard, venture, threaten. ANT. safeguard, protect, defend.

endangered a. imperiled, facing extinction, jeopardized, at risk, threatened. ANT. secure.

endearing a. lovable, charming, captivating, winning, adorable, sweet, dear, cuddly. ANT. repulsive.

endeavor n. attempt, effort, try, striving, venture, enterprise, undertaking, trial, *shot, crack, *whack, exertion.

endeavor v. attempt, try, strive, venture, make an effort, struggle, tackle, undertake, essay, labor, *have a go, *take a crack at.

endemic a. local, regional, localized, restricted to, confined to, peculiar to. ANT. unconfined, international.

ending n. finish, closing, close, completion, finale, denouement, resolution, outcome, curtains, termination, windup, last gasp, final word.

endless a. interminable, neverending, eternal, infinite, forever, unending, ceaseless, perpetual, continuous, incessant, relentless, *Sisyphean, everlasting. ANT. finite, limited, temporary.

endorphin n. hormone, natural painkiller, opiate.

endorse v. sanction, approve, recommend, support, back, back up, vouch for, certify, advocate, stand behind, warrant, *give one's stamp of approval. ANT. reject, repudiate.

endorsement n. sanction, approval, recommendation, support, backing, certification, advocacy, warranty, *stamp of approval, authorization, okay.

endow v. provide, grant, fund, contribute, equip, bestow, bequeath, enrich, favor, furnish, supply, appoint, vest. ANT. divest, deprive.

endowment n. 1. GIFT grant, contribution, bestowal, bequest, funding, donation, provision, subsidy, benefaction. 2. ATTRIBUTE natural gift, genius, quality, talent, asset, aptitude.

endurance n. stamina, fortitude, perseverance, grit, *guts, *stick-to-itiveness, backbone, staying power, tenacity, *starch, *moxie, *heart, strength, hardiness.

endure v. **1.** BEAR hold out, live through, withstand, tolerate, *stick it out, brave, suffer, weather, stand, *ride out, take it, *go through the mill, *hang in, brook. **2.** CONTINUE persist, last, abide, perdure, sustain, go on, outlast, survive, prevail. ANT. *1. give out, cave in, collapse, quit. 2. peter out, die, end.*

enemy n. foe, adversary, antagonist, opponent, rival, villain, contestant, hostile party, contender, nemesis, archenemy, *bad guy. "[One who] strengthens our nerves and sharpens our skill."—Edmund Burke. "An injured friend."—Thomas Jefferson.

energetic a. vigorous, peppy, active, lively, industrious, *zippy, tireless, spirited, full of vim and vigor, *bright-eyed and bushytailed, vibrant, sprightly, *high octane. ANT. *tired, slothful, lethargic.*

energize v. activate, invigorate, stimulate, spark, enliven, electrify, pep up, refresh, turn on, *pump up. ANT. *exhaust, sap, tire.*

energy n. power, force, steam, strength, juice, vigor, zip, *get-up-and- go, vitality, pep, zest, verve, life, punch.

ENERVATE v. [EN ur vate] to weaken or debilitate. *Smoking tends to enervate the immune system.* SYN. weaken, debilitate, sap, enfeeble, tire, exhaust, wear out, prostrate, fatigue, devitalize. ANT. *fortify, strengthen, invigorate.*

enfeeble v. weaken, deplete, enervate, debilitate, deplete, sap, emasculate, fatigue, exhaust, diminish, *take the starch out of.

enfilade n. barrage, gunfire, rake, sweeping fire.

enfold v. embrace, wrap.

enforce v. compel, impose, press, make, crack down, coerce, implement, oblige, *clamp down, prosecute, *strong-arm, bully.

enforcement n. compulsion, imposition, press, crackdown, coercion, implementation, obligation, prosecution, *strong-arm tactics, bullying, control, duress.

engage v. **1.** CONTRACT FOR employ, hire, enlist, commission, sign on, retain, enroll, secure, appoint, charter. **2.** ENGROSS occupy, captivate, absorb, hold, grip, rivet, arrest, interest, preoccupy, fascinate. **3.** PLEDGE promise, bind, commit, obligate, contract, betroth, affiance.

engaged a. **1.** BETROTHED pledged, spoken for, affianced, committed, plighted, bound. **2.** BUSY occupied, working, involved, employed, preocccupied, *tied up, operating, diverted. ANT. *1. single, unattached. 2. idle, free.*

engagement n. **1.** BETROTHAL pledge, promise, commitment, plight, troth. "In war, a battle. In love, the salubrious calm that precedes the hostilities."—Gideon Wurdz. **2.** APPOINTMENT date, meeting, commitment, tryst. **3.** BATTLE encounter, combat, conflict, confrontation, skirmish, action.

engaging a. charming, pleasing, attractive, magnetic, agreeable, sweet, appealing, winning, likable, fetching, captivating, pleasant. ANT. *unattractive, repellant, unappealing.*

ENGENDER v. [en JEN dur] to bring about; cause. *Understanding will engender peace.* SYN. produce, bring about, cause, give rise to, effect, arouse, stimulate, generate, create, spawn, breed.

engine n. motor, turbine, dynamo, power plant, powerhouse, *workhorse, generator, mechanism. SEE MOTOR

engineer n. builder, manager, architect, designer, planner, inventor, operator, tinkerer, troubleshooter, innovator.

engineer v. plan, devise, scheme, arrange, swing, set up, direct, *rig, mastermind, *call the shots, finagle, concoct.

engorged a. congested, full, filled, swollen, distended, bloated. ANT. *empty.*

engrave v. etch, cut, incise, carve, inscribe, scratch, chisel, imprint, ingrain.

engross v. absorb, occupy, rivet, fascinate, involve, engage, captivate, enthrall, grip, spellbind.

engrossed a. absorbed, rapt, lost in, riveted, involved, engaged, captivated, enthralled, deep in, *wrapped up in, gripped, fascinated. ANT. *distracted.*

engrossing a. absorbing, riveting, involving, engaging, captivating, enthralling, gripping, fascinating, occupying. ANT. *boring, dull, tiresome.*

engulf v. surround, swallow up, overwhelm, overflow, envelop, enclose, deluge, submerge, inundate, bury.

enhance v. augment, better, improve, strengthen, embellish, complement, raise, increase, beautify, aggrandize, magnify. ANT. *diminish, strip, weaken.*

ENIGMA n. [ih NIG muh] a riddle, mystery or puzzle. *The origin of the universe remains an enigma.* SYN. riddle, mystery, puzzle, conundrum, question, secret, perplexity, *tough nut to crack, *mind-boggler, unknown.

enigmatic a. mysterious, puzzling, perplexing, questionable, unknown, mind-boggling, baffling, incomprehensible, unfathomable, inscrutable, bewildering, unexplainable. ANT. *known, obvious, clear, plain.*

enjoin *v.* **1.** COMMAND impose, order, dictate, prescribe, demand, ordain, decree, charge. **2.** PROHIBIT forbid, ban, proscribe, outlaw, interdict. ANT. 2. *allow, permit.*

enjoy *v.* take pleasure in, delight in, relish, appreciate, revel in, savor, luxuriate in, *eat up, *get a kick out of.

enjoyable *a.* delightful, satisfying, fun, pleasing, pleasant, amusing, entertaining, delicious, gratifying, *a lot of laughs, wonderful. ANT. *miserable, rotten, unpleasant.*

enjoyment *n.* pleasure, delight, fun, amusement, relish, happiness, entertainment, gratification, satisfaction, *laughs, diversion, gusto, recreation, delectation.

enlarge *v.* increase, expand, extend, spread, augment, magnify, broaden, lengthen, stretch, inflate, grow, swell, blow up, branch out, snowball. ANT. *shrink, diminish, lessen, decrease.*

enlargement *n.* increase, expansion, extension, spreading, augmentation, magnification, broadening, lengthening, stretch, inflation, growth, swelling, snowballing. ANT. *shrinkage, decrease, lessening.*

ENLIGHTEN *v.* [en LITE un] to inform or instruct. *Obedience school will enlighten you and your dog.* SYN. inform, instruct, fill in, teach, edify, make one aware, apprise, school, illuminate, indoctrinate, ground, *open one's eyes. ANT. *put one in the dark, cloud, obfuscate, mystify.*

enlightened *a.* informed, aware, learned, educated, knowledgeable, apprised, grounded, knowing, open-minded, cultivated, *hip. ANT. *uninformed, *in the dark, ignorant.*

enlist *v.* sign up, enroll, draft, recruit, induct, conscript, join, volunteer, muster, register, engage.

enliven *v.* stimulate, spark, animate, *jumpstart, excite, invigorate, charge up, electrify, energize, vitalize, inflame, kindle. ANT. *dampen, extinguish, quiet.*

en masse *adv.* together, as a body, in a group, jointly, as one, ensemble. ANT. *individually, separately.*

enmesh *v.* entangle, catch, snarl, trap, knot, engage.

ENMITY *n.* [EN muh tee] hatred, deep hostility. *There was obvious enmity between the divorcing couple.* SYN. hatred, hostility, antagonism, animosity, malevolence, acrimony,

spite, bitterness, loathing, venom, malice, *bad blood. ANT. *love, adoration, affection.*

ENNUI *n.* [AN WEE] boredom and the listlessness that accompanies it. *The students suffered from a severe case of ennui.* SYN. boredom, listlessness, restlessness, languor, weariness, lassitude, malaise, blahs, tedium, doldrums. ANT. *excitement.*

enormity *n.* **1.** WICKEDNESS outrageousness, evil, monstrousness, atrocity, viciousness, ferocity, savagery, ruthlessness. **2.** HUGENESS largeness, vastness, size, bulk, greatness, magnitude, prodigiousness. ANT. 1. *morality, goodness, virtue.* 2. *smallness, triviality.*

enormous *a.* huge, gigantic, stupendous, immense, vast, gargantuan, mammoth, Brobdingnagian, prodigious, massive, astronomical, colossal, titanic, monstrous, towering. ANT. *tiny, pint-sized, pocket-sized, diminutive.*

enough *a.* sufficient, ample, plenty, adequate, acceptable, satisfactory, abundant. ANT. *short, wanting, scant, deficient.*

enquire *v.* look into, explore, query. SEE INQUIRE

enquiry *n.* inquest, probe. SEE INQUIRY

enrage *v.* incense, anger, infuriate, inflame, *piss off, madden, *make blood boil, *burn up, *tee off *get Irish up, rile. SEE ANGER, ANGRY

enraged *a.* furious, incensed, irate, angry, infuriated, inflamed, mad, *gone ballistic, *pissed, *boiling. ANT. *pleased, delighted, happy.*

enrich *v.* enhance, add, upgrade, improve, endow, cultivate, embellish, aggrandize, *sweeten, refine, *beef up. ANT. *degenerate, cheapen, impoverish.*

enroll *v.* register, record, enter, enlist, sign up, join, matriculate, admit.

ensconce *v.* settle, fix, curl up, nestle, seat, place, conceal, shelter, hide, cover.

ensemble *n.* **1.** UNIT collection, group, whole, aggregate. **2.** OUTFIT *getup, suit, coordinates. **3.** ENTERTAINMENT GROUP trio, quartet, group, orchestra, band, troupe, company, repertory.

enshrine *v.* cherish, sanctify, exalt, consecrate, hallow, deify, revere, immortalize, glorify.

enshroud *v.* shroud, cover, veil, conceal, cloak, mask.

ensign *n.* flag, standard, banner, pennant, streamer, insignia.

enslave *v.* subjugate, dominate, control, enthrall, indenture, subject, yoke, fetter, master, *jackboot into submission, coerce, subdue.

ensnare v. snare, catch, trap, bag, snag, net, entrap, entangle, take in.

ensue v. follow, succeed, result, come to pass, come out of, derive, spring from.

ensuing a. following, succeeding, resulting, subsequent, consequent, next, after. ANT. *preceeding, prior, earlier.*

ensure v. assure, make sure, guarantee, warrant, insure, certify, secure, safeguard, confirm.

entail v. involve, necessitate, require, call for, occasion, include, contain, incorporate.

entangle v. enmesh, tangle, snarl, entrap, involve, embroil, mix up, rope in, intertwine, trap, catch up, *suck in.

entanglement n. knot, snare, difficulty, problem, quandary, predicament, embroilment, web, mess, involvement, mix-up.

entente n. understanding, agreement, accord, rapprochement, settlement, arrangement, conciliation.

enter v. **1.** COME OR GO IN gain entree, make an entrance, infiltrate, intrude, set foot in, penetrate, *burst in, *breeze in, trespass. **2.** BEGIN start, commence, set out, launch. **3.** JOIN enlist in, enroll, embark on, sign up. **4.** RECORD register, log in, sign up, post, inscribe. ANT. *1. exit, leave.*

enterprise n. **1.** UNDERTAKING venture, project, job, campaign, adventure, concern, scheme, operation, task, endeavor, cause, business, crusade. **2.** EFFORT initiative, drive, determination, ambition, gumption, intensity, aggressiveness, industry, boldness, hustle. ANT. *2. sloth, laziness.*

enterprising a. ambitious, industrious, aggressive, bold, venturesome, audacious, earnest, resourceful, driving, hustling, inventive, energetic. ANT. *lazy, indolent, slothful, passive.*

entertain v. **1.** AMUSE interest, divert, engross, engage, absorb, rivet, beguile, *wow, pique, stimulate, enthrall. **2.** TO SHOW HOSPITALITY TO receive, host, accommodate, *wine and dine, feed, treat, regale, fete, have guests, give a party. **3.** CONSIDER think about, ponder, contemplate, muse over, deliberate, mind, weigh, heed.

entertainment n. amusement, diversion, recreation, fun, distraction, *ball, *laughs, enjoyment, merrymaking, pastime, divertissement, good time, *high time.

enthrall v. captivate, hold spellbound, charm, fascinate, rivet, beguile, bewitch, mesmerize, entrance, thrill, hypnotize, transfix.

enthusiasm n. eagerness, keenness, feeling, fervor, interest, zeal, passion, vivacity, ardor, relish, exuberance, verve, spirit, elan. "Energy that boils over and runs down the side of the pot."—Arnold Glasow. "A distemper of youth."—Ambrose Bierce. "Fire under control."—Norman Vincent Peale. "The great hill-climber."—Elbert Hubbard. ANT. *apathy, indifference, passivity.*

enthusiast n. zealot, fan, devotee, aficionado, fanatic, disciple, addict, buff, *freak, *nut, *bug.

enthusiastic a. eager, keen, fervent, interested, zealous, passionate, ardent, exuberant, spirited, wholehearted, avid, hot, rabid. ANT. *apathetic, indifferent, halfhearted.*

entice v. tempt, lure, tantalize, allure, inveigle, seduce, bait, draw, attract, persuade, cajole, coax.

entire a. total, whole, complete, full, aggregate, all, thorough, undivided, uncut, intact, unmitigated, uncompromised. ANT. *partial, incomplete.*

entitle v. authorize, allow, qualify, license, warrant, empower, enable, sanction.

entitlement program n. benefit program, government benefit, government assistance, social security, relief program, welfare program, social program, *safety net. SEE GOVERNMENT, POLITICS

entity n. being, thing, it, individual, soul, unit, existence, life, object, creature, essence.

entomb v. bury, inter, sepulcher, inhume, *lay to rest.

entourage n. attendants, train, followers, retinue, staff, court, cortege, escort, bodyguards, *toadies.

entrails n. intestine, viscera, internal organs, guts, bowels, innards, vitals.

entrance n. **1.** DOORWAY ingress, portal, access, gate, inlet, porch, vestibule, foyer, portico, threshold. **2.** ADMISSION admittance, ingress, passage, entry, approach, access.

entrance v. captivate, bewitch, charm, hypnotize, mesmerize, spellbind, enchant, enthrall, allure.

entrant n. competitor, contestant, entry, player, opponent.

entrap v. lure, allure, tempt, entice, *suck in, *set up, *lead on, trap, bait, inveigle, implicate, incriminate, nail.

entreat v. implore, beseech, beg, plead, petition, appeal, supplicate, pray.

entreaty n. plea, appeal, supplication, solicitation, prayer, bid, cry, request, petition, imploration.

entrée n. **1.** ADMITTANCE access. SEE ENTRY **2.**

DISH main course, meal, supper, dinner, pièce de résistance.

entrenched *a.* fixed, secured, established, deeprooted, deep-seated, embedded, ingrained, ensconced, dug in, grounded, settled. ANT. *capricious, changeable, inconstant, temporary.*

ENTREPRENEUR *n.* [on truh pruh NUR] one who starts and runs her own business. *Several entrepreneurs moved in to revitalize the downtown district.* SYN. businessman/woman, industrialist, go-getter, producer, promoter, impresario, undertaker, enterpriser, developer, capitalist, tycoon, venture capitalist, magnate, employer.

ENTROPY *n.* [EN truh pee] the ongoing deterioration of everything, but especially systems and societies. *The delapidated camp was a prime example of entropy at work.* SYN. deterioration, degeneration, regression, worsening, going from bad to worse, slipping away, falling apart, decline, disintegration, decay, transformation.

entrust *v.* commit, confide, turn over, consign, charge, vest, assign, delegate, invest, hand over, authorize.

entry *n.* **1.** ENTRANCE access, door, ingress, inlet, passageway, portal, opening, gate, foyer, approach. **2.** ADMITTANCE admission, access, entre e, intrusion, trespass.

entwine *v.* braid, intertwine, wind. SEE TWIST

enumerate *v.* count off, list, number, tally, itemize, calculate, sum, compute, inventory, name, run down, tick off.

ENUNCIATE *v.* [e NUN see ayt] to pronounce clearly. *She enunciated each word with great care.* SYN. pronounce, articulate, form words, express, utter, intone, voice, mouth, accentuate, modulate, frame each word carefully, inflect.

envelop *v.* enclose, encase, surround, engulf, enfold, contain, sheathe, wrap, shroud, overlay.

envelope *n.* wrapper, cover, case, jacket, sheath, casing, skin, shell, hull, mailer, *jiffy bag.

envious *a.* covetous, jealous, resentful, begrudging, yearning, *drooling over, green with envy, emulous, discontent. ANT. *contented, satisfied, fulfilled.*

environment *n.* surroundings, habitat, setting, environs, milieu, domain, terrain, turf, neighborhood, territory, *stomping grounds, world, atmosphere, climate, element, medium.

environmentalist *n.* conservationist, ecologist, naturalist, *tree hugger.

environs *n.* surroundings, environment, vicinity, neighborhood, territory, outskirts, suburbs.

envisage *v.* visualize, conceive of, see, imagine, envision, conceptualize, picture, fancy, think of.

ENVOY *n.* [ON voy] a representative or messenger. *The United States sent a special envoy to its embassy in Iran.* SYN. representative, messenger, agent, emissary, courier, delegate, diplomat, ambassador, attaché, minister.

envy *n.* covetousness, jealousy, grudgingness, rivalry, *green-eyed monster, resentment, spite, lusting, wanting, longing, greed. "The sincerest form of flattery."—John C. Collins. "The green sickness."—Shakespeare. "Self-made hurts."—Shaikh Saadi. "The tax which all distinction must pay."—Emerson.

envy *v.* covet, begrudge, grudge, resent, be green with envy, be jealous of, lust after, want, desire, *eat one's heart out, *drool over.

eon *n.* age, eternity, ages, years.

EPHEMERAL *a.* [i FEM ur al] lasting only a short time. *Fads are usually ephemeral.* SYN. short-lived, transient, brief, fleeting, temporary, transitory, of short duration, evanescent, momentary, *gone in a heartbeat. ANT. *long-lived, permanent, everlasting.*

epic *a.* huge, grand, legendary, mythical, exaggerated, fabulous, Homeric, heroic, majestic, sublime. ANT. *small, insignificant, shortlived, modest.*

epicure *n.* gourmet, epicurian, gourmand, gastronome, connoisseur, glutton, bon vivant, hedonist.

epidemic *n.* spread, contagion, infection, disease, plague, pestilence, endemic, pandemic.

epidemic *a.* spreading, contagious, infectious, catching, widespread, endemic, pandemic, rampant, rife, prevalent. ANT. *local, limited, confined.*

epigram *n.* observation, witticism, aphorism, quip, adage, slogan, bon mot, pun, motto, saying. "A light vessel carrying a heavy load."—Jacob Klatzkin. "A dash of wit and a jigger of wisdom, flavored with surprise."—Elbert Hubbard.

epilepsy *n.* seizure disorder, catalepsy, convulsions, fits, neurological disorder.

WORD FIND
major seizure and loss of consciousness: grand mal
medication: Dilantin
momentary unconsciousness without convulsions: petite mal
symptom of impending seizure: aura
SEE DISEASE, MEDICINE

epilogue n. afterword, conclusion, last word, follow-up, postscript, addendum, swan song, coda. SEE BOOK

EPIPHANY n. a great revelatory experience or insight; an illumination of a truth. *I experienced a great epiphany the first time I meditated; this was a great way to seek spiritual bliss.* SYN. insight, revelation, realization, illumination, grasp, understanding; appearance, manifestation.

episode n. incident, event, occurrence, happening, occasion, experience, action, installment, chapter, part.

episodic a. intermittent, sporadic, segmented, irregular, sequential. ANT. *frequent, recurrent, regular.*

epistle n. communication, message, composition, missive. SEE LETTER

epitaph n. inscription, memorial, legend, commemoration, hic jacet, *last word. *"An inscription showing that virtues acquired by death have a retroactive effect."*—Ambrose Bierce.

epithet n. nickname, name, label, pet name, appellation, designation, tag, sobriquet.

EPITOME n. [i PIT uh mee] the perfect representation of something. *Michael Jordan is the epitome of a great athlete.* SYN. representation, archetype, example, embodiment, typification, ultimate, quintessence, *last word, model.

epitomize v. typify, represent, exemplify, embody.

epoch n. era, period, time, age, span, interval.

equable a. even, steady, uniform, unvarying, consistent, regular, unchanging, constant, stable, serene, tranquil. ANT. *unequal, fluctuating.*

equal n. peer, counterpart, equivalent, compeer, coequal, double, fellow, match, alter ego.

equal v. match, accord with, line up with, align, correspond, parallel, *stack up against, mirror.

equal a. even, same, identical, balanced, uniform, alike, commensurate, parallel, *even Stephen, level, matching, comparable, *on common footing, *on a level playing field. ANT. *unequal, uneven, dissimilar, disparate.*

equality n. parity, par, sameness, equivalence, likeness, evenness, balance, uniformity, fairness. *"The centre and circumference of all democracy."*—Herman Melville. ANT. *inequality, disparity, unfairness, injustice.*

EQUANIMITY n. [EE kwuh NIM i tee] composure, calm. *He handled the crisis with equanimity.* SYN. composure, calmness, sangfroid, serenity, nonchalance, coolness, placidity, aplomb, tranquility, poise, presence of mind. ANT. *hysteria, panic.*

equate v. liken, associate, compare, relate, parallel.

EQUILIBRIUM n. [EE kwuh LIB ree um] balance, stability, composure. *The disaster challenged her equilibrium.* SYN. balance, stability, equanimity, calmness, levelheadedness, poise, sangfroid, composure, aplomb. ANT. *instability.*

equip v. outfit, furnish, rig, supply, gird, fit out, accoutre, arm, gear, appoint, *heel, provision.

equipment n. gear, apparatus, accessories, furnishings, supplies, contrivances, tools, rigging, trappings, appliances, fittings, tackle, machinery, paraphernalia.

EQUITABLE a. [EK wi tuh bul] fair, just. *The mediator helped the two sides reach an equitable agreement.* SYN. fair, just, equal, impartial, square, evenhanded, proportionate, honest, *even Stephen, unbiased, rightful, proper. ANT. *inequitable, unfair, unjust, partial.*

equity n. fairness, justice, impartiality, evenhandedness, honesty, fair play, objectivity, neutrality, rightness.

equivalent n. equal, counterpart, same, twin, match, mirror image, double, fellow, peer, *carbon copy.

equivalent a. equal, same, alike, synonymous, tantamount, analogous, identical, even, commensurate, *six of one, half dozen of another, correlative, comparable. ANT. *unequal, differing.*

equivocal a. ambiguous, vague, duplicitous, uncertain, indefinite, unclear, misleading, evasive, undecided, hazy, indeterminate. ANT. *definite, clear, plain.*

EQUIVOCATE v. [i KWIV uh kate] to use vague or ambiguous language, usually to evade. *The politician would equivocate to avoid the tough questions.* SYN. hedge, evade, waffle, hem and haw, dodge, *weasel out, *beat around the bush, *cloud the issue, double-talk, mince words, sidestep, *dance around the issue, *perform a verbal hatdance around.

ER *n.* emergency room, trauma center, critical care facility, triage room, medical crisis unit, intensive care unit. SEE HOSPITAL, MEDICINE

era *n.* period, time, age, epoch, days, interval, span. SEE TIME

eradicate *v.* annihilate, uproot, erase, remove, eliminate, extirpate, exterminate, destroy, expunge, abolish, do away with, obliterate.

erase *v.* rub off, expunge, remove, wipe out, delete, efface, strike, obliterate, nullify, scratch, blue-pencil, wash out.

erect *v.* construct, build, assemble, *slap together, fabricate, raise, frame, pitch, put up, devise, form.

erect *a.* upright, straight up, standing, perpendicular, vertical. ANT. *flaccid, flat, horizontal.*

erection *n.* **1.** CONSTRUCTION building, assembly, fabrication, framework, formation, structure, edifice. **2.** TUMESCENCE *hard-on. SEE PENIS

ergo *adv.* consequently, therefore, thus, accordingly.

ERGONOMICS *n.* [ur go NOM iks] the science of designing spaces and equipment that facilitiate human comfort and productivity, especially for work. *An ergonomic study showed that back problems decreased when chairs were adjusted to the proper height.* SYN. design science, efficiency science, science of productivity and design, streamlining, injury-proofing, accident-proofing.

erode *v.* wear away, corrode, waste, gnaw, consume, eat away, abrade, disintegrate, deteriorate.

EROGENOUS *a.* [i ROJ uh nus] pertaining to parts of the body that can be aroused by sexual stimulation. *Erogenous zones are rich in nerve endings.* SYN. erotogenic, erotic, sexual, amatory, sensuous, sensual, *hot, rousing, X-rated, libidinal, carnal.

Eros *n.* **1.** GOD OF LOVE son of Aphrodite. **2.** LOVE sex drive, libido, sexual urge, *urge to merge, desire, yearning, hunger, eroticism.

erosion *n.* wear, deterioration, corrosion, disintegration, destruction, attrition, abrasion, wasting.

erotic *a.* amatory, sexual, carnal, lusty, sensual, erogenous, romantic, libidinous, arousing, amorous, *hot, fleshly, *blue, titillating, spicey, *kinky, lascivious, passionate.

erotica *n.* pornography, sexual imagery, X-rated materials, sexually explicit art/literature, adult materials.

eroticism *n.* sexual excitement, arousal, stimulation, titillation, *horniness, erotomania.

err *v.* make a mistake, miscalculate, misjudge, misstep, *slip up, blunder, *goof, *blow it, *muff, go astray, misconstrue, misunderstand.

errand *n.* task, mission, chore, trip, jaunt, *run.

errant *a.* wrong, deviant, erring, astray, *off the straight and narrow, wayward, wandering. ANT. *right, straight, on course.*

erratic *a.* straying, inconsistent, deviating, eccentric, irregular, unpredictable, unreliable, shifting, peculiar, wayward. ANT. *consistent, predictable, unchanging.*

ERRONEOUS *a.* [i RO nee us] mistaken, wrong. *The theory of green cheese on the moon is erroneous.* SYN. mistaken, wrong, incorrect, false, amiss, in error, inaccurate, *all wet, fallacious, unfounded, misguided, faulty. ANT. *correct, right, accurate.*

error *n.* mistake, inaccuracy, miscalculation, wrong, erratum, blunder, flub, *slip-up, boner, blooper, lapse, gaffe, wrongdoing, *howler, *boo-boo, misconception. "The best teachers."—James A. Froude.

ersatz *a.* substitute, artificial, synthetic, fake, simulated, man-made, imitation, *bogus, counterfeit. ANT. *genuine, real, actual, *the real McCoy.*

erstwhile *a.* former, bygone, past, late.

ERUDITE *a.* [ER yoo DITE, ER oo DITE] highly educated, learned. *The college town was a bastion of erudite professors.* SYN. educated, scholarly, learned, intellectual, well-read, well-schooled, pedantic, highbrow, brainy, literate, well-versed, bookish. ANT. *uneducated, ignorant, illiterate, unschooled.*

erudition *n.* learning, scholarship, schooling, knowledge, book learning, refinement, wisdom, brains, education, higher education, pedantry, literacy.

erupt *v.* burst forth, explode, blow up, discharge, spout, rupture, gush, eject, emit, vent, spew, belch. SEE VOLCANO

eruption *n.* ejection, explosion, blowup, outburst, upheaval, expulsion, cataclysm, blast, detonation, gushing, outpouring, surge, paroxysm. SEE VOLCANO

escalate *v.* increase, rise, mount, climb, intensify, heighten, grow, enlarge, deepen, worsen. ANT. *decrease, shrink, lessen.*

escapade *n.* prank, adventure, antic, caper,

practical joke, stunt, tomfoolery, high jinks, *shenanigans.

escape n. getaway, fast break, flight, evasion, *the slip, breakout, extrication, dodging, departure, desertion, *disappearing act.

escape v. get away, break out, extricate, loose, liberate, break, bolt, *fly the coop, cut loose, elude, dodge, abscond, elope, *take on the lam, skip, flee, decamp, disappear.

escapee n. fugitive, runaway, refugee, evacuee.

ESCHEW v. [es CHOO] stay away from, avoid, shun. *He has chosen to eschew smoking for health reasons.* SYN. avoid, shun, forego, abstain, swear off, forswear, renounce, give up, shy away from, refrain from, *turn up one's nose at. ANT. *take up, indulge in, embrace.*

escort n. attendant, chaperon, guardian, accompaniment, companion, body guard, guide, protector, retinue, cortege, entourage, convoy.

escort v. accompany, attend, protect, guide, usher, chaperone, guard, conduct, look after, convoy, defend.

escrow n. pledge, collateral, security, account, insurance, surety, guarantee, bond, deed.

Eskimo n. Innuit, Alaskan, Aleut, Yuit.

WORD FIND
boat: umiak, oomiac, kayak
boot: mukluk
dog: husky, malamute
hooded jacket: anorak, parka
house: igloo, topek
sledge: komatik

esophagus n. gullet, food tube, throat.

ESOTERIC a. [ES uh TER ik] understood by only a few, hard to understand. *Einstein's theories are esoteric.* SYN. abstruse, arcane, recondite, profound, deep, obscure, inscrutable, mysterious, incomprehensible, occult. ANT. *understandable, simple, obvious.*

especially adv. specifically, particularly, exclusively, expressly, principally, specially, chiefly.

espionage n. spying, intelligence, undercover work, surveillance, shadowing, tailing, wiretapping, *cloak and dagger, secret service.

esplanade n. walk, walkway, promenade, avenue, road, sidewalk, lane, mall.

ESPOUSE v. [e SPOUZ] to support or take up. *The group claims to espouse environmentalism, but the president holds stock in an oil company.* SYN. take up, support, advocate, adopt, abet, champion, embrace, back, stand up for, uphold, advance. ANT. *reject, detract, spurn.*

ESPRIT DE CORPS n. [es SPREE de COHR] group spirit or group loyalty, common bond between members of a group. *Good companies foster a certain esprit de corps.* SYN. group spirit, common bond, group loyalty, solidarity, team morale, camaraderie, fellowship, fraternity.

essay n. 1. COMPOSITION article, paper, discourse, treatise, theme, think piece, editorial, exposition, study, thesis. "A loose sally of the mind."—Samuel Johnson. SEE WRITING 2. TRY attempt, endeavor, bid, trial, *shot, *whack, venture.

essay v. try, attempt, endeavor, bid, venture, *take a shot, *take a whack, *take a stab at.

essence n. 1. HEART soul, core, kernel, distillate, marrow, root, spirit, *meat, *nitty-gritty, gist, nature, quintessence, crux. 2. CONCENTRATE distillate, distillation, extract, elixir.

essential n. necessity, must, fundamental, basic, prerequisite, requirement, rudiment, cornerstone, indispensable element. ANT. *nonessential, extra.*

essential a. fundamental, important, vital, crucial, basic, prime, cardinal, necessary, elementary, indispensable, requisite. ANT. *incidental, unessential, peripheral, superfluous.*

establish v. 1. SET UP found, institute, create, make, organize, build, construct, erect, enact, install, place, originate. 2. PROVE demonstrate, substantiate, verify, authenticate, show, validate, corroborate.

establishment n. 1. FOUNDING formation, instituting, creation, organization, construction, origin. 2. INSTITUTION business, enterprise, concern, foundation, firm, company, corporation, association.

estate n. 1. ASSETS property, holdings, resources, wealth, fortune, belongings, possessions. 2. MANOR acreage, holdings, dominion, domain, residence, plantation.

esteem n. regard, respect, admiration, approval, repute, liking, affection, veneration, reverence. ANT. *disrespect, contempt, disdain.*

esteem v. regard highly, respect, look up to, admire, idolize, value, prize, appreciate, revere, venerate. ANT. *disrespect, disdain, scorn.*

estimable a. worthy, respectable, admirable, deserving, esteemed, honorable, reputable, valued, exemplary, revered. ANT. *disrespected, disregarded, scorned, disliked.*

estimate n. guess, *guesstimate, calculation, rough figure, educated guess, *ballpark figure, projection, evaluation, judgment.

estimate v. guess, *guesstimate, calculate, give a rough figure, give an educated guess, *give a ballpark figure, project, evaluate, judge, reckon, appraise, gauge, suppose.

ESTRANGED *a.* [e STRANJD] alienated, removed from the friendship of others. *The worker quit and soon became estranged from his colleagues.* SYN. alienated, removed, dissociated, separated, at odds, distant, disaffected, *turned off, hostile, *at arm's length.

estuary *n.* mouth, outlet, waterway, drain, arm, tidewater, tideway.

etch *v.* engrave, carve, burn into, eat into, impress, inscribe, ingrain, corrode.

eternal *a.* endless, neverending, everlasting, unending, ageless, infinite, timeless, perpetual, enduring, interminable, undying, immortal. ANT. *finite, fleeting, ephemeral, temporary.*

eternity *n.* forever, infinity, immortality, world without end, timelessness, afterlife. "Where there is no where and no when."—Arthur Schopenhauer. "The sum of all sums."—Lucretius.

ETHEREAL *a.* [i THIR ee ul] otherworldly, celestial or heavenly. Also, light, airy and delicate. *His musical compositions were haunting and ethereal.* SYN. otherworldly, celestial, heavenly, divine, unearthly, sublime, supernal, light, airy, delicate, gossamer, exquisite, tenuous. ANT. *earthly, mundane, heavy, ponderous.*

ethical *a.* right, moral, righteous, fair, just, honest, good, honorable, upright, pure, conscientious, square, decent, noble, correct. ANT. *unethical, immoral, dishonest, dishonorable, corrupt.*

ethics *n.* principles, values, standards, morality, moral code, integrity, honesty, honor, *Ten Commandments, *Golden Rule, mores, conscience, decency. "The obligations of morality."—Lajos Kossuh. "The doctrine of manners."—Maunder.

ethnic *a.* cultural, racial, tribal, folk.

etiquette *n.* manners, courtesy, civility, politeness, decorum, proper conduct, propriety, formalities, protocol, social graces. "Behaving yourself a little better than is absolutely essential."—Will Cuppy.

EUGENICS *n.* [yoo JEN iks] the study or science of improving the human population through selective breeding. *Eugenics advocates fear the human population is deteriorating due to unchecked breeding.* SYN. hereditary control, selective breeding, selective sterilization, genetic purification, reproductive control, selective reproduction, study, science, school, movement. SEE SCIENCE

eulogize *v.* praise, extol, laud, pay tribute, honor, celebrate, extol, pay homage to, glorify. ANT. *damn, condemn, defame.*

eulogy *n.* praise, encomium, tribute, homage, panegyric, laudation, extolment, honor, acclamation. "Praise that is too much and too late."—Anon. ANT. *damning, condemnation, defamation.*

EUPHEMISM *n.* [YOO fuh miz um] a polite word or phrase used in place of an offensive word or phrase. *"Heck" is a euphemism for "hell."* SYN. polite word, delicacy, pretense, *prudism, *nice-nellyism, substitution, mild word, *weasel word. ANT. *crude term, crass term, *gutter word.*

euphonious *a.* harmonious, melodious, mellifluous, pleasing. ANT. *discordant.*

EUPHORIA *n.* [yoo FOR ee uh] high spirits, elation. *Spring always brings on a curious euphoria.* SYN. high spirits, happiness, joy, glee, elation, ecstasy, bliss, jubilation, rapture, *seventh heaven. ANT. *misery, depression, unhappiness.*

EUTHANASIA *n.* [yoo than AY szhuh] mercy killing. *Euthanasia proponents allow for suicide as a permanent treatment for misery.* SYN. mercy killing, assisted suicide, *putting out of misery, *putting to sleep, *pulling the plug, easing of death, *playing God.

WORD FIND

advocate, pioneer: Dr. Jack Kevorkian
doctor-assisted suicide: patholysis

SEE SUICIDE

evacuate *v.* **1.** LEAVE withdraw, vacate, abandon, *run for the hills, hightail, clear out, *skedaddle, *bail out, decamp. **2.** EMPTY discharge, remove, void, excrete, eliminate.

evade *v.* elude, dodge, sidestep, avoid, escape, *give the slip, bypass, duck, *steer clear of, *shake off, shirk, circumvent. ANT. *confront, face, meet.*

evaluate *v.* appraise, assess, size up, judge, grade, estimate, measure, assay, gauge, determine, rate, weigh.

evaluation *n.* appraisal, assessment, judgment, grading, estimate, measurement, assay, gauging, determination, rating, ranking.

evanescent *a.* transient, fleeting, ephemeral, vanishing. ANT. *permenant, solid.*

evangelism *n.* preaching the gospel, proselytizing, *bible thumping, *spreading the word, testifying, bearing witness.

evangelist n. preacher, revivalist, minister, missionary, crusader for God. SEE RELIGION

evaporate v. vaporize, dehydrate, dry up, dissipate, desiccate, vanish, disappear, disperse, evanesce.

evasion n. avoidance, dodge, elusion, escape, subterfuge, circumvention, shirking, equivocation, *song and dance. ANT. *confrontation, meeting.*

evasive a. deceitful, elusive, slippery, equivocal, shifty, hedging, tricky, shuffling, dissembling, misleading, dodging, prevaricative. ANT. *direct, forthright, straightforward.*

even v. equalize, balance, level, align, square, make flush, smooth, straighten.

even a. **1.** LEVEL, UNIFORM flat, straight, smooth, plumb, balanced, plane, flush, proportional. **2.** EQUAL same, balanced, fifty-fifty, on a par, parallel, fair, identical, uniform, *even Stephen. **3.** CALM tranquil, serene, peaceful, even-tempered, placid, steady, stable. ANT. *1. uneven, crooked, unbalanced. 2. unequal, disparate. 3. unstable, excitable.*

even-handed a. fair, impartial, just, equitable. ANT. *biased, one-sided.*

evening n. nightfall, twilight, dusk, sundown, sunset, eve, eventide, gloaming.

event n. happening, occurrence, incident, episode, affair, circumstance, situation, matter, experience, phenomenon.

even-tempered a. easy going, calm, relaxed, type B, cool. ANT. *anxious, hot-headed.*

eventful a. busy, active, lively, exciting, momentous, outstanding. ANT. *uneventful, slow.*

eventual a. ultimate, future, final, destined, coming, ensuing, inevitable, concluding, succeeding, resultant, consequent, imminent. ANT. *avoidable, escapable, preventable.*

eventually adv. ultimately, in the future, finally, inevitably, sooner or later, in the long run, consequently, in the end.

everlasting a. eternal, agelong, unending, enduring, infinite, immortal, timeless, undying, never ending, unremitting, interminable. ANT. *temporary, ephemeral, fleeting, finite.*

everyday a. **1.** DAILY diurnal, circadian. **2.** ROUTINE regular, ordinary, commonplace, customary, usual, run-of-the-mill, household, stock, workaday, *garden variety, normal. ANT. *special, rare, occasional.*

evict v. eject, remove, throw out, *show the door, expel, oust, kick out, dispossess.

evidence n. proof, substantiation, confirmation, documentation, corroboration, testimony, support, verification, indication, grounds, *smoking gun, clue.

WORD FIND

hiding of: suppression of evidence

inconclusive, indirect or inferred: circumstantial evidence

physical evidence displayed in court: exhibit

what someone other than the witness has said: hearsay

SEE COURT, LAW

evident a. obvious, clear, plain, manifest, express, visible, *plain as the nose on one's face, apparent, incontestable, palpable, conspicuous, *open and shut. ANT. *hidden, uncertain, obscure, unknown.*

evidently adv. apparently, ostensibly, seemingly, as far as one can tell, doubtless, to all appearances.

evil n. badness, immorality, sinfulness, indecency, criminality, wickedness, villainy, diabolism, iniquity, viciousness, vileness, lawlessness, cruelty, misfortune, ruin, affliction, harm, woe, catastrophe, disaster. "Whatever springs from weakness."—Nietzsche. "Good tortured by its own hunger and thirst."—Kahil Gibran. ANT. *morality, goodness, righteousness.*

evil a. immoral, bad, wicked, depraved, demonic, sinful, villainous, heinous, malicious, iniquitous, atrocious, foul, black, damnable, nefarious, malevolent. ANT. *good, moral, righteous, virtuous.*

evildoer n. criminal, devil, sociopath, psychopath, felon, *Hitler, murderer, sinner, lawbreaker, gangster, servant of Satan, gangbanger.

evince v. show, indicate, disclose, prove, display.

eviscerate v. disembowel, gut, clean.

evoke v. summon, call forth, conjure up, extract, elicit, invite, cause, stimulate, rouse, awaken.

evolution n. *survival of the fittest, phylogeny, development, progression, succession, transformation, change, growth, mutation, adaptation, social Darwinism, metamorphosis. "The preservation of favored races in the struggle for life."—Herbert Spencer. "Men risen out of the mire."—Don Marquis. "Natural selection."—Charles Darwin.

evolve v. develop, progress, transform, grow, mutate, metamorphose, *reinvent oneself, advance, emerge, adapt.

EXACERBATE v. [ek ZAS ur bate] to make worse, aggravate. *Lashing out will only exacerbate the situation.* SYN. make worse, aggravate, intensify, worsen, inflame, *fan the flames, provoke, deepen, *rub salt into the wound, *add insult to injury, heighten. ANT. *mitigate, mollify, soften, ease.*

exact v. insist on, demand, require, compel, force, extort, extract, wring, *put the squeeze on.

exact a. **1.** PRECISE accurate, *on the button, *on the money, correct, true, *on the mark, faithful, *right on, *dead on, *bullseye, perfect, literal. **2.** CAREFUL rigorous, meticulous, exacting, painstaking, punctilious, methodical. ANT. *1. inexact, inaccurate, approximate, rough. 2. careless.*

EXACTING a. [ig ZAK ting] extremely demanding. *Defusing a bomb is an exacting task.* SYN. demanding, strict, difficult, meticulous, rigorous, painstaking, hard, particular, fastidious, strenuous, burdensome, trying.

exaggerate v. amplify, overstate, hyperbolize, *make a mountain out of a mole hill, *play up, embellish, *lay it on thick, color, embroider, *stretch the truth, puff, magnify, *blow out of proportion. ANT. *understate, play down, minimize.*

exaggeration n. amplification, overstatement, hype, hyperbole, embellishment, coloring, embroidery, *a stretch, magnification, tall tale, *fish story, *tempest in a teapot. "A branch of lying."—Baltasar Gracian.

EXALT v. [eg ZAWLT] to raise up, honor or glorify. *Americans tend to exalt sports figures and movie stars.* SYN. raise up, honor, glorify, *put on a pedestal, elevate, extol, praise, acclaim, revere, idolize, pay tribute to, worship. ANT. *condemn, put down, ridicule.*

exalted a. raised up, glorified, *put on a pedestal, elevated, extolled, praised, esteemed, acclaimed, venerated, idolized, revered. ANT. *condemned, put down, ridiculed, belittled.*

examination n. exam, test, inspection, analysis, scrutiny, study, investigation, checkup, probe, review, survey, *once-over, assessment, quiz, questionnaire.

examine v. **1.** LOOK OVER, TEST check out, inspect, analyze, scrutinize, study, investigate, probe, review, survey, *perform a once-over, *eyeball, assess, scan, peruse, appraise, *size up. **2.** QUIZ grill, question, interrogate, cross-examine, *pump, *give the third degree, catechize.

example n. sample, specimen, sampling, instance, exemplar, model, paradigm, stereotype. "The best sermon."—Ben Franklin.

EXASPERATE v. [eg ZAS puh RATE] to irritate profoundly. *Husband and wife tend to exasperate each other in divorce court.* SYN. irritate, annoy, ruffle, upset, madden, provoke, *get under one's skin, infuriate, rile, irk, *push one's buttons, peeve, needle, vex, rankle, *rattle one's cage, *pull one's chain. ANT. *mollify, pacify.*

excavate v. dig out, hollow out, unearth, burrow, dredge, scoop, tunnel, backhoe, channel, hoe, shovel out.

excavation n. pit, hollow, mine, ditch. SEE HOLE

excavator n. earth mover, *digger, backhoe.

exceed v. surpass, best, pass, transcend, eclipse, top, outdo, excel, outshine, overshadow, outrank, outdistance, overwhelm, *go above and beyond.

exceedingly adv. extremely, very, exceptionally, especially, greatly, highly, vastly, enormously.

excel v. surpass, transcend, best, eclipse, top, outdo, excel, outshine, overshadow, outrank, outdistance, trump, *smoke the competition.

excellence n. superiority, greatness, supremacy, distinction, fineness, quality, eminence, merit, virtue, perfection. ANT. *inferiority, imperfection, mediocrity.*

excellent a. superior, great, supreme, superlative, fine, exceptional, first-rate, peerless, world-class, capital, *premium, champion, superb, *top-drawer, transcendent, *tops, outstanding, *bang-up, *bad, *A-1, awesome, super, *bitchin', brilliant, *spot-on. *def. ANT. *inferior, poor, mediocre, *crappy.*

except v. leave out, omit, exclude, pass over, eliminate, overlook, reject, remove, bar.

exception n. **1.** OMISSION exclusion, barring, expulsion, rejection. **2.** IRREGULARITY anomaly, special case, exemption, departure, oddity, deviation, rarity, quirk. **3.** OBJECTION complaint, challenge, reservation.

exceptional a. irregular, anomalous, extraordinary, atypical, outstanding, unusual, special, abnormal, singular, rare, remarkable, freakish, unique. ANT. *normal, typical, common, everyday.*

excerpt n. passage, section, cut, selection, part, extract, citation, clip, scene, bit.

excess n. **1.** SURPLUS glut, overabundance, superabundance, overkill, fat, redundancy, surfeit, superfluity, overrun, *too much of a good thing, plethora. **2.** OVERINDULGENCE extravagance, indulgence, immoderation, intemperance, lack of restraint, exorbitance. ANT. *1. dearth, shortage, lack. 2. moderation, abstinence.*

excessive *a.* overdone, extreme, too much, inordinate, immoderate, extravagant, exorbitant, overmuch, undue, superfluous, redundant. ANT. *moderate, reasonable, called-for.*

exchange *n.* trade, barter, swap, transaction, reciprocation, interchange, truck, commutation, quid pro quo, substitution, alternate.

exchange *v.* trade, barter, swap, transact, reciprocate, interchange, *give and take, commute, substitute, alternate, bandy.

excise *n.* toll, duty, tax.

excise *v.* remove, cut out, exscind, extirpate.

excitable *a.* emotional, high-strung, temperamental, fiery, volatile, hotheaded, *high octane, explosive, passionate, skittish, tempestuous, hot-blooded. ANT. *unflappable, imperturbable, tranquil.*

excite *v.* arouse, stir, stimulate, *spark, *turn on, thrill, provoke, inspire, electrify, inflame, whet, titillate, incite, agitate, fluster, *charge up, impassion. ANT. *bore, tranquilize, calm.*

excited *a.* aroused, stirred, stimulated, *turned on, thrilled, provoked, electrified, *fired up, agitated, enthusiastic, energized, keyed up, impassioned, *hyper, *wired, electrified, *adrenalized, titillated, *charged up, flustered, frenzied, agog, *sparked, *hot, frenetic. ANT. *sedate, tranquil, bored, comatose.*

excitement *n.* agitation, stimulation, furor, arousal, electricity, passion, enthusiasm, energy, titillation, sensation, frenzy, tizzy, fever, commotion, ferment, *fireworks, flurry, *kicks, perturbation, tumult, *hubbub, *hullabaloo, *white heat, *to-do, *hoopla. ANT. *somnolence, dormancy, boredom, stagnation.*

exciting *a.* arousing, agitating, stirring, stimulating, thrilling, electrifying, energizing, inflaming, titillating, *adrenalizing, *hair-raising, invigorating, exhilarating, breathtaking, *spine-tingling, sensational. ANT. *somnolent, boring, dull.*

exclaim *v.* cry out, ejaculate, shout, burst out, cry, blurt, holler, clamor, interject.

exclamation *n.* cry, outburst, ejaculation, shout, clamor, yell, interjection.

exclude *v.* shut out, keep out, bar, reject, debar, *blackball, forbid, prohibit, ostracize, expel,

oust, eject, evict, throw out, omit, rule out, refuse. ANT. *include, welcome, invite.*

exclusive *a.* **1.** RESTRICTED selective, closed, *snobbish, discriminating, preferential, privileged, clannish, segregated, cliquish, undemocratic. **2.** HIGH-PRICED posh, luxurious, *ritzy, expensive, swank, fashionable, chic. **3.** SOLE single, individual, only, complete, entire, total. ANT. *1. open, public, unrestricted, democratic. 2. modest, cheap, *cutrate, pedestrian. 3. shared, limited.*

excommunicate *v.* exclude, censure, bar, shut out, blackball, reject, ostracize, freeze out, *kick out, cut off, ban, deny, close the door on, banish.

excoriate *v.* **1.** STRIP OFF scratch off, rub off, abrade, chafe, flay. **2.** DENOUNCE attack, censure, vilify, criticize, condemn, reproach, upbraid, chastise.

excrement *n.* feces, dung, waste, manure, stools, *squat, droppings, guano, fecal matter, excreta, bowel movement.

excrete *v.* discharge, eliminate, defecate, evacuate, void, expel, exude, eject, pass.

excruciating *a.* unbearable, agonizing, tortuous, painful, insufferable, consuming, unendurable, *teeth-gritting, *wincing, paralyzing, debilitating, racking, stabbing. ANT. *soothing.* SEE PAIN, PAINFUL

exculpate *v.* absolve, forgive, clear, exonerate, acquit, vindicate, pardon, liberate. ANT. *indict, condemn, convict.*

excursion *n.* trip, journey, jaunt, outing, tour, expedition, junket, cruise, trek, side trip, ride, drive, hike, run.

excusable *a.* forgivable, condonable, pardonable, allowable, venial, understandable, extenuating, justifiable, reasonable, justified. ANT. *inexcusable, unforgivable, indefensible.*

excuse *n.* defense, justification, explanation, reason, rationalization, grounds, alibi, *song and dance, extenuation, *cover story, *whitewash, plea.

excuse *v.* pardon, forgive, absolve, condone, overlook, make allowances for, exonerate, acquit, reprieve, exempt, spare, liberate, *let go, extenuate.

execrable *a.* detestable, abominable, contemptible, horrible, deplorable, revolting, loathsome, sickening, odious, atrocious, despicable. ANT. *great, superb, fabulous, first-rate.*

execute *v.* **1.** PERFORM do, carry out, follow out, discharge, accomplish, fulfill, achieve, effect, effectuate, complete. **2.** PUT TO DEATH kill, murder, assassinate, hang, behead, electrocute, lynch.

execution *n.* **1.** PERFORMANCE OF A DUTY implementation, discharge, accomplishment, fulfillment, achievement, completion, consummation. **2.** PUTTING TO DEATH death penalty, capital punishment, killing, hanging, beheading, lethal injection, electrocution, slaying, lynching, gassing, guillotining. **3.** STYLE manner, technique, touch, performance.

executive *n.* manager, administrator, chief executive officer (CEO), supervisor, director, head, *top brass, officer, *big wheel, *higher-up, boss, *white-collar worker, *big cheese, *big toad in the puddle. "[One] who isn't worried about his own career but rather the careers of those who work for him."—Henry Burns. "One who can delegate all the responsibility, shift all the blame, and appropriate all the credit."—Bobby Vinton.

WORD FIND

recruiter: headhunter

executive *a.* administrative, managerial, decision-making, directorial, authoritative, supervisory. ANT. *menial, servile.*

exemplar *n.* model, archetype, pattern, ideal, example, paradigm, standard, prototype, paragon, exemplification.

EXEMPLARY *a.* [eg ZEM pluh ree] serving as a model worth copying. *The exemplary student received a full scholarship to college.* SYN. model, worthy, admirable, ideal, praiseworthy, illustrative, laudable, superior, commendable, outstanding, classic, prototypical. ANT. *awful, poor, lousy, substandard.*

EXEMPLIFY *v.* [eg ZEM pluh FYE] to serve as a good example. *Youths often think that athletes exemplify only good characteristics.* SYN. epitomize, typify, represent, illustrate, demonstrate, symbolize, stand for, personify, embody.

exempt *a.* free from, excused, immune, unrestricted, discharged, privileged, unrestrained, excluded, spared from, absolved, *off the hook. ANT. *bound, liable, subject to.*

exercise *n.* **1.** WORKOUT aerobics, calisthenics, training, warm-up, gymnastics, drill, isometrics, regimen, bodybuilding, dancercise, push-up, sit-up, exertion, curls, extensions, pull-up, jumping jacks, skipjacks, crunch, *pumping iron, weightlifting. "A modern superstition, invented by people who ate too much, and had nothing to think about."—

George Santayana. **2.** USE execution, application, employment, utilization, practice.

exercise *v.* **1.** WORK OUT perform aerobics, perform calisthenics, train, drill, warm up, *pump iron. **2.** USE apply, employ, utilize, practice, execute, perform, exert.

exert *v.* **1.** USE exercise, employ, utilize, apply, employ. **2.** APPLY GREAT EFFORT push, drive, strain, struggle, *go all out, *dig deep, *bust a gut, strive, *pour it on, *pop a vein.

exertion *n.* effort, exercise, work, strain, labor, application, *muscle, pains, *elbow grease, toil, energy, struggle. ANT. *inertia, sloth, rest, relaxation.*

exfoliate *v.* flake off, scale off, peel.

exhale *v.* breathe, respire, blow. SEE BREATHE

exhaust *n.* discharge, fumes, gas, smoke, carbon monoxide, steam, outflow, outpouring, effluvium.

exhaust *v.* **1.** TIRE drain, fatigue, wear out, sap, *tucker out, *poop, enervate, *bush, tax, fag, *wear one's battery down, overtire. **2.** DEPLETE use up, empty, drain, consume, spend, clean out, expend, *blow, bankrupt. ANT. *1. energize, refresh, invigorate, revive. 2. restore, stock up, conserve.*

exhausted *a.* **1.** TIRED drained, fatigued, worn out, sapped, *tuckered out, *pooped, enervated, *bushed, fagged out, overtired, *trashed out, *wiped out, *beat, *dead, rundown, *out of juice, *dog-tired. **2.** DEPLETED used up, emptied, drained, consumed, spent, cleaned out, *blown, bankrupt, expended. ANT. *1. refreshed, invigorated, *charged up, energized. 2. restored, replenished, restocked, conserved.*

exhaustion *n.* weariness, fatigue, collapse, tiredness, enervation, *burnout, prostration, *physical bankruptcy, weakness, sleepiness, faintness, dissipation. ANT. *energy, *get-up-and-go, pep.*

EXHAUSTIVE *a.* [ex ZAWS tiv] thorough, painstaking. *The detectives made an exhaustive search of the crime scene.* SYN. thorough, painstaking, comprehensive, in-depth, complete, extensive, intensive, all-inclusive, sweeping, encyclopedic. ANT. *perfunctory, superficial, cursory.*

exhibit *n.* exhibition, showing, display, presentation, exposition.

exhibit *v.* show, display, present, expose, demonstrate, air, showcase, feature, illustrate, parade.

exhibition *n.* exhibit, showing, display, presentation, exposition, demonstration, spectacle, showcasing.

exhibitionism *n.* attention-seeking behavior, exposing oneself, indecent exposure, *flashing, compulsion, psychosexual disorder, neurosis.

exhilarate *v.* cheer, excite, gladden, enliven, stimulate, elate, animate, delight, *perk up, thrill, invigorate, uplift. ANT. *depress, sadden,* *bum out.

exhort *v.* urge, admonish, prod, persuade, egg, prompt, caution, warn, goad, prevail upon, recommend, advise.

exhume *v.* dig up, disinter, unearth, resurrect.

exigency *n.* urgency, demand, pressing need, crisis, requirement, imperative, necessity, emergency, dire circumstance, *pickle, *hot water.

exile *n.* **1.** BANISHMENT deportation, expatriation, expulsion, uprooting, separation, ostracism, relegation. **2.** BANISHED PERSON outcast, expatriate, refugee, deportee, pariah, displaced person. "One who serves his country by residing abroad, yet is not an ambassador."—Ambrose Bierce.

exile *v.* banish, deport, expatriate, expel, ostracize, uproot, separate, relegate, oust, displace.

exist *v.* be, live, endure, breathe, survive, subsist, abide, remain.

existence *n.* being, life, subsistence, presence, reality, actuality. ". . . a party, you join after it's started and you leave before it's finished."—Elsa Maxwell. "A series of footnotes to a vast, obscure, unfinished masterpiece."—Vladimir Nabokov.

exit *n.* **1.** DOORWAY egress, outlet, passage, escape-way. **2.** DEPARTURE leaving, withdrawal, egress, leave-taking, exodus, parting, farewell, goodbye, adieu.

exodus *n.* departure, going forth, flight, emigration, hegira, migration, fleeing, retreat, withdrawal.

EXONERATE *v.* [egg ZAWN ur rate] to free from charges or show that one is blameless. *The jury elected to exonerate the defendant on all counts.* SYN. acquit, clear, free, vindicate, absolve, excuse, exculpate, dismiss, let go. ANT. *convict, condemn, find guilty.*

EXORBITANT *a.* [eg ZORB uh tunt] excessive or unreasonable. *The prices for homes in Beverly Hills are exorbitant.* SYN. excessive, unreasonable, extravagant, outrageous, inordinate, out-of-line, unwarranted, disproportionate, extreme, *stiff, preposterous, ludicrous. ANT. *reasonable, modest, moderate.*

exorcise *v.* expel, purge, remove, cast out, banish, free from evil spirits.

exorcism *n.* ceremony, purging, expulsion, removal, banishment, casting out, ritual, incantation.

exotic *a.* foreign, alien, outlandish, unfamiliar, strange, peculiar, weird, unusual, different, extraordinary, imported, colorful. ANT. *native, ordinary, familiar.*

expand *v.* **1.** ENLARGE grow, magnify, inflate, widen, swell, distend, bloat, increase, fatten, broaden, puff up. **2.** ELABORATE detail, draw out, develop, expound upon, *flesh out. ANT. *1. shrink, contract, condense. 2. condense, shorten.*

expanse *n.* area, space, immensity, extent, plain, stretch, sweep, range, radius, territory, reach.

expansion *n.* enlargement, extension, increase, growth, development, magnification, spread, heightening, widening, broadening, lengthening. ANT. *contraction, downsizing, decrease.*

expansionism *n.* growth, development, progress.

expansive *a.* **1.** EXTENDED extensive, sweeping, broad, comprehensive, spacious, inclusive, voluminous, large. **2.** FRIENDLY open, demonstrative, sympathetic, generous, free, outgoing, unrestrained, effusive, talkative, unrestrained. ANT. *1. confined, restricted, cramped. 2. inhibited, reserved, restrained.*

expatriate *n.* outcast, displaced person, refugee. SEE EXILE

expect *v.* **1.** ANTICIPATE look for, count on, foresee, bargain for, envisage, look forward to, assume, presume, predict, imagine. **2.** WANT require, call for, demand, count on.

expectant *a.* anticipating, awaiting, anxious, watching, *on tenterhooks, *with bated breath, apprehensive, *on pins and needles.

expectation *n.* anticipation, outlook, prospect, belief, hope, fear, supposition, presumption, likelihood, assumption, forecast.

expecting *a.* *with child, *in a family way. SEE PREGNANT

expectorate *v.* SEE SPIT

expediency *n.* suitability, appropriateness, properness, usefulness, convenience, utility, advantage, effectiveness, opportunism.

EXPEDIENT *a.* [ek SPEE dee unt] serving one's immediate needs, useful. *It would be expedient to study if you want to pass the test.* SYN. useful, advantageous, practical, self-serving, prudent, profitable, fitting, sensible, proper, worthwhile, desirable. ANT. *impractical, useless, futile.*

expedient *n.* resource, makeshift, contrivance, means, measure, instrument, resort, device, scheme, stopgap.

EXPEDITE *v.* [EK spi DITE] to speed up or facilitate a process or action. *I'm going to expedite delivery by mailing the package first class.* SYN. speed up, facilitate, accelerate, hurry, quicken, hasten, precipitate, rush, *grease the wheels, advance, dispatch. ANT. *slow, bog down, hinder.*

expedition *n.* journey, voyage, trip, mission, march, tour, excursion, trek, campaign, exploration, crusade, safari, junket, enterprise.

expeditious *a.* quick, fast, speedy, prompt, efficient, swift, rapid, brisk, fleet, punctual, instant. ANT. *slow, leisurely, slothful.*

expel *v.* throw out, remove, banish, exile, dispel, eject, evict, get rid of, *bounce, oust, deport, *give the boot, *show the door, *give walking papers, expatriate. ANT. *invite, admit, welcome.*

expend *v.* use, consume, spend, exhaust, empty, drain, *blow, squander, dissipate, disburse, *shell out, deplete, *fritter away. ANT. *conserve, save.*

expendable *a.* dispensable, unimportant, replaceable, nonessential, spendable, extraneous, superfluous, crucial, essential, important.

expenditure *n.* expense, outlay, spending, payment, disbursement, outgo, cost, charge, overhead, investment, consumption, use. ANT. *income, receivable.*

expense *n.* cost, outlay, price, charge, amount, payment, price tag, *out of pocket cost, expenditure, fee, burden, *bottom line, overhead.

expensive *a.* costly, high-priced, *pricey, exorbitant, dear, steep, *sky-high, stiff, unreasonable, outrageous. ANT. *cheap, low-priced, cut-rate, economical.*

experience *n.* **1.** FIRSTHAND KNOWLEDGE exposure, familiarity, practice, understanding, participation, empiricism, involvement, seasoning, encountering, worldliness, wisdom. "A good school, but the fees are high."—Heinrich Heine. "The stern lights of a ship, which illumine only the track it has passed."—Samuel Taylor Coleridge "The fruit of the tree of errors."—Portuguese proverb. "The name everyone gives to their mistakes."—Oscar Wilde. **2.** AFFAIR event, ordeal, happening, adventure, encounter, incident, episode. ANT. *1. inexperience, naiveté.*

experience *v.* feel, undergo, encounter, taste, meet, sample, perceive, know, suffer, see, smell, hear, absorb.

experienced *a.* practiced, accomplished, seasoned, weathered, *battle-scarred, initiated, knowing, knowledgeable, worldly-wise, hardened, veteran, *been through the wringer, *been there, tested, mature. ANT. *inexperienced, green, unseasoned, naive, uninitiated.*

experiment *n.* test, trial, investigation, analysis, examination, assay, probe, inquiry, research, trial and error, try, study, *double-blind study. "A hard teacher because she gives the test first, the lesson afterwards."—Vernon Law. SEE SCIENCE

experiment *v.* test, try, investigate, analyze, examine, assess, assay, prove, probe, inquire, research, study, weigh, explore, scrutinize.

experimental *a.* trial, speculative, unproven, hypthothetical, conjectural, tentative, pilot, theoretical, exploratory, test, developmental. ANT. *proven, tested.*

expert *n.* authority, specialist, professional, master, virtuoso, connoisseur, scholar, *whiz, veteran, *crackerjack, journeyman, *guru, *shark, *old hand, *know-it-all, *maven. "A man who has made all the mistakes which can be made in a very narrow field."—Niels Bohr. "The one who predicts the job will take the longest and cost the most."—Arthur Bloch. ANT. *amateur, beginner, layman, apprentice.*

expert *a.* experienced, knowledgeable, *crack, proficient, masterful, schooled, practiced, virtuoso, dexterous, skilled, *whiz-bang, *ace. ANT. *inexperienced, unschooled, lay.*

expertise *n.* knowledge, know-how, skill, prowess, authority, proficiency, finesse, *knack, mastery, specialization.

expiration *n.* ending, closing, termination, death, cessation, passing, demise, finish, departure, conclusion, *last gasp.

expire *v.* **1.** RUN OUT OR DIE lapse, end, close, cease, discontinue, *kick the bucket, pass away, terminate. SEE DIE **2.** EXHALE respire. SEE BREATHE

explain *v.* clarify, clear up, illustrate, explicate, elucidate, expound, interpret, define, *make plain, spell out, describe, account for, justify.

explanation n. clarification, illustration, explication, elucidation, exposition, interpretation, definition, description, account, justification, answer, rationalization.

expletive n. curse, swear word, cuss word, *bad word, vulgarity, obscenity, profanity, oath.

EXPLICIT a. [eks PLIS it] clearly expressed, directly stated or shown. *The movie has explicit sex scenes.* SYN. clear, direct, unambiguous, definite, candid, exact, graphic, forthright, specific, frank, distinct, unequivocal, plain, straightforward. ANT. *indirect, vague, ambiguous.*

explode v. **1.** BLOW UP pop, burst, detonate, *blow, discharge, erupt, fulminate, blast, bang, thunder, burst into flames. **2.** DISCREDIT debunk, expose, refute, invalidate, *shoot down, belie, puncture.

exploit n. feat, deed, act, achievement, accomplishment, coup, stunt, adventure, maneuver.

EXPLOIT v. [EK sploit] to make use of or take advantage of. *He liked to exploit the talents of the younger members.* SYN. make use of, take advantage of, use, profit from, utilize, capitalize on, *milk, *cash in on, abuse, *walk on, impose upon, employ.

exploitation n. using, taking advantage, *milking, *bleeding, utilization.

exploration n. investigation, probe, *look-see, search, inspection, survey, canvass, examination, inquiry, scrutiny, reconnaissance, *trailblazing.

explore v. investigate, probe, look into, search out, inspect, scrutinize, survey, canvass, range over, examine, research, *blaze a trail.

explorer n. trailblazer, investigator, searcher, adventurer, researcher, probe, surveyor, map-maker, cartographer.

explosion n. blowup, detonation, blast, boom, outburst, eruption, pop, crack, fulmination, roar, report, concussion, percussion, shot, upheaval.

explosive n. bomb, dynamite, TNT, charge, gunpowder, nitroglycerine, warhead, blasting cap, cordite, dunnite, fuel-air explosive, Molotov cocktail, napalm, petard, plastic explosive. SEE AMMUNITION, BOMB, MISSILE, NUCLEAR BOMB, WAR, WEAPON

explosive a. volatile, charged, *at the boiling point, inflammable, fulminant, reaching critical mass, volcanic, eruptive, dangerous, perilous. ANT. *stable, relaxed.*

exponent n. spokesman, representative, proponent, interpreter, explainer, advocate, champion, expounder.

export v. transport, ship, trade, sell abroad, ship overseas.

exposé n. disclosure, uncovering, revelation, exposure, *kiss-and-tell, muckraking, explanation.

expose v. **1.** UNCOVER bare, reveal, show, disclose, unmask, *let the cat out of the bag, exhibit, unveil, air, divulge. **2.** LEAVE UNPROTECTED lay open, endanger, jeopardize, imperil, tempt fate, leave vulnerable, make defenseless. ANT. **1.** *cover up, hide, conceal.* **2.** *block, camouflage, protect.*

exposition n. explanation, commentary, explication, description, account, treatise, study, discourse, essay, exegesis, overview, elucidation.

expostulate v. reason, remonstrate, argue, advise, dissuade, admonish, plead, correct.

exposure n. uncovering, airing, disclosure, revelation, unmasking, exposé, unveiling, showing, exhibition, baring, divulging.

EXPOUND v. [eks POUND] to set forth detail by detail, explain. *She will expound her conservative views on the news.* SYN. detail, explain, describe, set forth, state, express, elucidate, spell out, illustrate, define, delineate, comment on.

express v. communicate, articulate, say, verbalize, enunciate, convey, put across, put into words, declare, voice, tell, pronounce, state.

express a. **1.** EXPLICIT clear, certain, plain, direct, precise, distinct, obvious, specific, exact. **2.** FAST quick, swift, fleet, prompt. ANT. **1.** *vague, ambiguous, indirect.* **2.** *slow, sluggish.*

expression n. **1.** COMMUNICATION articulation, verbalization, enunciation, conveyance, declaration, voicing, pronouncement, statement, utterance, elucidation, formulation, phrasing, wording. **2.** TERM phrase, word, idiom, saying, metaphor, simile. **3.** LOOK face, countenance, aspect, visage, cast, mien, *mug.

expressionless a. deadpan, poker-faced, blank, wooden, stony, vacuous, inscrutable, vacant, apathetic, *shark-eyed, unreadable. ANT. *animated, spirited, lively.*

expressive a. indicative, telling, eloquent, meaningful, evocative, revealing, vivid, pregnant, descriptive, pointed, graphic. ANT. *nondescript, empty, meaningless.*

expressly adv. **1.** PARTICULARLY purposely, precisely, strictly, exactly, especially, specifically. **2.** EXPLICITLY clearly, plainly, unambiguously, definitely, pointedly, unequivocally, categorically. ANT. *1. generally. 2. implicitly, indirectly, vaguely.*

expressway *n.* highway, freeway, beltway, turnpike, causeway, interstate, autobahn.

expulsion *n.* discharge, exile, banishment, ejection, eviction, ouster, *the boot, *history, expatriation, deportment, removal, exclusion. ANT. *inclusion, welcoming, receiving.*

expunge *v.* erase, blot out, delete, obliterate, efface, wipe out, cut, cancel, omit, extirpate, remove, eradicate.

expurgate *v.* censor, remove, expunge, cut, bowdlerize, clean up, sanitize, purge, soften.

exquisite *a.* delicate, lovely, fine, elegant, beautiful, dainty, precious, rare, consummate, superlative, splendid, ethereal, fragile. ANT. *clunky, rough, coarse, bulky, ponderous.*

extant *a.* existing, living, alive, surviving, around, present, current, remaining. ANT. *extinct, defunct, dead, gone.*

extemporaneous *a.* unrehearsed, offhand, unprepared, unpremeditated, impromptu, spontaneous, ad lib, *off the cuff, *spur of the moment, *on the spot. ANT. *rehearsed, prepared, premeditated.*

extemporize *v.* improvise, ad-lib, *perform offhand, *wing it, *play it by ear, *make up as one goes along, *do off the cuff.

extend *v.* **1.** STRETCH elongate, enlarge, expand, spread, lengthen, draw out, prolong, protract, unfurl, increase, continue. **2.** OFFER accord, grant, proffer, tender, present, submit, put forth. ANT. *1. contract, shorten, shrink. 2. withdraw, rescind.*

extension *n.* enlargement, lengthening, protraction, elongation, expansion, spread, prolongation, unfurling, increase, addition, augmentation, annex, attachment. ANT. *contraction, shortening, shrinkage.*

extensive *a.* broad, far-reaching, comprehensive, expansive, considerable, vast, sweeping, large-scale, widespread, out-and-out, wholesale, thorough, lengthy, protracted. ANT. *limited, restricted, small-scale.*

extent *n.* size, area, degree, magnitude, measure, proportions, range, expanse, amount, sweep, dimensions, scope.

EXTENUATE *v.* [ek STEN yoo ate] to lessen, mitigate or provide an excuse for a wrongdoing. *Mental illness is sometimes used in law to extenuate guilt.* SYN. lessen, mitigate, justify, soften, attenuate, moderate, diminish, palliate, qualify, make allowances for.

exterior *n.* surface, face, facade, outside, shell, skin, appearance. ANT. *interior, inside.*

exterior *a.* external, outside, outer, extrinsic, extraneous, superficial, foreign, surface, outward. ANT. *internal, inner, intrinsic.*

exterminate *v.* destroy, kill, wipe out, eradicate, annihilate, eliminate, abolish, slaughter, decimate, extirpate, massacre, extinguish.

external *a.* outer, extrinsic, outside, outward, surface, superficial, exterior, foreign, extraneous. ANT. *internal, intrinsic.*

extinct *a.* died out, dead, defunct, obsolete, nonexistent, vanished, vanquished, gone, wiped out, nonextant, *fossilized, *dead and forgotten, *history, outmoded. ANT. *living, existing, thriving.*

extinction *n.* dying out, death, downfall, destruction, annihilation, termination, *fossilization, obsolescence, disappearance, passing.

extinguish *v.* **1.** QUENCH douse, snuff out, put out, smother, *douse. **2.** DESTROY abolish, end, stifle, annihilate, quash, eliminate, exterminate, extirpate, eradicate, wipe out.

extirpate *v.* exterminate, destroy, eradicate, obliterate, annihilate, abolish, uproot, eliminate, root out, remove.

EXTOL *v.* [eks TOLE] to praise highly, laud. *Society tends to extol its athletes.* SYN. praise, laud, acclaim, glorify, cheer, commend, exalt, celebrate, applaud, honor, *sing the praises of. ANT. *put down, disparage, discredit, condemn.*

extort *v.* extract, blackmail, coerce, *strongarm, wrest, wring, *bleed, *milk, fleece, cheat, *put the screws to, squeeze, *armtwist, bully.

EXTORTION *n.* [eks TOR shun] the illegal means of getting money from one through intimidation, blackmail, etc. *The extortion ring threatened local businesses with arson.* SYN. blackmail, strong-arming, *arm-twisting, extraction, *bleeding, *milking, *the squeeze, bullying, wringing, shakedown, graft, hush money. SEE CRIME

extra *n.* accessory, spare, bonus, supplement.

extra *a.* additional, surplus, excess, more, accessory, extraneous, spare, superfluous, over. ANT. *enough, sufficient, lacking.*

extract *n.* **1.** EXCERPT clipping, quotation, citation, abstract, passage. **2.** DISTILLATION concentrate, distillate, essence, juice.

extract *v.* remove, withdraw, pull, pluck, yank, extirpate, glean, pry, wrench, cull, reap, derive, wrest.

extradite *v.* turn over, transfer, return.

EXTRANEOUS *a.* [ek STRAY nee us] inessential, unnecessary. *We ditched our extraneous gear to lighten the load.* SYN. inessential, unnecessary, irrelevant, extra, superfluous, incidental, peripheral, needless, immaterial. ANT. *essential, relevant, needed.*

extraordinary *a.* unusual, exceptional, remarkable, uncommon, rare, striking, singular, strange, odd, phenomenal, outstanding, marvelous, unprecedented, wondrous. ANT. *ordinary, usual, common.*

EXTRAPOLATE *v.* [ek STRAP uh late] to infer or draw conclusions from what is known. *Although it is not known for sure, many scientists extrapolate that life exists on other worlds.* SYN. infer, conclude, deduce, *put two and two together, figure, guess, hypothesize, postulate, theorize, assume, presume, *make an educated guess.

extrasensory perception *n.* ESP, psychic powers, *third eye, telepathy, clairvoyance, telesthesia.

extraterrestrial *n.* alien, space being, *E.T., unearthly visitor, *little green man, *visitor from another planet.

extravagance *n.* indulgence, excessiveness, lavishness, wastefulness, excess, immoderation, prodigality, frill, *overkill, superfluity, profligacy, exorbitance, *conspicuous consumption. "The way the other fellow spends his money."—Harry Thompson. ANT. *thrift, moderation, restraint, frugality.*

extravagant *a.* indulgent, excessive, lavish, wasteful, immoderate, prodigal, superfluous, profligate, exorbitant, conspicuous, ultra, unrestrained, spendthrift, ostentatious, extreme. ANT. *moderate, restrained, thrifty, reasonable.*

extreme *n.* outer limit, height, extremity, end, ultimate, maximum, ceiling, utmost, top, peak.

extreme *a.* drastic, beyond reason, excessive, utmost, severe, extraordinary, great, immoderate, extravagant, outrageous, imprudent, radical, overkill, undue. ANT. *conventional, normal, conservative, moderate.*

extremely *adv.* very, exceedingly, quite, exceptionally, excessively, greatly, immensely, highly, markedly, severely, intensely, inordinately.

extremist *n.* radical, fanatic, zealot, ultra, revolutionist, immoderate, *hard-liner.

extremity *n.* **1.** LIMIT edge, tip, boundary, outer limit, periphery, border, verge, terminus, margin, brink. **2.** APPENDAGE limb, leg, arm, hand, foot.

extricate *v.* free, get out of, extract, liberate, release, *get out from under, *wriggle out of, disentangle, relieve, save. ANT. *entangle, involve, embroil.*

extrinsic *a.* outer, outside, exterior, external, extraneous, foreign. ANT. *intrinsic, essential.*

extrovert *n.* outgoing person, socializer, *life of the party, gregarious person, *party animal, exhibitionist, *mixer. ANT. *introvert, loner, introspective person.*

extroverted *a.* outgoing, social, sociable, friendly, congenial, amicable, approachable, unreserved, cordial, party-loving, personable, people-loving. ANT. *introverted, aloof, reserved.*

extrude *v.* expel, push out, eject, force out.

exuberance *n.* **1.** HIGH SPIRITS liveliness, vitality, enthusiasm, ebullience, buoyancy, effervescence, zest, energy, vigor, bounce. **2.** ABUNDANCE luxuriance, lushness, profusion, lavishness, affluence, plenitude, richness. ANT. *1. depression, dullness, apathy, listlessness, low spirits. 2. scarcity, shortage.*

exuberant *a.* **1.** HIGH-SPIRITED lively, vital, enthusiastic, ebullient, buoyant, effervescent, effusive, zestful, energetic, vigorous, *full of bounce. **2.** ABUNDANT luxurious, lush, profuse, lavish, affluent, rich, flush, plentiful. ANT. *1. down, dispirited, *blue, listless. 2. short, scarce.*

exude *v.* emit, discharge, secrete, emanate, ooze, sweat, issue, well forth, excrete, trickle.

exult *v.* rejoice, jubilate, glory, celebrate, revel, *jump for joy, be joyful, make merry, crow.

EXULTANT *a.* [eg ZULT unt] jubilant, joyful, or jumping for joy. *The exultant partygoers sang for hours.* SYN. jubilant, joyful, triumphant, ecstatic, elated, gleeful, rejoicing, euphoric, overjoyed, transported, happy. ANT. *miserable, depressed, downhearted.*

exultation *n.* jubilation, rejoicing, joy, triumph, ecstasy, elation, glee, euphoria, happiness, exhilaration. ANT. *misery, depression, dejection.*

eye *n.* optical organ, eyeball, *peeper, orb, oculus, *winker, *baby blue. "The pulse of the soul; as physicians judge the heart by the pulse, so we by the eye."—Thomas Adams. "The traitor of the heart."—Thomas Wyatt. "Windows of the soul."—Guillaume Du Bartas. "Sentinels."—Cicero.

WORD FIND

blackened, bruised: shiner, mouse

blindness caused by loss of retina's rods: retinitis pigmentosa

blue eye, brown eye, having one of each: helerochroma iridis

bulging, protruding: exophthalmic

cavity: orbit, socket

close-up vision: nearsightedness, myopia

clouding of lens: cataract

color confusion: color blindness

color detectors, nerve cells: cones

colored portioned surrounding pupil: iris

corneal incisions that correct nearsightedness: radial keratotomy

crossed inwardly, one eye: esotropia, strabismus

crossed outward, one eye: exotropia

crossed outward, one eye or both: walleyed

cross-eyed, family of disorders: strabismus

dark spot that responds to light, dark: pupil

descriptive, shapes: almond, banjo, beady, bug, button, close-set, crescent, cue ball, deep-set, birdlike, fishy, goggle, hooded, lenticular, owlish, pop, rheumy, saucer, slanty, sloe, squinty, sunken, wide-set

discharge: rheum

distance vision: farsightedness, hyperopia

doctor: ophthalmologist, oculist

eyelid liner, inner: conjunctiva

feeling, showing deep: soulful

flashes of light, seeing: photopsia, scintillation

floating specks before: floaters (dead blood cells)

fluid between cornea and lens: aqueous humor

focusing body: lens

inflammation causing reddening of eyeball: pinkeye

inflammation of conjunctiva: conjunctivitis

inflammation on lid: sty

innermost layer where light rays are focused: retina

instrument: orthoscope

iris that is light-colored: walleye

jelly behind lens: vitreous humor

light sensitivity: photophobia

nerve to brain: optic nerve

Oriental skin fold: epicanthus

peripheral distortion: astigmatism

pertaining to: ocular

pressure build-up causing visual defects, blindness: glaucoma

pupil contraction: myosis

seeing double: diplopia

sunken: deep-set, cavernous

transparent outer membrane: cornea

velvety and dark: sloe-eyed

white of: sclera

eye *v.* look at, study, scrutinize, gaze at, *eyeball, scan, ogle, *give the once-over, regard, view.

eyeball *v.* SEE EYE

eyebrow *n.* brow, bree, *ceja.

WORD FIND

bushy, prominent: beetle-browed, caterpillar eyebrows

eye-catching *a.* noticeable, diverting, bold. ANT. *inconspicuous*.

eyeglasses *n.* glasses, spectacles, *specs, lenses, *eyes.

WORD FIND

circular, frameless glasses that pinch in place over nose: pince-nez

fake, nonprescription fashion glasses: planos

fancy, upscale: designer glasses

granny glasses worn on middle of nose: Ben Franklins

handle, held with a: lorgnette

heavy, dark brown frames: horn-rimmed

lenses divided for near and far sight: bifocals

mottled brown frames: tortoiseshell glasses

reading glasses with half-lenses for peering over: half-glasses

single lens hung from ribbon worn around neck: monocle

eyesight *n.* SEE VISION

eyesore *n.* ugliness, sight, fright, mess, pollution, monstrosity, pigsty, dump.

eyewash *n.* hogwash, *bull, flattery, bunk. SEE NONSENSE

eyewitness *n.* bystander, observer, spectator, onlooker, passerby, watcher.

F

fable *n.* myth, tale, parable, legend, allegory, story, yarn, fiction, old wives' tale, moral, fantasy.

fabled *a.* mythical, legendary, famous, storied, fanciful, fictitious, make-believe, fantastic.

fabric *n.* **1.** CLOTH material, textile, fiber, weave, dry goods, stuff.

WORD FIND

canvas: duckcloth, sailcloth

crinkled: crepe, seersucker

decorated with many small, colorful print designs: calico

drape, upholstery fabric of glazed cotton: chintz

dress fabric used in evening wear: faille

edging preventing raveling: selvage

filling: weft

fuzzy surface: nap

gingham, light: chambray

glossy: satin, etoile

goathair, angora: mohair

heavy, floral-patterned with metallic threads: brocade

heavy, used in tablecloths: damask

holes, full of: fishnet

hunting jacket fabric: mackinaw

jeans: denim, dungaree

leather, soft and napped: suede

leather, soft, goat: chamois

lustrous, tightly woven: broadcloth

man-made fiber known as artifical silk: rayon

metallic yarn fabric used in evening dresses: lamé

pile, thick and soft: velveteen

plush, velvet, corduroy: pile

puckered: plisse

quantity of, fifteen to twenty yards: bolt

rib, as of corduroy: wale

rabbit, goat: angora

raised design or bumpy surface on: blister

sample of: swatch

Scottish, handwoven: Harris tweed

silk, woven: tricot

sheer: gauze, organza, batiste, voile, chiffon, gossamer

sheets, bed: muslin, percale

shiny, imitation silk: poplin

shiny, rustling: taffeta

stretchy, synthetic: spandex

suit: tweed, serge

towel, robes: terry cloth

uniform, olive green: khaki

uniforms, twilled fabric for: cavalry twill, chino

wool, combed and smoothed: worsted

wool: fleece

wool, goat: cashmere

wool, nubby type used in suits: tweed

wool, soft and brushed: flannel

wool, unprocessed: virgin wool

wrinkle-resistant, man-made: polyester

2. MAKEUP substance, structure, framework, constitution, texture.

fabricate *v.* **1.** MAKE manufacture, construct, assemble, piece together, create, produce, fashion, devise. **2.** LIE prevaricate, *fudge, invent, make up, concoct, hatch, fib, contrive.

fabrication *n.* lie, concoction, invention, fib, prevarication, falsehood, *fish story, *cock and bull story, *tall tale, web. ANT. *truth, fact.*

fabulous *a.* **1.** INCREDIBLE OR GREAT astounding, wonderful, excellent, *out-of-this-world, super, *primo, marvelous, amazing, exceptional, superb, *aces, fantastic. **2.** MYTHICAL legendary, fictitious, fabled, imaginary, fantastic, make-believe, fanciful. SEE MONSTER ANT. *1. ordinary, run-of-the-mill, routine, everyday. 2. actual, real, factual.*

FACADE *n.* [fuh SAHD] the front or face of a person, place or thing, often with the implication of hiding something negative behind it. *His smiling face was just a facade; we knew he was really quite angry inside.* SYN. front, false front, face, mask, guise, veneer, show, *window dressing, *put-on, pretense, disguise, appearance.

face *n.* **1.** VISAGE countenance, features, physiognomy, *mug, *puss, front, profile, *kisser, head. "The portrait of the mind."—Samuel Coleridge. "The shorthand of the mind."—Jeremy Collier. "A book where men may read strange matters."—Shakespeare. "The title page which heralds the contents of the human volume."—William Matthews. "Oftentimes the true index of the heart."—James Howell. SEE EXPRESSION, EYE, FROWN, MOUTH, NOSE, OLD-FACED, SMILE **2.** FRONT exterior, surface, appearance, mask, semblance, disguise, facade.

face *v.* confront, meet, brave, encounter, beard,

withstand, bear, *fly in the face of, acknowledge, *meet head-on, brook, *bite the bullet.

face the music v. face up to it, look square in the eye, bite the bullet, grin and bear it, take one's lumps, take one's medicine, pay the piper.

facelift n. cosmetic surgery, plastic surgery.

facet n. aspect, side, point, angle, surface, feature, plane, side, detail, part, cut.

FACETIOUS a. [fuh SEE shus] jocular, flippant, tongue-in-cheek. *She was being facetious when she said I should run for president.* SYN. jocular, flippant, funny, humorous, playful, joking, kidding, tongue-in-cheek, not serious, *joshing, jesting, *wise, *pulling one's leg. ANT. *serious, grave, sober.*

facile a. 1. EASY simple, *cinchy, *a snap, *child's play, *a breeze, effortless. 2. FLUENT quick, ready, adroit, dexterous, smooth, superficial, glib. ANT. *1. difficult, hard, laborious. 2. awkward, halting.*

FACILITATE v. [fuh SIL uh tate] to simplify, make easier. *To facilitate mailing, please include a self-addressed stamped envelope.* SYN. simplify, ease, expedite, help, quicken, further, aid, smooth, speed up, *grease the wheels, advance. ANT. *hinder, complicate, hamper, burden.*

facility n. 1. ABILITY skill, ease, dexterity, adroitness, efficiency, fluency, proficiency, effortlessness, aptitude, knack. 2. ACCOMMODATION convenience, resource, means, appliance, building, room, office.

facsimile n. copy, reproduction, replica, duplicate, likeness, carbon copy, *Xerox, double, clone, twin, *ditto, fax.

fact n. truth, reality, datum, certainty, actuality, verity, gospel, law, scripture, particular, detail, specific, element, item.

FACTION n. [FAK shun] a group sharing a common cause, especially one within a larger group or body. *The liberal faction is working for stronger environmental controls.* SYN. group, bloc, clique, circle, part, sect, subdivision, side, camp, sector, pressure group, splinter group, coalition.

factious a. conflicting, quarrelsome, discordant, contentious, partisan, dissentious, divisive, warring, at odds, hostile, at loggerheads. ANT. *agreeing, consonant, harmonious.*

factor n. determinant, element, influence, cause, component, agent, means, instrument, circumstance, point, consideration, aspect.

factory n. manufactory, manufacturing facility, plant, mill, shop, firm, machine shop, works, foundry, assembly line.

factual a. true, actual, realistic, literal, authentic, faithful, correct, exact, sound, valid, credible, legitimate, certain, unquestionable. ANT. *untrue, false, fictitious, fanciful, made up.*

faculty n. 1. ABILITY capability, skill, aptitude, talent, facility, capacity, gift, knack, flair, instinct. 2. TEACHERS staff, instructors, academics, professors, body.

fad n. craze, vogue, mania, rage, *in thing, trend, fashion, *dernier cri, whim, furor, mode.

fade v. 1. LOSE COLOR pale, dim, wane, wash out, blanch. 2. DWINDLE disappear, vanish, slacken, wither, waste away, diminish, decline, recede, ebb, wane, languish, die out. ANT. *1. brighten, make vivid. 2. grow, increase, brighten.*

fail v. 1. NOT SUCCEED *blow it, *fall short, slip up, lose, go wrong, flop, *go down in flames, *choke, fizzle, *take a dive, go awry, miss, *bomb, *fall flat on one's face, flunk, *lay an egg, run aground, *strike out, *come a cropper. 2. WEAKEN deteriorate, dwindle, die away, wane, *collapse of one's own weight, sink, fade, *be on one's last legs, *circle the drain, decline, sicken. 3. DEFAULT back out, neglect, forsake, renege, let down, desert, slight, disregard, *abort, faulter, miscarry, ignore. 4. GO BANKRUPT crash, close, *lose one's shirt, *go belly up, *file for chapter eleven, *go broke, fold, go out of business, *drown in a sea of red ink. ANT. *1. succeed, win, achieve, triumph. 2. grow stronger, flourish, thrive. 3. carry out, follow through. 4. flourish, thrive, profit.*

failing n. fault, defect, weakness, imperfection, flaw, shortcoming, peccadillo, deficiency. ANT. *strength, strong point.*

failsafe a. foolproof, guaranteed, covered, protected, safeguarded, secure, supplied with a safety net, supplied with an escape.

failure n. 1. NONSUCCESS *washout, *bomb, fiasco, disappointment, defeat, *Edsel, stumble, botch, fumble, slip, miscarriage, mishap, *strikeout, abortion, misadventure, dud, loss, bust, *dog, *turkey, debacle. "A school in which the truth always grows strong."— Henry Ward Beecher. "Not the falling down, but the staying down."—Mary Pickford. "The highway to success."—John Keats. 2. LOSER *down-and-outer, *also-ran, flop, stiff, incompetent, *has-been, washout. **3.** WEAKENING deterioration, dwindling, fading, decline, loss. ANT. *1. success, achievement, triumph. 2. winner, success, champion. 3. strengthening, flourishing, thriving, growth.*

faint *v.* pass out, black out, collapse, lose consciousness, keel over, crumple, drop, swoon.

faint *a.* **1.** INDISTINCT vague, dim, pale, obscure, faded, soft, unclear, low, weak, ill-defined, distant. **2.** WEAK *woozy, lightheaded, dizzy, drooping, limp, feeble, enervated. ANT. *1. distinct, sharp, defined. 2. strong, invigorated, energetic.*

fainthearted *a.* timid, cowardly, *wimpy, *yellow, afraid, meek, spineless, *afraid of one's own shadow, mousy. ANT. *brave, courageous, bold.*

fair *a.* **1.** JUST evenhanded, equitable, unprejudiced, impartial, unbiased, *square, honest, clean, scrupulous. **2.** SUNNY bright, cloudless, clear, clement, pleasant, mild. **3.** MEDIOCRE adequate, intermediate, okay, satisfactory, good enough, *so-so, *not bad, tolerable, *comme ci, comme ca. **4.** ATTRACTIVE beautiful, good-looking, comely, handsome, pulchritudinous, lovely, pretty. **5.** LIGHT-COMPLEXIONED blonde, pale, peaches and cream, towheaded, alabaster, white. ANT. *1. unfair, one-sided, prejudiced, unjust, crooked. 2. stormy, cloudy, overcast, rainy. 3. excellent, superior, poor, inferior. 4. ugly, homely. 5. dark, swarthy, black.*

fairly *adv.* **1.** SOMEWHAT passably, moderately, sort of, tolerably, more or less. **2.** EQUITABLY justly, impartially, evenly, honestly, legitimately. ANT. *1. completely, entirely. 2. unfairly, unjustly, dishonestly.*

fairness *n.* justice, equity, evenhandedness, impartiality, honor, integrity, honesty, righteousness, *fair shake, *level playing field, equitableness. ANT. *unfairness, injustice, impartiality.*

fairy *n.* elf, pixie, nymph, leprechaun, brownie, gnome, sprite, dwarf, imp, puck, gremlin, sandman, Tinkerbell.

FAIT ACCOMPLI *n.* [fay tuh kon PLEE] an irreversible act, truth or accomplishment; a done deed. *There was nothing that could be done; it was a fait accompli.* SYN. done deed, irreversible act, irreversible truth, irreversible accomplishment, certainty, reality, grim reality, cold, hard facts.

faith *n.* **1.** BELIEF conviction, trust, confidence, certainty, sureness, credence, reliance, hope, dependence. "It is an instinct, for it

precedes all outward instruction."—Henry Amiel. "The response of our spirits to beckonings of the eternal."—George Buttrick. "The soul riding at anchor."—Josh Billings. "A bridge across the gulf of death."—Edward Young. "God felt by the heart, not by reason."—Blaise Pascal. **2.** RELIGIOUS BELIEF religion, persuasion, church, denomination, sect, doctrine, creed, dogma, teaching. SEE RELIGION

faithful *a.* **1.** LOYAL true, true-blue, trustworthy, devoted, allegiant, steadfast, staunch, patriotic, *tried and true, honorable, semper fidelis. **2.** ACCURATE exact, reliable, correct, literal, true, actual, perfect, authentic, precise. ANT. *1. disloyal, treacherous, backstabbing. 2. inaccurate, inexact, rough.*

fake *n.* phony, sham, counterfeit, fraud, imitation, imposture, hoax, *humbug, *three-dollar bill, forgery, fabrication, imposter, poseur, mountebank, charlatan. ANT. *genuine article, *real McCoy.

fake *v.* feign, counterfeit, falsify, sham, *put on, fabricate, pose, imitate, pretend, dissemble, affect, bluff.

fake *a.* counterfeit, phony, false, sham, fraudulent, *fakey, imitation, spurious, bogus, make-believe, pseudo. ANT. *real, genuine, authentic.*

fakir *n.* beggar, ascetic, dervish.

falderal *n.* nonsense, gibberish, blather, *gobbledegook, *crap.

fall *n.* **1.** DROP plunge, tumble, descent, dive, spill, *header, *nose dive, plummet. **2.** DECLINE decrease, drop, slump, reduction, dip, depreciation, lowering, recession, lessening. **3.** DEFEAT ruin, failure, downfall, collapse, destruction, submission. **4.** AUTUMN harvest time, October. SEE AUTUMN, OCTOBER, NOVEMBER ANT. *1. ascent, elevation. 2. increase, growth, appreciation. 3. victory, ascent, win.*

fall *v.* **1.** DROP plunge, tumble, descend, dive, spill, topple, plummet, *do a header, *nose-dive, cascade, trip, pitch, stumble, sprawl, flop. **2.** DECLINE decrease, drop, slump, reduce, dip, depreciate, lower, recede, lessen. **3.** BE RUINED OR DEFEATED succumb, be destroyed, fail, collapse, submit, capitulate, surrender, be overthrown. ANT. *1. ascend, rise, elevate. 2. increase, grow, appreciate. 3. win, ascend, be victorious.*

FALLACIOUS *a.* [fuh LAY shus] based on fallacy, erroneous, false. *His statements about green cheese on the moon were fallacious.* SYN. erroneous, incorrect, false, untrue, faulty, wrong, deceiving, unfounded, mistaken, spurious, invalid. ANT. *true, valid, substantiated*.

FALLACY n. [FAL uh see] a mistaken belief, false notion. *The belief that the moon is made of green cheese is a fallacy.* SYN. mistake, misconception, error, false notion, illusion, delusion, untruth, falsehood, sophistry, misapprehension, misinterpretation. ANT. *truth, fact, certainty*.

fall guy n. patsy, dupe, scapegoat, victim, *goat, whipping boy.

fallible a. imperfect, human, liable to make mistakes, faulty, unreliable, errant, mortal, defective, deficient. ANT. *perfect, *goof-proof, unerring, infallible*.

falling-out n. disagreement, fight, quarrel. SEE ARGUMENT

fallout n. 1. CONSEQUENCE backlash, reaction, repercussion, aftermath, result, wake, effect. 2. RAIN OF RADIOACTIVE PARTICLES settling, *rainout, contamination. SEE NUCLEAR BOMB

fallow a. inactive, idle, dormant, resting, inert, uncultivated, barren, neglected, unused, undeveloped. ANT. *productive, active, cultivated*.

false a. 1. UNTRUE wrong, erroneous, inaccurate, mistaken, fabricated, *full of hot air, *all wet, in error, bogus, fallacious, dishonest, fictitious, unfounded, spurious, invalid, misleading. 2. IMITATION fake, artificial, counterfeit, phony, ersatz, bogus, simulated, mock, sham, forged, pseudo. ANT. *1. true, factual, accurate. 2. real, genuine, authentic*.

falsehood n. lie, untruth, fib, fiction, fabrication, distortion, *whopper, prevarication, canard, *tall tale, perjury, fraud, *hogwash. ANT. *truth, fact, reality*.

false teeth n. dentures, implants, *choppers, partial.

falsify v. forge, fake, distort, misrepresent, adulterate, doctor, alter, misstate, dissemble, stretch, embroider.

falter v. 1. HESITATE waver, vacillate, flinch, oscillate, hang back. 2. STAMMER stumble, stutter, speak haltingly. 3. STUMBLE totter, stagger, shamble, reel, teeter, dodder.

fame n. renown, celebrity, prominence, notoriety, recognition, distinction, stardom, eminence, standing, repute, greatness, acclaim. "Vanity."—Marcus Aurelius. "Wind."—Thomas Coryate. "The perfume of heroic deeds."—Plato. "Footprints on the sands of time."—Longfellow. "A host of expendable sycophants, a lack of privacy and the alienation of old friends."—Morton Da Costa. ANT. *obscurity, anonymity, oblivion*.

familiar a. 1. WELL-KNOWN acquainted, accustomed, recognizable, intimate, *old hat, common, everyday, habitual, routine, ordinary, stock. 2. KNOWLEDGEABLE conversant with, informed, versed, aware of, apprised of, *up on, savvy, cognizant, au courant. 3. FRIENDLY intimate, informal, close, relaxed, neighborly, *free and easy, *buddy-buddy, cozy, genial, natural, at home. 4. BOLD over-familiar, presumptuous, forward, disrespectful, taking liberties, impudent. ANT. *1. unfamiliar, foreign, alien, extraordinary. 2. ignorant, unaware, oblivious. 3. formal, shy, aloof, stiff. 4. respectful, reserved, reticent*.

familiarity n. KNOWLEDGE acquaintance, association, intimacy, closeness, firsthand knowledge, conversance, understanding, cognizance, awareness, feel. "A magician that is cruel to beauty, but kind to ugliness."—Ouida 2. FRIENDLINESS informality, neighborliness, intimacy, closeness, naturalness.

familiarize v. acquaint, get to know, enlighten, accustom, make conversant, inform, school, *get a feel for, *get a handle on, acclimatize, habituate.

family n. 1. CLAN household, kin, tribe, kinfolk, relatives, relations, *blood, brethren, siblings, generation, dynasty, offspring, children, brood, kids, ancestry, bloodline, forebears, lineage, pedigree. "One of nature's masterpieces."—George Santayana. "The miniature commonwealth upon whose integrity the safety of the larger commonwealth depends."—Felix Adler. "The we of me."—Carson McCullers. "The first and essential cell of human society."—Pope John XXIII. "The nucleus of civilization."—Will Durant. 2. CLASS genus, classification, division, group, order, kind, species, type.

family tree n. genealogical chart, ancestral tree, lineage, pedigree, bloodline.

famine n. starvation, hunger, shortage, scarcity, privation, want.

famished a. starving, hungry, deprived, ravenous, *hungry enough to eat a horse. ANT. *satiated*.

famous a. well-known, prominent, renowned, celebrated, famed, eminent, notable, illustrious, glamourized, distinguished, exalted, glorified, acclaimed, recognized, notorious. ANT. *obscure, anonymous, unknown*.

fan n. enthusiast, devotee, *hound, *nut, *bug, *fiend, aficionado, addict, *freak, buff, fanatic, rooter.

fan n. blower, cooler, wind machine, ventilator, air conditioner.

fanatic n. zealot, extremist, radical, enthusiast, devotee, follower, militant, bigot, disciple, nut. "The gadflies that keep society from being too complacent."—Abraham Flexner. "The Devil's plaything."—Armenian proverb. "A lunatic with a hobby."—Leonard Levinson.

fanatical a. zealous, extreme, radical, devoted, militant, rabid, single-minded, monomaniacal, obsessive, fervent, dogmatic. ANT. *moderate, reasonable, open-minded.*

FANATICISM a. [fuh NAT uh siz um] excessive enthusiasm or zeal. *Her fanaticism led her into performing terrorist acts.* SYN. zeal, overenthusiasm, fervor, obsession, monomania, single-mindedness, devotion, passion, dogmatism, bigotry, militantism. "False fire of an overheated mind."—William Cowper. ANT. *moderation, apathy, indifference.*

fanciful a. imaginary, whimsical, unreal, made-up, romantic, capricious, fantastic, dreamy, fairy-tale, chimerical, illusory, flighty, quaint. ANT. *reality-based, real, down-to-earth, prosaic.*

fancy n. **1.** IMAGINATION fantasy, creation, illusion, visualization, whimsy, whim, conception, notion, vision, idea, picture, dream, daydream, figment, chimera, hallucination. **2.** LIKING fondness, *yen, desire, partiality, hankering, penchant, taste.

fancy a. fine, *done up, elegant, prime, extravagant, deluxe, ornate, embellished, frilly, special, showy, lavish, rich, elaborate, decorated. ANT. *plain, ordinary, simple.*

fanfare n. *hoopla, *ballyhoo, buildup, trumpeting, show, to-do, fuss, display, pomp, commotion, ruckus.

fang n. tooth, incisor, canine tooth.

fanny n. *Sl.* butt, ass, gluteus maximus, posterior, rump, seat, *tushy, buttocks.

fantasize v. envision, dream up, daydream, imagine, visualize, picture, invent, *take a flight of fancy, muse, *build castles in the air, moon, *trip.

fantastic a. **1.** EXCELLENT wonderful, great, super, awesome, sensational, marvelous, first-class, *primo, *out of this world. **2.** STRANGE weird, grotesque, odd, quaint, imaginary, outlandish, *out of this world, exotic, peculiar, freakish, queer, Kafkaesque, nightmarish, hallucinatory, incredible. ANT. *1. terrible, bad, lousy, awful. 2. normal, down to earth, ordinary, prosaic.*

fantasy n. imagination, imagining, visualization, envisioning, dream, daydream, invention, *flight of fancy, *castle in the air, reverie, whimsy, conception, hallucination, chimera, *fool's paradise. ANT. *reality, real world.*

far a. distant, remote, removed, far-off, far-flung, out-of-the-way, outlying. ANT. *near, close, at hand.*

farce n. **1.** COMEDY slapstick, burlesque, lampoon, satire, parody, *knee-slapper, absurdity, low comedy, travesty, silliness. **2.** ABSURDITY mockery, pretense, travesty.

FARCICAL a. [FARS i kul] absurd, laughable, ridiculous. *The solemn affair turned farcical when the speaker's pants fell down.* SYN. absurd, laughable, ludicrous, ridiculous, comical, funny, foolish, preposterous, droll, goofy. ANT. *serious, solemn, grave, deep.*

fare n. **1.** FOOD diet, menu, victuals, rations, table, edibles, spread, *munchies. **2.** CHARGE FOR TRANSPORTATION fee, price, passage, toll, token.

farewell n. goodbye, *see you later, *take care, *so long, adios, cheerio, adieu, auf Wiedersehen, bon voyage, *toodle-oo, *toodles, sayonara, ciao, ta-ta, hasta la vista, arrivederci, au revoir, Godspeed.

farfetched a. unlikely, doubtful, improbable, remote, strained, implausible, unbelievable, *hard to swallow, *stretching things, forced. ANT. *plausible, believable, likely.*

far-flung a. widespread, far-reaching, wide-ranging, remote, distant. ANT. *close, nearby, close at hand.*

farm n. farmstead, plantation, ranch, grange, barnyard, homestead, pasture, vineyard, orchard, acreage, tillage, croft, hacienda, patch, garden. "An irregular patch of nettles, bound by short term notes, containing a fool and his wife who didn't know enough to stay in the city."—S.J. Perelman.

WORD FIND
animal-raising: pastoral farming
animal used for pulling: draft animal
barren, as a field left unplanted: fallow
changing crop type grown in field periodically: crop rotation
channel cut into soil: furrow
chicken house: coop
corn storage structure: corncrib
cover crop and fodder: alfalfa
cow barn: byre
crops sold for money, not used as feed: cash crops

crop such as grass planted to prevent soil erosion: cover crop

cutting edge of moldboard plow: plowshare

cylindrical storage building for fodder: silo

descriptive: rolling patchwork; regiment of corn; pastoral quilting; stubble fields of Autumn; Irish green fields; weathered, swayback barn; plodding draft animals; rooting pigs; hens scratching in the dirt

farming: husbandry

farming to feed family only with crops: subsistence farming

feed for livestock: fodder

fertilizer: manure, compost, fish meal, bone meal

fodder that has been stored: silage

grain storage building: granary

grazing land for animals: pasture

harvesting machine that cuts, threshes, cleans, bags grain: combine

hay cutter: mower, sickle, scythe

hayfork: pitchfork

hay grass, most common in United States: timothy

hay pile (long) left to dry in field: windrow

hay pile shaped like cone: haycock

horse enclosure: corral

implement having spikes or disks for breaking clods, refining soil: harrow

implement having teeth, pulled by tractor to gather loose hay: rake

implement that breaks up soil, uproots weeds: cultivator

irrigation, farming without: dry farming

laborer: farm hand, migrant worker, bracero

natural farming without man-made pesticides, fertilizers: organic farming

pesticide spraying, especially by air: crop dusting

plant, scatter seeds: sow

rig that compresses and ties hay into blocks: baler

rig that separates seeds, grains from straw: thresher

rig that spreads manure, lime, other material: spreader

rotary blades for breaking up soil: tiller

separated husks of grain: chaff

separate seeds, grains from straw: thresh

shelf plowed into hill to prevent water run-off: terrace

silo that is horizontal: bunker silo

sowing grass to be used as pasture: ley farming

spread seeds: broadcast

stumps of crops left after harvest: stubble

subsistence farm, small: croft

tenant farmer who works for a share of the crop: sharecropper

unplowed strip of land at end of furrows: headland

wedge-shaped plow of yesterday: moldboard plow

SEE BARN, RANCH

farm v. cultivate, grow, sow, plow, till, raise crops, plant, practice husbandry, work the soil, *scratch out a meager existence, garden, homestead, ranch.

farmer n. agriculturist, cultivator, planter, grower, agrarian, agronomist, granger, sodbuster, rustic, *hayseed, *clodhopper, gardener, sharecropper, rancher, husbandman. "The staunchest soldiers."—Cato. "A handy man with a sense of humus."—Edward B. White.

farming n. husbandry, agriculture, agronomy, cultivation, crop-raising, sharecropping, harvesting, agribusiness, growing, tillage, working the land, homesteading, ranching. "The first and most precious of all the arts."—Thomas Jefferson. "A school of patience: you can't hurry the crops or make an ox in two days."—Emile C. Alain.

far-out a. Sl. wild, *cool, *groovy, weird, *rad *deep.

far-reaching a. extensive, wide-ranging, widespread, broad, sweeping, pervasive. ANT. limited, restricted, small scale.

farsighted a. foresighted, prescient, wise, shrewd, judicious, perceptive, provident, thoughtful. ANT. shortsighted, nearsighted, myopic, tunnel-visioned.

fart n. gas, flatulence, *barking spider, *ill wind, *call of the wood duck.

fart v. pass gas, *cut one, *rip one, *let her rip, *cut the cheese, *break wind.

fascinate v. spellbind, bewitch, charm, fix, attract, transfix, entrance, captivate, beguile, enthrall, engross, hypnotize.

fascinating a. spellbinding, bewitching, charming, attractive, transfixing, entrancing, captivating, beguiling, eye-popping, enthralling, engrossing, hypnotizing, riveting. ANT. boring, dull, prosaic.

fascination n. attraction, spellbinding, charm, bewitchment, captivation, trance, magnetism, enchantment, enthrallment.

fascism n. totalitarianism, nationalism. SEE DICTATORSHIP, GOVERNMENT

fascist n. Nazi, nationalist.

fashion n. style, mode, vogue, rage, dernier cri, trend, look, taste, fad, *latest thing, furor, way, craze, manner, design, cut. "What one wears himself; what is unfashionable is what other people wear."—Oscar Wilde. "Something that goes out of style as soon as most people have one."—Sylvia Bremer. "Beautiful things which always become ugly with time."—Jean Cocteau. "A despot whom the wise ridicule and obey."—Ambrose Bierce.

WORD FIND

calico dresses with long sleeves: prairie look

cowboy shirts, jeans, string ties, tooled-leather belts, Stetson: cowboy look

dashikis, selosos, bubas, Afros: African-American

1890-1910: leg-o-mutton sleeves, choker collars, pompadour hair: Gibson Girl

full skirts, hoop earrings, shawls: gypsy

historical fashion brought back: retro, vintage

Ivy League, upper-crust sweaters, chinos, cords, oxfords, loafers: preppy look

long torso dresses, ropes of pearls, 1920s: flapper look

male and female combined: androgynous

mod 1960s, miniskirts, polka dot shirts with white collars, bell-bottoms: Carnaby

mod 1960s, platform shoes, newsboy hats, faded dresses: funky

mohawks, spiked hair, black leather jackets, slitted skirts, safety pins, torn clothes: punk

nation, of a: ethnic

ruffled necks, wrists for both sexes, 1960s and 1970s: dandy

Scottish kilt like skirts, knee-socks, tam-o-shanter: kiltie look

tailored business or professional's clothes: Brooks Brothers

uncoordinated 1970s look, baggy pants, challis skirts: Annie Hall look

unkempt, long hair, tank tops, tie-dyed shirts, jeans, miniskirts, love beads: hippie, Grateful Dead look

fashion v. make, form, shape, create, devise, contrive, construct, forge, sculpt, *throw together, *slap together, fabricate, mold. SEE CLOTHING, DRESS

fashionable a. stylish, modish, in vogue, smart, chic, *on the cutting edge, *hot, trendsetting, *hip, mod, *all the rage, *happening, swank, a la mode, chi-chi, *in, *with it. ANT. unfashionable, old-fashioned, outmoded, dated, *out.

fast v. abstain, go hungry, refrain, starve, diet.

fast a. 1. QUICK rapid, swift, fleet, speedy, hasty, *snappy, *flying, *quicker than greased lightning, *breakneck, *in a heartbeat, *lickety-split, expeditious, instantaneous, brisk, supersonic, hypersonic, meteoric. 2. FIXED firm, stuck, unmovable, fastened, tight, secure, permanent, staunch, inextricable, steady, fortified. 3. WILD reckless, dissipated, loose, promiscuous, immoral, devil-may-care, lascivious, licentious, intemperate, unrestrained. ANT. 1. slow, leisurely, sluggish, slothlike. 2. movable, temporary, insecure. 3. moral, chaste, virtuous, celibate.

fast adv. 1. QUICKLY rapidly, swiftly, speedily, hastily, expeditiously, instantly, briskly, *in a flash, *in a heartbeat, *in short order, supersonically, hypersonically. 2. FIRMLY fixedly, securely, tight, solidly, steadfastly. ANT. 1. slowly, slothfully, leisurely. 2. loosely, insecurely.

fasten v. attach, secure, affix, hook, tie, join, couple, bind, lock, close, hitch, buckle, link, nail, weld, solder, rivet, cement. ANT. unfasten, detach, disconnect.

fastener n. holder, buckle, pin, latch, velcro, button, snap, catch, bolt, weld, rivet, lock, clasp.

FASTIDIOUS a. [fa STID ee us] discriminating, meticulous, picky. Also, overly dainty and easily disgusted. He was neat and fastidious; he was always picking lint from his clothing. SYN. discriminating, meticulous, picky, critical, fussy, finicky, hypercritical, dainty, overparticular, easily disgusted, squeamish, *persnickety. ANT. undiscriminating, uncritical, slack, sloppy.

fat n. adipose tissue, bulk, chubbiness, blubber, obesity, excess, *winter storage, flesh, *spare tire, *middle-aged spread, excess, beef, lard, grease.

fat a. 1. OVERWEIGHT obese, corpulent, chubby, plump, rotund, stout, portly, flabby, *porky, pudgy, fleshy, meaty, swollen, beefy, heavyset, elephantine, blubbery, lumpy, tubby, potbellied, paunchy, walruslike, roly-poly, *blimpy, thickset, full-figured, big-boned, *wide load. 2. RICH affluent, prosperous, well-to-do, moneyed, *well-heeled, comfortable, profitable, wealthy. ANT. 1. skinny, anorexic, bony, lean. 2. poor, poverty-stricken.

fatal *a.* deadly, lethal, mortal, destructive, killing, disastrous, terminal, calamitous, ruinous, death-dealing, catastrophic, pernicious. ANT. *harmless, benign.*

fatalism *n.* whatever will be will be, resignation, predestination, leaving it to the fates.

fatality *n.* death, casualty, victim, dead.

fate *n.* destiny, providence, fortune, kismet, lot, future, *wheel of fortune, end, predetermination, *the stars, luck, *lady luck, doom, God's will, karma, *handwriting on the wall. "What must be shall be."—Seneca. "The gunman that all gunmen dread."—Don Marquis.

fated *a.* destined, predetermined, preordained, doomed, predestined, in the stars, starcrossed, foreordained, dictated by karma or kismet. ANT. *up to chance, undetermined, undecided.*

fateful *a.* momentous, crucial, critical, important, decisive, portentous, apocalyptic, prophetic, deadly, lethal, fatal.

father *n.* 1. MALE PARENT dad, daddy, papa, pappy, pop, pa, *old man, parent, sire, head of the household, protector, forefather, progenitor, forebear. "A man who expects his son to be as good a man as he meant to be."—Franklin Clark. "He who brings up, not he who begets, is the father."—Bible. "One . . . is more than a hundred schoolmasters."—George Herbert. 2. FOUNDER inventor, originator, author, architect, creator, sire, initiator, maker, producer.

father *v.* sire, produce, beget, generate, procreate, engender, conceive, originate, create, invent, found.

fatherhood *n.* paternity, parenthood.

fatherland *n.* motherland, old country, homeland, native land.

fathom *v.* 1. UNDERSTAND comprehend, *get to the bottom of, grasp, get, sense, probe, interpret, figure out, penetrate. 2. SOUND plumb, measure.

fatigue *n.* tiredness, exhaustion, weariness, lassitude, listlessness, enervation, *burn-out, lethargy, malaise, weakness, languor. ANT. *energy, vigor, strength.*

fatigue *v.* tire, exhaust, wear out, enervate, *burn out, weaken, *poop, drain, wipe out, tucker out, deplete, debilitate, *bush.

fatty *a.* adipose, blubbery, lardy, tallowy, marbled, greasy, oily. ANT. *lean.*

fatuous *a.* stupid, silly, foolish, asinine, inane, moronic, *lamebrained, vacuous, idiotic, imbecilic. ANT. *brilliant, smart, wise.*

faucet *n.* spigot, valve, cock, tap.

fault *n.* 1. DEFECT imperfect, flaw, shortcoming, weakness, failing, *bug, blemish, stain. "The greatest . . . is to be conscious of none."—Thomas Carlyle. 2. MISTAKE error, slipup, lapse, blunder, *goof, blame, wrongdoing, liability, guilt, responsibility. ANT. *1. virtue, strength. 2. credit.*

fault *v.* blame, criticize, reproach, reprove, impugn, accuse, *wag one's finger at, shame.

faultfinder *n.* critic, nagger, nag, carper, caviler, *nitpicker, quibbler, Momus, *hairsplitter, *rag, *bellyacher, censor, grumbler, *backseat driver.

faultfinding *a.* critical, picky, nit-picking, captious, quibbling, *hairsplitting, caviling, hypercritical, overcritical. ANT. *easygoing, forgiving, tolerant.*

faultless *a.* flawless, perfect, impeccable, immaculate, clean, spotless, pure, ideal, unblemished, blameless, above reproach, innocent. ANT. *faulty, flawed, imperfect.*

faulty *a.* imperfect, flawed, defective, deficient, impaired, lacking, incorrect, wrong, unsound, malfunctioning. ANT. *perfect, flawless, sound.*

faux *a.* fake, artificial, synthetic, imitation, mock, ersatz, counterfeit, unnatural. ANT. *genuine, real.*

FAUX PAS *n.* [foh PAH] a social blunder, a mistake in etiquette. *Forgetting the host's name at a party is a faux pas.* SYN. social blunder, misstep, mistake, error, goof, impropriety, gaffe, indiscretion, transgression, lapse, offense, misconduct, slip.

favor *n.* 1. GOOD TURN service, courtesy, help, aid, accommodation, assistance, consideration, kindness, good deed, dispensation. 2. APPROVAL esteem, goodwill, liking, regard, approbation, backing, grace, patronage. ANT. *2. disfavor, ill will, disapproval.*

favor *v.* like, support, back, endorse, advocate, prefer, regard highly, fancy, *go for, sanction, pick, commend, indulge, pamper. ANT. *dislike, disfavor, frown upon, reject.*

favorable *a.* 1. APPROVING commending, friendly, good, kind, sympathetic, complimentary, affirmative, enthusiastic. 2. HELPFUL advantageous, beneficial, profitable, useful, auspicious, propitious, fortunate, convenient, timely, opportune, lucky. ANT. *1. disapproving, negative, unfriendly. 2. unfavorable, adverse, untimely.*

favorite *n.* preference, choice, selection, *number one, *apple of one's eye, pet, darling, ideal, dearest, idol, *pick of the litter.

favorite a. best-liked, preferred, pet, dear, choice, beloved, popular, selected, ideal, *fair-haired, dearest. ANT. *disliked, unwanted.*

favoritism n. partiality, bias, prejudice, discrimination, one-sidedness, preferential treatment, unfairness, partisanship, nepotism.

FAWN v. [FAWN] to flatter, cater to and generally fall all over someone in order to please. *Mary always fawns over the boss.* SYN. cringe, flatter, *kiss up to, *bootlick, *brownnose, toady, grovel, kowtow, bow and scrape, *apple polish, truckle to.

fawning a. servile, sycophantic, deferential, slavish, groveling, subservient, cringing, flattering, *brownnosing, kowtowing, submissive, obsequious. ANT. *forthright, domineering.*

fax n. facsimile, copy, transmission, reproduction, duplicate, document, image, electronic message.

fax v. copy, transmit, send, relay, deliver, forward, convey.

faze v. disturb, disconcert, bother, perturb, upset, rattle, embarrass, discompose, daunt, discomfit, *shake up, unnerve.

fear n. fright, terror, apprehension, foreboding, dread, alarm, anxiety, angst, panic, trepidation, nervousness, *butterflies, *the shakes, *cold feet, creeps, *chills, *cold sweat, *sweating bullets, awe, uneasiness, dismay, jitters, horror, cowardice, phobia, nightmare, *feeling of impending doom. "Nature's warning signal to get busy."—Henry Link. "The soul's signal for rallying."—Henry Ward Beecher. "A slinking cat I find beneath the lilacs of my mind."—Sophie Tunnel. SEE FEARFUL, PHOBIA

fear v. be afraid of, dread, apprehend, shudder at the thought of, be scared, *sweat bullets over, *get the shakes over, *get cold feet, feel alarm, *break out in a cold sweat, have qualms, cower, have butterflies, *break out in goosebumps, get jitters.

fearful a. 1. AFRAID frightened, scared, terrified, apprehensive, dreading, alarmed, anxious, frantic, panicky, discomposed, nervous, shaking, awed, uneasy, dismayed, intimidated, timorous, skittish, jittery, horrified, phobic, *sweating bullets. 2. FRIGHTENING terrifying, scary, frightful, dreadful, alarming, horrifying, chilling, nightmarish, distressing, creepy, shocking, horrible, *hairraising, bloodcurdling, formidable, *adrenalizing, *heart-pounding, paralyzing.

WORD FIND
Body reactions/language: hackles rise; small hairs at the back of the neck stir; prickling sensation up spine; skin crawling; icy chill down spine; skin blossoming with goosebumps; quaking knees; throat closes spastically; gulp; swallow dryly; swallow a lump in throat; knot constricting throat; breath raw in one's throat; shudder; heart fluttering/pounding/palpitating/hammering/performing flipflops; breath quickens; blood pounds in one's throat; trap door (sensation) opening in pit of belly; nauseating spurts of adrenalin coursing through veins; gasp; gulp air furiously; feel paralyzed; feel strangely semipresent or disembodied, as if in a dream; events appearing in slow motion; wring hands; sweat bullets; break out in cold sweat; skin turns clammy; stomach knots/clenches/shrivels/lurches; recoil in shock; reel; jumpy; feel weak and shaky from adrenalin

Facial expressions: gape pop-eyed, stare saucer-eyed with terror, stare catatonically, face ashen, face stricken, eyes take on a hunted look, nostrils dilate, face pales, blood drains from face, eyes dart maniacally, eyes widen in alarm, eyes transfixed, eyes watch with numbed horror, eyes watch with fascinated horror, peer wild-eyed, eyes blink with incredulity, lips form a silent O.

Voice: becomes high and hysterical, strangled cry, desperate, shrill with horror, hoarse shriek, mute, gargling scream, guttural scream, raw, constricted, strained, cracking, quavering, rises an octave. SEE ANXIETY

fearless a. courageous, bold, unafraid, brave, undaunted, unflinching, daring, valorous, stouthearted, bodacious, gutsy, confident, heroic, intrepid, spunky, *ballsy. ANT. *afraid, frightened, spineless, mousy, cowardly.*

feasible a. doable, possible, workable, attainable, achievable, practicable, viable, reachable, realistic. ANT. *impossible, unworkable, impractical.*

feast n. banquet, meal, spread, celebration, repast, dinner, supper, festival, eating and drinking, *feed.

feast v. banquet, eat, dine, wine and dine, indulge, partake, gorge, gormandize, regale, *stuff oneself, *pig out.

feat n. accomplishment, deed, act, exploit,

achievement, stunt, adventure, venture, triumph, coup.

feather *n.* plume, plumage, penna, quill, down, eider.

feathery *a.* downy, fluffy, soft, ticklish, gossamer, ethereal. ANT. *prickly, hard, sharp.*

feature *n.* **1.** CHARACTERISTIC aspect, component, element, point, item, quality, attribute, highlight, mark, trait, hallmark, property. **2.** MAIN SHOW headliner, highlight, drawing card, special attraction.

feature *v.* showcase, highlight, emphasize, spotlight, star, stress, play up, headline, give prominence to, underscore.

featureless *a.* nondescript, plain, unadorned, stark, minimalist, bland. ANT. *just, detailed, busy.*

febrile *a.* feverish, hot, flushed.

February *n.* "The most serious charge which can be brought against New England."—Joseph Krutch.

feces *n.* excrement, dung, stools, *crap.

feckless *a.* ineffective, futile, meaningless, worthless, purposeless. ANT. *purposeful.*

FECUND *a.* [FEE kund] fertile and productive. *A photograph of a fecund farmscape accompanied the article.* SYN. fertile, productive, fruitful, prolific, bounteous, rich, generating, teeming, potent. ANT. *sterile, barren, impotent.*

Fed *n.* *Sl.* government official, bureaucrat, politician, government regulator, government administrator, officeholder, government authority. SEE GOVERNMENT, POLITICS

federation *n.* confederacy, union, league, alliance, partnership, amalgamation, syndicate, fraternity, association.

fee *n.* charge, price, commission, payment, toll, due, bill, cost, expense, percentage, consideration, remuneration, compensation.

feeble *a.* weak, ineffective, frail, enervated, impotent, *wimpy, lame, powerless, fragile, inadequate, ineffectual, debilitated, sickly, slight, faint, meager. ANT. *powerful, potent, strong, effective.*

feebleminded *a.* mentally retarded, slow, dullwitted, imbecilic, stupid, dumb, moronic, *weak in the head, subnormal, *airheaded, bovine. ANT. *brilliant, *brainy, intelligent.*

feed *n.* food, fodder, ensilage, silage, forage, pasturage, vittles, *grub, provisions.

feed *v.* nourish, fuel, fill, sustain, provide, *wine and dine, serve, provision, foster, cater, maintain, give, *stuff, cram. SEE EAT

feedback *n.* response, answer, evaluation, reply,

observation, criticism, fallout, reverberation, echo, assessment, *pulse of the nation, barometer of public sentiment, *vibes.

feel *n.* flair, knack, aptitude, ability, faculty, gift, talent, hang.

feel *v.* **1.** TOUCH handle, finger, caress, palpate, stroke, fondle, grasp, squeeze, probe, grope, run hands over. **2.** SENSE experience, perceive, comprehend, know, understand, discern, notice, apprehend, detect, enjoy, suffer.

feeling *n.* **1.** SENSATION experience, perception, comprehension, understanding, consciousness, awareness, impression, response, reaction, emotion, sentiment. **2.** EMOTION passion, sensitivity, sympathy, depth, ardor, fervor, enthusiasm, zest, soul, heart, spirit, tenderness. "The emotion which drives the intelligence forward in spite of obstacles."—Henry Bergson. "The unconscious conversion of instinctual impulses."—Carl Jung. **3.** OPINION point of view, idea, sentiment, impression, sense, inclination, conviction, belief, evaluation, outlook, conception.

feelings *n.* emotions, sensibilities, passions, ego, impulses, susceptibilities, sentiments, sympathies, soul, spirit, drives, *plucking of heartstrings, instincts.

feet *n.* hooves, paws, pads, *dogs.

FEIGN *v.* [FANE] to make up, invent or fake. *Though he had never cared for his uncle, Joe decided to feign sympathy for him at the funeral.* SYN. make up, invent, fake, simulate, affect, pretend, assume, pose, bluff, *put on an act, sham, dissemble.

feint *n.* fake, diversion, sham, bluff, ruse, subterfuge, pretense, bait, snare, ploy, dodge, move, maneuver.

feisty *a.* spirited, spunky, lively, *high octane, fiery, courageous, hot-blooded, excitable, *full of it, strong-hearted, tough, touchy. ANT. *dispirited, meek.*

felicitous *a.* appropriate, apt, fitting, suitable, apropos, pertinent, relevant, timely. ANT. *inappropriate.*

felicity *n.* **1.** HAPPINESS bliss, joy, rapture, ecstasy, contentment. **2.** APPROPRIATENESS.

feline *a.* catlike, predatory, stealthy, sleek, graceful, slinky, sly, sneaky. SEE CAT

fell *v.* knock down, cut down, level, raze, hew, mow, prostrate. ANT. *raise.*

fellatio *n.* oral sex.

fellow *n.* **1.** MAN guy, person, boy, human, *chap, *dude, gentleman, individual, *hombre. **2.** PEER equal, companion, associate, compatriot, counterpart, friend, colleague, confrere, mate, twin, match.

fellowship n. companionship, friendship, association, comradeship, fraternity, camaraderie, togetherness, brotherhood, communion. "The ability to unite."—Berl Katznelson.

felon n. criminal, larcenist, lawbreaker, convict, outlaw, malefactor, miscreant, *hood, gangster, mafioso, crook, recidivist.

FELONIOUS a. [fuh LOW nee us] evil, wicked, designating serious criminal behavior. *Armed robbery is a felonious act.* SYN. evil, wicked, base, criminal, larcenous, villainous, vicious, corrupt, lawbreaking, illegal, immoral. ANT. *virtuous, law-abiding, moral, upstanding.*

felony n. crime, serious crime, offense, atrocity, evil, sin, violation, murder, rape, arson, assault, robbery. SEE LAW, POLICE, COURT

female n. girl, woman, lady, *she, femme, gal, matron, sister.

feminine a. female, womanly, girlish, ladylike, soft, gentle, genteel, effeminate. ANT. *masculine, manly, macho.*

femme fatale n. deadly woman, siren, seductress.

fence n. enclosure, barrier, barricade, boundary, wall, rail, paling, palisade, hedge.
WORD FIND
cattle-enclosing: barbed wire fence
fish-catching fence made of stakes: weir
post and rail: post and rail fence
screen of wood strips: lattice
stake fence: picket fence, paling
stake fence used for defense: palisade
sunken, in ditch: ha-ha
wire mesh: chain-link fence, *Cyclone fence
woven work of twigs, branches: wattle fence
zigzagging rail fence: Virginia fence, worm fence, snake fence

fence v. **1.** ENCLOSE surround, pen, confine, encircle, separate, bound, corral, wall, hem. **2.** FIGHT WITH SABERS OR FOILS duel, parry, engage in swordplay.
WORD FIND
deflect opponent's weapon: parry
faked movement to throw off opponent: feint
forward thrust and jump: lunge
grazing blow down opponent's blade: coulé
jump and lunge: balestra
leap: volt
offensive move made after parry: riposte

protective cup on weapon: guard
protective glove: gauntlet
protective jacket: fencing jacket, underplastron
readiness stance: on guard
run toward opponent with arm extended: fleché
score: hit
taking of opponent's blade, method of: croisé
term: touché
weapon: epee, foil, saber, rapier
SEE FEND OFF

fend off v. defend, parry, resist, ward off, dodge, repel, deflect, divert, shield from, keep at bay, protect, evade, repulse.

feng shui n. [literally, (wind/water)] geomancy, Chinese geomancy, furniture arranging, environmental balancing, interior design, natural alignment, Chinese art, space design, harmonizing, placement, layout modification, orientation, natural order.
WORD FIND
analysis methods: Eight House Theory; Flying School Theory
compass used to determine flow of cosmic energy or Chi, wooden: luo pan
divination related to, ancient Chinese system of: I Ching
elements, five: water, wood, fire, earth, metal
energy force: Chi, Chíi, cosmic breath
energy forces, opposing: Yin (negative), Yang (positive)
master or teacher of: Sifu; Shifu
measuring stick showing lucky measurements: Feng Shui ruler
octogonal amulet comprised of eight sections or trigrams: pakua
octogonal mirror reflecting Chi: Bagua
practitioner: geomancer

feral a. wild, untamed, undomesticated, fierce. ANT. *tamed.*

ferment n. agitation, excitement, commotion, uproar, turmoil, turbulence, stir, tumult, hubbub, disruption, to-do. ANT. *peace, calm, serenity.*

ferment v. agitate, excite, disturb, shake, stir, churn, provoke, foment, incite, inflame, *bring to a head, seethe, rouse. ANT. *soothe, quiet, calm.*

ferocious a. savage, fierce, violent, cruel, wild, beastly, brutish, predatory, bloodthirsty, brutal, rapacious, vicious, barbarous, merciless. ANT. *humane, gentle, mild, tame.*

ferocity *a.* savagery, fierceness, violence, cruelty, wildness, beastliness, brutality, bloodthirstiness, rapaciousness, viciousness, barbarity. ANT. *gentleness, passivity.*

ferret out *v.* search out, sniff out, root out, dig up, unearth, track down, chase down, hunt down, discover, probe, smoke out.

ferry *n.* boat, raft, barge, vessel, transport.

ferry *v.* carry, convey, cross, transport, *lug, ship, deliver, shuttle, pilot.

fertile *a.* productive, fecund, fruitful, reproductive, generative, potent, yielding, rich, teeming, prolific, bountiful. ANT. *sterile, barren, impotent, unproductive.*

fertility *n.* fecundity, potency, virility.

fertilize *v.* enrich, dress, compost, manure, germinate, inseminate, impregnate.

ferlizer *n.* soil enhancer, enrichment, dressing, compost, plant food, bone meal, manure, humus, muck, dung, green manure.

FERVENT *a.* [FUR vunt] passionate, intense, heated. *Because of her impoverished childhood, Jamie had a fervent desire to succeed.* SYN. passionate, intense, heated, ardent, fervid, burning, hot, earnest, raging, eager, flaming, zealous, feverish, fierce, spirited. ANT. *cool, lukewarm, apathetic, dispassionate.*

fervor *n.* passion, intensity, heat, ardor, warmth, fire, fever, eagerness, zeal, enthusiasm, gusto, spirit, zest, vigor. ANT. *apathy, indifference, coolness.*

fester *v.* **1.** SUPPURATE ulcerate, drain, run, putrefy, become inflamed. **2.** RANKLE rile, irk, annoy, irritate, gall, inflame, embitter.

festival *n.* celebration, feast, rite, observation, carnival, commemoration, fair, gala, jubilee, fiesta.

festive *a.* celebratory, merry, gay, mirthful, sportive, jolly, cheery, jubilant, lighthearted. ANT. *gloomy, dreary, somber.*

festivity *n.* merrymaking, celebration, gaiety, play, fun, revelry, party, mirth, jollity, carousal, sport, entertainment.

festoon *v.* adorn, decorate, deck, garland, trim, wreathe, ornament.

fetch *v.* **1.** GET bring, retrieve, deliver, tote, convey, obtain, transport, lug, grab. **2.** SELL FOR bring in, realize.

fetching *a.* attractive, charming, captivating, alluring, beautiful, winsome, fascinating, tantalizing, entrancing, enticing, lovely. ANT. *repulsive, unattractive, ugly.*

fetid *a.* stinking, putrid, *stinky, malodorous, foul, rank, rancid, smelly, rotten, tainted,

gamy, reeking. ANT. *fresh, floral, sweet.* SEE ODOR, SCENT, SMELL

fetish *n.* erotic fixation, obsession, idée fixe, *turn-on, mania, preoccupation.

fetter *n.* restraint, check, shackle, chain, binding, bond, irons, trammel, handcuffs, hobble, manacle.

fetter *v.* restrain, check, shackle, chain, bind, put in irons, trammel, manacle, handcuff, restrict, hold. ANT. *free, loose, liberate.*

fettle *n.* condition, shape, form, state, order, fitness.

fetus *n.* developing infant, unborn young.

feud *n.* fight, quarrel, conflict, combat, altercation, squabble, argument, contention, row, hostility, *falling-out. ANT. *peace, accord, harmony.*

feud *v.* fight, quarrel, combat, squabble, contend, clash, war, *lock horns, wrangle, dispute.

fever *n.* temperature, pyrexia, heat, glow, flush. SEE DISEASE

feverish *a.* **1.** RUNNING A TEMPERATURE warm, hot, fiery, *burning up, flushed, clammy, sweaty, delirious. **2.** EXCITED agitated, heated, passionate, frenetic, restless, fervid, worked up, frantic, ardent, frenzied. ANT. *1. cool, chilled, normal. 2. calm, cool, lukewarm.*

few *n.* some, a number, a handful, several, a bunch.

few *a.* not many, scant, scarce, rare, negligible, skimpy, sparse, thin, meager, limited, infrequent. ANT. *many, innumerable, countless.*

financé *n.* fiancée, wife-to-be, husband-to-be, betrothed, future mate, sweetheart, bride-to-be, groom-to-be, *future ball and chain. SEE MARRIAGE, WEDDING

fiasco *n.* failure, *turkey, disaster, *flop, *bomb, *dud, debacle, catastrophe, abortion, miscarriage, *washout, farce, *joke. ANT. *success, hit, triumph.*

fiat *n.* decree, command, act. SEE ORDER

fib *n.* lie, white lie, half-truth, untruth, falsehood, fabrication, *cock-and-bull story, prevarication, *whopper, *crock. ANT. *truth, fact.*

fib *v.* lie, tell a white lie, falsify, fabricate, prevaricate, *tell a whopper, *stretch the truth, fudge.

fiber *n.* strand, thread, filament, hair, string, fibril.

FICKLE *a.* [FIK ul] liable to change one's loyalties or affections, capricious. *Mary went through four boyfriends last month; she is very fickle.* SYN. capricious, changeable, unstable, inconstant, whimsical, variable, unpredictable, impulsive, *blowing hot and cold, vacillating, flighty, volatile. ANT. *stable, constant, faithful, steady.*

fiction n. story, fabrication, lie, yarn, tale, invention, fantasy. "The world of our dreams come true."—Courtney Cooper. "Imagining based on facts."—Margaret Banning. "Fact distorted into truth."—Edward Albee. ANT. *nonfiction, truth, fact.* SEE NOVEL, STORY

fictitious a. made up, imaginary, fabricated, concocted, untrue, unreal, *bogus, created, fanciful, fantastic, feigned, phony. ANT. *real, factual, true.*

fiddle v. fuss with, toy, diddle, tinker, adjust, finger, mess with, play.

FIDELITY n. [fi DEL i tee] faithfulness; loyalty. *She questioned her husband's fidelity after he stayed out all night.* SYN. faithfulness, loyalty, devotion, allegiance, constancy, dedication, fealty, reliability, integrity. ANT. *infidelity, faithlessness, disloyalty.*

fidget v. squirm, wiggle, twitch, twiddle, fret, jiggle, jitter, *get antsy, jump, *worm about.

fiduciary n. trustee, trusteeship, agent, depositary.

field n. **1.** MEADOW pasture, grassland, plain, green, clearing, glebe, range.

WORD FIND

descriptive: Audubonesque tableau of birds and flowers, tawny tussocks of fall, softly-flowered like a Monet canvas, profusion of flowers, mèlange of colors, soft heather meadow, sea of crested wheat, bluegrass meadow, golden alpine meadow, thatchy undergrowth, verdant, Irish green field, broad sweep, wildflower meadow, sprays of daisies and buttercups, the lush grasses of a miller's dreams

grasses: bluegrass, bunch grass, salt grass, foxtail, buffalo grass, crab grass, deer grass, fescue, orchard grass, June grass, red top, river grass, ribbon grass, cattail

grasslands of Eurasia: steppes

heather or other small shrubs: heath

marshy area covered with heather, bracken: moor

midwest plain: prairie

plain of South America: pampas

Siberian: tundra

South African grassland: veld, veldt

tropical/subtropical grassland: savanna

2. SPECIALTY line, profession, province, realm, domain, area, sphere, territory, bailiwick.

field trip n. outing, excursion, expedition, junket, jaunt, day trip, sightseeing tour.

fiend n. devil, demon, evil spirit, Satan, Lucifer, beast, monster, ogre, villain, savage, barbarian, scoundrel, sadist, *bad actor, *bastard, *creep. ANT. *angel, saint.*

fiendish a. evil, satanic, diabolical, demonic, monstrous, beastly, villainous, savage, barbarous, sadistic, *creepy, brutish. ANT. *angelic, saintly.*

fierce a. savage, wild, cruel, violent, ferocious, intense, furious, untamed, horrible, tempestuous, unbridled, vehement. ANT. *mild, tame, gentle.*

fiery a. passionate, burning, ardent, *hot, fervid, peppery, hot-blooded, blazing, feverish, angry, impassioned, excitable, high-strung, volatile. ANT. *cool, calm, lukewarm, dispassionate.*

fight n. battle, combat, clash, brawl, wrangle, bout, war, *scrap, fray, skirmish, encounter, scuffle, tussle, row, *fisticuffs, rumble, *free-for-all, donnybrook, altercation, set-to, dispute.

fight v. **1.** PHYSICALLY COMBAT battle, clash, brawl, wrangle, war, skirmish, rumble, contest, wrestle, altercate, assault, spar, box, *mix it up, *lock horns, tussle, *exchange blows, *slug it out, *go at it tooth and nail. **2.** OPPOSE BY ARGUMENT argue, contradict, dispute, contest, defy, *make a stand against, squabble, resist, *protest, repulse, bicker.

fighter n. battler, scrapper, warrior, combatant, boxer, pugilist, wrestler, brawler, soldier, aggressor, bruiser, bully, antagonist, contender.

figment n. fantasy, imagining, fancy, fiction, creation, invention, daydream, product of the imagination, fabrication, delusion. ANT. *reality, truth, fact.*

FIGURATIVE a. [FIG yur uh tiv] based on figures of speech, symbols, etc.; not literal; metaphorical. *"The show blew my mind" is a figurative statement; my brain is actually still intact.* SYN. metaphorical, symbolic, not literal, illustrative, allegorical, representative, emblematic, pictorial. ANT. *literal, exact.*

figure n. **1.** FORM outline, shape, configuration, cast, structure, conformation. **2.** PHYSIQUE build, body, frame, shape. **3.** ILLUSTRATION picture, diagram, drawing, depiction, sketch, pattern, design. **4.** PROMINENT PERSON celebrity, notable, personage, man, woman, character. **5.** NUMBER numeral, digit.

figure *v.* **1.** CALCULATE compute, reckon, add up, sum, tally, count. **2.** THINK reckon, believe, suppose, guess, reason, judge.

figure of speech *n.* expression, metaphor, simile, imagery, trope.

FIGUREHEAD *n.* [FIG yur hed] one with the appearance or rank of someone in charge, but who in reality has no power. *The president is just a figurehead; the real leadership comes from his cabinet members.* SYN. straw man, *front, *puppet, nominal head, *dummy, dupe, token.

figurine *n.* statuette, sculpture, knickknack.

filch *v.* steal, pilfer, lift, shoplift, swipe, *pinch, thieve, purloin, *power, *rip off, rob, misappropriate.

file *n.* record, documents, data, folder, dossier, information, cabinet, repository, directory, index.

file *v.* **1.** ORDER catalog, categorize, classify, alphabetize, organize, sort, index. **2.** APPLY petition, register, make an application. **3.** SMOOTH grind, rasp, abrade, grate.

filibuster *n.* speech, tirade, dissertation, monologue, exhortation, discourse, delaying tactic.

filigree *n.* ornamentation, tracery, delicate lines, flourish.

fill *v.* load, pack, cram, crowd, *top off, stuff, stock, replenish, squeeze in, glut, pad, heap, inflate, feed, gorge, saturate, pervade, suffuse. ANT. *empty, drain, deplete.*

film *n.* **1.** COATING layer, sheet, membrane, covering, scum, veil, cloud, haze, mistiness, blur, fog. **2.** MOVIE *flick, picture, cinema. SEE MOTION PICTURE, MOVIE

filmy *a.* veiled, hazy, cloudy, misty, foggy, blurred, milky, murky, gauzy. ANT. *clear, transparent, sharp.*

filter *n.* strainer, sieve, purifier, clarifier, screen, sifter.

filter *v.* strain, filtrate, screen, sift, clarify, purify, refine, stream, trickle, leak, drain, effuse.

filth *n.* **1.** DIRT muck, grubbiness, mud, scum, pollution, sewage, sludge, mire, *crap, *crud, grime, nastiness, slime, foulness, dung, excrement. **2.** OBSCENITY indecency, nastiness, pornography, smut, *raunch. ANT. *2. decency, wholesomeness, purity.*

filthy *a.* **1.** DIRTY mucky, grubby, muddy, scummy, polluted, gross, *sludgy, *crappy, *cruddy, grimy, nasty, slimy, foul, stinking,

soiled, begrimed. **2.** OBSCENE indecent, nasty, pornographic, *smutty, *raunchy, lewd. ANT. *1. clean, spotless, fresh, sanitary. 2. decent, *squeaky-clean, pure, wholesome.*

FINAGLE *v.* [fuh NA gul] arrange, maneuver or manipulate to get something. *Joe tried to finagle his way into the game without tickets.* SYN. arrange, maneuver, manipulate, wangle, trick, deceive, engineer, machinate, negotiate, contrive.

final *a.* last, end, concluding, closing, finishing, ultimate, terminal, completing, extreme, decisive, definitive. ANT. *first, opening, beginning.*

finale *n.* end, close, finish, cap, conclusion, termination, completion, culmination, consummation, swan song, windup, finis. ANT. *opening, beginning, start.*

finalize *v.* conclude, complete, close, cap, wind up, terminate, consummate, culminate, *sew up loose ends, *put on ice, *clinch.

finance *n.* money management, banking, investment, economics, fiscal matters.

finance *v.* pay for, back, underwrite, bankroll, subsidize, capitalize, support.

financial *a.* fiscal, monetary, pecuniary, economic, money.

financier *n.* banker, investor, venture capitalist, underwriter, tycoon, *fat cat, *angel, treasurer, merchant, *sugar daddy.

find *v.* discover, stumble upon, come upon, chance upon, uncover, spot, ferret out, see, locate, ascertain, espy, discern, sight, detect. ANT. *lose, misplace, lose sight of, overlook.*

finding *n.* judgment, conclusion, discovery, decision, verdict.

fine *n.* penalty, assessment, amercement, forfeit, punishment, damages, *slap on the wrist.

fine *a.* **1.** SUPERIOR excellent, very good, A-1, the best, first-class, first-rate, choice, prime, select, exceptional, great, supreme, refined. **2.** IN GOOD HEALTH well, okay, satisfactory. **3.** DELICATE light, gossamer, diaphanous, airy, fragile, dainty, flimsy, refined, exquisite. **4.** THIN slender, slight, narrow. **5.** GROUND powdered, pulverized, refined. **6.** SUBTLE slight, minute. ANT. *1. poor, inferior, mediocre. 2. sick, ill, *under the weather. 3. heavy, coarse, ponderous. 4. fat, broad, wide. 5. coarse, unrefined. 6. huge.*

fine *v.* levy, penalize, punish, charge, assess, amerce.

FINESSE *n.* [fi NES] delicate skill or maneuvering. *He pitched the ball with great finesse.*

SYN. skill, adroitness, delicacy, know-how, acumen, subtlety, sophistication, savvy, knack, shrewdness, savoir faire. ANT. *clumsiness, incompetence, bumbling, awkwardness.*

fine-tune *v.* adjust, calibrate, balance, tweak, align, set, attune.

finger *n.* digit, pointer, thumb, forefinger, ring finger.

finger *v.* touch, handle, squeeze, feel, palpate, poke.

finicky *a.* fussy, picky, overparticular, exacting, dainty, meticulous, choosy, fastidious, anal retentive, *persnickety, *hard to please. ANT. *easy, careless, sloppy.*

finish *n.* **1.** ENDING close, closing, completion, finale, termination, windup, fulfillment, consummation, culmination, finis, death, *curtains, cap, climax. **2.** COATING surface, shine, polish, refinement, patina, veneer, varnish, luster. **3.** REFINEMENT elegance, grace, polish, cultivation, sauvity, genteelness. ANT. *1. beginning, start, opening. 3. coarseness, roughness, crudity.*

finish *v.* **1.** COMPLETE end, close, finalize, stop, terminate, wind up, fulfill, consummate, culminate, die, cap off, *sew up loose ends. **2.** DEPLETE use up, exhaust, *knock off, consume, expend, dispose of, drain, dispatch. ANT. *1. start, begin, open. 2. refill, conserve, restock, replenish.*

FINITE *a.* [FI nite] limited, as distinguished from infinite. *Natural resources on earth are finite; they won't last forever.* SYN. limited, measureable, confined, bounded, countable, terminable, delimited, fixed, ephemeral, ending, exhaustable. ANT. *infinite, boundless, interminable, endless.*

fink *n. Sl.* informer, *rat, *tattletale, *snake, *weasel, *bastard.

fire *n.* **1.** FLAME blaze, conflagration, inferno, flare, sparks, embers, combustion, wildfire, bonfire, holocaust. "The symbol of civilization."—Joseph Hertz. "God's unfailing charity."—John Oxenham. "The most tolerable third party."—Thoreau.
WORD FIND
building that is a fire hazard: firetrap
causing fire: incendiary
door designed to withstand intense heat and flames: fire door
fear of fire: pyrophobia
firesetter with criminal intentions: arsonist, incendiary
firesetter with mental problems: pyromaniac, firebug

firesetting compulsion: pyromania
forecasting the future by peering into flames: pyromancy
god: Vulcan
intense, widespread fire caused by nuclear detonation: firestorm
strip of land cleared to stop fire spread: firebreak
wall designed to withstand intense heat and flames: fire wall
worshipper: pyrolater
2. ENTHUSIASM energy, drive, vigor, zeal, fervor, intensity, ardor, passion, verve, gusto, vehemence. **3.** GUNFIRE round, barrage, shelling, salvo, fusillade, volley, strafing. ANT. *2. apathy, indifference, dispassion.*

fire *v.* **1.** SHOOT discharge, shell, pull the trigger, let off, detonate. **2.** ROUSE arouse, excite, inflame, spark, stir, incite, electrify, inspire, quicken, galvanize. **3.** DISCHARGE FROM DUTIES *pink slip, lay off, dismiss, *give walking papers, *can, *show the door, *axe, *let go, give notice, *sack. ANT. *1. cease fire. 2. dampen, discourage. 3. hire.*

fire alarm *n.* smoke alarm, heat sensor, early warning system, emergency alarm.

firearm *n.* gun, pistol, revolver, rifle, *shooting iron, carbine, shotgun, sawed-off shotgun, assault rifle, *street sweeper, Uzi, *Saturday night special, *heat, derringer, six-shooter, .357 Magnum., .45, .38, .22, muzzleloader, musket, blunderbuss, flintlock. SEE GUN

fireball *n.* meteor, bolide. SEE METEOR

firebrand *n.* agitator, rabble-rouser, instigator, agent provocateur, troublemaker, rebel, revolutionist, anarchist, *sparkplug.

firecracker *n.* squib, *cherry bomb, petard, *noisemaker. SEE FIREWORKS

fireplace *n.* hearth, chimney, stove, grate, fireside, blaze, inglenook.

fireproof *a.* fire resistant, flameproof, incombustible, unburnable, nonflammable. ANT. *combustible, flammable, incendiary, explosive.*

firestorm *n.* **1.** CONFLAGRATION fallout. SEE FIRE **2.** CONTROVERSY protest, outburst, war, hostilties, riot, outcry, outbreak, uproar, hue and cry.

fireworks *n.* pyrotechnics, incendiary devices, rockets, feux d'artifice.
WORD FIND
arsenic sulfide used in: realgar
child's spark-maker: sparkler
hisses and sputters: fizgig, squib
pinwheellike: catherine wheel
rotating display: girandole

small rockets: bottle rockets
spiral, rises in a: tourbillion
star: star shell
tube ejecting balls of fire: Roman candle

firm *n.* company, corporation, business, enterprise, concern, outfit, institution, house, organization, conglomeration.

firm *a.* **1.** HARD solid, stiff, rigid, compressed, compact, unyielding, stony, inflexible, set. **2.** FIXED stationary, unmovable, stable, immovable, secure, immobile, anchored, sturdy, tight, unshakable, solid, rooted. **3.** CONSTANT, RESOLUTE consistent, enduring, steady, staunch, unshakable, fixed, persevering, unwavering, true, steadfast. ANT. *1. soft, loose. 2. unstable, mobile, movable. 3. wavering, unsteady, irresolute.*

firmament *n.* sky, heavens, vault, arch, *wild blue yonder, ether, infinity.

first *a.* **1.** EARLIEST original, beginning, front, opening, maiden, initial, premiere, preceding, prior, antecedent, primal, primeval, rudimentary, elementary. **2.** HIGHEST principal, chief, head, main, foremost, supreme, greatest, top, preeminent, dominant, capital, outstanding, ranking. **3.** BASIC fundamental, rudimentary, primary, elementary, beginning. ANT. *1. last, latest, end, subsequent. 2. lowest, least, smallest. 3. advanced.*

first-class *a.* best, superior, greatest, fine, excellent, superb, supreme, A-1, tops, *topdrawer, topnotch, *primo, peerless. ANT. *inferior, second-class, *bottom of the barrel.*

first-rate *a.* SEE FIRST-CLASS

fiscal *a.* financial, monetary, budgetary, revenue, money, spending and taxation. SEE MONEY

fish *v.* **1.** ANGLE troll, cast, flycast, trawl, seine, chum. **2.** SEARCH rummage, hunt, pick through.

fisherman *n.* angler, fisher, piscator, *gill-netter, lobsterman, aquaculturist.

fishing *n.* angling, casting, trolling, trawling. "That solitary vice."—Lord Byron.

WORD FIND
artificial bait: lure, jig, spinner, fly, nymph
bait: earthworm, night crawler, mayfly, nymph, baitfish, chum, herring, squid
basket used by fisherman: creel
chair in sport-fishing boat: fighting chair
dragging a line near surface behind boat: trolling
drag net along bottom: trawl
fence that corrals fish: weir
floating signal ball: bobber

gear box: tackle box
gear: tackle
illegal fishing: poaching
line with several hooks at intervals across stream: trotline
net drawn shut by two boats: purse seine
net that hangs from floats on surface: seine, gill net
rippled water showing where fish is rising to bait: rise
snarled line on reel caused by overrun: backlash, *bird's nest
spear: harpoon, gaff
taking of bait by fish: strike
up and down motion imparted on bait to lure fish: jigging
weight: sinker

fishwife *n.* bitch, scold, witch, hag, *battleax, nag, crab, complainer, grumbler.

fishy *a.* suspicious, doubtful, shady, unbelievable, incredible, shady, questionable, dubious, slippery, not kosher. ANT. *plausible, believable, credible.*

FISSION *n.* [FISH un] the splitting of an atom and its conversion to energy; nuclear fission. *Fission is what makes an atom go boom.* SYN. splitting, dividing, scission, parting, cleavage, nuclear fission, splitting the atom, atom smashing, atomic reaction. ANT. *fusion.* SEE NUCLEAR BOMB, AMMUNITION

fissure *n.* cleft, crack, groove, crevice, crevasse, crack, chasm, fracture, fault, rift, slit.

fit *n.* seizure, convulsion, paroxysm, spasm, attack, *spaz, throe, bout, conniption, outburst, spell, frenzy.

fit *v.* correspond, accord, jibe, harmonize, match, conform, agree, *dovetail, interlock, mesh.

fit *a.* **1.** SUITABLE fitting, apt, proper, seemly, right, correct, appropriate, befitting, decorous, germane. **2.** IN SHAPE healthy, well, robust, strong, hardy, hale, vigorous, hearty, strapping. ANT. *1. unsuitable, inappropriate. 2. sickly, weak, out of shape.*

fitful *a.* intermittent, irregular, spasmodic, restless, sporadic, erratic, unstable, spotty, fluctuating, random. ANT. *regular, constant, steady.*

fitness *n.* good health, healthiness, robustness, aerobic fitness, endurance, energy, cardiovascular fitness, strength, vigor, stamina, *steam, *juice, *zip, heartiness, vitality, *staying power, *pep, *get up and go. ANT. *sickness, weakness.* SEE EXERCISE

fitting n. fixture, part, accessory, component, attachment, *doohickey.

fitting a. proper, suitable, befitting, correct, appropriate, decorous, becoming, fit, comme il faut, right, seemly, *politically correct. ANT. improper, unsuitable, incorrect.

fix n. predicament, mess, jam, *stew, difficulty, plight, *hot water, *pickle, *between a rock and a hard place.

fix v. 1. REPAIR mend, patch up, doctor, remedy, restore, recondition, tune up, overhaul, adjust, correct. 2. ATTACH affix, secure, connect, fasten, plant, tie, couple, link, lock, implant, cement, nail. 3. DETERMINE set, decide, establish, settle. ANT. 1. break, bust. 2. detach, loosen, remove.

fixate v. focus, direct, lock on to, obsess, attach, become attached.

FIXATION n. [fiks A shun] a neurotic preoccupation with someone or something; an obsession. He has a fixation with blue-eyed blondes. SYN. obsession, preoccupation, monomania, mania, fetish, fascination, *thing, complex, crush, infatuation, compulsion, idée fixe.

fixed a. 1. FIRMLY ATTACHED unmovable, secured, anchored, firm, stable, solid, rooted, tight, made fast. 2. ESTABLISHED set, settled, unchangeable, decided, constant, steady, unvarying, firm, inflexible. ANT. 1. detached, loosened. 2. changeable, varying.

fixture n. fitting, part, accessory, component, attachment, appurtenance, *doohickey, device, contrivance.

fizz n. effervescence, carbonation, bubbles.

fizzle v. fail, *flop, *bomb, die, miscarry, fall short, *lay an egg, *sputter and die, come to nothing. ANT. succeed, triumph, *score.

flabbergasted a. surprised, amazed, astonished, taken aback, dumbfounded, astounded, struck dumb, rendered speechless, shocked, staggered, *bowled over, *blown away, confounded. ANT. nonchalant, calm, cool, unperturbed.

flabby a. flaccid, soft, limp, blubbery, *doughy, slack, droopy, fat, baggy, untoned, sagging, pendulous. ANT. firm, toned, rigid, *rockhard.

flaccid a. SEE FLABBY

flag n. banner, standard, ensign, colors, pennant, *Old Glory, *Stars and Stripes, *Union Jack, streamer, banderole, bunting. "The emblem of our unity, our power, our thought and purpose as a nation."—Woodrow Wilson. "The trademark of a nation."—Leonard Levinson.

WORD FIND
decorative cloth in the colors of a flag: bunting
military unit's: guidon
pirate's skull and crossbones: Jolly Roger
pole: staff, shaft
signaling pennant used on boats: burgee

flag v. weaken, wilt, tire, become limp, languish, wilt, droop, fade, wane, ebb, sink, diminish, die. ANT. strengthen, invigorate, energize.

flagellate v. flog, lash. SEE WHIP

FLAGRANT a. [FLA grunt] outrageous or glaring. He was ejected from the game after committing his second flagrant foul. SYN. outrageous, glaring, blatant, audacious, shameless, brazen, undisguised, gross, conspicuous, barefaced, flaunted, disgraceful, egregious, extreme. ANT. inconspicuous, subtle, slight, sneaky.

flagship n. leader, chief, mother ship, bellwether, queen, crown jewel, king.

flail v. strike, thrash, flog. SEE BEAT

flair n. 1. KNACK talent, aptitude, ability, genius, propensity, bent, feel, gift, faculty. 2. TASTE style, panache, dash.

flak n. criticism, disapproval, opposition, censure. SEE CRITICISM

flake n. scale, bit, fleck, chip, sliver, peel, shaving, sheet.

flake v. scale, peel, shave, exfoliate, chip, shed.

FLAMBOYANT a. [flam BOY unt] showy or ornate, loud. She wore flamboyant costumes to draw attention to herself. SYN. showy, ornate, loud, colorful, flashy, florid, gaudy, dazzling, ostentatious, garish, wild, theatrical, splashy, extravagant, glamorous. ANT. quiet, understated, modest, plain, inconspicuous, dull.

flame n. 1. FIRE flare, blaze, light, *tongue, flash. SEE FIRE 2. LOVER sweetheart, girlfriend, boyfriend.

flame v. burn, blaze, flare up, kindle, flash, spark, flicker, glow, sparkle.

flammable a. combustible, inflammable, incendiary, igneous, explosive. ANT. fireproof, nonflammable.

flap n. 1. FOLD cover, tab, wing, tail, fly, skirt. 2. CONTROVERSY agitation, commotion, brouhaha, to-do, fuss, hullabaloo, *tempest.

flap v. slap, whack, flutter, smack, swat, lash, whip.

flare v. 1. FLAME blaze, flash, flicker, glow, scintillate, sparkle, ignite, spark, glare. 2. BURST OUT erupt, explode, blow up, pop. 3. WIDEN broaden, spread, expand, dilate, splay. ANT. 2. *die down, dampen, cool.* 3. *contract, narrow.*

flare-up *n.* outbreak, outburst, explosion, rise, blowup, disruption, convulsion, epidemic, uprising, spurt, gush.

flash *n.* **1.** FLARE streak, burst, blaze, glint, flame, radiance, strobe, coruscation, illumination, spark, scintillation, glow, discharge, explosion. **2.** INSTANT second, *heartbeat, *blink of an eye, jiffy.

flash *v.* strobe, blink, fulgurate, flicker, flare, shine, scintillate, glow, glint, shimmer.

flashback *n.* memory, recurrence, remembrance, reliving, reminiscence, echo, recollection, recall, ghost from the past, *head trip.

flasher *n.* *Sl.* exhibitionist, pervert, *sicko, *dirty old man.

flash point *n.* moment of truth, critical mass, zero hour.

flashy *a.* showy, loud, flamboyant, gaudy, ostentatious, garish, glaring, blinding, glitzy, glittery, pretentious. ANT. *quiet, plain, understated, modest, sober.*

flask *n.* bottle, container, flagon, phial, vial, canteen.

flat *a.* **1.** LEVEL even, flush, horizontal, plane, smooth, lying down, recumbent, supine, prostrate, prone. **2.** ABSOLUTE unequivocal, unqualified, positive, definite, direct, plain, clear. **3.** TASTELESS, DULL insipid, stale, bland, dull, boring, flavorless, lackluster, blah, spiritless, drab, uninteresting. ANT. *1. uneven, rough, bumpy, round. 2. equivocal, qualified. 3. interesting, tasty, effervescent.*

flatten *v.* **1.** LEVEL plane, smooth, spread out, lie flat. **2.** KNOCK DOWN squash, crush, *steamroll, prostrate.

flatter *v.* compliment, praise, puff up, adulate, laud, extoll, inflate, *brownnose, *kiss up to, *apple polish, toady, cajole, fawn, *suck up to, *lay it on thick, *lay it on with a trowel, *butter up, *massage one's ego, *stroke, blandish, gush, *sweet talk.

flatterer *n.* complimenter, booster, trumpeter, sycophant, *yes-man, *brownnose, *sweet talker, *apple polisher, toady, *lickspittle, bootlicker. "Like cats, [they] lick and then scratch."—German proverb. "One who says things to your face that he would not say behind your back."—G. Millington. "A friend who is your inferior, or pretends to be so."—Aristotle.

flattery *n.* praise, compliment, adulation, tribute, eulogy, blarney, inflation, applause, sycophancy, blandishment, *brownnosing, *apple polishing, toadyism, *honeyed words, *snow job, gush, smarm, bootlicking, fawning, cajolery. "Something nice someone tells you about yourself that you wish were true."—Frank Malester.

flatulence *n.* gas, wind, bloating.

flatulent *a.* **1.** GASSY windy. **2.** PRETENTIOUS pompous, windy, long-winded, bombastic, verbose.

flaunt *v.* show off, strut, display, parade, wave, flash, exhibit, spotlight, swagger, peacock, broadcast, advertise, vaunt. ANT. *hide, cover up, conceal.*

flavor *n.* **1.** TASTE savor, sapor, tincture, piquancy, tang, zing, seasoning, spiciness, saltiness, sweetness, sourness, tartness. **2.** ESSENCE character, quality, nature, spirit, feel.

flavor *v.* season, spice, *liven up, salt, lace, infuse.

flaw *n.* defect, imperfection, fault, deformity, blemish, failing, weakness, pitfall, shortcoming, chink.

flawless *a.* faultless, defect-free. ANT. *faulty, flawed.* SEE PERFECT

fledgling *n.* beginner, *rookie, *greenhorn, *tenderfoot, freshman, *tyro, novice, neophyte.

flee *v.* run away, escape, bolt, *cut and run, *make a quick exit, take off, decamp, *split, *beat feet, *fly the coop, *make a getaway, *make tracks, *blow, *skeddadle, *vamoose, *scram.

fleece *v.* cheat, *rip off, swindle, rook, *flimflam, *take to the cleaners, *soak, *chisel, con, hustle.

fleet *n.* flotilla, armada, squadron, convoy, navy. SEE NAVY

fleet *a.* fast, swift, quick, rapid, speedy, mercurial, hasty, expeditious, meteoric, nimble. ANT. *slow, plodding, slothful, dragging.*

fleeting *a.* transient, brief, ephemeral, temporary, quick, short-lived, momentary, *flash in the pan, *here today gone tomorrow, meteoric. ANT. *enduring, lasting, permanent.*

flesh *n.* **1.** MEAT body tissue, muscle, fat, beef, brawn. **2.** BODY material person, human, man, woman, physical nature. ANT. *2. soul, spirit.*

fleshy *a.* fat, plump, beefy, obese, blubbery, corpulent, chubby, chunky, *tubby, meaty, porcine, portly, stout, paunchy, *jelly-bellied, pulpy. ANT. *skinny, anorexic, bony, rawboned.*

flex *v.* bend, crook, stretch, contract, tense.

flexible *a.* **1.** PLIABLE bendable, pliant, elastic, supple, springy, ductile, malleable, rubbery, willowy, lithe, limber. **2.** ADAPTABLE yielding, adjustable, manageable, compliant, docile, tractable, amenable. ANT. *1. rigid, stiff, inflexible. 2. rigid, obstinate.*

flick *v.* snap, flip, tap, brush.

flicker *v.* waver, flutter, dance, quiver, glimmer, glint, scintillate, flash, shimmer, flare, flame.

flier *n.* flyer, pilot, airman, aviator, aviatrix, navigator. SEE AIRCRAFT

flight *n.* soaring, air travel, hovering, gliding, planing, flying, aeronautics, volitation.

flighty *a.* frivolous, capricious, irresponsible, fickle, impulsive, scatterbrained, whimsical, harebrained, giddy, *airheaded, *ditzy, unstable. ANT. *stable, rational, thoughtful.*

flimflam *v.* cheat, swindle, *rip off, *con, deceive, trick, delude.

flimsy *a.* **1.** FRAGILE frail, easily broken, thin, delicate, slight, shoddy, unsubstantial, ethereal, diaphanous, gossamer, rickety, cheap. **2.** INADEQUATE ineffectual, feeble, weak, lame, shallow, unconvincing, trivial, poor, incredible, implausible. ANT. *1. solid, strong, *like the Rock of Gibraltar. 2. credible, solid, convincing, plausible.*

flinch *v.* recoil, wince, cringe, shrink, jump, cower, quail, start, blench, jerk, blink.

fling *v.* throw, pitch, cast, hurl, toss, sling, heave, flip, *chuck.

flinty *a.* hard, firm, stony, inflexible, rigid, unmerciful, coldhearted, hardened, heartless, unsympathetic. ANT. *soft, warmhearted, sympathetic.*

flip *n.* somersault.

flip *v.* toss, flick, throw, pitch, spin, snap.

flip-flop *n.* reversal, about-face, change, turnaround, change of heart, *fence-hopping.

flip out *v. Sl.* *go mental, *go berserk, *go ballistic, *go nuts, *lose it, *freak out, *flip one's lid.

flip side *n.* reverse side, obverse, back, opposite side, other side of the coin, *B-side.

FLIPPANT *a.* [FLIP unt] disrespectful, irreverent. *Tom was sent to the principal's office for being flippant.* SYN. disrespectful, irreverent, impudent, impertinent, insolent, brash, fresh, cheeky, *flip, *wise, cocky, rude, sassy. ANT. *respectful, reverent, polite.*

flirt *n.* tease, coquette, hussy, wolf, vamp, heartbreaker, *game-player.

flirt *v.* tease, lead on, entice, coquet, tantalize, toy, trifle, dally, vamp, *make eyes at, *wink at, *make a pass at, *hit on.

flirtatious *a.* teasing, enticing, tantalizing, provocative, coquettish, *on the make, *come-hither, alluring, *on the prowl, *making eyes at, inviting. ANT. *aloof, cold.*

flit *v.* dart, hop, flutter, hover, whisk, skim, fly, flitter, race, hurry, flap, wing.

float *v.* bob, buoy, levitate, hover, be borne along by current, ride, raft, drift, swim, waft, sail. ANT. *sink, go under, submerge.*

flock *n.* congregation, drove, pack, herd, group, gang, assemblage, band, swarm, colony, mass, throng, multitude. SEE ANIMAL

flog *v.* whip, thrash, lash, flagellate, horsewhip, beat, strap, flail, cane, flay, hide, tan.

flood *n.* deluge, inundation, torrent, overflow, outpouring, gush, rush, surge, wave, tsunami, downpour, cloudburst, gullywasher, *rain of biblical proportion, cataclysm.

flood *v.* deluge, inundate, overflow, gush, rush, surge, overwhelm, drown, engulf, submerge, swamp, flush, drench, saturate.

floor *n.* **1.** BOTTOM footing, base, flooring, planking, parquet, linoleum, rug, carpeting, walkway. **2.** STORY level, flight, tier, deck.

floor *v.* flabbergast, astound, stun, stagger, shock, throw, nonplus, dumbfound, astonish, confound.

flop *n.* failure, *bomb, *dud, *dog, loser, *turkey, disaster, *bust, fiasco, *clunker, *lemon, *lead balloon, *laugher. ANT. *success, hit, triumph, winner.*

flop *v.* **1.** FALL plop, collapse, flounder, *bellyflop, tumble, topple, *plunk down, *fall flat on one's face. **2.** FAIL *bomb, *go over like a lead balloon, *wash out, fizzle, *lay an egg, fold, *sputter and die. ANT. *2. succeed, triumph, win.*

florid *a.* ornate, showy, gaudy, ostentatious, flamboyant, flowery, elaborate, embellished, overdecorated, high-flown, garish, arabesque, rococo, baroque, ruddy, rosy, pink. ANT. *plain, simple, austere, stark, unadorned.*

flotilla *n.* fleet, armada, argosy, group, unit, squadrons, vessels.

flotsam *n.* wreckage, debris, cargo, odds and ends, castoffs, junk, jetsam.

flounder *v.* struggle, stumble, blunder, wallow, fumble, flop, thrash, stammer, stutter, falter, *flub one's lines.

flourish *n.* **1.** DECORATION embellishment, ornamentation, garnish, adornment, frill, curlicue. **2.** BRANDISHING wave, show, flaunting, exhibition, display.

flourish v. grow, thrive, prosper, blossom, flower, fatten, boom, burgeon, increase, wax, succeed, *go great guns, expand, mushroom. ANT. *wither, die, shrivel, fail.*

flout v. jeer, scoff, mock, scorn, ridicule, jeer at, spurn, insult, deride, taunt, *make fun of. ANT. *respect, honor, revere.*

flow n. current, course, gush, stream, drift, river, outpouring, spill, issuance, discharge, emanation, flux, trickle, progression, ebb, tide.

flow v. course, gush, stream, drift, issue, discharge, emanate, spout, trickle, progress, surge, run, roll, spew, ooze, ebb, proceed, cascade, well, spill.

flower n. bloom, blossom, ornamental, floweret, floret, bud, annual, perennial, spray, posy, nosegay, bouquet. "Heaven's masterpiece."—Dorothy Parker. "The sweetest thing God ever made, and forgot to put a soul into."—Henry Ward Beecher.

WORD FIND

bloom, blossom: effloresce

bouquet worn on shoulder: corsage

descriptive: teardrop petals, ruffles and lace, spikes like kitten tails, irridescent, radiant, creamy, flaming, blazing, dotting fields like fallen confetti, elegant profusion, heady perfumes of Spring

female organ that becomes fruit: pistil

grains of male germ cells: pollen

male organ: stamen

names: African violet, amaryllis, aster, azalea, baby's breath, begonia, black-eyed Susan, bleeding heart, bluebell, buttercup, camellia, candytuft, carnation, cat's paw, Chinese lantern, chrysanthemum, cockscomb, columbine, cornflower, cowslip, daffodil, dahlia, daisy, dandelion, dogwood, forget-me-not, forsythia, foxglove, foxtail, fuchsia, gardenia, gentian, geranium, gladiolus, goldenrod, heather, hibiscus, hollyhock, honeysuckle, hyacinth, impatiens, Indian paintbrush, iris, jack-in-the-pulpit, jonquil, lady's slipper, larkspur, lilac, lily, lily of the valley, lotus, lupine, magnolia, mallow, marigold, mayflower, mimosa, morning glory, narcissus, oleander, orchid, pansy, peony, petunia, phlox, poinsetta, poppy, primrose, Queen Anne's lace, rhododendron, rose, snapdragon, sunflower, sweet alyssum, sweet William, tulip, Venus flytrap, viola, violet, water lily, wolfbane, yucca, zinnia

native flowers of a region: flora

petals, collective term: corolla

science of growing: horticulture

sepals, or protective leaves of a flower: calyx

spike, dense: spadix, spike

spot of different color in center of some types: eye

sun, follows the: heliotropic, phototropic

SEE FIELD

fluctuate v. vary, waver, oscillate, vacillate, *run hot and cold, change, *seesaw, *yo-yo, alternate, shift, rise and fall.

flue n. pipe, channel, duct, vent, passage, tube, airway.

fluent a. flowing, smooth, easy, loose, fluid, articulate, eloquent, smooth-talking, practiced, effortless, glib, natural, *silvertongued. ANT. *halting, floundering, tongue-tied.*

fluff n. down, fleece, fuzz, eiderdown, wool.

fluffy a. downy, feathery, soft, fleecy, flossy, woolly, silky. ANT. *flat, hard.*

fluid n. liquid, water, juice, aqua.

fluid a. 1. LIQUID liquefied, watery, flowing, streaming, pouring, running, juicy, wet. 2. FLEXIBLE adaptable, unfixed, changeable, indefinite, adjustable. ANT. *1. solid. 2. fixed.*

fluke n. stroke of luck, good fortune, windfall, *one in a million, *lucky strike, break, fortuity, godsend, serendipity, accident, fate.

flume n. chute, channel, run.

flunk v. SEE FAIL

flunky n. lackey, servant, footman, toady, *yes man.

flurry n. 1. SUDDEN GUST OF WIND, SNOW OR RAIN shower, dusting, squall. SEE RAIN, SNOW 2. COMMOTION stir, bustle, fluster, *to-do, *ado, squall, turmoil, hubbub, ferment.

flush v. 1. BLUSH redden, color, glow, turn crimson, *burn, bloom, *turn rosy, *turn ruddy. 2. WASH OUT flood, rinse, drench, irrigate, spray, douche, douse. ANT. *1. blanch, whiten.*

flush a. 1. FLAT level, square, plane, plumb, straight. 2. ABUNDANT plentiful, affluent, rich, wealthy, well-supplied, well-to-do. ANT. *1. uneven, out of plumb. 2. poor, destitute, lacking.*

flushed a. red, pink, ruddy, florid, glowing, aglow, blushing, red-faced, burning, scarlet-faced, blooming, feverish. ANT. *pale, blanched, white.*

fluster n. confusion, befuddlement, agitation, nervousness, turmoil, *discombobulation, bewilderment, disturbance, excitement, commotion. ANT. *calm, composure, peace.*

fluster v. confuse, bewilder, perturb, befuddle, agitate, *discombobulate, disturb, *rattle, excite, stir, ruffle, disquiet. ANT. *calm, quiet, compose.*

flute n. SEE MUSICAL INSTRUMENT

fluting n. channels. SEE GROOVE

flutter v. flap, wave, beat, quiver, shake, sway, swing, shudder, tremble, bat, oscillate, wag, dance, flit, fly.

flux n. flow, current, course, stream, run, movement, tide, passage, surge, change, unrest, fluctuation. ANT. *stagnation, inertia, stasis.*

fly v. **1.** SOAR take wing, take flight, glide, flit, hover, jet, float, *ride the thermals, *wing, climb, dive, swoop, *hedgehop, waft, be borne along by the wind, scud, barnstorm. SEE AIRCRAFT, BIRD **2.** SPEED AWAY rush, hurry, *hightail, hustle, scoot, *make a mad dash, *go like the wind, scurry, *go off like a shot, *put the pedal to the metal, *beat feet. **3.** FLEE escape, *make a getaway, skedaddle, *cut and run, *split, *vamoose, *scram, *head for the hills, *blow.

fly-by-night a. unstable, unreliable, disreputable, unprofessional, untrustworthy, undependable, short-lived. ANT. *reputable, established.*

flying saucer n. unidentified flying object, UFO, bogey, spaceship, extraterrestrial vessel. SEE AIRCRAFT, SPACE

foam n. froth, lather, suds, scum, fizz, bubbles, spume, effervescence, spindrift, head.

foam v. froth, lather, fizz, bubble, spume, effervesce, ferment, cream.

foamy a. frothy, lathery, fizzy, bubbly, effervescent, spumy, soapy, sudsy, creamy. ANT. *flat, uncarbonated.*

focus n. focal point, center, target, hub, heart, spotlight, bull's eye, nucleus.

focus v. center on, center, zero in on, pinpoint, direct, fix, concentrate, *hone in on, spotlight, clear up, sharpen.

fodder n. feed, silage, food, hay, straw.

foe n. enemy, adversary, rival, opponent, antagonist, *bad guy, combatant, competitor. ANT. *friend, ally, *soul mate.*

fog n. **1.** MIST haze, cloud, brume, sea smoke, vapor, *pea soup, murk, smog, gloom.

WORD FIND

cooling point below which fog forms: dew point

dense mass of: fog bank

descriptive: diaphanous, gossamer, nubilous, ethereal, veils, gauzy, sea's breath, thick enough to curdle, as thick as New England clam chowder, thick enough to eat/shovel, creeping, dank, cloaking, shrouds, sheets of fog like the sails of Spanish galleons, ghosting over the water, wisps, fingers of fog clutching at ship riggings, soul-dampening

freezing fog that deposits frost: rime

ice crystals, containing: pogonip

surrounded by and prevented from sailing: fogbound

2. MUDDLE confusion, daze, bewilderment, haze, stupor, disorientation, perplexity, mystification.

foggy a. SEE FOG

foghorn n. siren, guide, diaphone fog signal, warning signal.

FOIBLE n. [FOY bul] a minor weakness or fault. *Reporters regularly expose the foibles of those in the public eye.* SYN. weakness, fault, shortcoming, deficiency, Achilles' heel, flaw, failing, frailty, imperfection, quirk, vice, chink. ANT. *asset, strength, strong point.*

foil n. contrast, complement, antithesis, background.

foil v. thwart, frustrate, balk, check, baffle, impede, outsmart, circumvent, stymie, prevent, checkmate, stop, outwit, counter, hamstring, spoil, *throw up a roadblock. ANT. *aid, assist, abet, advance.*

foist v. palm off, sneak in, fob, pass off, *pull a fast one.

fold n. crease, pleat, tuck, crimp, gather, dogear, overlap, layer, drape.

fold v. **1.** CREASE pleat, plait, tuck, crimp, gather, double over, dog-ear, overlap, drape, hem, enclose, envelop, wrap. **2.** GO OUT OF BUSINESS fail, close, go bankrupt, *go belly up, become insolvent.

folder n. file, binder, wrapper, envelope, sheath, covering.

foliage n. leaves, leafage, greenery, umbrage. SEE TREE, FOREST, JUNGLE

folklore n. myths, legends, fables, custom, tradition, superstition.

folks n. kin, relatives, parents, flesh and blood, family.

folksy a. *down-to-earth, friendly, informal, unassuming, rustic, natural, down-home, casual, unpretentious, simple, easygoing, corny. ANT. *sophisticated, pretentious, *la-di-da.*

follow v. **1.** COME AFTER ensue, succeed, supplant, supersede, proceed, replace, take the place of, result, issue, emanate. **2.** TRAIL stay behind, *bring up the rear, shadow, tail, track, *dog, hunt down, chase, pursue, go after. **3.** ABIDE BY obey, conform to, heed, regard, mind, comply with, do what is told, emulate, copy, imitate. ANT. *1. precede, antedate. 2. trailblaze, head up, lead. 3. disregard, ignore.*

follower *n.* disciple, fan, adherent, apostle, partisan, pupil, devotee, member, proponent, patron, votary, proselyte, henchman. ANT. *leader, mentor, detractor.*

following *n.* fans, supporters, patrons, devotees, adherents, coterie, entourage, retinue, train.

following *a.* afterward, successive, subsequent, next, ensuing, coming, *in the wake of, *on the horizon. ANT. *preceding.*

folly *n.* foolishness, silliness, nonsense, craziness, lunacy, absurdity, wackiness, senselessness, idiocy, fatuity. "A vigorous plant, which sheds abundant seed."—Isaac D'Israeli. ANT. *good sense, intelligence, wisdom, *wise move.*

foment *v.* instigate, incite, stir up, agitate, spark, fire, excite, arouse, provoke, spur, egg on, galvanize, *fan the flames. ANT. *extinguish, suppress, dampen, check.*

fond *a.* affectionate, loving, attached, tender, doting, close, warm, adoring, caring, devoted, *sweet on, enamored. ANT. *hostile, hating, uncaring, cool.*

fondle *v.* stroke, caress, pat, pet, embrace, rub, hug, hold, massage, squeeze.

font *n.* source, origin, wellspring, genesis, root, seed.

food *n.* nourishment, sustenance, foodstuffs, *eats, victuals, *chow, *grub, edibles, comestibles, cuisine, fare, *vittles, ration, provisions, subsistence, meal, meat and potatoes, fodder, feed. "The first enjoyment of life."—Lin Yutang.

food poisoning *n.* salmonella, ptomaine poisoning.

fool *n.* idiot, blockhead, ignoramus, moron, imbecile, ninny, nincompoop, simpleton, nitwit, harebrain, clown, ass, buffoon, *dingaling, *lunkhead, dupe, dunce, sap, oaf. "One who does not suspect himself."—José Ortega y Gasset. "The whetstone of the wits."—Shakespeare.

fool *v.* deceive, kid, trick, cheat, hoodwink, *pull the wool over one's eyes, mislead, dupe, *sucker, *scam, *take in, *bamboozle.

fool around *v.* **1.** WASTE TIME *horse around, fritter, *hang out, putter, diddle. **2.** MAKE LOVE *make out.

foolhardy *a.* reckless, rash, foolish, risk-taking, bold, Icarian, daring, stupid, impetuous, daredevil, imprudent, irrational, insane, adventuresome. ANT. *cautious, careful, wary.*

foolish *a.* stupid, idiotic, asinine, ignorant, imprudent, moronic, imbecilic, harebrained, clownish, oafish, *cockamamy, daft, unwise, silly, *nuts, ill-advised, *half-baked, fatuous, ludicrous, *screwy, childish. ANT. *wise, thoughtful, smart, rational, sensible.*

foolproof *a.* failsafe, *goofproof, *idiot-proof. ANT. *tricky, difficult.*

foot *n.* **1.** EXTREMITY hoof, pad, paw, *dog. **2.** BASE bottom, foundation, floor, pedestal. ANT. *2. crown, head.*

football *n.* sport.

WORD FIND

ball, slang for: pigskin

ball snapper: center

center of defensive line: nose guard, nose tackle

defends against passes and runs into the backfield: defensive back, safety, cornerback

defensive backfield: secondary

defensive players just behind linemen: linebackers

downing of ball in offense's end zone, two points to defense: safety

encroaching into opposing team's side before ball is snapped: offside, encroachment

extra point kick after touchdown: conversion

faking a handoff and running with ball hidden behind hip: bootleg

faking a handoff to running back, who pretends to run with ball hidden in arms, then passing: play-action pass

field: gridiron

five back defense: nickel defense

foul in which player without ball is hit from behind: clipping

imaginary line where ball is down: line of scrimmage

kickoff in which ball lands in receiving team's end zone: touchback

kickoff to opposing side: punt

kick that is low and tumbling, employed to force fumble: onside kick

know-it-all fan who criticizes players: armchair quarterback, Monday morning quarterback

lateral pass or handoff followed by surprise pass: flea-flicker

line-drive pass: bullet
line-of-scrimmage player: lineman
long pass requiring small miracle to be caught: Hail Mary, prayer
offensive alignment in which quarterback takes snap standing several yards back from center: shotgun
offensive back behind or near quarterback: fullback, halfback running back
passes, hands off, runs, calls plays: quarterback
pass that imparts spin on ball and keeps it from tumbling: spiral, bullet
play change called out at line of scrimmage: audible
quarterback's eluding of tacklers: scrambling
run and handoff to player running in opposite direction: reverse
score: touchdown
sideways or backwards pass: lateral
six back defense: dime defense
slamming ball down in end zone after scoring touchdown: spike
surprise run by quarterback: quarterback sneak
surprise rush: blitz
tackle with arm swung into opponent's neck or head: clothesline
tailback, halfback and fullback form a line behind quarterback: I formation
footing n. foot, foothold, foundation, establishment, position, toehold, basis, beachhead, bridgehead, vantage.
footloose a. free, unrestricted, fancy-free, unencumbered, unattached, roving, untethered, liberated, uninhibited. ANT. *restricted, bound, shackled.*
footprint n. track, footmark, impression, tread.
fop n. dandy, clotheshorse, dude, coxcomb, peacock, popinjay, fashion plate, Beau Brummel, poseur, *pretty boy.
for prep. **1.** IN THE INTEREST OF, on behalf of. **2.** IN FAVOR OF, in support of.
forage v. search, look for, hunt, sniff out, scavenge, rummage, explore, root out, seek, raid, plunder.
foray v. raid, plunder, pillage, ransack, loot, ravage, attack, invade, maraud, asault.
forbear v. refrain, avoid, resist temptation, abstain, lay off, desist, shun, eschew, go without, hold back, forgo, endure, tolerate, bear.
forbearance n. restraint, self-control, abstinence, refraining, avoidance, desistance, tolerance, patience, mercy. "To forgive an enemy who has been shorn of power."—Elbert Hubbard. ANT. *impatience, intolerance.*

forbid v. prohibit, proscribe, disallow, ban, outlaw, enjoin, restrict, veto, make off limits, taboo, interdict, stop. ANT. *allow, permit, approve.*
forbidden a. prohibited, proscribed, banned, outlawed, verboten, restricted, off limits, vetoed, taboo, disallowed. ANT. *allowed, permitted, approved of.*
forbidden fruit n. SEE TABOO
forbidding a. threatening, ominous, dangerous, frightening, scary, uninviting, foreboding, sinister, disagreeable, unfriendly. ANT. *inviting, friendly, alluring.*
force n. **1.** POWER strength, vigor, might, energy, velocity, momentum, pressure, horsepower, *muscle, drive, pull, weight, stress, potency, impetus. "The blind wild beast."—Alfred Lord Tennyson. **2.** COERCION compulsion, constraint, duress, bullying, arm-twisting, violence. **3.** MILITARY POWER army, navy, air power, troops, infantry, division, squadron, regiment. ANT. *1. impotence, weakness.*
force v. coerce, compel, oblige, arm-twist, strong-arm, constrain, pressure, press, make, *railroad, exact, push, drive, necessitate, wrest, *put the screws to.
forced a. **1.** COERCED involuntary, obligatory, compulsory, enforced, unwilling, constrained, pressured. **2.** NOT SPONTANEOUS strained, constrained, stiff, labored, contrived, unnatural, artificial, insincere, affected, self-conscious, studied. ANT. *1. voluntary, willing, unforced. 2. spontaneous, natural, genuine.*
forceful a. powerful, effective, vigorous, dynamic, potent, mighty, strong, robust, energetic, commanding, persuasive. ANT. *ineffectual, impotent, weak.*
fore a. front, first, forward, head, leading. ANT. *rear, last.*
forebear n. forefather, progenitor. SEE ANCESTOR
foreboding n. portent, bad feeling, omen, premonition, uneasiness, warning, prophecy, foreshadowing, *gut feeling, apprehension, *handwriting on the wall, *bad vibes, forewarning.
forecast n. prediction, prophecy, divination, prognostication, augury, projection, *reading of the cards, prognosis, conjecture, guess.
forecast v. predict, foresee, prophesy, foretell, divine, *read in the cards, augur, prognosticate, project, presage, envision, conjecture, guess, estimate.

forefather n. forbear, progenitor, forerunner, predecessor. SEE ANCESTOR

forefront n. front, head, *cutting edge, vanguard, fore. ANT. *rear, background.*

foregoing a. previous, former, aforesaid, preceding, prior, late, earlier. ANT. *following, ensuing.*

foreign a. **1.** NONDOMESTIC alien, exotic, unfamiliar, imported, faraway, distant, outlandish, unknown, nonnative, strange, overseas. **2.** UNCHARACTERISTIC aberrant, unnatural, abnormal, inconsistent, incompatible, unrelated, extraneous. ANT. *1. domestic, native, indigenous. 2. characteristic, compatible, natural.*

foreigner n. alien, nonnative, immigrant, outsider, stranger. ANT. *native.*

foreman n. boss, crew chief, overseer, supervisor, superintendent, spokesman, chair, foreperson.

foremost a. chief, first, leading, head, principal, primary, preeminent, main, paramount, supreme, first, uppermost. ANT. *bottom, least, lowest.*

forensic a. arguable, controversial, debatable, moot, judicial. ANT. *certain, incontrovertible.*

foreplay n. fondling, warm-up, sexual activity, heavy petting, cuddling, lovemaking. SEE SEX

forerunner n. **1.** PREDECESSOR precursor, ancestor, forebear, forefather, prototype, pioneer. **2.** HERALD announcer, harbinger, usher, messenger, portent, omen.

foresee v. anticipate, predict, prophesy, prognosticate, foretell, divine, envision, forecast, presage, augur.

foresight n. farsightedness, vision, anticipation, foreknowledge, precognition, forethought, preconception, prudence, preparedness, precaution, prophecy. ANT. *hindsight, unpreparedness.*

forest n. woods, woodland, timberland, weald, stand, grove, bush, copse, coppice, wilderness, wild, trees, habitat, *regiment of trees. **WORD FIND**
ancient, uncut: old-growth forest, virgin forest
cleared area littered with logging debris: slash
evergreen oak thicket: chaparral
grassy clearing in: glade
ground or floor material: litter, duff, mor
leaf-shedding trees: deciduous
logging, denuding method: clear-cutting
non-leaf-shedding trees: coniferous
pertaining to trees: arboreal
thickly treed: bosky
top of trees: canopy, crowns
trees of a forest region: sylva
tropical woods receiving heavy rainfall: rain forest
wind-toppled trees and branches: windthrow, windfall, deadfall
SEE JUNGLE, TREE

foretell v. predict, forecast, prophesy, foresee, divine, augur, presage, prognosticate, anticipate, forebode, portend, warn.

forethought n. planning, foresight, prudence, anticipation, farsightedness, preparedness, precaution, provision. ANT. *afterthought.*

forever adv. always, everlastingly, endlessly, eternally, incessantly, continually, unceasingly, for all time, interminably, *till hell freezes over. ANT. *never.*

foreword n. preface, introduction, prologue. ANT. *epilogue.*

forfeit n. penalty, fine, forfeiture, damages, fee, loss.

forfeit v. lose, surrender, give up, relinquish, sacrifice, yield.

forge v. **1.** FORM make, manufacture, shape, fabricate, mold, contrive, fashion, hammer out, cast, devise, invent. **2.** COUNTERFEIT copy, falsify, trace, reproduce, imitate, simulate.

forgery n. fake, counterfeit, fraud, copy, imitation, simulation, falsification, sham.

forget v. **1.** *DRAW A BLANK slip one's mind, overlook. **2.** LET PASS nevermind, disregard, ignore, write off, skip, drop. ANT. *1. remember, recall. 2. regard, consider.*

forgetful a. absentminded, amnesic, abstracted, distracted, *out to lunch, oblivious, inattentive, daydreaming, heedless, mindless, absent. ANT. *attentive, alert, focused.*

forgive v. pardon, excuse, absolve, overlook, condone, *wipe the slate clean, *let off the hook, *let bygones be bygones, exculpate, acquit. ANT. *condemn, convict, damn.*

forgiveness n. pardon, excusing, forbearance, absolution, amnesty, reprieve, dispensation, mercy, exoneration, clemency, acquittal. "The fragrance the violet sheds on the heel that has crushed it."—Mark Twain. "Man's deepest need and highest achievement."—Horace Bushnell. "The sweetest revenge."—Isaac Friedmann. ANT. *condemnation, conviction, revenge.*

forgo v. do without, give up, relinquish, abstain from, renounce, eschew, refrain from, forswear, pass up, quit. ANT. *take up, keep, indulge in.*

fork *n.* branching, division, split, divergence, bifurcation, parting.

FORLORN *a.* [for LORN] miserable and without hope. *After the funeral she was grim and forlorn.* SYN. miserable, hopeless, wretched, woebegone, pitiful, pathetic, abandoned, bereft, desolate, dismal, inconsolable, despairing, lonesome, deserted. ANT. *cheerful, happy, euphoric.*

form *n.* **1.** SHAPE configuration, contour, silhouette, outline, profile, cast, structure, figure, conformation, design, frame. **2.** BODY anatomy, figure, build, frame, physique, shape. **3.** MOLD cast, frame, model. **4.** TYPE kind, sort, variety, class, genus, species, order. **5.** PROCEDURE way, ceremony, formality, ritual, custom, decorum, motions, formula, protocol, method, mode, format. **6.** DOCUMENT application, sheet, questionnaire.

form *v.* **1.** SHAPE mold, cast, frame, design, make, produce, construct, build, fabricate, *hammer out, fashion, manufacture, invent, create, concoct. **2.** ORGANIZE found, establish, start, incept. **3.** MATERIALIZE arise, appear, *take shape, crystallize, come into being. **4.** COMPRISE compose, constitute, make up.

formal *a.* **1.** CEREMONIAL decorous, orderly, customary, proper, conventional, methodical, ritualistic, systematic, official, prescribed, correct, *by-the-book. **2.** STIFF stuffy, *starched, prim, ceremonious, stilted, straitlaced, punctilious, rigid, proper, self-conscious. ANT. *1. spontaneous, unconventional, uncustomary. 2. informal, relaxed, casual.*

formality *n.* **1.** CONVENTION form, tradition, observance, protocol, practice, decorum, officiality, *red tape. **2.** PROPRIETY etiquette, ceremony, decorum. ANT. *2. informality.*

format *n.* arrangement, layout, system, shape, size, form, setup, configuration, organization, scheme, method, formula, plan.

formation *n.* creation, establishment, development, genesis, generation, production, construction, manufacture, crystallization, evolution, structure, composition.

former *a.* previous, prior, earlier, aforementioned, first, past, antecedent, preceding, bygone. ANT. *later, following, ensuing.*

formfitting *a.* snug, body-hugging. ANT. *baggy, loose.* SEE TIGHT

FORMIDABLE *a.* [FOR muh duh bul] an intimidating thing or person that is difficult to face, surmount or overcome. *The rookie boxer met his formidable opponent—the World Heavyweight Champion.* SYN. intimidating, dreadful, frightening, scary, feared, awesome, difficult, hard, overwhelming, insurmountable, powerful, indomitable, staggering, tough, huge. ANT. *weak, manageable, tiny, insignificant.*

formless *a.* shapeless, amorphous, asymmetrical. ANT. *distinct, specific, defined.*

formula *n.* recipe, prescription, specifications, method, blueprint, code, system, principle, creed.

fornicate *v.* have sexual intercourse, have an affair, commit adultery, *sleep around, philander, *cheat. SEE SEX

fornication *n.* intercourse, copulation, sex, adultery. SEE SEX

forsake *v.* abandon, leave behind, renounce, give up, quit, discard, forswear, reject, desert, disown, disavow, repudiate, *spurn, *wash one's hands of, *kiss off. ANT. *embrace, take up.*

forswear *v.* renounce, disavow, deny, repudiate.

fort *n.* fortress, fortification, stronghold, citadel, garrison, defense, army post, battlement. SEE CASTLE

FORTE *n.* [FOR tay] something one does particularly well or excels at. *I'm not much of a tennis player; basketball is more my forte.* SYN. specialty, strong point, strength, *bag, *cup of tea, *thing, proficiency, skill, area of expertise, bent, talent, aptitude, *long suit, metier. ANT. *weakness, foible.*

forthcoming *a.* upcoming, *on the horizon, approaching, imminent, impending, prospective, expected, pending, awaited. ANT. *distant, past.*

forthright *a.* direct, straightforward, frank, blunt, candid, honest, plain, unambiguous, undisguised, heart-to-heart, *up front, bald. ANT. *indirect, dishonest, ambiguous, disguised, *sugar-coated.*

forthwith *adv.* immediately, at once, now, directly, without delay, tout de suite, *pronto, this instant, speedily. ANT. *eventually, gradually, slowly, later.*

fortification *n.* fort, fortress, stronghold, citadel, garrison, defense, army post, battlement, earthwork, outwork, palisade, bastion, bulwark, rampart. SEE CASTLE

fortify *v.* **1.** STRENGTHEN reinforce, brace, bulwark, secure, harden, shore up, steel, temper, buttress, build up, arm, shield, gird. **2.** REASSURE encourage, hearten, embolden, empower, strengthen, invigorate, *buck up.

3. ENRICH, enhance, improve. ANT. *1. weaken, strip down, expose, soften. 2. demoralize, undermine, discourage.*

FORTITUDE n. [FORT uh tood] courage and strength in the face of adversity. *Intestinal fortitude allowed him to press on, despite the death of his wife.* SYN. strength, courage, heart, grit, endurance, mettle, backbone, *guts, resoluteness, bravery, tenacity, pluck, hardiness, *stick-to-itiveness. ANT. *weakness, cowardice, spinelessness, mousiness.*

fortress n. stronghold, fort, citadel, defense, castle, garrison, safeguard, refuge.

FORTUITOUS a. [for TOO uh tus] occurring by chance, accidental. *A fortuitous discovery led to the invention.* SYN. chance, accidental, serendipitous, casual, random, *fluky, unforeseen, unintentional, haphazard, lucky, providential. ANT. *planned, *mapped out, arranged.*

fortunate a. lucky, blessed, happy, fortuitous, felicitous, propitious, favored, providential, advantageous, opportune, timely. ANT. *unfortunate, unlucky, untimely.*

fortune n. **1.** RICHES wealth, affluence, money, assets, treasure, estate, *miser's hoard. **2.** CHANCE luck, fate, destiny, providence, serendipity, fortuity, *wheel of fortune, happenstance, *toss of the dice. "A tide in the affairs of men."—Shakespeare. "That arrant whore."—Shakespeare. "Like glass, the brighter the glitter, the more easily broken."—Publius Syrus.

fortuneteller n. seer, soothsayer, augur, crystal ball gazer, diviner, palm reader, tarot reader, prophet, prognosticator, astrologer, psychic, sibyl.

forward a. bold, presumptuous, brazen, pushy, insolent, brash, impudent, cheeky, audacious, *nervy, *ballsy, fresh, pert. ANT. *backwards, shy, reserved, deferential.*

fossil n. remains, specimen, relic, impression, mineralized bone, remnant.

foster v. **1.** ADVANCE further, promote, feed, nurture, cultivate, boost, support, help, stimulate. **2.** REAR bring up, raise, care for, parent, mother, father, nurture, nurse, sustain, shelter. ANT. *1. hinder, hamper, undermine.*

foul n. infraction, violation.

foul v. **1.** MAKE DIRTY soil, defile, taint, pollute, dirty, stain, smear, contaminate. **2.** ENTANGLE catch, snarl, tangle, ensnare. ANT. *1. clean, wash. 2. untangle.*

foul a. **1.** DISGUSTING loathsome, stinking, dirty, *gross, disgraceful, repulsive, revolting, nasty, malodorous, rank, filthy, putrid, spoiled, polluted. **2.** INDECENT obscene, vulgar, indelicate, nasty, course, smutty, *raunchy, lewd, scatological, dirty, offensive. **3.** WICKED abominable, evil, villainous, monstrous, hellish, abhorrent, heinous, atrocious. ANT. *1. attractive, appealing, clean, pure. 2. wholesome, clean, *G-rated. 3. moral, good, virtuous.*

foul play n. SEE MURDER

found v. establish, organize, originate, develop, start, create, launch, institute.

foundation n. **1.** BASE basis, groundwork, bedrock, footing, underpinning, substructure, support, rudiment, fundamental, root, grounds. **2.** FINANCING ORGANIZATION institution, establishment, charity, endowment.

founder n. originator, creator, organizer, father, designer, architect, establisher.

founder v. **1.** TAKE ON WATER AND SINK go down, capsize, swamp, wallow, lurch, submerge, run aground, shipwreck. **2.** COLLAPSE fall, break down, fail, stumble, trip, go under, falter, bog down.

fountain n. **1.** SPOUT jet, fount, spray, gush, geyser, font, spring. **2.** SOURCE origin, wellspring, birthplace, root, beginning.

fountainhead n. spring, source.

foxy a. sly, wily, crafty, cunning, shrewd, tricky, artful, sharp, devious, deceitful, scheming, crazy, vulpine. ANT. *artless, stupid, naive.*

foyer n. hall, lobby, entrance, reception area, receiving area, waiting room, vestibule, anteroom.

fracas n. fight, brawl, quarrel, wrangle, argument, *scrap, row, melee, ruckus, uproar, scuffle, free-for-all, fistfight, donnybrook, altercation, *rumble.

fraction n. part, fragment, division, segment, piece, slice, portion.

FRACTIOUS a. [FRAK shus] unruly, troublemaking, irritable. *The fractious mob demanded a recount.* SYN. unruly, troublemaking, rebellious, irritable, cross, peevish, insubordinate, touchy, unmanageable, *ornery, petulant, huffy. ANT. *agreeable, peaceful, docile, easygoing.*

fracture n. crack, cleft, rent, split, fissure, rupture, breach, cleavage, slit, gash, chasm, cut.

fracture v. crack, split, break, shatter, rupture, cut, breach, rend, cleave.

fragile a. delicate, frail, breakable, brittle, flimsy, fine, frangible, flimsy, dainty, tender, unsubstantial. ANT. *unbreakable, sturdy, strong.*

fragment *n.* part, fraction, segment, piece, portion, slice, splinter, chip, shard, sliver, snippet, bit, shaving.

fragmentary *a.* incomplete, partial, piecemeal, broken, disconnected, choppy, separate, fractional, imperfect, sketchy. ANT. *complete, whole.*

fragrance *n.* scent, sweet smell, perfume, aroma, odor, incense, bouquet, essence, redolence. ANT. *stink, stench, reek.* SEE ODOR

fragrant *a.* sweet-smelling, aromatic, savory, redolent, spicy, balmy, heady, floral, intoxicating, ambrosial, tangy. ANT. **stinky, malodorous, foul, fetid, noxious.*

frail *a.* fragile, delicate, weak, dainty, flimsy, slight, breakable, feeble, decrepit, infirm, sickly, wispy. ANT. *strong, robust, sturdy.*

frailty *n.* weakness, failing, shortcoming, *chink in one's armor, *Achilles heel, deficiency, fallibility, foible, susceptibility. ANT. *strength, virtue.*

frame *n.* **1.** FRAMEWORK support, substructure, skeleton, underpinning, scaffolding, construction, mounting, staging, armature, rack. **2.** PICTURE FRAME mounting, casing, edging. **3.** PHYSIQUE build, body, figure, shape, anatomy.

frame *v.* **1.** BUILD construct, assemble, set up, stage, shape, fashion, form, erect, fabricate. **2.** COMPOSE conceive, create, concoct, devise, contrive, put into words, articulate.

frame of mind *n.* state of mind, disposition. SEE MOOD

franchise *n.* **1.** RIGHT due, privilege, authority, vote, prerogative. **2.** DEALERSHIP distributorship, chain store, enterprise, business, partnership, retail establishment, outfit, store, shop, business.

frank *a.* honest, straightforward, candid, open, *straight from the heart, direct, blunt, plain, explicit, outspoken, unequivocal, unambiguous, sincere, forthright. ANT. *indirect, mealymouthed, insincere, euphemistic, disguised.*

frankfurter *n.* hot dog, wiener, *weenie, *dog, frank, *footlong, sausage.

frantic *a.* frenzied, wild, excited, distraught, *unglued, agitated, *at wit's end, overexcited, beside oneself, crazy, berserk, *gone ballistic, raving, maniacal, *out of one's mind, furious, *freaked out, *wigged out. ANT. *calm, composed, serene, self-possessed, cool.*

fraternity *n.* brotherhood, brotherliness, fellowship, kinship, camaraderie, comradeship, society, club, *frat, order, house, clan.
WORD FIND
rite: rush, initiation, hazing

fraternize *v.* associate with, hang out with, rub shoulders with, socialize with, mingle with, *hobnob, run with, cosort with.

fraud *n.* **1.** DECEIT deception, trickery, cheating, swindle, *flimflam, ruse, *rip-off, con, extortion, scam, racket, hoax, double-dealing. **2.** CHEAT imposter, deceiver, *con artist, *rip-off artist, swindler, crook, charlatan, *shark, mountebank. ANT. *1. honesty, trustworthiness, integrity. 2. *honest John, *Dudley Do-right.*

fraudulent *a.* deceptive, deceitful, tricky, cheating, dishonest, crooked, criminal, illegal, bogus, shifty, treacherous, shady, *sham. ANT. *honest, moral, trustworthy.*

fraught *a.* loaded, filled, charged, full of, teeming with, laden, pregnant, replete. ANT. *empty, devoid of.*

fray *n.* fight, quarrel, brawl, *rumble, wrangle, melee, skirmish, battle, war, squabble, row, scuffle, clash.

fray *v.* shred, ravel, unravel, come apart, tear, tatter, rip.

frazzle *v.* stress out, exhaust, wear out, drain.

freak *n.* abnormality, anomaly, weirdo, aberration, mutant, *geek, monster, monstrosity, deformity, curiosity, oddity, *oddball. SEE MONSTER

freak *v. Sl.* *freak out, *flip out, *wig out, *go ballistic, *lose it.

freak *a.* anomalous, aberrant, weird, abnormal, unusual, irregular, atypical, extraordinary. ANT. *normal, typical, usual.*

freakish *a.* abnormal, anomalous, weird, aberrant, unusual, irregular, quirky, atypical, extraordinary, strange, outlandish, bizarre. ANT. *normal, regular, usual.*

freak out *v. Sl.* go crazy, *go nuts, *go bananas, *go ballistic, *lose one's mind, *see things, hallucinate, *flip out, *wig out.

free *a.* **1.** UNRESTRICTED liberated, at liberty, emancipated, footloose, independent, autonomous, self-governing, unrestrained, loose, unconfined, sovereign. **2.** COSTING NOTHING gratis, *on the house, complimentary, no charge. **3.** UNOCCUPIED clear, open, available, vacant, unused, empty, unengaged. **4.** GENEROUS lavish, liberal, openhanded, giving, munificent. ANT. *1. restricted, enslaved, dependent, imprisoned. 2.*

costing, *dear, expensive. 3. occupied, busy. 4. cheap, stingy, *tight.

free v. liberate, release, loose, let go, emancipate, unshackle, discharge, deliver, *spring, clear, extricate, unburden, disencumber, absolve. ANT. imprison, enslave, shackle, confine, restrict.

freedom n. liberty, independence, autonomy, sovereignty, self-government, emancipation, free will, license, carte blanche, privilege, *free reign, immunity, exemption, latitude, range, unrestraint. "Room to enlarge."—C.A. Bartol. "The right to be wrong, not the right to do wrong."—John Diefenbaker. ANT. slavery, bondage, restriction, confinement.

free-for-all n. fight, brawl, melee, *rumble, fray, donnybrook.

freelance a. independent, non-staff, on one's own, unaffiliated, free agent, autonomous, self-employed, at large, self-directed. ANT. associated, staff.

free spirit n. maverick, nonconformist, bohemian, eccentric.

freeway n. expressway, highway, superhighway, interstate, parkway, beltway, artery, road, autobahn.

free-wheeling a. free, unrestrained, unrestricted, uninhibited, unfettered. ANT. restrained, limited.

freezer n. ice box, ice chest, cooler, refrigerator.

freezing a. frigid, icy, cold, arctic, chilling, numbing, anesthetizing, *bone-chilling, biting, frosty, wintry, raw. ANT. hot, sweltering.

freight n. cargo, shipment, load, lading, tonnage.

frenetic a. frenzied, wild, overexcited. SEE FRANTIC

frenzy n. mania, madness, delerium, hysteria, fit, furor, outburst, rage, tantrum, spell, agitation, paroxysm, derangement. ANT. stability, composure, calmness, equanimity.

frequent a. numerous, regular, habitual, recurrent, common, continual, daily, everyday, incessant, periodic, usual, often. ANT. seldom, rare, infrequent.

frequent v. attend regularly, visit often, haunt, *hang out at, patronize.

fresh a. 1. NEW up-to-date, *hot, current, modern, newborn, recent, bright, sparkling, unused, *hot off the presses, untouched, vernal, *spring-fresh. 2. ADDITIONAL new, more, further. 3. VIGOROUS energetic, lively, vital, bright-eyed, rested, revived, full of vim and vigor, vibrant, alert, bouncing. 4. ORIGINAL imaginative, creative, new, unconventional, novel, untried, *cutting edge. 5. REFRESHING cool, clean, bracing, pure, invigorating. 6. INEXPERIENCED raw, green, untried, new, untrained, *wet behind the ears. 7. SASSY rude, smart-alecky, cheeky, flippant, disrespectful, *smartass, impudent, bold, *nervy, ballsy. ANT. 1. old, worn, dated, stale. 3. tired, exhausted, weary. 4. trite, hackneyed, clichéd. 5. stale, musty, polluted. 6. experienced, tried, veteran. 7. polite, shy, quiet, deferential.

freshman n. student, *frosh, beginner, novice, *greenhorn, *rookie.

fret v. worry, brood, agonize, stew, mope, anguish, fuss, lose sleep over, chafe, *work oneself up, *give oneself an ulcer, *eat one's heart out, fume. ANT. relax, ignore.

fretful a. discontented, irritable, annoyed, peevish, cross, grouchy, cranky, touchy, testy, *ornery, grumbling, anxious, whiny. ANT. relaxed, cheerful, good-humored, unperturbed.

friable a. crumbly, fragile, powdery, brittle.

friction n. 1. ABRASION rubbing, erosion, attrition, grinding, scraping, chafing, rasping, wearing. 2. DISAGREEMENT discord, conflict, opposition, animosity, antagonism, dispute, clash, hostility, strife. ANT. 2. agreement, accord, harmony.

friend n. confidant, pal, *buddy, companion, sidekick, alter ego, chum, playmate, *soul mate, *bro, crony, amigo. "A person with whom you dare to be yourself."—Frank Crane. "The medicine of life."—Bible. "The best mirror."—George Herbert. "One who walks in when the rest of the world walks out."—Walter Winchell. ANT. enemy, adversary, stranger.

friendly a. sociable, amiable, warm, approachable, amicable, *buddy-buddy, companionable, neighborly, affectionate, hospitable, *chummy, outgoing, intimate, close, familiar. ANT. hostile, distant, cool, aloof, standoffish.

friendship n. companionship, comradeship, fellowship, camaraderie, neighborliness, relationship, intimacy, amity, affection, rapport, affinity, pact, tie. "To feel as one while remaining two."—Anne Swetchine. "The wine of life."—Edward Young. "A holy tie."—John Dryden. ANT. hostility, distance, coolness.

fright n. fear, terror, alarm, apprehension, scare, panic, trepidation, horror, shock, awe, *the creeps, *the willies, dread. ANT. courage, calm, composure. SEE ANXIETY, FEAR, FEARFUL

frighten v. scare, terrify, panic, shock, fill with dread, petrify, awe, *adrenalize, horrify, unnerve, *send chills down spine, spook, alarm, startle, intimidate, *curdle one's blood, *paralyze. ANT. *encourage, embolden, reassure.*

frightening a. scary, terrifying, shocking, dreadful, petrifying, awesome, *adrenalizing, unnerving, chilling, *spooky, alarming, startling, intimidating, *bloodcurdling, *paralyzing, traumatic, horrifying. ANT. *encouraging, reassuring, heartening.*

frigid a. **1.** FREEZING icy, cold, arctic, frosty, wintry, hyperborean, *anesthetizing, biting, bitter, brisk, Siberian, polar, glacial, gelid. **2.** STIFF formal, cold, icy, cool, distant, remote, aloof, austere, unsociable. **3.** UNRESPONSIVE lifeless, unfeeling, passionless, inhibited, passive, cold, chilly, frosty. ANT. *1. hot, sweltering, warm. 2. warm, friendly, sociable. 3. passionate, *hot-blooded, orgasmic.*

frill n. ornament, trimming, decoration, extra, luxury, ruffle, extravagance, superfluity, embellishment, frippery.

fringe n. **1.** DECORATIVE EDGING border, margin, trimming, ruff, hem, skirting, flounce. **2.** BORDER margin, outskirts, edge, periphery, verge, perimeter.

frisk v. **1.** FROLIC gambol, romp, cavort, prance, dance, play, wiggle. **2.** Sl. SEARCH shake down, inspect.

frisky a. lively, playful, spirited, frolicsome, zippy, active, kittenish, *peppy, coltish, spry. ANT. *lifeless, dead, comatose.*

fritter v. waste, squander, *blow, spend, dissipate, throw away, lavish, *piss away. ANT. *save, conserve.*

frivolous a. trivial, trifling, silly, impractical, petty, unimportant, foolish, extravagant, shallow, *piddling, pointless, worthless, unnecessary. ANT. *important, vital, necessary.*

frock n. tunic, robe, gown, garment.

frog n. amphibian, bullfrog, toad.

frolic n. fun, play, sport, romping, merriment, antics, mirth, joking, game-playing, gaiety, amusement, tomfoolery.

frolic v. play, romp, make merry, have fun, joke, *cut up, *cut loose, *whoop it up, play games, frisk, gambol, cavort, *raise hell, *fool around.

front n. **1.** FORE face, facade, head, exterior, anterior, foreground, top, obverse, beginning. **2.** PRETENSE facade, mask, false front, look, air, demeanor, expression, countenance, guise, exterior. ANT. *1. rear, back.*

front a. fore, lead, first, forward, topmost, anterior. ANT. *back, posterior, end.*

frontier n. **1.** BORDERLAND boundary, far reaches, perimeter, limit, verge. **2.** UNCIVILIZED TERRITORY outskirts, remote region, far reaches, outland, hinterland, outpost, no-man's-land.

frost n. frozen condensation, frozen dew, rime, ice, snow, hoarfrost, ice crystals.

frosting n. icing, spread, topping, glaze.

frosty a. **1.** FREEZING hoary, rimy, icy, frigid, frozen, cold, raw, nippy, bone-chilling, anesthetizing. **2.** UNFRIENDLY cool, icy, aloof, distant, remote. ANT. *1. hot, sweltering. 2. friendly, warm.*

froth n. bubbles, foam, fizz, spume, suds, spray, head, lather, effervescence, spindrift, scum.

frothy a. **1.** BUBBLY foamy, fizzy, spumous, effervescent, *scummy, lathery, soapy. **2.** TRIFLING light, worthless, trivial, frivolous, shallow, foolish. ANT. *1. flat, uncarbonated. 2. important, deep, serious.*

frown v. **1.** SCOWL glower, *give a dirty look, glare, *shoot daggers, *scorch with one's eyes, *narrow eyes with contempt, lower, gloom. SEE ANGRY **2.** FROWN UPON *look down on, dislike, object to, disapprove of, *take a dim view of, discourage. ANT. *1. smile, grin. 2. approve of, accept, like.*

frozen a. icy, frigid, cold, chilled, iced, cooled, solidified, wintry, glacial, numb, arctic. ANT. *thawed, melted.* SEE COLD, SNOW

FRUGAL a. [FROO gul] careful not to be wasteful, thrifty. *He's so frugal he manages to pay for everything in cash.* SYN. thrifty, economical, unwasteful, conserving, sparing, saving, penny-pinching, stingy, scrimping, *nickel-squeezing, parsimonious, tight. ANT. *extravagant, wasteful, lavish, spending.*

fruit n. **1.** PRODUCE drupe, harvest, crop. **2.** REWARD return, yield, profit, benefit, result, consequence, outcome.

fruitful a. fertile, productive, rich, prolific, profitable, bounteous, advantageous, gainful, worthwhile, successful. ANT. *fruitless, worthless, unproductive.*

FRUITION n. [froo ISH un] a fulfillment, a bearing of fruit. *A number of her investments have come to fruition.* SYN. fulfillment, realization, consummation, maturity, achievement, ripeness, attainment. ANT. *incompletion, nonfulfillment.*

fruitless a. futile, vain, useless, unproductive, worthless, unsuccessful, unrewarding, pointless, barren, infertile. ANT. *fruitful, productive, worthwhile.*

frumpy *a.* dowdy, frumpish, dull, plain, unfashionable, colorless, slovenly, shabby, wrinkled, *as fashionable as a potato sack/burlap bag. ANT. *fashionable, stylish, chic.*

frustrate *v.* thwart, foil, check, balk, circumvent, hamstring, cripple, short-circuit, arrest, stymie, defeat, discourage, baffle, obstruct, impede, inhibit, exasperate. ANT. *advance, promote, encourage, abet.*

frustration *n.* defeat, circumvention, discouragement, obstruction, check, nonfulfillment, failure, disappointment, miscarriage, bafflement, dissatisfaction, thwarting. ANT. *success, advancement, encouragement, fulfillment.*

fry *v.* brown, singe, pan fry, sizzle, deep fry, sear, sauté, French fry, stir fry, blacken.

frying pan *n.* pan, skillet, wok, spider, fry pan.

fuddy-duddy *n.* *square.

fuel *n.* combustible, gas, oil, propellant, wood, kindling, coal.

fuel *v.* charge, stoke, fire, fan, *tank up, feed, nourish. ANT. *extinguish, quench, dampen.*

fugitive *n.* runaway, exile, absconder, escapee, refugee, truant, renegade, deserter, outlaw.

fugitive *a.* fleeing, runaway, escaped, wanted, evading. ANT. *caught, captured.*

fulfill *v.* complete, satisfy, realize, achieve, consummate, carry out, accomplish, bring to fruition, perfect, meet, make good, perform, effect. ANT. *fall short, *miss the mark, fail.*

fulfillment *n.* completion, satisfaction, realization, achievement, consummation, accomplishment, fruition, perfection, culmination, attainment. ANT. *failure, miscarriage, incompletion.*

full *a.* **1.** FILLED glutted, gorged, sated, brimming, crammed, stuffed, *chock-full, bursting, stocked, crowded, teeming, replete, chockablock, saturated, overflowing, bulging. **2.** COMPLETE whole, entire, thorough, comprehensive, exhaustive, maximum, total, integral. ANT. **1.** *empty, barren, vacant, hungry, starving.* **2.** *incomplete, partial.*

full-blooded *a.* purebred, thoroughbred, unmixed. ANT. *mongrel, half-breed, mutt.*

full-bodied *a.* rich, concentrated, strong, undiluted. ANT. *weak, diluted.*

full-fledged *a.* developed, trained, schooled, skilled, qualified, experienced. ANT. *unqualified, *green, inexperienced.*

full-grown *a.* adult, fully developed, ripe. ANT. *immature, young.* SEE MATURE

fully *adv.* **1.** COMPLETELY totally, entirely, comprehensively, wholly. **2.** ADEQUATELY sufficiently, amply.

fulminate *v.* denounce, denunciate, censure, criticize, damn, curse, shout down, *knock, condemn, remonstrate, thunder, swear at, revile.

fumble *v.* grope, mishandle, bungle, *drop the ball, *flub, botch, blunder, muff, flounder, bobble, mess up.

fume *n.* smoke, exhaust, gas, steam, vapor, effluvium, exhalation, pollution, reek, smog, stench, miasma.

fume *v.* rage, rant, rave, seethe, boil, blow up, explode, bluster, *get steamed, *blow one's stack, *fly off the handle, *go ballistic.

fumigate *v.* disinfect, *smoke out, poison, sanitize, sterilize.

fun *n.* amusement, entertainment, enjoyment, pleasure, diversion, play, sport, good time, romping, *blast, frolic, recreation, merriment, pastime, jollity, *jollies. ANT. *misery, torture, agony, monotony.*

function *n.* **1.** ROLE job, use, purpose, duty, task, business, occupation, employment, responsibility, activity, concern. **2.** AFFAIR ceremony, gala, social, formal, *get-together, reception, party.

function *v.* act, work, serve, operate, perform, run.

functional *a.* working, operative, serviceable, performing, practical, useful. ANT. *impractical, ineffective, *for show.*

fund *n.* reserve, savings, treasury, capital, nest egg, account, endowment, stock, mutual fund, *stash, hoard, pool, *kitty. SEE BANK, MONEY

fund *v.* pay for, finance, bankroll, endow, back, capitalize, grant, subsidize, contribute, underwrite, *pick up the check.

fundamental *n.* basic, essential, element, rudiment, principle, foundation, ABCs, cornerstone, *nitty-gritty, heart, nucleus. ANT. *extra, peripheral, supplement.*

fundamental *a.* basic, essential, primary, elementary, rudimentary, principal, underlying, cardinal, chief, indispensable, integral, foundational. ANT. *secondary, peripheral, auxiliary.*

fundraiser *n.* pledge drive, telethon, charity event, charity ball, philanthropic enterprise.

funds *n.* money, cash, capital, currency, finances, means, *dough, *bread, reserve, assets, resources, nest egg, *loot, *piggy bank, *stash. SEE MONEY, BANK

funeral *n.* obsequies, exequies, burial, inhumation, interment, entombment, last rites, services, cremation. "The last bedtime story."—Leonard Levinson. "A consolation to the living than of any service to the dead."—Saint Augustine.

WORD FIND

announcement: obituary

automobile/coach that carries coffin to cemetery: hearse

bell toll signaling death: knell

bugle call at military funeral: taps

burial at sea: deep six

burial cloth or sheet: shroud, winding sheet

Catholic Mass for: Requiem Mass

churchyard gateway sheltering coffin at service: lich gate

coffin carriers: pallbearers

euphemism, burying: lay to rest

friends, relatives of deceased: bereaved, mourners

mourn aloud by weeping, wailing, etc.: lament

pile of wood on which corpse is burned: pyre

praise for deceased: eulogy

prayer for deceased: requiescat

procession: cortege, death march

RIP: rest in peace

song of lament: dirge, elegy, requiem, threnody

undertaker: mortician

watch or viewing of the deceased, often with festivities: wake, vigil

SEE CEMETERY, COFFIN, DEATH, MOURNING

funereal *a.* somber, depressing, black, gray, grim, mournful, sepulchral, dreary, doleful, dismal, grave, lugubrious, gloomy, melancholy. ANT. *cheerful, euphoric, bright, upbeat.*

fungus *n.* thallophyte, mold, mildew, mushroom, parasite.

funk *n.* depression, blues, blue funk, melancholy, doldrums.

funnel *v.* channel, direct, conduct, siphon, pour, filter, focus, conduct.

funny *a.* **1.** HUMOROUS comical, hilarious, laughable, *side-splitting, amusing, *a scream, droll, absurd, riotous, hysterical, ludicrous, ridiculous, farcical, silly, jocular, *tickling. **2.** PECULIAR strange, odd, weird, bizarre, unusual, outlandish, abnormal, *offbeat, different, queer. ANT. *1. serious, grave, grim, morbid. 2. ordinary, normal, usual.*

furious *a.* **1.** ANGRY enraged, infuriated, outraged, irate, *beside oneself, *boiling, *pissed, *on the warpath, fuming, mad, inflamed, incensed, livid, *up in arms, *spitting tacks, *bent out of shape, rabid, *ripped. **2.** VIOLENT overpowering, intense,

fierce, wild, ferocious, stormy, turbulent, raging, vicious, savage. ANT. *1. calm, unperturbed, pleased. 2. mild, meek, weak.*

furlough *n.* leave, leave of absence, vacation, layoff.

furnace *n.* heater, burner, stove, warmer, oil burner, forge blast furnace, incinerator, smelter, kiln.

furnish *v.* supply, equip, provide, stock, outfit, provision, fit, turn out, rig, appoint, accouter, give.

furnishings *n.* gear, trappings, appointments, decor, fittings, equipment, accessories.

furniture *n.* furnishings, seating, cabinetry, shelving, tables, chairs. Armchair, armoire, buffet, bureau, cabinet, Canadian rocker, card table, chaise lounge, chest, chest of drawers, chiffonier, china cabinet, commode, console, couch, credenza, daybed, divan, etagereí, hassock, highboy, loveseat, lowboy, ottoman, recliner, rocking chair, roll-top desk, secretary, settee, sideboard, side chair, sleigh bed, slipper chair, Tambour desk, vitrine, wardrobe, windsor chair, wing chair.

WORD FIND

FURNITURE STYLES AND DESIGN ELEMENTS

American colonies to 1776, style of: Colonial

arcs, sleek lines, geometric shapes, 1920s and '30s style featuring: Art Deco

bulge or convex shape on chest or commode: bombe

cabinetmaker of 1700s, famous: Hepplewhite

carved foot, craneís claw, or dragonís claw element: ball-and-claw foot

column supporting a rail, turned: baluster

contrasting wood insert: marquetry

couch or sofa with no exposed wood, overstuffed: Chesterfield

curved lines, 1875 style featuring slightly: Art Nouveau

curved wood element: bentwood

eagle heads and talons, lion heads and claws, and satyrsí masks, 1700s style featuring: Georgian

folding, portable furniture: campaign furniture

goat-like legs, introduced in 17th century: cabriole

gothic revival: Neo Gothic

Greek, Roman or Egyptian styling revivals of late 1700s: Neoclassical

heavily carved, massive style of second half of 1500s England: Elizabethan heavy, massive and richly decorated style: Baroque

hinged panel which can be raised on a table: drop leaf

inserted wood, grain, mother of pearl, or other material of contrasting appearance: inlay

local or rural design stylings: Provincial

medieval style, heavy: gothic

mosaic of wood in geometric patterns: parquetry

motifs of animals, mythological creatures, garlands of flowers, early 1600s style featuring carved: Louis XIV

Napoleonís style decorated with bees, crowns, laurel leaves and mythological figures: Empire

oak, simple rectilinear style made mostly of: Mission

painted ornamentation, contrasting veneers, and inlays, 1700s style featuring: Sheraton

plain, blocky, German style, 19th century: Biedermeier

plain, simple style of the late 19th century: Arts and Crafts

plain, simple style sometimes featuring chrome and glass and mass produced in 20th century: yle

rococo style of mid-18th century, delicate: Chippendale

scrollwork on rich woods, style featuring highly ornate: Rococo

serpentine arms, cabriole legs, rounded frames and walnut veneers, style featuring: Queen Anne

sleek and polished style of 1930s: Moderne

unadorned, practical style built by Shakers: Shaker

veneer and inlay, style following American Revolution featuring brass feet: Federal

furor n. uproar, craze, excitement, frenzy, commotion, rage, outburst, mania, disturbance, *ado, *to-do, ruckus, *big stink. ANT. *apathy, indifference, dispassion.*

furrow n. channel, groove, rut, trench, ditch, cut, trough, track, line, seam, crease, wrinkle.

furry a. hairy, woolly, shaggy, bushy, downy. ANT. *bald, hairless.*

further v. advance, forward, assist, foster, facilitate, promote, aid, contribute to, abet. ANT. *hamper, hinder, thwart.*

further a. additional, more, added, supplementary, other, new. ANT. *fewer, scant.*

furthermore adv. in addition, additionally, also, moreover, what's more, too.

FURTIVE a. [FUR tiv] secret, sneaky. *He shot a furtive glance at his desk partner's notes.* SYN. secret, sneaky, stealthy, surreptitious, covert, clandestine, sly, wary, hidden, underhand, conspiratorial, skulking, concealed, shifty. ANT. *open, overt, aboveboard.*

fury n. anger, rage, wrath, furor, frenzy, indignation, madness, fire, ire, tantrum, fit, dudgeon, storm, squall, tempest, hot blood, huff, rampage, fierceness. ANT. *calm, serenity, tranquility, indifference.*

fuse v. merge, meld, smelt, combine, blend, compound, unite, integrate, commingle, weld, alloy, consolidate. ANT. *divide, separate, split.*

fusion n. union, amalgamation, coalescence, melding, blend, mixture, consolidation, compound, merger, combination, coalition. ANT. *separation, division, splitting.*

fusillade n. enfilade, salvo, volley, broadside, burst of fire.

fuss n. bother, ado, fluster, pother, trouble, turmoil, disturbance, agitation, stir, fretting, flutter.

fussy a. particular, picky, choosy, meticulous, persnickety, discriminating, finicky, fastidious, dainty, hard-to-please, nit-picking. ANT. *easy, careless.*

fustian a. bombastic, pompous, pretentious, extravagant, grandiose, lofty. ANT. *understated, low-key.*

futile a. vain, useless, hopeless, fruitless, ineffective, unproductive, for naught, pointless, unavailing, idle, *on a wild goose chase. ANT. *fruitful, productive, worthwhile.*

futility n. uselessness, pointlessness, emptiness, worthlessness, ineffectiveness, frivolousness.

futon n. mattress, bed, couch, sofa.

future n. tomorrow, offing, time to come, hereafter, *down the road, *over the horizon, prospect, fate, destiny. "The shape of things to come."—H.G. Wells. "That period of time in which our affairs prosper, our friends are true and our happiness is assured."—Ambrose Bierce. "The past returning through another gate."—Arnold Glasgow.

future a. coming, expected, prospective, anticipated, imminent, impending, next, *on the horizon, forthcoming, approaching, scheduled, eventual, projected, succeeding, subsequent. ANT. *past, former, bygone.*

futuristic *a.* visionary, cutting edge, innovative, ahead of one's time, on the horizon, up and coming, of tomorrow, ground breaking, pioneering. ANT. *antiquated, old fashioned.*

fuzz *n.* hair, fur, fluff, down, wool, nap, lint.

fuzzy *a.* **1.** HAIRY furry, fluffy, downy, woolly, napped, linty, frizzy. **2.** UNCLEAR blurry, vague, cloudy, dim, hazy, obscure, misty, out of focus. ANT. *1. smooth, hairless. 2. clear, focused, sharp.*

G

gab *n*. chatter, talk, jabber, conversation, babble, *chitchat, *tongue-wagging, *rap, prattle, palaver, gossip.

gab *v*. chatter, talk, jabber, converse, babble, *yak, *chitchat, *rap, prattle, *jaw, *shoot the breeze, gossip.

gabby *a*. talkative, loquacious, windy, garrulous, long-winded, voluble, wordy, verbose, *motor-mouthed, blabbermouthed, chatty, babbling. ANT. *reserved, taciturn, quiet, mute.*

gadabout *n*. wanderer, fun-seeker, rambler, roamer, playboy.

gadfly *n*. *pain in the neck, irritant. SEE PEST

gadget *n*. contraption, *widget, apparatus, appliance, device, mechanism, instrument, tool, *gizmo, contrivance, *doohickey, *thingamajig, machine, *Rube Goldberg device.

gadgetry *n*. mechanism, contraptions, works, appliances, instrumentation, machinery, *bells and whistles, robotics, peripherals, *Rube Goldberg devices.

gaffe *n*. blunder, goof, mistake, *boner, faux pas, *boo-boo, slip, misstep, indiscretion, lapse, transgression, pecadillo, error.

gag *n*. joke, practical joke, prank, trick, wisecrack, caper, jest, *leg-pulling.

gag *v*. **1.** CHOKE retch, heave, gasp, upchuck, vomit, puke. **2.** SILENCE muzzle, shut up, censor, squelch, hush, muffle, suppress, *put a lid on.

gaiety *n*. happiness, cheer, mirth, joy, high spirits, elation, revelry, merriment, lightheartedness, glee, joie de vivre, festivity, jollity, gladness, hilarity, jubilation, buoyancy. ANT. *somberness, depression, downheartedness, melancholy.*

gain *n*. profit, increase, proceeds, growth, earnings, yield, winnings, advancement, improvement, enrichment, progress, headway. ANT. *loss, decline.*

gain *v*. profit, increase, grow, earn, yield, acquire, attain, get, advance, improve, enrich, progress, win, make headway. ANT. *lose, decline, fall.*

gainful *a*. profitable, productive, worthwhile, rewarding, remunerative, paying, lucrative, fruitful, beneficial. ANT. *unprofitable, unrewarding.*

gainsay *v*. deny, contradict, controvert, dispute, refute, oppose, negate, disagree, repudiate. ANT. *affirm, uphold, *own up.*

gait *n*. stride, walk, step, carriage, motion, run, tread, pace, gallop, canter.

WORD FIND

descriptive: limp; hobble; lumber; plod; stagger; shuffle; totter; traipse; trudge; shamble; pert wiggle; military gait; goose-stepping; portly waddle; long, fluid stride; bowlegged stride; grace of a porteuse; loose-boned gait; willowy gait; strut; swagger; feline grace; voluptuous sway; mincing steps; authoritative gait

SEE WALK

gala *n*. celebration, festival, bash, fiesta, party, jubilee, *blowout, *blast, *wingding, *shindig.

galaxy *n*. *island universe, star cluster, star system, Milky Way, Andromeda. SEE ASTRONOMY, CONSTELLATION, MOON, PLANET, SPACE, STAR

gale *n*. wind, gust, squall, blow, blast, breeze, tempest, northeaster, hurricane, cyclone, tornado. SEE WIND

gall *n*. *nerve, brass, *chutzpah, *balls, impudence, insolence, brashness, sauciness, *cheek, audacity, *guts, effrontery. ANT. *timidity, deference, mousiness, shyness.*

gall *v*. irritate, annoy, *rub the wrong way, rankle, vex, irk, agitate, peeve, *piss off, provoke, inflame, chafe, nettle. ANT. *please, delight.*

gallant *a*. **1.** BRAVE daring, courageous, valorous, heroic, chivalrous, noble, valiant, lionhearted, intrepid, dauntless, high spirited, knightly. **2.** POLITE gracious, courteous, noble, mannerly, courtly, gentlemanly, kindly, well-bred, attentive, considerate. ANT. *1. cowardly, timid, mousy. 2. rude, impolite, discourteous, coarse, crude.*

gallantry *n*. **1.** BRAVERY daring, courage, valor, heroism, chivalry, nobility, dauntlessness, fearlessness, *derring-do, intrepidity. **2.** POLITENESS graciousness, courtesy, suavity, tact, nobility, manners, gentleness, kindness, courtliness, attentiveness, duty. "To remember one is a gentleman in spite of one's birth and training."—Elbert Hubbard. ANT. *1. cowardice, mousiness, timidity. 2. rudeness, crudeness, discourtesy.*

gallery *n*. **1.** WALKWAY passage, hall, corridor, veranda, porch, arcade, loggia, colonnade. **2.** BALCONY bleachers, grandstand. **3.** EXHIBIT art museum, exhibition hall, showplace, showroom, salon.

galling *a.* annoying, irritating, nettlesome, vexing, aggravating, chafing, rankling, irksome, peeving, exasperating. ANT. *pleasing, delightful.*

gallop *v.* run, race, sprint, hurdle, dash, bolt, *hightail, canter, lope, rack, trot, *clippety-clop. SEE HORSE

GALVANIZE *v.* [GAL vuh nize] to stimulate or rouse into action, to jolt. *The plight of the spotted owl galvanized the environmental movement.* SYN. stimulate, rouse, stir, spur, goad, excite, *fire, *spark, energize, electrify, jolt, wake up, vitalize, invigorate. ANT. *dampen, inhibit, deaden, *pull the plug.*

gambit *n.* maneuver, action, move, play, tactic, strategy, plan, ploy, stratagem, ruse, trick.

gamble *n.* bet, wager, stake, speculation, chance, risk, *shot in the dark, *outside chance, *long shot, *toss of the dice, *a ride on the wheel of fortune, *flier.

gamble *v.* bet, wager, chance, speculate, risk, *take a shot in the dark, *toss the dice, *take a flier, *spin the wheel of fortune, try one's luck, *shoot the works, *go for broke, hazard, prospect, *play the ponies, *play the numbers.

gambler *n.* wagerer, risk-taker.

gambling *n.* "The sure way of getting nothing for something."—Wilson Mizner. "This tyrant vice."—David Garrick.

gambol *v.* frolic, frisk, caper, romp, cavort, bounce, prance, spring, rollick, sport, dance about, leap about.

game *n.* **1.** CONTEST match, competition, tournament, tourney, meet, showdown, round, bout, test of skill. **2.** AMUSEMENT entertainment, pastime, diversion, play, sport, recreation, fun, merriment, romp, clowning, test of skill.

game *a.* brave, courageous, bold, dauntless, fearless, plucky, *gutsy, daring, spirited, eager, enthusiastic, willing. ANT. *unwilling, *chicken, afraid.*

gamely *adv.* bravely, courageously, boldly, dauntlessly, fearlessly, pluckily, eagerly, enthusiastically, willingly. ANT. *unwillingly, timidly, cowardly.*

gamut *n.* range, extent, sweep, scope, area, reach, compass, spectrum.

gamy *a.* strong-smelling, strong-tasting, tainted, ripe, foul, stinky, dirty, wild, reeking, malodorous, spoiled, rank. ANT. *ambrosial.*

gang *n.* group, band, pack, mob, tribe, party, squad, herd, company, clique, crowd, crew, troop, coterie, club, ring, league, fraternity, *boys in the hood, juvenile delinquents.

gangling *a.* lanky, tall, thin, awkward, skinny, spindly, rangy, loosely built. ANT. *husky, stout, brawny, obese.*

gangrene *n.* decay, rot, putrefaction, wasting away.

gangster *n.* mobster, Mafioso, criminal, *soldier, thug, hoodlum, *hood, racketeer, *goon, crook, godfather, *consigliere, hit man, gunman, tough. SEE CRIME

gap *n.* opening, break, hole, aperture, breach, cleft, separation, rent, crevice, chasm, space, crack, fissure, hiatus, lacuna, void, interruption.

gape *v.* gawk, look saucer-eyed, stare, ogle, stare at goggle-eyed, *rubberneck, peer, stare openmouthed, stare in astonishment.

garage *n.* **1.** SHELTER, car barn, stall, building, hangar, car port. **2.** REPAIR FACILITY, shop.

garb *n.* clothes, clothing, apparel, outfit, dress, wear, vestments, costume, attire, gear, *duds, *threads.

garb *v.* dress, clothe, outfit, attire, fit out, apparel, clad, deck, vest, array.

garbage *n.* waste, refuse, scraps, leavings, remains, rubbish, trash, offal, *slop, dregs, *crap.

garble *v.* confuse, mix up, distort, jumble, slur, mumble, misrepresent, twist, misstate, misunderstand.

garden *n.* vegetable garden, flower garden, herb garden, plot, bed, patch, nursery. "The richer realm."—Alice Brown. "The purest of human pleasures."—Francis Bacon. "The best place to seek God . . . you can dig for Him there."—George Bernard Shaw.

WORD FIND

cultivation science: horticulture

enclosed garden: garth

fertilizer: bone meal, manure, compost

first: Eden

glass container, small garden in: terrarium

greenhouse display: conservatory

greenhouse-like box, small: cold frame

Japanese teahouse, bonsai, water: tea garden, Japanese garden

pest: aphid, cutworm, borer, Japanese beetle, slug

pleasure ground or garden on an estate: pleasance

protective organic cover of straw, leaves, peat moss: mulch

rock: rock garden, rockery
section: bed, plot
sheltered from elements: greenhouse, hothouse
shrubs sculpted into shapes of animals, objects: topiary
skill for growing: green thumb
soil: humus, loam
soilless growing method using nutrient-rich solution: hydroponics
tool: hoe, trowel, rake, sprinkler
tree and shrub: arbor, arboretum
wartime garden grown to boost food production: victory garden
watering: irrigation

gargantuan *a.* gigantic, huge, colossal, enormous, immense, monstrous, Brobdingnagian, Herculean, mammoth, stupendous, towering, massive, elephantine, prodigious, *humongous. ANT. *tiny*, *pint-sized, miniature*, *Lilliputian*.

garish *a.* flashy, showy, gaudy, glaring, loud, ostentatious, cheap, blatant, ornate, tawdry, glittering, bright. ANT. *subtle, understated, plain, modest, conservative*.

garland *n.* wreath, festoon, laurel, crown, coronet. SEE FLOWER

garlic *n.* herb, clove, bulb, seasoning.

garment(s) *n.* clothing, attire, outfit, dress, costume, vestment, apparel, wear, *duds, *threads, *getup, uniform, *rags.

garner *v.* collect, reap, harvest, store, gather, assemble, *squirrel away, amass, accumulate.

garnish *n.* embellishment, adornment, ornament, decoration, dressing, enhancement, trimming.

garnish *v.* embellish, adorn, ornament, decorate, dress, enhance, bedeck, trim.

garrison *n.* fort, fortification, military post, command post, fortress, stronghold, troop station.

GARRULOUS *a.* [GAR uh lus] talkative. *They're a garrulous family; they'll talk your ear off.* SYN. talkative, loquacious, long-winded, windy, verbose, *motor-mouthed, *loose-lipped, babbling, windy, effusive, wordy, glib. ANT. *quiet, reserved, taciturn*.

gas *n.* **1.** VAPOR fume, air, exhalation, steam, smoke, effluvium, miasma, oxygen, carbon dioxide, carbon monoxide, methane, propane, hydrogen, nitrogen. **2.** GASOLINE fuel, petrol, flammable liquid, propellant, combustible, gasahol.

gash *n.* cut, slice, slash, slit, tear, rent, split, laceration, incision, wound.

gash *v.* cut, slice, slash, slit, tear, rent, split, lacerate, incise, wound, rend, hack, hew.

gasket *n.* seal, packing.

gasoline *n.* SEE GAS 2.

gasp *n.* heave, pant, sharp intake of air, huff, gulp.

gasp *v.* heave, pant, huff, inhale sharply, gulp.

gassy *a.* flatulent, bloated.

gastronomy *n.* ecpicurism.

gate *n.* entry, entrance, door, opening, gateway, portal, access, egress, ingress, turnstile.

gatekeeper *n.* sentry, guard, monitor, watchman, custodian.

gather *v.* **1.** MASS amass, collect, accumulate, assemble, reap, harvest, muster, garner, glean, stockpile, hoard. **2.** INFER assume, guess, surmise, reckon, deduce, presume, conclude, judge. ANT. *1. disperse, scatter*.

gathering *n.* congregation, assembly, collection, crowd, mass, throng, bunch, concentration, gang, band, meeting, convention, muster, conference, convocation, council, caucus.

GAUCHE *a.* [GO/SH] tactless, lacking social grace. *Telling the queen a dirty joke is considered gauche.* SYN. tactless, clumsy, boorish, uncultured, uncouth, ill-mannered, crude, unrefined, cloddish, crass, unsophisticated, ignorant, graceless. ANT. *gracious, refined, cultured, suave*.

gaudy *a.* showy, flashy, cheap, garish, ostentatious, loud, tacky, tasteless, eye-catching, tawdry, glaring, pretentious. ANT. *tasteful, understated, modest, conservative*.

gauge *n.* measure, standard, yardstick, criterion, test, touchstone, barometer, indicator, benchmark, guideline.

gauge *v.* measure, evaluate, appraise, assess, estimate, guess, calculate, judge, weigh, quantify, figure, compute, calibrate.

GAUNT *a.* [GAWNT] emaciated and hollow-eyed, as if from starvation, old age, sickness etc. *The old man looked gaunt on his death bed.* SYN. emaciated, thin, haggard, hollow-eyed, bony, sickly, cadaverous, spindly, rawboned, wasted, scrawny, skeletal, drawn, *like death warmed over, anorexic. ANT. *strapping, robust, well-fed, fat*.

GAUNTLET, RUN THE *v.* [GONT lit] an outmoded form of punishment in which a soldier was forced to run between two lines of men, who would hit him with clubs, knotted ropes, etc., as he passed. In modern use, any multidirectional ordeal, punishment criticism, etc. *Politicians with unpopular ideas are forced to run the gantlet of public opinion.* SYN. face one's punishment, take potshots, be a target, be a whipping boy, face criticsm, *run an emotional minefield.

GAUNTLET, THROW DOWN THE [GONT lit] to challenge another, as to a fight or debate. *She questioned his credibility and thus officially threw down the gauntlet.* SYN. challenge, dare, invite to debate, invite to do battle, contest, start trouble, defy, invite for a face-off, provoke, confront, accost, stand up to. ANT. *back off, acquiesce.*

gauzy *a.* sheer, diaphanous, *see-through, transparent, gossamer, filmy, hazy, unsubstantial, translucent. ANT. *opaque, heavy, thick.*

gavel *n.* mallet.

gawk *v.* gape, stare in astonishment, stare saucer-eyed, ogle, look goggle-eyed, *rubberneck.

gawky *a.* clumsy, ungainly, awkward, oafish, graceless, bumbling, bungling, cloddish, maladroit, uncoordinated. ANT. *coordinated, graceful.*

gay *a.* **1.** HAPPY joyous, joyful, cheerful, sunny, festive, merry, mirthful, jolly, in high spirits, gleeful, vivacious, lighthearted, buoyant, animated, effervescent. **2.** BRIGHT brilliant, vivid, intense, showy, flashy, colorful. **3.** HOMOSEXUAL lesbian.

gaze *v.* stare, peer, ogle, eye, *eyeball, look, scrutinize, inspect, watch, survey, scan, regard, study, admire, glare, *scorch with one's eyes.

gazebo *n.* summerhouse, shelter, structure, bandstand, platform.

gear *n.* **1.** EQUIPMENT apparatus, rigging, accessories, tools, implements, paraphernalia, outfit, kit, trappings, accoutrement, *stuff, effects. **2.** MACHINE PART cog, toothed wheel, sprocket, flywheel, cam. **3.** CLOTHING apparel, outfit, attire, costume, *togs, *duds.

geek *n.* *Sl.* freak, goon, weirdo, mutant, oddball, one who belongs in a carnival sideshow.

geisha *n.* companion, hostess.

geld *v.* castrate, neuter, sterilize, emasculate, alter, *fix.

gem *n.* jewel, precious stone, semiprecious stone, *rock, *ice, bauble.

WORD FIND

blue: sapphire, aquamarine, turquoise, hyacinth

carved in relief: cameo
cutting device: lap
diamond look-alike: zircon
engraving: glyptics
expert, cutter, polisher, dealer: lapidary
fake: paste, rhinestone
flaw: feather
imperfectly transparent gem: loupe
iridescent: pearl, moonstone, opal, cat's eye
green: emerald, beryl, aquamarine, jade, peridot
magnifying glass used by jeweler: loupe
oblong shape, cut in: baguette
plane or individual cut: facet, culet, bezel, bezel
purple: amethyst
red: ruby, garnet, carnelian, sard, avena
setting, groove and flange: bezel
study of: gemology
transparent: diamond
weight: carat, karat
yellow: topaz
SEE JEWELRY

gender *n.* sex, classification.

genealogy *n.* descent, pedigree, lineage, family tree, ancestry, blood line, extraction, parentage.

general *a.* **1.** COMMON popular, regular, conventional, routine, normal, everyday, familiar, usual, prevalent, accepted, widespread. **2.** COMPREHENSIVE universal, all-inclusive, catholic, blanket, sweeping, extensive, broad, worldwide. **3.** INEXACT approximate, vague, unspecific, ill-defined, indefinite. ANT. *1. uncommon, irregular, unconventional. 2. exclusive, restricted. 3. exact, specific, defined.*

generality *n.* generalization, loose statement, broad statement, sweeping statement, abstraction.

generalize *v.* speculate, hypothesize, make sweeping statement, make broad statement, *paint with a broad brush.

generally *adv.* **1.** COMMONLY regularly, conventionally, usually, routinely, normally, typically, ordinarily. **2.** MAINLY mostly, for the most part, chiefly, ordinarily, on the whole, as a rule. ANT. *1. rarely, seldom, irregularly.*

generate *v.* produce, create, start, give rise to, invent, fashion, make, cause, initiate, originate, spawn, father, mother, found, give birth to, beget.

generation *n.* **1.** CREATION production, formation, invention, inception, fashioning, making, initiation, origination, spawning, founding, genesis. **2.** AGE period, era, epoch, eon, day, span.

generator *n.* dynamo, alternator.

generic *a.* general, universal, common, comprehensive. ANT. *specific.*

generous *a.* **1.** GIVING charitable, unselfish, big-hearted, openhanded, lavish, munificent, beneficent, benevolent, philanthropic, liberal, unstinting. **2.** PLENTIFUL bounteous, abundant, copious, ample, rich, lavish, liberal, overflowing. ANT. *1. cheap, stingy, *tight. 2. scanty, spare, meager.*

genesis *n.* origin, beginning, birth, creation, inception, start, generation, formation, dawn, commencement. ANT. *death, finish.*

genial *a.* cheerful, friendly, amiable, warm, sympathetic, cordial, sunny, pleasant, agreeable, good-natured, nice, convivial, sociable. ANT. *unfriendly, moody, standoffish, grouchy.*

genie *n.* jinni, supernatural being, spirit, wizard, conjurer.

genitals *n.* sexual organs, genitalia, reproductive organs, pudendum, privates, private parts. MALE: penis, phallus, *tool, testicles, testes, gonads. FEMALE: vagina, vulva, labia, clitoris.

genius *n.* **1.** MENTAL GIANT *brain, *whiz, intellectual, *wunderkind, prodigy, savant, *Edison, master, *Einstein, expert, virtuoso, *egghead, *rocket scientist. **2.** GREAT ABILITY OR INTELLECT talent, gift, facility, knack, endowment, brilliance, intelligence, astuteness, acumen, understanding, insight, creativity, imagination, aptitiude, brains, smarts, flair, wisdom, ingenuity, propensity, grasp, inventiveness. "Nothing more than our common faculties refined to a greater intensity."—Benjamin Haydon. "Nothing but labor and diligence."—William Hogarth. "Perseverance in disguise."—Henry Austin. "Originality, the opening of new frontiers."—Arthur Koestler. ANT. *1. moron, imbecile, ignoramus, idiot.*

GENOCIDE *n.* [JEN uh SIYD] the extermination or attempted extermination of an entire ethnic group, originally of the Jews by Nazi Germany, but now any mass ethnic extermination. *Ethnic cleansing is a form of genocide.* SYN. mass extermination, ethnic cleansing, holocaust, annihilation, eradication, ethnic elimination, massacre, slaughter, bloodbath, mass murder, decimation, carnage. SEE MURDER

GENRE *n.* [ZHAHN ruh] a type, kind or category. *Stephen King writes primarily within the horror genre.* SYN. type, kind, category, class, sort, classification, school, variety, style, genus.

GENTEEL *a.* [jen TEEL] refined and polite. Also, affectedly refined. *He never burped out loud; he was too genteel for that.* SYN. refined, polite, cultured, respectable, mannerly, civil, courtly, behaved, gentlemanly, ladylike, formal, prudish, pretentious, *la-di-da, *highfalutin, affected, pompous, *stuffy, hoity-toity. ANT. *unrefined, coarse, crude, uncultured, rude, earthy, *down-home.*

gentile *n.* non-Jew, goy.

gentility *n.* refinement, politeness, manners, civility, courtliness, courtesy, polish, sophistication, culture, respectability, nobility. ANT. *coarseness, vulgarity.*

gentle *a.* **1.** SOFT light, delicate, calm, quiet, easy, tender, slight, mellow, faint, temperate. **2.** KINDLY agreeable, mild, docile, tender, soft, quiet, placid, peaceful, meek, serene, tame. ANT. *1. rough, hard, violent. 2. violent, vicious, rough.*

gentleman *n.* **1.** MAN fellow, *guy, chap, *dude. **2.** REFINED MAN OR RICH MAN patrician, lord, aristocrat, nobleman, *gent, *blue-blood, courtier. "To speak as the common people do, to think as wise men do."—Roger Ascham.

gentlemanly *a.* genteel, mannerly, courtly, refined, polite, courteous, gallant, civil, honorable, cultivated, noble.

gentry *n.* aristocracy, upper class, *upper crust, nobility, gentlefolk, elite.

genuine *a.* **1.** REAL authentic, legitimate, *the real McCoy, bona fide, certified, actual, honest, true, unadulterated. **2.** SINCERE honest, frank, ingenuous, forthright, heartfelt, unaffected, earnest, natural. ANT. *1. counterfeit, fake, bogus. 2. insincere, affected, disingenuous.*

genus *n.* class, classification, sort, kind, type, category, order.

germ *n.* **1.** MICROBE microorganism, *bug, virus, bacterium, bacillus, pathogen, infectious agent, rhinovirus, retrovirus, streptococcus, spirochete. **2.** SOURCE root, beginning, origin, seed, embryo, fountainhead, spark.

GERMANE *a.* [jur MANE] relevant, pertinent. *Your comment is not germane to the subject at hand.* SYN. relevant, pertinent, related, appropriate, applicable, to the point, apropos, related, material, apt. ANT. *irrelevant, immaterial, unrelated.*

germicide *n.* antiseptic, germ killer, disinfectant, antibiotic, fumigant, bactericide.

germinate *v.* sprout, bud, flower, grow, develop, spring up, shoot, generate.

gerontology *n.* geriatrics, study of aging.

gestation *n.* pregnancy, incubation, maturation, development.

gesticulate *v.* SEE GESTURE

gesture *v.* gesticulate, motion, signal, wave, pantomime, mime, express with hands, *use body language, *use body English, sign.

get *v.* **1.** OBTAIN acquire, attain, come by, secure, net, take, *bag, gain, receive, seize, earn, win, procure, reap, harvest, gather, achieve. **2.** UNDERSTAND comprehend, grasp, see, follow, fathom, take in, apprehend. **3.** BE AFFLICTED WITH catch, *come down with, contract.

geyser *n.* spout, fountain, jet, blast, gusher, thermal spring.

ghastly *a.* **1.** FRIGHTFUL horrible, hideous, gruesome, shocking, dreadful, horrendous, appalling, revolting, macabre, grisly. **2.** CADAVEROUS ghostly, pale, haggard, blanched, corpselike, deathly, ashen. ANT. *1. lovely.*

ghetto *n.* slum, inner city, rundown quarter, public housing district.

ghost *n.* spirit, specter, apparition, phantom, *spook, phantasm, poltergeist, wraith, doppelganger, shade, shadow. "The outward and visible sign of an inward fear."—Ambrose Bierce.

ghostly *a.* spectral, phantom, spiritual, phantasmic, spooky, spiritual, haunted, unearthly, wraithlike, supernatural, ghastly, eerie, illusory.

ghoul *n.* evil spirit, demon, graverobber, fiend, devil, bogeyman, goblin, creep, vampire, monster.

ghoulish *a.* monstrous, hideous, fiendish, vampiric, gruesome, diabolical, necrophilic, cold-blooded, horrible.

GI *n.* government issue, soldier, member of the service, marine, army man, army woman, sailor, *grunt, *dogface, *leatherneck. SEE AIR FORCE, ARMY, NAVY

giant *n.* titan, Gargantua, colossus, behemoth, *whopper, *bruiser, hulk, Goliath, Brobdingnagian, Amazon, Cyclops, ogre, giantess. ANT. *midget, dwarf, *shrimp, *Lilliputian.*

giant *a.* huge, gigantic, gargantuan, mammoth, colossal, enormous, prodigious, Brobdingnagian, titanic, Herculean, elephantine, towering. ANT. *tiny, microscopic, *Lilliputian.*

gibberish *n.* babble, gibber, *gobbledegook, mumbo jumbo, jabber, chatter, nonsense, twaddle, drivel, blather, prattle, jargon.

gibe *v.* taunt, jeer, mock, scoff, ridicule, tease, *ride, deride, make fun of, sneer at, heckle, *razz, rib.

giddy *a.* **1.** DIZZY light-headed, *woozy, reeling, unsteady, faint, vertiginous. **2.** FLIGHTY frivolous, fickle, *bubbleheaded, capricious, silly, *airheaded, scatterbrained, *ditzy. ANT. *1. steady, strong, energetic. 2. level-headed, sober, stable, serious.*

gift *n.* **1.** PRESENT gratuity, donation, giveaway, contribution, offering, token, gesture, favor, benefaction, bonus, grant, tip. **2.** TALENT natural ability, knack, faculty, aptitude, endowment, flair, bent, genius.

gifted *a.* talented, endowed, skilled, expert, accomplished, masterly, proficient, adept, ingenious, intelligent, blessed. ANT. *dense, inept, slow.*

gig *n.* show, performance, play date, engagement, job, appearance, concert, recital.

gigantic *a.* huge, big, titanic, gargantuan, colossal, *whopping, Brobdingnagian, Herculean, enormous, stupendous, towering, prodigious. ANT. *tiny, microscopic, Lilliputian.*

giggle *v.* laugh, titter, snigger, chuckle, snicker, *teehee, chortle, cackle.

gigolo *n.* escort, lover, *pro, *professional, paramour, paid date, lady-killer, paid companion, *sex machine, Lothario, Don Juan, Cassanova, love buddy.

gild *v.* embellish, decorate, gloss over, embroider, dress up, enhance, touch up, garnish, whitewash, sugarcoat.

gimcrack *n.* knickknack, bauble, gew gaw, trinket, doodad, novelty, whatnot, bagatelle.

gimmick *n.* device, scheme, catch, subterfuge, artifice, wrinkle, ruse, ploy, trick, contrivance, *dodge.

gingerly *adv.* delicately, lightly, carefully, cautiously, gently, warily, guardedly, discreetly, charily, timidly. ANT. *recklessly, boldly, rashly.*

gingivitis *n.* gum inflammation, gum disease, bleeding gums.

gird *v.* encircle, surround, enclose, circumscribe, band, encompass, secure, reinforce, fortify.

girder *n.* beam, joist, timber, support.

girdle *n.* corset, undergarment, truss.

girl *n.* female, lass, lassie, maiden, miss, *filly, damsel, wench, *chick, *babe, *dame, mademoiselle, debutante, belle, tomboy, *muchacha. "Innocence playing in the mud, beauty standing on its head, and motherhood dragging a doll by the foot."—Allan Beck.

gist n. essence, substance, main point, pith, crux, heart, core, point, drift, thrust, *bottom line.

give v. **1.** CONTRIBUTE, BESTOW donate, present, hand over, confer, award, dispense, deliver, transmit, provide, *fork over, convey, *shell out, entrust. **2.** IMPART express, communicate, send, deliver, offer, announce, state. **3.** CONCEDE yield, bend, surrender, relinquish. **4.** COLLAPSE buckle, cave in, fall.

give-and-take n. compromise, cooperation, reciprocity, *mutual back-scratching, interchange, trade-off, collaboration, exchange, swap.

gizmo n. device, appliance, mechanism, tool, gadget, thingamajig, thingamabob, contraption, widget, machine, *Rube Goldberg device.

glacial a. icy, snowy, frozen, gelid, frigid, frosty, arctic, polar, wintry. ANT. *tropical, warm, sunny.*

WORD FIND

altering of land mass by glacier: glaciation
boulder pushed far from its native land by: glacial erratic
bowl-like gouge carved out of mountain side by glacier: cirque
breaking away of large chunks from head of glacier: calving
cave in a glacier: glaciere
chunks of glacier floating in ocean: iceberg
epoch: pleistocene
expert: glaciologist
form: glaciate
gravel and rocks deposited by: drift, till, drumlin, esker, kame, moraine
mountain peak surrounded by: nunatak
period of cold in which glaciers grow and expand: ice age
pinnacle of ice on: serac
scratches, grooves left on bedrock by passing glacier: striations
snow that gradually becomes glacial ice: neve, firn
study of: glaciology
SEE SNOW, WINTER

glacier n. ice mass, snow mass, ice cap, snow pack.

glad a. **1.** HAPPY delighted, *tickled, *tickled to death, *tickled pink, pleased, thrilled, gratified, cheerful, joyous, upbeat. **2.** DELIGHTFUL happy, pleasing, gratifying, cheering. **3.**

WILLING eager. ANT. *1. sad, depressed, unhappy. 2. miserable, awful, terrible. 3. unwilling, reluctant.*

gladden v. cheer, make happy, hearten, please, brighten, delight, *tickle pink, *raise one's spirits, elate. ANT. *bring down, *bum out, depress.*

gladiator n. swordsman, fighter, combatant.

glamorous a. fascinating, charismatic, alluring, captivating, charming, magnetic, bewitching, enchanting, dazzling, provocative. ANT. *humdrum, prosaic, every day.*

glamour n. allure, charm, appeal, fascination, *razzle-dazzle, charisma, magnetism, attraction, bewitchment, *star power.

glance n. look, glimpse, peek, peep, gander, *once-over.

glance v. **1.** LOOK glimpse, peer, peek, peep, view, observe, *get a load of, *take a gander, *give a once-over, eye, *eyeball. **2.** GRAZE sideswipe, brush, carom, kiss, ricochet, skim, bounce off, touch.

gland n. organ, secreting organ, lymph gland, thymus, thyroid, parotid, adrenal gland, sweat gland, pituitary gland, liver, pancreas.

glare v. **1.** SHINE flash, gleam, blaze, dazzle, light, radiate, blind, flame, glow. **2.** SCOWL frown, *stare down, glower, lower, *scorch with one's eyes, *look at piercingly, *stare icily. SEE ANGRY

glaring a. **1.** BRIGHT blinding, dazzling, brilliant, intense, overpowering, shining, harsh, flashy, blazing. **2.** FLAGRANT obvious, conspicuous, blatant, extreme, open, overt, prominent, undisguised. ANT. *1. dim, subdued. 2. subtle, covert, negligible, inconspicuous.*

glass n. cup, tumbler, goblet, mug, chalice, beaker, pony.

glasses n. *specs, spectacles, corrective lenses, lenses. SEE EYE GLASSES

glassy a. **1.** TRANSPARENT clear, crystal, glossy, vitreous, lucid, smooth, slick. **2.** EXPRESSIONLESS glazed, lifeless, vacuous, empty, dazed, deadpan, fixed. ANT. *1. opaque, clouded. 2. expressive.*

glaze n. varnish, lacquer, gloss, coat, finish, patina, luster.

glaze v. varnish, lacquer, gloss, coat, finish, polish, paint.

gleam n. flash, beam, light, brilliance, sparkle, glimmer, glow, twinkle, scintillation, shimmer.

gleam v. shine, beam, flash, light, radiate, sparkle, glimmer, glow, twinkle, scintillate, shimmer.

glean *v.* collect, gather, harvest, reap, cull, take in, extract.

glee *n.* joy, gaiety, happiness, merriment, exultation, elation, verve, mirth, gladness, jubilation, felicity. ANT. *depression, misery, melancholy.*

gleeful *a.* joyous, gay, happy, merry, exultant, elated, mirthful, glad, jubilant, exhilarated, blithe. ANT. *depressed, miserable, melancholy.*

GLIB *a.* [GLIB] spoken or given too easily, too offhandedly or too superficially to be taken seriously, as a piece of advice. *His glib response to Marcia's earnest question left her unsatisfied.* SYN. facile, superficial, shallow, smooth-tongued, quick, ready, slick, smooth-talking, fluent, fast-talking, voluble. ANT. *thoughtful, sincere, deep, profound.*

glide *v.* slide, glissade, float, skim, plane, waft, coast, drift, skate, slip, flow, wing.

glimmer *v.* gleam, glow, flicker, sparkle, glare, coruscate, beam, glitter, twinkle, scintillate, flash.

glimpse *n.* look, peek, peep, glance, fleeting look, flash.

glimpse *v.* catch a peek, peep, look, glance, see, eye, *eyeball, spot, *get a load of, take in, spy.

glint *n.* sparkle, gleam, flash, glitter.

glisten *v.* shine, sparkle, flash, glimmer, shimmer, gleam, glint, scintillate, glitter.

glitch *n. Sl.* error, malfunction, *bug, snag, *snafu.

glitter *n.* sparkle, glint, glimmer, gleam, sheen, shine, brilliance, radiance, scintillation, luster, twinkle.

glitter *v.* sparkle, glint, glimmer, gleam, shine, radiate, scintillate, twinkle, coruscate.

glitz *n.* showiness, ostentation, gaudiness, garishness.

gloaming *n.* dusk, twilight, nightfall, sundown.

gloat *v.* crow, exult, strut, brag, vaunt, triumph, *rub it in, boast, *lord over, *take malicious pleasure in. ANT. *downplay, deprecate.*

glob *n.* lump, chunk, hunk, mass, blob, globule, drop, ball, gob.

global *a.* worldwide, international, intercontinental, universal, planetary, pandemic, widespread, extensive, far-reaching. ANT. *local, regional, confined.*

globe *n.* sphere, orb, spheroid, earth, planet, world, ball, *spaceship Earth, biosphere.

gloom *n.* **1.** DARKNESS dimness, murk, shadow, obscurity, shade, dusk, blackness, cloudiness. **2.** SADNESS depression, hopelessness, melancholy, despair, woe, grief, sorrow, dejection, unhappiness, desolation, heavy-heartedness. ANT. **1.** *brightness, sunniness, light, radiance.* **2.** *happiness, cheerfulness, joy.*

gloomy *a.* **1.** DARK dim, murky, shadowy, dismal, obscure, dusky, gauzy, black, cloudy, dreary, somber. **2.** SAD depressed, depressing, hopeless, dismal, melancholy, woeful, glum, sorrowful, dejected, unhappy, desolated, joyless, heavyhearted, despondent, saturnine, black, bleak, funereal. ANT. **1.** *bright, light, radiant, sunny.* **2.** *happy, elated, euphoric, bright.*

glorify *v.* **1.** EXALT honor, idolize, revere, worship, deify, elevate, venerate, immortalize, beatify, sanctify. **2.** PRAISE extol, celebrate, honor, *put on a pedestal, *talk up, *sing the praises of, hail, acclaim, celebrate, flatter, lionize. ANT. *degrade, condemn, dishonor, disgrace.*

glorious *a.* divine, splendid, magnificent, wonderful, grand, marvelous, superb, excellent, heavenly, sublime, spectacular, resplendent. ANT. *lowly, humble, modest, plain.*

glory *n.* **1.** HONOR admiration, fame, renown, celebrity, praise, acclaim, esteem, adoration, veneration, prestige, notoriety. "Goads and spurs to virtue."—Francis Bacon. "A torch to kindle the noble mind."—Silius Italicus. **2.** BEAUTY splendor, magnificence, radiance, grandeur, resplendence, majesty, brilliance. ANT. **1.** *dishonor, degradation, disgrace.* **2.** *ugliness.*

gloss *n.* shine, luster, sheen, shimmer, glow, gleam, polish, brilliance.

gloss *v.* **1.** SHINE make lustrous, polish, buff, rub, burnish, varnish. **2.** SMOOTH OVER cover up, mask, disguise, *sugarcoat, soft-pedal, *whitewash, doctor.

glossary *n.* lexicon, word list, nomenclature, vocabulary, dictionary.

glossy *a.* shiny, lustrous, shimmering, gleaming, glowing, polished, burnished, sleek, silky, glassy. ANT. *dull, tarnished.*

glow *n.* radiance, light, gleam, brightness, glimmer, shine, luminosity, illumination, incandescence, effulgence, phosphorescence. SEE BLUSH

glow *v.* radiate, light, gleam, glimmer, shine, illuminate, incandesce, shimmer, glare. SEE BLUSH

glower *v.* frown, scowl, glare, lower, stare blackly, *shoot a dirty look, *scorch with one's eyes. SEE ANGRY

glowing *a.* **1.** RADIANT aglow, luminous. **2.** COLORED red, ruddy, rosy, flushed, florid, radiant, aglow, blooming. **3.** ENTHUSIASTIC complimentary, laudatory, favorable. ANT. *1. dull, dim. 2. pale, blanched, pallid. 3. negative, unenthusiastic, critical.*

glue *n.* cement, paste, fixative, adhesive, *stickum, mucilage.

glum *a.* sullen, gloomy, morose, down, low, dispirited, long-faced, sulky, dismal, cheerless, lugubrious, sad. ANT. *cheerful, happy, joyous, elated.*

glut *n.* excess, surplus, overabundance, superfluity, surfeit, surplus, flood, inundation, overflow, plethora, repletion. ANT. *dearth, scarcity, lack, shortage.*

glut *v.* fill, flood, surfeit, sate, satiate, inundate, clog, choke, oversupply, stuff, congest, overload.

glutton *n.* *pig, *hog, gourmand, *garbage disposal, eater, epicure, *garbage gut, *chow hound, overeater. "One who digs his grave with his teeth."—French proverb.

gluttonous *a.* voracious, gourmandizing, insatiable, ravenous, *piggish, *hoggish.

gnarled *a.* knotted, knotty, twisted, contorted, tortured, crooked, distorted, arthritic, wrinkled. ANT. *smooth.*

gnash *v.* grind, grit, grate, rasp, clamp.

gnaw *v.* **1.** MUNCH nibble, chew, bite, champ, eat away. **2.** BOTHER nag, *eat at, trouble, worry, plague, torment.

gnome *n.* fairy, elf, dwarf, troll, pixie, leprechaun, imp.

go *n.* **1.** ENERGY animation, drive, vigor, zest, pep, life, force. **2.** TRY attempt, whirl, stab, shot, crack.

go *v.* **1.** PROCEED advance, begin, move, start, set out, get the ball rolling, travel, make headway, progress. **2.** LEAVE depart, retire, run, *split, *scram, decamp, withdraw, slip away, *hit the road, vamoose, quit, *shove off, *beat it, *blow. **3.** FUNCTION perform, run, work, operate, act. **4.** PASS elapse, slip away, transpire, expire. **5.** EXTEND lead, stretch, span, reach. ANT. *1. stop, stay, freeze. 2. remain, stay.*

goad *n.* stimulus, spur, prod, inducement, impetus, catalyst, urge, motive, incentive, *kick in the pants, *swift kick.

goad *v.* stimulate, spur, prod, induce, urge, motivate, impel, incite, spark, egg on, coerce, prompt, *kickstart, provoke.

goal *n.* aim, ambition, end, purpose, objective, target, design, intention, destination.

goat *n.* scapegoat, *fall guy, whipping boy, butt, *patsy.

gobble *v.* bolt, wolf, gulp, stuff, cram, choke down, devour, *shovel, gorge, *suck up, swallow whole.

gobbledygook *n.* gibberish, jargon, cant, *officialese, claptrap, legalese, nonsense, *bunk, *rot, *bafflegab.

go-between *n.* intermediary, middleman, medium, second, arbitrator, mediator, agent, broker, referee.

goblin *n.* spirit, bogeyman, *spook, hobgoblin, imp, elf, puck, gnome, kobold.

God/god *n.* **1.** GOD Supreme Being, Father in Heaven, Heavenly Father, the Almighty, the All-Powerful, the All-Wise, the All-Merciful, the All-Seeing, Lord of Lords, King of Kings, the Creator, Brahma, Allah, Adonai, Lord, Jehovah, Holy Spirit, the Man Upstairs. "Love."—The Bible. "A superior reasoning power . . . revealed in the incomprehensible universe."—Albert Einstein. "Conscience."—Mohandas Gandhi. "A light that is never darkened."—Francis Quarles. "A mighty fortress."—Martin Luther. "Personified incomprehensibility."—George Lichtenberg. "That which has no definition."—Joseph Albo. "A vengeful, pitiless, and almighty fiend."—Percy Bysshe Shelley. "An infantile fantasy . . . necessary when men did not know what lightning was."—Edward Anhalt. "A gaseous vertebrate."—Ernst Haeckel. **2.** DEITY goddess, divinity, spirit, idol. ANT. *1. the Devil, Satan, Lucifer, Prince of Darkness. 2. mortal, physical being.*

WORD FIND

appearance of: theophany

belief in god other than that of Jewish, Christian or Muslim faith: paganism

cry of praise to God: hosanna

disbelief in: atheism

disbeliever: atheist

half god, half human: demigod

Hindu deity on earth: avatar

human traits imagined in: anthropomorphism

humans created by God not evolved, belief that: creationism

Latin: Deus

one, belief in more than: polytheism

one, belief in only: monotheism

questioner of God's existence: agnostic

questioning of God's existence: agnosticism
Son of God: Jesus Christ
study of: theology
universe and its natural laws are God, belief
that: pantheism
SEE CHURCH, MYTHICAL DEITIES, RELIGION

God-fearing *a.* pious, devout, faithful, devoted, reverent, holy, religious. ANT. *atheistic, godless, heathen.*

godforsaken *a.* desolate, forlorn, lonely, abandoned, wretched, cheerless, forgotten, condemned. ANT. *lush, hospitable.*

godless *a.* atheistic, heathen, impious, pagan, sacrilegious, blasphemous, freethinking, agnostic, wicked, unholy. ANT. *pious, devout, God-fearing.*

godly *a.* religious, God-fearing, devout, pious, righteous, holy, spiritual, reverent, born-again, saintly, good, moral. ANT. *godless, sinful, atheistic, blasphemous, sacrilegious.*

godsend *n.* blessing, gift, windfall, miracle, manna, benediction, boon.

Godspeed *n.* good luck, good fortune, success, God's blessings, prosperity, God's favor.

gofer *n. Sl.* errand boy, errand girl, *go getter, gal Friday, man Friday, *grunt.

gold *n.* **1.** COLOR yellow, gilt, straw, tawny, flaxen, blond, honey, auric. **2.** METAL precious metal, nugget. "The touchstone whereby to try men."—Thomas Fuller.
WORD FIND
bar: ingot, bullion
fool's: pyrite
of gold: aurous
glacial deposit: placer mine
overlay: gild, gilt
weight: carat

goldbrick *v. Sl.* shirk, loaf, *goof off, malinger.

gold digger *n.* user, parasite, bloodsucker, leech, sponge, opportunist, exploiter.

golden *a.* **1.** SEE GOLD **2.** ADVANTAGEOUS best, opportune, favorable, auspicious, timely, propitious, providential, rosy. ANT. **2.** *black, unfavorable.*

gold mine *n.* bonanza, mother lode, Eldorado, *cash cow, *goose that layed the golden egg.

golf *n.* sport, pastime. "A plague invented by the Calvinistic Scots as a punishment for man's sins."—James Reston. "A good walk spoiled."—Mark Twain.
WORD FIND
aid: caddy
average number of shots deemed necessary for each hole: par

ball position after coming to rest: lie
closely cropped green around hole: putting green
club: baffy, blade, brassie, chipping iron, cleek, iron, mashie, niblick, putter, driver, wood, wedge, spoon
curving drive: hook, slice
curving fairway: dogleg
extra shot allowed in casual game: Mulligan
fee to play: greens fee
flagstick: pin
grounds: fairway, green, links, course
hole made in one stroke: ace, hole in one
lockers, club building: clubhouse
long grass area: rough
par, scoring one stroke over: bogey
par, scoring one stroke under: birdie
par, scoring three strokes under: albatross, double eagle
par, scoring two strokes over: double bogey
par, scoring two strokes under: eagle
plug that ball sits on: tee
poor golfer: duffer, hacker
sand hazard: sand trap, bunker; *beach
shots: drive, putt, chip shot, loft, pitch, hook, slice
shouted warning: fore!
turf hacked out by club: divot

gone *a.* departed, left, removed, away, absent, vanished, missing, extinct, *AWOL, out, off, lost, used up, consumed, finished. ANT. *present, arrived, here.*

gonzo *a. Sl.* strange, odd, bizarre, weird, *far out, experimental, unconventional. ANT. *straight-laced, conventional.*

good *n.* **1.** ADVANTAGE benefit, welfare, profit, gain, interest, well-being. **2.** VIRTUE goodness, morality, value, worth, uprightness.

good *a.* **1.** SATISFACTORY adequate, acceptable, worthy, OK, all right, fine, excellent, first-rate, choice, super, great, commendable, prime, marvelous, select, sufficient, beneficial, reputable, recommended, effective. **2.** MORAL virtuous, righteous, wholesome, honorable, upright, conscientious, exemplary, respectable, noble, chaste. **3.** KIND humane, benevolent, sympathetic, compassionate, giving, charitable, merciful, altruistic. **4.** WELL-BEHAVED mannerly, respectful, polite, considerate. **5.** UNSPOILED fresh, uncontaminated, untainted, fit, sound. **6.** SKILLED able, proficient, competent, accomplished, adept, capable, talented. **7.** GENUINE authentic, real, bona fide, valid, true, sound, *kosher.

8. CONSIDERABLE big, large, sizable, respectable, substantial, extensive. ANT. *1. unsatisfactory, bad, poor, second-rate. 2. immoral, sinful, wicked. 3. cruel, mean, vicious. 4. rude, impolite, unruly. 5. spoiled, tainted. 6. unskilled, bad, inadequate. 7. fake, counterfeit, phony. 8. scant, trivial, piddling.*

goodbye *interj.* farewell, bye-bye, *so long, Godspeed, *toodle-oo, *toodles, *ta-ta, adieu, adios, ciao, sayonara, hasta la vista, arrivederci, au revoir, auf Wiedersehen, see you later, *later, *see you later alligator, vaya con dios, aloha, shalom.

good-humored *a.* SEE GOOD-NATURED

good-looking *a.* attractive, beautiful, handsome, pretty, cute, comely, lovely, becoming, fair, *nice, *foxy, *bonny. ANT. *ugly, repulsive.*

good-natured *a.* easygoing, cheerful, amiable, genial, pleasant, good-humored, agreeable, nice, even-tempered, complaisant, kindly. ANT. *grouchy, touchy, standoffish.*

goodness *n.* virtue, excellence, righteousness, uprightness, morality, integrity, kindness, wholesomeness, benevolence. ANT. *badness, wickedness, evil.*

goods *n.* **1.** PERSONAL PROPERTY belongings, possessions, things, stuff, effects. **2.** MERCHANDISE wares, stock, inventory, commodities.

goodwill *n.* benevolence, kindliness, altruism, favor, friendliness, humanitarianism, graciousness, goodness. ANT. *ill will, hostility.*

goody-goody *a.* straight-laced, upright, politically correct, nice, pious, moral, prudish, prissy, Victorian, Puritan, no-nonsense. ANT. *wild, rowdy, immoral.*

gooey *a.* sticky, *gloppy, tacky, viscous, gelatinous, gummy. ANT. *dry.*

goof *v. Sl.* bungle, mess up, blunder, fail, *screw up, miscalculate.

goofy *a. Sl.* silly, foolish, stupid, sophomoric, childish, *nerdy, *ditzy, *daffy, dopey. ANT. *serious, respected.*

goon *n.* *geek, *bozo, clown, *boob, *dork, *goober, lummox, freak, moron, *throwback, *Neanderthal.

GORDIAN KNOT *n.* SEE CUT THE GORDIAN KNOT

gore *n.* bloodshed, slaughter, carnage. SEE MURDER

gore *v.* pierce, puncture, stab, impale, gouge, horn, hook.

gorge *n.* canyon, chasm, pass, valley, gap, ravine, gully, defile.

gorge *v.* bolt, stuff, cram, wolf, swallow whole, gulp, gobble, devour, *shovel in, overeat, satiate, glut.

gorgeous *a.* beautiful, magnificent, splendid, sumptuous, attractive, stunning, lovely, ravishing, exquisite, luxurious, resplendent. ANT. *repulsive, hideous, plain.* SEE GOOD-LOOKING

gorilla *n.* **1.** GREAT APE beast, primate, mammal, simian, *King Kong, *Mighty Joe Young. **2.** THUG beast, bruiser, goon, hoodlum, brute, animal.

gormandize *v.* devour, gorge, *pig out, overeat, stuff, gobble, wolf.

gospel *n.* fact, truth, God's word, simple truth, reality, actuality, chapter and verse, *what's what.

gory *a.* bloody, bloodstained, sanguinary, murderous, savage, horrible.

gossamer *a.* delicate, diaphanous, airy, fine, feathery, cobwebby. ANT. *strong, solid, well-built.*

gossip *n.* **1.** RUMORS hearsay, chatter, talk, scandal, *dirt, *lowdown, *scuttlebutt, report, mudslinging, *grapevine, *small talk, *buzz. "Foul whisperings."—Shakespeare. "Murder by language."—Roland Barthes. **2.** RUMORMONGER tattler, tattletale, *big mouth, *blabbermouth, busybody, snoop, prattler

gouge *n.* groove, channel, hole, scratch, furrow, score, gash, excavation, striation.

gouge *v.* scratch, scrape, excavate, dig, scoop out.

gourmet *n.* epicure, epicurean, gastronome, connoisseur, bon vivant, gourmand. "Just a glutton with brains."—Philip Haberman.

govern *v.* **1.** RULE administer, direct, supervise, manage, oversee, dictate, run, reign, order, occupy the throne, regulate, *lay down the law, hold sway, *pull the strings, exercise authority. **2.** HOLD IN CHECK curb, inhibit, bridle, restrain, control, arrest, regulate.

government *n.* regulation, administration, governing body, control, *Big Brother, Washington, *Uncle Sam, the state, *powers that be, management, supervision, guidance, bureaucracy, rule, command, reign, authority, leadership, dictatorship, regime, senate, congress, ministry. "The biggest organized social effort for dealing with social problems."—Felix Frankfurter. "The people."—John Quincy Adams. "The Santa Claus of something-for-nothing and something-for-everyone."—Barry Goldwater. "A kind of gangsterism."—Frank Lloyd Wright.

WORD FIND

absence of: anarchy
authoritarian: totalitarianism
autonomy: sovereignty
betrayal of: treason
citizens in authority: commonwealth, democracy, republic
clergy, headed by: hierocracy, theocracy, hagiarchy
dictated by one ruler or small group: dictatorship, despotism, tyranny
experts, by: technocracy
female: matriarchy, gynarchy, gynecocracy
king's: monarchy
male lineage, handed down through: patriarchy
Medieval system of lords and vassals: feudalism
military, by: stratocracy, martial law
oppressive, one-party system: fascism
preserving cultural diversity: pluralism
privileged class, by: aristocracy, oligarchy, plutocracy
secret police, controlled by: police state
seizure of: coup d'etat
self-governing: autonomous
without: acracy
SEE CONGRESS, ELECTION, POLITICS

governor n. ruler, regulator, director, administrator, supervisor, head, bureaucrat, magistrate.

gown n. dress, frock, robe, negligee.

grab v. snatch, seize, clutch, grasp, pluck, catch, capture, bag, nab, take, latch on to, get one's hands on.

grace n. 1. BEAUTY AND CHARM loveliness, attractiveness, elegance, appeal, pulchritude. 2. GOOD FORM fluidity, symmetry, finesse, ease, *poetry in motion, form, agility, dexterity, poise, refinement, coordination. 3. MANNERS thoughtfulness, savoir faire, decorum, tact, charm, cultivation, etiquette. 4. MERCY forgiveness, clemency, leniency, compassion, reprieve, quarter, good will. 5. PRAYER benediction, thanksgiving, request for blessings. 6. GOD'S FAVOR love, virtue, divine influence, holiness. "The outward expression of the inward harmony of the soul."—William Hazlitt. ANT. 1. ugliness, repulsiveness. 2. clumsiness, awkwardness. 3. boorishness, rudeness, bad manners. 4. condemnation, damnation, ill will.

grace v. decorate, adorn, beautify, bedeck, ornament, enhance, garnish, dignify, honor, distinguish.

graceful a. 1. HAVING GOOD FORM fluid, coordinated, poised, dexterous, agile, refined, adroit, nimble, lissome, lithesome, supple, *graceful as a porteuse, smooth, balanced, elegant. 2. CHARMING appealing, attractive, elegant, mannerly, cultivated, winsome, tactful, urbane. ANT. 1. clumsy, awkward. 2. rude, obnoxious, boorish, unrefined.

gracious a. kind, courteous, hospitable, cordial, polite, benevolent, accommodating, considerate, well-mannered, friendly, affable, charitable. ANT. ungracious, rude, inconsiderate.

grade n. 1. SLOPE incline, gradient, slant, rise, pitch, ascent, descent. 2. RANK status, standing, position, class, station, stage, increment, rating, mark.

grade v. 1. RANK rate, evaluate, classify, sort, brand, order, label. 2. LEVEL flatten, smooth.

gradient n. grade, slope, incline, slant, rise, pitch, ascent, descent.

gradual a. progressive, successive, slow, incremental, piecemeal, step-by-step, bit-by-bit, leisurely, measured, steady, by degrees. ANT. abrupt, sudden, instantaneous.

graduate n. alumnus, alumna, grad, bachelor.

graduate v. 1. COMPLETE SCHOOL receive a diploma, receive a degree, complete one's education. 2. GRADE measure, calibrate, mark off.

graduation n. commencement, advancement.
SEE COLLEGE, SCHOOL

graffiti n. slogans, graphics, defacement, graffita, epigrams, obscenities, scribbles, ceremony, inscriptions, sophomoric, philosophy, epithets, doodles.

graft n. 1. TRANSPLANT implant, scion, splice, slip. 2. CORRUPTION spoils, *take, *payola, bribe, *hush money, *skimming, kickback, boodle.

graft v. implant, transplant, splice, insert, affix.

grain n. 1. SEED kernel, grist, cereal, wheat, oats, barley, rice, rye, millet. 2. PARTICLE granule, bit, speck, fleck, mote, dot. 3. TEXTURE surface, weave.

grammar n. composition, language, language rules, syntax, semantics.

grand a. 1. MAGNIFICENT impressive, great, majestic, imposing, striking, glorious, splendid, excellent, superb, ambitious, marvelous, sumptuous, monumental, stately, august, awesome, huge, palatial, lofty. 2. MAIN principle, head, chief, leading, supreme, preeminent. 3. EXCELLENT great, good, superb, fabulous, first-rate. ANT. 1. lowly, pedestrian, paltry, modest. 2. secondary, lesser, minor. 3. poor, lousy, second-rate.

grandeur n. magnificence, greatness, splendor, majesty, glory, resplendence, vastness, augustness, beauty, distinction, eminence. ANT. insignificance, modesty.

GRANDILOQUENT a. [gran DIL uh kwent] using big words to try to impress, bombastic. Many politicians are grandiloquent but have little to say. SYN. bombastic, pompous, pretentious, high-flown, fustian, *windy, inflated, verbose, magnific, turgid, rhetorical. ANT. plainspoken, *folksy, simple, unpretentious.

grandiose a. grand, magnificent, impressive, imposing, extravagant, ambitious, cosmic, epic, homeric, pompous, theatrical, *highfalutin. ANT. down to earth, modest, humble.

grandstand n. bleachers, seating, stands, decking, box seats.

grandstand v. showoff, *hot dog, *showboat, play to the crowd.

grant n. gift, contribution, donation, present, endowment, award, bestowal, charity, scholarship.

grant v. 1. GIVE confer, transfer, bestow, award, impart, present, contribute, donate. 2. CONCEDE acknowledge, admit, accede, yield, go along with. ANT. refuse, deny.

grape n. berry, fruit.

graphic a. vivid, clear, lifelike, striking, pictorial, picturesque, realistic, explicit, descriptive, effective, expressive. ANT. vague, obscure.

graphics n. pictorials, pictures, drawings, art, imagery, illustrations, visuals, representations.

grapple v.1. STRUGGLE wrestle, scuffle, battle, tussle, combat, *lock horns, confront, fight. 2. GRIP hold, seize, clutch, snatch, squeeze, catch.

grasp n. 1. GRIP hold, clutch, clasp. 2. COMPREHENSION understanding, perception, mastery, knowledge, cognition.

grasp v. 1. GRIP grab, hold, clutch, clasp, catch, snatch, clinch, grapple, nab. 2. COMPREHEND understand, get, see, sense, follow, apprehend, appreciate. ANT. 1. loose, release, let go.

grasping a. avaricious, greedy, acquisitive, hungry, covetous, rapacious, miserly, *grabby, venal, desirous. ANT. generous, giving.

grass n. lawn, turf, sward, pasture, meadow, alfalfa, barley, Bermuda grass, bluegrass, broomcorn, buckwheat, bulrush, bunch grass, cane, crab grass, darnel, eelgrass, fescue, foxtail, hay, horsetail, lemon grass, millet, oat, orchard grass, redtop, ribbon grass, rice, rush, rye, sedge, sorghum, timothy, wheat, witch grass. "The hair of the earth."—Thomas Dekker.

WORD FIND
clump: hassock, tussock, tuft
decaying matter beneath: thatch
dried: hay
hay: timothy
individual: blade, spear, shoot, leaf
new growth: fog
SEE FIELD

grassland n. meadow, field, prairie, pasture, range, pampas, campo, savanna, plain, steppe, veldt.

GRASS ROOTS n. the common people, ordinary taxpayers. The movement began among the grass roots of America. SYN. common people, taxpayers, the masses, middle class, rank and file, *little guys, hoi polloi, electorate, Middle America.

grate v. 1. SHRED grind, rasp, fray, mince, abrade, grit, file. 2. IRRITATE *rub the wrong way, annoy, *get on one's nerves, irk, nettle, peeve, fret.

grateful a. thankful, appreciative, indebted, beholden, obliged, much obliged. ANT. ungrateful, unappreciative.

gratification n. satisfaction, enjoyment, pleasure, fulfillment, contentment, delight, happiness, reward, gratuity.

gratify v. please, satisfy, fulfill, content, make happy, delight, gladden, favor, oblige, indulge. ANT. displease, dissatisfy, disappoint.

gratifying a. pleasing, satisfying, fulfilling, contenting, delightful, gladdening, rewarding, enjoyable. ANT. displeasing, disappointing.

grating n. framework, grille, grid, latticework, grate.

grating a. 1. HARSH rasping, jarring, grinding, strident, scraping, screeching, piercing. 2. IRRITATING annoying, irksome, nettlesome, vexatious, exasperating, abrasive. ANT. 1. fluid, melodious, pleasing. 2. pleasing, agreeable.

gratis a. free, complimentary, *on the house, no charge, gratuitous. ANT. for a fee, costing extra.

gratitude n. appreciation, thankfulness, gratefulness, thanks, acknowledgement, recognition, sense of obligation. "The exchequer of the poor."—Shakespeare.

GRATUITOUS a. [gruh TOO i tus] uncalled

for or unjustified, also, given freely or without charge. *Movies today are filled with gratuitous violence.* SYN. **1.** UNCALLED FOR unjustified, unnecessary, unwarranted, needless, superfluous, inessential, unprovoked, baseless. **2.** FREE gratis, complimentary, *on the house. ANT. *1. necessary, relevant, justified, warranted.*

gratuity *n.* gift, tip, present, fee, extra, *perk, lagniappe, recompense, bonus, offering, vail, cumshaw.

grave *n.* tomb, resting place, crypt, vault, sepulcher, burial pit, mausoleum, catacomb, God's acre, burial grounds, barrow. "The last inn of all travelers."—William Davenant. "The footprints of angels."—Longfellow. "The threshold of eternity."—Robert Southey. SEE CEMETERY, COFFIN, FUNERAL, MONUMENT

grave *a.* **1.** SERIOUS important, momentous, weighty, critical, crucial, *life and death, vital, pivotal, urgent, ominous, grievous, dangerous, threatening. **2.** SOLEMN grim, somber, dignified, serious, sedate, gloomy, sober, subdued, staid, dour, quiet, saturnine. ANT. *1. trivial, unimportant, insignificant, inconsequential. 2. cheerful, beaming, silly, merry.*

graveyard *n.* necropolis, *boneyard. SEE CEMETERY

gravitate *v.* be drawn to, be attracted, head toward, converge, incline, fall, settle, sink.

gravity *n.* **1.** GRAVITATION pull, attraction, pressure, force, weight. **2.** SERIOUSNESS importance, weightiness, consequence, magnitude, significance, urgency, import, enormity. ANT. *1. repulsion. 2. insignificance, triviality, frivolity.*

gravy *n.* drippings, natural juices, sauce.

gray *a.* **1.** SILVERY ash, leaden, pearly, smoky, gunmetal, battleship gray, stone, slate, dovecolored, salt and pepper, grizzled. **2.** OVERCAST gloomy, dismal, dim, dreary, somber. ANT. *2. bright, sunny.*

graze *v.* **1.** TOUCH scrape, brush, glance, kiss, skim, skin, scratch. **2.** FEED forage, browse, crop, munch, pasture.

grease *n.* fat, oil, lard, tallow, drippings, lubricant.

grease *v.* lubricate, oil.

greasy *a.* oily, fatty, buttery, lardy, oleaginous, slick, slippery, waxy, unctuous, smeared.

great *a.* **1.** LARGE big, huge, grand, immense, prodigious, gigantic, massive, tremendous, stupendous, enormous, gargantuan, extensive, boundless, voluminous, countless, extreme, prolonged, numerous. **2.** INTENSE strong, pronounced, extraordinary, considerable, powerful. **3.** IMPORTANT significant, momentous, consequential, influential, critical. **4.** CELEBRATED eminent, illustrious, famed, distinguished, esteemed, prominent, exalted, noted, renowned, heroic. **5.** EXCELLENT superb, super, fantastic, exceptional, awesome, first-rate, outstanding, terrific, wonderful, *crack, *aces, proficient, skilled. ANT. *1. small, lesser, tiny, miniscule. 2. mild, minor, light, weak. 3. insignificant, unimportant, inconsequential. 4. obscure, unknown, ordinary. 5. mediocre, terrible, lousy, awful.*

greed *n.* avarice, *grabbiness, acquisitiveness, covetousness, gluttony, rapaciousness, insatiability, graspingness, cupidity, want, hunger. ANT. *generosity, charity.*

greedy *a.* avaricious, covetous, *grabby, *piggish, *hoggish, acquisitive, gluttonous, rapacious, insatiable, grasping, hungry, selfish, stingy. ANT. *generous, giving, charitable.*

green *a.* **1.** COLOR aquamarine, emerald, grass, kelly, pea, lime, beryl, sap, apple, moss, sea green. **2.** YOUNG AND GROWING youthful, blooming, budding, developing, vigorous, robust, fresh, spreading, flourishing, burgeoning, verdant. **3.** INEXPERIENCED unseasoned, untried, *wet behind the ears, naive, new, untrained, ignorant, raw. ANT. *2. withered, wilted, dying. 3. experienced, veteran, seasoned, mature.*

greenhorn *n.* newcomer, tenderfoot, novice, amateur, *babe in the woods, neophyte, beginner, tyro, rookie, pup. ANT. *veteran, *old hand.*

greenhouse effect *n.* global warming, trapped heat.

greet *v.* welcome, hail, receive, salute, meet, wave to, usher in, address, recognize.

greeting *n.* salutation, acknowledgement, respects, hello, hail, nod, welcome, *how do, salute, bow, reception.

GREGARIOUS *a.* [gri GAIR ee us] outgoing and sociable, liking the company of others. *Gregarious partygoers.* SYN. sociable, outgoing, friendly, social, extroverted, companionable, affable, genial, *chummy, folksy. ANT. *introverted, reclusive, aloof.*

gridlock *n.* jam, entanglement, Gordian knot, obstruction, logjam, block, congestion, squeeze, clog, bottleneck, impasse, dead end, constipation.

grief *n.* sorrow, sadness, heartache, anguish, woe, misery, bereavement, desolation, mourning, melancholy, agony, despair, despondency. "An iron chain."—Stephen Vincent Benet. ANT. *joy, euphoria, happiness.*

grief-stricken *a.* sad, heartsick, anguished, heavyhearted, devastated, despairing, heartbroken, desolate, melancholy, miserable, despondent. ANT. *happy, joyful, cheerful.*

grievance *n.* complaint, gripe, wrong, injustice, injury, hardship, *axe to grind, *stink, objection, *beef, *bone to pick.

grieve *v.* **1.** MOURN lament, ache, sorrow, rue, bewail, bemoan, *eat one's heart out, weep, cry, shed tears, be heartsick. **2.** AFFLICT WITH GRIEF aggrieve, hurt, sadden, pain, break one's heart, wound, crush. ANT. *1. rejoice, revel, *party. 2. cheer, hearten.*

grievous *a.* serious, severe, harmful, appalling, atrocious, deplorable, egregious, flagrant, heinous, intolerable, outrageous, monstrous, grave, distressing, sad, sorrowful. ANT. *harmless, trivial, insignificant.*

grift *n.* swindle, *con game, confidence game, *rip-off, extortion, sting, scam, *racket, hustle, fraud.

grill *v.* **1.** BROIL sear, flame-broil, barbecue, fry, cook. **2.** QUESTION cross-examine, quiz, interrogate, pump, *give the third degree.

grim *a.* gloomy, harsh, severe, stern, sullen, somber, hard, morose, surly, miserable, dour, menacing, bleak, hopeless, forbidding, sinister, horrible, ghastly, gruesome, resolute, determined. ANT. *bright, cheerful, pleasant.*

grimace *n.* pained expression, wry face, face, twisted face, scowl, frown, glare, look of distaste.

grime *n.* dirt, soot, grit, smudge, filth, soil, mud, dust, *crud, *gook.

grimy *a.* dirty, filthy, *grungy, sooty, smudged, soiled, muddy, *cruddy, befouled, begrimed, dingy. ANT. *clean, spotless, bright, unsoiled.*

grin *v.* smile, beam, smirk, simper, *grin like a Cheshire cat. SEE SMILE, TEETH

grind *n.* drudgery, tedium, treadmill, routine, rut, chore.

grind *v.* **1.** PULVERIZE crush, mash, grit, grate, rasp, powder, mill, granulate, triturate, crush, disintegrate. **2.** SHARPEN hone, smooth, whet, polish, burnish. **3.** GNASH grit, grate, rasp, crunch.

grip *n.* **1.** HOLD clasp, clutch, clench, grasp. **2.** COMPREHENSION understanding, perception, mastery, grasp. **3.** CONTROL mastery, command.

grip *v.* grasp, hold, clasp, clutch, clench, squeeze.

gripe *n.* complaint, *beef, grumble, protest, grouch, grievance, pain, grouse.

gripe *v.* complain, *beef, grumble, protest, grouch, grouse, nag, whine, cry, bellyache.

grisly *a.* terrifying, horrible, ghastly, frightful, hideous, dreadful, gruesome, sickening, shocking, macabre, gory. ANT. *pleasant, heartwarming, lovely.*

grit *n.* **1.** DIRT sand, dust, soot, particles, powder. **2.** COURAGE perseverance, toughness, pluck, determination, tenacity, mettle, backbone, heart, fortitude, *guts, *moxie. ANT. *2. cowardice, weakness, mousiness.*

gritty *a.* **1.** DIRTY sandy, dusty, sooty, granular, powdery. **2.** COURAGEOUS persevering, tough, plucky, determined, tenacious, *gutsy, steadfast, resolute, game, mettlesome. ANT. *1. clean. 2. cowardly, weak, mousy.*

grizzled *a.* gray, salt and pepper, silvery.

groan *n.* moan, grumble, whine, complaint, mutter, gripe, howl, murmur, lament, whimper.

groan *v.* moan, grumble, whine, complain, mutter, gripe, howl, murmur, lament, whimper.

grocery store *n.* market, supermarket, food mart, Mom and Pop store, convenience store, franchise.

groggy *a.* dazed, *dopey, dizzy, *punch-drunk, *punchy, shaky, sluggish, stupefied, numbed, sleepy, *out of it, woozy, reeling, confused. ANT. *lucid, alert, steady.*

groin *n.* crotch.

groom *n.* bridegroom, husband, spouse, partner.

groom *v.* **1.** CLEAN UP tidy, neaten, prepare, dress, freshen up, brush, comb, curry, primp, *fix up, preen, tend to one's toilette. **2.** TRAIN prepare, educate.

groove *n.* **1.** CHANNEL score, rut, furrow, canal, cut, striation, scratch, flute, trench, indentation, line. **2.** RUT habit, routine, custom, *same old thing.

groovy *a.* *Sl.* *cool, excellent, great, *neat, *far-out, wonderful.

grope *v.* feel about, finger, seek blindly, paw, probe, fumble, fish for, poke around, grabble.

gross *a.* **1.** DISGUSTING, INDELICATE vulgar, foul, crude, indecent, obscene, *out of the gutter, *barnyard, unseemly, tasteless, offensive. **2.** TOTAL whole, aggregate, comprehensive, all, before taxes. **3.** FLAGRANT blatant, obvious, glaring, apparent, outrageous, egregious, shocking, heinous, plain, shameful. **4.** OBESE fat, overweight, big, corpulent, stout, burly, *blubbery. ANT. 1. *seemly, tasteful, decent*. 2. *net, after taxes, take-home*. 3. *subtle, minor*. 4. *skinny, anorexic*.

grotesque *a.* strange, ridiculous, fantastic, bizarre, freakish, odd, incongruous, distorted, weird, peculiar, fanciful, surrealistic, misshapen, ugly, *gross, deformed, monstrous. ANT. *normal, ordinary, realistic*.

grotto *n.* cavern. SEE CAVE

grouch *n.* complainer, faultfinder, grumbler, nag, whiner, crab, curmudgeon, *sourpuss, *bear, *grump.

grouch *v.* complain, find fault, grumble, nag, whine, crab, *grump, sulk, gripe, grouse, bellyache, growl.

grouchy *a.* *grumpy, grumbling, complaining, whining, crabby, sulky, surly, testy, cross, cantankerous, *like a bear. ANT. *good-humored, easygoing, agreeable*.

ground *n.* earth, soil, land, terra firma, turf, sand, terrain, real estate.

ground *v.* teach, educate, train, base, familiarize, prime, instruct, indoctrinate.

groundbreaking *a.* pioneering, spearheading, trendsetting, innovating, cutting edge, trailblazing. ANT. *old fashioned, obsolete*.

groundless *a.* baseless, unjustified, unwarranted, idle, unsupported, conjectural, gratuitous, unfounded. ANT. *substantiated, corroborated, verified*.

grounds *n.* 1. AREA land, estate, holding, lot, acreage, terrain, property, tract, surroundings. 2. BASIS base, foundation, rationale, premise, reason, argument, cause, motive.

groundswell *n.* wave, tsunami, force to be reckoned with, surge, upsurge, uprising, rush, sweep, landslide, avalanche.

groundwork *n.* preparation, foundation, footing, underpinning, infrastructure, fundamentals, preliminaries, base, planning.

group *n.* 1. ASSEMBLAGE body, mass, collection, party, bunch, band, crowd, gang, pack, crew, congregation, herd, flock, throng, aggregation. 2. CLASS classification, variety, category, division, branch, set, circle.

group *v.* classify, categorize, divide, sort, assign, grade, systematize, arrange, bunch.

grouse *v.* grumble, complain. SEE GROUCH

grove *n.* stand, orchard, wood, copse, coppice, thicket, boscage.

grovel *v.* *bow and scrape, kowtow, cringe, beg, *kiss up, *brownnose, toady, *fall all over, demean oneself, fawn, *bootlick, *kiss feet,

cower, *suck up to, wheedle, cower, *apple-polish, kneel before, worm. ANT. *defy, challenge, dominate*.

grow *v.* 1. DEVELOP spread, increase, enlarge, expand, lengthen, double, flourish, thrive, mature, burgeon, progress, sprout, spring up, germinate, blossom, mushroom. 2. PRODUCE cultivate, raise, generate, nurture, propagate. ANT. 1. *die, wither, shrink*.

growl *v.* snarl, grumble, rumble, gnarl, howl, *give a throaty warning, roar, bark, make a guttural noise.

grown-up *a.* mature, adult, full-grown, of age. ANT. *immature, childish*.

growth *n.* 1. DEVELOPMENT spread, increase, expansion, lengthening, branching out, maturing, burgeoning, progress, germination, blossoming, blooming, evolution. 2. TUMOR mass, lump, cancer.

grub *v.* dig, root, poke, probe, forage, unearth, search, hunt, ferret about, dig, delve, uproot.

grubby *a.* messy, dirty, grimy, soiled, unclean, filthy, *grungy, foul, begrimed, slovenly, *scuzzy, squalid. ANT. *clean, tidy, fresh*.

grudge *n.* resentment, grievance, malice, spite, hard feelings, bitterness, *bone to pick, ill will, *axe to grind, rancor. ANT. *good will, benevolence*.

grudge *v.* begrudge, resent, mind, envy, hold against.

grueling *a.* exhausting, trying, arduous, backbreaking, hard, taxing, draining, strenuous, laborious, fatiguing, demanding, punishing. ANT. *easy, effortless, *no sweat*.

gruesome *a.* grisly, horrifying, repulsive, disgusting, hideous, frightful, ghastly, revolting, repellant, appalling, monstrous, horrific, repugnant. ANT. *lovely, charming, delightful*.

gruff *a.* 1. RUDE brusque, surly, blunt, grouchy, grumpy, abrupt, rough, curt, sour, bearish, nasty, short. 2. HOARSE throaty, harsh, croaking, husky, rough, gutteral. ANT. 1. *genial, polite, sweet*. 2. *resonant, smooth*.

grumble *v.* complain, groan, gripe, bellyache, fuss, grouch, growl, squawk, snarl.

grump *n.* complainer, whiner, *one who isn't happy unless he is miserable, curmudgeon, griper, grouch, *crab, sulker, *sourpuss.

grumpy *v.* grouchy, surly, crabby, bearish, cross, cranky, peevish, cantankerous, testy, moody, irritable, touchy. ANT. *cheerful, happy, good-humored*.

grungy *a.* grimy, dirty, dingy, messy, *scuzzy, foul. ANT. *clean*.

guarantee *n.* warranty, pledge, assurance, bond, promise, contract, word of honor, covenant, surety, security, oath.

guarantee *v.* warrant, promise, pledge, assure, *give one's word of honor, back, certify, *stand behind, vouch for, ensure, insure, protect, contract, underwrite.

guarantor *n.* warrantor, sponsor, backer, insurer, bondsman, underwriter.

guard *n.* security officer, protector, guardian, watchman, sentinel, sentry, lookout, escort, custodian, warder, cordon.

guard *v.* watch, protect, defend, attend, cover, shield, lookout, secure, safeguard, place under surveillance, screen, escort, *ride shotgun, patrol.

guarded *a.* wary, cautious, circumspect, careful, mindful, leery, watchful, apprehensive, suspicious, reserved, discreet. ANT. *careless, reckless, rash.*

guerrilla *n.* bushfighter, resistance, soldier, freedom fighter, warrior, mercenary, soldier of fortune, volunteer soldier, mujahadeen.

guess *n.* estimate, *guesstimate, conjecture, hypothesis, calculation, presumption, speculation, assumption, supposition, *shot in the dark, *ballpark figure, reckoning, hunch.

guess *v.* estimate, *guesstimate, calculate, hypothesize, conjecture, presume, speculate, assume, suppose, *take a shot in the dark, *give a ballpark figure, reckon, figure, deduce, infer, theorize, gather, imagine.

guest *n.* visitor, company, caller, roomer, renter, boarder, lodger, client, customer. "[Those who] are often welcomest when they are gone."—Shakespeare. "A nuisance after three days."—Plautus.

guffaw *n.* roar, howl, burst of laughter. SEE LAUGH

guidance *n.* counseling, counsel, advice, direction, instruction, word to the wise, suggestion, recommendation, leadership, navigation.

guide *n.* leader, director, captain, pilot, navigator, escort, chaperon, mentor, guru, teacher, example, exemplar, model, beacon, landmark, lodestar.

guidebook *n.* manual, guide, field guide, handbook, reference book, how-to book, itinerary, tome, volume, vade mecum, bible.

guild *n.* society, association, union, fraternity, sorority, federation, league, club, group, company, alliance, coalition, brotherhood.

guideline *n.* direction, guide, instruction, indication, rule, code, mark, marker, clue, key, signal.

GUILE *n.* [GILE] slyness, craftiness, artfulness. *He managed a passing grade through pure guile; he used crib notes.* SYN. slyness, craftiness, artfulness, cunning, trickery, artifice, deceit, duplicity, fraud, dishonesty, treachery. ANT. *honesty, naivete, candor.*

guileless *a.* open, honest, frank, candid, naive, innocent, artless, ingenuous, sincere, truthful, unsophisticated. ANT. *sly, crafty, artful.*

guilt *n.* 1. BLAME culpability, culpa, reprehensibility, criminality, guiltiness, crime, sin, wrongdoing, liability, 2. REMORSE regret, shame, conscience, contrition, disgrace, self-reproach, penitence, compunction. "The avenging fiend that follows us behind with whips and stings."—Nicholas Rowe. ANT. *1. innocence, *clean hands, clear conscience.*

guilty *a.* 1. TO BLAME culpable, responsible, blameworthy, at fault, wrong, reprehensible, *caught red-handed, in flagrante delicto, sinful, liable. 2. REMORSEFUL regretful, ashamed, conscience-stricken, contrite, disgraced, compunctious, sorry, sheepish, hangdog. ANT. *1. innocent, faultless, blameless. 2. proud, remorseless.*

guinea pig *n.* test subject, victim, testee, examinee, cavy, rodent, lab animal, *pharmaceutical pincushion.

guise *n.* appearance, semblance, aspect, cover, facade, disguise, form, mode, pretense, garb, dress, costume.

guitar *n.* SEE MUSICAL INSTRUMENT

gulch *n.* channel, ravine, trench, gulley, wash, ditch, arroyo, cut.

gulf *n.* 1. INLET bay, estuary, harbor, cove, sound. 2. CHASM abyss, gap, rift, cleft, void, canyon, breach, hollow.

GULLIBLE *a.* [GULL uh bul] easily fooled, credulous. *Gullible people believe anything told them by the media.* SYN. credulous, naive, easily fooled, trusting, innocent, unsophisticated, unsuspicious, *born yesterday, green, *wet behind the ears. ANT. *wary, skeptical, wise, suspicious.*

gully *n.* ditch, ravine, culvert, channel, trench, gutter, watercourse, gorge, valley, gulch.

gulp *v.* swallow, bolt, wolf, gobble, choke down, guzzle, swill, *chugalug, swig, quaff.

gummy *a.* sticky, gooey, viscid, tacky.

gumption *n.* courage, boldness, initiative, *starch, resourcefulness, enterprise, *get up and go, hustle, drive.

gun *n.* firearm, revolver, pistol, *six-shooter,

*shooting iron, rifle, carbine, shotgun, *peashooter, *Saturday night special, *.38 special, *.45, *equalizer, *rod, *piece, *enforcer, *heater, *roscoe. "[That which] makes men equal, a citizen's musket fires as well as a nobleman's."—Heinriche Heine.

WORD FIND

ammunition receptacle: clip, magazine, cylinder
antique: blunderbuss, breechloader, Colt six-shooter, flintlock, Gatling gun, musket, muzzle loader
attack rifle: assault rifle
back explosion: backfire
barrel end: muzzle
barrel portion receiving bullet: chamber
bead: sight
bore: caliber, gauge
brush: swab
butt: stock
case: holster
cock: hammer
colored finish on metal parts: blueing
gunfire: fusillade, enfilade, volley, salvo
handle: grip
knife mounting: bayonet
locking mechanism: safety
manufacturer: Colt, Magnum, Luger, Winchester, Smith and Wesson, Beretta, Remington, Uzi
plug placed in muzzle for safety: tampion
quieting attachment: silencer, suppressor
rear portion: breech
recoil after firing: kick
revolver's ability to shoot without first cocking hammer: double-action
revolving cartridge holder: cylinder
trigger needing only slight pull: hair trigger
single-shot pistol: derringer
sliding rod that pushes cartridge into firing chamber: bolt
SEE AMMUNITION, ARMY, BULLET, CANNON, WAR, WEAPON

gunfire n. gunshot, discharge, shot, detonation, enfilade, gunplay, fusillade, backfire, volley, salvo.

gung ho a. Sl. enthusiastic, eager, *fired up, ardent, fanatical. ANT. blasé, nonchalant, jaded.

gunman n. killer, triggerman, assassin. SEE MURDERER

gurgle v. burble, babble, murmur, tinkle, ripple, bubble.

guru n. advisor, mentor, teacher, guide, leader, master, maharishi, swami, spiritual leader.

gush n. outpouring, flow, spurt, cascade, flood, rush, flush, surge, stream, spill, jet, discharge.

gush v. 1. POUR OUT flow, spurt, cascade, flood, rush, flush, surge, stream, spill, jet, spew. 2. EXAGGERATE *lay it on thick, *get carried away, be effusive, blather, bubble over, overstate, *carry on. ANT. 2. understate, restrain oneself.

gust n. wind, rush, blow, burst, breeze, surge, squall, gale, blast, puff, draft. SEE WIND

gusto n. enjoyment, appreciation, zest, relish, exhilaration, enthusiasm, delight, pleasure, passion, ardor. ANT. apathy, indifference.

gut n. stomach, belly, abdomen, *tummy, innards, intestines, bowels, *spare tire, *beer gut, *middle-aged spread, paunch.

gut v. eviscerate, clean out, disembowel, dress, decimate.

gut a. instinctual, intuitive, inner, internal, visceral, deep, heartfelt, emotional. ANT. fact-based, literal, unemotional.

gutless a. cowardly, timid, fearful, mousy, *wimpy, fainthearted, spineless, *chicken, *yellow, *lily-livered, weak. ANT. brave, courageous, *gutsy, *ballsy.

guts n. Sl. courage, bravery, backbone, pluck, nerve, *balls, heart, spunk, daring, boldness, *spine, *grit, *moxie, fortitude. ANT. cowardice, timidity, faintheartedness.

gutsy a. Sl. courageous, brave, plucky, *nervy, *ballsy, spunky, daring, bold, *gritty, intrepid, game. ANT. cowardly, fainthearted, spineless.

gutter n. channel, trough, trench, ditch, conduit, drain, culvert, sewer, canal, watercourse, runnel, gully.

guttural a. throaty, harsh, rasping, hoarse, gruff, *whiskey-voiced, croaking, deep, glottal, gravelly, thick. ANT. high-pitched, shrill, soprano.

guy n. man, fellow, gentleman, chap, *dude, person, teen, boy, lad, *bro, *buddy.

guzzle v. swill, swig, *chug-a-lug, *down, quaff, tipple, *knock back, gulp, drain, *polish off, *choke down.

gym n. gymnasium, workout facility, court, indoor sport facility, fitness center, weight room, basketball court, arena, hall, auditorium. SEE FITNESS

gymnastics n. athletics, acrobatics, vaulting, calisthenics, exercises, somersaults, handstands, headstands, handsprings, floor exercises, pommel horse, the vault, parallel bars, uneven bars, balance beam, rings, tumbling, aerobics.

gyp *v.* *rip-off, cheat, swindle, defraud, bilk, trick, bamboozle, hoodwink, rook, *gull.

gypsy *n.* wanderer, nomad, roamer, vagrant, vagabond, migrant, drifter, rover, gadabout, Bohemian.

WORD FIND

known for: fortunetelling

language of: Romany

gyrate *v.* revolve, spin, twirl, whirl, rotate, circle, wheel, gyre, pirouette, spiral.

H

habit *n.* routine, custom, practice, tendency, convention, way, rut, pattern, mode, proclivity, manner, mannerism, inclination. "A cable. We weave a thread of it everyday, and at last we cannot break it."—Horace Mann.

habitat *n.* natural environment, home, terrain, haunt, natural element, *stomping grounds, biosphere, range, domain, realm, natural surroundings, dwelling.

habitation *n.* home, dwelling, lodging, residence, domicile, abode, quarters, house, chambers, roost, place, *pad, shelter. SEE HOUSE

habitual *a.* routine, usual, customary, established, fixed, set, hardened, inveterate, regular, everyday, accustomed, chronic, repetitious, persistent, ingrained, rooted. ANT. *irregular, unusual, infrequent.*

habituated *a.* inurred, used to, accustomed, familiar, acclimated, seasoned, adapted, hardened, conditioned. ANT. *unfamiliar, new.*

hacienda *n.* estate, plantation, house, mansion, ranch.

hack *v.* chop, slice, axe, cleave, slash, cut, sever, hew, gash, lop off, shear, fell.

hacker *n.* computer programmer, computer nerd, *cracker, *cyber punk, *internaut, *computer crackerjack, *computer wiz, computer prodigy, encryption expert, *computer brain. SEE COMPUTER, INTERNET

HACKNEYED *a.* [HAK need] commonplace; dull from overuse, trite. *Clichés are hackneyed expressions.* SYN. commonplace, trite, banal, pedestrian, unimaginative, unoriginal, stock, overworked, tired, shopworn, inane, threadbare, clichéd, stale. ANT. *fresh, original, imaginative.*

hag *n.* witch, crone, harridan, ogress, virago, demon, enchantress, beldam, battle-ax, shrew.

HAGGARD *a.* [HAG urd] having a wild-eyed, drawn or gaunt appearance from exhaustion, sickness, etc. SYN. wild-eyed, wild, drawn, gaunt, wasted, drained, unruly, exhausted, careworn, run-down, hollow-cheeked, emaciated, ghastly, mad, insane. ANT. *fresh, rested, vigorous.*

haggle *v.* argue, bargain, wrangle, dicker, higgle, deal, *drive a hard bargain, chaffer, barter, *hash out a deal, quibble.

hail *v.* greet, wave to, call to, hello, accost, salute, welcome, *tip one's hat to, nod to, flag down, signal.

hair *n.* locks, mane, tress, down, *mop, fur, strand, tuft, curls, fuzz, fringe, bristle, whiskers. "The only thing that will really prevent baldness."—Drew Berkowitz.

WORD FIND

African-American, puffy, 1960s, 1970s: Afro

arrange: coif, set, style, perm

auburn dye: henna

back comb: tease

bald crown surrounded by ring of fringe: tonsure

bald: glabrous

baldness, common: male pattern baldness

band: filet, snood

beehive-like style of 1950s, 1960s: beehive

bowl-like: Beatle cut, *Moe

braided rows close to head: cornrows

braid: plait, cue, cueue, pigtail, tress, fishbone braid, French braid

colors: ash, ash blond, auburn, black, bleach blond, blond, blue-gray, brown, brunet, carrot, chestnut, cinnamon, coal black, cocoa, copper, dusky, fair-haired, fiery, flaxen, frosted, ginger, golden, gray, grizzled, hoary, honey, jet-black, nutbrown, nutmeg, peroxide blond, platinum blond, polished wood, premature gray, raven, russet, rust, sable, salt and pepper, silver, snowy, strawberry blond, tawny, technicolor (dyed, punk), titian, towheaded, violent red, washed out, white

curl: ringlet, corkscrew

curled-ends style with bangs: flip

curl pressed against face with saliva: spit curl

curly like a poodle: poodle cut

cut short: crop

Dorothy Hamill style of 1970s: wedge

ducktail-like style of 1950s: ducktail

fake: toupee, *rug, wig, implant

forehead fringe: bangs

graying, premature: poliosis

hairy, abnormally: hirsute, hirsutism

high sweep of hair combed back from forehead: pompadour

Jamaican braids: dreadlocks, Rastafarian dreadlocks, dreads

knot: chignon, bob, bun

mass, tangled or bushy: shock

matted, tangled hairs: elflocks

neck hairs: hackles

point of hair tapering to forehead: widow's peak

puffed-out mass, style: bouffant

punk: mohawk, porcupine, spiked, shaved, dyed

remove: epilate, depilate, bob

remover: depilatory, electrolysis

roll: bun, chignon

shaved trails in a slanted or sculpted buzz cut: *fade, *gumby

short haircut for men: buzz, flattop, crew cut, butch, *fade

short haircut for women: bob

short on sides, nearly shoulder-length in back: mullet

standing cone ending in ponytail: empire cone

stick-up tuft: cowlick

straight-cut style with bangs: page boy

textures: billowing, bouncy, bristly, bushy, coarse, cornsilk, crimped, crinkly, dollish, downy, eiderdown, fine (baby fine), fleecy, flowing, flyaway, frazzled, frizzy, fuzzy, greasy, kinky, knotted, lacquered, listless, lustrous, luxurious, matted, nappy, oily, rat's nest, rigid, ropey, satiny, shaggy, shocked, silky, snarled, stringy (like twine), thatched, wispy, withered, wizened, woolly.

waves style: marcel

hairdresser n. hair stylist, barber, coiffeur, beautician.

hairless a. SEE BALD, HAIR

hairsplitting n. nitpicking, pettiness, quibbling, caviling, fault-finding.

hair-raising a. bloodcurdling, breathtaking, frightening, terrifying, hackle-raising, spine-tingling, electrifying, shocking, chilling, horrifying. ANT. *reassuring, encouraging, emboldening.*

hairy a. hirsute, shaggy. SEE HAIR

halcyon a. calm, peaceful, tranquil, serene, untroubled. ANT. *agitated, turbulent.*

hale a. vigorous, sound, healthy, robust, fit, hearty, spry, hardy, well, *in the pink, *full of vim and vigor, *in fine fettle. ANT. *sickly, weak, frail, failing.*

half-baked a. stupid, sophomoric, harebrained, premature, crude, impractical, *birdbrained, idiotic, imbecilic, uninspired, moronic, dumb. ANT. *practical, brilliant, well-formulated.*

halfhearted a. unenthusiastic, lukewarm, blasé, indifferent, apathetic, dispassionate, cool, perfunctory, tepid, spiritless. ANT. *enthusiastic, eager, ardent, wholehearted.*

half-wit n. dimwit, nitwit, *pea brain. SEE MORON

halitosis n. bad breath, *dragon breath, foul breath, *garbage breath, offensive breath.

hall n. hallway, corridor, passageway, entrance, foyer, vestibule, gallery.

HALLMARK n. [HALL mark] an identifying characteristic or telltale sign. *The hallmark of a sluggish economy is a drop in interest rates.* SYN. characteristic, telltale sign, identifying mark, sign, symbol, indicator, badge, earmark, index.

hallowed a. holy, sacred, venerated, revered, sanctified, worshipped, honored, consecrated, blessed, beatified, divine.

hallucination n. vision, illusion, hypnogogic image, delusion, fantasy, figment of the imagination, apparition, delirium, mirage, phantasmagoria.

WORD FIND

alcoholic's: delirium tremens

amputee's false perception of limb: phantom limb pain

crossed senses: synesthesia

induces: hallucinogen

odor: phantosmia

halo n. nimbus, aureole, glory, ring, circle, radiance. SEE ANGEL

halt n. stop, end, close, termination, pause, freeze, stay, recess, standstill, break, discontinuance.

halt v. stop, end, close, terminate, pause, freeze, stay, recess, stand still, take a break, discontinue, cease and desist, suspend.

halting a. hesitant, *jerky, unsteady, disconnected, stuttering, stammering, faltering, stumbling, tentative, clumsy. ANT. *assured, decisive, unfaltering.*

halve v. divide, split, cut in two, bisect.

hamlet n. small town, crossroads. SEE VILLAGE

hammer n. beetle, clawhammer, sledge, maul, mallet, gavel, ball-peen hammer.

hammer v. pound, beat, batter, bang, hit, pummel, drive, tap, strike, nail, *clobber, fashion, form, forge.

hamper v. impede, hinder, handicap, hamstring, slow, inhibit, encumber, obstruct, frustrate, retard, restrict, hobble, curb. ANT. *help, assist, facilitate.*

hamstring v. cripple, handicap, hobble. SEE DISABLE

hamstrung a. crippled, handicapped. SEE DISABLED

hand n. **1.** FIST palm, *mitt, *paw, *duke. **2.** HELPER worker, employee, laborer, aide, assistant, help. **3.** HELP assistance, aid, lift, support, boost.

handbook n. manual, guide, how-to book, reference book, field guide, bible.

handicap n. disability, impediment, encumbrance, disadvantage, impairment, limitation, millstone, difficulty, burden, restriction, stumbling block.

handicap v. disable, impede, hamstring, cripple, encumber, impair, limit, burden, restrict, inhibit, weigh down, hamper.

handkerchief n. kerchief, bandanna, neckerchief, hanky, *snot rag.

handle n. grip, haft, hilt, butt, knob, holder, crank, stock, pull.

handle v. 1. TOUCH feel, examine, finger, poke, hold, fondle, stroke, caress, rub, palpate. 2. MANAGE take care of, direct, supervise, oversee, govern, control, administer, deal with, steer.

hand-me-down a. passed down, second-hand, used, previously-owned, old. ANT. new, latest.

hand out vt. distribute, dispense, disburse, deal out, parcel, mete, give out, deliver.

handsome a. 1. ATTRACTIVE good-looking, *hunky, comely, fine, fair, manly, dignified, gorgeous, majestic, statuesque, *foxy, luscious, macho, beautiful. 2. GENEROUS liberal, considerable, abundant, princely, magnanimous, ample. ANT. 1. ugly, repulsive, *gross. 2. meager, small, niggardly.

handwriting n. script, penmanship, calligraphy, chirography, *hen scratching, manuscript, scribbling, hand.

WORD FIND

poor: cacography
slip of the pen: lapsus calami
study of: graphology
style: cursive, block lettering
time and word-saving: shorthand

handy a. 1. CONVENIENT accessible, close at hand, nearby, at one's fingertips, within reach. 2. DEXTEROUS deft, clever, adroit, skilled, adept, proficient, masterful, *crackerjack. ANT. 1. inconvenient, inaccessible. 2. unskilled, inept, clumsy.

hang v. 1. SUSPEND dangle, drape, depend, stick, pin, affix, sling, fall, swing, be pendent. 2. EXECUTE lynch, *string up, *send to the gallows, *invite to a necktie party, gibbet, noose.

hangdog a. shamefaced, cringing, crestfallen, cowering, browbeaten, abject, miserable, wretched, conscience-stricken. ANT. saintly, triumphant, innocent.

hangout n. haunt, stomping ground, home away from home, club, club house, retreat, meeting place.

hang-up n. Sl. problem, inhibition, difficulty, quirk, disturbance, preoccupation, phobia, fear.

hankering n. desire, craving, yearning, want, thirst, itch, yen, ache, longing, *fire in one's belly, drive.

hanky-panky n. Sl. 1. TRICKERY *funny business. 2. AFFFAIR *fooling around, romance, fling, liaison, dalliance, *thing, amour. SEE MISCHIEF

haphazard a. unmethodical, unorganized, slapdash, uncoordinated, aimless, casual, *willy-nilly, indiscriminate, *hit or miss, careless, random, arbitrary. ANT. planned, organized, designed.

hapless a. unfortunate, cursed, unlucky, star-crossed, jinxed, hopeless, luckless, wretched, woeful. ANT. fortunate, lucky.

happen v. occur, take place, befall, transpire, materialize, come about, come to pass, develop, ensue, spring, pass, result, arise.

happening n. event, occurrence, incident, experience, occasion, episode, incidence, affair, circumstance.

happiness n. joy, gladness, contentment, bliss, delight, jubilation, pleasure, cheer, high spirits, peace of mind, elation, rapture, euphoria, *seventh heaven, exuberance, felicity, ecstasy. "It is all within yourself, in your way of thinking."—Marcus Aurelius. "[Something that] makes up in height for what it lacks in length."—Robert Frost. "Tranquility and occupation."—Thomas Jefferson. "Freedom from suffering."—Arthur Schopenhauer. "The mastery of passions."—Alfred Lord Tennyson. "Good friends, good books and a sleepy conscience."—Mark Twain. ANT. misery, depression, melancholia.

happy a. 1. GLAD joyful, content, blissful, delighted, jubilant, pleased, cheerful, in high spirits, at peace, elated, euphoric, in *seventh heaven, exuberant, ecstatic, gleeful, *tickled pink, *walking on air, chipper, overjoyed, *high. 2. FORTUNATE lucky, felicitous, auspicious, opportune, favorable, propitious, timely. ANT. 1. depressed, miserable, downhearted, suicidal, sad, glum. 2. inauspicious, inopportune, unlucky.

happy-go-lucky a. carefree, untroubled, *devil-may-care, lighthearted, casual, easy, easygoing, nonchalant, insouciant, *living the life of Riley, unconcerned. ANT. *stressed, worried, anxious, careful, concerned.*

hara kiri *n.* ritual suicide, disembowelment.

harangue *n.* tirade, diatribe, exhortation, lecture, *chewing-out, speech, sermon.

harangue *v.* exhort, *chew out, lecture, spout off, rant, sermonize, preach, declaim, rant and rave, go on about, *get on one's soapbox.

harass *v.* disturb, trouble, torment, pester, plague, bother, *bug, badger, distress, worry, *pull one's chain, *rattle one's cage, irritate, attack, intimidate, persecute, hound, harry, vex, ride, beset.

HARBINGER *n.* [HAR binj ur] a sign of things to come, a forerunner, herald. *April rain is a harbinger of May flowers.* SYN. sign of things to come, forerunner, herald, precursor, omen, usher, messenger, premonition, portent, signal.

harbor *n.* 1. ANCHORAGE port, dock, pier, mooring, wharves, landing, bay, inlet, cove. 2. HAVEN refuge, retreat, shelter, sanctuary, port, port in a storm.

harbor *v.* 1. SHELTER house, lodge, quarter, berth, hide, protect, secrete, conceal, cover, shield, guard. 2. TO ENTERTAIN IN THE MIND hold, maintain, believe, cling to, foster, imagine, indulge, nurse.

hard *a.* 1. FIRM rigid, stiff, rock-solid, stony, inflexible, concrete, set, compacted, like iron, like steel, unyielding, impregnable. 2. DIFFICULT arduous, demanding, tough, laborious, burdensome, exhausting, strenuous, backbreaking, rigorous, painstaking, Herculean, *murder, draining. 3. COMPLICATED complex, knotty, involved, incomprehensible, perplexing, bewildering, thorny. 4. STRONG powerful, severe, heavy. 5. UNFEELING callous, unfriendly, hostile, cold, merciless, harsh, cruel, hard-boiled, hard-hearted, unsympathetic, pitiless, ruthless, unrelenting. 6. HARSH rough, severe, trying, intolerable, unbearable, torturous, insufferable, difficult, bad. ANT. *1. soft, pliable, flexible. 2, 3. easy, simple, effortless. 4. weak, light. 5. warm, sympathetic, compassionate. 6. soft, easy, mild.*

hard-and-fast *a.* set, invariable, strict, binding, unalterable, exacting, unbending, inflexible, incontrovertible. ANT. *flexible, variable, changeable.*

hard-boiled *a.* SEE HARD, TOUGH

hard-core *a.* 1. ABSOLUTE express, unqualified. 2. FIRM unyielding, resistant, rigid, staunch, steadfast, stubborn, inveterate, die-hard, unwavering. ANT. *2. pliant, unresistant, waffling.*

harden *v.* 1. STIFFEN solidify, thicken, set, toughen, indurate, compact, cement, temper, steel, freeze, petrify. 2. ACCUSTOM strengthen, steel, inure, season, case harden, toughen, acclimatize, gird, callous. ANT. *1. soften, weaken, thin.*

hard-hearted *a.* cold, callous, cruel, merciless, pitiless, unsympathetic, unfeeling, *coldhearted, inhuman, uncaring, *icewater in one's veins. ANT. *compassionate, sympathetic, warmhearted.*

hard-line *a.* uncompromising, unyielding, adamant, firm, intractable, hardcore, unbending. ANT. *submitting, yielding.*

hardly *adv.* scarcely, barely, just, rarely, only.

hard-nosed *a.* hardheaded, stubborn, bullheaded, mulish, pigheaded, obstinate, tough, uncompromising, indomitable. ANT. *flexible, open-minded.*

hardship *n.* adversity, misfortune, suffering, privation, burden, affliction, *hard knock, trial, tribulation, bad luck, grief, infelicity, trouble, hard times, disaster, catastrophe, rigor, travail. ANT. *good fortune, blessing, boon.*

hardware *n.* 1. TOOLS metalware, equipment, gear, utensils, cutlery, implements, machinery, applicances. 2. COMPUTER COMPONENTS microprocessor, peripherals, keyboard, modem, monitor. SEE COMPUTER

hardy *a.* robust, vigorous, strong, tough, rugged, powerful, strapping, fit, healthy, *tough as nails, hearty, hale, sound, in good shape. ANT. *weak, sickly, frail.*

harebrained *a.* stupid, reckless, rash, foolish, idiotic, imbecilic, silly, half-witted, brainless, scatterbrained. ANT. *smart, *brainy, sensible.*

harem *n.* seraglio.

WORD FIND

male attendant: eunuch

slave woman: odalisque

harlot *n.* whore, prostitute, strumpet, hussy, slut, tramp, loose woman, wench, trollop, streetwalker, *hooker, lady of the evening.

harm *n.* injury, hurt, damage, destruction, adversity, waste, wrong, detriment, abuse, loss, ruin. ANT. *help, good, benefit.*

harm *v.* hurt, injure, damage, wound, cripple, maim, molest, impair, destroy, wrong, abuse, ruin, misuse, wreck, spoil. ANT. *help, benefit, do good.*

harmful *a.* injurious, hurtful, damaging, destructive, detrimental, wounding, crippling, abusive, adverse, noxious, deleterious, inimical, pernicious, ruinous, disastrous. ANT. *beneficial, helpful, harmless.*

harmless *a.* benign, innocuous, safe, innocent, unoffensive, powerless, impotent, *a pussycat, gentle, *defanged. ANT. *harmful, deleterious, noxious, injurious.*

harmonica *n.* mouth organ, SEE MUSICAL INSTRUMENT

harmonious *a.* compatible, agreeable, in rapport, peaceable, amicable, friendly, in accord, congenial, in tune, simpatico, likeminded, unified, blending. ANT. *discordant, clashing, incompatible.*

harmonize *v.* correspond, agree, unify, get in tune, attune, blend, coincide, *be of one mind, jibe with, accommodate, accord, integrate. ANT. *disagree, clash.*

harmony *n.* agreement, correspondence, unification, blending, accord, integration, concurrence, rapport, consonance, rapprochement, coordination, compatibility. ANT. *discord, dissonance, disagreement.* SEE MUSIC

harp *n.* lyre. SEE MUSICAL INSTRUMENT

harpsichord *n.* clavichord. SEE MUSICAL INSTRUMENT

harried *a.* pressured, stressed, troubled, *at wit's end, beset, agitated, put-upon, overtaxed, plagued, harassed. ANT. *relaxed, calm, unwound.*

HARROWING *a.* [HAIR o wing] frightening, distressing. *The child found the roller coaster ride a harrowing experience.* SYN. frightening, distressing, upsetting, traumatic, disturbing, terrifying, bloodcurdling, hair-raising, tormenting. ANT. *soothing, pacifying, tranquilizing, relaxing.*

harry *v.* torment, harass, worry, agitate, beset, trouble, plague, pester, pressure, annoy, bother, *stress out, nag, bug, weary.

harsh *a.* **1.** ROUGH coarse, jagged, craggy, rugged, sharp, unpleasant, grinding, jarring, discordant, grating, clashing. **2.** SEVERE cruel, unfeeling, hard, tough, merciless, stern, brutal, hard-boiled, unbending, cold-blooded. ANT. **1.** *smooth, pleasant, melodious, musical.* **2.** *soft, mild, easy, gentle.*

harvest *n.* gathering, reaping, return, yield, crop, fruit, profit, product.

harvest *v.* reap, gather, pick, collect, amass, glean.

hash *n.* mixture, hodgepodge, mess, jumble, potpourri, mishmash, medley, miscellany, muddle.

hashish *n.* narcotic, cannabis, cannabis resin, hash. SEE DRUG, NARCOTIC, MARIJUANA

hassle *n.* *Sl.* problem, difficulty, bother, *pain, dispute, squabble, argument, disagreement, tussle.

hassle *v.* bother, harass, *give a hard time, annoy, plague, pester, *bug, hound, harry.

haste *n.* speed, swiftness, quickness, fleetness, dispatch, celerity, hurry, hustle, rapidity, rush, velocity, promptness. ANT. *slowness, sluggishness, delay.*

hasten *v.* hurry, rush, speed, race, *step on it, *get a move on, go quickly, scurry, *ride like the wind, hustle, fly, accelerate, expedite, sprint, *get the lead out, *beat feet. ANT. *slow, delay, *drag one's feet, procrastinate.*

hasty *a.* quick, fast, swift, rushed, fleet, rapid, expeditious, abrupt, prompt, *on the double, *pronto, brisk, instantaneous, *quick as a wink, *in a heartbeat, brief, rash, impetuous, reckless. ANT. *slow, leisurely, careful.*

hat *n.* cap, chapeau, headgear, headdress, *lid.

WORD FIND

Australian cowboy hat with brim turned up on one side: bush hat

bejeweled, decorated skullcap for evening wear, weddings: Juliet

beret with pompom in the middle: tam, tam-o-shanter

bowler: derby

box: bandbox

brimless, round, small hat of 1920s: pillbox

collapsible opera hat: gibus

cowboy: Stetson, ten-gallon hat

Crockett's, Davy: coonskin cap

derby: bowler

French Foreign Legion cap with havelock: kepi, Legionnaire's

graduate's square with tassel: mortarboard

high-domed hat worn by English police: bobby

high-domed hat worn by polo players: chukka

Jewish embroidered skullcap: yarmulka

knitted winter hat: watch cap

knitted winter hat with a long tail sometimes fitted with pompom: stocking cap

marching band's tall hat with feather cockade: shako

Mexican broad hat made of straw or felt: sombrero

pancakelike cap: beret, tam

pith helmet: topee

scarf wound around head: turban

Scottish Highland Military's creased cloth cap with badge and black ribbons: glengarry

seventeenth-century tall black hat, silver buckle: Puritan

Sherlock Holmes's tweed hat: deerstalker

snap-brim hat with low, flat crown: porkpie

snap-brim hat with puffed crown: newsboy

soft, domelike hat pulled down over forehead, for women: cloche

soft, felt hat creased down middle of crown: fedora, homburg

soft hat that can be crushed, carried in pocket: crusher

stovepipelike hat with tall crown, silky finish: top hat

straw hat, man's: Panama

straw hat with oval crown: boater, picture hat

straw, parasol-like hat worn by Chinese: coolie

straw, yellow and broad: leghorn

tall, fur hat worn by British army: busby

three-cornered: tricorne

Turkish hat shaped like truncated cone, decorated with tassel: fez

World War II folding dress cap, olive or khaki-colored: garrison cap

SEE CAP

hatch v. create, concoct, bring forth, devise, design, produce, *cook up, conceive, invent, originate, formulate, *dream up.

hate n. loathing, dislike, abhorrence, detestation, odium, aversion, scorn, disgust, contempt, venom, repugnance, enmity, hostility, animosity, malice. ANT. love, liking, affection.

hate v. loathe, dislike, abhor, detest, scorn, regard with disgust, regard with contempt, feel hostile toward, despise, be sickened by, abominate, shrink from, disdain, have an aversion to. ANT. love, like, admire.

hateful a. loathsome, detestable, despicable, abhorrent, abominable, odious, nasty, mean, damnable, repugnant, foul, heinous, malicious. ANT. loving, nice, wonderful.

hatred n. loathing, dislike, abhorrence, detestation, odium, aversion, scorn, disgust, contempt, venom, repugnance, enmity, hostility, animosity, malice. "Self-punishment."—Hosea Ballou. "Burning down your own house to get rid of a rat."—Harry Emerson Fosdick. "The coward's revenge."—George Bernard Shaw. ANT. love, affection, friendliness.

HAUGHTY a. [HAWT ee] arrogant and disdainful of others, high and mighty. She had a haughty way of peering down her nose at us. SYN. arrogant, disdainful, high and mighty, snobbish, lordly, condescending, patronizing, stuck-up, self-important, vain, conceited, imperious, superior, *hoity-toity, supercilious, *sniffy, *above it all. ANT. modest, humble, down to earth, folksy.

haul v. pull, drag, tow, draw, lug, move, carry, truck, transport, convey, cart, take.

haunt n. purlieu, hangout, stomping gound, gathering place.

haunt v. 1. FREQUENT hang out at. 2. TROUBLE worry, torment, plague, disquiet, disturb. 3. *SPOOK inhabit, appear, possess, manifest, terrorize, materialize, scare.

haunting a. unforgettable, spooky, ethereal, supernatural.

HAUTEUR n. [ho TUR] haughtiness, arrogance. He regarded us with his usual hauteur. SYN. haughtiness, arrogance, disdain, snobbishness, condescension, pride, self-importance, imperiousness, superiority, presumptuousness, conceit, airs. ANT. modesty, folksiness.

have v. 1. BE IN POSSESSION possess, hold, own, retain, keep, enjoy. 2. EXPERIENCE endure, suffer, entertain, bear, undergo, know.

haven n. refuge, asylum, safe harbor, sanctuary, shelter, sanctum, port in a storm, retreat, hideaway.

havoc n. destruction, devastation, ruin, disaster, catastrophe, demolition, waste, chaos, desolation, shambles, calamity.

hawk n. 1. RAPTOR bird of prey. 2. WARMONGER.

hawker n. peddler, huckster, street vendor, salesman, pitchman.

hayseed n. Sl. yokel, bumpkin, hick, clodhopper, rustic, farmer, hillbilly, hobnail, *rube, *goat-roper, *Bubba, *Arky, *Clem, *Okie, *brush ape. ANT. *city slicker, sophisticate, cosmopolitan.

haywire a. Sl. crazy, confused, *bonkers, berserk, amok, disordered, *out of kilter, *out of whack, *psycho, out of order. ANT. functioning, normal.

hazard n. danger, threat, peril, risk, jeopardy, pitfall, *thin ice, *house of cards, insecurity, endangerment, cause for alarm, quicksand.

hazard v. risk, chance, venture, wager, gamble, stake, dare, attempt, try, *go out on a limb, *go for broke.

hazardous a. dangerous, threatening, perilous, imperiling, endangering, life-threatening, risky, unsafe, chancy, menacing, *hairy, *dicey, precarious. ANT. *safe, secure, harmless.*

hazardous waste n. toxic waste, pollution, nuclear waste, *toxic soup, poison, contaminated materials, pathogenic materials.

haze n. vapor, fog, smog, smoke, mist, murk.

haze v. persecute, humiliate, tease, test, initiate.

hazy a. 1. CLOUDY foggy, misty, murky, nebulous, dim, gauzy, steamy, smoky, veiled, blurred, filmy, fuzzy. 2. VAGUE obscure, indefinite, confused, indistinct, dim, muddled, unintelligible, nebulous. ANT. *1. clear, sunny. 2. clear, distinct, lucid.*

head n. 1. SKULL cranium, brain, noggin, *belfry, *noodle, *bean, dome. "The palace of the soul."—Lord Byron. "The dupe of the heart."—La Rochefoucauld. 2. CROWN top, summit, peak, tip, apex, acme, pinnacle, cap, crest, vertex, height. 3. LEADER boss, chief, president, director, CEO, commander, ringleader, principal, chairman, *big cheese, *biggest toad in the puddle, *top dog, captain, ruler. ANT. *2. foot, base. 3. follower, underling.*

head v. lead, direct, command, boss, preside, chair, captain, run, rule, control, govern, supervise, oversee.

headache n. 1. migraine. 2. DIFFICULTY *pain, *pain in the neck, trouble, bother, annoyance, nuisance, problem.

headhunting n. recruiting, talent search.

heading n. 1. TITLE caption, headline, line. 2. COURSE bearing, direction.

headline n. caption, heading, title, banner, screamer. SEE NEWSPAPER

headlong a. reckless, dangerous, incautious, rash, foolhardy, breakneck, impetuous, uncontrolled, at full tilt, ungoverned. ANT. *cautious, careful, prudent.*

headquarters n. HQ, command post, nerve center, home office, main office, base, center of operations.

headstrong a. stubborn, self-willed, pigheaded, bullheaded, willful, obstinate, mulish, unyielding, wayward, defiant, intractable. ANT. *docile, obedient, yielding.*

headway n. advance, improvement, procession. SEE PROGRESS

heady a. intoxicating, stimulating, powerful, inebriating, exhilarating, exciting, arousing.

heal v. cure, make well, mend, restore, remedy, repair, treat, recover, alleviate, patch up, fix,

doctor, nurse, revive, renew, medicate, rejuvenate.

healer n. physician, shaman, medicine man. SEE DOCTOR

health n. fitness, soundness, well-being, vitality, strength, vigor, hardiness, shape, condition. "To eat what you don't want, drink what you don't like and do what you'd rather not."—Mark Twain.

healthy a. 1. GOOD FOR YOU salubrious, healthful, wholesome, salutary, beneficial, nutritious, nourishing, invigorating, restorative, sustaining, energizing. 2. IN GOOD SHAPE fit, strong, sound, well, vital, vigorous, hardy, hearty, *bright-eyed, robust, hale, trim, *in the pink, *in fine fettle, lusty, lively, energetic. ANT. *1. unhealthy, noxious, pernicious, deleterious. 2. failing, sickly, diseased, weak.*

heap n. pile, mound, stack, mass, bank, accumulation, clump, load, agglomeration, stockpile, jumble, bunch, abundance, *lots, plenty.

heap v. pile, mound, stack, amass, bank, accumulate, clump, load, gather, group, cluster.

hear v. listen, heed, pay attention to, receive, hearken.

hearing n. interview, audience, inquiry, day in court, inquisition, inquest, review, trial, presentation.

hearsay n. rumor, gossip, *grapevine report, scuttlebutt, word of mouth, talk, second-hand information, *talk of the town.

heart n. 1. BLOOD-PUMPING ORGAN muscle, *pump, *ticker.

WORD FIND

angina drug used to widen blood vessels: nitroglycerin

artery, large: aorta

artery-repairing procedure: angioplasty, bypass

chest pain from lack of blood flow: angina pectoris

damage to heart muscle due to insufficient blood supply: heart attack, myocardial infarction

decreased blood flow to: ischemia

defect sign: murmur

device used to regulate heartbeat: pacemaker

drug used to strengthen heartbeat: digitalis

enlarged heart caused by strenuous exercise: athletic heart syndrome

fluttering or pounding beat: palpitation

inflammation: pericarditis

occluded arteries: atherosclerosis

out-of-control heart contractions: fibrillation

pertaining to: cardiac

pumping failure or weakening: congestive heart failure

rapid heartbeat: tachycardia

readout of electrical impulses: electrocardiogram (EKG)

rhythm disturbance: arrhythmia

stoppage: cardiac arrest

study of: cardiology **2.** CENTRAL CORE nucleus, pith, center, kernel, essence, crux, seat, hub. **3.** EMOTIONS compassion, love, sympathy, feeling, passion, soul, humanity, sensitivity, affection, pity. "The tabernacle of the human intellect."—Moses Maimonides. "The organ that sees better than the eye."—Yiddish proverb. "A free and fetterless thing—a wave of the ocean, a bird on the wing."—Longfellow. **4.** COURAGE *guts, bravery, spirit, *spunk, valor, grit, nerve, backbone, mettle, fortitude. ANT. *2. periphery, outskirts, edge. 3. coldness, hatred, indifference. 4. cowardice, timidity.*

heartache n. heartbreak, anguish, grief, sorrow, misery, sadness, despair, broken heart, agony, heartsickness, desolation, woe, suffering, melancholy.

heart attack n. SEE HEART

heartbreak n. grief, anguish. SEE HEARTACHE

heartbreaking a. sad, pitiful, heart-wrenching, heartrending, painful, agonizing, disappointing, tragic, grievous, poignant, bitter, unendurable, crushing, devastating. ANT. *cheering, heartening.*

heartbroken a. sad, disappointed, crushed, devastated, heartsick, desolate, dejected, miserable, disheartened, despondent, depressed, crestfallen. ANT. *cheered, heartened, buoyed.*

heartburn n. reflux, pyrosis.

hearten v. encourage, cheer up, embolden, buoy, raise one's spirits, fortify, *give a shot in the arm, boost up, buck up, comfort. ANT. *discourage, dishearten, *take the wind out of one's sails.*

heartfelt a. sincere, feeling, real, deep, genuine, serious, ardent, fervent, honest, impassioned, profound. ANT. *insincere, phony, feigned.*

heartless a. cold, cruel, brutal, inhuman, callous, merciless, pitiless, unfeeling, *thick-skinned, uncaring, mean, insensitive, hard. ANT. *compassionate, sympathetic, feeling.*

heartrending a. painful, distressing, agonizing, mournful, touching, moving, grievous, anguishing, saddening, excruciating, soul-stirring. ANT. *heartwarming.*

heartsick a. sad, mournful, grieving, nostalgic, despondent, disappointed, inconsolable, despairing, depressed, blue, down, lost. ANT. *euphoric, gleeful.*

heartwarming a. loving, affectionate, sweet, heartfelt, heartening, joyous. ANT. *heartrending, chilling, unpleasant.*

hearty a. **1.** WARM friendly, genial, cordial, affectionate, jovial, enthusiastic, wholehearted, passionate, unrestrained, effusive. **2.** STRONG healthy, robust, hardy, vigorous, sturdy, energetic, stout, *in fine fettle. ANT. *1. cool, reserved, restrained, half-hearted. 2. frail, feeble, weak, sickly.*

heat n. **1.** HIGH TEMPERATURE warmth, hotness, fever, fire, torridity, sultriness. **2.** ANGER passion, rage, ardor, zeal, fervor, intensity, excitement, vehemence. ANT. *1. coldness, frigidity. 2. indifference, apathy, coolness.*

heated a. passionate, hot, raging, angry, ardent, fervent, intense, excited, vehement, violent, fiery, volcanic. ANT. *cool, calm, mild.*

heathen n. pagan, non-Christian, non-Jew, non-Muslim, infidel, nonbeliever, atheist, idolater, agnostic, skeptic. ANT. *believer, Christian, Jew, Muslim.*

heave v. **1.** RAISE, THROW hurl, cast, toss, hoist, lift, fling, shoot, fire, pitch, chuck. **2.** VOMIT throw up, puke, *ralph, disgorge, discharge, *upchuck, spew, spit up, *blow chunks.

heaven n. **1.** HEREAFTER paradise, afterworld, bliss, kingdom of God, glory, providence, ecstasy, utopia, *Shangri-la, *happy hunting ground, nirvana, city of light, Elysium, transport, happiness. "To be one with God."—Confucius. "Fulfilled desire."—Edward Fitzgerald. **2.** SKY cosmos, universe, firmament, celestial sphere, *the wild blue yonder. ANT. *1. hell, Hades, purgatory, torment.* SEE GOD

heavenly a. blissful, glorious, divine, beautiful, holy, sublime, wonderful, extramundane, spiritual, beatific, ethereal. ANT. *hellish, horrible, demonic.*

heavy a. **1.** HEFTY weighty, burdensome, overweight, unmanageable, ponderous, substantial, massive, huge, titanic, obese. SEE FAT **2.** INTENSE great, large, strong, abundant, extreme, powerful, overwhelming, violent, rough, deep, extensive, prolonged, profound. **3.** SERIOUS profound, grave, weighty, important, critical, vital, crucial. **4.** BURDEN-SOME oppressive, distressing, hard, harsh, onerous, intolerable, harsh. ANT. *1. light, weightless, featherlike. 2. light, mild, weak, brief. 3. trivial, unimportant, petty. 4. easy, light, tolerable.*

heckle v. harass, annoy, hassle, pester, *wise off, jeer, bait, taunt, tease, *ride, bother, *give a hard time, *bug.

hectic a. feverish, confused, rushed, chaotic, frenzied, frenetic, excited, wild, riotous, furious, tumultuous. ANT. *relaxed, calm, tranquil.*

hector v. bully, browbeat, pester, bait, badger, bother, torment, threaten, intimidate, harry, plague, menace, dominate.

hedge n. bush, hedgerow, boundary, shrubbery, windbreak, fence, barrier.

hedge v. avoid, lessen, evade, dodge, sidestep, equivocate, *stonewall, *hem and haw, temporize, *pass the buck, *waffle, duck.

HEDONIST n. [HEE dun ist] a pleasure-seeker, one who indulges. *He partied every Saturday night; he was a dyed-in-the-wool hedonist.* SYN. pleasure-seeker, bon vivant, indulger, *party animal, profligate, glutton, voluptuary, epicure, gourmand, debauchee. ANT. *prude, Puritan, bluenose.*

heed n. attention, mind, notice, consideration, regard, thought.

heed v. mind, regard, pay attention to, consider, take notice, note, follow, hear, look at.

heedless a. inattentive, unmindful, careless, unobservant, thoughtless, reckless, rash, negligent, disregardful. ANT. *attentive, mindful, observant.*

hefty a. heavy, weighty, large, massive, powerful, bulky, gigantic, ample, husky, brawny, rugged, muscular. ANT. *puny, weak, wispy.*

heifer n. calf, yearling.

height n. **1.** ALTITUDE elevation, tallness, highness, loftiness. **2.** TOP, CLIMAX crest, crowning point, acme, zenith, high point, limit, peak, summit, pinnacle, apex, culmination.

heighten v. increase, intensify, enlarge, magnify, amplify, raise, lift, elevate, augment, strengthen, extend. ANT. *lower, lessen, shorten.*

HEINOUS a. [HAY nus] evil or wicked to the extreme, abominable. *The heinous war crimes will never be forgotten.* SYN. evil, wicked, abominable, atrocious, hellish, monstrous, loathsome, ghastly, horrid, shocking, unspeakable, revolting, outrageous, damnable,

sickening, despicable, grisly. ANT. *saintly, angelic, good, moral.*

heir n. heiress, inheritor, beneficiary, recipient, successor, heir apparent, heir presumptive.

heirloom n. hand-me-down, cherished possession, legacy, inheritance, bequest.

heist n. Sl. holdup, *stickup. SEE ROBBERY

helicopter n. aircraft, *chopper, *eggbeater, *whirlybird, *copter, autogyro.

hell n. Hades, Gehenna, nether world, abyss, fire and brimstone, inferno, underworld, Pandemonium, Abaddon, abode of the damned, limbo, eternal punishment, abode of the dead, abode of Satan, infernal regions, purgatory, pit, perdition, torment, depths. "Where their worms die not, and the fire is not quenched."—Bible. "A vast, unbottom'd, boundless pit."—Robert Burns. "A brimstone sea of boiling fire."—Francis Quarles. "Every man is his own."—Henry Louis Mencken. "God's penitentiary."—Charles Jaynes. ANT. *heaven, paradise, bliss.*

WORD FIND

halfway to: purgatory, limbo

hell-bent a. determined, driven, reckless, obsessed, resolute, bound and determined, single-minded. ANT. *wavering, unsure.*

hellion n. troublemaker, rascal, *rowdy, devil, rogue.

hellish a. infernal, satanic, demonic, diabolical, fiendish, horrible, black, evil, wicked, stygian, terrible, cruel, pitiless. ANT. *heavenly, blissful.*

helm n. wheel, driver's seat, tiller, control, leadership, seat of power.

helmet n. headgear, head protector, hard hat.

help n. assistance, aid, hand, succor, support, boost, contribution, lift, service, guidance.

help v. **1.** ASSIST aid, lend a hand, support, boost, contribute, lift, serve, guide, accommodate, do a favor, succor, abet, *pitch in, oblige, *go to bat for, *stick up for, back, promote, rescue, save, extricate, *throw a lifeline. **2.** IMPROVE alleviate, ameliorate, mitigate, relieve, remedy, cure, allay, better, benefit. ANT. *1. hinder, hamper, *throw up a roadblock. 2. make worse, aggravate.*

helper n. assistant, aide, hand, helpmate, *right-hand man, *gofer, laborer, handmaid, henchman, subordinate, girl/man Friday, colleague, partner.

helpful a. useful, beneficial, constructive, accommodating, of service, valuable, conducive, invaluable, profitable, practical. ANT. *harmful, useless, worthless.*

helpless a. powerless, impotent, useless, inadequate, incompetent, incapable, weak, vulnerable, defenseless, infirm, dependent, spineless, lost. ANT. *capable, independent, powerful.*

helter-skelter a. disorderly, arbitrary, confused, random, haphazard, hurried, pell-mell, hit-or-miss, jumbled, chaotic. ANT. *orderly, arranged.*

hem n. edge, border, edging, skirt, trim, fringe, verge, ruff.

hemorrhage v. bleed, shed blood.

henchman n. follower, helper, underling, aide, flunky, bodyguard, subordinate, *yes-man, hatchet man, advisor, attendant.

hen-peck v. nag, *ride, dominate, *bug, pester, *pick on.

herald n. messenger, usher, forerunner, harbinger, precursor, omen, sign, indication, portent, symptom.

herald v. usher in, announce, foretell, harbinger, portend, trumpet, precede, presage, broadcast.

herbicide n. poison, defoliant, weed killer.

Herculean a. powerful, courageous, strong, mighty, formidable, tough, brawny, muscular, *built, gigantic, colossal, heroic, laborious, arduous, hard, rough, backbreaking, strenuous. ANT. *puny, weak, easy.*

herd n. drove, flock, bunch, drift, mass, swarm, mob, bevy, crush, crowd, throng, horde.

hereditary a. inborn, inherited, congenital, genetic, inbred, ancestral, innate, inherent. ANT. *acquired, learned.*

heresy n. apostasy, unorthodoxy, nonconformity, freethinking, blasphemy, heterodoxy, infidelity, dissension, atheism, agnosticism. "Only another word for freedom of thought."—Graham Greene. "Experiments in man's unsatisfied search for truth."—H.G. Wells.

heretical a. unorthodox, infidelic, nonconforming, unbelieving, freethinking, heterodox, impious, schismatic, heathen. ANT. *orthodox, faithful.*

heritage n. legacy, inheritance, ancestry, tradition, birthright, lot. "Scriptures . . . which have been absorbed into our blood."—Sholom Asch.

hermit n. recluse, solitary, loner, *lone wolf, anchorite, misanthrope.

hero n. heroine, champion, idol, conqueror, victor, star, role model, principal, public figure, lion, protagonist, leading man. "One

who is afraid to run away."—English proverb. "The shortest lived profession on earth."—Will Rogers. "One who thinks slower than a coward."—William Rotsler.

heroic a. brave, courageous, fearless, bold, noble, gallant, valiant, lionhearted, manly, *gutsy, *bigger than life, virile, gritty, altruistic, exalted, epic. ANT. *cowardly, fainthearted, dastardly.*

heroin n. narcotic, drug, *horse, *snow, *smack, *Big H, *black pearl, *Charley, *DOA, *Hazel, *joy powder, *junk, *Mexican brown, *mojo, *parachute, *poppy, *scag, *sweet Jesus, *the beast, *white nurse, *wings, *witch.

WORD FIND
cocaine and heroin mixed: *Belushi, *goofball, *speedball, *snowball
crack and heroin: *moonrock
inject into someone else: *give wings
lethal dose: *hot load
low purity heroin: flea powder
marijuana and heroin mixture: *atom bomb
marijuana, heroin and cocaine mixture: *el diablo
PCP and heroin mixed: *whack
SEE DRUN, NARCOTIC

heroism n. bravery, courageousness, fearlessness, boldness, nobility, gallantry, valiance, valor, manliness, *gutsiness, virility, grit, altruism. "Unbounded courage and compassion joined."—Joseph Addison. "Endurance for one moment more."—George Kennan. "It is always either doing or dying."—Roswell Hitchcock.

hesitant a. reluctant, irresolute, faltering, undecided, balking, tentative, wavering, halting, unsure, stalling, dallying. ANT. *decided, firm, confident.*

hesitate v. pause, hem and haw, falter, balk, waver, stall, wait, *dillydally, *waffle, dither, hang back, pussyfoot, *drag one's feet.

HETEROGENEOUS a. [HET ur o GEE nee us] made up of dissimilar elements, different, incongruous. *America is known for its heterogeneous society.* SYN. dissimilar, different, incongruous, diverse, motley, varied, mixed, miscellaneous, disparate, unrelated. ANT. *homogeneous, like, same, uniform.*

heterosexual a. *straight. ANT. *gay, homosexual.*

hex n. curse, spell, jinx, whammy, evil eye.

HIATUS n. [hi AYE tus] a break, gap or rest, often in one's work. SYN. break, interruption, lapse, discontinuity, interim, gap, pause, blank, rest, suspension, time out.

hibernate v. winter, sleep, hole up, lie low, lie dormant.

hick n. yokel, *hayseed, farmer, rustic, bumpkin, *hillbilly, *rube, clodhopper, *Okie, *Arky, *Clem.

hidden a. concealed, covered, covert, secret, under wraps, cloaked, clandestine, veiled, undercover, secreted, indiscernible, obscure, latent, occult, cryptic, invisible. ANT. open, exposed, *in the spotlight, overt.

hide v. conceal, secrete, cover, *put under wraps, cloak, veil, obscure, lie low, cache, shield, mask, camouflage, disguise, *drop out of sight, *hole up. ANT. expose, reveal, show.

hideous a. horrible, dreadful, appalling, terrible, ugly, awful, monstrous, grotesque, sickening, repulsive, gruesome, frightful, ghastly, grisly, repugnant, macabre. ANT. lovely, beautiful, attractive.

HIERARCHY n. [HYE uh RAHR kee] an order of rank, pecking order. He was second in command in the company hierarchy. SYN. order, pecking order, ranking, grouping, strata, *chain of command, *ladder, caste system.

high a. **1.** LOFTY tall, towering, soaring, steep, sky-high, *cloud-kissing, *cloud-piercing, elevated, skyward, alpine, vertiginous. **2.** IMPORTANT powerful, superior, prominent, excellent, exalted, ranking, eminent, chief, leading, uppermost. **3.** EXTREME excessive, great, intensified, dear, expensive, exorbitant, extravagant, costly, *steep. **4.** HIGH-PITCHED soprano, shrill, treble, piercing. **5.** HAPPY euphoric, elated, ecstatic, joyful, cheerful, exuberant, rhapsodic. **6.** UNDER THE INFLUENCE OF DRUGS OR DRINK *buzzed, under the influence, intoxicated, *stoned, *flying, *hammered, *baked, *blitzed, *coked out, delirious, *fried, *hopped up, *out of it, *tripping, *wired, *spaced out. ANT. 1. low, short. 2. low, insignificant, piddling. 3. modest, low, cheap. 4. low, bass. 5. low, depressed, *down in the dumps. 6. sober, lucid, clearheaded.

high and mighty a. lordly, arrogant, presumptuous. SEE HAUGHTY

highbrow n. longhair, thinker, *egghead, scholar. "The kind of person who looks at a sausage and thinks of Picasso."—Alan Herbert. "A person educated beyond his intelligence."—Brander Mathews. SEE INTELLECTUAL

highbrow a. erudite, scholarly, intellectual, learned, cultivated, bookish, cultured. ANT. lowbrow, unread, uncultured.

high-class a. superior, first-rate, best, supreme, *tops, upper-class, *upper-crust, top-flight, select, deluxe, quality, plush. ANT. low-class, ordinary, mediocre.

highfalutin a. pretentious, high-flown. SEE POMPOUS

high-flown a. high-sounding, bombastic, grandiloquent, lofty, grandiose, pretentious, stilted, inflated, extravagant, turgid, showy, flowery. ANT. folksy, down to earth, plain.

high-handed a. overbearing, domineering, imperious, tyrannical, dictatorial, arbitrary, oppressive, ironhanded, authoritarian. ANT. cooperating, helpful, just.

highlight n. high point, memorable part, feature, focus, focal point, peak, climax, best part.

highlight v. spotlight, underline, underscore, feature, play up, headline, punctuate, accentuate, emphasize, stress. ANT. downplay, obscure.

high-minded a. ethical, moral, principled, honorable, noble, upright, conscientious, virtuous, honest, righteous. ANT. unethical, immoral, unprincipled.

high society n. cultured class, upper class, upper crust, moneyed class, beau monde, *jet set, society, haut monde, privileged class, *beautiful peple, aristocracy, elite, crème de la crème, glitterati.

high-strung a. nervous, tense, uptight, wound up, *hyper, *wired, edgy, skittish, jumpy, excitable, taut, temperamental, snappy. ANT. calm, relaxed, placid.

highway n. road, street, freeway, drive, parkway, turnpike, expressway, thoroughfare, boulevard, *main drag, causeway, autobahn, toll road, beltway. SEE AUTOMOBILE

hijack v. seize control, commandeer, steal, *hold up, skyjack, *carjack.

hijacker n. robber, skyjacker, *carjacker, kidnapper, abductor.

hike n. walk, journey, walkabout, ramble, trek, march, tramp, odyssey.

hike v. walk, journey, ramble, backpack, trek, march, tramp, rove, *hoof it, range.

hilarious a. funny, side-splitting, *hysterical, humorous, *a riot, *a scream, uproarious, amusing, merry, boisterous, gay, jolly, mirthful, gleeful, noisy. ANT. grim, grave, sad, depressing.

hill n. elevation, rise, knoll, hillock, hummock, knob, hump, bluff, gradient, slope, highland, prominence, mound, tor, dune. ANT. *crater, canyon, hollow, valley.*

WORD FIND

hilly: rolling, tumulose

land between hills: intervale

SEE MOUNTAIN

hillbilly *n.* *hayseed, *Clem, clodhopper. SEE HICK

hillock *n.* SEE HILL

hinder *v.* obstruct, block, impede, slow, stop, prevent, check, deter, thwart, frustrate, hamper, interfere, foil, forestall, stand in the way, *hamstring. ANT. *help, enable, facilitate, free.*

hindrance *n.* impediment, obstruction, encumbrance, stumbling block, obstacle, restriction, restraint, constraint, snag, handicap.

hindsight *n.* retrospect, *Monday morning quarterbacking, experience, wisdom, knowledge, seasoned perception, looking back.

Hinduism *n.* SEE RELIGION

hinge *v.* depend, be contingent, rest, hang, revolve.

hint *n.* **1.** CLUE indication, tip, *tip-off, suggestion, telltale, implication, allusion, sign, lead, innuendo, intimation. **2.** TRACE tinge, touch, suggestion, taste, sprinkling.

hint *v.* give a clue, suggest, indicate, intimate, imply, indicate, allude to, insinuate, *put a bug in one's ear, infer, tip, cue.

hinterland *n.* backcountry, outback, *boonies, *sticks, remote region, wilderness, frontier, wilds, bush country.

hip *a. Sl.* *with it, sophisticated, *in the know, aware, stylish, savvy, au courant, worldly-wise, experienced, astute, *cool. ANT. *ignorant, *out of it, unaware.*

hip hop *n.* rap, black urban music, *gangsta rap. SEE RAP

hippie *n.* nonconformist, *long-hair, *freak, free spirit, Bohemian, *Deadhead, flower child, beatnik, deviant, *60s dropout.

hire *v.* employ, engage, enlist, take on, commission, secure, appoint, delegate, put to work, retain, contract for, rent, charter, lease. ANT. *fire, let go, *pink slip.*

Hispanic *a.* Spanish, Latino, Hispano.

historic *a.* momentous, consequential, important, notable, significant, unforgettable, famous, celebrated, renowned, outstanding, extraordinary. ANT. *unimportant, insignificant, inconsequential, obscure.*

historical *a.* documented, factual, real, actual,

authentic, true, recorded, verifiable, chronicled, past, bygone, former. ANT. *mythical, fictitious, made-up, contemporary, modern.*

history *n.* **1.** CHRONICLE record, documentation, account, annals, saga, chronology, memories, diary, memoirs. "The witness of the times . . . the messenger of antiquity."— Cicero. "A voice forever sounding across the centuries the laws of right and wrong."—James Froude. "A sort of mask, richly colored."—John Quincy Adams. "The great dust heap."—Augustine Birrell. "A fraud agreed upon."—Napoleon I. "That terrible mill in which sawdust rejoins sawdust."—Edith Sitwell. **2.** THE PAST yesteryear, bygone era, *good old days, *water under the bridge, antiquity.

HISTRIONIC *a.* [HISS tree AWN ik] theatrical, overly dramatic. *His histrionic show of temper made him the center of attention.* SYN. theatrical, dramatic, melodramatic, overplayed, overacted, affected, stagy, thespian, forced, unnatural, *put-on. ANT. *natural, unaffected, understated.*

histrionics *n.* theatrics, melodramatics, dramatics, show, acting, affectation, display, playacting, performing.

hit *n.* **1.** BLOW strike, knock, bump, impact, smack, whack, tap, rap, thump, *conk, cuff, punch, slap, swat. **2.** SUCCESS triumph, winner, *smash, sensation, best-seller, sellout.

hit *v.* strike, knock, bump, smack, whack, tap, rap, thump, *conk, cuff, punch, slap, swat, belt, bang, wallop, sock, pound, bash, beat, bop, slug.

hitch *n.* problem, snag, impediment, hindrance, stumbling block, *snafu, catch, difficulty, *glitch, bug, complication.

hitch *v.* join, connect, fasten, link, bind, attach, harness, couple, yoke, unite.

hitchhike *v.* *thumb a ride.

hit man *n. Sl.* *triggerman, *hired gun, assassin. SEE KILLER, MURDERER

hit-or-miss *a.* random, haphazard, careless, inaccurate, luck of the draw, trial and error, casual. ANT. *precise, accurate.*

hoard *n.* stockpile, store, cache, supply, reserve, stash, *nest egg, collection, accumulation.

hoard *v.* stockpile, store, cache, put away, *squirrel away, amass, stash, hide, save, collect, accumulate. ANT. *squander, waste, spend.*

hoarse *a.* husky, throaty, rough, harsh, rasping, gravelly, croaking, *whiskey-voiced, scratchy, roupy, guttural, ragged.

hoary *a.* **1.** WHITE OR GRAY salt and pepper, grizzled, snowy-haired. **2.** OLD elderly, ancient, aged, venerable.

hoax *n.* prank, trick, *put-on, *fake-out, joke, *spoof, ruse, fraud, deception, *crock, *humbug.

hoax *v.* trick, *put on, *fake out, deceive, *con, *hoodwink, fool, delude, *pull the wool over one's eyes, *sucker, dupe.

hobble *v.* **1.** LIMP hitch, shamble, falter, dodder, walk lamely, stumble, stagger, *shortleg. **2.** RESTRICT fetter, hinder, hamper, *hamstring, cripple, impede, handicap, inhibit.

hobby *n.* pastime, avocation, diversion, sideline, *thing, leisure time activity, pursuit, play, *bag, fun, *cup of tea.

hobgoblin *n.* bogey, bugbear, apparition, evil spirit, *spook, puck, elf, imp, fairy.

hobo *n.* tramp, *bum, transient, drifter, vagrant, derelict, *stiff, migrant worker, rover.

hock *v.* pawn.

hockey *n.* ice hockey, field hockey, sport.

WORD FIND

ICE HOCKEY

avoid being scored against while shorthanded: kill a penalty

bumping opponent away from play: check, body check

cup: Stanley

disk: puck

drop of puck by referee between two players: face-off

fake a move to shake off opponent: deke

free shot on goal: penalty shot

goaltender: goalie

hard, driving shot: slapshot

holding crook of opponent's stick to stop movement: hooking

illegally striking opponent with stick: slashing, spearing, high sticking

illegal shot from behind center red line: icing

penalty situation in which team has a one-man advantage: power play

positions: center, forwards, wings, backline, defensemen

rectangle in front of goal: crease

roughness penalty, excessive: roughing

three goals scored by one player in a single game: hat trick

vehicle that restores ice surface: Zamboni

hocus-pocus *n.* magic, trickery, legerdemain, sleight-of-hand, prestidigitation, hoax, conjuring, deception, incantation, *abracadabra, mumbo jumbo, gibberish.

hodgepodge *n.* mixture, miscellany, jumble, melange, potpourri, medley, patchwork, *goulash, mess, *mishmash, hash, *mixed bag.

hoe *n.* garden implement, tool, weeder, cultivator, digger.

hog *n.* **1.** PIG swine, *oinker, shoat, piglet, sow, boar. **2.** GLUTTON gourmand.

hog *v.* *Sl.* be greedy, take all, monopolize.

hogwash *n.* *BS, *baloney, balderdash, *bilge. SEE NONSENSE

hoi polloi *n.* the common people, the masses, commoners, rank and file, the working class, the crowd, citizenry, plebians, proletariat, *Middle America. ANT. *aristocracy, high society, upper class.*

hoist *v.* raise, lift, pull up, elevate, raise aloft, jack up, erect.

hokey *a.* SEE CORNY

hold *n.* influence, grip, control, sway, pull, effect, *clout.

hold *v.* **1.** GRIP clutch, grasp, clasp, clench, carry, embrace, squeeze, palm, cradle, handle, wield. **2.** POSSESS have, retain, keep, own, secure, maintain, contain. **3.** BELIEVE maintain, think, feel, reckon, view, deem, assume, surmise, espouse, swear by. **4.** CHECK restrain, restrict, suspend, postpone. **5.** PERSIST continue, last, endure, stay, remain. **6.** SUPPORT uphold, bear, shoulder.

hold up *n.* **1.** ARMED ROBBERY *stickup, heist. **2.** DELAY gridlock, red tape, wait, pause, stoppage, bottleneck, congestion. SEE CRIME

hole *n.* **1.** OPENING space, aperture, gap, orifice, vent, cavity, rift, slot, break, puncture, perforation, excavation, hollow, crater, pit, dugout, well, burrow. **2.** PREDICAMENT *box, *pickle, jam, dilemma, fix, spot, bind, plight, *hot water, *tight squeeze.

holiday *n.* celebration, festival, commemoration, fiesta, jubilee, holy day, observance, anniversary, vacation, day off, day of rest, long weekend. "Overrated disturbances of routine."—Edward Lucas.

HOLIER-THAN-THOU *a.* acting as if one is more virtuous than another, self-righteous. *We were sickened by his hypocritical, holier-than-thou judgments.* SYN. sanctimonious, self-righteous, pious, self-satisfied, smug, snobbish, *squeaky clean, judgmental.

holiness *n.* sanctity, sacredness, godliness, divinity, blessedness, grace, saintliness, piety, virtue. "A sweet, pleasant, charming, serene, calm nature."—Jonathan Edwards. "A fire whose outgoing warmth pervades the universe."—Plotinus. ANT. *sinfulness, sin.*

HOLISTIC *a.* [ho LIS tik] encompassing an entire integrated system, as opposed to an individual part. *Holistic medicine seeks to look at the entire mind/body connection in addition to the disease site.* SYN. complete, whole, one, comprehensive, entire, total, integral, universal, full, integrated, systemic, multi-dimensional. ANT. *partial, individual.*

holler *v.* yell, bellow, thunder. SEE SHOUT

hollow *n.* depression, concavity, indentation, cavity, dent, dimple, sink, bowl. SEE HOLE

hollow *a.* **1.** EMPTY vacant, void, unfilled. **2.** CONCAVE deep-set, indented, sunken, cavernous. **3.** MEANINGLESS empty, vain, futile, worthless, useless, insincere. ANT. *1. full, teeming, replete. 2. convex. 3. meaningful, important, profound.*

holocaust *n.* destruction, annihilation, genocide, mass killing, massacre, carnage, extermination, catastrophe, disaster, devastation, conflagration, firestorm, inferno.

holy *a.* godly, divine, sacred, hallowed, sacrosanct, consecrated, blessed, saintly, virtuous, religious, righteous, pious, faithful, spiritual. ANT. *ungodly, unholy, profane, diabolical, demonic.*

HOMAGE *n.* [xfí(H) ÄM - ij] something done, said or given to honor or show respect for another. *We paid homage to the president with our salute.* SYN. honor, respect, tribute, exaltation, esteem, admiration, reverence, allegiance, obeisance, deference, recognition.

home *n.* **1.** RESIDENCE house, domicile, abode, habitation, dwelling, quarters, place, castle, lodging, roost, *diggings, *pad. "Where we love."—Oliver Wendell Homes. "A place where you can scratch any place you itch."—Henry Ainsley. "The abode of the heart."—Elbert Hubbard. **2.** HOME BASE OR ORIGIN birthplace, native land, fatherland, habitat. SEE HOUSE

homebody *n.* introvert, *house cat, *stick in the mud, *couch potato. ANT. *extrovert.*

homeboy *n.* Sl. friend, buddy, neighbor, acquaintance, *homie, *brother, *sister.

homegrown *a.* native, homespun, homemade. ANT. *foreign.*

homeless *a.* destitute, *down-and-out, vagrant, displaced, derelict, evicted, dispossessed, exiled, forsaken, impoverished. ANT. *affluent, well-off, comfortable.*

homely *a.* **1.** UGLY plain, unattractive, *short on looks. **2.** SIMPLE plain, unpretentious, unsophisticated, homey, modest, folksy, informal, comfortable. ANT. *1. beautiful, pretty, handsome. 2. pretentious, sophisticated, showy.*

homemade *a.* homespun. ANT. *storebought.*

homemaker *n.* housewife, house husband, housekeeper, mother, domestic, household manager, domestic manager.

homesick *a.* nostalgic, wistful, heartsick, longing, yearning, pining, lonely for home, alienated, estranged.

homespun *a.* plain, unpretentious, homemade, homely, simple, unsophisticated, folksy, simple, down-home, modest, informal. ANT. *sophisticated, pretentious, refined.*

homestead *n.* farm house.

homey *a.* comfortable, cozy, relaxed, familiar, informal, folksy, domestic, intimate, friendly, unpretentious. ANT. *sophisticated, formal.*

homicidal *a.* murderous, bloodthirsty, violent, maniacal. ANT. *pacifistic, peaceful.*

homicide *n.* murder, killing, manslaughter, slaughter, slaying, assassination, *hit, shooting. SEE MURDER

homily *n.* sermon, lecture, lesson.

hominid *n.* hominoid, human ancestor, Homo sapien, primate.

HOMOGENEOUS *a.* [HO mo JEE nee us] made of like or similar elements. *A nation with only one ethnic group is a homogeneous society.* SYN. similar, like, identical, kindred, uniform, consistent, unmixed, the same. ANT. *heterogeneous, dissimilar.*

homosexual *n.* gay man, gay woman, lesbian, invert, bisexual, transsexual. ANT. *heterosexual.*

homosexual *a.* gay, lesbian, *queer, bisexual, transsexual, inverted.

hone *v.* sharpen, file, whet, grind.

honest *a.* **1.** TRUTHFUL trustworthy, upstanding, scrupulous, moral, ethical, veracious, reputable, straight, *on the level, honorable, aboveboard, conscientious, principled, credible, believable. **2.** CANDID frank, direct, straightforward, forthright, sincere, genuine, real, outspoken, outright, blunt. ANT. *1. dishonest, deceitful, disreputable. 2. indirect, insincere.*

honesty *n.* **1.** TRUTHFULNESS veracity, integrity, trustworthiness, scrupulousness, probity, principle, morality, virtue, conscientiousness, credibility. "The ability to resist small temptations."—John Ciardi. **2.** CANDOR frankness, directness, straightforwardness, forthrightness, sincerity, outspokenness, bluntness. ANT. *1. dishonesty, deceit, deception. 2. indirectness, insincerity.*

honeyed *a.* sweetened, sugarcoated, candied, syrupy, flattering, smooth-tongued, ingratiating, cajoling.

honk *v.* beep, toot, blast, blare, blow, sound.

honor *n.* **1.** REGARD respect, esteem, admiration, veneration, reverence, dignity, glory, deference, homage, exaltation, recognition, approval. **2.** INTEGRITY character, honesty, morality, virtue, principles, decency, righteousness, rectitude, nobility, dignity. "The moral conscience of the great."— William D'Avenant. "The morality of superior men."—Henry Louis Mencken. "A mistress all mankind pursue."—Paul Whitehead. ANT. *1. dishonor, shame, disgrace, 2. dishonor, dishonesty, immorality, perfidy, treachery.*

honorable *a.* virtuous, scrupulous, honest, moral, ethical, principled, decent, righteous, noble, trustworthy, upright, good. ANT. *dishonorable, disreputable, dishonest.*

honorary *a.* honorific, titular, in name only. ANT. *actual, earned.*

hood *n.* punk, thug. SEE HOODLUM

hoodlum *n.* *hood, criminal, thug, ruffian, gangster, mobster, *tough, *goon, *hooligan, *punk, rowdy, troublemaker.

hoodwink *v.* dupe, mislead, deceive, confuse, trick, *pull the wool over one's eyes, delude, cheat, fool, bamboozle.

hook *n.* **1.** GRAPPLE grapnel, crook, catch, hasp. **2.** BEND crook, dogleg, curve, angle, loop, arc, hairpin turn.

hook *v.* hitch, catch, gaff, grab, seize, snag, secure, fasten, couple.

hooked *a. Sl.* *having a monkey on one's back. SEE ADDICTED

hooker *n. Sl.* whore, lady of the evening, streetwalker. SEE PROSTITUTE

hooligan *n.* rowdy, *punk, *tough. SEE HOODLUM

hoopla *n. Sl.* excitement, to-do, fuss, fireworks, brouhaha, bustle, furor, ballyhoo.

hoot *v.* jeer, shout in disapproval, scorn, catcall, deride, boo, *razz, howl, mock, scoff at.

hop *v.* jump, leap, bound, hurdle, vault, spring, bounce, skip, dance, romp, caper, prance, gambol.

hope *n.* optimism, faith, confidence, trust, expectation, wish, desire, want, aspiration, dream, anticipation, expectancy, prospect,

belief, fancy. "The poor man's bread."— George Herbert. "Eating the air on promise of supply."—Shakespeare. ANT. *hopelessness, despair, pessimism.*

hope *v.* have faith, trust, be optimistic, expect, wish, desire, want, aspire, dream, anticipate, believe, fancy, look forward to, count on. ANT. *despair, doubt.*

hopeful *a.* **1.** OPTIMISITC *keeping the faith, looking forward to, anticipating, expectant, confident, sanguine. **2.** PROMISING encouraging, bright, favorable, heartening, reassuring, auspicious, propitious. ANT. *1. pessimistic, hopeless. 2. black, bleak, hopeless, foreboding.*

hopeless *a.* **1.** FUTILE lost, desperate, irrevocable, bleak, discouraging, vain, foreboding, incurable, threatening, grave, unobtainable, impossible. **2.** DESPAIRING desperate, demoralized, lost, disconsolate, miserable, heartbroken, depressed, suicidal, *broken, dispirited. ANT. *1. hopeful, bright, promising. 2. hopeful, optimistic, confident, encouraged.*

horde *n.* crowd, mass, throng, multitude, mob, pack, swarm, bunch, gang, group, band, press.

horizon *n.* skyline, vista, purview, field of vision, limit, range, offing, azimuth.

horizontal *a.* flat, level, flush, plane, straight, supine, prone, recumbent. ANT. *vertical, upright.*

horn *n.* **1.** OUTGROWTH tusk, antler, spike, cornu. **2.** SEE MUSICAL INSTRUMENTS

horny *a. Sl.* *hot, lustful, *turned on, amorous, passionate, lascivious, erotic, goatish, feverish, salacious, libidinous, sex-crazed, randy, *hot as a three-dollar pistol. ANT. *turned off, frigid.*

horoscope *n.* **1.** celestial positioning. **2.** DIAGRAM chart, forecast, astrological forecast.

horrendous *a.* SEE HORRIBLE

horrible *a.* horrendous, terrible, awful, frightful, horrid, appalling, dreadful, horrifying, abominable, hideous, ghastly, shocking, gruesome, disgusting, terrifying, repulsive, atrocious. ANT. *wonderful, lovely, charming, delightful.*

horrid *a.* SEE HORRIBLE

horrify *v.* dismay, shock, frighten, terrify, appall, scare, *curdle one's blood, *curl one's hair, *scare the daylights out of, *make one's skin crawl, *send chills up one's spine, sicken, nauseate, disgust, revolt, fill with morbid fascination, paralyze, petrify. ANT. *calm, soothe, reassure.*

horror *n.* fear, terror, fright, dread, trepidation, dismay, revulsion, repulsion, disgust, loathing, abhorrence, aversion.

hors d'oeuvre *n.* tidbit, finger sandwich, canape. SEE APPETIZER

horse *n.* equine, steed, mount, nag, pony, *bronc, stallion, mare, *plug, *crowbait.

WORD FIND

COLORS AND MARKINGS

beige with black mane: buckskin

beige with brown or light mane: dun

black and white: piebald

black speckles: medicine hat

bluish gray: grulla, smokey

bronze or coppery: chestnut, sorrel

brownish sprinkled with gray and white: roan

palomino color: buttermilk, golden

patches of white over any coat color except black: skewbald

piebald or spotted: calico, pinto, dappled, paint

reddish brown with black mane: bay

stripe extending down back: eel stripe, dorsal stripe

white above fetlock: stocking

white below fetlock: sock

white marking around nostril: snip

white marking between eyes: star

white streak on face: blaze, race

white with white mane: palomilla

yellowish cross of sorrel and dun: claybank

BREEDS

Appaloosa, Arabian, Cleveland bay, Clydesdale, Dartmoor, Exmoor, French Trotter, Hackney, hunter, Lipizzaner, Morgan, palomino, Percheron, quarter horse, saddlebred, Shetland, Shire, standardbred, Suffolk, Tennessee Walking Horse, thoroughbred

GENERAL

back, highest portion of: withers

bangs: forelock

barnyard play area: paddock

bent-backed: swaybacked, hogbacked

breeding mare: brood mare

breeding period of mare: heat

bushy tail: broomtail

care and feeding of, for a fee: livery

castrated male: gelding

cattle horse: cutting horse

comb: currycomb

command to turn left: haw

command to turn right: gee

cry of: neigh, whinny, snort

disease: staggers, distemper, loco, spavin, heaves

equipment: appointments, breastplate, bridle, bit, cheek straps, crownpiece, throatlatch, headband, blinder, caveson, reins, saddle, halter, hackamore

feeding trough: manger

female under age four: filly

gait: walk, trot, lope, canter, gallop, rack, volt, fox trot

gentle farm horse: dobbin

half-turn: caracole

Indian: pinto, cayuse, mustang

joint above hoof: fetlock

leap, playful four-legged: gambado

leap straight up: capriole

male under age four: colt

measurement of four inches: hand

mythological: Pegasus, centaur

nervous movement sideways or backwards: jib

newborn: foal

nose and mouth area: muzzle

pen: corral

pertaining to: equestrian, equine

race: steeplechase, derby

riding competition: gymkhana

riding pants, boots: jodhpurs

rising and falling in English riding style: posting

shelter: stall, stable

short-legged horse: cob

sideways gait: volt

smooth, refined gait for show: dressage

stand up on rear legs: rear

strong horse used for pulling: draft horse

stud's herd: harras

sweat: lather

trained: broken, bridlewise

trot in place for show: piaffe

upjerk of head: bridle

wild or half-wild: mustang, bronco

winker: blinder

horseman *n.* equestrian, rider, jockey, roughrider, cowboy, broncobuster.

horseplay *n.* clowning, foolishness, antics, fun, hijinks, tomfoolery.

horticulture *n.* gardening, cultivation, agriculture, farming, vegetable growing, floriculture.

hose *n.* hosiery, stockings.

hospice *n.* hostel, lodging, shelter.

hospitable *a.* gracious, accommodating, sociable, friendly, welcoming, neighborly, convivial, genial, cordial, helpful. ANT. *unwelcoming, inhospitable, unfriendly.*

hospital *n.* medical center, infirmary, clinic, sanatorium, sick bay, dispensary, ward, institution, treatment facility, hospice. "That blend of penitentiary and third-class hotel."—Henry Sigerist. SEE DOCTOR, MEDICINE, NURSE, OPERATION, SURGERY

hospitality *n.* accommodation, welcome, friendliness, graciousness, sociability, neighborliness, geniality, cordiality, warmth. "A genial hearth, a hospitable board, and a refined rusticity."—William Wordsworth.

host *n.* multitude, group, throng, legion, horde, flock, myriad.

hostage *n.* pawn, captive, security. SEE PRISONER

hostile *a.* unfriendly, antagonistic, malevolent, bellicose, belligerent, enemy, contrary, aggressive, nasty, contentious, warring, pugnacious, cold. ANT. *friendly, warm, amiable, peaceful.*

hostility *n.* **1.** UNFRIENDLINESS antagonism, malevolence, hatred, ill will, enmity, animus, opposition, aggression, venom, bellicosity, virulence, bad blood, anger, nastiness. **2.** HOSTILITIES war, conflict, dispute, clash. ANT. *1. friendliness, good will. 2. amity, peace.*

hot *a.* **1.** TORRID blazing, fiery, burning, scorching, steaming, boiling, blistering, roasting, sweltering, feverish, sizzling, sultry, tropical. **2.** SPICY peppery, sharp, biting, burning, piquant, zesty, pungent. **3.** PASSIONATE ardent, fiery, intense, fervent, vehement, impassioned, angry, raging, furious, violent. **4.** AROUSED SEXUALLY *horny, lustful, lascivious, salacious, libidinous, randy. **5.** NEW AND POPULAR trendy, fresh, in vogue. ANT. *1. cold, wintry, frigid. 2. bland, mild. 3. indifferent, apathetic, lukewarm. 4. turned off, repulsed, cold.*

hot dog *n.* **1.** FRANKFURTER wiener, *weenie, *dog, *foot long. **2.** SHOWOFF crowd-pleaser, grandstander.

hotel *n.* motel, inn, motor inn, resort, lodging, tavern, hostel, *flophouse.

hotheaded *a.* hot-tempered, quick-tempered, touchy, explosive, volatile, testy, *short-fused, combustible, rash, impetuous. ANT. *even-tempered, levelheaded, easygoing.*

hothouse *n.* greenhouse, nursery, conservatory.

hound *v.* chase, nag, badger, harass, pester, pursue, dog, *bug, ride, *hassle, persecute, go after.

house *n.* home, residence, shelter, abode, habitation, domicile, homestead, castle, mansion, duplex.

WORD FIND
attic access hole: scuttle
beam supporting floor or ceiling: joist
board siding: clapboard
flooring of wood forming geometric pattern: parquet
foundation without basement: slab
frame made of heavy timbers: post-and-beam construction
framing member, vertical: stud
glass-enclosed lookout on top of roof: belvedere
glass: glazing
ornamentation, elaborate: gingerbread
passage between garage and house: breezeway
projection, with window, on sloping roof: dormer
roof dome or domelike structure: cupola
roof framing member: rafter, purlin, ridgeboard
roof overhang: eaves
roof walkway: widow's walk
roof with double slope on each side: gambrel
roof with four sides, no gables: hip roof
roof with two slopes on all four sides: mansard roof
stair railing spindles: balusters
styles: adobe, bothy, brownstone, bungalow, cabin, cajun cottage, Cape Cod, chateau, colonial, cottage, Creole townhouse, Dutch Colonial, Elizabethan, English magpie, Federal, gambrel, Georgian, gingerbread, Gothic Revival, Greek Revival, Italianate, octagon, pueblo, Queen Anne, Romanesque, row house, saltbox, Second Empire, split level, Tudor, Victorian
tile mortar: grout
upper wall portion between slopes of roof: gable
wall not requiring plaster: drywall, sheetrock, gypsum wallboard
window framework: sash
window strips or bars: mullions
window that projects: bay window
SEE ARCHITECTURE, CASTLE, HOME

housekeeper *n.* homemaker, housewife, house husband, domestic, maid, cleaner.

housewife *n.* homemaker, lady of the house, matron, domestic manager.

hovel *n.* shed, hut, shack, cabin, shanty, lean-to, *dump, *rattrap, *hole.

hover v. float, hang, linger, flutter, stay suspended.

howl v. wail, waul, bay, bellow, yowl, cry out, bawl, moan, whine, ululate, caterwaul.

hub n. center, axis, core, pivot, focal point, *nerve center, heart, middle.

hubbub n. noise, uproar, tumult, commotion, clamor, racket, confusion, pandemonium, hullaballoo, stir, fuss, *ruckus, unrest. ANT. *quiet, silence, stillness.*

hubris n. arrogance, insolence. SEE PRIDE

huckster n. salesman, peddler, tradesman, hawker, vendor, concessionaire, merchant.

huddle v. mass, gather, pack, crowd, cluster, bunch, converge, herd, confer, *powwow.

hue n. color, tint, shade, tone, tinge, cast.

hue and cry n. outcry, protest, outrage, clamor, uproar, hullabaloo, brouhaha.

huff n. snit, bad mood, *stew, tiff, rage, resentment, fit of anger, tantrum.

huffy a. touchy, irritable, easily offended, testy, sensitive, hypersensitive, petulant, peevish, cross, crabby, waspish, nettled, irate. ANT. *cheerful, good-humored.*

hug n. embrace, squeeze, clasp, clinch, *bear hug. "A roundabout way of expressing emotion."—Gideon Wurdz.

hug v. embrace, squeeze, clasp, clinch, hold, clutch, *bear hug, take in one's arms, cuddle.

huge a. gigantic, colossal, immense, enormous, gargantuan, prodigious, humongous, great, whopping, tremendous, king-size, titanic, monstrous, massive, jumbo, stupendous, Brobdingnagian, mountainous, monumental, towering, elephantine, staggering, *eclipsing. ANT. *tiny, small, miniature, Lilliputian, microscopic.*

hulking a. heavy, large, clumsy, bulky, unwieldy, ponderous, massive, awkward, cumbersome, weighty, unmanageable. ANT. *compact, petite.*

hullabaloo n. uproar, noise, confusion. SEE HUBBUB

hum v. drone, buzz, whir, croon, intone, purr, murmur, sound, throb, bombinate.

human n. man, woman, person, Homo sapiens, being, *naked ape, creature. "A pair of pincers set over a bellows and a stewpan, the whole fixed upon stilts."—Samuel Butler. "A proper engine for the soul to work with."—Joseph Addison. "A little cave-dwelling virus mutated."—John D. MacDonald.

human a. 1. ANTHROPOID anthropomorphic, manlike, hominine, bipedal, civilized, mortal. 2. SEE HUMANE

humane a. compassionate, kind, sympathetic, merciful, good, understanding, humanitarian, forgiving, pitying, tolerant, magnanimous. ANT. *inhumane, cruel, unfeeling, vicious, merciless.*

humanitarian n. good Samaritan, philanthropist, do-gooder, *Robin Hood, altruist, benefactor.

humanity n. 1. HUMAN RACE mankind, humankind, men and women, people, the masses, society, man. 2. COMPASSION kindness, goodness, sympathy, benevolence, mercy, magnanimity, goodwill, brotherly love.

humankind n. humanity, mankind, human race, anthropoid population, Homo sapiens, family of man, civilized species. "A tribe of animals, living by habits and thinking in symbols; and it can never be anything else."—George Santayana. "A farce."—Mark Twain.

humble a. 1. MODEST self-effacing, unassuming, unpretentious, reserved, deferential, meek, demure, self-conscious, subservient, diffident, obsequious, lowly. 2. LOWLY shabby, simple, plain, ordinary, poor, undistinguished, rough, plebian, humdrum, unrefined, inconsequential. ANT. 1. *arrogant, pretentious, haughty, proud, conceited.* 2. *rich, superior, ostentatious, illustrious, distinguished.*

humble v. degrade, deflate, *take the wind out of one's sails, *bring down a peg, shame, humiliate, demean, disgrace, *make one feel small, *make one eat crow, *make one eat humble pie. ANT. *exalt, *put on a pedestal, inflate, puff up.*

humbug n. baloney, *BS, nonsense, balderdash, *eyewash, *bunk, claptrap, poppycock, *hogwash, rubbish, *rot.

humdrum a. monotonous, boring, tedious, *ho-hum, dull, tiresome, routine, prosaic, uninteresting, *blah, flat, insipid, somnolent. ANT. *interesting, stimulating, fascinating, riveting, exciting.*

humid a. moist, damp, wet, vaporous, muggy, steamy, clammy, sticky, *close, dank, sultry, foggy, misty. ANT. *dry, arid.*

humiliate v. embarrass, mortify, shame, disgrace, chagrin, *make a fool out of, abash, put to shame, degrade, deflate, demean, humble, abase. ANT. *honor, exalt, *put on pedestal.*

humiliation n. embarrassment, mortification,

shame, disgrace, chagrin, degradation, deflation, humbling, humble pie, losing face, *put-down, belittling. ANT. *honor, exaltation.*

HUMILITY n. [hyoo MIL uh tee] humbleness, modesty, the absence of arrogance or pride. *She accepted the award with great humility.* SYN. humbleness, modesty, unpretentiousness, lowliness, meekness, reserve, diffidence, sheepishness, obsequiousness, self-abasement. "Nothing else but a right judgment of ourselves."—William Law. "A noble mind in a low estate."—Jane Porter. ANT. *arrogance, pride, haughtiness.*

humor n. **1.** COMEDY funniness, jest, wit, facetiousness, jocularity, buffoonery, slapstick, drollery, whimsy, parody, satire. **2.** MOOD temperament, disposition, spirits, frame of mind, bent. "Truth in an intoxicated condition."—George Jean Nathan. "Pleasantry in pain."—Moritz Saphir. "Playful aggression."—Emil Draitser.

humorist n. comedian, comedienne, *stand-up, joker, comic, jester, wit, clown, caricaturist, mimic.

humorous a. funny, comical, laughable, ludicrous, hilarious, *side-splitting, facetious, tickling, farcical, amusing, droll, jocular, whimsical. ANT. *serious, grave, somber.*

hump n. bulge, protuberance, hunch, swelling, lump, mound, bump, knob, swell, hummock, hill.

hunch n. feeling, suspicion, guess, idea, premonition, inkling, intuition, notion, foreboding, impression.

hunch v. hump, bend, bow, huddle, crouch.

hunchbacked a. humpbacked, crookbacked, buffalo humped, deformed, gibbous.

WORD FIND
elderly, in: dowager's hump

hunger n. appetite, starvation, famine, ravenousness, voraciousness, famishment, *sweet tooth, *munchies, stomach pangs, desire, craving, longing, yen, want, need, lust, drive, thirst. "The best sauce in the world."—Miguel de Cervantes. ANT. *satiety.*

hungry a. starving, famished, ravenous, malnourished, peckish, voracious, hankering, *got the munchies, *could eat a horse, craving, salivating. ANT. *full, sated, gorged.*

hunk n. **1.** CHUNK lump, piece, clod, slab, block, portion, square, loaf, glob, slice. **2.** ATTRACTIVE MALE *stud, *beefcake, Adonis, sex symbol, *looker, *he-man, *dreamboat, Greek god.

hunt n. search, chase, pursuit, trailing, quest, coursing.

hunt v. **1.** LOOK FOR search high and low, ferret out, scour, seek, quest for, leave no stone unturned, turn everything upside down, rummage, probe, fish for, investigate. **2.** PURSUE AND KILL hound, trail, chase, track, *beat the bushes, stalk, course, poach.

hurdle n. obstacle, obstruction, stumbling block, barrier, impediment, difficulty, complication, block, snag.

hurdle v. jump over, clear, vault, leap, spring, hop, bound, negotiate.

hurl v. throw, chuck, fling, sling, heave, toss, pitch, lob, launch, catapult, propel.

hurricane n. tropical cyclone, cyclone, tempest, monsoon, typhoon, *blow, windstorm, rainstorm.

WORD FIND
calm center: eye
tide rise, rapid: storm surge

hurried a. hasty, quick, rushed, speedy, swift, breakneck, superficial, cursory, perfunctory, slapdash. ANT. *slow, leisurely, careful.*

hurry n. haste, speed, swiftness, rush, celerity, hustle, dispatch, expeditiousness, bustle.

hurry v. hasten, quicken, pick up the pace, *step on it, rush, run, lose no time, hustle, *get a move on, zip, fly, race, speed, scurry, *make tracks, expedite, *get the lead out, *beat feet. ANT. *slow, decelerate, delay.*

hurt n. injury, harm, pain, wound, trauma, soreness, ache, pang, *boo-boo, sting, stitch, pinch, twinge, throb.

hurt v. **1.** PHYSICALLY injure, harm, pain, torture, wound, damage, punish, abuse, sting, pinch, ache, throb, bite, sear, gnaw, stab, chafe, smart, pierce. **2.** EMOTIONALLY insult, wound, cut to the quick, grieve, anguish, sadden, depress, affront, offend, abuse, distress, upset, torment, crush, *rake over the coals.

hurt a. injured, harmed, pained, wounded, traumatized, sore, aching, stinging, throbbing, bleeding, bruised, stricken, damaged, offended, crushed, devastated, distressed.

hurtful a. injurious, harmful, painful, wounding, traumatizing, deleterious, pernicious, damaging, destructive, cutting, nasty, cruel, spiteful, mean. ANT. *helpful, benign, beneficial.*

hurtle v. fly, rush, plunge, charge, hurl, scramble, *zip, tear.

husband n. spouse, groom, *hubby, *old man, mate, alter ego, sidekick, *ball and chain, companion. "A hero in his own home until the company leaves."—Warren Goldberg.

husband *v.* preserve, manage, economize. SEE CONSERVE

hush *n.* silence, stillness, peace, quiet, lull, quietude, vacuum.

hush *v.* silence, quiet, mute, shut up, stifle, muffle, mute, suppress, gag, shush.

husk *n.* shell, hull, pod, shuck, peel, covering, case, bark.

husky *a.* **1.** HOARSE harsh, rough, throaty, rasping, croaking, whiskey-voiced, gruff, raucous, guttural. **2.** BRAWNY muscular, stout, beefy, burly, *Herculean, powerful, strapping, strong, athletic, hefty. ANT. *1. clear, fluid, fluting, shrill. 2. anorexic, scrawny, puny.*

hussy *n.* loose woman, wench, *tart, Jezebel, strumpet, slut, whore, trollop, minx.

hustle *v.* **1.** HURRY *get a move on, bustle, scramble, rush, *hotfoot, make haste, fly, run, *step on it, *work like hell, *move. **2.** PUSH shove, jostle, force, knock about, elbow, nudge, shoulder.

hustler *n.* *Sl.* con artist, *rip-off artist, flim-flam man, scam artist, grifter, swindler, *shark, thief, fast talker, enterpriser, go-getter.

hut *n.* shelter, shack, camp, cabin, cottage, lean-to, shed, hovel, shanty, hutch.

hutch *n.* **1.** PEN coop, cote, shed, cage, confine. **2.** CHEST box, cabinet, locker, trunk.

hybrid *n.* cross, crossbreed, half-breed, mixed breed, mongrel, *mutt, composite, mixture, conglomerate, combination, mulatto. ANT. *thoroughbred.*

hygiene *n.* cleanliness, hygienics, sanitation, washing, regimen.

hygienic *a.* clean, sanitary, healthful, pure, disinfected, aseptic, sterile, germfree, prophylactic, wholesome. ANT. *dirty, infected, germinfested.*

hymn *n.* spiritual, psalm, paean, choral, anthem, song of praise, canticle. SEE SONG

hype *n.* *Sl.* exaggeration, promotion. SEE HYPERBOLE

hyperactive *a.* overactive, wild, unfocused, frenetic, unrestrained, uncontrollable, unruly. ANT. *calm, sedate, tranquil.*

WORD FIND
related disorder: attention deficit disorder (ADD)

HYPERBOLE *n.* [hi PUR bul ee] an exaggeration, often used in figures of speech. *"I'm so hungry I could eat an elephant" is a statement illustrating the use of hyperbole.* SYN. exaggeration, overstatement, aggrandizement, *hype, embellishment, *PR, enlargement, inflation, magnification. ANT. *understatement.*

hypercritical *a.* overcritical, hard to please, severe, fussy, exacting, rigid, strict, overparticular, captious, persnickety, hairsplitting, finicky. ANT. *easy to please, unparticular.*

hypnotic *a.* soporific, somnolent, sleep-inducing, sedative, numbing, spellbinding, mesmerizing, mesmeric, entrancing, stupefying. ANT. *invigorating, awaking.*

hypnotize *v.* spellbind, entrance, mesmerize, stupefy, bewilder, enchant, enthrall, charm, bewitch, sedate, put to sleep.

hypocrisy *n.* lip service, pretense, insincerity, phoniness, imposture, falsity, pietism, sanctimoniousness, Pharisaism, duplicity, two-facedness, crocodile tears. *"A mouth that prays, a hand that kills."—Arabian proverb.* ANT. *sincerity, genuineness, honesty.*

hypocrite *n.* pretender, *con, Pharisee, fake, dissembler, phony, tartuffe, deceiver, Janus, whited sepulchre, Holy Willie, poser.

hypocritical *a.* insincere, phony, hollow, dishonest, Janus-faced, deceptive, fake, Pecksniffian, pretending, sanctimonious, unnatural, pious, self-righteous, dissembling, artificial, duplicitous, pretentious. ANT. *sincere, genuine, real, honest.*

hypothesis *n.* theory, supposition, proposition, assumption, conjecture, speculation, guess, thesis, inference, deduction, idea, *shot in the dark.

HYPOTHETICAL *a.* [hye puh THET i kul] assumed, unproven, uncertain. *There are numerous hypothetical explanations for UFOs.* SYN. assumed, unproven, uncertain, conjectural, speculative, supposed, presumed, inferred, guessed, academic, theoretical, presumptive. ANT. *factual, established, actual, confirmed.*

hysteria *n.* hysterics, frenzy, madness, delirium, craze, panic, mania, anxiety, agitation, fit, outburst.

hysterical *a.* **1.** OUT OF CONTROL wild, crazed, frenzied, mad, delirious, panicked, manic, agitated, raving, carried away, rabid, *nuts, berserk. **2.** COMICAL funny, *side-splitting, uproarious, ludicrous, *a riot. ANT. *1. calm, rational, composed.*

I

icky *a. Sl.* *yucky, *gross, disgusting, distasteful, sickening, repulsive, sticky, gluey. ANT. *pleasant, *yummy.*

ICONOCLAST *n.* [iye KON uh KLAST] one who attacks popular institutions, beliefs, public figures, etc., or who views such modern icons with skepticism and cynicism. *The true iconoclast believes that nothing is sacred.* SYN. cynic, skeptic, critic, detractor, nonconformist, image-shatterer, denouncer, dissenter, nonbeliever.

ice *n.* glaze, icicle, glacier.

icon *n.* image, representation, picture, likeness, symbol, idol.

icy *a.* **1.** FREEZING frozen, frigid, frosty, gelid, glacial, chilly, wintry, biting, cold. **2.** UNFRIENDLY cold, aloof, distant, chilly, frigid, hostile, stony. ANT. *1. tropical, warm. 2. friendly, warm, genial.*

idea *n.* thought, notion, concept, view, plan, design, inkling, scheme, theory, insight, belief, understanding, *brainstorm, inspiration.

ideal *n.* model, archetype, epitome, paragon, standard, example, acme, ne plus ultra, exemplar, ultimate, inspiration.

ideal *a.* **1.** PERFECT model, supreme, consummate, exemplary, optimal, classic, faultless, best, excellent, utopian. **2.** CONCEPTUAL imaginary, visionary, fanciful, abstract. ANT. *1. imperfect, flawed. 2. real, actual.*

idealist *n.* dreamer, visionary, optimist, Pollyanna, romantic, utopian. "One who, on noticing that a rose smells better than a cabbage, concludes that it will also make a better soup."—H. L. Mencken. ANT. *realist, cynic, skeptic, pragmatist.*

idealistic *a.* unrealistic, visionary, optimistic, utopian, Pollyannish, dreaming, romantic, naive. ANT. *realistic, skeptical, cynical.*

identical *a.* matching, alike, same, indistinguishable, twin, duplicate, corresponding, exact, synonymous, uniform, *carbon copy. ANT. *different, distinct, dissimilar.*

identify *v.* recognize, determine, distinguish, know, pick out, place, *tag, *spot, *peg, name, label, earmark.

identity *n.* individuality, self, oneself, ego, personality, character, identification, uniqueness.

idiocy *n.* foolishness, stupidity, imbecility, lunacy, craziness, madness, wackiness, absurdity, silliness.

idiom *n.* language, tongue, dialect, vernacular, lingo, parlance, jargon, colloquialism, expression, phrasing.

idiosyncrasy *n.* peculiarity, mannerism, quirk, singularity, characteristic, bent, trait, distinction, habit, quality, eccentricity.

idiot *n.* moron, imbecile, *retard, fool, nincompoop, simpleton, half-wit, lamebrain, *numskull, *chowderhead, *airhead, *dufus, *boob, blockhead, *pinhead. ANT. *genius, *Rhodes scholar, *brain, rocket scientist.*

idiotic *a.* moronic, stupid, retarded, foolish, imbecilic, simple, half-witted, *lamebrained, *numb, ignorant, dumb, asinine. ANT. *brilliant, intelligent, clever.*

idle *a.* **1.** WORTHLESS useless, vain, futile, frivolous, unproductive, pointless, irrelevant. **2.** UNUSED inactive, out of action, down, still, unemployed, quiet, dead, mothballed, empty, vacant. **3.** LAZY unemployed, slothful, shiftless, indolent, lethargic, loafing, sluggish, resting. ANT. *1. useful, valuable, productive. 2. in use, active, working. 3. active, busy, employed.*

idol *n.* hero, god, role model, star, superstar, celebrity, luminary, favorite, darling, icon.

idolize *v.* look up to, admire, revere, worship, venerate, deify, hero-worship, honor, *put on a pedestal, *worship the ground one walks on.

IDYLLIC *a.* [iye DIL ik] pastoral and peaceful; rustic and simple. *They chose an idyllic spot to build their house.* SYN. rustic, charming, peaceful, pastoral, unspoiled, romantic, simple, picturesque, heavenly, blissful. ANT. *urban, frenetic, noisy.*

iffy *a.* uncertain, unsettled, doubtful, questionable, *up in the air, dubious, unresolved, tentative, chancy. ANT. *certain, settled, sure.*

ignite *v.* **1.** LIGHT set fire, burst into flames, touch off, kindle, blow up, put a match to, flare up, burn. **2.** EXCITE arouse, agitate, spark. ANT. *douse, extinguish, smother.*

ignoble *a.* dishonorable, base, low, contemptible, despicable, shameful, corrupt, rotten, mean, disgraceful, vile, deplorable. ANT. *noble, honorable, admirable, good.*

IGNOMINY *n.* [IG num MIN ee] shame and dishonor. *He suffered the ignominy of a jail sentence.* SYN. shame, dishonor, disgrace, infamy, disrepute, discredit, odium, degradation, loss of face, humiliation. ANT. *honor, glory.*

ignoramus *n.* idiot, moron, *retard, simpleton, dunce, fool, half-wit, *airhead, bonehead, dolt, *dummy, *pea-brain. ANT. *intellectual,* *Rhodes scholar, *brain.

ignorance *n.* stupidity, inexperience, unenlightenment, illiteracy, denseness, naivete, unfamiliarity, unconsciousness, emptyheadedness, innocence, nescience, greenness. "The only slavery."—Ralph Ingersoll. ANT. *knowledge, experience, intelligence.*

ignorant *a.* uneducated, inexperienced, unschooled, stupid, retarded, unenlightened, illiterate, dense, *thick, naive, unfamiliar, unaware, unconscious, empty-headed, innocent, unlettered, obtuse, oblivious, mindless, moronic, sophomoric, nescient, green, *dense as a post, *numb as a hake. "Confident in everything."—Charles Spurgeon. "What everybody is, only on different subjects."—Will Rogers. ANT. *educated, aware, experienced, schooled, conscious.*

ignore *v.* disregard, overlook, skip, *pass over, slight, nevermind, discount, *turn a deaf ear on, neglect, pay no attention to, *bury one's head in the sand, *give the cold shoulder. ANT. *regard, mind, heed.*

ilk *n.* sort, kind, class, type.

ill *n.* harm, injury, hurt, pain, trouble, misfortune, damage, evil, misery, calamity, bad luck, tribulation. ANT. *good fortune.*

ill *a.* **1.** SICK ailing, sickly, unwell, afflicted, *laid low, *green around the gills, *under the weather, *out of sorts, *off one's feed, *out of commission, bedridden, feverish, nauseated, diseased. **2.** EVIL bad, wicked, harmful, malicious, sinful, wrong, nefarious, immoral, foul, nasty. ANT. *1. healthy, well, sound. 2. good, moral, kind.*

ill-advised *a.* unwise, imprudent, misguided, stupid, foolish, short-sighted, harebrained, *half-baked, rash, injudicious. ANT. *wise, prudent.*

ill-at-ease *a.* uncomfortable, self-conscious, anxious, nervous, uneasy, apprehensive, awkward, insecure, shy, bashful. ANT. *relaxed, calm, confident.*

illegal *a.* against the law, unlawful, prohibited, forbidden, criminal, banned, illicit, outlawed, wrongful, felonious, shady, *black market. ANT. *legal, lawful, licit.*

illegible *a.* unreadable, indecipherable, unintelligible, *hard to make out, scrawled, scribbled, *clear as mud, *hen scratching. ANT. *legible, readable.*

WORD FIND
illegible handwriting: griffonage
poor handwriting: cacography

illegitimate *a.* *born out of wedlock, misbegotten, bastard, baseborn, *love child, illegal, unlawful.

ill-fated *a.* doomed, unlucky, star-crossed. SEE UNFORTUNATE

illicit *a.* unlawful, prohibited, improper. SEE ILLEGAL

illiterate *a.* uneducated, unschooled, unlettered. SEE IGNORANT

ill-mannered *a.* rude, beastly, discourteous, impolite, crude, coarse, uncivil, boorish, tacky, rough, vulgar. ANT. *courteous, mannerly, civil.*

ill-natured *a.* moody, ill-tempered, contentious, ill-humored, grouchy, irritable, crabby, touchy, sour, surly, waspish, cantankerous. ANT. *good-natured, easygoing, amiable.*

illness *n.* sickness, affliction, disorder, malady, ailment, disease, infirmity, syndrome, indisposition, poor health, complaint, *bug, virus. "A great leveler. At its touch, the artificial distinctions of society vanish away."—Max Thorek.

illogical *a.* unscientific, unsound, fallacious, senseless, wacky, *screwy, inconsistent, invalid, incongruous, unreasonable, wrong, irrational, *cockeyed. ANT. *sound, correct, logical.*

ill-suited *a.* unsuitable, incompatible. SEE INAPPROPRIATE

ill-tempered *a.* nasty, moody, explosive, ill-natured, contentious, grouchy, irritable, crabby, touchy, sour, surly, waspish, cantankerous. ANT. *even-tempered, easygoing, good-natured.*

illuminate *v.* **1.** LIGHT UP brighten, spotlight, radiate, beam, shine. **2.** EXPLAIN elucidate, clarify, throw light on, shed light on, clear up, define, enlighten, expound. ANT. *1. darken, dim. 2. obfuscate, muddy, obscure.*

illumination *n.* **1.** LIGHT luminescence, radiation, radiance, glow, shine. **2.** EXPLANATION elucidation, clarification, enlightenment, knowledge, instruction, wisdom, insight, understanding.

illusion *n.* apparition, mirage, hallucination, misconception, pipe dream, vision, phantasm, figment of the imagination, delusion, fallacy, deception.

illusory *a.* unreal, deceptive, imaginary, false, delusory, visionary, hallucinatory, fanciful, spurious, chimerical. ANT. *real, concrete, true.*

illustrate *v.* **1.** MAKE CLEAR explain, demonstrate, illuminate, cite, elucidate, expound, clear up, make plain, describe, clarify, give an example, exemplify. **2.** DRAW depict, paint, portray, sketch, diagram, delineate, decorate, adorn.

illustration *n.* **1.** DEMONSTRATION exemplification, example, anecdote, story, analogy, sampling, case in point, instance. **2.** DRAWING depiction, painting, portrayal, sketch, diagram, cartoon, reproduction, design, figure, artwork, picture.

illustrious *a.* famous, renowned, distinguished, celebrated, prominent, eminent, notable, well-known, outstanding, acclaimed, esteemed. ANT. *obscure, unknown, undistinguished.*

ill will *n.* hostility, animosity, hate, malice, dislike, enmity, antipathy, hard feelings, spite, venom, grudge. ANT. *goodwill, friendliness, love.*

image *n.* **1.** REPRESENTATION picture, form, likeness, resemblance, imitation, copy, *carbon copy, mirror image, reproduction, facsimile, replica. **2.** IMPRESSION concept, idea, conception, mental picture, perception, thought.

imaginary *a.* fantasized, fancied, unreal, fantastic, visionary, invented, fictitious, *dreamed-up, made-up, conceived, mythical, hypothetical. ANT. *real, actual, true.*

imagination *n.* mind's eye, mental imagery, fabrication, visualization, *mental gymnastics, fantasy, illusion, reverie, dream world, figment, fancy, *castle in Spain, delusion, creativity, enterprise, inventiveness. "The true magic carpet."—Norman Vincent Peale. "A ladder to the fourth dimension."—Elbert Hubbard. "A warehouse of facts, with poet and liar in joint ownership."—Ambrose Bierce.

imaginative *a.* creative, inventive, original, innovative, *far-out, artistic, visionary, clever, ingenious, inspired, fanciful, fantastic, surreal. ANT. *unimaginative, unoriginal, prosaic, shallow.*

imagine *v.* **1.** PICTURE think of, fantasize, conceive, visualize, envision, conceptualize, dream, invent, fancy, create, conjure up. **2.** ASSUME believe, think, deduce, expect, conjecture, suspect, infer, surmise, suppose, guess.

imbecile *n.* idiot, moron, *retard, cretin, *pinhead, simpleton, dimwit, fool, dolt, *mental midget, *dummy, *chowderhead, dope, blockhead, ignoramus. ANT. *genius, *Rhodes scholar, *rocket scientist, *brain.* SEE MORON

imbibe *v.* drink, partake, consume, quaff, swallow, guzzle, sip, *swig, *swill, *tipple, *chug-a-lug, *hit the sauce.

IMBROGLIO *n.* [im BROL yo] a confusing or complicated situation causing misunderstanding and, sometimes, a fight. *The police are experts at disentangling neighborhood imbroglios.* SYN. predicament, entanglement, confusion, disagreement, mess, complication, confusion, problem, difficulty, dilemma, quandary, trouble, *Catch-22, stalemate, squabble.

imbue *v.* infuse, saturate, suffuse, permeate, steep, fill, impregnate, instill, pervade, inspire.

imitate *v.* copy, mimic, match, emulate, follow suit, ape, impersonate, clone, simulate, replicate, mirror, parrot, caricature, model after.

imitation *n.* simulation, copy, fake, replica, likeness, facsimile, *phony, counterfeit, *sham, fraud, clone, parody, caricature, impersonation, impression. "The sincerest form of flattery."—Charles Colton. ANT. *genuine article, *the real McCoy, original.*

imitation *a.* simulated, fake, artificial, synthetic, ersatz, phony, bogus, mock. ANT. *authentic, genuine, real.*

immaculate *a.* clean, pure, flawless, *squeaky clean, uncorrupted, spotless, unsoiled, faultless, sinless, untainted, perfect, above reproach, pristine, virginal. ANT. *dirty, unclean, tainted, sinful, defiled.*

immaterial *a.* irrelevant, impertinent, unimportant, insignificant, trivial, inconsequential, meaningless, extraneous. ANT. *important, vital, central, relevant.*

immature *a.* young, undeveloped, incomplete, unfinished, imperfect, unseasoned, *green, infantile, babyish, childish, juvenile, sophomoric, inexperienced, *wet behind the ears, raw, unfledged, callow, puerile. ANT. *mature, adult, experienced, seasoned.*

immeasurable *a.* infinite, boundless, vast, inestimable, incalculable, limitless, unfathomable, inexhaustible, countless, neverending. ANT. *finite, measurable, limited.*

immediate *a.* **1.** INSTANTANEOUS instant, now, present, current, sudden, prompt, swift, hasty, without delay. **2.** NEAR next, close, direct, neighboring, adjacent, adjoining, contiguous. ANT. *1. slow, leisurely, eventual. 2. distant, remote.*

immediately *a.* instantly, at once, without delay, now, presently, *in a wink, *in a heartbeat, *licketysplit, forthwith, *pronto, directly, *PDQ, *in a New York minute, *tout de suite, *before you can say "Jack Robinson," *before you can say "Bob's your uncle," *in a jiffy. ANT. *eventually, later.*

immense *a.* huge, gigantic, colossal, gargantuan, prodigious, vast, enormous, massive, towering, Brobdingnagian, tremendous, stupendous, staggering, *humongous, monstrous. ANT. *tiny, miniature, microscopic.*

immerse *v.* 1. DIP submerge, sink, dunk, douse, duck, plunge, soak, baptize. 2. ABSORB engross, involve, engage, occupy.

imminent *a.* impending, approaching, threatening, at hand, on the verge, close, immediate, looming, nearing, on the horizon. ANT. *far, distant.*

immobile *a.* stationary, unmovable, fixed, stable, motionless, rooted, riveted, still, frozen, paralyzed. ANT. *mobile, movable.*

immoderate *a.* excessive, unreasonable, extreme, extravagant, unrestrained, too much, inordinate, overblown, unwarranted. ANT. *moderate, reasonable, just enough.*

immodest *a.* bold, shameless, unseemly, indecent, unblushing, risqué, unrestrained, brazen, *cheeky. ANT. *modest, restrained, shy.*

immoral *a.* wrong, evil, sinful, bad, wicked, nasty, depraved, unethical, unprincipled, corrupt, unscrupulous, degenerate, *loose, debauched, perverted, disreputable. ANT. *moral, upright, virtuous, good.*

immortal *n.* SEE GOD

immortal *a.* deathless, everlasting, eternal, undying, indestructible, enduring, lasting, timeless, never ending, ageless, perpetual. ANT. *mortal, temporary, ephemeral.*

immortality *a.* 1. DEATHLESSNESS everlastingness, indestructiblility, endurance, eternity, infinity. "To rise upon some fairer shore."—J.L. McCreery. 2. FAME renown, celebrity, glorification, commemoration. "When a man dies but his words live."—Carl Crow. "The genius to move others long after you yourself have stopped moving."—Franklin Rooney. ANT. *mortality, death, obscurity, oblivion.*

immune *a.* invulnerable, resistant, safe, protected, exempt, unsusceptible, defended, inoculated, spared. ANT. *vulnerable, susceptible, liable.*

immunity *n.* protection, resistance, defense, inoculation, safety, exemption, privilege, exception, impunity. ANT. *vulnerability, liability, susceptibility.*

IMMUTABLE *a.* [i MYOO tuh bul] unchangeable. *The rules of the club are strict and immutable.* SYN. unchangeable, unalterable, inflexible, permanent, fixed, irreversible, unbreakable, stable, *carved in stone. ANT. *changeable, variable, flexible.*

imp *n.* devil, demon, brat, troublemaker, puck, sprite, hellion, hobgoblin, rascal, hellcat, scamp, tyke, mischievous child. ANT. *angel, little saint.*

impact *n.* 1. COLLISION crash, bang, striking, slam, bump, smash, blow, whack, crunch, jolt, concussion, thump, rock, meeting, percussion. 2. EFFECT repercussion, force, influence, power, consequences, results, brunt.

impair *v.* injure, damage, weaken, hinder, debilitate, harm, hurt, lessen, worsen, diminish, undermine, deteriorate, disable, enfeeble. ANT. *strengthen, improve, fortify.*

impale *v.* pierce, transfix, stab, run through, lance, spear, stick, prick, spike, puncture, skewer.

impart *v.* communicate, make known, inform, tell, announce, pass on, relate, transmit, proclaim, convey, divulge.

IMPARTIAL *a.* [im PAR shul] completely fair and unbiased. *We need an impartial judge to make the right decision.* SYN. fair, unbiased, neutral, disinterested, just, unprejudiced, objective, detached, equitable, dispassionate, nonpartisan. ANT. *partial, biased, partisan.*

impasse *n.* dead end, cul-de-sac, deadlock, stalemate, gridlock, *Catch-22, morass, standstill, standoff, dead stop.

impassioned *a.* passionate, ardent, fervent, intense, fiery, vehement, enthusiastic, excited, burning, torrid, powerful, rousing, emotional. ANT. *indifferent, apathetic, cool, dispassionate.*

impassive *a.* emotionless, calm, placid, stoic, stony, cool, indifferent, apathetic, stolid, dispassionate, unfeeling, matter-of-fact, reserved, phlegmatic. ANT. *impassioned, ardent, fervent.*

impatience *n.* restlessness, eagerness, agitation, expectancy, *ants in one's pants, restiveness, itchiness, excitement. ANT. *patience, calm.*

impatient *a.* restless, eager, agitated, expectant, restive, itching, *antsy, *chomping at the bit, hurried, nervous, anxious, edgy, annoyed. ANT. *patient, nonchalant, calm.*

impeach v. accuse, charge, indict, discredit, incriminate, denounce, impugn, point the finger at.

IMPECCABLE a. [im PEK uh bul] flawless, without fault or sin. *The general's record was impeccable.* SYN. flawless, faultless, perfect, immaculate, spotless, unblemished, irreproachable, virtuous, sinless, pure. ANT. *flawed, imperfect, defective.*

impede v. block, hinder, obstruct, delay, hamper, check, thwart, bar, foil, inhibit, slow, stymie, stop, hold up, retard. ANT. *help, facilitate, advance.*

impediment n. barrier, obstacle, hindrance, block, stumbling block, obstruction, restriction, bar, check, holdup, delay, deterrent. ANT. *help, advancement, aid.*

impending a. imminent, coming, approaching, close, at hand, nearing, on the horizon, in the offing, forthcoming, looming, threatening. ANT. *far, distant.*

impenetrable a. 1. IMPERVIOUS dense, hard, solid, thick, bulletproof, impassable, unaccessible. 2. INCOMPREHENSIBLE unfathomable, inscrutable, unknowable, arcane, baffling, inexplicable, esoteric, mysterious. ANT. *1. penetrable, accessible, passable. 2. knowable, understandable, clear, simple.*

imperative a. necessary, urgent, compelling, pressing, important, mandatory, obligatory, requisite, essential. ANT. *unnecessary, voluntary, unimportant.*

imperfect a. flawed, faulty, defective, deficient, unfinished, insufficient, below par, substandard, immature. ANT. *perfect, flawless.*

imperfection n. flaw, fault, defect, deficiency, failing, blemish, shortcoming, malformation, weakness, inadequacy, disfigurement. ANT. *perfection, faultlessness.*

imperil v. endanger, jeopardize, hazard, *play with fire, risk, chance it, expose, *put one's life on the line. ANT. *safeguard, protect.*

IMPERIOUS a. [im PEER ee us] domineering and overbearing. *He peered down his nose at us with his usual imperious expression.* SYN. domineering, overbearing, lordly, arrogant, haughty, high-handed, tyrannical, bossy, authoritarian, commanding. ANT. *deferential, mousy, bashful.*

IMPERMEABLE a. [im PERM ee uh bul] water or air-tight; impenetrable. *An impermeable membrane inside the container kept liquids*

from leaking out. SYN. impenetrable, watertight, airtight, waterproof, impervious, impassable, nonporous, sealed, leak-proof. ANT. *permeable, porous.*

impersonal a. unfriendly, detached, remote, distant, cold, businesslike, formal, cool, disinterested, objective, neutral. ANT. *friendly, warm, personal.*

impersonate v. imitate, ape, caricature, do an impression, mimic, double as, represent, mock, parody, pretend to be.

impertinent a. 1. IRRELEVANT not germane, immaterial, unrelated, extraneous, beside the point. 2. INSOLENT rude, impudent, disrespectful, saucy, brash, inappropriate, fresh, *smart-alecky, *flip, *mouthy. ANT. *1. relevant, germane. 2. polite, respectful.*

impervious a. inaccessible, dense. SEE IMPENETRABLE

IMPETUOUS a. [im PECH oo us] acting thoughtlessly or without careful consideration. *The impetuous youth drove without brakes and crashed into a wall.* SYN. rash, impulsive, headlong, hasty, careless, spontaneous, reckless, foolhardy, precipitate, spur-of-the-moment. ANT. *thoughtful, careful, prudent, cautious.*

impetus n. incentive, stimulus, spur, motive, spark, instigation, motivation, goad, catalyst, drive, force.

impinge v. trespass, encroach, infringe, invade, intrude.

impious a. irreverent, sacrilegious, blasphemous, ungodly, atheistic, irreligious, agnostic, sinful, iconoclastic, profane, immoral. ANT. *pious, religious, devout.*

impish a. mischievous, troublesome, naughty, prankish, devilish, *bratty, rascally, roguish, puckish, pert. ANT. *angelic, saintly.*

implacable a. inflexible, inexorable, unappeaseable, unforgiving, relentless, merciless, vengeful, vindictive, unbending. ANT. *placable, merciful, forgiving.*

implausible a. unbelievable, improbable, unlikely, incredible, questionable, doubtful, dubious, inconceivable, farfetched. ANT. *plausible, believable, likely, credible.*

implement n. tool, utensil, instrument, device, contrivance, mechanism, apparatus, appliance, gadget, contraption. SEE TOOL

implement v. start, fulfill, carry into effect, perform, accomplish, bring about, execute, enable.

implicate v. involve, point the finger at, accuse,

embroil, name, incriminate, entangle, insinuate, connect, associate. ANT. *exclude, acquit, exonerate.*

implication n. association, involvement, connection, link, inference, incrimination, suggestion, assumption, ramification.

IMPLICIT a. [im PLIS it] not expressed explicitly but implied or suggested. *There was an implicit understanding that Joe was guilty.* SYN. implied, suggested, unspoken, tacit, inferred, understood, unexpressed, deduced, hinted. ANT. *explicit, spoken.*

implied a. suggested, implicit, unspoken, inferred, hinted at, tacit, deduced, alluded to, indicated, insinuated.

implode v. collapse, cave in, fall in, fold.

implore v. beg, beseech, ask, plead, entreat, appeal to, request, pray, supplicate.

imply v. suggest, hint, infer, allude to, indicate, point to, refer, insinuate, signify, mean.

impolite a. rude, discourteous, ill-mannered, unrefined, disrespectful, boorish, crude, indelicate, ungracious, uncivil. ANT. *polite, courteous, respectful.*

importance n. consequence, significance, weight, moment, substance, value, magnitude, gravity, greatness, seriousness.

important a. consequential, significant, weighty, *heavy, momentous, substantial, valuable, great, serious, critical, vital, crucial, paramount, far-reaching, big, huge, influential, *major league, decisive. ANT. *unimportant, trivial, insignificant, inconsequential.*

impose v. place, set, dictate, charge, enjoin, assign exact, demand, lay, force, prescribe, fix, order, require, obtrude, *shove down one's throat, intrude.

IMPOSING a. [im PO zing] grand, awesome, having a powerful presence. *New York has many imposing skyscrapers.* SYN. grand, awesome, impressive, powerful, majestic, monumental, towering, massive, commanding, striking, magnificent, mighty, stupendous. ANT. *unimpressive, insignificant.*

impossible a. inconceivable, unachievable, unfeasible, unobtainable, insurmountable, unreachable, beyond reason, unthinkable, preposterous, absurd, hopeless. ANT. *possible, conceivable, feasible.*

impostor n. pretender, masquerader, fake, phony, fraud, con man, mountebank, impersonator, charlatan, humbug.

IMPOTENT a. [IM puh tunt] powerless, weak, ineffective. Also, unable to engage in sexual intercourse. *The marshall was impotent without his six-shooter.* SYN. powerless, weak, ineffective, helpless, debilitated, incapacitated, emasculate, prostrate, inadequate, worthless. ANT. *potent, strong, powerful.*

impound v. confine, hold, retain, keep, imprison, pen, confiscate, seize, take.

impoverished a. poor, destitute, poverty-stricken, indigent, penniless, impecunious, ruined, needy, broke, insolvent, bankrupt, *strapped, *hard up, receiving welfare, receiving food stamps, living hand to mouth. ANT. *rich, wealthy, affluent.*

impractical a. unworkable, impracticable, unrealistic, useless, wild, starry-eyed, chimerical, impossible, unfeasible, speculative, ideal. ANT. *practical, workable, viable, realistic, down-to-earth.*

impregnable a. unyielding, firm, secure, invincible, invulnerable, indestructible, impenetrable, strong, indomitable. ANT. *pregnable, yielding, vulnerable.*

impregnate v. inseminate, fertilize, fecundate, procreate, make pregnant, *knock up.

impresario n. producer, manager, sponsor, director.

impress v. **1.** AFFECT influence, move, sway, stir, touch, grab, faze, strike, overwhelm, inspire, excite. **2.** IMPRINT dent, indent, stamp, mold, engrave, emboss, mark.

impression n. **1.** EFFECT influence, mark, impact, feeling. **2.** FEELING notion, sense, inkling, hunch, idea, suspicion, belief, sensation, perception. **3.** IMPRINT dent, indentation, stamp, mold, engraving, mark.

impressionable a. susceptible, moldable, gullible, receptive, vulnerable, suggestible, inexperienced, naive, pliable, malleable, easily brainwashed, sensitive. ANT. *worldly-wise, impervious, sophisticated, hardened.*

impressive a. effective, powerful, striking, awesome, extraordinary, profound, dramatic, imposing, moving, wondrous, admirable, momentous, breathtaking. ANT. *unimpressive, *blah, *ho-hum, ordinary.*

imprint n. impression, stamp, signature, trademark, seal.

imprison v. jail, incarcerate, immure, lock up, confine, cage, impound, put behind bars, *throw in the slammer, hold in custody, hold captive, *send up the river, detain. ANT. *release, free, liberate.*

improbable a. unlikely, doubtful, questionable, implausible, dubious, unrealistic, unbelievable, impossible, farfetched, unheard of. ANT. *probable, likely, reasonable.*

impromptu a. unrehearsed, extemporaneous, improvised, ad-lib, off the cuff, unprepared, spontaneous, offhand, *off the top of one's head, spur-of-the-moment. ANT. *rehearsed, prepared, planned.*

improper a. unsuitable, inappropriate, unfitting, wrong, out of place, inapt, imprudent, uncalled for, incorrect, indecent, unseemly, indecorous, impolite, indelicate, offensive. ANT. *proper, correct, appropriate, fitting.*

impropriety n. slip, faux paus, gaffe, mistake, blunder, indecency, misstep, fault, bad taste, bad form.

improve v. make better, better, upgrade, reform, rework, correct, *touch up, *doctor, revise, enhance, mend, fix, refine, polish, enrich, ameliorate, promote, heal. ANT. *worsen, damage, impair.*

improvement n. enhancement, enrichment, amelioration, betterment, change for the better, progression, advance, upgrade, rectification, furtherance, revision. ANT. *worsening, impairment, decline.*

improvident a. thriftless, shortsighted, incautious, happy-go-lucky. ANT. *prudent, cautious.*

improvise v. invent, *wing it, *play by ear, make do, fake it, extemporize, make up, contrive, ad-lib, jury-rig.

imprudent a. unwise, rash, careless, indiscreet, thoughtless, foolhardy, reckless, injudicious, unthinking, irresponsible, impulsive, impetuous, unwary. ANT. *prudent, wise, cautious.*

IMPUDENT a. [IM pyoo dunt] boldly disrespectful, impertinent. *The impudent student was removed from the classroom.* SYN. bold, disrespectful, impertinent, shameless, insolent, saucy, rude, cheeky, brazen, audacious, fresh, *mouthy, *smart-alecky. ANT. *respectful, reverent, deferential.*

IMPUGN v. [im PYOON] to attack or criticize, especially for dishonesty or lack of integrity, to refute. *The attorney impugned the witness for stretching the truth.* SYN. attack, criticize, refute, call into question, vilify, challenge, assail, negate, cast aspersions, rebuke, impeach.

impulse n. urge, drive, instinct, itch, spur, goad, desire, feeling, whim, notion, impetus, incitement, want, wish, inclination, reflex.

impulsive a. spontaneous, impetuous, spur-of-the-moment, extemporaneous, precipitate, unpremeditated, offhand, sudden, thoughtless, rash, hasty, whimsical. ANT. *premeditated, cautious, planned.*

IMPUNITY n. [im PYOO ni tee] freedom from penalty or punishment. *The looters thought they could steal with impunity.* SYN. exemption, freedom, immunity, license, privilege, without liability, *free hand, amnesty. ANT. *punishment, liability, comeuppance.*

impure a. 1. CONTAMINATED polluted, dirty, adulterated, tainted, infected, sullied, foul, defiled, unclean. 2. IMMORAL unchaste, defiled, indecent, corrupted, degenerate, sinful, depraved, unvirginal. ANT. *1. pure, clean, untainted. 2. moral, upright, wholesome.*

impurity n. contaminant, pollutant, foreign matter, defilement.

impute v. attribute, ascribe, blame, charge, assign, credit, cite, implicate, accuse, associate.

inaccessible a. unreachable, remote, removed, distant, far away, beyond one's grasp, out-of-the-way, godforsaken, unattainable. ANT. *nearby, close at hand.*

inaccuracy n. error, mistake, fault, blunder, defect, miscalculation, bungle, slip, flub, *screwup, *boo-boo, *boner.

inaccurate a. inexact, imprecise, wrong, incorrect, false, faulty, erroneous, mistaken, slipshod, *way off, flawed, fallacious, *wide of the mark, unreliable, *all wet. ANT. *accurate, precise, correct.*

inactive a. idle, inert, immobile, down, inoperative, dormant, disengaged, still, unemployed, lazy, lethargic, sedentary, slothful. ANT. *active, busy, bustling.*

inadequate a. deficient, unsatisfactory, lacking, unfit, wanting, insufficient, too little, short, scanty, scarce, incompetent, impotent, incapable, unqualified. ANT. *adequate, satisfactory, sufficient, capable.*

inadmissible a. not allowed, unacceptable, unfitting, inappropriate, unsuitable, objectionable, immaterial, unqualified, untenable, restricted. ANT. *permitted, approved.*

inadvertent a. accidental, unplanned, unintentional, undeliberate, unwitting, undesigned, not on purpose, involuntary. ANT. *on purpose, designed, intentional, deliberate.*

inadvisable a. unwise, ill-advised, foolish, wrong, imprudent, inexpedient, unrecommended, injudicious, impulsive, inopportune, reckless, irrational, illogical, senseless, unintelligent, crazy. ANT. *wise, opportune.*

INANE a. [i NANE] empty, silly or foolish, pointless. *The TV show was poorly written* *and inane.* SYN. empty, silly, foolish, senseless, pointless, fatuous, insipid, thoughtless, ludicrous, stupid, idiotic, mindless. ANT. *deep, profound, intelligent, meaningful.*

inanimate *a.* lifeless, dead, nonliving, inert, nonmoving, dull. ANT. *alive, animated.*

inapplicable *a.* unsuited, unfit, inapt, irrelevant, immaterial, impertinent, incompatible, inappropriate. ANT. *applicable, suitable, relevant.*

inappropriate *a.* unsuitable, unfitting, improper, incompatible, inapt, incorrect, out of line, wrong, unseemly, indecorous. ANT. *appropriate, fitting, suitable.*

inapt *a.* SEE INAPPROPRIATE

inarticulate *a.* mute, incoherent, indistinct, garbled, unintelligible, tongue-tied, speechless, taciturn, reticent, shy. ANT. *articulate, expressive, intelligible.*

inattentive *a.* absentminded, daydreaming, *out to lunch, negligent, distracted, unobservant, faraway, preoccupied, unconscious, heedless. ANT. *sharp, observant, *on the ball, aware.*

inaudible *a.* silent, soundless, noiseless, unintelligible, imperceptible, indistinct, low, muffled, out of earshot, below the threshold of hearing, quiet, still, stone silent, silent as a tomb, silent as the depths of space. ANT. *loud, deafening.*

inaugurate *v.* **1.** INDUCT install, invest, instate. **2.** BEGIN commence, start, initiate, launch, set in motion, get under way.

inauguration *n.* **1.** INDUCTION installation, investiture, instatement, *swearing in. **2.** BEGINNING commencement, start, initiation, launch, outset, institution.

inborn *a.* innate, inbred, congenital, natural, indigenous, inherent, inherited, native, in the genes, in the blood. ANT. *acquired, learned.*

inbred *a.* genetic, congenital. SEE INBORN

incalculable *a.* inestimable, immeasurable, countless, infinite, innumerable, unfathomable, endless, limitless, unknowable. ANT. *measurable, finite, limited.*

incantation *n.* magic spell, magic charm, magic formula, hocus-pocus, abracadabra, conjuration, chant, invocation, mumbo-jumbo, hex, jinx. SEE MAGIC

incapable *a.* unable, inept, incompetent, unskilled, inadequate, insufficient, helpless, impotent, ineffective, unfit, powerless. ANT. *capable, able, competent.*

incapacitated *a.* disabled, crippled, handicapped, debilitated, unfit, disarmed, put out of action, *hamstrung, paralyzed, immobilized. ANT. *hale, healthy.*

incarcerate *v.* jail, imprison, lock up, *throw in the slammer, confine, hold in custody, impound. ANT. *free, release, liberate.*

incautious *a.* unwary, careless, rash, reckless, imprudent, impetuous, injudicious, *devil-may-care, bold, unthinking, impulsive. ANT. *careful, wary, prudent, judicious.*

incendiary *a.* rebellious, troublemaking, rabble-rousing, inflammatory, agitating, provocative, stirring, ardent, electrifying, fiery. ANT. *pacifying.*

incense *n.* aromatic, scent, pastille, tablet, stick, spice, essence, fragrance, perfume, joss stick, sandalwood, frankincense.

incensed *a.* enraged, angry, outraged, furious, wrathful, infuriated, *up in arms, mad, *pissed, irate, peeved, rankled, indignant, *ticked off, fired up. ANT. *calm, unruffled, composed.* SEE ANGRY

incentive *n.* motivation, motive, inducement, stimulus, goad, provocation, impetus, spur, consideration, enticement, lure.

inception *n.* start, beginning, origin, outset, birth, commencement, debut, conception, initiation. ANT. *end, close, finish, death.*

INCESSANT *a.* [in SES unt] never ceasing, nonstop. *I'm sick of your incessant complaining.* SYN. unceasing, neverending, relentless, constant, perpetual, continual, unremitting, unending, persistent. ANT. *infrequent, sporadic, intermittent, occasional.*

incest *n.* sexual abuse, molestation, statutory crime.

incident *n.* event, occurrence, happening, experience, affair, episode, occasion, circumstance, matter, scene, encounter.

incidental *a.* casual, accidental, chance, random, odd, *fluky, coincidental, secondary, minor, subordinate, unimportant, insignificant, negligible. ANT. *main, central, basic.*

incidentally *adv.* by the way, parenthetically, speaking of that, by the by.

incinerate *v.* burn, cremate, consume, reduce to ashes.

incinerator *n.* burner, furnace, crematory, crematorium, gas chamber.

incipient *a.* beginning, commencing, developing, newborn, nascent, initial, embryonic, developing, early.

incision *n.* slit, slash, scratch, score, gash. SEE CUT

INCISIVE a. [in SYE siv] sharp, penetrating to the heart of a matter. *An incisive newspaper story on the homeless changed his attitude.* SYN. sharp, penetrating, trenchant, acute, cutting, biting, piercing, to the point, keen, crisp, probing. ANT. *shallow, superficial, dull.*

incite v. instigate, spark, prompt, rouse, stir, spur, provoke, goad, inflame, whip up, agitate, encourage, *egg on. ANT. *dissuade, dampen, stop.*

incivility n. rudeness, discourtesy, disrespect, impoliteness, bad manners, tactlessness, roughness, coarseness. ANT. *civility, courtesy, politeness.*

inclement a. rough, stormy, harsh, severe, raw, nasty, foul, violent. ANT. *clement, mild, nice.*

inclination n. disposition, tendency, proclivity, bent, penchant, propensity, leaning, drift, bias, predilection, preference.

incline n. slant, slope, grade, cant, tilt, leaning, rise, pitch, ramp.

incline v. slant, slope, cant, tilt, lean, pitch, grade, rise, recline, list.

inclined a. disposed, prone, tending, liable, likely, predisposed. ANT. *unwilling, reluctant, disinclined.*

include v. involve, incorporate, comprise, hold, embody, contain, comprehend, take into account, number, accommodate, embrace. ANT. *exclude, preclude, omit.*

incognito a. in disguise, masked, concealed, clandestine, anonymous. ANT. *exposed, revealed, unmasked.*

incoherent a. unintelligible, illogical, disjointed, disconnected, incohesive, indistinguishable, rambling, muddled, inarticulate, mumbling. ANT. *coherent, intelligible, understandable, clear.*

income n. revenue, profit, gross, net, earnings, pay, *take-home, wages, salary, yield, receipts, gain, proceeds.

incomparable a. peerless, unequaled, matchless, unrivaled, superior, supreme, beyond compare, superlative, second to none. ANT. *run-of-the-mill, average, *just another brick in the wall.*

incompatible a. unsuited, incongruous, clashing, contrary, contradictory, mismatched, inharmonious, conflicting, opposite, *different as night and day. ANT. *compatible, harmonious, suited, *like hand in glove.*

incompetent a. inadequate, incapable, unskilled, inept, unfit, bumbling, useless, unable, out of one's league, out of one's element, inexperienced, ignorant, *all thumbs,

unqualified, bungling, inexpert. ANT. *competent, skilled, capable, expert.*

incomplete a. unfinished, lacking, deficient, wanting, imperfect, immature, short, insufficient, rough, fragmentary. ANT. *complete, finished, done.*

incomprehensible a. beyond comprehension, unintelligible, baffling, *beyond me, bewildering, *over one's head, unfathomable, unexplainable, deep, profound, mysterious, *clear as mud. ANT. *clear, plain, understandable.*

inconceivable a. unimaginable, unthinkable, unbelievable, incredible, incomprehensible, *mind-boggling, hard to grasp, unheard of, fantastic. ANT. *believable, reasonable, plausible.*

inconclusive a. undetermined, indefinite, unresolved, *up in the air, ambiguous, vague, open, uncertain, doubtful. ANT. *conclusive, definite, certain.*

INCONGRUOUS a. [in KON groo us] not fitting together, incompatible, inharmonious. *The new sports dome looked incongruous among the Victorian mansions.* SYN. incompatible, inharmonious, incongruent, discordant, conflicting, odd, inconsistent, discrepant, clashing, out of place, jarring, unsuited, inappropriate. ANT. *congruous, suitable, compatible, consistent.*

inconsequential a. insignificant, unimportant, immaterial, neglible, *small time, *no great shakes, trivial, trifling, piddling. ANT. *consequential, significant, important.*

inconsiderate a. thoughtless, insensitive, unthinking, rude, inattentive, boorish, ungracious, discourteous, self-centered. ANT. *considerate, sensitive, thoughtful.*

inconsistent a. **1.** IRREGULAR erratic, variable, unstable, changing, fickle, inconstant. **2.** INCOMPATIBLE contradictory, contrary, incongruous, divergent, out of step, conflicting, at odds, incoherent. ANT. *1. regular, steady, consistent. 2. compatible, harmonious, congruent.*

INCONSPICUOUS a. [in kon SPIK yoo us] not standing out, attracting little attention. *The shoplifter tried to remain as inconspicuous as possible.* SYN. undistinguished, unapparent, indistinct, unnoticeable, low-profile, invisible, hidden, unostentatious, plain, unobtrusive, *fading into the woodwork, *like another brick in the wall. ANT. *conspicuous, distinguished, obvious, *standing out like a sore thumb.*

inconstant *a.* irregular, erratic, variable, unstable, changing, intermittent, unsteady, fickle. ANT. *constant, steady, stable.*

incontrovertible *a.* indisputable, beyond doubt, established, certain, incontestable, solid, undeniable, irrefutable. ANT. *debatable, questionable, doubtful.*

inconvenient *a.* bothersome, troublesome, inopportune, untimely, burdensome, disadvantageous, cumbersome, discommoding. ANT. *convenient, advantageous, timely.*

incorporate *v.* include, involve, embody, comprise, unite, join, integrate, consolidate, merge, combine, associate.

incorrect *a.* wrong, in error, inaccurate, erroneous, faulty, false, inexact, fallacious, *way off. ANT. *correct, right, accurate.*

INCORRIGIBLE *a.* [in KAWR i juh bul] incapable of improving or becoming reformed. *The incorrigible youth was destined for the county jail.* SYN. hardened, hopeless, beyond help, irreformable, irredeemable, lost, intractable, incurable, recidivous, *unbreakable, *dyed in the wool. ANT. *correctable, reformable, curable.*

incorruptible *a.* honest, moral, honorable, virtuous, noble, principled, ethical, righteous, irreproachable, innocent, *squeaky clean. ANT. *corrupt, dishonest, immoral, dishonorable.*

increase *n.* growth, rise, enlargement, addition, expansion, enhancement, escalation, upsurge, intensification, broadening, burgeoning. ANT. *decrease, reduction, shrinkage.*

increase *v.* grow, rise, enlarge, add, expand, enhance, escalate, surge, intensify, broaden, burgeon, amplify, swell, advance, heighten, augment, *snowball, mushroom, multiply, build, inflate, double, triple. ANT. *decrease, reduce, shrink, deflate.*

incredible *a.* unbelievable, improbable, inconceivable, farfetched, unimaginable, extraordinary, fantastic, awesome, miraculous, wonderful, astonishing, fabulous, *unreal. ANT. *credible, believable, ordinary.*

INCREDULOUS *a.* [in KREJ oo lus] unbelieving, skeptical. *The cop looked incredulous; clearly he didn't believe the driver's story.* SYN. unbelieving, doubting, skeptical, suspicious, dubious, distrusting, mistrusting, unconvinced, cynical. ANT. *credulous, trusting, believing, gullible.*

increment *n.* addition, accession, step, increase, rise, gain, augmentation, accretion.

incriminate *v.* accuse, charge, *point the finger at, blame, involve, implicate, *blow the whistle on, *squeal.

incubus *n.* evil spirit, demon, devil, sex demon, fiend, goblin, hobgoblin, nightmare.

incur *v.* contract, acquire, get, gain, come into, bring upon oneself, bargain for.

incurable *a.* fatal, deadly, terminal, uncorrectable, hopeless, inoperable. ANT. *curable, remedial.*

incursion *n.* inroad, infiltration, encroachment, advance, penetration, invasion, raid, foray.

indebted *a.* obligated, beholden, bound, owing, appreciative, thankful, grateful. ANT. *free, unbound, independent.*

indecency *n.* obscenity, foulness, offensiveness, vulgarity, filthiness, *raunchiness, vileness, incivility, crudity, impropriety.

indecent *a.* obscene, foul, offensive, vulgar, filthy, *raunchy, vile, crude, *dirty, *X-rated, pornographic, lewd, unseemly, indecorous, indelicate, improper. ANT. *decent, modest, *clean, wholesome.*

indecisive *a.* **1.** UNCERTAIN wavering, faltering, vacillating, waffling, irresolute, wishy-washy, hesitant, undecided, *of two minds. **2.** INCONCLUSIVE unclear, indeterminate, unsettled, *up in the air. ANT. *1. certain, positive, resolute. 2. conclusive, settled.*

indeed *adv.* truly, certainly, surely, verily, by all means, positively, really.

indefatigable *a.* tireless, untiring, inexhaustible, unflagging, energetic, unfaltering, dogged, unremitting, persevering, diligent, tenacious. ANT. *slothful, sluggish, anemic.*

indefensible *a.* inexcusable, unjustifiable, unforgivable, untenable, weak, insupportable. ANT. *defensible, excusable, justifiable.*

indefinite *a.* uncertain, imprecise, ambiguous, undetermined, inexact, vague, indeterminate, unspecific, unknown, indistinct, ill-defined. ANT. *definite, specific, precise, unambiguous.*

INDELIBLE *a.* [in DEL uh bul] leaving a lasting impression. *The Kennedy assassination left an indelible impression on the minds of millions of Americans.* SYN. fixed, permanent, enduring, indestructible, unforgettable, ingrained, nonerasable, unfading, fast. ANT. *erasable, temporary, fading.*

indelicate *a.* coarse, rough, crude, gross, offensive, indecorous, tactless, unrefined, indecent, immodest, rude, lewd. ANT. *delicate, refined, decent.*

indent v. dent, depress, dimple, push in, mark, impress, hollow.

independence n. self-determination, self-government, self-reliance, self-sufficiency, autonomy, freedom, liberty. "Resistance to the herd spirit."—Daniel Mason. "The privilege of the strong."—Friedrich Nietzsche. "To live after your own nature."—Thoreau. ANT. dependence, subordination, subjugation.

independent a. self-determining, self-governing, self-reliant, self-sufficient, autonomous, sovereign, free, nonpartisan, separate. ANT. dependent, subordinate, controlled.

indescribable a. beyond words, inexpressible, nondescript, extraordinary, incredible, strange, wondrous.

indestructible a. unbreakable, lasting, durable, permanent, enduring, immortal, deathless. ANT. fragile, delicate, mortal.

indeterminate a. indefinite, inexact, vague, uncertain, inconclusive, unclear, unspecified. ANT. exact, specific, precise.

indicate v. signify, denote, mark, show, point out, express, tell, suggest, demonstrate, imply, designate, specify, symbolize.

indication n. sign, signal, symptom, hint, testimony, evidence, manifestation, intimation, clue, telltale, suggestion, attestation, warning, portent.

indicator n. pointer, dial, gauge, register, sign, guide, index, barometer.

INDICT v. [in DITE] to charge with a crime, accuse. He was indicted by the grand jury. SYN. charge, accuse, arraign, cite, incriminate, impute, prosecute, impeach.

INDICTMENT n. [in DITE munt] a formal charge of a crime, a written accusation. The grand jury handed down an indictment against three gang members. SYN. charge, accusation, imputation, arraignment, incrimination, implication, complaint, blame, allegation, summons, prosecution, impeachment.

indifference a. apathy, disinterest, unconcern, nonchalance, impassiveness, lack of interest, detachment, stoniness, disregard, insensitivity. "The worst sin toward our fellow creatures."—George Bernard Shaw. ANT. interest, concern, passion.

INDIFFERENT a. [in DIF ur unt] unconcerned, not interested, apathetic. She didn't care who won the election; she was indifferent. SYN. unconcerned, disinterested, apathetic, impassive, detached, nonchalant, cool, lukewarm, removed, blasé, uninvolved. ANT. interested, concerned, passionate, involved.

INDIGENOUS a. [in DIJ uh nus] originating in a specific region, native. Cactus is indigenous to the American southwest. SYN. native, aboriginal, natural, endemic, original, homegrown, domestic, innate, inherent, intrinsic. ANT. foreign, imported, naturalized.

INDIGENT a. [IN di junt] poor. The indigent family had no money for luxuries. SYN. poor, poverty-stricken, needy, impoverished, penniless, destitute, *bad off, *hard up, *broke, *down and out, *struggling to keep the wolf from the door. ANT. wealthy, rich, well off.

indignant a. angry, incensed, irate, peeved, *sore, furious, wrathful, miffed, *bent out of shape, fuming, resentful, exasperated. ANT. pleased, happy, joyful.

indignation n. anger, fury, wrath, rage, resentment, offense, displeasure, ire, exasperation, irritation, gall. ANT. delight, pleasure. SEE ANGER

indignity n. insult, affront, humiliation, embarrassment, outrage, *slap in the face, abuse, slur, disrespect, *snub.

indirect a. 1. ROUNDABOUT circuitous, wandering, divergent, tortuous, digressive, deviating, oblique, sidelong. 2. INCIDENTAL secondary, unintentional, ancillary, circumstantial. 3. DISHONEST backhanded, deceitful, sneaky. ANT. 1. direct, straight. 2. primary, direct. 3. direct, honest, straightforward.

indiscreet a. imprudent, unwise, injudicious, careless, thoughtless, inconsiderate, insensitive, hasty, rash. ANT. discreet, sensitive, considerate.

indiscretion n. imprudence, injudiciousness, blunder, impropriety, mistake, gaffe, misstep, faux pas, lapse, *slip, gaucherie, transgression, offense.

indiscriminate a. random, careless, unparticular, casual, uncritical, undiscriminating, haphazard, promiscuous, unmethodical, hit-or-miss, unselective. ANT. discriminating, selective.

indispensable a. necessary, essential, vital, needed, requisite, required, crucial, fundamental, basic, critical. ANT. extraneous, dispensable, superfluous.

indisposed a. ill, sick, *under the weather, ailing, *laid up, *out of sorts, *out of action, *feeling crappy. ANT. hale, vigorous, robust, well.

indisputable a. irrefutable, incontestable, undeniable, clear, beyond doubt, incontrovertible, unquestionable, *open and shut, solid. ANT. questionable, debatable, dubious.

indistinct a. vague, fuzzy, ambiguous, obscure, faint, dim, hazy, unclear, unintelligible, blurry, undefined, out of focus, nebulous, undecipherable. ANT. *distinct, clear, sharp, defined.*

individual n. person, human being, body, soul, character, man, woman, guy, girl, boy, personality.

individual a. single, separate, distinctive, sole, lone, exclusive, peculiar, particular, unique, singular, characteristic, specific, special, personal. ANT. *group, general, common, universal.*

individuality n. personality, character, distinction, difference, uniqueness, singularity, idiosyncrasy, peculiarity, originality, self, temperament.

INDOCTRINATE v. [in DAWK truh nate] to teach or instruct, to transfer one's beliefs to another. *The cult thoroughly indoctrinates new members with its beliefs.* SYN. teach, instruct, school, imbue, enlighten, train, implant, instill, *beat into one's head, brainwash, program. ANT. *deprogram.*

INDOLENT a. [IN duh lunt] lazy. *He was homeless because he was indolent, not unlucky.* SYN. lazy, idle, slothful, *allergic to work, listless, inactive, shiftless, do-nothing. ANT. *industrious, bustling, *go-getting.*

indomitable a. invincible, unyielding, unconquerable, undefeatable, unbeatable, insurmountable, dogged, steadfast, staunch, resolute, tough. ANT. *yielding, weak, *wimpy.*

indubitably adv. certainly, unquestionably, undoubtedly, surely, undeniably, definitely.

induce v. bring on, persuade, encourage, produce, influence, talk into, instigate, incite, prompt, cause, abet, prevail upon, sway, effect.

inducement n. incentive, motive, *carrot, stimulus, spur, enticement, instigation, reason, cause, *come-on.

induct v. bring in, install, instate, swear in, inaugurate.

indulge v. gratify, humor, satisfy, spoil, pamper, coddle, accommodate, splurge, treat oneself, *baby oneself.

indulgence n. luxury, self-gratification, immoderation, extravagance, treat, excess, satisfaction, *wishfulfillment, intemperance, spoiling, pampering, *babying, catering, splurging.

indulgent a. immoderate, extravagant, excessive, *weak, intemperate, pampering, *babying, splurging, lenient, overpermissive.

industrious a. hardworking, bustling, on the go, busy, *busy as a bee, hustling, *high octane, aggressive, productive, assiduous, diligent, dynamic, vigorous, constructive. ANT. *indolent, lazy, slothful.*

industry n. **1.** BUSINESS manufacturing, enterprise, trade, commerce. **2.** HARD WORK effort, industriousness, labor, toil, diligence, enterprise, activity.

inebriated a. drunk, intoxicated, tipsy, *bombed, *smashed, *loaded, *hammered, *sloshed, *drunk as a lord, *lit to the gills, *under the table. ANT. *sober.*

ineffective a. ineffectual, impotent, useless, inadequate, incompetent, vain, futile, unproductive, powerless, fruitless. ANT. *effective, powerful, potent.*

ineffectual a. SEE INEFFECTIVE

inefficient a. deficient, unfit, inapt, inept, incompetent, *below par, ineffective, wasteful, time-wasting, slow, disorganized, sloppy. ANT. *efficient, effective.*

INEPT a. [in EPT] awkward, clumsy, incompetent; unsuitable. *Every beginning carpenter is inept.* SYN. awkward, clumsy, incompetent, unfit, unskilled, bungling, *all thumbs, ungraceful, oafish, maladroit, wrong, unsuitable, inappropriate. ANT. *competent, skilled, graceful, appropriate.*

inequitable a. unequal, unfair, uneven, unjust, unbalanced, biased, partial, one-sided. ANT. *equal, fair.*

INERT a. [in URT] inactive, motionless. *The substance had completed its chemical reaction and was now inert.* SYN. inactive, still, motionless, lifeless, dead, unresponsive, quiescent, dormant, passive, static, sleepy, sluggish. ANT. *active, moving, reactive.*

inertia n. inactivity, stillness, lifelessness, quiescence, passivity, stasis, stagnation, paralysis, sluggishness, laziness. ANT. *activity, motion, business.*

inevitable a. unavoidable, inescapable, inexorable, assured, certain, irrevocable, unpreventable, ordained, fated, destined, predetermined. ANT. *avoidable, escapable, preventable.*

inexcusable a. unforgivable, unpardonable, unacceptable, outrageous, indefensible, unjustifiable, reprehensible, intolerable. ANT. *forgivable, understandable, acceptable.*

inexhaustible a. **1.** UNLIMITED limitless, boundless, infinite, bountiful, measureless, endless. **2.** TIRELESS unflagging. ANT. *1. limited, finite. 2. tiring.*

INEXORABLE *a.* [in EK sur uh bul] unchangeable and unrelenting, inevitable. *Americans have two inexorable fates: death and taxes.* SYN. unchangeable, unalterable, inescapable, inevitable, *carved in stone, unmovable, inflexible, unremitting, unyielding. ANT. *changeable, alterable, flexible.*

inexpensive *a.* cheap, reasonable, bargain, low-priced, *dime-a-dozen, nominal, economical, sale-priced, *budget. ANT. *expensive, costly, exorbitant.*

inexperienced *a.* green, unseasoned, unfamiliar, unschooled, virgin, unfledged, immature, innocent, young, untrained, raw, callow, ignorant, *wet behind the ears, rookie, naive, unsophisticated. ANT. *practiced, veteran, seasoned, sophisticated.*

inexplicable *a.* unexplainable, mysterious, baffling, puzzling, bewildering, incomprehensible, undecipherable, inscrutable. ANT. *explainable, understandable, explicable.*

infallible *a.* unerring, accurate, unfailing, flawless, perfect, reliable, dependable, trustworthy, foolproof, impeccable. ANT. *fallible, inaccurate, imperfect, erring.*

INFAMOUS *a.* [IN fuh mus] having a bad or scandalous reputation, notorious. *The infamous gangster went on trial today.* SYN. notorious, disreputable, disgraceful, scandalous, villainous, dishonorable, shameful, wicked, evil, low, wretched, reprehensible, despicable. ANT. *virtuous, illustrious, noble, revered.*

infamy *n.* bad reputation, scandalous reputation, disgrace, dishonor, disrepute, shame, villainy, evil, wickedness, notoriety, ignominy, opprobrium. ANT. *honor, nobility, repute.*

infant *n.* newborn, tot, toddler. SEE BABY

infantile *a.* babyish, childish, juvenile, immature, spoiled. ANT. *adult, mature, dependable.*

infatuated *a.* enamored, smitten, charmed, bewitched, beguiled, taken with, spellbound, in love, *stuck on, *hung up on, *gaga over, *hot for, *having a crush on, *carried away with. ANT. *repulsed, disgusted, repelled.*

infect *v.* contaminate, poison, taint, pollute, affect, disease, defile, corrupt, befoul.

infectious *a.* catching, contagious, spreading, communicable, transmittable, transferable, epidemic, pestilent, poisonous, toxic, virulent. ANT. *nontoxic, benign.*

INFER *v.* [in FUR] to deduce or come to a conclusion, to suppose something from a set of facts. *The police infer that a lack of eye contact may point to a guilty conscience.* SYN. deduce, conclude, gather, suppose, assume, presume, *put two and two together, figure, arrive at, guess, surmise, reckon, judge.

inference *n.* deduction, conclusion, assumption, presumption, corollary, supposition, figuring, guess, reckoning, judgment, interpretation, reasoning.

inferior *a.* poor, bad, awful, second-rate, *bush-league, lousy, mediocre, substandard, low, *junky, *two-bit, subordinate, minor, junior. ANT. *superior, first-rate, *top-drawer, senior.*

infernal *a.* hellish, diabolic, Stygian, fiendish, demonic, satanic, devilish, hateful, outrageous, evil, damned, damnable. ANT. *heavenly, angelic, saintly, godly.*

inferno *n.* hellfire, conflagration. SEE HELL

infertile *a.* barren, sterile, unproductive, unfruitful, infecund, impotent, depleted, exhausted, fallow. ANT. *fertile, productive, fecund.*

infest *v.* overrun, swarm, populate, spread, pervade, flood, fill, overwhelm, teem.

infidel *n.* nonbeliever, atheist, non-Christian, non-Muslim, pagan, heathen, heretic, dissenter, idolater, agnostic. ANT. *believer, follower.*

infidelity *n.* unfaithfulness, disloyalty, betrayal, treachery, perfidy, adultery, cheating, *two-timing. ANT. *fidelity, loyalty, faithfulness.*

infiltrate *v.* pass through, creep in, penetrate, intrude, invade, impregnate, permeate.

infinite *a.* endless, boundless, limitless, unlimited, countless, immeasurable, innumerable, inexhaustible, astronomical, vast, immense, never ending, eternal, ceaseless, perpetual. ANT. *finite, limited, ending.*

INFINITESIMAL *a.* [IN fin i TES uh mul] infinitely small, microscopic. *The odds of winning the contest were infinitesimal.* SYN. infinitely small, microscopic, tiny, minute, imperceptible, negligible, inappreciable, atomic, miniscule, slight. ANT. *gigantic, huge, enormous, great.*

infinity *n.* endlessness, limitlessness, continuum, eternity, inexhaustibility, infinitude, immeasurability, forever, perpetuity, vastness. "A fathomless gulf, into which all things vanish."—Marcus Aurelius. "A dark illimitable ocean, without bound."—John Milton.

infirm *a.* weak, feeble, sick, faint, shaky, fragile, ailing, frail, debilitated, unsound, powerless, faltering, decrepit. ANT. *strong, robust, sound, powerful.*

infirmary *n.* hospital, dispensary, treatment

center, clinic, pharmacy, nurse's station, sick bay, medical facility. SEE HOSPITAL

infirmity *n.* weakness, ailment, sickness, illness, handicap, condition, disease, frailty, affliction, malady. SEE DISEASE, MEDICINE

inflame *v.* fire, spark, ignite, agitate, excite, incite, impassion, fan the fire, aggravate, enrage, rile, intensify. ANT. *dampen, extinguish.*

inflammable *a.* combustible. SEE FLAMMABLE

inflammation *n.* redness, swelling, pain, immune response, tissue irritation, tenderness.

inflammatory *a.* fiery, explosive, incendiary, provocative, inciting, rabble-rousing, riotous, instigative. ANT. *conciliatory, pacific, mollifying.*

inflate *v.* blow up, swell, increase, dilate, distend, expand, puff up, bloat, stretch, grow, balloon. ANT. *deflate, contract, shrink.*

inflation *n.* increase, runaway prices, oversupply of currency, stagflation. SEE ECONOMY

inflexible *a.* 1. HARD unyielding, rigid, firm, stiff, unmalleable. 2. STUBBORN unyielding, adamant, firm, uncompromising, obstinate, rigid, unbending, intractable, fixed, pigheaded. ANT. *1. flexible, soft, malleable. 2. compromising, yielding.*

inflict *v.* impose, deal out, administer, visit upon, wreak, bring to bear, mete out.

influence *n.* power, pull, control, clout, weight, authority, leadership, pressure, force, effect, dominance, sway.

influence *v.* sway, control, persuade, move, incline, affect, act on, impact upon, impress, direct, turn, shape, *pull strings, manipulate.

influential *a.* powerful, persuasive, weighty, compelling, authoritative, effective, consequential, potent, inspiring, charismatic, forceful, important. ANT. *unimportant, trivial, meaningless.*

influenza *n.* flu, *bug, virus, viral infection, respiratory virus, grippe, chills and fever, Hong Kong flu, Asian flu, disease, illness, sickness, bacterial pneumonia, bronchitis.

WORD FIND
widespread: epidemic, pandemic, outbreak
SEE DISEASE

influx *n.* inflow, arrival, incoming, infusion, inpouring, tide.

inform *v.* tell, let know, advise, apprise, fill in, enlighten, notify, communicate to, *squeal, *rat on, tattle, snitch, fink.

informal *a.* casual, relaxed, unofficial, unceremonious, simple, workaday, down-home, breezy, *laid-back, loose, natural. ANT. *formal, ceremonious, stiff, official.*

information *n.* data, facts, intelligence, knowledge, *dope, *lowdown, news, communication, *skinny.

informative *a.* educational, enlightening, instructive, edifying, informational, illuminating, explanatory. ANT. *unredeeming, unhelpful.*

informed *a.* educated, knowing, in the know, advised, savvy, up-to-date, au courant, briefed, *up to speed, knowledgeable, enlightened, *up on, conversant with, abreast of. ANT. *ignorant, unaware.*

informer *n.* informant, tattletale, *rat, *fink, snitch, *stool pigeon, *squealer, *weasel, whistle-blower, betrayer.

infraction *n.* violation, infringement, breach, lawbreaking, transgression, offense, malfeasance, trespass. SEE LAW

infrastructure *n.* foundation, base, framework, underpining, support, structure.

infrequent *a.* rare, seldom, occasional, odd, unusual, exceptional, irregular, limited, *few and far between. ANT. *frequent, often.*

infringe *v.* trespass, violate, transgress, intrude, encroach, contravene.

infuriate *v.* enrage, anger, *make one's blood boil, outrage, madden, *burn up, incense, rile, inflame, *get one's dander up. ANT. *pacify, mollify.*

infuse *v.* instill, impart, imbue, inspire, inculcate, fill, ingrain, infect, implant, suffuse, permeate, introduce.

ingenious *a.* clever, brilliant, intelligent, resourceful, creative, inventive, shrewd, imaginative, skillful, proficient, *crack. ANT. *uncreative, stupid, unimaginative, *lame.*

ingenue *n.* innocent, naif, juvenile, *babe in the woods, young woman, debutante.

ingenuity *n.* cleverness, brilliance, intelligence, resourcefulness, creativity, inventiveness, shrewdness, imagination, skill, proficiency, genius.

INGENUOUS *a.* [in JEN yoo us] unsophisticated, unworldly, naive, artless and honest. *Most young children are naturally ingenuous.* SYN. unsophisticated, unworldly, naive, artless, honest, simple, up-front, innocent, childlike, open, sincere, genuine, candid, frank, direct. ANT. *disingenuous, artful, sophisticated, deceitful, insincere.*

ingest *v.* swallow, consume, eat.

inglorious *a.* shameful, dishonorable, disgraceful, ignominious, odious, scandalous, disreputable, infamous, reprehensible. ANT. *honorable, commendable.*

ingrained *a.* deep-rooted, fixed, planted, inherent, intrinsic, innate, *built-in, indelible, dyed-in-the-wool, permanent. ANT. *surface, superficial.*

INGRATIATE *v.* [in GRA she ate] to court favor with someone or purposely try to get on his or her good side. *After the argument she attempted to ingratiate herself with her boyfriend by preparing a special dinner.* SYN. court, blandish, *kiss up, *brownnose, charm, flatter, *get on one's good side, *butter up, curry favor, cajole, kowtow.

ingratitude *n.* ungratefulness, unthankfulness.

ingredient *n.* element, component, part, constituent, item.

inhabit *v.* live, abide, reside, lodge, dwell, occupy, stay at, populate.

inhabitant *n.* resident, occupant, lodger, tenant, renter, boarder, citizen, native, denizen.

inhale *v.* breathe, draw a breath, gasp, inspire, sniff.

INHERENT *a.* [in HEER unt, in HER unt] existing naturally, as an inborn trait, innate, native. *The drive to survive is inherent in every living thing.* SYN. natural, inborn, innate, native, existing, instinctive, hereditary, built-in, ingrained, fundamental, essential. ANT. *extrinsic, alien, foreign, unnatural.*

inheritance *n.* legacy, bequest, estate, birthright, endowment, gift heirloom.

inherited *a.* genetic, inbred, in the genes, hereditary, connate, in the blood, inborn, passed down, innate. ANT. *acquired, learned.*

inhibit *v.* hinder, restrain, check, repress, arrest, cramp, hold back, obstruct, constrict, impede, forbid, prohibit. ANT. *free, encourage, let.*

inhibited *a.* shy, withdrawn, self-conscious, reticent, reserved, guarded, uptight, bashful, self-censoring, stiff. ANT. *spontaneous, outgoing, uninhibited.*

inhibition *n.* **1.** SHYNESS self-consciousness, withdrawal, reticence, reserve, guardedness, uptightness, bashfulness, self-censorship, stiffness. **2.** RESTRAINT restriction, hindrance, check, constriction, blockage, prohibition. ANT. *1. spontaneity, outgoingness, unrestraint. 2. freedom, liberty.*

inhospitable *a.* unfriendly, forbidding, unkind, ungracious, hostile, cold, unwelcoming, aloof, unsociable. ANT. *hospitable, friendly, warm.*

inhuman *a.* beastly, cruel, inhumane, brutal, cold-blooded, merciless, pitiless, heartless, savage, animal, vicious, barbaric, unfeeling, ferocious, malicious. ANT. *human, humane, compassionate, kind.*

inhumane *a.* SEE INHUMAN

inhumanity *n.* beastliness, cruelty, brutality, cold-bloodedness, savagery, viciousness, barbarity, maliciousness. ANT. *humanity, compassion, kindness.*

inimitable *a.* unequaled, unmatched, preeminent, incomparable, unparalleled, unrivaled, unsurpassed, peerless, supreme. ANT. *comparable, similar, surpassed.*

iniquity *n.* wickedness, evil, injustice, sinfulness, wrong, immorality, wrongdoing, godlessness, abomination, infamy, crime. ANT. *virtue, righteousness, morality, justice.*

initial *a.* first, original, primary, beginning, earliest, inaugural, opening, commencing, maiden, embryonic. ANT. *last, final, closing.*

initiate *v.* **1.** START originate, begin, commence, introduce, usher in, institute, launch, establish, kick off, pioneer. **2.** TEACH instruct, train, acquaint with, familiarize with, tutor, train, indoctrinate, inculcate. **3.** INDUCT instate, enroll.

initiation *n.* start, beginning, commencement, entrance, introduction, institution, launch, kickoff, inception, debut, induction.

initiative *n.* **1.** FIRST STEP first move, start, lead, beginning, kickoff. **2.** ENTERPRISE ambition, resourcefulness, hustle, drive, *get up and go, dynamism, push, aggressiveness.

inject *v.* insert, introduce, put in, implant, infuse, imbue, inoculate, *shoot up, *mainline.

injection *n.* shot, booster shot, inoculation, vaccine, vaccination, infusion, dose.

injure *v.* harm, damage, hurt, wound, maim, bruise, impair, cripple, weaken, disfigure, mangle, afflict, mutilate, abuse.

injurious *a.* harmful, damaging, hurtful, wounding, maiming, bruising, impairing, crippling, pernicious, weakening, deleterious, disfiguring, destructive. ANT. *healing, helpful, reconstructive.*

injury *n.* harm, damage, hurt, wound, impairment, *boo-boo, indignity, disfigurement, mutilation, trauma, bruise, cut, gash, contusion, laceration, sprain, break, fracture, hemorrhage, scar, abrasion, concussion, dislocation, whiplash.

injustice *n.* unfairness, inequity, mistreatment, inequality, wrong, injury, crime, miscarriage, outrage, offense, inequity, discrimination, bias, grievance. ANT. *justice, fairness, equity.*

inkling *n.* hint, suggestion, indication, glimmer, idea, clue, notion, suspicion, trace.

inn *n.* lodging, hotel, motel, motor inn, motor court, bed and breakfast, hostel, resort, roadhouse.

INNATE *a.* [i NATE] naturally present, as from birth. *Infants have an innate ability to grasp.* SYN. inborn, natural, native, hereditary, in the blood, inherent, inherited, intrinsic, indigenous, inbred. ANT. *acquired, foreign, alien, learned, unnatural.*

inner *a.* **1.** INTERIOR inside, internal, inward, central, middle. **2.** PRIVATE personal, intimate, mental, psychic, interior, *gut, spiritual, emotional, psychological, secret. ANT. *1. outer, external, exterior. 2. outer, public, surface.*

innocence *n.* **1.** FREEDOM FROM GUILT blamelessness, clean hands, virtue, inculpability, clear conscience, purity, righteousness. **2.** SIMPLICITY naivete, harmlessness, unsophistication, unworldliness, ingenuousness, artlessness, gullibility, unfamiliarity. "The unbounded hope, the heavenly ignorance."—Lord Byron. ANT. *1. guilt, unclean hands, corruption. 2. artfulness, worldliness, sophistication, disengenuousness.*

innocent *a.* **1.** FREE FROM GUILT blameless, pure, *clean, inculpable, above suspicion, sinless, unimpeachable, guilt-free, guiltless, uncorrupt, immaculate, irreproachable. **2.** SIMPLE, AS A CHILD naive, childlike, harmless, unsophisticated, unworldly, ingenuous, artless, gullible, guileless, pure of heart. "Those who not only are guiltless themselves but who think others are."—Josh Billings. ANT. *1. guilty, to blame, culpable, corrupt. 2. sophisticated, worldly, artful, disengenuous.*

INNOCUOUS *a.* [i NOK yoo us] harmless, dull, or causing no controversy or offense. *Her comments were largely innocuous.* SYN. harmless, benign, inoffensive, innocent, painless, insipid, banal, dull, bland, mild, safe, *blah. ANT. *harmful, malignant, noxious, offensive.*

innovation *n.* change, invention, novelty, *new wrinkle, modernization, *new thing, *latest thing, *cutting edge, *last word.

innovator *n.* creator, pioneer, inventor, groundbreaker, father, architect, trailblazer, discoverer, trendsetter, pacesetter, avant-gardist.

INNUENDO *n.* [IN yoo EN do] a remark or reference made indirectly that implies something negative. *He never insulted the company directly, but by innuendos and subtle hints.* SYN. insinuation, oblique remark, intimation, suggestion, hint, allusion, implication, reference, overtone, *winking compliment, veiled sarcasm.

innumerable *a.* countless, numberless, myriad, *umpteen, incalculable, infinite, untold. ANT. *finite, limited, measurable.*

inoculation *n.* immunization, injection, shot, vaccination. SEE DISEASE

inoffensive *a.* unobjectionable, innocuous, harmless, clean, innocent, quiet, unobtrusive, wholesome. ANT. *offensive, objectionable.*

inopportune *a.* untimely, inconvenient, ill-timed, unseasonable, disadvantageous, inauspicious, unfavorable. ANT. *opportune, timely.*

inordinate *a.* excessive, immoderate, extravagant, unreasonable, disproportionate, uncalled for, exorbitant, unwarranted. ANT. *reasonable, proportionate, moderate.*

INQUEST *n.* [IN kwest] a legal inquiry, such as that made by a coroner to determine the cause of death of one who has died under suspicious circumstances. *The inquest officially termed the death suspicious.* SYN. inquiry, probe, investigation, hearing, inquisition, examination.

inquire *v.* **1.** ASK question, query, quiz, interrogate, pry, feel out, grill, pump, seek information, cross-examine. **2.** LOOK INTO investigate, probe, examine, scrutinize, inspect, *sniff out, study, track down, *leave no stone unturned.

inquiry *n.* **1.** QUESTIONING query, quiz, interrogation, inquisition, *Q and A, grilling, *third degree, cross-examination. **2.** INVESTIGATION probe, examination, scrutiny, inspection, study, analysis, exploration.

inquisitive *a.* curious, prying, nosy, inquiring, questioning, interested, *dying to know, probing, intrusive, *snooping, *hungry for knowledge. ANT. *uninterested, indifferent.*

inroad *n.* advance, encroachment, incursion, intrusion, trespassing, infiltration, foray, onslaught, infringement.

insane *a.* mentally ill, psychotic, *psycho, *nuts, deranged, crazy, demented, schizophrenic, *cracked, *loony, maniacal, paranoid, mad, *mental, *out of one's mind, *off one's rocker, lunatic, *loco, scatterbrained, not of sound mind, *cuckoo, *flipped out, sick, touched, *wigged out, daft, unbalanced, *one brick short of a load, irrational, delusional, non compos mentis. ANT. *sane, rational, normal.*

insanity *n.* mental illness, psychosis, derangement, dementia, schizophrenia, paranoia, madness, lunacy, craziness, unbalance, psychopathy, diseased mind, loss of reason. "A perfectly rational adjustment to the insane world."—R.D. Laing.

WORD FIND

alcoholic's: delirium tremens, hallucinosis, Korsakoff's psychosis

amnesic flight from reality: fugue state

brain lobe removal treatment: prefrontal lobotomy

conscience, without: antisocial personality, sociopathic

corpse, sexual attraction to: necrophilism

delusion that one is great or powerful: delusions of grandeur

deteriorating behavior due to long-term stress: decompensation

emotional agitation, extreme: hysteria

excessive, irrational talking: logorrhea

hands, delusion one has lost one or both: achiria

memory loss, profound: amnesia

mood swings disorder: manic-depressive psychosis

multiple personality: multiple personality, split personality

nonstop talking: logomania

odor hallucination: phantosmia

overeating, pathologic: hyperphagia

perception of sights, sounds, smells that aren't there: hallucination

persecution, delusions of: paranoia

pregnant, delusion that one is: pseudocyesis

primitive behavior, reverting to: atavism

psychosis involving thought processes, moods, emotion: schizophrenia

schizophrenia marked by constant silly grin: hebephrenia

shock therapy: electroconvulsive therapy

stupor marked by muteness, motionlessness: catatonia

unstable or rapidly changing moods: lability

SEE DISEASE, MANIA, NEUROSIS, PHOBIA

insatiable *a.* unquenchable, ravenous, voracious, unappeasable, gluttonous, greedy, unsatisfiable, wanting, desiring, *hungry for more. ANT. *satiable, satisfiable.*

inscribe *v.* write, print, engrave, carve, sign, mark, imprint, impress, autograph.

inscription *n.* wording, message, statement, epitaph, epigraph, blurb, imprint, impression, signature, autograph, dedication, engraving.

inscrutable *a.* unfathomable, mysterious, enigmatic, impenetrable, unknowable, indecipherable, hidden, incomprehensible, unreadable, secret. ANT. *knowable, readable, obvious.*

insect *n.* bug, *creepy crawler, vermin, pest, louse, cootie, flea, gnat, mite, aphid, fly, ant, tick, mosquito, beetle, termite, weevil, horsefly, bee, wasp, hornet, cockroach, midge, no-see-um, earwig, cricket, grasshopper, katydid, praying mantis, ladybug.

insecure *a.* **1.** UNSURE uncertain, anxious, lacking confidence, doubtful, diffident, timid, shy, apprehensive. **2.** UNSAFE defenseless, vulnerable, unprotected, unguarded, exposed, dangerous, hazardous, perilous, precarious. ANT. *1. confident, sure. 2. safe, guarded, defended, invulnerable.*

insensitive *a.* unfeeling, thoughtless, inconsiderate, indifferent, obtuse, callous, unconcerned, hardened, thick-skinned, unrefined. ANT. *sensitive, considerate, thoughtful.*

insert *v.* put in, inject, implant, introduce, pop in, tuck in, enter, imbed, place, stick, root, inlay, *shoehorn. ANT. *remove, extract.*

inside *n.* interior, middle, innards, soul, guts, heart.

INSIDIOUS *a.* [in SID ee us] working in a treacherous or sneaky way and quietly producing severe results. *Cancer is frequently insidious; by the time victims learn they have it, it may be too late.* SYN. treacherous, sneaky, sly, tricky, quietly damaging, guileful, underhanded, subtle, stealthy, slippery, covert, shady, Machiavellian. ANT. *overt, blatant, innocuous.*

insight *n.* awareness, observation, wisdom, sensitivity, intuitiveness, intuition, understanding, grasp, perception, discernment, sagacity, ken.

insightful *a.* perceptive, intelligent, wise, smart, thoughtful, sharp, understanding, discerning, aware, sensitive, observant. ANT. *ignorant, oblivious.*

insignia *n.* emblem, badge, mark, patch, decoration, regalia.

insignificant *a.* inconsequential, unimportant, trivial, trifling, meaningless, petty, negligible, *no great shakes, inappreciable, not worth mentioning, piddling, picayune, minor. ANT. *important, weighty, meaningful.*

insincere *a.* ungenuine, *fake, dishonest, phony, disingenuous, *put-on, deceitful, hypocritical, two-faced, pretended, slick, pretentious, fulsome. ANT. *sincere, genuine, honest, *real.*

insinuate *v.* imply, suggest, indicate, hint, intimate, allude, cast innuendos.

INSIPID *a.* [in SIP id] dull, lifeless, bland. *Television programming is growing ever more insipid.* SYN. dull, lifeless, bland, vapid, tasteless, prosaic, flavorless, *blah, uninteresting, boring, tiring, colorless, weak, *lame. ANT. *interesting, stimulating, exciting, colorful.*

insist *v.* demand, require, command, *lay down the law, stand firm, urge, contend, maintain, aver.

insistent *a.* demanding, commanding, tenacious, laying down the law, won't take no for an answer, determined, persistent, standing firm, urging, pushy, dogged. ANT. *wishy-washy, undemanding.*

insolence *n.* disrespect, boldness, impertinence, impudence, arrogance, nerve, gall, cheek, effrontery, back talk, *lip, *guff, haughtiness. ANT. *respect, deference, courtesy.*

INSOLENT *a.* [IN suh lunt] boldly disrespectful, arrogant. *Insolent youths disrupted the class.* SYN. disrespectful, bold, impertinent, impudent, arrogant, *nervy, *smart-alecky, *wise, *flip, cheeky, insulting. ANT. *respectful, deferential, courteous.*

insomnia *n.* sleeplessness, insomnolence, restlessness, wakefulness, sleep disorder, sleep deprivation, sleep latency, tossing and turning, *curse of Hypnos.

INSOLVENT *a.* [in SAWL vunt] unable to pay one's bills or debts. *The company became insolvent and declared bankruptcy.* SYN. indebted, ruined, *behind, *broke, wiped out, bankrupt, penniless, in arrears, *in the red, *in the hole, *strapped, *hard up. ANT. *solvent, in the black, profitable.*

insouciant *a.* carefree, lighthearted, buoyant, happy-go-lucky, untroubled, devil-may-care, airy, free and easy, sunny. ANT. *anxious, troubled, worried.*

inspect *v.* examine, scrutinize, look over, check, eye, scan, study, survey, peruse, probe, *give the once-over.

inspection *n.* examination, scrutiny, check, scan, study, survey, perusal, probe, *once-over, audit, inventory.

inspector *n.* examiner, tester, checker, investigator, detective, sleuth, private eye, police officer, assessor, reviewer, auditor.

inspiration *n.* motivation, stimulus, provocation, prompting, spur, sparking, igniting, idea, *flash, spark, flight of fancy, vision, insight.

inspire *v.* influence, stimulate, impel, arouse, prompt, motivate, spur, encourage, spark, stir, excite, ignite, inflame, trigger, give rise to. ANT. *discourage, stifle, dampen.*

instability *a.* unstableness, unsteadiness, shakiness, imbalance, precariousness, insecurity, variability, inconstancy, impermanence, vacillation, fickleness, capriciousness, volatility. ANT. *stability, equilibrium, steadiness.*

install *v.* put in, place, fix, set, situate, position, locate, establish, induct, instate, inaugurate, invest.

installment *n.* **1.** INSTALLATION emplacement, fixing, positioning, locating, establishment. **2.** SEGMENT portion, section, part, fragment, division, chapter, serial.

instance *n.* example, case, situation, sampling, exemplification, time, particular, occasion.

instant *n.* moment, split second, *heartbeat, *wink/blink of an eye, *flash, *jiffy, *twinkling, *nothing flat.

instant *a.* immediate, quick, sudden, direct, fast, prompt, swift, instantaneous, split second, quick, direct, abrupt. ANT. *slow, delayed.*

instantly *adv.* immediately, at once, instantaneously, now, directly, tout de suite, *PDQ, without delay, forthwith.

instigate *v.* incite, foment, initiate, urge on, egg on, spur, prompt, goad, start, begin, encourage, *whip up, kindle, spark, rally. ANT. *discourage, stop, check, quell.*

instigator *n.* troublemaker, *spark, *sparkplug, spur, rabble-rouser, initiator, fomenter, incendiary, *provocateur, *agent provocateur.

instill *v.* infuse, imbue, implant, impart, inculcate, indoctrinate, introduce, engender, brainwash, program, inject, impress.

instinct *n.* **1.** DRIVE intuition, impulse, *gut feeling, urge, sense, prompting. **2.** APTITUDE tendency, bent, knack, talent, proclivity.

instinctive *a.* innate, inborn, inbred, inherent, natural, reflexive, automatic, impulsive, intuitive, unthinking, involuntary, *gut. ANT. *acquired, learned, unnatural.*

institute *n.* institution, organization, company, establishment, society, association, union, school, academy, college.

institute v. begin, establish, set up, found, originate, develop, *usher in, create, organize, launch, fix, introduce.

institution n. **1.** SEE INSTITUTE **2.** CUSTOM law, practice, convention, principle, system, code, tradition, bylaw.

instruct v. **1.** TEACH school, train, show how, educate, tutor, enlighten, edify, indoctrinate, inform, drill, acquaint. **2.** ORDER command, direct, charge, enjoin.

instruction n. **1.** EDUCATION teaching, direction, training, grounding, tutelage, drilling, enlightenment, edification, indoctrination. **2.** COMMAND demand, direction, order, directive, mandate, charge.

instructive a. educational, informative, enlightening, edifying.

instructor n. teacher, educator, trainer, tutor, coach, mentor, master, professor, counselor, guide, pedagogue.

instrument n. **1.** TOOL implement, appliance, apparatus, contrivance, device, mechanism, utensil, machine, contraption, *gizmo. **2.** SEE MUSICAL INSTRUMENT **3.** MEANS agent, vehicle, medium, tool, way, mechanism.

instrumental a. helpful, useful, effectual, valuable, serviceable, of assistance, contributory, influential, vital, determining. ANT. unimportant, trivial, useless.

insubordinate a. disobedient, defiant, rebellious, uncompliant, contrary, refractory, uncooperative, dissentious, *too big for one's britches. ANT. subordinate, deferential, obedient, compliant.

insubordination n. disobedience, defiance, rebellion, noncompliance, noncooperation, dissension, revolt, insurrection, resistance. ANT. subordination, obedience, deference.

insubstantial a. **1.** SLIGHT flimsy, airy, tenuous, light, gossamer, ethereal, delicate, weak. **2.** IMAGINARY unreal, immaterial, intangible, phantom, illusive, impalpable. ANT. 1. substantial, hefty. 2. real.

insufferable a. intolerable, unbearable, unendurable, agonizing, impossible, too much, excruciating, torturous. ANT. tolerable, bearable.

insufficient a. deficient, lacking, inadequate, wanting, short, not enough, incomplete, shy, scant, missing, unsatisfactory, incommensurate. ANT. enough, sufficient, plenty.

INSULAR a. [IN suh lur] isolated like an island, detached. The hermit lived an insular lifestyle in the woods. SYN. isolated, detached, separated, sequestered, insulated, lonely, cloistered, secluded, cut off, provincial, narrow-minded. ANT. connected, urban, *in touch, broad-minded.

insult n. affront, *put-down, slight, *slap in the face, dig, offense, snub, denigration, abuse, attack, *cheap shot, slam, impudence. ANT. compliment, praise, *pat on the back.

insult v. affront, *put down, slight, cut, *slap in the face, dig, offend, snub, denigrate, abuse, attack, slam, *cut to the quick, ridicule, *dump on, belittle. ANT. compliment, praise, flatter.

insulting a. offensive, abusive, hurtful, disparaging, cutting, disrespectful, derogatory, ridiculing, denigrating, insolent. ANT. complimentary, flattering, respectful.

insurance n. security, protection, guarantee, pledge, assurance, warranty, backing, indemnity, safeguard.

insure v. **1.** ASSURE secure, make sure, make certain, warrant, guarantee. **2.** UNDERWRITE cover, protect, financially safeguard.

insurgent n. rebel, revolutionist, mutineer, insurrectionist, agitator, malcontent, subversive.

insurmountable a. insuperable, unconquerable, invincible, unassailable, unbeatable, formidable, impossible, hopeless, impassable. ANT. surmountable, superable.

INSURRECTION n. [in suh REK shun] a rebellion or revolt against established authority. The insurrection of the masses stunned the king. SYN. rebellion, revolt, uprising, revolution, mutiny, sedition, insubordination, coup, overthrow.

intact a. whole, undamaged, all together, unbroken, sound, unimpaired, complete, unharmed, unscathed, all in one piece. ANT. broken, damaged, shattered.

INTANGIBLE a. [in TAN juh bul] that which cannot be physically perceived, impalpable. The soul is intangible. SYN. impalpable, imperceptible, invisible, nonphysical, insubstantial, untouchable, incorporeal, unapparent, immaterial, indefinite, elusive. ANT. tangible, palpable, physical.

integral a. essential, central, basic, indispensable, fundamental, elemental, necessary, component. ANT. inessential, unnecessary.

integrate v. unify, unite, combine, mix, merge, consolidate, combine, amalgamate, fuse, desegregate. ANT. divide, separate, segregate.

integrity n. **1.** UPRIGHTNESS goodness, honesty, honor, morality, virtue, character, incorruptibility, rectitude, probity, decency. **2.**

COMPLETENESS wholeness, unity, soundness. ANT. 1. *improbity, immorality, dishonor, corruption.* 2. *fragmentation, unsoundness.*

intellect *n.* brain power, reason, sense, intelligence, *brains, comprehension, understanding, wits, judgment, cognition, intuition, aptitude, genius, *smarts, mental agility.

intellectual *n.* *brain, *egghead, thinker, scholar, genius, *Einstein, pundit, academic, savant, mental giant, philosopher, highbrow, *walking encyclopedia, *know-it-all. "A person educated beyond his intellect."—Horace Porter. "A man who takes more words than necessary to tell us more than he knows."—Dwight D. Eisenhower. ANT. *moron, imbecile, ignoramus, idiot.*

intellectual *a.* smart, intelligent, *brainy, cerebral, learned, scholarly, educated, well-schooled, literate, bookish, erudite. ANT. *ignorant, unschooled, illiterate.*

intelligence *n.* **1.** SMARTNESS intellect, mind, brain power, brains, *smarts, *gray matter, *IQ, reasoning, sense, comprehension, understanding, wits, judgment, aptitude, genius, brilliance, cleverness, acumen, wisdom, astuteness, sagacity, creativity. "The thing that enables a man to get along without an education."—Albert Wiggam. **2.** INFORMATION news, report, data, facts, *lowdown, surveillance.

intelligent *a.* smart, intellectual, *brainy, brilliant, bright, wise, astute, clever, sharp, knowledgeable, ingenious, perceptive, witty, resourceful, creative, quick, sagacious, *having a good head on one's shoulders, sensible. ANT. *stupid, moronic, dense, ignorant.*

intelligentsia *n.* literati, brains, geniuses, brain trust, intellectuals, academia.

intelligible *a.* clear, comprehensible, understandable, plain, distinct, unmistakable, unambiguous. ANT. *unintelligible, unclear, incomprehensible.*

intend *v.* plan, have in mind, mean, aim at, aspire to, propose, expect, design, figure on, plot, scheme, devise.

intended *a.* planned, designed, meant, devised, intentional, expected, set, prearranged, deliberate, premeditated. ANT. *unintentional, accidental, unplanned.*

intense *a.* concentrated, acute, strong, severe, powerful, deep, extreme, violent, sharp, fierce, potent, high, vivid, passionate, earnest, ardent, fervent, vigorous. ANT. *mild, light, weak, gentle.*

intensify *v.* concentrate, strengthen, deepen, sharpen, heighten, magnify, amplify, escalate, raise, *beef up, step up, redouble. ANT. *weaken, lighten, diminish.*

intensity *n.* force, concentration, strength, power, magnitude, severity, potency, vigor, depth, volume, ferocity, violence, sharpness, passion, earnestness, ardor, fervor. ANT. *weakness, lightness, emptiness.*

intensive *a.* concentrated, thorough, profound, exhaustive, strengthened, stepped-up, increased, heightened, comprehensive, in-depth. ANT. *weakened, diluted, diminished.*

intent *n.* intention, purpose, goal, aim, design.

intent *a.* determined, resolved, resolute, intense, concentrated, set, steadfast, committed, *hell-bent. ANT. *irresolute, wavering, hesitant.*

intention *n.* purpose, intent, goal, aim, design, plan, object, end, target.

intentional *a.* deliberate, planned, intended, designed, calculated, meant, willful, on purpose, premeditated, voluntary. ANT. *unintentional, accidental, unplanned.*

inter *v.* bury, entomb, lay to rest, inhume, consign to the grave. ANT. *exhume, dig up.*

intercede *v.* mediate, arbitrate, advocate, plead for, petition for, step in, intervene, interpose.

intercept *v.* stop, head off, cut off, catch, seize, arrest, check, confiscate, impound.

interchangeable *a.* switchable, identical, same, equal, convertible, synonymous, reciprocal, mutual.

intercourse *n.* **1.** COPULATION sexual relations, coitus, lovemaking, mating, carnal knowledge, "Making the beast with two backs."—Shakespeare. **2.** COMMUNICATION exchange, interchange, interplay, correspondence, connection, liaison.

interest *n.* **1.** CURIOSITY engagement, attention, engrossment, attraction, notice, regard, concern. **2.** SHARE claim, stake, investment, right, involvement, percentage. **3.** ADVANTAGE benefit, welfare, profit, gain. ANT. 1. *indifference, boredom, apathy.*

interesting *a.* engaging, engrossing, fascinating, riveting, entertaining, diverting, absorbing, stimulating, intriguing, enthralling, provocative, gripping. ANT. *boring, dull, insipid.*

interfere *v.* *butt in, intervene, meddle, intercede, obtrude, intrude, interpose, horn in, hinder, impede, obstruct.

interim *n.* meantime, interval, interlude, break, pause, interruption, hiatus, intermission.

interim *a.* temporary, stopgap, intervening, provisional, makeshift. ANT. *permanent, stable.*

interior *n.* inside, center, innards. ANT. *exterior.*

interior *a.* inner, internal, inside, inward, innermost, central. ANT. *exterior, outer.*

interject *v.* throw in, insert, interrupt, interpose, introduce.

interloper *n.* intruder, meddler, trespasser, busybody, outsider.

interlude *n.* pause, recess, break, intermission, rest, lull, interval, interim.

intermediary *n.* go-between, mediator, middleman, agent, medium, negotiator, arbitrator, intermediate, referee, interceder, broker.

intermediate *a.* intervening, in-between, halfway, middle, median, midway, intervening, compromising. ANT. *beginning, ending.*

interment *n.* burial, entombment, inhumation.

interminable *a.* endless, eternal, neverending, everlasting, limitless, ceaseless, continuous, incessant, nonstop, infinite, constant. ANT. *fleeting, finite, limited.*

intermingle *v.* mix, blend, combine, commingle, compound, merge, amalgamate, fuse.

intermission *n.* break, pause, recess, interim, interlude, breather, time-out, rest, lull, interruption.

intermittent *a.* sporadic, irregular, periodic, off and on, broken, now and then, occasional, alternate, infrequent. ANT. *regular, constant.*

internal *a.* inner, interior, within, inside, gut, innate, intrinsic. ANT. *external, outer.*

international *a.* worldwide, multinational, global, intercontinental, universal, cosmopolitan. ANT. *domestic, local.*

INTERNET *n.* [IN tur net] a national or international network of computers and computer networks. *Many people are making connections over the Internet.* SYN. computer network, *information superhighway, World Wide Web, the Web, the Net, medium, online network, cyberspace, *Infobahn, *virtual city, *virtual village, *global village.

WORD FIND

abandoned Web site no longer maintained: ghost site, orphan annie

ACK: chatting shorthand for "acknowledge address abreviation," such as .com or .org, at end of URL: domain

address, Web site: URL (Uniform Resource Locator)

advertisement, Web page: banner ad, pop-up ad

advertisement trading between Web sites: banner exchange

AFK: chatting shorthand for "away from keyboard"

animation and computation program: applet

articles, collection of related: newsgroup

ASAP: chatting shorthand for "as soon as possible"

BAK: chatting shorthand for "back at the keyboard"

BBN: chatting shorthand for "bye bye now"

BBS: bulletin board system

BCNU: chatting shorthand for "be seeing you"

BRB: chatting shorthand for "be right back"

blinking line on computer screen marking next character location: cursor

browse, search or move about on the Web: navigate, *surf, *cruise

browsing aid: browser

BTW: chatting shorthand for "by the way"

BWL: chatting shorthand for "bursting with laughter"

business deriving income via the Internet: e-business

button that brings one to previous Web page: back button

C&G: chatting shorthand for "chuckle and grin"

CNP: chatting shorthand for "continued in next post"

CYA: chatting shorthand for "see ya"

CYAL8R: chatting shorthand for "see ya later"

decoding of encrypted messages: decryption

device for photographing hard documents or graphics and transmitting them on to the Intenet: scanner

devious marketing trick using false keywords such as "sex" to draw search engines to a Web site: bait and switch

café with computers and Internet access: cybercafé

camera used to send video or pictures over Web: webcam

Capital letters, e-mailing or chatting using all: shouting

coding data into math for security: encryption

coding mathematics used to secure transactions: cryptography

college or other classroom learning over the Internet: distance learning

commands for creating Web pages, formatting: HTML (Hypertext Markup Language)

compressed file, Windows-based: Zip file, .zip file

communications allowing direct contact, two-way: interactive

connect to a network or Web site: log in, log on

connected to server or Internet: online

connector of networks, electronic: router

conversations, online medium where users can have real time: chat room

converse online in real time: chat; instant message

correspondence, electronic: e-mail

criminal destruction or disruption of Internet communications: cyberterrorism

decompress or open a Zip file: unzip

disconnected from server or Internet: offline

discussion forum: newsgroup

discussions, reading but not participating in: lurking

e-mail which must be downloaded, file sometimes sent with: attachment

failure of network resulting in frozen mouse or keyboard: crash; meltdown

fight between two or more people, online: *flame war

fighting verbally online: flaming

file page, online: Web page

fraud, online: cyberfraud

FYEO: chatting shorthand for "for your eyes only"

FYI: chatting shorthand for "for your information"

GG: chatting shorthand for "gotta go"

G/S?: chatting shorthand for "gay or straight?"

IC: chatting shorthand for "I see"

identification file automatically created and stored on hard drive after visiting Web site: cookie

identification marker used to legally protect original documents from unauthorized use: digital fingerprinting

ILY: chatting shorthand for "I love you"

IM: chatting shorthand for "instant message"

IMHO: chatting shorthand for "in my humble opinion"

IMO: chatting shorthand for "in my opinion"

frequent traveler through: *cybernaut, *internaut

identification number assigned to every computer on Internet: IP address

identify person online from e-mail address, program or utility that can: finger

FAQS: frequently asked questions

format change, rewriting to create a: encoding

handwriting recognition software: Graffiti

head page of Web site: home page

host computer, network's: server

image or the mechanism that creates it, standardized, compressed: JPG (Joint Photographic Experts Group), .jpg

image transformation effects: morphing

inaccessible due to technical difficulty: down

inexperienced newcomer to: *newbie

interconnection of two or more computers: network

junk e-mail, unwanted advertisements or: spam

K: chatting shorthand for "kiss"

KIT: chatting shorthand for "keep in touch"

know-it-all, Internet: geek

large or very powerful computer: mainframe, Cray

L8R: chatting shorthand for "later"

lettering style: font

library of stored files: archive

link leading directly to a favorite site: bookmark

link made up of glowing text or graphics that when clicked leads directly to another Web page or site: hyperlink, hotlink

links to related documents, text system used to create: hypertext

list of options to choose on screen: menu, drop-down menu

log of Web sites recently visited: history list

LOL: chatting shorthand for "laughing out loud"

loss of data during transmission: bitloss

M/F?: chatting shorthand for "male or female?"

magazine, electronic: e-zine

mail downloading tool and clock setter: bot, autobot

mailing list server: Listserve

mail sorter used to block unwanted advertisements: mail filter

mailing to a single recipient to wreak havoc on server, intentional mass: flooding, mail bomb

mail that is undeliverable, to return: bounce

manners, online: *netiquette

medium, computer: cyberspace

meeting with participants on video, Internet: video conferencing message medium: bulletin board

message, put up a: post

miniaturized picture clicked on to display a larger version: thumbnail

money, electronic: *cybercash, e-money

motion picture file: MPEG (Motion Picture Experts Group)

multimedia links allowing the downloading of graphcis, videos, or audio files: hypermedia

music storage and transmission in digital format, standard of: MP3

music (MP3 files) downloading and trading application: Napster

network confined to a single building or floor: LAN (Local Area Network)

network computer providing multiple services, such as e-mail, for other computers: host

network of discussion groups called newsgroups: USENET

network, in-house company: intranet

network, individual computer connected to a: node

network, international: World Wide Web, the Web

networking method used in small areas: ethernet

netgroups, giant network of: Usenet

NTMY: chatting shorthand for "nice to meet you"

OIC: chatting shorthand for "oh, I see"

OMG: chatting shorthand for "oh my god!"

online journal or forum with links to communicate with participants: blog, Web log

overloaded data path resulting in no or slow response from server: congestion

PM: chatting shorthand for "private message"

PMJI: chatting shorthand for "pardon my jumping in"

portion of data transmitted or received, one: packet

programming wizard: *hacker, *cracker

protocol for transmission and reception, data: HTTP (Hypertext Transfer Protocol)

protocol of Internet, standard communications: TCP/IP (Transmission Control Protocol/Internet)

record of activity on a Web site: log

reload Web page for updated content: refresh

representation or picture of specific item that is clicked to activate program or link: icon

ROTF: chatting shorthand for "rolling on the floor"

screen portion one must scroll down to see: below the fold

screen presentation without toolbars, menus, borders: kiosk mode; presentation mode

search system: search engine

searches new Internet resources, program that: crawler, bot, spider

section of a Web page, separate or divided: frame

sex on, pseudo: *cybersex

sexual materials found on: *cyberporn

shopping mall, online: e-mall

simulation: virtual

simulation of reality: virtual reality

software copying, illegal: piracy

software, free: shareware

stealing a Web page and its files for unauthorized use: pagejacking

storage disk, data and graphics: Zip Disk

storage and shrinkage, data: compression

store, compress multiple files as one: archive

storehouse of related data: database

store of Web files on hard drive used for quicker access to previously visited Web sites: cache

symbols illustrating sender's emotional state, shorthand: emoticons

SYS: chatting shorthand for "see you soon"

talk medium and meeting place: chat room

talking with others online in real time: chatting, instant messaging

television online service: WebTV

transfer file from another's computer to yours: download

transfer file to another's computer from yours: upload

transmission channel using fiber-optic or coaxial cable, high speed, high capacity: broadband

transmission circuit superior to regular phone circuit: DSL (Digital Subscriber Line)

transmission service via telephone lines: dial-up

TTYL: chatting shorthand for "talk to you later"

video data transfer technique, live: streaming

Web sites, related and linked: Web ring

virus disguised as a program, hard drive-erasing: Trojan Horse

viruses, program that weeds out: anti-virus

virus-safe programming language used for Internet use: Java

virus, self-replicating: worm

visits to Web site, tallied: hits

WB: chatting shorthand for "welcome back"

Web site architect or graphics designer: Web designer

Web site manager: Webmaster

wire-free Internet access: wireless

wireless Internet access unit: wi-fi

WWW: World Wide Web

SEE COMPUTER

interpret v. 1. CONSTRUE read, understand, view, define, explain, explicate, clarify, shed light on, spell out, illuminate. 2. TRANSLATE transcribe, paraphrase.

interpretation n. understanding, reading, slant, perception, meaning, definition, explanation, view.

interrogate v. question, ask, probe, cross-examine, quiz, query, grill, pump, *give the third degree, inquire, *pick one's brains.

interrupt v. 1. INTRUDE *butt in, break in, cut in, *chime in, interject, inject, horn in, speak out of turn, obtrude, disturb, interfere. 2. STOP suspend, halt, discontinue, break off.

intersect v. cross, traverse, bisect, divide, cross-cut.

intersperse v. sprinkle, strew, scatter, pepper, distribute, diffuse, disseminate, broadcast.

intertwine v. entwine, tie, interweave, braid, crisscross, cross, mesh, reticulate.

interval n. pause, rest, break, recess, intermission, hiatus, interim, gap, space, period, spell, lull.

intervene v. step in, intercede, interfere, mediate, arbitrate, interpose, come between, obtrude, meddle.

interview n. *Q and A, inquiry, press conference, probe, talk, conference, exchange, meeting, parley, dialogue, *tête-à-tête, examination, hearing.

interviewer n. questioner, interrogator, inquirer, inquisitor, prober.

intestines n. bowels, guts, viscera, entrails, innards, alimentary canal.

intimacy n. closeness, fellowship, communion, friendship, understanding, acquaintance, confidentiality, sharing, disclosing, chumminess, familiarity, affection. ANT. *alienation, isolation, aloofness, estrangement*.

intimate v. suggest, announce, state, *tip off, hint at, tell, *let the cat out of the bag, *spill the beans, leak, insinuate, imply, allude.

intimate a. 1. PERSONAL private, confidential, privy, secret, innermost, *gut. 2. CLOSE familiar, friendly, acquainted, dear, chummy, personal, bosom. 3. COZY romantic, quiet, comfortable, warm, snug. 4. SEXUAL carnal, adulterous, erotic, impure, lustful. ANT. *1. public. 2. distant, remote, aloof, formal. 3. crowded, loud, uncomfortable*.

intimation n. suggestion, hint, clue, inkling, allusion, insinuation, implication, tip, innuendo.

intimidate v. scare, frighten, cow, threaten, daunt, bully, unnerve, terrify, terrorize, awe, appall, silence, coerce, strong-arm, twist one's arm, put the fear of God into.

intimidating a. threatening, inhibiting, demoralizing, scary, frightening, daunting, terrifying, unnerving, emasculating, silencing, powerful, formidable, commanding respect. ANT. *reassuring, conciliatory*.

intolerable a. insufferable, unbearable, unendurable, agonizing, excruciating, unacceptable, too much, extreme, monstrous, unreasonable, outrageous. ANT. *tolerable, acceptable*.

intolerant a. bigoted, illiberal, closed-minded, narrow-minded, prejudiced, uncharitable, inconsiderate, biased, chauvinistic, sexist, racist, *homophobic, xenophobic, misanthropic, contemptuous, disdainful, arrogant. ANT. *tolerant, liberal, open-minded*.

intonation n. modulation, inflection.

intoxicated a. drunk, inebriated, tipsy, besotted, soused. ANT. *sober, *on the wagon*.

INTRACTABLE a. [in TRAK tuh bul] unmanageable, uncontrollable or stubborn. *The two-year-old is famous for his intractable demeanor.* SYN. unmanageable, uncontrollable, stubborn, disobedient, rebellious, obstinate, ungovernable, difficult, headstrong, contrary, unruly, wild, intransigent. ANT. *obedient, docile, compliant, easy*.

INTRANSIGENT a. [in TRAN si junt] uncompromising and stubborn. *Smith was intransigent; nobody could negotiate with him and win.* SYN. uncompromising, stubborn, obstinate, mulish, pigheaded, unbending, unyielding, rigid, steadfast, die-hard, resolute, *hard-nosed, persistent. ANT. *compromising, yielding, flexible, *easy*.

INTREPID a. [in TREP id] fearless, courageous. *The intrepid explorers bushwhacked their way deeper into the jungle.* SYN. fearless, courageous, brave, dauntless, bold, daring, *gutsy, *ballsy, adventurous, valiant, lionhearted, game, plucky, heroic. ANT. *cowardly, frightened, mousy, *wimpy, craven*.

intricate *a.* complex, complicated, involved, convoluted, knotty, labyrinthine, elaborate, sophisticated, thorny, perplexing, tough. ANT. *simple, uninvolved, easy.*

intrigue *n.* plotting, scheme, machination, conspiracy, maneuver, finagling, manipulation, trickery, double-dealing, cabal.

intrigue *v.* **1.** PLOT scheme, machinate, conspire, maneuver, finagle, manipulate, trick, double-deal. **2.** INTEREST fascinate, pique one's interest, attract, grab, captivate, excite, appeal, draw, arouse.

intriguing *a.* interesting, fascinating, captivating, exciting, arousing curiosity, thought-provoking, enthralling, provocative, riveting. ANT. *boring, mundane.*

INTRINSIC *a.* [in TRIN sik] naturally or inherently belonging. *His success was partially due to an intrinsic aggressiveness.* SYN. inherent, natural, essential, innate, internal, inbred, native, inherited, built-in, basic, fundamental, constitutional. ANT. *extrinsic, external, outer.*

introduce *v.* **1.** ACQUAINT present, familiarize. **2.** START begin, open, *get the ball rolling, launch, set in motion, usher in, lead off, *kick off, initiate. **3.** PUT IN insert, add, inject, interject, work in, enter, instill, infuse.

introduction *n.* **1.** START beginning, opening, lead, commencement, *intro, launching, initiation. **2.** PREFACE foreword, prologue, preamble, prelude. ANT. *1. end. 2. afterword.*

introductory *a.* opening, beginning, starting, initial, preliminary, first, inaugural, preparatory, prefatory. ANT. *concluding, final.*

INTROSPECTIVE *a.* [IN truh SPEC tiv] observing one's own thoughts, feelings, inner self, etc. *Joe was always analyzing his own mind; he was introspective.* SYN. introverted, self-analyzing, self-examining, soul-searching, pensive, contemplative, meditative, self-occupied, consciousness-raising, in deep thought. ANT. *outer-directed, extroverted.*

introvert *n.* bookworm, loner, *lone wolf, *wallflower, quiet person. ANT. *extrovert.*

introverted *a.* introspective, reserved, bookish, retiring, shy, bashful, taciturn, quiet, solitary, preferring one's own company. ANT. *extroverted, outgoing.*

intrude *v.* obtrude, invade, interfere, barge in, *horn in, infringe, meddle, *butt in, interpose, *gate-crash, encroach, trespass, interlope.

intruder *n.* interloper, trespasser, thief, burglar, prowler, infiltrator, *gate-crasher, invader, unwelcome visitor.

intrusive *a.* obtrusive, invasive, unwelcome, unwanted, meddlesome, interfering, *nosy, officious, *overstepping one's bounds. ANT. *welcome, invited, wanted.*

intuition *n.* sense, sixth sense, hunch, feeling, instinct, insight, *feeling in one's bones, *gut instinct, *vibes, inkling, perception, discernment, apprehension.

intuitive *a.* instinctive, *gut, innate, natural, inherent, automatic, *seat of the pants, perceptive, psychic. ANT. *learned, practiced, dense.*

inundate *v.* flood, deluge, engulf, drown, swamp, submerge, overwhelm, overpower, glut, bury.

inure *v.* habituate, accustom, harden, desensitize, season, toughen, temper, acclimate.

invade *v.* encroach, trespass, attack, assault, assail, strike, storm, swarm, blitz, occupy, overrun, intrude, interlope, *gate-crash.

invalid *n.* sick person, convalescent, cripple, shut-in, patient.

invalid *a.* **1.** NULL AND VOID unenforceable, impotent, nonviable, inoperative, useless, worthless, not binding. **2.** FALSE unfounded, wrong, untrue, fallacious, baseless, unsubstantiated, unproven. **3.** SICKLY weak, feeble, bedridden, disabled, crippled, infirm, frail. ANT. *1. valid, viable, binding. 2. true, substantiated, correct. 3. strong, able-bodied.*

invalidate *v.* void, nullify, annul, cancel, repeal, countermand, revoke, negate, disqualify, quash. ANT. *validate.*

invaluable *a.* valuable, priceless, precious, indispensable, helpful, *worth its weight in gold. ANT. *worthless.*

invariable *a.* unvarying, unchanging, constant, steady, consistent, unwavering, stable, regular, uniform, unbroken, undeviating. ANT. *variable, varying, changing, inconstant.*

invasion *n.* attack, assault, strike, storm, encroachment, trespass, incursion, intrusion, onslaught, infringement, offensive, blitz.

INVECTIVE *n.* [in VEK tiv] a verbal attack, insults, criticism. *He continued his invective until she was in tears.* SYN. verbal attack, verbal abuse, censure, tongue-lashing, vilification, diatribe, tirade, disparagement, condemnation, harsh words, sarcasm.

inveigh *v.* verbally attack, rail against, assail, vituperate, censure, denounce, vilify, criticize, scold, castigate, condemn, remonstrate.

inveigle *v.* entice, lure, seduce, *suck in, tempt,

tantalize, manipulate, cajole, bait, *string along, *rope in, *lead on.

invent v. **1.** CREATE devise, come up with, think up, originate, design, shape, conceive, forge, fabricate, improvise, concoct, develop, fashion. **2.** LIE fabricate, fib, prevaricate, *tell a white lie, distort, trump up, make up.

invention n. **1.** CREATION innovation, concoction, *brainchild, original, design, composition, fabrication, construction, contrivance, formulation, discovery. "Bringing out the secrets of nature and applying them for the happiness of man."—Thomas Edison. **2.** LIE fabrication, fib, prevarication, white lie, distortion, falsehood, *tall tale.

inventive a. creative, ingenious, imaginative, resourceful, artistic, gifted, *brainy, visionary, clever, constructive, productive, fertile, *having a Da Vinci-like mind. ANT. unimaginative, unoriginal.

inventor n. creator, originator, father, discoverer, designer, deviser, innovator, craftsman, builder, tinkerer, pioneer.

inventory n. stock, goods, supply, reserve, backlog, stockpile, store, backlist, catalog, itemized list, survey, record, itemization, tally, count, tabulation, census, account, register.

invert v. reverse, turn inside out, convert, upend, overturn, transpose, flip over.

inverse a. reversed, inverted, opposite, back to front, turned, contrary, transposed. ANT. obverse.

invest v. **1.** INVEST MONEY venture, speculate, risk, put money into, *plow profits back into, entrust, *salt away. **2.** GRANT POWER empower, authorize, confer, sanction, enable, license, entrust, ordain, charge. ANT. 1. divest. 2. divest, strip of power.

investigate v. look into, inquire, probe, examine, explore, inspect, research, delve into, review, nose around, scrutinize, sift, muckrake, *check out, *case.

investigation n. inquiry, probe, inspection, inquest, *fact-finding mission, search, analysis, review, exploration, scrutiny, study.

investigator n. examiner, analyst, reviewer, inspector, inquirer, inquisitor, fact finder, researcher, detective, *sleuth, *private eye.

investment n. financial venture, security, speculation, hedge against inflation, risk, down payment on one's future, stocks, bonds, mutual fund, commodities, retirement fund, IRA. SEE BANK, ECONOMY, MONEY

investor n. venture capitalist, capitalist, backer, banker, shareholder, stockholder, financier, speculator, developer, risk-taker.

INVETERATE a. [in VET ur it] habitual, long-standing, chronic. She was an inveterate liar. SYN. habitual, long-standing, chronic, deeply rooted, long-established, ingrained, deep-seated, incurable, entrenched, hardcore, dyed-in-the-wool. ANT. reformed, cured.

invidious a. insulting, offensive, hateful, malicious, spiteful, hostile, odious, slighting, baleful, discriminatory. ANT. complimentary, flattering, sweet.

invigorating a. energizing, enlivening, refreshing, stimulating, vitalizing, restorative, bracing, strengthening, animating. ANT. tiring, somnolent, weakening.

invincible a. unconquerable, unbeatable, indestructible, indomitable, invulnerable, insuperable, impregnable, mighty, powerful, inviolable. ANT. vulnerable, weak, conquerable.

invisible a. imperceptible, imperceivable, impalpable, intangible, hidden, indiscernible, out of sight, unseen, transparent. ANT. visible, perceivable, palpable.

invitation n. bidding, summons, call, request, solicitation.

invite v. ask for, beckon, summon, request, solicit, bid, court, woo, petition.

inviting a. alluring, enticing, tempting, attractive, captivating, magnetic, seductive, appealing, welcoming, beguiling. ANT. repulsive, repellent, forbidding.

in vitro a. outside the womb, test-tube, artificial.

invoice n. bill, itemized bill, account, bill of lading, statement, manifest, itemization.

invoke v. call on, call forth, summon, petition, entreat, request, implore, supplicate, appeal to, conjure, solicit.

involuntary a. unintentional, reflexive, automatic, instinctive, spontaneous, unpremeditated, unthinking, uncalculated, forced. ANT. voluntary, intentional, calculated.

involve v. include, comprise, engage, contain, incorporate, concern, affect, entail, encompass, comprehend, implicate.

invulnerable a. indestructible. SEE INVINCIBLE

iota n. jot, speck, scintilla, bit, shred, whiff, mite, smidgen, atom, dot, particle, fleck.

IRASCIBLE a. [i RAS uh bul] quick-tempered or easily angered. Mike was irascible; we walked on eggshells around him. SYN. quick-tempered, easily angered, touchy, testy, irritable, bad-tempered, *short-fused, grouchy, cantankerous, grumpy, ornery, crabby, snappish. ANT. *easygoing, good-humored, mild-mannered, serene.*

irate *a.* angry, mad, furious, infuriated, incensed, *up in arms, livid, indignant, wrathful, inflamed, *foaming at the mouth, *gone ballistic. ANT. *placated, euphoric, joyful.* SEE ANGRY

ire *n.* anger, rage, fury, indignation, wrath, displeasure, choler, vexation, dudgeon, passion, irritation, *Irish. SEE ANGER

irk *v.* annoy, irritate, *bug, aggravate, nettle, peeve, bother, harass, fret, gall, *get on one's nerves, *try one's patience, *get under one's skin.

irksome *a.* annoying, irritating, aggravating, nettlesome, bothersome, vexing, troubling, troublesome, wearisome, tiring, problematic. ANT. *simple, solvable.*

iron *a.* hard, strong, powerful, tough, firm, unyielding, unbending, rigid, steel, stony, cruel, merciless. ANT. *soft, weak, yielding.*

ironclad *a.* unalterable, fixed.

IRONIC *a.* [i RON ik] opposite of or incongruous with what is expressed or expected. *He said he loved steamed clams, but he was being ironic—clams really disgusted him.* SYN. sarcastic, mocking, contradictory, paradoxical, double-edged, sardonic, satirical, unexpected, surprising. ANT. *straightforward, frank, earnest.*

irony *n.* double meaning, contradiction, sarcasm, incongruity, paradox, satire, mocking, lampoon, twist, wit. "Jesting hidden behind gravity."—John Weiss.

irrational *a.* senseless, unthinking, unreasonable, foolish, illogical, crazy, mindless, unwise, stupid, unsound, unscientific, half-baked, *cockamamy, idiotic. ANT. *rational, sane, sensible, wise.*

irreconcilable *a.* irreparable, unresolvable, conflicting, hostile, incompatible, contrary, at odds, intransigent, inflexible. ANT. *resolvable, compatible.*

irrefutable *a.* undeniable, unquestionable, certain, indisputable, sure, proven, incontrovertible, beyond a shadow of a doubt. ANT. *debatable, questionable, moot.*

irregular *a.* **1.** VARIABLE erratic, uneven, fitful, random, sporadic, inconsistent, changeable, disordered, spasmodic. **2.** ANOMALOUS abnormal, deviant, unusual, odd, unexpected, strange, eccentric, singular, peculiar, quirky. **3.** UNEVEN asymmetrical, crooked, variable.

ANT. *1. regular, consistent, even. 2. normal, typical, usual. 3. even, symmetrical.*

irrelevant *a.* impertinent, immaterial, unrelated, beside the point, not germane, unconnected, inapplicable, neither here nor there, extraneous. ANT. *relevant, pertinent, germane.*

irreligious *a.* atheistic, impious, faithless, agnostic, unholy, ungodly, profane, heathen, pagan. ANT. *religious, pious, faithful.*

irreparable *a.* beyond repair, irrevocable, ruined, irretrievable, *consigned to the scrap heap, *done, *shot, *kaput, hopeless. ANT. *repairable, salvageable.*

irrepressible *a.* unrestrainable, insuppressible, uncontrollable, uninhibited, unbridled, vivacious, lively, effervescent, buoyant. ANT. *disheartened, dispirited, *down.*

irreproachable *a.* beyond reproach, blameless, faultless, inculpable, unblemished, above suspicion, *squeaky clean, virtuous, innocent, pure, upright. ANT. *reproachable, to blame.*

irresistible *a.* overwhelming, overpowering, powerful, potent, compelling, invincible, unconquerable, fascinating, charming, alluring, captivating, seductive. ANT. *resistible, powerless.*

irresolute *a.* wavering, indecisive, vacillating, undecided, dubious, wishy-washy, doubtful, hesitant, undetermined, *hot and cold, half-hearted. ANT. *resolute, resolved, firm, determined.*

irresponsible *a.* careless, unreliable, undependable, devil-may-care, untrustworthy, lax, immature, unaccountable, reckless, capricious. ANT. *responsible, dependable, reliable.*

IRREVERENT *a.* [ir REV ur unt] disrespectful. *With today's irreverent comedians, even the pope is the subject of dirty jokes.* SYN. disrespectful, contemptuous, mocking, sneering, *wise, rude, impudent, insolent, insulting, *smart-alecky, impious, blasphemous, profane. ANT. *reverent, respectful, civil.*

irrevocable *a.* irreversible, unchangeable, fixed, final, unalterable, permanent, irretrievable, *carved in stone. ANT. *reversible, changeable.*

irrigate *v.* water, bathe, wash, flush, flood, sprinkle, soak, drench.

irritable *a.* grouchy, touchy, cantankerous, irascible, crabby, testy, moody, snappy, grumbling, quick-tempered, petulant, grumpy. ANT. *good-humored, good-natured, even-tempered.*

irritate v. **1.** ANNOY *bug, agitate, nettle, disturb, *get under one's skin, try one's patience, exasperate, irk, *drive one up a wall, peeve, *get on one's nerves, plague. **2.** MAKE SORE inflame, aggravate, hurt, chafe, sting, rub, worsen. ANT. *1. please, delight, humor. 2. relieve, soothe.*

Islamic a. Muslim, Moslem, Muhammadan, Mohammedan, Shiite, Sunni. SEE RELIGION

island n. land mass, atoll, islet, isle, cay, key, reef, sand bar.

WORD FIND
group of: archipelago
river, in a: holm

isolate v. seclude, separate, segregate, dissociate, sequester, set apart, confine, remove, quarantine.

isolated a. secluded, separated, segregated, dissociated, sequestered, confined, set apart, alone, lonely, removed, remote, cloistered, in quarantine. ANT. *public, central.*

isolation n. seclusion, separation, segregation, dissociation, sequestration, loneliness, solitude, confinement, removal, quarantine, cloister.

issue n. **1.** SUBJECT topic, matter, question at hand, bone of contention, controversy, problem. **2.** RESULT consequence, outcome, end, upshot, conclusion, effect. **3.** INSTALLMENT copy, number.

issue v. **1.** PUT OUT give out, distribute, circulate, dispense, disseminate, deliver. **2.** EMIT pour forth, emanate, exude, gush, effuse, stream, ooze.

itch n. **1.** URGE TO SCRATCH prickling sensation, tickling, irritation, crawling sensation. **2.** DESIRE craving, urge, yen, thirst, hunger, appetite, hankering, passion.

item n. article, thing, part, piece, bit, element, matter, paragraph, story, feature.

itemize v. detail, enumerate, count, inventory, tally, list, record, specify, spell out, codify.

itinerant a. wandering, roaming, traveling, roving, transient, rambling, journeying, wayfaring, vagabond, nomadic, migratory. ANT. *rooted, settled.*

itinerary n. route, course, way, tour, path, plan, schedule, agenda, *game plan.

J

jab v. poke, thrust, punch, hit, strike, prod, stab.

jabber v. chatter, gibber, prattle, babble, *run off at the mouth, yak, prate, palaver.

jacket n. **1.** COVER case, wrapper, wrapping, sheath, skin, envelope. **2.** COAT blazer, windbreaker.

WORD FIND

black, waist-length, wide-lapelled: Eton jacket

Eskimo: anorak

fringed deerskin: buckskin jacket

khaki-colored with four large front pockets: safari jacket, bush jacket

knitted, sweaterlike: cardigan

leather flight jacket: bomber jacket

lightweight jacket of waist-length: golf jacket, windbreaker

parka with hood: snorkel

plaid wool: lumber jacket

seaman's: pea jacket, pea coat, reefer

sleeveless: bolero

winter, insulated: parka

woman's loose jacket: paletot

wool with blanket-like patterns: mackinaw

World War II army jacket: Eisenhower jacket, battle jacket

SEE COAT

JADED a. [JAY did] wearied or worn out, as from overindulgence. *He saw it all and grew jaded.* SYN. wearied, worn out, tired, sated, played out, exhausted, cloyed, surfeited, dulled, gorged, inured, bored. ANT. *enthusiastic, interested.*

jagged a. broken, serrated, rough, uneven, ragged, notched, saw-toothed, crenelated, ridged, denticulate. ANT. *smooth, even, level.*

jail n. prison, penitentiary, house of correction, *slammer, lockup, brig, stockade, hoosegow, *clink, *cooler, penal institution, *the big house, *pokey, *the academy.

jail v. imprison, lock up, incarcerate, put behind bars, cage, hold, confine, intern, impound. ANT. *release, free, liberate.*

jailer n. warden, correctional officer, guard, turnkey, gaoler.

jalopy n. automobile, car, *bucket of bolts, *junker, *clunker, *boat, wreck, *wheezer, *flivver, derelict, *heap, *lemon, *rattletrap. SEE AUTOMOBILE

jam n. trouble, scrape, bind, *hot water, *pickle, hole, predicament, mess, plight.

jam v. **1.** SQUEEZE IN cram, ram, pack, stuff, press, wedge, tamp, *squish, squash, overcrowd, *stuff to the gills. **2.** CLOG plug, obstruct, congest, stick, *gum up the works, *bottleneck.

jamboree n. celebration, party, gathering, revelry, festival, outing, carnival, jubilee, *wingding.

jangle n. clang, rattle, ring, reverberation, jingle, clatter, clangor, cacophony, racket.

jangle v. clang, rattle, ring, reverberate, jingle, clatter, chime, crash.

janitor n. custodian, caretaker, cleaning man, *super, handyman, maintenance man, superintendent.

jar n. vessel, container, bottle, receptacle, jug.

jar v. **1.** SHAKE vibrate, jog, jounce, jolt, shock, jerk, rattle, rock, jiggle. **2.** *FAZE shock, disquiet, disturb, upset, unsettle, shake up, surprise, discompose.

jargon n. **1.** LINGO vernacular, cant, argot, parlance, tongue, slang, idiom, dialect, phraseology, shop talk, *officialese, legalese. **2.** GIBBERISH gobbledygook, mumbo jumbo, nonsense, blather, babble, drivel, twaddle.

jaundiced a. prejudiced, biased, partial, narrow-minded, warped, embittered, jealous, envious, hostile, critical. ANT. *impartial, fairminded.*

jaunt n. short trip, excursion, outing, drive, tour, cruise, stroll, *spin, day trip, airing.

jaunty a. sprightly, carefree, buoyant, self-confident, bouncy, frisky, pert, lighthearted, lively, breezy, debonair.

jazz n. music, bop, bebop, fusion jazz, improvisational music, swing, Dixieland, jive, ragtime, barrelhouse, hot jazz, cool jazz, boogie-woogie. "A thrilling communion with the primitive soul, or an earsplitting bore."—Winthrop Sargent. "Music that will endure as long as people hear it through their feet instead of their brains."—John Sousa.

WORD FIND

nonsensical vocalizations: scat singing

SEE MUSIC

jealous a. **1.** ENVIOUS green-eyed, green with envy, begrudging, resentful, desirous, covetous. **2.** WATCHFUL guarded, proprietary, possessive, protective, vigilant, wary. ANT. *2. trusting.*

jealousy n. envy, *green-eyed monster, resentment, grudge, begrudging, covetousness, spite, distrust, paranoia, suspicion. "Jealousy is all the fun you think they had."—Erica Jong. "The fear or apprehension of superiority."—William Shenstone.

jeans *n.* pants, Levis, Lees, dungarees.

jeer *v.* mock, taunt, hoot, heckle, scoff, ridicule, sneer, laugh at, tease, hector, deride, boo, hiss. ANT. *cheer, applaud, praise.*

jeopardize *v.* endanger, imperil, hazard, risk, put in jeopardy, chance, threaten, tempt fate.

jeopardy *n.* danger, hazard, peril, trouble, *double-trouble, threat, menace, insecurity, exposure, vulnerability, liability. ANT. *safety, security.*

jerk *n. Sl.* *dink, fool, *bozo, *chump, *creep, *dork, *dweeb, *goober.

jerk *v.* pull, yank, twist, move, thrust, tug, push, shove, jolt, start.

jerrybuilt *a.* shoddy, flimsy, defective, rickety, unstable, *junky, faulty, unsound, thrown together, cheap. ANT. *solid, sturdy, sound.*

jest *n.* joke, gag, wisecrack, witticism, *funny, bon mot, *one-liner, prank, banter, riposte.

jest *v.* joke, kid, fool, quip, poke fun at, *josh, *pull one's leg, wisecrack, tease, banter, gibe.

jester *n.* joker, clown, comic, comedian, buffoon, humorist, wit, *card, zany, prankster, *cutup, *stand-up.

Jesus Christ *n.* Son of God, Savior, teacher, prophet, Messiah, Lord, spiritual leader. SEE GOD, RELIGION

jet *n.* **1.** SEE AIRCRAFT **2.** SPURT gush, stream, fountain, spout, spray, squirt, spring, geyser, spritz.

jet *v.* spurt, gush, stream, spout, spew, spray, squirt, spring, shoot, discharge, issue.

jet set *n.* beautiful people, high society, glitterarti, fashionable society, beau monde, elite, *upper crust.

jettison *v.* eject, dump, get rid of, chuck, expel, cast off, discard, unload, *deep-six, heave.

jetty *n.* breakwater, sea wall, barrier, groin, riprap.

Jew *n.* Semite, Israelite, Hebrew, Judaist, Hasid. SEE RELIGION

jewel *n.* **1.** GEM stone, precious stone, semiprecious stone, *rock, birthstone, bauble, baguette, bijou, diamond, emerald, opal, ruby, sapphire, pearl. SEE GEM **2.** RARITY treasure, prize, find, pride and joy, work of art, one in a million.

jewelry *n.* jewels, gems, precious stones, semiprecious stones, bauble, ornament, chain, necklace, choker, locket, cameo, brooch,

pin, ring, earring, nose ring, tiara, crown, bracelet, anklet, beads, bijou, chatelaine, rhinestone, adornment, trinket, gewgaw, gimcrack, *ice. "Orators of love."—Samuel Daniel. SEE GEM

Jewish *a.* Semitic, Hebrew, Israelite, Hasidic. SEE RELIGION

WORD FIND

languages of Ashkenazic Jews: Yiddish

Jezebel *n.* whore, hussy, strumpet, harlot, loose woman, wanton, trollop, witch, harridan.

jibe *v.* harmonize, correspond, match, fit, accord, agree, dovetail, conform, square, go together.

jiffy *n.* instant, moment, second, *blink of an eye, *heartbeat, *two shakes of a lamb's tail, flash, twinkling. ANT. *eternity, lifetime.*

jiggle *v.* wiggle, shake, shimmy, twitch, joggle, jig, bib, vibrate, rock, bounce.

jilt *v.* reject, dump, cast off, drop, *give the mitten, spurn, break off, forsake, *give the brush off, ditch, *drop a bomb on.

jingle *v.* clang, tinkle, tingle, jangle, ring, clang, chime, ding, tintinnabulate.

jinx *n.* curse, spell, hex, invocation, evil eye, *whammy, *double whammy, voodoo, hoodoo, black magic, *bête noire.

jitterbug *n.* dance, Lindy Hop, swing dance.

jitters *n.* shakes, shivers, anxiety, nervousness, trembling, quaking, *heebie-jeebies, *willies, quivering.

jittery *a.* shaky, nervous, anxious, trembling, quaking, quivering, tense, uptight, uneasy. ANT. *relaxed, calm.*

job *n.* **1.** TASK chore, work, project, business, assignment, mission, responsibility, duty, obligation, role, charge, function, errand, venture, commission, burden. **2.** EMPLOYMENT occupation, business, livelihood, career, trade, post, position, vocation, profession, craft, *racket.

jobless *a.* unemployed, out of work, laid off, idle, collecting unemployment benefits. ANT. *employed.*

jock *n. Sl.* **1.** ATHLETE *macho man, letterman. **2.** JOCK STRAP athletic supporter.

jockey *n.* rider, equestrian.

jockey *v.* race, ride, steer, maneuver, direct, position, push, jostle.

jocular *a.* joking, humorous, funny, jesting, playful, comical, fun, prankish, droll, jocose, lighthearted, jovial, sportive. ANT. *serious, grave, grim, solemn.*

jocund *a.* cheerful, gay, blithe, in high spirits,

lighthearted, breezy, happy-go-lucky, optimistic, buoyant, genial, merry. ANT. *depressed, sad, miserable.*

jog *v.* **1.** RUN trot, speedwalk, dash. SEE RUN **2.** SHAKE jerk, nudge, jostle, poke, jab, prod, bump, tap.

John Hancock *n.* autograph, name. SEE SIGNATURE

join *v.* **1.** CONNECT fasten, unite, fuse, link, couple, merge, attach, combine, unify, hitch, splice, tie, consolidate, bind. **2.** ENROLL sign up, enlist, associate with, become a member, subscribe to. ANT. *1. disconnect, detach, divide, separate.*

joint *n.* connection, hinge, coupling, junction, link, union, articulation, bend. ANT. *single, individual.*

joint *n. Sl.* marijuana cigarette, *reefer, *doobie, *joy stick, *goofbutt, *J, *jay, *mooter, *ju-ju, *log, *number, *twist. SEE MARIJUANA
WORD FIND
burned-down end piece requiring clip to hold: *roach
cigar filled with marijuana or marijuana and cocaine: *blunt
cigar filled with marijuana and crack: *woolah
cigar laced with marijuana and dipped in malt liquor: *B-40
clip used to hold burned-down end: *roach clip
smoke, to: *fly Mexican airlines, *puff the dragon, *toke, *toke up

joint *a.* combined, mutual, cooperative, shared, united, concerted, allied, collaborative, collective, hand in hand.

joke *n.* **1.** JEST *one-liner, gag, witticism, wisecrack, quip, humor, bon mot, *funny, drollery, pun, *rib-tickler, prank, *knee-slapper. "The cayenne of conversation."—Paul Chatfield. "Sport to one . . . death to another."—William Hazlitt. **2.** LAUGHING-STOCK butt, object of ridicule, target, clown, goat. SEE LAUGHTER

joker *n.* jester, clown, comic, comedian, *stand-up, humorist, wisecracker, prankster, *card, *cutup, wit, *punster.

jolly *a.* high-spirited, merry, jovial, cheerful, playful, mirthful, jocular, joyous, glad, gleeful, gay, lively, exuberant. ANT. *depressed, miserable, somber.*

jolt *n.* jerk, shake, blow, jar, start, jump, jounce, bump, jog, slam, lurch, shock, surprise, *bolt out of the blue, bombshell.

jolt *v.* jerk, shake, jar, start, jounce, bump, jog,

slam, jostle, rock, shock, surprise, stun, stagger, *take one's breath away, shake up, startle.

jostle *v.* bump, push, elbow, shove, nudge, crash, shoulder, crowd, scuffle, *bulldoze, herd.

journal *n.* chronicle, record, diary, narrative, history, memoir, log, daybook, account, minutes, ledger, register.

journalism *n.* news-gathering, reporting, writing, news, print media, fourth estate. "The first power in the land."—Samuel Bowles. SEE NEWSPAPER, MAGAZINE

journalist *n.* reporter, newspaperman/woman, correspondent, writer, newshound, columnist. "Alarmists."—George Riddell. "Puppets. They simply respond to the pull of the most powerful strings."—Lyndon Johnson. SEE NEWSPAPER, MAGAZINE

journey *n.* trip, wayfaring, tour, excursion, travel, expedition, odyssey, voyage, drive, journey, peregrination, trek, cruise, safari, adventure, junket, hike.

journey *v.* travel, take a trip, tour, voyage, drive, cruise, trek, roam, globe-trot, ramble, range, wander.

jovial *a.* playful, genial, cheerful, merry, mirthful, happy, gleeful, blithe, jocund, glad, high-spirited, effervescent. ANT. *miserable, depressed, somber.*

jowl *n.* cheek, jaw.

joy *n.* happiness, delight, euphoria, high spirits, gladness, bliss, glee, elation, cheer, jubilance, rapture, transport. ANT. *misery, depression, desolation, despair.*

joyful *a.* happy, delightful, euphoric, elated, high-spirited, glad, blissful, gleeful, cheerful, jubilant, rapturous, transported, ecstatic, high. ANT. *miserable, depressed, despondent.*

joyous *a.* SEE JOYFUL

jubilant *a.* joyful, elated, overjoyed, rejoicing, exultant, exhilarated, triumphant, celebrating, thrilled, euphoric, *beside oneself, *on cloud nine. ANT. *miserable, dejected, despondent, downhearted.*

Judaism *n.* SEE RELIGION

Judas *n.* betrayer, backstabber, traitor, Judas Iscariot, snake in the grass, rat, weasel, two-timer, Benedict Arnold.

judge *n.* **1.** JUSTICE magistrate, jurist, *his Honor. "Nothing but the law speaking."—Benjamin Whichcote. "A law student who marks his own papers."—Henry Louis Mencken. SEE COURT **2.** ARBITRATOR arbiter, adjudicator, mediator, referee, umpire, conciliator.

judge v. **1.** ADJUDICATE try, adjudge, hear, sit, rule, give a verdict, decide, settle, determine, arbitrate, mediate, referee, umpire. **2.** ESTIMATE guess, surmise, reckon, infer, deduce, gather, arrive, size up. **3.** APPRAISE rate, assess, rank, evaluate, value, size up.

judgment n. **1.** SENSE common sense, wisdom, intelligence, prudence, discernment, understanding, savvy, brains, acumen, reasoning. **2.** LEGAL DECISION order, decree, ruling, decision, adjudication, sentence, verdict, award, damages. **3.** OPINION estimate, determination, appraisal, assessment, deduction, conclusion, conviction.

judgemental a. critical, disapproving, censorious, fault-finding, appraising, holier-than-thou, self-righteous, discriminating, discerning. ANT. accepting, liberal-minded.

judicial a. **1.** LEGAL judiciary, juristic, forensic. **2.** CRITICAL careful, thoughtful, analytical, discriminating, discerning, perceptive, keen. **3.** Unbiased. ANT. 2. obtuse, undiscriminating. SEE FAIR

JUDICIOUS a. [joo DISH us] having or using sound judgment. We rely on the Supreme Court to make judicious decisions. SYN. wise, sound, sensible, sage, sagacious, mindful, careful, well-considered, rational, thoughtful, astute, keen, persipacious, discriminating. ANT. injudicious, senseless, thoughtless, irrational, careless.

judo n. martial art, self-defense technique, throws.

WORD FIND

martial arts: jujitsu, karate, tae kwon do

jug n. vessel, receptacle, container, pitcher, jar, bottle, vase.

JUGGERNAUT n. [JUG ur not] any large, powerful force or institution, sometimes followed with blind devotion. The cult had become a religious juggernaut, sometimes pressuring its followers into selling all they owned. SYN. god, idol, object of worship, institution, force to be reckoned with, religion, crusade, movement, tidal wave, monster, colossus, titan, giant, engine, tidal wave.

juice n. fluid, extract, distillation, liquid, serum, sap, nectar, essence, secretion.

juicer n. food processor, blender, mixer, liquefier.

juicy a. **1.** MOIST succulent, dripping, watery, liquid, saturated. **2.** INTERESTING provocative, racy, sexy, spicy, sensational, fascinating, colorful, risqué. ANT. 1. dry, dehydrated. 2. dry, dull, bland.

juke joint n. bar, roadhouse, club, tavern, pool hall.

jumble n. mixture, hodgepodge, mishmash, medley, melange, tangle, miscellany, mess, confusion, assortment, goulash, hash.

jumbled a. mixed, scrambled, strewn about, disorganized, cluttered, thrown together, disarranged, tangled, confused, in disarray. ANT. organized, ordered.

jumbo a. huge, gigantic, king-size, industrial size, oversized, immense, prodigious, elephantine, Brobdingnagian. ANT. little, *mini, small, Lilliputian.

jump n. **1.** LEAP hop, bound, vault, hurdle, spring, pounce, rise, leapfrog, buck, frolic, bounce. **2.** INCREASE upsurge, advance, upturn, boost.

jump v. **1.** LEAP hop, bound, vault, hurdle, spring, dive, pounce, rise, leapfrog, bounce, lunge, buck. **2.** RECOIL start, flinch, wince, bolt, jerk. **3.** INCREASE surge, advance, escalate, rise, gain, boost.

jumpy a. nervous, restless, jittery, skittish, edgy, on edge, fidgety, *on pins and needles, *having hair-trigger nerves, uneasy, tense. ANT. relaxed, calm, tranquil.

junction n. juncture, convergence, joining, meeting, union, link, connection, crossing, intersection, crossroads, confluence.

juncture n. **1.** CONNECTION joint, joining, junction, coupling, hookup, link, seam, convergence, meeting, union. **2.** POINT OF TIME moment, point, stage, period. **3.** CRITICAL MOMENT crisis, turning point, crossroad, *zero hour, exigency, emergency.

jungle n. rain forest, forest, woods, bush, *the wild, the wilderness.

WORD FIND

descriptive: lush, moss-bearded trees, festooned and encrusted with parasites, tangled gardens, steaming, rampant foliage, leafy mosaic, ferns like lacy parasols, soaring monoliths

flowering parasite growing from cracks of trees: bromeliad, orchid, epiphyte

misty jungle: cloud forest

rotting floor debris: litter

uppermost story: canopy

vine, great: liana

vine, killer: strangler

vines, slang: bush rope

junior a. lower, lesser, subordinate, inferior, minor, secondary. ANT. senior, superior.

junk n. trash, scrap, refuse, waste, rubbish, debris, castoffs, salvage, garbage, crap, remnants, bits and pieces.

junk v. throw out, scrap, heave, dump, discard, dispose of, trash.

junket n. outing, trip, tour, fact-finding junket, excursion, party, banquet.

junk food n. snacks, fast food, processed food.

junkyard n. scrap yard, auto graveyard, dump, salvage yard, refuse yard, recycling facility.

jurisdiction n. 1. AUTHORITY authorization, power, command, sanction, control, dominion, rule, sovereignty. 2. REALM OF AUTHORITY domain, sphere, bounds, province, bailiwick, district, area, territory, reach.

jurist n. lawyer, attorney, attorney-at-law, counsel, counselor, legal advisor, judge, justice, magistrate.

jury n. peers, panel, judges, grand jury, petit jury, inquest, jury of one's peers.

WORD FIND
spokesperson: foreman, forewoman
SEE COURT

just a. 1. FAIR impartial, unbiased, equitable, evenhanded, dispassionate, objective, nonpartisan, right. 2. RIGHTEOUS upright, decent, virtuous, moral, ethical, honorable, proper, scrupulous, principled, good. 3. DESERVED justified, worthy, merited, earned, due, fitting, rightful. 4. ACCURATE right, correct, precise, sound, valid, true. ANT. 1. unfair, partial, biased. 2. corrupt, immoral, unprincipled. 3. undeserved, unearned. 4. inaccurate, imprecise.

just adv. 1. ONLY merely, simply. 2. BARELY hardly, narrowly, *by the skin of one's teeth.

justice n. 1. RIGHTEOUSNESS virtue, rectitude, uprightness, integrity, honor, honesty, morality, goodness. 2. FAIRNESS impartiality, equity, evenhandedness, fair play, objectivity. "To give everyone his due."—Cicero. 3. LAWFULNESS rightness, legitimacy, validity, legality. 4. PENALTY OR REWARD recompense, compensation, reparation, just deserts, redress, retribution. ANT. 1. immorality, dishonor, corruptness. 2. unfairness, partiality, bias.

justice of the peace n. magistrate, official, witness, notary public. SEE LAW

justify v. vindicate, absolve, warrant, legitimize, show just cause, substantiate, answer for, defend, rationalize, support, exonerate, excuse.

jut v. project, protrude, stick out, extend.

juvenile n. youngster, kid, boy, girl, youth, minor, teenager, adolescent, lad, lass.

juvenile a. childish, young, immature, childlike, babyish, teenaged, adolescent, pubescent, undeveloped, inexperienced, naive, *wet behind the ears. ANT. adult, old, experienced.

juvenile delinquent n. punk, hooligan, hoodlum, malefactor, rowdy, gangbanger. "Other people's children in trouble."—Jerry Dashkin.

JUXTAPOSE v. [JUK stuh POSE] to place side by side. He had to juxtapose the pieces in order to see where they fit. SYN. appose, place side by side, pair, place parallel to one another.

K

KAFKAESQUE *a.* [KAHF kuh ESK] surreal or nightmarish, as the writings of Franz Kafka. *As the drug took effect, the captive's surroundings took on an increasingly Kafkaesque quality.* SYN. surreal, nightmarish, weird, bizarre, fantastic, freakish, monstrous, unbelievable, dreamy.

keen *a.* **1.** SHARP cutting, razor-sharp, knife-edged, honed, pointed. **2.** PIERCING cutting, incisive, penetrating, trenchant. **3.** ASTUTE acute, sharp, bright, perceptive, intelligent, discerning, quick, shrewd, wise, clever, discriminating. **4.** ENTHUSIASTIC eager, interested, avid, *gung ho, ardent, zealous, *psyched. ANT. *1. dull, blunt. 2. shallow, superficial. 3. dull, obtuse, dense, stupid. 4. indifferent, apathetic, lukewarm.*

keep *v.* **1.** HOLD retain, possess, have, own, save, store. **2.** TAKE CARE OF maintain, tend, look after, support, board, provide for, protect, mind, guard, watch over. **3.** CELEBRATE observe, commemorate, memorialize, regard. **4.** RESTRAIN keep back, hold in check, prevent, curb, check, obstruct, detain, arrest, stop. ANT. *1. throw out, discard, release. 2. neglect, ignore. 3. disregard, ignore. 4. free, let loose, liberate.*

keeper *n.* guardian, protector, custodian, watchman, warden, caretaker, conservator, curator.

keepsake *n.* memento, reminder, souvenir, memorial, token, remembrance.

keg *n.* barrel, cask, drum, hogshead, container, tank, butt, firkin, tun.

ken *n.* perception, understanding, knowledge, cognizance, grasp, comprehension, range of vision.

kernel *n.* seed, grain, pit, stone, germ, nut, core, essence, heart, gist, center, crux, marrow.

kettle *n.* cauldron, pot, boiler, vessel, vat, stewpot, teakettle.

key *n.* **1.** SOLUTION answer, clue. **2.** GUIDE manual, code.

keyboard *n.* organ, synthesizer. SEE MUSICAL INSTRUMENTS

keystone *n.* principle, cornerstone, linchpin, support, foundation, ground, basis.

kick *n.* **1.** THRILL *bang, *charge, *rush, enjoyment. **2.** THRUST jolt, recoil. **3.** COMPLAINT gripe, objection. **4.** STIMULATION zing, bite, punch, snap, potency, power, sharpness.

kick *v.* **1.** BOOT punt, drop-kick. **2.** OBJECT complain, gripe, protest, remonstrate, grumble. **3.** *Sl.* QUIT give up, *go cold turkey, stop.

kickback *n. Sl.* percentage, payment, *payola, payoff, graft, cut, bribe, *money under the table.

kid *n.* child, juvenile, adolescent, youth, teenager, boy, girl, youngster, tot, lad, lass.

kid *v.* tease, fool, *pull one's leg, *put on, make fun of, *josh, play a joke on, make sport of, *rib.

kidnap *v.* abduct, *shanghai, *snatch, seize, hold for ransom, hijack, skyjack, pirate.

kill *v.* **1.** MURDER put to death, execute, slay, do in, dispatch, get rid of, assassinate, exterminate, *waste, slaughter, *rub out, destroy. SEE MURDER **2.** END stop, abort, halt, cease, terminate, turn off, cancel. **3.** VETO defeat, reject, *give thumbs down, turn down, negate.

killer *n.* murderer, slayer, assassin, executioner, ripper, homicidal maniac, *hit man, serial killer, gunman. SEE MURDERER

killing *n.* murder, homicide, slaying, manslaughter, execution, extermination, assassination, slaughter, foul play, death, fatality.

killjoy *n.* *wet blanket, spoilsport, *gloomy Gus, *partypooper, *prophet of doom, naysayer, *stick in the mud.

kin *n.* relatives, kinsfolk, kindred, sibling, family, blood relative, relations.

kind *n.* type, sort, variety, class, order, category, breed, strain, genus, brand, genre.

kind *a.* nice, compassionate, considerate, good, benevolent, generous, charitable, bighearted, understanding, loving, sympathetic, humane, gentle, *bleedingheart, friendly, soft, merciful, forgiving, Christian, tenderhearted. ANT. *mean, cruel, cold, brutal.*

kindhearted *a.* SEE KIND

kindle *v.* **1.** SET ON FIRE ignite, burn, torch, fuel, inflame. **2.** AROUSE excite, inflame, *fire up, agitate, incite, egg on, stir up, stimulate, fan the fire.

kindly *a.* kind, nice, compassionate, considerate, good, benevolent, generous, charitable, bighearted, understanding, gracious, loving, sympathetic, humane, gentle, friendly, softhearted, merciful, forgiving, Christian. ANT. *mean, cruel, cold, brutal.*

kindly *adv.* nicely, compassionately, benevolently, generously, charitably, bigheartedly, understandingly, lovingly, sympathetically, humanely, gently, mercifully, agreeably. ANT. *meanly, cruelly, coldly, brutally.*

kindness n. **1.** NICENESS compassion, consideration, goodness, benevolence, generosity, charity, bigheartedness, understanding, graciousness, love, magnanimity, sympathy, humanity, gentleness, friendliness, mercy, forgiveness. "The golden chain by which society is bound together."—Johann Goethe. **2.** GOOD TURN good deed, service, accommodation, helping hand, generosity, charity, assistance, relief. ANT. *1. meanness, cruelty, coldness, brutality.*

kindred a. similar, like, related, matching, corresponding, parallel, close, allied. ANT. *different, opposite, unrelated.*

kinetic a. energetic, dynamic, active, lively, in motion. ANT. *static, motionless, stationary.*

king n. monarch, His Majesty, crowned head, sovereign, ruler, emperor, czar, overlord, chief, leader, boss, *top dog, *kingpin, *head honcho, *big cheese, *biggest toad in the puddle. "A name of dignity and office, not of person."—John Milton. "A highly paid model for postage stamps."—Anon.

kingdom n. monarchy, realm, empire, dominion, domain, sovereignty, country, nation, territory, turf, sphere.

kink n. **1.** CURL twist, bend, screw, coil, curlicue, crinkle, knot, crimp. **2.** MUSCLE SPASM cramp, *charley horse, knot, stitch, twinge, crick. **3.** ECCENTRICITY peculiarity, quirk, idiosyncrasy, singularity. **4.** DIFFICULTY defect, hitch, knot, snarl, *glitch, complication.

kinky a. **1.** CURLY snarled, knotted, frizzy, tangled, twisted, matted. **2.** PERVERTED bizarre, strange, eccentric, twisted, peculiar, depraved, warped, sick, outlandish, unconventional. ANT. *1. straight, smooth. 2. normal, conventional, ordinary.*

kinship n. relationship, kin, blood ties, close connection, affinity, association.

kiosk n. booth, stand, stall.

KISMET n. [KIZ met] fate; destiny. *His early death was attributed to kismet.* SYN. fate, destiny, fortune, Providence, *what is written in the stars, predestination, lot, portion.

kiss n. peck, *smack, *French kiss, osculation, smooch, buss, *soul kiss. "A word invented by the poets as a rhyme for "bliss.""—Ambrose Bierce. "The sure, sweet cement, glue and lime of love."—Robert Herrick.

kiss v. peck, *smack, *smooch, *neck, osculate.

kit n. gear, outfit, set, equipment, implements,

rigging, supplies, tools, utensils, instruments, tackle, case, bag, pack.

klutz n. clumsy oaf, lummox, bungler, *butterfingers, *bull in a china shop.

knack n. ability, skill, talent, dexterity, aptitude, gift, propensity, genius, flair, command, *head, know-how.

knave n. rascal, bastard, villain, rogue, cad, scoundrel, cur, louse, fiend, snake, *SOB, scamp, cheater, blackmailer, extortionist, *bum.

knead v. press, work, fold over, mix, rub, massage, manipulate, squeeze.

knickknack n. bric-a-brac, ornament, *whatnot, bauble, gewgaw, trinket, doodad, gimcrack, bibelot, objet d'art, conversation piece.

knife n. dagger, switchblade, blade, dirk, stiletto, scalpel, bowie knife, butter knife, jackknife, penknife, Swiss Army knife, cutlery. SEE DAGGER, SWORD

knife v. stab, run through, stick, cut, slash, impale, pierce, wound, lance.

knit v. purl, crochet, loop, cable, knot, intertwine, bind, weave.

knob n. protuberance, lump, bump, projection, nub, node, bulge, tumor, prominence, swelling.

knock v. **1.** STRIKE bump, strike a blow, hit, bang, punch, pound, pummel, batter, thump, rap, *slug, slap, smack, floor. **2.** CRITICIZE *pan, find fault, belittle, pick apart, *slam, *badmouth, disparage, *rake over the coals. ANT. *1. caress, pat. 2. praise, laud, applaud.*

knoll n. hillock, hill, mound, rise, hummock, hump, elevation, swell.

knot n. **1.** TIE twist, loop, bow, braid, plait, intertwinement, tangle, entanglement, mat, kink, snarl. **2.** LUMP bump, protuberance, knob, gnarl, nub, node. **3.** BUNCH group, aggregation, mob, swarm, gathering, mass, assemblage. **4.** COMPLEX PROBLEM complexity, Gordian knot, puzzle, difficulty, horns of a dilemma, labyrinth.

knotty a. complex, puzzling, baffling, perplexing, complicated, troublesome, labyrinthine, intricate, thorny, involved. ANT. *simple, easy, elementary.*

know v. **1.** UNDERSTAND apprehend, comprehend, grasp, realize, *get it, fathom, recognize, appreciate, see, *have the hang of, *have down pat, have memorized, *know backward and forward, *have down cold. **2.**

BE ACQUAINTED WITH be familiar with, be intimate with, be close to, be on good terms with, associate with. **3.** DISTINGUISH discern, recognize, discriminate, differentiate.

know-how n. expertise, skill, capability, ability, experience, savvy, talent, proficiency, knack, flair, command, mastery, *the right stuff. ANT. *ignorance, inexperience, incompetence.*

knowing a. knowledgeable, informed, aware, conscious, perceptive, astute, schooled, educated, learned, enlightened, intelligent, sophisticated, worldly, shrewd, clever, bright, insightful, wise. ANT. *unenlightened, ignorant, obtuse, dense.*

know-it-all n. *walking encyclopedia, *brain, intellectual, *professor, *blowhard, *windbag.

knowledge n. **1.** ACQUAINTANCE familiarity, awareness, understanding, apprehension, conversance, appreciation, consciousness, cognizance, realization, perception, enlightenment, experience, recognition, memory. "The wing wherewith we fly to heaven."—Shakespeare. "An unending adventure at the edge of uncertainty."—Jacob Bronowski. "The only instrument of production

that is not subject to diminishing returns."—J.M. Clark. **2.** EDUCATION schooling, erudition, learning, scholarship, instruction, enlightenment. **3.** INFORMATION facts, data, *low-down, lore, science, wisdom. ANT. *ignorance, unfamiliarity, unconsciousness.*

knowledgeable a. learned, schooled, well-read, erudite, educated, scholarly, literate, conversant, au courant, experienced, informed, knowing, abreast of, wise, worldly, sophisticated. ANT. *ignorant, unaware, unschooled.*

knurled a. knotty, knobby, bumpy, gnarled, warty. ANT. *smooth.*

kook n. Sl. *nut case, *loony tune, *fruitcake, *wacko, weirdo, *screwball, eccentric, character, *ding-a-ling.

kosher a. Sl. all right, okay, proper, correct, acceptable, approved, fitting, permissible, legitimate, permitted. ANT. *unacceptable.*

kowtow v. bow, kneel, stoop, genuflect, bow and scrape, kiss feet, *kiss up, *brownnose, toady, cringe, grovel, fawn.

KUDOS n. [KOO doz] praise for an outstanding accomplishment. *The restaurant critic gave kudos to the chef for a magnificent dinner.* SYN. credit, praise, honor, glory, fame, acclaim, applause, laudation, esteem, plaudits, recognition, prestige.

L

lab n. SEE LABORATORY

label n. **1.** TAG sticker, ticket, stamp, sign, brand, name, logo, trademark, seal, identification. **2.** CHARACTERIZATION stereotype, classification, generalization, epithet.

label v. **1.** TAG classify, differentiate, identify, name, designate, ticket, stamp, mark, brand. **2.** CHARACTERIZE stereotype, classify, generalize, brand.

labor n. **1.** WORK effort, toil, *sweat of one's brow, exertion, struggle, *plugging, *blood, sweat and tears, energy, *grind, strain, *grunt work, *elbow grease. "The grand conqueror, enriching and building up nations more surely than the proudest battles."—William Channing. "The capital of our workingmen."—Grover Cleveland. **2.** BIRTH PROCESS contractions, parturition. SEE BIRTH, BABY, PREGNANCY ANT. *1. rest, leisure, relaxation.*

laboratory n. lab, testing room, testing ground, analysis lab, chemistry lab, workshop. SEE SCIENCE

labored a. strained, with great effort, forced, excessive, overworked, overwrought, stiff, studied, unnatural. ANT. *effortless, natural, spontaneous.*

laborer n. worker, blue-collar worker, hand, *grunt, unskilled worker, drudge, peon, *hardhat, wage earner, employee.

laborious a. hard, arduous, difficult, backbreaking, strenuous, burdensome, heavy, ponderous, tough, *Herculean, demanding. ANT. *easy, light, effortless,*child's play.*

labyrinth n. maze, convolution, network, complexity, intricacy, knot, tangle, winding way, Gordian knot.

lace n. netting, mesh, tatting, openwork, web, embroidery, macramé, braid, filigree.

lacerate v. tear, rip, cut, gash, slash, rend, mutilate, stab, mangle, slice, wound.

laceration n. tear, jagged tear, rip, cut, gash, slash, scratch, rent, slice, mutilation, wound.

lack n. want, deficiency, need, dearth, insufficiency, shortage, shortfall, paucity, privation. ANT. *overflow, excess, abundance.*

lack v. miss, need, want, fall short, be found wanting, require.

lackadaisical a. listless, languid, spiritless, indifferent, apathetic, unmotivated, languorous, impassive, lethargic, careless, laid-back,

halfhearted, lazy. ANT. *eager, spirited, enthusiastic, energetic.*

lackey n. toady, servant, footman, slave, stooge, *brownnose, *yes-man, flunky, underling, inferior.

lackluster a. dull, drab, colorless, bland, flat, *blah, boring, lifeless, dead, *ho-hum. ANT. *vivid, radiant, colorful, interesting.*

LACONIC a. [luh KON ik] employing few words, terse. *The laconic waiter grunted a one-word reply.* SYN. terse, brief, short, concise, to the point, succinct, short and sweet, pithy, curt, taciturn, quiet, reticent. ANT. *loquacious, talkative, wordy, garrulous.*

lacquer n. finish, coating.

lacy a. filigreed, webbed, tatted, delicate, meshy, frilly.

lad n. boy, young man, youth, fellow, kid, chap, guy, *dude.

lady n. woman, female, gal, gentlewoman, matron, girl, senorita, mademoiselle. "One who makes a man behave like a gentleman."—Russel Lynes.

ladylike a. refined, cultured, well-bred, genteel, proper, feminine, courtly, dignified, matronly, polite, well-mannered, prim. ANT. *rough, crude, uncouth, boorish, *gross.*

lag v. fall behind, wane, ebb, flag, slow, linger, poke, drag, stall, dawdle, delay, trail, dally, procrastinate, *take one's sweet time. ANT. *rush, race, accelerate, surpass.*

lagoon n. pool, body of water, shallow, tidal pond.

laggard n. straggler, slowpoke, dawdler, lagger, dallier, *slug.

lair n. den, hole, burrow, cave, nest, hideaway, hideout, retreat, lie, refuge, sanctuary.

LAISSEZ-FAIRE n. [LESS ay FEHR] allowance to do as one pleases without interference, regulation or control, a "hands-off" government policy. *The government's laissez-faire policy allows some businesses to set their own rules.* SYN. *hands-off policy, free enterprise, nonintervention, noninterference, permissiveness, deregulation, inaction, free hand, latitude, *enough rope to hang oneself with.

lake n. pond, tarn, pool, basin, reservoir, loch, Great Salt Lake, Erie, Ontario, Superior, Michigan, Huron, Tahoe, Geneva, Champlain, Mead, Loch Ness, Titicaca, Victoria,

Baikal, Crater, Dead Sea. "The earth's eye."—Thoreau.

WORD FIND
bend of a river, cut off: oxbow lake
crater lake: caldera
desert, temporary, shallow: playa
diminishing process from lake to pond to marsh to swamp: eutrophication, succession
epoch when most lakes formed: Pleistocene
expert on: limnologist
glacial: ice scour, kettle, moraine lake
glacial series of, resembling beads: paternoster lakes
Great Lakes forming glacier: Wisconsin ice sheet
mountain lake: tarn
mountainside basin: cirque
oscillations of: seiche
outlet: bayou
pertaining to: lacustrine
skimming insect: boatman
SEE MARSH, POND, RIVER, SWAMP

lambaste v. scold, berate, dress down, *rake over the coals, reprimand, castigate, cuss out, censure, rebuke, *chew out, *jump down one's throat.

lame a. **1.** DISABLED crippled, handicapped, gimpy, hamstrung, limping, hobbled, sidelined, impaired, stiff, sore. **2.** WEAK feeble, poor, inferior, ineffectual, inadequate, unsatisfactory, insufficient, flimsy. ANT. *1. fleet-footed, agile, nimble. 2. sound, strong, effective.*

lament v. mourn, grieve, weep, wail, cry, sob, shed tears, sorrow, commiserate, bewail, deplore, rue, *eat one's heart out.

lamentable a. grievous, deplorable, regrettable, woeful, pitiable, heartbreaking, distressing, sad, sorrowful, wretched. ANT. *happy, fortunate, welcome.*

lamentation n. lament, grieving, mourning, wailing, weeping, crying, sobbing, moaning, commiseration, plaint, dirge.

lamp n. lantern, beacon, illuminant. SEE LIGHT

LAMPOON v. [lam POON] to satirize or parody, to ridicule. *The comedy troupe loves to lampoon the president.* SYN. satirize, parody, mock, ridicule, make fun of, caricature, burlesque, *send up, pasquinade.

lance v. pierce, cut open, incise, stick, prick, puncture, stab.

land n. **1.** GROUND earth, soil, terra firma, turf, sand, loam, dirt. **2.** TERRAIN expanse,

stretch, sweep, topography, lowland, highland. **3.** PROPERTY real estate, grounds, acreage, plot, lot, parcel, holding. **4.** COUNTRY, AREA nation, region, motherland, fatherland, old country, district, territory.

land v. **1.** SET DOWN touch down, alight, dock, drop anchor, arrive. **2.** OBTAIN *bag, get, win, secure, catch, acquire, *collar.

landfill n. dump, toxic waste site, disposal area, hazardous waste dump.

landlord n. landholder, lessor, proprietor, slumlord.

landmark n. guide, marker, milestone, guidepost, beacon, benchmark, watershed.

landscape n. expanse, view, panorama, sweep, vista, scene, scenery, surroundings, prospect.

landslide n. avalanche, mudslide, rockslide, collapse.

lane n. way, path, route, passage, alley, avenue, course, access, road, trail.

language n. verbalization, vocalization, communication, linguistics, speech, parlance, tongue, expression, articulation, wording, vernacular, vocabulary, idiom, idiolect, phraseology, prose, lingo, jargon, cant, slang, slanguage, dialect, diction, colloquialism, localism, Americanism, syntax. "A man's language is an unerring index of his nature."—Laurence Binyon. "The armory of the human mind."—Samuel Taylor Coleridge. "Man's deadliest weapon."—Arthur Koestler. "A city to the building of which every human being brought a stone."—Ralph Waldo Emerson. "A series of squeaks."—Alfred North Whitehead.

LANGUID a. [LAN gwid] lacking vitality or energy, weak. *The day after the party, we sat around languidly.* SYN. weak, drooping, listless, faint, enervated, lethargic, languorous, sluggish, dull, slow, apathetic, indifferent. ANT. *vigorous, vital, energized.*

LANGUISH v. [LAN gwish] to grow weak, listless or dull, flag. *After the drought, the delicate flowers languished, then died.* SYN. weaken, flag, grow listless, tire, fade, wilt, wither, droop, decline, ebb, sicken, *fizzle out, *go downhill. ANT. *flourish, revive, thrive, strengthen.*

languor n. weakness, listlessness, sluggishness, languidness, faintness, lethargy, torpor, fatigue, apathy, indifference. ANT. *vigor, strength, zest, vitality.*

lanky a. tall, skinny, lean, bony, slender, spare, twiggy, gangling, skin-and-bones, spindly, *lean as linguine, *built like a broomstick, *could fall through a flute and not sound a note. ANT. *stout, hulking, fat, Herculean.*

lantern n. lamp, torch, flashlight. SEE LIGHT

lap v. lick, splash, slosh, slap, ripple.

lapse n. **1.** SLIP error, fault, flub, blunder, mistake, omission, oversight, *screwup. **2.** GAP passage, break, pause, lull, interval, interim.

larceny n. stealing, theft, petty larceny, burglary, robbery, shoplifting, pilfering, embezzlement, swindling, fraud. SEE CRIME, LAW

larder n. store, storage, pantry, supply room; supplies, provisions, stock.

large a. big, sizable, great, huge, gigantic, immense, colossal, prodigious, hefty, towering, enormous, *jumbo, voluminous, *whopping, massive, gargantuan, vast, extensive, expansive, roomy, spacious, commodious, capacious, generous. ANT. *tiny, small, microscopic, minute, sparse, paltry.*

largely adv. mostly, chiefly, mainly, for the most part, principally, by and large, to a great extent, overall, generally.

larger than life a. legendary, storybook, mythical, towering, imposing, impressive, awesome, extraordinary, fabulous, ANT. *ordinary, down-to-earth.*

largess a. generosity, charity, giving, gift-giving, philanthropy, benefaction. ANT. *stinginess, cheapness, penny-pinching.*

LASCIVIOUS a. [luh SIV ee us] lustful, expressing lust, lewd. *Her lascivious glance spoke volumes.* SYN. lustful, lewd, wanton, licentious, *horny, lecherous, *hot, libidinous, carnal, goatish, salacious, blue, *raunchy, lurid, obscene. ANT. *celibate, pure, chaste, frigid.*

lash v. **1.** THRASH whip, beat, flog, switch, strike, flail, flagellate, swat, scourge. **2.** CENSURE rebuke, attack, criticize, tongue-lash, berate, scold, chastise, lambaste, *chew out.

lass n. girl, female, young woman, maid, maiden, lassie, miss, *filly, colleen, mademoiselle.

lassitude n. fatigue, weariness, languor, torpor, lethargy, listlessness, exhaustion, malaise, sluggishness, tiredness. ANT. *vigor, energy, vitality.*

lasso n. lariat, rope, thong, noose.

last v. endure, survive, persist, persevere, keep on, remain, continue, outlast, hold out. ANT. *die, wear out, give out.*

last a. **1.** FINAL ending, closing, concluding, terminal, ultimate, climactic, finishing, trailing, rearmost. **2.** LATEST newest, current, recent, up-to-the-minute. ANT. *1. first, beginning, opening. 2. oldest, earliest.*

lasting a. enduring, permanent, continuing, durable, undying, persisting, everlasting, indestructible, immortal, abiding, perdurable. ANT. *short-lived, fleeting, temporary, ephemeral.*

lastly adv. finally, in closing, ultimately.

latch n. lock, catch, hook and eye, bolt, fastening, hasp, clasp.

latch v. lock, bolt, fasten, secure, hook, close.

late a. **1.** TARDY overdue, behind, delayed, lagging, slow, held up. **2.** RECENT new, modern, current, up-to-the-minute, fresh. **3.** DECEASED dead, extinct, defunct, bygone, former, past, previous. ANT. *1. punctual, on time. 2. early, old. 3. existing, living.*

lately adv. of late, recently, a short time ago, now.

LATENT a. [LAYT unt] existing or present beneath the surface, hidden. *He possessed a latent talent that only occasionally emerged.* SYN. dormant, hidden, under the surface, inactive, quiescent, *closet, slumbering, potential, smoldering, undeveloped. ANT. *apparent, obvious, active, developed.*

lateral a. sideways, sidewise, sidelong, oblique, slanting, glancing, flanking. ANT. *perpendicular.*

lather n. foam, froth, suds, spume, cream, bubbles.

LATITUDE n. [LAT uh tood] freedom to act without restrictions. *The governor was given complete latitude to choose the state's fate.* SYN. freedom, liberty, free hand, carte blanche, license, leeway, *slack, room, play, run, independence. ANT. *restriction, confinement.*

lattice n. framework, openwork, screen, trellis, grid, grating, fretwork.

LAUD v. [LAWD] to praise or acclaim. *The critics lauded his latest work.* SYN. praise, acclaim, applaud, extol, hail, compliment, sing the praises of, cheer, celebrate, commend. ANT. *disparage, criticize, denigrate.*

laudable a. praiseworthy, commendable, admirable, excellent, exceptional, good, exemplary, superb, worthy, meritorious. ANT. *awful, contemptible, terrible, shameful.*

laudatory a. commendatory, praising, approving, eulogizing, complimentary, favorable, acclamatory, flattering. ANT. *condemning, critical.*

laugh n. chuckle, giggle, snigger, snicker, chortle, guffaw, roar, cackle, *tee-hee, horselaugh, belly laugh, *great gust/gale of laughter, howl, fit of laughter, titter, snort, hoot, *raspy chuckle, *wheezing chuckle, shriek, scream, squeal, unrestrained laughter.

laugh *v.* chuckle, giggle, snigger, snicker, chortle, guffaw, roar, cackle, *tee-hee, convulse with glee, double over with laughter, howl, titter, snort, hoot, chuckle hoarsely, shriek, scream, squeal.

laughable *a.* absurd, ridiculous, hilarious, ludicrous, comical, funny, stupid, silly, sidesplitting, amusing, *a scream, hysterical, nonsensical. ANT. *serious, sad, depressing.*

laughter *n.* giggling, chuckling, *great gales of laughter, howling, squealing, shrieking, tittering, snickering, merriment, hilarity, mirth, glee, jollity. "A smile that burst."—Patricia Nelson. "A noisy smile."—Steven Goldberg. "A universal bond that draws all men closer."—Nathan Ausubel. "A tranquilizer with no side effects."—Arnold Glasow.

launch *v.* **1.** START inaugurate, begin, commence, institute, *start the ball rolling, usher in, break ground, open. **2.** SET OFF send forth, propel, discharge, fire off, catapult, set afloat.

launder *v.* wash, clean, cleanse, scrub, rinse.

laurels *n.* fame, honor, credit, kudos, renown, glory, praise, laudation, tribute, commendation, recognition.

lavatory *n.* washroom, toilet, rest room. SEE BATHROOM

lavish *v.* shower, spend, squander, deluge, heap, give, waste, pour, fritter, be generous with. ANT. *limit, stint.*

lavish *a.* generous, liberal, extravagant, profuse, abundant, bountiful, immoderate, excessive, unsparing, lush, prodigal. ANT. *sparing, scant, meager.*

law *n.* regulation, code, ordinance, rule, principle, statute, restriction, control, act, commandment, enactment, mandate, legislation. "Reason free from passion."—Aristotle. "The embodiment of the moral sentiments of the people."—William Blackstone. "The expression and the perfection of common sense."—Joseph Choate. "The backbone which keeps man erect."—S.C. Yuter.

WORD FIND

evidence that incriminates oneself, refusal to give: taking the Fifth

habitual lawbreaker: scofflaw, recidivist

ignorance of the law is no excuse: ignorantia legis non excusat

jargon, law: legalese

lawlessness: anarchy

lured into a crime by police: entrapment

punishment, laws regarding: penal code

puritanical or overly strict laws: blue laws

reading of rights rule on arrest: Miranda rule

science and philosophy of law: jurisprudence

second prosecution, law against: double jeopardy

time limit for judicial action: statute of limitations

unjust imprisonment, writ preventing: habeas corpus

SEE COURT, MURDER

lawbreaker *n.* criminal, violator, felon, offender, outlaw, transgressor, miscreant, delinquent, culprit, malefactor, scofflaw, recidivist.

lawful *a.* legal, allowable, legitimate, licit, within the law, sanctioned, permissible, constitutional, rightful. ANT. *illegal, unlawful, illicit.*

lawless *a.* anarchic, ungoverned, unchecked, unruly, felonious, criminal, nihilistic, barbarous, uncivilized, savage, chaotic. ANT. *lawful, civilized, law-abiding.*

lawn *n.* yard, grass, grounds, turf, sward, greensward, green.

lawsuit *n.* suit, action, litigation, case, claim, prosecution, dispute. "A machine which you go into as a pig and come out as a sausage."—Ambrose Bierce. SEE COURT

lawyer *n.* attorney, counselor, counsel, legal advisor, advocate, jurist, member of the bar, public defender, solicitor, barrister. "Perilous mouths."—Shakespeare. "A learned gentleman who rescues your estate from your enemies and keeps it himself."—Henry Brougham. "Those who earn a living by the sweat of their browbeating."—James Huneker. "One skilled in the circumvention of the law."—Ambrose Bierce. SEE COURT, LAW

lax *a.* slack, loose, remiss, careless, negligent, inattentive, devil-may-care, sloppy, casual, inexact, *asleep at the wheel. ANT. *careful, conscientious, strict.*

laxative *n.* cathartic, purging agent, physic.

lay *n.* position, layout, arrangement, configuration, form, orientation.

lay *v.* **1.** PUT place, set, set down, leave, deposit, rest, position. **2.** KNOCK DOWN fell, level, flatten, floor. **3.** PRODUCE bear, bring forth, generate, deposit. **4.** IMPOSE place, exact, assess, levy. **5.** *Sl.* COPULATE.

lay *a.* amateur, nonprofessional, ordinary, secular, unschooled. ANT. *professional.*

layer *n.* stratum, thickness, bed, course, tier, ply, fold, overlap, sheet, row, zone.

layman *n.* amateur, nonprofessional, laic, neophyte, novice. ANT. *professional, expert.*

layoff *n.* dismissal, discharge, firing, *downsizing, cutback, unemployment.

lazy *a.* indolent, slothful, unwilling to work, *allergic to work, idle, shiftless, malingering, sleepy, loafing, inert, unindustrious, unmotivated. ANT. *industrious, enterprising, hard-working, hard-driving, *busy as a beaver.*

leach *v.* drain, pass, percolate out, drip, filter, empty.

lead *n.* **1.** FIRST PLACE edge, top spot, vanguard, jump, head, spearhead, cutting edge. **2.** CLUE tip, hint, indication, sign. ANT. *1. rear, tail.*

lead *v.* **1.** GUIDE direct, show the way, conduct, usher, shepherd, escort. **2.** HEAD command, direct, govern, supervise, run, *take the helm, rule, dominate, take charge. **3.** INFLUENCE persuade, incline, guide, direct, affect, *sell on, prevail upon, prompt, cause. **4.** PRECEDE go before. **5.** EXCEL surpass, outdo, outshine, outperform, head the pack, rank first, stand head and shoulders above.

leader *n.* head, chief, commander, director, boss, supervisor, manager, captain, maestro, ruler, general, governor, dean, *biggest toad in the puddle, *big cheese, bellwether, pacesetter, pioneer, trailblazer, groundbreaker, vanguard. "A man who has the ability to get other people to do what they don't want to do and like it."—Harry S. Truman. "The wave pushed ahead by the ship."—Leon Tolstoy.

leadership *n.* command, control, direction, guidance, influence, domination, sway, mastery, charisma, potency, authority, counsel, management, supervision, rulership, government, shepherding, pacesetting, trailblazing, supremacy, dominace. "Action, not position."—Donald McGannon. ANT. *subservience, subordination, obedience.*

leading *a.* foremost, preeminent, chief, main, dominant, supreme, outstanding, greatest, ranking, most important. ANT. *secondary, minor, lesser.*

league *n.* alliance, association, confederation, federation, coalition, organization, union, affiliation, partnership, fraternity.

leak *n.* seepage, drip, trickle, oozing, stream, dribble, discharge, opening, rupture, crack, puncture, gash, break, breach.

leak *v.* **1.** DISCHARGE seep, drain, drip, trickle, ooze, stream, spurt, dribble, flow. **2.** DIVULGE reveal, *spill the beans, disclose.

lean *v.* **1.** INCLINE slant, slope, cant, bend, tilt, pitch, list. **2.** RELY ON depend on, count on for support. **3.** TEND incline, be disposed, gravitate toward, have a preference for.

lean *a.* **1.** THIN spare, emaciated, anorexic, skin and bones, rawboned, gaunt, slim, slender, svelte, skinny, *lean as linguine, malnourished. **2.** UNPRODUCTIVE meager, poor, scanty, unprofitable. ANT. *1. fat, plump, rotund. 2. productive, profitable, rich.*

leaning *n.* tendency, inclination, disposition, preference, proclivity, propensity, bias, weakness, mindset, penchant.

leap *n.* jump, spring, vault, hop, bound, bounce, hurtle.

leap *v.* jump, spring, vault, hop, bound, bounce, hurtle, soar, rise, leapfrog.

learn *v.* **1.** ACQUIRE KNOWLEDGE *pick up, master, understand, comprehend, apprehend, grasp, realize, absorb, become educated, memorize, become versed in, *get the hang of, study, pore over, *cram. **2.** DISCOVER find out, hear, detect, determine, stumble upon.

learned *a.* educated, schooled, erudite, scholarly, literate, well-read, knowledgeable, lettered, intellectual, pedantic, bookish. ANT. *ignorant, unschooled, illiterate.*

learning *n.* education, schooling, enlightenment, study, edification, erudition, research, training, scholarship, cultivation, inquiry, questioning, growth, knowledge. "Dust shaken out of a book and into an empty skull."—Ambrose Bierce. "A companion on a journey to a strange country . . . a strength inexhaustible."—Hitopadesa.

learning disability *n.* learning disorder, learning deficit, learning impairment, dyslexia, ADD (attention deficit disorder).

lease *v.* let, rent, hire out, sublease, lend.

leash *n.* lead, line, rein, tether, rope, choker.

leash *v.* tie, restrain, tether, hitch, chain, collar, restrict.

least *a.* smallest, slightest, fewest, minimum, poorest, lowest, minutest, last. ANT. *greatest, largest, most.*

leave *n.* **1.** PERMISSION okay, consent, authorization, allowance, liberty, concession, indulgence, tolerance. **2.** TIME OFF furlough, leave-of-absence, sabbatical, break, *R&R. ANT. *1. refusal, denial.*

leave *v.* **1.** GO depart, exit, *split, take one's

leave, vacate, withdraw, *shove off, decamp, flee, *cut out, bid farewell, run along, take off. **2.** ABANDON drop, desert, quit, give up, relinquish, forsake. ANT. *1. arrive, come.*

lecherous *a.* lustful, lewd, lascivious, libidinous, salacious, carnal, wanton, *horny, licentious, randy, *dirty-minded, *raunchy. ANT. *chaste, pure, celibate.*

lechery *n.* lewdness, lust, lasciviousness, salaciousness, carnality, *horniess, nymphomania, *dirty-mindedness, *raunchiness. ANT. *chastity, purity, celibacy.*

lectern *n.* desk, stand, support, ambo.

lecture *n.* **1.** TALK address, speech, discussion, discourse, oration, disquisition, sermon, lesson, instruction. **2.** SCOLDING *dressing down, reprimand, rebuke, criticism, reproach, *talking-to, remonstrance, admonishment, sermon.

lecture *v.* **1.** TALK give a speech, address, discuss, discourse, orate, give a lesson, give instruction, expound, preach, hold forth. **2.** SCOLD *dress down, reprimand, rebuke, criticize, reproach, remonstrate, admonish, sermonize, preach.

ledge *n.* shelf, overhang, projection, ridge, mantle, shoulder, outcrop.

ledger *n.* account book, record book, journal.

leech *n.* parasite, bloodsucker, sponge, golddigger, blackmailer, extortionist, *bum.

leer *n.* salacious look, lascivious look, ogle, lustful stare, stare, once-over, lecherous look, sidelong glance, sneer.

leer *v.* eye lustfully, eye salaciously, eye lasciviously, eye lecherously, stare, give once-over, eye hungrily, ogle, look sidelong, smirk.

leery *a.* wary, guarded, suspicious, distrusting, cautious, chary, skeptical, uncertain. ANT. *trusting, unsuspecting.*

leeway *n.* room, margin, space, latitude, breathing space, elbow room, freedom, slack, range.

LEFT-HANDED *a.* [LEFT HAND ED] referring to an insincere or dubious compliment, one that is actually insulting. *She told him he had the ability to sing semiprofessionally, another of her subtle left-handed compliments.* SYN. insincere, dubious, backhanded, ambiguous, questionable, ironic, veiled, sardonic, mocking. ANT. *sincere, unambiguous, genuine.*

leftover *n.* remnant, remainder, surplus, leaving, scrap, remains, oddments.

LEFT-WING *a.* [LEFT WING] liberal, leftist, radical. *Left-wing activists wanted to preserve* the entire forest, regardless of the jobs lost. SYN. liberal, leftist, radical, progressive, far left, red, communistic. ANT. *right-wing, conservative, rightist.*

LEGACY *n.* [LEG uh see] something passed down from a previous generation or ancestor. *Drug abuse is now commonplace, a legacy of the "anything goes" 1960s.* SYN. inheritance, bequest, heritage, *hand-me-down, gift, heirloom, birthright, carryover.

legal *a.* lawful, licit, allowable, sanctioned, permitted, constitutional, right, just, authorized, legitimate, judicial. ANT. *illegal, illicit, unlawful.*

legalize *a.* make lawful, legitimize, allow, sanction, authorize, decriminalize, permit, license, legislate. ANT. *outlaw, prohibit.*

legend *n.* **1.** MYTH fable, lore, tale, story, fiction, narrative, allegory. **2.** CELEBRITY giant, star, superstar, hero, prodigy.

legendary *a.* **1.** MYTHICAL fabled, fanciful, fantastic, fictional, imaginary, traditional, romantic, epic. **2.** REMARKABLE immortal, great, celebrated, extraordinary, acclaimed, renowned, heroic. ANT. *1. actual, real, true-to-life. 2. commonplace, unremarkable.*

legerdemain *n.* sleight of hand, deceit.

legible *a.* readable, decipherable, clear, plain, easy-to-read, intelligible. ANT. *illegible, unreadable.*

legion *n.* mass, multitude, crowd, throng, pack, army, swarm, horde, mob, scores.

legislation *n.* bill, act, law, statute, code, ordinance, rule, regulation, charter, constitution. SEE GOVERNMENT, POLITICS

legislator *n.* lawmaker, lawgiver, politician, representative, congressman, senator, selectman, assemblyman, councilman. SEE POLITICIAN, ELECTION

legislature *n.* congress, senate, house of representatives, parliament, assembly, council. SEE CONGRESS, POLITICS

legitimate *a.* **1.** LAWFUL legal, licit, *legit, statutory, constitutional. **2.** GENUINE authentic, *for-real, true, *legit, *on the level, *kosher, *OK. ANT. *1. unlawful, illegal, illicit. 2. fake, dishonest, fraudulent.*

leisure *n.* repose, ease, freedom, liberty, rest, recreation, relaxation, unemployment, idle hours, respite, *downtime. "The time you don't get paid for and enjoy spending."— Hyman Berston. ANT. *labor, work, employment.*

leisurely *a.* slow, unhurried, deliberate, casual,

relaxed, laid-back, easy, lazy, *poky. ANT. *hurried, breakneck, rushed.*

lemon n. *dud, *dog, loser, *piece of crap, *hunk of junk, reject. ANT. *piece of work, success.*

lend v. **1.** LOAN entrust, let use, accommodate, advance, oblige. **2.** IMPART give, provide, furnish, contribute.

length n. **1.** DISTANCE span, extent, reach, measure, size, dimension, expanse. **2.** DURATION span, period, term.

lengthen v. stretch, elongate, protract, extend, expand, increase, prolong. ANT. *shorten, cut.*

lengthy a. long, protracted, drawn out, extended, prolonged, extensive, elongated, interminable, long-winded. ANT. *brief, short.*

lenient a. soft, mild, easy, merciful, tolerant, permissive, liberal, indulgent, charitable, kind, forgiving, compassionate. ANT. *strict, harsh, tough, unforgiving.*

leprechaun n. fairy, elf, little old man, dwarf, gnome, brownie, sprite, pixie, goblin.

lesbian n. homosexual, sapphist, gay woman.

lesbian a. homosexual, gay, sapphist. ANT. *heterosexual.*

lesion n. injury, damage, hurt, wound, sore, trauma, cut, laceration, bruise, contusion, impairment, *boo-boo.

less a. fewer, smaller, slighter, shorter, lower, not as great, inferior, minor, subordinate, lower, secondary. ANT. *more, greater, superior.*

lessen v. decrease, diminish, reduce, lower, abate, slacken, dwindle, shrink, fall off, cut, contract, downsize, pare, fade, subtract, moderate. ANT. *increase, multiply, expand.*

lesson n. instruction, class, exercise, lecture, assignment, drill, study, homework, teaching.

let v. **1.** ALLOW permit, authorize, enable, grant, *give the go-ahead, *give the green light, give permission, license. **2.** LEASE rent, sublease, hire out, charter.

letdown n. disapointment, disillusionment, anticlimax, disenchantment, *comedown, frustration, *washout, blow, *bubbleburster. ANT. *fulfillment, satisfaction, dreamcome-true.*

lethal a. fatal, deadly, mortal, killing, death-dealing, murderous, dangerous, poisonous, pernicious, malignant. ANT. *harmless, benign.*

lethargic a. drowsy, sluggish, tired, weary, fatigued, listless, sleepy, torpid, languid, *out of it, lazy, slothful, apathetic, somnolent, dragging, comatose. ANT. *energized, lively, hyperactive.*

lethargy n. drowsiness, sluggishness, tiredness, fatigue, listlessness, sleepiness, somnolence, torpor, languor, malaise, laziness, slothfulness, apathy. ANT. *liveliness, vigor, *get-up-and-go.*

letter n. note, dispatch, message, missive, communication, memo, reply, acknowledgement, billet-doux, *fax. "Servant of parted friends."—Charles Eliot. "An unannounced visit."—Friedrich Neitzsche.

letters n. belles lettres, learning.

letup n. stopping, pause, cessation, interlude, break, lapse, lull, recess.

levee n. bank, embankment, dam, mound, breakwater.

level n. **1.** HEIGHT elevation, altitude, story, floor, stratum, extent. **2.** RANK position, grade.

level v. **1.** GRADE smooth, plane, flatten, even out. **2.** RAZE flatten, knock down, fell, wreck, demolish, destroy.

level a. even, flat, flush, plane, uniform, straight, smooth, balanced, equable, proportionate, in line. ANT. *uneven, tilted.*

levelheaded a. sensible, reasonable, prudent, composed, even-tempered, cool, calm, self-possessed, unruffled, unflappable, poised. ANT. *unreasonable, thoughtless, irrational, wild.*

leverage n. weight, influence, *pull, *clout, power, control, upper hand, advantage.

leviathan n. giant, colossus, monster, behemoth, titan, hulk, mammoth, whale, sea monster. ANT. *shrimp, midget, gnat.*

LEVITY n. [LEV i tee] light or unserious behavior, frivolity. *His jokes added much-needed levity to the occasion.* SYN. lightness, frivolity, lightheartedness, foolishness, silliness, buoyancy, mirth, merriment, whimsy, giddiness. ANT. *seriousness, gravity, somberness.*

levy n. tax, tariff, toll, assessment, duty, revenue, dues, fee, collection, imposition.

levy v. impose, exact, assess, tax, fix, lay on, charge, collect, wrest, tithe.

lewd a. lascivious, lecherous, lustful, libidinous, salacious, licentious, obscene, vulgar, indecent, immodest, suggestive, X-rated, lurid. ANT. *chaste, pure, upright, wholesome, clean.*

lexicon n. dictionary, thesaurus, glossary, word book, vocabulary.

liability n. **1.** RESPONSIBILITY accountability, burden, blame, obligation. **2.** DEBT indebtedness, obligation, due, debit. **3.** DRAWBACK disadvantage, hindrance, handicap, impediment, encumbrance, millstone, burden.

ANT. *1. immunity. 2. asset. 3. advantage, plus.*
liable *a.* **1.** RESPONSIBLE accountable, answerable, obligated, subject, bound. **2.** LIKELY apt, probable, prone, disposed, given, subject, open, susceptible. ANT. *1. immune, exempt. 2. unlikely.*

liaison *n.* **1.** ALLIANCE connection, affiliation, hookup, union, association, linkup, communication. **2.** LOVE AFFAIR romance, fling, amour, tryst, *hanky-panky.

liar *n.* prevaricator, fabricator, fibber, deceiver, perjurer, cheater, dissembler, *con artist.

LIBEL *n.* [LYE bul] published statements that are untrue, malicious, and damaging to one's reputation. *The tabloid was recently sued for libel.* SYN. slander, defamation, smear, malicious gossip, falsehood, dirty lie, yellow journalism, innuendo, aspersion. SEE LAW, NEWSPAPER

libel *v.* slander, defame, smear, scandalize, malign, denigrate, *drag through the mud, slur, discredit, *give a black eye.

libelous *a.* slanderous, defamatory, scandalous, denigrating, untrue, false, malicious, injurious, maligning, discrediting, made up. ANT. *true, proven, accurate.*

liberal *n.* progressive, reformer, leftist, left-winger, libertarian, radical. *bleeding heart, *sucker for a sob story. "A man too broad-minded to take his own side in a quarrel."—Robert Frost.

liberal *a.* **1.** GENEROUS giving, free-handed, charitable, openhanded, lavish, philanthropic, bountiful, unsparing. **2.** ABUNDANT plentiful, ample, copious, rife, rich, lavish, large. **3.** NONRESTRICTIVE loose, unrestrictive, free, unstrict. **4.** TOLERANT broadminded, open-minded, unprejudiced, accepting, unbiased, indulgent. **5.** PROGRESSIVE reformist, left-wing, leftist, radical. ANT. *1. stingy, cheap, tightfisted. 2. sparse, skimpy. 3. strict, literal. 4. intolerant, prejudiced, closeminded. 5. conservative, right-wing.*

liberal arts *n.* academic disciplines, studies, general education, the trivium and quadrivium, language, literature, philosophy, history, mathematics, science.

liberate *v.* free, release, emancipate, loose, unshackle, deliver, manumit, unbind, extricate, rescue. ANT. *enslave, subjugate, shackle.*

liberation *n.* freedom, liberty, release, emancipation, unshackling, deliverance, manumission, salvation, extrication, rescue. ANT. *enslavement, subjugation, imprisonment.*

liberty *n.* freedom, release, emancipation, liberation, autonomy, self-determination, nonrestriction, independence, privilege, license, sovereignty, latitude, unrestraint. "A power to do as we would be done by."—John Quincy Adams. ANT. *enslavement, restriction, restraint.*

libidinous *a.* lustful, *hot, *horny, lascivious, lewd, randy, sensual, carnal, lecherous, turned on. ANT. *turned off.*

libido *n.* sex drive, urge, lust, desire, *horniness, *hot pants, hot blood, sexuality, Eros, biological drive.

library *n.* book depository, institution, reference center, athenaeum, atheneum, bibliotheca, book collection, media center, lending library. "The true university."—Thomas Carlyle. "The ruins of an antique world and the glories of a modern one."—Longfellow. "The diary of the human race."—George Dawson. SEE BOOK

license *n.* **1.** PERMIT permission, authorization, entitlement, privilege, grant, right. **2.** FREEDOM liberty, latitude, free hand, indulgence, presumption, immoderation, unrestraint, looseness, excess, boldness. ANT. *1. prohibition, restriction. 2. restriction, restraint.*

license *v.* permit, authorize, allow, sanction, warrant, certify, accredit.

licentious *a.* lascivious, lewd, immoral, libidinous, wanton, abandoned, lecherous, carnal, promiscuous, lustful, debauched, smutty, unrestrained. ANT. *chaste, prudish, wholesome, restrained.*

lick *n.* **1.** HIT punch, *whack, smack, blow, slap, jab. **2.** MUSICAL PHRASE *riff.

lick *v.* **1.** LAP tongue, kiss, graze, brush. **2.** BEAT whip, defeat, trounce, overpower, *shellac, trample.

lid *n.* cover, top, cap.

lie *n.* prevarication, fabrication, fib, falsehood, story, *cock-and-bull story, little white lie, *whopper, untruth, perjury, fiction, deceit, misrepresentation, distortion, stretching of the truth, barefaced lie. "The refuse of fools and cowards."—Lord Chesterfield. "An art in a lover."—Helen Rowland. ANT. *truth, gospel truth, fact.*

lie *v.* **1.** PREVARICATE fabricate, fib, falsify, *tell a little white lie, perjure, deceive, misrepresent, distort, stretch the truth, fudge, con. **2.** REST recline, stretch out, be recumbent, be prone, be supine, sprawl, lounge. ANT. *2. stand.*

life *n.* **1.** EXISTENCE being, vitality, animation,

viability, consciousness, flesh and blood, organism. "A vapor, that appeareth for a little time, and then vanisheth away."—Bible. "A little gleam of time between two eternities."—Thomas Carlyle. "A play. It's not in its length, but its performance that counts."—Seneca. **2.** LIVELINESS vigor, spirit, energy, animation, zest, vivacity, heart, enthusiasm. **3.** LIFE SPAN life expectancy, duration, longevity, course, length, period. **4.** TRIALS AND TRIBULATIONS peaks and valleys, the human condition, vicissitudes, *hand one is dealt, survival of the fittest. "A bridge of groans across a stream of tears."—Philip Bailey. "One long process of getting tired."—Samuel Butler. "Like eating artichokes—you've got to go through so much to get so little."—T.A. Dorgan. "A B-picture script."—Kirk Douglas. "An onion, and one peels it crying."—French proverb. ANT. *death, nonexistence, oblivion.*

life-and-death *a.* life or death, critical, crucial, important, vital, consequential, earth-shaking, emergent, pivotal, climactic. ANT. *inconsequential, trivial.*

lifeless *a.* **1.** DEAD deceased, extinct, *dead as a coffin nail, *stone dead, defunct, *down for the count, comatose, unconscious, inanimate, inert. **2.** COLORLESS dull, lackluster, flat, *blah, insipid, wooden, tiresome, spiritless. ANT. *1. alive, living, vital. 2. spirited, lively, colorful.*

lifestyle *n.* way of life, behavior, habits, conduct, orientation, inclinations. SEE LIFE

lifetime *n.* lifespan, life expectancy, duration, day, age, being, *threescore years and ten.

lifelike *a.* natural, realistic, true-to-life, faithful, true, graphic. ANT. *unnatural.*

lift *n.* **1.** HOIST heave, raising, boost, pull up. **2.** RAISING OF SPIRITS boost, *shot in the arm, *pick-me-up, encouragement.

lift *v.* **1.** HOIST elevate, heave, raise, boost, jack up, erect, upraise, hike, heft. **2.** STEAL swipe, pinch, pocket, shoplift, pilfer. **3.** REMOVE cancel, annul, rescind. ANT. *1. drop. 3. impose.*

liftoff *n.* launch, take-off, blast-off, ignition, firing.

light *n.* **1.** RADIANCE luminescence, illumination, radiation, glow, shine, incandescence, effulgence, flash, glare, brilliance, glimmer. **2.** LAMP beacon, lantern, candle, torch, flare. ANT. *1. dark, gloom, blackness.*

light *v.* **1.** ILLUMINATE spotlight, shine, irradiate, brighten. **2.** IGNITE kindle, spark, set fire to,

inflame. **3.** GET DOWN descend, alight, land, settle, perch. ANT. *1. darken, dim. 2. extinguish, douse.*

light *a.* **1.** BRIGHT illuminated, radiant, brilliant, shining, luminous, glowing, aglow, well-lit, lambent, sunny, gleaming. **2.** PALE faded, fair, bleached, blanched, washed-out. **3.** OF WEIGHT weightless, slight, ethereal, *featherlight, wispy, insubstantial, airy, lighter than air, unheavy, sheer, scant. **4.** WEAK mild, slight, soft, faint, gentle. **5.** SIMPLE easy, effortless, undemanding, untaxing, *no sweat. **6.** CHEERFUL humorous, amusing, gay, merry, blithe, funny, entertaining, frivolous, trifling. ANT. *1. dark, black, gloomy. 2. dark, deep, vivid. 3. heavy, hefty, massive. 4. strong, powerful, hard, harsh. 5. hard, demanding, taxing. 6. *heavy, deep, serious.*

lighten *v.* **1.** REDUCE decrease, ease, unload, remove, lessen, empty, disencumber, alleviate, mitigate. **2.** LIFT cheer, perk up, buoy, gladden. **3.** BRIGHTEN illuminate, light up, irradiate. ANT. *1. increase, burden, weigh down. 2. depress, discourage. 3. darken.*

lighthearted *a.* carefree, cheerful, happy, buoyant, sunny, jovial, playful, upbeat, blithe, glad, untroubled, joyous. ANT. *downhearted, heavyhearted, grave, depressed.*

lightly *adv.* slightly, softly, faintly, gently, daintily, delicately, sparingly, gingerly, easily, carefully. ANT. *heavily, ponderously.*

lightning *n.* electrical discharge, bolt, thunderbolt, flash, chain lightning, stroke, jag. SEE CLOUD, THUNDER

likable *a.* winning, agreeable, charming, attractive, nice, pleasing, pleasant, appealing, sweet, good-natured, warmhearted, friendly. ANT. *repellent, mean, unappealing.*

like *v.* **1.** FANCY enjoy, care for, delight in, *get a kick out of, be partial to, *dig, love, adore, take pleasure in, be fond of, appreciate, relish, *have a soft spot for, esteem. **2.** WANT choose, prefer, care, feel inclined. ANT. *1. dislike, hate, abhor, detest.*

like *a.* similar, alike, uniform, approximating, much the same, comparable, corresponding, close, equivalent, homologous, akin. ANT. *different, unlike.*

likelihood *n.* probability, good chance, prospect, possibility, potentiality.

likely *a.* probable, apt, promising, liable, expected, anticipated, presumable, plausible, *in the cards, destined. ANT. *unlikely, improbable, doubtful.*

like-minded *a.* simpatico, similar, of one mind,

of like mind, compatible, in ageement, in accord, en rapport, unanimous. ANT. *at odds, opposite, clashing.*

liken *v.* relate, link, equate. SEE COMPARE

likeness *n.* **1.** RESEMBLANCE semblance, similarity, correspondence, sameness, uniformity, analogy. **2.** FACSIMILE replica, image, representation, depiction, portrait, picture, photo, copy, model. ANT. *1. difference, dissimilarity.*

liking *n.* fondness, fancy, affinity, taste, appetite, inclination, partiality, preference, attraction, *soft spot. ANT. *aversion, hatred.*

limb *n.* appendage, member, part, extremity, leg, arm, wing, branch, bough.

limber *a.* flexible, pliant, elastic, supple, agile, loose, pliable, malleable. ANT. *stiff, rigid, inflexible.*

limbo *n.* nowhere. SEE OBLIVION

limit *n.* boundary, end, extent, margin, maximum, ceiling, border, brink, utmost, farthest reach, termination.

limit *v.* restrict, bound, confine, put a ceiling on, inhibit, restrain, constrict, hem in, curb, ration, check, circumscribe.

limitation *n.* restriction, check, curb, impediment, stumbling block, stricture, bar, block, hindrance, handicap, qualification.

limited *a.* restricted, bound, confined, restrained, checked, circumscribed, controlled, curbed, fixed. ANT. *unlimited, unrestricted.*

limitless *a.* unlimited, boundless, unrestricted, infinite, neverending, immeasurable, incalculable, innumerable, vast. ANT. *limited, finite.*

limp *v.* hobble, falter, favor one leg, drag one foot, walk lamely, stagger, shuffle, hitch, move haltingly, hop, totter, take mincing steps.

limp *a.* flaccid, drooping, wilted, soft, slack, flabby, weak, lax. ANT. *rigid, firm, stiff, strong.*

limpid *a.* clear, transparent, pellucid, crystal, like glass, translucent. ANT. *cloudy, muddy.*

line *n.* **1.** LONG MARK score, underscore, underline, stripe, stroke, dash, streak, slash, demarcation. **2.** ROW course, column, series, succession, queue, procession, chain, series, train, string, file, tier. **3.** CORD string, twine, rope, cable, filament, thread, strand. **4.** LINE OF WORK business, calling, specialty, interest, vocation, profession, *racket. **5.** LINEAGE ancestry, descent, breed, stock, pedigree.

lineage *n.* descent, ancestry, stock, family,

strain, bloodline, genealogy, heredity, succession, extraction.

linger *v.* stay, remain, hang back, hang around, loiter, dawdle, dillydally, poke about, wait, procrastinate, delay, hesitate.

lingerie *n.* underclothes, undergarments, underwear, *undies, underthings, panties, bra, teddy, camisole, chemise, garterbelt, negligee.

lingo *n.* language, dialect, jargon, vocabulary, vernacular, argot, tongue, speech, slang, idiom.

linguist *n.* polyglot, bilinguist, translator, interpreter.

liniment *n.* ointment, salve, balm, lotion, embrocation, unguent.

link *n.* **1.** CONNECTION component, section, coupling. **2.** ASSOCIATION attachment, tie, connection, bond, contact.

link *v.* associate, connect, attach, unite, tie, bond, couple, join, splice, bind, relate.

lion *n.* lioness, king of beasts, carnivore, predator, meat-eater, mammal, quadriped, cub, wildcat, puma, mountain lion, cougar.

WORD FIND

group: pride

hair: mane

lionize *v.* celebrate, acclaim, glorify, exalt, elevate, idolize, immortalize, worship, revere.

lip *n.* **1.** RIM brim, edge, verge. **2.** *Sl.* IMPUDENCE *mouth, back talk, insolence, rudeness, *sass, *wising off.

LIP SERVICE *n.* [LIP SER vis] insincere agreement, empty talk or gesture. *Politicians pay a lot of lip service to their constituents.* SYN. insincerity, empty talk, empty gesture, token agreement, tokenism, show, hollow words, flattery, smooth talk, duplicity.

liquefy *v.* dissolve, thaw, melt.

liquid *n.* fluid, water, solution, aqua, juice, extract, broth, soup.

liquid *a.* fluid, running, flowing, aqueous, wet, moist, watery, juicy, molten. ANT. *solid, dry.*

liquidate *v.* **1.** SETTLE pay off, dispose of, make good, square, satisfy, discharge. **2.** CLOSE OUT sell out, convert to cash, sell stock. **3.** KILL murder, *knock off, slay, *rub out, *bump off, exterminate, assassinate.

liqueur *n.* liquor, alcohol, flavored drink, cordial, aperitif, appetizer.

WORD FIND

almond-flavored: amaretto

bourbon and spice: Wild Turkey

cherry and almond: maraschino

chocolate and vanilla: crème de cacao

coconut and rum: ron coco
coffee flavor with vanilla: Kahlúa
cognac and orange: grand marnier
French cherry: crème de cerise
French raspberry: framboise
Greek, anise-flavored: ouzo
green, licorice flavor: absinthe
herbed brandy: benedictine, chartreuse
Irish whiskey, honey and orange: Irish mist
Israeli, chocolate and orange: sabra
Jamaican, coffee and spice: tia maria
Japanese, honeydew melon: midori
licorice-flavored: anise, pernod, sambuca
mint and menthol: crème de menthe
peach: Southern Comfort
plum gin: sloe gin
scotch, heather, honey and herbs: drambuie
SEE ALCOHOL, COCKTAIL, DRINK, LIQUOR, MOON-
SHINE, WINE

liquor *n*. alcohol, booze, spirits, whiskey, *hard
stuff, firewater, *rotgut, demon rum, intoxicant, inebriant, potation, rum, gin, vodka,
Scotch, rye. SEE ALCOHOL, COCKTAIL, LIQUEUR,
MOONSHINE, WINE

lissom *a*. lithe, limber, supple, agile, flexible,
pliant, loose, graceful, light on one's feet.
ANT. *stiff, heavy, awkward*.

list *n*. checklist, rundown, inventory, roll, roster, directory, tally, lineup, schedule, index,
series, menu.

list *v*. 1. INVENTORY record, tally, schedule, tabulate, itemize, note, post, index, record, file.
2. LEAN tilt, slant, incline, pitch, slope, tip.

listen *v*. hear, absorb, harken, pay attention,
prick up one's ears, catch, *tune in, monitor,
heed, overhear, eavesdrop. "The only way to
entertain some folks."—Kin Hubbard. ANT.
ignore, disregard, turn a deaf ear on.

listless *a*. languid, weary, apathetic, indifferent,
lethargic, sluggish, *out of it, passive, fatigued, drowsy, dead, torpid, leaden, spiritless, *blah. ANT. *energetic, lively, spirited*.

litany *n*. list, listing, repetition, recital, rendition, rundown, account, compilation.

literal *a*. exact, true, actual, word-for-word,
faithful, real, accurate, verbatim, *to the letter, undeviating, precise. ANT. *figurative,
metaphorical, loose, imprecise, paraphrased*.

literally *adv*. exactly, actually, word-for-word,
real, nonfiguratively, faithfully, verbatim,
*to the letter, precisely. ANT. *figuratively,
metaphorically, imprecisely, loosely*.

literary *a*. bookish, literate, scholarly, erudite,
cerebral, formal, artistic, stuffy.

literate *a*. schooled, educated, well-read, able

to read and write, scholarly, lettered, knowledgeable, cultured. ANT. *illiterate, ignorant,
uneducated*.

lithe *a*. flexible, limber, pliant, supple, bendable, lithesome, lissome, loose, agile, nimble.
ANT. *stiff, rigid*.

lithesome *a*. SEE LITHE

LITIGATE *v*. [LIT uh GATE] to take a dispute to court, to sue. *The damaged party
threatened to litigate*. SYN. try in court, contest in court, file suit, bring suit, sue, prosecute, bring legal action.

litigation *n*. lawsuit, suit, legal action, legal proceedings, prosecution, filing of charges,
court case, trial. "A machine which you go
into as a pig and come out of as a sausage."—
Ambrose Bierce. SEE LAW, COURT

LITIGIOUS *a*. [li TIJ us] quick to threaten
with or file lawsuits, contentious, quarrelsome. *America has become one of the most litigious societies on earth*. SYN. contentious,
quarrelsome, argumentative, combative,
belligerent, given to filing lawsuits, *sue-
happy, *lawsuit happy. ANT. *accommodating,
compromising, peaceful*.

litter *n*. trash, rubbish, refuse, garbage, *crap,
debris.

litter *v*. strew, clutter, mess, scatter.

little *a*. **1.** SMALL tiny, wee, diminutive, miniature, pint-sized, undersized, dinky, shrimpy,
Lilliputian, itsy-bitsy, minute, puny, microscopic. **2.** SCANT insufficient, few, meager,
skimpy. **3.** BRIEF fleeting, passing, short, momentary, limited. **4.** WEAK insignificant, inconsequential, ineffective, faint, feeble,
powerless, trivial, slight. **5.** YOUNG immature, juvenile, undeveloped. ANT. *1. big,
huge, gigantic. 2. ample, sufficient. 3. protracted, prolonged. 4. strong, powerful. 5. big,
adult*.

liturgy *n*. ritual, service, rite, ceremony, worship.

livable *a*. habitable, comfortable, satisfactory,
adequate, tolerable, homey, *equipped with
creature comforts. ANT. *uninhabitable, intolerable*.

live *v*. **1.** EXIST live and breathe, draw breath,
survive, be alive, function, subsist, persist,
endure, last. **2.** RESIDE dwell, inhabit, occupy, lodge, *hang one's hat. ANT. *1. die,
expire, perish*.

live *a*. **1.** LIVING alive, breathing, animate, vital,
conscious, *alive and kicking, viable. **2.**
LIVELY energetic, dynamic, hot, operative,

active, vigorous, spirited. ANT. *1. dead, inanimate, lifeless. 2. dead, cold.*

livelihood n. living, occupation, job, work, employment, trade, profession, vocation, business, source of income, subsistence.

lively a. full of life, energetic, active, *peppy, bustling, vivacious, vigorous, *hyper, frisky, spry, effervescent, perky, *bubbly, *high octane. ANT. *dead, sluggish, leaden, listless.*

livid a. **1.** BLACK AND BLUE bruised, discolored. **2.** FURIOUS enraged, infuriated, irate, mad, beside oneself with rage, incensed, indignant, red in the face. ANT. *2. calm, peaceful, composed.*

living n. livelihood, subsistence, source of income, job, support, *bread and butter, occupation.

living a. alive, existing, animated, breathing, vital, vigorous, lively, conscious, viable, active. ANT. *dead, extinct, inanimate.*

load n. **1.** FREIGHT cargo, shipment, lading, haul, payload, consignment, burden, contents, goods. **2.** BURDEN weight, encumbrance, millstone, cross, albatross, hardship, worry, care, oppression, *excess baggage.

load v. fill, pack, stack, stuff, lade, pile, cram, weigh down, saddle, burden, encumber. ANT. *unload, empty, unburden.*

loaf v. lounge about, *goof off, laze, idle, *sit on one's butt, *not lift a finger, vegetate, *lie down on the job, shirk, malinger.

loafer n. idler, *lazybones, *layabout, *couch potato, *sofa spud, deadbeat, slacker, *goof-off, do-nothing, ne'er-do-well, shirker, malingerer. ANT. *hustler, go-getter, doer.*

loan n. advance, credit, allowance, mortage, *fronting. SEE MONEY

loathe v. dislike, hate, abhor, look upon with disgust, regard contemptuously, feel sick at the sight of, despise, detest, reject, scorn. ANT. *like, love, admire.*

loathing n. hatred, dislike, abhorrence, disgust, revulsion, repugnance, contempt, aversion, distaste. ANT. *love, admiration, adoration.*

loathsome a. abhorrent, disgusting, revolting, despicable, detestable, contemptible, distasteful, abominable, hateful, repugnant, deplorable. ANT. *admirable, likable, wonderful.*

lob v. toss, throw, loft, flip, pitch, fling.

lobby n. **1.** HALL entrance, corridor, foyer, vestibule, reception area, anteroom. **2.** PRESSURE GROUP special interest group, political action group, influence peddlers, lobbyists.

LOBBY v. [LAH bee] to try to influence others, especially politicians and their votes.

The paper companies plan to lobby in Washington for stronger lumbering rights. SYN. influence, *influence-peddle, *pull strings, persuade, pressure, sway, solicit votes, sell, push, politick.

lobbyist n. special interest representative, pressure group representative, influence peddler, string-puller, power-broker, mover and shaker, persuader. SEE POLITICS

local a. regional, neighborhood, community, municipal, divisional, district, close to home, civic, parochial, provincial, native, limited, narrow, confined. ANT. *national, international, worldwide, foreign.*

locality n. locale, spot, place, area, neighborhood, position, site, point, region, zone, district.

localize v. confine, limit, narrow, restrict.

locate v. **1.** FIND detect, come across, uncover, discover, place, track down, pinpoint, unearth, root out, sniff out, ferret out. **2.** ESTABLISH settle, occupy, take root, house, take up residence, squat.

located a. situated, stationed, placed, positioned, based.

location n. place, spot, site, position, point, zone, locale, locality, area, neighborhood, district, neck of the woods.

lock n. **1.** bolt, catch, padlock, latch, hook, bar, deadbolt, clamp. **2.** tress, curl, ringlet, tuft. SEE HAIR

lock v. secure, latch, bolt, padlock, bar, close, shut.

locker n. chest, footlocker, trunk, cabinet, compartment, closet.

locomotion n. motion, movement, progression, traveling, driving, walking. ANT. *inertia, stasis.*

locution n. phrasing, phraseology, language, ideolect, dialect, pronunciation, accent, brogue.

lodestar n. **1.** NORTH STAR pole star, Polaris. **2.** GUIDE ideal.

lodge n. summer house, cabin, camp, cottage, chalet, hostel, resort hotel, hunting lodge.

lodge v. **1.** STAY room, house, abide, *put up, reside, live, bunk, *hole up, sojourn. **2.** BECOME STUCK stick, wedge, fix, catch.

lodger n. guest, tenant, boarder, renter, roomer.

lodging n. accommodation, hotel, motel, inn, bed and breakfast, hostel, boarding house, rooming house, quarters, room and board, pied-à-terre, billet.

loft n. attic, garret, storeroom, upper level, studio, gallery, clerestory.

loft v. throw, toss, launch skyward.

lofty a. **1.** VERY HIGH sky high, elevated, soaring, towering, vertiginous, tall, aerial, cloud-kissing, heavenly, celestial. **2.** NOBLE OR SUBLIME exalted, elevated, great, grand, esteemed, renowned, celebrated, distinguished, majestic. **3.** HAUGHTY arrogant, high and mighty, lordly, supercilious, self-important, *snotty, *stuck-up, *on one's high horse, *uppity, pompous, proud. ANT. *1. low, earthbound, short. 2. ignoble, low, common. 3. modest, humble, down to earth.*

log n. **1.** TREE LIMB OR TRUNK stump, timber, branch, block, pole, beam, wood. **2.** RECORD BOOK journal, register, account, daybook, diary, chronicle.

WORD FIND

game, knock opponent off rolling log: birling

logger: lumberjack

logging slope run: flume, sluice

mass of in river: drive

pile: rollway

log v. record, report, enter, note, register, chronicle, take down, keep an account, tally.

loge n. box, balcony, compartment, stall.

logger n. lumberjack, woodcutter, forest worker.

logic n. reasoning, argumentation, deduction, induction, syllogization, analysis, rationale, sense, good sense, sound judgment. "The anatomy of thought."—John Locke. "The architecture of human reason."—Evelyn Waugh. "The armory of reason."—Thomas Fuller.

logical a. reasonable, sensible, commonsensical, rational, sound, analytical, intelligent, smart, deductive, scientific, plausible. ANT. *illogical, nonsensical, unscientific.*

LOGISTICS n. [lo JIS tiks] management of any large operation, military or otherwise, and particularly dealing with procurement, distribution, transport and maintenance of materials and personnel. *The logistics of feeding, moving and lodging 100,000 troops in two days is nightmarish.* SYN. management, organization, coordination, maintenance, procurement, upkeep, systematization, governance, handling, direction, husbandry, methodization.

logo n. trademark, logogram, logotype, name, symbol, trade name, emblem, colophon.

loiter v. hang around, linger, idle, lounge, tarry, hover, mill around, poke, *hang, loaf, vegetate, dawdle.

loll v. **1.** LOUNGE lean, recline, sprawl, relax, slouch, lie on, repose, hang. **2.** DROOP hang, dangle, trail, sag.

lone a. solitary, sole, isolated, lonely, single, individual, unaccompanied, deserted, forsaken. ANT. *paired, accompanied.*

loneliness n. isolation, emptiness, aloneness, alienation, detachment, remoteness, seclusion, lack of intimacy, heartache, longing for compaionship. ANT. *intimacy, camaraderie, fellowhip.*

lonely a. **1.** FRIENDLESS feeling empty, lonesome, companionless, lone, forsaken, isolated, solitary, secluded, reclusive, *like a hermit, forlorn, lovelorn, desolate, deserted, abandoned, forgotten, estranged, shut in. **2.** REMOTE out of the way, unfrequented, uninhabited, deserted, isolated, secluded, unpopulated, sequestered, cloistered. ANT. *1. befriended, popular. 2. crowded, mobbed, frequented.*

loner n. *lone wolf, solitary, hermit, recluse, introvert, outcast, misanthrope.

lonesome a. SEE LONELY

long a. **1.** EXTENSIVE extended, expanded, lengthy, elongated, protracted, prolonged, stretched out, drawn out. **2.** TAKING TOO MUCH TIME overlong, interminable, long-winded, unending, endless, dragging, tedious. ANT. *1. short, brief. 2. brief, short, concise.*

long v. yearn, hunger, desire, crave, thirst, want, hanker, wish for, pine, *lust after, *have the hots for.

longevity n. long life, endurance, staying power, durability.

longing n. yearning, desire, hunger, craving, thirst, want, hankering, yen, wish, *itch.

longing a. yearning, desirous, wanting, craving, hungry, wishful, pining. ANT. *content, satisfied.*

longshot n. outside shot, outside chance, one in a million chance, *a snowball's chance in hell.

long-standing a. long-established, deeply rooted, long-lived. ANT. *short-lived, new.*

long-winded a. wordy, verbose, prolix, *windy, diffuse, rambling, circumlocutory, overlong, endless, interminable. ANT. *brief, short, to the point.*

look n. **1.** EXPRESSION appearance, face, aspect, bearing, guise, impression, air, fashion. **2.** GLANCE glimpse, eye, regard, stare, gander, inspection, *once-over, scrutiny, examination.

look v. **1.** SEE regard, behold, check out, inspect, examine, view, observe, scrutinize, notice, *take a gander, *feast one's eyes on, survey, watch, *eyeball, *get a load of, gaze, stare, glimpse, glance. **2.** APPEAR seem, strike one as, exhibit, resemble, manifest.

look-alike n. twin, double, carbon copy, clone, mirror image, *dead ringer, match, *spitting image, duplicate.

lookout n. **1.** WATCH guard, eye, vigilance, heed, surveillance. **2.** SENTINEL guard, sentry, watchman, patrol, spotter. **3.** LOOKOUT STATION tower, perch, crow's nest, watchtower, observatory.

loom v. appear, take shape, materialize, rise up, emerge, threaten, menace, impend, cast a long shadow. ANT. *disappear, vanish, recede.*

loony a. Sl. crazy, nutty, demented, lunatic, *daffy, *cuckoo, *wacky, mad, daft, foolish, stupid, *out of one's gourd, irrational. ANT. *sane, rational, sober.*

loony bin n. Sl. mental health institution, mental health treatment facility, psychiatric hospital, psychiatric ward, recovery center, mental hospital, insane asylum, *nuthouse, *madhouse, *laughing academy, *funny farm, *psycho ward, *booby hatch, *nut college, *rubber room.

loop n. circle, ring, hoop, bow, noose, spiral, coil, eyelet, bend, circuit.

loop v. circle, encircle, ring, wind, coil, curl, knot.

loophole n. escape, evasionary route, way out.

loose v. SEE LOOSEN

loose a. **1.** NOT TIGHT slack, relaxed, lax, limp, baggy, unbinding. **2.** UNRESTRAINED unbound, unfastened, untied, undone, unrestricted, unconstrained, unsecured, unattached, free. **3.** INEXACT indefinite, imprecise, vague, broad, roundabout. **4.** SEXUALLY IMMORAL lascivious, licentious, promiscuous, lewd, lecherous, abandoned, debauched, unrestrained, libidinous, perverted, *having the morals of an alley cat. ANT. *1. tight, snug, binding. 2. restrained, bound, tied. 3. exact, precise. 4. chaste, celibate, moral.*

loosen v. **1.** SLACKEN relax, unbind, ease up, moderate, relieve tension. **2.** FREE untie, unbind, let go, liberate, unfasten, untether, undo, unlock. ANT. *1. tighten, restrict, bind. 2. tie, bind, fasten.*

loot n. plunder, spoils, stolen goods, booty, take, haul, pillage.

loot v. plunder, rob, steal, despoil, pillage, *rip off, swipe, lift, ransack, pilfer, burglarize.

looter n. thief, plunderer, pillager, criminal, grabber, raider, ravager, ransacker, pilferer, opportunist.

lop v. trim, cut, remove, prune, sever, truncate, chop off, clip, shear, pare.

lope v. stride, spring, *move right along. SEE WALK

lopsided a. uneven, asymmetrical, one-sided, unbalanced, disproportional, top-heavy, *cockeyed, awry, irregular. ANT. *even, symmetrical, balanced.*

LOQUACIOUS a. [loh KWAY shus] talkative, gabby. *Talk show hosts are naturally loquacious.* SYN. talkative, gabby, garrulous, chatty, longwinded, voluble, babbling, verbose, *bigmouthed, *motor-mouthed, *having the gift of gab. ANT. *taciturn, reticent, reserved.*

lord n. nobleman, master, ruler, monarch, governor, baron, viscount, king.

lordly a. **1.** NOBLE grand, stately, dignified, gracious, lofty, princely, regal, royal. **2.** HAUGHTY arrogant, overbearing, high and mighty, imperious, domineering, insolent, condescending, supercilious, *snotty, superior. ANT. *1. low, common, humble. 2. modest, humble, down to earth, subservient.*

lose v. **1.** MISLAY misplace, lose track of, lose sight of. **2.** BE DEFEATED fail, fall, *blow it, *flunk, *go belly up, be outclassed, be outdistanced, fall short, surrender, *eat one's dust, *meet one's Waterloo, *take a beating, be humbled, *take a dive, *bomb, flop, *lay an egg, *take a bath. **3.** ELUDE evade, escape, avoid, *give the slip, rid, *throw off the trail, outdistance, *leave in one's wake. ANT. *1. find, stumble upon, locate. 2. win, defeat, triumph, outclass, vanquish.*

loser n. failure, *Charlie Brown, *schlemiel, also-ran, *dud, *flop, *dog, *sad sack, *foul ball, *turkey, *poor slob. ANT. *winner, champion, hero.*

loss n. **1.** COST debit, deficit, debt, forfeiture. **2.** SEE DEFEAT **3.** DAMAGE deprivation, detriment, disadvantage, harm, injury, impairment, privation, misfortune, destruction, removal. ANT. *1. profit, gain, surplus. 2. win. 3. gain, return.*

lost a. **1.** MISPLACED mislaid, missing, disappeared, vanished, gone, strayed, down the drain, irretrievable. **2.** OFF TRACK disoriented, astray, *going around in circles, offcourse, adrift. **3.** DESTROYED ruined, wiped out, wrecked, obliterated. **4.** WASTED squandered, misspent, exhausted. **5.** DEEP IN THOUGHT absorbed, dreaming, rapt, preoccupied, engrossed, abstracted, far away. **6.** BEWILDERED confused. ANT. *1. found, uncovered, retrieved. 2. oriented, on course, having one's bearings. 3. preserved, saved.*

lot n. **1.** PARCEL OF LAND plot, acreage, tract, real estate, subdivision. **2.** PORTION share, allotment, allowance, interest, part, percentage. **3.** FORTUNE fate, *hand one is dealt, destiny, portion, status, doom, *the way the cookie crumbles. **4.** A GREAT DEAL much, quantity, piles, slews, loads, scores, tons, abundance, plenty, oodles.

lothario n. womanizer, lady-killer, seducer, rake, lover, *wolf, philanderer, Don Juan, Casanova, Romeo.

lotion n. cream, ointment, balm, salve, embrocation, conditioner, liniment, unguent.

lottery n. drawing, game of chance, Lotto, sweepstakes, raffle, numbers game, gambling.

loud a. **1.** BLARING earsplitting, deafening, piercing, thundering, booming, stentorian, intense, clamorous, noisy, vociferous, *enough to wake the dead, powerful, roaring, cacophonous. **2.** GAUDY flashy, garish, blinding, splashy, ostentatious, vivid, cheap. ANT. *1. quiet, low, soft, silent. 2. tasteful, understated.*

loudmouthed a. bigmouthed, obnoxious, blustering, bellowing, vociferous, boisterous, strident, clamorous. ANT. *reticent, shy, quiet, taciturn.*

lounge n. **1.** LOBBY waiting room, reception room, anteroom. **2.** COCKTAIL LOUNGE club, bar, saloon, disco.

lounge v. relax, recline, lie about, repose, stretch out, sprawl out, loll, loaf, vegetate, idle, laze.

lousy a. Sl. poor, rotten, inferior, awful, terrible, *crappy, shoddy, inadequate, shabby, bad, disgusting, contemptible, atrocious. ANT. *good, great, high class.*

lout n. boor, oaf, clodhopper, clod, bumpkin, hayseed, dolt, clown, *lug, *slob, yahoo, *lummox.

loutish a. boorish, clumsy, stupid, oafish, cloddish, dense, rough, churlish, *like a bull in a china shop. ANT. *refined, gracious, urbane, suave.*

lovable a. endearing, adorable, sweet, dear, warmhearted, winning, amiable, cute, cuddly, lovely, likable, charming, angelic. ANT. *repugnant, nauseating, loathsome.*

love n. endearment, devotion, adoration, fondness, affection, warmth, esteem, friendship, closeness, intimacy, attachment, regard, passion, infatuation, crush, enchantment, amour, ardor, rapture, desire, longing, *hots. "Our highest word, and the synonym of God."—Ralph Waldo Emerson. "An alliance of friendship and animalism."—Charles Colton. "Friendship set on fire."—Jeremy Taylor. "The heart's immortal thirst to be completely known and all forgiven."—Henry Van Dyke. "Spiritual fire."—Emanuel Swedenborg. "Two minds without a single thought."—Philip Barry. "A perpetual hyperbole."—Francis Bacon. "When another' person's needs are as important as your own."—Abe Burrows. ANT. *hate, disgust, contempt, repulsion.*

love v. **1.** ADORE be fond of, cherish, worship, hold dear, treasure, idolize, think the world of, like, be crazy about, long for, desire. **2.** *MAKE OUT hug, kiss, cuddle, neck, embrace, make love, romance, have sex, engage in foreplay, *have the hots for. ANT. *1. hate, dislike, loathe, detest.*

love affair n. affair, fling, romance, intrigue, liaison, relationship, tryst, adultery, amour.

love child n. bastard, illegitimate child, whoreson.

love handle n. Sl. fat, flab, *spare tire, *middle age spread.

lovelorn n. loveless, forsaken, lovesick, spurned, bereft, rejected, jilted.

lovely a. beautiful, pretty, attractive, exquisite, fair, gracious, winning, charming, handsome, good-looking, comely, fetching, captivating, pleasing, graceful, nice, personable. ANT. *ugly, repulsive, hideous.*

lovemaking n. *making out, foreplay, intercourse, coitus, copulation, sexual union, passion, pair-bonding, mating, cuddling, fondling, kissing. SEE SEX

lover n. **1.** SWEETHEART flame, steady, *honey, *significant other, mate, sex partner, suitor, paramour, stud, Romeo, beau, boyfriend, girlfriend, mistress, lothario, Don Juan, Casanova, heartthrob. **2.** FAN aficionado, devotee, enthusiast, buff, *freak, *bug, *nut.

lovesick a. longing, pining, *out of it, *gone, lovelorn, *having it bad. ANT. *repulsed, *over it.*

loving *a*. affectionate, warm, tender, giving, fond, devoted, caring, doting, kind, friendly, demonstrative, solicitous, passionate, amorous, romantic, sexual, erotic, ardent. ANT. *hateful, mean, cold, brutal.*

low *a*. **1.** CLOSE TO THE GROUND ground-level, low-lying, low-hanging, low-slung, short, squat, bottommost. **2.** DECREASED diminished, drained, depleted, dried up, exhausted, shallow, expended, running out. **3.** UNHAPPY depressed, melancholy, *bummed out, miserable, blue, downhearted, dejected, glum, discouraged, sad, heavyhearted. **4.** SMALL little, paltry, slight, modest, slim, puny, deficient, humble. **5.** MEAN despicable, bad, evil, base, depraved, contemptible, disgraceful, wretched, reprehensible, ignoble, vulgar, nasty. **6.** QUIET hushed, subdued, soft, muted, muffled, whispered, murmured. **7.** POOR plebian, humble, lowborn. ANT. *1. high, tall, skyscraping, towering. 2. full, replenished, overflowing. 3. high, happy, joyous. 4. large, generous, high. 5. honorable, noble, nice. 6. loud, amplified. 7. wealthy, highborn, aristocratic.*

low-browed *a*. uneducated, uncultivated, unsophisticated, vulgar, unschooled, ignorant, illiterate. ANT. *refined.*

lower *v*. **1.** DROP bring down, let down, let fall, depress, descend, submerge, dip, sink. **2.** REDUCE decrease, diminish, lessen, downgrade, depreciate, modify, cut, slash, shorten, soften, abate, relieve. **3.** HUMBLE degrade, dishonor, shame, humiliate, disgrace, debase, demean. ANT. *1. raise, lift, elevate. 2. increase, boost, add, extend. 3. respect, honor, exalt.*

lower *a*. inferior, under, lesser, secondary, minor, subordinate, junior. ANT. *higher, superior.*

low-key *a*. subdued, understated, subtle, restrained, toned down, mellow, muted, quiet. ANT. *loud, intense, blatant.*

lowly *a*. inferior, humble, modest, common, ordinary, plain, simple, poor, plebian, proletarian, baseborn, obscure. ANT. *superior, high-born, lofty.*

loyal *a*. faithful, trustworthy, true, allegiant, *tried and true, *true-blue, devoted, patriotic, dedicated, staunch, reliable, dependable. ANT. *disloyal, unfaithful, treacherous.*

loyalty *n*. faithfulness, allegiance, devotion, dedication, patriotism, fidelity, duty, honor, reliability, dependability, steadfastness, staunchness, trustworthiness. ANT. *disloyalty, backstabbing, treachery, perfidy.*

LSD *n*. lysergic acid diethylamide, hallucinogen, drug, *acid, *blotter, *blue cheer, *California sunshine, *dots, *electric Koolaid, *mellow yellows, *pearly gates, *tabs, *strawberry fields, *yellow, *beast, *blue heaven, *blue microdot, *blue moons, *Lucy in the sky with diamonds, *Zen, *barrels. SEE DRUG

WORD FIND

supplier: *travel agent

user: *acid head

lubricant *n*. grease, oil, coating.

lubricate *v*. grease, oil, slicken.

LUCID *a*. [LOO sid] clear, easy to understand. Also, clearheaded. *The report was straightforward and lucid.* SYN. clear, crystal-clear, transparent, understandable, comprehensible, plain, intelligible, easy to grasp, distinct, apparent, obvious, unambiguous, clearheaded, rational, of sound mind, sensible. ANT. *unclear, cloudy, unintelligible, irrational.*

Lucifer *n*. Satan, archangel. SEE DEVIL

luck *n*. **1.** FORTUNE fate, chance, lot, destiny, wheel of fortune, fortuity, happenstance, *fickle finger of fate, *toss of the dice, providence, kismet. **2.** GOOD FORTUNE *break, success, windfall, godsend, opportunity, serendipity, fluke. "An explanation of the other fellow's success."—Harry Thompson. ANT. *2. misfortune, bad break.*

lucky *a*. fortunate, blessed, auspicious, providential, propitious, fortuitous, by chance. ANT. *unlucky, unfortunate.*

LUCRATIVE *a*. [LOO kruh tiv] producing profit or riches. *His oil business turned out to be highly lucrative.* SYN. profitable, profit-producing, wealth-producing, income-producing, remunerative, money-making, high-paying, gainful, prosperous, rewarding, worthwhile. ANT. *unprofitable, money-losing, unprosperous, income-draining.*

lucre *n*. money, riches, wealth.

LUDICROUS *a*. [LOO di krus] laughable, absurd. *The medical beliefs of the early Victorians were often ludicrous.* SYN. laughable, absurd, ridiculous, stupid, preposterous, comical, hilarious, outlandish, crazy, silly, uproarious, nonsensical, *cockamamy. ANT. *serious, sensible, respectable.*

lug *v*. carry, drag, haul, tow, *schlep, hump, tug, pull, tote.

luggage *n*. baggage, trunks, carry-on, suitcases, valises, packs, bags, gear, effects.

lukewarm *a.* unenthusiastic, halfhearted, cool, apathetic, indifferent, tepid, impassive, uncaring, uninterested. ANT. *enthusiastic, passionate, hot.*

lull *n.* quiet period, calm, pause, letup, break, quiet, respite, hush, spell, breather, silence.

lull *v.* calm, soothe, reassure, sedate, pacify, quiet, put to sleep, tranquilize, allay. ANT. *agitate, arouse, excite.*

lulu *n. Sl.* *dilly, *corker, *dandy, *humdinger, *doozy, *ripsnorter, *something to write home about.

lumber *n.* timber, wood, planks, boards, two-by-fours, milled wood, studs, posts, beams.

lumber *v.* clump, plod, stump, trudge, stamp, *clomp, drag, waddle, move heavily, move awkwardly.

lumberjack *n.* logger, woodcutter.

luminary *n.* celebrity, star, *superstar, *VIP, notable, personality, dignitary, *big name, *bigshot, *bigwig, *toast of the town. ANT. *nobody.*

luminous *a.* **1.** BRIGHT glowing, aglow, shining, illuminated, lighted, brilliant, radiant, lit, resplendent, luminescent, lustrous. **2.** CLEAR understandable, lucid, comprehendable, intelligible, perspicuous, plain, obvious. ANT. *1. dark, dim, black. 2. cloudy, confusing, vague.*

lummox *n.* oaf, clod, *klutz, *big ape, lunkhead, lout, clodhopper.

lump *n.* clump, chunk, mass, gob, ball, hunk, piece, bulk, scrap, bump, protuberance, swelling, bulge, prominence, node, knot.

lunacy *n.* craziness, insanity, psychosis, madness, dementia, folly, foolishness, idiocy, *wackiness, *nuttiness, stupidity, silliness, imbecility. ANT. *sanity, rationality, sensibleness.*

lunatic *n.* psychopath, maniac, madman, psychotic, sociopath, *schizo, *psycho, *whacko, *nut, *kook, *loony, *screwball, crackbrain. SEE INSANITY

lunatic *a.* SEE CRAZY

lunch *n.* luncheon, dinner, bite to eat, brunch, meal, déjeuner.

lung *n.* respiratory organ.

lunge *n.* thrust, plunge, charge, pounce, jump, rush, spring, leap, pass, jab, stab.

lunge *v.* thrust, plunge, charge, pounce, jump, rush, spring, leap, pass, jab, stab.

lurch *v.* pitch, jerk, heave, slip, roll, stagger, sway, lunge, plunge, toss, reel, tilt.

lure *n.* enticement, bait, temptation, *carrot, *magnet, *come-on, attraction, tease, inducement, allurement, draw, hook, bribe. ANT. *repellent.*

lure *v.* entice, bait, tempt, *hold out a carrot, attract, tease, induce, draw, hook, bribe, allure, seduce. ANT. *repel.*

LURID *a.* [LOOR id] shocking, horrifying or sensational, as a grisly crime. *The news show provided all the lurid details of the murder.* SYN. shocking, horrifying, sensational, startling, vivid, graphic, horrid, gruesome, appalling, grisly, revolting.

luscious *a.* delicious, delightful, delectable, *scrumptious, tasty, flavorful, toothsome, palatable, sumptuous, heavenly, succulent, savory, *out of this world, mouth-watering, ambrosial, *yummy, rich. ANT. *disgusting, nauseating, sickening.*

lush *a.* rich, luxurious, luxuriant, profuse, dense, thick, flourishing, prolific, abundant, green, verdant. ANT. *sparse, scanty, thin.*

lust *n.* desire, *burning desire, passion, libido, want, hunger, longing, craving, urge, Eros, sex drive, hot blood, itch, licentiousness, lechery, heat. "The brutish passion."—Robert Burton. "A means for the satisfaction of animal needs."—Mohandas Gandhi. "A honeyed poison."—John Taylor.

lust *v.* desire, want, hunger for, long for, crave, itch for, pant after, *have the hots for, ache for, be consumed with desire.

luster *n.* shine, glow, gloss, sheen, radiance, shimmer, gleam, burnish, glint, brilliance, dazzle. ANT. *dullness, drabness.*

lustrous *a.* shining, glowing, bright, glossy, radiant, shimmering, gleaming, burnished, glinting, brilliant, dazzling. ANT. *dull, drab.*

lusty *a.* vigorous, hearty, strong, robust, hardy, full of life, hale, energetic, healthy, vital, virile. ANT. *weak, sickly, frail.*

luxuriant *a.* **1.** LUSH teeming, vigorous, abundant, profuse, rich, luxurious, dense, thick, copious, overgrown. **2.** EXTRAVAGANT excessive, florid, ornate, busy, overdone, rococo, showy, sumptuous. ANT. *1. sparse, thin, scanty. 2. understated, plain.*

luxurious *a.* rich, extravagant, sumptuous, splendid, plush, ostentatious, fancy, indulgent, posh, lush, immoderate, *ritzy, comfortable, sensuous. ANT. *poor, shoddy, shabby.*

luxury *n.* extravagance, indulgence, riches, wealth, affluence, superfluity, opulence, *bed of roses, sumptuousness, abundance, lavishness, comfort, ease, immoderation, *high living, hedonism, treat, frill, extra.

"Positive hindrances to the elevation of mankind."—Thoreau. ANT. *poverty, want, deprivation, bare necessity.*

lying *n.* dishonesty, untruthfulness, prevarication, deceit, fibbing, dissembling, fabrication, storytelling, insincerity, mendacity. "A form of creativity; talking the truth is being only a reporter."—Eric Hoffer. ANT. *honesty, truth-telling.*

lying *a.* dishonest, untruthful, deceitful, fibbing, dissembling, mendacious, fabricating, insincere, prevaricating. ANT. *truthful, honest.*

lynching *n.* hanging, *stringing up, *necktie party, execution, *mob justice, murder, vigilante justice.

lyric *a.* songlike, poetic, musical, melodic, melodious, tuneful, mellifluous.

lyrical *a.* expressive, emotional, soulful, deep, heartfelt, rhapsodic.

lyricist *n.* songwriter, songsmith, poet, composer.

M

MACABRE *a.* [muh KAHB ruh] gruesome, ghastly, denoting the horrors of death. *The macabre account of torture and murder was a bestseller.* SYN. gruesome, ghastly, horrifying, horrible, grim, grisly, deathly, morbid, frightful, lurid, eerie, ghostly, spooky, unearthly.

marcaroni *n.* pasta, shells. SEE PASTA

MACHIAVELLIAN *a.* [MAK ee uh VEL ee un] deceitful and crafty, wily. *The politician was Machiavellian in his dealings with rivals.* SYN. deceitful, crafty, wily, duplicitous, expedient, cunning, scheming, conniving, devious, sly, unscrupulous. ANT. *honorable, straightforward, honest.*

MACHINATION *n.* [mak uh NAY shun] a plot or scheme, especially of devious intent. *He won the nomination through behind-the-scenes machinations.* SYN. plot, plotting, scheme, scheming, engineering, string-pulling, design, contrivance, ploy, maneuver, artifice, *skulduggery, *backdoor dealing, device.

machine *n.* mechanism, apparatus, device, appliance, engine, motor, contraption, vehicle, *workhorse, automoton, robot, gadget.

machinery *n.* SEE MACHINE

machismo *n.* masculinity, virility, manliness, dominance, strength, fierceness, aggressiveness, fearlessness, potency, toughness.

macho *a.* masculine, virile, dominant, strong, fierce, fearless, manly, aggressive, potent, tough, swaggering, cocky. ANT. *weak, effeminate,* *wimpy.

macrocosm *n.* world, cosmos, universe, all creation. ANT. *microcosm.*

mad *a.* **1.** INSANE crazy, psychotic, psychopathic, schizophrenic, *nuts, deranged, demented, *out of one's mind, unstable, unbalanced, *loony, *off one's rocker, *mental, *wacky, foolish, harebrained. SEE INSANITY **2.** ANGRY enraged, furious, infuriated, incensed, irate, peeved, irritated, annoyed, vexed, *ticked, enflamed, *pissed, livid, *gone ballistic. SEE ANGRY ANT. *1. sane, rational, stable, of sound mind. 2. pleased, delighted, happy.*

madcap *a.* reckless, wild, impulsive, crazy, rash, imprudent, foolish, foolhardy. ANT. *prudent, sensible, cautious.*

maddening *a.* infuriating, aggravating, exasperating, enraging, galling, provoking, riling, troubling, irritating, annoying, outrageous, frustrating. ANT. *encouraging, settling, fulfilling.*

made-up *a.* fictional, fictitious, invented, fabricated, contrived, thought up, dreamed up, concocted. ANT. *true, factual, real.*

madhouse *n.* insane asylum, *loony bin, mental hospital, *laughing academy, mental institution, psychiatric hospital, *nuthouse, *booby hatch, chaos, bedlam.

madman *n.* psychopath, psychotic, *psycho, lunatic, schizophrenic, maniac, sociopath, *sicko, *kook, *nut.

madness *n.* insanity, craziness, psychosis, lunacy, schizophrenia, dementia, derangement, mental illness, *nuttiness, mania, delusion of grandeur. "That reckless fire."— Edmund Gosse. "A common calamity; we are all mad at some time or other."—Johannes Mantuanus. SEE NEUROSIS, MANIA, PHOBIA, INSANITY

maelstrom *n.* **1.** WHIRLPOOL vortex, eddy, swirl, Charybdis. **2.** AGITATION turmoil, turbulence, uproar, madness, confusion, unbalance.

maestro *n.* master, conductor, composer, master musician, music teacher, instructor.

Mafia *n.* *the mob, Cosa Nostra, organized crime, the underworld, Black Hand, the Syndicate, gangland.

WORD FIND

advisor to chief: consigliere

arrested: pinched

blackmail or scare someone for money: shakedown

business enterprises: loan sharking, money laundering, drug trafficking, gambling, labor racketeering, counterfeiting, extortion, prostitution, gangland killings

chief: boss, capo, chairman, don

code of silence: omerta

crime family: borgata, brugad

euphemism: waste management business, garbage business

gambling profits without declaring on taxes, to take: skim

gun: piece

gun, carrying a: heavy, packing

inducted into the Mafia: made

informer: canary, rat, squealer

interest paid to loan sharks: juice

intimidates, threatens, beats up, or kills; one who: enforcer

legal protection for testifying against: Witness Protection Program

loans money at exorbitant interest rate: loanshark

low-ranking member: soldier

member of: goodfella, Mafioso, mobster, wiseguy

mistress of Mafia member: comare

murder, to: whack, hit, burn, put a contract out on.

second-in-command: caporegime, underboss

slipping away by various means from someone who may be following on foot or in a car: cleaning

soldiers, group of: crew

stolen goods: swag

stolen goods, one who receives or sells: fence

underling, stupid: babbo

magazine n. periodical, publication, journal, digest, monthly, weekly, quarterly, *rag, review, *slick.

magic n. **1.** SUPERNATURAL POWERS wizardry, witchcraft, sorcery, black magic, necromancy, conjuring, mysticism, voodoo, hoodoo, occultism, diabolism. **2.** TRICKERY legerdemain, sleight-of-hand, prestidigitation, hocus-pocus, *smoke and mirrors, conjuring.

WORD FIND

gold from metal art: alchemy

magic words: incantation, abracadabra, presto, mumbo jumbo, sesame

symbol: pentacle

SEE OCCULT

magical a. enchanting, bewitching, charming, spellbinding, mesmerizing, entrancing, fascinating, hypnotic, seductive. ANT. *ordinary*.

magician n. **1.** ONE WITH SUPERNATURAL POWERS wizard, sorcerer, witch, necromancer, mystic, conjurer, warlock, Merlin, shaman. **2.** TRICKSTER prestidigitator, illusionist, legerdemainist, sleight-of-hand expert, Houdini.

magistrate n. civil officer, administrator, justice of the peace, judge, justice.

MAGNANIMOUS a. [mag NAN uh mus] high-minded or noble, quick to forgive and not hold grudges. *John was magnanimous in his loss, conceding that his opponent was the better man.* SYN. noble, forgiving, high-minded, big, generous, liberal, tolerant, charitable, ungrudging, benevolent, chivalrous. ANT. *grudging, petty, unforgiving*.

MAGNATE n. [MAG nate] a powerful or influential business person. *The oil magnate made a large donation to the library.* SYN. *big shot, *bigwig, tycoon, capitalist, industrialist, baron, leader, power, giant, VIP, *big-time operator, *biggest toad in the puddle.

magnetic a. drawing, pulling, attractive, irresistible, arresting, tugging, grabbing, seductive, alluring, captivating, charismatic. ANT. *repellent, repulsive*.

magnetism n. attractiveness, charisma, drawing power, hold, irresistibility, charm, appeal, dynamism, animal magnetism, sex appeal, pull.

magnificent a. grand, beautiful, stately, glorious, exalted, spectacular, grandiose, wonderful, splendid, majestic, imposing, awe-inspiring, elegant, gorgeous, sumptuous, breathtaking. ANT. *modest, humble, *nothing to write home about*.

magnify v. enlarge, blow up, intensify, enhance, increase, expand, amplify, *beef up, heighten, concentrate, exaggerate, blow out of proportion, overstate. ANT. *minimize, reduce, diminish*.

magnitude n. **1.** SIZE extent, greatness, bigness, dimensions, vastness, measure, mass, volume, expanse, bulk. **2.** IMPORTANCE influence, consequence, weight, degree, moment, significance, import, enormity, prominence. ANT. *1. smallness. 2. insignificance*.

maharishi n. guru, spiritual guide, mystic, teacher.

maiden n. maid, girl, miss, lass, virgin, school girl, damsel, *jailbait, *chick.

maiden a. new, untried, virgin, fresh, first, inaugural, initial, original. ANT. *old, hackneyed, *old hat*.

mail n. letters, postcards, correspondence, post, packages, parcel post, *junk mail, circulars, *snail mail, dispatch.

mail v. post, send, dispatch, address, ship, transmit, *fax, send it UPS, e-mail, *snail mail.

mailman n. letter carrier, mail carrier, postal carrier, mailwoman, postman.

maim v. cripple, handicap, mutilate, disable, hurt, injure, wound, incapacitate, mangle, hamstring, dismember, damage, break.

main a. principal, chief, primary, central, prime, major, critical, important, head, predominant, foremost, essential, crucial, outstanding. ANT. *secondary, minor, subordinate, lesser*.

mainly *adv.* principally, chiefly, primarily, predominantly, essentially, mostly.

mainstay *n.* chief support, backbone, anchor, pillar, strength, prop, staff, foundation, buttress.

mainstream *a.* prevailing, general, average, typical, standard, predominant, main, principle, middle-of-the-road, primary. ANT. *extreme, fringe, radical.*

maintain *v.* **1.** KEEP UP look after, service, repair, mend, care for, take care of, sustain, preserve, conserve. **2.** CONTINUE WITH carry on, prolong, keep, keep going, keep alive, sustain, perpetuate, support. **3.** ASSERT declare, hold, contend, state, claim, testify, affirm, insist, argue. ANT. *1. neglect, let go, destroy, ruin. 2. stop, quit, kill, end. 3. deny, disavow.*

maintenance *n.* **1.** UPKEEP servicing, repair, care, grooming, preservation, conservation. **2.** SUSTENANCE support, livelihood, income, allowance, alimony, child support.

majestic *a.* grand, stately, lofty, dignified, regal, princely, kingly, imperial, distinguished, palatial, imposing. ANT. *modest, humble, lowly.*

majesty *n.* grandeur, stateliness, loftiness, dignity, regalness, magnificence, nobility, splendor.

major *a.* **1.** BIGGER larger, greater, chief, superior, dominant, main, principal. **2.** IMPORTANT chief, principal, primary, foremost, top, critical, outstanding, significant. ANT. *1. smaller, lesser. 2. minor, secondary.*

majority *n.* **1.** THE MOST greater part, preponderance, bulk, more than half, mass, lion's share. **2.** ADULTHOOD voting age, age of consent, maturity, manhood, womanhood, drinking age. ANT. *1. minority, less than half, few. 2. minority, childhood.*

make *n.* brand, kind, variety, model, style.

make *v.* **1.** FORM construct, fabricate, create, originate, concoct, manufacture, build, assemble, compose, produce, devise, shape, fashion, *slap together, cook up, brew. **2.** CAUSE bring about, effect, effectuate, start, generate, produce, do, accomplish. **3.** FORCE compel, impel, coerce, prevail upon, press, pressure, oblige, railroad, arm twist, *strongarm, require. **4.** ELECT appoint, vote in, designate, name, assign, install. **5.** EARN bring in, clear, *take home, gross, net, reap, gain. ANT. *1. disassemble, dismantle, destroy, obliterate. 5. spend, pay, *blow, lose.*

make-believe *n.* fantasy, imagination, pretending, dream, fancy, fiction, invention, pretense.

makeshift *a.* temporary, expedient, *slapdash, emergency, stopgap, thrown-together, jury-rigged, improvised, on-the-spot, substitute. ANT. *permanent.*

make-up *n.* **1.** COSMETICS foundation, rouge, blush, greasepaint, beauty aid, mascara, face paint. **2.** CHARACTER genetic heritage, nature, personality, disposition, temperament, individuality, composition, sums of one's parts.

maladjusted *a.* maladapted, unadapted, unfit, neurotic, disturbed, *messed up, *warped, abnormal, stressed. ANT. *adjusted, adapted, normal, fit.*

maladroit *a.* awkward, clumsy, bumbling, *klutzy, blundering, bungling, *having two left feet, *all thumbs, *like a bull in a china shop, uncoordinated, cloddish, inadequate, oafish. ANT. *graceful, coordinated, adroit, dexterous.*

malady *n.* disease, disorder, illness, sickness, ailment, affliction, infirmity, disability, complaint, infection, *bug.

MALAISE *n.* [ma LAYZ] uneasiness or queasiness, especially that which manifests itself at the start of an illness. *He fell into a state of malaise and rarely got off the couch.* SYN. uneasiness, queasiness, weakness, sickness, tiredness, exhaustion, *the blahs, discomfort, lassitude. ANT. *vigor.*

malaria *n.* infectious disease, mosquito-borne disease, illness, sickness, malady, ague.

malarky *n. Sl.* rot, poppycock, baloney, bull. SEE NONSENSE

malcontent *n.* complainer, faultfinder, grumbler, whiner, *bellyacher, grouch, rebel.

malcontent *a.* discontented, dissatisfied, unsatisfied, unhappy, disgruntled, rebellious, complaining, faultfinding. ANT. *content, satisfied.*

male *n.* man, gentleman, guy, fellow, buck, *dude, boy, brother, father. ANT. *female, woman.*

male *a.* masculine, manly, *macho, virile. ANT. *female, feminine.*

malediction *n.* curse, damning, imprecation, execration, anathema, vilification. ANT. *blessing, best wishes.*

MALEVOLENT *a.* [mu LEV uh lunt] malicious, wishing harm on others. *He was severely abused as a child and had a malevolent disposition.* SYN. malicious, mean, vicious, nasty, hostile, spiteful, evil, malignant, vindictive, hateful, wicked, venomous, bitter. ANT. *kind, benevolent, warm, big-hearted.*

malformation *n.* abnormality, deformity, anomaly, mutation, irregularity, freak, monster, monstrosity.

malformed *a.* deformed, misshapen, distorted, mutated, grotesque, irregular, crooked, misproportioned, freakish, stunted, hunchbacked. ANT. *well-formed, perfect, impeccable.*

malfunction *n.* breakdown, *glitch, *bug, *gremlin, *SNAFU, failure, snag, foul-up, jam, *computer virus.

MALICE *n.* [MAL iss] the desire to hurt others, ill will. *The humiliating loss filled him with malice.* SYN. ill will, spite, maliciousness, hatred, malevolence, evil intent, malignance, venom, animosity, bitterness, vengefulness, viciousness, bad blood, meanness. ANT. *love, compassion, kindness.*

malicious *a.* spiteful, hurtful, vicious, malignant, malevolent, hateful, bitter, venomous, nasty, mean, wicked, pernicious, vengeful, harmful. ANT. *loving, kind, compassionate, benevolent.*

malign *v.* defame, slander, denigrate, disparage, vilify, run down, *bad-mouth, mudsling, insult, smear, revile, *drag one's name through the mud, slur.

malignant *a.* 1. DEADLY lethal, fatal, harmful, virulent, metastatic, cancerous, pernicious. 2. MALICIOUS malevolent, hostile, hurtful, harmful, evil, wicked, spiteful, vicious. ANT. *1. benign, harmless. 2. kind, helpful, friendly.*

malingerer *n.* shirker, slacker, loafer, clock-watcher, idler, *faker.

mall *n.* 1. SHOPPING CENTER shopping complex, shopping mecca, shopping plaza, strip mall, marketplace. 2. PROMENADE walk, alameda, esplanade.

malleable *a.* 1. PLIABLE flexible, movable, plastic, moldable, yielding, soft. 2. IMPRESSIONABLE changeable, moldable, adaptable, susceptible, teachable, *like putty in one's hands, tractable, docile. ANT. *1. rigid, inflexible, hard. 2. intractable, unchangeable.*

malnutrition *n.* nutrient deficiency, protein deficiency, malnourishment.

malodorous *a.* stinking, *stinky, smelly, noxious, offensive, foul, fetid, nasty, strong, reeking, putrid, rotten, rank, vile, nauseating. ANT. *sweet-smelling, flowery.*

malpractice *n.* incompetence, negligence, unprofessional conduct, misconduct, impropriety, carelessness, maltreatment, abuse, egregious error, mistake, ineptitude, irresponsibility.

mammal *n.* warm-blooded animal, creature, beast.

mammoth *a.* huge, gigantic, elephantine, colossal, gargantuan, immense, enormous, stupendous, monstrous, titanic, prodigious, massive, Brobdingnagian. ANT. *tiny, minute, microscopic, Lilliputian.*

man *n.* 1. MALE fellow, guy, gentleman, boy, chap. 2. HUMANKIND mankind, human being, human, Homo sapiens, hominid, person, creature, soul, mortal, earthling. "An ape with possibilities."—Roy Andrews. "An intelligence served by organs."—Ralph Waldo Emerson. "An ingenious assembly of portable plumbing."—Christopher Morley. "The bad child of the universe."—James Oppenheim. "The only joker in the deck of nature."—Fulton Sheen. "The organ of the accumulated smut and sneakery of 10,000 generations of weaseling souls."—Philip Wylie. "An omnivorous biped that wears breeches."—Thomas Carlyle.

manacle *n.* handcuff, shackle, iron, chain, bond.

manage *v.* 1. OVERSEE direct, govern, supervise, control, take charge of, lead, regulate, administer, conduct, guide, pilot, command, captain, quarterback. 2. ACCOMPLISH work, succeed, contrive, bring about, cause, effect, finagle, swing, engineer, wangle.

manageable *a.* controllable, governable, tractable, docile, obedient, compliant, tame, submissive, meek. ANT. *uncontrollable, unmanageable, noncompliant.*

management *n.* 1. ADMINISTRATION overseeing, direction, government, supervision, control, leadership, regulation, guidance, operation, command. 2. ADMINISTRATORS administration, executives, supervisors, bosses, superiors, directors, leaders.

manager *n.* administrator, boss, overseer, director, governor, supervisor, controller, leader, regulator, commander, foreman, officer, executive, CEO, *biggest toad in the puddle. ANT. *subordinate, employee, laborer.*

MANDATE *n.* [MAN dayt] the will or order of the people, as expressed through a vote or referendum, any order backed by authority. *The governor received a clear mandate from his constituents.* SYN. order, directive, command, charge, decree, edict, dictate, *word, ruling, instruction, authorization, commission.

mandatory *a.* required, obligatory, necessary, requisite, compulsory, demanded, needed, essential, imperative, *a must. ANT. *elective, optional, unnecessary.*

man-eater n. cannibal, anthropophagite. SEE MONSTER

maneuver n. **1.** MOVE strategy, scheme, artifice, gambit, tactic, ruse, dodge, feint, subterfuge, ploy, play, machination. **2.** MILITARY MANEUVER exercise, deployment, war game, tactics, movements, operations, flanking maneuver.

maneuver v. **1.** MANIPULATE scheme, engineer, machinate, plot, intrigue, contrive, *finagle, *pull strings. **2.** GUIDE direct, handle, steer, drive, navigate, negotiate, pilot, jockey.

mangle v. mutilate, cut, tear, hack, rip, lacerate, slice, slash, disfigure, crush, bruise, maim, damage.

mangy a. shabby, filthy, dingy, dirty, ragged, scruffy, seedy, sordid, wretched, poor. ANT. *fine, new.*

manhandle v. strong-arm, dominate, abuse, arm-twist, rough up, bully, beat up, mistreat, *belt, *slug, batter, push around.

mania n. craze, obsession, mental disorder, compulsion, fixation, preoccupation, desire, passion, fascination, madness.

WORD FIND
alcohol: dipsomania
animals: zoomania
books: bibliomania
cats: ailuromania
children: pedomania
dancing: choreomania
death: necromania
dogs: cynomania
eating: sitomania
fire: pyromania
flowers: anthomania
food: phagomania
genius, delusion one is: sophomania
horses: hippomania
kill, desire to: dacnomania
money: chrematomania
nakedness: gymnomania
night: noctimania
pleasure: hedonomania
sex: nymphomania, aphrodisiomania
sleep: hypnomania
solitude: automania
stealing: kleptomania
sun: heliomania
talking: logomania
travel: hodomania
washing: ablutomania
wealth: plutomania
women: gynemania

woods: hylomania

maniac n. madman, lunatic, psychotic, *psycho, psychopath, sociopath, *nut, *nutcase, *mental case, *sicko, *loony. SEE INSANITY, NEUROSIS, PHOBIA

maniacal a. crazy, insane, raving, *out of one's mind, demented, deranged, crazed, psychotic, *psycho, *flipped out, *nuts, *wigged out. ANT. *sane, rational, stable.*

manic a. excited, agitated, *wired, *hyper, hyperactive, *worked-up, frantic, frenzied, *high, hysterical. ANT. *calm, tranquil, depressed, down.*

manifest v. show, reveal, make plain, expose, exhibit, materialize, display, illustrate, express, bring to light, demonstrate. ANT. *hide, conceal, cover up.*

MANIFEST a. [MAN uh FEST] obvious, visible, evident. *That he was sincere was manifest.* SYN. obvious, visible, evident, clear, plain, apparent, distinct, showing, glaring, in full view, unmistakable, prominent. ANT. *invisible, unapparent, uncertain, ambiguous.*

manifestation n. form, demonstration, evidence, exhibition, display, indication, example, illustration, expression, proof, testimony.

MANIFESTO n. [MAN uh FES toh] a public declaration of political doctrine and intentions. *The new government produced a written manifesto of their beliefs.* SYN. proclamation, declaration, promulgation, notice, notification, announcement.

manifold a. varied, various, multifold, multifarious, multiple, multifaceted, diverse, miscellaneous, numerous. ANT. *simple, one-dimensional.*

manipulate v. **1.** HANDLE operate, work, wield, use, finger. **2.** FINAGLE *pull strings, contrive, influence, plot, scheme, machinate, engineer, jockey, trick, *wangle, *wheel and deal.

mankind n. SEE MAN

manly a. masculine, brave, strong, courageous, macho, virile, tough, potent, red-blooded, *two-fisted, daring, unflinching, heroic, gritty, fearless, aggressive, chivalrous, muscular, husky. ANT. *effeminate, *wimpy, mousy, feminine, weak.*

man-made a. artificial, synthetic, manufactured, fabricated, handmade, unnatural, fake. ANT. *natural, real.*

manner n. **1.** STYLE way, mode, fashion, method, system, pattern, custom, practice. **2.** BEHAVIOR air, way, conduct, deportment, aspect, bearing, mien, posture, appearance, demeanor.

mannered *a.* affected, unnatural, pretentious, put-on, posed, phony, artificial, *fake, studied, calculated. ANT. *natural, genuine.*

mannerism *n.* habit, idiosyncrasy, quirk, peculiarity, trait, tic, characteristic gesture, affectation, put-on.

mannerly *a.* polite, courteous, well-behaved, civil, gracious, considerate, refined, nice, proper, respectful, gentlemanly, ladylike, polished. ANT. *rude, ill-mannered, discourteous.*

manners *n.* courtesy, civilities, decorum, graciousness, etiquette, politeness, formalities, social graces, good form, refinement, gentility. "The final and perfect flower of noble character."—William Winter. "The art of making those people easy with whom we converse."—Jonathan Swift. "Oil that lubricates social contacts."—Leon Harrison. ANT. *rudeness, bad manners, impoliteness, roughness.*

mansion *n.* manor, estate, chateau, villa, palazzo, castle, stately home, *showplace, *dream house, *spread. SEE HOUSE

manslaughter *n.* killing, slaying, homicide. SEE MURDER

manual *n.* handbook, guidebook, instructions, directions, *how-to, bible, reference, primer, textbook. SEE BOOK

manufacture *v.* **1.** MAKE produce, mass-produce, fabricate, assemble, build, create, formulate, construct, fashion, hammer out, turn out, cast, forge. **2.** CONCOCT make up, invent, think up, fabricate, devise, lie, embellish, *tell a tall tale.

manufacturer *n.* maker, builder, producer, mill, assembler, assembly plant.

manure *n.* dung, excrement, *crap, droppings, mulch, waste matter, *do do, *cow chips, fertilizer, compost.

manuscript *n.* script, text, book, composition, story, document, article, typewritten pages, hard copy.

many *n.* a lot, abundance, scores, tons, *scads, a bunch, multitude, myriad, *galaxy, *heaps, profusion. ANT. *a few, none.*

many *a.* abundant, several, numerous, countless, multitudinous, innumerable, plentiful, copious, *umpteen. ANT. *few.*

map *n.* chart, plan, plot, graph, relief map, atlas, street guide.

maple *n.* tree, acer, deciduous tree.

mapmaker *n.* cartographer, mapper, topographer, surveyor.

mar *v.* disfigure, spoil, damage, impair, injure, blemish, deface, deform, mangle, ruin, wreck, scar, crack.

marathon *n.* cross-country race, footrace, endurance run, long distance race.

maraud *v.* raid, plunder, ransack, pillage, loot, ravage, prey upon, wreak havoc on, despoil, assault.

marauder *n.* raider, attacker, plunderer, pillager, looter, pirate, ransacker, thief, robber.

march *v.* step in time, pace, tramp, tread, parade, goose-step, walk, promenade, file, plod, strut.

WORD FIND

manner of: lockstep

marching in formations: close-order drill

Mardi Gras *n.* festival, parade, carnival, celebration, masquerade party.

margin *n.* border, edge, perimeter, verge, periphery, brink, brim, lip, hem, skirt, fringe, limit.

marginal *a.* borderline, slight, minimal, limited, negligible, insignificant, trivial. ANT. *significant, considerable.*

marijuana *n.* cannabis, hemp, *pot, *weed, *grass, *dope, *ganja, *Columbian, *Indian hay, *Jamaican, *Kona gold, *Mary Jane, *Panama red, *sinsemilla, *smoke, *Maui wowie, *Thai stick.

WORD FIND

active substance: tetrahydrocannabinol, THC

block of pressed: brick

bundle weighing one kilogram: *kilo

butt end of cigarette: *roach

cigarette holding clip: *roach clip

cigarette: *reefer, *doobie, *jay, *joint, *number, *bomb

five-dollar bag: *nickel bag

ounce of: *lid

resin product: hashish, *hash

ten-dollar bag: *dime bag

water pipe: bong

SEE COCAINE, DRUG, NARCOTIC

marina *n.* harbor, dock, dockage, boat basin, moorings, berth, slip, landing, boat yard, pier, wharf. SEE BOAT, SAIL, SHIP

marinate *v.* pickle, steep, soak.

marine *n.* SEE ARMY, MILITARY, NAVY

marine *a.* oceanic, sea, aquatic, pelagic, maritime, nautical.

mariner *n.* sailor, seafarer, seaman, *sea dog, *salt, bluejacket, navy man, skipper, mate, helmsman, boatswain, deckhand. SEE NAVAL OFFICER, NAVY, SHIP, BOAT

marionette n. dummy, doll. SEE PUPPET

marital a. wedded, matrimonial, married, conjugal, connubial, nuptial. ANT. *single.*

maritime a. oceanic, sea, aquatic, pelagic, nautical, seagoing, oceangoing, naval, marine.

mark n. **1.** LINE, SPOT OR BLEMISH streak, tick, blot, impression, trace, blotch, dot, stain, smudge, imprint, score, scratch, cut. **2.** CHARACTERISTIC sign, hallmark, indication, symptom, symbol, brand, badge, signature, proof, evidence. **3.** STANDARD norm, rule, criterion, scale, yardstick, gauge. **4.** TARGET goal, aim, end, objective, object, bull's-eye.

mark v. **1.** BLEMISH streak, blot, leave an impression, blotch, dot, stain, smudge, splotch, mar, imprint, score, scratch, cut. **2.** CHARACTERIZE distinguish, brand, stamp, imprint, identify, label, indicate, symbolize, denote.

marked a. noticeable, obvious, distinct, conspicuous, clear, apparent, prominent, outstanding, striking, glaring, pronounced. ANT. *indistinct, undistinguished.*

market n. store, mart, shopping center, grocery store, outlet, mall, stall, stand, emporium, exchange.

market v. sell, peddle, hustle, offer for sale, hawk, wholesale, retail, exchange, trade, advertise.

marksman n. sharpshooter, crack shot, dead shot, good shot.

maroon v. strand, abandon, leave behind, cast away, desert, put ashore, forsake, isolate.

marriage n. union, wedding, matrimony, coupling, wedlock, tie, bond, nuptials, *wedded bliss, *tying the knot, merger. "An armed alliance against the outside world."—Gilbert Keith Chesterson. "The high sea for which no compass has yet been invented."—Heinrich Heine. "Fever in reverse: it starts with heat and ends with cold."—German proverb. "A field of battle, not a bed of roses."—Robert Louis Stevenson.

WORD FIND

after death of first spouse: digamy

broker, Jewish: schatchen

divorce: dissolution

estrangement: alienation of affections

failing: *on the rocks

forced, due to sexual misconduct: *shotgun wedding

hater of: misogamist

hatred of: misogamy

interracial: miscegenation, mixed marriage

invalidation of: annulment

long-term cohabitation without benefit of wedding: common-law marriage

loveless couple joined for benefits other than affection: marriage of convenience

man uninterested in: confirmed bachelor

man who has sexually unfaithful wife: cuckold

married to more than one spouse: bigamy, polygamy

married to one spouse: monogamy, monogyny, monandry

outside the bonds of marriage: extramarital

property brought into by woman: dowry

seventh-year temptation: *seven-year itch

unfaithfulness in: infidelity

vow: troth

with others: open marriage

SEE DIVORCE, WEDDING

marry v. wed, *tie the knot, exchange wedding vows, unite in holy wedlock, *say "I do," *hitch up, *walk down the aisle, *settle down. ANT. *divorce, *split up, separate.*

marsh n. bog, swamp, fen, bayou, everglade, estuary, moor, wetland, quagmire, slough.

WORD FIND

gas: methane

hollow: swale

plant: reed, sedge, cattail, bulrush

SEE LAKE

marshal v. order, arrange, array, manage, direct, coordinate, organize, distribute, deploy, dispose, guide.

marshy a. boggy, swampy, fenny, wet, soggy, spongy, mucky. ANT. *dry, arid.*

martial a. military, militant, warlike, hostile, combative, aggressive, bellicose, antagonistic. ANT. *peaceful, civil.*

martinet n. disciplinarian, drillmaster, taskmaster, *whip, tyrant, slavedriver, authoritarian, stickler.

martyr n. sufferer, self-sacrificer, *poor me.

martyrdom n. suffering, torment, torture, anguish, self-sacrifice, persecution, crown of thorns, crucifixion, hell, vale of tears, ordeal. "Proof of the intensity, never of the correctness of a belief."—Arthur Schnitzler. "The only way in which a man can become famous without ability."—George Bernard Shaw.

marvel n. wonder, miracle, prodigy, sensation, spectacle, *sight to behold, *mindblower, phenomenon, rarity.

marvel v. wonder at, stand in awe, be awestruck, be astonished, gape at, stare at with wonder, be amazed.

marvelous a. **1.** WONDERFUL sensational, phenomenal, miraculous, amazing, astonishing, surprising, extraordinary, awesome, wondrous, stunning, supernatural. **2.** GREAT excellent, fabulous, fantastic, fine, splendid, superb, *super, terrific, *out of this world, wonderful. ANT. *1.* *ho-hum, ordinary, banal, everyday.* *2.* *lousy, terrible, bad.*

masculine a. manly, macho, virile, male, strong, tough, powerful, muscular, dominant, potent, butch, bold, *gutsy. ANT. *effeminate, feminine, *wimpy, weak.*

mash v. smash, crush, pulp, squash, scrunch, grind, press, pulverize.

mask n. disguise, cover-up, facade, masquerade, veil, concealment, false front.

mask v. disguise, cover up, hide, conceal, veil, camouflage, cloak, screen, masquerade.

mason n. stoneworker, bricklayer, stone mason.

masquerade n. disguise, costume, facade, put-on, guise, getup, mask, mummery, ball, costume party, *Mardi Gras, imposture, pose, pretense.

mass n. **1.** MATTER body, lump, solid, hunk, chunk, pile, bulk, mound, load, block, heap, deposit, gob, wad, accumulation, collection, aggregation, conglomeration, assemblage, host, number, assortment, crowd. **2.** SIZE magnitude, bulk, weight, volume, dimension, greatness.

massacre n. slaughter, mass killing, bloodbath, indiscriminate killing, wholesale slaughter, carnage, butchery, decimation, annihilation, genocide. SEE MURDER

massacre v. slaughter, kill, butcher, slay, annihilate, decimate, kill off, liquidate, wipe out, exterminate, eliminate. SEE MURDER

massage n. rubdown, back rub, kneading, manipulation, *Rolfing.

massage v. rub, knead, stroke, press, roll, flex.

masses n. common people, working class, lower class, peasantry, plebeians, proletariat, hoi polloi. "Mute, inglorious men and women who made no nuisance of themselves in the world."—Philip Howard. "The nondistinctive bulk of human kind—the average man."—Robert Zwickey. ANT. *upper class, aristocracy, elite, royalty, *upper crust.*

massive a. huge, large, tremendous, stupendous, colossal, enormous, prodigious, extensive, immense, gigantic, gargantuan, staggering, monstrous, monumental, towering. ANT. *tiny, microscopic, miniscule.*

master n. **1.** EXPERT pro, professional, *ace, authority, *whiz, veteran, *old hand, master hand, proficient, mentor, teacher. **2.** CHIEF overseer, boss, commander, director, ruler, manager, governor, leader, head, lord, *top dog, *biggest toad in the puddle. ANT. *1. amateur, beginner, tyro, rookie.* *2. subordinate, employee, underling.*

master v. learn, *get the hang of, *get down, understand, *know backwards and forwards, *know inside and out, become proficient in.

master a. **1.** EXPERT proficient, skilled, experienced, professional, accomplished. **2.** MAIN principal, great, dominant, chief, leading, ruling, commanding. ANT. *1. unskilled, rookie, inexperienced, amateur.* *2. secondary, subordinate, minor.*

masterful a. expert, proficient, skilled, accomplished, experienced, crack, *crackerjack, virtuoso, dexterous, adroit. ANT. *amateurish, bumbling, inept.*

mastermind n. architect, author, engineer, leader, ringleader, wizard, genius, *brains, designer, orchestrator, instigator.

masterpiece n. masterwork, magnum opus, chef d'oeuvre, pièce de résistance, tour de force, *jewel in the crown, showpiece.

mastery n. **1.** CONTROL command, rule, domination, authority, power, sway, upper hand, influence. **2.** EXPERTISE proficiency, command, skill, prowess, knowledge, ability, facility, virtuosity. ANT. *1. submission, subservience.* *2. ineptness, ignorance.*

masturbation n. self-gratification, onanism, autoeroticism, self-abuse.

match n. **1.** EQUAL equivalent, mate, double, twin, fellow, duplicate, peer, counterpart. **2.** COUPLE pair, pairing, partnership, duet. **3.** CONTEST competition, meet, bout, game, tournament, duel, rivalry.

match v. equal, go together, look alike, parallel, correspond, make a pair, mirror one another. ANT. *clash, oppose.*

matching a. twin, paired, like, coordinating, corresponding, identical, duplicate, of a set. ANT. *clashing, opposing, unlike.*

matchless a. unequaled, unparalleled, peerless, incomparable. ANT. *comparable, akin, *on par with.*

mate n. partner, twin, counterpart, fellow, double, equal, one of a pair, peer, sidekick, alter ego, companion, *buddy, friend, lover, spouse, colleague.

mate v. pair up, couple, join up, marry, wed, breed, procreate, copulate.

material n. 1. SUBSTANCE matter, stuff, medium, components, constituents, ingredients, elements, stock. 2. TEXTILE fabric, cloth, dry goods. 3. DATA facts, information, notes, text, documentation.

material a. 1. PHYSICAL palpable, tangible, touchable, solid, concrete, corporeal, bodily, real, nonspiritual. 2. IMPORTANT relevant, significant, consequential, weighty, fundamental, germane, momentous, vital, crucial. ANT. 1. spiritual, impalpable. 2. immaterial, irrelevant, unimportant.

materialistic a. acquisitive, greedy, *keeping up with the Joneses, *like a yuppie.

materialize v. appear, take shape, come to be, emerge, turn up, rise, issue, come about, develop, form, manifest, accomplish, realize. ANT. disappear, vanish, fade away.

maternal a. motherly, parental, nurturing, protecting, caring, devoted, doting, sheltering, loving. ANT. uncaring, cruel.

mathematics n. math, arithmetic, calculation, figures, numbers, multiplication, addition and subtraction, division, algebra, calculus, geometry, equations, trigonometry. "The music of reason."—James Sylvester.

matriarch n. mother, grandmother, matron, dame, dowager, queen, empress, *ruler of the roost, *battle-ax.

matrimony n. holy wedlock. SEE MARRIAGE

matron n. 1. MATURE WOMAN middle-aged woman, matriarch, dame, dowager, widow. 2. WARDEN head mistress, supervisor, housemother, governess.

matronly a. dignified, sedate, mellow, mature, serious, motherly.

matted a. tangled, snarled, twisted, knotted, full of snags, *like a rat's nest, uncombed, messy, disheveled.

matter n. 1. SUBSTANCE material, stuff, body, medium, element, object. 2. AFFAIR issue, concern, situation, question, subject, doing, business, topic, happening, episode. 3. CONSEQUENCE importance, weight, significance, import, gravity, magnitude. 4. TROUBLE difficulty, problem, dilemma, upset, distress.

matter-of-fact a. unemotional, prosaic, dry, businesslike, dull, plain, unexciting, *cold-blooded, sober, phlegmatic, impassive, straightforward, direct. ANT. emotional, passionate.

mature v. grow, season, develop, ripen, bloom, flower, *come of age, grow up, evolve, settle down, mellow.

mature a. 1. ADULT fully grown, full-grown, full-fledged, ripened, in bloom, seasoned, developed, in one's prime. 2. WISE AND EXPERIENCED seasoned, practiced, responsible, dependable, independent, self-sufficient, settled. ANT. 1. immature, juvenile, young. 2. immature, dependent, callow.

maturity n. 1. ADULTHOOD manhood, womanhood, majority, age of consent, full bloom, full growth, development, completion, perfection. 2. WISDOM AND EXPERIENCE responsibility, dependability, reliability, independence, self-sufficiency, seasoning, sophistication, refinement. "The ability to live in someone else's world."—Oren Arnold. "The day you don't need to be lied to about anything."—Frank Yerby. "The ability to postpone gratification."—Sigmund Freud. "The day you have your first real laugh at yourself."—Ethel Barrymore. ANT. 1. immaturity, childhood, infancy. 2. imperfection, incompletion, dependence, irresponsibility.

MAUDLIN a. [MAWD lin] overly sentimental to the point of silliness. The drunk embraced everyone and grew increasingly maudlin. SYN. sentimental, overly sentimental, mawkish, mushy, cow-eyed, *drippy, unrestrained, teary, weepy, *schmaltzy, *cornball, overemotional, *laying it on thick, *laying it on with a trowel. ANT. cold, matter-of-fact, emotionless.

maul v. beat, injure, tear, lacerate, bruise, pound, batter, pummel, rough up, *clobber, trounce, thrash, manhandle.

mausoleum n. tomb, sepulchre. SEE GRAVE, CEMETERY

maverick n. independent, nonconformist, vanguard, trendsetter, trailblazer, pioneer, dissenter, eccentric, rebel, individual, *lone voice in the wilderness. ANT. follower, *one of the herd, conformist.

mawkish a. sickeningly sentimental, maudlin, nauseating, mushy, emotional, *schmaltzy, teary, *gushy, *sappy. ANT. emotionless, cold, matter-of-fact.

MAXIM n. [MAK sim] a saying that illustrates a basic truth. "Blood is thicker than water" is a popular maxim. SYN. saying, truth, principle, truism, adage, aphorism, proverb, axiom, tenet, saw, *bromide, cliche. "Little sermons."—Gelett Burgess. "The condensed good sense of nations."—James Mackintosh.

maximum n. top, height, zenith, peak, pinnacle, climax, culmination, high point, extreme, most, optimum, limit. ANT. minimum, bottom.

maximum *a.* highest, greatest, biggest, top, most, maximal, supreme, utmost, paramount. ANT. *minimum, least, smallest.*

maybe *adv.* possibly, perhaps, perchance.

mayhem *n.* destruction, violence, brutality, injury, chaos, pandemonium, havoc, disorder, confusion. ANT. *calm, order.*

maze *n.* labyrinth, convolution, meander, tangle, knot, puzzle, jungle, confusion, perplexity, muddle, bewilderment.

meadow *n.* field, grassland, pasture, range, prairie, plain, lea, veldt, mead.

WORD FIND

descriptive: Audubonesque tableau of birds and flowers, grasses undulating in the breeze, windblown timothy, Irish green meadow, tawny tussocks of Autumn.

open spot in a forest: glade

SEE GRASS, FLOWER

meager *a.* scanty, sparse, scarce, thin, bare, lean, insufficient, inadequate, poor, lacking, skimpy. ANT. *plentiful, abundant.*

meal *n.* repast, *feed, feast, banquet, fare, *grub, breakfast, lunch, dinner, supper, brunch, *eats, spread, food, mess, chow, K ration, entree.

mealymouthed *a.* euphemistic, insincere, indirect, mincing, delicate, overnice, prim, oversubtle, roundabout, honeyed, vague. ANT. *direct, blunt, straightforward.*

mean *n.* average, norm, happy medium, par, middle, rule, median. ANT. *extreme.*

mean *v.* **1.** HAVE IN MIND intend, plan, think of, expect, propose, aim, anticipate, want. **2.** SIGNIFY denote, indicate, designate, stand for, represent, symbolize, express, imply.

mean *a.* **1.** NASTY unpleasant, obnoxious, cruel, vicious, hurtful, rude, malicious, *dirty, rotten, rough, sour, unkind, contemptible, hostile, insulting, petty, ignoble, spiteful, brutal. **2.** STINGY miserly, cheap, penny-pinching, ungenerous, tight, parsimonious, grudging, niggardly. **3.** POOR shabby, low, second-rate, humble, modest, squalid, paltry, mediocre, menial, small. **4.** AVERAGE normal, medium, middle, median, mid, intermediate. ANT. *1. noble, nice, kind. 2. generous, giving. 3. rich, first-rate, superior.*

meander *v.* wind, convolute, twist, snake, take a serpentine path, *switchback, zigzag, corkscrew, wander, go in roundabout fashion, range, ramble, *go all over the place, follow a tortuous course. ANT. *make a beeline.*

meaning *n.* intent, intention, purport, signification, denotation, sense, definition, connotation, drift, suggestion, point, thrust, interpretation, essence, content.

meaningful *a.* important, deep, profound, consequential, significant, weighty, momentous, purposeful. ANT. *meaningless, insignificant, empty.*

meaningless *a.* empty, vacuous, senseless, nonsensical, useless, worthless, pointless, inconsequential, purposeless, hollow, trivial, futile. ANT. *meaningful, deep, profound, important.*

means *n.* **1.** WAY method, resources, modus operandi, system, apparatus, mechanism, power, instrumentation, medium, expedient, agent. **2.** MONEY wealth, resources, assets, capital, cash, finances, *bucks, income.

meanwhile *adv.* meantime, at the same time, simultaneously, while, during, concurrently.

measles *n.* viral disease, contagious disease, illness, affliction, sickness.

measly *a. Sl.* paltry, skimpy, meager, scanty, poor, puny, trifling. ANT. *large, substantial, generous.*

measurable *a.* quantifiable, quantitative, calculable, assessable, computable, gaugeable, determinable. ANT. *immeasurable, infinite.*

measure *n.* **1.** EXTENT share, portion, part, allowance, allotment, division, quantity, quota, sum, ration, extent, dimension, scope, span, capacity, volume, magnitude. **2.** STANDARD rule, gauge, benchmark, model, yardstick, scale. **3.** ACTION act, step, course, procedure, means, expedient, move.

measure *v.* gauge, weigh, take dimensions, survey, quantify, figure, calculate, compute, appraise, size, figure, calibrate, judge.

measurement *n.* measuring, gauging, estimation, calculation, computation, assessment, dimension, volume, depth, capacity, height, width, weight, mass, density, length, magnitude.

meat *n.* **1.** FLESH beef, veal, fat, pork, chicken, ham, bacon, sausage, venison, mutton, pastrami, hamburger, blubber, chop, loin, roast, cut, flank, steak, cutlet, rasher, sirloin, food. **2.** GIST heart, crux, essence, core, nub.

meaty *a.* meaningful, rich, *heavy, full of substance, profound, rich, pithy, weighty, deep. ANT. *trivial, frivolous, light.*

meat-eating *a.* carnivorous, flesh-eating, predacious, bloodthirsty. ANT. *herbivorous, vegetarian.*

mecca *n.* center, hub, destination, goal.

mechanical *a.* **1.** TECHNOLOGICAL power-driven, motor-driven, machine-driven, automated, *robotic. **2.** SKILLED WITH ONE'S HANDS dexterous, deft, proficient, handy. **3.** EXPRESSIONLESS automatic, robotlike, emotionless, unfeeling, impersonal, matter-of-fact, lifeless. ANT. *1. manual, hand-powered. 2. inept, bumbling, clumsy. 3. emotional, feeling, spontaneous.*

mechanism *n.* machine, motor, generator, device, contrivance, servomechanism, apparatus, gear, component, instrument, gadget.

mechanize *v.* automate, motorize, rig, equip.

medal *n.* medallion, decoration, citation, ribbon, award, badge, testimonial, recognition.

meddle *v.* interfere, *stick one's nose in where it doesn't belong, *butt in, intrude, interlope, intervene, impose, horn in, *kibitz. ANT. *mind one's business, *stick to one's own knitting.*

meddlesome *a.* interfering, intrusive, meddling, officious, obtrusive, presumptuous, busybody, *snoopy, *kibitzing. ANT. *removed, restrained, indifferent.*

media *n.* press, communications industry, news industry, radio, television, publishing, reporters, paparazzi. SEE NEWSPAPER, MAGAZINE, RADIO, TELEVISION, BOOK, INTERNET

median *a.* middle, mid, central, mean. ANT. *outer, extreme.*

MEDIATE *v.* [MEE dee ATE] to take an intermediate position and help settle differences between two or more parties. *Better to have a third party mediate than to call in expensive lawyers.* SYN. settle, conciliate, compromise, reconcile, bring to terms, negotiate, referee, umpire, resolve differences, moderate.

mediation *n.* settlement, peaceful intervention, conciliation, compromise, reconciliation, negotiation, refereeing, moderating, making peace.

medicine *n.* medication, medicament, remedy, cure, elixir, preparation, drug, wonder drug, pharmaceutical, antibiotic, pill, inoculation, vaccine, physic, dose, treatment, therapeutics. "Consists of amusing the patient while nature cures the disease."—Voltaire. "A conjectural art."—Celsus.

WORD FIND

MEDICINES AND DRUGS

acid neutralizer: antacid, bicarbonate of soda
alcohol, solution of: tincture
allergy reliever that counters histamine: antihistamine
analgesic: acetaminophen, aspirin, codeine, ibuprofen, morphine, opium
angina, relieves: nitroglycerin
antibiotic: amoxicillin, ampicillin, erythromycin, penicillin, streptomycin, sulfa drug, sulfonamide, tetracycline
bacterial infection treatment derived from fungus: antibiotic
blood clotting, prevents: anticoagulant, heparin
blood serum containing antibodies: gamma globulin
blood vessel constrictor: vasoconstrictor
blood vessel widener: vasodilator
body's natural immune protein: antibody
book listings of: pharmacopoeia
breathing passages, opens: bronchodilator
cancelling out of one drug's effects by another: antagonism
circulation, steps up: epinephrine, adrenalin
cough suppressant: antitussive, codeine
cure-all: panacea, catholicon
diabetes victim's blood sugar regulator: insulin
dropper: pipette
epilepsy, seizure medication: diazepam, Dilantin
fever reducer: antipyretic, febrifuge
heart activity, decreases: beta blocker
heart stimulant: digitalis
itch reliever: antipruritic
laxative: cathartic, purgative
malaria drug: quinine
motion sickness reliever: Dramamine
muscle-building hormone: steroid
nonprescription: over-the-counter
ointment: salve, unguent, balm, emollient
organ transplant, fights rejection of: immunosuppressant
painkiller: analgesic, Demerol, methadone
Parkinson's disease, controls: L-dopa
phlegm, helps bring up: expectorant
poison counteractant: antidote, antivenin
polio vaccine: Sabin vaccine, Salk vaccine
quack: patent medicine, nostrum
reduced effectiveness of medicine over time: tolerance
relieves symptoms but does not cure disease: palliative
simulated: placebo
skin, applied to: topical
sleep, induces: hypnotic, soporific
spasm reliever: antispasmodic
study of medicines: pharmacology
tranquilizer: Librium, Miltown, Thorazine

ulcer medicine: Xantac, antacid
urine, increases excretion of: diuretic
vaccine for diptheria, pertussis and tetanus: DPT
vaccine for measles, mumps and rubella: MMR
vessel: ampule, phial, vial
vomiting, induces: emetic
PROCEDURES, SEE ALSO OPERATION
alcohol, drug, toxin removal from body: detoxification, *detox
allergy test: patch test, scratch test
blood cell count: blood count
blood filtering to aid kidney function: dialysis
brain scan by tomography: PET scan, positron emission tomography
brain's electrical activity reading: electroencephalogram, EEG
breast X-ray or imaging: mammography
broken bone alignment by force: traction
cancer treatment with X-rays, beta rays, gamma rays: radiation therapy
chemical or drug treatment for cancer: chemotherapy
choking maneuver: Heimlich maneuver
CPR: cardiopulmonary resuscitation
determination of disease: diagnosis
EEG: electroencephalogram
EKG: electrocardiogram
enhanced radiology imaging: CAT scan (computerized axial tomography)
evaluation, general: workup, physical
fat sucked out, plastic surgery method: liposuction
feeling for body abnormalities by hand: palpation
heart exam through ultrasound imaging: echocardiography
heart fitness test: stress test
heart's electrical activity reading: electrocardiogram, EKG
imaging internal body with magnetic field: magnetic resonance imaging, MRI
intravenous introduction of blood: transfusion, IV
microorganisms, lab examination of body's: culture
prediction of disease outcome: prognosis
prioritizing of most critical patients first: triage
stone destruction by sound waves: lithotripsy
tapping body part to aid in diagnosis: percussion

tissue removal for examination: biopsy
tube insertion in body part for drainage, diagnosis, etc.: intubation
uterine fluid removal during pregnancy: amniocentesis
uterine or cervical cancer test: Pap test
X-ray image live on screen: fluoroscopy
MEDICAL EQUIPMENT
bladder probe: cytoscope
bleeding, stops profuse: hemostat
blood filtering machine aiding kidney function: dialysis machine
blood pressure cuff: sphygmomanometer
breathing apparatus: respirator, resuscitator
colon discharge bag: colostomy bag
colon probe: sigmoidoscope
decompression chamber: hyperbaric chamber
ear probe: otoscope
electrocardiogram machine: electrocardiograph
gown, green surgical: *scrubs, scrub suit
grasper: forceps
hammer used to check reflexes: plessor, percussion hammer
holds body cavity open: speculum
internal probe: endoscope
joint probe: arthroscope
knife: bistoury, lancet, scalpel
knife, electrical: radio knife
larynx probe: lyngoscope
listening device, diaphragm: stethoscope
needle and syringe: hypodermic
photographs internal body by radiation: X-ray machine
pole on which medicinal fluids are hung: IV pole, *ivy pole
pump used in heart surgery: heart-lung machine
rectal probe: proctoscope, sigmoidoscope
respitory recorder: spirograph
sterilizer, instrument: autoclave
stretcher: gurney
stomach probe: gastroscope
tissue retractor: retractor
tissue scraper: curette
tongue, moves out of the way: tongue depressor
trachea probe: bronchoscope
tube drain: catheter
X-ray screen: fluoroscope
FIELDS OF MEDICINE
aging: geriatrics, gerontology
anesthesia: anesthesiology
animal: veterinary medicine

behavioral effects of drugs: psychopharmacology
birth: obstetrics, tocology
blood: hematology
bones: osteology, osteopathy, orthopedics
children: pediatrics
cosmetic and reconstructive surgery: plastic surgery
digestive system: gastroenterology
disease identification: diagnostics
disease: pathology, etiology
ears, nose and throat: otorhinolaryngology
ears: otology
epidemics: epidemiology
eyes: ophthalmology, optometry
feet: podiatry
female reproductive system: gynecology
gums: periodontics
hearing: audiology
heart: cardiology
hormones, glands: endocrinology
immune system: immunology
internal disease, noninvasive treatment of: internal medicine
joints: arthrology
kidneys: nephrology
liver: hepatology
lungs and breathing: pulmonology
malformations: teratology
mental diseases, disorders: psychopathology, psychiatry
muscles: myology, orthopedics
needles, Chinese: acupuncture
nervous system: neurology
newborns: neonatology
obstetrics and gynecology: ob-gyn
poisons: toxicology
rectum, anus and colon: proctology
rheumatic disease: rheumatology
sexually transmitted diseases: venereology
skin: dermatology
skull: craniology
spinal alignment: chiropractic
stomach: gastrology
teeth: dentistry, orthodontics
tumors: oncology
urinary tracts: urology
veins: phlebology
viruses: virology
whole body teatment: holistic medicine
X rays, radiation: radiology
SEE ALSO BIRTH, DISEASE, DOCTOR, HOSPITAL, OPERATION, PREGNANCY

medieval *a.* of the Middle Ages, of the Dark Ages, Gothic, feudal, archaic. ANT. *modern.*

WORD FIND
catapult: mangonel, trebuchet
chemistry: alchemy
duty and loyalty owed to lord by vassal: fealty
garden, villager's: croft
land grant made by lord in exchange for services: fief
land unit of eighteen to thirty-two acres supporting peasant: virgate
lord's tenant pledging military service: vassal
manager of lord's manor: bailiff
musical instrument: lute, lyre, rebec
peasant: serf, villein
political and social system: feudalism
singer: minstrel, troubador
sport: tilting, jousting
tax paid to a lord: tallage
town, village: bourg
tunic: gipon, jupon
yard: toft
SEE CASTLE

mediocre *a.* fair, okay, ordinary, middling, so-so, okay, passable, tolerable, run-of-the-mill, garden-variety, *fair to middling, secondrate, poor, pedestrian, undistinguished. ANT. *superior, first-rate, exceptional, outstanding.*

meditate *v.* think, reflect, muse, contemplate, ruminate, ponder, brood, chew over, deliberate, focus on, cogitate, weigh, mull over.

meditation *n.* deep thought, reflection, contemplation, musing, rumination, cogitation, concentration, reverie, chewing over, mulling over.

medium *n.* 1. MEANS vehicle, agency, mode, channel, way, instrument, mechanism. 2. ATMOSPHERE air, environment, element, climate, surroundings, setting. 3. CLAIRVOYANT psychic, telepathist, necromancer, seer, mindreader.

medium *a.* mean, middle, midway, intermediate, median, average, moderate, par, standard, fair, ordinary, normal. ANT. *extraordinary, extreme, unusual.*

medley *n.* mixture, hodgepodge, miscellany, jumble, mélange, assortment, potpourri, mishmash, variety, assortment, mixed bag.

meek *a.* mild, gentle, docile, compliant, peaceful, passive, tame, patient, timid, shy, spineless, deferential, submissive. ANT. *aggressive, pugnacious, rebellious, domineering.*

meet *n.* competition, match, tournament, contest, game.

meet *v.* 1. ENCOUNTER happen upon, come

upon, run across, *bump into, chance upon, face, see. **2.** MAKE ACQUAINTANCE shake hands with, get to know, say hello to, greet. **3.** JOIN connect, touch, converge, unite, cross, abut, intersect. **4.** ASSEMBLE gather, congregate, convene, get together, muster, collect. **5.** FULFILL satisfy, execute, handle, perform, carry out, discharge. dispose of. ANT. *1. miss, avoid. 3. separate, disconnect. 4. disperse, break up. 5. shirk, fall short, renege.*

meeting n. **1.** ENCOUNTER engagement, confrontation, rendezvous, collision, convergence. **2.** ASSEMBLY gathering, conference, *powwow, congregation, convention, gettogether, discussion, council, *confab. ANT. *avoidance, parting.*

melancholy n. depression, unhappiness, downheartedness, blues, sadness, gloom, low spirits, funk, woe, misery, sorrow, despondency. "A hell upon earth."—Robert Burton. "The mind's disease."—John Ford. "The pleasure of being sad."—Victor Hugo. ANT. *happiness, elation, euphoria.*

melancholy a. depressed, downhearted, blue, dejected, sad, dispirited, low, glum, *down in the mouth, *down in the dumps, *bummed out, heartsick, forlorn, disconsolate, gloomy, miserable, despondent. ANT. *happy, elated, euphoric.*

mélange n. mixture, hodgepodge, miscellany. SEE MEDLEY

meld v. blend, unite, merge, combine, mix, fuse, incorporate, mingle, amalgamate, compound. ANT. *separate, split.*

melee n. riot, fight, free-for-all, *rumble, brawl, fracas, donnybrook, tussle, scuffle, pandemonium, *ruckus, scrap, hubbub.

MELLIFLUOUS a. [muh LIF loo us] sweetsounding and smooth. *The mellifluous tones echoed quietly across the stage.* SYN. smoothsounding, sweet-sounding, honeyed, dulcet, euphonic, liquid, fluid, silver-toned, resonant. ANT. *harsh, grating, rough, discordant.*

mellow a. **1.** GENTLE mild, softened, easygoing, placid, seasoned, wise, mature. **2.** RIPE soft, sweet, aged, smooth, full-flavored, rich. ANT. *1. immature, aggressive, hard, troubled. 2. green, unripe, immature.*

melodious a. tuneful, musical, melodic, songlike, harmonious, euphonic, symphonic, sweet, pleasing to the ear, mellifluous. ANT. *cacophonous, discordant, unmusical.*

MELODRAMATIC a. [MEL o druh MAT ik] exaggerated or sensational, theatrical. *The teenager was being melodramatic when he said* *he'd die without a new pair of jeans.* SYN. exaggerated, sensational, theatrical, stagy, overemotional, histrionic, overacted, maudlin, mawkish, gushing. ANT. *understated, subtle, matter-of-fact.*

melody n. tune, song, *ditty, musical arrangement, refrain, line, run, lyric, passage, *hook.

melt v. liquefy, dissolve, soften, deliquesce, thaw, defrost.

member n. associate, enrollee, constituent, fellow, brother, sister, affiliate, part, element, component, segment.

membership n. members, associates, enrollment, constituency, rolls, roster, rank and file, fellowship, brotherhood, sisterhood, society, club, body, fraternity.

membrane n. layer, sheet, covering, lining, film, tissue, skin, sheath, mucosa.

memento n. souvenir, keepsake, remembrance, reminder, token, memorabilia, record, memorial.

memo n. SEE MEMORANDUM

memoirs n. autobiography, biography, diary, life story, reminiscences, recollections, journal, chronicle, history, *bio. "When you put down the good things you ought to have done, and leave out the bad ones you did do."—Will Rogers.

memorabilia n. mementos, token, souvenir, keepsakes, remembrance, collectible, reminder, records, archives, annals.

memorable a. unforgettable, important, momentous, critical, crucial, historic, powerful, leaving an indelible image, noteworthy, extraordinary, striking, remarkable, *red-letter, meaningful, *once in a lifetime. ANT. *forgettable, unimportant, ordinary, everyday.*

memorandum n. memo, note, reminder, message, notice, dispatch, minute, tickler.

memorial n. monument, statue, shrine, marker, monolith, reminder, commemoration, record, inscription.

memorial a. remembering, commemorative, retrospective.

memorize v. remember, commit to memory, store, learn by rote, learn by heart, retain, imprint on one's mind.

memory n. **1.** RECALL recollection, remembrance, retention, retrospection, reminiscence, photographic memory, eidetic memory, hypermnesia, calling to mind. "The library of the mind."—Francis Fauvel-Gouraud. "What God gave us so that we might have roses in December."—James Barrie.

"The warder of the brain."—Shakespeare.
2. REMINDER image, recollection, picture, thought, vision. ANT. *amnesia.*

menace *n.* threat, danger, hazard, peril, danger, troublemaker, sword of Damocles.

menace *v.* threaten, scare, frighten, intimidate, terrorize, endanger, daunt, imperil.

menacing *a.* threatening, scary, frightening, intimidating, terrorizing, dangerous, hazardous, looming, hanging over one's head. ANT. *reassuring, calming.*

menagerie *n.* zoo, collection, zoological collection, exhibition.

mend *v.* fix, repair, restore, correct, patch up, doctor, rectify, recondition, remedy, heal, cure, right.

mendacious *a.* dishonest, lying, false, deceptive, misleading, deceitful, fraudulent, untruthful, dissembling. ANT. *honest, truthful.*

menial *a.* low, servile, mean, humble, common, subservient, unskilled, abject, ignoble, obsequious. ANT. *highborn, superior, noble, arrogant.*

menopause *n.* change of life, climacteric.

mental *a.* **1.** INTELLECTUAL cerebral, cognitive, thinking, phrenic, reasoning, of the mind, psychic, psychological. **2.** OF MENTAL ILLNESS mentally ill, disturbed, deranged, psychotic, insane, mad, neurotic, psychiatric, phobic, *nutty, crazy.

mentality *n.* attitude, outlook, view, opinion, state of mind, *mind-set, way of thinking, reasoning.

mental hospital *n.* psychiatric hospital, insane asylum, mental health treatment facility, recovery center, psychiatric ward, *madhouse, *nuthouse, *loony bin, *laughing academy.

mental illness *n.* emotional disorder, personality disorder, neurosis, psychosis, maladjustment, schizophrenia, delusions, phobia, mania, insanity, nervous breakdown. SEE INSANITY, PHOBIA, MANIA

mention *n.* reference, remark, referral, utterance, comment, note, acknowledgement, statement, indication, suggestion.

mention *v.* refer, remark, speak of, allude to, cite, bring up, comment on, touch on, make note of, acknowledge, indicate.

MENTOR *n.* [MEN tur] a teacher, guide, coach or advisor. *She couldn't have succeeded without her mentor.* SYN. teacher, guide, coach, advisor, guru, master, instructor, trainer.

menu *n.* bill of fare, selection.

mercenary *n.* soldier of fortune, *hired gun, professional soldier, legionnaire, hired hand.

MERCENARY *a.* [MUR suh ner ee] working for monetary gain and no other reason. *His motivation for fighting in the war was purely mercenary.* SYN. monetary, selfish, money-grubbing, greedy, venal, acquisitive, for financial gain. ANT. *altruistic, idealistic.*

merchandise *n.* goods, products, wares, stock, commodities, vendibles, line, stuff.

merchandise *v.* buy and sell, trade, advertise, *move, market, deal in, traffic, distribute, wholesale, do business in.

merchant *n.* trader, wholesaler, retailer, dealer, shopkeeper, salesman, businessman, jobber, vendor, hawker.

merciful *a.* compassionate, forgiving, humane, humanitarian, kind, charitable, sympathetic, sparing, lenient, pitying, mild, gentle, soft-hearted. ANT. *merciless, unfeeling, brutal, pitiless.*

merciless *a.* uncompassionate, unforgiving, inhumane, unfeeling, brutal, coldhearted, hardhearted, heartless, pitiless, stony, mean, callous, cruel, ruthless. ANT. *merciful, compassionate, kind.*

MERCURIAL *a.* [mur KYOOR ee ul] quick or quick to change, volatile. *She was known for her fickle, mercurial manner.* SYN. quick, changeable, volatile, unstable, quick to change, flighty, unpredictable, erratic, *blowing hot and cold, capricious, *up and down, lively. ANT. *stable, predictable, constant.*

mercy *n.* compassion, forgiveness, humanity, kindness, charity, sympathy, pity, lenience, clemency, softheartedness, quarter. "Nobility's true badge."—Shakespeare. ANT. *cruelty, meanness, cold-bloodedness.*

mere *a.* nothing more than, insignificant, trifling, little, small, minor, only, simple, bare. ANT. *significant, great, major.*

merge *v.* unite, combine, blend, consolidate, become partners, unify, marry, join, fuse, mix, confederate, join forces. ANT. *separate, split, diverge.*

merger *n.* consolidation, incorporation, alliance, combination, partnership, unification, union, marriage, joining, fusion. ANT. *separation, split-up, parting.*

meridian *n.* zenith, apex, highest point, crowning point, acme, peak, pinnacle, summit, climax, culmination. ANT. *low point, nadir.*

merit *n.* worth, worthiness, value, quality, virtue, excellence, integrity, credit.

merit *v.* deserve, be worthy of, earn, have coming to, be entitled to, rate.

meritorious *a.* praiseworthy, commendable, honorable, good, worthy, admirable, laudable, deserving, exemplary, noble. ANT. *unworthy, reprehensible, despicable.*

merriment *n.* fun, gaiety, frolic, joy, celebration, good times, enjoyment, mirth, laughter, joviality, jollity, sport. ANT. *misery, gloom, depression.*

merry *a.* fun, cheerful, gay, mirthful, joyful, celebratory, jovial, jolly, laughing, happy, rollicking, festive, blithe, carefree. ANT. *miserable, gloomy, depressed.*

merry-go-round *n.* carousel.

mesa *n.* plateau, tableland, butte.

mesh *n.* net, netting, network, web, webbing, screen, strainer, plexus, openwork, grid, grille, lattice.

mesh *v.* engage, fit, interlock, come together, enmesh, dovetail, interweave, entangle.

mesmerize *v.* hypnotize, spellbind, entrance, enthrall, *cast a spell on, put under, enchant, bewitch, fascinate, *do a Svengali.

mess *n.* **1.** CLUTTER jumble, disorder, disarray, litter, eyesore, debris, unsightliness, dump, mayhem, pigpen, filth, *rat's nest. **2.** PREDICAMENT trouble, plight, difficulty, *pickle, *jam, fix, stew, *fine kettle of fish, quandary. ANT. *1. order, neatness, tidiness.*

message *n.* **1.** COMMUNICATION note, word, communiqué, notice, memo, wire, dispatch, bulletin, missive, intelligence. **2.** THEME meaning, idea, moral, point.

messenger *n.* courier, runner, carrier, bearer, emissary, envoy, herald, delivery person.

messy *a.* cluttered, jumbled, disordered, in disarray, littered, unsightly, filthy, dirty, chaotic, untidy. ANT. *clean, neat, tidy.*

METAMORPHOSIS *n.* [MET uh MOR fuh sis] a change of form, transformation. *We studied the metamorphosis of a caterpillar to a butterfly.* SYN. change, transformation, transmutation, conversion, metastasis, alteration, evolution, transmogrification, mutation, rebirth.

METAPHOR *n.* [MET uh for] a figure of speech comprised of a word or phrase that transfers its meaning to another use, as a means of illustration. *We are 'drowning in paperwork' is a metaphor and not meant to be taken literally.* SYN. figure of speech, analogy, likening, image, simile, trope, symbol. "The language of poetry."—Raphael Kraus.

metaphorical *a.* figurative, symbolic, analogous, poetic. ANT. *literal, actual.*

METAPHYSICAL *a.* [met uh FIZ i kul] not of the physical world, supernatural. *The astronomer uses hard science along with the metaphysical to understand the universe.* SYN. incorporeal, supernatural, transcendental, philosophical, abstract, theoretical, immaterial, impalpable, speculative, spiritual. ANT. *physical, concrete, material.*

metaphysics *n.* "The attempt of the mind to rise above the mind."—Thomas Carlyle. "The art of bewildering oneself methodically."—Jules Michelet.

meteor *n.* meteorite, fireball, bolide.

meteoric *a.* dazzling, brilliant, flashing, fleeting, ephemeral, short-lived, brief, sudden, swift.

meteorology *n.* weather science, weather forecasting, weather prediction. SEE CLOUD, STORM

method *n.* **1.** TECHNIQUE way, system, mode, style, formula, process, manner, means, procedure, program, course. **2.** DESIGN order, arrangement, plan, scheme, regularity.

methodical *a.* systematic, orderly, ordered, constant, efficient, regular, precise, machinelike, robotic, routine, step by step, structured. ANT. *loose, unmethodical, casual.*

methodology *n.* methods, procedures, practices, science, designs, programs, processes, techniques, mode, systems.

meticulous *a.* careful, detail-oriented, scrupulous, painstaking, precise, finicky, exact, particular, demanding, perfectionist. ANT. *lax, casual, careless, sloppy.*

metier *n.* trade, profession, line of work. SEE OCCUPATION

metropolis *n.* capital, city, municipality, downtown, urban sprawl, megalopolis. SEE CITY, NEW YORK

mettle *n.* character, courage, heart, *what one is made of, spirit, *guts, strength, spunk, *grit, makeup, nerve, backbone, resolve.

miasma *n.* effluvium, vapor, gas, fog, cloud, mist, pollution, smog, stench, reek, methane.

microbe *n.* SEE MICROORGANISM

MICROCOSM *n.* [MYE kruh KOZ um] a miniature world or reality. *Bangladesh is a microcosm of a much greater population problem.* SYN. miniature world, miniature reality, little world, miniature universe. ANT. *macrocosm.*

microorganism *n.* microbe, germ, *bug, bacillus, bacterium, virus, pathogen.

microscopic *a*. tiny, minute, infinitesimal, invisible to the naked eye, miniscule, imperceptible, *wee. ANT. *macroscopic, immense*.

microwave *v*. heat, cook, *zap, *nuke.

middle *n*. center, midpoint, halfway point, midsection, mean, epicenter, bull's-eye, thick of things, core, focal point. ANT. *periphery, margin, extreme*.

middle *a*. central, median, center, mean, halfway, intermediate, between, inside, equidistant. ANT. *outer, peripheral*.

middle age *n*. mid-life, middle years, forties. "The old age of youth and youth of old age."—Nunally Johnson.

middle class *n*. bourgeoisie, bourgeoise, common people, hoi polloi, Middle America, citizenry, working class. "The backbone of a country."—Robert Zwickey.

middleman *n*. go-between, intermediary, broker, agent, mediator, wholesaler.

middle-of-the-road *a*. moderate, *on the fence, neutral, noncommittal, nonpartisan. ANT. *radical, leftist, rightist, liberal, conservative*.

middling *a*. okay, so-so, fair, medium, adequate, moderate, mediocre, tolerable, nothing to brag about, run-of-the-mill. ANT. *exceptional, outstanding, first-class*.

midget *n*. dwarf, homunculus, pygmy, gnome, *Lilliputian, midge, Tom Thumb, runt, shrimp, pipsqueak. ANT. *giant, titan, monster*.

midnight *n*. twelve o'clock, *witching hour, *dead of night. "Fairy time."—Shakespeare. "The outpost of advancing day."—Longfellow.

midst *n*. middle, core, thick of things, hub, nucleus, heart, center, interior. ANT. *edge, periphery, outskirt*.

mien *n*. manner, bearing, air, demeanor, carriage, deportment, act, expression, look, presence, attitude, aura.

miff *v*. insult, hurt, irritate, annoy, offend, irk, bother, *bug, aggrieve, upset, vex.

might *n*. strength, power, force, muscle, potency, command, energy, brawn, vigor, steam. ANT. *weakness, impotency*.

mighty *a*. **1.** STRONG powerful, forceful, potent, commanding, influential, muscular, omnipotent, vigorous, puissant, *strong as an ox. **2.** HUGE gigantic, colossal, immense, titanic, enormous, gargantuan, massive, monstrous. ANT. *1. weak, feeble, impotent. 2. tiny, small, wee*.

migrant *n*. drifter, vagrant, nomad, mover, wanderer, rover, itinerant, gypsy, transient, tramp, *hobo.

migrate *v*. emigrate, immigrate, drift, move, wander, rove, travel, range, relocate, pull up stakes, *hit the road. ANT. *remain, put down roots*.

mild *a*. **1.** GENTLE soft, easygoing, docile, good-natured, meek, tame, mellow, peaceful, tender, pacific, kind, passive. **2.** TEMPERATE moderate, balmy, clement, gentle, fair, sunny, halcyon. ANT. *1. harsh, severe, hard, aggressive. 2. stormy, rough, wild*.

mildew *n*. fungi, growth, mold.

milestone *n*. landmark, turning point, high point, climax, achievement, accomplishment, event.

MILIEU *n*. [mil YOO] environment, setting. *The classical musician was out of his milieu at the heavy metal concert*. SYN. environment, setting, surroundings, element, medium, arena, theatre, background, scene.

militant *n*. fighter, troublemaker, agitator, firebrand, aggressor, attacker, combatant, warrior. ANT. *dove, pacifist, peacemaker*.

militant *a*. combative, aggressive, contentious, belligerent, pugnacious, hostile, fierce, antagonistic, warlike, offensive. ANT. *peaceful, pacific, passive*.

military *n*. army, armed forces, soldiers, troops, defense, service, air force, navy, marines, militia. SEE AIR FORCE, AMMUNITION, ARMY, BOMB, GUN, MISSILE, NAVY, NUCLEAR BOMB, WAR, WEAPON

military *a*. fighting, armed, combative, warring, militant, martial, soldierly, militaristic, militant. ANT. *peaceful, pacific*.

milksop *n*. *wimp, mouse, *chicken, *wuss, coward, pansy, sissy, baby, pantywaist, milquetoast. ANT. *macho man, he-man, hero*.

Milky Way *n*. galaxy, *backbone of the night, *starry trail, *island universe. SEE ASTRONOMY, CONSTELLATION, STAR

mill *n*. factory, plant, manufactory, works, foundry, shop.

millenium *n*. one thousand years, one-thousandth anniversary, golden age, heaven, utopia, Second Coming.

millstone *n*. burden, weight, load, cross, affliction, encumbrance, albatross.

milquetoast *n*. SEE MILKSOP

mimic *n*. impersonator, imitator, mime, caricaturist, pantomimist, *copycat, ape, parrot.

mimic *v*. impersonate, imitate, mime, caricature, pantomime, copy, ape, parrot, burlesque, parody, mock.

mince *v*. **1.** CUT UP chop up, dice, cube, hash, slice, fragment. **2.** SPEAK EUPHEMISTICALLY speak delicately, euphemize, *water down, minimize, soften, gloss over, moderate.

mind *n.* **1.** INTELLIGENCE intellect, seat of consciousness, brains, head, thought, mentality, cognitive power, perception, wisdom, reason, wits, intuition, psyche. "That little world."—Samuel Rogers. "An empire."—Robert Southwell. **2.** MEMORY recollection, remembrance. **3.** OPINION belief, view, outlook, attitude, feeling, sentiment, way of thinking, conviction, notion. **4.** SANITY reason, rationality, stability, wits, judgment, soundness of mind, *marbles.

mind *v.* **1.** HEED observe, pay attention to, notice, attend to, watch, abide by, follow. **2.** LOOK AFTER care for, tend, babysit, protect, nurse. **3.** CARE dislike, disapprove of, object, be opposed to, detest, care one way or another. ANT. *1. ignore, overlook. 2. neglect, ignore.*

mind-blowing *a.* mind-bending, stunning, staggering, mind-altering, hallucinatory, psychedelic, breathtaking. ANT. *soporific, boring.*

mind-boggling *a.* overwhelming, mind-blowing, stunning, staggering, astonishing, amazing. ANT. *believable.*

mindful *a.* aware, conscious, attentive, heedful, cognizant, regardful, careful, alert, wary, on the lookout. ANT. *unaware, heedless, oblivious.*

mindless *a.* brainless, stupid, witless, imbecilic, oblivious, unintelligent, asinine, idiotic, moronic, sophomoric, *bubble-headed. ANT. *intelligent, brainy, brilliant.*

mind reader *n.* psychic, mentalist, telepathist, clairvoyant.

mindset *n.* attitude, disposition, view, opinion, perspective, leaning, way of thinking, feeling, sentiment, position, stance.

mine *n.* quarry, deposit, excavation, shaft, tunnel, pit, vein, lode, claim, diggings, bonanza.

WORD FIND

claim: stake
coal cart: corf
coal dust: culm
combustible gasses in: firedamp
discovery of ore: strike
drain: sump
entranceway: adit, portal
flume for washing out gold ore: sluice
fraudulently scatter minerals about to deceive prospective buyer: salt

glacial mineral deposit of loose particles: placer
largest vein: mother lode
lung disease caused by coal dust: black lung disease
ore deposit: vein, lode
oxygen, absence or low level in shaft: chokedamp
passageway, main: gangway
potential area containing ore: prospect
residue of: tailings
rich vein: bonanza
search for ore: prospect
stratum: seam
waterway: tailrace
SEE CAVE

mine *v.* dig, quarry, excavate, tunnel, prospect, extract, pan, delve.

mingle *v.* **1.** MIX blend, unite, merge, intermingle, combine, join, marry. **2.** SOCIALIZE associate, hobnob, *work the room, mix, fraternize, circulate, join. ANT. *1. separate, divide. 2. snub, remain aloof, stay at arm's length.*

miniature *a.* mini, small, tiny, baby, midget, toy, dwarf, pint-sized, pocket-sized, small-scale, bantam, minute, wee. ANT. *giant, jumbo, oversized.*

minimal *a.* SEE MINIMUM

minimum *n.* least, lowest, bottom, slightest. ANT. *maximum.*

minimum *a.* minimal, least, smallest, lowest, slightest, bottom. ANT. *maximum, maximal, greatest.*

minion *n.* follower, sycophant, dependent, subordinate, flunkey, *lap dog, *kiss-up, *brownnose, *yes-man, fawner, lackey, toady.

miniscule *a.* tiny, small, wee, minute, microscopic, micro, mini, miniature, little, trifling, trivial, insignificant, pint-sized, infinitesimal. ANT. *gargantuan, gigantic.*

minister *n.* **1.** CLERGYMAN cleric, pastor, preacher, parson, deacon, priest, ecclesiastic, man of the cloth, reverend, servant of God, rabbi, father. SEE CLERGYMAN, RELIGION **2.** ADMINISTRATOR diplomat, ambassador, envoy, consul, cabinet member, official, delegate, secretary.

minister *v.* administer, tend, attend, serve, care for, accommodate, wait on, help, comfort, relieve, nurse.

minor *n.* child, juvenile, youth, adolescent, teenager, *teenybopper, kid, schoolboy, schoolgirl. ANT. *adult.*

minor *a.* small, trivial, insignificant, slight, light, low grade, trifling, piddling, bush-league, secondary, inconsequential. ANT. *major, severe, extreme, significant.*

minstrel *n.* troubador, singer, musician, lyricist, bard, balladeer, poet.

minute *n.* sixty seconds, moment, instant, twinkling, jiffy, wink of an eye, *two shakes of a lamb's tail. SEE TIME

minute *a.* tiny, miniscule, microscopic, infinitesimal, teeny, atomic, molecular, small, wee, micro, mini, little, trifling, trivial, insignificant, pint-sized. *itsy-bitsy, puny, miniature, negligible. ANT. *huge, gigantic, massive, gargantuan.*

MINUTIAE *n.* [mi NOO shee uh] trivial details. *Don't be so concerned with minutiae.* SYN. trivia, trivial details, unimportant details, trifles, minor details, inessentials, nonessentials, useless information.

miracle *n.* act of God, divine act, supernatural event, marvel, wonder, spectacle, phenomenon, sensation. "The dearest child of faith."—Johann W. Goethe. "An event which creates faith; that is the purpose . . . of miracles."—George Bernard Shaw. "Life itself."—Christopher Fry. "Every cubic inch of space."—Walt Whitman.

WORD FIND

location of several: Lourdes
study of: thaumatology
SEE GOD, RELIGION, FAITH

miraculous *a.* divine, supernatural, marvelous, wonderful, wondrous, phenomenal, sensational, anomalous, supermundane, magical, superhuman, unearthly, freakish, extraordinary, mind-blowing, *unreal. ANT. *ordinary, everyday, pedestrian.*

mirage *n.* optical illusion, refraction of light, delusion, vision, specter, phantom, apparition, hallucination, fantasy.

mire *n.* bog, mud, ooze, soggy ground, slush, marsh, fen, swamp, quagmire.

mire *v.* bog down, sink, stick, flounder, slow, wallow, get involved.

mirror *n.* looking glass, reflector. "A device which tells us the truth is a terrible thing."—Abraham Pollock.

mirror *v.* copy, imitate, mimic, reflect, simulate, personify, emulate, ape, mock, caricature.

mirth *n.* merriment, gaiety, joyousness, cheer, frolic, high spirits, glee, jollity, good times, lightheartedness, laughs, hilarity, sport. ANT. *depression, gloom, misery.*

mirthful *a.* merry, gay, joyous, cheerful, gleeful, jolly, lighthearted, hilarious, jocular, blithe, happy, glad. ANT. *depressed, gloomy, sad.*

misadventure *n.* mishap, accident, disaster, miscarriage, misfortune, *screw-up, slip, catastrophe, tragedy, calamity.

misanthrope *n.* man-hater, woman-hater, people-hater, cynic, hermit, loner, recluse, misogynist, grouch.

misappropriate *v.* steal, swindle, embezzle, pocket, defalcate, *rip off, filch, cheat.

misbegotten *a.* illegitimate, bastard, out of wedlock, illegal, unlawful, disreputable. ANT. *legitimate.*

misbehave *v.* act out, make trouble, get out of line, offend, be bad, disobey, *raise hell, *raise dickens, transgress. ANT. *behave, show good manners.*

misbehavior *n.* acting out, naughtiness, transgression, offensiveness, bad manners, rudeness, impropriety, misconduct, *hell-raising.

miscalculate *v.* err, misjudge, miscompute, make a mistake, *mess up, blunder, misconstrue, underestimate, overestimate.

miscarriage *n.* 1. ABORTION spontaneous abortion, stillbirth, premature delivery. 2. FAILURE malfunction, misfire, mistake, miss, nonfulfillment, washout, disappointment, debacle. ANT. 2. *success, achievement, fruition.*

miscellaneous *a.* varied, assorted, mixed, sundry, diversified, heterogenous, multiform, motley. ANT. *uniform, homogenous.*

miscellany *n.* assortment, collection, combo, variety, potpourri, medley, mélange, anthology, compilation, mixture, pastiche.

mischief *n.* 1. PRANKS playfulness, trick, misbehavior, trouble, devilment, deviltry, *hell, shenanigans, naughtiness, funny business, horseplay, espièglerie. 2. HARM damage, injury, destruction, sabotage, nuisance.

mischievous *a.* naughty, impish, devilish, prankish, roguish, playful, troublemaking, rascally, sportive, boyish, puckish. ANT. *angelic, well-behaved, saintly.*

misconception *n.* erroneous notion, wrong idea, misunderstanding, distortion, misinterpretation.

misconduct *n.* misbehavior, bad behavior, transgression, wrongdoing, misstep, delinquency, malfeasance, impropriety.

misconstrue *v.* misunderstand, misinterpret, misjudge, mistake, distort. ANT. *understand.*

miscreant *n.* criminal, evildoer, villain, sinner, felon, hoodlum, outlaw, scoundrel, rogue, rascal.

misdeed *n.* crime, sin, wrongful act, misdemeanor, transgression, offense, malefaction, malfeasance, felony, violation.

misdemeanor *n.* misdeed, offense, misbehavior, misconduct, indiscretion, infringement, violation, naughtiness, wrong.

miser *n.* hoarder, penny-pincher, skinflint, cheapskate, *tightwad, *money-grubber, *Scrooge, curmudgeon, misanthrope. ANT. *spendthrift, philanthropist.*

miserable *a.* **1.** UNHAPPY anguished, troubled, depressed, blue, forlorn, desolate, despondent, suicidal, inconsolable, dejected, sad, melancholy, heartbroken, woebegone, glum, mournful, wretched. **2.** BAD poor, inferior, rotten, lousy, disgraceful, wretched, pathetic, pitiful, sorry, deplorable, second-rate, abysmal. ANT. *1. happy, joyous, euphoric, elated. 2. good, excellent, superb.*

miserly *a.* hoarding, cheap, penny-pinching, tight, money-grubbing, misanthropic, stingy, parsimonious, niggardly. ANT. *generous, charitable, philanthropic.*

misery *n.* **1.** SUFFERING pain, anguish, depression, melancholy, unhappiness, woe, agony, sadness, distress, torment, hardship, sorrow, heartache, desolation, despair. "A communicable disease."—Martha Graham. "Almost always the result of thinking."—Joseph Jourbert. **2.** ADVERSITY affliction, trouble, ordeal, trial, tribulation, problem, curse. ANT. *1. happiness, pleasure, euphoria. 2. good fortune.*

misfire *v.* fail, fizzle, miss, *shoot a blank, backfire.

misfit *n.* nonconformist, lone wolf, *square peg in a round hole, individual, *queer duck, *fish out of water, oddball.

misfortune *n.* bad luck, adversity, trouble, *bad break, trial, tribulation, setback, calamity, affliction, reversal, hardship, blow, disaster, tragedy. "Knives, that either serve us or cut us, as we grasp them by the blade or the handle."—Herman Melville. ANT. *good luck, fortune, blessing, godsend.*

misgiving *n.* uncertainty, apprehension, qualm, doubt, hesitation, uneasiness, question, fear, distrust, suspicion. ANT. *certainty, trust, confidence.*

misguided *a.* misled, ill-advised, misinformed, led astray, mistaken, faulty, wrong, erroneous, *led up the garden path, *barking up the wrong tree, *off. ANT. *well-advised, correct.*

mishandle *v.* botch, *screw up, *flub, mismanage, mess up, bungle, fumble, *muff, blow, *foul up, *drop the ball. ANT. *succeed, master.*

mishap *n.* accident, miscarriage, misadventure, *screw-up, blunder, mistake, misfortune, calamity, casualty.

mishmash *n.* hodgepodge, jumble, conglomeration. SEE MISCELLANY

misinform *v.* mislead, lead astray, misstate, misguide, misrepresent, distort, lie, deceive.

misinterpret *v.* misconstrue, misread. SEE MISUNDERSTAND

misjudge *v.* miscalculate, misread, overestimate, underestimate, overrate, underrate, err, mistake, misconstrue, misunderstand.

mislead *v.* lead astray, misinform, misguide, deceive, *lead down the garden path, bamboozle, delude, *give the bum steer, take in, *pull the wool over one's eyes.

mismanage *v.* SEE MISHANDLE

mismatch *n.* SEE DISPARITY

misogynist *n.* woman-hater, male chauvinist, misanthrope, sexist.

misplace *v.* lose, lose track of, mislay, displace.

misrepresentation *n.* distortion, misstatement, falsification, fabrication, misquote, *stretch, perversion, adulteration, lie, exaggeration. ANT. *truth, accuracy.*

miss *n.* young lady, girl, lass, maiden, gal, young woman, mademoiselle.

miss *v.* **1.** FAIL fall short, pass over, overlook, *drop the ball, miscalculate, bobble, *blow it, *choke, muff. **2.** LONG FOR pine for, yearn for, ache with nostalgia, think of fondly. ANT. *1. succeed, catch, see.*

misshapen *a.* deformed, malformed, grotesque, distorted, misproportioned, contorted, monstrous, ugly. ANT. *well-formed, perfect.*

missile *n.* rocket, projectile, trajectile, ballistic missile, air-to-air missile, ground-to-air missile, guided missile.

WORD FIND
air-to-air: Sidewinder, Falcon, Sparrow
anti-armor, wire-guided: TOW missile
antiship cruise missile: Harpoon
antitank: Hellfire missile, Maverick
camera-guided: AGM-142, Have Nap missile
electronic beam, guided by: beam rider
explosive portion: warhead
guided missile: cruise missile, Tomahawk
intercepts enemy missiles: Patriot

intercontinental missile: MX, Titan
multiple warhead missile: MIRV
propulsion unit, additional: booster
radar installations, homes in on: HARM
shoulder-fired: Stinger
silo-deployed, three-stage nuclear missile:
Minuteman
tank-mounted: Shillelagh
underwater, launched from: Polaris, Poseidon, Trident II
SEE AMMUNITION, BOMB

missing *a.* lacking, absent, elsewhere, lost, gone, away, wanting, removed, mislaid, out of sight, unaccounted for, *AWOL. ANT. *here, present.*

mission *n.* task, undertaking, assignment, object, objective, charge, duty, quest, errand, job, enterprise, calling.

missionary *n.* evangelist, proselytizer, preacher, clergyman, minister, messenger.

missive *n.* letter, message, note, dispatch, communication, memo, report, word, bulletin, *fax.

misspent *a.* wasted, squandered, misapplied, thrown away, *down the drain, *blown, prodigal. ANT. *well spent, productive.*

misstatement *n.* misrepresentation, innacuracy, misquote, distortion, mistake, falsification, perversion, lie, *blooper.

misstep *n.* error, slip, mistake, wrong move, gaffe, lapse, faux pas, trip, transgression, blunder, oversight.

mist *n.* vapor, fog, drizzle, fine rain, cloud, steam, spray, brume, moisture, haze, smog.
SEE CLOUD, FOG, RAIN

mistake *n.* error, inaccuracy, fault, blunder, gaffe, *boo-boo, *flub, slip, miscalculation, boner, misinterpretation, goof, omission, oversight, failure.

mistake *v.* err, blunder, *flub, miscalculate, misinterpret, goof, omit, overlook, misunderstand, underestimate, overestimate, *botch, miss, misconstrue, confuse.

mistaken *a.* wrong, incorrect, inaccurate, off, inexact, imprecise, erroneous, in error, fallacious, *wide of the mark, confused, *all wet, *off base, misinformed, unsound. ANT. *correct, right, accurate.*

mistreat *v.* abuse, maltreat, wrong, rough up, manhandle, brutalize, disrespect, *step on, *walk all over, bully. ANT. *coddle, dote on.*

mistreatment *n.* abuse, maltreatment, disrespect, cruelty, brutality, torment, torture, manhandling, rough treatment. ANT. *coddling, kindness.*

mistress *n.* **1.** MATRON madam, authority, head, matriarch, head of the household. **2.** LOVER concubine, courtesan, sweetheart, kept woman, girlfriend, *other woman.

mistrust *n.* distrust, suspicion, doubt, uncertainty, skepticism, apprehension, misgiving, wariness, qualm, leeriness. ANT. *trust, confidence, faith.*

mistrust *v.* distrust, suspect, doubt, have misgivings, question, apprehend, fear, have reservations. ANT. *trust, believe in, have faith in.*

misty *a.* vaporous, drizzling, foggy, moist, gauzy, cloudy, filmy, murky, steamy, hazy, fuzzy, shrouded, nebulous. ANT. *clear, transparent.*

misunderstand *v.* misinterpret, misconstrue, misapprehend, misconceive, get the wrong idea, misread, misjudge, miscalculate, *get signals crossed. ANT. *understand, get, see.*

misunderstanding *n.* **1.** MISINTERPRETATION misapprehension, the wrong idea, confusion, mix-up, misconception, mistake, misreading, false impression. **2.** ARGUMENT disagreement, difference, dispute, rift, quarrel, dissension, squabble, *falling-out.

misuse *n.* misapplication, abuse, misusage, corruption, misemployment, perversion.

misuse *v.* misapply, misemploy, abuse, corrupt, pervert, mistreat, wrong.

MITIGATE *v.* [MIT uh GATE] to lessen the effect or severity of something. *Mitigate the pain of a sprain by elevating the injured ankle.* SYN. moderate, lessen, diminish, soften, reduce, alleviate, allay, lighten, check, blunt, ease. ANT. *exacerbate, aggravate, worsen.*

mix *n.* mixture, blend, combination, combo, compound, amalgamation, composite, variety, potpourri, goulash, mélange, medley.

mix *v.* **1.** BLEND combine, mingle, compound, amalgamate, jumble, suffuse, conglomerate, unite, join, merge. **2.** SOCIALIZE fraternize, hobnob, *work the room, mingle. ANT. *1. separate, divide. 2. be aloof, snub, *be a wallflower.*

mixed bag *n.* assortment, miscellany, odds and ends, medley, hodgepodge, melange, mishmash, jumble, potpourri.

mixed-up *a.* confused, muddled, lost, befuddled, perplexed, puzzled, confounded, misunderstanding. ANT. *clear, *with it.*

mixture *n.* SEE MIX

moan *n.* groan, cry, lament, wail, sigh, plaint.

moan *v.* groan, cry, lament, wail, sigh, grumble, complain, grieve.

moat *n.* trench, fosse, foss, ditch, gully, defense.
SEE CASTLE

mob *n.* **1.** CROWD throng, mass, legion, flock, multitude, horde, collection, crush, host. "Man voluntarily descending to the nature of a beast."—Ralph Waldo Emerson. "Many heads, but no brains."—Thomas Fuller. "A many-headed beast."—Horace. **2.** GANG Mafia, underworld, syndicate, Cosa Nostra.

mob *v.* crowd, throng, swarm, surround, jostle, elbow, descend upon, attack.

mobile *a.* movable, moving, portable, locomotive, fluid, transportable, on the move, traveling. ANT. *stationary, immobile.*

mobilize *v.* ready, organize, summon, muster, assemble, call up, call to arms, round up, marshal, rally, activate. ANT. *immobilize, disperse.*

mobster *n.* goon. SEE GANGSTER

mock *v.* **1.** RIDICULE make fun of, taunt, challenge, laugh at, *poke fun at, kid, tease, scoff, jeer, burlesque, *thumb nose at. **2.** IMITATE mimic, impersonate, caricature, ape, parrot, *do, burlesque, lampoon, parody. ANT. *1. show respect, honor, *put on a pedestal.*

mock *a.* imitation, fake, artificial, counterfeit, simulated, mimic, *bogus, make-believe, substitute, sham. ANT. *true, genuine, real.*

mockery *n.* **1.** JOKE laughingstock, farce, travesty, *butt, fool, sham. **2.** RIDICULE taunting, kidding, disrespect, derision, scoffing, contempt, sport. ANT. *2. respect, honor, reverence.*

mode *n.* **1.** WAY manner, method, technique, style, practice, approach, procedure, methodology, form. **2.** FASHION style, look, vogue, trend, rage, craze.

model *n.* **1.** REPLICA mockup, dummy, prototype, miniature, copy, imitation, facsimile. **2.** IDEAL standard, exemplar, archetype, pattern, paragon, mold, role model, prototype. **3.** FASHION OR ARTIST'S MODEL poser, sitter, subject, dummy.

model *v.* **1.** FASHION shape, mold, design, construct, base, cast. **2.** SHOW show off, wear, display, parade.

model *a.* ideal, standard, exemplary, classic, perfect, archetypal. ANT. *flawed, imperfect.*

modem *n.* modulator/demodulator, electronic device, peripheral, data converter, translator. SEE COMPUTER

moderate *n.* *middle-of-the-roader, nonliberal, nonconservative, centrist. ANT. *radical, conservative, liberal.*

moderate *v.* **1.** LESSEN soften, mitigate, restrain, check, tone down, control, regulate, reduce,

slacken, ease, blunt. **2.** PRESIDE OVER control, oversee, chair, mediate, referee, lead, emcee, govern, supervise. ANT. *1. intensify, increase, aggravate.*

moderate *a.* **1.** TEMPERATE reasonable, sensible, judicious, balanced, equable, conservative, restrained, neutral, unexceptional, middling, not extreme. **2.** MILD calm, gentle, soft, low-key, quiet. **3.** AVERAGE medium, mediocre, so-so, fair, middling, ordinary, intermediate, mean, common. ANT. *1. extreme, severe, excessive. 2. harsh, severe, violent. 3. exceptional, outstanding, extraordinary.*

moderation *n.* temperance, happy medium, middle ground, discretion, restraint, judiciousness, forbearance, sobriety, golden mean. "Nothing to excess."—Anacharsis. "The silken string running through the pearl—chain of all virtues."—Thomas Fuller.

moderator *n.* master of ceremonies, emcee, chairperson, referee, speaker, presiding officer, mediator.

modern *a.* contemporary, up-to-date, new, neo, now, current, today, *cutting edge, *leading edge, *mod, fresh, late, up-to-the-minute, *hot, fashionable, modish, trendy, *in, in vogue, progressive. ANT. *out of date, outdated, old-fashioned, antiquated, ancient, antique, passé.*

modernize *v.* update, renovate, remodel, revamp, redesign, streamline, retool. ANT. *antiquate.*

modest *a.* **1.** UNASSUMING humble, self-effacing, reserved, demure, unpretentious, down to earth, shy, blushing, bashful. **2.** ORDINARY humble, limited, moderate, medium, simple, plain, small, unpretentious, homely, adequate, middling, fair, unexceptional. ANT. *1. arrogant, pretentious, *full of oneself, vain. 2. exceptional, extravagant, ostentatious.*

modesty *n.* **1.** HUMILITY humbleness, unpretentiousness, moderation, reserve, reticence, shyness, bashfulness, simplicity, plainness. "The only sure bait when you angle for praise."—Lord Chesterfield. "Meekness and wisdom combined."—Solomon Ibn Gabirol. "An index to nobility."—Solomon Ibn Gabirol. **2.** DECENCY decorum, propriety, seemliness. ANT. *1. arrogance, pretentiousness, vanity. 2. indecency, unseemliness.*

modicum *n.* bit, small amount, speck, little, iota, shred, snippet, drop, ounce, atom, whit, particle. ANT. *lot, *truckload.*

modify v. **1.** CHANGE alter, rework, correct, adjust, vary, innovate, reshape, reform, convert, moderate, transform, tweak, *fiddle with. **2.** LESSEN limit, moderate, reduce, soften, tone down. ANT. *2. increase, intensify.*

modish a. fashionable, stylish, in vogue, chic, trendy, *in, up-to-the-minute, *hot, *all the rage, smart, fresh. ANT. *old-fashioned, dated, passé.*

modulate v. adjust, regulate, tune, fine-tune, attune, balance, moderate, equalize, soften, tone down.

modus operandi n. mode of operation, method, technique, system, workings, means, way.

mogul n. *big shot, *bigwig, *power, magnate, tycoon, baron, *VIP, personage, *mover and shaker, *heavy hitter, *heavyweight. ANT. *nobody, *zero, peasant.*

moist a. damp, wet, watery, humid, muggy, dewy, dank, steamy, misty, foggy, drizzly, rainy, clammy. ANT. *dry, arid, dehydrated.*

moisten v. dampen, wet, moisturize.

moisture n. dampness, wetness, humidity, mugginess, dew, steam, mist, fog, drizzle, rain, liquid. ANT. *dryness, aridity.*

moisturizer n. cream, lotion, oil, salve, emollient.

mold n. **1.** FORM cast, pattern, stamp, shape, impression, die, outline, cut, model. **2.** FUNGUS mildew.

mold v. **1.** SHAPE form, cast, make, fashion, forge, sculpt, model, construct. **2.** INFLUENCE model, shape, guide.

moldy a. musty, stale, decayed, rotting, moldering, crumbling, mildewed, decomposing. ANT. *fresh, new, in good shape.*

mole n. spot, nevus, blemish, birthmark, freckle, blotch, discoloration, beauty mark.

molest v. **1.** PHYSICALLY OR SEXUALLY ABUSE violate, rape, *feel up, accost, fondle, make an advance, solicit, approach, *paw, assault, mistreat. **2.** BOTHER trouble, annoy, besiege, torment, plague, harass, upset, beset, irritate, pester, disturb.

MOLLIFY v. [MOL uh FYE] to soothe, soften or appease. *We gave the toddler a stick of gum to mollify him.* SYN. soothe, soften, appease, pacify, tranquilize, mellow, calm, tame, gentle, tone down, mitigate, blunt, ease. ANT. *aggravate, intensify, exacerbate.*

mollycoddle v. pamper, coddle, baby, cosset, indulge, wait on, spoil.

molt v. shed, cast off, slough off, exuviate, exfoliate, peel.

molten a. melted, liquefied, red-hot, smelted, igneous, volcanic. ANT. *frozen, hardened.*

mom n. SEE MOTHER

moment n. **1.** INSTANT minute, second, hour, point in time, *twinkling, time, *jiffy, short time, *wink of an eye, flash, *two shakes of a lamb's tail, date. **2.** IMPORTANCE consequence, weight, significance, import, gravity, concern, substance, magnitude. ANT. *2. unimportance, insignificance.*

momentarily adv. shortly, in a second, immediately, briefly, any moment now.

momentary a. brief, fleeting, short-lived, transitory, ephemeral, transient, instantaneous, passing. ANT. *long-lived, long, prolonged.*

momentous a. important, consequential, weighty, of great moment, significant, decisive, critical, crucial, pivotal, earthshaking, vital. ANT. *insignificant, trivial, unimportant.*

momentum n. impetus, force, push, drive, thrust, energy, impulse, go, speed.

monarch n. ruler, king, queen, autocrat, emperor, empress, sovereign, crowned head.

monarchy n. kingdom, sovereign state, autocracy, absolute monarchy.

monastery n. abbey, friary, cloister, religious community, convent, nunnery, priory, retreat, hermitage.

monetary a. pecuniary, financial, capital, fiscal.

money n. currency, legal tender, cash, *bucks, *dough, *bread, medium of exchange, *wad, *loot, *scratch, *wampum, coin, specie, change, almighty dollar, funds, wealth, capital, riches. "A good servant but a bad master."—Henry Bohn. "Slave or master."—Horace. "A good soldier."—Shakespeare. "An eel in the hand."—Welsh proverb.
WORD FIND
Afghanistan: afghani
Algeria: dinar
Argentina: Peso
Australia: dollar
Austria: Euro
Barbados: dollar
Belgium: Euro
Bermuda: dollar
Bolivia: Boliviano
Brazil: real
Britain: pound
Bulgaria: lev
Cambodia: riel
Canada: dollar
Chile: peso
Columbia: peso
Costa Rica: colon

Croatia: Kuna
Cuba: peso
Cyprus: pound
Czech Republic: koruna
Denmark: krone
Dominican Republic: peso
Ecuador: sucre
Egypt: pound
El Salvador: colon
Estonia: kroon
Ethiopia: birr
Finland: Euro
France: Euro
Germany: Euro
Greece: Euro
Guatemala: quetzal
Guinea: Franc
Haiti: gourde
Honduras: lempira
Hong Kong: dollar
Hungary: forint
Iceland: krona
India: rupee
Indonesia: rupiah
Iran: rial
Iraq: dinar
Ireland: Euro
Israel: shekel
Italy: Euro
Jamaica: dollar
Japan: yen
Jordan: dinar
Kazakhstan: tenge
Kenya: shilling
Kuwait: dinar
Lao: kip
Latvia: lats
Lebanon: pound
Libya: pound
Lithuania: litas
Luxembourg: Euro
Macau: pataca
Malaysia: ringgit
Malta: lira
Mexico: peso
Mongolia: tugrik
Morocco: dirham
Mozambique: metical
Myanmar: kyat
Namibia: dollar
Nepal: rupee
Netherlands: Euro
New Zealand: dollar
Nicaragua: cordoba oro
Nigeria: naira

North Korea: won
Norway: kroner
Oman: rial
Pakistan: rupee
Panama: balboa
Paraguay: guarani
Peru: nuevo sol
Philippines: peso
Poland: zloty
Portugal: Euro
Qatar: rial
Romania: leu
Russia: rouble
Samoa: tala
Saudi Arabia: riyal
Singapore: dollar
Somalia: shilling
South Africa: rand
South Korea: won
Spain: Euro
Sri Lanka: rupee
Sudan: dinar, pound
Sweden: krona
Switzerland: franc
Syria: pound
Taiwan: dollar
Tanzania: shilling
Trinidad/Tobago: dollar
Tunisia: dinar
Turkey: lira
Uganda: shilling
Ukraine: hryvnia
United Arab Emirates: dirham
United States of America: dollar
Uruguay: peso
Venezuela: bolivar
Vietnam: dong
Yugoslavia: dinar
Zambia: kwacha
Zimbabwe: dollar

moneyed *a.* rich, wealthy, affluent, *loaded, *well-off, *well-to-do, *flush. ANT. *poor, destitute*.

money-making *a.* profitable, lucrative, paying, gainful, successful. ANT. *unprofitable*.

mongrel *n.* mixture, crossbreed, mutt, hybrid, half-blood, half-breed, cur. ANT. *purebred, thoroughbred*.

moniker *n. Sl.* nickname. SEE NAME

monitor *n.* overseer, watchdog, supervisor, observer, advisor.

monitor *v.* oversee, watch over, observe, *keep an eye on, check, supervise, police, scan.

monk *n.* brother, monastic, friar.

monkey *n.* simian, primate, ape, chimpanzee,

rhesus monkey, spider monkey, orangutan. "An organized sarcasm upon the human race."—Henry Ward Beecher.

monkey business *n. Sl.* foolishness, mischief, misbehavior, impishness, antics, high jinks, *monkeyshines, horseplay. ANT. *serious business.*

monolith *n.* slab, stone, block, monument, obelisk

MONOLITHIC *a.* [MON uh LITH ik] huge, massive, and permanent, as a monolith. *Our monolithic government has hundreds of sub-bureaucracies.* SYN. massive, huge, like a rock, unyielding, gigantic, permanent, unchanging, immovable, immobile. ANT. *tiny, portable, yielding.*

monologue *n.* soliloquy, talk, discourse, lecture, speech, oration, one-man show, one-woman show. ANT. *dialogue, give and take.*

monopolize *v.* corner, appropriate, own, dominate, *hog, keep for oneself, control. ANT. *share, divide equally.*

monopoly *n.* control, corner, domination, cartel, bloc, exclusive possession. "The octopus."—Frank Norris.

monotonous *a.* boring, tiresome, wearisome, repetitious, unstimulating, unvarying, dull, ho-hum, tedious, dry, *dull as dishwater, *blah, flat, somnolent, droning. ANT. *varying, changing, stimulating.*

monotony *n.* sameness, uniformity, boredom, dullness, tedium, routine, humdrum, repetition, dreariness, flatness. ANT. *change, variation, excitement.*

monster *n.* **1.** UNNATURAL BEAST creature, mutant, miscreation, ogre, freak of nature, monstrosity, boogieman, brute, thing, *it, *lab experiment, dragon, drake, sea serpent, kraken, hydra, Loch Ness Monster (Nessie), Champ (Lake Champlain), yeti, Bigfoot, abominable snowman, Frankenstein, werewolf, vampire, ghoul, goblin, hobgoblin, zombie, incubus, succubus, troll, basilisk, harpy, centaur, griffin, gargoyle, chimera, Gorgon, Medusa, Minotaur, Phoenix, Cerberus, Argus, Cyclops, Pluto, Sphinx, Orthos, Python, Pan, roc, demon, orc, satyr, hellhound, alien, extraterrestrial, little green man, man-eater, Godzilla, the Blob, B-movie monster (Roger Corman Creation). **2.** GIANT colossus, behemoth, Gargantua, Goliath, titan, leviathan, mammoth, Brobdingnagian. ANT. *2. dwarf, midget, runt, baby.*

monstrosity *n.* SEE MONSTER

monstrous *a.* **1.** GROTESQUE hideous, abnormal, mutated, unnatural, repulsive, freakish, teratoid, weird, wild, outlandish, bizarre, otherworldly, beastly, frightful, shocking. **2.** HUGE gigantic, gargantuan, colossal, stupendous, hulking, enormous, titanic, immense, mammoth, towering. **3.** EVIL atrocious, satanic, revolting, heinous, hateful, gruesome, loathsome, vile, horrible. **4.** OUTRAGEOUS shocking, incredible, ridiculous, astonishing. ANT. *1. normal, natural, beautiful. 2. tiny, wee, small. 3. good, moral, angelic. 4. normal, reasonable.*

montage *n.* hodgepodge, jumble, patchwork, mosaic, mishmash, potpourri, miscellany, arrangement, scheme.

monument *n.* **1.** MEMORIAL statue, pillar, column, monolith, obelisk, tower, stone, plinth, shrine, pyramid, tombstone, headstone, marker, cross, mausoleum, cenotaph, effigy, ossuary, sepulchre, solium, weeper. SEE CEMETERY **2.** NOTABLE ACHIEVEMENT landmark, magnum opus, masterpiece, masterwork, chef d'oeuvre, watershed.

monumental *a.* massive, huge, prodigious, colossal, towering, grand, exalted, enduring, permanent, outstanding, exceptional. ANT. *tiny, microscopic, insignificant, forgettable.*

moo *v.* low, bellow.

mooch *v. Sl.* cadge, beg, *sponge, *bum off, *leach off, *panhandle, pilfer.

mood *n.* state of mind, frame of mind, spirit, temper, humor, vein, mind, disposition, caprice. SEE ANGER, ANXIETY, DEPRESSION, FEAR, HAPPINESS, SADNESS

moody *a.* temperamental, touchy, grouchy, labile, gloomy, glum, petulant, unpredictable, cranky, *running hot and cold. ANT. *stable, predictable, even-tempered, constant.*

moon *n.* satellite, orb, planetoid, celestial body, sphere, *dustball, Luna, Selene, Diana. "Magnificent desolation."—Edwin Aldrin. "A corpse upon the road of night."—Robert Burton. "A golden sickle reaping darkness down."—James B. Hope. "The passionless bright face."—Dinah Craik.

WORD FIND
crater: Alphonsus, Copernicus, Kepler, Plato, Tycho
descriptive: sickle, wan, albescent, sallow, sterile, stark, surrealistic
goddess: Luna, Selene, Diana, Phoebe, Astarte, Cynthis, Lucina, Hecate
halo around: nimbus
hole from meteorite impact: crater

horn of crescent: cusp
landing site, original: Sea of Tranquility
line or crack from meteorite impact: ray
line where light and dark meet: terminator
mares: (maria): Mare Imbrium, Mare Nubium, Oceanus Procellarum, Mare Tranquilititis (sea of tranquility)
mound: dome
mountains: Alps, Apennines, Caucasus, Doerfel, Leibnitz
narrow trench or valley: rill(e)
orbital point farthest from earth: apogee
orbital point nearest to earth: perigee
phases: new, crescent, quarter, gibbous, full
plain originally mistaken for sea: mare (maria)
reflected sunlight: albedo
seasonal: harvest, hunter's
shadow: umbra
study of: selenology
waxing, waning

moon v. Sl. **1.** DROP ONE'S DRAWERS *flash, *salute. **2.** DREAM daydream, fantasize, *go off into one's own world.

moonlight n. moonshine, moonbeams, albedo, effulgence, luminescence, radiance.

moonshine n. Sl. corn liquor, contraband, home brew, bootleg, *white lightning, *mountain dew, *rotgut, *stump liquor, *bathtub gin, *the stuff that looks like water and kicks like a mule.

moonstruck v. crazed, deranged, demented, possessed, loony, insane.

moor n. heath, peat bog, scrubland, swamp, tundra, wasteland, marsh, prairie.

moorings n. slip, port, harbor, anchorage, dock, marina, wharf, berth, landing, pier.

WORD FIND
deck posts around which mooring lines are secured: bitt
dock or pier post around which mooring lines are secured: bollard

moose n. deer, elk, mammal.

WORD FIND
feeding place: yard
female: cow
kin: reindeer, caribou
male: bull
sexual season: rut
young: calf

MOOT a. [MOOT] subject to discussion or debate. *Whether or not abortion is morally acceptable is a moot question.* SYN. debatable, arguable, disputable, contestable, questionable,

open to question, controversial, at issue, unsettled, theoretical, academic, conjectural. ANT. *indisputable, uncontestable, resolved.*

mop n. swab, duster, *squeegee.

mop v. swab, wipe up, sponge up, dust, *squeegee.

mope v. sulk, pout, brood, grumble, put on a long face, fret, pine, moon, languish, lose heart.

moral n. lesson, principle, truism, adage, proverb, teaching.

moral a. **1.** RIGHTEOUS virtuous, ethical, good, upright, scrupulous, honorable, honest, principled, trustworthy, fair, decent, conscientious, correct, aboveboard, just. **2.** SEXUALLY VIRTUOUS chaste, immaculate, pure, innocent, respectable, *squeaky clean. ANT. *1. immoral, unethical, unprincipled, corrupt, evil. 2. promiscuous, loose, wild.*

morale n. spirit, resolve, attitude, confidence, mood, state.

morality n. righteousness, goodness, integrity, virtue, decency, fairness, honesty, conscientiousness, honor, respectability, responsibility. "A terribly thin covering of ice over a sea of primitive barbarity."—Karl Barth. "To enjoy and give enjoyment, without injury to yourself or others."—Nicolas Chamfort. "Feeling temptation but resisting it."—Sigmund Freud. ANT. *immorality, evil.*

moralize v. preach, sermonize, pontificate, lecture, pass judgment, *climb on one's moral soapbox, *look down one's holier-than-thou nose.

morals n. ideals, standards, mores, scruples, principles, ethics, ethos, manners.

morass n. **1.** MARSH bog, swamp, fen, quagmire, wetland, mire, slough, wallow. **2.** ENTANGLEMENT mess, mix-up, jam, predicament.

MORATORIUM n. [MOR uh TOR ee um] a suspension or delay of an activity. *The city has placed a moratorium on new real estate development.* SYN. suspension, delay, deferment, postponement, discontinuance, stop.

MORBID a. [MOR bid] unhealthy, unwholesome, gloomy or gruesome. *He had a morbid fascination with death.* SYN. unhealthy, sickly, pathological, morose, gloomy, black, depressed, somber, melancholy, neurotic, sick, gruesome. ANT. *healthy, wholesome, happy.*

mordant a. biting, cutting, caustic, bitter, sarcastic, acid, scathing, acerbic, venomous, pungent, acrimonious, pointed, sharp.

more n. additional amount, supplement, replenishment, increase, extra.

more *a.* additional, extra, further, greater, added. ANT. *fewer, less.*

more or less *a.* approximately, about, roughly, generally, thereabouts, in round numbers.

moreover *adv.* in addition, furthermore, over and above, also.

mores *n.* customs, codes, manners, standards, conventions, ethos.

morgue *n.* mortuary, funeral parlor, charnel house, crematorium.

moribund *a.* dying, expiring, failing, wasting away, on one's deathbed, terminal, *circling the drain, *sinking fast, *at death's door. ANT. *robust, healthy, vital.*

morning *n.* dawn, daybreak, sunup, sunrise, A.M., forenoon, the holy light of dawn.

moron *n.* imbecile, idiot, simpleton, retardate, dope, dolt, nitwit, dullard, dunce, dummy, lamebrain, *lunkhead, *meathead, *chowderhead, *airhead, *maroon, *one with the IQ of a woodchuck, *one who cuts with a dull tool, *one who is one or two bricks shy of a load, *one slower than a glacier, *one as dense as a post, *one as numb as a flounder, *one who is dead from the neck up. ANT. *genius, savant, Rhodes scholar, Mensa member, rocket scientist.*

moronic *a.* dumb, addle-brained, bovine, asinine. SEE STUPID

morose *a.* gloomy, glum, sullen, melancholy, sour, dour, ill-humored, austere, saturnine, stern, scowling, lugubrious, surly. ANT. *cheerful, upbeat, sunny.*

morphine *n.* narcotic, pain killer, pain reliever, anesthetic, opiate, *bang, *hocus, *joy dust, *white nurse. SEE DRUG, NARCOTIC

morsel *n.* bite, tidbit, spoonful, bit, a taste, mouthful, scrap, piece, shred, speck, chunk, hunk, lump, smidgen.

mortal *a.* **1.** SUBJECT TO DEATH human, earthly, perishable, temporal, transient, fleeting, finite, ephemeral, transitory. **2.** CAUSING DEATH fatal, lethal, malignant, deadly. **3.** TO THE DEATH homicidal, murderous, death-dealing, suicidal, bloodthirsty, fatal, deadly, unrelenting. ANT. *1. immortal, permanent, everlasting. 2. benign, harmless.*

mortality *n.* **1.** IMPERMANENCE transience. **2.** DEATH ON A LARGE SCALE slaughter, carnage, bloodbath, holocaust, extermination, fatality. **3.** DEATH RATE

mortally *adv.* gravely, seriously, fatally. ANT. *superficially, slightly.*

mortgage *n.* contract, pledge, title, deed, lease, loan agreement. SEE MONEY

mortician *n.* undertaker, funeral director, embalmer. SEE FUNERAL

mortification *n.* humiliation, shame, embarrassment, chagrin, humbling, humble pie, disgrace, loss of face.

mortify *v.* humiliate, embarrass, shame, humble, disgrace, dismay, deflate, bring down, *take down a notch, belittle. ANT. *honor, exalt, worship.*

mortuary *n.* funeral home, funeral parlor, morgue, charnel house, crematorium. SEE FUNERAL

mosaic *n.* inlay, collage, tile-work, marquetry, parquetry, miscellany, jumble, hodgepodge.

mosey *v.* shuffle, saunter, pad, amble, stroll. SEE WALK

Moslem *n.* Muslem, Muslim, Mohammedan. SEE RELIGION

mosque *n.* temple, church, house of worship, house of God, sanctuary.

WORD FIND

prayer tower: minaret

moss *n.* lichen, liverwort, Irish moss, Spanish moss, club moss, peat moss.

mossback *n.* *old fogy, *fuddy-duddy, fossil, mid-Victorian, ultraconservative.

most *a.* greatest, largest, nearly all, majority, *lion's share, maximum, utmost, unsurpassed, unequaled, furthest. ANT. *least, smallest, lowest.*

mostly *adv.* for the most part, principally, chiefly, mainly, by and large, on the whole.

mot *n.* witticism, quip, bon mot, repartee, riposte.

mote *n.* speck, particle, fragment, bit, flake, grit.

motel *n.* motor court, inn, motor inn, roadhouse, *stop and drop. SEE HOTEL

moth-eaten *a.* **1.** THREADBARE tattered, ragged, *holey, worn-out, decrepit. **2.** OLD-FASHIONED outmoded, outdated, antiquated, out of style, obsolete. ANT. *1. fresh, new, pristine. 2. recent. contemporary.*

mother *n.* **1.** MOM matriarch, parent, matron, nurturer, caregiver, *hand that rocks the cradle, foster mother, adoptive mother, mother-in-law, *mama, *mum, *mumsy, *old lady. **2.** SOURCE origin, originator, womb, cradle. "What God made because He could not be everywhere."—Adapted from Jewish proverb. "God's deputy on earth."—Rahel Varnhagen. SEE FAMILY

mother *v.* nurture, raise, rear, bring up, parent, foster, nourish, protect, nurse, care for, overprotect, spoil, smother, coddle.

motherhood n. maternity, mothership.
motherland n. native land, home land, *the old country.
motherly a. maternal, nurturing, doting, protective, solicitous. ANT. *neglectful, abusive.*
motif n. theme, pattern, subject, leitmotif, idea, strain, device, form, concept.
motion n. **1.** ACTION movement, change, moving, transition, drift, shift. **2.** A PROPOSAL recommendation, suggestion, proposition, submission, offering.
motion v. gesture, gesticulate, point, nod, beckon, shrug, pantomime.
motionless a. unmoving, still, inert, static, lifeless, tranquil, dead, frozen, paralyzed, inanimate, stationary, immobile, becalmed, fixed, quiet, idle.
motion picture n. picture show, *flick. SEE MOVIE
motivate v. impel, induce, move, stimulate, spur, goad, encourage, challenge, incite, prompt, inspire, start, arouse, *hold out a carrot, *light a fire under, galvanize, serve as a catalyst, *give a good, swift kick. ANT. *discourage, deflate, *take the wind out of one's sails, dishearten.*
motivation n. incentive, enticement, reason. SEE MOTIVE
motive n. motivation, purpose, reason, incentive, stimulus, rationale, driving force, grounds, enticement, aim, instigation, goal, spur, bribe.
motley a. heterogenous, diverse, many-colored, assorted, miscellaneous, varied, varicolored, variegated, kaleidoscopic, patchwork, jumbled, multifarious. ANT. *similar, uniform, homogeneous.*
motor n. engine, power plant, dynamo, turbine, generator, transformer, transducer, *workhorse; TYPES internal combustion motor, diesel, Wankel, rotary, steam, double-overhead cam, two-stroke, four-stroke, V-6, V-8, four-barrel, slant, transverse, supercharged, turbocharged, inboard-outboard.
WORD FIND
alternating current producer: alternator
carburetor replacement system: fuel injection
closes air to carburetor: choke
coolant: antifreeze, ethyl glycol
cooling system: fan, radiator, thermostat, water jackets, water pump
cylindrical plugs that move up and down, compresses air-fuel mix: pistons

distributes electricity to spark plugs: distributor
drive train: clutch, transmission, driveshaft, differential
energy unit: horsepower, rpm (revolutions per minute)
exhaust burner: catalytic converter, afterburner, turbocharger
filters dirt and dust: air filter, fuel filter, oil filter
frame: chassis
friction reducers: bearings
fuel vaporizer: carburetor
heat exchanger: radiator
knocking: ping, detonation
main framework containing cylinders: engine block
main rotating shaft: crankshaft
overtaxing of: red-lining
piston housing: cylinder
sputtering after ignition turned off: dieseling
turning force of motor: torque
valve operator: camshaft
SEE AIRCRAFT, AUTOMOBILE, MACHINERY
motor v. drive, cruise, ride, tour, steer.
motorboat n. speedboat, power boat, outboard, cruiser. SEE BOAT, SHIP
motorcade n. parade, procession, caravan, cavalcade.
motorcycle n. motor bike, dirt bike, motor scooter, minibike, moped, *hog, *wheels, *chopper, *iron horse, *rice burner, *bike, *sled. SEE MOTOR
WORD FIND
accelerator: throttle
engine shutoff: kill switch
model: Honda, Harley Davidson, Kawasaki, Suzuki, Triumph, Indian
safety bar, passenger: sissy bar
seat: saddle
motor home n. trailer, mobile home, RV, camper, *tin can.
motorist n. driver, commuter.
motorized a. powered, mechanized, automatic. ANT. *manual.*
mottled a. variegated, streaked, dappled, piebald, pied, spotted, shaded, motley, splotchy, marble-patterned, flecked, particolored. ANT. *monochrome, uniform.*
motto n. maxim, adage, aphorism, saying, proverb, axiom, truism, principle, slogan, epigram, saw.
mound n. heap, pile, mass, knoll, hump, hummock, hillock, dune. SEE HILL
mount v. **1.** ASCEND climb, go up, scale, surmount. **2.** INCREASE grow, pile up, burgeon,

accrue, swell, mushroom, multiply, proliferate, balloon, accumulate.

mountain *n.* peak, alp, mount, summit, pinnacle, highland, elevation, ridge, pike, seamount, volcano, butte, mesa, plateau, massif, matterhorn, monadnock, nunatak, uprising, cliff. FAMOUS MOUNTAINS Aetna, Annapurna, Blanc, Everest, Fuji, Godwin Austen (K²), Grand Teton, Hood, Kilamanjaro, Krakatoa, Matterhorn, McKinley, Pelee, Pike's Peak, Rainier, Sinai, St. Helens, Vesuvius, Washington, Whitney. (Ranges) Adirondacks, Alps, Andes, Appalachian, Appenines, Canadian Rockies, Cascades, Caucasus, Himalayas, Karakoram, Pyrenees, Rockies, Sierra Madre, Sierra Nevada, Tetons, Urals, White Mountains. "The palaces of nature."—Lord Byron. ANT. *valley, dale, dell, crater.*

WORD FIND
air: rarefied
base: piedmont
bowllike hollow carved by glacier: cirque
chain: cordillera, range, sierra
cloud: banner
crest: areête
descriptive: bell-shaped, flinty, spired
elevation above 4800 ft.: alpine
erosion resistant: monadnock
flat-topped: butte, mesa, plateau
formation: orogeny
frozen fog: rime ice, verglas
glacial ice, surrounded by: nunatak
glow at sunrise/sunset: alpenglow
gully: couloir
humpback: shoulder
lake: tarn
leeward side: rain shadow
low between summits: saddle
needlelike peak: aiguille, matterhorn
nymph: oread
oxygen deprivation: mountain sickness
pass: col, defile
peak: horn, summit
ranges, multiple: cordillera
ridge: areête, hogback, sawback, spur
rounded: knob
rubble: scree, talus
saddle: col
sea: seamount
shadow illusion: specter of the brocken
side: flank
snow collapse: avalanche
steep, weathered rock: crag
study: orography

vestigial nubbin: inselberg
SEE HILL, MOUNTAINEER, MOUNTAINEERING, MOUNTAINOUS, VOLCANO

mountaineer *n.* highlander, uplander, Sherpa, mountain climber, rock climber, adventurist.

mountaineering *n.* mountain climbing, ascending, surmounting, scaling, rock climbing.

WORD FIND
climbing without mechanical aids: freeclimbing
dangerous overhang of ice and snow: cornice
descend by rope: rappel
diagonal ascent: slab
makeshift shelter: bivouac
narrow, vertical passageway: chimney
oxygen deprivation: mountain sickness
ring that connects ropes to pitons: carabiner
securing or playing out rope: belaying
short rope ladder: etrier
sideways movement across slope: traverse
sideways rope traverse: pendulum
spike, wedge or peg used to secure climber: piton
staff: alpenstock
toothed, metal traction attachment: crampon
zigzag to counter steep slopes: switchback

mountainous *a.* alpestrine, alpine. ANT. *flat, level.*

WORD FIND
descriptive: rugged, towering, lofty, vertiginous, cloud-capped, supernal, washboard
ranges: cordillera, sierra

mountebank *n.* charlatan, swindler, quack, *rip-off artist, *con man, *grifter, cheat, imposter, *huckster, *snake oil salesman.

mounted *a.* **1.** SEATED astride, in the saddle. **2.** FITTED attached, seated, backed. ANT. *1. dismounted. 2. unattached, loose.* SEE MOUNTING

mounting *n.* frame, backing, support, seating.

mounting *v.* growing, piling up, expanding, accruing, burgeoning, mushrooming, proliferating, accumulating, multiplying, snowballing. ANT. *diminishing, shrinking.*

mourn *v.* grieve, lament, bemoan, pine, bewail, rue, despair, miss, deplore, languish, agonize, yearn, ache, suffer, anguish.

mourner *n.* the bereaved, griever, survivor.

mournful *a.* sorrowful, bereft, desolate, woeful, heavyhearted, downhearted, forlorn, griefstricken, anguished, heartsick, inconsolable, aching with nostalgia, disheartened, prostrate. ANT. *cheerful, sunny, joyous.*

mourning n. grieving, sorrowing, lamentation, lamenting, bereavement, grief, anguish. ANT. *rejoicing, celebrating.*
WORD FIND
dress of: black, veil, sackcloth, mourning band, widow's weeds. SEE DEATH, FUNERAL
mouse n. **1.** RODENT vermin, field mouse, pocket mouse, vole. **2.** SISSY coward, milquetoast, shrinking violet, weakling, *wimp, *wuss.
mousy a. timid, quiet, shy, timorous. ANT. *bold, aggressive.*
mouth n. **1.** ORAL CAVITY lips, maw, orifice, muzzle chops, *choppers, *kisser. SEE LIPS, SMILE, TEETH **2.** END OF A RIVER outlet, estuary, delta, drain. SEE RIVER **3.** OPENING entrance, aperture.
mouthful n. bite, spoonful, morsel.
mouth off v. spout off, vociferate, vituperate, harangue, taunt, rant, rave, sass, *wise off.
mouthpiece n. spokesman, spokeswoman, PR person, attorney.
mouthwash n. mouth rinse, breath freshener, gargle.
mouth-watering a. salivary, appetizing, savory, succulent. ANT. *unappetizing, distasteful.*
mouthy a. loudmouthed, vociferous, ranting, obnoxious, sassy. ANT. *meek, quiet, mute.*
movable a. portable, transportable, fluid. SEE MOBILE
move v. **1.** SET OR BE IN MOTION transport, change places, impel, propel, advance, lug, haul, budge, relocate, push, pull, go, come, travel, proceed, walk, run, fly. **2.** CHANGE RESIDENCES relocate, transfer, pull up roots, vacate, emigrate, migrate, fly the coop. **3.** AFFECT THE EMOTIONS touch, stir, arouse, play on one's sympathies, pluck or tug at the heartstrings, strike a nerve, melt the heart, stimulate, disturb. **4.** PROPOSE put forth, recommend, urge, offer, submit.
movement n. **1.** MOTION action, stirring, activity, advancement, propulsion, ascension, descension, retraction, flight. **2.** CAMPAIGN grassroots movement, crusade, undertaking, drive popular front, fundraiser, push. **3.** MUSICAL PASSAGE section, part, sequence, division, piece.
mover n. shipper, trucker, moving company.
mover and shaker n. doer, producer, *player, *heavy hitter, instigator, catalyst, generator, *whip, *wheeler and dealer, *spark plug, *lightning rod, *go-getter, enterpriser, entrepreneur, *biggest toad in the puddle, *big

cheese, *chairman of the board, *kingpin, pathfinder, bellwether.
movie n. motion picture, moving picture, film, picture, show, screenplay, cinema, photoplay, silver screen, video, *talkie, *flick, documentary, docudrama, melodrama, epic, *spaghetti western, horse opera, B movie, blue movie, stag film, *skin flick. "Life with the dull parts cut out."—Alfred Hitchcock.
WORD FIND
actor/small role: bit player, cameo appearance, extra
actor who is partially created by computer make-up effects: synthespian
advertising/promotional clip: trailer
aerial shot: crane shot
award: Academy Award, Oscar
black-and-white to color process: colorization
box office smash: *boffo
captioned drawings of planned camera shots: storyboard
clapper: slate
daytime run movie: matinee
digital special effect that metamorphoses person or thing: morphing
directs actors and technicians: director
double scene effect: split screen
electrician assistant: best boy
electrician in charge of lights: gaffer
end of shooting for the day: wrap
fade out effect: dissolve
gunshot wound effect: squib
head of financing and hiring: producer
joining of two pieces of film: splice
journals of the industry: trades, *Variety, Hollywood Reporter*
library film: stock footage
lip synchronization on short loops of film: looping
location finder: location scout
moving shot: dolly shot, trucking shot
music of: score
object: prop
past, scene from character's: flashback
photographer, motion picture: cinematographer
prints from day's shooting: dailies, rushes
proposal of movie to financiers: pitch
publicity: publicist
record dialogue and sound effects: dub, Foley
rolling credits at end of movie: crawl, closing credits
script continuity: script supervisor

set or prop assistant: grip
sets and costumes head: art director
sound effects room: Foley studio
sound recorder: sound technician, Foley artist
stop-action photography: pixillation
superimposition effect: blue screen, matte shot
studio and outside shooting area: lot, backlot
wardrobe assistant: dresser
widening shot: pull-back
wide-screen film process: Cinemascope
wide side-to-side shot: pan
writer: screenwriter, script doctor
writer's outline: treatment
zooming in effect: zoom shot

moving *a.* 1. IN MOTION going, coming, motioning, transporting, proceeding, advancing, ascending, descending, retracting, reversing. 2. RELOCATING transferring, vacating, pulling up roots, emigrating, migrating, flying the coop. 3. EFFECTING THE EMOTIONS touching, stirring, rousing, stimulating, striking a nerve, plucking at the heartstrings, heart-wrenching, gut-wrenching. ANT. *1. stationary. 2. settled, fixed. 3. blunt, soporific, unemotional.*

mow *v.* cut, trim, shear, clip, scythe, hack, reap. SEE HARVEST

moxie *n. Sl.* courage, pluck, guts, mettle, chutzpah, *balls.

much *n.* great quantity, a lot, abundance, profusion, plethora, myriad, deluge, scores, wealth, bonanza, tons, *oodles, *all the tea in China. ANT. *nothing, zero, pittance.*

much *a.* 1. TO A GREAT DEGREE OR EXTENT important, remarkable, considerable, significant, paramount, impressive, critical, of consequence. 2. IN GREAT QUANTITY abundant, plentiful, ample, sufficient, profuse, lavish, generous, considerable, copious, liberal, sizable.

muck *n.* 1. MANURE dung, compost, fertilizer, *crap, ooze. 2. SCANDALOUS INFORMATION lowdown, *skinny, slander, gossip, *dirt, *goods. SEE MUCKRAKING

muck-a-muck *n. Sl.* big shot, *big gun, *big cheese, *high muckety-muck, *pooh-bah, *VIP, *bigwig, *biggest toad in the puddle.

MUCKRAKER *n.* [MUCK raker] one who investigates and reports corruption. *Newspapers train their best reporters to be muckrakers.* SYN. *whistle-blower, investigative journalist, *keyhole journalist, exposer, gossipmonger, scandalmonger, mudslinger, debunker.

MUCKRAKING *n.* [MUCK raking] investigating and reporting corruption. *Muckraking can sometimes be a journalist's most dangerous job.* SYN. whistle-blowing, investigating, exposing, *digging for dirt, gossipmongering, scandalmongering, *dragging through the mud, defaming, character assassinating.

mud *n.* mire, muck, ooze, sludge, slime, clay, slush, silt, dirt, wallow, organic matter.

muddle *v.* mix up, stir up, jumble, disorder, fumble, blunder, puzzle, scramble, ensnarl, confuse, turn upside-down, mess up, foul. ANT. *order, organize, neaten, clarify.*

muddled *a.* confused, befuddled, incoherent, addled, bewildered, disoriented. ANT. *lucid, clear-headed.*

muddy *a.* mucky, miry, sloppy, silty, slimey, slushy, gooey, dirty, oozy, soggy, swampy, boggy, soiled, filthy, grubby, organic, sedimentary. ANT. *clean, pristine, spotless.*

mudslinging *n.* smear campaign, slander, defamation, scandalizing, libeling, name-calling, dragging one's name through the mud, *political parry and jab. ANT. *compliment, praise, tribute.*

muff *v.* bungle, botch, fumble, drop the ball, *blow it, stumble, *choke, fail, miscalculate, slip, trip up, *screw up. ANT. *succeed, accomplish.*

muffin *n.* bread, roll, biscuit, scone, bran muffin, corn muffin.

muffle *v.* stifle, deaden, dampen, mute, tone down, silence, soften.

muffler *n.* 1. CLOTHING scarf, neckerchief, ascot. 2. NOISE-ABSORBING DEVICE baffle, mute, silencer.

mug *n.* 1. DRINKING VESSEL stein, tankard, flagon, cup, toby, goblet. 2. FACE countenance, puss, grimace, mug shot. SEE FACE

mug *v.* hold up, assault, rob, purse-snatch, strong-arm, *jump, *stick up.

mugging *n.* holdup, assault, robbery, purse-snatching, *stick-up.

muggy *a.* humid, damp, moist, sticky, close, clammy, steamy, sultry, dank, sweltering, oppressive. ANT. *dry, arid.*

mulatto *n.* mixed breed, half-breed, hybrid, creole, octoroon, quadroon.

mule *n.* hinny, jackass, donkey, burro, jenny.

mulish *a.* obstinate, headstrong. SEE STUBBORN

mull v. ponder, reflect, think, consider, meditate, weigh, ruminate, deliberate, contemplate, marshal one's thoughts, chew, brood, muse, cogitate.

multicolored a. polychromatic, parti-colored, spectral, variegated, kaleidoscopic, mottled, dappled, striped, streaked. ANT. *monochromatic*. SEE COLORED

multifaceted a. **1.** MANY-SIDED many-faced, manifold. **2.** INTRICATE complex, complicated. ANT. *1. one-sided. 2. simple.*

multifarious a. manifold, diverse, multitudinous, various, multifaceted, heterogeneous, multiplex. ANT. *limited.*

multinational a. international, global, continental, worldwide, multicultural. ANT. *local.*

multiple a. many, manifold, numerous, multitudinous, several, plural, various, duplex, triplex, sundry, myriad. ANT. *single, lone.*

multiply v. **1.** TO ADD increase, compound, duplicate, triple, quadruple, burgeon, proliferate, grow, spread, mushroom. **2.** PRODUCE OFFSPRING propagate, procreate, generate, breed. SEE REPRODUCE

multitude n. mass, throng, bunch, horde, legion, flock, mob, crowd, swarm.

mum a. silent, mute, tight-lipped, speechless. ANT. *effusive, talkative.*

mumble v. mutter, maunder, murmur, speak indistinctly, whisper, talk to oneself, *talk into one's chin/beard, drone. ANT. *project, articulate, shout, roar.*

mummify v. dry, shrivel, preserve, desiccate, embalm, swaddle.

mummy n. corpse, cadaver, the embalmed, the entombed, *stiff.

munch v. chew, bite, crunch, snack, nosh, chomp, nibble, gnaw. SEE CHEW, EAT

munchies n. Sl. **1.** SEE SNACK **2.** SEE APPETITE, HUNGER

mundane a. **1.** ORDINARY everyday, common, banal, trite, humdrum, routine, prosaic, stale, pedestrian. **2.** EARTHLY worldly, terrestrial, material, physical, human. ANT. *1. extraordinary, rare, exceptional. 2. spiritual, divine, out of this world.*

municipal a. civic, civil, metropolitan, city, urban, local, community, town; self-governing. SEE CITY, TOWN

municipality n. city, town, village, metropolis, district, borough, suburb, bedroom community, precinct, parish, hamlet. SEE CITY

munificent a. generous, lavish, extravagant, bountiful, openhanded, philanthropic, liberal. ANT. *cheap, niggardly, tightfisted.*

munitions n. ammunition, weapons, bombs, ordnance, arsenal.

mural n. wall painting, panorama.

murder n. homicide, manslaughter, slaying, killing, assassination, shooting, execution, knifing, lynching. "One murder makes a villain, millions a hero."—Beilby Porteus.

WORD FIND

accidental or unintentional: involuntary manslaughter

automobile, from: drive-by shooting

brother: fraticide

ethnic group or race, of: genocide

father: patricide

gang-related: gangland killing, drive-by shooting, contract killing, *hit

hired: contract killing

infant: infanticide

(in the) heat of passion without malice aforethought: manslaughter, crime of passion

mass slaughter: massacre

mother: matricide

planned: premeditated, first-degree murder

rage, motivated by sudden: crime of passion, manslaughter

random act: *wilding

self: suicide

serial: serial killing

sister: sororicide

surprise, politically motivated: assassination

suspected: foul play

unplanned with malice aforethought: second-degree murder

murder v. kill, slay, slaughter, assassinate, shoot, gun down, knife, run through, lynch, strangle, suffocate, decapitate, butcher, hack to death, bludgeon to death, asphyxiate, poison, dismember, disembowel, dispatch, silence, *waste, *finish off, *rub out, *wax, *hit, *ice, *smoke, *exterminate, *grease, *eighty-six, *blow away, *pump full of lead, *take out, *put out of misery, *bump off.

murderer n. killer, assassin, slayer, strangler, psychopath, sociopath, sniper, lunatic, serial killer, madman, thug, executioner, *ripper, *trigger man, *gun, *hired gun, *liquidator, *hit man, terrorist.

murderous a. homicidal, bloodthirsty, deranged, frenzied, maniacal, savage, sociopathic, psychopathic, cannibalistic, violent, *rabid, *in a spitting rage. ANT. *tranquil, at peace.*

murk n. darkness, gloom, shadow, haze, fog, mist, brume. SEE FOG

murky *a.* **1.** GLOOMY dark, dismal, dusky, dreary, gauzy, funereal, somber, hazy, misty, foggy, brumous. **2.** OBSCURE unclear, vague, nebulous, esoteric, veiled, hidden, obfuscated, occult, mysterious, arcane, impenetrable. ANT. *1. sunny, bright, clear. 2. clear, distinct, in plain view.*

murmur *n.* mutter, whisper, sigh, coo, purr, mumble, sough, purl.

murmur *v.* mutter, whisper, sigh, coo, speak softly, purr, mumble.

muscle *n.* abductor, adductor, flexor, constrictor, extensor, tendon, sinew, fiber, tissue, thew, brawn.

WORD FIND

abdominal support: abdominal obliques, rectus abdominus, transversus abdominus

ankle bender: plantaris

anus: sphincter ani

arm extension, rotation, flexion: lattissimus dorsi, pectoral, supinator

back/body bender: rectus abdominus

back straightener: longissimus

breathing: diaphragm, serratus

chewing, clenching: masseter

disease of muscle wasting: muscular dystrophy

elbow straightener: triceps

eye focusing: ciliary

finger benders: flexor digitorum

finger straighteners: extensor digitorum

forehead/brow: corrugator, epicranial

frowning mouth: depressor, risorious

goosebumps: erector pili

head bender: longus capitus, rectus capitus

head rotator: head oblique

jaw: buccinator

kissing (puckered) lips: orbicularis oris

knee flexor: hamstring

lack of muscle coordination: ataxia

leg muscle aiding balance: soleus

leg/thigh extender: quadriceps

muscle pain: myalgia

penis erector: erector penis

rump: gluteus maximus, medius and minimus

shoulder: deltoid, trapezius

swallowing: constrictor of pharynx

testicle elevator: cremaster

tongue extender: genioglossus

upper arm: biceps, triceps

vocal cords: cricothyroid

withering muscles from lack of use: atrophy

wrist benders: flexor carpi radialis, flexor carpi ulnaris

wrist straighteners: extensor carpi radialis, extensor carpi ulnaris

2. STRENGTH power, force, weight, brawn, heft, might, leverage, *elbow grease, *oomph. ANT. *2. weakness, flaccidity, impotence.*

muscle *v. Sl.* jostle, *bull, ram, shoulder, shove, cow, buffalo, plow through, bulldoze, elbow one's way, strong-arm.

muscular *a.* brawny, sinewy, husky, thewy, strapping, rippling, slabbed, muscle-bound, chiseled, Herculean, sculpted, corded, *cut, *pumped, *bull-necked, Olympian, *washboardlike stomach, *hamlike biceps. ANT. *skinny, flabby, frail, undeveloped.*

muse *n.* inspiration, genius, creativity, talent.

muse *v.* ponder, meditate, reflect, ruminate, consider, mull over, brood, cogitate, chew, weigh, study, think about, turn over in one's mind, deliberate, speculate.

museum *n.* gallery, institute, archives, treasury, exhibit, collection, repository, depository, library, storehouse, *gallery of the Muses, *nation's attic, *history's attic. "Cemeteries of the arts."—Alphonse de Lamartine.

mush 1. BOILED MEAL corn meal, hasty pudding, porridge, cereal, gruel, mash. **2.** EXCESSIVE SENTIMENT treacle, pap, schmaltz, melodrama, bathos, *corn.

mushroom *n.* fungus, toadstool, meadow mushroom, truffle, champignon, chanterelle, death cup, shiitake, morel.

mushroom *v.* burgeon, spread, sprout up, grow, proliferate, thrive, pop up, boom, swell, snowball, multiply.

mushy *a.* sentimental, maudlin, gushy, *lovey-dovey, saccharine. ANT. *unfeeling, cold.*

music *n.* melodies, rhythms, vocals, instrumentals, harmonies, singing, orchestrations, arrangements, tunes, sounds, tones, compositions, *canned, Muzak, longhair, rock, funk, rhythm and blues (R&B), rap, hip hop, punk, acid rock, heavy metal, top forty, boogie woogie, jazz, bebop, Dixieland, ragtime, folk, country and western, bluegrass, zydeco, swing, soul, reggae, pop, easy listening, salsa, bossa nova, classical, opera, ethnic, polka, march, baroque, primitive, new age, gangsta rap. "The speech of angels."—Thomas Carlyle. "A fluid architecture of sound."—Roy Harris. "The universal language of mankind."—Longfellow. SEE MUSICAL INSTRUMENTS, OPERA, SING, SONG, RAP

WORD FIND

GENERAL MUSIC TERMS

above correct pitch: sharp

arrangement: composition
bar: measure
beats per measure: meter
below correct pitch: flat
changing key of composition: transposing
chord with notes played individually in quick succession: arpeggio, broken chord
closing passage: coda
connection between two musical passages: bridge
dual melody: counterpoint
emphasis on a particular note: accent
highly skilled musician: virtuoso
horizontal lines on which notes are written: staff
informal rock or jazz session: jam
in-tune, pleasant-sounding: consonance
key and meter signs: signature
lowest notes or voice: bass
multiple notes played simultaneously: chord
multiple rhythms played simultaneously: polyrhythmic
out of tune, harsh-sounding: dissonance, discord
pause or silence: rest
performance of multiple song portions: medley
performing music on sight: sight reading
performing rights society: BMI
performing without notes: by ear
return to the original theme: reprise
school of music: conservatory
science of sound properties: acoustics
second or third highest voice class: alto
section or verse repeated: refrain
short composition: bagatelle
short melodic phrase on jazz or rock guitar: riff, lick
study of music: musicology
teaching of pitch and rhythm recognition: ear training
trumpeting intro: fanfare
words of song: lyrics
written music for movie or play: score

SYMPHONIC TERMS
composition of arias, duets, choruses in several movements: cantata
final movement: finale
instrumental composition preceding opera, oratorio or play: overture
instrumental composition with movements in varied keys, tempos: sonata
instrumental composition with several movements of dance music: suite
one section of a composition: movement

orchestra or musical society: philharmonic
polyphonic composition sung sequentially by two or more vocalists: fugue
work or composition of a composer: opus

MUSIC DIRECTIVES
boldly: fiero
comically: burlesco
decrease in volume: decrescendo
delicately: delicato
fast tempo: allegro, presto
loudly, very: fortissimo
moderate tempo: andante
mournfully: funerale
slow: adagio
slow, extremely: adagissimo
softly: sotto voce
softly, sweetly: dolce
softly, very: pianissimo
spoken: parlato
volume, half the singer's normal: mezza voce
volume, increase in: crescendo
wildly: furioso

musical *n.* revue, musical comedy, burlesque, Broadway production, show.

musical *a.* melodic, rhythmic, harmonious, lyrical, soulful, choral, spiritual, mellifluent, symphonic, sonorous, euphonic. ANT. *dissonant, cacophonous, discordant, noisy.*

musical instrument *n.* woodwind, stringed instrument, percussive instrument, keyboard instrument, brass, *noisemaker.

WORD FIND

KEYBOARD INSTRUMENTS
accordion with button keyboard: concertina
automatic piano: player piano
bell-like soundmaker in "Dance of the Sugar Plum Fairy": celesta
electronic sound recreator: synthesizer
organ, steam whistle: calliope
piano, full-sized: grand piano
piano, largest: concert piano
piano, predecessor: clavichord, harpsichord
piano, slang: *eighty-eights, *ivories
piano, small grand: baby grand
piano, space-saving: upright
plucked instead of struck by hammers: harpsichord
squeezebox, handheld: accordion, *squeezebox
wind or electric-generated keyboard: organ

PERCUSSION INSTRUMENTS
bell: campanella
block, wooden: wood block, clog box
Caribbean tinkling drum: steel drum
clackers, wooden stick: claves

clappers clicked rhythmically: castanets
cow's bell: cowbell
crash, sizzlemaker: cymbal
Cuban drums played with fingers, hands: bongos
drum for rolls, flourishes, fills: tom-tom
hanging cymbal struck with mallet: gong
kettle drum: timpani
largest, booming drum: bass drum, *kick drum
rasping gourd: guiro
rat tat tat beatkeeper: snare drum
rattling skeleton-soundmaker: xylophone
seed-filled gourd: maraca
xylophonelike with resonant tubes: marimba
xylophonelike with steel bars: glockenspiel, bell lyre
STRINGED INSTRUMENTS
Appalachian lap instrument: dulcimer, zither
barrel organ: hurdy gurdy
bowed, quivering four-string: violin
country twanger: banjo
dulcimer struck with small hammers: hammered dulcimer
electric guitar, slang: *axe
guitar, hollow-bodied: acoustic
guitar, low-voiced four-string: bass
guitar, very small: ukelele
harplike: lyre
Hawaiian guitar with nasal tone: Hawaiian guitar
heavenly-sounding 46-string: harp
Japanese national instrument: koto
lute, East Indian long-necked: sitar
lute, small four string: mandolin
middle ages guitar: lute
rasper, husky: cello
violin, large, velvety or husky-sounding: viola
zither: dulcimer
WIND INSTRUMENTS
Alps horn: alpenhorn
alto clarinet with upcurving bell: basset horn
bass tuba: helicon, sousaphone
brass instrument with three keys, flaring bell: trumpet
clarinet nickname: *licorice stick
clarion blasters: brass
cornet with wider bore: flugelhorn
double-reeded woodwind: oboe
elephant tusk horn: oliphant
English flute: recorder

flute, small: fife, piccolo
flute, whistlelike: recorder, flageolet, fipple flute
jazz woodwind: saxaphone
*licorice stick, reeded: clarinet
military horn: bugle, cornet
pan pipes: pan flute
potatolike whistle: ocarina
sad, comedic soundmaker: bassoon
Scottish skirling and droning windbag: bagpipes
slide horn: trombone
trumpet with high pitch: Bach trumpet
tuba, tenor: euphonium
wooden: woodwind
music hall n. auditorium, concert hall, amphitheater, dance hall.
musician n. performer, player, artist, singer, vocalist, instrumentalist, minstrel, session artist, studio musician, longhair, bard, drummer, guitarist, bassist, flutist, violinist, troubador. SEE SINGER
musing a. meditative, thoughtful, reflective. ANT. *oblivious*.
musket n. breechloader, flintlock, blunderbuss. SEE GUN
muss v. mess up, tousle, tangle, disarrange, ruffle, rumple, crumple, wrinkle, dishevel, scramble, disorder, throw into disarray. ANT. *neaten, order, organize, smooth*.
must n. **1.** REQUIREMENT imperative, necessity, need, prerequisite, obligation, essential, exigency, fundamental. **2.** MUSTINESS mold, mildew, fungus, dry rot.
must v. have to, obligated to, required to, should, have no choice, compelled, forced, have no alternative, doomed to, bound. SEE NECESSARY
mustache n. moustache, moustachio, whiskers, *soupstrainer, *tickler, *cookie duster.
WORD FIND
descriptive: wings of a B-52, twitchy, rat's nest
dual crescents: mistletoe
long and drooping over chin: horseshoe, Fu Manchu
long and thick with turned-up ends: Hindenburg
M-shaped: regent
neat, thin line: pencil line, Clark Gable
rectangular with squared ends: boxcar, toothbrush, Charlie Chaplin, Hitler
T, forms with chin tuft: Roman T
thick and overgrown over lip: walrus, soupstrainer

turned-up: handlebar, Hindenburg, Kaiser, waxed, waxed and twiddled
V-shaped: chevron

mustang *n.* range horse, wild horse, bronco, bronc, cayuse.

muster *n.* assembly, gathering, congregation, turnout, review, line up, group, bunch, troupe, company.

muster *v.* assemble, gather, summon, call the roll, mobilize, convoke, marshal, convene, rally, collect, congregate, huddle, line up. ANT. *disperse, fallout, scatter, disband.*

muster, pass *v.* *make the grade, *come up to snuff, pass inspection, *measure up, *come through with flying colors, *stand the test, *come up to scratch.

musty *a.* **1.** MOULDY fusty, dusty, stale, decaying, crumbling, tainted, rancid, spoiled. **2.** WORN OUT, ANTIQUATED stale, old, aged, moss-grown, obsolete, old-fashioned, moth-eaten, passé. ANT. *1. fresh, unspoiled, vibrant. 2. new, modern, fresh.*

mutant *n.* deviation, mutation, alteration, miscreation, freak of nature.

mutation *n.* deviation, mutant, alteration, variation, modification, miscreation, metamorphosis, transformation, accident of nature.

mute *v.* muffle, deaden, dampen, silence, stifle, tone down, still, quiet. ANT. *amplify.*

mute *a.* speechless, silent, aphonic, wordless, mum, voiceless, tongue-tied, uncommunicative, closedmouthed, still. ANT. *talkative, loquacious, communicative.*

mutilate *v.* tear apart, dismember, disfigure, maim, deform, rip to shreds, amputate, cut up, hack, butcher, castrate, tear limb from limb.

mutilated *a.* dismembered, amputated, torn limb from limb, castrated, disfigured, maimed, deformed.

mutinous *a.* rebellious, subversive, riotous, insurrectionary, insurgent, revolutionary, seditious, traitorous, insubordinate, malcontent. ANT. *dutiful, subservient, compliant, cooperative.*

mutiny *n.* rebellion, revolt, riot, uprising, insurrection, overthrow, takeover, coup, strike.

mutiny *v.* rebel, revolt, rise up, riot, subvert, overthrow.

mutt *n.* **1.** MONGREL cur. **2.** FOOL dull witted person, muttonhead. SEE DOG

mutter *v.* murmur, mumble, grumble, whisper, grunt, maunder, *talk into one's beard/chin, talk under one's breath, grouse, complain.

mutual *a.* reciprocal, give-and-take, interchangeable, common, joint, related, shared, communal. ANT. *singular, sole.*

mutual fund *n.* stock fund, bond fund, growth fund, investment fund. SEE MONEY

muzzle *n.* **1.** SNOUT jaws, nose, mouth, chops. **2.** RESTRAINT bind, bit, bridle, strap.

muzzle *v.* restrain, restrict, stifle, silence, censor, shut up, mute, suppress, still, inhibit, squelch, harness.

myopic *a.* SEE NEARSIGHTED

myriad *n.* ten thousand, a thousand and one, infinity, host, profusion, multitude, abundance, *truckload, *slew, *passel, *lots, *galaxy.

mysterious *a.* unknowable, unexplainable, inexplicable, enigmatic, inscrutable, cryptic, unfathomable, secret, mystical, weird, arcane, esoteric, puzzling, dark. ANT. *knowable, obvious, clear, explainable.*

mystery *n.* **1.** AN UNKNOWN puzzle, enigma, perplexity, conundrum, secret, closed book, question mark. **2.** INSCRUTABILITY obscurity, imperceptibility, secret, inexplicability, insolvability. **3.** NOVEL/PLAY police procedural, detective story, *whodunit, *cat and mouse, *cloak and dagger, *cozy. ANT. *1. open book, answer, explanation, clarification.*

mystic *n.* seer, soothsayer, palm reader, prophet, astrologer, sorcerer, witch, astral projectionist, new age follower, *past-lifer.

mystic *a.* occult, esoteric, mystical, oracular, magical, arcane. ANT. *out in the open, scientific.*

mystical *a.* inscrutable, inexplicable, intuitive, spiritual, ethereal, metaphysical, transcendental, incorporeal, extramundane, otherworldly, supernatural. ANT. *corporeal, earthly, scientific.*

mysticism *n.* occultism, supernaturalism, cabalism.

mystify *v.* bewilder, perplex, puzzle, confuse, baffle, confound, hoodwink, *bamboozle, *buffalo. ANT. *clarify, explain, clear up.*

mystique *n.* aura, air, charisma, character, glamour, ambience, persona, charm, attraction, fascination, appeal, magnetism.

myth *n.* **1.** STORY legend, tale, fable, allegory, fiction, parable. **2.** UNTRUTH foolishness, fiction, nonsense, old wive's tale, misconception, fallacy, superstition, falsehood.

mythical *a.* mythological, fabled, fictitious, fabulous, imaginary, fanciful, fantastical, storybook. ANT. *actual, true, real, factual.*

WORD FIND

Argonauts leader who retrieved Golden Fleece: Jason
arts, nine goddesses of the: Muses
beautiful man: Adonis
bisexual: Hermaphroditus
dawn, goddess of: Aurora, Eos
dog with three heads guarding underworld: Cerberus
dreams, god of: Morpheus
earth, goddess of: Gaea
earth on his shoulders: Atlas
ecstasy, god of: Dionysus
eyed beast, hundred: Argus
fire, god of: Vulcan
fire, stole from gods: Prometheus
fish and man combined, controlled waves: Triton
flowers, goddess of: Flora
flying horse created from Medusa's blood: Pegasus
forbidden box of human misery, opened by: Pandora
forever reaching for fruit and water: Tantalus
giants, race of: Titans
giant with one eye: Cyclops
god ruler: Zeus
gold, touch turned things to: Midas
gorgon, most famous: Medusa
heel, hero with vulnerable: Achilles
horse and human combined: centaur
laurel tree, turned into: Daphne
loved his own reflection and was changed to a flower: Narcissus

love, goddess of: Venus
love, god of: Cupid, Eros
marriage, god of: Hymen
Medusa, slew: Perseus
messenger of gods: Mercury
minotaur, slew: Theseus
moon and forest goddess: Diana
moon, goddess of: Luna, Diana, Selene
mother, married his: Oedipus
oracle of Apollo: Delphic oracle
prophetess who was never believed: Cassandra
punishment, goddess of: Nemesis
Rome, founder of: Romulus
sea, god of: Poseidon
sisters of hideous form who turned onlookers to stone: Gorgons
sisters three who control human destiny: the Fates
sleep, god of: Hypnus, Somnus
stone, rolled incessantly up hill: Sisyphus
strongman: Hercules
sun, flew too near and melted wings: Icarus
sun, god of: Helios
twin protectors of seagoers: Castor and Pollux
unavenged crimes, three snake-haired females who punish guilty: Furies
underworld, god of: Hades, Pluto
victory, goddess of: Nike
war, god of: Mars
whirlpool, turned into: Charybdis
wisdom, goddess of: Minerva
Zeus, beautiful daughters of: Graces
SEE MONSTER

N

nab v. grab, snatch, seize, catch, grasp, snare, steal, snag, arrest, collar, apprehend, trap, *nail. ANT. release.

nadir n. low point, base, depth, floor, bottom.

nag n. 1. COMPLAINER *battle-ax, whiner, needler, kvetch, faultfinder, *pain, fishwife, witch. 2. OLD HORSE plug, swayback, *bag of bones, dobbin, *crowbait, *dogfood.

nag v. 1. COMPLAIN scold, needle, badger, whine, carp, harass, grouse, henpeck, heckle, berate, irritate, find fault. 2. TROUBLE distress, worry, prey on, torment, bother, disturb.

nail n. 1. FINGERNAIL claw, talon. 2. FASTENER spike, brad, pin, rivet, tack, staple, hobnail, tenpenny, box nail, finishing nail, roofing nail.

nail v. 1. DRIVE pound, anchor, fix, bolt. 2. CATCH catch red-handed, nab, apprehend, seize, *pinch.

naive a. unsophisticated, innocent, unsuspecting, uneducated, simple, ingenuous, childlike, inexperienced, unseasoned, unworldly, unschooled, trusting, gullible, immature, *wet behind the ears. ANT. sophisticated, experienced, wise, worldly.

NAIVETÉ n. [ni eev TAY] or [ni EEV uh TAY] childlike innocence or unsophistication, lack of insight and experience. The con man took advantage of her obvious naiveté. SYN. inexperience, childishness, innocence, simplicity, ingenuousness, artlessness, simplemindedness, credulity, gullibility. ANT. sophistication, worldliness, experience.

naked a. nude, unclothed, bare, undressed, exposed, stripped, disrobed, uncovered, *in the buff, *in the raw, *without a stitch, *in one's birthday suit, *wearing nothing but goosebumps, defenseless, vulnerable.

namby-pamby n. sissy, pansy, mama's boy, weakling, milquetoast, *wimp, *wuss.

name n. 1. APPELLATION nickname, given name, surname, Christian name, epithet, designation, title, sobriquet, *moniker, *handle, *pet name, diminutive, pseudonym, pen name, non de plume. 2. REPUTATION character, repute.

name v. 1. CHRISTEN dub, call, title, nickname, denominate, style, self-style. 2. DESIGNATE delegate, appoint, nominate, pick.

namedropper n. status seeker.

nameless a. anonymous, untitled, unknown. ANT. named, known.

namely adv. specifically, to wit, that is, i.e.

nanny n. nursemaid, nurse, wet nurse, mammy, babysitter, governess.

nap n. 1. SNOOZE doze, siesta, catnap. SEE SLEEP 2. FIBER fuzz, weave, fluff.

nap v. snooze, doze, catnap, *catch forty winks, *catch some shuteye, *drop off. SEE SLEEP

napalm n. incendiary, explosive, flammable gel, *Zippo.

nape n. scruff.

napkin n. linen, wipe, serviette, moist towelette.

nappy a. hairy, downy, shaggy, fuzzy, kinky, woolly, fleecy.

narcissist n. egotist, braggart, peacock.

NARCISSISTIC a. [nar sis SIS tic] vain, excessively interested in one's self. An egotistical, narcissistic man won't make a good husband. SYN. vain, self-centered, egotistical, egocentric, conceited, self-worshipping, self-infatuated, egomaniacal, self-absorbed, *wrapped up in oneself.

narcotic n. drug, opiate, soporific, sedative, tranquilizer, anesthetic, pain reliever, hypnotic, depressant, *downer, morphine, heroin, codeine, opium, hashish. SEE DRUG, MARIJUANA

narrate v. recount, tell, describe, recite, chronicle, report, portray, relate, detail.

narration n. recounting, telling, description, chronicling, portrayal, detailing, account, summary.

narrative n. account, description, tale. SEE STORY

narrator n. storyteller, chronicler, reporter, author, relater, recounter, raconteur, *voiceover.

narrow v. attenuate, hone, diminish, thin, lessen, contract, constrict, compress, squeeze.

narrow a. 1. SLIM slender, thin, lean, spare, slight, attenuated. 2. CONFINED cramped, tight, scant, sparse, meager, incapacious, close, incommodious, pinched. 3. NARROWMINDED prejudiced, bigoted, intolerant, small-minded. ANT. 1. fat, broad, wide. 2. capacious, roomy, spacious. 3. liberal, openminded, tolerant.

narrow-minded a. small-minded, closedminded, bigoted, prejudiced, blind, myopic, short-sighted, tunnel-visioned, one-sided, intolerant, pigheaded, biased, deaf to reason. ANT. *broad-minded, liberal, tolerant.*

nasty *a.* **1.** DIRTY filthy, foul, soiled, unclean, revolting, gross, offensive. **2.** INDECENT obscene, immoral, slutty, sleazy, lewd, licentious, offensive, vulgar, coarse, crude, raunchy, *morals of an alley cat. **3.** MEAN ill-tempered, disagreeable, ugly, surly, malicious, spiteful, hateful, vicious. ANT. *1. clean, unsoiled, washed. 2. decent, wholesome, pure, chaste. 3. good-humored, good-natured, kindhearted, friendly, amiable.*

nation *n.* **1.** COUNTRY state, federation, republic, commonwealth, union, empire, sovereignty. **2.** PEOPLE race, populace, natives, tribe, ethnic group. SEE POLITICS

national *a.* federal, nationwide, interstate, coast-to-coast. ANT. *local, regional.*

nationalism *n.* provincialism, isolationism, independence. "A silly cock crowing on its own dunghill."—Richard Aldington.

nationality *n.* nativity, citizenship, tribe, clan, race, extraction, native home, lineage, bloodline, ancestry.

native *a.* aboriginal, innate, indigenous, domestic, native-born, local, *homegrown. ANT. *foreign, distant.*

native land *n.* homeland, motherland, mother country, fatherland, the old country, birthplace.

natty *a.* dapper, neat, trim, smart, spruce, chic, sharp, *spiffy, *snazzy, *dressed to the teeth, *dressed to the nines. ANT. *sloppy, unfashionable.* SEE FASHION

natural *a.* **1.** MADE BY NATURE organic, wild, pure, untouched, untamed, unspoiled, uncultivated, unrefined, primitive, primordial. **2.** REAL genuine, authentic, true. **3.** INHERENT instinctive, innate, genetic, inherited, natural-born. **4.** UNAFFECTED unstudied, unpretentious, spontaneous, real, sincere, earthy, down to earth, ingenuous. "A very difficult pose to maintain."—Oscar Wilde. **5.** NORMAL typical, usual, characteristic. ANT. *1. unnatural, refined, processed, man-made, synthetic. 2. phony, unreal, unnatural. 3. learned, extrinsic. 4. affected, studied, pretentious, phony.*

naturalist *n.* zoologist, botanist, field observer, environmentalist.

naturally *adv.* **1.** BY NATURE innately, instinctively. **2.** OF COURSE as one would expect, characteristically, normally.

natural selection *n.* survival of the fittest, evolution, Darwinian law.

nature *n.* **1.** CHARACTER makeup, constitution, personality, essence, identity. **2.** DISPOSITION temperament, temper, spirit, personality. **3.** PHYSICAL WORLD cosmos, universe, creation, environment, ecology, evolution, chaos, regeneration, natural forces, the wild, the great outdoors, Mother Nature. "The never idle workshop."—Mathew Arnold. "The art of God eternal."—Dante. "The living, visible garment of God."—Johann W. Goethe "God under a disguise."—A.E. Taylor. **4.** KIND class, type, sort, species, stripe, category, brand.

naughty *a.* **1.** BAD mischievous, disobedient, prankish, impish, full of the devil, wayward, unruly, unmanageable, disrespectful. **2.** INDECENT nasty, lewd, obscene, improper, offensive, immoral. ANT. *1. good, well-mannered, angelic. 2. decent, moral.*

nausea *n.* queasiness, qualm, indigestion, sickness, upset stomach, bellyache, motion sickness. SEE VOMIT

nauseate *v.* sicken, disgust, *gross out, turn one's stomach, revolt, disgust, *make one want to vomit.

nauseating *a.* SEE NAUSEOUS

nauseous *a.* nauseating, unsettling, sickening, revolting, repulsive, loathsome, disgusting.

nautical *a.* maritime, marine, naval, oceangoing, seagoing. SEE NAVIGATION, NAVY, OCEAN, SAIL, SHIP

navel *n.* umbilical, *belly button, *innie, *outie.

navigable *a.* passable, boatable. SEE NAVIGATE

navigate *v.* steer, direct, plot, con, pilot, skipper, guide.

navigation *n.* course plotting, course charting, guiding, piloting, steering, conning, manning the helm, taking bearings, seamanship, celestial navigation, dead reckoning.

navigator *n.* course plotter, pilot, chartsman, helmsman, seaman, aviator, explorer. SEE SAILOR

navy *n.* fleet, armada, flotilla, sea force, argosy, convoy, marine defense, squadron, task force, merchant marine.

WORD FIND

aircraft carrier runway: flight deck
aircraft carrier, slang: *flattop, *floating city
antimine vessel: minesweeper
antitorpedo defense: torpedo defense net
battleship nickname: floating fortress

boundary marker for mineswept area: dan buoy
disguised as merchant ship: Q ship
fuel ship: oiler, tanker
group of ships: convoy, squadron
guns/weapons of the same size or caliber: battery
heavily armed vessel: battleship
high-speed warship: destroyer
hostile shore position: beachhead
medical ship: hospital ship
mine clearing: mine sweeping
mining ship: mine
missile-armed: guided missile cruiser, guided missile destroyer
multipurpose vessel: ocean station ship
nuclear-powered submarine: Trident
officer: chief warrant officer, ensign, lieutenant, lieutenant commander, commander, captain, rear admiral, vice admiral, admiral, fleet admiral
patrol torpedo boat: PT boat
readiness condition: general quarters
simultaneous gunfire on target: salvo
sonic locator device: sonar
submarine detector: sonobuoy
two or more ship divisions: squadron
underwater vessel: submarine, U-boat
vessel that lays dan buoys: dan runner
warship capable of acting independently: frigate
SEE SHIP, SUBMARINE

naysayer n. pessimist, oppositionist, dissenter, opponent, critic, prophet of doom, defeatist.

Nazi n. fascist, nationalist.

Neanderthal n. barbarian, savage, brute, *animal, troglodyte, caveman.

near v. approach, close in, advance, move toward.

near adv. close, nearby, close at hand, nigh, at close range, within shouting distance, proximate, neighboring, *cheek by jowl. ANT. distant, far.

nearing a. approaching, coming toward, closing in on, converging, impending. ANT. receding, leaving.

nearly adv. almost, not quite, just about, all but, virtually, well-nigh, roughly, about.

near miss n. near hit, close call, narrow escape.

nearsighted a. myopic, shortsighted, *blind as a mole, *blind as a post, *blind as a bat. SEE VISION

neat a. **1.** ORDERLY tidy, trim, shipshape, spotless, spruce, immaculate, spic-and-span. **2.** FASTIDIOUS meticulous, exacting, natty, spiffy. **3.** GREAT Sl. *cool, *neato, good, excellent. ANT. 1. disorderly, untidy, sloppy, messy. 2. sloppy, unkempt. 3. bad, awful. SEE CLEAN

neaten v. tidy, arrange, order, fix up, clean up, smooth out, spruce up.

neatly adv. orderly, tidily, in good order, uniformly, smoothly, cleanly.

NEBULOUS a. [NEB u luss] cloudy, vague or unclear. The paper was filled with nebulous guidelines. SYN. cloudy, misty, hazy, obscure, unclear, shrouded, veiled, vague, indistinct. ANT. clear, distinct.

necessarily adv. inevitably, of necessity, as a matter of course, perforce, like it or not, unavoidably, inescapably.

necessary a. essential, vital, needed, required, called for, requisite, prerequisite, mandatory, imperative, compulsory, fundamental, obligatory. ANT. unnecessary, unneeded, unessential.

necessity n. must, essential, vital component, requirement, obligation, requisite, prerequisite, need, want, basic, fundamental, dire necessity, exigency. ANT. extra, luxury, inessential.

necking n. Sl. kissing, *making love, *making out, cuddling, *smooching, *sucking face, *parking.

necklace n. chain, strand, choker, beads, pearls, locket, pendant, lavalier, torque, collar. SEE JEWELRY

necktie n. tie, ascot, cravat, bow tie, string tie, jabot, four-in-hand, Windsor, half-Windsor.

necromancy n. sorcery, communing with the dead, black magic, conjuring, mysticism, Satan worshipping, demonology.

necropolis n. graveyard. SEE CEMETERY

need n. **1.** POVERTY destitution, indigence, penury, privation. **2.** REQUIREMENT requisite, prerequisite, necessity, essential, obligation. **3.** LACK want, dearth, paucity, insufficiency, shortage.

need v. require, must have, want, call for, lack, have use for, hunger for, desire, covet, got to have, can't live without.

needle v. pester, annoy, goad, heckle, provoke, nag, badger, *rag on, *bug.

needless a. unnecessary, pointless, uncalled for, unwanted, nonessential.

needlework n. needlepoint, embroidery, sewing, stitching, darning, knitting, crocheting, tatting, quilting, point lace, gros point, petit point, cross-stitch, weaving.

needy *a.* **1.** POOR impoverished, destitute, indigent, penniless, lacking, *hard up, *broke, *down and out, *in dire straits. **2.** EMOTIONALLY INSECURE *clingy, clinging, desperate.

ne'er do well *n.* *loser, wastrel, failure, good-for-nothing, *do-nothing, *bum, *slug, loafer.

NEFARIOUS *a.* [ni FAIR ee us] evil, wicked. *They committed murders and other nefarious acts.* SYN. evil, wicked, villainous, heinous, iniquitous, detestable, vicious, infamous, sinister, bad, abominable, shameful. ANT. *good, moral, decent.*

negate *v.* invalidate, nullify, cancel out, counteract, neutralize, void, annul, repeal.

negation *n.* contradiction, denial, repudiation, refutation, cancellation.

negative *n.* no, nay, not.

negative *a.* denying, nullifying, voiding, invalidating, opposing, vetoing, contradictory, contrary, conflicting, inverse.

negative attitude *n.* pessimism, cynicism, *chip on one's shoulder, doubt, prophecy of doom, lack of confidence.

neglect *n.* laxness, disregard, thoughtlessness, inattentiveness, carelessness, slackness, oversight, negligence, dereliction, indifference. ANT. *care, regard, conscientiousness.*

neglect *v.* disregard, ignore, overlook, slight, shirk, omit, pass over, discount, make light of, be remiss, *lie down on the job, forget, let slip, let slide, brush aside, *blow off. ANT. *regard, consider, care for.*

neglectful *a.* careless, remiss, derelict, negligent, inattentive, slack, lax, inconsiderate, delinquent, sloppy. ANT. *careful, conscientious, mindful.*

negligee *n.* nightgown, nightie, chemise, robe, peignoir, deshabille.

negligence *n.* disregard, carelessness, dereliction, laxness. SEE NEGLECT

negligent *a.* careless, derelict, inattentive, delinquent, lax, slack, remiss, disregardful, thoughtless, inconsiderate, forgetful, casual, nonchalant, devil-may-care. ANT. *caring, responsible, fostering, conscientious, attentive.*

negligible *a.* minute, minimal, insignificant, inconsequential, trifling, nominal, piddling, paltry, imperceptible, unimportant, minor, trivial, microscopic. ANT. *sizable, significant, considerable.*

negotiate *v.* **1.** BARGAIN deal, dicker, haggle, arbitrate, mediate, settle, arrange, transact, conciliate, compromise, come to terms, finagle, work out, *give one's shirt but keep one's pants, *hash out a deal. **2.** PASS THROUGH OR OVER surmount, get around, cross, clear, forge through, ford, maneuver, step nimbly around.

negotiation *n.* mediation, arbitration, bargaining, give and take, dickering, compromise, haggling, counteroffering.

negotiator *n.* mediator, arbitrator, diplomat, haggler, middleman, go-between, intermediary, *wheeler-dealer.

Negro *n.* black, colored person, negroid, negress, African American, Afro-American.

neigh *n.* whinny, nicker, whicker.

neighborhood *n.* community, vicinage, suburb, block, district, borough, *housing complex, *development, street, *hood, *projects, *home turf, *neck of the woods.

neighborly *a.* friendly, sociable, hospitable, personable, harmonious, helpful, convivial. ANT. *inhospitable.* SEE FRIENDLY

neither here nor there irrelevant, beside the point, impertinent, not germane, immaterial.

nemesis *n.* **1.** JUST PUNISHMENT retribution, comeuppance, just deserts, vindication, revenge, vengeance, ruin, downfall, Waterloo. **2.** AVENGER bane, adversary, opponent, rival.

neologism *n.* new word, new term, new expression, *buzz word, new meaning, new interpretation.

neophyte *n.* beginner, novice, tyro, amateur, debutant, *rookie, *greenhorn, *tenderfoot, *new kid on the block, freshman, intern, trainee, apprentice. ANT. *veteran, *old hand, expert, master.*

NEPOTISM *n.* [NEP uh tizm] favoritism shown to relatives in work, politics. *Joe got work through his father's nepotism.* SYN. favoritism, partiality, bias, discrimination. "A $10 word meaning to stow your relatives in a soft berth."—Ilka Chase.

nerd *n. Sl.* *dork, *goofball, *geek, *jerk, *dweeb, *goober, *goon, *nebbish, *schlepper, *wimp, *trekkie.

nerve *n.* **1.** COURAGE bravery, strength, spirit, spunk, spine, mettle, pluck, *grit, *guts, *gumption, *balls, *chutzpah. **2.** IMPUDENCE effrontery, insolence, gall, brazenness, *balls. **3.** SENSORY PATHWAY sensor, impulse pathway, neuron. ANT. *1. cowardice, timidity, spinelessness. 2. shyness, reserve, reticence.*

nerve center *n.* control center, headquarters, HQ, command post, plexus.

nerveless *a*. **1.** WEAK impotent, powerless, helpless. **2.** MEEK spineless, cowardly, timid, reticent. **3.** COOL nonchalant, collected, unruffled, imperturbable, undisturbed, self-possessed, self-controlled. ANT. *1. potent, powerful. 2. bold, brash, cheeky. 3. ruffled, upset, a nervous wreck.*

nerve-racking *a*. distressing, stressful, disturbing, trying, grating on the nerves, aggravating, frazzling, jarring, irritating, disquieting. ANT. *soothing, calming, relaxing.*

nerves *n*. tension, stress. SEE ANXIETY

nervous *a*. anxious, tense, stressed, uneasy, *uptight, *antsy, *jittery, jumpy, excited, *keyed up, *wound up, *on edge, highstrung, flustered, ruffled, *wired, *hyper, *butterflies in the stomach, shaky. ANT. *calm, relaxed, composed, cool.* SEE ANXIOUS, FEARFUL

nervous breakdown *n*. nervous prostration, emotional collapse, *burnout, nervous exhaustion, clinical depression, hysteria.

nervous Nellie *n*. *Sl.* *Caspar Milquetoast, *chicken, *'fraidy cat, *pantywaist, *wuss, *wimp.

nervousness *n*. anxiety, tension, stress, excitement, fluster, jitters, *butterflies, apprehension, uneasiness, angst, stage fright, *the shakes. ANT. *relaxation, calm, serenity, tranquility.*

WORD FIND

descriptive/symptoms: throat-clearing, gulping, teeth-grinding, hand-wringing, pacing, nail-biting, stomach-knotting, hyperventilation, nervous tics and twitches, sweating.

nervy *a*. **1.** INSOLENT rude, bold, brash, forward, cocky, brassy, *cheeky, impudent, fresh, flip, flippant. **2.** BRAVE courageous, daring, plucky, valiant, *ballsy, *gutsy, intrepid. ANT. *1. reticent, shy, polite. 2. cowardly, spineless, *chicken.*

nest *n*. aerie, roost, *wattle and daub construction. SEE BIRD

nest egg *n*. savings, investment, *something for a rainy day, piggy bank, *the oink in one's piggy bank, *stash, *mad money, *stake.

nestle *v*. curl up against, snuggle, cuddle, huddle, nuzzle, *spoon together.

net *n*. **1.** MESH webbing, seine, screen, trawl, network, lacework, dragnet, purse net, butterfly net, snare. **2.** PROFIT earnings, gain, take-in, take-home, remainder. **3.** INTERNET *information superhighway, *infobahn.

net *a*. take-home, after taxes, ultimate, final, remaining.

nettle *v*. irritate, annoy, vex, needle, irk, aggravate, *get on one's nerves, *bug, *get under one's skin, hassle, *ride, rile, *drive up a wall, *rattle one's cage, *pull one's chain, pester, pick on.

nettlesome *a*. irritating, annoying, aggravating, vexatious, vexing, disturbing, perturbing, irksome, rankling, thorny. ANT. *pleasing, delightful, relieving.*

network *n*. **1.** INTERLACING netting, mesh, webbing, lacework, latticework, reticulum. **2.** ORGANIZATION affiliations, chain, system, order, interconnection, relationship. **3.** CHANNELS labyrinth, circuitry, plexus, terminal system.

network *v*. associate, make connections, hobnob, connect, fraternize, *rub elbows, *drum up leads, interconnect, affiliate, consort with, enterprise.

neurosis *n*. nervous disorder, personality disorder, emotional disorder, mental illness, disordered thinking, maladjustment, dysfunction, anxiety. "The result of a conflict between the ego and the id; the person is at war with himself."—Sigmund Freud.

WORD FIND

accidental nature: accident-prone

aversion to people: misanthropy

aversion to women: misogyny

collapse, nervous: nervous breakdown

combat neurosis: shell shock, Post Traumatic Stress Syndrome

daughter's sexual attraction to father: Electra Complex

death, excessive fear of: necrophobia

depression, seasonal: SAD, seasonal affective disorder

dieting to the point of emaciation: anorexia nervosa

dieting with binging and forced vomiting: bulimia

fantasizing to escape reality: escapism

fault-finding, passively hostile character: passive-aggressive personality

fear, irrational: phobia

fire-setting, fascination with: pyromania

genitals, compulsion to expose: exhibitionism

health and symptoms, dwelling excessively on: hypochondria

heart attack, excessive fear of: cardioneurosis

infant or childlike behavior, return to: infantilism

inferiority, feelings of: inferiority complex, low self-esteem

isolation from others: withdrawal

obsession or crazed desire: mania

panic, prone to: panic disorder, panic attack

passive acceptance of another's vices and abuse: codependency

past, dwelling excessively on the: alethia

poor-me personality: martyrdom

pregnancy, imagined: pseudocyesis

psychological disturbances converted to physical symptoms: conversion disorder

rapid breathing due to anxiety: hyperventilation

reality, denial of: denial, defense mechanism

repeated thoughts, rituals: obsessive-compulsive disorder

ritual that must be carried out: compulsion

self-love, excessive: narcissism

steal, compulsion to: kleptomania

SEE FEAR, INSANITY, MANIA, NEUROTIC, PHOBIA

neurotic *a.* emotionally disturbed, mentally ill, irrational, unstable, paranoid, anxious, obsessive, compulsive, phobic, maladjusted, hypochondriacal, manic, accident-prone, dysfunctional, *screw loose, *splinters in the windmills of one's mind, *loopy, *twisted, *warped, *off kilter. ANT. *stable, rational, of sound mind.*

neuter *n.* eunuch, gelding.

neuter *v.* castrate, emasculate, geld, *fix, *cut, spay.

neutral *a.* **1.** IMPARTIAL uninvolved, nonpartisan, unbiased, nonaligned, uncommitted, indifferent, *riding the fence, dispassionate, disinterested, unaffiliated, detached. **2.** NONCOMBATIVE uninvolved, peaceful, pacifistic. **3.** COLORLESS uncolored, drab, achromatic, pale, vague, white, black, gray. ANT. *1. partial, biased, involved. 2. combative, taking sides. 3. colorful.*

neutralize *v.* counteract, offset, negate, cancel, dilute, counterbalance, nullify, disarm, deactivate.

neverending *a.* perpetual, infinite, timeless, everlasting, forever, eternal, endless, relentless, persistent, continual. ANT. *finite, ending.*

nevertheless *adv.* nonetheless, notwithstanding, in any event, still, yet, be that as it may.

new *a.* **1.** CURRENT recent, fresh, up-to-date, up-to-the-minute, contemporary, novel, modern, latest, *cutting edge, *hot. **2.** PRISTINE fresh, virginal, green, maiden, newborn. **3.** UNFAMILIAR unheard of, unknown, strange, peculiar, untried, untested, unexplored, experimental. **4.** RENEWED restored, revised, remodeled, revived. **5.** ADDITIONAL further, more, supplementary. ANT. *1. out-of-date, old, dated. 2. old, used, stale. 3. familiar, known, tried-and-true.*

newborn *n.* infant, neonate, weanling, suckling, nursling, babe, baby, *bambino.

newfangled *a.* modern, new, novel, state of the art, *cutting edge. ANT. *obsolete, passé.*

news *n.* reportage, report, bulletin, information, message, account, announcement, communication, communique, dispatch, flash, press release, publication, broadcast, *scoop, lowdown, *skinny, *dope, *straight poop. "News is almost by definition bad news."—Marquis W. Childs. "When a dog bites a man that is not news, but when a man bites a dog that is news."—Charles A. Dana. "The first rough draft of history."—Philip Graham. SEE NEWSPAPER

newscast *n.* broadcast, telecast, dispatch, bulletin.

newscaster *n.* broadcaster, reporter, news anchor, announcer. SEE NEWSMAN

newsletter *n.* bulletin, report, journal, publication.

newsman/newswoman *n.* reporter, journalist, investigative reporter, anchor, stringer, correspondent, photojournalist, muckraker, *newshound.

newspaper *n.* journal, publication, chronicle, daily, weekly, tabloid, scandal sheet, *rag, special edition, press, Gazette, Tribune, Herald, Examiner, Express, Telegram, extra. "A circulating library with blood pressure."—Arthur Baer. "A device for amusing one half of the world with the other half's troubles."—Leonard Levinson.

WORD FIND

beat the competition to a story: scoop

cancel a story: kill, spike

checks for errors: copy editor

city news supervisor: city editor

correction of an inaccuracy: retraction

early edition: bulldog, bullpup

hawking of: bootjacking

large print headline: screamer, second coming type

large story: feature

light, human interest story: bright

London press: Fleet Street

material to be printed: copy

nonstaff reporter: freelancer

number of copies sold each day: circulation

personal opinion piece: editorial
prepare for printing: put to bed
reporter's name line: byline
reference room/files: morgue
short news item: squib
short stock item: filler
story in pictures: photojournalism
story's point of origin: dateline
story's point of view: slant
syndicated pieces, press releases, prewritten
material: canned copy
trite publicity piece: puff piece
trivial news period: silly season
wire services: Associated Press, Reuters

newsworthy a. notable, important, remarkable, momentous, significant, consequential, weighty. ANT. *insignificant, trivial.*

New York City n. the Big Apple, Manhattan, Gotham, metropolis, Brooklyn, the Bronx, Queens, Harlem, Staten Island. "A city where everyone mutinies but no one deserts."—Harry Hershfield. "A beautiful catastrophe."—Charles Jeanneret.

next adv. following, succeeding, successively, ensuing, later, upcoming, coming up, *on the horizon.

nibble v. chew, munch, snack, nosh, bite, pick at, peck at, gnaw.

nice a. 1. APPEALING pleasing, attractive, agreeable, pleasant, satisfactory, desirable, enjoyable. 2. LIKABLE charming, kind, considerate, gracious, amiable, sweet, well-mannered, genial, cordial, kind, thoughtful, good-hearted. 3. UPRIGHT virtuous, moral, chaste, genteel, seemly. 4. REFINED delicate, proper, correct, seemly, appropriate. ANT. *1. unpleasant, unattractive, undesirable. 2. unlikable, rude, mean, nasty. 3. immoral, unseemly. 4. unrefined, indelicate.*

niche n. notch, corner, cranny, nook, pigeonhole, cubbyhole, recess, hollow.

nick n. notch, slit, gouge, indentation, scratch, cut, score, slit, gash, scrape.

nickname n. pet name, moniker, *handle, diminutive, cognomen, appellation.

niggardly a. cheap, miserly, stingy, pennypinching, tightfisted, parsimonious, *nickel-squeezing, penurious, small, grudging. ANT. *generous, giving.*

night n. evening, after dusk, midnight, twilight, sundown, moonrise, bedtime, *wee hours, witching hour. "A stealthy evil raven."—Thomas Bailey Aldrich. "Vast sin-concealing chaos."—Shakespeare.

nightclub n. night spot, club, lounge, disco, discotheque, dance club, cabaret, supper club, comedy club, roadhouse, music hall, singles bar, honky-tonk, speakeasy, casino, *juke joint, *watering hole. "A place where the tables are reserved and the guests aren't."—Fred Casper.

nightmare n. 1. BAD DREAM incubus, succubus, phantasmagoria, hallucination, hypnogogic imagery, night terrors, night sweats, *night frights. 2. ORDEAL hell, horror, calamity, trial, tribulation, *horror show. SEE DREAM

nightmarish a. surreal, terrifying, ethereal, horrific, creepy, ghastly, otherworldly, unreal, weird, hallucinatory, Kafkaesque, hellish. ANT. *comforting, soothing.*

night stick n. *billy club, *billy, *hickory, *shill, cudgel.

nihilism n. 1. DENIAL AND REJECTION renunciation, disbelief, atheism. 2. ANARCHY lawlessness, subversion. 3. NOTHINGNESS nonexistence, void.

nil n. nothing, zero, null, *nada, *zip, *zilch, *diddly.

nimble a. 1. AGILE spry, sprightly, deft, quick, lithe, light-footed, surefooted, swift, facile. 2. QUICK-WITTED alert, quick, sharp, quick-thinking. ANT. *1. clumsy, plodding, slow. 2. dull, slow, *dense.*

nip n. drink, dram, sip, jiggerful, *taste, *swallow, shot, swig, *snort.

nip v. bite, nibble, pinch, cut, snip, squeeze.

NIRVANA n. [nur VAHN uh] a state of absolute bliss or sprititual enlightnment. *Achievement of nirvana was the mystic's goal.* SYN. enlightenment, awakening, bliss, oneness, perfection, tranquility, heaven, blessedness, paradise, ecstasy. SEE HEAVEN

nit-pick v. split hairs, quibble, pettifog, niggle, *make a federal case out of nothing.

nitty-gritty n. Sl. heart of the matter, crux, core, the facts, gist, kernel, root, *brass tacks, *bottom line.

nitwit n. dimwit, idiot, simpleton. SEE MORON

nobility n. 1. EMINENCE prominence, fame, rank, aristocracy, pedigree, peerage, upper class, noblesse, blue blood, elite, ruling class, First Family, king, queen, emperor, empress, prince, princess, marquis, earl, duke, lord, viscount, baron, baroness, knight, chevalier, squire, count, countess. 2. INTEGRITY gentility, honor, morality, virtue, chivalry, character, moral fiber. SEE ANCESTRY, ARISTOCRACY, ROYALTY

noble a. 1. EMINENT renowned, famous, illustrious, distinguished, preeminent, esteemed, acclaimed, celebrated. 2. OF HIGH MORAL

CHARACTER moral, virtuous, chivalrous, idealistic, magnanimous, lofty, heroic, honorable, principled, decent, forthright, gallant, exemplary, ethical, scrupulous, humane, benevolent, valorous. "All nobility in its beginnings was somebody's natural superiority."—Ralph Waldo Emerson. **3.** BELONGING TO NOBILITY aristocratic, highborn, princely, royal, blue-blooded, pedigreed, to the manor born, regal, titled, patrician. **4.** HAVING EXCELLENT QUALITIES superior, grand, stately, splendid, majestic, regal, august, superb. ANT. *1. unknown, obscure. 2. immoral, low, dishonorable, ignoble. 3. plebian, common, lower class, working class. 4. inferior, poor, shoddy.*

nobody n. nothing, zero, nonentity, flunky, *lightweight, *small fry, *bush-leaguer, *nebbish, *nobody to write home about, *bench-warmer, *second stringer, *just another brick in the wall. ANT. *somebody, *bigwig, bigshot.*

nocturnal a. night, nighttime, nightly, night-prowling, night-roaming, night-loving.

nod n. greeting, acknowledgement, gesture, signal, consenting nod. SEE GREETING

nod v. **1.** GREET OR ACKNOWLEDGE recognize, salute, incline the head, bow. **2.** CONSENT agree, concur. **3.** FALL ASLEEP doze off, drop off, nap.

noise n. clamor, din, uproar, racket, cacophony, ruckus, disturbance, blare, babel, ballyhoo, hullabaloo, outcry, tumult, crack, boom, bang, thud, crash, thump, blast, thunder, roar, bellow, rip, eruption, rumble, explosion, shot, detonation, reverberation, pop, clang, clank, clunk, twang, jingle, jangle, ring, tone, plop, kerplop, plunk, trill, peep, tinkle, whistle, ululation, warble, chirp, rattle, screech, scream, wail, shriek, squeal, shout, snap, crackle, crunch, sizzle, buzz, hiss, fizzle, honk, bleat, trumpeting, whir, clatter, scrape, grate, rasp, tick, grind, drone, hum, murmur, purr, sigh, ripple, swish, splash, whoosh, honk, echo, static, white noise, feedback, distortion. ANT. *silence, peacefulness, stillness, hush.* SEE LOUD, SOUND

noiseless a. silent, still, soundless, hushed, noiseless as the vacuum of space, noiseless as a tomb. ANT. *loud, boisterous.* SEE QUIET, SILENCE

noiseproof a. soundproof, insulated.

noisome a. **1.** HARMFUL injurious, hurtful. **2.** MALODOROUS foul-smelling, stinky, smelly,

fetid, reeking, rank, rancid, putrid. ANT. *1. beneficial, benign. 2. fragrant.*

noisy a. clamorous, cacophonous, blaring, strident, shrill, uproarious, riotous, turbulent, deafening, ear-shattering, nerve-racking. ANT. *peaceful, silent.* SEE LOUD

nomad n. Bedouin, wanderer, gypsy, itinerant, rover, roamer, rambler, vagabond, transient. SEE TRAVELER

nomadic a. wandering, roving, rambling, migratory, vagrant, drifting.

nom de plume n. pseudonym, pen name, assumed name, nom de guerre.

nomenclature n. terminology, classification, naming, vocabulary, taxonomy.

nominal a. **1.** IN NAME ONLY titular, so-called, professed, self-styled, purported, supposed. **2.** SLIGHT minor, small, trivial, minimal, inconsequential, trifling, insignificant. ANT. *1. actual, real, genuine. 2. considerable, large, exorbitant.*

nominate v. choose, select, appoint, propose, suggest for election, submit for approval, delegate, name, designate, denominate.

nomination n. selection, choice, proposal, naming, designation. SEE APPOINTMENT

nominee n. candidate, appointee, aspirant, office-seeker, runner, party favorite.

nonagression n. pacifism, nonviolence, passivity, irenicism, *dovishness.

NONCHALANT a. [non shuh LAUNT] having a cool or casual attitude, lacking concern. *Fred's nonchalant manner proved he wasn't nervous at all.* SYN. blasé, casual, cool, devil-may-care, lackadaisical, composed, detached, apathetic, insouciant, self-possessed, poised, carefree, disinterested, unconcerned. ANT. *earnest, anxious, concerned, wary.*

noncommittal a. undecided, guarded, cautious, *on the fence, equivocal, playing it safe, *playing it close to the vest, indecisive, wary. ANT. *committed, decisive, definite.*

noncompliant a. incompliant, disobedient, rebellious, insubordinate, unruly, rejecting, dissenting. ANT. *compliant, assenting, agreeable.*

nonconforming a. independent, *straying from the herd, individualistic, *marching to the beat of a different drummer, unorthodox, radical, disobedient, nonadhering, deviant. ANT. *conforming, *falling in step, obedient.*

nonconformist n. maverick, rebel, insubordinate, Bohemian, dissenter, heretic, individual, free spirit, eccentric, deviant, renegade, hippie, yippie, beatnik, *skinhead, *square peg in a round hole. ANT. *conformist*, *sheep, lamb, follower.*

nondescript *a.* **1.** INDESCRIBABLE undistinguished, unclassifiable, amorphous, undistinctive, hard to describe, plain, vague, *blending into the woodwork, *as distinctive as a plain, brown wrapper. **2.** DRAB unremarkable, colorless, common, dull, bland, *blah, prosaic. ANT. *1. distinctive, distinguished, eye-catching. 2. remarkable, colorful, eye-catching.*

nonessential *a.* unnecessary, extraneous, unimportant, unneeded, uncalled for, unrequired, superfluous, expendable, dispensable, extra. ANT. *essential, required, basic, indispensable.*

nonexistent *a.* inexistent, fictitious, null, void, made-up, make-believe, imaginary, mythical, groundless, extinct, dead, defunct, hypothetical, immaterial. ANT. *real, tangible.*

nonpartisan *a.* independent, unbiased, neutral, impartial, nonaligned, unaffiliated, objective, unprejudiced, *on the fence, openminded, individualistic. ANT. *partisan, aligned, left wing, right wing, conservative, liberal.*

nonplus *v.* perplex, bewilder, flummox, confound, baffle, *put at a loss, dumbfound, disorient, fluster, rattle, daze, disconcert, discompose, take aback.

nonprofit *a.* not for profit, funded, underwritten, supported, sponsored, public service, subsidized, charitable, philanthropic, benevolent. ANT. *profitable, lucrative.*

nonsense *n.* **1.** SILLINESS foolishness, absurdity, poppycock, folly, balderdash, rot, twaddle, drivel, blather, prattle, moonshine, *monkeyshines, *hooey, *baloney, *bunk, *applesauce, *crock, *crap, *malarkey, *hogwash. **2.** TRIVIALITY garbage, trash, junk, gimcrackery, trifle. ANT. *1. sense, logic, wisdom, sound thinking.*

nonsensical *a.* **1.** UNINTELLIGIBLE meaningless, incomprehensible, senseless. **2.** ABSURD silly, foolish, scatterbrained, ridiculous, preposterous. ANT. *1. comprehensible. 2. meaningful, intelligent.*

nonstop *a.* endless, relentless, ceaseless, neverending, perpetual, everlasting, around the clock, continuous, ongoing, interminable, incessant. ANT. *finite.*

nonviolence *n.* peace, peacefulness, pacifism, passiveness, nonaggression, dovishness, passive resistance.

nook *n.* niche, recess, cranny, corner, inglenook, retreat, alcove, cubbyhole.

noon *n.* midday, twelve o'clock, high noon, meridian. SEE TIME

noose *n.* loop, snare, hangman's loop.

WORD FIND
cowboy rope: lariat, lasso

norm *n.* standard, rule, accepted practice, criterion, the usual, benchmark, yardstick, average, mean.

normal *a.* **1.** STANDARD usual, typical, conventional, universal, traditional, regular, customary, accepted, average, *par for the course, orthodox, established. **2.** MENTALLY HEALTHY well-adjusted, sane, stable, *having all one's marbles, *all there, *together. "The only normal people are the ones you don't know very well."—Joe Ancis. ANT. *1. abnormal, unusual, atypical. 2. abnormal, sick, *twisted.*

normally *adv.* usually, typically, conventionally, traditionally, regularly, customarily, generally, as a rule, under normal circumstances.

Northern Lights *n.* aurora borealis, solar wind.

North Star *n.* Polaris, polestar, lodestar.

nose *n.* snout, olfactory organ, proboscis, *beak, *honk, *hooter, *snoot, *bazoo, *schnozzle, *schnozzola, *bugle. "The bone and gristle penthouse."—Stewart Robertson.

WORD FIND
blocked nasal passage disorder: deviated septum
descriptive: skewed, gumdrop, potatolike
flattened, somewhat turned-up: pug, snub
hooked like an eagle: aquiline
large: bulbous
red and grossly enlarged: rum nose, whiskey nose, toper's nose, rhinophyma
redness: rosacea
turned-up: retrousse

nose job *n.* rhinoplasty, plastic surgery, cosmetic surgery.

nosh *v.* snack, nibble, taste, pick at, munch. SEE EAT

NOSTALGIA *a.* [nuh STAL juh] a longing for the past or for one's home, homesickness. *We drove through our childhood neighborhood and ached with nostalgia.* SYN. longing, yearning, sentimentality, reminiscence, pining, remembering, mourning, aching, wistfulness. "A seductive liar."—George Ball. "Yesterdaze."—Leonard Bossard.

nostalgic *a.* reminiscent, homesick, wistful,

sentimental, longing, yearning, pining, romantic. ANT. *forward-looking.*

nostrum *n.* medicine, quack medicine, cure-all, panacea, *snake oil.

nosy *a.* snooping, prying, eavesdropping, curious, inquisitive, sniffing around, meddlesome, *goggle-eyed, *fence-peeping. ANT. *indifferent, unconcerned, oblivious, *minding one's own business.*

notable *a.* noteworthy, of note, special, important, remarkable, outstanding, of distinction, exceptional, momentous, of consequence. ANT. *inconsequential, unimportant, insignificant.*

notarize *v.* certify, attest, authenticate, endorse, witness, validate, register, sign and seal.

notary (public) *n.* registrar, certifier, signatory, witness, scrivener, recorder, clerk, public official.

notation *n.* **1.** NOTE memo, reminder, annotation, footnote, transcription, shorthand, entry, log note. **2.** MUSIC score, musical symbols.

not born yesterday *a. Sl.* wise, experienced, *been around the block, savvy, seasoned, battle-scarred, *been through the mill, worldly, been around, sophisticated.

notch *n.* nick, gouge, groove, cleft, slice, scratch, crenel. SEE CUT

notched *a.* crenelated, serrated, saw-toothed, grooved, serriform. ANT. *smooth, inlined.* SEE CUT

note *n.* **1.** MEMO reminder, letter, jotting, acknowledgement, RSVP, transcription, entry, footnote, *Post-it. **2.** MUSIC tone, sharp, flat, whole note, half note. SEE MUSIC

note *v.* take note, record, regard, pay heed to, observe, notice, give thought to, consider, pay attention to.

notebook *n.* writing tablet, binder, chronicle, diary, memo book, blotter, scratch pad, journal, log, daybook, ledger.

notes *n.* shorthand, transcription, scribblings, outline, rough draft, briefs, thumbnail sketch, jottings.

noteworthy *a.* notable, of note, important, significant, of distinction, remarkable, outstanding, prominent, newsworthy. ANT. *unimportant, insignificant.*

not for profit *a.* nonprofit, charitable, philanthropic, publicly funded. ANT. *lucrative, money-making.*

nothing *n.* **1.** ZERO naught, none, nil, *nix, *zip, *zilch, *nada, *diddly, *squat, *goose egg,

*scratch. "A good thing to say, and always a clever thing to say."—Will Durant. **2.** NONEXISTENCE void, vacuum, oblivion, nothingness, inexistence, emptiness, nonentity, nullity. ANT. *1. infinity, *scads, a lot. 2. existence, being.*

nothingness *n.* nonexistence, nihility, emptiness, void, vacuum, vacancy. SEE NOTHING

nothing to it *a. Sl.* effortless, easy, piece of cake, *easy as pie, *easy as ABC, *no-brainer, *cinchy, *a snap, *a breeze, *duck soup.

notice *n.* announcement, notification, bulletin, communique, warning, caution, pronouncement, mention, information, *tip, advisory.

notice *v.* observe, heed, take note of, regard, pay attention to, recognize, perceive, look at, behold, discern.

noticeable *a.* perceivable, conspicuous, observable, discernible, distinct, in plain view, palpable, obvious, *standing out like a sore thumb, *plain as the nose on one's face. ANT. *imperceivable, inconspicuous, out of sight, camouflaged, hidden.*

notification *n.* announcement, communiqué, warning, message, notice, statement, advisory.

notify *v.* inform, give notice, advise, warn, caution, let one know, apprise, serve notice, *tip off. SEE COMMUNICATE, TELL

notion *n.* **1.** THOUGHT idea, concept, conception, opinion, view, belief, feeling. **2.** DESIRE inclination, whim, intention, fancy, caprice.

notional *a.* **1.** IMAGINARY abstract, conceptual, visionary, dreamed, fanciful. **2.** WHIMSICAL fanciful, capricious, frivolous. ANT. *1. real, proven, tangible, sensory. 2. practical, down to earth.*

notoriety *n.* infamy, ill repute, renown, stardom, eminence, prominence.

NOTORIOUS *a.* [no TOR ee us] infamous, known for something bad. *The notorious criminal was released, much to the dismay of the community.* SYN. infamous, disreputable, of ill repute, scandalous, ignominious, opprobrious, discredited, stigmatized, gossiped about, prominent, famous, celebrated, touted, eminent. ANT. *reputable, respectable, uncorrupt.* SEE FAMOUS

nourish *v.* feed, nurture, fortify, sustain, foster, promote, suckle, support.

nourishing *a.* nutritious, fulfilling, filling, fortifying, sustaining, alimentary. ANT. *inedible, unhealthy.*

nourishment *n.* nutriment, food, sustenance,

subsistence, vitamins and minerals, aliment, viands, daily bread, feed.

nouveau riche *n.* new rich, parvenu, upstart, *yuppie, status seeker, arriviste.

novel *n.* narrative, story, fiction, saga, tale, yarn, chronicle, dime novel, best-seller, paperback, novelette, novella. "A short story padded."—Ambrose Bierce.

WORD FIND

characters are real persons under fictitious names: roman à clef

cheap novel of yesteryear: dime novel, penny dreadful

highbrow: literary novel

historical romance: gothic, bodice ripper, Regency romance

imaginative: sword and scorcery, fantasy, sci-fi, space opera

lengthy chronicle of a family or society: roman-fleuve

mystery: whodunit, police procedural

rags to riches: Horatio Alger story

real events, based on: docudrama

ridiculing life: satire

young person's maturation: Bildungsroman, come-of-age story

SEE BOOK

novel *A.* new, first of its kind, unusual, newfangled, fresh, original, unfamiliar, innovative, offbeat, unique, unprecedented, unheard of. ANT. *old hat, old-fashioned, trite.*

novelist *n.* storyteller, fiction writer, creative writer, freelance writer, wordsmith, teller of tales, *hack. SEE AUTHOR, WRITER

novelty *n.* **1.** SOMETHING NEW innovation, departure, original. **2.** FAD craze, *all the rage, *the "in" thing, *the latest thing. **3.** GADGET *doodad, *whim-wham, trifle, knickknack, trinket, *gimcrack.

November *n.* autumn, fall, month, hunting season. "The gloomy month . . . when the people of England hang and drown themselves."—Joseph Addison.

novena *n.* prayers, devotions, recitations.

novice *n.* beginner, neophyte, tyro, apprentice, trainee, rookie, *greenhorn, *tenderfoot, *virgin. ANT. *veteran, expert, *old hand.* SEE AMATEUR

novitiate *n.* **1.** TRIAL PERIOD training period, probation, initiation, apprenticeship, indoctrination. **2.** NOVICE beginner, amateur, neophyte.

now *adv.* **1.** THE PRESENT at this moment, today, this instant. **2.** IMMEDIATELY at once, this minute, this instant, straightaway, without delay, *chop chop.

now and then *adv.* once in awhile, occasionally, now and again, from time to time, *once every blue moon, intermittently, sometimes.

nowhere *a.* no place, *nowheresville, *boonies, *sticks, *East Jesus, *podunk, *North Overshoe, outback, *noplaceville.

NOXIOUS *a.* [NOK shus] harmful, injurious. *The car emitted noxious exhaust fumes.* SYN. harmful, toxic, poisonous, injurious, hurtful, obnoxious, pernicious, deleterious, unhealthful. ANT. *innocuous, benign, harmless.*

nozzle *n.* spout, valve, conduit, snout, sprinkler head.

NUANCE *n.* [NOO ahns] a subtle difference, variation or gradation. *The color nuances in the painting became more apparent the closer we looked.* SYN. subtlety, gradation, shade, shading, variation, distinction, refinement.

nub *n.* knob, protuberance, lump, bump, bulge.

nubby *a.* lumpy, knotted, studded, knobbed, textured. ANT. *smooth, slick.*

nubile *a.* **1.** MARRIAGEABLE of age, ripe. **2.** SEXUALLY ATTRACTIVE sexy, sexual, captivating, tempting, seductive, foxy, shapely, curvy. ANT. *1. underage, prepubescent, *jailbait. 2. unattractive.*

nuclear *a.* atomic, subatomic, thermonuclear.

nuclear bomb *n.* atomic bomb, A-bomb, hydrogen bomb, H-bomb, thermonuclear bomb, fission bomb, nuclear warhead, neutron bomb, megaton weapon, kiloton weapon, *nuke, *the big one, *physics package, *peacekeeper.

WORD FIND

absorption of radioactive material after blast: contamination

billowing cloud after blast: mushroom cloud

blast effect that causes damaging electrical surges: electromagnetic pulse

bomb portion of missile: warhead

bomb with blast yield equivalent of millions of tons of TNT: megaton weapon

bomb with blast yield equivalent of thousands of tons of TNT: kiloton weapon

fiery side effect of blast: firestorm

illness from fallout: radiation sickness

kills people, leaves buildings intact: neutron bomb

location of detonation at, below or above ground: ground zero

minimum fissionable material necessary for chain reaction: critical mass

penetrate deep underground, able to: earth penetrator

precipitation of radioactive material: fallout, rainout
splitting of atom: fission
spreads radiation only, low-cost, low-tech bomb that: dirty bomb
unit of radiation: rem
weapon with augmented radiation properties: salted weapon
SEE EXPLOSION, MISSILE, NUCLEAR FISSION, NUCLEAR FUSION

nuclear energy *n.* atomic power, fission power.

nuclear fission *n.* atom-splitting, atom smashing, atomic reaction.

nuclear fusion *n.* atomic fusion.

nuclear physics *n.* particle physics, quantum physics, atomic science, quantum mechanics.

nuclear reactor *n.* atomic reactor, core reactor, breeder reactor.

nuclear weapons *n.* weapons of mass destruction, atomic weapons. SEE NUCLEAR BOMB

nucleus *n.* core, kernel, center, heart, pith, nut, deuteron, proton.

nude *A.* naked, unclothed, bare, stripped, *au naturel, disrobed, *in the buff, *in the raw, *without a stitch, *in one's birthday suit, *wearing nothing but goosebumps.

nudge *v.* push, poke, prod, shove, jerk, elbow, tap. SEE TOUCH

nudist *n.* naturist, Adamite, gymnosophist, *free spirit.

nudity *n.* nakedness, *the buff, *the altogether, *undress.

nugget *n.* lump, chunk, hunk, piece, bit, clump. SEE GOLD, ROCK

nuisance *n.* 1. ANNOYANCE irritation, plague, vexation, trouble, inconvenience, bother, pain, thorn in one's side. 2. PEST *pain in the neck, *nudnik, bane, bore. ANT. *1. pleasure, joy.*

nuke *n.* *Sl.* nuclear bomb, nuclear reactor, nuclear power plant. SEE NUCLEAR BOMB

nuke *v.* *Sl.* 1. BOMB destroy, wipe out, obliterate, *blow back to the stone age, incinerate, *fry, *grease, *wax, *smoke. 2. *Sl.* MICROWAVE cook, heat, warm.

null *A.* invalid, not binding, inconsequential, ineffectual, worthless, valueless, insignificant. ANT. *valid, effectual, valuable.* SEE VOID

nullify *v.* cancel, annul, negate, invalidate, repeal, revoke, veto, kill, neutralize, counteract.

numb *A.* 1. BENUMBED unfeeling, deadened, dead, insensate, anesthetized, insensitive, paralyzed, stunned, narcotized, stupefied. 2.

INSENSITIVE apathetic, unfeeling, indifferent, uncaring. ANT. *1. feeling, sensitive, responsive. 2. empathetic, feeling, receptive.*

number *n.* 1. DIGIT numeral, integer, cipher, round number, whole number, fraction. 2. AMOUNT sum, total, count, aggregate, tally, quantity, score.

number *v.* count, tally, enumerate, add up, paginate, reckon, tick off, compute, figure up, calculate, account, audit. SEE ADD

number cruncher *n.* *Sl.* statistician, *bean counter, accountant, tabulator, calculator, computer, adding machine, *stat basher.

numberless *A.* innumerable, countless, infinite, incalculable, myriad, endless, many, *umpteen, measureless, copious. ANT. *numbered, finite, limited.*

numerous *A.* many, myriad, copious, plentiful, innumerable, a lot, profuse, numberless, plenty, *scads, several, manifold, *umpteen, considerable, rife. ANT. *few, little, sparse.*

numskull *n.* dolt, idiot, *blockhead. SEE MORON

nun *n.* sister, prioress, ecclesiast, abbess, virgin, contemplative, mother superior, reverend mother.

nunnery *n.* convent, abbey, cloister, sisterhood, priory.

nuptial *A.* matrimonial, marital, bridal, conjugal, connubial.

nuptials *n.* marriage ceremony, marriage, wedding, matrimony, espousal.

nurse *n.* medical technician, medical assistant, caregiver, attendant, registered nurse (R.N.), licensed practical nurse (L.P.N.), certified nurse's aid (C.N.A.), nurse practitioner, charge nurse, scrub nurse, orderly, therapist, *candystriper.

nurse *v.* 1. CARE FOR tend, attend, treat, aid, minister to, medicate, cater to, provide therapy, medicate, *provide TLC. 2. BREASTFEED suckle, wet-nurse.

nursemaid *n.* nanny, wet nurse, babysitter, governess.

nursery *n.* 1. CHILD CARE CENTER day care center, nursery school, preschool. 2. MATERNITY WARD 3. GREENHOUSE hothouse, cold frame, hot bed.

nursing home *n.* convalescent home, *old folks home, rest home, retirement facility.

nurture *n.* raising, fostering, guidance, care, rearing, training, education.

nurture *v.* nourish, care for, sustain, cultivate, foster, raise, bring up, rear, mother, educate. SEE FEED

nut *n.* 1. SEED kernel, fruit, peanut, *goober,

acorn, chestnut, hazelnut, walnut, pinon, Brazil nut, almond, beechnut, pecan, filbert, cashew, pistachio, butternut, coconut, hickory nut. **2.** FANATIC buff, *freak, enthusiast, fan, aficionado, devotee, zealot. **3.** ECCENTRIC *kook, *flake, *butterfly case, *weirdo, *foul ball, *loon, *nutter, *crackpot, mental case, *screwball, *ding-a-ling. SEE ECCENTRIC

nut house n. *Sl.* insane asylum, *booby hatch, *loony bin, *bughouse, *funny farm, *laughing academy, *nut college, *nut hatch, *rubber room.

nutrient n. vitamin, mineral, nutriment, food, protein, carbohydrate.

nutrition n. nourishment, sustenance, balanced diet, alimentation.

nutritionist n. dietician, diet consultant.

nutritious a. nourishing, sustaining, nutritive, body-building, alimentary, fortifying,

healthy, wholesome, *good for you. ANT. *unwholesome, unhealthy.*

nuts a. *Sl.* crazy, insane, *wacko, *bonkers, *crackers, demented, deranged, *gone 'round the bend, cracked, *loony, *bananas, *cuckoo, *food for squirrels, *gaga, *googoo, *haywire, *loco, *mental, *not tightly wrapped, *off one's nut, *off one's trolley, *out of one's gourd, *potty, *psycho, *schizo, *spacey, non compos mentis, *off in the twilight zone. ANT. *sane, rational, normal.*

nuzzle v. snuggle, cuddle, nestle, lie close, hug, embrace.

nylons n. stockings, hosiery, hose.

nymph n. spirit, sprite, goddess, maiden, dryad, oread, naiad, mermaid. SEE FAIRY

nymphomania n. lustfulness, goatishness, erotomania, carnal desire, prurience, concupiscence, libidinousness, satyriasis.

O

oaf *n.* lummox, dolt, dunce, lout, simpleton, rustic, ignoramus, clod, clodhopper, ninny, *klutz, *boob. ANT. *intellectual, sophisticate, genius.*

oafish *a.* clumsy, awkward, *klutzy, stupid, ignorant, simple, rustic. ANT. *sophisticated, intelligent, *smooth.*

oak *n.* acorn tree, shade tree, hardwood. SEE FOREST, TREE

oar *n.* paddle, scull, pole, blade, rudder pole.

oasis *n.* **1.** SPRING watering hole, wadi, fertile area, desert arbor, *island Eden. **2.** REFUGE sanctuary, retreat, haven, sanctum, asylum.

oath *n.* **1.** PLEDGE promise, vow, declaration, swearing, word of honor, guarantee, affirmation. **2.** SWEAR WORD curse, profanity, expletive.

obdurate *a.* hardened, hard, hard-hearted, callous, heartless, unsympathetic, unmovable, stubborn, obstinate, unyielding, intractable, inflexible, dogged. ANT. *feeling, tractable, flexible.*

obedience *n.* compliance, acquiescence, submission, deference, subservience.

obedient *a.* obeying, submissive, compliant, acquiescent, tractable, obsequious, amenable, dutiful, nonresistant, servile, subservient, scraping, prostrate, docile, *at one's beck and call, *wrapped around one's little finger, *under one's thumb, *whipped, conforming. ANT. *disobedient, insubordinate, rebellious.*

obeisance *n.* **1.** GESTURE OF RESPECT bow, curtsy, genuflection, salaam, kneeling, salute. **2.** DEFERENCE homage, worship, respect, reverence, subservience, servility, obsequiousness, fawning, sychophancy. ANT. *1. *thumbing one's nose. 2. disrespect, irreverence, insolence.*

obeisant *a.* deferential, respecting, reverent, servile, worshipping, obsequious. ANT. *disrespectful, irreverent, insolent.*

obelisk *n.* monolith, shaft, column, monument, pillar, pylon, needle, tower.

obese *a.* fat, overweight, corpulent, plump, rotund, stout, chubby, roly-poly, blubbery, paunchy, pleasingly plump, full-figured, elephantine, *sleek as a walrus. ANT. *slim, lithe, skinny.* SEE FAT

obesity *n.* corpulence, plumpness, rotundness, stoutness, paunchiness, portliness, chubbiness, overweight, fatness. SEE FAT

obey *v.* comply, follow orders, acquiesce, submit, yield, mind, heed, abide, relent, concur, serve, do one's bidding, carry out one's wishes, toe the line, *bend over backwards, knuckle under. ANT. *disobey, defy, rebel.*

OBFUSCATE *v.* [ob FUS kate] to darken, obscure or make unclear, confuse. *His irrelevant arguments served only to obfuscate the issue.* SYN. obscure, confuse, muddle, darken, cloud, conceal, confound, bewilder, cover up, hide, camouflage. ANT. *clear up, clarify, elucidate.*

obituary *n.* obit, death notice, necrology. SEE DEATH, EULOGY

object *n.* **1.** THING item, subject, article, entity. **2.** PURPOSE aim, intent, goal, objective, target, end.

object *v.* disapprove, protest, oppose, demur, inveigh, except, remonstrate. ANT. *approve, assent, agree, support.*

objection *n.* disapproval, protest, remonstrance, disagreement, exception, complaint, criticism, admonition, dispute, opposition, grievance, dissatisfaction, gripe, *kick. ANT. *acceptance, agreement, approval.*

objectionable *a.* offensive, revolting, disagreeable, unbefitting, undesirable, unpleasant, inappropriate, uncalled for, unsatisfactory, out of line, unacceptable. ANT. *acceptable, agreeable.*

objective *n.* purpose, goal, intent, end, aim, target, object, quarry, point.

objective *a.* unbiased, fair, unprejudiced, unemotional, disinterested, detached, indifferent, impersonal. ANT. *biased, partial.* SEE FAIR

objectivity *n.* disinterest, neutrality, detachment, indifference, distance, fairness, evenhandedness, dispassion.

objector *n.* resister, protester, dissenter, naysayer, detratctor, challenger, rebel, critic, opponent, dissident.

objet d' art *n.* object of art, figurine, vase, curio. SEE KNICKKNACK

objurgate *v.* scold, rebuke, berate, chastise, chide, upbraid, reproach.

obligate *v.* bind, pledge, compel, force, constrain, commit, require, necessitate, behold, indebt, contract. ANT. *free, release.*

obligated *a.* bound, beholden, indebted, required, constrained, committed, obliged, pledged, contracted. ANT. *released, freed, unbound.*

obligation n. duty, promise, pledge, contract, responsibility, requirement, charge, commitment, bond, liability, burden.

obligatory a. required, necessary, binding, requisite, mandatory, imperative, essential, compulsory, peremptory. ANT. unrequired, optional, unnecessary.

oblige v. 1. ACCOMMODATE serve, help out, favor, aid, lend a hand, cater to, gratify. 2. NECESSITATE compel, force, bind.

obliged a. 1. REQUIRED compelled, bound, forced. 2. INDEBTED.

oblique a. 1. SLANTING sloping, inclined, tilting, leaning, angled, deviating, askew, canted, crooked, diagonal, listing. 2. INDIRECT evasive, devious, sly, underhanded, disingenuous, surreptitious, deceptive. ANT. 1. straight, level, horizontal. 2. straightforward, honest, open.

obliterate v. 1. ERASE expunge, wipe out, rub out, deface, scratch out, delete, blot out, remove. 2. DESTROY annihilate, eliminate, eradicate, exterminate, do away with, incinerate, wipe out, decimate. ANT. 1. put in, enter, put in bold print, insert. 2. build up, fortify, create.

OBLIVION n. [uh BLIV ee un] the state of being totally lost and forgotten. Most people fear that their names will be lost to oblivion after death. SYN. the forgotten, nothingness, void, *never-never land, nihility, nonexistence, space, obscurity, inexistence, extinction, unconsciousness. "The swallowing gulf."— Shakespeare. ANT. prominence, fame, notoriety. SEE EMPTINESS

oblivious a. unconscious, unaware, forgetful, absentminded, abstracted, absorbed, mindless, amnesic, preoccupied, thoughtless, *out to lunch, *off in space, *out of it. ANT. conscious, aware, focused.

oblong a. elliptical, oval, egg-shaped, elongated, rectangular.

obloquy n. censure, vituperation, verbal abuse, defamation, insult, discredit, dressing-down, belittlement. ANT. compliment, praise, adulation.

obnoxious a. offensive, objectionable, loathsome, odious, unpleasant, disagreeable, disgusting, revolting, hateful, insulting, repugnant, deplorable. ANT. pleasant, agreeable, pleasing.

obscene a. 1. OFFENSIVE repulsive, foul, gross, indecent, unsavory, lewd, shameless, vulgar, revolting, distasteful, indelicate, lurid. 2. INCITING LUST libidinous, pornographic, salacious, lewd, lascivious, nasty, smutty, *raunchy, prurient, licentious, naughty. ANT. 1. respectable, inoffensive, decent. 2. pure, chaste, prudish, puritanical.

obscenity n. 1. INDECENCY vulgarity, smut, lewdness, indelicacy, vileness, *raunch, filth, ribaldry. 2. SWEAR WORD four-letter word, oath, cuss word, curse, expletive. ANT. 1. delicacy, decency, propriety. 2. euphemism, polite word.

obscure v. 1. MAKE INDISTINCT conceal, obstruct, hide, camouflage, muddy, obfuscate, cloud, confuse. 2. DARKEN dim, cloud, shadow. ANT. 1. make distinct, define, make clear, spotlight, expose. 2. lighten, brighten.

obscure a. 1. INDISTINCT vague, faint, ambiguous, inconspicuous, unclear, indiscernible, imperceptible, hazy, nebulous, undistinguished, hard to make out. 2. DARK gloomy, dusky, murky, dim, hazy, shadowy. 3. LITTLE KNOWN unknown, unseen, elusive, inconspicuous, unheard of, remote, unsung, insignificant. ANT. 1. distinct, clear, defined. 2. bright, sunny, light. 3. famous, well-known, notorious.

OBSEQUIOUS a. [ub SEE kwee us] servile, fawning or overly compliant. The bully and his obsequious underlings started a brawl. SYN. servile, fawning, abject, abasing, submissive, sycophantic, deferential, compliant, *brownnosing, *apple-polishing, *kissing up, *bootlicking, *ring-kissing, toadying, *falling all over oneself to please, ingratiating. ANT. domineering, lordly, disrespectful.

obsequy n. funeral rite, ceremony, service. SEE EULOGY, FUNERAL

observable a. perceptible, perceivable, palpable, noticeable, obvious, evident, in plain view, distinct. ANT. hidden, obscure, camouflaged.

observance n. 1. CUSTOM rite, ritual, ceremony, celebration, commemoration, remembrance, memorial. 2. OBSERVATION watching, notice, attention, scrutiny, lookout, inspection, examination. 3. ABIDING BY adherence, compliance, heeding, obeying, regarding. ANT. 3. disregard, breach, noncompliance.

observant a. watchful, attentive, noticing, perceptive, keen-eyed, aware, sharp-eyed, alert, mindful. ANT. overlooking, daydreaming, ignoring.

observation n. 1. OBSERVING noticing, seeing,

perception, observance, examination, attention, viewing. **2.** REMARK comment, assertion, sentiment, opinion, observance, account, declaration, thought, judgment. **3.** NOTING recording, sizing up, measuring, scrutiny, assessment.

observatory *n.* observation post, lookout, watchtower. SEE ASTRONOMY

observe *v.* **1.** WATCH see, look at, notice, view, eye, examine, study, behold, *get a load of, *take a gander at. **2.** ABIDE BY adhere, respect, recognize, follow, obey, heed, honor, maintain, regard, acknowledge, comply. ANT. *1. ignore, neglect, overlook. 2. disregard, disrespect, ignore.*

observer *n.* lookout, watcher, eyewitness, spectator, onlooker, bystander, examiner.

obsess *v.* preoccupy, haunt, beset, possess, hound, harass, torment, plague, occupy, dominate, *prey on one's mind. ANT. *ignore, forget, exorcise.*

obsessed *a.* preoccupied, haunted, beset, possessed, fixated, dominated, *hung up, troubled, immersed in, *gaga over, gripped, crazed.

obsession *n.* preoccupation, fixation, compulsion, fascination, mania, delusion, fetish, infatuation, possession, passion. SEE INSANITY, MANIA, NEUROSIS, PHOBIA

obsolete *a.* **1.** DISCARDED useless, abandoned, cast off, defunct, extinct, retired, forgotten. **2.** OLD-FASHIONED outmoded, antiquated, dated, passé, out of date, primitive, *old hat, ancient, worn out, Victorian. ANT. *fresh, new, modern, *cutting edge.*

obstacle *n.* impediment, hindrance, block, obstruction, barrier, snag, check, deterrent, impasse, bar, hurdle, restriction, stumbling block.

obstetrics *n.* tocology, midwifery, childbirth, labor and delivery. SEE BIRTH, PREGNANCY

obstinate *a.* stubborn, firm, inflexible, adamant, unyielding, resistant, tenacious, headstrong, unwavering, bullheaded, mulish, pigheaded, hardnosed, dogged, unbending, stiff-necked, cussed, *stubborn as a bobtail mule, *stubborn as crabgrass. ANT. *flexible, tractable, yielding.*

obstreperous *a.* noisy, boisterous, vociferous, unruly, rowdy, unmanageable, uproarious, riotous, clamorous. ANT. *peaceful, quiet.*

obstruct *v.* **1.** BLOCK impede, stop up, clog, check, retard, hinder, bar, preclude. **2.** HIDE block, camouflage, screen, curtain, cover up, obscure. ANT. *1. open up, release, unstop,*

broach, clear. **2.** *reveal, expose, spotlight, unveil.*

obstruction *n.* impediment, obstacle, bar, barricade, block, check, stumbling block, hindrance, restriction, bottleneck, stop. ANT. *opening, gap, hole, passage.*

obtain *v.* get, acquire, procure, gain possession, seize, attain, net, capture, *get one's hands on, pick up, harvest. ANT. *lose, forfeit, give up.*

obtainable *a.* available, acquirable, attainable, winnable. ANT. *unobtainable, *out of reach.*

obtrude *v.* **1.** INTRUDE impose, *barge in, meddle, interrupt, *butt in, *stick one's nose in, *pry, *horn in. **2.** EXTRUDE stick out, protrude, push out, eject, thrust forward.

obtrusive *a.* **1.** PROJECTING protruding, prominent, protuberant, jutting out, sticking out. **2.** INTRUSIVE forward, brash, pushing, meddlesome, interfering, bold, invasive, interruptive. **3.** CONSPICUOUS glaring, overt, blatant, flagrant, striking, obvious, bald-faced, outrageous. ANT. *1. flattened, smoothed, planed. 2. retiring, reticent, shy, unobtrusive. 3. inconspicuous, subtle, hidden.*

obtuse *a.* **1.** BLUNT dull, rounded. **2.** STUPID dull, slow, thick, dense, vapid, vacuous, pea-brained, insensitive. ANT. *1. sharp, pointed. 2. sharp, intelligent, quick.* SEE MORONIC, STUPID

obverse *a.* **1.** FACE front, top, head. **2.** COUNTERPART opposite, reverse.

obviate *v.* preclude, prevent, forestall, avert, avoid, evade, circumvent.

obvious *a.* apparent, evident, visible, plain to see, clear, conspicuous, manifest, overt, noticeable, perceivable, glaring, palpable, patent, prominent, unambiguous, *sticking out like a sore thumb, *goes without saying. ANT. *imperceivable, mysterious, vague, inconspicuous.*

obviously *adv.* unmistakably, apparently, evidently, certainly, overtly, clearly.

occasion *n.* **1.** EVENT happening, affair, function, happening, incident. **2.** OPPORTUNITY chance, opening, golden opportunity, *shot, *crack. **3.** CELEBRATION holiday, festival, gala, carnival. **4.** TIME juncture, instance, point, case.

occasion *v.* cause, give occasion to, produce, bring about, prompt, induce, effect, create, bring to pass. ANT. *stop, end, quit.*

occasional *a.* irregular, once in awhile, sporadic, infrequent, every now and then, periodic, casual, odd, from time to time. ANT. *frequent, regular, continuous.*

occasionally *adv.* now and then, once in awhile, from time to time, periodically, sometimes, infrequently, irregularly, once in a blue moon, sporadically. ANT. *regularly, frequently, constantly.*

occlude *v.* obstruct, close off, shut off, seal, plug, stop, clog, choke, block, fill. ANT. *open, clear, unstop.*

occlusion *n.* blockage, obstruction, seal, plug, stop, clog, block. ANT. *opening, hole, clearance.*

occult *n.* mystical arts, cabalism, mysticism, occultism, channeling, astrology, voodoo, alchemy, tarot, Ouija board, psychic powers, clairvoyance, exorcism, satanism, devil worshipping, sorcery, witchcraft, telekinesis, telepathy, reincarnation, possession. SEE MAGIC

occult *a.* supernatural, secret, hidden, magical, unexplainable, unfathomable, arcane, mystical, cryptic, esoteric, orphic. ANT. *earthly, tangible, explainable, known.* SEE MYSTERIOUS

WORD FIND

affected or demented by unseen forces: touched

assembly headed by a medium who summons spirits: seance

ball of glass hung in window to ward off evil spirits: witch ball

beetle talisman of Egypt: scarab

black magic: black arts, sorcery, witchcraft, wizardry

black magic, one who practices: sorcerer, sorceress, witch, wizard

board game used to summon the spiritual world and answer questions: Ouija board

cards, fortune-telling: tarot cards

castle mirage: fata morgana

celestial bodies, divining one's fate by position of: astrology

celestial bodies used to predict one's fate, a chart of: horoscope

celestial pathway divided into 12 astrological signs: zodiac

celestial bodies at a precise time to predict one's fate, the plotting of: horoscope

Celtic order of priests who acted as prophet or sorcerer, member of a: druid

charm to ward off evil: amulet, talisman

coincidence, hidden meaning and interconnectedness of: synchronicity

communications, acting as a medium to receive spiritual: channeling

corpse brought back to life: zombie

crystal ball, read the future by gazing into a: scry

curse or spell: hex, whammy

dead, returns from: revenant

demon through prayers and incantations, casting out of: exorcism

evil, magic used for: black magic

evil spirit, occupied by an: possessed

feeling that one has experienced or visited a place before in a past life, eerie: deja vu

formula or incantation causing trance state or other prescribed behavior: spell

future by various means, reading the: divination

future, knowledge of what will transpire in the: prescience

future, one who has the ability to predict the: prophet, psychic, seer

future, prediction of what will occur in the: prophesy

future will bring, one who tells what the: soothsayer

future, seeing the: precognition

ghost, noisy: poltergeist

ghost who haunts its living twin: doppelganger

ghostly visitations or appearances: haunting

glass ball used to peer into the future: crystal ball

Haitian religion employing charms and fetishes: voodoo

healing through prayer alone: faith healing

hear the spirit world, ability to: clairaudience

intuition, understanding the spiritual world through: gnosis

intuition, pre-Christians who believed spiritual world could be understood through: Gnostics

language without studying, acquiring of foreign: xenoglossia

letters and characters, mystical: runes

love potion: philter

luck, bad: hoodoo

luck, one who brings bad: hoodoo

luck, thing that brings bad: jinx

magic used for good: white magic

meaning, having a hidden: cabalistic

memory of experiences before one's existence: past life memories

metal into gold, stone or substance once believed could turn: philosopher's stone

mind reader: psychic

misfortune, invocation of: curse

move objects with one's mind, ability to: psychokinesis, telekinesis

Native American mysticism and magic: shamanism

numbers to determine one's fate, study of: numerology

object, such as a rabbit's foot, thought to have magical power: charm, fetish

omens and signs, study of: augury

otherworldly: ethereal

palm reader: chiromancer

perceive what cannot be physically seen, ability to: clairvoyance

perceive what cannot be physically seen, one who can: clairvoyant

perception, all things beyond explanation or human: paranormal; the supernatural

psychic ability: ESP, extra sensory perception, sixth sense, third eye

psychic powers, referring to: psi

psychic or other powers, study of: parapsychology

quartz or other transparent mineral used in healing: crystal

radiance surrounding some people or objects, mystical: aura

reader of omens and signs, ancient Roman: augur

receives spiritual messages, person or thing that: medium, channeler, oracle

release of one's soul from physical body, temporary: out-of-body experience

Satan worship: diabolism, Satanism

Satan worshippers, group of: Satanic cult

science, phony: pseudoscience

sign, magical: sigil

sign of things to come: omen, portent

sorcery and witchcraft: black arts

soul, belief that nature has a: animism

spellbinding: hypnotism, mesmerism

spell utterance: incantation

spiritual world, belief in: mysticism

summon a spirit, to: conjure

thought transference to another: telepathy

time and space eddy through which one may travel to another dimension: vortex

trance, put someone in a: spellbind

travel, spiritual, out-of-body: astral projection

voodoo, form of Brazilian: macumba

voodoo priestess, Haitian: mambo

water by forked divining rod, searching for underground: dowsing

water by forked divining rod, one who searches for: dowser

werewolf, ability to change oneself into a: lycanthropy

witchcraft practiced for the good of the earth and the environment: Wicca

witches, group of 13: coven

witch, male: warlock

written word, spirit communication through medium through: spirit writing SEE DIVINATION.

occupancy *n.* residence, residency, occupation, living, tenancy, inhabitance, inhabitation, stay, tenure, lodging, possession. ANT. *leave, vacancy, absence.* SEE HOUSE

occupant *n.* resident, inhabitant, tenant, leaseholder, renter, lodger, dweller, homeowner, owner, lessee.

occupation *n.* **1.** VOCATION job, work, career, trade, profession, business, livelihood, calling, pursuit, employment. SEE JOB, WORK **2.** OCCUPANCY tenancy, possession, inhabitation. **3.** CONQUEST seizure, takeover, overthrow, subjugation, defeat, possession, rule.

occupied *a.* **1.** ENGAGED busy, preoccupied, engrossed, absorbed, employed, diverted. **2.** INHABITED lived in, settled, taken. **3.** CONQUERED seized, overthrown, possessed, defeated, taken, over, subjugated. ANT. *1. idle, inactive, unoccupied, at leisure. 2. uninhabited, vacant, empty. 3. sovereign, independent, self-ruled.*

occupy *v.* **1.** ENGAGE busy, preoccupy, engross, absorb, employ, divert, entertain. **2.** INHABIT live in, settle, take, reside in, take up residence. **3.** CONQUER seize, overthrow, possess, defeat, take over, subjugate, rule. ANT. *1. disengage, make idle, bore. 2. vacate, *fly the coop, leave, relinquish. 3. retreat, relinquish, evacuate.*

occurrence *n.* happening, incident, event, episode, transaction, circumstance, matter, action, experience, affair.

ocean *n.* sea, the deep, the abyss, deep blue sea, brine, *the drink, *Davy Jones locker, high seas, the seven seas, *bounding main, Neptune, Poseidon, expanse, *unbridgeable horizon, Arctic, Antarctic, Atlantic, North Atlantic, South Atlantic, Pacific, North Pacific, South Pacific, Indian. "The wavy waste."—Thomas Hood. "A highway between the doorways of the nations."—Franklin Lane.

WORD FIND

bottom and its creatures: benthic realm, benthos

bottom, one region of: province

circular currents: gyres

current of Atlantic: Gulf Stream

current of Pacific that disrupts weather patterns: El Niño

depression in floor: cauldron

depth between one hundred and one thousand meters: bathyal zone

depth between one thousand and six thousand meters: abyssal zone

depth from six thousand meters down: hadal zone

depth, greatest trench: Marianas Trench

depth measurement of six feet: fathom

eddy that breaks off from main current: meander, ring

flat calm, no wind region: doldrums

foam: spume

glow of sea creatures: bioluminescence

god: Neptune

graveyards of ships: Bermuda Triangle, graveyard of the Atlantic

hills: abyssal hills

measurement of depth: bathymetry, sounding

mile, nautical: 6,082.2 feet

mountain chain in Atlantic: mid-Atlantic ridge

mountain chain in Pacific: Emperor Seamounts

mountain: seamount

seaweed region in North Atlantic: Sargasso Sea

sediment deposit, large offshore: submarine fan

shallow area, navigational hazard: shoal

spray: spindrift

study of: oceanography

tide, maximal low and high: spring tide

tide, minimal low and high: neap tide

turbulence involving bottom mud: benthic storm

waves, crash and crest of opposing: cross seas

waves: plunger, spiller, graybeard, swell, eagre (tidal bore), tsunami

wave, tidal: tsunami

wind distance and relationship to wave height: fetch

SEE BEACH

oceanic *a.* marine, maritime, deep-sea, aquatic, pelagic, abyssal, nautical. ANT. *terrestrial.*

ocean liner *n.* cruise ship, luxury liner.

oceanographer *n.* marine scientist, oceanologist, hydrographer.

October *n.* month, harvest time, autumn, fall, Indian summer.

odd *a.* **1.** STRANGE unusual, weird, unconventional, out of the ordinary, offbeat, unnatural, bizarre, atypical, peculiar, singular, irregular, queer, unique. **2.** UNMATCHED lone,

single, unpaired, mateless. ANT. *1. usual, typical, ordinary, regular. 2. matched, paired.*

oddball *n. Sl.* *weirdo, eccentric, misfit, *crackpot, *freak, *nut, *screwball, *character, *queer duck, nonconformist. ANT. *regular Joe, *average Joe, conformist.*

oddity *n.* curiosity, rarity, quirk, peculiarity, eccentricity, anomaly, freak.

odds *n.* **1.** PROBABILITY chances, likelihood, expectation, prospect. **2.** ADVANTAGE handicap, edge. **3.** AT ODDS at sixes and sevens, at loggerheads, in disagreement, misunderstanding, difference of opinion.

odds and ends *n.* bits and pieces, oddments, miscellany, mishmash, hodgepodge, mélange, mixed bag, assortment, patchwork, remnants.

oddsmaker *n.* statistician, gambler, bettor, tout.

odds-on-favorite *n.* front-runner, best bet, chalk horse.

ode *n.* poem, lyric, hymn, song. SEE POEM, SONG

odious *a.* offensive, abhorrent, repugnant, disgusting, hateful, repulsive, detestable, revolting, loathsome. ANT. *pleasing, delightful, nice.*

odium *n.* **1.** HATRED ill will, loathing, disgust, repugnance. **2.** DISGRACE opprobrium. ANT. *1. love, goodwill, benevolence. 2. grace, honor.*

odometer *n.* distance indicator, instrument, mileage meter, gauge.

odor *n.* scent, smell, aroma, fragrance, essence, effluvium, redolence, fume, emanation, whiff, stench, stink, bouquet, perfume.

WORD FIND

types: foul, fetid, rank, goaty, musty, spring-fresh, herbal, floral, pungent, spicy, chemical, organic, fruity, sweet, sour, rancid, incense, civet, musk, potpourri, frankincense, sandalwood, myrrh, balsam, antiseptic, dank, stale, honeysuckle, lilac, putrid, carbolic, spindrift, ozone, fishy, diesel, ambrosial.

SEE PERFUME, SMELL

odorless *a.* nonfragrant, neutral, unscented, deodorized. ANT. *scented, fragrant, odorous.*

odorous *a.* fragrant, smelly, stinky, distinct-smelling, redolent, odoriferous, aromatic, scented. ANT. *unscented, odorless.*

odyssey *n.* wandering, trek, journey, quest, sojourn, voyage, travels. SEE TRAVEL

off *a.* **1.** AWAY OR DETACHED removed, above, below, aside, behind, distant, not touching, separated. **2.** SHUT OFF, INOPERABLE stopped, malfunctioning, disconnected, shut down, defunct, unpowered, down. **3.** MISTAKEN incorrect, in error, wrong, inaccurate, erroneous, miscalculated. **4.** OFF DUTY on holiday, not working, on liberty, on leave. ANT. *1. on, attached, touching, astride. 2. on, functioning, running. 3. correct, accurate, right. 4. on duty, working.*

offal n. entrails, guts, refuse, rubbish, waste. SEE GARBAGE

off and on adv. intermittent, alternately, variably, fluctuating, vacillating, starting and stopping, sporadically, irregularly.

off-balance a. **1.** OFF-CENTER uncentered, unbalanced. **2.** UNSTEADY *tippy, tipping, uncoordinated, leaning, toppling, inclining. ANT. *1. centered, balanced. 2. steady, balanced, stable, counterpoised.*

offbeat a. unconventional, unorthodox, unusual, *off-center, strange, novel, *kinky, *freaky, *oddball, different, weird, atypical, *far out. ANT. *conventional, orthodox, traditional, normal.*

off-center a. misaligned, off-balanced, askew, eccentric. ANT. *aligned, centered.*

off-color a. risqué, improper, tasteless, indecent, inappropriate, suggestive, lewd, racy, *raunchy, dirty, offensive, indelicate, gross. ANT. *tasteful, prudish, respectable, clean.*

off course a. strayed, drifted, lost, lost one's bearings. SEE LOST

offend v. **1.** INSULT affront, annoy, slight, spite, disgust, outrage, mortify, vex, *ruffle one's feathers, *pull one's chain, *rattle one's cage, *rub one the wrong way. **2.** DO A MISDEED break the law, violate, transgress, sin. ANT. *1. please, honor, compliment, praise.*

offender n. perpetrator, culprit, lawbreaker, sinner, violator, malefactor. SEE CRIMINAL

offense n. **1.** INSULT affront, slight, injury. **2.** UMBRAGE resentment, pique, displeasure. **3.** MISDEED transgression, violation, infraction, misdemeanor, felony, wrongdoing, peccadillo, sin, charge. **4.** ATTACK, ATTACKERS assault, siege, invasion, charge, raid, offensive, blitzkrieg, blitz, run, attackers, aggressors, invaders, opposing side. ANT. *1. courtesy, compliment. 2. delight, honor. 3. good deed, benevolence. 4. defense, retreat, submission.* SEE CRIME, LAW

offensive n. attack, invasion, raid, assault, siege, charge, counteroffensive, bombing run, flanking maneuver, blitzkrieg, enfilade.

offensive a. **1.** INSULTING rude, obnoxious, revolting, disgusting, hateful, repugnant, outrageous, discourteous, distasteful, sickening,

disagreeable, affronting, abominable, objectionable. SEE MEAN, OBSCENE, VULGAR **2.** AGGRESSIVE warlike, invading, pugnacious, hostile, attacking, belligerent. ANT. *1. pleasing, honoring, respectful, nice. 2. peaceful, pacific, passive, appeasing.*

offer n. proffer, proposal, proposition, overture, bid, tender, offering, submission.

offer v. proffer, present, tender, bid, propose, submit, put forward, advance, lay at one's feet, suggest, counteroffer. ANT. *withdraw, renege, take back.* SEE PROPOSE

offering n. contribution, donation, oblation, tithe, sacrifice, grant. SEE GIFT

off-guard a. unprepared, unalert, asleep, napping, *flat-footed, unwary, daydreaming, lost in thought, *zoned out, *spaced out. ANT. *alert.*

offhand a. **1.** IMPROMPTU unprepared, casual, *at the spur of the moment, unplanned, extemporaneous, unrehearsed, unpremeditated, ad-lib. **2.** BRUSQUE curt, blunt, abrupt, informal, terse, casual. ANT. *1. rehearsed, prepared, studied. 2. tactful, mannered, polite.*

office n. **1.** PLACE OF BUSINESS OR WORK AREA department, headquarters, precinct, bureau, command center, practice, suite, *nerve center, *boiler room, base, room, work station, cubicle, compartment, niche, cubbyhole, pigeonhole, closet. **2.** POST position, service, role, function, charge, appointment.

officer n. **1.** POLICEMAN constable, magistrate, deputy, sheriff, peace officer, patrolman, *cop, *fuzz, *John Law. SEE POLICE **2.** OFFICIAL functionary, officeholder, bureaucrat, commissioner, director, minister, civil servant, secretary, commissar, corporate officer. **3.** MILITARY OFFICER MP, commissioned officer, noncommissioned officer, NCO. SEE AIR FORCE, ARMY, NAVY

office worker n. *desk jockey, *pencil driver, *bean counter, *number cruncher, *hacker, secretary, receptionist, accountant, computer programmer, controller, comptroller, clerk, payroll clerk, VP, Chief Executive Officer (CEO), file clerk, typist, word processor, billing clerk, data processor.

official n. **1.** OFFICER functionary, dignitary, administrator, public official, bureaucrat. **2.** REFEREE judge.

official a. authorized, sanctioned, certified, endorsed, approved, vested, accredited. ANT. *unofficial, unauthorized, not recognized.* SEE LEGAL

officialese n. doublespeak, *gobblydegook,

*federalese, jargon, *bloated English, *gassy prose, *verbosity, *mush, *tapioca, *departmental murk.

officiate v. oversee, preside over, chair, supervise, direct, emcee, referee, judge. SEE MEDIATE.

OFFICIOUS a. [uh FISH us] offering help or advice when it is not wanted, meddlesome, especially in a domineering way. *His mother-in-law is particularly officious.* SYN. meddlesome, obtrusive, intrusive, pushy, interfering, forward, prying, domineering, bossy, overbearing, high-handed, pragmatic. ANT. *reserved, unobtrusive, knowing one's place.*

offing n. 1. horizon, far distance. SEE FUTURE

off-key a. flat, sharp, out of tune, discordant, dissonant. ANT. *in tune.*

off-limits a. restricted, prohibited, forbidden, barred, out of bounds, banned, taboo, unlawful, illegal. ANT. *unrestricted, open, free.*

off-line a. disconnected, logged off, detached, separated. ANT. *on-line.*

offset v. counter, counteract, compensate, balance, neutralize, equalize, even out, cancel out, level out.

offshoot n. branch, stem, tendril, sprout, descendant, offspring, heir, *spinoff.

offshore a. seaward, the offing, *the high seas, out to sea.

offspring n. children, progeny, descendants, brood, heirs, clutch, litter, spawn, seed, young.

offstage n. wings, backstage, green room, dressing room.

off the cuff a. impromptu, offhand, unrehearsed, extemporaneous, ad-lib, improvised. ANT. *rehearsed.*

off the record a. confidential, not for publication, on the QT, unofficial, *between you, me and the bedpost. ANT. *quotable, public.*

off-white a. antique white, ivory, blond.

often adv. frequently, repeatedly, quite a bit, oft, time and again, regularly, habitually, generally. ANT. *seldom, rarely.*

ogle v. stare, leer, goggle, gawk, gaze, *stare bug-eyed, *stare saucer-eyed, *eye salaciously, gape at.

ogre n. giant, brute, man-eater, boogieman. SEE MONSTER

oil n. crude oil, petroleum, lubricant, motor oil, machine oil, *black gold, *Texas tea, sludge, grease, ooze, lard, oleo, fat, vegetable oil, corn oil, olive oil, linseed oil, cod-liver oil, mineral oil.

oily a. 1. VISCOUS greasy, slippery, unctious, oleaginous, fatty, lardy, tallowy, slick. 2. EXCESSIVELY SUAVE slick, smooth, unctuous, honey-tongued, flattering. ANT. *2. sincere, artless, unpolished.*

ointment n. emollient, salve, unguent, medicament, balm.

okay a. all right, correct, fine, *okey dokey, copacetic.

okay interj. yes, sure, *okey dokey, *righto, *sure thing, *no problem.

old a. 1. AGED elderly, venerable, advanced in years, matured, past one's prime, patriarchal, vintage, seasoned, *at a ripe old age, senior, retirement age. SEE OLD AGE 2. WORN OUT decrepit, dilapidated, crumbling, decayed, deteriorated, shabby, enfeebled, senile. 3. FORMER previous, early, past, bygone, once. 4. LONG-STANDING age-old, of the past, from time immemorial. ANT. *1. young, newborn, immature, unseasoned. 2. new, fresh, 3. later, future. 4. recent, new.*

old age n. retirement age, senescence, declining years, *winter of one's life, enfeeblement, dotage, senility. "To take in sail."—Emerson. "To be left alone at a banquet—the lights dead and the flowers faded."—Gilbert Chesterson. "Whenever a man's friends begin to compliment him about looking young."—Washington Irving. "The road's last turn."—Henry Van Dyke.

old country n. motherland, native land, mother country, Europe.

old days n. olden times, *yesteryear, horse and buggy days, days gone by, *good old days, days of yore.

old-faced a. cadaverous, careworn, timeworn, rawboned, craggy, crow's-feet, fleshy wattle under the chin, gap-toothed, goat-skinned, haggard, hollowed cheekbones, hollowed eye sockets, jaundiced, leathery, liver-spotted, mirthful crinkles about the eyes, skin like scalded milk, mottled, prune-faced, rheumy-eyed, weathered. ANT. *youthful, fresh-faced.*

old-fashioned a. outdated, outmoded, dated, obsolete, out of style, moss-grown, passé, fusty, antiquated, behind the times, Victorian, *horse and buggy, oldfangled, prehistoric, traditional, conservative, stodgy. ANT. *modern, fresh, fashionable, *cutting edge, new, chic.*

old maid n. spinster, maiden, single woman, virgin.

old man n. SEE OLD-TIMER

old school *a.* traditional, conservative, old-fashioned, old line, ingrained. ANT. *innovative, nontraditional.*

old-timer *n.* veteran, old hand, senior, mossback, *antique, *fossil, Methuselah, graybeard, centenarian, nonagenarian, octogenarian, sexagenarian, golden-ager, *codger, *geezer, *old fart, *duffer, *old buzzard, *gramps, *grandma, *old girl, *old hen.

old wives' tale *n.* superstition, lore, folklore, belief, myth, fallacy.

Olympian *n.* athlete, world-class athlete, medalist, competitor, champion.

Olympics *n.* Olympic Games, world championships, tournament, contest, challenge, international competition, Olympiad.

omen *n.* augury, portent, sign, precursor, warning, harbinger, forewarning, token, handwriting on the wall, foreboding, premonition, *storm cloud on the horizon.

OMINOUS *a.* [OM un us] pertaining to omens, portentous, foreboding. *A dark cloud on the horizon is particularly ominous to one on a sailboat.* SYN. portentous, foreboding, dreadful, prophetic, menacing, boding evil, inauspicious, threatening, sinister, cautionary. ANT. *boding well, encouraging, heartening, reassuring.*

omission *n.* exclusion, oversight, exception, deletion, neglected item. ANT. *inclusion, admission.*

omit *v.* leave out, exclude, delete, cut, overlook, erase, edit out, forget, preclude, skip, pass over, expunge, neglect, strike out, ignore. ANT. *include, put in, add to.*

omitted *a.* excluded, left out, deleted, overlooked, erased, precluded, forgotten, passed over, expunged. ANT. *included, put in, added.*

omnibus *n.* anthology, compilation, collection, collected works, volume, edition. SEE BOOK

OMNIPOTENT *a.* [om NIP uh tent] having unlimited or infinite power. *Many dictators strive to be as omnipotent as God.* SYN. all-powerful, almighty, supreme, unlimited, godlike. ANT. *ineffectual, powerless, weak.* SEE GOD, OMNISCIENT

omnipresent *a.* all-present, pervasive, ubiquitous. SEE GOD

omniscient *a.* all-knowing, all-seeing, god-like. ANT. *ignorant, unseeing, blind, unknowing.* SEE GOD, OMNIPOTENT

on *prep.* **1.** UPON above, touching, in contact with, atop, covering, attached to. **2.** NEAR by, around, beside. ANT. *1. off, away from, detached from. 2. away from, distant from.*

on *adv.* **1.** ONWARD forward, ahead. **2.** OPERATING running, going, engaged, working, functioning, powered. ANT. *1. stop, backward, behind. 2. off, stopped, unpowered.*

on and off *adv.* now and then, intermittently, start and stop. ANT. *constant, uninterrupted.*

on and on *adv.* constantly, continuously, never-ending, relentless, forever, unremitting. ANT. *finitely.*

onanism *n.* masturbation, self-gratification.

on a roll *a.* *hot, *on one's game, *in a groove, *cooking, *on fire, *in a zone, *hot-handed, *smoking, *rolling. ANT. *cold, ice cold, in a rut, in a slump.*

on call *a.* standing by, on alert, accessible, at hand, at one's beck and call, at one's disposal, at the ready.

once *adv.* one time, one time only, never again. ANT. *repeatedly.*

once *a.* formerly, previously, in the past, at one time, long ago. ANT. *currently.*

once and for all *adv.* finally, decisively, conclusively, positively, at long last.

once, at *adv.* immediately, now, this instant, *pronto, straightaway, forthwith, posthaste, *before you can say Jack Robinson/Bob's your uncle, *lickety-split.

once in awhile *adv.* every now and then, every so often, occasionally, periodically, sometimes, *once every blue moon.

once-over *n.* sizing up, inspection, examination, appraising glance, scrutiny, probe, *the eye, *critical eye, *piercing look.

oncoming *a.* approaching, nearing, looming, impending, onrushing, emerging, bearing down. ANT. *leaving, receding, retreating.*

on duty *a.* on, working, *clocked in, *punched in. ANT. *off the clock, off duty.*

one *a.* **1.** SINGLE individual, solitary. SEE NUMBER **2.** UNITED undivided, complete, whole. ANT. *1. multiple. 2. divided, incomplete.*

one by one *adv.* in succession, one at a time, individually.

on edge *a.* jittery, anxious, wired, *hyper. ANT. *relaxed, calm.* SEE NERVOUS

one-horse *a.* insignificant, small, *tinhorn, *two-bit, limited, *bush, inferior, *small-townish, *piddling. ANT. *significant, of consequence, *big-time.*

one-horse town *n.* whistlestop, one stoplight town, *a U-turn and a mayor, tank town, *podunk, *filling station, *jerk town, *wide place in the road.

one-liner *n.* joke, crack, wisecrack, bon mot, witty remark. SEE JOKE

oneness *n.* unity, singleness, togetherness, co-alescence.

one-night stand *n.* **1.** ONE-NIGHT SEXUAL AFFAIR tryst, *quickie, liaison. **2.** ENTERTAINMENT BOOKING engagement, one-nighter, *road gig.

ONEROUS *a.* [OHN ur us] burdensome, laborious or oppressive. *We were given the onerous task of mowing all thirty acres.* SYN. burdensome, laborious, oppressive, troublesome, difficult, arduous, formidable, demanding, wearisome. ANT. *easy, effortless, painless, trouble-free.*

one-sided *a.* biased, partial, prejudiced, unfair, narrow-minded, partisan. ANT. *fair-minded, democratic.*

one-track mind *n.* obsession, fixation, passion, preoccupation, fascination, single-mindedness.

one-upmanship *n.* rivaling, bettering, outsmarting, outfoxing, outwitting, outgaming, cutthroat, domination, gamesmanship, resourcefulness, artfulness, finesse, cunning, cageyness, outmaneuvering. ANT. *submission, concession, quitting.*

on guard *a.* defensive, guarded, alert, on one's toes, vigilant, watchful, cautious. ANT. *asleep, oblivious, nonchalant, carefree.*

onion *n.* shallot, scallion, leek, bulb.

on-line *a.* connected, wired, networked, linked, auxiliary, peripheral, plugged in, engaged. ANT. *off-line, disconnected, independent.* SEE INTERNET

onlooker *n.* spectator, eyewitness, bystander, observer.

only *a.* sole, single, lone, solitary.

only *adv.* singly, solely, alone, solitarily.

on paper *adv.* theoretically, hypothetically, in theory, in the abstract.

on purpose *adv.* deliberately, knowingly, intentionally, purposefully, wittingly, consciously, by intent, by design. ANT. *accidently, unwittingly, unintentionally.*

onrush *n.* rush, stampede, *blitz, storm, headlong dash, tidal wave, deluge, flood, avalanche.

onset *n.* **1.** START beginning, outset. **2.** ATTACK assault.

onslaught *n.* attack, rush, charge, assault, invasion, *blitz, offensive, strike, incursion, storming.

on tap *a.* *Sl.* handy, at hand, in stock, available, at one's fingertips.

on the ball *a.* *Sl.* *on the stick, *with it, sharp,

quick, *on one's toes, ready, alert, *plugged in. ANT. *slow, unprepared, asleep.*

on the blink *a.* *Sl.* broken, *out of whack, *out of kilter, *on the fritz, *out of commission, in disrepair. ANT. *functioning, in good repair, working.*

on the brink *a.* *Sl.* on the verge, on the edge, at the threshold, at the limit.

on the double *a.* *Sl.* *double quick, *pronto, *lickety-split, *chop chop.

on the fence *a.* *Sl.* undecided, neutral, nonpartisan, noncommitted, half-and-half, *torn, divided, *in the middle of the road, impartial. ANT. *one-sided, biased, partial, liberal, conservative, left, right.*

on the house *a.* *Sl.* gratis, free, *on one, no charge, *freebie, compliments of the house.

on the level *a.* *Sl.* *on the up-and-up, *for real, legitimate, square, fair, straight, aboveboard, authentic. ANT. *dishonest, illegitimate, *BS, on the make, *on the prowl, out for.*

on the nose *a.* *Sl.* bulls-eye, precisely, exactly, *on the money.

on the wagon *a.* *Sl.* sworn off, sober, *dry, abstinent, abstemious.

on the whole *a.* *Sl.* for the most part, mostly.

on trial *adv.* under examination, in litigation, before the court, up for investigation.

onus *n.* burden, responsibility, load, weight, duty, task, obligation.

onward *adv.* ahead, forward, forth, on beyond, frontward, advancing, along.

oodles *n.* slews, lots, piles, *scads, *zillions. SEE MANY

oomph *n.* *Sl.* **1.** ENERGY vigor, muscle, power, *elbow grease, exertion. **2.** SEX APPEAL *it.

ooze *n.* mud, sludge, muck, mire, slime, *goo, *crap.

ooze *v.* exude, flow, seep, percolate, squeeze out, discharge, bleed.

opalescent *a.* irridescent, rainbowlike.

OPAQUE *a.* [o PAKE] impossible to see through or impossible to understand. *The windows in the limo were opaque; nobody could see through them.* SYN. impervious, clouded, murky, misty, blurred, nebulous, filmy, hazy, foggy, nontransparent, obscure, vague, abstruse, unclear. ANT. *transparent, clear, translucent, lucid.*

open *v.* **1.** TO MAKE AN OPENING unlock, unlatch, undo, unseal, unscrew, uncork, loosen, free, untie, breach, broach, tear down, puncture, slit, pierce, rupture. **2.** SPREAD unfold, unfurl, unroll, lay out. **3.** BEGIN commence, start, inaugurate, initiate, launch, *get the ball rolling. ANT. 1. *close, shut, cover, stop up, seal.* 2. *fold, roll up, ball up.* 3. *end, close, finalize.*

open *a.* **1.** UNCLOSED unsealed, accessible, agape, unlocked, unobstructed, ajar, clear, yawning. **2.** EXPOSED uncovered, unprotected, open to view, unenclosed, unconcealed. **3.** SPREAD OUT unfolded, unfurled, unrolled, laid out. **4.** OPEN TO THE PUBLIC accessible, open for business, in operation, ready to serve. **5.** FAIR-MINDED receptive, open-minded, unbiased, unprejudiced. **6.** HONEST OR CANDID frank, sincere, blunt, communicative, revealing, disclosing, intimate, *real. ANT. 1. closed, shut, sealed, unaccessible.* 2. *covered, hidden, enclosed, concealed.* 3. *folded, bunched up.* 4. *closed.* 5. *close-minded, narrow-minded, biased.* 6. *reserved, uncommunicative, secretive.*

open-air *a.* outdoors, outside, alfresco.

open-and-shut *a.* simple, easy, obvious, incontrovertible, cut and dried, guaranteed, clearcut, beyond argument, indisputable, *in the bag, *sewn up, cinched. ANT. *arguable, moot, disputable, complex, convoluted, difficult.*

open-ended *a.* unlimited, undetermined, unrestricted.

opener *n.* **1.** MECHANICAL OPENER key, skeleton key, can opener, corkscrew, drill, punch, gouge, awl, borer, reamer, trepan, jimmy, crowbar, glasscutter, *jaws of life. **2.** OPENING ACT warmup act, supporting act.

open-eyed *a.* **1.** WATCHFUL vigilant, hawk-eyed, eagle-eyed, awake, alert, wary. **2.** WIDE-EYED saucer-eyed, pop-eyed, goggle-eyed, spellbound, enthralled, wonderstruck, thunderstruck, bug-eyed. ANT. *1. inattentive, lax, sleepy-eyed, unguarded.* 2. *sleepy-eyed, droopy-eyed.*

openhanded *a.* generous, charitable, giving, unselfish, munificent, altruistic, beneficent, magnanimous. ANT. *stingy, tightfisted, pennypinching, cheap.*

openhearted *a.* **1.** CANDID frank, sincere, open, straightforward, honest, ingenuous, genuine, *from the heart, *real. **2.** KINDHEARTED good-hearted, softhearted, benevolent, compassionate, warm, humane, *Christian. ANT. *1. aloof, insincere, dishonest.* 2. *mean, cruel, cold, brutal.*

opening *n.* **1.** HOLE gap, orifice, slot, aperture, chasm, crack, rift, hollow, lacuna, gateway, doorway. **2.** BEGINNING start, commencement, initiation, introduction, inauguration, launch, *kickoff. **3.** VACANCY position, chance, availability. ANT. *1. closure, occlusion, blockage, seal.* 2. *ending, closing, finale.*

opening *a.* beginning, starting, commencing, initiating, introducing, inaugurating, launching, *kicking off. ANT. *closing, ending, finalizing.*

open-minded *a.* receptive, amenable, unbiased, impartial, broad-minded, tolerant, understanding, liberal-minded, sympathetic, reasonable. ANT. *close-minded, narrow-minded, intolerant, dogmatic, bigoted.*

opera *n.* musical, melodrama, libretto, drame lyrique. "When a guy gets stabbed in the back and instead of bleeding, he sings."—Edward Gardner. "A magic scene contrived to please the eyes and the ears at the expense of the understanding."—Lord Chesterfield.

WORD FIND

bass voice, sweet and light: basso cantante
booming bass voice: basso profundo
brilliant and pure vocal tone: bel canto
comical opera: buffa
composition with several arias, duets, choruses: cantata
false high pitch of male: falsetto
highest range of male voice: tenor
highest singing voice: soprano
lead female singer: prima donna, diva
lead male singer: prima uomo
light opera: operetta
long composition of religious theme presented without scenery, costumes: oratorio
long vocal solo piece: aria
low, comical voice: basso buffo
lowest female voice: contralto
lowest male voice: bass
male castrated in seventeenth, eighteenth centuries to retain high singing voice: castrato
manager or director of opera company: impresario
midrange male voice: baritone
repetition of theme sung in succession by two or more: call and answer
short vocal solo: cavatina
SEE MUSIC, SINGING, SONG, VOICE

operable *a.* viable, serviceable, workable, feasible. ANT. *inoperable.*

operate *v.* **1.** FUNCTION work, perform, act, conduct, manage, carry on, do, run. **2.** PERFORM SURGERY amputate, incise, excise, transplant, cauterize, cut open, explore, bypass, suture, stitch up. SEE OPERATION

operation *n*. **1.** EXERCISE project, action, campaign, maneuver, organization, venture. **2.** RUNNING performance, working, discharge, functioning. **3.** SURGICAL PROCEDURE surgery, incision, excision.

WORD FIND

anesthetic used in localized area: local anesthetic

appendix removal: appendectomy

birth delivery through abdomen: Caesarian section, C-section

blood vessel graft to improve blood flow: bypass

boring hole in skull: trepanning

brain, removal of front portion: lobotomy

brain, spinal cord or nerve surgery: neurosurgery

breast removal: mastectomy

burning away of abnormal tissue: cauterization

bypass: shunt

cornea incisions to improve vision: radial keratotomy

cutting nerve to relieve pain: denervation

cutting surgically: incising

cyst removal: cystectomy

esophagus removal: esophagectomy

exploratory: exploratory surgery

exposure of brain: craniotomy

extreme cold used to destroy abnormal tissue: cryosurgery

fallopian tube closure to prevent pregnancy: tubal ligation

gallbladder removal: cholecystectomy

general pain blocker, unconsciousness inducer: general anesthesia

gum surgery: gingivectomy

inhaled anesthetic agent: ether

joint exploration: arthroscopy

kidney removal: nephrectomy

large intestine removal: colectomy

local anesthetic agent: lidocaine, procaine

lung removal: pneumorectomy

nose enhancement: rhinoplasty

pancreas removal: pancreatectomy

passage of tube into body part: intubation

prostate gland removal: prostatectomy

removal of tissue or organ: excision

replacement of organ: transplant

restoring blood vessel flow: angioplasty

scraping of tissue: curettage

sex change: transsex surgery

sperm-blocking surgery: vasectomy

spleen removal: splenectomy

stitching of wound: suturing

tissue sampling: biopsy

tonsil removal: tonsillectomy

transplant from one body part to another: graft

tumor or mass removal: lumpectomy

uterus removal: hysterectomy

violent reaction to transplanted foreign organ: rejection reaction

operational *a*. functional, fit, viable, workable, in working order, operative, usable. ANT. *out of service, disfunctional*.

operative *a*. functioning, operating, running, working. ANT. *broken*.

operator *n*. **1.** TECHNICIAN worker, engineer, driver, handler, processor, keypunch operator, switchboard operator, PBX operator. **2.** SWINDLER *con artist, fraud, *ripoff artist, *flim-flam man, *shark, *hot shot, *snake.

opiate *n*. soporific, narcotic, tranquilizer, sedative, hypnotic, *downer. SEE DRUG, NARCOTIC, OPIUM

opine *v*. think, reckon, of the opinion, believe, imagine, maintain, suppose, assume, guess.

opinion *n*. conviction, belief, notion, thought, conclusion, view, idea, judgment, inference, sentiment, feeling, theory, point of view, impression, conception, finding, estimation. "Truth filtered through the moods, the blood, the disposition of the spectator."— Wendell Phillips.

opinionated *a*. biased, prejudiced, dogmatic, headstrong, obstinate, pigheaded, convinced, close-minded, narrow-minded, one-sided. ANT. *open-minded, broad-minded, tractable, neutral*.

opium *n*. narcotic, opiate, soporific, laudanum, *dope, *downer, *hop, *black snake, *leaf, *tar, *mud, *poppy hops. SEE DRUG, OPIATE

opponent *n*. adversary, enemy, rival, competitor, antagonist, foe, contender, nemesis, *sparring partner. SEE ENEMY

opportune *a*. timely, favorable, advantageous, fortuitous, felicitous, expedient, auspicious, suitable, appropriate, fitting, apropos, apt, seasonable, correct, right. ANT. *inopportune, unfavorable, untimely, unseasonable*.

opportunism *n*. exploitation, expediency, *go-getting, *making hay while the sun shines, *striking while the iron is hot.

opportunist *n*. *gold digger, operator, *go-getter, adventurer, enterpriser.

opportunity *n*. opening, chance, occasion, *window of opportunity, possibility, contingency, *shot, golden opportunity.

oppose v. resist, conflict, repulse, confront, repel, counter, contest, refute, dispute, contradict, disapprove, reject, contravene, go up against. ANT. support, embrace, advance, advocate, concur.

opposite n. reverse, contrary, inverse, antithesis, counterpart, *other side of the coin, *flipside. ANT. twin, mirror image, duplicate.

opposite a. facing, face to face, vis à vis, inverse, obverse, contrary, contradictory, antithetical, reverse. ANT. corresponding.

opposition n. 1. OPPOSING INDIVIDUAL OR GROUP adversary, opponent, rival, antagonist, competitor. 2. RESISTANCE repulsion, antagonism, conflict. 3. OBSTRUCTION hindrance, impediment, restriction, check. ANT. 1. proponent, advocate, partnership, collaboration. 2. attraction, acceptance. 3. opening, clearance, help, aid.

OPPRESS v. [uh PRESS] to force or keep down, especially by abuse of power, to tyrannize. The dictator tries to oppress the populace through threats of violence. SYN. subjugate, suppress, persecute, tyrannize, *step on, depress, harass, crush, stifle, burden, saddle, weigh down, dominate, subdue, squelch, *rule by yoke and whip, *rule with an iron fist, *straitjacket into conformity, *jackboot. ANT. liberate, free, emancipate.

oppressed a. downtrodden, harassed, tormented, persecuted, tyrannized, enslaved, misused, subdued, dominated, saddled, weighed down, burdened, abused. ANT. liberated, honored, respected.

OPPRESSION n. [uh PRESH un] the keeping or forcing down, especially by abuse of power; tyranny. The inferior leader rules by oppression. SYN. tyranny, subjugation, persecution, suppression, enslavement, domination, coercion, torment, martial law, heavy-handedness, *bullied obeisance. ANT. freedom, liberty, justice.

oppressive a. tyrannical, despotic, domineering, heavy-handed, iron-fisted, severe, harsh, burdensome, ruthless, brutal, abusive. ANT. liberating, just, fair.

oppressor n. tyrant, despot, dictator, persecutor, master, slavedriver, martinet, disciplinarian, authoritarian, bully, tormentor, puppet-master. ANT. emancipator.

opprobrious a. 1. DISGRACEFUL shameful, infamous, despicable, dishonorable, hateful. 2. ABUSIVE offending, insulting, contemptuous, reproachful. ANT. 1. honorable, commendable. 2. complimentary, flattering.

opprobrium n. disgrace, infamy, shame, dishonor, discredit, reproach, stigma. ANT. honor, regard, esteem.

oppugn v. criticize, attack, oppose, controvert, *shoot down, *blast, *light into, *rake over the coals. ANT. concur, compliment, agree.

opt v. choose, elect, decide, pick, elect.

optical a. visual, ocular.

optician n. optometrist, oculist.

optimal a. best, optimum, favorable, greatest, superlative. ANT. worst, terrible.

optimism n. hopefulness, rosy outlook, positive attitude, great expectations, enthusiasm, cheerfulness, anticipation, bullishness, buoyancy, confidence, encouragement. ANT. pessimism, negative outlook, gloomy outlook, cynicism.

optimist n. idealist, dreamer, Pollyanna, hoper, *ray of sunshine, positive thinker. "Someone who tells you to cheer up when things are going his way."—Edward R. Murrow. ANT. pessimist, defeatist, killjoy, *gloomy Gus.

optimistic a. hopeful, forward-looking, sanguine, cheerful, upbeat, expectant, assured, sunny, bullish, confident, anticipating, positive, *up, Pollyannish. ANT. pessimistic, gloomy, cynical, negative.

optimum a. optimal, greatest, foremost, most, highest, ideal, utmost, champion, consummate, prime, select, superior, tiptop. ANT. worst, lowest, poorest.

option n. 1. CHOICE selection, alternative, decision, substitute, preference, election, predilection. 2. THE RIGHT TO BUY OR SELL claim, grant, privilege, prerogative, franchise.

optional a. elective, discretionary, voluntary, free, open, volitional. ANT. obligatory, compulsory, mandatory.

optometrist n. optician, eye specialist, oculist.

OPULENCE n. [OP yuh lence] wealth or luxury. The opulence of Beverly Hills is evident in the homes, stores and people one observes. SYN. wealth, affluence, riches, prosperity, fortune, luxury, abundance, money, capital, excess, *easy street. ANT. poverty, squalor, indigence, privation.

opulent a. rich, wealthy, affluent, prosperous, moneyed, well-to-do, well-off, *loaded, *rolling in dough, *on easy street, *in clover, *high on the hog, abundant. ANT. poor, penniless, indigent, destitute.

opus n. composition, score, creation, work, piece, production, volume, title. SEE BOOK

or conj. else, otherwise, alternatively.

oracle *n.* prophet, seer, soothsayer, augur, diviner, fortune-teller, prognosticator, sage, priest, authority, judge.

oracular *a.* prophetic, prognostic, Delphic, augural, authoritative, wise, knowing.

oral *a.* spoken, verbal, said, voiced, verbalized, articulated, vocalized, uttered. ANT. *written, mental, telepathic.*

orange *a.* reddish-yellow, flaming, salmon, fox, tangerine, peach, pumpkin, tarnished sunset, ocher, tiger, apricot, burnt orange, burnt sienna, mandarin, marigold, yellow carmine, Titian, old gold, carrot.

orangutan *n.* ape, great ape, primate, *man of the forest.

orate *v.* speak, speechify, lecture, preach, sermonize, pontificate, *get up on one's soapbox, *get up on one's moral soapbox, hold forth, declaim, rhapsodize, moralize, vociferate, bluster, talk, *grandstand.

oration *n.* speech, address, lecture, talk, discourse, recitation, declamation, recital, disquisition, monologue.

orator *n.* speaker, lecturer, preacher, reciter, declaimer, sermonizer, pontificator, rhetorician, elocutionist. "One who can make men see with their ears."—Arabian proverb.

oratorical *a.* rhetorical, eloquent, declamatory, grandiloquent, bombastic, fustian, blustering, *rabble rousing, blatherous, silvertongued.

oratory *n.* rhetoric, platform rhetoric, public speaking, declamation, eloquence, grandiloquence, speechifying, preaching, sermonizing, elocution, articulation.

orb *n.* sphere, spheroid, globe, ball, heavenly body, celestial body, moon.

orbit *n.* circuit, revolution, cycle, circle, course, path, ellipse, ring, flight path, gravitational path, *gravitational tether.

orbit *v.* circle, round, circuit, revolve around, gravitate around, cycle around.

orc *n.* killer whale, grampus, cetacean, whale.

orchard *n.* plantation, grove, stand, vineyard, garden.

orchestra *n.* symphony, ensemble, band, philharmonic, quintet, quartet, combo, group. SEE MUSIC

orchestrate *v.* arrange, organize, conduct, lead, coordinate, direct, manage, guide, marshal, command, *hold the reins, oversee.

orchestrator *n.* conductor, director, manager, arranger, organizer, leader, coordinator, commander, overseer, stage manager.

orchid *n.* epiphyte, flower, *moccasin, *lady's slipper, *puttyroot, *Adam and Eve. SEE FLOWER

ordain *v.* 1. TO INVEST WITH AUTHORITY install, pronounce, appoint, frock, induct, instate, swear in, consecrate. 2. ARRANGE prepare, put in order. 3. TO DETERMINE predetermine, preordain, predestine, prearrange, fate, doom.

ordeal *n.* trial, tribulation, trying experience, difficulty, hardship, nightmare, trial by fire, torture, hell, test, strain, trouble, torment, misery, fiasco. ANT. *treat, *walk on the beach, joy, pleasure.*

order *n.* 1. A COMMAND direction, directive, dictate, demand, mandate, prescription, assignment, bid, enjoinder, fiat, charge. 2. ARRANGEMENT organization, system, sequence, progression, succession, alignment, grouping, classification. 3. CONDITION state, disposition, shape, repair. 4. RESERVATION TO PURCHASE requisition, request, booking, layaway. 5. SOCIETY OR CLUB guild, fraternity, sorority, fellowship, lodge, council, Masons, Knights of Columbus. ANT. *2. disorder, jumble, mess.*

order *v.* 1. GIVE A COMMAND direct, dictate, demand, mandate, prescribe, remand, enjoin, assign, bid, charge, instruct, *bark out an order. 2. RESERVE FOR PURCHASE request, tender, bid, secure, buy, requisition, layaway. 3. TO ARRANGE organize, systemize, put in sequence, align, group, classify, alphabetize, index, codify. ANT. *1. request, ask for nicely, beg, supplicate. 3. disorganize, disarrange, mess, jumble, mix up, scramble.*

order about *v.* dominate, badger, nag, command, *ride, lord over, henpeck, control, dictate, master, bully, *put under one's thumb. ANT. *supplicate, *cave in, defer.*

ordered *a.* orderly, arranged, well-ordered, systematic, in good form, organized, methodical, shipshape, tidy, neat. ANT. *disordered, in disarray, disorganized, messy.*

orderly *n.* hospital attendant, staff, assistant, nurse's aid.

orderly *a.* 1. ORGANIZED systematic, arranged, well-ordered, in good form, in apple pie order, methodical, shipshape, neat, tidy, trim, uncluttered. 2. PEACEFUL behaved, law-abiding, well-mannered, civil. ANT. *1. disorderly, in disarray, disorganized, messy. 2. rowdy, ill-mannered, riotous, uncivil.*

order, out of *a.* 1. INOPERATIVE broken, out of commission, busted, in disrepair, *on the fritz, *shot, *out of whack. 2. INAPPROPRIATE out of place, out of turn, indecorous, improper. ANT. 1. *functioning,* *running like a Swiss watch,* *humming.* 2. *appropriate, proper.*

ordinance n. order, command, decree, law, rule, edict, injunction, regulation, fiat, sanction, prescription.

ordinarily adv. usually, normally, as a rule, most of the time, customarily, generally, by and large, regularly, routinely. ANT. *rarely, seldom, infrequently.*

ordinary a. 1. COMMON everyday, usual, commonplace, conventional, typical, average, normal, medial, routine, customary, general. 2. MEDIOCRE run of the mill, so-so, nothing to write home about, banal, humdrum, pedestrian, plain, household, prosaic, bourgeois, undistinguished, garden-variety. ANT. 1. *uncommon, unconventional, unusual, out of the ordinary.* 2. *distinguished, exceptional, extraordinary, significant.*

ordinary, out of the a. unusual, uncommon, strange, bizarre, odd, exceptional, off the beaten track, unheard of, incredible, wonderful, unique, one of a kind. ANT. *ordinary, normal, typical,* *par for the course.*

ordination n. ordainment, holy orders. SEE CHURCH, RELIGION

ordnance n. artillery, weapons, armor, guns, bombs. SEE ARMS, MUNITIONS

ordure n. excrement, dung, feces, manure, muck, droppings, guano, cow flop, filth, *crap.

ore n. unrefined earth, rock, metal, iron ore, bauxite, lodestone, magnetite, pyrite, tinstone, zincite.

oread n. nymph, fairy, mountain nymph.

organ n. 1. MUSICAL INSTRUMENT keyboard, synthesizer, pipe organ, melodeon, reed organ, calliope, harmonium, barrel organ, hurdygurdy, accordion. SEE MUSICAL INSTRUMENT 2. PUBLICATION journal, newsletter, newspaper, periodical, communique, vehicle, mouthpiece, bulletin. 3. LIVING COMPONENT part, member, element, heart, lungs, brain, liver, kidneys, bladder, gallbladder, pancreas, large intestine, small intestine, appendix, stomach, uterus.

organic a. 1. LIVING alive, animate, biological. 2. NATURAL nonchemical, untouched by man. 3. INHERENT intrinsic, innate, native, natural. ANT. 1. *inanimate, inorganic, mineral.* 2. *unnatural, man-made, synthetic.*

organism n. life-form, being, creature, animal, plant, cell.

organization n. 1. A UNITED GROUP association, corporation, federation, syndication, union, alliance, company, league, institute, club, guild, corps, confederation, sorority, fraternity, cartel, brotherhood, sisterhood, coalition, affiliation, network, consortium, team. 2. ARRANGEMENT order, systemization, classification, coordination, ordering, construction, assembling, institution, disposition, standardization. SEE ORDER

organization man n. *corporate clone, *another brick in the wall, *sheep, follower, *corporate disciple, *company man.

organize v. 1. ORDER arrange, systematize, coordinate, methodize, align, collate, *get it together, *get one's ducks in a row, *get one's act together. SEE ORDER 2. FORM formulate, develop, create, bring together, give rise to, found, originate, establish. ANT. 1. *disorder, jumble, scramble, disorganize.* 2. *disband, dissolve, break up, disorganize, fold.*

organized a. 1. ORDERED arranged, systematized, coordinated, methodized, aligned, collated, classified, categorized, *ducks in a row, *got one's act together. SEE ORDERED 2. FORMED developed, created, brought together, founded, originated, established. ANT. 1. *disordered, jumbled, scrambled, disorganized.* 2. *disbanded, dissolved, broken up, disorganized, folded.*

organized crime n. Mafia, Cosa Nostra, mob, underworld, the syndicate, gang, Black Hand.

organized movement n. campaign, drive, crusade, popular front, grassroots movement, lobby, ground swell.

organizer n. coordinator, arranger, developer, creator, originator.

orgasm n. ejaculation, climax, spasm, convulsion, throes, paroxysm, peak, consummation, frenzy, shudder, shiver, quiver, *unfurling waves of pleasure. SEE LOVE, PASSION, SEX

orgasmic a. frenzied, abandoned, exhilarated, rapturous, elated, breathless, overcome, blissful, *on cloud nine, *in seventh heaven, flying, *in orbit. ANT. *unstimulating, frigid.*

orgiastic a. bacchanalian, Dionysian, debauched, wild, abandoned, wanton, saturnalian, unrestrained, out of control. ANT. *reserved, peaceful, chaste.*

Orient n. Far East, Asia, mysterious east, East Indies, Eastern Hemisphere.

orient *v.* **1.** TAKE ONE'S BEARINGS orientate, situate, align, locate, position, fix, face, turn, get the lay of the land. **2.** FAMILIARIZE adjust, acquaint, adapt, acclimate, accustom, reconcile, conform, get used to, habituate, condition.

Oriental *a.* Eastern, Asian, Far Eastern, Asiatic, Chinese, Japanese, Tai, Korean, Indian.

orientation *n.* **1.** BEARINGS placement, fixing, locating, position, coordination. **2.** FAMILIARIZATION adjusting, adapting, conforming, acclimating, accommodation, acculturation. **3.** INTRODUCTION initiation, breaking in, indoctrination, reception, *showing the ropes, welcoming.

orifice *n.* mouth, aperture, vent, opening, hole, lacuna, pore, cavity, slot, crack, gap, hollow.

origin *n.* **1.** INCEPTION source, root, birth, beginning, genesis, commencement, start, fountain. **2.** PARENTAGE ancestry, lineage, pedigree, extraction, descent, line. ANT. *1. end, death, closing.*

original *n.* **1.** PROTOTYPE archetype, model, exemplar, standard, mold, first draft, template. **2.** CHARACTER eccentric, oddball, nonconformist.

original *a.* **1.** FIRST initial, primary, earliest, fundamental, rudimentary, beginning, starting, opening, introductory. **2.** CREATIVE visionary, imaginative, resourceful, inventive, ingenious. **3.** FRESH OR UNIQUE new, groundbreaking, visionary, unusual, unconventional, novel, *cutting edge, *new wave, *new school, *new age, extraordinary, unorthodox, singular. ANT. *1. last, final, ending, ultimate. 2. banal, unoriginal, pedestrian, imitative, trite. 3. old, old hat, tired, dull, banal, hackneyed.*

originality *n.* ingenuity, inventiveness, vision, creativity, freshness, creative spark, imagination, novelty, newness, ingeniousness, genius, *blowing fresh wind through a stale art. "Simply a fresh pair of eyes."—Thomas W. Higginson. ANT. *imitation, plagiarism, orthodoxy, unoriginality.*

originally *adv.* initially, first, in the beginning, at the start, *from the word go.

original sin *n.* disobedience, fall from grace, eating the apple.

originate *v.* start, begin, emerge, spring forth, initiate, commence, inaugurate, generate, arise.

origination *n.* origin, source, birthplace. SEE ORIGIN

originator *n.* creator, inventor, father, mother, innovator, instigator, *spark, catalyst, architect.

ornament *n.* decoration, embellishment, adornment, beautification, dressing, accessory, trimming, garnish, garnishment, festoon, bauble, gewgaw, torsade, tassel, trinket, spangle, knickknack, gimcrack, frill, flounce, filigree, tracery, filet, gilding, fleur-de-lis, fretwork, storiation, fluting, tooling, finial, beading, acanthus, palmette, embossing, molding, inlay, relief work, scroll work, checker-work, diamond work, floriation, astragal, swag, mosaic, wainscotting. SEE DECORATION

ornament *v.* decorate, adorn, dress, garnish, festoon, trim, finish, embellish, beautify.

ornamental *a.* decorative, garnishing, enhancing, adorning, beautifying.

ornate *a.* elaborate, showy, flamboyant, florid, aureate, flowery, busy, fussy, fancy, flashy, gaudy, baroque, rococo, arabesque, rich, lush. ANT. *stark, plain, simple.*

ornery *a.* mean, nasty, ugly, irritable, feisty, surly, cranky, crabby, short-tempered, *short-fused, testy, cantankerous, grouchy, obstinate, stubborn, cussed, mulish, *ornery as an underfed grizzly. ANT. *sweet, good-natured, nice, pleasant.*

orotund *a.* **1.** RESOUNDING sonorous, booming, resonant, projecting, stentorian, reverberating, thundering, powerful, mighty, rich. **2.** GRANDIOSE IN SPEECH pompous, bombastic, fustian, bloated, grandiloquent. SEE ORATION, VOICE ANT. *1. quiet, feeble. 2. simple, understated.*

orphan *n.* waif, foundling, stray, motherless child, fatherless child, castaway.

orphanage *n.* foster home, group home, institution, asylum, refuge.

orphaned *a.* left motherless, left fatherless, deprived, abandoned, forsaken.

ORTHODOX *a.* [ORTH uh DOKS] adhering to a particular standard, convention or doctrine, as in religion or politics; approved, recognized. *Their religious practices are orthodox; they are not at all unusual.* SYN. **1.** ACCEPTED traditional, approved, customary, conventional, sound, standard, established, proper, correct, official, right, recognized. **2.** ULTRACONSERVATIVE OR DOGMATIC strict, straitlaced, purist, puritanical, devout, faithful, fundamental. ANT. *1. unorthodox, radical, unconventional. 2. liberal, flexible, open-to-change, radical, unconventional.*

orthodoxy *n.* **1.** BELIEF faith, creed, credo. **2.**

CONFORMITY compliance, obedience. **3.** CONSERVATISM ultraconservatism, fundamentalism, puritanism, strictness, inflexibility, rigidness. ANT. *2. nonconformity, disobedience, noncompliance. 3. liberalism, flexibility, openmindedness, tolerance.*

Oscar *n.* Academy award, statuette.

oscillate *v.* **1.** MOVE BACK AND FORTH swing, alternate, vibrate, pulsate, librate. **2.** BE INDECISIVE vacillate, fluctuate, waver, hem and haw, change one's mind, do an about-face, equivocate, be on the fence, blow hot and cold, shilly-shally. ANT. *2. decide, resolve, choose.*

oscillation *n.* **1.** MOVING BACK AND FORTH swinging, alternating, vibrating, vibration, pulsating, pulsation, librating. **2.** INDECISION vacillation, wavering, hemming and hawing, changing one's mind, equivocating, blowing hot and cold, shilly-shallying, fickleness, fence-sitting. ANT. *2. decisiveness, settling, resolving.*

osmose *v.* diffuse, dissolve, mix, undergo osmosis.

osmosis *n.* diffusion, absorption, mixing, comixing, blending, comingling, dissolving.

ossified *a.* hardened, hard, rigid, stiffened, bony.

ossuary *n.* urn, receptacle, vault.

OSTENSIBLE *a.* [uh STEN suh bul] seeming or outwardly apparent but possibly misleading. *The Peeping Tom's ostensible motivation was to make money washing windows.* SYN. seeming, apparent, professed, outward, evident, manifest, pretended, external, assumed, implied, inferred.

ostentation *n.* showiness, pretentiousness, exhibitionism, pomp, display, gloss, affectation, flashiness, flamboyance, swank, putting on airs, immodesty, *glitz, foppery, flaunting. ANT. *modesty, plainness, inconspicuous, humbleness, restraint, understatement, blending into the woodwork.*

OSTENTATIOUS *a.* [AWS ten TAY shus] showiness, pretentiousness, overly ornate. *Her ostentatious finery drew stares as she entered the room.* SYN. showy, pretentious, pompous, affected, flashy, flamboyant, swank, immodest, grandiose, ornate, gaudy, glittery, *glitzy, foppish, garish, spotlight-seeking, *showboating. ANT. *understated, subtle, modest.*

ostracism *n.* banishment, exclusion, exile, excommunication, ejection, rejection, expulsion, shunning, blackballing, relegation, disgrace. ANT. *inclusion, acceptance, welcoming, embracing.*

OSTRACIZE *v.* [AWS truh SIZE] to banish, bar or shun. *Society tends to ostracize nonconformists.* SYN. banish, bar, shun, exclude, eject, isolate, excommunicate, blackball, relegate, shut out, oust, *give the cold shoulder, cast out, *freeze out, blacklist. ANT. *include, embrace, welcome, accept.*

other *a.* **1.** DIFFERENT dissimilar, distinct, separate, unrelated, disparate, variant. **2.** ADDITIONAL extra, further, supplementary, more, another. ANT. *1. same, alike, similar. 2. fewer, less.*

otherwise *adv.* **1.** IN ANOTHER WAY differently. **2.** UNDER DIFFERENT CIRCUMSTANCES elsewise, if not, on the other hand.

otherworldly *a.* alien, extraterrestrial, unearthly, unworldly, ethereal, mystical, transcendent, spiritual, supernatural, out of this world, heavenly.

otiose *a.* **1.** LAZY idle, indolent, slothful, *do-nothing. **2.** USELESS ineffective, futile, worthless, impotent, powerless. ANT. *1. ambitious, active, busy, *go-getting. 2. effective, powerful, useful.*

ottoman *n.* footstool, hassock, divan.

ought *v.* should, is fitting, is natural, behoove.

oust *v.* eject, remove, throw out, expel, banish, depose, dismiss, overthrow, unseat, evict, discharge, *send packing, *show the door, *give the boot, *bounce. ANT. *install, induct, admit.*

ouster *n.* ejection, removal, expulsion, eviction, banishment, dismissal, discharge, overthrow. ANT. *installment, admittance, induction.*

out *a.* **1.** ABSENT away, elsewhere, gone, not here. **2.** EXTINGUISHED extinct, dead, expired, inoperable, finished, over, done. **3.** OUTMODED obsolete, old-fashioned, passé, out-of-date. **4.** UNCONSCIOUS out cold, *out like a light, *down for the count, comatose, anesthetized. ANT. *1. in, here, present. 2. alive, functioning, living and breathing. 3. in, *cutting edge, newfangled, modern. 4. conscious, alert, awake.*

out *n.* alibi, escape, excuse, explanation, loophole, dodge.

out *v.* *Sl.* unmask, reveal, *bring out of the closet, disclose, bring out into the open, tip off, publicize, announce, unburden oneself, *blow the whistle on, blab, tattle, expose. ANT. *keep secret, keep hush-hush, keep in the closet.*

outage *n.* blackout, brownout, power failure.

out-and-out *a.* outright, complete, thorough,

total, utter, absolute, arrant, unmitigated, flagrant, blatant, dyed-in-the-wool, downright.

outback n. back country, hinterland, wilderness, wilds, *boonies, *sticks, howling wilderness, desert, barrens, wasteland. SEE DESERT

outbreak n. **1.** DISEASE SPREAD epidemic, pandemic, manifestation, contagion. **2.** OUTBURST eruption, flare up, upheaval, uproar. **3.** CIVIL DISCONTENT riot, insurrection, revolt, uprising, mutiny.

outbound a. outward bound, outgoing, out flowing, departing, leaving. ANT. inbound, coming in, incoming, arriving.

outbuilding n. auxiliary building, shed, shack, barn, outhouse.

outburst n. eruption, explosion, outbreak, outpouring, flare-up, outcry.

outcast n. pariah, exile, castaway, outsider, derelict, untouchable, vagabond, outlaw, orphan, refugee, runaway, *reject.

outcast a. driven out, banned, shunned, cast out, rejected, exiled, ostracized.

outclass v. surpass, outperform, outshine, outdo, outdistance, better, eclipse, overshadow, outmuscle, dwarf, dominate, *leave in the dust, beat, defeat, rise above, *smoke the competition, outhustle, *leave others swirling in one's wake. SEE OUTDO

out of the closet a. out, exposed, revealed, disclosed, out into the open, divulged, brought to light, uncovered, unveiled.

out cold a. unconscious, *down for the count, anesthetized. SEE OUT

outcome n. result, consequence, aftermath, end, upshot, *payoff, effect, aftermath, wake, repercussion.

outcrop n. rock shelf, mantel, protrusion, obtrusion, bedrock, *knuckle of rock.

outcry n. clamor, uproar, protest, outburst, exclamation, shout, scream, cry, hue and cry, howl, holler, hullabaloo.

outdated a. obsolete, old, antiquated. SEE OLD-FASHIONED

outdistance v. outrun, outmuscle, outdo, outclass, surpass, overtake, leave behind, *leave in the dust, *smoke the competition. SEE OUTDO

outdo v. outperform, outshine, outdistance, outmuscle, excel, eclipse, dwarf the competition, *leave others swirling in one's wake, dominate, beat, defeat, run circles around, do one better, out-Herod Herod.

outdoor a. out-of-doors, outside, open-air, out in the open, alfresco.

outdoorsman n. sportsman, woodsman, naturalist, environmentalist, camper, hunter, fisherman, trapper, adventurer.

outer a. outside, external, exterior, outlying, peripheral, outward, remote, fringe, extrinsic. ANT. inner, intrinsic, proximal.

outermost a. outer, outlying, peripheral, outmost, furthest out, remote, fringe. ANT. innermost.

outer space n. universe, cosmos, space, infinity, heavens, interstellar space, intergalactic space, void, vacuum, firmament, *great beyond, *wild blue yonder, all creation, macrocosm, nebulous void, galactic realm, solar system. SEE COMET, GALAXY, MILKY WAY, MOON, PLANET, STAR, SUN, UNIVERSE

outfield n. playing field, left field, right field, center field, warning track, *deep, *shallow left, *shallow right. SEE BASEBALL

outfit n. rig, gear, kit, trappings, equipment, accoutrements, trousseau, getup, turnout, garb, attire, *togs, duds. SEE CLOTHING, SUIT **2.** GROUP company, unit, crew, business, enterprise, battalion, troop, corps, detachment.

outfit v. rig, fit out, turn out, equip, provision, furnish, supply, appoint.

outflank v. outmaneuver, outfox, outwit, thwart.

outflow n. efflux, flow, effluence, effusion, outpouring, outwelling, emanation, gush, stream, spring.

out-front a. straight, *on the level, *on the square, honest, up front.

outfox v. outwit, outsmart, outguess, *run circles around, outdistance.

outgo n. **1.** EXPENDITURE expenses, bills, outlay, disbursement, cost. ANT. income, profit, earnings.

outgo v. outdistance, outhustle, outrun. SEE OUTDO

outgoing a. **1.** GREGARIOUS sociable, extroverted, friendly, amiable, congenial, affable, convivial, companionable, unreserved. SEE FRIENDLY **2.** OUTBOUND departing, leaving. ANT. **1.** introverted, reserved, solitary, aloof. **2.** incoming, inbound.

outgrowth n. product, byproduct, offshoot, *spinoff, offspring, result, consequence, upshot, aftermath.

outhouse n. privy, toilet, latrine, backhouse, outbuilding, *necessary, *crapper.

outing n. excursion, trip, expedition, *spin,

jaunt, junket, ride, drive, walk, hike, stroll.

outlandish *a.* bizarre, weird, strange, odd, queer, freakish, out of the ordinary, alien, quaint, exotic, wild, peculiar, *far-out. ANT. *ordinary, everyday, usual.*

outlast *v.* outlive, prevail, hold out, endure, stand the test of time, survive, outdistance. SEE OUTDO

outlaw *n.* criminal, felon, *bad guy, desperado, fugitive, brigand, highwayman, crook, robber, bandit, killer, gunman.

outlaw *v.* ban, stop, prohibit, bar, proscribe, forbid, make illegal, disallow, restrict, limit. ANT. *legalize, allow.*

outlay *n.* expenditure, expense, disbursement, cost, outgo, charge, payment, price, fee. ANT. *income, gain, profit.*

outlet *n.* exit, opening, passage, port, vent, mouth, spout, egress, release, channel, race, conduit. ANT. *entrance, ingress, intake.*

outline *n.* **1.** PROFILE form, configuration, shape, contour, silhouette, figure. **2.** SYNOPSIS breakdown, *rundown, plan, draft, framework, rough draft, sketch, *thumbnail sketch.

outline *v.* rough out, sketch, delineate, summarize, draft, abstract, synopsize, frame.

outlive *v.* SEE OUTLAST

outlook *n.* **1.** LOOKOUT observation post, observation tower. **2.** VIEW vista, panorama, sweep, perspective. **3.** ATTITUDE point of view, *mind-set, viewpoint, standpoint, perspective, frame of mind, interpretation. **4.** PROSPECT expectation, hope, anticipation, forecast, future, horizon, probability.

outlying *a.* remote, distant, peripheral, frontier, rural, suburban, out-of-the-way, secluded, isolated, outer, backcountry, God-forsaken. ANT. *nearby, neighboring, next-door.*

outmoded *a.* antiquated, obsolete, outdated, old-fashioned, displaced, dated, passé, horse and buggy, old school. ANT. *new, newfangled, *cutting edge.*

output *n.* production, productivity, yield, harvest, quantity, work, efficiency, turnout, product, amount.

outrage *n.* **1.** ATROCITY vicious act, violent act, crime, act of savagery, evil, abomination, monstrosity, disgrace, horror, barbarity, wrong. **2.** INSULT offense, affront, blow, *slap in the face, indignity, *put down, injury, abuse. **3.** ANGER fury, indignation, wrath, rage, *spitting rage. SEE ANGER

outrage *v.* enrage, anger, incense, infuriate, fill with wrath, madden, *make one's blood

boil, provoke, gall, affront, insult, offend. ANT. *pacify, tickle, delight.*

outrageous *a.* **1.** ATROCIOUS monstrous, vicious, savage, criminal, evil, abominable, disgraceful, inhuman, barbaric, wrong, unspeakable, heinous, wicked. **2.** UNREASONABLE excessive, ridiculous, preposterous, exorbitant, unconscionable, immoderate, uncalled for, unrestrained. ANT. *1. normal, standard. 2. reasonable, within reason, fair, moderate.*

outright *a.* out-and-out, downright, complete, total, whole, entire, wholesale, unqualified, unmitigated. ANT. *partial.*

outside *n.* outdoors, exterior, face, facade, front, surface, veneer, shell, covering.

outside *a.* **1.** EXTERIOR outer, external, surface, extrinsic, superficial. **2.** SLIGHT marginal, slim, remote, unlikely, faint, small. ANT. *1. inside, internal, intrinsic. 2. probable, certain.*

outsider *n.* stranger, alien, foreigner, interloper, *fifth wheel.

outspoken *a.* vocal, unreserved, frank, blunt, straightforward, candid, plainspoken, uninhibited, unrestrained, *not backwards about coming forward. ANT. *shy, reticent, reserved, tactful.*

outstanding *a.* **1.** EXCEPTIONAL extraordinary, superior, distinguished, superb, excellent, standout, great, phenomenal, remarkable, impressive, marvelous, prominent, renowned, noteworthy, sensational, *out of this world. **2.** UNRESOLVED overdue, unpaid, unsettled, due, owing, in arrears. ANT. *1. ordinary, mediocre, so-so, fair, poor. 2. paid, settled.*

outward *a.* outer, outside, external, exterior, surface, superficial, visible, apparent, evident. ANT. *inward, internal.*

outwardly *adv.* apparently, evidently, superficially, visibly, ostensibly, to the eye. ANT. *inwardly, secretly.*

outweigh *v.* surpass, transcend, exceed, dominate, take precedence, overshadow, eclipse, override, *tip the scales, overrule.

outwit *v.* outsmart, outfox, outthink, beat, *put one over on, *get the better of, outdo, outshine, fool, trick, euchre.

oval *a.* elliptical, ovoid, oviform, egg-shaped.

ovation *n.* applause, cheers, clapping, *hand, outburst, acclamation, laudation, tribute, curtain call, encore. ANT. *boos, *Bronx cheer.*

over *a.* finished, done, completed, closed, terminated, concluded, ended. ANT. *beginning, opening, commencing.*

over *adv.* above, overhead, aloft, high. ANT. *below, earthward.*

overabundance *a.* excess, glut, surplus, overflow, overkill, plethora, overage, spate, flood, too much, superfluity. ANT. *shortage, dearth.*

overall *a.* general, complete, from end to end, blanket, sweeping, comprehensive, long-range.

overbearing *a.* arrogant, domineering, dictatorial, high and mighty, supercilious, lordly, high-handed, tyrannical, disdainful, pompous, bossy, imperious. ANT. *shy, humble, modest, deferential.*

overblown *a.* excessive, exaggerated, inflated, puffed up, overdone, overworked, immoderate, disproportionate. ANT. *modest, moderate.*

overcast *a.* cloudy, foggy, murky, *smoggy, hazy, gray, dreary, gloomy, sunless, leaden. SEE CLOUD, CLOUDY

overcome *v.* defeat, beat, vanquish, conquer, subdue, *get the better of, triumph over, rise above, win, outlast, survive, weather, prevail over, surmount.

overconfident *a.* arrogant, cocky, cocksure, swaggering, strutting, boastful, egotistical, pompous, headed for a fall, complacent, smug, *full of oneself. ANT. *insecure, unsure, self-doubting.*

overflow *v.* spill over, slop over, flood, run over, deluge, drown, swamp, brim, gush, cascade, inundate, engulf.

overhaul *v.* restore, repair, service, fix, recondition, revamp, rebuild, check, inspect.

overhead *n.* expenses, costs, outlay, upkeep, disbursement.

overjoyed *a.* ecstatic, joyous, jubilant, thrilled, happy, elated, euphoric, delirious, *tickled, rapturous. ANT. *depressed, miserable, *bummed out.*

overlook *v.* **1.** DISREGARD neglect, pass over, ignore, fail to notice, miss, slight, omit, forget. **2.** EXCUSE *look the other way, disregard, *wink at, let go, let ride, make allowances for, condone, ignore. **3.** LOOK DOWN UPON front on, tower above, have a view of.

overly *adv.* excessively, too, exceedingly, unduly, inordinately, immoderately. ANT. *insufficiently, inadequately.*

overpower *v.* overcome, beat, crush, overwhelm, subdue, get the upper hand, get the better of, conquer, vanquish, master, *outmuscle, immobilize, dominate. ANT. *give in, *say uncle, surrender.*

overrated *a.* overvalued, overesteemed, overestimated, *blown out of proportion, overpraised, exaggerated, oversold, puffed up, *hyped.

override *v.* surpass, prevail over, take precedence, overrule, predominate, outweigh, supersede, cancel.

overrule *v.* rule against, disallow, override, overturn, annul, reverse, countermand, nullify, invalidate.

overrun *v.* infest, swarm over, invade, spread over, permeate, cover, saturate, inundate, engulf, choke.

oversee *v.* supervise, manage, watch over, run, look after, direct, operate, boss, govern, rule, regulate, administer.

overshadow *v.* eclipse, dwarf, tower over, outshine, outclass, outdo, dominate, *stand head and shoulders above, *leave in one's wake, *steal the spotlight/limelight.

oversight *n.* omission, mistake, negligence, carelessness, inattention, lapse, slip, blunder, slight, slackness.

overstate *v.* exaggerate, inflate, *blow out of proportion, magnify, embroider, hyperbolize, *hype, embellish, play up. ANT. *downplay, understate.*

overt *a.* open, unconcealed, undisguised, obvious, patent, manifest, plain to see, bald, naked, explicit. ANT. *covert, undercover, concealed.*

overtake *v.* pass, *leave swirling in one's wake, catch up to, outdistance, leave in the dust, reach, gain on, *blow one's doors off. ANT. *fall behind, lag behind, drop back.*

overthrow *v.* defeat, vanquish, conquer, remove from power, unseat, unhorse, dethrone, depose, overcome, topple, bring down, overpower.

overture *n.* proposal, offer, introduction, opening, bid, tender, presentation, suggestion, approach.

overturn *v.* **1.** CAPSIZE turn over, knock over, flip, upset, tip, topple, upend. **2.** DEFEAT conquer, vanquish, overthrow, overpower.

overview *n.* survey. SEE REVIEW

overweening *a.* arrogant, proud, cocky, cocksure, overconfident, presumptuous, haughty, disdainful, overbearing, imperious. ANT. *modest, quiet, timid.*

overweight *a.* fat, obese, roly-poly, heavy, corpulent, stout, plump, rotund, blubbery, hefty. ANT. *anorexic, skeletal, emaciated.*

overwhelm *v.* **1.** BURY flood, drown, inundate, swamp, engulf, crush, smother, overpower, overflow. **2.** OVERCOME crush, devastate, overpower, *blow away, stun, *bowl over, floor, paralyze, stagger, *knock off one's feet, dumbfound.

overwhelming *a.* overpowering, staggering, crushing, devastating, stunning, paralyzing, dumbfounding, irresistible, awe-inspiring.

overwrought *a.* nervous, excited, agitated, overexcited, *wired, *strung out, *hyper, worked up, in a dither, wound up, riled. ANT. *relaxed, calm, tranquil.*

owe *v.* be in debt, be bound, be under obligation, be in arrears, have a debt to pay.

own *v.* **1.** POSSESS have, hold, keep, retain, have the rights to. **2.** ADMIT acknowledge, allow, concede, confess, grant, recognize, come clean.

owner *n.* proprietor, possessor, landlord, holder, titleholder, keeper, deed holder.

P

pace n. **1.** STEP gait, walk, run, stride, carriage. **2.** SPEED velocity, clip, rate, momentum, progress.

pace v. walk back and forth, *wear a rut in the carpet. SEE WALK

pacesetter n. pacemaker, leader, bellwether, pacer.

pacific a. peaceful, appeasing, peace-making, peace-loving, dove-like, gentle, tranquil, serene. ANT. *hawk-like, pugancious, belligerent.*

PACIFIST n. [PAS uh fist] one who refuses to use force or violence; a peace lover. *She was a dyed-in-the-wool pacifist who believed in peaceful resistance.* SYN. peace-lover, dove, peacemaker, appeaser, *bridge-builder, concilitator, *peacenik, *lover not a figher, antiwar demonstrator, passive resistor. ANT. *hawk, fighter, warmonger.*

pacify v. appease, mollify, quiet, lull, soothe, calm, tranquilize, placate, assuage, cool, soften. ANT. *enrage, agitate, infuriate.*

pack n. **1.** PACKAGE parcel, load, bundle, packet, load, knapsack, bale. **2.** BUNCH group, mass, collection, crowd, throng, number, mob, flock, herd.

pack v. load, fill, stuff, cram, jam, stow, insert, pile, crowd, compress, ram.

package n. pack, parcel, box, carton, container, bundle, bale, receptacle.

packed a. full, stuffed, crammed, jammed, compressed, chock-full, chock-a-block, filled, overflowing, *bursting at the seams, wall-to-wall, standing room only. ANT. *empty, vacant.*

packet n. parcel, package, bundle, bale, envelope, sheaf.

pact n. agreement, compact, covenant, treaty, contract, understanding, alliance, league, arrangement, deal.

pad n. **1.** CUSHION pillow, mat, padding, bolster. **2.** WRITING TABLET notepad, notebook, scratch pad, memo pad.

pad v. **1.** STROLL saunter. SEE WALK **2.** FILL OUT stretch, expand, protract, elaborate.

paddle n. oar, blade, scull, pole.

paddle v. row, scull, oar, pole.

padre n. father, priest, chaplain, parson, minister, cleric.

pagan n. heathen, nonbeliever, infidel, atheist, idolater. SEE RELIGION

page n. attendant, servant, errand-runner, messenger, *gopher.

pageant n. exhibition, parade, spectacle, show, extravaganza, display, procession, gala, presentation.

pageantry n. exhibition, parade, spectacle, show, extravaganza, display, procession, gala, grandeur, splendor, festivity, glitter, ostentation, pomp.

pager n. *beeper, receiver, communication device.

pagoda n. Buddhist tower, memorial, shrine, temple.

pain n. **1.** PHYSICAL HURT ache, suffering, agony, discomfort, sensation, irritation, torture, torment, soreness, tenderness, smarting, twinge, pang, spasm, throbbing, stabbing, burning, sharp pain, chafing, clamping, cramping, searing pain, stitch. **2.** MENTAL ANGUISH distress, anguish, misery, torment, anxiety, worry, grief, woe, heartache, travail. **3.** Sl. PAIN IN THE NECK pest, bother, headache, annoyance, trouble, nuisance. ANT. *ease, comfort, relief.*

WORD FIND

PHYSICAL PAIN

facial expressions: wince, grimace, teeth-gritting, teeth-clamping, snarl of agony, cringe, clamp eyes shut, pout, wounded look in the eyes, face drawn and pinched, pale, blanched, twisted/contorted in pain, brows furrowed deeply

body language: writhing, thrashing, stiffening, convulsing, throes, doubling over, squirming, cringing, balling fists, gulping, recoiling, rocking in fetal position

pain v. hurt, smart, sting, bother, irritate, harm, excruciate, distress, wound, torture, torment, afflict, annoy.

painful a. hurtful, agonizing, excruciating, torturous, sore, smarting, distressing, tender, aching, stinging, biting, searing, sharp, uncomfortable, unpleasant, disagreeable, difficult, grievous, trying. ANT. *comfortable, delightful, enjoyable.*

painkiller n. analgesic, anesthetic, palliative, anodyne, morphine, opiate. SEE MEDICINE

painstaking a. thorough, demanding, exacting, meticulous, careful, precise, fussy, strict, *persnickety, assiduous, conscientious, *going the extra mile. ANT. *slack, negligent, lazy.*

paint n. pigment, dye, coloring, tint, oil paint,

latex paint, acrylic, enamel, stain, varnish, primer.

paint *v.* coat, color, tint, daub, dye, brush on, stipple, wash, stain, varnish, prime.

painter *n.* artist, portrait artist, watercolorist, old master.

painting *n.* picture, portrait, landscape, depiction, illustration, work of art, composition, masterpiece, watercolor, still life, fresco, mural, canvas, oil. "Silent poetry."—Simonedes. "A poem without words."—Confucius. "The art of protecting flat surfaces from the weather and exposing them to the critic."—Ambrose Bierce. SEE ART

pair *n.* couple, twosome, duo, couplet, matched set, twins, combo, two of a kind.

pair *v.* match, mate, couple, yoke, marry, team.

pajamas *n.* PJs, *jammies, bedclothes, *nightie.

pal *n.* buddy, chum, friend, *bro, alter ego, sidekick, crony, comrade, companion, amigo, *partner in crime.

palace *n.* king's residence, castle, mansion, royal home, manor, alcazar, chateau. SEE CASTLE

palatable *a.* edible, agreeable, acceptable, potable. ANT. *distasteful.*

palatial *a.* magnificent, luxurious, rich, ornate, majestic, grand, sumptuous, stately, huge, monumental, imposing, noble. ANT. *humble, mean, plain, poor.*

pale *v.* whiten, blanch, turn white. ANT. *flush, bloom, blush.*

pale *a.* colorless, blanched, white, bloodless, pallid, wan, cadaverous, ashen, sallow, sickly, lackluster. ANT. *ruddy, rosy, deeply-hued.*

pall *n.* cloud, smoke, covering, cloak, gloom, shadow, darkness, shroud, black cloth, spirit of depression, spirit of desolation.

pall *v.* bore, cloy, become tiresome, become dull, satiate, tire, weary, jade.

pallid *a.* pale, faint, wan, sallow, ashen, anemic, white, colorless, sickly, pasty. ANT. *glowing, flushed, rosy, ruddy.*

pallor *n.* paleness, whiteness, colorlessness, wanness, sallowness, pastiness, lack of color. ANT. *glow, ruddiness.*

PALPABLE *a.* [PAL puh bul] that which can be physically touched or felt, tangible, perceivable. *She had no palpable evidence of conspiracy, only her own suspicions.* SYN. perceivable, tangible, touchable, physical, solid, real, obvious, evident, visible, conspicuous, discernible, plain. ANT. *imperceptible, spiritual, abstract, invisible.*

palpitate *v.* flutter, throb, beat, pound, pulsate, quiver, quaver, shake, twitter, pump, hammer.

paltry *a.* trifling, worthless, measly, insignificant, petty, cheap, slight, piddling, meager, inconsequential, pitiful. ANT. *considerable, significant.*

pamper *v.* indulge, overindulge, coddle, mollycoddle, spoil, baby, cater to, *wait on hand and foot, *make things cushy for.

pamphlet *n.* booklet, brochure, circular, leaflet, bill, *flier, book, tract.

PANACEA *n.* [PAN us SEE uh] cure-all. *Scientists are still looking for a panacea to stop aging.* SYN. cure-all, catholicon, remedy, *fix-all, *magic bullet, elixir, nostrum, magic potion.

PANACHE *n.* [puh NASH] a dashing or flamboyant style. *The dancer had great panache.* SYN. dashing manner, flamboyance, style, self-confidence, razzle-dazzle, flair, jauntiness, spirit, élan, je ne sais quoi.

pancake *n.* flapjack, batter cake, griddle cake, crepe, blintz, fritter.

pandemonium *n.* disorder, chaos, uproar, turmoil, confusion, bedlam, anarchy, *hullabaloo, tumult, ruckus. ANT. *peace, calm, order.*

pander *v.* cater to, satisfy, *suck up to, indulge, gratify, attend, *play up to, serve, humor.

panel *n.* **1.** BOARD sheet, plywood, plank, wall, partition, section, divider. **2.** COMMITTEE council, jury, review board, group, round table, conference, tribunal.

pang *n.* pain, spasm, twinge, ache, stab, throe, twitch, distress, discomfort, misgiving, anguish.

panhandle *v.* *bum, cadge, *hit up, scrounge. SEE BEG

panic *n.* terror, fear, alarm, fright, hysteria, loss of composure, *shakes, frenzy, consternation, *cold sweat, *sweating bullets, *rush of adrenalin. SEE FEAR, FEARFUL

panic *v.* be overcome with fear, *break out in a cold sweat, become hysterical, become paralyzed with fear, freeze up, become unnerved, *sweat bullets, soil one's drawers, become adrenalized, lose control, *lose it, be filled with a sense of impending doom. ANT. *relax, calm, breathe easy.* SEE FEAR

panic disorder *n.* panic attack, anxiety attack, hyperventilation, psychological disorder.

panorama *n.* scene, view, picture, landscape, sweep, perspective, vista, range, stretch, spectacle.

panoramic *a.* sweeping, far-ranging, far-reaching, extensive, bird's-eye, broad, all-encompassing. ANT. *limited, short-sighted, focused.*

pant *v.* gasp, breathe, puff, blow, wheeze, huff, huff and puff.

pantheon *n.* temple.

panther *n.* leopard, mountaion lion, cougar, puma, cat.

panties *n.* underwear, undies, underpants, briefs.

pantomime *v.* mime, act out, gesture, communicate nonverbally, use body language.

pantry *n.* larder, room, closet, store room, buttery, cupboard.

pants *n.* trousers, breeches, pantaloons, jeans, dungarees, slacks, *britches, overalls, *cords, corduroys, *Levis.

WORD FIND
army work pants: fatigues
athletic: sweat pants, *sweats
bullfighter's: toreador pants
calf-length, slitted, tight-fitting: capri pants
cowboy leggings: chaps
Indian loincloth-like with broad legs tapering to ankles: dhoti
jockey: jodhpurs
khaki-colored sport pants: chinos
knee-lengths: surfers, *clamdiggers
leather: buckskins
1960s favorites: bell-bottoms, hip huggers
puffy pants gathered at waist and ankles: harem pants
shorts: Bermuda shorts, *cutoffs, *hot pants, lederhosen
skirtlike pants of various lengths: culottes
straight-cut and tight: stovepipe pants
straight-cut, cuffed, bike-riding pants of the 1940s and 1950s: pedal pushers
stretch pants: spandex pants

pantywaist *n.* sissy, *wimp, *wuss, *wussy, crybaby.

paparazzi *n.* photographers, photojournalists, freelance photographers, celebrity stalkers.

paper *n.* **1.** SHEET piece, stationery, letterhead, parchment, note paper, vellum, bond, onion skin, construction paper. **2.** DOCUMENT certificate, instrument, title, credentials, affidavit, deed, contract, charter, license, warrant. **3.** SEE NEWSPAPER **4.** ESSAY dissertation, thesis, composition, article, treatise, report, monograph, study.

par *n.* average, standard, norm, usual, equal footing, mean, parity, equality.

parable *n.* story, allegory, morality play, fable, tale.

parade *n.* procession, march, train, cavalcade, promenade, column, pageant, spectacle, autocade, motorcade, exhibition.

PARADIGM *n.* [PAIR uh dime] a model or example serving as a base for instruction. *The real estate magnate's investment strategy serves as a paradigm of successful wealth-building.* SYN. model, example, pattern, standard, archetype, ideal, original, prototype, exemplar, standard, classic example.

paradise *n.* heaven on earth, heaven, utopia, Shangri-la, *cloud nine, *Eden, bliss, rapture, joy, euphoria.

PARADOX *n.* [PAR uh DAWKS] a contradictory statement that is nevertheless true. *It was a paradox, the more money he made, the less happy he grew.* SYN. contradiction, self-contradiction, incongruity, inconsistency, anomaly, enigma, reverse, puzzle.

PARAGON *n.* [PAR uh gawn] a model of excellence. *Stephen King is a paragon of the horror fiction genre.* SYN. model, exemplar, standard, ideal, paradigm, archetype, prototype, pattern, role model, cream of the crop, crème de la crème.

parallel *n.* analogy, correspondence, match, twin, mirror image, counterpart, equal, equivalent, duplicate, kin.

parallel *v.* mirror, match, equal, equate, agree, correspond, double, imitate, approximate.

parallel *a.* **1.** SIDE-BY-SIDE aligned, abreast, alongside. **2.** SIMILAR correspondent, matching, alike, akin, analogous. ANT. *1. perpendicular. 2. dissimilar.*

paralysis *n.* immobility, incapacitation, palsy, disability, prostration, loss of sensation, spinal cord damage, insensitivity.

WORD FIND
complete from neck down: quadriplegia
lower half of body: paraplegia

paralyze *v.* immobilize, incapacitate, disable, cripple, freeze, prostrate, debilitate, numb, anesthetize, *put out of commission.

paramedic *n.* emergency medical technician, EMT, ambulance attendant, medical assistant. SEE HOSPITAL, MEDICINE

paramount *a.* dominant, supreme, main, foremost, chief, leading, outstanding, principal, prime, highest ranking. ANT. *minor, secondary, least.*

paramour *n.* lover, mistress, concubine, courtesan, kept woman, suitor, swain, *stud, Don Juan, Casanova, beau, boyfriend, gigolo.

paranoia n. psychosis, delusions, mental disorder, psychiatric disorder, mental illness, delusions of persecution, delusions of grandeur, distrust, suspicion, wariness.

paranoid a. psychotic, mentally ill, delusional, feeling persecuted, suffering from delusions of grandeur, psychopathic, suspicious, distrusting, wary. ANT. *trusting.*

paranormal a. supernatural, metaphysical, occult, beyond explantion, mysterious. ANT. *mundane.*

parapet n. barricade, barrier, breastwork. SEE CASTLE

paraphernalia n. equipment, gear, accoutrements, tackle, stuff, things, apparatus, instruments, rigging, belongings, effects.

paraphrase v. reword, restate, transcribe, translate, rephrase, interpret, rehash, repeat roughly, summarize, abridge.

parasite n. leech, bloodsucker, *freeloader, *sponge, dependant, *moocher.

parcel n. 1. PACKAGE packet, pack, bundle, box, carton, bale. 2. PLOT OF LAND tract, acreage, lot, division.

parcel v. apportion, dole, divide, mete, allot, distribute, *divvy up.

parched a. arid, dry, dried up, *dry as a bone, *dry as a fossil, roasted, dehydrated, withered, wilted, scorched, evaporated, desiccated, baked. ANT. *wet, watery, waterlogged, saturated.*

pardon n. forgiveness, clemency, amnesty, reprieve, release, grace, excusal, acquittal, lenience, mercy, forbearance, exemption. ANT. *condemnation, damnation, punishment.*

pardon v. forgive, condone, excuse, indulge, *look the other way, *wink at, absolve, overlook, tolerate, acquit, let off, exonerate, exculpate. ANT. *punish, condemn, damn.*

pare v. trim, peel, skin, clip, crop, cut down, cut back, decrease, slash, curtail. ANT. *increase.*

parent n. mother, father, nurturer, sire, creator, folks, progenitor, *old man, *old lady, genitor, procreator, forerunner, predecessor, ancestor, begetter, author, inventor, architect. "The bones on which children cut their teeth."—Peter Ustinov. SEE FATHER, MOTHER

pariah n. outcast, *reject, castaway, exile, refugee, Ishmael, expatriate, undesirable, leper, untouchable.

parish n. parishioners, congregation, churchgoers, fold, assembly, flock, brethren, archdiocese, diocese, church, district.

parity n. equality, equivalence, balance, sameness, evenness, par, likeness, symmetry, uniformity, affinity. ANT. *inequality, disparity.*

park n. common, green, village green, promenade, garden, square, playground, grounds, quad, plaza.

parlance n. language, idiom, lingo, speech, tongue, vernacular, talk, wording, ideolect.

parlay v. bet, wager, invent.

parliament n. legislature, congress, assembly, House of Lords, House of Commons. SEE GOVERNMENT

parlor n. living room, sitting room, front room, drawing room, salon.

PAROCHIAL a. [puh ROH kee ul] limited in scope, narrow, provincial. *She had a parochial perspective and cared little about the larger view.* SYN. limited, narrow, provincial, restricted, local, regional, small-town, insular, myopic, prejudiced. ANT. *worldly, national, international, broad.*

PARODY n. [PAR uh dee] a satirical or humorous imitation of a literary or musical work. *The canine sex magazine,* Playdog, *was a parody of* Playboy. SYN. imitation, lampoon, takeoff, mockery, satire, spoof, *send-up, burlesque, mimicry, travesty.

parody v. imitate, mock, mimic, ape, lampoon, caricature, satirize, ridicule, *take off on, send up, burlesque.

parole n. release, early release, trial release.

paroxysm n. convulsion, spasm, outburst, seizure, attack, flareup, fit, eruption, throe, spell.

parrot v. echo, repeat, mimic, imitate, copy, ape.

parry v. ward off, deflect, turn aside, fend off, defend against, avert, sidestep, dodge, elude.

PARSIMONIOUS a. [PAR suh MOH nee us] miserly, stingy. *The parsimonious old fool recycled everything.* SYN. miserly, stingy, cheap, thrifty, penny-pinching, nickel-squeezing, close, *tightfisted, sparing, economical, frugal. ANT. *generous, giving, charitable, free-spending.*

parson n. cleric, rector, clergyman, minister, preacher, pastor, man of the cloth.

part n. 1. PIECE component, portion, unit, ingredient, constituent, element, section, division, segment, fraction, department. 2. ROLE function, job, duty, responsibility, involvement. 3. ACTING ROLE character, bit part, lead, supporting role. ANT. *1. whole, total, aggregate.*

part v. 1. DIVIDE separate, disunite, split, sever, cleave, dissect, break, splay, branch out. 2. LEAVE go, depart, withdraw, break away, go separate ways, take one's leave, *split.

partake v. take part, participate, join in, share in, eat, *have a taste, consume.

partial a. **1.** INCOMPLETE limited, fragmentary, deficient, unfinished, halfway. **2.** BIASED prejudiced, one-sided, partisan, discriminatory, unbalanced, unfair, unjust. ANT. *1. complete, whole. 2. fair, impartial, neutral, objective.*

partiality n. bias, prejudice, favoritism, preference, one-sidedness, unfairness, leaning, partisanship, predilection, predisposition, weakness, affinity, fondness, liking. ANT. *impartiality, objectivity, fairness.*

partially adv. partly, incompletely, somewhat, halfway.

participant n. member, contributor, accessory, player, actor, partaker, a party to.

participate v. take part, join in, partake, be a party to, contribute, engage in, play, have a hand in. ANT. *forego, beg off.*

particle n. bit, speck, piece, grain, fleck, atom, molecule, whit, mote, fragment, dot, trace, iota.

particular a. **1.** SPECIFIC exact, precise, single, special, distinct, definite, peculiar, lone, express. **2.** FUSSY demanding, exacting, critical, finicky, picky, *persnickety, hard to please, overparticular. ANT. *1. general, unspecified. 2. unparticular, easy to please, careless.*

particularly adv. specifically, especially, notably, distinctly, markedly, exceptionally, explicitly, expressly.

partisan n. adherent, party member, supporter, devotee, follower, backer, disciple, champion, stalwart, upholder. ANT. *opponent, independent, nonconformist.*

partisan a. partial, biased, prejudiced, one-sided, factional, sectarian, limited, bigoted, myopic, close-minded. ANT. *nonpartisan, unbiased, open-minded, bipartisan.*

partition n. divider, wall, barrier, panel, screen, division, separation, dermarcation, segregation.

partition v. separate, divide, wall off, segregate, screen, subdivide, section, apportion.

partly adv. partially, incompletely, somewhat, halfway.

partner n. ally, collaborator, colleague, associate, counterpart, accomplice, cohort, confederate, teammate, sidekick, compatriot. SEE FRIEND

partnership n. alliance, collaboration, cooperative, association, union, confederacy, marriage, team, affiliation, company.

party n. **1.** CELEBRATION *bash, revelry, gala, festivity, *blowout, get-together, *beer bash, social gathering, soiree, *do, reception, *wingding, fun and games, orgy, shindig, stag party, bachelor party. **2.** GROUP band, bunch, assemblage, assembly, company, crew, troupe. **3.** INDIVIDUAL person, participant, man, woman, human being. **4.** SECT faction, group, side, wing, denomination, alliance, set, bloc, league, confederacy, camp.

pass n. **1.** PASSAGE opening, defile, gap, canyon, gorge, trail. **2.** TICKET admission, permit, license, furlough, *free ride. **3.** PROPOSITION advance, flirtation, overture.

pass v. **1.** GO BY, MOVE THROUGH go past, proceed, cross, progress, move, leave, depart, advance, flow, course, fly. **2.** OVERTAKE outdistance, leave behind, *leave in one's wake, *blow by, outrun, exceed, surpass, beat. **3.** ELAPSE flow, drag, slip by, race, proceed. **4.** DIE pass on, expire, run out, terminate, *peter out, run its course, fade, dissolve, wane, succumb. **5.** SATISFY meet requirements, pass muster, make the grade, qualify, graduate. **6.** ENACT legislate, endorse, certify, authorize, legalize, ratify, adopt, sanction. **7.** DELIVER hand over, throw, give, transfer, convey. **8.** DECLINE refuse, skip, pass up, overlook, omit. ANT. *1. stop, hold up. 2. lag, fall behind, trail. 5. fail, flunk, *blow it. 6. veto, vote down, defeat. 8. accept, take.*

passable a. **1.** TRAVERSABLE crossable, clear, free, unobstructed, navigable, unimpeded, accessible, penetrable. **2.** ACCEPTABLE okay, fair, mediocre, adequate, good enough, satisfactory, tolerable, so-so. ANT. *1. impassable, blocked, impenetrable. 2. unacceptable, intolerable, unsatisfactory.*

passage n. **1.** ACCESS path, course, corridor, hall, thoroughfare, way, door, exit, entrance, passageway, route, channel. **2.** EXCERPT section, extract, quotation, portion, selection, sentence, paragraph, verse, page, chapter. **3.** PROGRESSION passing, movement, advance, transit, trip. **4.** ENACTMENT acceptance, adoption, legislation, legalization, ratification. ANT. *3. obstruction, stoppage, blockage. 4. veto, defeat.*

passageway n. hall, corridor, alley, aisle, passage, gallery, path, walkway, gangway.

PASSÉ a. [pa SAY] old-fashioned, out-of-date. *This year's fashions will soon be passé.* SYN. old-fashioned, out-of-date, outdated, outmoded, démodé, antiquated, obsolete, stale, old, dated, discredited, unfashionable. ANT. *fashionable, stylish, *chic, *hip, in vogue, fresh.*

passenger *n.* rider, commuter, *fare, traveler.

passion *n.* **1.** INTENSE EMOTION fervor, ardor, intensity, zeal, fire, heat, frenzy, vehemence, enthusiasm, devotion. "The winds necessary to put everything in motion, though they often cause storms."—Bernard de Fontenelle. **2.** ANGER rage, fury, towering rage, *lather, wrath, *dither, hot blood. **3.** LOVE adoration, fondness, affection, amour, infatuation, ardor, lust, desire, sex drive, eroticism, appetite, aching. **4.** INTENSE INTEREST obsession, mania, fixation, fancy, infatuation, liking, craze.

passionate *a.* **1.** IMPASSIONED ardent, fervid, fervent, excited, burning, hot, fiery, heartfelt, eager, emotional, enthusiastic, vehement, vigorous. **2.** LUSTFUL aroused, *turned on, desirous, *hot, *horny, erotic, amorous, libidinous, romantic, sensual. ANT. *1. apathetic, indifferent. 2. turned off.*

passive *a.* inactive, unresponsive, dispassionate, lifeless, apathetic, impassive, unemotional, uninterested, spiritless, submissive, yielding, docile, meek, unassertive. ANT. *active, passionate, responsive.*

passport *n.* identification, I.D., proof of citizenship, travel permit, official document, authorization, credentials, visa.

password *n.* code word, secret word, key phrase, countersign, watchword.

past *n.* yesterday, *yesteryear, history, olden days, antiquity, days of old, *good old days, yore, horse and buggy days, dark ages. "The best prophet of the future."—Lord Byron. "The misty black and bottomless pit of time."—Thomas Duffett. "A funeral gone by."—Edmund Gorse. "What's past is prologue."—Shakespeare. ANT. *future, tomorrow, days to come.*

past *a.* gone, bygone, over, forgotten, finished, old, historical, ancient, former, passed, never to return, extinct, dead and buried. ANT. *future, upcoming.*

pastime *n.* hobby, diversion, amusement, recreation, avocation, leisure time activity, sport, fun.

pastor *n.* minister, priest, clergyman, reverend, rector, chaplain, preacher, ecclesiastic.

PASTORAL *a.* [PAS tuh rul] referring to the peace and simplicity of rural life. *Many New Englanders still live a pastoral life.* SYN. rural, country, countrified, peaceful, simple, rustic, bucolic, agrarian, natural, arcadian, idyllic. ANT. *urban, metropolitan, citified, sophisticated.*

pastry *n.* baked good, sweet roll, cake, pie, tart, cream puff, Danish, turnover, croissant, éclair, doughnut.

pasture *n.* field, meadow, grazing land, grass, grassland, vegetation, pasturage.

pat *n.* tap, stroke, slap, touch, rap, caress, poke.

pat *v.* tap, stroke, fondle, slap, touch, rap, caress, poke.

pat *a.* glib, easy, facile.

patch *n.* spot, piece, plot, tract, ground, lot, strip.

patch *v.* repair, fix, mend, cover, recondition, sew up, stitch.

patchwork *n.* jumble, hodgepodge, mixture, miscellany, mishmash, conglomeration, mélange, potpourri, pastiche.

PATENT *a.* [PATE unt] evident, obvious. *We all recognized his statement as a patent lie.* SYN. evident, obvious, plain, conspicuous, apparent, clear, open, blatant, glaring, manifest, overt, flagrant, unconcealed, transparent. ANT. *covert, concealed, subtle.*

patent *n.* grant, right, protection, title, registration, license, certificate of origination.

WORD FIND
protected right covering literary, musical or artistic work: copyright

paternal *a.* fatherly, fatherlike, patriarchal, protective, solicitous. ANT. *maternal.*

path *n.* **1.** TRAIL walkway, footpath, walk, way, course, track, shortcut, rut, passage. **2.** TRAJECTORY.

pathetic *a.* pitiful, piteous, sorrowful, moving, wretched, grievous, deplorable, lamentable, heartbreaking, poignant, miserable, woeful. ANT. *worthy, deserving, meritous.*

pathological *a.* **1.** MORBID unhealthy, diseased, disease-borne, infected, contaminated. **2.** HABITUAL unhealthy, sick, compulsive.

pathology *n.* infection, growth, contamination, immune response, immune breakdown, disease, manifestation, malignancy, contagiousness, spread.

pathos *n.* pity, sadness, poignancy, suffering, heartache, sentiment, bathos.

patience *n.* endurance, perseverance, *staying power, stamina, stick-to-itiveness, tenacity, diligence, forbearance, tolerance, understanding, *long fuse, *type B behavior, even temper, composure. "Passion tamed."—Lyman Abbott. "The life-long martyrdom."—Longfellow.

patient *n.* sick person, case, outpatient, victim, convalescent, invalid, client.

patient *a.* steady, enduring, persistent, perseverant, tenacious, diligent, long-suffering, tolerant, imperturbable, easygoing, even-tempered, calm, long-fused, composed, resigned, stoical. ANT. *impatient, restless, irritable, exasperated, *intolerant.*

patio *n.* courtyard, barbecue area, deck.

PATRIARCH *n.* [PAY tree AHRK] the male head of a family or group. *The tribesmen consulted their patriarch for guidance.* SYN. head of household, chief, father, grandfather, elder, senior, ruler, sage, graybeard, wise man, master.

patrician *n.* aristocrat, nobleman, *blue blood, lord, *silk stocking.

patrician *a.* aristocratic, highborn, noble, blue-blooded, upper-class, genteel, royal. ANT. *plebian, common, lower-class.*

patriot *n.* loyalist, *flag waver, nationalist, statesman, jingoist, chauvinist. "The seed of freedom's tree."—Thomas Campbell. "The dupe of statesmen and the tool of conquerors."—Ambrose Bierce. ANT. *traitor, subversive, *turncoat, *Benedict Arnold.*

patriotism *n.* nationalism, *flag-waving, *flag-kissing, allegiance, loyalty, jingoism, chauvinsim. "A lively sense of collective responsibility."—Richard Aldington. "The passion of fools and the most foolish of passions."—George Santayana. "That pernicious sentiment, 'Our country right or wrong.' "—James Russell Lowell. ANT. *treason, subversion, *flag-burning, disloyalty.*

patrol *v.* police, secure, observe, reconnoiter, *walk a beat, safeguard, eyeball, keep watch, make the rounds, inspect, *scope out, guard.

patron *n.* 1. CUSTOMER shopper, client, buyer, subscriber, regular. 2. SUPPORTER backer, sponsor, booster, benefactor, financer, champion, advocate, *angel.

patronage *n.* 1. SUPPORT backing, sponsorship, benefaction, financing, aid, subsidy, advocacy, promotion. 2. BUSINESS trade, purchasing, buying, shopping, commerce, clients, customers, clientele.

patronize *v.* do business with, buy at, deal with, trade at, frequent, shop at.

PATRONIZE *v.* [PAY truh nize] to talk down to as an inferior; to condescend. *He always patronizes those without college degrees.* SYN. *talk down to, talk to as an inferior, indulge, condescend, regard loftily, *look down one's nose at, regard superciliously, humor, suffer,

endure. ANT. *look up to, flatter, *kiss up to, *brownnose.*

patsy *n.* sucker, scapegoat, *whipping boy, *fall guy, dupe, *easy mark, *pushover.

patter *n.* *spiel, pitch, *line, chatter, talk, monologue, recitation.

pattern *n.* 1. DESIGN motif, theme, arrangement, composition, figure, scheme, device, decoration, form. 2. MODEL guide, sample, example, exemplar, standard, prototype, mold, archetype, template.

PAUCITY *n.* [PAW si tee] scarcity, lack. *A paucity of funds motivated him to find work.* SYN. scarcity, lack, dearth, shortage, deficiency, insufficiency, absence, sparsity, rarity. ANT. *wealth, surplus, excess, glut.*

paunch *n.* potbelly, *beer belly, *beer gut, *spare tire, *middle-aged spread, *bay window, stomach, *blubbergut, bulge. ANT. *washboard stomach.*

pauper *n.* poor person, *down-and-outer, homeless person, indigent, beggar, hobo, tramp, *bum, debtor, *panhandler, *street person. ANT. *millionaire.*

pause *n.* break, stop, rest, time out, beat, delay, wait, gap, suspension, respite, halt, cessation. ANT. *continuation.*

pause *v.* break, stop, rest, take time out, delay, wait, suspend, halt, cease, take a breather. ANT. *continue, carry on, proceed.*

pave *v.* surface, blacktop, resurface, tar, overlay, lay asphalt, macadamize, level, cobble.

pavement *n.* blacktop, asphalt, concrete, surface, road, tar, cobble, paving stones, macadam.

pavilion *n.* tent, shelter, gazebo, summerhouse, belvedere.

pawn *n.* tool, instrument, hostage, puppet, dupe, *stooge, patsy, medium, cat's paw.

pawn *v.* pledge, give as security, *hock, deposit, mortgage, borrow on, venture, gamble.

pay *n.* wages, salary, earnings, income, *take-home, profit, remuneration, fee, compensation, commission, cut, percentage. SEE MONEY

pay *v.* 1. REMIT compensate, disburse, settle, *cough up, *foot the bill, spend, expend, *shell out, *fork over, *pick up the tab, contribute, bankroll, finance, remunerate, recompense. 2. BE WORTHWHILE be profitable, benefit, profit, serve, be advantageous. 3. SUFFER FOR *pay the piper, answer, atone, be punished. 4. GIVE offer, extend.

payback *n.* return, payment due, benefit, rebate.

payment n. remittance, installment, fee, expenditure, payout, outlay, remuneration, settlement, defrayal, recompense, sum, restitution.

peace n. **1.** HARMONY accord, friendship, concord, friendliness, armistice, truce, treaty, detente, brotherhood, amity, goodwill. "Liberty in tranquility."—Cicero. "War in masquerade."—John Dryden. "A short pause between wars for enemy identification."—Clemens Kirchner. "The white space between the chapters in the history books."—Leonard Levinson. **2.** QUIET stillness, silence, hush. **3.** TRANQUILITY serenity, peacefulness, quiet, placidity, relaxation, contentment. ANT. *1. war, hostilities, conflict. 2. noise, clamor. 3. discontent, agitation, disturbance.*

peaceable a. peaceful, friendly, gentle, nonviolent, amicable, conciliatory, peace-loving, irenic, mild, pacific, accommodating, dovish, lamblike, easygoing, agreeable. ANT. *hostile, belligerent, contentious, aggressive.*

peaceful a. **1.** HARMONIOUS friendly, pacific, agreeable, peaceable, nonviolent, nonaggressive, conciliatory, accommodating, dovish, easygoing, irenic. **2.** QUIET still, silent, hushed, noiseless, tranquil, serene, placid, undisturbed. ANT. *1. warring, hostile, contentious, belligerent. 2. noisy, clamorous, cacophonous.*

peacemaker n. diplomat, pacifist, dove, makepeace, conscientious objector, conciliator, negotiator, mediator, intermediary. ANT. *hawk, warmonger.*

peacock n. pea fowl, peahen.
WORD FIND
eyelike spot: ocellus
walk: strut

peak n. top, pinnacle, summit, mountaintop, crest, height, roof, tip, ridge, head, climax, zenith, limit, apex, maximum, acme, high point, crown. ANT. *low point, depression, foot.*

peak v. crest, climax, *come to a head, culminate, top, reach the zenith, crown. ANT. *bottom out.*

peaked a. thin, wan, pale, sickly, gaunt, haggard, emaciated, wizened. ANT. *healthy, robust, hearty.*

peal n. ringing, reverberation, thunder, boom, rumble, roar, crack, blast, chime, clang, tintinnabulation, clangor, toll.

peal v. resound, ring, reverberate, resonate, sound, clang, chime, toll, knell, bong, tintinnabulate, rumble, thunder.

peasant n. farmer, laborer, farmhand, serf, vassal, rustic, provincial, commoner, *hick, *hayseed. ANT. *aristocrat, nobleman.*

pebble n. stone, gravel. SEE ROCK

PECCADILLO n. [PEK uh DIL oh] a minor fault, sin or offense. *The media has a way of flushing out a politician's every peccadillo.* SYN. minor fault, petty offense, infraction, slip, lapse, misdemeanor, indiscretion, transgression, false step, shortcoming, sin, faux pas. ANT. *capital offense.*

peck v. pick, bite, poke, nibble, dig, prick, jab, rap, flick.

pecking order n. hierarchy, line of dominance, natural order, chain of command, corporate ladder.

peculiar a. **1.** UNIQUE distinctive, singular, characteristic, individual, exclusive, special, personal, particular, limited. **2.** ODD queer, strange, weird, offbeat, different, curious, unusual, bizarre, outlandish, quaint, *off-the-wall. ANT. *1. common. 2. normal, predictable, unsurprising.*

peculiarity n. characteristc, singularity, trait, feature, oddity, mark, idiosyncrasy, distinction, quirk.

pecuniary a. financial, monetary, fiscal, money.

pedagogic a. educational, academic, professorial, teaching, scholastic, instructional, tutorial, pedantic.

PEDANTIC a. [puh DAN tik] overly precise or scholarly, nit-picking with facts and rules. *She was meticulously accurate with facts but had little common sense; she was pedantic.* SYN. scholarly, didactic, academic, learned, overprecise, pretentious, pompous, professorial, meticulous, bookish, nit-picking, *hairsplitting.

peddler n. salesman, hawker, vendor, costermonger.

PEDESTRIAN a. [puh DES tree un] unimaginative, dull, ordinary. *The story was trite and pedestrian.* SYN. unimaginative, dull, prosaic, ordinary, trite, mediocre, run-of-the-mill, flat, banal, uninspired, uninteresting, mundane, inane. ANT. *imaginative, original, profound, interesting.*

pedigree n. family tree, ancestral record, genealogy, descent, lineage, line, bloodline, parentage, stock, roots, dynasty.

peek v. peep, spy, glimpse, eye surreptitiously, glance, peer, *have a gander.

peel v. pare, skin, husk, strip, scale, exfoliate, decorticate, shuck, shell.

peep v. **1.** SEE PEEK **2.** CHEEP chirp, tweet, pip, twit, chirrup. SEE BIRD

peeping Tom n. SEE VOYEUR

peer n. equal, fellow, compatriot, compeer, counterpart, equivalent, *bird of a feather.

peer v. look closely, squint, focus in on, *eyeball, scrutinize, inspect, peep, stare, gaze, gawk.

peerless a. unequaled, unmatched, second to none, incomparable, superior, unparalleled, supreme, best, preeminent, greatest. ANT. *inferior, second-rate, mediocre.*

peeve v. irk, annoy, irritate, *bug, bother, aggravate, *rub the wrong way, nettle, vex, gall, *burn one up.

peevish a. irritable, touchy, cross, cranky, grouchy, snappish, moody, impatient, cantankerous, waspish, ugly, petulant. ANT. *good-humored, cheerful, easygoing.*

PEJORATIVE a. [pi JOR uh tiv] disparaging, negative. *His pejorative remarks upset the teacher.* SYN. disparaging, negative, derogatory, deprecatory, belittling, depreciatory, uncomplimentary, demeaning, degrading. ANT. *complimentary, flattering, favorable.*

pell-mell adv. helter-skelter, hastily, carelessly, recklessly, heedlessly, slapdash, hurriedly, abruptly, impetuously, wildly. ANT. *methodically, orderly, thoughtfully.*

pellucid a. transparent, limpid, crystal. SEE CLEAR

pelt n. skin, hide, coat, fur.

pelt v. throw things at, bombard, hurl at, shower, pepper, stone, beat, pound, wallop, belt, pummel, punch, sock, whack, thrash.

pen n. **1.** WRITING INSTRUMENT ballpoint, quill, style, fountain pen. "That mighty instrument of little men."—Lord Byron. "Wit's plough."—John Clarke. **2.** ENCLOSURE cage, pound, confine, corral, sty, coop, jail, prison.

penalize v. punish, discipline, correct, fine, impose a penalty on, *throw the book at, sentence, amerce, castigate, handicap, put at a disadvantage, disable, hamstring. ANT. *reward.*

penalty n. punishment, discipline, correction, fine, retribution, sentence, imprisonment, forfeit, damages, handicap, disadvantage.

penance n. repentance, reparation, self-punishment, confession, remorse, retribution, penalty, absolution, atonement, mea culpa.

PENCHANT n. [PEN chunt] a strong fondness for something. *She had a penchant for cream cheese and bagels.* SYN. fondness, liking, taste, inclination, partiality, weakness,

leaning, affinity, propensity, attraction, bent, predisposition.

pendent a. hanging, suspended, dangling.

pending a. upcoming, impending, about to happen, imminent, in the offing, forthcoming, on the horizon, coming, approaching, unsettled, unresolved, *up in the air. ANT. *past, former.*

pendulous a. hanging, suspended, drooping, pendent, dangling.

penetrate v. **1.** GO THROUGH pierce, pass into, puncture, prick, bore through, break through, encroach, broach. **2.** SPREAD THROUGH permeate, pervade, diffuse, infiltrate, saturate, fill, infuse, suffuse.

penetrating a. **1.** PIERCING sharp, intrusive, cutting, biting, mordant, strong, earsplitting. **2.** DISCERNING acute, sharp, perceptive, keen, astute, sensitive, aware, intelligent, deep. ANT. *1. dull, blunt, muted. 2. imperceptive, shallow, superficial.*

penis n. sexual organ, male organ, genitalia, genitals, member, organ of copulation.

penitence n. repentance, sorrow, contrition, remorse, regret, penance, compunction, shame, self-reproach, regret.

PENITENT a. [PEN i tunt] sorry, contrite, regretful. *The truly penitent shall be forgiven their misdeeds.* SYN. sorry, sorrowful, contrite, regretful, repentant, remorseful, conscience-stricken, ashamed, compunctious, atoning. ANT. *unrepentant, impenitent, conscienceless.*

penitentiary n. jail, federal prison, penal institution, *slammer. SEE PRISON

pen name n. pseudonym, nom de plume, alias.

pennant n. banner, flag, pennon, streamer, banderole, bunting, colors.

penniless a. impoverished, destitute, poor, *broke, poverty-stricken, bankrupt, indigent, homeless. ANT. *rich, wealthy.*

pension n. annuity, retirement benefits, payment, social security, disability income. SEE MONEY

PENSIVE a. [PEN siv] in deep thought, especially about sad things. *We remained pensive long after the funeral.* SYN. deep in thought, meditative, contemplative, melancholy, withdrawn, ruminative, troubled, wistful, brooding. ANT. *carefree, untroubled.*

penthouse n. apartment, dwelling, residence.

pent-up a. confined, restrained, curbed, held in check, repressed, suppressed, held-in, bottled-up. ANT. *released, relieved, vented.*

penurious a. miserly, stingy, hoarding, frugal,

thrifty, penny-pinching, cheap, parsimonious, tightfisted, mean. ANT. *extravagant, wasteful, generous.*

peon *n.* laborer, drudge, farmhand, peasant, worker, menial, toiler, serf, slave.

people *n.* **1.** HUMANS human beings, folks, humankind, human race, mankind, man, persons, populace, individuals, Homo sapiens, mortals. **2.** MASSES community, electorate, rank and file, working class, society, citizens. "A many-headed beast."—Alexander Pope. "The vulgar popular cattle."—Robert Buchanan. "A wild beast."—Niccolo Machiavelli.

pep *n.* energy, vim, vitality, life, zip, vigor, get-up-and-go.

pepper *v.* shower, rain on, pelt, bombard, sprinkle.

peppy *a.* lively, energetic, *zippy, snappy, vigorous, spirited, perky. ANT. *sluggish, lethargic, slothful.*

perceive *v.* **1.** SEE notice, discern, make out, observe, spot, detect, recognize, apprehend, sense, distinguish. **2.** UNDERSTAND comprehend, read, see, grasp, appreciate, conclude, decipher, judge. ANT. *1. miss, overlook.*

percentage *n.* portion, part, fraction, share, section, cut.

perceptible *a.* discernible, noticeable, apparent, visible, observable, detectable, distinguishable, obvious, conspicuous, palpable. ANT. *imperceptible, unapparent, impalpable.*

perception *n.* awareness, sense, feeling, discernment, apprehension, impression, insight, understanding, comprehension, recognition, cognition.

perceptive *a.* sensitive, sharp, alert, acute, cognizant, conscious, intelligent, insightful, wise, penetrating, intuitive, *tuned in, *on the ball. ANT. *obtuse, thick, dense, dull.*

perch *n.* roost, stand, seat, post.

perch *v.* light, alight, roost, rest, settle, sit, squat, nest.

percolate *v.* filtrate, filter, seep, strain, leach, drip, exude, ooze.

perdition *n.* damnation, hell, fire and brimstone, destruction, punishment, ruination, loss of the soul.

PEREMPTORY *a.* [per EMP tuh ree] final, as of the last word, with no further argument or action. *He made a peremptory order and the meeting was concluded.* SYN. final, absolute, ultimate, decisive, imperative, dictatorial, commanding, irrevocable, incontrovertible, unquestionable, authoritative, obligatory, autocratic. ANT. *wishy-washy, tentative, inconclusive, indecisive.*

PERENNIAL *a.* [puh REN ee ul] continuous, perpetual, returning again and again. *The Wizard of Oz is a perennial favorite with children.* SYN. continuous, continual, perpetual, everlasting, recurrent, returning, enduring, unfailing, eternal, undying, immortal. ANT. *dying, short-lived, temporary.*

perfect *v.* finish, polish, smooth, *get the bugs out of, *put finishing touches on, refine, accomplish, achieve, realize, complete, consummate, fulfill, effect, culminate.

perfect *a.* **1.** FLAWLESS faultless, immaculate, spotless, unblemished, untarnished, superlative, extraordinary, supreme, ideal, exemplary, pure, impeccable, consummate. **2.** COMPLETE whole, intact, finished, realized, utter. **3.** ACCURATE precise, exact, correct, true, right, unerring, letter-perfect, *on target, *dead on. ANT. *1. faulty, flawed, imperfect. 2. deficient. 3. inaccurate, imprecise, wrong.*

perfection *n.* **1.** FLAWLESSNESS excellence, ne plus ultra, precision, idealism, faultlessness, highest form, exacting standard. **2.** DEVELOPMENT achievement, accomplishment, consummation, completion, realization, fulfillment, honing, maturing.

perfectionist *n.* stickler, nitpicker, fussbudget, quibbler, pedant.

perfidious *a.* treacherous, traitorous, faithless, unfaithful, disloyal, two-faced, backstabbing, treasonous, double-dealing, dishonorable. ANT. *loyal, faithful.*

perforate *v.* pierce, puncture, prick, penetrate, punch, slit, bore, cut, make a hole in.

perform *v.* **1.** DO execute, carry out, fulfill, accomplish, act, complete, satisfy, meet, *pull off, discharge. **2.** ACT put on, take on a role, enact, present, exhibit, *ham it up, depict, portray.

performance *n.* **1.** EXECUTION carrying out, fulfillment, accomplishment, completion, doing, discharge, realization. **2.** SHOW entertainment, presentation, production, exhibition, spectacle, portrayal, depiction, rendition, characterization.

perfume *n.* fragrance, essence, scent, cologne, bouquet, emanation, aroma. "Any smell that is used to drown out a worse one."—Elbert Hubbard.
WORD FIND
bag of: sachet
case: pomander

East Indian: patchouli
smoking: incense
sprayer: atomizer
substance used in: musk, ambergris, myrrh, attar, civet, bergamot, castor, orris
SEE ODOR

PERFUNCTORY *a.* [pur FUNK tuh ree] performed superficially and unenthusiastically, often as part of a routine. *The bank clerk gave me a perfunctory smile.* SYN. routine, unenthusiastic, superficial, disinterested, automatic, blasé, unthinking, apathetic, mechanical, cursory. ANT. *enthusiastic, intense, careful.*

perhaps *adv.* maybe, possibly, conceivably, perchance.

peril *n.* danger, hazard, risk, jeopardy, threat, vulnerability, insecurity, endangerment, pitfall, *sword of Damocles. ANT. *security, safety.*

perilous *a.* dangerous, hazardous, risky, *putting one in jeopardy, threatening, *playing with fire, *playing Russian roulette, *playing with a hair trigger, *treading on thin ice, ticklish, precarious, life-threatening, chancy, *dicey, menacing. ANT. *safe, secure, harmless.*

perimeter *n.* border, periphery, circumference, boundary, limit, outline, skirt, rim, edge. ANT. *center, middle.*

period *n.* time, interval, span, epoch, age, eon, era, days, season, course.

periodic *a.* recurrent, repeating, at intervals, sporadic, every so often, intermittent, regular, cyclical, daily, seasonal, weekly, monthly, annually.

peripatetic *a.* traveling, roving, itinerant, walking, moving, migrant, wandering, nomadic, roaming. ANT. *stable, static, stationary.*

peripheral *a.* outside, side, sideline, external, surrounding, neighboring; secondary, minor, incidental. ANT. *primary, main.*

peripheral *n.* auxiliary device, component, module, adjunct; modem, printer, monitor.

periphery *n.* perimeter, outskirts, border, circumference, boundary, limit, outline, skirt, rim, edge. ANT. *center, middle, core.*

perish *v.* die, expire, pass away, pass on, *croak, *bite the dust, *buy the farm, *kick the bucket, be destroyed, be killed, meet death, vanish, disappear. ANT. *survive, thrive.* SEE DIE

perishable *a.* liable to spoil, liable to rot, short-lived. ANT. *nonperishable, inorganic.*

PERJURY *n.* [PUR jur ee] lying while under oath in a court of law. *He committed perjury on the witness stand.* SYN. lying, dishonesty, false testimony, deception, falsification, bearing false witness, untruthfulness, prevarication. SEE LAW, COURT

perky *a.* lively, jaunty, spirited, energetic, vigorous, vivacious, animated, dynamic, cheerful, lighthearted. ANT. *dispirited, plodding, sedate.*

permanent *a.* fixed, lasting, eternal, everlasting, endless, long-lived, perennial, immortal, perpetual, constant, stable, unchangeable, immutable, durable. ANT. *temporary, impermanent, short-lived.*

PERMEATE *v.* [PUR mee ATE] to penetrate and spread throughout. *Her perfume permeated the room.* SYN. penetrate, pervade, spread throughout, saturate, imbue, diffuse, overrun, fill, osmose, suffuse, choke. ANT. *dissipate.*

permissible *a.* permitted, allowed, okay, legal, lawful, authorized, acceptable, approved, sanctioned, proper, *kosher. ANT. *forbidden, taboo, off limits, wrong.*

permission *n.* authorization, okay, say-so, consent, nod, go-ahead, license, permit, allowance, approval, sanction, endorsement, liberty. ANT. *prohibition, denial, refusal, proscription.*

permissive *a.* lenient, indulgent, soft, easy, lax, liberal, accommodating, agreeable, obliging. ANT. *strict, restrictive.*

permit *n.* license, permission slip. SEE PERMISSION

permit *v.* allow, authorize, license, consent, sanction, let, endorse, tolerate, entitle, grant, give the go-ahead, *okay. ANT. *prohibit, refuse, deny, ban.*

PERNICIOUS *a.* [pur NISH us] destructive, deadly, very harmful. *The pernicious disease affected half the community.* SYN. destructive, lethal, deadly, fatal, harmful, ruinous, injurious, hurtful, devastating, mortal, noxious, malignant. ANT. *harmless, benign, innocuous.*

perpetrate *v.* do, perform, carry out, commit, transact, *pull off, execute.

perpetual *a.* neverending, everlasting, unending, eternal, continuous, permanent, immortal, nonstop, incessant, ceaseless, ongoing, infinite. ANT. *temporary, short-lived, finite.*

perplex *v.* confuse, puzzle, mix up, *discombobulate, confound, muddle, befuddle, mystify, baffle, bewilder, dumbfound. ANT. *clarify, enlighten, *show the light.*

PERQUISITE n. [PUR kwi zit] a special privilege or fringe benefit that comes with a job. *Having unlimited use of the company car was a nice perquisite.* SYN. *perk, fringe benefit, privilege, right, extra, bonus, reward, employee benefit.

persecute v. harass, oppress, torment, afflict, victimize, plague, ill treat, crucify, torture, mistreat, abuse, bully, trouble. ANT. *put on a pedestal, honor, *kiss up to, serve.

perseverance n. *stick-to-itiveness, persistence, tenacity, steadfastness, grit, resolve, doggedness, diligence, dedication, stamina, drive, backbone. "The mother of good luck."—Ben Franklin. "Patience concentrated."—Thomas Carlyle. "The greatest of all teachers."—Arabian proverb. ANT. *lack of resolve.*

persevere v. persist, be steadfast, continue, *keep chipping away, *never say die, *never say never, carry on, stick to it, *hang in there, be resolved, *keep plugging, *tough it out, *stay the course, be tenacious, *hammer away. ANT. *give up, quit, admit defeat.*

persist v. persevere, continue, carry on, endure, *stick to it, keep up, be steadfast, *hang in there, survive. ANT. *quit, give up, die.*

persistent a. persevering, determined, dogged, tenacious, unrelenting, steadfast, resolute, diligent, untiring, stalwart, stubborn, sustained, incessant. ANT. *quitting, irresolute.*

personable a. friendly, nice, pleasant, warm, charming, people-pleasing, winning, agreeable, amiable, congenial, good-humored, attractive, magnetic. ANT. *unfriendly, aloof.*

personage n. VIP, notable, *big shot, somebody, celebrity, dignitary, public figure, star, luminary, *bigwig. ANT. *nobody, *zero, unknown.*

personal a. private, individual, own, intimate, familiar, inner, secret, confidential. ANT. *public, outer.*

personal computer n. PC, microcomputer. SEE COMPUTER

personality n. 1. CHARACTER temperament, disposition, traits, makeup, identity, individuality, self, ego, psyche. 2. CHARISMA charm, magnetism, attractiveness, *star quality.

personify v. embody, symbolize, incarnate, represent, exemplify, anthropomorphize, humanize, illustrate.

personnel n. staff, employees, crew, workers, members, faculty, work force, labor force.

perspective n. 1. VISTA panorama, outlook, lookout, prospect, view, aspect. 2. POINT OF VIEW viewpoint, standpoint, position, angle, outlook, frame of reference, turn of mind, *mind-set.

perspire v. sweat, *break a sweat, glow, secrete, drip, lather, swelter, *sweat bullets.

persuade v. talk into, prevail upon, influence, motivate, induce, cajole, sell on, wear down, urge, *twist one's arm, coax, sway, prompt, brainwash. ANT. *dissuade, talk out of, discourage.*

persuasive a. influential, convincing, compelling, effective, powerful, inducing, enticing, seductive, winning, forceful, swaying. ANT. *ineffective, unconvincing.*

pert a. impudent, forward, bold, insolent, saucy, fresh, brazen, cheeky, nervy. ANT. *polite, shy, deferential.*

pertain v. regard, apply, relate, connect, refer, bear upon.

PERTINENT a. [PUR tuh nunt] relevant. *Stick to the subject at hand; your side comments aren't pertinent.* SYN. relevant, germane, material, applicable, fitting, pertaining, connected, related, apt. ANT. *irrelevant, impertinent, immaterial.*

PERTURB v. [pur TURB] to disturb or trouble, to upset greatly. *The student would perturb the teacher with his rebellious attitude.* SYN. disturb, trouble, upset, agitate, distress, disconcert, discompose, unsettle, *rattle one's cage, bother. ANT. *calm, pacify, quiet.*

PERUSE v. [puh ROOZ] to read or study carefully, to scrutinize. Also, to read through casually. *She made it a habit to peruse the classifieds each morning.* SYN. scrutinize, study, read, examine, pore over, scan, inspect, review, skim, *flip through.

PERVADE v. [pur VADE] to spread throughout, permeate. *The odor of cooking fish will pervade an entire household.* SYN. spread throughout, permeate, diffuse, saturate, fill up, penetrate, imbue, osmose, disseminate. ANT. *dissipate, dispel.*

PERVASIVE a. [pur VAY siv] spreading throughout, widespread. *The weak economy gave rise to a pervasive disillusionment among the American people.* SYN. spreading, widespread, permeating, extensive, far-reaching, broad, general, rampant, epidemic, prevalent.

perverse a. 1. DEVIANT wrong, aberrant, abnormal, odd, strange, weird, warped, backward, corrupt, wicked, depraved, perverted, immoral, degenerate, evil, bad, nasty. 2. CONTRARY AND STUBBORN obstinate, intractable, difficult, disobedient, mulish, ornery, cantankerous, wrongheaded, unruly. ANT. *1. normal, proper, correct, moral. 2. accommodating, yielding, tractable.*

perversion n. sexual deviation, *kink, fetish, depravity, twist, sickness, abomination.

pervert n. sexual deviant, *sex freak, sex fiend, sadist, masochist, fetishist, pedophile, voyeur, *flasher, exhibitionist, *weirdo.

pervert v. corrupt, debase, subvert, warp, degrade, debauch, lead astray; distort, twist, butcher, slant, misconstrue, misuse, misapply.

perverted a. abnormal, deviant, depraved, warped, twisted, distorted, corrupt, immoral, debauched, sick, unnatural. ANT. *normal, healthy, proper.*

pesky a. annoying, irritating, bothersome, troublesome, aggravating, irksome, disturbing, nettlesome, tormenting, obnoxious. ANT. *agreeable, welcome, pleasing.*

pessimism n. negative thinking, negative attitude, gloom, gloom and doom, hopelessness, doubt, cynicism, skepticism, belief in Murphy's Law, *black outlook, despair. "The name that men of weak nerves give to wisdom."—Bernard De Voto. ANT. *optimism, hopefulness, positive outlook.*

pessimist n. prophet of doom, gloomy Gus, defeatist, naysayer, doubter, doubting Thomas, cynic, *killjoy, *worrywart, *wet blanket. "One who builds dungeons in the air."—Walter Winchell. "[One who] burns his bridges before he gets to them."—Sidney Ascher. ANT. *optimist, *Pollyanna.*

pest n. annoyance, *pain, *pain in the neck, nuisance, irritant, *headache, bother, gadfly, bore, *thorn in one's side.

pester v. annoy, bother, irritate, plague, *bug, hassle, harass, torment, hound, *drive nuts, *drive up the wall, bedevil, nag, get on one's nerves.

pestilence n. epidemic, pandemic, virus, plague, disease, contagion, infection, visitation, scourge. SEE DISEASE

pet v. pat, stroke, caress, fondle.

pet a. favorite, beloved, preferred, special, dear.

petite a. small, little, slight, tiny, diminutive, wee, dainty, trim, pint-sized. ANT. *huge, extra large, big.*

petition n. appeal, request, application, solicitation, entreaty, invocation, supplication, prayer.

petition v. appeal, request, ask for, apply for, solicit, entreat, pray for, supplicate.

petrified a. **1.** HARDENED solidified, calcified, mineralized, turned to stone, fossilized. **2.** PARALYZED WITH FEAR terrified, stunned, *scared stiff, transfixed, immobilized, frightened, shocked, stupefied. ANT. *1. softened, dissolved. 2. emboldened, driven to action.*

petrol n. gasoline, gas, fuel, petroleum.

petroleum n. oil, gas, natural gas, fuel, hydrocarbon, diesel, butane, propane, kerosene.

petty a. **1.** UNIMPORTANT trivial, insignificant, minor, piddling, frivolous, inconsequential, *two-bit, picayune, trifling. **2.** SMALL-MINDED mean, unreasonable, ungenerous, grudging. ANT. *1. important, weighty, consequential. 2. *big, broad-minded.*

PETULANT a. [PECH uh lunt] irritable, moody. *The hot weather made her petulant.* SYN. irritable, moody, cranky, ill-tempered, grouchy, crabby, *bitchy, peevish, touchy, snappish, waspish. ANT. *good-humored, good-natured, lighthearted.*

phantom n. apparition, spirit, vision, phantasm, presence, specter. SEE GHOST

pharmacist n. druggist, apothecary, *chemist.

pharmacy n. drug store, apothecary, chemist, dispensary.

phase n. **1.** PERIOD stage, time, point. **2.** ASPECT side, level, angle.

phenomenal a. extraordinary, remarkable, outstanding, unusual, exceptional, rare, wondrous, uncommon, astonishing, unbelievable, miraculous, out of this world. ANT. *ordinary, everyday, *ho-hum.*

phenomenon n. wonder, rarity, miracle, spectacle, marvel, sight, sensation, *one in a million, *one for the books, prodigy, happening.

philanderer n. adulterer, *swinger, flirt, *make-out artist, *wolf, Don Juan.

philanthropic a. charitable, benevolent, giving, humane, humanitarian, altruistic, kind, generous, beneficent, magnanimous. ANT. *selfish, miserly, misanthropic.*

philanthropist n. humanitarian, giver, benefactor, Good Samaritan, donor, contributor, sponsor, booster, financier. "A rich . . . old gentleman who has trained himself to grin while his conscience is picking his pocket."—Ambrose Bierce. ANT. *miser, *tightwad, misanthrope.*

PHILANTHROPY n. [fi LAN thruh pee] the giving to charity or doing of good deeds for society. *She will long be remembered for her philanthropy.* SYN. humanitarianism, charity, benefaction, altruism, munificence, generosity, public service, assistance, donation. "The wish to scatter joy and not pain around us."—Ralph Waldo Emerson. ANT. *selfishness, miserliness, misanthropy.*

philharmonic *a.* symphonic, orchestral.

philistine *n.* ignoramus, boor, *yahoo, *lowbrow, barbarian. ANT. *highbrow.*

philosopher *n.* deep thinker, logician, Aristotle, Plato, savant, sage, wise man/woman, theorist. "One who aspires to explain away all mysteries, to dissolve them into light."—Henry Amiel. "A blind man in a dark room looking for a black cat which isn't there."—Lord Bowen.

philosophical *a.* **1.** DEEPLY THOUGHTFUL meditative, logical, cogitative, pensive, reflective, contemplative, deep, profound, learned, abstract, metaphysical. **2.** CALM AND RATIONAL composed, reasonable, tranquil, unruffled, impassive. ANT. *1. shallow-minded, thoughtless. 2. irrational, ruffled.*

philosophy *n.* knowledge, logic, pursuit of truth, wisdom, deep thought, reason, metaphysics, theory. "Unintelligible answers to insoluble problems."—Franklin Adams. "The purple bullfinch in the lilac tree."—T.S. Eliot. "Common sense in a dress suit."—Oliver Braston. "A route of many roads leading from nowhere to nothing."—Ambrose Bierce.

phlegm *n.* mucous, secretion, *loogie, *lunger.

PHLEGMATIC *a.* [fleg MAT ik] dull, hard to excite, lethargic. *Tired old Fred couldn't be moved to action; he was hopelessly phlegmatic.* SYN. unexcitable, dull, apathetic, indifferent, disinterested, dormant, unemotional, flat, unresponsive, impassive, lifeless, passive. ANT. *excitable, passionate, fervid, responsive.*

phobia *n.* irrational fear, obsessive fear, anxiety, dread, *hang-up, aversion, *thing, neurosis, maladjustment, horror.

WORD FIND

alone, being: eremiophobia
animal skin or fur: doraphobia
animals: zoophobia
blood: hemophobia
blushing: erythrophobia
bridges: gephyrophobia
burial alive: taphephobia
cancer: cancerphobia
cats: ailurophobia
children: pedophobia
cold: psychrophobia
confinement in enclosed space: claustrophobia
crowds: demophobia, agoraphobia
dark: nyctophobia
dead bodies, death: necrophobia
death: thanatophobia, necrophobia
defecation: rhypophobia
depths: bathophobia
dirt: mysophobia
disease: pathophobia
dogs: cynophobia
eating: phagophobia
fire: pyrophobia
flood: antlophobia
foreigners, strangers: xenophobia
germs: microphobia
ghosts: phasmophobia
heights: acrophobia
homosexuals: homophobia
horses: hippophobia
insects: entomophobia
knives: aichmophobia
lice: pediculophobia
marriage: gamophobia
medicine: pharmacophobia
men: androphobia
mice: musophobia
missiles: ballistophobia
money: chrematophobia
monsters: teratophobia
night: nyctophobia
noise: phonophobia, acousticophobia
number 13: triskaidekaphobia
ocean: thalassophobia
old age: gerontophobia
open spaces: agoraphobia
pain: alophobia
poison: toxicophobia
precipices: cremnophobia
responsibility: hypengyophobia
ridicule: catagelophobia
robbers: harpaxophobia
sex: coitophobia, genophobia
sharp objects: aichmophobia
sin, committing: peccatiphobia
sleep: hypnophobia
snakes: ophidiophobia
snow: chionophobia
solitude: autophobia
speaking: lalophobia
spiders: arachneophobia
stars: astrophobia
strangers: xenophobia
sunlight: heliophobia
thunderstorms: astraphobia, brontophobia

touched, being: haptephobia
water: hydrophobia
women: gynophobia
work: ergophobia
SEE NEUROSIS, FEAR, INSANITY, MANIA

phobic *a.* anxious, fearful, afraid, irrational, apprehensive, neurotic, conditioned to fear, disturbed, disordered, terrified, scared. ANT. *fearless, at ease.*

phony *n.* fake, fraud, counterfeit, sham, forgery, imposter, hoax.

phony *a.* fake, counterfeit, sham, fraudulent, bogus, imitation, spurious, specious. ANT. *real, genuine, authentic.*

photocopy *v.* copy, run off, reproduce, duplicate, replicate, reprint, Xerox.

photograph *n.* photo, picture, print, still, snapshot, close-up, portrait, blowup, shot, *pix, negative, slide, *Polaroid, glossy, composite, photocopy.

photograph *v.* shoot, take, capture on film, snap, film, tape.

photographer *n.* *shutterbug, paparazzo, cinematographer, photojournalist.

photography *n.* picture-taking, still photography, portraiture, cinematography. "Instantaneous art."—M.F. Agha. "A form of voyeurism."—Joseph Strick.

WORD FIND
altering photos with dye: airbrushing, retouching
border for photo: matte
borderless or faded border photo: vignette
brushup work in lab: airbrush, retouch
chemical solution used in developing: fixer, stop bath
converts light to electricity in scanners, copiers, camcorders: charged coupled device (CCD)
dawn and dusk hours: magic hour
details, bringing out: computer enhancement
dual-image photo: double exposure
electronic: digital photography
electronic memory chip for storing images: card
enlargement for photo: blowup
enlarges photos: enlarger
exposure, long: time exposure
focus range of image: depth of field
glaring photo imperfection: overexposure
illuminate subject from behind: backlight
lab: darkroom
lens aperture setting: F-stop
lens, effects: filter, anamorphic lens, fisheye,

long-focus lens, portrait lens, telephoto lens, wide angle lens, zoom lens
lens for photographing tiny objects: macro lens
light facing camera technique: contre jour
light-measuring device: light meter, photometer, exposure meter
microscopic photography: photomicrography
opening in camera lens: aperture
photographers, freelance celebrity: paparazzo, paparazzi
photographs well, subject that: photogenic
room: studio, darkroom
points, individual electronic image: pixels
sensitivity of film to light: film speed
stand, camera: tripod, high hat
three-dimensional photography: holography
three-dimensional photo: hologram, anaglyph

phrase *n.* expression, figure of speech, clause, idiom, saying, catchphrase, wording, saying, motto, slogan.

physical *n.* medical examination, checkup, workup.

physical *a.* material, tangible, solid, concrete, substantial, palpable, corporeal, corporal, bodily, somatic, fleshly, mortal. ANT. *spiritual, mental.*

physician *n.* doctor, M.D., general practitioner, GP, health care provider, D.O., *sawbones, specialist, resident, intern, surgeon, *bones, medic, specialist, surgeon. SEE DOCTOR, MEDICINE

physique *n.* build, anatomy, body, shape, physiognomy, frame, makeup, configuration, musculature.

piano *n.* *ivories, keyboard. SEE MUSICAL INSTRUMENT

picayune *a.* trivial, trifling. SEE PETTY

pick *n.* choice, selection, preference, favorite, prize, elite, cream.

pick *v.* 1. CHOOSE select, opt for, take, settle on, single out, cull, favor, prefer. 2. PLUCK harvest, collect, reap. ANT. *1. reject, spurn.*

picket *n.* 1. STAKE pale, paling, post, palisade, upright. 2. GUARD lookout, sentinel, sentry, patrol, watch.

picket *v.* demonstrate, strike, boycott, protest, sit in, march, rally, *make a stink.

pickle *n.* bind, jam, *between a rock and a hard place, predicament, *hot water, *sticky situation, fix, scrape.

picky *a.* fussy, choosy, discriminating, finicky,

hard to please, particular, fastidious, meticulous. ANT. *easy to please, undiscriminating.*

picnic n. outing, cookout, barbecue, clambake.

picture n. **1.** REPRESENTATION illustration, painting, drawing, likeness, sketch, draft, image, portrait, photo, photograph. **2.** SEE MOVIE **3.** EPITOME perfect example, embodiment, model, essence.

picture v. imagine, envision, see, call to mind, conceive of.

picturesque a. scenic, idyllic, vivid, striking, quaint, unique, charming, breathtaking, arresting, colorful, photographic, photogenic. ANT. *dull, ordinary, *as interesting as a brown paper bag, nondescript.*

piece n. part, portion, component, bit, fragment, segment, fraction, chunk, hunk, slice, parcel.

pièce de résistance n. **1.** MAIN COURSE main dish. **2.** MASTER WORK accomplishment, masterpiece, feat, great performance, achievement, master stroke, tour de force, consummation.

pier n. wharf, dock, landing, quay, anchorage, slip, mooring.

pierce v. puncture, penetrate, perforate, stick, cut, bore, stab, slit, incise, run through, prick.

piercing a. **1.** SHRILL loud, earsplitting, deafening, high, blaring, screeching, strident, intense, penetrating. **2.** SHARP, AS A GLANCE penetrating, intense, scorching, glaring, acute, boring, mesmerizing, withering. ANT. *1. quiet, low. 2. cool inexpressive.*

piety n. religious devotion, faith, devoutness, religion, belief, loyalty, godliness, holiness, zeal, reverence. ANT. *irreverence, ungodliness, unholiness.*

piffle n. foolishness, nonsense, futile talk, useless words.

pig n. hog, swine, porker, piglet, shoat, sow, boar.

pigeonhole n. compartment, niche, hole, recess, nook, cranny, opening, cubbyhole, cell, slot.

pigheaded a. stubborn, obstinate, headstrong, bullheaded, mulish, unyielding, intractable. ANT. *tractable, yielding, flexible.*

pigment n. coloring, dye, tint, shade, paint, stain.

pigpen n. pigsty, dump, mess, *disgraceland, cesspool, refuse heap, hovel, hole, swamp, rathole, hazardous waste dump, wallow.

pile n. **1.** HEAP mass, load, mound, stack, collection, accumulation, stockpile, quantity, bulk, bank. **2.** SEE POST

pile v. heap, mass, load, stack, stockpile, amass, bunch, mound, pyramid, hoard.

pilfer v. filch, steal, thieve, lift, pocket, appropriate, *walk off with, *palm, *rip off.

pilgrimage n. journey, expedition, sojourn, mission, trip, excursion, *hadj, trek.

pill n. capsule, tablet, lozenge, drop, pellet, dose.

pillage n. plundering, plunder, booty, loot, spoils, looting, stealing, robbery, rapine.

pillage v. plunder, loot, rob, sack, despoil, steal, thieve, maraud, desecrate.

pillar n. **1.** COLUMN post, upright, support, pier, piling, shaft, colonnade, pylon. **2.** LEADER supporter, backbone, mainstay, upholder, *tower of strength.

pillow n. cushion, pad, bolster, head support.

pilot n. navigator, flyer, aviator, helmsman, coxswain, captain, wheelman.

pilot v. navigate, fly, steer, direct, guide, *man the helm, drive control.

pimp n. whoremonger, agent, procurer, panderer, *flesh peddler, madam, *hustler.

pimple n. papule, pustule, *zit, eruption, inflammation, boil, blemish, blackhead, acne.

pin n. **1.** FASTENER safety pin, straight pin, bobby pin, hat pin, catch, needle. **2.** JEWELRY brooch, clasp, breast pin, stud, badge.

pin v. **1.** FASTEN fix, affix, secure, bind, attach. **2.** HOLD DOWN OR BACK restrain, hold fast, immobilize.

pinch n. **1.** TWEAK squeeze, nip, grasp, clamp, cramp, twinge. **2.** TINY AMOUNT *smidgen, *tad, touch, bit. **3.** EMERGENCY crisis, plight, predicament, exigency, jam, pickle.

pinch v. **1.** SQUEEZE compress, clamp, crush, tweak, nip, grasp, cramp, crimp. **2.** Sl. ARREST nab, *collar, catch, apprehend, *bust.

pine v. long for, desire, yearn, want, hunger, thirst, crave, ache for, *carry a torch for.

pinnacle n. peak, summit, top, zenith, crown, apex, crest, height, high point, acme, eminence.

pinpoint v. locate, spot, *get a fix on, *home in on, *zero in on, triangulate, identify.

pioneer n. **1.** FRONTIER PERSON colonist, immigrant, settler, homesteader, squatter, trailblazer, explorer, forerunner, founder. **2.** DEVELOPER innovator, inventor, father, founder, trailblazer, groundbreaker, trendsetter. "A nail, driven wherever the country demands."—Vladimir Jabotinsky.

pioneer v. found, trailblaze, invent, father, lead, innovate, break new ground.

PIOUS *a.* [PYE us] devoutly religious, sometimes hypocritically so. *He was always looking down his holier-than-thou nose; he was annoyingly pious.* SYN. devout, devoted, religious, holy, zealous, faithful, reverent, spiritual, righteous, self-righteous, holier-than-thou, sanctimonious, hypocritical, unctuous. ANT. *impious, irreverent, blasphemous.*

pipe *n.* **1.** CONDUIT tube, pipeline, main, duct, line, conveyor, cylinder, passage, drain. **2.** SMOKING INSTRUMENT corncob pipe, meerschaum, calumet, hookah, water pipe, *bong.

pipe dream *n.* fantasy, *castle in the sky, *castle in Spain, daydream, flight of fancy, *fool's paradise, chimera, delusion, *pie in the sky, wishful thinking.

pipeline *n.* conduit, tube, passageway, sewer line.

PIQUANT *a.* [PEE kunt] sharp or stimulating, especially to the taste buds. Also, stimulating to the mind. *The sauce and the conversation were delightfully piquant.* SYN. sharp, stimulating, pungent, biting, flavorful, zesty, spicy, lively, heavily seasoned, peppery, hot, *having a kick, provocative, exciting, racy, interesting, titillating. ANT. *bland, mild, dull, uninteresting, tasteless.*

pique *v.* **1.** IRRITATE resent, affront, offend, wound, hurt one's feelings, gall, irk, nettle, displease. **2.** AROUSE excite, whet, stimulate, provoke, *turn on.

piracy *n.* robbery, hijacking, thievery, stealing, banditry, marauding, commandeering, looting, raiding, swashbuckling.

pirate *n.* buccaneer, privateer, corsair, freebooter, hijacker, sea robber, sea wolf, algerine.

WORD FIND
famous: Long John Silver, Blackbeard, Captain Kidd
flag: Jolly Roger, skull and crossbones
ship: privateer, brigantine, picaroon

pistol *n.* revolver, six-shooter, firearm, *rod, *Saturday night special. SEE GUN

pit *n.* excavation, hole, abyss, chasm, mine, burrow, cavity, hollow, tomb, grave.

pit *v.* **1.** GOUGE nick, dent, scratch, pock. **2.** PLAY OFF match, vie, oppose, counter.

pitch *n.* **1.** INCLINE slope, slant, grade, steepness, cant, tilt. **2.** TONE timbre, key. **3.** SALES PITCH spiel, patter. **4.** THROW delivery, toss, fling, sling, fastball, curve ball, knuckleball, spitball.

pitch *v.* **1.** THROW deliver, hurl, fling, sling, lob, cast, *smoke one by, *throw smoke, *gun. **2.** PLUNGE HEADLONG dive, dip, fall, drop, toss, topple, lurch, tumble. **3.** ERECT put up, raise.

pitcher *n.* **1.** JUG container, vessel, cruet, pot, ewer, bottle. **2.** BASEBALL PITCHER hurler, *fireballer, reliever, *closer, ace, *lefty, *southpaw. SEE BASEBALL

pitch in *v.* help, *chip in, participate, lend a hand, contribute, work.

piteous *a.* pitiful, pitiable, pathetic, heartbreaking, miserable, sad, wretched, deplorable, grievous, poignant. ANT. *honorable, proud, jubilant.*

pitfall *n.* trap, snare, booby trap, danger, peril, drawback, stumbling block, hazard, risk, *catch.

pithy *a.* concise, to the point, brief, succinct, meaningful, pointed, *meaty, tight, focused. ANT. *rambling, wordy, digressive.*

pitiful *a.* pathetic, piteous, pitiable, miserable, wretched, sad, heartrending, heartbreaking, sorry, low, deplorable, grievous, lamentable. ANT. *happy, joyful, bright, humorous.*

pitiless *a.* hard, cruel, cold, unfeeling, merciless, uncompassionate, sociopathic, inhumane, inhuman, ruthless, barbarous, savage. ANT. *compassionate, merciful, caring.*

pittance *n.* *chicken feed, *drop in the bucket, *slave wages, insufficiency, modicum, small change, *peanuts. ANT. *wealth, *miser's hoard, bounty.*

pity *n.* **1.** COMPASSION mercy, feeling, sympathy, humanity, brotherly love, understanding, commiseration, tenderness, heart, ruth, softheartedness. "The scavenger of misery."—George Bernard Shaw. **2.** *CRYING SHAME shame, misfortune, crime, sorry situation, *bummer. ANT. *1. mercilessness, coldness, cruelty, ruthlessness. 2. good fortune, congratulation.*

pity *v.* feel sorry for, sympathize, feel compassion for, *bleed for, ache for, commiserate, grieve for, condole, have mercy on.

pivot *n.* hub, turning point, axis, axle, center, fulcrum, swivel.

pivot *v.* turn, twirl, wheel, revolve, swing, rotate, spin, twist, circle.

pivotal *a.* critical, crucial, vital, focal, important, determining, decisive, paramount. ANT. *unimportant, insignificant, trivial.*

pixie *n.* imp, elf, sprite. SEE FAIRY

placard *n.* sign, notice, poster, posting, bill, announcement, advertisment.

PLACATE *v.* [PLAY kate] to pacify or soothe one's anger, appease. *To placate the screaming* *baby, we gave him a bottle.* SYN. pacify, soothe, appease, quiet, mollify, assuage, propitiate, moderate, conciliate. ANT. *aggravate, exacerbate, intensify, infuriate.*

place *n.* **1.** LOCATION locale, locality, spot, site, point, whereabouts, space, position, *corner of the world, station. **2.** REGION territory, zone, district, neighborhood, area, city, town, village. **3.** RESIDENCE house, dwelling, abode, *pad, home, domicile, apartment, room, habitation. **4.** POSITION standing, rank, pecking order, station, grade, footing. **5.** ROLE function, job, responsibility, affair, duty.

place *v.* **1.** PUT locate, position, situate, lay, plant, fix, set, install, stand. **2.** IDENTIFY recognize, remember, recall, *put one's finger on.

placebo *n.* sugar pill, inert pill, fake, inactive medicine, preparation, control substance, test substance. SEE MEDICINE

placenta *n.* organ, afterbirth, fetal life support system.

placid *a.* peaceful, tranquil, calm, relaxed, serene, composed, imperturbable, self-possessed, quiet, gentle. ANT. *agitated, highstrung, fiery, turbulent.*

plagiarism *n.* copying, stealing, imitation, lifting, cribbing, borrowing, cheating. "Stealing a ride on someone else's train of thought."—Russel Curran.

plague *n.* **1.** AFFLICTION scourge, epidemic, pandemic, outbreak, pestilence, contagion, bubonic plague, Black Death, calamity. **2.** ANNOYANCE nuisance, irritant, *thorn in one's side, aggravation, bother, *pain, headache. SEE DISEASE

plague *v.* annoy, irritate, trouble, bother, harass, torment, hound, vex, irk, disturb.

plaid *a.* tartan, check patterned, checkered, crossbarred.

plain *n.* level land, expanse, grassland, field, meadow, prairie, steppe, tundra, savannah, *land as flat and featureless as a Euclidian plane.

plain *a.* **1.** CLEAR evident, obvious, apparent, visible, transparent, open, unmistakable, distinct. **2.** UNDERSTANDABLE simple, straightforward, clear. **3.** STRAIGHTFORWARD honest, frank, blunt, undisguised, unvarnished, outspoken, forthright, direct. **4.** UNEMBELLISHED unadorned, undecorated, austere, stark, colorless, severe, simple, *no frills, bare, restrained, understated. **5.** HOMELY ugly, unattractive, *not much to

look at, *short on looks. ANT. *1. unapparent, unclear, ambiguous. 2. indecipherable, incomprehensible. 3. disguised, indirect. 4. ostentatious, showy, colorful. 5. beautiful, attractive, pretty.*

PLAINTIVE *a.* [PLANE tiv] expressing sadness. *The lost fawn gave a plaintive cry.* SYN. sad, sorrowful, melancholy, mournful, pathetic, piteous, pitiful, heartrending, wistful, doleful, heartsick. ANT. *happy, cheery, perky.*

plan *n.* scheme, strategy, design, outline, idea, plot, course, agenda, schedule, program, proposal, blueprint, scenario, intention.

plan *v.* **1.** SCHEME design, outline, plot, set agenda, work out, schedule, program, propose, blueprint, organize, draft, project, map out, ready. **2.** INTEND aim, mean, count on, propose.

plane *n.* aircraft, jet. SEE AIRCRAFT

planet *n.* world, celestial body, heavenly body, planetoid, sphere, globe, Mercury, Venus, Mars, Earth, Saturn, Jupiter, Uranus, Neptune, Pluto

WORD FIND

forming body: planetesimal
pathway: orbit
shadow of: umbra
study of: planetology
SEE ASTRONOMY, MOON, SPACE

plank *n.* board, stud, two-by-four, beam.

plant *n.* **1.** VEGETABLE herb, flower, weed, grass, greenery, perennial, annual, shrub, tree, seedling, shoot, cutting. **2.** FACTORY manufactory, mill, works, yard, foundry, assembly line.

plant *v.* sow, seed, set, scatter, implant, start, root, transplant, embed, install.

plantation *n.* farm, cropland, orchard, agricultural site, estate, hacienda.

plastic *a.* flexible, malleable, pliable, pliant, supple, moldable, yielding, resilient. ANT. *hard, unyielding, rigid.*

plastic surgery *n.* cosmetic surgery, reconstructive surgery, facelift, *nose job, rhinoplasty, tummy tuck, eye tuck, chemical peel, liposuction, dermabrasion. SEE MEDICINE

plate *n.* dish, platter, china, saucer.

plateau *n.* mesa, tableland, highland, upland.
SEE MOUNTAIN

platform *n.* **1.** STAGE dais, rostrum, podium, stand, scaffold, soapbox. **2.** PROGRAM policies, beliefs, plan, party line, stance, manifesto.

PLATITUDE *n.* [PLAT i tood] a trite or clichéd remark, often given as original. *Politicians spewed platitudes to a jaded audience.*

SYN. trite remark, cliché, banality, bromide, *chestnut, *saw, *familiar tune, *twice-told tale, *spent horse, *same old same-old, *corn, truism.

PLATONIC a. [pluh TAWN ik] referring to a love relationship based only on emotion, not sex. *They had a strictly platonic relationship.* SYN. nonphysical, nonsexual, emotional, spiritual, idealistic, celibate. ANT. *physical, sexual, lustful.*

platoon n. unit, two squads, group, detachment. SEE ARMY

plaudits n. applause, praise, approval, cheers, kudos, acclaim, raves, standing ovation.

plausible a. believable, credible, reasonable, likely, probable, tenable, sound, possible, feasible. ANT. *implausible, unlikely, impossible.*

play n. **1.** SHOW drama, stage play, production, performance, entertainment, melodrama, musical, comedy, farce, tragedy. **2.** FUN amusement, recreation, entertainment, sport, relaxation, game-playing, diversion, frolic, romping, pastime.

play v. **1.** HAVE FUN recreate, romp, amuse oneself, engage in sport, *cut loose, *let down one's hair, clown around, kid around, frolic, cavort. **2.** COMPETE vie, go up against, contend, pit oneself against. **3.** PERFORM portray, take the part of.

playboy n. pleasure seeker, *swinger, stud, partyer, *pick up artist, flirt, philanderer, smooth operator, womanizer, hedonist, debauchee, libertine, rake, Lothario, Don Juan, Casanova, *skirt-chaser, ladies' man, *make-out artist.

player n. **1.** COMPETITOR team member, athlete, *jock, contestant, opponent, participant. **2.** ACTOR actress, performer, thespian, trouper, *ham.

playful a. frisky, frolicsome, fun, coltish, childish, spirited, lively, jaunty, impish, prankish, mirthful. ANT. *sober, serious, grave.*

playgirl n. pleasure seeker, party girl, *Cosmo girl, lover girl, hedonist, debauchee, flirt, swinger, seductress.

playground n. recreation area, field, yard, park.

playwright n. author, writer, dramatist, screenwriter.

plaza n. square, open area, court, quadrangle, piazza, green, marketplace, mall.

plea n. **1.** EXCUSE defense, explanation, justification, alibi, apology, argument. **2.** REQUEST appeal, entreaty, begging, petition, solicitation, prayer, supplication.

plead v. beg, appeal, implore, beseech, entreat, solicit, pray, supplicate, petition.

pleasant a. pleasing, pleasurable, enjoyable, gratifying, agreeable, nice, delightful, good, welcome, likable, friendly, sweet, charming, kindly, amicable, cheering, warm, gracious, good-natured. ANT. *unpleasant, painful, miserable, disagreeable.*

pleasantry n. quip, kidding, jest, joke, banter, repartee, crack, bon mot, witticism, polite remark, small talk.

please v. **1.** MAKE HAPPY gratify, satisfy, gladden, *tickle, suit, delight, cheer, warm. **2.** CHOOSE want, like, desire, be inclined.

pleasing a. pleasurable, gratifying, pleasant, delightful, agreeable, enjoyable, winning, charming, likable, cheering, friendly, sweet, kindly, amiable, warm, gracious, goodnatured. ANT. *displeasing, disagreeable, unpleasant.*

pleasure n. enjoyment, delight, happiness, contentment, elation, euphoria, amusement, joy, bliss, gratification, good feeling. ANT. *displeasure, pain, misery.*

plebian, plebeian n. commoner, proletarian, peasant, *plebe, man on the street, woman on the street, *John Q. Public, *Joe Blow.

PLEBIAN, PLEBEIAN a. [pluh BEE un] common, lower-class, vulgar. *He objected to her plebeian lifestyle.* SYN. common, low, ignoble, humble, working-class, proletarian, pedestrian, mean, uncultivated, coarse, vulgar. ANT. *aristocratic, noble, highborn.*

pledge n. **1.** PROMISE vow, word of honor, oath, guarantee, contract, assurance, agreement. **2.** SECURITY bond, collateral, guaranty, surety, stake, earnest money.

pledge v. promise, vow, give one's word, guarantee, swear, contract, pawn.

plentiful a. abundant, bountiful, overflowing, full, *chock-full, profuse, ample, teeming, fat, great, thick, bumper, prolific, swarming, copious, replete. ANT. *scant, scarce, sparse.*

plenty n. abundance, *loads, wealth, profusion, lots, bunch, quantity, volume, scores, mountains, overabundance, surplus, plethora, glut, *oodles, whole slew, *miser's hoard. ANT. *shortage, scarcity, dearth.*

PLETHORA n. [PLETH ur uh] an overabundance. *The politician made a plethora of promises.* SYN. overabundance, excess, profusion, flood, overflow, deluge, surfeit, overkill, *too much of a good thing, glut. ANT. *shortage, scarcity.*

pliable a. pliant, flexible, bendable, malleable,

supple, yielding, plastic, elastic, moldable, impressionable. ANT. *rigid, unyielding, hard.*

plight *n.* predicament, situation, state of affairs, circumstances, trouble, tribulation, dilemma, *fix, *scrape, *pickle.

plod *v.* **1.** TRUDGE walk heavily, tramp, slog, drag one's feet, stamp, stomp, move laboriously, lumber. **2.** WORK STEADILY drudge, plug away, grind away, slave, sweat, toil.

plot *n.* **1.** AREA OF LAND lot, tract, parcel, subdivision, piece, patch, acreage. **2.** SCHEME conspiracy, plan, machination, design, intrigue. **3.** STORY theme, narrative, design, action, story line.

plot *v.* **1.** SCHEME conspire, plan, design, machinate, intrigue, collude, maneuver, *make backdoor arrangements. **2.** MAP OUT chart, draft, lay out, outline.

plow *v.* break ground, turn over, till, harrow, furrow, cultivate, hoe, dig up, *rototill.

ploy *n.* maneuver, device, action, trick, move, play, tactic, gambit, stratagem, subterfuge, goal, complication.

pluck *n.* courage, fortitude, guts, mettle, spunk, backbone, spine, boldness, *balls, nerve.

pluck *v.* pick, pull out, yank, jerk, harvest, gather.

plucky *a.* courageous, brave, *gutsy, *ballsy, *nervy, spunky, bold, tough, determined, tenacious. ANT. *meek, cowardly.*

plug *n.* **1.** STOPPER cork, bung. **2.** GOOD WORD blurb, advertisement, mention.

plumb *v.* fathom, probe, explore, sound, *get to the bottom of, delve, penetrate, investigate.

plumb *a.* vertical, straight down, upright, perpendicular. ANT. *horizontal.*

plummet *v.* plunge, fall, dive, drop, nose-dive, descend, crash, tumble, *rocket earthward. ANT. *ascend, rise, go up.*

plump *a.* fat, chubby, endomorphic, corpulent, *chunky, rotund, full-figured, stout, obese, zaftig, obese, tubby, moon-faced. ANT. *anorexic, thin, slender.* SEE FAT

plunder *n.* pillage, robbery, loot, booty, spoils, prize.

plunder *v.* rob, take, loot, pillage, ransack, appropriate, raid, despoil, sack, rape.

plunge *n.* drop, fall, dive, descent, nosedive, jump.

plunge *v.* **1.** DIVE rush, descend, fall, drop, nose-dive, plummet, hustle, pitch, swoop. **2.** THROW ONESELF INTO charge, lunge, dash, leap, shoot, surge, pounce, spring, jump headlong. ANT. *1. ascend, rise, go up. 2. proceed slowly, move with caution.*

plunk *v.* throw down, plop.

plural *a.* more than one, multiple, numerous, many. ANT. *single, singular.*

plus *n.* extra, bonus, asset, advantage, benefit. ANT. *liability, negative.*

plus *a.* additional, added, extra, supplementary. ANT. *minus, negative.*

plush *a.* luxurious, rich, lush, opulent, sumptuous, posh, deluxe, elegant. ANT. *stark, austere, plain.*

ply *v.* work at, practice, engage in, carry on, pursue, follow, employ, use, wield.

pneumonia *n.* lung inflammation, acute infection, viral infection, disease, pulmonary disease, bacterial infection, illness, sickness. SEE DISEASE, MEDICINE

poach *v.* trespass, encroach, take game illegally, steal.

poacher *n.* thief, pilferer, scofflaw, intruder, trespasser, hunter.

pocket *n.* **1.** POUCH fob, sack, bag. **2.** HOLLOW opening, hole, cavity.

pocket *v.* take, filch, steal, nab, lift, pilfer, shoplift, appropriate, *walk off with.

pocketbook *n.* purse, handbag, wallet, billfold, clutch.

pockmark *n.* pit, gouge, crater.

podium *n.* platform, dais, rostrum, stage.

poem *n.* verse, rhyme, composition, ode, sonnet, lyric, limerick.

WORD FIND

fifteen-line, three stanza with only two rhymes: rondeau
four line: quatrain
heroic narrative: epic
Japanese: haiku
love: madrigal
pastoral or rural theme: idyll
rhyme and meter, without: free verse
rhythm: meter
satirical, witty and short: epigram
study of: prosody
talentless poet: poetaster
two line: couplet
SEE POETRY

poet *n.* versifier, rhymer, lyricist, bard, poetaster, author. "The painter of the soul."— Isaac D'Israeli. "A nightingale who sits in darkness and sings to cheer its own solitude with sweet sounds."—Percy Bysshe Shelley.

poetic *a.* romantic, flowery, idyllic, symbolic, metaphoric, musical, melodic, songlike, lyrical, singsong. ANT. *prosaic.*

poetry *n.* verse, rhyme, poems, song, composition, balladry. "Vocal painting."—Simonides. "The impish attempt to paint the color of the wind."—Maxwell Bodenheim. "Talking on tiptoe."—George Meredith. "Life distilled."—Gwendolyn Brooks. "The best words in their best order."—Samuel Taylor Coleridge. SEE POEM

POIGNANT *a.* [POIN yunt] moving or touching, especially in a painful way. *The poignant final scene moved the audience to tears.* SYN. moving, touching, painful, emotional, heartrending, heartbreaking, soulstirring, sad, pitiful, pathetic, agonizing. ANT. *insipid, vapid, flat, emotionless.*

point *n.* **1.** MARK dot, spot, period. **2.** LOCATION spot, place, position, site. **3.** TIME instant, moment, juncture, stage. **4.** TIP end, top, nib, head, prick, spike. **5.** FOCUS thrust, meaning, idea, core, heart, essence, theme, issue, gist, object. **6.** PURPOSE aim, object, goal, end, use, sense, value. **7.** ARGUMENT fact, idea.

point *v.* direct, aim, train, level, guide, draw a bead on.

pointed *a.* sharp, to the point, piercing, penetrating, incisive, cutting, insinuating, trenchant. ANT. *vague, meaningless, wishy-washy.*

pointless *a.* meaningless, senseless, irrelevant, inconsequential, vain, stupid, nonsensical, purposeless, worthless, inane. ANT. *meaningful, useful, purposeful.*

poise *n.* **1.** BALANCE stability, equilibrium, equipoise. **2.** DIGNITY self-assurance, aplomb, coolness, confidence, sangfroid, serenity, composure, savoir faire, equanimity, presence of mind. "The ability to be ill at ease inconspicuously."—Earl Wilson. "The art of raising your eyebrows instead of the roof."—Howard Newton. ANT. **1.** *imbalance, instability.* **2.** *insecurity,* *loss of cool, panic.*

poison *n.* toxin, deadly chemical, venom, germ, miasma, toxic substance, carcinogen, strychnine, cyanide, arsenic, hemlock, lead, carbon monoxide, caustic soda, mustard gas, nerve gas, nightshade. ANT. *antidote.*

poison *v.* contaminate, infect, taint, envenom, make ill, kill, *slip a mickey, adulterate, pervert, defile.

poisonous *a.* toxic, venomous, virulent, carcinogenic, noxious, deadly, lethal, malignant, pernicious, vitriolic, caustic. ANT. *healthy, beneficial, benign.*

poke *v.* **1.** HIT nudge, prod, push, jab, punch, shove, butt, finger. **2.** DAWDLE loiter, putter, lag, mosey along, drag one's feet.

poker *n.* card game, draw poker, stud poker, strip poker.
WORD FIND
facial expression: deadpan, poker-faced, wooden, stony
sequence, five cards in: straight
show hands: call
stake: pot, ante, chips, kitty
suit, five cards of same: flush, royal flush
suit, four cards of same: four flush
three of a kind and a pair: full house
withdraw: fold

POLARIZE *v.* [POH luh RIZE] to take opposing sides. *Certain issues have the tendency to polarize Americans.* SYN. split, oppose, counter, contradict, take side, conflict, *be on the opposite ends of the spectrum, differ, diverge. ANT. *join forces, ally, confederate, merge, unite.*

pole *n.* post, shaft, staff, rod, standard, stick, mast.

police/policeman/woman *n.* law enforcement, *arm of the law, force, law, *heat, *cops, bobby, *John Law, *fuzz, constable, officer, keeper of the peace, patrolman, highway patrol, state trooper, *badge, sheriff, marshal, deputy.
WORD FIND
arrest: *collar, *bust, apprehend
baton: billy club, nightstick
book of recorded arrests: blotter
bulletin or criminal alert: APB, all points bulletin
criminal running free: at large
cruiser's rotating roof light: cherry, beacon
defensive spray: pepper spray, Mace
DNA identification technique: DNA fingerprinting
drugs and prostitution squad: vice squad
fingerprinting system: Bertillon system
French: gendarme
informer: *snitch, *fink, *rat, *canary, *stool pigeon
interrogation of criminal: third degree
investigates crime-related deaths: coroner
lie detector: polygraph
London police: Scotland Yard
massive, organized crackdown of crime in one area: sweep
method of operation, criminal's: MO, modus operandi
microphone, carrying a concealed: *wired
military: MP
narcotics officer: *narc
navy ship officer: master-at-arms

Policy–Politics

networking search for criminal: dragnet, manhunt
paramilitary squad: S.W.A.T., Special Weapons and Tactics
photo of criminal: mug shot
plaster cast taken of object for evidence: moulage
reading of rights, rule: Miranda rule
record of criminal's arrests, convictions: rap sheet
register criminal at jail: book
search criminal's body: frisk
search, permission to: search warrant
section of city covered by one station: precinct
surveillance: stakeout
take law into their own hands: vigilantes
vehicle: cruiser, squad car, prowl car, *paddy wagon, Black Maria
SEE COURT, LAW

policy n. custom, code, course, procedure, *the book, rule, guideline, method, line of action, way, system.

polish n. **1.** SHINE sheen, brilliance, gloss, finish, luster, buff, glaze, varnish. **2.** REFINEMENT cultivation, finish, grace, elegance, poise, savoir faire, suavity. ANT. *1. tarnish, grime. 2. imperfection, awkwardness, coarseness.*

polite a. well-mannered, courteous, gracious, civil, considerate, thoughtful, courtly, behaved, gentlemanly, ladylike, refined, nice, diplomatic. ANT. *rude, discourteous, boorish, ill-mannered.*

politeness a. "One half good nature and the other half good lying."—Mary Little. "Consists in being easy about oneself, and in making everyone about one as easy as one can."—Alexander Pope.

politic a. diplomatic, prudent, tactful, discreet, delicate, shrewd, smooth, judicious. ANT. *tactless, rude, cloddish.*

political a. governmental, civic, civil, bureaucratic, administrative, legislative, executive.

political action committee n. PAC, special interest group, lobby, lobbyist, power brokers, influence peddlers, backers, bankrollers. SEE POLITICS, GOVERNMENT

politically correct a. socially acceptable, inoffensive, sensitive, sanitized, multiculturally sensitive, oversensitive, emphatic, considerate, diplomatic, teactful, politic, self-censoring, mealy-mouthed. ANT. *politically incorrect, offensive.*

politician n. public servant, office holder, politico, civil servant, statesman, legislator, lawmaker, democrat, republican, congressman,

senator, representative, bureaucrat, *baby kisser. "Trustees of the people."—Grover Cleveland. "A dealer in promises."—Gabriel Chevallier.
WORD FIND
appeals to prejudices of people to win them over: demagogue
attacks opponents, associate who: hatchetman
candidate who already holds office: incumbent
candidate who is unlikely to win: dark horse
conservative party member: Republican
conserver of the past: conservative, mossback
extremist: radical
liberal: democratic
middle-of-the-roader: moderate
older, respected politician: elder statesman
outsider who is resented: carpetbagger
party leader: whip
party, member of neither: independent
progress and reform, advocates: liberal
serves party interests over his/her own: good soldier
skilled, respected politician: statesman
sob story suckers: bleeding heart liberals
southern conservative democrats: boll weevils
veterans: old guard
weakened politician after loss of election: lame duck
SEE CONGRESS, ELECTION, GOVERNMENT, POLITICS

politics n. government, political science, legislature, civics, affairs of state, statesmanship. "War without bloodshed."—Mao Tse-tung. "The diplomatic name for the law of the jungle."—Ely Culbertson. "The moral man's compromise, the swindler's method, and the fool's hope."—John Ciardi.
WORD FIND
ambiguous language used by politicians: doublespeak, weasel words
analyst, observer, political: pundit
appointment, cushy political: political plum
backscratching, reciprocal political: logrolling
breaking the law to make a point, protest: civil disobedience
cause, one who works for a: activist
corruption, profit from: graft
demand of the people to carry out some action: mandate
dissenting group within larger body: faction, splinter group

Roget's Superthesaurus 443

engage in: politick

expert investigative panel: blue-ribbon panel

group with common cause or goal: bloc

hands-off economic policy: laissez-faire

heartland of America, how issue is received in: play in Peoria

hedge or be wishy-washy on issue: waffle

hysterical investigation, finger-pointing: McCarthyism, witch hunt

influence group or attempt to influence vote: lobby

influences politician's vote on issue: lobbyist, pressure group

insults, trading of between politicians: mudslinging, smear campaign

issue used to distract public from more important issue: red herring

local projects that are sometimes wasteful, treasury for: pork barrel

member, supporter of organization, referring to serious: card carrying, dyed-in-the-wool

minding one's own business internationally: isolationism

multiculturally sensitive: politically correct

negotiating concession: bargaining chip

neutral: nonpartisan

nonmilitary hostility between nations: cold war

opponents, bad guys: black hats

party, dual: bipartisan

party ideology: party line

party line, following: singing from the party hymnal

passing responsibility, burden or blame to someone else: buck passing

pocketbooks, issue that affects voters': bread and butter issue

popular issue jumped on to make politician look good or to help party: bandwagon, political football

popular support for an issue: ground swell, grassroots support

powerless nation that makes threats: paper tiger

project that wastes taxpayers' money: boondoggle

research trip taken by politician: junket, fact-finding trip

speech, argument, persuasion: rhetoric

speech, crowd-rousing: stemwinder

speech, long-winded: filibuster

tactfulness, negotiation, art of: diplomacy

threat of military action: saber-rattling

uproar, controversy: brouhaha

warming of relations between two formerly hostile nations: detente

SEE ELECTION, CONGRESS, GOVERNMENT

poll *n.* survey, sampling, census, canvass, tally.

poll *v.* survey, sample, take a census, canvass, question, tally.

pollster *n.* survey taker, surveyor, poll-taker, public opinon gatherer.

pollutant *n.* contaminant, toxin, toxic waste, hazardous waste, scum, filth, runoff, pollution.

pollute *v.* contaminate, poison, dirty, taint, adulterate, foul, sully, spoil, corrupt, defile.

pollution *n.* contamination, toxic waste, hazardous waste, poison, taint, adulteration, fouling, defilement, sewage, runoff, smog. "The reek that shall inherit the earth."—Anon.

Pollyanna *n.* optimist, blind optimist, idealist, Dr. Pangloss, *one who wears rose-colored glasses.

poltergeist *n.* ghost, *thing that goes bump in the night, *spook, doppelganger. SEE GHOST

polygamy *n.* bigamy, group marriage, polygyny. SEE MARRIAGE

pomp *n.* splendor, show, display, grandeur, spectacle, pageantry, ceremony, ostentation, pomposity. ANT. *simplicity, modesty.*

pompous *a.* pretentious, egotistic, self-important, arrogant, haughty, supercilious, overbearing, condescending, patronizing, inflated, overblown, ostentatious. ANT. *modest, humble, down to earth.*

poncho *n.* cloak, raincoat, garment.

pond *n.* marsh, bog, lagoon, pool, fish pond. SEE LAKE

ponder *v.* think about, weigh, consider, deliberate, contemplate, meditate, ruminate, reflect, cogitate, evaluate.

ponderous *a.* heavy, bulky, unwieldy, massive, prodigious, awkward, cumbersome, clumsy, laborious. ANT. *handy, lightweight, pocket-sized.*

PONTIFICATE *v.* [pawn TIF i KATE] to preach or lecture, especially in a dogmatic way; sermonize. *He liked to pontificate on the dangers of beer.* SYN. preach, lecture, sermonize, harangue, hold forth, moralize, *get up on one's moral soapbox, admonish, declaim.

pool *n.* **1.** PUDDLE pond, lagoon, spring, swimming hole, reservoir. SEE LAKE **2.** COMBINATION association, collective, trust, consortium, union, collation. **3.** FUNDS *pot, *kitty, bank, reserves.

pool v. combine, share, consolidate, merge, ally, join together.

pooped adv. exhausted, tired, drained, sapped, worn out, fatigued, *out of gas, *beat, weary, tuckered out. ANT. energized, invigorated.

poor a. **1.** DESTITUTE poverty-stricken, impoverished, indigent, *strapped, *broke, bankrupt, *down and out, *hard up, needy, homeless. **2.** INADEQUATE lacking, deficient, unsatisfactory, subpar, second-rate, inferior, insufficient, sorry, low grade, substandard, cheap, pitiable, wanting, shoddy, shabby. **3.** UNFORTUNATE pitiful, pitiable, pathetic, hapless, miserable, unlucky, wretched. ANT. 1. rich, wealthy, well-off. 2. superior, first-rate, superb. 3. lucky, fortunate, blessed.

pop v. bust, explode, blow up, bang, crack, report, blow, go off.

pope n. pontiff, bishop of Rome, patriarch, vicar of Christ.

WORD FIND
ambassador: nuncio
answer to question of doctrine: rescript
cape: fanon; mozetta
court: Curia
court office: datary
crown: tiara
decree: decretal
electing group: Sacred College of Cardinals
envoy: legate
head piece: miter
letter to bishops: encyclical
meeting to elect new pope: conclave
office or jurisdiction of: papacy
residence: Vatican
succession of popes: papacy
SEE CHURCH, RELIGION.

poppycock n. *bull, rot, baloney, hogwash, rubbish, bunk, nonsense, balderdash, *horsefeathers, malarkey.

popular a. **1.** WELL-LIKED favorite, in demand, sought after, crowd-pleasing, in style, in vogue, *all the rage, beloved, *boffo, celebrated, renowned. **2.** COMMON general, public, standard, conventional, universal, prevailing. ANT. 1. unwanted, outmoded, disliked. 2. uncommon, limited.

popularity n. approval, esteem, regard, acclaim, favor, adoration, acceptance, appeal, idolization, demand, fame.

population n. inhabitants, residents, populace, census, citizenry, people.

populous a. crowded, dense, overpopulated, *crawling with people, mobbed, *wall to wall, *elbow to elbow, swarming. ANT. vacant, unpopulated.

porch n. veranda, stoop, steps, portico, gallery, deck.

pore v. read, study, peruse, look over, examine, review, scrutinize.

pornographic a. obscene, sexually explicit, X-rated, indecent, dirty, filthy, lewd, titillating, salacious, erotic, blue, sexy, lascivious. ANT. wholesome, G-rated, *clean.

pornography n. smut, obscene materials, X-rated materials, erotica, adult material, sexually explicit material, filth, dirt magazines, blue movie, *skin flick.

port n. harbor, dock, pier, wharf, berth, anchorage, landing, mooring, quay, haven.

portable a. transportable, movable, transferable, conveyable, light, compact, pocket-sized, handy. ANT. immovable, fixed, unwieldy.

portal n. entrance, doorway, gate, ingress, passageway, threshold.

portend v. bode, foretell, predict, presage, forewarn, foreshadow, augur, herald, harbinger, point to, bespeak.

PORTENT n. [POR tent] a sign of things to come, a forewarning. A storm cloud on the horizon is one portent sailors should take seriously. SYN. sign of things to come, forewarning, omen, harbinger, herald, augury, indication, threat, presage, *handwriting on the wall.

portentious a. ominous, foreboding, threatening, menacing, doomed, prophetic, inauspicious, unpromising. ANT. reassuring, encouraging.

portion n. part, share, cut, section, division, ration, measure, segment, parcel, hunk, chunk, serving, allotment.

portion v. divide, apportion, segment, allocate, section, ration, dispense, dole out, mete out.

portly a. stout, large, heavy, corpulent, fat, rotund, plump, spherical, obese, pudgy. ANT. thin, anorexic, skinny.

portray v. depict, represent, characterize, limn, caricature, profile, mimic, delineate, simulate.

pose n. position, posture, stance, attitude, air, mien, guise, pretense, facade.

pose v. **1.** STRIKE A POSE position, posture, stand, model, sit for, assume an attitude. **2.** AFFECT pretend, put on, feign, posture, put on an act, show off, *put on airs, *peacock. **3.** PUT FORTH ask, offer, assert, posit, propound.

posh a. luxurious, elegant, grand, *ritzy, deluxe, sumptuous, rich, opulent, *swanky, fancy. ANT. humble, modest, low-class.

position *n.* **1.** LOCATION site, placement, place, locality, situation, *whereabouts, spot, point, bearings. **2.** ATTITUDE stand, point of view, viewpoint, outlook, opinion. **3.** POSTURE pose, stance, attitude. **4.** JOB post, office, function, duty, responsibility, appointment. **5.** STATUS standing, class, eminence, station, stature, prestige.

positive *a.* **1.** CERTAIN absolute, express, explicit, definite, unqualified, categorical, sure, emphatic, precise, specific, firm. **2.** BENEFICIAL useful, good, constructive, helpful, practical. ANT. *1. uncertain, qualified, equivocal. 2. negative, deleterious.*

positively *adv.* absolutely, certainly, surely, definitely, undeniably, categorically, doubtlessly, unquestionably, emphatically.

possess *v.* have, own, hold, enjoy, control, retain, occupy, be blessed with, keep, maintain.

possessed *a.* bedeviled, bewitched, haunted, cursed, crazed, entranced, under a spell, enthralled, demonized.

possession *n.* **1.** OWNERSHIP custody, control, hold, proprietorship, title, occupancy. **2.** PROPERTY belonging, effect, holding, *things, *stuff, worldly good.

possessive *a.* greedy, grasping, acquisitive, proprietary, controlling, dominating. ANT. *generous.*

possibility *n.* chance, likelihood, odds, feasibility, prospect, probablity, plausibility, eventuality, hazard.

possible *a.* feasible, doable, conceivable, attainable, imaginable, obtainable, viable, potential, probable, likely. ANT. *impossible, unlikely, unthinkable.*

post *n.* **1.** UPRIGHT shaft, pile, column, stake, support, prop, stud. **2.** JOB position, office, duty, appointment, situation, role, assignment. **3.** STATION lookout, beat.

post *v.* put up, display, affix, publicize, announce, notify, report, circulate.

poster *n.* placard, bill, advertisement, picture, artistic work, print, lithograph, illustration, reproduction.

posterior *n.* backside, rump, rear, buttock, *butt, bottom, tail, *tush. ANT. *anterior, fore.*

posterior *a.* rear, back, hind, after, last.

posterity *n.* descendants, following generations, successors, heirs, offspring, progeny. ANT. *ancestors.*

postman *n.* mailman, mailwoman, letter carrier.

postpone *v.* delay, defer, suspend, put off, put on hold, shelve, *issue a rain check, cancel.

postscript *n.* P.S., P.P.S., epilogue, appendix, addendum, conclusion, closing thought, afterthought.

postulate *n.* assumption, supposition, presumption, theory, hypothesis, guess, speculation, fundamental.

POSTULATE *v.* [POS chuh LATE] to assume without proof. *Astronomers postulate that extraterrestrial life exists in the universe.* SYN. assume, suppose, guess, theorize, hypothesize, figure, posit, surmise, take for granted, speculate.

posture *n.* **1.** STANCE position, pose, carriage, bearing, aspect, attitude, deportment. **2.** OPINION attitude, frame of mind, point of view, outlook. **3.** CIRCUMSTANCES condition, situation, state of affairs.

pot *n.* **1.** KETTLE saucepan, cauldron, boiler, vessel, pressure cooker. **2.** MARIJUANA *dope, *weed, *grass. SEE MARIJUANA

potable *n.* drink, beverage.

potable *a.* drinkable, fit to drink, palatable, pure, non-toxic, clean. ANT. *toxic.*

potato *n.* tuber, *spud, yam.

potent *a.* effective, powerful, strong, fertile, vital, dynamic, cogent, vigorous, compelling, forceful, *packing a punch, virile, influential, moving, weighty, efficacious. ANT. *impotent, weak, powerless, helpless, ineffectual.*

potentate *n.* ruler, monarch, sovereign, emperor, king, prince, crowned head, president, chieftain, dictator.

potential *n.* capability, untapped ability, capacity, *makings, possibility, promise, prospect, *sleeping giant.

potential *a.* possible, latent, unrealized, *sleeping, dormant, promising, budding, future, lurking, developing.

pothole *n.* rut, chuckhole, frost heave, pit, crater, pocket, cavity, fracture, chasm.

potion *n.* elixir, concoction, brew, drink, dose, medicine, *love potion, tonic, remedy, mixture.

potpourri *n.* mixture, hodgepodge, medley, miscellany, assortment, *mixed bag, mélange, *combo, mishmash, hash.

pouch *n.* bag, sack, pocket, holder, receptacle, poke.

pounce *v.* spring, leap, swoop, jump, assault, descend upon, surprise.

pound *n.* enclosure, pen, holding pen, kennel.

pound *v.* **1.** BANG beat, strike, batter, drub, wallop, hammer, hit, pelt, thump. **2.** PULSATE palpitate, beat, throb, hammer, flutter.

pour *v.* **1.** LET FLOW spill, decant, slosh, drop, drip, trickle, dribble, spew, splash, funnel, stream, gush, flow, cascade. **2.** RAIN HARD *rain cats and dogs, drench, flood, *come down in buckets, *come down in sheets, soak, splatter.

pout *v.* sulk, mope, put on a long face, roll out one's lip, brood, *feel sorry for oneself, sniffle. ANT. *smile, grin, laugh.* SEE CRY

poverty *n.* poorness, want, need, destitution, indigence, penuriness, privation, penury, financial distress, *wolf at the door, *Dickensian poverty, *hand-to-mouth existence, homelessness, lack, scarcity, paucity, insufficiency. "The parent of revolution and crime."—Aristotle. "The reward of honest fools."—Colley Cibber. "Life near the bone, where it is sweetest."—Henry Thoreau. ANT. *wealth, riches, affluence, plenty, abundance.*

poverty-stricken *a.* impoverished, strapped, broke. SEE POOR

power *n.* **1.** PHYSICAL FORCE energy, strength, might, brawn, muscle, horsepower, potency, *punch, virility, vigor, *oomph. **2.** ABILITY capacity, capability, aptitude, *what it takes, faculty, skill, endowment. **3.** CONTROLLING FORCE mastery, authority, domination, sway, clout, weight, command, might, influence, *pull, importance, *friends in high places. "The application of intelligence to force."—Arthur Corey. "A drug, the desire for which increases with the habit."—Bertrand Russell. ANT. *weakness, impotency, powerlessness, helplessness.*

powerful *a.* **1.** PHYSICALLY STRONG mighty, potent, energetic, brawny, muscular, *built, *strapping, robust, vigorous, hulking, massive, *built like an ox. **2.** AUTHORITATIVE, EFFECTIVE commanding, dominant, in control, influential, controlling, potent, capable, forceful, preeminent, important, *carrying a lot of weight, *having a lot of clout, puissant. ANT. *1. weak, feeble, *wimpy, emasculated. 2. powerless, unimportant, submissive, helpless.*

powerless *a.* weak, impotent, helpless, prostrate, incapacitated, emasculated, debilitated, ineffectual, incapable, paralyzed. ANT. *powerful, potent, effective.*

powwow *n.* meeting, council, conference.

practical *a.* useful, realistic, utilitarian, sensible, down-to-earth, sane, workable, practicable, functional, serviceable, pragmatic. ANT. *impractical, unworkable, unrealistic.*

practically *adv.* just about, nearly, almost, virtually.

practice *n.* **1.** TRAINING repetition, drilling, rehearsal, discipline, preparation, conditioning. **2.** HABIT routine, way, custom, fashion, manner, method, system, procedure, mode, wont, convention. **3.** PROFESSION occupation, firm, business, work, trade, clientele.

practice *v.* **1.** TRAIN drill, rehearse, prepare, condition, discipline, perfect, exercise, polish, refine. **2.** CARRY OUT do, perform, observe, follow, employ. **3.** WORK AT be employed with, pursue, ply, specialize.

practitioner *n.* professional, expert, specialist, master, pro, agent, artist, novice, hobbyist, doctor, nurse, scientist.

PRAGMATIC *a.* [prag MAT ik] actual, practical, real-world, as opposed to the theoretical or speculative. *He looked for pragmatic solutions, not daydreamed ideals.* SYN. actual, practical, real-world, down-to-earth, utilitarian, workable, sensible, sober, hard, hard-nosed. ANT. *theoretical, idealistic, unrealistic.*

prairie *n.* grassland, plain, meadow, veldt, pasture, tundra. SEE FIELD

praise *n.* compliments, commendation, applause, acclaim, good words, approval, tribute, recognition, laudation, extolment, cheers. "That which makes good men better and bad men worse."—Thomas Fuller. "The sweetest of all sounds."—Zenophon. ANT. *condemnation, disapproval.*

praise *v.* commend, compliment, flatter, applaud, acclaim, approve, pay tribute, laud, extol, hail, boost, put in a good word for. ANT. *condemn, criticize, disparage.*

praiseworthy *a.* commendable, admirable, laudable, meritorious, worthy, fine, honorable, sterling, excellent. ANT. *contemptible, despicable, awful.*

prank *n.* practical joke, trick, antic, mischief, *cheap trick, gag, caper, sport, shenanigans.

prattle *n.* chatter, babble, blather, twaddle, drivel, jabber, blabbing.

pray *v.* plead, petition, bow one's head, appeal, supplicate, implore, solicit, entreat, say grace, ask forgiveness, give thanks.

prayer *n.* pleading, petition, appeal, supplication, imploring, entreaty, request, thanksgiving, grace, benediction, worship, litany, communion with God. "A window to heaven."—Israel Baal Shem Tob. "A ladder on which thoughts mount to God."—Abraham Heschel. "A direct approach to the throbbing heart of the universe."—Israel Bettan.

WORD FIND

beads: rosary

enemy, prayer calling for a calamity to befall one's: imprecation

evening: vesper

Islam call to adhan: azan

Islam prayer mat: seggadeh

Jewish mourning prayer: kaddish

Jewish "standing" prayer: amidah

knee, get down on one: genuflect

meal: grace

mosque's prayer leader: imam

nine day: novena

saint's prayer made on behalf of others: intercession

shawl, Jewish: tallith

sung or spoken supplications with congregational replies: litany

synagogue's prayer leader: cantor

trust, to: amen

SEE CHURCH, CLERGY, RELIGION

preach v. deliver a sermon, sermonize, spread the gospel, moralize, teach, lecture, pontificate, evangelize, minister, exhort, get up on one's moral soapbox, counsel, admonish.

preacher n. clergyman, minister, evangelist, pastor, reverend, man of the cloth, parson, ecclesiastic, rabbi, cleric. "God's ambassador."—William Cowper. "A messenger, not an actor."—Ralph Sockman.

precarious a. insecure, risky, dangerous, chancy, unsafe, slippery, perilous, unstable, shaky, *out on a limb, *hanging by a thread, treacherous, unpredictable. ANT. secure, safe, stable.

precaution n. caution, case, safety measure, safeguard, insurance, provision, foresight, preparation, wariness, heedfulness, circumspection.

precede v. go before, antedate, antecede, usher in, preface, lead, predate, forerun, head up. ANT. follow, succeed, ensue.

PRECEDENCE n. [PRES uh duns] priority. The baby's welfare took precedence over all other matters. SYN. priority, preeminence, importance, preference, supremacy, rank, superiority, right, *front seat, *front burner. ANT. *back seat, *back burner, second place.

PRECEDENT n. [PRES uh dunt] a prior instance that serves as an example, model or guideline, especially an earlier case in a law matter. The lawyer found numerous precedents to help support his case. SYN. example, model,

guideline, standard, prior instance, classic example, pattern, paradigm, exemplar.

preceding a. previous, prior, earlier, foregoing, antecedent, former, aforementioned, preliminary, erstwhile. ANT. following, upcoming, succeeding.

PRECEPT n. [PREE sept] a rule to live by; maxim. He lived by the precept, "Live and let live." SYN. rule to live by, maxim, principle, direction, commandment, rule, axiom, canon, tenet, motto, guideline.

precinct n. division, subdivision, district, neighborhood, section, quarter, zone, ward, *neck of the woods.

precious a. 1. COSTLY valuable, priceless, inestimable, expensive, high-priced, rich. 2. BELOVED dear, loved, adored, treasured, cherished, worshipped, idolized, darling, esteemed, favorite. 3. FASTIDIOUS overrefined, particular, finicky, overnice, fussy, affected, unnatural, pretentious, flowery, dainty. ANT. 1. cheap, worthless. 2. despised, hated. 3. sloppy, careless, cloddish.

precipice n. drop-off, cliff, ledge, height, brink, *vertiginous overlook, bluff, escarpment.

PRECIPITATE v. [pri SIP i TATE] to cause to happen sooner than desired or expected. The embargo precipitated the rise of oil prices. SYN. hasten, quicken, speed, expedite, accelerate, advance, trigger, instigate, drive, impel.

precipitate a. hasty, rash, headlong, rushed, hurried, sudden, abrupt, impetuous, reckless, impatient. ANT. considered, planned, expected.

precipitous a. sheer, high, vertiginous. SEE STEEP

precise a. 1. EXACT accurate, specific, pinpoint, correct, *on the button, *on the nose, right, *on the mark, definite, faithful, literal, flawless. 2. FASTIDIOUS finicky, fussy, scrupulous, particular, meticulous, exacting, punctilious. ANT. 1. imprecise, inexact, approximate, rough, loose. 2. careless, casual.

precision n. exactness, accuracy, perfection, correctness, fidelity, faithfulness, rectitude, *Swiss watch accuracy, attention to detail. ANT. inaccuracy, approximation.

PRECLUDE v. [pree KLOOD] to prevent something from happening. A felony conviction precludes any chance for running for public office. SYN. prevent, stop, make impossible, foil, avert, thwart, check, rule out, forestall, hinder, inhibit. ANT. facilitate, allow.

PRECOCIOUS a. [pre KO shus] advanced or mature for one's years. The precocious child composed a symphony by the time he was ten-years-old. SYN. advanced, mature, premature, ahead of one's peers, progressive, bright, early-blooming, intelligent, gifted, developed. ANT. *immature, behind, slow to develop, late-blooming*.

precognition n. clairvoyance, vision, ESP, extra sensory perception, premonition, sixth sense, intuition, fortunetelling, divination, prophecy, prediction.

preconception n. preconceived notion, prejudgment, assumption, presumption, prejudice, predisposition.

PRECURSOR n. [pree KUR sur] something that comes before, forerunner. *A rainy April is the precursor of May flowers.* SYN. forerunner, harbinger, herald, predecessor, usher, vanguard, antecedent, groundbreaker, trailblazer.

predator n. hunter, carnivore, meat-eater, stalker, victimizer, killer, beast, prowler, raptor, bird of prey.

predatory a. eating, attacking, hunting, carnivorous, bloodthirsty, predacious, bestial, voracious, rapacious, omnivorous. ANT. *pacifistic, peaceful*.

predecessor n. forerunner, precursor, antecedent, ancestor, forebear, forefather. ANT. *descendant, successor*.

predestination n. predetermination, fate, God's plan, God's design, God's will, destiny, karma, kismet, doom.

predetermined a. preplanned, fixed, arranged, fated, destined, doomed, preordained, preset, settled, decided. ANT. *uncertain, *up for grabs*.

predicament n. difficulty, scrape, bind, mess, plight, trouble, jam, pickle, hole, strait, *hot water, pinch, corner.

predict v. prophecy, forecast, foresee, foretell, divine, prognosticate, augur, envision, read the signs, guess.

prediction n. prophecy, forecast, prognostication, prognosis, guess, augury, divination, expectation, intuition.

PREDILECTION n. [PRED uh LEK shun] a natural liking or preference. *She had a predilection for ginger snaps.* SYN. liking, fondness, preference, partiality, predisposition, inclination, propensity, penchant, leaning, bias, prejudice. ANT. *aversion, dislike*.

predispose v. make susceptible, influence, bias, sway, prejudice, impress, prime, affect, bend.

predominant a. dominant, superior, leading,

ruling, controlling, paramount, top, preeminent, ranking, supreme, chief. ANT. *subordinate, secondary, minor, inferior*.

preeminent a. dominant, superior, surpassing, unsurpassed, unrivaled, foremost, major, supreme, peerless, incomparable, unparalleled, number one, top. ANT. *inferior, second-rate, minor*.

PREEMPT v. [pree EMPT] to take the place of another beforehand by rights. *The World Series will preempt normal TV programming.* SYN. appropriate, take away, usurp, claim, bump, assume, seize, commandeer.

prefabricate v. preconstruct, preassemble.

preface n. foreword, prologue, introduction, prelude, preamble, overture, opening. ANT. *epilogue, postscript*.

preface v. introduce, begin, start, open, initiate. ANT. *close, end*.

prefer v. favor, choose, select, pick, opt for, be partial to, lean toward, desire, single out. ANT. *reject, pass on, dislike*.

preference n. 1. FIRST CHOICE favorite, choice, selection, desire, inclination, pick, leaning, partiality. 2. PRIORITY advantage, precedence, edge, *leg up.

pregnancy n. gestation, fertilization, incubation, *the family way, parturiency.

WORD FIND

abortion, spontaneous: miscarriage

before labor: antepartum

blood discharge before labor: bloody show

brown patches on pregnant woman's skin: *mask of pregnancy, chloasma

dark line on pregnant woman's belly: linea nigra

embryo, earliest form of: blastocyst

false pregnancy: pseudocyesis

fetal movement, mother's first perception of: quickening

fluid: amniotic fluid

fluid secreted from breast prior to birth: colostrum

fluid withdrawal from uterus, test: amniocentesis

genetic test sampling of placenta: chorionic villus sampling

implantation of fertilized eggs, mechanical: in vitro fertilization

nausea: morning sickness

optical examination of fetus through scope: fetoscopy

organ providing nutrients and oxygen to fetus from mother: placenta

premature birth, abnormality leading to: incompetent cervix

semen, artificial deposit of: artificial insemination

sympathetic pregnancy symptoms of father: couvade

three-month division: trimester

ultrasound picture of fetus: sonogram

uterus, development of egg outside of: ectopic pregnancy

SEE BABY, BIRTH

pregnant *a.* **1.** EXPECTING *in a family way, gravid, *with child, parturient, gestating, carrying. **2.** MEANINGFUL important, weighty, significant, telling.

prehistoric *a.* early, primitive, primeval, antediluvian, ancient, antiquated, pleistocene, pliocene, miocene, oligocene, eocene, paleocene, cretaceous, jurassic, triassic, permian, paleozoic, cambrian, pre-cambrian. ANT. *future, modern.*

prejudice *n.* bias, preconceived idea, preconception, predisposition, jaundiced eye, foregone conclusion, bigotry, racism, sexism, chauvinism, homophobia, intolerance, partiality, discrimination, narrow-mindedness. "An opinion without judgment."—Voltaire. "Weighing the facts with your thumb on the scales."—Leon Aikman. "The child of ignorance."—William Hazlitt. ANT. *openmindedness, objectivity, fairness, tolerance.*

prejudicial *a.* encouraging preconceptions, damaging, misleading, delusive, misguiding, presumed, biased, predetermined. ANT. *unbiased.*

preliminary *a.* introductory, preparatory, initial, first, preceding, antecedent, opening, precursory. ANT. *ending, final.*

prelude *n.* introduction, preface, preamble, beginning, opening, overture, warmup, prologue.

premature *a.* early, too soon, unready, green, immature, undeveloped, unripe, precipitate, hurried, *half-baked, *jumping the gun, untimely. ANT. *late, overdue, behind.*

premeditated *a.* planned, prearranged, calculated, mapped out, studied, conscious, thought-out, intentional, deliberate, willful. ANT. *spur-of-the-moment, in the heat of the moment, spontaneous, impulsive, unplanned.*

premiere *n.* debut, opening night, first showing.

premise *n.* hypothesis, argument, postulate, proposition, foundation, theory, supposition, basis, assertion.

premium *n.* reward, bonus, prize, gift, incentive, *carrot, extra, *gravy, fringe benefit, *perk.

premonition *n.* foreboding, presentiment, forewarning, feeling, *gut feeling, hunch, apprehension, intuition, *bad vibes, omen, portent.

preoccupied *a.* busy, occupied, engaged, involved, immersed, absorbed, *wrapped up, engrossed, removed, *lost in thought, *deep in thought.

preparation *n.* **1.** MAKING READY arrangement, development, priming, establishment, groundwork, anticipation, *prep work, provision, framework, setting up, grooming, training. **2.** CONCOCTION compound, mixture, composition, drug, prescription.

prepare *v.* ready, prime, groom, arrange, do groundwork, *prep, set up, anticipate, plan, develop, smooth the way, train.

preponderance *n.* dominance, supremacy, bulk, weight, predominance, *lion's share, biggest part, majority, prevalence. ANT. *lesser part, minority.*

preposterous *a.* absurd, ridiculous, outrageous, ludicrous, asinine, foolish, silly, nonsensical, crazy, insane, impossible, unbelievable, unthinkable. ANT. *logical, reasonable, sensible.*

PREREQUISITE *a.* [pree REK wuh zit] required, necessary. *Math may always be a prerequisite course.* SYN. required, necessary, demanded, essential, imperative, called for, obligatory, mandatory, needed. ANT. *elective, unnecessary.*

PREROGATIVE *n.* [pree ROG uh tiv] a right or privilege. *It was her prerogative to close the store whenever she wished.* SYN. right, privilege, choice, authority, liberty, freedom, advantage, license, exemption.

preschool *n.* nursery school, day care center, kindergarten.

prescribe *v.* direct, order, ordain, set down, recommend, dictate, assign, select, advocate, exact, rule.

prescription *n.* order, direction, recommendation, directive, instruction, requirement, preparation, concoction, medicine, drug, dose.

presence *n.* **1.** ATTENDANCE existence, occupancy, being, residence, proximity. **2.** POISE confidence, bearing, air, demeanor, charisma, personality, carriage, self-assurance, aura.

presence of mind *n.* calm, coolness, coolheadedness, clearheadedness.

present *n.* **1.** HERE AND NOW today, now, this instant. **2.** GIFT offering, favor, benefaction, donation, premium, gratuity, give-away, bonus.

present v. **1.** INTRODUCE have one meet, acquaint. **2.** EXHIBIT display, show, demonstrate. **3.** PUT FORWARD advance, pose, submit, proffer, *trot out for inspection, offer, profess, declare. **4.** GIVE hand over, confer, bestow, award, entrust, donate, submit.

present a. **1.** CURRENT contemporary, existing, immediate, at hand, present-day, modern, at this moment. **2.** HERE at hand, in attendance, nearby, on hand, within reach. ANT. *1. past, bygone, previous. 2. absent, away.*

presentable a. groomed, dressed, neat and clean, fit to be seen, acceptable, respectable, suitable, *decent, passable. ANT. *sloppy, disreputable, unsuitable.*

presentation n. performance, exhibition, show, production, demonstration, display, offering, gift, bestowal, award, pitch.

presentiment n. foreboding, feeling, *bad vibes, premonition, apprehension, *gut feeling, intuition, hunch, presage.

presently adv. shortly, soon, directly, now, immediately, forthwith.

preservation n. conservation, maintenance, protection, conservancy, safekeeping, saving, sustenance, upkeep, perpetuation.

preserve n. reserve, game reserve, sanctuary, zoo, refuge, haven, park, conservation area.

preserve v. **1.** PROTECT save, conserve, maintain, sustain, keep up, safeguard, perpetuate. **2.** TO KEEP FRESH can, pickle, salt, cure, smoke, dry, corn, refrigerate, freeze. ANT. *1. ruin, neglect. 2. let spoil, let rot.*

preside v. chair, oversee, direct, control, supervise, run, officiate, *be in the driver's seat, *hold the reins, conduct, head.

president n. chief executive, head of state, commander-in-chief, first citizen, chief executive officer, CEO, chairman. "Chief servant."—Mohandas Gandhi. "A link in the long chain of his country's destiny, past and future."—Herbert Hoover. SEE CONGRESS, ELECTION, GOVERNMENT, POLITICS

press n. **1.** MEDIA reporters, newsmen, newswomen, fourth estate, TV, radio, journalists, photojournalists. SEE NEWSPAPER **2.** CROWD throng, mob, pack, swarm, horde, crush.

press v. **1.** PUSH squeeze, depress, crush, clamp, compress, bear down, flatten, squash, put weight on, cramp, compact, hug, embrace. **2.** IRON smooth, steam. **3.** FORCE compel, impel, constrain, move. **4.** REQUEST entreat, plead, petition, importune, solicit.

pressing a. urgent, importunate, high-priority, crucial, exigent, critical, vital, imperative, important, compelling, momentous. ANT. *unimportant, inconsequential, trivial.*

pressure n. **1.** COMPRESSION squeezing, tension, load, heaviness, weight, force, gravity. **2.** STRAIN stress, duress, demand, tension, burden, load, cross, millstone. **3.** INFLUENCE force, power, coercion, persuasion, pull, sway, compulsion, obligation, necessity, arm-twisting.

pressure v. compel, influence, force, push, persuade, coerce, press, drive, arm-twist, constrain, *lean on, *railroad, *put the screws to, *put the squeeze on.

prestige n. status, reputation, repute, stature, standing, fame, prominence, esteem, distinction, notoriety, rank, influence, power.

prestigious a. esteemed, distinguished, renowned, reputable, notable, eminent, great, famous, illustrious, impressive, influential. ANT. *unknown, disrespected.*

presumably adv. probably, ostensibly, likely, in all probability.

presume v. **1.** ASSUME take for granted, think, guess, surmise, suppose, believe, take it, postulate, consider. **2.** DARE venture, take liberties, have the audacity, overstep, go too far.

presumption n. **1.** ASSUMPTION thinking, supposition, guess, belief, suspicion, conjecture, hypothesis, premise. **2.** FORWARDNESS effrontery, audacity, gall, boldness, daring, *cheek, nerve, insolence.

PRESUMPTUOUS a. [pree ZUMP choo us] overly bold or confident and taking too much for granted. *It was quite presumptuous of her to take the blue ribbon before the winner was even announced.* SYN. bold, nervy, confident, audacious, forward, *ballsy, rude, cocksure, brazen, lordly, arrogant, egotistical, insolent, pompous. ANT. *unassuming, modest, humble.*

pretend v. **1.** MAKE BELIEVE play act, imagine, put on, suppose. **2.** FEIGN fake, bluff, simulate, *put on, dissemble, fool, deceive, act, sham, counterfeit, affect.

PRETENSE n. [PREE tens] a falsification, put-on, show or affectation. *His claim of being rich was only a pretense to impress women.* SYN. falsification, put-on, show, affectation, imposture, fake, display, act, charade, showing off, facade, simulation, masquerade, posing, ruse, trick. ANT. *truth, reality, honest.*

PRETENTIOUS a. [pree TEN shus] putting

on airs, especially of importance or grandness, ostentatious. *They were a bunch of pretentious snobs.* SYN. affected, self-important, bragging, showy, ostentatious, boastful, pompous, assuming, conceited, *la-di-da, vainglorious, snobbish, *highfalutin. ANT. *down-to-earth, unassuming, natural, modest, humble.*

pretext *n.* excuse, front, *story, alibi, cover, alleged reason, *song and dance, subterfuge, guise.

pretty *a.* attractive, comely, beautiful, lovely, nice-looking, cute, appealing, eye-catching, foxy, becoming, ravishing, fair, handsome. ANT. *ugly, plain, homely.*

pretty *adv.* fairly, moderately, reasonably, passably, adequately.

prevail *v.* **1.** WIN OVER overcome, dominate, best, succeed, triumph, conquer, master, *come out on top. **2.** PREDOMINATE be widespread, be prevalent, abound, preponderate. ANT. *1. lose, fail, give up. 2. be rare.*

prevailing *a.* superior, dominant, affective, prevalent, widespread, general, preponderant, predominant, universal, popular, current, principal, reigning, in style. ANT. *outmoded, disappearing, failing.*

prevalent *a.* prevailing, common, widespread, abundant, extensive, general, popular, pervasive, rampant. ANT. *rare, uncommon, infrequent.*

prevaricate *v.* equivocate, evade the truth. SEE LIE

prevent *v.* stop, prohibit, preclude, avert, stave off, arrest, *nip in the bud, thwart, bar, check, restrict, block. ANT. *allow, facilitate, cause.*

prevention *n.* stoppage, prohibition, preclusion, arrest, restriction, blockage, deterrence, obstruction, forestalling, interception.

previous *a.* prior, earlier, preceding, past, antecedent, anterior, erstwhile, aforementioned. ANT. *future, succeeding, upcoming, ensuing.*

previously *adv.* earlier, in the past, before, hitherto, formerly, once, at one time, a while ago.

prey *n.* victim, the hunted, mark, quarry, kill, spoil, *sitting duck.

prey *v.* hunt, kill, victimize, eat, devour, feed on, attack, pounce, consume, exploit, use.

price *n.* cost, asking price, sticker price, charge, retail, wholesale, bill, expense, value, rate, assessment, appraisal, outlay, *damage.

priceless *a.* invaluable, precious, valuable, dear,

expensive, *worth its weight in gold, *worth all the oil in Arabia, costly, prized, treasured. ANT. *cheap, *dime a dozen, worthless.*

prick *v.* pierce, stick, puncture, impale, jab, stab, cut, perforate, lance.

pride *n.* **1.** SELF-ESTEEM self-respect, self-worth, dignity, satisfaction, self-confidence, healthy ego, *amour propre. **2.** ARROGANCE conceit, hauteur, haughtiness, egotism, self-importance, vainglory, overconfidence, smugness, presumption, cockiness. "Cap and bells for a fool."—Alfred Lord Tennyson. "Pampered vanity."—Joanna Baillie.

priest *n.* father, minister, clergyman, man of the cloth, ecclesiastic, vicar, padre, chaplain, pastor, deacon. "Crutches for the crippled life of the soul."—Franz Kafka. SEE CLERGYMAN, PREACHER

priesthood *n.* ministry, clergy, the cloth. SEE CHURCH, RELIGION

prim *a.* formal, proper, demure, correct, Victorian, straitlaced, prissy, prudish, upright, stiff, decorous. ANT. *loose, wild, unrefined, informal, casual.*

PRIMA DONNA *n.* [PREE muh DONN uh] a moody, complaining and egotistical person. Also, the lead female vocalist in an opera. *Her success made her an unappealing prima donna.* SYN. **1.** SPOILED BRAT crybaby, *snot, witch, grouch, loudmouth, temperamental whiner, princess, egotist, *hell on wheels, *jerk. **2.** STAR headliner, soloist, lead vocalist.

primal *a.* primeval, original, prehistoric, primitive, aboriginal.

primarily *adv.* mainly, in the first place, fundamentally, first and foremost, principally, chiefly, largely.

primary *a.* **1.** FIRST original, earliest, primal, primordial, introductory, initial, beginning. **2.** MAIN principal, chief, basic, essential, fundamental, first, capital, major. ANT. *1. secondary, succeeding. 2. minor, secondary.*

primate *n.* simian, hominid, ape, monkey, prosimian, chimpanzee, gorilla.

prime *n.* best days, youth, springtime of life, heyday, peak, height, spring, summer.

prime *v.* prepare, *prep, ready, groom, train, break in, coach.

prime *a.* SEE PRIMARY

prime minister *n.* premier, cabinet head, head, leader, chief executive, office holder, chief minister. SEE GOVERNMENT

primer *n.* textbook, how-to, reference, introductory volume, reader. SEE BOOK

primeval *a.* primal, primordial, prehistoric, primitive, ancient, earliest, antediluvian, pristine. ANT. *later, recent, modern.*

primitive *a.* **1.** ANCIENT original, earliest, primal, primordial, primeval, primary, elemental, rudimentary. **2.** CRUDE rough, undeveloped, simple, uncivilized, unsophisticated, wild, natural, barbaric. ANT. *1. modern, contemporary, late. 2. refined, sophisticated, civilized.*

primordial *a.* SEE PRIMITIVE

primp *v.* groom, preen, beautify, dress up, *gussy up, *doll up, *spruce up.

principal *n.* **1.** CHIEF head, actor, performer, player, star, combatant. **2.** HEADMASTER dean.

principal *a.* main, major, chief, leading, primary, dominant, foremost, supreme, star, key, most important. ANT. *secondary, supporting, minor.*

principle *n.* **1.** TRUTH law, doctrine, fundamental, standard, rule, foundation, basis, criterion, precept, theory, canon. **2.** PRINCIPLES/ MORALS ethics, code, policies, guiding principle, belief, tenet, dogma, standards, credo, scruples, conscience.

print *v.* compose, write, imprint, run off, type, stamp, hand-letter.

printer *n.* typesetter, publisher, photocopier.

prior *a.* previous, earlier, former, antecedent, anterior, preceding, preexisting, erstwhile, aforementioned. ANT. *following, upcoming, subsequent.*

priority *n.* precedence, leading concern, rank, urgency, preference, weight, preeminence, seniority.

prison *n.* penitentiary, penal institution, jail, house of detention, house of correction, lockup, cell, *cooler, *clink, *poky, *can, *hoosegow, *slammer, *big house. "Stones of law."—William Blake.

WORD FIND

castle: dungeon
cell search by guards: shakedown
convicts chained together for work detail: chain gang
death penalty: capital punishment
division: ward
drunks, overnight cell for: drunk tank
early release for good behavior: parole
famous: Alcatraz, Sing Sing, Newgate
head: warden
informer: *rat, fink
inmates: convicts, *cons
isolation cell: solitary confinement

jailer: turnkey
legal expert, prisoner who becomes: jailhouse lawyer
life term, prisoner serving: *lifer
military: stockade
reforming of prisoner: rehabilitation
return to life of crime after prison: recidivism
section holding those sentenced to death: death row
ship: brig
smuggler of contraband: *mule
spousal relations visit: conjugal visit
transfer of prisoner to other jurisdiction: extradition
youth: reformatory, reform school
war camp: concentration camp

prisoner *n.* SEE PRISON

prissy *a.* *goody-goody, straitlaced, prudish, prim, *goody two shoes, overnice, fussy, fastidious, particular, puritanical. ANT. *wanton, unruly, loose.*

PRISTINE *a.* [pris TEEN] unspoiled or pure, as something in its original state. *The pristine mountains of Alaska should be left forever wild.* SYN. unspoiled, pure, untouched, virginal, natural, primitive, primordial, unsullied, uncorrupted, clean. ANT. *spoiled, ruined, sullied.*

privacy *n.* solitude, separation, concealment, secrecy, isolation, sequestration, seclusion.

private *a.* **1.** PERSONAL secret, internal, confidential, intimate, individual, nonpublic, own. **2.** SECLUDED isolated, sequestered, reclusive, secret, concealed, cloistered, hermitic, remote, solitary. **3.** UNDISCLOSED secret, *under wraps, quiet, confidential, *hush-hush. **4.** RESTRICTED off-limits, closed to the public, exclusive. ANT. *1. public. 3. public, announced, out in the open. 4. public, unrestricted, open.*

privation *n.* deprivation, need, want, scarcity, lack, poverty, hardship, destitution, indigence. ANT. *wealth, affluence.*

privilege *n.* right, advantage, due, favor, entitlement, perquisite, liberty, prerogative, benefit, birthright.

privileged *a.* entitled, favored, empowered, exempt, immune, sanctioned, authorized, accommodated, given preferential treatment. ANT. *disadvantaged, underprivileged.*

privy *n.* latrine, toilet. SEE OUTHOUSE

prize *n.* award, winnings, reward, title, blue ribbon, medal, trophy, loving cup, decoration, laurel, honors, jackpot, haul, stake, spoils, booby prize.

prize v. value, regard highly, esteem, appreciate, hold dear, cherish, treasure.

prize a. award-winning, winning, choice. SEE BEST

probability n. likelihood, chance, prospect, possibility, odds, expectation, outlook.

probable a. likely, *odds-on, reasonable, expected, anticipated, possible, presumed, plausible, *in the cards, foreseeable. ANT. unlikely, improbable, implausible.

probation n. trial period, test period, suspension of sentence.

probe n. investigation, examination, inquiry, inquisition, exploration, study, scrutiny, feeler.

probe v. investigate, examine, inquire, look into, explore, study, scrutinize, analyze, check out, poke about, interrogate.

problem n. 1. DIFFICULTY complication, knot, trouble, dilemma, quandary, mess, *pickle, predicament, *can of worms, *headache, *pain in the neck, *hassle. 2. PUZZLE brainteaser, question, riddle, conundrum, *stumper, *head-scratcher, *hard nut to crack.

problematic a. 1. DIFFICULT hard, tricky. 2. QUESTIONABLE doubtful, debatable, uncertain, unsettled, dubious, disputable, moot, suspect, hard to believe, *full of holes, undetermined. ANT. 1. easy, simple. 2. certain, settled.

procedure n. method, manner, process, course, sequence, steps, mode, practice, formula, way.

proceed v. go, go ahead, go on, continue, progress, move on, carry on, get on with. ANT. stop, halt, suspend.

proceedings n. business, matters, *doings, activities, affairs, transactions, agenda, minutes.

proceeds n. take, earnings, income, profit, receipts, gain, revenue, gross, net, gate, box office. SEE MONEY

process n. method, workings, operation, modus operandi, procedure, course, sequence, technique, formula, way, steps, stages, mechanism.

process v. work, refine, handle, prepare, treat, convert, cook, cure, deal with.

procession n. parade, train, column, caravan, cavalcade, file, march, cortege, motorcade.

proclaim v. announce, declare, state, make

known, profess, voice, broadcast, herald, advertise. ANT. hush up, cover up.

proclamation n. announcement, declaration, pronouncement, notice, statement, profession, manifesto, decree, edict.

proclivity n. inclination, tendency, propensity, disposition, predilection, penchant, weakness, leaning, bias. ANT. aversion, dislike.

procrastinate v. put off, stall, delay, *drag one's feet, *shilly-shally, postpone, dawdle, temporize, prolong, protract, play for time. ANT. *get cracking, *get a move on, expedite. "The art of keeping up with yesterday."—Don Marquis.

procreate v. produce, beget, reproduce, breed, parent, propagate, spawn, mother, father, engender, bear.

procure v. get, obtain, acquire, secure, come by, get one's hands on, get hold of, pick up, appropriate, buy, purchase, score.

prod v. poke, jab, shove, elbow, finger, punch, *goose, nudge, shove, goad, urge, rouse, motivate, spur, provoke, incite, move.

PRODIGAL a. [PROD uh gul] extremely wasteful or extravagant. *Joe's prodigal grandson spent his entire inheritance within a week.* SYN. wasteful, extravagant, excessive, squandering, spendthrift, lavish, immoderate, improvident, reckless. ANT. *thrifty, frugal, penny-pinching.*

PRODIGIOUS a. [pruh DIJ us] huge, powerful, spectacular or astounding. *Climbing Mt. Everest is a prodigious undertaking.* SYN. huge, massive, enormous, colossal, stupendous, Herculean, immense, monumental, tremendous, powerful, extraordinary, astounding, spectacular, phenomenal, impressive, amazing. ANT. *tiny, trivial, pint-sized, common, ordinary.*

PRODIGY n. [PROD i jee] a child of rare and exceptional talent or intelligence, a young genius. *The young prodigy attended college at the age of twelve.* SYN. wonder, genius, *whiz kid, wunderkind, sensation, marvel, *freak, phenomenon, gifted student. "A child who plays the piano when he ought to be in bed."—John Morton.

produce v. 1. MAKE manufacture, create, bear, generate, form, fabricate, construct, invent, devise, fashion, frame, turn out. 2. CAUSE effect, bring about, generate, result in, breed. 3. SHOW FOR INSPECTION display, present, offer, exhibit, show, disclose.

product n. good, commodity, creation, work,

handiwork, production, turnout, merchandise, result, end, yield, outcome, issue.

production *n.* manufacture, creation, fabrication, generation, formation, assembly, construction, invention, outpost.

productive *a.* fertile, rich, fecund, fruitful, prolific, profitable, gainful, creative, rewarding, worthwhile. ANT. *unproductive, barren, worthless.*

productivity *n.* output, turnout, capacity, yield, production.

PROFANE *a.* [pro FANE] irreverent and disrespectful, especially toward religion. Also, that which is outside of religion. *His profane sense of humor got him in trouble with the church.* SYN. irreverent, disrespectful, blasphemous, impious, sacrilegious, irreligious, ungodly, sinful, crude, nasty. ANT. *religious, pious, devout, Christian.*

profane *v.* desecrate, defile, debase, disrespect, violate, blaspheme, corrupt, taint, abuse. ANT. *revere, respect, worship.*

profanity *n.* swear word, swearing, cuss word, cussing, bad word, *four-letter word, dirty word, oath, expletive, obscenity, blasphemy, irreverence. ANT. *polite word, euphemism, reverence.*

profess *v.* **1.** AFFIRM declare, assert, admit, proclaim, tell, state, acknowledge, confess, avow, announce. **2.** TO CLAIM INSINCERELY purport, allege, pretend, feign, fake, simulate, *swear up and down.

profession *n.* **1.** OCCUPATION line of work, trade, vocation, calling, work, career, business, employment, specialty, job, field, métier. **2.** AFFIRMATION announcement, declaration, assertion, admission, proclamation, statement, confession, claim, pretense.

professional *n.* expert, master, pro, *old hand, veteran, specialist, virtuoso, mavin, journeyman, *crackerjack. ANT. *amateur, dabbler, hobbyist.*

professional *a.* expert, schooled, experienced, trained, masterly, learned, proficient, accomplished, pro, practiced, big league, au fait, accredited. ANT. *amateur, inexperienced, unschooled, incompetent.*

professor *n.* teacher, academic, instructor, educator, *prof, faculty member, doctor, lecturer, fellow, sage, *brain. SEE COLLEGE

professorial *a.* pedantic, pedagogic, scholarly. SEE ACADEMIC, COLLEGE

PROFICIENT *a.* [pro FISH unt] highly competent, skillful, able. *He was a proficient*

craftsman. SYN. competent, skilled, able, talented, masterful, adept, expert, *crack, *crackerjack, capable, accomplished. ANT. *incompetent, incapable, inept.*

profile *n.* **1.** OUTLINE side view, figure, contour, form, silhouette, delineation. **2.** BIOGRAPHY review, sketch, thumbnail sketch, characterization, portrait.

profit *n.* gain, income, proceeds, net, revenue, return, yield, benefit, *take, earnings, *bottom line, *take-home. ANT. *loss, red ink.* SEE MONEY

profit *v.* gain, benefit, yield, take, earn, make money, clear, *clean up, *make a killing, reap, *make a bundle, advance, better, learn. ANT. *lose, suffer, go bankrupt.*

profitable *a.* lucrative, money-making, paying, cost-effective, worthwhile, rewarding, productive, gainful, fruitful, remunerative. ANT. *unprofitable, costly, unproductive.*

PROFLIGATE *a.* [PROF luh git] shamelessly immoral. Also, extravagant and wasteful. *His profligate lifestyle left him penniless and miserable.* SYN. immoral, shameless, debauched, wild, wanton, degenerate, promiscuous, fast, loose, abandoned, unbridled, extravagant, wasteful, excessive, prodigal, lavish, immoderate. ANT. *moral, virtuous, principled, thrifty, economical.*

PROFOUND *a.* [pro FOUND] deep or intense, either physically, intellectually or emotionally. *Her theory of galactic formation was quite profound. She remembered the profound sadness of the day.* SYN. **1.** INTELLECTUAL deep, intelligent, thoughtful, wise, insightful, abstruse, heavy, penetrating, esoteric, enlightened, scholarly, difficult, complex. **2.** EMOTIONAL heartfelt, deep, intense, acute, sincere, keen, heartrending, soul-stirring, moving. **3.** THOROUGH comprehensive, complete, utter, far-reaching, total, absolute. **4.** BOTTOMLESS sunken, fathomless, abysmal. ANT. *1. superficial, shallow, mindless. 2. insincere, unfeeling. 3. partial, slight. 4. shallow.*

PROFUSE *a.* [pro FYOOS] pouring out freely or excessively. *Her profuse apologies fell on deaf ears.* SYN. pouring forth freely, abundant, excessive, free-flowing, overflowing, generous, copious, plentiful, extravagant, lavish, immoderate, prodigal. ANT. *sparse, thin, limited, meager, moderate.*

PROFUSION *n.* [pro FYOO zhun] a great pouring forth, or a great amount. *A profusion* *of daisies colored the meadow.* SYN. outpouring, overflow, great amount, abundance, lavish amount, extravagant supply, bounty, quantity, cornucopia, multitude, excess, flood, plethora. ANT. *dearth, lack, scarcity.*

progeny n. children, offspring, young, issue, descendants, successors, lineage, stock, posterity. ANT. *parents, ancestors, forebears.*

prognosis n. forecast, prognostication, projection. SEE PREDICTION

prognosticator n. seer, diviner, forecaster. SEE PROPHET

program n. **1.** AGENDA schedule, order of business, card, bill, slate, lineup, plan, docket, calendar, timetable. **2.** BROADCAST show, production, presentation, performance, telecast, drama, sitcom, musical. SEE TELEVISION **3.** PROCEDURE plan, course, scheme, way, approach. **4.** COMPUTER PROGRAM software, instructions. SEE COMPUTER

progress n. advance, development, improvement, furtherance, headway, strides forward, progression, march of progress, evolution, breakthrough, gain, growth. ANT. *regression, retreat, recession.* "The law of life."—Robert Browning. "Man's ability to complicate simplicity."—Thor Heyerdahl.

progress v. move forward, develop, grow, gain, improve, make headway, evolve, advance, upgrade, improve, perfect. ANT. *regress, decline, recede, retreat.*

progression n. progress, succession, sequence, cycle, forward march, headway, continuance. ANT. *regression, recession.*

progressive a. forward-looking, modern-minded, prodevelopment, cutting edge, twenty-first century, advancing, liberal, visionary, revolutionary, evolutionary, reformist, dynamic. ANT. *conservative, unchanging, static, abiding, regressive.*

prohibit v. forbid, disallow, proscribe, interdict, ban, outlaw, restrict, prevent, stop, preclude, constrain, block, restrain, deny, put a stop to, *put a lid on. ANT. *allow, authorize, sanction, permit.*

prohibition n. ban, interdiction, proscription, nix, embargo, restriction, outlawing, disallowance, blockage, taboo. ANT. *permission, allowance, authorization.*

project n. venture, undertaking, enterprise, job, work, campaign, occupation, assignment, task, plan, scheme, proposal.

project v. **1.** PLAN propose, calculate, predict, estimate, forecast, scheme, envision, conceive, draft, outline. **2.** JUT bulge, stick out, overhang, protrude. **3.** THROW hurl, cast, shoot, propel, fling, launch.

projection n. **1.** ESTIMATE calculation, prediction, forecast, guess, approximation, figure. **2.** JUT protrusion, overhang, prominence, bump, bulge, extension, shelf.

PROLETARIAT n. [PROH li TAIR ee ut] the industrial working class or working class. *The proletariat are speaking out against higher taxes.* SYN. industrial working class, working class, laborers, blue-collar workers, commoners, lower class, rank and file, plebians, bourgeoisie, the masses, hoi polloi. ANT. *upper class, ruling class, nobility, royalty, aristocrats.*

PROLIFERATE v. [proh LIF uh RATE] to multiply, increase or spread at a fast rate. *Mushrooms proliferate on moist ground.* SYN. multiply, increase, spread, reproduce, breed, *mushroom, grow rampant, *run riot, burgeon, escalate, teem, *snowball, metastasize. ANT. *decrease, die out.*

PROLIFIC a. [proh LIF ik] richly productive, fertile. *A prolific author, he once wrote three books in one year.* SYN. productive, fertile, fruitful, generative, creative, fecund, bountiful. ANT. *sterile, unproductive, barren.*

prologue n. preface, introduction, foreword, opening.

prolong v. extend, draw out, drag out, protract, stretch, lengthen, expand, sustain, perpetuate. ANT. *shorten, curtail, cut short.*

promenade n. walk, walkway, avenue, footpath, course, mall, stroll.

prominence n. **1.** RENOWN fame, distinction, eminence, reputation, notability, standing, importance, greatness, celebrity. **2.** JUTTING bump, projection, bulge, extrusion, eminence, peak, swelling, protrusion, protuberance, hump, lump. ANT. **1.** *obscurity, anonymity.* **2.** *depression, indentation, hole.*

prominent a. **1.** RENOWNED famous, eminent, distinguished, notable, celebrated, well-known, important, great, acclaimed. **2.** STICKING OUT jutting, projecting, conspicuous, standing out, outstanding, glaring, obvious, striking, bulging. ANT. **1.** *obscure, unknown, anonymous.* **2.** *inconspicuous, indented.*

promiscuous a. sexually active, sexually indiscriminate, oversexed, fast, loose, easy, wild, whorish, of easy virtue, wanton, lustful. ANT. *celibate, chaste, virginal.*

promise n. **1.** WORD OF HONOR word, vow, pledge, oath, commitment, assurance, warranty, guarantee, contract, swearing. **2.** POTENTIAL hope, prospect, expectation.

promise v. **1.** GIVE ONE'S WORD pledge, vow, swear, commit, assure, *cross one's heart and hope to die, take an oath, warrant, guarantee. **2.** GIVE HOPE OF suggest, indicate, portend, bode, bespeak, show signs of.

promising a. encouraging, hopeful, full of promise, favorable, bright, up-and-coming, auspicious, rosy, *shaping up, heartening. ANT. *discouraging, disheartening, black.*

promontory n. headland, head, point, cape, projection, bluff, hill, height.

promote v. **1.** PUBLICIZE sell, advertize, *talk up, plug, tout, back, *hype, push, ballyhoo, trumpet, sing praises. **2.** FURTHER advance, foster, boost, support, cultivate, lift. **3.** UPGRADE ONE'S RANK advance, raise, *kick upstairs, move up, graduate. ANT. *1. criticize, condemn, censor, *bad-mouth. 2. retard, inhibit, discourage. 3. demote, downgrade.*

promoter n. supporter, backer, advocate, organizer, publicist, booster, champion, sponsor, proponent.

promotion n. **1.** PUBLICITY selling, advertisement, plugging, touting, backing, *hype, ballyhoo, hoopla. **2.** UPGRADE IN RANK graduation, *kick upstairs, move up, advance, raise. ANT. *1. condemnation, criticism, *bad-mouthing, censoring. 2. demotion, downgrade.*

prompt v. urge, provoke, incite, goad, evoke, cue, stimulate, induce, spur, initiate, prod, arouse, push.

prompt a. quick, punctual, timely, swift, rapid, immediate, expeditious, meteoric. ANT. *late, slow, leisurely.*

promptly adv. at once, immediately, quickly, swiftly, in timely fashion, punctually, pronto, expeditiously, directly, *PDQ. ANT. *eventually, sooner or later, slowly.*

PROMULGATE v. [PROM ul gate] to proclaim or state publicly, publish. *The company will promulgate its new policies soon.* SYN. proclaim, announce, make known, publish, broadcast, declare, communicate, spread the word, present, herald.

prone a. **1.** LYING FLAT prostrate, recumbent, supine, horizontal, face-down. **2.** INCLINED disposed, given, bent, likely, of a mind to, liable, apt. ANT. *1. erect, upright, vertical. 2. disinclined.*

pronounce v. **1.** DECLARE announce, say, assert, decree, proclaim, report, state. **2.** ARTICULATE enunciate, say, vocalize, utter, sound, express, frame a word.

pronounced a. distinct, unmistakable, conspicuous, clear, striking, outstanding, prominent, bold, plain, obvious. ANT. *inconspicuous, subtle, concealed, hidden.*

pronouncement n. declaration, statement, announcement, assertion, proclamation, decree, notification, manifesto.

proof n. evidence, verification, confirmation, authentication, corroboration, validation, certification, substantiation, testimony, facts.

proofread v. copyedit, blue pencil, edit, read, check for errors.

prop n. support, brace, buttress, pillar, stanchion, upright, beam, post, column, joist.

prop v. hold up, carry, support, shoulder, brace, gird, buttress, shore, stand, lean against.

propaganda n. disinformation, brainwashing, indoctrination, lies, distortion, deception, dissemination, psychological manipulation, subversive PR. "Polished lying."—Lin Yutang. "A polite euphemism for deception."—Walter Lippmann.

propagate v. **1.** BREED reproduce, multiply, generate, beget, engender, raise, mother, father, proliferate. **2.** SPREAD disseminate, promulgate, broadcast, publish, circulate, dispense.

propel v. drive, impel, push, shoot, move, launch, throw, thrust, force, send, actuate, hurl.

propellor n. prop, screw, blade, rotor, driver.

PROPENSITY n. [pruh PEN si tee] a natural inclination. *She had a propensity for Swedish meatballs.* SYN. tendency, leaning, bent, partiality, taste, liking, weakness, penchant, predilection, disposition, proclivity. ANT. *aversion, dislike.*

proper a. **1.** SUITABLE appropriate, suited, befitting, apt, right, fit, apropos, correct, sensible. **2.** SEEMLY decent, genteel, polite, correct, *politically correct, mannerly, nice, decorous, acceptable, fitting, comme il faut, refined. **3.** PECULIAR distinctive, distinguishing, own, individual, specific, personal. ANT. *1. unsuitable, ill-fitting, wrong. 2. unseemly, rude, impolite.*

property n. **1.** POSSESSIONS belongings, *things, *stuff, holdings, effects, goods, assets, wealth. **2.** REAL ESTATE land, acreage, estate, plot, lot, house. **3.** CHARACTERISTIC quality, feature, attribute, trait, distinction, mark, trademark.

prophecy *n.* prediction, foretelling, forecast, augury, divination, soothsaying, presage, prognostication, presentiment, second sight, revelation. "Dreaming on things to come."—Shakespeare. SEE DIVINATION

prophesy *v.* predict, foretell, forecast, augur, divine, presage, prognosticate, soothsay, foresee, portend.

prophet *n.* predictor, fortuneteller, forecaster, augur, diviner, prognosticator, soothsayer, seer, astrologer, oracle, prophet of doom, Cassandra. "He who conjectures well."—Euripides.

prophetic *a.* predictive, oracular, foretelling, mantic, premonitory, augural, prognostic, prescient, portentous, ominous.

PROPITIOUS *a.* [pro PISH us] favorable, auspicious. *Some claim that a full moon is a propitious time to plant.* SYN. favorable, auspicious, promising, opportune, timely, good, advantageous, fortunate, conducive, providential. ANT. *adverse, inopportune, unfortunate, bad.*

PROPONENT *n.* [pro PO nunt] a supporter, backer or advocate. *The politician is a vocal proponent of environmental protection.* SYN. supporter, backer, advocate, exponent, champion, upholder, endorser, defender, friend, booster. ANT. *opponent, detractor, critic.*

proportion *n.* **1.** RATIO amount, size, dimension, portion, scale, volume, fraction, measure, degree, division, percentage, quota, relationship. **2.** BALANCE symmetry.

proportions *n.* measurements, size, area. SEE DIMENSIONS

proposal *n.* suggestion, recommendation, presentation, idea, proposition, pitch, tender, plan, scheme, offer, bid.

propose *v.* **1.** SUGGEST recommend, present, pitch, tender, submit, proffer, advance, offer, proposition, make a bid, put forth for consideration. **2.** ASK FOR HAND IN MARRIAGE *pop the question, affiance.

proposition *n.* **1.** OFFER proposal, suggestion, submission, presentation, deal, proffer. **2.** FLIRTATION sexual overture, *come-on, *move.

proprietor *n.* owner, landlord, landlady, deed holder, master, lord of the manor.

PROPRIETY *n.* [pro PRYE i tee] proper behavior, decorum, good manners. *The children conducted themselves with unexpected propriety.* SYN. properness, proper behavior, decorum, good manners, conformity, seemliness, appropriateness, politeness, good form, gentility, etiquette. ANT. *impropriety, rudeness, bad manners.*

propulsion *n.* force, driving force, energy, power, thrust, accelerating force, push.

pro rata *adv.* proportionately, in proportion.

PROSAIC *a.* [proh ZAY ik] dull, ordinary, flat. *His was a prosaic story, the normal details of a quiet life.* SYN. dull, ordinary, flat, unimaginative, *ho-hum, blah, colorless, stale, humdrum, monotonous, trite, tedious. ANT. *interesting, colorful, imaginative.*

PROSCRIBE *v.* [proh SCRIBE] to outlaw, ban, condemn. *The church proscribes pornography.* SYN. outlaw, ban, prohibit, condemn, denounce, forbid, reject, exile, boycott, embargo, banish. ANT. *accept, allow, permit.*

prosecute *v.* file legal proceedings against, try, bring suit, sue, bring to trial, litigate, take to court, seek redress, arraign, indict. SEE COURT, LAW, LAWYERS.

proselytize *v.* espouse, persuade, talk into, convert, convince

prospect *n.* **1.** OUTLOOK expectancy, possibility, likelihood, anticipation, chance, speculation, probability, hope. **2.** VIEW panorama, scene, vista, outlook, aspect, lookout, perspective.

prospect *v.* search, explore, look for, seek, probe, pan.

prospective *a.* future, expected, likely, forthcoming, anticipated, possible, potential, coming, on the horizon, destined, probable. ANT. *unlikely, far-fetched.*

prospector *n.* mineral hunter, rock hunter, rockhound, miner, gold panner, sourdough, wildcat driller, wildcatter, forty-niner.

prospectus *n.* financial statement, investment summary, program, plan.

prosper *v.* succeed, grow, thrive, make a fortune, do well, get ahead, get rich, bear fruit, arrive, *make a killing, *hit the jackpot. ANT. *fail, go bankrupt, *go belly up.*

prosperity *n.* success, growth, fortune, wealth, riches, affluence, boom times, *life of luxury, *easy street, plenty. "An instrument to be used, not a deity to be worshipped."—Calvin Coolidge. ANT. *poverty, failure, bankruptcy.*

prosperous *a.* successful, flourishing, thriving, growing, booming, fortunate, well-off, fat, wealthy, rich, affluent, *in the money, *on easy street. ANT. *failing, *going bankrupt, *going belly up, *drowning in red ink.*

prostitute *n.* whore, hooker, call girl, street

walker, woman of ill repute, lady of the evening, working girl, harlot, slut, *hustler, fille de joie, strumpet, trollop, demimondaine, tart, tramp, *ho.

WORD FIND

act, one sexual: *trick
agent: pimp
bought off, willingness to be: venality
customer: *john, *trick
district: red-light district
euphemism: adventuress, escort
group: demimonde
group of concubines: harem
homosexual: *chicken
homosexual's old male customer: *chicken hawk
hostess mistakenly thought to be, Japanese: geisha
house: brothel, *cathouse, house of ill repute, *joy house, *sporting house, bordello, bawdy house, massage parlor
male, upper class: gigolo
mistress: concubine
mistress of rich man: courtesan
proprietor of brothel: madam
ring of prostitution featuring kidnapped girls: white slavery
solicit customers: pander
undercover: escort service, massage parlor

prostitute *v.* sell one's body, sell oneself out, lower oneself, demean oneself, debase, degrade, cheapen, misuse, abuse.

prostrate *a.* **1.** LYING FACE DOWN prone, recumbent, horizontal, flat, supine, in a position of humility, lying in submission, laid out. **2.** OVERCOME helpless, overwhelmed, overpowered, crushed, paralyzed, humbled, powerless, exhausted, weak, spent, fatigued, worn out, tired. ANT. *1. standing, upright, erect. 2. powerful, emboldened, invigorated.*

protagonist *n.* principal, lead, central figure, hero, heroine, star, exponent, champion.

protect *v.* shield, defend, take care of, safeguard, fend, cover, stick up for, escort, screen, shelter, mother, father. ANT. *expose, leave vulnerable.*

protection *n.* shielding, defense, care, safeguarding, cover, escort, screen, shelter, security, preservation, safety, refuge. ANT. *exposure, vulnerability.*

protective *a.* protecting, shielding, defensive, safeguarding, covering, sheltering, securing, preserving, maternal, paternal. ANT. *unprotective, unsafe, insecure, damaging.*

protégé *n.* student, star pupil, dependent,

charge, understudy, protégée, ward, apprentice.

protest *n.* objection, remonstrance, complaint, grievance, march, demonstration, strike, riot, boycott, rally, sit-in, *stink, fuss, picketing, challenge.

protest *v.* object, remonstrate, complain, file a grievance, march, picket, demonstrate, strike, riot, rally, sit in, boycott, *put up a stink, fuss, challenge, squawk.

protocol *n.* code of conduct, rules of conduct, formalities, conventions, custom, propriety, good form, etiquette, decorum, diplomatic code, manners.

prototype *n.* model, pattern, original, archetype, standard, exemplar, paradigm, first, forerunner, antecedent, *mockup.

PROTRACT *v.* [proh TRACT] to prolong, stretch out, lengthen. *They expect another protracted war in the Middle East.* SYN. prolong, stretch out, draw out, lengthen, extend, *drag out, elongate, sustain, keep going, pad.

protrude *v.* stick out, jut out, project, extrude, stand out, obtrude, bulge, swell, pop, overhang.

protuberance *n.* bump, projection, prominence, jut, protrusion, outgrowth, bulge, swelling, node, lump, excrescence.

proud *a.* **1.** PLEASED WITH ONESELF self-satisfied, self-respecting, *swollen with pride, honored, dignified, great, big, puffed up, *standing tall, winning. **2.** ARROGANT *full of oneself, *cocky, egotistical, pretentious, vainglorious, lordly, pompous, conceited, haughty, *bigheaded, strutting. ANT. *humble, modest, ashamed, low, humiliated.*

prove *v.* confirm, verify, evince, demonstrate, corroborate, affirm, validate, substantiate, establish, show, bear out, document, authenticate. ANT. *disprove, discredit, invalidate.*

proverb *n.* adage, maxim, aphorism, saying, epigram, axiom, truism, bromide, saw, cliché. "The wisdom of the streets."—William Benham. "A short sentence based on long experience."—Miguel de Cervantes.

provide *v.* supply, furnish, contribute, cater, provision, outfit, equip, stock, offer, bring, produce, accommodate, take care of, give, lend, render, donate.

provident *a.* prepared, farsighted, ready, precautious, foresighted, prudent, shrewd, economical, frugal. ANT. *unprepared, shortsighted.*

province *n.* **1.** TERRITORY division, district, region. **2.** RESPONSIBILITY duties, functions, bailiwick, sphere, concern, jurisdiction, department.

PROVINCIAL *a.* [pruh VIN shul] having a narrow outlook, as one from a small town or province, rustic. *Their provincial concerns excluded the needs of outsiders.* SYN. narrow, limited, small-town, unsophisticated, rustic, rural, countrified, insular, parochial, local. ANT. *worldly, universal, metropolitan, cosmopolitan.*

provision *n.* **1.** SUPPLY furnishing, accoutrement, outfitting, providing, giving, stock, stores, food. **2.** PREPARATION prearrangement, readiness, forearming. **3.** PROVISO clause, stipulation, specification, term, requirement, restriction, obligation, *fine print.

proviso *n.* condition, stipulation, clause, article, specification, term, requirement, restriction, obligation, rider, provision.

provocation *n.* provoking, incitement, cause, instigation, stimulus, motivation, inducement, grounds, offense, irritation, agitation.

PROVOCATIVE *a.* [pro VAWK uh tiv] provoking, stimulating, exciting. *The show was so provocative, it incited a riot.* SYN. provoking, stimulating, exciting, disturbing, aggravating, inciting, prodding, goading, offensive, instigating, angering, infuriating, arousing, erotic, sexy, seductive, titillating. ANT. *inane, insipid, dull.*

provoke *v.* **1.** STIMULATE excite, arouse, incite, stir up, instigate, goad, prod, generate, start, bring about, produce, evoke, kindle. **2.** ANGER infuriate, irritate, annoy, enrage, *piss off, offend, insult, *get on one's nerves, perturb, incense. ANT. 1. *throw cold water on, inhibit, smooth over. 2. mollify, appease, pacify.*

prowess *n.* **1.** BRAVERY courage, valor, fearlessness, daring, gallantry, spunk, *guts, mettle, heroism. **2.** ABILITY skill, expertise, talent, mastery, facility, know-how, proficiency, knack, command. ANT. *1. cowardice, weakness, timidity. 2. incompetence, inability.*

prowl *v.* lurk, skulk, hunt, move with stealth, stalk, lie in wait, sneak, slink, steal, tiptoe.

prowler *n.* predator, lurker, hunter, stalker, *sneak, thief, burglar, *peeping Tom.

proximity *n.* nearness, closeness, immediacy, vicinity, propinquity, adjacence.

proxy *n.* agent, substitute, surrogate, fill-in, deputy, alternate, second.

prude *n.* *goody two shoes, *goody-goody, Victorian, Mrs. Grundy, puritan, prig.

PRUDENT *a.* [PROOD unt] using good judgment, wise, cautious. *The prudent thing to do is buckle your seatbelts.* SYN. wise, sensible, cautious, judicious, thoughtful, discreet, sound, reasonable, careful, sage, practical. ANT. *irrational, reckless, thoughtless, mindless.*

prudish *a.* *goody-goody, prissy, squeamish, Victorian, puritanical, strict, overnice, *uptight, straitlaced, prim, starchy, priggish. ANT. *wild, loose, wanton, abandoned.*

prune *v.* trim, clip, thin, reduce, dock, lop, snip, cut, crop, shorten.

prurient *a.* lustful, lewd, libidinous, salacious, lascivious, sexual, lecherous, *horny, carnal. ANT. *prudish, puritanical, prim.*

pry *v.* **1.** *STICK ONE'S NOSE IN interfere, meddle, intrude, snoop, be nosy, *butt in, interlope. **2.** OPEN wrest, force open, pull apart, lift off, raise, lever, prize, jimmy.

psalm *n.* hymn, song.

pseudonym *n.* assumed name, alias, pen name, nom de plume, a.k.a., stage name, professional name.

psyche *n.* soul, intellect, mind, self, ego, spirit, subconscious, anima.

psyched *a.* *Sl.* excited, *pumped, aroused, *rarin' to go, inspired, charger, eager, *fired up, *wired, roused, *on fire, stimulated. ANT. *discouraged, demoralized.*

psychiatrist *n.* doctor, psychoanalyst, psychotherapist, psychologist, *head doctor, therapist, *shrink, *headshrinker, mental health practitioner. "Someone who will listen to you as long as you don't make sense."— Maxwell Hyman.

psychic *n.* one having extrasensory perception, mind-reader, telepathic, clairvoyant, medium, supersensory, superhuman, prophet, telepathist, telekinetic, preternatural, mystic, occult.

psychobabble *n.* jargon, lingo, vernacular, vocabulary, phraseology, *gobbledegook, mumbo jumbo.

psychological *a.* mental, of the mind, conscious, subconscious, unconscious, psychic, cognitive, intellectual, emotional, cerebral.

psychology *n.* SEE INSANITY, MANIA, NEUROSIS, PHOBIA

psychopath *n.* sociopath, antisocial person, lunatic, *loony, *nut case, *psycho, deranged person, psychotic, madman, madwoman, mentally ill person.

psychopathic *a.* psychotic. SEE INSANE, PSYCHOTIC

psych out *v. Sl.* intimidate, trouble, *play with one's head, confuse, unnerve, demoralize.

psychotic *a.* psychopathic, mentally ill, deranged, demented, disturbed, *nuts, delusional, unstable. ANT. *clear-headed, sane, healthy.* SEE INSANE

pub *n.* tavern, bar, public house, saloon, alehouse.

puberty *n.* adolescence, teen years, sexual maturation, development, awkward years, pubescence.

WORD FIND
boy's change of voice: ponticello

public *n.* community, people, society, citizens, populace, masses, nation, *man/woman in the street, everyone.

public *a.* **1.** COMMON community, communal, popular, mutual, general, universal, open, unrestricted, accessible. **2.** KNOWN not private, open, plain as day, visible, overt, undisguised, disclosed, publicized. ANT. **1.** *private, restricted, exclusive.* **2.** *private, confidential, secret.*

publication *n.* book, magazine, newspaper, newsletter, periodical, journal, bulletin, printing, pamphlet, report, dissemination.

publicity *n.* attention, promotion, notice, ballyhoo, advertisement, puffery, spotlight, hype, *plug, *blurb, *hoopla.

publicize *v.* promote, hype, get attention, announce, tout, advertise, sell, trumpet, promulgate, *plug, air, spotlight. ANT. *hush up, conceal, censor.*

publish *v.* issue, print, circulate, put out, distribute, promulgate, report, broadcast.

pucker *v.* purse, crease, wrinkle, contract, fold, crinkle.

puddle *n.* pool, wallow, drink, run-off, plash.

pudgy *a.* fat, dumpy, podgy, tubby, stout, roly-poly, chubby, squat, overweight, chunky. ANT. *thin, skinny, anorexic.*

puerile *a.* childish, immature, young, juvenile, infantile, babyish, callow, silly, sophomoric, foolish. ANT. *mature, adult, serious.*

puff *n.* breath, whiff, huff, wind, gust, draft, waft, blow, expulsion, cloud, smoke, vapor.

puff *v.* blow, breathe, inhale, exhale, huff, pant, wheeze, gust, draw, suck.

puffy *a.* swollen, baggy, inflated, bulging, puffed up, distended, bloated, billowy. ANT. *deflated, flat.*

PUGNACIOUS *a.* [pug NA shus] given to fighting, combative. *The pugnacious bully*

was the terror of the school. SYN. combative, quarrelsome, belligerent, given to fighting, aggressive, contentious, bellicose, antagonistic, militant. ANT. *peaceful, passive, pacifist, meek.*

pulchritude *n.* prettiness, attractiveness, loveliness. SEE BEAUTY

pull *n.* **1.** TUG yank, tow, jerk. **2.** INFLUENCE clout, power, weight, sway, authority.

pull *v.* tug, yank, tow, wrench, drag, haul, jerk, pluck, remove, withdraw, extract, rip out.

pulpit *n.* lectern, platform, podium, dais.

puke *v.* vomit, throw up, upchuck, *toss one's cookies, *blow lunch, *hurl, *ralph, *barf, heave, retch.

pulsate *v.* vibrate, quiver, beat, throb, pulse, palpitate, oscillate, flutter, thrum, ebb and flow.

pulse *n.* vibration, beat, rhythm, throb, pulsation, palpitation, oscillation, flutter, thrum, ebb and flow, contraction, cadence.

pulverize *v.* grind, smash, crush, crumble, powder, break up, granulate, fragment, pound, shatter, atomize.

pummel *v.* pommel, beat, pound, punch, hit, strike, drub, whale on, thrash, use as a punching bag.

pump *v.* **1.** DRAIN remove, suction, suck out, siphon, draw. **2.** INFLATE blow up, expand, fill. **3.** QUESTION interrogate, *grill, cross-examine, quiz, *give the third degree, probe.

pun *n.* play on words, witticism. "A low species of wit."—Noah Webster.

punch *n.* **1.** HIT belt, blow, uppercut, jab, *one-two, *Sunday punch, cuff, *clip, thump, *clout, *smack, *sockdolager. **2.** FORCE wallop, impact, bite, *oomph.

punch *v.* hit, belt, jab, cuff, *clip, thump, pummel, *clout, *smack, *one-two, uppercut.

punctilio *n.* nicety, convention. SEE FORMALITY

punctilious *a.* careful, exact, fussy, finicky, strict, detail-oriented, meticulous, precise, scrupulous. ANT. *slack, careless, slipshod.*

punctual *a.* on time, prompt, on schedule, *on the dot, timely, dependable, reliable. ANT. *late, tardy.*

punctuate *v.* emphasize, accentuate, stress, underscore, underline, accent, mark.

puncture *n.* hole, opening, cut, slit, perforation, rupture, leak, *flat, *blowout.

puncture *v.* pierce, prick, cut, open, rupture, slit, perforate, put a hole in.

PUNDIT *n.* [PUN dit] one who is an authority, a learned man or woman. *The political pundit gave a witty and insightful lecture to a* *delighted audience.* SYN. authority, expert, learned man/woman, sage, scholar, know-it-all, professional observer, master, savant.

PUNGENT *a.* [PUN junt] sharply flavorful or sharp-smelling. Also, sharp or biting in language or speech. *Both the meal and the conversation were pungent.* SYN. **1.** SPICY sharp, biting, acrid, harsh, bitter, acid, stinging, strong, acerbic, piquant, flavorful, peppery. **2.** BITING acid, penetrating, piercing, pointed, salty, spicy, hot, peppery, scathing, caustic, sharp-tongued. ANT. *bland, mild, dull.*

punish *v.* penalize, discipline, correct, chasten, chastise, teach a lesson, castigate, reprove, *come down hard on, *lower the boom on, fine, sentence, whip, flog, beat, thrash, torture, *slap one's wrist. ANT. *reward, praise, commend.*

punishment *n.* penalty, discipline, disciplinary action, chastening, chastisement, retribution, *one's due, comeuppance, *just deserts, castigation, penance, *the rod, reparation, fine, sentencing, whipping, beating, torture, *slap on the wrist. "A sort of medicine."—Aristotle. "Justice for the unjust."—Saint Augustine. "Sin is a suppurating wound; punishment is the surgeon's knife."—Saint John Chrysostom. ANT. *reward, praise, commendation.*

WORD FIND
beheader: guillotine
board with head and hand holes to lock in and humiliate offender in public: pillory
eye for an eye, tooth for a tooth: talion
frame with ankle, wrist holes to lock in offender: stocks
hanging, instrument of: gallows, gibbet
illegal: cruel and unusual
isolation from others: solitary confinement
neck, iron collar tightened around: garrote
ruler or stick to punish children: ferule
soles of feet, beating with stick: bastinado
stretching device: rack
tar and feather: tar and feather
vigilantes, execution by: lynching
yoke fastened around neck, Chinese: cangue
SEE PRISON, TORTURE

punitive *a.* penalizing, disciplinary, correctional, punishing, penal, harsh, hard, severe, strict. ANT. *lenient, merciful.*

punk *n.* hoodlum, *hood, hooligan, juvenile, delinquent, troublemaker, brat, *snot-nosed kid.

puny *a.* tiny, small, slight, pint-sized, little, undersized, inconsequential, trifling, runty, weak, underdeveloped, insignificant. ANT. *massive, huge, gigantic.*

pupil *n.* student, schoolboy, schoolgirl, first-grader, junior, sophomore, undergraduate, senior, scholar, disciple, apprentice.

puppet *n.* marionette, *muppet, doll, dummy, pawn, *stooge, *patsy, instrument, tool, figurehead.

purchase *n.* buy, acquisition, acquirement, procurement, bargain.

purchase *v.* buy, pay for, acquire, obtain, invest in, procure, bargain for, order, pick up.

pure *a.* **1.** UNMIXED clean, untainted, unadulterated, clear, unalloyed, undiluted, natural, genuine, real, clean, immaculate, unsullied, unpolluted, pristine. **2.** UTTER absolute, stark, out and out, sheer, downright, thorough. **3.** SINLESS, CHASTE virgin, virtuous, clean, *squeaky-clean, *pure as the driven snow, immaculate, celibate, decent, good, wholesome, moral, blameless, innocent, guiltless. ANT. *1. impure, tainted, mixed, diluted, dirty. 2. rather, somewhat, a little. 3. sinful, wicked, impure, unchaste.*

purgatory *n.* limbo, punishment, torment, hell, atonement, living hell, penance, suffering, retribution, expiation.

purge *v.* cleanse, remove, clean out, eliminate, clear, purify, excrete, expel, banish, *dump, eradicate, get rid of, exorcise.

purify *v.* clean, cleanse, sanitize, sterilize, clarify, purge, decontaminate, wash, filter, refine, distill.

puritanical *a.* straitlaced, strict, severe, austere, rigid, stiff, stuffy, prim, narrow. ANT. *wild, loose, fast, permissive.*

purloin *v.* filch, thieve, pilfer. SEE STEAL

purple *a.* violet, plum, lavender, lilac, amethyst, mauve, orchid, dahlia, fuchsia, royal, raisin, magenta, hyacinth, heliotrope.

purport *v.* mean, claim, profess, allege, hold, maintain, pretend.

purpose *n.* **1.** INTENTION aim, intent, object, objective, motivation, motive, goal, design, reason, plan, driving force, point. **2.** DETERMINATION resolve, will, single-mindedness, drive, persistence, tenacity.

purposeful *a.* resolved, determined, deliberate, intent, committed, decided, resolute, fixed, persistent, tenacious. ANT. *unintentional, purposeless.*

purposely *adv.* on purpose, deliberately, intentionally, consciously, by design, knowingly, willingly, calculatedly. ANT. *unintentionally, unknowingly, accidentally.*

purse *n.* **1.** POCKETBOOK handbag, clutch, wallet, pouch. **2.** PRIZE award, sum, winnings, jackpot, stake.

purse *v.* close, press, pucker, contract.

pursue *v.* **1.** CHASE go after, run down, *tail, follow, give chase to, track, trail, hunt down, *bird dog, stalk, *shadow. **2.** STRIVE FOR seek, work for, go after, contend for, aspire to, aim for, try for.

push *n.* **1.** SHOVE thrust, propulsion, nudge, prod, poke, advance, drive, force. **2.** AMBITION drive, aggressiveness, determination, *oomph, vigor, energy.

push *v.* **1.** SHOVE thrust, propel, nudge, prod, poke, advance, drive, force, butt, press, ram, muscle, shoulder. **2.** URGE impel, goad, incite, prod, egg on, spur, pressure, motivate, compel, provoke. ANT. *1. pull, yank, tow.*

pushover *n.* weakling, *wimp, *wussy, mouse, invertebrate, *lightweight.

pushy *a.* aggressive, bumptious, obnoxious, domineering, bossy, controlling, officious, overbearing. ANT. *passive, submissive, deferential.*

put *v.* **1.** SET place, position, deposit, stick, rest,

lay, plunk, plop, drop, insert, park, situate, center. **2.** EXPRESS phrase, word, present, state, say, articulate, pose.

putrefy *v.* rot, decompose, spoil, decay, *go bad, deteriorate, taint, molder, *die.

putrid *a.* rotten, decomposing, spoiled, decayed, *gone bad, deteriorated, tainted, rancid, moldy, stinking, rank. ANT. *fresh, sweet, preserved.*

putter *v.* tinker, fiddle, *poke about, *mess about, trifle, *monkey with, toy, dawdle, fritter.

puzzle *n.* mystery, conundrum, problem, poser, riddle, enigma, maze, labyrinth.

puzzle *v.* perplex, confuse, bewilder, stump, baffle, mystify, confound, befog, *bamboozle.

puzzling *a.* perplexing, confusing, bewildering, stumping, baffling, mystifying, confounding, mysterious, enigmatic. ANT. *decipherable, understandable.*

pygmy *n.* Negrillo, nomad, Akka, Batwa, Mbuti.

pygmy *a.* miniature, dwarf, midget, tiny, small, undersized, toy, stunted, Lilliputian.

pyramid *n.* monument, memorial, landmark, architectural wonder, mausoleum, burial shrine, heap, construction, ziggurat.

Q

quack *n.* charlatan, fraud, fake, pretender, masquerader, humbug, *phony, imposter, mountebank, *con artist.

quagmire *n.* **1.** BOG mire, morass, slough, fen, swamp, marsh, quicksand, ooze. **2.** DIFFICULT OR INEXTRICABLE SITUATION hole, predicament, quandary, plight, corner, impasse, pinch, strait, mess, entanglement.

quail *v.* cower, draw back, flinch, cringe, recoil, wince, shrink.

quaint *a.* unusual, curious, strange, peculiar, charming, old-fashioned, antique, picturesque, whimsical, eccentric. ANT. *modern, usual.*

quake *v.* tremble, shudder, shiver. SEE SHAKE

qualification *n.* **1.** MODIFICATION restriction, limitation, stipulation, condition, requirement, proviso, caveat. **2.** ABILITY capability, skill, *the right stuff, attribute, competence, aptitude, eligibility, requisite.

qualified *a.* **1.** ABLE capable, skilled, *having the right stuff, competent, well-grounded, eligible, adequate, proficient, fit, certified, trained. **2.** MODIFIED limited, conditional, provisional, contingent, dependent, confined, circumscribed. ANT. *1. unqualified, incompetent, inadequate, ineligible. 2. unconditional, unqualified.*

qualify *v.* ready, measure up, certify, make fit, entitle, make eligible, prepare, *make the cut, suit, ground, endow, enable, license.

QUALIFY *v.* [KWOL uh FYE] to modify or restrict. *She qualified her answer.* SYN. modify, restrict, limit, soften, confine, tone down, temper, mitigate.

quality *n.* **1.** ATTRIBUTE feature, characteristic, mark, trait, element, nature, property, peculiarity, quirk. **2.** EXCELLENCE value, superiority, distinction, worth, merit, perfection, eminence, caliber, stature, standing, class, virtue.

qualm *n.* uneasiness, misgiving, doubt, twinge, anxiety, sick feeling, uncertainty, pang, apprehension, compunction, scruple.

quandary *n.* predicament, dilemma, plight, fix, bind, strait, *pickle, corner, *Catch-22, jam.

quantify *v.* gauge, count, measure, put a number on, determine, calculate.

quantity *n.* amount, number, measure, volume, sum, mass, bulk, portion, lot, magnitude, dose, extent, total.

quarantine *v.* isolate, sequester, confine, seclude, restrict.

quantum *n.* quantity, portion, amount, mass, percentage, fraction.

QUANTUM LEAP* *n.* [KWAN tum LEEP] a radical change, departure or new direction. *The discovery took us a quantum leap forward.* SYN. radical change, sea change, departure, new direction, advance, jump, progress, reverse, flip flop, shift.

quarrel *n.* dispute, disagreement, argument, fight, difference of opinion, spat, contention, row, altercation, squabble, controversy, tiff, debate, bickering, run-in, falling-out. ANT. *agreement, accord.*

quarrel *v.* dispute, disagree, argue, fight, differ, clash, *lock horns, bicker, squabble, debate, battle, wrangle, feud, contend. ANT. *agree, *see eye-to-eye, accommodate.*

quarrelsome *a.* argumentative, contentious, belligerent, combative, controversial, fiery, peppery, pugnacious, contrary, disagreeable. ANT. *peaceful, agreeable, accommodating.*

quarry *n.* **1.** PREY target, victim, prize, game, the hunted. **2.** PIT mine, excavation, rock quarry.

quarter *n.* **1.** DISTRICT neighborhood, barrio, precinct, section, region, zone. **2.** MERCY compassion, clemency, lenience, pity, forgiveness.

quarters *n.* lodging, accommodations, abode, shelter, housing, dwelling, domicile, room, place, residence, barracks.

quash *v.* quell, suppress, crush, put down, subdue, squelch, stamp out, squash, defeat.

queasy *a.* nauseated, qualmish, sickly, seasick, *green around the gills, *under the weather, out of sorts.

queer *a.* **1.** ODD strange, weird, bizarre, unusual, abnormal, out of the ordinary, singular, funny, *off the wall, quaint, extraordinary. **2.** HOMOSEXUAL gay, lesbian. ANT. *1. normal, ordinary, usual. 2. heterosexual.* SEE HOMOSEXUAL

quell *v.* subdue, crush, put down, defeat, stamp out, conquer, suppress, quash, vanquish, end, silence.

quench *v.* **1.** EXTINGUISH put out, douse, smother, snuff out, subdue, suppress, quash, quell. **2.** SATISFY ONE'S THIRST slake, satiate, *hit the spot, sate, refresh, cool.

querulous *a.* fault-finding, complaining, critical, hard to please, caviling, grumbling, whining, fretful, petulant. ANT. *easy to please, content, easygoing.*

query *n.* question, inquiry, enquiry, interrogatory.

query *v.* ask, question, inquire, look into, interrogate, enquire, quiz, probe, pump, investigate, cross-examine.

quest *n.* search, seeking, hunt, pursuit, enterprise, adventure, exploration, expedition, mission, crusade.

question *n.* **1.** INQUIRY enquiry, query, interrogatory, examination, investigation, poser. **2.** UNCERTAINTY doubt, controversy, misgiving, hesitation, debate, confusion. **3.** ISSUE matter, subject, problem. ANT. *1. answer, reply. 2. certainty, confidence.*

question *v.* **1.** ASK inquire, enquire, query, seek an answer, interrogate, examine, quiz, probe, investigate, grill, cross-examine, pump. **2.** DOUBT challenge, mistrust, suspect, disbelieve, wonder about, call into question. ANT. *1. answer, reply. 2. trust, have confidence in.*

questionable *a.* **1.** DOUBTFUL debatable, in question, controversial, unsettled, indeterminate, controvertible, ambiguous, moot, unsure. **2.** SUSPECT fishy, shady, suspicious. ANT. *1. certain, settled. 2. believable, legitimate, unimpeachable.*

quibble *v.* *split hairs, *nit-pick, cavil, evade, bicker, equivocate, carp, haggle, prevaricate.

quick *a.* **1.** FAST swift, rapid, speedy, fleet, expeditious, prompt, mercurial, *breakneck, *on the double, hasty, immediate, sudden. **2.** INTELLIGENT smart, quick to catch on, sharp, astute, bright, *on the ball, acute, savvy, alert, receptive, keen. ANT. *1. slow, slothful, sluggish. 2. slow, dense, stupid.*

quicken *v.* **1.** SPEED UP accelerate, expedite, hurry, speed, hasten, hustle. **2.** ENLIVEN stimulate, invigorate, stir, arouse, revive, animate, awaken, strengthen. ANT. *1. slow down, mire, bog down. 2. kill, deaden.*

quickly *adv.* speedily, fast, expeditiously, swiftly, hastily, rapidly, hurriedly, briskly, full-tilt, pronto, *quicker than greased lightning. ANT. *slowly, slothfully.*

quick-tempered *a.* irritable, touchy, *short-fused, grouchy, cantankerous, volatile, temperamental, hot-blooded, testy, waspish, fiery. ANT. *easygoing, placid, long-fused.*

quick-witted *a.* alert, *on the ball, nimble,

sharp, smart, acute, shrewd, savvy, bright, intelligent, quick on the uptake, clever. ANT. *dull, stupid, dense.*

quiet *n.* silence, peace, hush, stillness, calm, soundlessness, noiselessness, tranquility, serenity, lull. "Noise you don't mind."—Leonard Levinson. ANT. *noise, racket, uproar, din.*

quiet *v.* hush, shush, silence, shut up, muffle, tone down, soften, squelch, muzzle, *put a lid on, *keep down to a low roar.

quiet *a.* **1.** SOUNDLESS silent, still, peaceful, hushed, soft, quiescent, inaudible, low, muted, noiseless, *as silent as the vacuum of space, *as silent as a crypt, *quiet enough to hear a pin drop. **2.** NOT TALKATIVE close-mouthed, silent, taciturn, reserved, mute, tightlipped, not big on small talk. **3.** CALM tranquil, peaceful, motionless, undisturbed, still, serene, placid, halcyon. ANT. *1. noisy, loud, deafening. 2. loquacious, talkative, *motor-mouthed. 3. turbulent, wild, agitated.*

quintessence *n.* **1.** ESSENCE heart, pith, soul, distillation. **2.** PARAGON model, exemplar, cream, *crème de la crème.

quip *n.* witty remark, witticism, jest, gibe, crack, bon mot, wisecrack, joke, retort, repartee. SEE JOKE

quirk *n.* peculiarity, oddity, characteristic, trait, mannerism, idiosyncrasy, eccentricity, twist, kink.

quit *v.* **1.** STOP give up, discontinue, break off, end, *call it a day, cease, desist, *knock off, *halt, *pack in, *hang it up, give notice. **2.** LEAVE depart, abandon, withdraw, *cut out, take off, relinquish, surrender, bow out, walk out on, drop, leave flat, forsake, resign from. ANT. *1. start, begin, commence. 2. take up, remain, maintain, sustain.*

quite *adv.* completely, entirely, totally, fully, wholly, very, really, truly, surely.

quiver *n.* tremor, tremble, shake, vibration, twitch, shudder, shiver, quaver, flutter, throb, palpitation.

quiver *v.* shake, tremble, vibrate, shudder, shiver, twitch, quaver, flutter, throb, palpitate.

QUIXOTIC *a.* [kwik SOT ik] idealistic or romantic in a foolish or impractical way, like the fictional character Don Quixote. *He had long entertained the quixotic notion of giving children the vote.* SYN. idealistic, romantic, foolish, impractical, unrealistic, dreamy, utopian, fanciful, chimerical, *starry-eyed, visionary, chivalrous. ANT. *practical, down-to-earth, realistic.*

quiz *n.* test, exam, examination, pop quiz, questioning, multiple choice, Q&A, catechism.

quiz *v.* test, examine, question, grill, ask, query, pump, inquire, interrogate, cross-examine.

quizzical *a.* **1.** QUESTIONING perplexed, inquisitive, confused, puzzled, inquiring, curious, searching, unbelieving, bewildered, lost. **2.** TEASING ridiculing, mocking, derisive, impudent, insolent, joking.

quota *n.* portion, share, cut, ration, allowance, percentage, lot, part, piece, dole, measure.

quotation *n.* quote, passage, citation, excerpt, saying, selection, extract, reference.

quote *v.* cite, parrot, recite, paraphrase, repeat, excerpt, refer to, extract, reference.

R

rabbi *n.* master, teacher, clergyman, clergywoman.
WORD FIND
school: yeshiva
SEE RELIGION
rabbit *n.* bunny, jackrabbit, hare, doe, buck.
rabble *n.* crowd, mob, the masses, commoners, common people, lower classes, proletariat, rank and file, hoi polloi, horde. "The dregs of the people."—Cicero. "The venal herd."—Juvenal. ANT. *upper class, ruling class, aristocracy.*
rabid *a.* raging, berserk, maniacal, crazed, deranged, mad, zealous, extreme, *nuts, violent, fanatical, *foaming at the mouth. ANT. *sane, reasonable, moderate.*
race *n.* **1.** PEOPLE ethnic group, nationality, line, tribe, breed, stock, clan, folk, strain. **2.** SPRINT dash, run, marathon, footrace, heat, relay, contest, meet, steeplechase, derby.
WORD FIND
AUTO RACING
aerodynamic wing or wedge that improves car handling: spoiler
broadside crash into competitor's car or wall: T-bone
bumper-to-bumper pressure tactic: dogging
coveted front inside position at start: pole position
curve or tight turn: ess-turn, hairpin turn, chicane
custom-built, nonstock race car: formula car, Indy car
drag race, beat competitor in: shut down
drag racing car: dragster, rail, funny car
driving directly behind lead car to create fuel-conserving vacuum: drafting, slipstreaming
flag alerting hazardous car to leave the track: black flag
flag, end of race: checkered flag
flag, final lap: white flag
flag, go: green flag
flag, hazard: yellow flag
flag, stop: red flag
flag warning of competitor on one's tail: blue flag
formula car race: Grand Prix
long-distance competition: rally
low edge of track: apron
NASCAR: National Association for Stock Car Auto Racing

noncompeting pacesetter at start of race: pace car
parachute, release at end of drag race: *hang out the laundry
passing method creating vacuum on lead car: slingshot
pass one track-length ahead of competitor: lap
pit crew's head mechanic: crew chief
production car: stock car
racing tires: *shoes, *slicks
running start: flying start
service area: pit
service mechanics: pit crew
steel support network protecting inside of car: roll cage
steel support tube protecting inside of car: roll bar
straightaway in front of grandstand: chute
straightaway race: drag race
THOROUGHBRED HORSERACING
barrier: starting gate, post
betting away from the track: offtrack betting
betting system: pari-mutuals
bugle call: Boots and Saddles
castrated male horse: gelding
close finish: photo finish, blanket finish
costumes, riders': colors, silks
crouching riding posture: monkey crouch
drug horse illegally: hop
escorts horses to post: outrider
exercise or practice run: airing
favored to win: chalk horse
first two finishers, bet on: quinella
hold back horse to keep it from winning: stiff
horse that does well on muddy track: mudder
info sheet: dope sheet
insider with "inside" information on horse: tout
length: eight to nine feet
mile, one-eighth of a: furlong
money, horse that fails to finish in the: also-ran
money-losing horse: hayburner
observation ring: walking ring
odds board: tote board
officials: clerk of the scales, stewards
pasture or saddling enclosure: paddock
peripheral visions blockers, horse's: blinkers
rider: jockey

saddle and other horse equipment, collective term: tack
short race: sprint
stable assistant: groom
straightaway, farside: backstretch
straightaway in front of grandstand: homestretch
surrounded position: pocket
three-year-old horse: sophomore
three-year-olds, race for: derby
track condition, broken into clods and hoofprints: cuppy
track condition, freshly harrowed: deep
track condition, hard and fast: pasteboard track
two-year-old horse: juvenile
underrated horse: sleeper, dark horse
weight, adding to equalize competition: handicap
weight assigned to horse in handicap race: impost
weighing of jockeys with tack: weigh-in, weigh-out
whip: gad, leather
winners of two races, correctly picking: daily double
winning Kentucky Derby, Preakness Stakes and the Belmont Stakes: Triple Crown
winning of three races by same jockey on one program: hat trick
win one's first race: break maiden, graduate
win without prodding or whipping the horse: armchair ride
withdrawal of entrant: scratch

racism n. prejudice, discrimination, bigotry, bias, segregation, apartheid, intolerance, white supremacy.

racist n. bigot, white supremacist, black supremacist, xenophobe, Ku Klux Klan member, klansman.

racist a. bigoted, prejudiced, white supremacist, anti-Semitic, xenophobic, intolerant.

rack n. frame, framework, stand, holder, scaffolding, grating, hack, flake.

racket n. 1. NOISE din, clamor, uproar, commotion, clatter, disturbance, pandemonium, hubbub, babel, cacophony. 2. CRIMINAL ACTIVITY bootlegging, fraud, swindling, loansharking, graft, extortion, corruption, bribery, blackmail.

raconteur n. storyteller, teller of tales, spinner of yarns. SEE AUTHOR, NOVELIST

racy a. 1. SUGGESTIVE risqué, spicy, bawdy, immodest, off-color, dirty, indecent, pornographic, ribald. 2. LIVELY spirited, energetic, vigorous, zesty, exciting, peppy, vivacious. ANT. 1. modest, wholesome, G-rated. 2. dull sluggish, *dead.

RADAR n. Radio Detecting and Ranging System, tracking device, scanning system.
WORD FIND
air surveillance, early warnings system: AWACS, Airborne Warning and Control System
image: blip
police radar detection device: *fuzzbuster
sound: beep, racon
SEE AIR FORCE, AIRPLANE, AIRPORT, AUTOMOBILE

radiant a. 1. SHINING bright, glowing, beaming, gleaming, luminous, refulgent, resplendent, brilliant, incandescent. 2. HAPPY bright, beaming, glowing, joyous, joyful, cheerful, sunny. ANT. 1. dull, dim, dark. 2. gloomy, black.

radiate v. shine, illuminate, glow, beam, pour out, send out, shoot out, spread out, diffuse, throw off.

radiation n. emission, energy, particle stream, nuclear decay, fallout, nuclear energy.

radical n. extremist, fanatic, zealot, revolutionist, leftist, left-winger, iconoclast, nonconformist. "A man with both feet firmly planted in the air."—Franklin Delano Roosevelt. ANT. conservative, moderate.

radical a. 1. FUNDAMENTAL basic, rudimentary, elemental, foundational. 2. EXTREME thorough, extremist, severe, progressive, fanatical, drastic, revolutionary, complete, whole, sweeping, far left. ANT. 1. peripheral, unimportant. 2. modest, partial, moderate.

radio n. receiver, *boom box, *ghetto blaster, Marconi, CB, crystal set, ham radio, walkie-talkie. "Television without eyestrain."—Max Gralnik.
WORD FIND
AM: amplitude modulation
amateur two-way radio enthusiast: ham
brief quote from someone in the news: soundbite
broadcast sent from other station or network: feed
DJ: disc jockey
FM: frequency modulation
identification letters: call letters
morning and evening time when commuters listen: drive time
obnoxious radio show: shock radio
overseas political radio of United States: Voice of America

range of radio frequencies: band
station that only rebroadcasts other stations' shows: translator
switch used by DJ to block cough or sneeze from going over the air: cough button
type of programming: format
unlicensed station: pirate station

radius *n.* extent, range, scope, sphere, compass.

raffish *a.* careless, unconventional, casual, wild, bohemian, rakish, vulgar, low, tawdry. ANT. *prim, conventional, *straight-laced.*

ragamuffin *n.* tramp, *bum, *street person, urchin, derelict, guttersnipe, waif, tatterdemalion.

rage *n.* **1.** FURY anger, wrath, tantrum, fit, ferocity, high dudgeon, hysterics, rampage, furor, *piss hemorrhage, uproar, hot blood. SEE ANGER **2.** FAD craze, *in thing, fashion, *latest thing, *latest wrinkle, vogue, dernier cri. ANT. **1.** *delight, calm, passivity.*

rage *v.* *blow up, *explode, *go ballistic, be furious, fume, rant and rave, *fly off the handle, *blow a fuse, boil, *blow one's top, become livid, *turn purple, *spit tacks, *see red, *blow a gasket, *flip out, *get into a lather, *get one's Irish up, *go apeshit, *have a conniption fit, storm.

ragged *a.* tattered, frayed, in shreds, worn, threadbare, shaggy, moth-eaten, torn, full of holes, seedy, shabby, jagged. ANT. *smooth, whole, new.*

raid *n.* attack, invasion, onslaught, incursion, offensive, foray, assault, charge, *bust.

raid *v.* attack, invade, storm, strike, launch an offensive, charge, sweep, maraud, assail, loot, plunder, *bust.

rail *v.* complain, criticize, *tongue-lash, assail, denounce, condemn, censure, castigate, chastise, *chew out. ANT. *praise, compliment, approve.*

railing *n.* baluster, balustrade, banister, handhold, fence, parapet.

railroad *n.* rail line, tracks, railway, subway, monorail, *el. "Only a device for making the world smaller."—John Ruskin.
WORD FIND
barrier or stop at end of track: bumper
bed in a sleeping car: berth
brake operator: brakeman
bridge: trestle
cars owned by one company: rolling stock
crew's tail car: caboose, *doghouse, *shanty, *buggy, *van, *penthouse, *doodlebug
driver: engineman, engineer
driving compartment of locomotive: cab

elevated: *el
engine employed to clear cars in yard: trimmer, *yard goat
engine: locomotive
fast train: bullet train, express train
freight car: boxcar, flatcar, gondola, hopper, livestock car, platform car, refrigerator car (*reefer), tank car, *wagon
hitching clamp: coupler
holding area for train, cars: yard
locomotive's front bumper: cowcatcher
lover of railroads: ferrophiliac
magnetically levitated train: Maglev
meal car: dining car
mountain track employing cogs to increase traction: cog railway
passenger car: coach, dining car, Pullman sleeper, lounge car, observation car, smoking car
porter at station: redcap
rail layers: *steel gang, *spikers
rotating platform used to turn locomotives: turntable
second engine used in steep areas: booster, *rammer
shunting mechanism: switch
sidetrack dead-end: spur
signaling apparatus: semaphore
signaling framework over tracks: gantry
single rail track: monorail
sleeper, luxury: palace car
slip off tracks: derail
sorting cars in freight yard: marshaling
steam whistle's peep: crow
supervisor, fare collector: conductor
supervisor of yard: yardmaster
switching tracks: shunting
tie: sleeper, crosstie
turntable facility for switching locomotives: roundhouse
wheeled trucks that support cars: bogies
width of track: gauge
worker's hand-pumped transport: handcar
X-like railroad crossing sign: crossbuck

railroad *v.* push through, force through, rush through, expedite.

rain *n.* precipitation, rainfall, mist, drizzle, mizzle, sprinkle, spit, shower, cloudburst, downpour, squall, thundershower, *gully washer, deluge, drencher, *cats and dogs, torrent, *rain of biblical proportion, sleet, hail.
WORD FIND
moisture content of air: humidity
precipitation, all types of: hydrometeors
rain and evaporation cycle: hydrologic cycle

rain driven by wind: scud
study of: hyetography
sudden heavy rain: spate
temperature at which moisture condenses
  into rain: dewpoint
SEE CLOUD, FOG, SNOW

rain *v.* precipitate, fall, pour, drop, sprinkle, shower, spit, mist, *come down in buckets, drizzle, weep, *rain pitchforks.

rainbow *n.* spectrum, arc, band.

raise *n.* increase, advance, pay hike, boost, promotion, jump.

raise *v.* **1.** LIFT elevate, hoist, erect, run up, jack up, heighten, heave, loft. **2.** INCREASE escalate, inflate, enlarge, heighten, magnify, amplify, boost, *jack up, double, triple, quadruple. **3.** AROUSE stir up, rouse, start, activate, awaken, whip up, provoke, spur, incite. **4.** REAR bring up, parent, cultivate, nurture, foster, breed. ANT. *1. lower. 2. decrease, devalue, lower. 3. dampen, inhibit. 4. abandon.*

RAISON D'ÊTRE *n.* [ray ZON DET ruh] reason for being. *Protection of the company's proprietary interests was given as the security's system raison d'être.* SYN. reason for being, justification for being.

rake *n.* roué, playboy, lecher, swinger, *makeout artist, womanizer, Casanova, Don Juan, Lothario, wolf, philanderer.

RAKISH *a.* [RAKE ish] dashing, jaunty. Also, highly sexual or debauched. *A rakish gentleman entered the room, and all the women stared at him.* SYN. dashing, jaunty, sporty, stylish, debonair, dapper, chic, sharp, debauched, oversexed, wanton, lecherous, flirtatious. ANT. *frumpy, out of style, unkempt, upright, gentlemanly, chaste, virginal.*

rally *n.* **1.** GATHERING meeting, pep rally, assembly, meet, convention, revival, session, celebration. **2.** COMEBACK resurgence, revival, recovery, renewal, road to recovery, renaissance, rebound. ANT. *2. collapse, decline, loss, death, turn for the worse.*

rally *v.* **1.** GATHER meet, convene, assemble, reassemble, mobilize, summon together, collect, get together, unite, call to arms. **2.** RECOVER come back, surge, resurge, rise again, revive, renew, rebound, bounce back, turn around, come around, rejuvenate, *get a second wind. ANT. *1. disperse, break up. 2. decline, lose, die, take a turn for the worse.*

ram *v.* drive, hammer, slam, bang, smash, butt, crash into, hit head-on, beat, tramp.

ramble *v.* roam, wander aimlessly, drift, rove,

range, stroll, traipse, meander, stray, walk, saunter, hike.

rambling *a.* digressive, discursive, circuitous, wordy, verbose, prolix, circumlocutory, roundabout, desultory. ANT. *concise, to the point.*

RAMBUNCTIOUS *a.* [ram BUNK shus] unruly, disorderly, raucous, noisy. *Most two-year-olds are rambunctious.* SYN. unruly, disorderly, raucous, noisy, unrestrained, wild, unmanageable, boisterous, *hyper, hyperactive. ANT. *docile, well-behaved, quiet.*

RAMIFICATION *n.* [RAM uh fuh KA shun] a consequence, effect or result. *One ramification of unbridled terrorism is outright war.* SYN. consequence, effect, result, outgrowth, offshoot, product, end, upshot, complication.

ramp *n.* slope, incline, rise, grade.

rampage *n.* outbreak, fury, uproar, blowup, rage, tempest, storm, running amuck, *warpath, furor. ANT. *calm, peace, contentment.*

rampant *a.* growing, spreading, uncontrolled, rife, widespread, out of hand, unchecked, out of control, unbridled, epidemic. ANT. *contained, limited, under control.*

rampart *n.* fortification, bulwark, defense, barrier, embankment, earthwork, wall, breastwork. SEE CASTLE

ramshackle *a.* rickety, falling apart, shaky, broken down, tumble-down, dilapidated, crumbling, derelict, decrepit. ANT. *sound, solid, rock-solid.*

ranch *n.* cattle farm, range land, grange, plantation, *spread.

rancid *a.* spoiled, rotten, stale, rank, reeking, bad, fetid, stinking, sour, foul, disgusting, putrid. ANT. *sweet, fresh, mouth-watering.*

RANCOR *n.* [RANG kur] long-lasting hatred and ill will. *The two parties were divided by rancor.* SYN. hatred, ill will, malice, spite, bitterness, animosity, enmity, malevolence, resentment, vindictiveness. ANT. *goodwill, friendliness, affection, love.*

random *a.* haphazard, casual, chance, accidental, unplanned, arbitrary, fortuitous, desultory, blind, hit-or-miss, aimless. ANT. *planned, designed, premeditated.*

range *n.* scope, extent, reach, limit, sphere, sweep, parameters, boundary, area, radius, expanse, territory. SEE MOUNTAIN

range *v.* roam, travel, wander, meander, rove, traverse, drift, cross, ramble.

rangy *a.* gangling, lank, lanky, slender, long-legged, *split high, leggy, thin, skinny. ANT. *squat, stout, fat.*

rank v. classify, align, group, station, grade, arrange, order, rate, position, sort.

rank a. **1.** OFFENSIVE stinking, strong, rancid, foul, bad, fetid, reeking, nauseating, revolting, rotten. **2.** LUXURIANT luxurious, lush, rich, vigorous, overgrown, flourishing, dense, proliferating, coarse. ANT. *1. sweetsmelling, sweet-tasting, mild, pleasant, fresh. 2. sparse, barren.*

rankle v. anger, inflame, infuriate, gall, embitter, irritate, *rub the wrong way, irk, *piss off, *fill with venom, *make blood boil, fill with resentment. ANT. *delight, pacify, mollify.*

ransack v. search, *tear place apart, *turn inside out, rummage, look over, rifle, *leave no stone unturned, overhaul, scour, plunder, pillage, rob.

rant v. rave, *sound off, shout, yell, roar, holler, *spout off, fume, vociferate, bluster, declaim. ANT. *whisper, murmur, *talk under one's breath.*

rap n. **1.** KNOCK tap, hit, blow, stroke, slap, cuff, punch, belt. **2.** MUSIC *hip hop, urban black music, street music, inner city music. **3.** Sl. CONVERSATION dialogue, spoken word, talk. **4.** Sl. BLAME punishment, flak, responsibility. SEE PUNISHMENT

WORD FIND

STREET, RAP, AND HIP HOP SLANG

ad libbed rap lyrics: freestyle

agree or be friends with: down on, down with

attractive: fly

bigot, white: cracker

breakdancer: b-boy, b-girl

bullet: cap

crazy: wack

crimes as part of a gang, commit: gangbang

dance: breakdancing, hip hop, popping and locking

disrespect: dis

fight or kill, to: bang

friend from the neighborhood: homeboy, homegirl, homey

good: def, fresh

group one hangs out with: crew, homeboys, homeys, posse

home: crib

lowrider: car that rides low due to altered suspension

neighborhood: hood

playboy: player

prostitute: ho

qualities, having several great qualities: all that

rear: booty

relax: chill

rich, excellent: phat

rob someone: jack

music with violent or ganster-related lyrics: gangsta rap

sexually, a woman who is promiscuous or aggressive: freak

sexual relations, have: freak

up, what's: word up

rap v. **1.** KNOCK tap, hit, deliver a blow, slap, cuff, punch, belt. **2.** CONVERSE talk, chat, have a dialogue, confabulate.

RAPACIOUS a. [ruh PAY shus] plundering, predatory. *The rapacious pirates stole everything of value.* SYN. plundering, predatory, thieving, marauding, pillaging, greedy, grasping, ravenous, voracious, savage. ANT. *generous, kind-hearted, kindly.*

rape n. sexual assault, molestation, forcible intercourse, ravishment, overpowering, violation, *date rape, deflowering, plundering, pillage, sacking.

rape v. molest, sexually assault, ravish, *force oneself on, attack, overpower, violate, deflower, defile, *have one's way with, plunder, pillage, sack.

rapid a. fast, swift, quick, fleet, speedy, expeditious, mercurial, hasty, winged, *quicker than greased lightning. ANT. *slow, slothful, leisurely.*

rapport n. harmony, agreement, *seeing eye-to-eye, *common ground, closeness, understanding, affinity, compatibility, *simpatico, *good vibes. ANT. *hostility, alienation, *bad vibes, disagreement.*

rapt a. **1.** ENRAPTURED carried away, transported, rapturous, ecstatic, euphoric, emotional, joyous. **2.** ENGROSSED absorbed, captivated, preoccupied, deep, *wrapped up, spellbound, enthralled, oblivious, fascinated. ANT. *1. depressed, dejected, downhearted. 2. distracted, bored, disinterested.*

rapture n. ecstasy, euphoria, elation, joy, happiness, bliss, transport, heaven, exultation. ANT. *depression, misery, melancholy.*

rare a. **1.** UNCOMMON infrequent, scarce, unusual, unique, exceptional, *few and far between, extraordinary, singular, *once in a blue moon, at a premium, *scarce as hens' teeth, seldom found. **2.** EXCELLENT superlative, superior, fine, exquisite, select, choice, first-class, priceless, precious. **3.** UNDERCOOKED half-cooked, bloody, red, raw, underdone. ANT. *1. common, frequent, abundant, usual. 2. poor, inferior, bad. 3. welldone, burned.*

rarely *adv.* seldom, hardly ever, almost never, *once in a blue moon, once in awhile, infrequently, scarcely. ANT. *often, frequently.*

rascal *n.* scoundrel, scamp, rogue, knave, imp, rapscallion, devil, cad, cur, *bastard, *SOB.

rash *a.* incautious, reckless, impulsive, thoughtless, careless, hasty, injudicious, devil-may-care, unwary, foolhardy. ANT. *cautious, careful, judicious.*

rasp *v.* scrape, grate, scratch, rub, file, grind, scour, abrade.

raspy *a.* scratchy, rough, whiskey-voiced, hoarse, harsh, gritty, grating, gravelly. ANT. *smooth, soothing, pleasant.*

rat *n.* 1. RODENT vermin, pest, mammal, scavenger. 2. INFORMER squealer, fink, stool pigeon, backstabber.

rate *n.* 1. AMOUNT degree, proportion, ratio. 2. PRICE fee, charge, cost, value, expense, levy, duty. 3. SPEED tempo, pace, velocity, progress, flow.

rate *v.* appraise, estimate, evaluate, assess, rank, score, grade, weigh, value, deem, classify.

rather *adv.* moderately, pretty, somewhat, fairly, relatively, kind of, more or less.

RATIFY *v.* [RAT uh fi] to approve or pass officially. *They plan to ratify the amendment today.* SYN. approve, pass, sanction, support, affirm, endorse, authorize, back, warrant, *rubber stamp. ANT. *disapprove, veto, invalidate.* SEE POLITICS

rating *n.* rank, score, grade, mark, class, classification, evaluation, assessment.

ratio *n.* proportion, relationship, percentage, quota, distribution.

ration *v.* apportion, allot, allocate, mete out, dole out, divide, *divvy up, split up.

rational *a.* sane, reasonable, of sound mind, clear-thinking, sensible, levelheaded, sober, *with it, lucid, logical. ANT. *irrational, unreasonable, nonsensical, insane.*

rationale *n.* basis, reason, grounds, excuse, rationalization, motive, justification, logic, explanation.

rationalize *v.* justify, explain away, account for, make excuses for, intellectualize.

rattle *v.* clatter, vibrate, jangle, clink, clang, clank, knock, jiggle, bang.

raucous *a.* loud, noisy, rowdy, boisterous, riotous, strident, vociferous, blaring, uproarious, clamorous. ANT. *quiet, still, silent.*

raunchy *a.* sexual, pornographic, lustful, dirty, X-rated. ANT. *chaste, wholesome, pure.* SEE LEWD

ravage *v.* destroy, ruin, devastate, wreck, demolish, lay waste, plunder, pillage, ransack, despoil.

rave *v.* 1. TALK WILDLY rant, carry on, *run off at the mouth, speak deliriously, rattle on, speak incoherently. 2. PRAISE gush, speak highly of, enthuse, carry on, rhapsodize, go on about. 3. RAGE roar, thunder, explode, storm, fume, sputter, *holler, *flip out. ANT. *1. rationalize, explain, intone. 2. criticize, disparage. 3. please, pacify, placate.*

ravenous *a.* hungry, famished, voracious, starved, starving, *could eat a horse, gluttonous, insatiable, greedy, predatory. ANT. *satiated, full, sated.*

ravine *n.* gully, gorge, gulch, arroyo, valley, ditch, wash, chasm, coulee.

ravishing *a.* attractive, enchanting, alluring, entrancing, gorgeous, bewitching, beautiful, captivating. ANT. *repulsive, ugly, disgusting.*

raw *a.* 1. UNCOOKED rare, bloody, underdone. 2. NATURAL unrefined, unprocessed, virgin, crude, rough, undressed, unfinished. 3. INEXPERIENCED untrained, green, unseasoned, immature, callow, unfledged, new, ignorant, unschooled. 4. SORE inflamed, tender, sensitive, abraded, exposed, open, bare, chafed. 5. COLD chilly, bitter, damp, bleak, freezing, nippy, biting. ANT. *1. cooked, well-done. 2. refined, processed, milled. 3. experienced, trained, seasoned. 4. healthy, calloused, numb. 5. warm, pleasant, balmy.*

rawboned *a.* lean, gaunt, wasted, hollow-cheeked. ANT. *corpulent, obese.* SEE THIN

raze *v.* tear down, level, flatten, destroy, topple, demolish, wreck, knock down, fell, *total.

reach *n.* distance, extent, range, grasp, span, stretch, sweep, compass, play.

reach *v.* 1. ARRIVE AT come to, enter, *hit town, get in, get to, land. 2. EXTEND THE HAND thrust out, stretch out, outstretch, strain. 3. TOUCH grasp, get hold of, clutch, grab, seize, make contact, secure. 4. AMOUNT TO extend, attain, arrive at.

react *v.* respond, act, counter, recoil, reciprocate, answer, return, acknowledge, reply.

reaction *n.* response, comeback, answer, feedback, counteraction, return, reflex, reciprocation, acknowledgement, recoil, backlash, fallout, repercussion.

reactionary *a.* retrogressive, right wing. SEE CONSERVATIVE

read *v.* 1. TO INTERPRET THE PRINTED WORD comprehend, understand, construe, interpret, decipher, translate, peruse, scan, skim, pore over, flip through. **2.** UTTER recite, deliver.

readable *a.* legible, decipherable, intelligible, understandable, clear, plain. ANT. *illegible, incomprehensible.*

readily *adv.* quickly, without delay, unhesitatingly, immediately, promptly, *at the drop of a hat, willingly, cheerfully, freely, *on the spur of the moment. ANT. *hesitantly, slowly, reluctantly.*

ready *v.* prepare, set up, prime, equip, prep, fit, gear up, warm up.

ready *a.* **1.** PREPARED in place, primed, set, equipped, *all systems go, *on one's toes, on call, expectant. **2.** UNHESITANT willing, eager, prompt, enthusiastic, cheerful, inclined, game. **3.** CLEVER sharp, keen, intelligent, bright, smart, astute, quick. ANT. *1. unprepared, *flat-footed, ill-equipped. 2. hesitant, unwilling, slow. 3. slow, dull.*

real *a.* actual, genuine, authentic, true, factual, valid, legitimate, bona fide, honest-to-goodness, tangible, physical, material, sincere. ANT. *unreal, fictitious, counterfeit, phony, insincere.*

realistic *a.* **1.** PRACTICAL down-to-earth, pragmatic, reasonable, *having both feet on the ground, unromantic, sober, sane. **2.** REPRESENTATIONAL lifelike, true-to-life, faithful, photographic, graphic, exact. ANT. *1. impractical, idealistic, unrealistic. 2. fake, rough.*

realize *v.* **1.** UNDERSTAND apprehend, comprehend, get, recognize, be cognizant of, grasp, appreciate, perceive, conceive, discern, see. **2.** ACHIEVE fulfill, accomplish, effectuate, complete, actualize, *pull off, attain, carry out.

really *adv.* truly, honestly, in fact, certainly, surely, literally, indeed, verily.

realm *n.* area, domain, sphere, region, empire, kingdom, dominion, territory, zone, field, reach, world, arena, orbit.

reap *v.* gather, harvest, collect, bring in, pick, pluck, cut, gain, obtain.

rear *v.* raise, bring up, grow, nurture, foster, breed, parent, train, groom.

rear *a.* back, posterior, hind, tail, aft, last. ANT. *front, fore, first.*

reason *n.* **1.** EXPLANATION justification, grounds, motive, rationale, cause, why, occasion, excuse, basis. **2.** THINKING ABILITY analysis, intellect, intelligence, wisdom, sense, smarts, logic, judgment, deduction, wit, brains. "The only oracle of man."—Ethan Allen. "A harmony among irrational impulses."—George Santayana.

reason *v.* think, deduce, analyze, apply logic, judge, cogitate, draw conclusions, use one's head, deliberate, rationalize.

reasonable *a.* **1.** SENSIBLE rational, sane, logical, intelligent, sound, thoughtful, levelheaded, judicious, commonsensical, well-advised. **2.** MODERATE fair, within reason, conservative, judicious, equitable, evenhanded, right, unextreme, temperate. ANT. *1. unreasonable, irrational, nonsensical. 2. extreme, immoderate.*

reasoning *n.* analysis, deduction, induction, thinking, thought, logic, inference, rationale, deliberation, cogitation, ratiocination.

reassure *v.* assure, fill with confidence, encourage, bolster, hearten, buck up, embolden, put one's mind at ease, comfort. ANT. *unnerve, frighten, discourage, shake one's confidence.*

rebate *n.* reimbursement, bonus, discount. SEE REFUND

rebel *n.* revolutionary, insurrectionist, malcontent, nonconformist, dissenter, insurgent, mutineer, iconoclast, anarchist, independent, opponent, traitor, young Turk. ANT. *conformist, follower, *sheep.*

rebel *v.* revolt, defy, disobey, resist, fight, dissent, rise up, oppose, mutiny, riot, overthrow.

rebellion *n.* revolt, revolution, defiance, insurrection, disobedience, insurgency, resistance, dissent, opposition, uprising, mutiny. "A medicine necessary for the sound health of government."—Thomas Jefferson.

rebellious *a.* revolutionary, defiant, disobedient, resistant, iconoclastic, nonconforming, insurgent, insurrectionary, mutinous, recalcitrant, seditious, riotous, ungovernable. ANT. *conforming, passive, *following the herd, docile, obedient.*

rebound *v.* bounce back, spring back, recover, return, recoil, ricochet, boomerang.

rebuff *v.* refuse, snub, brush off, reject, spurn, slight, repel, check, repulse, *give the cold shoulder, *cut. ANT. *embrace, accept, welcome.*

REBUKE *v.* [ri BYOOK] to reprimand or criticize harshly. *He was rebuked for losing the documents.* SYN. criticize, reprimand, admonish, *chew out, berate, reprove, reproach, censure, scold, *call on the carpet, *jump down one's throat, *rake over the coals. ANT. *praise, laud, honor, *pat on the back.*

rebut *v.* contradict, argue, controvert, refute, disprove, invalidate, discredit, *shoot down, retort. ANT. *support, prove, validate.*

rebuttal n. counterargument, contradiction, refutation, invalidation, discrediting, retort, riposte, *comeback, disproof.

RECALCITRANT a. [ri KAL si trunt] defiant, disobedient. *The recalcitrant mule had to be gently coaxed.* SYN. defiant, disobedient, insubordinate, rebellious, resistant, refractory, intractable, fractious, contrary, stubborn. ANT. *obedient, tractable, submissive.*

recall n. recollection, memory, remembrance, reminiscence. ANT. *forgetfulness, mental block, amnesia.*

recall v. 1. REMEMBER recollect, reminisce, call to mind, think back, evoke, look back on, review, summon. 2. CALL BACK withdraw, repeal, rescind, revoke, retract, take back. ANT. 1. *forget, suffer amnesia, *have a mental block. 2. support, *allow to stand, *stand behind.*

RECANT v. [ri KANT] to take back statements formerly made. *He recanted his story in view of the overwhelming evidence against him.* SYN. take back, withdraw, disavow, retract, back down, disclaim, recall, *eat one's words, reverse, revoke. ANT. *acknowledge, confirm, *own up, admit.*

recap n. recapitulation, summary, rehash.

recap v. SEE RECAPITULATE

recapitulate v. repeat, summarize, recount, review, restate, rehash, recap, go over again.

recede v. withdraw, back away, go down, diminish, dwindle, decline, retreat, wane, shrink, fade, ebb, regress, drain. ANT. *rise, advance, increase.*

receipt n. 1. SALES SLIP proof of purchase, voucher, stub. 2. RECEIVING reception, arrival, delivery, acquisition, acceptance.

receive v. 1. GET take possession, acquire, collect, be given, obtain, pocket, gain, come by, inherit. 2. EXPERIENCE undergo, encounter, suffer, endure, bear, sustain, meet with. 3. TAKE IN VISITORS accommodate, greet, admit, accept, welcome, host, entertain.

recent a. late, now, current, fresh, modern, today, present-day, hot, new, up-to-date. ANT. *past, old, bygone, ancient.*

receptacle n. holder, container, vessel, repository, box, basket, bin, bag.

reception n. 1. RECEIVING acknowledgement, welcome, greeting. 2. PARTY function, gathering, levee, soiree.

receptionist n. receiver, greeter, secretary, office worker.

receptive a. open, accepting, open-minded, accessible, favorable, amenable, inclined, hospitable. ANT. *closed, close-minded, unreceptive, cold.*

recess n. 1. BREAK rest, intermission, halt, respite, breathing spell, *breather, hiatus, interlude. 2. HOLLOW niche, indentation, nook, slot, cranny, hole, bay, alcove.

recession n. receding, withdrawal, retreat, reversal, regression, decline, downturn, slump, *hard times, economic slowdown, depression. ANT. *progression, advance, growth, *boom times.*

recharge v. reenergize, revive, renew, revitalize, rejuvenate, regenerate, bring back to life, resurrect.

recipe n. formula, prescription, directions, compound, ingredients, list, blueprints, specifications.

reciprocal a. mutual, interchangeable, exchanged, alternate, interdependent, *give-and-take, corresponding, shared. ANT. *independent, autonomous.*

reciprocate v. give and take, interchange, exchange, return in kind, trade, repay, share, swap, retaliate, *scratch each other's back.

recital n. narration, account, report, reading, telling, performance, solo performance.

recite v. repeat, read, deliver, narrate, speak, tell, perform, report, relate.

reckless a. incautious, careless, devil-may-care, heedless, headlong, breakneck, wild, daring, foolhardy, rash, negligent. ANT. *cautious, careful, responsible.*

reckon v. 1. FIGURE UP add up, count, compute, total, tally, calculate, estimate. 2. SUPPOSE think, surmise, imagine, gather, guess, presume, figure, fancy.

reckoning n. count, computation, figuring-up, totaling, tally, calculation, estimate, bill, account, statement, charge.

recline v. lean back, lie back, lounge, stretch out, lie down, repose, sprawl.

recluse n. hermit, loner, *lone wolf, solitary, anchorite, monk, misanthrope, troglodyte. ANT. *socialize, *social animal, *people person.*

reclusive a. solitary, secluded, isolated, lone, hermitic, cloistered, unsocial, withdrawn, misanthropic. ANT. *social, gregarious, outgoing, friendly.*

recognition n. 1. IDENTIFICATION realization, detection, discovery, placing, recall, perception, notice, acknowledgement. 2. APPRECIATION acknowledgement, approval, gratitude, esteem, notice, *pat on the back.

recognize v. **1.** IDENTIFY know, place, *peg, distinguish, detect, realize, recall, discover. **2.** APPRECIATE acknowledge, show gratitude, honor, salute, approve.

recoil v. draw back, shrink back, pull back, jump, withdraw, cringe, flinch, wince, start, reel.

recollect v. remember, recall, call to mind, reminisce, summon, place, evoke. ANT. *forget, draw a blank.*

recommend v. suggest, advise, back, endorse, approve, favor, prescribe, tout, *put in a good word for, advocate, sanction, counsel. ANT. *disapprove, reject, advise against.*

recommendation n. suggestion, advice, endorsement, approval, prescription, *good word, counsel, testimonial, reference, plug, *word to the wise.

recompense n. payment, repayment, compensation, remuneration, restitution, reward, reparation, return.

recompense v. repay, compensate, pay back, remunerate, make restitution, reimburse, reward, return.

reconcile v. **1.** HARMONIZE settle, resolve differences, make up, make peace, conciliate, win over, appease, compromise, accord, *bury the hatchet, mediate. **2.** RESIGN ONESELF TO accept, let go, adjust to, take in stride, make the best of it, *roll with the punches. **3.** MAKE AGREE square, harmonize, equalize, rectify, straighten out. ANT. *1. war, aggravate, antagonize, offend.*

RECONDITE a. [REK un DITE] beyond the average person's understanding, difficult. *Her theories of creation were recondite.* SYN. difficult, abstruse, hard, deep, erudite, pedantic, complex, complicated, *over one's head, arcane, incomprehensible. ANT. *easy, simple, *child's play.*

reconnaissance n. survey, *look-see, scouting mission, observation, reconnoitering.

reconsider v. rethink, reevaluate, reexamine, *look at in a different light, change one's mind, think twice, review, amend.

record n. **1.** HISTORY register, account, chronicle, transcription, log, journal, minutes, archives, documentation, diary. **2.** PERFORMANCE HISTORY track record, book, resumé, *stats. **3.** RECORDING disc, album, *45, *hot wax, single, LP, CD. SEE MUSIC

record v. register, chronicle, transcribe, take down, write down, log, take minutes, document, enter, set down, keep an account of. ANT. *erase, delete.*

recording n. tape, CD, audio tape, record, LP, cassette.

recount v. tell, narrate, repeat, describe, *recap, detail, run down, relate, review.

recoup v. recover, get back, regain, make up for, compensate, reimburse, replace.

recover v. **1.** GET BACK reclaim, retrieve, win back, retake, recoup, resume. **2.** GET BETTER get well, restore one's health, regain one's strength, convalesce, heal, recuperate, come around, rally, *pull through. ANT. *1. lose. 2. take a turn for the worse, relapse, fail.*

recreation n. amusement, leisure, activity, relaxation, *R&R, play, fun, games, exercise, sport, diversion, hobby.

recruit v. enlist, enroll, draft, induct, round up, muster, hire, sign up.

rectify v. correct, adjust, right, amend, fix, remedy, revise, straighten out, square, calibrate.

recumbent a. lying down, reclining, prone, flat, supine, prostrate, stretched out, sprawled. ANT. *erect, standing, upright.*

recuperate v. get better, get well, recover, convalesce, heal, come around, mend, rally, *pull through, get back on one's feet. ANT. *take a turn for the worse, relapse, fail, *circle the drain.*

recur v. repeat, happen again, reappear, reoccur, return, come back, persist.

recurrent a. repeating, repetitive, reappearing, returning, persistent, frequent, regular, periodic, cyclical, chronic. ANT. *infrequent, erratic, *out-of-the-ordinary.*

red a. crimson, blood, cherry, brick, ruby, vermillion, wine, blush, coral, ruddy, scarlet, rose, salmon, fuchsia, maroon, carmine.

redeem v. **1.** CASH IN recover, collect on, trade in, exchange, claim, turn in, convert. **2.** DELIVER FROM SIN atone, reform, rehabilitate, absolve, save, make up for, make amends.

RED HERRING n. something that diverts attention away from another issue; an object of deliberate distraction. *The threat of communism was a red herring employed to make the voters forget about the president's misconduct.* SYN. distractor, distraction, smokescreen, show-stealer, diversion, diversionary tactic, dodge, false trail, attention-grabber.

redneck n. Sl. *good old boy, ignoramus, bigot, *yahoo, Neanderthal, hick, farmer, caveman, *Archie Bunker, peckerwood, *white trash, *cracker, conservative, southern blue collar worker.

REDOLENT a. [RED uh lunt] fragrant. *We closed our eyes and inhaled the smells of the* *redolent sea shore.* SYN. fragrant, aromatic, scented, sweet-smelling, odoriferous, smelling, evocative, reminiscent. ANT. *reeking, putrid, fetid.*

REDRESS *n.* [REE dress] a setting right, compensation for a wrong. *They will seek redress for the damages done.* SYN. compensation, reparation, amends, recompense, satisfaction, righting, restitution, correction, payment.

redress *v.* rectify, set right, correct, remedy, compensate, make reparations, make restitution, satisfy, put right, square.

red tape *n.* bureaucracy, *bureaucrap, *paper shuffling, delay, *jumping through hoops, *aligning ducks in a row, documentation, officialese, inefficiency, proper channels.

reduce *v.* **1.** LOWER lessen, decrease, cut, diminish, scale down, shorten, lighten, subtract, contract, trim, deflate. **2.** DEMOTE downgrade, lower in rank. **3.** SOFTEN temper, ease, moderate, dilute, mitigate, mellow, modify. **4.** SUBDUE conquer, vanquish, crush, overpower, put down, break. ANT. *1. increase, heighten. 2. promote, upgrade. 3. intensify, strengthen. 4. surrender, retreat.*

REDUNDANT *a.* [ri DUN dunt] more than what is needed, repetitive, wordy. *His speech was long-winded and redundant.* SYN. excessive, unnecessary, superfluous, repetitious, more than enough, inessential, long-winded, *de trop, wordy, verbose. ANT. *necessary, indispensable, concise.*

reef *n.* bank, bar, sand bar, ridge, shoal, atoll shelf, ledge, coral reef.

reek *n.* smell, stench, odor, stink, fetor.

reek *v.* stink, smell, *smell to high heaven, steam, vaporize, permeate.

reel *v.* stagger, sway, lurch, spin, pitch, waver, teeter, whirl, rock, fall back.

refer *v.* **1.** MAKE REFERENCE cite, allude, point to, touch on, mention, quote, speak of, bring up. **2.** SEND direct, point, assign, recommend. **3.** REGARD relate, deal with, involve, concern, apply, pertain, cover.

referee *n.* *ref, umpire, judge, arbitrator, mediator, intermediary, go-between, moderator.

reference *n.* **1.** MENTION citation, allusion, quotation, notice, implication, intimation. **2.** RECOMMENDATION testimonial, endorsement, good word, certification.

refined *a.* **1.** CULTIVATED cultured, polished, perfected, finished, civilized, genteel, gentlemanly, courtly, ladylike, polite, well-bred,

elegant. **2.** CLEANED purified, washed, filtered, strained, processed, clarified, distilled. ANT. *1. unrefined, coarse, crude. 2. unrefined, unpure, rough, raw.*

refinement *n.* cultivation, culture, polish, perfection, finish, elegance, civility, gentility, graciousness, good breeding, urbanity, delicacy. ANT. *roughness, coarseness, crudeness, vulgarity.*

reflect *v.* **1.** THROW BACK mirror, echo, reverberate, rebound, resonate, repercuss, resound, return. **2.** CONSIDER think, contemplate, ponder, ruminate, deliberate, weigh, meditate, cogitate, muse.

reflection *n.* **1.** MIRROR IMAGE image, counterpart, impression. **2.** CONSIDERATION contemplation, meditation, deliberation, rumination, thought, cogitation, pondering, musing. "Wisdom's best nurse."—John Milton.

reform *n.* correction, change for the better, improvement, advancement, betterment, renovation, progress, rectification.

reformatory *n.* penal institution, correctional facility, reform school, training center. SEE PRISON

refrain *v.* do without, forgo, forbear, abstain, eschew, stop, resist, pass on, *swear off, desist. ANT. *indulge, take up.*

refresh *v.* **1.** RENEW freshen, rejuvenate, invigorate, revitalize, restore, revive, breathe new life into, vivify. **2.** STIMULATE jog, activate, arouse, awaken, prompt, remind, cue. ANT. *1. wear out, drain, tire, sap. 2. dull, inhibit.*

refreshing *a.* **1.** RENEWING freshening, rejuvenating, invigorating, revitalizing, restoring, reviving, bracing, energizing. **2.** NEW fresh, different, original, novel. ANT. *1. tiring, draining, sapping. 2. old, unoriginal.*

refreshment *n.* fortification, *pick-me-up, nourishment, sustenance, food, drink, bite, snack.

refrigerate *v.* chill, cool, ice, freeze, aircondition.

refuge *n.* shelter, retreat, safe haven, hiding place, hideout, asylum, sanctuary, cover, security, protection.

refugee *n.* emigrant, expatriate, defector, emigré, runaway, evacuee, outcast, alien, fugitive.

refund *n.* reimbursement, rebate, return, repayment.

refund *v.* pay back, reimburse, rebate, return, repay, settle, recompense, satisfy.

refurbish *v.* renovate, fix up, freshen up,

brighten up, clean up, recondition, restore, renew, rejuvenate, revamp.

refusal *n.* no, rejection, *thumbs down, nix, veto, nonacceptance, denial, turndown.

refuse *n.* waste, trash, rubbish, litter. SEE GARBAGE

refuse *v.* say no, reject, *give thumbs down, nix, veto, deny, turn down, decline, demur, disapprove, spurn. ANT. *okay, accept, agree.*

REFUTE *v.* [ri FYOOT] to prove or argue to be wrong. *They refuted his theories.* SYN. disprove, prove false, confute, controvert, contradict, rebut, discredit, *shoot full of holes, counter. ANT. *support, corroborate, prove.*

regal *a.* royal, stately, kingly, majestic, noble, princely, august, queenly, lordly. ANT. *lowly, plebian.*

REGALE *v.* [ri GALE] to delight, amuse or entertain. *He regaled us with his adventures during the war.* SYN. delight, amuse, entertain, enthrall, enchant, divert, captivate, humor, charm.

regalia *n.* finery, attire, outfit, dress, livery.

regard *n.* **1.** LOOK gaze, attention, heed, stare, mind, glance. **2.** CONSIDERATION thought, concern, care, attention, heed, awareness. **3.** ESTEEM respect, affection, liking, fondness, approval, admiration, appreciation. **4.** MATTER aspect, point, detail. ANT. *2. thoughtlessness. 3. disregard, disrespect, dislike.*

regard *v.* **1.** LOOK AT heed, watch, see, behold, eye, observe, take in, notice, pay attention to. **2.** CONSIDER take into account, think of, look upon, deem, view, judge.

regardless *adv.* in any event, anyway, anyhow, at any rate, nevertheless, nonetheless.

regime *n.* administration, government, leadership, rule, command, party, management, power.

regiment *v.* organize, systematize, coordinate, standardize.

region *n.* area, territory, zone, locality, location, district, place, ward, quarter, province, vicinity, spot, realm.

register *n.* record, list, book, entry, ledger, roll, daybook, registry, roster, diary.

REGRESS *v.* [ree GRESS] to go back, reverse, progress backwards. *His behavior began to regress to that of a child.* SYN. retrogress, go back, revert, retreat, degenerate, backslide, retrograde, ebb. ANT. *progress, advance.*

regret *n.* self-reproach, remorse, penitence, sorrow, self-condemnation, contrition, pangs of guilt, conscience, second thought, qualm.

"The beginning of a new life."—George Eliot.

regret *v.* be sorry for, *look back and kick oneself for, lament, bemoan, rue the day, have pangs of conscience, have second thoughts, never forgive oneself, repent, hate oneself for.

regretful *a.* sorry, contrite, ashamed, apologetic, conscience-stricken, guilty, penitent, self-reproachful, *sadder but wiser. ANT. *unrepentant, *having no qualms, brazen.*

regrettable *a.* lamentable, unfortunate, shameful, grievous, deplorable.

regular *a.* **1.** NORMAL usual, customary, conventional, typical, routine, everyday, traditional, average, stock, ordinary, standard. **2.** ORDERLY symmetrical, balanced, ordered, harmonious, even, aligned, straight, uniform. **3.** CONSISTENT habitual, fixed, undeviating, recurrent, set, established, daily. ANT. *1. irregular, abnormal, unconventional. 2. disorderly, asymmetrical, uneven. 3. sporadic, irregular, infrequent.*

regulate *v.* **1.** GOVERN control, manage, direct, administer, run, maintain, oversee. **2.** BALANCE equalize, adjust, time, moderate.

regulation *n.* **1.** CONTROL government, management, adjustment, supervision, direction, moderation, tuning, timing. **2.** RULE law, ordinance, statute, code, requirement, order, commandment, instruction, canon.

regurgitate *v.* throw up, heave, puke. SEE VOMIT

rehabilitate *v.* restore, reclaim, *rehab, straighten out, improve, reform, change, transform, save, redeem, change one's ways.

rehearse *v.* practice, go over, run through, prepare, perfect, drill, train, *have a dry run, tune up, *jam.

reign *n.* rule, power, dominance, dominion, sovereignty, sway, dynasty, governance, leadership, tenure, control, regime.

reign *v.* rule, hold power, be in power, govern, command, manage, administer, hold sway, lead, control, dominate, run the show.

reimburse *v.* pay back, repay, recompense, compensate, refund, make restitution, make good, settle, indemnify.

rein *n.* harness, bridle, control, restraint, guide.

rein *v.* stop, slow, restrain, control, guide, bridle, curb, check.

reinforce *v.* strengthen, fortify, *beef up, harden, stiffen, bolster, buttress, prop, toughen, support. ANT. *weaken, soften, undermine, cripple.*

REITERATE *v.* [ree IT uh RATE] to go over

again, repeat. *Some students nodded off when the professor reiterated for the second time.* SYN. go over again, repeat, *recap, recapitulate, restate, rehash, belabor, retell.

reject *n.* castoff, outcast, discard, second, irregular, pariah, loser.

reject *v.* *nix, refuse, repulse, pass on, turn down, *give thumbs down, brush off, *give the cold shoulder, *turn one's nose up at, spurn, shun, repudiate, veto, rebuff, *spit upon, *kiss off, jilt. ANT. *accept, embrace, approve, *give thumbs up.*

rejoice *v.* be full of joy, be happy, be glad, celebrate, revel, be elated, exult, jump for joy, glory, delight. ANT. *grieve, lament.*

rejoinder *n.* answer, reply, comeback, response, retort, repartee, rebuttal, countering.

rejuvenate *v.* renew, restore, revive, invigorate, *breathe new life into, regenerate, revitalize, refresh, reanimate. ANT. *tire, sap, drain.*

relapse *n.* recurrence, reappearance, *turn for the worse, setback, decline, regression, fall, deterioration. ANT. *remission, improvement, progress.*

relate *v.* **1.** RECOUNT tell, narrate, detail, state, report, communicate, describe, give an account of, repeat. **2.** CONNECT correspond, correlate, associate, link, pertain, apply, have to do with, concern, bear upon. **3.** IDENTIFY WITH empathize, understand, *stand in another's shoes.

related *a.* associated, connected, correlated, linked, allied, affiliated, akin, kindred, cognate. ANT. *independent, unrelated, unlike.*

relation *n.* association, connection, affiliation, link, relationship, kinship, alliance.

relationship *n.* association, friendship, alliance, kinship, affiliation, marriage, liaison, connection, rapport.

relative *n.* relation, kin, family member, kinsman, sibling, blood relative, cognate, mother, father, brother, sister, *kissing cousin, niece, nephew, aunt, uncle, in-law. ANT. *stranger.*

relative *a.* **1.** COMPARATIVE proportional, comparable, relating to, respective. **2.** PERTAINING pertinent, relative, germane. ANT. *1. dissimilar, unlike. 2. unrelated, *like apples and oranges.*

relax *v.* **1.** LOOSEN UP be at ease, *take it easy, rest, unwind, let oneself go, calm down, *let one's hair down, take a break, laze. **2.** SLACKEN soften, let up, lessen, ease off, loosen, diminish, relieve, lighten, moderate.

ANT. *1. get wound up, tense, labor, *drive oneself into the grave. 2. tighten, tense up, wind up.*

relaxation *n.* **1.** REST recreation, *R&R, fun, unwinding, *cutting loose, leisure, quiet time, holiday, lounging, repose, *decompression. **2.** LOOSENING slackening, easing. ANT. *1. work, labor, toil, stress. 2. tightening, intensification.*

release *n.* liberation, emancipation, liberty, freeing, deliverance, discharge, loosing, dismissal, acquittal, letting go. ANT. *imprisonment, incarceration, capture.*

release *v.* let go, discharge, free, liberate, emancipate, deliver, loose, dismiss, acquit, untie, unshackle.

relegate *v.* consign, assign, delegate, entrust, commission.

relent *v.* soften, let up, yield, give up, slow, ease off, mitigate, relax, slacken, drop, come around, bend, reduce.

RELENTLESS *a.* [ri LENT liss] unremitting, incessant, pitiless. *The enemy bunkers took a relentless pounding.* SYN. unremitting, incessant, persistent, sustained, pitiless, merciless, unrelenting, hard, cruel, unflagging. ANT. *relenting, brief, mercifully short, sparing.*

relevant *a.* relating, pertinent, applicable, germane, to the point, material, relative, apropos, connected, apt. ANT. *irrelevant, beside the point, unrelated.*

reliable *a.* dependable, trustworthy, responsible, conscientious, faithful, unfailing, constant, steady, trusty. ANT. *unreliable, undependable, irresponsible.*

reliance *n.* confidence, dependence, trust, belief, credit, certainty, security. ANT. *distrust, insecurity.*

relic *n.* ruin, antique, antiquity, artifact, remnant, remains, vestige, keepsake, souvenir.

relief *n.* release, alleviation, easing, relaxation, mitigation, soothing, amelioration, succor, letup, respite, palliation, balm, help. ANT. *intensification, aggravation, worsening.*

relieve *v.* **1.** EASE alleviate, release, comfort, free, relax, mitigate, soothe, palliate, assuage, diminish, quell. **2.** SET FREE unburden, take over, stand in for, substitute for, replace, release, spell.

religion *n.* belief in God, faith, spirituality, devotion, godliness, worship, piety, theology, persuasion, devoutness. "The life of God in the soul of man."—Lyman Abbott. "The opium of the people."—Karl Marx. "The elder sister of philosophy."—Walter Savage

Landor. "A universal obsessional neurosis."—Sigmund Freud. "The soul of civilization."—Will Durant.

WORD FIND

CHRISTIANITY

abandonment of one's faith: apostasy

Adam and Eve's sin of eating from tree of knowledge: Original Sin

admitting sins to priest in Roman Catholic Church: confession

amending sacrament: penance

amends for sins: atonement

amen: to trust

angel, high: archangel

angel, second order: cherubim

ascent to heaven, Christ's: Ascension

battle, location of final: Armageddon (mountain of Megiddo)

biblical texts questioned by some denominations: apocrypha

birth of Christ or Second Coming: Advent

blessed with gift of tongues, healing, or prophecy: charismatic

blessing at end of service: benediction

bread and wine, body and blood of Christ, sacrament of: Eucharist, Communion, Holy Communion, Mass

bread wafers: host

casting out of church due to transgressions: excommunication

container or chest holding Ten Commandments: Ark of the Covenant

crucifixion of Christ, commemoration: Good Friday

cursing of God: blasphemy

declaration by Pope that deceased person is blessed and worthy to pray to: beatification

declaration by Pope that deceased person is saint following beatification: canonization

dissenter: heretic

enemy of Christ: Antichrist, the beast

faith, statement of: Apostle's Creed

fellowship: communion

forgiveness of sins: absolution

forty-day period before Easter: Lent

funeral mass, Roman Catholic: requiem

God, seeing: beatific vision

gospel, one of twelve who spread: apostle

guardian or protector of specific group: patron saint

healing illness through prayer: faith healing, laying on of hands

Hebrew Bible: Old Testament

Holy Land: Israel, Palestine

kneel in worship: genuflect

laws, ecclesiastical: canon

Lamb of God icon: Agnus Dei

Last Supper, day of: Maundy Thursday

Lent, first day of: Ash Wednesday

literal interpretation of Bible, believing in: fundamentalism

nonbeliever: atheist

non-Christian: infidel

offense to God: abomination

oil, apply: anoint

oil used in Catholic confirmation: chrism

Old Testament scrolls: Dead Sea Scrolls

overlooking of transgressions in Roman Catholic Church: dispensation

prayer: Angelus

prayer beads: rosary

presiding priest at Holy Communion: celebrant

questioner or doubter: agnostic

repentance for sins: contrition

revelation of future in Bible: Apocalypse

rising of soul after death: resurrection

rites: sacraments

sacred, make: consecrate

Second Coming will arrive soon, denomination believing: Seventh Day Adventist, Second Adventists

sect: denomination

sex, priest's vow to abstain from: vow of celibacy

song from biblical text: canticle

spread of word throughout the world: evangelism

study of religion: theology

tongues, denomination known for some members who speak in: Pentecostal Church

tongues, speaking in: glossolalia

Virgin Mary: Madonna

washing before ceremonies: ablutions

water immersion ceremony: baptism

wise men's visit to Christ's birth, commemoration of: Epiphany

JUDAISM

candelabra used to mark Chanukah: menorah

discrimination against Jews: antisemitism

eight-day festival commemorating exodus of Jews from Egypt: Passover

festival of lights commemorating victory of Maccabees over the Syrians: Chanukah

food fit to be eaten: kosher

God, name of: Jehovah, Elohim, Yahweh, YHWH, Adonai

holy day devoted to prayer, fasting: Yom Kippur

Jewish New Year: Rosh Hashanah

minister: rabbi

morning and evening prayer: Shema

non-Jew: gentile

Old Testament of Bible: Hebrew Bible, Torah

prayer leader in synagogue: cantor

rabbinical writings, interpretations and the Torah collectively: Talmud

skullcap worn by Jewish men: yarmulka

strict, orthodox Jews known for earlocks, black coats: Chasidim, Hasidim

thirteen-year-old's rite of adulthood: bar mitzvah

twelve- or thirteen-year-old girl's rite of adulthood: bat mitzvah

ISLAM

adherent: Moslem, Muslim

authority on Muslim law: ayatollah

call to prayer from minaret of mosque: azan

daily call to prayers: adhan

fit to eat, according to dietary laws: halal

God: Allah

holy war, fighting for Islam: jihad

month of fasting: Ramadan

Muhammad's birthplace: Mecca

night of forgiveness: Lailat-ul-Bara'h

non-Moslem: infidel

"Peace be upon you": Salam Alaikum

pilgrimage to Mecca: hajj

prayer leader in mosque: imam

prayers required five times per day: Salat

prophet of God and founder of Islam: Muhammad

requirements of Islamic religion: five pillars of Islam

rule that women must keep covered in public: purdah

sacred stone at Mecca: Black Stone

sacred text: Koran

HINDUISM

black god, avatar of Vishnu: Krishna

communal house: ashram

elephant-headed god, symbol of luck: Ganesha

incarnation of a god: avatar

god of creation: Brahma

god of life and death: Shiva

god of love and desire: Kamadeva

god of rain and war: Indra

god who will come to destroy the world: Kalki

guidance book, "The Song of the Lord": Bhagavad Gita

meditation word or phrase repeated to clear head: mantra

mental, physical exercises to achieve well-being: yoga

merchant caste: Vaisyas

nonviolence doctrine: ahimsa

peasant, servant caste: Sudras

peasants outside of caste system: Untouchables

priestly caste: Brahmin

release from endless reincarnation: moksha

spiritual teacher: guru

supreme being: Vishnu

yoga adherent: yogi

warrior caste: Kshatriyas

what goes around comes around, doctrine of: karma

worship: puja

BUDDHISM

Chinese Buddhism, enlightenment through meditation: Zen

domed Buddhist shrine: stupa

enlightenment, path to: dharma

enlightenment, sudden achievement of: satori

festival: Wesak

moral rules: five precepts

nonviolence doctrine: ahimsa

one devoted to seeking enlightenment: bodhisattva

spiritual awakening, bliss: enlightenment, bodhi, nirvana

spiritual leader of Tibetan Buddhism: Dalai Lama

suffering, belief that everything leads to: dukkha

word or phrase repeated during meditation: mantra

SEE BIBLE, CHURCH, CLERGYMAN, GOD, PRAYER

religious *a.* **1.** PIOUS devout, godly, spiritual, faithful, churchgoing, theological, righteous, God-fearing, reverent, saintly. **2.** CAREFUL scrupulous, exact, conscientious, rigorous, meticulous. ANT. *1. atheistic, nonbelieving, impious. 2. careless, slack.*

RELINQUISH *v.* [ri LING kwish] to give up, let go or renounce. *He will relinquish his office in thirty days.* SYN. give up, let go, renounce, abandon, quit, drop, surrender, forswear, leave, forsake, surrender, abdicate, resign. ANT. *hold, keep, maintain.*

relish *n.* pleasure, enjoyment, appreciation, liking, love, fondness, fancy, zest, satisfaction, gusto.

relish *v.* enjoy, take pleasure in, like, love, be

fond of, appreciate, savor, adore, revel in, luxuriate in, *dig. ANT. *hate, find distasteful, detest.*

reluctant *a.* hesitant, unwilling, disinclined, slow, unenthusiastic, hanging back, leery, wary, cautious, averse, loath. ANT. *eager, willing, enthusiastic.*

rely *v.* depend, count on, bank on, have confidence in, trust, entrust, put faith in, bet on, swear by. ANT. *doubt, mistrust.*

remain *v.* stay, wait, sit tight, stay put, hold, endure, continue, abide, keep on, persist. ANT. *go, leave, change.*

remainder *n.* the rest, leftover, remnant, remains, balance, surplus, residue, overage.

remark *n.* comment, commentary, word, observation, statement, note, thought, mention, utterance, reflection.

remarkable *a.* outstanding, extraordinary, noteworthy, noticeable, unusual, exceptional, phenomenal, unique, striking, impressive, rare. ANT. *usual, ordinary, common, everyday.*

remedial *a.* healing, corrective, restorative, curing, therapeutic, curative. ANT. *harmful, detrimental.*

remedy *n.* cure, treatment, medicine, restorative, cure-all, panacea, corrective, therapy, relief, antidote, elixir, prescription, drug.

remedy *v.* cure, treat, medicate, fix, restore, correct, relieve, revive, counteract, neutralize, alleviate, help, doctor. ANT. *aggravate, exacerbate, poison, infect.*

remember *v.* **1.** RECALL recollect, call to mind, reminisce, think back, retrospect, conjure up, summon, memorize, commit to memory, retain, learn. **2.** KEEP IN MIND bear in mind, don't forget. ANT. *1. forget, draw a blank, have amnesia.*

remind *v.* bring back, bring to mind, spur one's memory, refresh memory, make remember, *ring a bell, awaken memories.

reminisce *v.* think back, retrospect, recollect, remember, *ache with nostalgia, live in the past.

REMISS *a.* [ri MISS] lax or negligent in performing one's responsibilities. *He has long been remiss in his duties.* SYN. negligent, careless, lax, slack, neglectful, sloppy, lazy, inattentive, delinquent, irresponsible, derelict. ANT. *responsible, careful, dutiful.*

remission *n.* abatement, arrestment, lessening, subsiding, reduction, reprieve, letup, diminution, waning, quelling, stoppage, alleviation.

remit *v.* send, forward, transmit, mail, discharge.

remnant *n.* remainder, leftover, remains, excess, extra, surplus, leaving, residue, scrap, odds and ends, relic, vestige.

remodel *v.* make over, redesign, rebuild, refurbish, redo, renovate, overhaul, retrofit.

REMONSTRATE *v.* [ri MON strate] to object to or protest against. *The demonstrators continued to remonstrate outside the mayor's door.* SYN. object, protest, argue against, challenge, criticize, take issue, expostulate, take exception, oppose, denounce. ANT. *go along with, assent, agree.*

remorse *n.* guilt, penitence, self-reproach, compunction, contrition, regret, sorriness, repentance, shame, rue. "The pain of sin."— Theodore Parker. "The echo of a lost virtue."—Edward Bulwer Lytton. "The fatal egg by pleasure laid."—William Cowper. ANT. *indifference, hard-heartedness, glee, pride.*

remote *a.* **1.** DISTANT far-off, far-flung, isolated, secluded, God-forsaken, outlying, lonely, removed, out-of-the-way, inaccessible. **2.** UNLIKELY slight, faint, slim, small, improbable, outside. **3.** ALOOF distant, removed, cold, detached, faraway, withdrawn, uninterested. ANT. *1. close, at hand, nearby. 2. likely, significant, probable. 3. intimate, warm, close.*

remove *v.* **1.** TAKE OFF eject, expel, extract, throw off, cut off, move, transfer, get rid of, oust, withdraw, uproot, disconnect, erase, expunge. **2.** DO AWAY WITH kill, assassinate, take out, eliminate, execute, dismiss, depose, oust, discharge, unseat, unhorse, eject, fire, *can. ANT. *1. keep, maintain, retain. 2. hire, install.*

remunerate *v.* pay, compensate, repay, reward, recompense, reimburse, indemnify.

RENAISSANCE *n.* [REN i SAHNS] a rebirth, resurgence or revival. *The agency is hoping for a renaissance in space exploration.* SYN. rebirth, resurgence, revival, reawakening, resurgence, new day, renewal, rejuvenation, regeneration.

rend *v.* rip, split, cleave. SEE TEAR

render *v.* **1.** PRESENT deliver, give, hand over, furnish, submit, tender, provide, impart. **2.** CAUSE TO BE make. **3.** PERFORM recite, represent, interpret, portray, play, treat, depict.

rendezvous *n.* meeting place, gathering place, appointment, engagement, date, meeting, tryst.

rendition *n.* rendering, version, interpretation,

performance, presentation, arrangement, depiction, portrayal.

renegade *n.* rebel, turncoat, traitor, apostate, betrayer, double-crosser, defector, deserter, revolutionist, Benedict Arnold.

RENEGE *v.* [ri NIG] to go back on one's word, to fail to follow through on an agreement. *If they renege on the deal, we will sue for breach of contract.* SYN. go back on one's word, break promise, default, back out, *weasel out, *change one's tune, *cop out, backpedal. ANT. *fulfill, make good, satisfy.*

renew *v.* begin again, resume, make a fresh start, restore, rejuvenate, refresh, recondition, revitalize, replenish, regenerate, reinvigorate, *breathe new life into.

RENOUNCE *v.* [ri NOUNCE] to give up, repudiate, wash one's hands of. *She renounced her belief in astrology.* SYN. give up, abandon, reject, *swear off, relinquish, quit, desert, disavow, forswear, disown, repudiate, *turn one's back on, *divorce oneself from. ANT. *embrace, hold dear, claim.*

renovate *v.* renew, revive, clean up, fix up, recondition, restore, remodel, refurbish, redecorate, *give a face-lift, modernize, update.

renown *n.* celebrity, fame, reputation, prominence, notoriety, stardom, eminence, popularity, illustriousness. ANT. *obscurity, anonymity.*

renowned *a.* celebrated, famous, prominent, noted, eminent, popular, acclaimed, illustrious, distinguished, notorious, outstanding. ANT. *obscure, unknown.*

rent *n.* opening, split, rip, tear, hole, slit, fissure, rift.

rent *v.* lease, let, sublet, hire, charter, contract for.

renunciation *n.* renouncement, rejection, abandonment, relinquishment, repudiation, disavowal, spurning, forswearing. ANT. *acceptance, embracement.*

repair *n.* fixing, mending, restoration, service, reconditioning, patching, alignment, overhaul, correction, tune-up.

repair *v.* **1.** FIX mend, restore, recondition, patch, rebuild, reconstruct, align, overhaul, adjust, tinker with. **2.** GO move, head for, proceed, retire.

REPARTEE *n.* [REP ar TAY] witty comebacks, a series of quick and witty replies, clever conversational exchange. *He was famous for his brilliant repartee.* SYN. witty

comebacks, snappy comebacks, witty replies, witty rejoinders, banter, quip, sally, lively exchange, badinage, give-and-take, jesting, riposte, mot. "A duel fought with the points of jokes."—Max Eastman. "Something we think of 24 hours too late."—Mark Twain.

repast *n.* meal, food and drink, feast, banquet, eats, *feed, spread, *bite.

repay *v.* pay back, reimburse, return, make up for, compensate, square, requite, refund, rebate, settle, even the score, reciprocate.

repeal *n.* revocation, abrogation, rescission, annulment, nullification, voiding, invalidation, withdrawal, cancellation.

repeal *v.* withdraw, revoke, cancel, declare null and void, rescind, abrogate, invalidate, annul, abolish.

repeat *n.* repetition, replay, rebroadcast, rerun, rehash.

repeat *v.* **1.** REITERATE restate, say again, recap, recapitulate, parrot. **2.** DO AGAIN duplicate, remake, reproduce, redo, echo. **3.** TELL recount, relate.

repel *v.* **1.** REPULSE push back, force back, ward off, resist, drive away, fend off, check, refuse, spurn, reject, snub, *give cold shoulder. **2.** DISGUST *turn off, sicken, revolt, appall, *turn one's stomach, *gross out, *make one's flesh crawl. ANT. *1. welcome, embrace, accept. 2. attract, delight, please.*

repellent *a.* repulsive, disgusting, revolting, appalling, sickening, nauseating, offensive, repugnant, obnoxious.

repent *v.* feel sorry, be remorseful, be contrite, be conscious-stricken, rue the day, apologize, ask forgiveness, lament, deplore, be penitent.

repentance *n.* penitence, sorrow, remorse, contrition, guilt, compunction, sorriness, regret, pangs of conscience. "The voice of God."—Israel Baal Shem Tob. ANT. *pride, self-satisfaction.*

REPERCUSSION *n.* [REE pur KUSH un] an effect or consequence of some action. *Opening the borders to free trade will create serious repercussions.* SYN. effect, consequence, result, reaction, fallout, outcome, aftermath, impact, backlash, echo.

repetition *n.* duplication, repeat, rerun, replay, reiteration, recapitulation, recurrence, *broken record, rote, reprise.

repetitious *a.* repetitive, redundant, tautological, wordy, long-winded, verbose, boring, tedious, recurring. ANT. *concise, to the point, spare.*

replace *v*. **1.** TAKE THE PLACE OF succeed, follow, supersede, supplant, stand in, *step into one's shoes, fill in for. **2.** RETURN put back.

replenish *v*. fill, supply, refill, stock, restore, replace, provision, top off, reload.

REPLETE *a*. [ri PLEET] filled, full, plentiful. *The cellar was replete with wine bottles.* SYN. full, filled, plentiful, abundant, crammed, stuffed, packed, glutted, *chock-full, loaded. ANT. *empty, vacant, bare.*

replica *n*. reproduction, copy, imitation, look-alike, *knockoff, duplicate, facsimile, clone, photocopy.

reply *n*. answer, response, reaction, acknowledgement, comeback, return, rejoinder, retort.

reply *v*. answer, respond, react, acknowledge, come back, return, rejoin, *shoot back, retort.

report *n*. **1.** ACCOUNT statement, news, exposition, message, detailing, *blow by blow, communication, story, *word, rundown, summary, communiqué, bulletin, announcement. **2.** RUMOR gossip, talk, *word, *grapevine, *buzz, *scuttlebutt, hearsay. **3.** LOUD NOISE boom, explosion, bang, blast, detonation, crash, shot, crack, reverberation.

report *v*. **1.** COMMUNICATE give an account, state, give news, give message, detail, *give blow by blow, bring word, give rundown, summarize, announce, describe, tell, recount, relate. **2.** TURN IN tell on, *rat on.

reporter *n*. newsman, newswoman, journalist, member of the press, member of the media, correspondent, newscaster, feature writer, snoop, scribe. SEE NEWS

repose *n*. rest, sleep, ease, relaxation, quiet, respite, peace, tranquility, leisure, break.

repository *n*. depository, warehouse, vault, storehouse, store room, archives, museum, depot, magazine, library, safe, safe deposit box.

repossess *v*. reclaim, take back, recover, regain, retrieve.

REPREHENSIBLE *a*. [REP ri HEN suh bul] that which deserves criticism or rebuke. *The criminals' actions were reprehensible.* SYN. blameworthy, reproachable, sinful, shameful, felonious, villainous, criminal, heinous, wicked, unforgivable, disgraceful, ignoble, despicable. ANT. *praiseworthy, honorable, virtuous, noble.*

represent *v*. **1.** STAND FOR symbolize, denote, express, exemplify, typify, embody, personify, betoken, act as, serve as. **2.** DEPICT portray, render, picture, evoke, describe, mirror, illustrate. **3.** SERVE AS AN AGENT act on behalf of, speak for, stand for, be proxy for, *go to bat for.

representative *n*. agent, proxy, stand-in, spokesperson, *mouthpiece, advocate, delegate, envoy, emissary, surrogate, congressman, councilman.

representative *a*. characteristic, typical, illustrative, model, symbolic, exemplary, indicative. ANT. *atypical, unusual, different.*

repress *v*. keep down, hold down, control, hold in, check, restrain, contrain, crush, curb, suppress, stifle, subdue, shut up.

reprieve *n*. postponement, suspension, escape, relief, stay, stay of execution, remission, delay, abeyance.

reprimand *n*. rebuke, scolding, admonishment, reproach, *bawling out, censure, chastisement, *tongue-lashing, upbraiding, castigation. ANT. *approval, praise.*

reprimand *v*. rebuke, scold, admonish, reproach, *bawl out, censure, chastise, *give a tongue-lashing, upbraid, castigate, *rake over the coals. ANT. *approve, praise, commend.*

reprisal *n*. retaliation, *eye for an eye, revenge, vengeance, retribution, redress, vindication, counterattack.

REPROACH *n*. [ri PROACH] blame, criticism. *She was above reproach.* SYN. blame, criticism, shame, discredit, rebuke, scolding, condemnation, reprimand, censure, disapproval, disgrace. ANT. *approval, credit, praise.*

reproach *v*. accuse, blame, rebuke, criticize, shame, discredit, scold, condemn, reprimand, censure, disapprove, find fault. ANT. *approve, credit, praise.*

reprobate *n*. sinner, criminal, villain, *bad guy, lost soul, profligate, miscreant, degenerate, scoundrel, evildoer, lowlife. ANT. *angel, saint.*

reprobate *a*. bad, immoral, corrupt, unprincipled, wicked, depraved, evil, miscreant, foul. ANT. *good, virtuous, moral.*

reproduce *v*. **1.** COPY duplicate, replicate, redo, photocopy, reprint, clone, imitate, counterfeit. **2.** PROPAGATE breed, spawn, multiply, engender, procreate, proliferate.

reproduction *n*. **1.** COPY duplicate, replication, photocopy, reprint, clone, imitation, counterfeit, *mirror image, twin. **2.** PROPAGATION procreation, breeding, proliferation. ANT. *1. original, model, master.*

reproof *n.* rebuke, censure. SEE REPROACH

REPROVE *v.* [ri PROOV] to give or show one's disapproval. *She reproved the workers for making too much noise.* SYN. disapprove, rebuke, reproach, scold, admonish, censure, reprimand, condemn. ANT. *approve, praise, credit.*

REPUDIATE *v.* [ri PYOO dee ATE] to reject, have nothing to do with. *She repudiated his views.* SYN. reject, renounce, have nothing to do with, disown, cast off, disapprove, spurn, refuse, disavow, disclaim, deny. ANT. *embrace, accept, support.*

repugnant *a.* offensive, distasteful, obnoxious, repulsive, repellent, revolting, disgusting, foul, sickening, nauseating. ANT. *delightful, pleasing, appealing.*

repulse *v.* **1.** REPEL drive back, hold off, resist, check, defend, defeat. **2.** DISGUST offend, repel, revolt, sicken. **3.** REJECT rebuff, refuse, spurn, snub, *give cold shoulder. ANT. *1. embrace, welcome, pull in, draw.* 2. *delight, please, appeal.* 3. *invite.*

repulsive *a.* repellent, offensive, revolting, disgusting, foul, distasteful, *sickening, nauseating, *gross, repugnant. ANT. *appealing, delightful, attractive.*

reputable *a.* respectable, in good repute, esteemed, well thought of, acclaimed, honorable, honest, legitimate, principled, *on the up and up, reliable. ANT. *disreputable, questionable, shady.*

reputation *n.* repute, character, name, regard, stature, renown, *word of mouth, standing, *approval rating, estimation, *credit rating. "A bubble which a man bursts when he tries to blow it for himself."—Emma Carleton. "What people gossip behind your back."—Henry Banks.

repute *n.* SEE REPUTATION

reputed *a.* supposed, regarded, believed, assumed, presumed, alleged, thought, rumored. ANT. *proven, actual.*

request *n.* petition, solicitation, question, application, want, desire, behest, plea, demand.

request *v.* ask, petition, solicit, apply, appeal for, seek, *put in for, beg, demand.

requiem *n.* mass, service, memorial, eulogy, elegy, dirge, hymn, compostion.

require *v.* **1.** NEED want, lack, miss, be short of, be deficient in, desire. **2.** DEMAND order,

command, obligate, call for, insist on, compel, direct, dictate.

requirement *n.* necessity, must, essential, need, imperative, requisite, prerequisite, condition, term, provision, dictate.

requisite *n.* SEE REQUIREMENT

requisite *a.* required, essential, prerequisite, needed, necessary, imperative, obligatory, called for. ANT. *optional, elective, voluntary.*

RESCIND *v.* [ri SIND] to repeal or abolish. *They rescinded the order.* SYN. repeal, abolish, revoke, cancel, reverse, invalidate, declare null and void, annul, recall. ANT. *uphold, confirm, defend, shore up.*

rescue *n.* saving, recovery, delivery, extrication, relief, release, liberation, salvation, heroics.

rescue *v.* save, recover, deliver, extricate, relieve, release, liberate, free, bail out, retrieve, *save one's bacon.

research *n.* fact-finding, investigation, inquiry, *digging, legwork, study, probing, sifting, *detective work, delving, *R&D. "The process of going up alleys to see if they are blind."—Marston Bates. "If you steal from one, it's plagiarism, if you steal from many, it's research."—Wilson Mizner.

researcher *n.* prober, investigator, data specialist, analyst, scientist, experimenter, medical detective, scientific detective, medical sleuth, tester, clinician, scholar.

resemblance *n.* likeness, similarity, sameness, correspondence, closeness, semblance, parallel, uniformity, affinity, analogy. ANT. *difference, dissimilarity, contrast.*

resemble *v.* look alike, mirror, double, be similar to, match, bear a resemblance to, approximate, mimic, echo. ANT. *contrast.*

resent *v.* take offense, be offended, be indignant over, take exception to, dislike, bristle, harbor resentment, *get one's nose out of joint, seethe over. ANT. *appreciate, like, delight in.*

resentment *n.* offense, indignation, displeasure, annoyance, outrage, disgust, umbrage, rancor, bitterness, pique, hard feelings.

reservation *n.* **1.** RESERVE preserve, sanctuary, territory, enclave, tract, habitation, settlement. **2.** BOOKING retaining, place, *lock. **3.** QUALIFICATION condition, limitation, stipulation, reluctance, qualm, second thoughts, hesitancy.

reserve *n.* **1.** STORE cache, savings, *nest egg, stockpile, backlog, reservoir, *ace in the hole, *something for a rainy day. **2.** QUIET-NESS silence, self-restraint, aloofness, reticence, shyness, inhibition, guardedness, distance, coolness.

reserve *v.* **1.** SAVE hold, hoard, store, stockpile, lay up, stash, *keep for a rainy day, conserve, *squirrel away. **2.** BOOK retain, secure, engage.

reserved *a.* self-restrained, quiet, silent, aloof, taciturn, reticent, shy, bashful, inhibited, guarded, distant, cool. ANT. *loud, demonstrative, loquacious.*

reside *v.* **1.** LIVE dwell, stay, inhabit, lodge, abide, domicile, occupy, take up residence, *hang one's hat. **2.** EXIST IN be inherent, be present, lie in, dwell.

residence *n.* home, inhabitation, house, abode, domicile, place, living quarters, address, dwelling, lodging, apartment, condo. SEE HOUSE

resident *n.* inhabitant, occupant, lodger, tenant, citizen, denizen, inmate.

residue *n.* remainder, rest, remnant, leftovers, dregs, scum, refuse, leavings.

resign *v.* **1.** QUIT step down, leave, abdicate, give notice, drop out, bail out, walk out, *hang it up, renounce. **2.** RESIGN ONESELF TO accept, live with, submit, endure, comply, *grin and bear it, tolerate.

resignation *n.* **1.** QUITTING retirement, termination, withdrawal, leaving, notice, abdication. **2.** ACCEPTANCE submission, acquiescence, tolerance, endurance, reconciliation, passivity.

resigned *a.* accepting, submissive, acquiescent, tolerant, enduring, reconciled, passive, unresisting, stoical, long-suffering. ANT. *unaccepting, rebellious, resisting.*

resilient *a.* elastic, flexible, rebounding, springy, pliable, rubbery, bouncy, supple, recovering quickly. ANT. *rigid, inflexible, stiff.*

resist *v.* fight, oppose, withstand, defy, repel, repulse, hold off, stand up against, thwart, check, weather. ANT. *surrender to, yield, give in, *cave in to.*

resistance *n.* fight, opposition, defiance, repulsion, withstanding, repellance, rebuff, refusal, blocking.

RESOLUTE *a.* [REZ uh LOOT] determined, resolved. *When it came to quitting smoking, Frank was resolute.* SYN. determined, resolved, fixed, firm, intent on, steady, tenacious, decided, purposeful, strong-willed, *dead set on, earnest, persevering. ANT. *weak-minded, irresolute, *wishy-washy.*

resolution *n.* **1.** DETERMINATION decidedness, purpose, resolve, tenacity, perseverance, dedication, willpower, earnestness. **2.** RESOLVING solution, sorting out, working out, outcome, end, upshot, settlement, finding. **3.** PLAN proposition, proposal, motion, objective.

resolve *n.* determination, resolution, purpose, decidedness, intention, earnestness, firmness, steadfastness, will, stick-to-itiveness.

resolve *v.* **1.** DETERMINE decide, make up one's mind, fix, intend, settle, will, *stick to one's guns. **2.** SETTLE solve, straighten out, clear up, harmonize, work out, *iron out, answer.

resonant *a.* resounding, reverberant, vibrant, echoing, loud, ringing, booming, full, rich, sonorous. ANT. *tinny, tinkling, muted.*

resonate *v.* echo, reverberate, resound, ring, vibrate, boom, have far-reaching effects, impact, have deep consequences.

resort *n.* vacation spot, hotel, motel, *tourist trap, mineral springs, park, club, retreat.

resort *v.* turn to, use, utilize, take up, employ, have recourse to.

resound *v.* echo, reverberate, ring, repeat, clang, resonate, peal, vibrate, thunder.

resourceful *a.* inventive, clever, creative, ingenious, handy, quick, imaginative, capable, versatile, adaptable. ANT. *unimaginative, incapable, helpless, inefficient.*

respect *n.* **1.** REGARD honor, esteem, deference, admiration, reverence, consideration, fear, veneration, awe, appreciation. **2.** POINT detail, sense, aspect, way, regard. **3.** REFERENCE relation. ANT. *1. disrespect, disregard, contempt.*

respect *v.* **1.** REGARD HIGHLY honor, esteem, defer to, idolize, admire, revere, look up to, fear, venerate, view with awe, appreciate. **2.** OBEY comply. ANT. *1. disrespect, *dis.*

respectable *a.* **1.** WORTHY OF RESPECT admirable, estimable, worthy, reputable, honorable, dignified, good, esteemed, strong, decent, principled, correct, proper. **2.** FAIRLY LARGE appreciable, substantial, decent, sizable, tolerable, goodly. ANT. *1. disreputable, despicable, bad. 2. tiny, small, paltry.*

respectful *a.* deferential, regardful, courteous, reverential, submissive, obeisant, polite, well-mannered, obliging, obedient. ANT. *disrespectful, irreverent, disobedient.*

RESPITE *n.* [RES pit] a rest or break from something. *The rain provided respite from the heat.* SYN. rest, break, relief, lull, breather, letup, time-out, recess, reprieve, remission.

respond v. act, react, answer, come back, reply, acknowledge, feedback, retort.

response n. reaction, answer, comeback, reply, acknowledgement, feedback, retort.

responsibility n. **1.** DUTY charge, obligation, burden, onus. **2.** ACCOUNTABILITY liability, culpability, answerability. **3.** CONSCIEN-TIOUSNESS dependability, reliability, maturity, trustworthiness. "The price of greatness."—Winston Churchill. "A detachable burden easily shifted to the shoulders of God, Fate, Fortune, Luck, or one's neighbor."—Ambrose Bierce.

responsible a. **1.** ACCOUNTABLE liable, culpable, answerable, at fault, to blame, incumbent, duty-bound, beholden, bound. **2.** CONSCIEN-TIOUS dependable, reliable, mature, dutiful, trustworthy, adult, grown up, sensible, rational. ANT. *1. *off the hook, unaccountable, irresponsible. 2. immature, unreliable, undependable.*

responsive a. reactive, reacting, active, respondent, reflexive, reciprocal, receptive, answering. ANT. *unresponsive, inactive.*

rest n. **1.** RELAXATION inactivity, break, ease, respite, recess, sleep, slumber, nap, repose, breather, time-out, lull, pause, *downtime. "The end and reward of toil."—James Beattie. **2.** REMAINDER balance, remains, excess, surplus. **3.** BASE stand, holder, seat, bed, cradle.

rest v. **1.** RELAX take a break, recess, sleep, slumber, nap, repose, take a breather, take a time-out, lounge, stop, hold up, pause, *put feet up, retire, *crash, catch one's breath, *recharge one's batteries. **2.** LIE lay, sit, stand, set, lean, prop. **3.** DEPEND rely, hinge, hang. ANT. *1. hustle, bustle, *do double-time, work, *break a sweat.*

restful a. quiet, peaceful, relaxing, tranquil, recharging, restorative, serene, calming. ANT. *restless, stressful, tiring, exhausting.*

restitution n. reparation, compensation, recompense, redress, amends, reimbursement, remuneration, indemnity.

restaurant n. eatery, dining establishment, steakhouse, cafe, *greasy spoon, luncheonette, diner, cafeteria, drive-in, hamburger stand, commissary, *fast-food joint, nightclub, supper club, bistro.

restless a. troubled, disturbed, uneasy, stressed, *wired, unsettled, edgy, restive, fidgety, ill at ease, *uptight, anxious, agitated, uncomfortable, *ants in the pants, *hyper. ANT. *restful, quiet, content, relaxed.*

restore v. renew, bring back, fix, recondition, rejuvenate, rehabilitate, revive, refresh, put in good repair, regenerate, overhaul.

restrain v. hold, limit, check, arrest, contain, restrict, muzzle, suppress, bridle, hamper.

restrict v. limit, confine, check, restrain, curb, impede, inhibit, constrain, hamper, circumscribe, bind, hem in.

restriction n. limit, limitation, circumscription, proscription, check, curb, control, confinement, restraint, *no-no, rule, regulation, provision, condition.

result n. outcome, effect, consequence, upshot, product, byproduct, end, aftereffect, fruit, outgrowth, fallout, denouement.

result v. issue, arise, happen, develop, ensue, eventuate, stem, occur, come about.

resumé n. employment history, vita, curriculum vita, work history, biographical outline, *bio.

resume v. continue, proceed, go on, begin again, carry on, return, pick up where one left off, restart.

resurgence n. revival, rise, return, rebirth, renewal, resurrection, renaissance. ANT. *death, petering out, decline.*

resurrection n. rising from the dead, return to life, rebirth, revival, regeneration, restoration, *Lazarus effect.

resuscitate v. revive, bring back, revitalize, breathe life into, perform artificial respiration, perform CPR, give mouth-to-mouth resuscitation, bring around.

retain v. keep, hold, maintain, possess, save, own, hang on to, secure, grasp.

retainer n. fee, allowance, charge, stipend.

retaliate v. strike back, get even, pay back, avenge, revenge, *even the score, reciprocate, *give tit for tat, pay back in kind, give measure for measure, *take an eye for an eye. ANT. *turn the other cheek, overlook.*

retard v. hinder, slow, delay, obstruct, block, impede, check, detain, hamper, restrict, handicap.

retch v. gag, vomit, heave, *barf, *puke, *hurl, *ralph, have dry heaves, *upchuck.

RETICENT a. [RET i sunt] reserved, quiet, restrained. *He tended to be reticent and barely spoke more than three words at a time.* SYN. reserved, quiet, restrained, taciturn, close-mouthed, shy, bashful, silent, uncommunicative, *clammed up, retiring. ANT. *loquacious, *motor-mouthed, talkative.*

retinue n. entourage, train of attendants, cortege, court, personnel, escort, following.

retire v. leave, retreat, withdraw, depart, exit, part, run along, turn in, go to bed, *call it a day, *hit the sack, quit, resign.

retiring a. shy, bashful, backward, withdrawn, unsociable, shrinking, quiet, reserved, reclusive, keeping to oneself, private, solitary, preferring one's own company. ANT. *outgoing, gregarious, sociable.*

retort n. reply, answer, comeback, snappy comeback, counter, rejoinder, repartee, rebuttal, riposte.

retort v. reply, answer, come back, respond, counter, rebut, rejoin, fire back, *return fire.

retract v. take back, recant, withdraw, backtrack, disavow, recall, *eat one's words, disclaim, back down, forswear, reverse, repeal.

retreat n. **1.** WITHDRAWAL flight, departure, pull-out, evacuation, escape, volte-face, *backpedaling, getaway, retirement. **2.** SAFE, QUIET PLACE sanctuary, asylum, haven, refuge, hideaway, shelter, cloister.

retreat v. withdraw, flee, depart, pull out, evacuate, escape, *head for the hills, do an about-face, backpedal, get away, escape, *beat a hasty retreat. ANT. *charge, advance, progress.*

retribution n. requital, *payback, revenge, retaliation, punishment, vengeance, comeuppance, reprisal, *just deserts, *tit for tat, talion.

retrieve v. get, get back, fetch, recover, regain, reclaim, recoup, reacquire.

retrospect n. looking back, reminiscence, review, remembering, reexamination, hindsight, reflection, afterthought, *Monday morning quarterbacking.

return n. **1.** REAPPEARANCE rebound, comeback, homecoming, recurrence, rebirth, revival, renaissance, resurrection, reinstatement. **2.** PROFIT yield, interest, proceeds, net, income, gain, revenue. **3.** RESPONSE comeback, answer, rebuttal, retort, reply, rejoinder, riposte, repartee.

return v. **1.** COME BACK go back, put back, reappear, rebound, recoil, boomerang, reverse, retreat, backtrack, recur, revive, resurrect, reinstate, restore, replace, double back, retrace one's steps. **2.** PAY BACK reciprocate, requite, retaliate, replace, reimburse, recompense. **3.** GAIN show a profit, yield, earn, gain, net. **4.** RESPOND answer, come back, rebut, retort, reply, rejoin.

reunion n. reuniting, homecoming.

revamp v. renovate, revise, fix up, repair, make over, refurbish.

reveal v. disclose, expose, show, divulge, uncover, bring to light, make known, lay bare, bring out into the open, tell, confess, *let the cat out of the bag, *spill the beans, declare, announce, *blab. ANT. *conceal, cover up, keep secret.*

revel v. celebrate, delight in, *party, *party hearty, take pleasure, *cut loose, rejoice, make merry, *whoop it up, enjoy, *get a kick out of, be festive, carouse, *have a ball, bask.

revelation n. disclosure, eye-opener, exposé, exposition, news, divulgement, announcement, broadcast, bombshell, *bolt from the blue, flash, shock.

revelry n. merry-making, partying, celebration, rejoicing, festivity, gaiety, carousal, romping, carrying on, *good times.

revenge n. vengeance, retaliation, retribution, talion, *eye for an eye, reprisal, vindication, requital, *payback, *tit for tat, avenging, *getting even, countering, measure for measure. "That recoil of Nature."—Ralph Waldo Emerson. "Nothing which we don't invite."—Ralph Waldo Emerson.

revenge v. retaliate, take vengeance, avenge, *even the score, *take an eye for an eye, give measure for measure, repay, reciprocate, vindicate, settle accounts, get back at.

revenue n. return, income, gain, yield, proceeds, net, gross, earnings, receipts, profit, cash flow, wages, salary. SEE MONEY

reverberate v. echo, reecho, resound, resonate, ring, vibrate, have repercussions, have an aftereffect, recoil, rebound, bounce back.

REVERE v. [ri VEER] to look up to, respect and honor highly. *The mayor was greatly revered in the community.* SYN. respect, honor, look up to, esteem, worship, venerate, idolize, *put on a pedestal, admire, exalt, think highly of, *kiss up to. ANT. *disrespect, despise, look down on.*

reverence n. respect, honor, esteem, worship, veneration, idolization, admiration, exaltation, awe, homage, regard. ANT. *irreverence, disrespect, contempt.*

reverent a. respectful, deferential, honoring, admiring, awed, reverential, venerating, adoring, worshipping. ANT. *disrespectful, irreverent, impertinent.*

REVERIE n. [REV ur ee] daydreaming, fantasizing. *I called her name twice, but she was deep in reverie.* SYN. daydreaming, fantasizing, musing, contemplation, deep thought, woolgathering, flight of fancy, trance, abstraction.

reversal n. repeal, overturning, upset, withdrawal, retraction, about-face, turnaround, switch.

reverse n. **1.** OPPOSITE inverse, converse, counterpart, antithesis, other side of the coin, mirror image, back, rear, *flip side. **2.** SETBACK defeat, check, reversal, turnabout, misfortune, misadventure, mishap, disaster, catastrophe, contretemps. ANT. *1. front, obverse. 2. promotion, help, boon.*

reverse v. **1.** GO OR TURN BACKWARDS back, *flip-flop, revert, upend, turn over, overturn, invert, transpose, *turn inside out, backtrack, backpedal, *do an about-face. **2.** CHANGE revoke, annul, repeal, withdraw, counter, overturn, rescind, recant, *change one's tune.

reverse a. backward, opposite, inverse, converse, contrasting, contrary.

revert v. go back, return, regress, backslide, degenerate, retrogress, relapse, deteriorate, hark back.

review n. **1.** EXAMINATION reexamination, reassessment, second look, another look, rundown, survey, inspection, reevaluation, retrospection. **2.** CRITIQUE evaluation, commentary, appraisal, report, *write-up, criticism, blurb, notice, rave, *pan. **3.** FORMAL INSPECTION exhibition, parade, procession, exposition, demonstration.

review v. **1.** EXAMINE reexamine, reassess, have a second look, have another look, run down, survey, inspect, reevaluate, go over again, retrospect. **2.** CRITIQUE evaluate, comment on, appraise, report on, *write up, criticize, rave, *pan, *trash, *slam.

reviewer n. critic, analyst, commentator, judge, evaluator, appraiser, connoisseur, summarizer, faultfinder, reporter, scrutinizer, nitpicker.

revile v. scold, abuse, tongue-lash, curse, *jump down one's throat, *rip up one side and down the other, lambaste, upbraid, vilify, disparage. ANT. *commend, praise, compliment.*

revise v. correct, improve, change, amend, edit, *blue pencil, tighten, rewrite, polish, rectify, redraft, modify.

revision n. second draft, corrected version, amended version, editing, tightening, cutting, rewriting, polishing, modification.

revival n. rebirth, return, restoration, renaissance, rejuvenation, revitalization, resurrection, new dawn, new day, reawakening.

revive v. breathe life into, resuscitate, bring back to life, rescue from the brink of extinction, *bring around, wake up, reawaken, rejuvenate, renew, recharge, refresh, vivify, rally, recover.

revoke v. abolish, repeal, withdraw, rescind, annul, cancel, abrogate, nullify, void, declare null and void, recall. ANT. *maintain, uphold, *beef up.*

revolt n. rebellion, refusal, revolution, insurrection, uprising, mutiny, resistance, protest. SEE REVOLUTION

revolt v. **1.** REBEL refuse to cooperate, rise up against, resist, protest, mutiny, riot, oppose, defy, insurrect, boycott. **2.** DISGUST sicken, turn one's stomach, appall, nauseate, *make one's flesh crawl, repulse. ANT. *1. comply, obey, accept. 2. delight, please.*

revolting a. disgusting, repulsive, sickening, repugnant, gross, offensive, abhorrent, *stomach-turning, foul, obnoxious. ANT. *delightful, pleasing, appetizing.*

revolution n. **1.** REBELLION uprising, mutiny, revolt, insubordination, insurrection, outbreak, uproar, riot, anarchy, coup, coup d'état, takeover, overthrow, unrest, turmoil. "A phoenix rising like a flame from the bodies of the wretched."—Luis Cernuda. "An abrupt change in the form of misgovernment."—Ambrose Bierce. "A thought in one man's mind."—Ralph Waldo Emerson. **2.** ROTATION circle, orbit, lap, circuit, cycle, spin.

revolutionary a. **1.** REBELLIOUS mutinous, insubordinate, riotous, resistant, insurrectionary, subversive. **2.** NEW progressive, radical, innovative, *cutting edge, novel, advanced.

revolve v. circle, orbit, go around, rotate, spin, wheel, gyrate, twirl, whirl.

revulsion n. disgust, repugnance, aversion, loathing, nausea, detestation, distaste, abhorrence, hatred. ANT. *liking, attraction.*

reward n. prize, payment, award, winnings, return, compensation, recompense, dividend, honor, bonus, requital, remuneration. ANT. *punishment, penalty.*

reward v. pay, award, compensate, recompense, honor, remunerate, reimburse, tip. ANT. *penalize, punish.*

rewarding a. compensating, worthwhile, enriching, fulfilling, satisfying, paying dividends, productive. ANT. *unrewarding, unfulfilling.*

rhapsodize v. gush, rave, speak with passion, wax poetic, dramatize, deliver breathlessly, get carried away, play up, ham it up, enthuse.

RHETORIC n. [RET ur ik] words and their artful employment in speech or writing. Also, high-blown language that says nothing. *The crowd listened to the usual political rhetoric.* SYN. expressiveness, eloquence, command of language, articulateness, fluency, elocution, *way with words, grandiloquence, magniloquence, bombast, *hot air, fustian, verbosity, *BS.

rhetorical a. **1.** EXPRESSIVE articulate, eloquent, fluent, persuasive, well-said, *silver-tongued. **2.** GRANDILOQUENT magniloquent, bombastic, fustian, verbose, pretentious, high-sounding, oratorical, inflated. ANT. *1. inarticulate, awkward, stumbling. 2. understated, simple, subtle.*

rhyme n. poem, verse, lyric, limerick, ode, alliteration.

rhythm n. beat, meter, cadence, swing, tempo, pulse, downbeat, backbeat, throb, flow.

RIBALD a. [RIB uld] vulgar, earthy or coarse, especially with sexual humor. *The men sat around the bar and told ribald jokes.* SYN. vulgar, earthy, lewd, dirty, obscene, risqué, off-color, indecent, pornographic, X-rated, gross. ANT. *wholesome, decent, G-rated, *clean*

rich a. **1.** WEALTHY affluent, *well-off, *well-to-do, *well-heeled, *on easy street, *rolling in dough, opulent, flush, comfortable, mon-eyed, *filthy rich. **2.** ABUNDANT abounding, replete, well-supplied, well-stocked, over-flowing, copious, plentiful, prodigal. **3.** LUX-URIOUS elegant, costly, lavish, sumptuous, elaborate. **4.** FILLING heavy, sweet, *fatty, fattening. **5.** DEEP intense, full, vivid, striking, vibrant. **6.** FUNNY comical, amusing, absurd, *wacky, ludicrous, ridiculous, laughable. ANT. *1. poor, indigent, penniless. 2. scarce, scant, meager. 3. plain, poor. 4. light. 5. light, subtle, slight. 6. grave, grim, serious.*

riches n. wealth, money, affluence, opulence, possessions, fortune, *big bucks, treasure, property, abundance, resources. "A great slavery."—Seneca. "A contented mind."—Mohammed. "Not the end, but a change of worries."—Epicurus. ANT. *poverty, indigence, want.* SEE MONEY

rickety a. shaky, wobbly, unstable, unsteady, teetering, tottering, fragile, *jerry-built, *tumble-down. ANT. *stable, sturdy, rock-solid, sound.*

ricochet v. rebound, bounce off, recoil, glance, deflect.

rid v. free, do away with, get rid of, purge, throw out, clear, clean, evict, disencumber, relieve, remove.

riddle n. puzzle, question, poser, *brainteaser, *stumper, mind-boggler, complexity, conundrum, knot, rebus, enigma, mystery.

ride n. drive, cruise, trip, excursion, spin, jaunt, outing.

ride v. **1.** TRAVEL cruise, tour, motor, commute, tool, move, float, journey, be carried along. **2.** TEASE torment, harass, *give a hard time, pester, make fun of, plague, ridicule, *kid.

rider n. addition, amendment, supplement, clause, attachment, appendix, codicil.

ridge n. **1.** CREST hill, spine, hogback, pinnacle, rise. **2.** RAISED AREA line, wale, rib, seam, cord, corrugation, seam, wrinkle, fold.

ridicule n. mocking, joking, taunting, teasing, making fun of, derision, poking fun at, laughter, needling, caricature, sarcasm. "The fume of little hearts."—Alfred Lord Tennyson. "These paper bullets of the brain."—Shakespeare. "The weapon of those who have no other."—Hubert Pierlot. ANT. *honor, veneration, respect, homage.* SEE JOKE

ridicule v. make fun of, laugh at, poke fun at, mock, make the butt of a joke, taunt, tease, deride, needle, caricature, belittle, lampoon, roast. ANT. *honor, venerate, respect, pay homage to.*

ridiculous a. preposterous, absurd, ludicrous, laughable, stupid, foolish, nonsensical, senseless, idiotic, mindless, moronic, insane, crazy, *nuts, *wacky, farcical, outrageous. ANT. *sensible, rational, sober, sound.*

RIFE a. [RIFE] abounding, widespread, commonly occurring. *The show was rife with black humor.* SYN. widespread, abounding, abundant, plentiful, copious, profuse, numerous, bursting, overflowing, prevalent, teeming, rampant, thick. ANT. *scarce, scant, rare.*

riffraff n. rabble, *dregs of society, peasantry, commoners, hoi polloi, rank and file, lower class, *scum of the earth.

rifle n. carbine, shotgun, musket, firearm. SEE GUN

rifle v. search, rummage, turn inside out, ransack, steal, strip, loot, thieve.

rift n. **1.** OPENING fissure, cleft, crack, rent, split, crevice, fracture, breach, fault, split, tear. **2.** FALLING-OUT BETWEEN FRIENDS parting of the ways, split, separation, schism, break, disagreement, estrangement, breakup.

rig *n.* equipment, outfit, gear, tackle, apparatus, rigging.

rig *v.* **1.** EQUIP fit out, gear up, furnish, outfit, supply, set up, accoutre, clothe, appoint, array, slap together. **2.** MANIPULATE fix, tamper with, falsify, finagle, arrange, machinate, contrive.

right *n.* **1.** PRIVILEGE authority, prerogative, power, claim, license, title, birthright, say, favor, freedom, due. **2.** GOOD virtue, morality, morals, righteousness, justness, justice, integrity, uprightness, honor, correctness. "The greatest good to the greatest number."—Jeremy Bentham. **3.** CONSERVATISM rightism, orthodoxy. ANT. *2. wrong, immorality, incorrectness. 3. left, liberalism.*

right *v.* **1.** CORRECT fix, straighten out, amend, make right, mend, repair, doctor, rectify, adjust, remedy, redress, balance. **2.** PUT BACK IN UPRIGHT POSITION turn over, flip over. ANT. *1. *mess up, *screw up, ruin. 2. capsize, upend, upset.*

right *a.* **1.** VIRTUOUS upright, moral, good, righteous, honorable, scrupulous, just, honest, ethical, fair, proper, *politically correct, socially acceptable. **2.** CORRECT accurate, precise, *on the money, *on the mark, *on target, *on the nose, exact, true, perfect, valid, sound, faithful, flawless, unerring, factual. **3.** FITTING suitable, appropriate, befitting, correct, seemly, favorable, desirable, preferable, opportune. **4.** NORMAL sound, rational, sensible, sane, competent, lucid, sober. **5.** CONSERVATIVE right-wing, rightist, traditional, reactionary, orthodox, *old-line. ANT. *1. immoral, bad, unethical, wicked. 2. incorrect, inaccurate, wrong. 3. unsuitable, inappropriate. 4. irrational, insane, not of sound mind. 5. liberal, left, leftist.*

right *adv.* **1.** VIRTUOUSLY morally, righteously, honorably, justly, honestly ethically, fairly, properly. **2.** CORRECTLY accurately, precisely, *on the money, *on the mark, *on target, exactly, truly, perfectly, faithfully, flawlessly, unerringly. ANT. *1. immorally, dishonorably, unjustly. 2. incorrectly, inaccurately, imperfectly.*

righteous *a.* good, right, virtuous, moral, ethical, honest, honorable, just, fair, upright, noble, saintly, innocent, angelic. ANT. *bad, wicked, immoral, wrong.*

rightful *a.* right, just, fair, moral, ethical,

proper, fitting, appropriate, legitimate, authorized, lawful. ANT. *wrong, illegitimate.*

right stuff *n.* qualifications, credentials, experience, courage, *guts, bravery, drive, talent, abilities, skills.

rigid *a.* **1.** UNYIELDING inflexible, hard, stiff, unbending, firm, nonpliant, unmalleable. **2.** STRICT severe, exacting, harsh, uncompromising, inflexible, unaccommodating, stern, stringent, *bullheaded. ANT. *1. yielding, flexible, pliable. 2. *easy, compromising, accommodating, flexible.*

rigmarole *n.* babble, blather, gobbledygook, drivel, *bunk, *rot, claptrap, *bilge, hogwash, bull, twaddle. SEE NONSENSE

rigor *n.* harshness, severity, hardness, hardship, rigidity, roughness, toughness, difficulty, trial, strictness, inflexibility.

RIGOROUS *a.* [RIG ur us] harsh, severe, strict. *Life in the Arctic is rigorous.* SYN. harsh, severe, strict, hard, tough, rough, brutal, stringent, trying, austere. ANT. *easy, undemanding, soft.*

rile *v.* anger, annoy, irritate, peeve, *rub the wrong way, irk, aggravate, nettle, *get under one's skin, *get one's dander up, *get one's Irish up. ANT. *pacify, mollify, appease.*

rim *n.* edge, border, margin, perimeter, brink, fringe, verge, ring, hem, lip, brim, skirt.

rind *n.* peel, peeling, skin, husk, hull, outer layer.

ring *n.* **1.** CIRCLE band, loop, hoop, orbit. **2.** FINGER JEWELRY band, wedding band. **3.** ARENA rink, circus ring, bowl, coliseum. **4.** GROUP OR GANG mob, band, circle, party, bloc, association, bunch, syndicate, outfit, coterie, clan. **5.** CLANG ding, chime, reverberation, knell, peal, tintinnabulation, tinkle, toll, jingle.

ring *v.* **1.** CLANG ding, dong, bong, chime, reverberate, knell, peal, tintinnabulate, tinkle, toll, jingle, sound, vibrate, resonate. **2.** ANNOUNCE herald, signal, trumpet, broadcast. **3.** CIRCLE loop, orbit, encircle, circumscribe, encompass, surround, go around, gird.

ringleader *n.* leader, chief, boss, *head honcho, *big cheese, instigator, orchestrator.

rinse *v.* wash, wet, cleanse, clean, soak, flush, irrigate, drench, splash, immerse.

riot *n.* **1.** UPRISING disorder, outburst, demonstration, anarchy, uproar, protest, melee, commotion, turbulence, ruckus, rebellion, revolt, insurgence, donnybrook, free-for-all,

distemper, civil unrest. **2.** SOMETHING HILARI-
OUS *scream, *laugh-a-minute, panic, howl.
ANT. *1. peace, order.*

riot *v.* rise up, erupt, demonstrate, protest, raise
a ruckus, *rumble, rebel, revolt, engage in a
free-for-all, go on the rampage, engage in
civil disobedience.

riotous *a.* disorderly, run amuck, boisterous,
loud, out of control, wild, chaotic, rebellious, rambunctious, rowdy, anarchic. ANT.
peaceful, orderly, placid.

rip *n.* tear, split, rend, slash, slit, cut, rift, rent,
gash, hole.

rip *v.* tear, split, rend, slash, slit, cut, sever,
hack, divide, cleave, shred.

ripe *a.* **1.** MATURE fully developed, ready, full-
grown, seasoned, aged, soft, prime, mellow.
2. READY timely, favorable, primed, set, prepared, opportune. ANT. *1. green. 2. untimely.*

ripen *v.* mature, develop, grow, season, age,
soften, mellow.

rip-off *n. Sl.* *gyp, thievery, theft, stealing,
cheat, larceny, fraud, robbery, gouging,
swindle, *con.

ripoff *v. Sl.* *gyp, thieve, steal, cheat, commit
larceny, commit fraud, rob, gouge, swindle,
*con, *stiff, *take one to the cleaners,
*screw.

RIPOSTE *n.* [ri POST] a quick retort; after the
quick thrust made in fencing. *His unexpected
riposte took the mayor by surprise.* SYN. quick
retort, snappy comeback, rejoinder, repartee, return, sally, reply, response, zinger, *returned fire, rebuttal.

ripple *n.* wave, wavelet, riffle, undulation, lap,
purl, ridge, wrinkle.

ripple *v.* wave, riffle, undulate, lap, purl, swish,
splash, wash.

riptide *n.* undertow.

rise *n.* **1.** ASCENT ascension, climb, lift, advancement, progression. **2.** HILL elevation,
ridge, humpback, mound, knoll. **3.** INCREASE
growth, jump, gain, upswing, hike, enlargement, expansion, upsurge, raise. ANT. *1. descent, plunge. 2. depression, hole. 3. drop, dip,
loss.*

rise *v.* **1.** ASCEND go up, climb, lift, elevate, levitate, mount, scale, soar, go skyward, stand,
get up. **2.** INCREASE grow, jump, gain, enlarge, expand, surge, raise, inflate, swell, intensify, heighten, double, triple, multiply. **3.**
ADVANCE *climb the corporate ladder, *step
up, progress, be promoted, get ahead, arrive.
ANT. *1. descend, plunge. 2. decrease, shrink,
dip. 3. recede, get demoted.*

risk *n.* danger, hazard, threat, peril, jeopardy,
uncertainty, *thin ice, vulnerability, exposure, gamble, chance, insecurity. ANT. *safety,
assurance, security.*

risk *v.* endanger, hazard, face a threat, imperil,
put oneself in jeopardy, face uncertainty, expose oneself, leave oneself vulnerable, gamble, chance it, *take a shot in the dark, *roll
the dice.

risky *a.* dangerous, hazardous, threatening, perilous, uncertain, chancy, a gamble, dicey,
*treading on thin ice, *hairy, *out on a
limb, ticklish, *playing with fire, insecure,
venturesome. ANT. *safe, risk-free, secure,
guaranteed.*

risqué *a.* suggestive, racy, daring, dirty, improper, ribald, off-color, indecent, vulgar,
bawdy, *spicy, *blue, crude, provocative,
lewd. ANT. *clean, G-rated.*

rite *n.* ceremony, ritual, exercise, observance,
solemn act, procedure, practice, custom, formality, liturgy.

ritual *n.* ceremony, rite, exercise, observance,
solemn act, procedure, practice, custom, formality, tradition.

ritzy *a. Sl.* elegant, luxurious, posh, sumptuous,
*classy, high-class, deluxe, *swank, *snazzy,
fancy. ANT. *low-class, shabby, poor.*

rival *n.* competitor, opponent, combatant, adversary, contestant, contender, challenger,
match, equal, enemy. ANT. *colleague, partner,
confederate, friend, ally.*

rival *v.* compete with, equal, match, *go head
to head against, *come up to, oppose, vie,
contend, contest, challenge, emulate.

rival *a.* competing, combating, contesting, con-
tending, opposing, vying. ANT. *allied, supporting.*

rivalry *n.* competition, contest, vying, opposition, match, equaling, struggle, clash, contention, one-on-one, *fight for supremacy,
emulation.

river *n.* waterway, tributary, branch, estuary,
stream, brook, creek, feeder, torrent, rapids,
freshet, rill. "A wet highway."—Leonard
Levinson.

WORD FIND
artificial channel: sluice
brook, tiny: rill, runnel
cross a: ford
dam: weir
deposits of silt left behind by: alluvium
eddy that is foaming and violent: souse hole
embankment protecting against flooding:
levee

fear of water: hydrophobia

flooding, area nearby that is susceptible to: floodplain

intertwined with several branches: braided river

island in: holm

loop of water sometimes separated from main river: oxbow

mill wheel, turns: millrace

ocean between high banks: fiord

passage of smooth water between rocks: tongue

rate of descent: gradient

referring to riverbank area: riparian

referring to rivers: fluvial

ridge of sand or silt: bar

rotating current: eddy

science of water in motion: hydraulics

sediment left in triangular mound at mouth of: delta

shallow area surrounded by deeper water: shoal

shallow stream with ripples made by cobbles or rocks: riffle

slow-moving deep water: pool

standing wave among rapids: *rooster, *haystack

steep, narrow stretch of descending water: chute

surrounding area contributing water: watershed

tidal: estuary

underground: aquifer, groundwater

upwelling or mounding water current: boil

waterfall: cataract

winding section: meander, bend

SEE LAKE, WATERFALL

rivet v. 1. FASTEN bolt, pin, tack, secure, link, couple. 2. FIX ONE'S ATTENTION fascinate, enthrall, grip, engross, occupy.

riveting a. gripping, fascinating, enthralling, engrossing, occupying, spellbinding, mesmerizing, keeping one's attention, entrancing. ANT. *boring, dull, bland*.

road n. street, avenue, lane, thoroughfare, track, boulevard, highway, freeway, parkway, causeway, expressway, turnpike, interstate, route, *main drag, artery, alley, pavement.

WORD FIND

bump to check speed: speedbump

circle: rotary, cloverleaf, roundabout, circus

cliff edge road: corniche

concrete highway divider: jersey barrier

curve: ess, hairpin

dead-end: cul-de-sac, blind alley, impasse

descriptive: ribbon

dividing area of highway: median strip, island

edge: shoulder

elevated: skyway

French: rue

German expressway with no speed limit: autobahn

German: strasse

hole: chuckhole, pothole

overhead crossover: overpass

paving material: macadam, cobblestone, gravel, blacktop, asphalt

ringing a city: beltway

shoulder: berm

smoothing vehicle: grader, steamroller

Spanish: via

traffic jam: gridlock

zigzagging mountain road: switchback

SEE AUTOMOBILE

roam v. wander, travel, wander aimlessly, ramble, rove, range, meander, stray, drift, gad about.

roar n. howl, bellow, yowl, growl, shriek, bay, cry, yell, bawl, thunder, rumble, explosion, boom, detonation, report.

roar v. howl, bellow, yowl, growl, shriek, bay, cry, yell, bawl, thunder, rumble, explode, boom, detonate, blast.

roast v. 1. BAKE cook, brown, broil, barbecue, sear. 2. RIDICULE make fun of, make sport of, put down, *rib, *kid, insult, slam, tease, taunt.

rob v. 1. STEAL burglarize, burgle, hold up, stick up, *mug, *heist, thieve, filch, *swipe, loot, purloin, pilfer. 2. DEPRIVE withhold, do out of.

robber n. crook, thief, *mugger, bandit, criminal, petty thief, *second-story man, housebreaker, hijacker.

robbery n. stealing, thievery, burglary, mugging, armed robbery, theft, *holdup, *stickup, *heist, looting, break-in, piracy.

robe n. bathrobe, gown, cassock, garment, vestment, kimono, caftan, toga, frock.

robot n. automaton, mechanical man, android, automated machine, golem, cyborg.

robust a. hale, hardy, strong, vigorous, healthy, sturdy, fit, hearty, tough, potent, strapping, muscular, virile. ANT. *weak, sickly, fragile*.

rock n. 1. STONE boulder, pebble, rubble, cobblestone, gravel, bedrock, crag, granite, ore.

WORD FIND

broken rock layer used as breakwater or bank: riprap

conglomeration: breccia, conglomerate
digestion aid for animal: gastrolith
drawing or carving on: petroglyph
glacier-deposited rock: till, drift, boulder train
ground layer: bedrock
layers of: strata
mass containing gems or fossils: matrix
metamorphosed by heat, pressure: metamorphic rock
mineral-lined: geode
molten: magma, lava
projecting: outcrop, ledge, knuckle, shelf
sand, silt, organic material, made from: sedimentary rock
study of: petrology
volcanic rock: igneous, pumice, obsidian, basalt
windblown sand, shaped by: ventifact
2. ROCK AND ROLL rhythm and blues (R&B), metal, heavy metal, disco, rockabilly, acid rock, punk rock, boogie, doo-wop, funk, fusion, hip-hop, rap, new wave, Motown, pop, psychedelic, reggae, surf music. SEE MUSIC

rock *v.* roll, pitch, swing, wobble, sway, seesaw, jiggle, lurch, teeter, totter, undulate.

rocket *n.* missile, projectile, spaceship, spacecraft, space capsule. SEE MISSILE, SPACECRAFT

rocket *v.* soar, shoot up, fly skyward, skyrocket, climb, *take off like a shot, whiz, zoom.

rock the boat *v. Sl.* *make waves, disturb, protest, *make a stink, complain, stir things up, challenge the status quo, *upset the apple cart, agitate, rebel.

rocky *a.* **1.** STONY flinty, craggy, rugged, jagged, petrous, gravelly, pebbly, bouldered, cobbled. **2.** *TIPPY shaky, teetering, wobbly, tottering, unsteady, unstable. ANT. *2. stable, steady.*

rococo *a.* ornate, ornamented, florid, *busy, profuse, involved, elegant, baroque, overdone, tasteless. ANT. *simple, plain, unadorned.*

rod *n.* stick, pole, staff, shaft, cane, baton, bar, switch, mace, scepter.

rogue *n.* scoundrel, rascal, cad, knave, bastard, creep, scamp, villain, rapscallion, *SOB, ne'er-do-well, cur, *cheat. ANT. *goody-two-shoes, *choirboy, *Dudley Do-Right.*

roguish *a.* unscrupulous, cheating, dishonest, unprincipled, knavish, villainous, two-timing, crooked, mischievous, impish, devilish, prankish, fun-loving. ANT. *scrupulous, upstanding, honest, principled.*

roil *v.* cloud, muddy, agitate, stir up, disturb, churn up.

role *n.* function, office, character, characterization, impersonation, part.

role model *n.* hero, heroine, good example, mentor, god, goddess, idol, star, superstar, one to look up to.

roll *n.* bread, bun, brioche, scone, bagel, biscuit.

roll *v.* **1.** SPIN revolve, rotate, twirl, gyrate, circle, wheel, twist, spiral, reel, pivot, trundle. **2.** THUNDER reverberate, rumble, roar, resound, resonate, boom. **3.** WIND coil, ball, furl, twine.

rollicking *a.* lively, frisky, playful, jolly, carefree, mirthful, jovial, spirited, rip-roaring, romping, boisterous. ANT. *subdued, sad, depressed.*

roly-poly *a.* plump, pudgy, dumpy. SEE FAT

Roman *a.* Latin, Italian.

WORD FIND

ampitheater, large: coliseum
arena: hippodrome
assembly: forum
commander: centurion
commoner: plebeian
fighter: gladiator
garment: toga, tunic
hall or court: atrium
highway: via, Appian Way
hospital: valetudinarium
jar: amphora
merchandise house: emporium
sidewalk: crepido
stadium: circus
temple dedicated to the gods: pantheon
vehicle: chariot
wine room: apotheca

romance *n.* **1.** LOVE AFFAIR relationship, *fling, liasion, amour, pair bonding, *affaire d'amour, courtship. **2.** LOVE STORY novel, melodrama, *bodice-ripper, story, fantasy, fairy tale, fiction, epic. **3.** ADVENTURE love, excitement, glamour, fantasy, exoticism, mystery.

romantic *a.* **1.** LOVING amorous, passionate, sentimental, demonstrative, affectionate, tender, ardent, *hot, lustful, overemotional, *cow-eyed, *mushy, saccharine. **2.** ADVENTUROUS exotic, exciting, fabulous. **3.** NOT PRACTICAL quixotic, fanciful, unrealistic, idealistic, dreamy, farfetched, starry-eyed, visionary, fantastic. ANT. *1. antagonistic, warring, hateful. 2. humdrum, boring. 3. practical, realistic, down-to-earth.*

romp *v.* play, frolic, cavort, frisk, rollick, gambol, prance, fool around, revel.

roof *n.* ceiling, top.

WORD FIND

lookout: belvedere
types: mansard, gambrel, shed, *catslide, dome, cupola, shingle, slate, thatch
walkway: widow's walk
window: skylight, dormer
SEE HOUSE

rookie n. Sl. fresh recruit, *greenhorn, *tenderfoot, beginner, newcomer, freshman, *frosh, raw recruit, *Johnny-come-lately, *boot, *snotnose.

room n. **1.** COMPARTMENT chamber, cubicle, living space, cell. **2.** SPACE clearing, clearance, expanse, play, elbowroom, opening, range, leeway, latitude.

roomy a. spacious, large, capacious, commodious, voluminous, extensive, sizable, broad, wide, long, open. ANT. cramped, tiny, confined.

roost n. perch. SEE NEST

root n. **1.** TAPROOT rootstock, radix, tuber. **2.** SOURCE basis, seat, germ, heart, soul, nub, essence, nucleus, foundation, mainspring, origin, fountain.

root v. **1.** DIG UP unearth, forage, nose about, sniff out, uncover, pry out, grub. **2.** CHEER support, back, boost, applaud, hail, *egg on.

roots n. ancestry, lineage, background, heritage, birthplace, genealogy, family tree.

rope n. cord, cordage, line, strand, hemp rope, cable, painter, hawser, lanyard, shroud, ratline, guy, bungee cord, lariat, lasso, bola, tether, jump rope, hangman's noose.

roster n. list, roll, inventory, register, index, muster, schedule, agenda.

rostrum n. platform, stage, dais, podium, pulpit, lectern, *stump, soapbox.

rosy a. **1.** PINK ruddy, reddish, blushing, blooming, glowing, flushed, roseate, rubicund, sunburned, *apple-cheeked. **2.** OPTIMISTIC encouraging, positive, promising, hopeful, favorable, auspicious, bright, sunny. ANT. 1. pale, sallow, wan, pallid, ashen. 2. pessimistic, bleak, black, gloomy.

rot n. **1.** DECAY spoilage, putrefaction, putrescence, decomposition, corrosion, deterioration, mold, blight. **2.** Sl. NONSENSE rubbish, *crap, *baloney, *twaddle, *hogwash. SEE NONSENSE

rot v. spoil, decay, putrefy, decompose, *go bad, corrode, deteriorate, mold, *stink, rust, crumble.

rotary a. revolving, turning, spinning, twirling, gyrating, rolling. ANT. stationary.

rotate v. **1.** GO ROUND revolve, spin, twirl, gyrate, wheel, turn, pivot, roll, circle, twist. **2.** ALTERNATE switch, replace, exchange places.

rote (by) adv. from memory, by heart, mechanically, by routine.

rotten a. **1.** DECAYED spoiled, putrefied, putrid, decomposed, *gone bad, rancid, sour, tainted, foul, rank, stale, stinking, corroded. **2.** IMMORAL nasty, corrupt, dishonest, evil, disgraceful, vicious, unscrupulous, bad, despicable, dirty, mean. ANT. 1. fresh, good. 2. good, honest, nice.

rotund a. **1.** PLUMP stout, round, fat, obese, big, spherical, roly-poly, corpulent, *tubby, pudgy, full-figured, burly. **2.** SONOROUS full-toned, booming, stentorian, rich, resonant. ANT. 1. skinny, thin. 2. weak, unsupported, thin.

roué n. rake, debauchee, womanizer, *swinger, *wolf, *skirt-chaser, profligate, playboy, Casanova, Don Juan, Lothario, philanderer.

rough a. **1.** IRREGULAR bumpy, uneven, course, jagged, scaly, craggy, lumpy, wrinkled, corrugated, broken, shaggy, fuzzy, bristly. **2.** VIOLENT stormy, tempestuous, fierce, riotous, ferocious, intense, wild, furious, bumpy, rocky, choppy. **3.** RUDE coarse, unrefined, crude, impolite, uncouth, vulgar, boorish, indelicate, bad-mannered, ungentlemanly, unladylike, gruff. **4.** UNFINISHED unrefined, raw, basic, crude, imperfect, unprocessed, rough-hewn, inexact, preliminary. **5.** APPROXIMATE imprecise, inexact, *ballpark, *thumbnail, sketchy, quick. ANT. 1. regular, smooth, level. 2. smooth, mild, easy, gentle. 3. polite, refined, cultured, genteel. 4. finished, refined, perfected. 5. exact, precise.

roughhouse n. rowdiness, horseplay, frolic, sport, *bull in a china shop, misbehavior, wildness, unruliness, *hell-raising, scuffle.

roughly adv. about, approximately, more or less.

round n. **1.** BOUT OR CYCLE course, series, circuit, sequence, turn, cycle, tour. **2.** GUNFIRE load, burst, salvo, barrage, enfilade, volley, fusillade.

round v. circle, encircle, go around, circumnavigate, make a circuit, gird, flank, encompass.

round a. **1.** CIRCULAR spherical, cylindrical, globular, hooplike, ringlike, ball-like, oval, ovoid, elliptical. **2.** ROTUND roly-poly, spherical, fat, plump, *chubby, stout, obese. **3.** RESONANT full, sonorous, rich. **4.** COMPLETE full, whole, unbroken, entire. ANT. 1. square, *straight.* **2.** *angular, thin, slender.* **3.** *thin.* **4.** *incomplete, broken.*

roundabout *a.* **1.** INDIRECT wandering, rambling, winding, circuitous, meandering, straying, deviating, circumlocutory, long. **2.** NOT STRAIGHTFORWARD indirect, evasive, oblique, digressive, devious, ambiguous, hinting. ANT. **1.** *direct, straight, short.* **2.** *direct, blunt, straightforward.*

round up *v.* gather, assemble, corral, muster, herd, amass.

rouse *v.* stir, arouse, stimulate, wake, awaken, get going, *fire, rally, move, motivate, spur, prod, excite, goad, electrify. ANT. *tranquilize, put to sleep.*

rousing *a.* stirring, lively, brisk, spirited, energized, electrifying, enthusiastic, vigorous, stimulating. ANT. *sleepy, tired, dead.*

rout *n.* defeat, humiliating loss, beating, conquest, *drubbing, whipping, thrashing, shutout, debacle, retreat, flight, *turning-tail.

rout *v.* defeat overwhelmingly, overwhelm, conquer, humiliate, beat, whip, thrash, shut out, vanquish, *skunk, *wipe the floor with, *shellac.

route *n.* way, course, passage, road, street, highway, path, trail, beat, round, itinerary, shortcut.

route *v.* direct, steer, dispatch, guide, channel, conduct.

routine *n.* custom, habit, pattern, treadmill, matter of course, convention, *beaten path, rut, *grind, method.

routine *a.* usual, daily, everyday, regular, habitual, customary, accustomed, normal, typical, standard, predictable. ANT. *unusual, irregular, abnormal.*

rove *v.* ramble, wander, roam, range, drift, stray, meander, gad about, travel aimlessly, hike.

row *n.* **1.** LINE chain, file, column, series, sequence, succession, course, rank, queue. **2.** QUARREL argument, fight, altercation, disagreement, dispute, *run-in, controversy, *falling-out, wrangle, conflict, *set-to, tiff.

row *v.* **1.** QUARREL argue, fight, disagree, dispute, *have a run-in, *have a falling-out, wrangle, conflict, *have a tiff. **2.** PADDLE scull, oar, stroke. SEE BOAT

rowdy *n.* hoodlum, tough, punk, *loudmouth, ruffian, *roughneck, *bad actor, *rabblerouser, thug, hellion, troublemaker, bully, *yahoo. ANT. *gentleman, lady, choirboy.*

rowdy *a.* rough, quarrelsome, loud, noisy, boisterous, unruly, coarse, raucous, wild, roughhouse, rambunctious, trouble-making. ANT. *mild, quiet, gentle.*

royal *a.* regal, kingly, queenly, princely, noble, lordly, majestic, aristocratic, imperial, monarchical, stately, sovereign. ANT. *plebian, common.*

royalty *n.* sovereignty, kingship, queenship, regality, majesty, aristocracy, nobility, stateliness.

rub *n.* **1.** MASSAGE rubdown, stroke, kneading, caress, patting, petting, friction. **2.** OBSTACLE hindrance, check, barrier, obstruction, difficulty, catch, snag.

rub *v.* massage, rubdown, stroke, knead, caress, pat, pet, apply friction, brush, buff, wipe, burnish, abrade, scour, scrub.

rubber-stamp *v.* approve, okay, endorse.

rubbish *n.* **1.** TRASH refuse, garbage, waste, junk, litter, debris, rubble, sweepings, scraps, dregs. **2.** NONSENSE foolishness, *poppycock, *hogwash, *baloney, *hooey, *rot, *bunk, *horsefeathers, *crap, *bilge, *balderdash, humbug.

rubdown *n.* kneading. SEE MASSAGE

RUBE GOLDBERG DEVICE *n.* any overly-elaborate contraption, especially that employed for a very simple procedure, named after the cartoonist who drew such devices. *The young inventor constructed an elaborate Rube Goldberg device to make lemonade automatically.* SYN. contraption, contrivance, rig, apparatus, mechanism, appliance, gadget, *whatchamacallit, *thingamabob, *thingamajig.

rub the wrong way *v.* annoy, *bug, *ruffle one's feathers. SEE IRRITATE

ruckus *n.* disturbance, uproar, commotion, hubbub, rumpus, upheaval, turbulence, racket, outburst.

ruddy *a.* red, reddish, healthy, glowing, pinkish, *apple-cheeked, blooming, flushed, rosy, rubicund, rosy-cheeked, sunburned. ANT. *pale, pallid, wan, ashen.*

rude *a.* **1.** DISCOURTEOUS bad-mannered, unmannerly, impolite, ungracious, inconsiderate, coarse, insulting, ungentlemanly, unladylike, crude, vulgar, tactless, fresh, indelicate, brutal, brusque, rough. **2.** CRUDE, ROUGHLY FASHIONED rough-hewn, primitive, unfinished, unrefined, raw, simple, ill-formed, makeshift. **3.** BARBAROUS ignorant, savage, unrefined, uncivilized, uncultured, uncouth, wild, brutish. **4.** VIOLENT harsh, abrupt, rough, fierce, uproarious, savage. ANT. *1. courteous, polite, mannerly, gracious, tactful. 2. finished, refined, fully developed. 3. civilized, cultured. 4. gentle, mild, soft.*

rudeness n. discourtesy, bad manners, impoliteness, inconsideration, coarseness, lack of grace, conduct unbefitting a gentleman/lady, crudeness, vulgarity, tactlessness, freshness, brutality, impudence, insolence. "The weak man's imitation of strength."—Eric Hoffer. ANT. *courtesy, politeness, good manners, consideration.*

rudimentary a. elementary, basic, fundamental, primary, beginning, initial, original, embryonic, early, undeveloped, incomplete. ANT. *advanced, developed.*

rudiments n. fundamentals, first principles, elements, basics, essentials, ABCs, beginnings.

rue v. regret, be remorseful, lament, *be sick about, deplore, repent, bemoan, fret over, be sorry for, grieve.

rueful a. mournful, regretful, sorry, grieving, contrite, remorseful, *sick at heart over, heartsick, doleful, lugubrious, woeful. ANT. *happy, proud, joyous.*

ruffian n. hoodlum, *hood, tough, rowdy, punk, criminal, *roughneck, thug, goon, bully, *bad actor, troublemaker, *animal.

ruffle n. frill, trim, edging, flounce, pleat, border, ruff.

ruffle v. **1.** WRINKLE mess up, rumple, crinkle, crease, ripple, tousle, dishevel, disturb. **2.** IRRITATE annoy, disturb, *rattle one's cage, *rub the wrong way, *get on one's nerves, *get under one's skin, *pull one's chain, upset, aggravate, unsettle, nettle, chafe. ANT. *1. smooth, arrange.*

rug n. carpet, mat, runner, floor covering, broadloom, area rug, throw rug, braided rug, shag carpeting.

rugged a. **1.** UNEVEN, ROUGH irregular, bumpy, jagged, wrinkled, broken, craggy, unlevel, rocky, weathered. **2.** ROUGH-FACED weathered, wrinkled, lined, stony, strong, leathery, hard. **3.** STORMY tempestuous, violent, rough, harsh, severe, inclement. **4.** STRONG powerful, robust, brawny, stout, hearty, big, tough, muscular, burly. ANT. *1. smooth, flat, level. 2. baby-faced. 3. calm, balmy, mild. 4. weak, *wimpy, skinny.*

ruin n. **1.** REMAINS OF A COLLAPSED OR DECAYED BUILDING OR CITY remnants, wreckage, vestige, relics, debris, rubble. "Time's slow finger written in the dust."—Anna Barbauld.

2. DESTRUCTION downfall, collapse, ruination, undoing, failure, decay, devastation, doom, fall, desolation, skids, extinction, Waterloo.

ruin v. destroy, wreck, devastate, wipe out, demolish, decimate, desolate, smash, crush, lay waste, bankrupt, defeat.

ruinous a. destructive, devastating, decimating, desolating, crushing, catastrophic, cataclysmic, disastrous, fatal, deadly, bankrupting. ANT. *prosperous, fruitful.*

ruins n. SEE RUIN

rule n. **1.** REGULATION law, statute, bylaw, ordinance, guideline, practice, policy, code, order, edict, tenet, principle, doctrine, precept, maxim. **2.** CUSTOM habit, routine, practice. **3.** REIGN control, authority, command, leadership, sovereignty, dominion, domination, government, power, administration.

rule v. **1.** GOVERN reign, control, assert authority, command, lead, hold power, administer, *lay down the law, *run the show, *hold the reins, *be in the driver's seat, *call the shots, supervise, dominate. **2.** DETERMINE judge, adjudicate, settle, find, deem, hand down a decision.

rule out v. exclude. SEE ELIMINATE

ruler n. leader, governor, administrator, sovereign, king, queen, prince, monarch, dictator, chief, tyrant, autocrat. SEE GOVERNMENT

ruling n. judgment, determination, decision, settlement, verdict, adjudication, finding.

rumble n. **1.** ROLL thunder, reverberation, roar, peal, grumble. **2.** GANG FIGHT fight, donnybrook, street fight, free-for-all, riot, melee.

RUMINATE v. [ROO muh NATE] to think over or meditate on. *He went to his room to ruminate.* SYN. think over, meditate, turn over in one's mind, deliberate, *chew over, weigh, ponder, contemplate, cogitate, reflect on, muse.

rummage v. search through, fish for, go through, ransack, turn over, hunt, *turn inside out, root, comb.

rummy n. Sl. drunkard, drunk, lush. SEE ALCOHOLIC

rumor n. talk, *word on the street, gossip, hearsay, *grapevine talk, *scuttlebutt, report, tattle, *scoop, *lowdown. "A pipe blown by surmises, jealousies, conjectures."—Shakespeare.

rumor v. gossip, tell, tattle, *buzz, whisper, *pass on, leak.

rump n. rear, bottom, backside, hindquarters,

posterior, butt, buttocks, seat, derriere, haunches, *tush, *bum, ass, *duff.

rumple v. wrinkle, mess up, muss up, crinkle, crumple, crease, ripple, fold, furrow, bedraggle, dishevel.

rumpus n. disturbance, commotion, uproar, ruckus, tumult, stir, upheaval, noise, ado, storm.

run n. **1.** SPRINT race, footrace, jog, dash, rush, clip, burst of speed, flight, bound, trot, gallop. **2.** TRIP, ESPECIALLY ONE TAKEN REGULARLY journey, route, tour, round, spin, excursion, circuit. **3.** PERIOD course, spell, span, interval, stretch, term. **4.** COURSE progression, passage, flow.

run v. **1.** SPRINT race, jog, dash, rush, bound, *beat feet, *clip, bolt, *hotfoot it, scurry, scramble, hustle, trot, gallop. **2.** FLEE *skedaddle, *make tracks, escape, *beat it, *blow, take flight. **3.** ASSOCIATE WITH consort, *hang out with. **4.** GO, MOVE FREELY flow, roll, spill, discharge, gush, stream, surge, cascade. **5.** OPERATE drive, control, work, maneuver, propel, direct, pilot. **6.** CAMPAIGN FOR OFFICE *throw one's hat in the ring. **7.** SUPERVISE direct, manage, administer, control, head, boss, oversee, regulate, conduct, operate, *be in the driver's seat. **8.** LAST continue, elapse.

runaround n. evasion, delay, *buck-passing, excuses, *migraine merry-go-round.

runaway n. fugitive, escapee, deserter, refugee, truant.

rundown n. summary, outline, recap, synopsis, sketch, briefing, abstract, short version.

run-down a. **1.** TIRED fatigued, weary, exhausted, *dead, drained, enervated, sickly, *pooped, peaked, out of shape. **2.** IN DISREPAIR dilapidated, broken down, tumbledown, ramshackle. ANT. 1. energized, energetic, strong, fit. 2. intact, sound, solid.

run-in n. fight, quarrel. SEE ARGUMENT

run-of-the-mill a. average, ordinary, common, mediocre, fair, everyday, routine, so-so, regular, *comme ci, comme ça. ANT. extraordinary, superlative, unique.

run out v. deplete, expire, exhaust, finish, end, close, stop, dry up.

runt n. dwarf, pygmy, midget, *shrimp, *halfpint, Lilliputian, pipsqueak, peewee.

runway n. airstrip, landing strip, taxiway. SEE AIRPORT

rupture n. break, crack, burst, split, fracture, tear, rift, rip, cleavage, fissure, rent.

rupture v. break, crack, burst, split, fracture, tear, rip, cleave, rend, *bust, breach.

rural a. country, rustic, backwoods, countrified, pastoral, farm, agricultural, undeveloped, sylvan, idyllic, bucolic. ANT. urban, metropolitan, citified.

ruse n. trick, artifice, stratagem, deception, deceit, subterfuge, feint, *sham, maneuver, wile, contrivance.

rush n. **1.** HURRY speed, swiftness, haste, race, expedition, bustle, dispatch, flurry, hustle, quickness. **2.** RUN dash, charge, sprint, storm, stampede, scramble, race. ANT. 1. crawl, *snail's pace, *glacial pace.

rush v. **1.** HURRY race, hustle, bustle, dash, make haste, *step on it, *get the lead out, *zoom, fly, sprint, scurry, scamper, *hotfoot it, tear. **2.** ATTACK assault, blitz, storm. **3.** PRESSURE push, hurry. ANT. 1. crawl, *go at a snail's pace, *move slower than a glacier.

rust n. oxidation. SEE CORROSION

rust v. oxidize, decay, crumble. SEE CORRODE

rustic n. country person, country cousin, farmer, *hick, yokel, bumpkin, hillbilly, *hayseed.

RUSTIC a. [RUS tik] rural, simple, plain. They lived a rustic lifestyle. SYN. rural, backwoods, country, agrarian, pastoral, bucolic, Arcadian, simple, plain, unrefined, unsophisticated, natural. ANT. urban, sophisticated, citified.

rustle v. shuffle, swish, crackle, crinkle, crepitate, sigh, brush, whisper, flutter.

rusty a. **1.** CORRODED oxidized, decayed. **2.** OUT OF PRACTICE stiff, impaired, out of shape, below par, unfit. ANT. 2. practiced, trained, skilled.

rut n. **1.** FURROW track, groove, trench, cut, trough, score, channel, ditch. **2.** ROUTINE same-old same-old, pattern, treadmill, grind.

ruthless a. cruel, pitiless, merciless, heartless, brutal, vicious, mean, cold, unfeeling, savage, hard, callous, barbarous, ferocious. ANT. compassionate, caring, merciful, soft.

S

Sabbath n. Saturday, Sunday, day of rest. "The attuning of the heart to the comprehension of God."—Moses Maimonides. "A sponge to wipe out all the sins of the week."—Henry Ward Beecher. SEE RELIGION

sabbatical n. leave, rest, vacation, holiday, break. SEE VACATION

sabre n. fencing weapon, cutlass, blade. SEE SWORD

sable a. black, dark brown, ebony, jet, raven, dark.

sabotage n. destruction, demolition, treachery, obstruction, wrecking, impairment, undermining.

sabotage v. destroy, demolish, wreck, *blow up, obstruct, impair, undermine, cripple, *gum up the works, *put out of commission, *put out of action, subvert.

saboteur n. agent provocateur, terrorist, bomber, subversive, demolition expert, revolutionist, anarchist, fifth columnist.

SACCHARINE a. [SAK uh rin] excessively or sickeningly sweet. *The happy ending was too saccharine for me.* SYN. sweet, excessively sweet, sickeningly sweet, sugary, syrupy, honeyed, nauseating, cloying, maudlin, *mushy. ANT. *bitter, sour, acid.*

sack n. bag, pouch, satchel, knapsack.

sack v. 1. FIRE discharge, *ax, *give pink slip, dismiss, *send packing, *give walking papers, lay off. 2. Sl. TACKLE down, bring down. 3. PLUNDER loot, pillage, ransack, despoil, rob.

sacrament n. rite, ceremony, ritual, vow, pledge, oath, baptism, confirmation, the Eucharist, penance, holy orders, matrimony.

sacred a. 1. HOLY consecrated, sanctified, blessed, divine, godly, hallowed, venerated, religious. 2. INVIOLABLE protected, guarded, defended, immune, sacrosanct. ANT. *1. profane, unsanctified. 2. violable, unprotected.*

SACRED COW n. something granted immunity from attack or disparagement. *Social Security is the politican's sacred cow.* SYN. idol, sensitive issue, juggernaut, object of worship, hero, god, goddess, protected interest, protected institution, taboo object.

sacrifice n. offering, concession, loss, relinquishment, surrendering.

sacrifice v. give up, trade off, forfeit, let go, offer, surrender, relinquish, dispose of, cede, forgo.

SACRILEGE n. [SAK ruh lij] violation of something held sacred. *Taking the Lord's name in vain is a sacrilege.* SYN. violation, desecration, profanation, blasphemy, disrespect, mockery, impiety, irreverence, sin.

sacrilegious a. in violation, profane, impious, blasphemous, disrespectful, irreverent, godless, unholy, sinful. ANT. *holy, reverent, pious.*

SACROSANCT a. [SAK roh SANGKT] holy, sacred. *The teachings of Jesus are sacrosanct.* SYN. sacred, holy, divine, godly, consecrated, hallowed, venerated, sanctified, religious, untouchable, inviolable, inviolate. ANT. *profane, impious, sacrilegious.*

sad a. 1. DOWNHEARTED *blue, depressed, dejected, unhappy, sorrowful, mournful, *bummed out, despondent, *down in the dumps, woebegone, melancholy, heartsick, forlorn, *out of sorts, dispirited, brokenhearted, glum. 2. HEARTBREAKING woeful, pitiful, tearful, poignant, moving, touching, depressing, tragic, joyless, miserable. ANT. *1. happy, joyful, euphoric, elated. 2. joyful, happy, uplifting.*

sadden v. depress, *bring down, grieve, dispirit, deject, dampen one's spirits, *break one's heart, *make blue, distress, *bum out, *make one's heart heavy. ANT. *cheer, uplift, gladden.*

saddle n. seat, western saddle, English saddle, mount, pad, perch.

WORD FIND

part: pommel, cinch, cantle, girth, stirrup, latigo

SEE HORSE

SADISTIC a. [suh DIS tik] enjoying or being sexually aroused from dominating or inflicting pain on others. *The sadistic dictator liked to torture his detractors.* SYN. cruel, domineering, bossy, strict, harsh, dictatorial, aggressive, commanding, disciplinary, severe, nasty, dirty, perverse, *raunchy, sadomasochistic. ANT. *masochistic.*

sadness n. downheartedness, sorrow, depression, melancholy, misery, unhappiness, cheerlessness, woefulness, gloom, despondency, broken heart, heavy heart, *the blues. ANT. *happiness, joy, euphoria, elation.*

safari n. hunting expedition, hunt, journey, trek, caravan, shoot, campaign.

safe n. strongbox, safety-deposit box, money box, vault.

safe a. **1.** SECURE *out of harm's way, out of danger, *out of the woods, safe and sound, sheltered, protected, guarded, invulnerable, *home free, *in the clear, impregnable. **2.** HARMLESS innocent, innocuous, tame, risk-free, okay, secure, sure. **3.** CAUTIOUS careful, conservative, wary, prudent, reliable, dependable, circumspect, guarded. ANT. *1. in danger, in peril, *on thin ice, vulnerable. 2. harmful, dangerous, risky. 3. imprudent, out of control.*

safeguard n. protection, shield, security, defense, precaution, guard, screen, safety measure, sure.

safeguard v. protect, shield, secure, defend, take a precaution, guard, screen, take a safety measure, assure, insure.

safekeeping n. protection, security, preservation, care, custody, guardianship.

safety n. security, protection, shelter, invulnerability, sanctuary, refuge, safe haven, safe harbor, immunity. ANT. *danger, hazard, peril.*

sag v. droop, sink, hang, wilt, slump, bow, dip, settle, bend.

saga n. story, narrative, adventure, tale, legend, myth, epic, chronicle, history, romance, roman-fleuve.

SAGACIOUS A. [suh GAY shus] shrewd, sharp, having a keen power of judgment. *The sagacious police officer sized up the situation quickly.* SYN. shrewd, sharp, judicious, intelligent, acute, keen, discerning, wise, sage, smart, quick, perceptive, savvy, insightful. ANT. *stupid, undiscerning, slow.*

sagacity n. intelligence, good judgement, sharpness, astuteness, judiciousness, wisdom, perceptiveness, insight. ANT. *stupidity, dullness, dull-wittedness.*

sage n. wise man, *brain, learned man, scholar, intellectual, authority, savant, philosopher, guru, Solomon. ANT. *moron, imbecile, *retard, idiot.*

sage a. wise, intelligent, smart, savvy, learned, astute, sagacious, sensible, judicious, sapient, discerning. ANT. *stupid, imbecilic, dense.*

sail v. ply the seas, cruise, ride the bounding main, pilot, navigate, skipper, tack, float, drift, shove off, cast off.

WORD FIND

change tack: come about
close to the wind: luffing, close-hauled
come about: hard alee
crew member: hand

dead calm area of sea: doldrums
fin used in place of keel: centerboard, daggerboard
lean of vessel while sailing: heel
line fitting on deck: chock
line fixture with prongs: cleat
lines and wires: rigging
line used to hoist sail: lanyard
mast, aft-most: mizzenmast
mast, angle of: rake
mast housing on deck: tabernacle
mooring bow line: painter, bowline
overhead: aloft
pennant, yacht club: burgee
race: regatta
rigging, mast: forestay
roll up sail: furl
rope stairway to aloft: ratlines
sail, adjust angle of: trim
sail, aftermast, rigged fore-and-aft: spanker
sail, forward, triangular: foresail, jib
sail, large forward: Genoa
sail, largest: mainsail
sail, large, three-cornered: spinnaker
sail, lower a: strike, take in
sail, L-shaped: blooper
sail, raise a: hoist, set
sail, reduce main: reef
sail set forward of mast, any: headsail
sail, square, set abeam: square-rigged
sail, triangular, fore-and-aft-rigged: Bermuda-rigged, Marconi-rigged
sail used in weak winds: drifter
seat used for worker aloft: bosun's chair
shallow water, sailing in: gunkholing
sideways, moving: crabbing, making leeway
spar, large vertical sail: mast
spar on bow to which headsail is attached: bowsprit
spar on which bottom of sail is attached: boom
steers, crew member who: helmsman
tack downwind: jibe
tack upwind: beat
vessel, tri-hulled: trimaran
vessel, twin-hulled: catamaran
wind indicators made of yarn tied to shrouds: telltales
wind-protected side of vessel: lee, leeward
wind, run before the: scud
wind, sail with the: run
wind, side of boat taking: windward
wires that stabilize mast: shrouds
world, sail around the: circumnavigate
zigzagging course to counter wind: tacking

SEE BOAT, NAVY, SAILBOAT, SHIP
sailboat *n.* boat, vessel, craft, pleasure craft, yacht, windjammer.

WORD FIND

TYPES

fast nineteenth century freight and transport: clipper

fifteenth-sixteenth century Spanish: caravel

fishing vessel: smack

fore-and-aft-rigged vessel with two or three masts: schooner

Oriental: sampan, junk

single-masted: sloop, cutter

small, two-masted vessel: ketch

Spanish square-rigger of fifteenth-eighteenth century: galleon

square-rigged warship of eighteenth-nineteenth century: frigate

square-rigger with three or four masts: bark

tri-hulled: trimaran

twin-hulled: catamaran

two-masted: brigantine

warship, fast, small: corvette

SEE BOAT, NAVY, SAIL, SHIP

sailor *n.* mariner, seafarer, seaman, navy man, sea dog, navigator, salt, shellback, skipper, helmsman, hand, first mate, midshipman, quartermaster, petty officer, bosun.

WORD FIND

bag: ditty bag

dance: hornpipe

hat: sou'wester, watchcap

inexperienced: lubber

kidnap: shanghai

living quarters: forecastle

one who brings bad luck: Jonah

rebellion: mutiny

song: shanty, chantey

yes: aye-aye

SEE NAVY

saint *n.* holy person, Christian, angel, martyr. "A dead sinner, revised and edited."—Ambrose Bierce. ANT. *sinner, devil, evil-doer.*

WORD FIND

declare a: canonize

image: icon

patron saint of children: Nicholas

patron saint of sailors: Elmo

patron saint of the handicapped: Giles

qualify one for sainthood: beatify

study of: hagiography

tomb: shrine

worship: hagiolatry

SEE RELIGION, CHURCH, GOD

saintly *a.* Christian, good, faithful, godly, pious, holy, angelic, spiritual, religious, devout, moral, pure, righteous, virtuous. ANT. *unholy, immoral, sinful, wicked.*

sake *n.* **1.** BEHALF welfare, good, gain, interest, advantage, regard. **2.** PURPOSE reason, object, end, goal, aim.

salacious *a.* lustful, *horny, lecherous, libidinous, lewd, prurient, obscene. ANT. *chaste, virginal, celibate, abstinent.*

salad *n.* greens, vegetarian fare, lettuce and tomato, cress salad, endive salad, coleslaw, tossed salad, fruit salad, potato salad.

salary *n.* pay, wages, earnings, income, compensation, remuneration, *take-home, stipend.

sale *n.* **1.** SELLING trade, exchange, transfer, vending, marketing, transaction. **2.** REDUCTION IN PRICES discount, cut, clearance sale, bargain pricing.

salesman/woman *n.* merchandiser, peddler, pitchman, solicitor, vendor, drummer, clerk.

SALIENT *a.* [SAYL yunt] standing out, prominent, outstanding. *He wrote down the most salient points of the lecture.* SYN. prominent, outstanding, conspicuous, striking, important, weighty, noticeable, primary, significant, glaring. ANT. *inconspicuous, unimportant, insignificant.*

saliva *n.* spit, spittle, drool, sputum, salivation, slobber, slaver.

sallow *a.* pale yellow, yellowish, sickly, jaundiced, pale, pallid, wan. ANT. *rosy, glowing, ruddy.*

sally *n.* **1.** RUSH charge, attack, assault, blitz, foray, sortie, raid, offensive, onslaught, thrust. **2.** QUICK REMARK witticism, quip, *comeback, banter, repartee, mot.

sally *v.* rush out, charge, storm, raid, assault, attack, blitz, drive.

salon *n.* **1.** SOCIAL ROOM front room, reception area, saloon, drawing room, hall, living room. **2.** HAIR-DRESSING ESTABLISHMENT parlor, beauty shop, spa, hairdresser's.

saloon *n.* bar, pub, drinking establishment, *beer joint, taproom, alehouse, beer garden, tavern, *watering hole, *speakeasy, *honkytonk, *ginmill, grogshop, rathskeller.

salty *a.* **1.** SALINE brackish, briny, heavily seasoned. **2.** SHARP piquant, pungent, biting. **3.** EARTHY coarse, ribald, off-color, risqué, dirty, racy. ANT. *1. fresh, clean, potable. 2. bland, mild. 3. decent, G-rated, proper.*

salubrious *a.* healthful, wholesome, salutary, beneficial, good for. ANT. *unhealthy, harmful.*

salutary *a.* healthy, healthful, wholesome, salubrious, beneficial, good for one. ANT. *unhealthy, harmful.*

salutation *n.* greeting, hail, hello, salute, *howdy, address.

salute *n.* recognition, respects, greeting, obeisance.

salute *v.* **1.** RECOGNIZE show one's respect, greet, *snap to attention, show one's obeisance. **2.** PAY TRIBUTE honor, praise, commend, applaud, recognize.

salvage *v.* save, rescue, recover, retrieve, reclaim, recondition, redeem, recycle. ANT. *dump, waste, squander.*

salvation *n.* saving, rescue, deliverance, redemption, release, liberation, emancipation, conversion.

salve *n.* ointment, balm, emollient, unguent, cream, lotion, liniment.

salve *v.* soothe, ease, assuage, smooth over, relieve, alleviate, heal.

salvo *n.* discharge, firing, gunfire, broadside, fusillade, volley, cannonade, bombardment, hail, shower.

same *a.* **1.** IDENTICAL alike, ditto, equal, matching, twin, duplicate, comparable, equivalent, similar, corresponding. **2.** UNCHANGED changeless, constant, steady, unvarying. ANT. *1. contrasting, different, unlike. 2. changed, varied.*

sample *n.* part, piece, bit, example, fragment, segment, cross section, portion, *swatch, *demo, bite, taste.

sample *v.* try, experience, partake, test, taste, *take a cross section.

sanctify *v.* make holy, consecrate, bless, anoint, hallow, glorify, exalt, beatify, canonize, dedicate. ANT. *desecrate, profane.*

SANCTIMONIOUS *a.* [SANGK tuh MOH nee us] pretending to be holy and righteous. *We were sick of his sanctimonious preaching and left.* SYN. self-righteous, holier-than-thou, hypocritical, *up on one's moral soapbox, affected, overpious, unctuous, preachy, *goody-goody, false.

sanctimony *n.* self-righteousness, hypocrisy, sanctimoniousness, pietism, *goody-goodyness, pretense, affectation, *lip service.

sanction *n.* authorization, approval, permission, confirmation, endorsement, *okay, accreditation, warrant, license, consent. ANT. *veto, *no, disapproval.*

sanction *v.* authorize, approve, permit, confirm, endorse, *give the okay, accredit, warrant, license, consent. ANT. *veto, disapprove, prohibit.*

sanctioned *a.* authorized, approved, permitted, confirmed, *okayed, accredited, warranted, licensed, consented. ANT. *prohibited, rejected, vetoed.*

sanctity *n.* holiness, sacredness, saintliness, godliness, inviolability, spirituality, righteousness, piety, purity. ANT. *wickedness, godlessness.*

sanctuary *n.* **1.** HOLY PLACE church, temple, chapel, sanctum, altar, shrine. **2.** REFUGE asylum, haven, retreat, safe harbor, hideaway, shelter. **3.** ANIMAL CONSERVATION AREA reserve, reservation, preserve, game preserve, wild animal park.

sandwich *n.* club, grinder, hero, Italian, BLT, hoagie, poor boy, Reuben, *Dagwood, submarine, canapé, PB&J, open-faced sandwich, doubledecker, *fluffernutter, grilled cheese sandwich.

sane *a.* of sound mind, rational, lucid, clear-thinking, right-minded, compos mentis, possessing all of one's faculties, *having all one's marbles, *playing with a full deck, stable, *in one's right mind, *all there, sober, sensible, reasonable. ANT. *insane, crazy, *out of one's mind, deranged.*

SANG-FROID *n.* [sahn FRWAH] composure, cool blood, coolness. *Even in a crisis, she had a certain sang-froid that people respected.* SYN. composure, coolness, cool-headedness, cool, cool blood, equanimity, calmness, presence of mind, equilibrium, poise, grace under pressure. ANT. *anxiety, tenseness, hysteria.*

sanguinary *a.* **1.** BLOODY bloodied, bloodstained, gory. **2.** BLOODTHIRSTY murderous, savage, predatory, homicidal, out for blood, brutal, slaughterous.

SANGUINE *a.* [SAN gwin] cheerful, upbeat, optimistic. Also, reddish or ruddy, as a complexion. *She appeared sanguine most of the day.* SYN. **1.** cheerful, upbeat, optimistic, buoyant, happy, positive, spirited, hopeful, lighthearted, confident. **2.** reddish, ruddy, rubicund, glowing, blooming, scarlet, florid. ANT. *1. miserable, depressed, pessimistic, hopeless. 2. pale, pallid.*

sanitarium *n.* sanitorium, resort, health spa, hospital, institution, baths, asylum.

sanitary *a.* clean, hygienic, healthy, uncontaminated, antiseptic, disinfected, germ-free, sterile, sterilized, wholesome. ANT. *dirty, germ-ridden, unsanitary, unhealthy.*

sanitize v. clean, sterilize, disinfect, make antiseptic.

sanity n. saneness, sound mind, rightmindedness, mental stability, mental health, *all one's marbles, rationality, sense, levelheadedness, good judgment, lucidity, *both oars in the water. ANT. *insanity, psychosis, craziness, instability.*

Santa Claus n. Saint Nicholas, Saint Nick, Kriss Kringle, Father Christmas.

sap v. weaken, exhaust, undermine, drain, wear out, enervate, enfeeble, deplete, impair, bleed dry, suck dry, debilitate. ANT. *invigorate, energize, strengthen.*

sapient a. sagacious, sage, discerning, intelligent, smart. ANT. *dim-witted, stupid, unwise.* SEE WISE

sappy a. Sl. silly, foolish, corny, fatuous, sentimental, *mushy, maudlin. ANT. *unfeeling, cold-hearted.*

sarcasm n. mockery, jeering, snideness, ridicule, scorn, irony, satire, contempt, *cut, *dig, wisecrack, put-down. ANT. *compliment, praise, approval.*

sarcastic a. mocking, snide, ridiculing, scornful, ironic, satiric, contemptuous, *cutting, *digging, *wise, *smart-alecky, sardonic, nasty, caustic, sneering, jeering. ANT. *complimentary, approving, positive.*

SARDONIC a. [sar DON ik] mocking or sarcastic, bitter. *She has had enough of his sardonic observations.* SYN. mocking, sarcastic, bitter, nasty, disdainful, contemptuous, *cutting, cynical, jeering, *smart-mouthed, *smart-alecky, *wise, *wise-ass, acid, biting. ANT. *complimentary, positive, sweet.*

sash n. band, ribbon, belt, tie, scarf, cummerbund.

sashay v. strut, swagger, parade, glide, roll one's hips, wiggle pertly, slink, sway, bounce. SEE WALK

sass n. impudence, insolence, *mouth, *lip, back talk, effrontery, disrespect, cheek, *sauce. ANT. *respect, silence.*

sass v. talk back, *mouth off, *give lip, be impudent, be insolent, be disrespectful, *get smart, *wise off. ANT. *respect, *button one's lip, defer.*

sassy a. saucy, flippant, *mouthy. SEE IMPUDENT

Satan n. the Devil, Lucifer, Prince of Darkness, Beelzebub, Mephistopheles, fiend, demon, Lord of the Flies, Old Harry, Apollyon. SEE DEVIL

satanic a. demonic, devilish, evil, wicked, hellish, infernal, diabolical, fiendish, black-hearted, malevolent, vicious. ANT. *godly, angelic, saintly.*

satchel n. bag, valise, sack, suitcase.

sate v. satisfy, fill. SEE SATIATE

satellite n. moon, planetoid, orbiter, space station, weather satellite, spacecraft, *Sputnik, *Skylab.

satiate v. fill, satisfy, sate, slake, stuff, gorge, gratify, quench, glut, overload, *pig out, cloy.

satire n. caricature, ridicule, mockery, lampoon, *takeoff, parody, burlesque, *spoof, irony, sarcasm. "Moral outrage transformed into comic art."—Philip Roth.

satirical a. ridiculing, mocking, lampooning, sarcastic, ironic, *kidding, smart-alecky, tongue-in-cheek, farcical, burlesque, cynical. ANT. *earnest, solemn, sincere.*

satirize v. ridicule, mock, lampoon, parody, caricaturize, *kid, burlesque, *take off on, make fun of, make sport of.

satisfaction n. **1.** FULFILLMENT gratification, pleasure, contentment, enjoyment, delight, happiness, reward. **2.** SETTLEMENT compensation, restitution, reparation, recompense, reimbursement, redress, indemnity. ANT. *1. dissatisfaction, discontent.*

satisfactory a. okay, acceptable, good enough, all right, sufficient, adequate, pleasing, fulfilling, suitable, up to scratch. ANT. *unsatisfactory, insufficient, unacceptable.*

satisfy v. **1.** FULFILL gratify, please, content, delight, make happy, reward, *fill the bill, quench, appease. **2.** MEET fulfill, answer, equal, match, comply. **3.** ASSURE convince, persuade. **4.** SETTLE discharge, make up for, compensate, make restitution, clear, pay off. ANT. *1. dissatisfy, discontent. 2. come up short, *miss the mark.*

satisfying a. fulfilling, gratifying, pleasing, contenting, delightful, rewarding, quenching, satiating, *filling the bill, *hitting the spot. ANT. *unfulfilling, lacking, unsatisfying.*

saturate v. soak, imbue, fill, drench, souse, wet through, permeate, impregnate, suffuse, pervade, drown. ANT. *drain, dehydrate, dry.*

saturnine a. gloomy, morose, depressed, sorrowful, glum, sullen, sulky, downhearted, hopeless, dour, moody. ANT. *happy, cheerful, sunny.*

satyr n. lech, debaucher, playboy, *horny little devil, profligate, rake, wolf, womanizer, Don Juan, Casanova. ANT. *choir boy, celibate.*

sauce n. gravy, dressing, relish, condiment, soy sauce, Worcestershire sauce, Mornay sauce, white sauce, soubise.

saucy a. rude, impudent, *smart-mouthed, *mouthy, *wise, impertinent, flippant, disrespectful, insolent, *sassy, bold, fresh. ANT. *respectful, shy, courteous, diplomatic.*

saunter v. stroll, walk leisurely, *mosey along, amble, pad, shuffle, promenade, dawdle, stray, meander. SEE WALK

sauté v. quick fry.

savage n. primitive, aborigine, brute, barbarian, beast, monster, animal, cave man, Neanderthal, wild man, killer. "Animals in human shape."—Bernard de Fontenelle.

savage v. attack, brutalize, tear apart, maul, rip apart, *beat to a pulp, kill, murder, torture.

savage a. wild, fierce, ferocious, untamed, beastly, vicious, brutal, inhuman, barbaric, bloodthirsty, predatory, animalistic, brutish, cruel. ANT. *tame, gentle, civilized, broken.*

savagery n. barbarity, brutality, brutishness, beastliness, monstrosity, wildness, cruelty, viciousness.

savannah n. plain, grassland, pampas, steppe. SEE FIELD

savant n. scholar, *brain, intellectual, learned person, sage, *walking encyclopedia, wise man, expert, authority. ANT. *moron, imbecile, idiot.*

save v. **1.** RESCUE liberate, deliver, bail out, *save one's bacon, *save one's neck, recover, free, emancipate. **2.** SQUIRREL AWAY hoard, lay aside, stash, *sock away, *put away for a rainy day, salt away. **3.** CONSERVE preserve, be thrifty, be frugal, *pinch pennies, scrimp, economize, *tighten one's belt. ANT. *1. put at risk, imperil. 3. spend, expend, squander, *blow.*

savings n. security, reserve, *something for a rainy day, hoard, investment, *nest egg, bank account, pile, treasure, amassed wealth.

savior n. liberator, deliverer, lifesaver, emancipator, messiah, Jesus Christ.

SAVOIR FAIRE n. [SAV wahr FEHR] social know-how. *He always knew what to say; he had great savoir faire.* SYN. social know-how, sophistication, cultivation, worldliness, graciousness, suavity, smoothness, social grace, poise, urbanity, tactfulness, diplomacy. ANT. *tactlessness, clumsiness, awkwardness.*

savor n. taste, flavor, tang, scent, odor, aroma, smell.

savor v. taste, smell, enjoy, relish, *smack one's lips over, luxuriate in, appreciate.

savory a. **1.** TASTY appetizing, delicious, mouthwatering, delectable, toothsome, ambrosial, luscious, flavorful, agreeable. **2.** RESPECTABLE reputable, decent, moral, upright, virtuous. ANT. *1. unsavory, *gross, disgusting, unappetizing. 2. unsavory, disreputable.*

savvy n. Sl. know-how, *smarts, understanding, shrewdness, intelligence, knowledge, experience, proficiency, grasp, awareness. ANT. *stupidity, ignorance.*

savvy a. Sl. in the know, knowledgeable, shrewd, astute, sharp, *on the ball, educated, experienced, intelligent, *hip, proficient. ANT. *ignorant, uneducated, stupid.*

saw n. **1.** CUTTING TOOL cutting instrument, blade, handsaw, circular saw, crosscut saw, bucksaw, hacksaw, coping saw. **2.** SAYING maxim, proverb, truism, adage, aphorism, epigram, cliché.

saw v. rend, rip. SEE CUT

saw-toothed a. jagged, serrated, serrate, notched. ANT. *smooth.*

say v. utter, speak, tell, assert, give voice, mouth, pronounce, vocalize, remark, phrase, state, articulate.

saying n. maxim, proverb, truism, adage, aphorism, epigram, cliché, slogan, saw, motto.

scab n. crust, incrustation, scale.

scaffold n. framework, platform, staging, gallows, gantry.

scald v. heat, injure. SEE BURN

scale n. **1.** SKIN layer, covering, crust, plate, scurf. **2.** GAUGE progression, order, gradation, succession, degrees, measure, calibration, ratio.

scale v. climb, ascend, mount, clamber up. ANT. *descend.*

scalp v. cheat, rob, *rip off.

scamp n. rascal, mischief-maker, troublemaker, imp, rogue, scoundrel, scalawag, knave, prankster, *little devil.

scamper v. run, hurry, scurry, scramble, dash, rush, sprint, dart, scuttle, scoot. ANT. *saunter, *mosey along, creep.*

scan v. look at, scrutinize, study, survey, examine, inspect, search, scour, peruse, check, glance at, skim, *flip through, *thumb through, browse, *give the once-over.

scandal n. disgrace, shocker, sin, atrocity, transgression, vice, outrage, wrongdoing, crime, infamy, *skeleton in the closet, impropriety, misconduct. "Vice enjoyed vicariously."—Elbert Hubbard.

scandalous *a.* disgraceful, shocking, sinful, atrocious, outrageous, wrong, criminal, infamous, improper, shameful, odious.

scant *a.* meager, inadequate, lacking, sparse, insufficient, deficient, tight, wanting, poor, spare, limited. ANT. *plentiful, bountiful, overflowing.*

scapegoat *n.* *fall guy, whipping boy, *goat, *patsy, victim, butt, dupe.

scar *n.* **1.** DISFIGUREMENT scab, pockmark, scar tissue, scratch, line, cut, gash, cicatrix, mark. **2.** EMOTIONAL DAMAGE psychological wound, trauma, reminder, stigma, flashbacks.

scar *v.* **1.** DISFIGURE scratch, cut, gash, blemish, mar, wound, lacerate. **2.** EMOTIONALLY DAMAGE wound psychologically, traumatize, stigmatize, brand, hurt.

scarce *a.* rare, uncommon, scanty, scant, insufficient, in short supply, *scarce as hens' teeth, not enough, meager, inadequate, at a premium, tight. ANT. *plentiful, abundant, bountiful.*

scarcely *adv.* barely, merely, only, just, hardly.

scantiness *n.* rareness, insufficiency, shortage, short supply, meagerness, inadequacy, dearth, paucity, need, poverty, sparsity.

scare *n.* fright, shock, turn, panic, terror.

scare *v.* frighten, unnerve, terrify, alarm, panic, daunt, shock, appall, *put the fear of God into, petrify, paralyze, *send chills down one's spine, *make one's hair stand on end, spook, *scare the bejeesus out of, *curl one's hair, *make one's blood run cold, *adrenalize, intimidate, horrify, fill with dread. ANT. *reassure, encourage, embolden.*

scarecrow *n.* malkin, straw man.

scarf *n.* muffler, neckpiece, bandanna, ascot, boa, tippet.

scary *a.* frightening, unnerving, terrifying, alarming, panic-inducing, daunting, shocking, appalling, petrifying, paralyzing, *bone-chilling, *bloodcurdling, *spine-tingling, *hair-curling, *hair-raising, *adrenalizing, intimidating, horrifying, creepy. ANT. *reassuring, encouraging, emboldening.*

scathing *a.* harsh, searing, caustic, biting, acid, bitter, severe, vitriolic, cutting, sharp, nasty, pointed, brutal. ANT. *mild, bland, gentle.*

scatter *v.* **1.** STREW sprinkle, litter, spread, broadcast, distribute. **2.** SEPARATE rout, disperse, diffuse, dispel. ANT. *gather, assemble, amass.*

scatterbrained *a.* flighty, giddy, brainless, frivolous, *bubbleheaded, *airheaded, *dizzy, *a

space case, *off in the ozone, harebrained, *ditzy, *like duh. ANT. *on the ball, *with it, *savvy, sharp.

scenario *n.* outline, synopsis, script, sketch, concept, plot, story, plan.

scene *n.* **1.** SETTING place, location, locale, backdrop, site, spot. **2.** VIEW scenery, panorama, vista, landscape, prospect. **3.** SEGMENT act, bit, episode, part. **4.** DISPLAY OF EMOTION tantrum, fit, *spectacle, *blowup, outburst.

scenic *a.* picturesque, beautiful, panoramic, breathtaking, grand, spectacular, awe-inspiring, quaint. ANT. *nondescript, ugly, unsightly.*

scent *n.* odor, smell, fragrance, aroma, essence, bouquet, stink, whiff, trace, redolence, incense.

scented *a.* odorous, smelling, aromatic. SEE FRAGRANT

schedule *n.* agenda, program, timetable, calendar, roster, docket, plan, lineup, itinerary, slate.

scheme *n.* **1.** PLAN plot, stratagem, ploy, machination, intrigue, conspiracy, maneuver. **2.** SYSTEM arrangement, organization, order.

scheming *a.* crafty, underhanded, sneaky, artful, tricky, conniving, calculating, sly, foxy, slippery. ANT. *artless, innocent.*

SCHISM *n.* [SIZ um] a separation within a group, due to disagreement over a particular issue. A *schism* has formed in the church over the abortion issue. SYN. separation, split, division, rift, splintering, break, faction, disjunction, fragmentation. ANT. *unification, union, harmony.*

schlemiel *n. Sl.* loser, bungler, *schlimazel, *Charlie Brown, *zero, dupe, victim, *sap, *patsy, *stooge, *sucker, fool.

schlep *v. Sl.* drag oneself, drag, lug, carry.

schlock *n. Sl.* *crap, garbage, trash, *cheap stuff, junk, *dreck.

scholar *n.* learned person, educated person, intellectual, *brain, man of letters, *egghead, highbrow, professor, teacher, student, pupil, *walking encyclopedia, *know-it-all, authority, expert, pundit, savant, polymath. "A man long on advice but short on action."—Elbert Hubbard. ANT. *ignoramus, idiot, *airhead, imbecile.*

scholarly *a.* learned, knowledgeable, educated, studious, erudite, literate, well-read, intellectual, academic, bookish, pedantic, *brainy. ANT. *ignorant, uneducated, stupid, empty-headed.*

scholarship *n.* **1.** KNOWLEDGE education, erudition, learning, schooling, edification, enlightenment, pedantry. **2.** GRANT student aid, gift, endowment, fellowship.

school *n.* **1.** EDUCATIONAL INSTITUTE academy, high school, elementary school, university, college, institution of higher learning, alma mater, seminary. **2.** SYSTEM method, style, mode, belief system, doctrine.

school *v.* educate, teach, instruct, train, enlighten, edify, indoctrinate, tutor.

science *n.* hard facts, physical laws, truths, body of knowledge, discipline. "Trained and organized common sense."—Thomas Huxley. "A knowledge of matter."—Fulton Sheen. "Pearls strung on a cord of faith."—Joshua Steinberg. "Only the tools in a box."—Frank Lloyd Wright.

WORD FIND

agriculture: geoponics, agrology
air, moving objects through: aerodynamics
air: pneumatics
animal, prebirth development: embryology
animals: zoology
aviation: aeronautics
birds: ornithology
building design: architecture
caves: speleology
cells: cytology
chemicals, applied: chemical engineering
chemistry of life processes: biochemistry
civilization, uncovering facts about early: archeology
classification, plant and animal: taxonomy
climate: climatology
color: chromatology
crime: criminology
cycles, natural: chronobiology
earth: geology
earthquakes: seismology
earth's moving plates: tectonics
energy and heat: thermodynamics
energy and matter: physics
epidemics: epidemiology
fish: ichthyology
fluids: hydraulics
fossils, animal: paleontology
heredity and genes: genetics
human beings: anthropology
human beings, extinct: paleoanthropology
gene manipulation: genetic engineering, eugenics
life processes: biology
lines, angles, planes, etc.: geometry
machinery: mechanics

mapping of terrain: topography, cartography
metals: metallurgy
monsters: teratology
motion: kinetics, dynamics
plants: botany
plants, ornamental: horticulture
population studies: demography
primitive societies: ethnography
societies and social behavior: sociology
sound: acoustics
space, study of: astronomy, astrophysics, cosmography, cosmology
time: chronometry, horology
water: hydrography
weather: meteorology

scientific *a.* systematic, provable, exact, empirical, physical, material, observable, mathematical, technical, technological. ANT. *unscientific, spiritual.*

scientist *n.* researcher, expert, authority, investigator, analyst, scientific detective, prober, scholar, inquirer, examiner, tester, scientific sleuth, experimenter, lab technician. SEE SCIENCE

scintilla *n.* particle, trace, iota, hint, bit, speck, atom, whit, drop, spark.

SCINTILLATING *a.* [SIN tuh late ing] sparkling, flashing. Also, brilliant, as of wit. *The scintillating conversation made the party a success.* SYN. **1.** SPARKLING glittering, brilliant, glinting, glimmering, twinkling, gleaming, shimmering, flashing. **2.** WITTY clever, brilliant, effervescent, lively. ANT. *dull, lackluster.*

scion *n.* offspring, descendant, child, heir, successor, offshoot, shoot.

scoff *v.* jeer, mock, ridicule, deride, snicker at, laugh at, gibe, dismiss, belittle, *pooh-pooh, discount, knock. ANT. *respect, accept, praise.*

scold *v.* berate, rebuke, upbraid, reprimand, reproach, *blast, *jump down one's throat, find fault, vituperate, *chew out, *give hell, *take to task, castigate, *rake over the coals, *rip into, *let have it with both barrels, *bawl out. ANT. *commend, praise, give a pat on the back.*

scoop *n.* **1.** SHOVEL spade, spoon, bail, trowel, ladle. **2.** HOT NEWS *inside information, *skinny, *poop, exclusive, *lowdown.

scoot *v.* dart, scurry, skedaddle, hurry, *move it.

scope *n.* area, range, extent, span, reach, compass, radius, breadth, sphere.

scorch *v.* burn, blacken, char, singe, parch, sear, shrivel, brown, toast, blister.

score *n.* **1.** TALLY count, points, sum, total. **2.** GRADE mark. **3.** MUSICAL COMPOSITION arrangement, chart. **4.** GROOVE nick, notch, cut, gash.

score *v.* **1.** SUCCEED triumph, achieve, win, *rack up, *chalk up, *nail it, *hit it. **2.** CUT crosshatch, gouge, nick, notch, gash, slit.

scores *n.* many, multitude, lots, throng, mass, myriad, crowd, legion. ANT. *few, hardly any.*

scorn *n.* contempt, disdain, hatred, loathing, disgust, distaste, derision, sneering, arrogance, scoffing, mocking. ANT. *admiration, respect, esteem.*

scorn *v.* regard with contempt, disdain, despise, detest, hate, loathe, look down on, reject, spurn, revile, mock, ridicule. ANT. *admire, look up to, respect, like.*

scoundrel *n.* rascal, villain, rogue, *SOB, *bastard, cad, dog, knave, *creep, *rat, dastard, wretch, *bad egg, *bad actor.

scour *v.* **1.** SCRUB clean, wash, rub, abrade, brush, wipe. **2.** SEARCH OUT comb, rummage, range over, pass over, *turn upside-down, *leave no stone unturned, look high and low.

scourge *n.* punishment, torture, torment, affliction, plague, misery, tribulation, curse.

scourge *v.* punish, torture, torment, afflict, plague, chastise, curse, beat, whip, flog, thrash.

scout *n.* spy, patrol, outrider, advance man, reconnoiterer, picket, lookout.

scout *v.* spy, reconnoiter, *have a look-see, survey, investigate, explore, observe, patrol, *check out.

scow *n.* barge, flatboat.

scowl *n.* angry look, irritated look, frown, glower, *black look, *dirty look, glare, knitted brow, nasty look, lower. SEE ANGRY

scowl *v.* frown, glower, glare, shoot an angry look, shoot an irritated look, *give a dirty look, *shoot daggers. SEE ANGRY

scraggly *a.* scrubby, ragged, uneven, irregular, straggly, rough, *like a rat's nest, ungroomed. ANT. *neat, trim.*

scraggy *a.* skinny, lean, scrawny, bony, thin, slender, gaunt. ANT. *hefty, husky.*

scramble *n.* run, dash, struggle, climb, race, scuffle, competition.

scramble *v.* **1.** CLAMBER climb, crawl, struggle, rush, dash, run, race, scuffle, compete for, strive for. **2.** MIX jumble, stir up, disorder, mingle, tangle, confuse.

scrap *n.* **1.** BIT fragment, piece, shred, chip, speck, slice, hunk, chunk, particle, end. **2.**

SALVAGE junk. **3.** FIGHT argument, quarrel, *tiff, conflict, tussle, altercation, disagreement, squabble, brawl.

scrap *v.* throw out, drop, ditch, get rid of, discard, junk, *deep-six, jettison.

scrape *n.* **1.** SCRATCH scuff, abrasion, graze, scar. **2.** DIFFICULT SITUATION predicament, trouble, dilemma, quandary, fix, pickle, *mess, *hole.

scrape *v.* scratch, scuff, abrade, graze, scar, scour, rasp, shave, skin.

scrappy *a.* game, aggressive, pugnacious, plucky, gritty, contentious. ANT. *wimpy, meek.*

scratch *n.* cut, laceration, incision, scar, abrasion, scrape, gash, line, score.

scratch *v.* **1.** CUT lacerate, incise, scar, abrade, scrape, gash, score, graze. **2.** ELIMINATE cancel, drop, delete, erase, withdraw, strike.

scrawl *v.* scribble, scratch, *hen-scratch, doodle.

scrawny *a.* skinny, thin, lean, slender, *skin and bones, emaciated, anorexic, bony, gaunt, malnourished, spare, rawboned, *could slip through a flute and not sound a note. ANT. *brawny, big, beefy, fat.*

scream *n.* cry, shriek, yelp, yell, hysterical cry, strangled cry for help, wail, squeal, squall.

scream *v.* cry, shriek, yelp, cry out hysterically, wail, screech, ululate, let out a strangled cry, sing out, bawl, howl, squeal, squall.

screech *v.* SEE SCREAM

screen *n.* **1.** PARTITION divider, shield, covering, wall, fence, curtain, veil. **2.** MESH net, strainer, grating, lattice.

screen *v.* **1.** PARTITION divide, shield, cover, block, wall off, fence off, veil. **2.** SORT OUT cull, *weed out, sift, sieve, filter, strain, eliminate, winnow.

screw *v.* **1.** TWIST wind, turn, wrench, corkscrew, crank. **2.** *Sl.* CHEAT *rip off, take advantage of, defraud, *give the shaft, swindle, extort, chisel. **3.** *Sl.* HAVE SEXUAL INTERCOURSE mate, *make love, copulate.

screw up *v.* mess up, bungle, blow it, muff, botch, *flub up, goof up, mismanage, mishandle, *drop the ball, *choke.

screwy *a.* *Sl.* odd, queer, peculiar, eccentric, *nuts. SEE CRAZY

scribble *v.* scrawl, scratch, *hen-scratch, doodle, dash.

scribe *n.* scrivener, transcriber, calligrapher, writer, clerk.

scrimp *v.* be frugal, economize, save, be cheap, *pinch pennies, *squeeze nickels, skimp, be stingy, stint. ANT. *squander, *blow, spend.*

script *n.* **1.** HANDWRITING writing, longhand, cursive, calligraphy, penmanship. **2.** STORY dialogue, text, screenplay, manuscript.

Scrooge *n.* misanthrope, *tightwad, cheapskate, *penny-pincher, skinflint, miser, hoarder, *miserable cuss, curmudgeon. ANT. *philanthropist, giver, altruist.*

scrounge *v.* dig for, hunt for, beg, scare up, forage for, bum, track down, *scrape up, panhandle.

scrub *n.* shrubs, bushes, trees, brush, thicket, bush.

scrub *v.* scour, wash, clean, rub, swab, brush, *clean with elbow grease, wipe, mop.

scruffy *a.* shabby, grubby, straggly, unkempt, ungroomed, untrimmed, unwashed, mangy, ragged, bedraggled, *like a rat's nest. ANT. *neat, tidy, trim, groomed.*

scrumptious *a.* tasty, mouth-watering, pleasing. SEE DELICIOUS

scruple *n.* hesitancy, doubt, qualm, misgiving, second thought, pang, apprehension, caution, reluctance, *little voice.

SCRUPULOUS *a.* [SKROO pyuh lus] proper and highly principled, careful to do the right thing, meticulous. *He was a scrupulous businessman.* SYN. proper, principled, moral, upright, ethical, honest, upstanding, careful, meticulous, punctilious, painstaking, exacting, particular, fussy. ANT. *unscrupulous, unprincipled, dishonest, sloppy.*

SCRUTINIZE *v.* [SKROOT uh NIZE] to look at very closely. *She scrutinized the will for her name.* SYN. look at, examine, inspect, study, pore over, *eyeball, peruse, explore, probe, *scorch with one's eyes. ANT. *overlook, pass over, disregard.*

scrutiny *n.* inspection, close look, examination, treatment, surveillance, study, probing, perusal, investigation, *eyeballing, search, exploration. ANT. *quick glance, quick glimpse.*

scuba diving *n.* skin diving, snorkeling.

scuff *v.* SEE SCRAPE

scuffle *n.* struggle, fight, tussle, scrap, *set-to, commotion, *ruckus, fray, *rumble, brawl.

scuffle *v.* struggle, fight, tussle, scrap, *rumble, brawl, *mix it up.

sculpture *n.* **1.** STATUE statuary, bust, figure, figurine, bronze, carving, abstract. **2.** CARVING chiseling, molding, stonecutting. "An art that takes away superfluous material."—Michelangelo. "Mud pies which endure."—Cyril Connolly.

WORD FIND

bizarre human or animal figure: grotesque

chip off stone: stun

frame, framework: armature, butterfly

Greek statue of marble: acrolith

larger than life-size sculpture: heroic, colossal

low relief: bas-relief

medium: marble, clay, bronze

projection: relief

smaller than life-size sculpture: statuette

tool: bushhammer, calipers, mallet, rasp

trim: fettle

scum *n.* **1.** DROSS refuse, film, layer, froth, residue. **2.** LOWLIFE *sleazebag, riffraff, *dregs of society.

scurrilous *a.* vulgar, indecent, abusive, offensive, insulting, obscene, gross, foulmouthed, dirty, raunchy, *gutter-mouthed, nasty.

scurry *v.* scamper, run, race, hurry, scuttle, dash, scoot, sprint, dart, hasten, bolt, fly.

scurvy *a.* mean, contemptible, despicable, low. ANT. *admirable.*

scuttle *v.* **1.** RUN scurry, scamper, race, hurry, dash, scoot, sprint, dart, hasten, bolt, *beat feet. **2.** ABANDON scrap, scrub, scratch, quit, desert.

scuttlebutt *n.* *Sl.* rumor, gossip, word, grapevine news, talk.

sea *n.* ocean, the deep, *briny deep, *bounding main, *Davy Jones's locker, high seas, surf, rolling sea. SEE BEACH, OCEAN

seafarer *n.* seaman, mariner. SEE SAILOR

seal *n.* **1.** STAMP symbol, emblem, imprint, impression, logo, authentication, insignia, imprimatur. **2.** FASTENING adhesive, sealant.

seal *v.* **1.** FASTEN secure, shut tight, lock in, waterproof, make airtight, plug. **2.** SETTLE assure, determine, decide, ensure, clinch, make certain, confirm.

seam *n.* closure, connection, juncture, junction, stitches, suture.

seaman *n.* seafarer, mariner. SEE SAILOR

seamy *a.* sordid, unpleasant, squalid, disagreeable, rough, unwholesome, unsavory, objectionable, revolting, dirty. ANT. *pleasant, decent, good.*

seance *n.* communion with the dead, spiritual contact, session, sitting, conjuring.

sear *v.* scorch, burn, brown, singe, toast, char, sizzle, wither, dry up, parch, shrivel, wilt.

search *n.* hunt, exploration, quest, probe, inquisition, *shakedown, *frisking, scrutiny, investigation, study, rummaging, foraging, research.

search v. seek, look, hunt, explore, quest, probe, *shake down, *frisk, scrutinize, investigate, study, rummage, forage, *sniff out, *go over with a fine-tooth comb, *leave no stone unturned, *turn inside out, research, ferret, delve, ransack.

searching a. penetrating, piercing, probing, sharp, intent, deep, inquisitive, curious, quizzical. ANT. *cursory, uninterested.*

sea serpent n. giant squid, oarfish, kraken, Loch Ness monster. SEE MONSTER

seashore n. coast, strand. SEE BEACH

seasickness n. motion sickness, queasiness. SEE NAUSEA

season n. period, term, spell, interval, quarter, month, summer, spring, fall, winter, Indian summer.

season v. **1.** FLAVOR spice, salt, pepper, lace, marinade, smoke, cure, corn, devil. **2.** HARDEN OR SOFTEN toughen, weather, temper, acclimate, accustom.

seasonable a. opportune, fitting, suitable, right. ANT. *inopportune.* SEE TIMELY

seasoned a. hardened, softened, toughened, weathered, experienced, tempered, acclimated, accustomed, inured. ANT. *green, immature, inexperienced.*

seasoning n. flavoring, spice, salt, pepper, marinade, dressing, condiment, sauce, gravy, relish, hot sauce, mustard, garlic, onion powder, herbs.

seat n. **1.** CHAIR bench, couch, sofa, recliner, lounge, loveseat, stool, settee, throne, perch. **2.** CENTER core, location, capital, heart, hub, headquarters, place. **3.** BUTTOCKS rear, behind, rump, derriere, posterior, *tush, *duff.

seaweed n. kelp, sargasso, wrack, dulse.

SECEDE v. [si SEED] to formally withdraw or break off from a group, organization, government, etc. *The islands seceded from the mainland government.* SYN. withdraw, break off, defect, quit, renounce, separate from, split from, expatriate, pull out, disaffiliate, *wash one's hands of. ANT. *join, merge, confederate.*

secession n. withdrawal, breakup, defection, renunciation, separation, split, expatriation, pullout, disaffiliation. ANT. *union, joining, merger, confederation.*

seclude v. isolate, sequester, hide, segregate, insulate, go into retreat, withdraw, quarantine.

secluded a. isolated, sequestered, segregated, insulated, cloistered, reclusive, private, hidden, sheltered, lonesome, remote, deserted, solitary, quarantined. ANT. *public, open, frequented.*

seclusion n. isolation, sequestration, segregation, privacy, hiding, shelter, solitude, sanctuary, retreat, quarantine.

second n. instant, tick of the clock, wink, *heartbeat, moment, flash, twinkling, jiffy, *nothing flat.

second v. support, back, root for, side with, abet, advocate, further. ANT. *oppose, contradict, dispute.*

secondary a. lesser, inferior, subordinate, minor, ancillary, subsidiary. ANT. *main, first, primary.*

second-hand a. previously-owned, used, handed down, old, broken-in, pre-owned. ANT. *new.*

second-rate a. inferior, cheap, *crappy, poor, shabby, *two-bit, low-grade, middling, fair, so-so, second class. ANT. *first-rate, superior, *top drawer.*

secrecy n. concealment, covertness, confidentiality, privacy, surreptitiousness, stealth, hiding, underhandedness, sneakiness, silence. ANT. *overtness, publicity, openness.*

secret n. confidence, classified information, privileged information, *skeleton in the closet, mystery, enigma.

secret a. concealed, hidden, covert, confidential, private, surreptitious, furtive, stealthy, underhanded, sneaky, quiet, silent, hush-hush, under wraps, classified, undisclosed, clandestine, mysterious, cryptic, secluded, sequestered, out-of-the-way, undercover. ANT. *overt, public, open.*

secretary n. office worker, typist, word processor, receptionist, filer, stenographer, bookkeeper, *guy/gal Friday, *desk jockey. SEE OFFICE WORKER

secrete v. **1.** HIDE conceal, stow away, closet, seclude, shroud, veil, bury, harbor, stash. **2.** RELEASE discharge, emit, excrete, ooze, exude.

secretive a. private, tight-lipped, close-mouthed, silent, evasive, surreptitious, furtive, covert, clandestine, sneaky, backdoor, stealthy, cryptic, mysterious. ANT. *open, overt, public.*

sect n. faction, party, group, denomination, body, order, cult, division, clique, splinter group.

sectarian a. partisan, party-minded, factional,

denominational, cultish, cliquish, parochial, provincial, narrow-minded. ANT. *broad-minded, nonpartisan.*

section n. part, segment, piece, component, slice, hunk, chunk, parcel, quarter, division, fragment, fraction, unit, share, district, region, neighborhood, community, ward, precinct, borough.

sector n. section, segment, division, group, class, district, area, zone, region.

SECULAR a. [SEK yuh lur] unrelated to religion or the church, worldly. *The church organist sometimes played secular music.* SYN. worldly, nonreligious, laic, lay, profane, earthly, temporal, mundane. ANT. *religious, ecclesiastical, spiritual.*

secure v. 1. GET obtain, procure, acquire, pick up, attain. 2. BIND tighten, tie down, lock up, fasten, fix, attach, set, anchor, stabilize. 3. SAFEGUARD defend, shield, shelter, protect.

secure a. 1. SAFE sheltered, protected, defended, immune, out of harm's way, unassailable, invulnerable, in the clear, in safekeeping. 2. CONFIDENT self-assured, carefree, untroubled, certain, definite, settled. 3. FIRM stable, strong, fast, locked, set, tight, fastened, bound, anchored, tied down. ANT. *1. unsafe, insecure, unprotected, vulnerable. 2. insecure, troubled, doubting. 3. loose, unsecured, unlocked.*

security n. 1. CONFIDENCE fearlessness, assurance, peace of mind, certainty, freedom from worry. 2. PROTECTION defense, shield, shelter, safeguard, safety, immunity, refuge, invulnerability. 3. GUARANTEE pledge, assurance, collateral, bond, surety, escrow.

sedate a. calm, quiet, staid, serious, serene, impassive, sober, dignified, tranquil, placid, grave. ANT. **a nervous wreck, excited, agitated.*

sedative n. tranquilizer, hypnotic, sleeping pill, soporific, depressant, opiate, Demerol, Nembutal.

sedative a. tranquilizing, calming, relaxing, sleep-inducing, tension-relieving, sedating. ANT. *stimulating, exciting.*

SEDENTARY a. [SED un tair ee] inactive, sitting around. *She lives a sedentary lifestyle.* SYN. inactive, *couch-potato-like, *couchbound, *chair-bound, sitting, stationary, unmoving, vegetative. ANT. *active, busy, *on the move.*

sediment n. dregs, grounds, deposit, settlings, lees, precipitate.

sedition n. rebellion, treason, incitement, rabble-rousing, mutiny, insurrection, revolt, subversion.

seditious a. rebellious, rabble-rousing, inciting, mutinous, insurrectionary, revolutionary, subversive. ANT. *loyal, subservient.*

seduce v. lure, tempt, persuade, lead astray, entice, trap, snare, beguile, *lead on, tease, debauch.

seduction n. persuasion, enticement, temptation, allurement, tantalizing, trap, beguilement, tease.

seductive a. persuasive, enticing, tempting, alluring, tantalizing, beguiling, attractive, flirtatious, sexy, bewitching. ANT. *repellent, repulsive.*

sedulous a. diligent, hard-working, busy, industrious, assiduous, tireless, constant, persistent, plodding, dogged, intense. ANT. *lazy, lagging, lax.*

see v. 1. BEHOLD discern, eye, *eyeball, perceive, regard, spot, *lay eyes on, notice, detect, look, view, peer, watch, glimpse, distinguish, *get a load of, peep, stare, make out. 2. UNDERSTAND comprehend, get it, appreciate, catch on, *catch one's drift, fathom, recognize, perceive, grasp. 3. IMAGINE visualize, picture, conceive, think, envisage, envision. 4. LOOK INTO find out, discover, ascertain. 5. MEET encounter, run into, come face to face, speak with, visit.

seed n. source, wellspring, beginning, start, nucleus, grain, kernel, nut, sperm, egg, germ.

seedy a. shabby, run-down, broken-down, dilapidated, neglected, squalid, scruffy, unkempt, mangy, bedraggled, poor. ANT. *luxurious, well-kept, groomed, sparkling.*

seek v. 1. LOOK FOR search for, hunt, *look high and low, cast about for, quest, *fish for, *sniff out, *ferret out, *leave no stone unturned. 2. INQUIRE request, question, ask for. 3. PURSUE aim, set one's sights for, aspire to.

seem v. appear, have the appearance of, look like, give the impression.

seeming a. ostensible, apparent, outward, external, assumed, presumable, professed, illusory, quasi. ANT. *actual, real.*

seemly a. proper, fitting, suitable, appropriate, right, correct, becoming, decorous, prudent, in good taste. ANT. *improper, unsuitable, rude.*

seep v. leak, ooze, exude, percolate, bleed, drip, dribble, issue, sweat, weep, permeate.

seer n. prophet, prognosticator, predictor, psychic, oracle, fortuneteller, forecaster, diviner, medium, soothsayer.

seesaw *n.* teeter-totter.

seethe *v.* **1.** BOIL bubble, froth, roll, surge. **2.** RAGE *see red, *get steamed, *do a slow burn, *boil over, *blow one's top, fume, be livid, *storm, *foam at the mouth.

segment *n.* section, piece, part, portion, fragment, fraction, division, parcel, bit, element, component, quarter.

segregate *v.* separate, set apart, isolate, divide, insulate, split up, dissociate, quarantine. ANT. *unite, join, integrate, desegregate.*

segregation *n.* separation, apartheid, isolation, division, insulation, splitting up, setting apart, exclusion, quarantine.

seize *v.* **1.** GRAB take, snatch, grasp, grip, clasp, pluck, catch, embrace, *jump on. **2.** CONFISCATE capture, apprehend, arrest, *nail, *collar, *nab, commandeer, impound, take by force, appropriate, usurp, kidnap, hijack.

seizure *n.* **1.** APPREHENSION arrest, capture, confiscation, commandeering, impounding, appropriation, kidnapping, hijacking. **2.** CONVULSION fit, attack, throe, paroxysm, epileptic episode, stroke.

seldom *adv.* rarely, infrequently, hardly ever, *once in a blue moon. ANT. *often, frequently.*

select *v.* pick, choose, elect, opt for, single out, prefer, vote for, favor, cull, weed out. ANT. *reject, *turn one's nose up at, shun.*

select *a.* choice, preferred, best, top-notch, A-1, prime, finest, handpicked, cream, crème de la crème. ANT. *second-rate, mediocre, run-of-the-mill.*

selection *n.* pick, choice, preference, election, favorite, choosing, culling, weeding out, vote. ANT. *reject.*

selective *a.* choosy, picky, discriminating, particular, fussy, finicky, *persnickety, discerning. ANT. *undiscriminating, *easy.*

self *n.* ego, individuality, entity, soul, mind, personality, being, character.

self-assured *a.* confident, self-confident, sure of oneself, cocky, *full of oneself, secure, self-possessed, cool. ANT. *insecure, lacking self-esteem.*

self-centered *a.* selfish, self-absorbed, narcissistic, *thinks the world revolves around one, conceited, self-serving, egocentric, egotistical. ANT. *other-directed, giving, generous.*

self-confidence *n.* self-assurance, inner strength, positive self-image, coolness, aplomb. "The first requisite to great undertakings."—Samuel Johnson. SEE CONFIDENCE

self-conscious *a.* shy, bashful, ill at ease, awkward, self-aware, *redfaced, blushing, embarrassed, anxious, sheepish. ANT. *self-confident, self-assured.*

self-control *n.* self-discipline, self-restraint, willpower, self-constraint, abstemiousness, fortitude, strength. "The hardest victory."— Aristotle. ANT. *impulsiveness, weakness.*

self-defeating *a.* *shooting oneself in the foot, *cutting off one's nose to spite one's face, defeating its own purpose.

self-esteem *n.* pride, self-respect, healthy ego, self-regard, confidence, self-love, self-assurance, amour propre, dignity, belief in oneself. "The most voluble of the emotions."— Frank M. Colby.

self-evident *a.* evident, obvious, apparent, clear, manifest, self-explanatory, undeniable, plain, uncontestable, axiomatic. ANT. *questionable, doubtful, uncertain.*

self-image *n.* conception of oneself, self-esteem, self-regard.

self-important *a.* conceited, overbearing, arrogant, *bigheaded, egotistical, pompous, swaggering, smug, snobbish, *snotty, *high and mighty. ANT. *self-effacing, modest, humble.*

selfish *a.* self-centered, self-serving, greedy, egocentric, egotistical, *wrapped up in oneself, narcissistic, *looking out for number one, *thinks the world revolves around one, *piggish. ANT. *giving, other-directed, generous.*

selfishness *n.* self-centeredness, greediness, egocentricity, narcissism. "Consuming happiness without producing any."—Joan Tepperman.

self-reliant *a.* independent, *standing on one's own two feet, self-sufficient, autonomous, strong. ANT. *dependent, needy.*

self-respect *n.* self-esteem, pride, self-regard, self-worth, dignity, *the ability to hold one's head up, *the ability to stand tall. "The corner-stone of all virtue."—John Herschell. "The noblest garment."—Samuel Smiles.

self-righteous *a.* holier-than-thou, sanctimonious, complacent, smug, hypocritical, preachy, *goody-goody, pious, self-satisfied. ANT. *humble.*

self-satisfied *a.* complacent, smug, pleased with oneself, proud, arrogant, *full of oneself, swelled-headed, bigheaded, content. ANT. *self-effacing, humble, modest.*

self-sufficient *a.* SEE SELF-RELIANT

sell v. deal, trade, market, wholesale, retail, peddle, vend, offer for sale, unload, auction, barter, hustle. ANT. *buy, purchase.*

seller n. dealer, trader, marketer, wholesaler, retailer, peddler, vendor, merchant, auctioneer, hustler, broker, agent.

sell out v. betray, double-cross, *stab in the back, sell one's soul, do anything for money.

SEMANTICS n. [suh MAN tiks] dealing with language and the meanings of words, phrases, etc. *They were no longer arguing over hard issues, but semantics.* SYN. meanings, semiotics, lexicology, lexicography, linguistics, interpretations, connotations.

semblance n. appearance, look, aspect, air, aura, resemblance, bearing, show, face, facade, image.

semen n. seminal fluid, sperm.

semester n. term, period, interval, session, half-year.

SEMINAL a. [SEM uh nul] the first, originating or developmentally important, basic. *Little Richard is regarded as a seminal rock and roll singer.* SYN. first, originating, germinal, innovative, developmental, first of its kind, fresh, pioneering, trailblazing.

seminar n. group discussion, workshop, panel discussion, forum, conference, symposium, meeting, review.

send v. transport, transmit, deliver, transfer, convey, direct, remit, mail, post, ship, relay, wire, shoot, propel, throw, fire off, broadcast. ANT. *receive, get.*

send packing v. show the door, dismiss, discharge, give walking papers.

senile a. disoriented, mentally deficient, forgetful, demented, feebleminded, *slipping, confused, in one's dotage, deteriorating. ANT. *sharp, lucid, clear-thinking.*

senior n. elder, senior citizen, retiree, matriarch, patriarch, grandmother, grandfather, firstborn, doyen, superior, dean. ANT. *junior, inferior, subordinate.*

senior a. ranking, superior, chief, preeminent, elder, older, higher, veteran. ANT. *junior, inferior, lesser.*

sensation n. **1.** FEELING sense, sensitivity, perception, reaction, response, sound, sight, smell, pain, tingle, itch. **2.** EXCITEMENT public interest, fuss, uproar, hit, wonder, phenomenon. ANT. *1. insentientness, anesthesia. 2. apathy, indifference, *hardly a ripple.*

WORD FIND

disorder causing confused sensations, as sight for sound: synesthesia

extreme sensitivity: hyperesthesia

sensational a. **1.** EXCELLENT exceptional, good, superb, *out of this world, fantastic, fabulous, outstanding, extraordinary, marvelous, terrific, wonderful. **2.** STARTLING shocking, thrilling, exciting, *mind-blowing, spine-tingling, hair-raising, breathtaking, electrifying, staggering. **3.** EXAGGERATED melodramatic, lurid, *tabloid, cheap, *yellow, scandalous. ANT. *1. awful, lousy, second-rate. 2. boring, dull. 3. understated, dry.*

sensationalism n. exaggeration, melodrama, luridness, *tabloid journalism, *keyhole journalism, *yellow journalism, scandal, shock reporting.

sense n. **1.** SENSATION feeling, perception, sensitivity, responsiveness, stimulus reception, sight, hearing, smell, taste, touch. **2.** AWARENESS perception, realization, impression, feeling, consciousness, premonition. **3.** INTELLIGENCE wisdom, judgment, reason, common sense, logic, brains, *smarts, sharpness, understanding, *savvy, intuition. **4.** MEANING substance, point, content, gist, interpretation, thrust, essence, core, significance, definition.

sense v. feel, perceive, pick up, get the impression, have a feeling, discern, *catch some vibes, notice, *have a gut feeling, suspect.

senseless a. nonsensical, stupid, brainless, idiotic, foolish, insane, crazy, *nuts, mindless, *wacky, ludicrous, ridiculous, irrational. ANT. *sensible, rational, smart.*

sensibility n. ability to feel, sensitivity, sentience, responsiveness, receptivity, perception, perceptiveness.

sensible a. smart, intelligent, judicious, prudent, rational, logical, sober, sound, level-headed, realistic, sane, reasonable, down-to-earth. ANT. *senseless, nonsensical, stupid.*

sensitive a. **1.** IMPRESSIONABLE responsive, acute, keen, receptive, reactive, conscious, feeling, sentient, sympathetic. **2.** EASILY HURT easily offended, touchy, hypersensitive, testy, thin-skinned, ticklish, irritable. **3.** SORE tender, painful, hurting, raw. **4.** SYMPATHETIC compassionate, understanding, empathetic, enlightened. considerate. ANT. *1. insentient, unresponsive. 2. thick-skinned. 3. calloused, numb. 4. insensitive, inconsiderate, dense.*

sensitivity n. **1.** RESPONSIVENESS feeling, sense, receptiveness, acuteness, keenness. **2.** SYMPATHY understanding, compassion, empathy, enlightenment, consideration. ANT. *1.*

unresponsiveness, insentience. 2. *insensitivity, lack of understanding.*

sensual *a.* physical, of the body, bodily, fleshly, voluptuous, sexual, sensuous, carnal, lustful, erotic, lascivious, libidinous, *horny, licentious, lewd. ANT. *spiritual, cerebral, of the mind.*

sensuous *a.* stimulating, sensory, luxurious, pleasurable, pleasant to the touch, pleasant to the eye, rich, sumptuous, voluptuous.

sentence *n.* judgment, decision, punishment, penalty, time, prison term, *stretch up the river, doom.

sentence *v.* judge, rule, punish, penalize, give a prison term, condemn, term, doom, mete out, imprison, *send up the river, *throw the book at.

sententious *a.* 1. CONCISE short, pithy, succinct. 2. APHORISTIC grandiloquent, bombastic, pompous, moralizing, trite. ANT. *1. wordy, long-winded. 2. sensible, meaningful.*

sentient *a.* feeling, sensitive, conscious, perceptive, receptive, responsive. ANT. *insensient, unfeeling.*

sentiment *n.* 1. FEELINGS attitude, opinion, thought, leaning, idea, way of thinking, view, emotion, judgment. 2. SENTIMENTALITY romanticism, *mushiness, feeling, tenderness, emotion, *hearts and flowers. "Jam without bread."—Sydney Harris. "The poetry of the imagination."—Alphonse Lamartine.

sentimental *a.* tender, romantic, maudlin, mawkish, *mushy, emotional, softhearted, misty-eyed, weepy, nostalgic, *saccharine, *corny, *schmaltzy, *gushy, sloppy. "Having a good cry for its own sake."—Myron Schueller. ANT. *unfeeling, cold, hard, stony.*

sentimentality *n.* mawkishness, *mush, softheartedness, weepiness, nostalgia, *corniness, *schmaltz, *gush, sloppiness. "Ostentatious parading of excessive and spurious emotion."—James Baldwin.

sentinel *n.* sentry, guard, watch, lookout, picket, patrol, scout.

sentry *n.* SEE SENTINEL

separate *v.* remove, break off, divide, disconnect, detach, split, sever, divorce, take apart, single out, segregate, secede, isolate. ANT. *connect, attach, join, unite.*

separate *a.* unconnected, detached, disconnected, unattached, apart, divided, single, individual, distinct, sole, lone, independent, autonomous. ANT. *connected, attached, together, joined.*

separation *n.* division, detachment, disconnection, parting, removal, breakup, split, divorce, segregation, dissassociation, rift, secession. ANT. *union, connection, attachment.*

septic *a.* infective, putrid, putrified, rotting, contaminated. ANT. *antiseptic, sterile.*

sepulcher *n.* vault, grave, tomb, mausoleum, crypt, resting place, catacomb. SEE CEMETERY

SEPULCHRAL *a.* [suh PUL krul] gloomy, dark, dismal, as of the grave. *A sepulchral silence fell over the proceedings.* SYN. gloomy, dark, dismal, black, like the grave, funereal, deathly, morbid, mournful, dreary, heavy, Stygian. ANT. *bright, sunny, cheerful.*

sequel *n.* part two, follow-up, continuation, consequence, aftermath, outcome, epilogue, *spin-off, offshoot.

sequence *n.* series, order, succession, lineup, progression, array, cycle, train, course, string, round.

SEQUESTER *v.* [si KWEST ur] to set apart or isolate, separate. *The jury will be sequestered during the trial.* SYN. set apart, separate, isolate, seclude, hide away, secrete, remove oneself, withdraw, confine, quarantine.

SERENDIPITY *n.* [SER un DIP uh tee] accidental good fortune. *We located the treasure by pure serendipity.* SYN. good fortune, fortuity, chance, *Lady Luck, *wheel of fortune, luck, happy chance, happenstance, *toss of the dice, *fluke. ANT. *design, plan.*

serene *a.* 1. PEACEFUL tranquil, placid, calm, untroubled, quiet, sedate, halcyon, undisturbed, still, composed. 2. CLEAR unclouded, bright, fair, sunny. ANT. *1. wild, violent, agitated. 2. stormy, cloudy.*

serenity *n.* peace, peacefulness, tranquility, placidity, calm, quiet, stillness, composure, coolness, relaxation, imperturbability. ANT. *wildness, violence, agitation.*

serf *n.* slave, villein, vassal.

serial *a.* in series, successive, continuing, consecutive, ongoing, sequential, progressive. ANT. *single, lone.*

series *n.* chain, string, order, succession, array, procession, sequence, round, line, cycle, run.

serious *a.* 1. SOMBER earnest, grave, sober, *meaning business, unsmiling, humorless, dour, stern, stony-faced, *no-nonsense, grim, staid. 2. WEIGHTY important, crucial, *heavy, no laughing matter, consequential, life-and-death, momentous, grave, grim, critical, dangerous. 3. SINCERE earnest, honest. ANT. *1. silly, foolish, lighthearted. 2. trivial, trifling, silly, inconsequential. 3. kidding.*

sermon *n.* lecture, speech, preaching, lesson, moralizing, homily, exhortation, *fire and brimstone, discourse, exemplum.

serpent *n.* viper. SEE SNAKE

serpentine *a.* winding, twisting, coiled, snaking, tortuous, meandering, sinuous, slinky, labyrinthine. ANT. *straight, direct.*

serrated *a.* saw-toothed, jagged, serrulated, notched, crenelated. ANT. *smooth.*

servant *n.* domestic, butler, maid, housekeeper, cook, help, valet, chauffeur, attendant, menial, slave, *guy/gal Friday.

serve *v.* **1.** WAIT ON provide, tend to, *be at one's beck and call, waitress, cater, deliver, minister to, help, assist, *be a gopher. **2.** BE OBEDIENT obey, respect, honor, be dutiful to. **3.** WORK perform, carry out, do one's duties. **4.** PASS spend, do. **5.** FUNCTION be used, perform for.

service *n.* **1.** ASSISTANCE work, help, labor, employment, duty, use, benefit. **2.** ARMED FORCES military, army, navy, marines, air force, active duty. **3.** WAITING ON catering, waitressing, *gophering, serving, accommodation. **4.** CHURCH FUNCTION ceremony, worship, sermon, observance, prayer meeting. **5.** MAINTENANCE repair, upkeep, servicing.

service *v.* repair, maintain, fix, tune up, overhaul, restore.

serviceable *a.* usable, ready, operative, functional, workable, durable, utile. ANT. *inoperable, unworkable.*

SERVILE *a.* [SUR vile] submissive or subservient, like a servant or slave. *He smiled and nodded in the proper servile manner.* SYN. submissive, subservient, yielding, slavish, obsequious, fawning, groveling, deferential, cringing, sycophantic, toadying. ANT. *rebellious, defiant, domineering.*

servitude *n.* slavery, bondage, enslavement, indenture, serfdom, service, yoke, subjugation, serfdom. ANT. *freedom, liberty.*

session *n.* **1.** MEETING assembly, discussion, hearing, conference, council, legislative session, convention. **2.** TERM period, semester, course.

set *n.* **1.** OUTFIT collection, assemblage, array, assortment, arrangement, pair, group, series. **2.** THEATRICAL SETTING scenery, backdrop, props. **3.** GROUP clique, circle, class, pack, crowd, gang, clan, fraternity.

set *v.* **1.** PLACE position, put, stick, lay, plant, plop, situate, locate, rest, deposit, station, install, insert, mount. **2.** SETTLE UPON agree

on, determine, decide, arrange, prearrange, fix, schedule, specify, establish, designate. **3.** ADJUST fix, position, ready. **4.** HARDEN stiffen, solidify, thicken, congeal. ANT. *1. pick up, remove, lift. 4. soften, loosen, liquefy.*

set *a.* **1.** SETTLED agreed on, determined, decided, arranged, prearranged, fixed, scheduled, specified, ordained, ready. **2.** USUAL routine, normal, conventional, fixed, customary, regular. **3.** HARDENED fixed, firm, rigid, stiff, locked, positioned, secured, rooted. ANT. *1. unsettled, undecided. 2. different, unconventional. 3. soft, loose.*

setback *n.* reversal, disappointment, *stumbling block, defeat, blow, loss, trouble, relapse, upset, check, regression, *one step forward and two steps back, *square one. ANT. *advance, progress, leap forward.*

setting *n.* scene, scenery, backdrop, environment, surroundings, locale, site, milieu, mise-en-scène, time, place, period.

settle *v.* **1.** PUT IN ORDER arrange, fix, straighten out, resolve, rectify, *iron out, satisfy, clear, end. **2.** SIT sink, sag, droop, plant oneself, lay, repose. **3.** TAKE UP RESIDENCE move to, locate, colonize, populate, set up housekeeping, reside, come to roost, *put down roots, inhabit. **4.** SINK clear out, clarify, precipitate. **5.** RELAX calm, quiet, soothe, tranquilize, compose, lull, sedate. **6.** MEDIATE arbitrate, resolve, negotiate, compromise. ANT. *1. mess up, confuse. 2. rise. 3. pull up roots, *fly the coop, leave. 5. agitate, stress, *put on edge. 6. stir up, unsettle.*

settlement *n.* **1.** COMMUNITY colony, village, outpost, peopling. **2.** AGREEMENT arrangement, resolution, compromise, negotiation, arbitration, disposition. **3.** PAYMENT OF DEBT satisfaction, clearance, liquidation.

settler *n.* colonist, homesteader, frontiersman, pioneer, squatter, *sooner.

settlings *n.* dregs, sediment, lees.

set-to *n.* fight, fistfight, struggle. SEE FIGHT

setup *n.* arrangement, configuration, structure, system, organization, format, plan.

set up *v.* **1.** CONSTRUCT erect, raise, build, put together, assemble. **2.** CREATE start, originate, organize, establish, found, institute. ANT. *1. tear down, disassemble, dismantle, raze. 2. terminate, end.*

sever *v.* **1.** CUT cleave, split, divide, separate, cut in two, slice, rend, chop off. **2.** DISSOCIATE break off, separate, cut off, split up, discontinue, drop, divorce, disband. ANT. *1. join, attach. 2. join, unite, reunite.*

several *a.* **1.** A LOT a number, quite a few, a handful, considerable, numerous, some. **2.** SEPARATE distinct, individual, single, respective, particular, personal. ANT. *1. none, few. 2. joint.*

severe *a.* **1.** HARSH stern, strict, hard, *hard-nosed, uncompromising, unsparing, rigid, unfeeling, merciless, pitiless. **2.** SERIOUS grave, forbidding, stern, unsmiling, grim, austere, cold, stony. **3.** GRIEVOUS serious, acute, violent, nasty, critical, dire, life-threatening, bad, dangerous, fierce, intense, extreme. **4.** PLAIN unornamented, spare, bare, stark, austere, undecorated. ANT. *1. softhearted, easy, compassionate. 2. light-hearted, smiling, jovial. 3. mild, minor, trivial. 4. ornate, rococo, luxurious.*

sew *v.* stitch, mend, tailor, seam, hem, embroider.

sewage *n.* waste, discharge, runoff, foul water, pollution.

sex *n.* **1.** GENDER **2.** COPULATION intercourse, coitus, mating, marital relations, fornication, *making love, *making out, *birds and the bees, reproduction, procreation, *facts of life, *roll in the hay, *sleeping with someone. "The formula by which one and one makes three."—Leonard Levinson. "An emotion in motion."—Mae West. "An appetite placed in humans to insure breeding."—Jonathan Benter. "The poor man's polo."—Clifford Odets.

WORD FIND

abstinence: celibacy

anal or oral sex on a male: sodomy

aphrodisiac from beetle juice, alleged: Spanish fly

assault: molestation, rape

baby, pleasure derived by acting like a helpless: infantilism

condom, slang for having sex without a: riding bareback

counselor: sex therapist, sex surrogate

dominant woman as sexual pleasurer: dominatrix

ejaculation period when no new ejaculation is possible, post-: refractory period

ejaculation, removal of penis from vagina before: coitus interruptus

erection, medical condition of permanent: priapism

erection drug aid: Viagra™

expose oneself: flash

exposes himself, one who: flasher

family member, sex with: incest

feces, pleasure from: coprophilia

find a partner and have sex: score

forbidden: taboo

Freudian notion of daughter's attraction to father, hostility toward mother: Electra Complex

frustration in males due to lack of ejaculation, severe sexual: blue balls

group sex: ménage à tois, orgy, threesome, three-way, gang bang, daisy chain

hole through which two males participate: glory hole

hormone, sex drive: testosterone

hymen, slang for: cherry

impotence: erectile dysfunction

insatiable female: nymphomaniac

insatiable desire in females: nymphomania

kissing of another's entire body as a prelude to: around the world

lesbian sex, referring to: Sapphic

male or female, enjoys sex with: bisexual

murder for sexual pleasure, film showing real: snuff film

nocturnal emission of semen: wet dream

one partner for life, sex with: monogamy

oral sex position, dual: 69

orgasms, exercises to improve: kegel exercises

orgasms, incapable of: anorgasmic

overpowering behavior for pleasure, giving in to another's: submission

overpowering behavior that brings pleasure: dominance

own sex, physically attracted to one's: homosexual; lesbian; gay

opposite sex, attracted only to: heterosexual

partners, interested in having sex with multiple: polyamorous

perversion or fetish, any: paraphilia

pleasure derived from viewing erotic photos: scopophilia

pornography, explicit: hardcore

pornography showing naked models or limited sex acts: softcore

potency, sexual: virility

scent attractant, hormonal: pheremones

sheath to protect against impregnating female, male's: condom, rubber

standard, woman-on-back position: missionary position

stimulation: titillation

strangling or suffocating oneself for pleasure: autoerotic strangulation, sexual hanging, autoerotic asphyxia

text, ancient Indian sex: Kama Sutra

tiring of sex, never: insatiable
urinating on partner, sex act of: golden shower
urine, pleasure from drinking of: urolagnia
vaginal pleasure spot: G-spot (Granfenberg Spot)
virgin, to have sex with a: deflower
warm, relaxed feeling after orgasm: afterglow
warm-up activities: foreplay
watches others for pleasure, secretly: peeping Tom, voyeur
whipping, pleasure: flagellation

sex appeal *n.* sexiness, charm, erotic charm, *oomph, magnetism, charisma, curvaceousness, virility, allure, *come-hither look.

sexism *n.* discrimination, prejudice, chauvinism, sex bias.

sexless *a.* **1.** ASEXUAL neuter. **2.** HAVING NO SEX DRIVE frigid, anaphrodisic. ANT. *1. male, female. 2. *horny, hot, nymphomaniacal, satyriasic.*

sexual *a.* reproductive, procreative, generative, coital, carnal, erotic, *hot, *horny, lustful. ANT. *chaste, platonic.*

sexual assault *n.* rape, molestation, date rape, ravishment, violation, *gang bang.

sexual harassment *n.* impropriety, flirtation, obscenity, pressure, sexual advances, inappropriate behavior, abuse of power, abuse of office, unprofessional behavior, misconduct, overtures, suggestive comments, exploitation, teasing, indiscreet advances, intimidation, blackmail.

sexually transmitted diseases *n.* STD, venereal disease, gonorrhea, syphilis, HIV, herpes, chancroid, chlamydia, *clap, crabs, yeast infection.

sexy *a.* *hot, *foxy, charming, alluring, enticing, seductive, magnetic, charismatic, erotic, sensual, attractive, curvaceous, voluptuous, titillating, flirtatious, desirable, irresistible. ANT. *repellant, repulsive, *gross, disgusting.*

shabby *a.* **1.** DETERIORATED run down, ragged, dilapidated, poor, threadbare, mangy, grungy, ragged, scraggly, scruffy, ratty, seedy. **2.** LOUSY disgraceful, poor, mean, shameful, terrible, bad, miserable, despicable, cheap, shoddy. ANT. *1. new, fresh, sparkling. 2. excellent, good.*

shack *n.* shanty, hut, shed, cabin, hovel, shelter.

shackle *n.* restraint, handcuff, manacle, fetter, irons, chain, hobble, leg-iron.

shackle *v.* restrain, fetter, handcuff, *cuff, manacle, chain, hobble, tie. ANT. *free, loose, release.*

shade *n.* **1.** DARKNESS shadows, cover, dimness, umbra, penumbra. **2.** HUE tone, color, tint, gradation. **3.** BLIND visor, shutter, drape, curtain, screen. **4.** SLIGHT DIFFERENCE hint, trace, touch, suggestion, tiny degree, nuance.

shade *v.* darken, dim, cover, veil, shroud, mask, protect, hide, obscure, blacken.

shadow *n.* **1.** DARKNESS dimness, shade, gloom, cover, umbra, penumbra, silhouette. **2.** TRACE hint, suggestion, breath.

shadow *v.* follow, trail, tail, track, watch.

shady *a.* **1.** SHADOWY dark, cool, covered, shaded. **2.** DISREPUTABLE crooked, questionable, devious, underhanded, dishonest, suspect, slippery, fishy. ANT. *1. sunny, bright. 2. reputable, honest, honorable.*

shaggy *a.* hairy, woolly, furry, hirsute, unkempt, ungroomed, untrimmed, uncombed, snarled, tangled. ANT. *neat, trimmed, bald.*

shake *v.* **1.** VIBRATE rock, tremble, quiver, quake, jog, wobble, shiver, convulse, wiggle, tremble, shudder, jounce, rattle, flutter. **2.** MIX jumble, combine, churn. **3.** UNNERVE upset, discompose, disturb, disconcert, distress, rattle, unsettle, disquiet, daze. ANT. *1. stabilize. 3. calm, soothe, put one's mind at ease.*

shaky *a.* **1.** UNSTABLE unsteady, wobbly, rickety, precarious, loose, wiggly, jerry-built, teetering, unreliable. **2.** NERVOUS quivering, tremulous, shivering, jittery, trembling, quaking. **3.** QUESTIONABLE doubtful, uncertain, dubious, speculative, unreliable, undependable, suspect. ANT. *1. stable, secure, steady. 2. calm, relaxed. 3. certain, sure.*

shallow *a.* superficial, surface, lacking depth, skin-deep, slight, weak, lacking character, meaningless, empty, frivolous. ANT. *deep, profound, in-depth.*

sham *n.* counterfeit, fake, imitation, fraud, phony, forgery, humbug, hoax, deception, pretense. ANT. *the genuine article, *the real McCoy.

sham *a.* counterfeit, false, fake, pretended, imitation, fraudulent, *bogus, phony, simulated, artificial, ersatz, spurious. ANT. *genuine, real, authentic.*

shaman *n.* priest, medicine man.

shambles *n.* mess, disorder, destruction, chaos, disaster area, disarray, pigsty, wreck, devastation, *bomb crater.

shame *n.* disgrace, dishonor, humiliation, embarrassment, loss of face, chagrin, stigma, scandal, infamy, degradation, ill-repute, ignominy, pain, mortification, guilt, remorse. ANT. *pride, self-respect.*

shame *v.* disgrace, dishonor, humiliate, embarrass, degrade, ridicule, mortify, fill with guilt, *take down a notch, debase, scandalize, *take the wind out of one's sails. ANT. *fill with pride, compliment, honor.*

shamefaced *a.* embarrassed, ashamed, disgraced, mortified, red-faced, blushing, hangdog, crestfallen, chagrined, abashed. ANT. *proud.*

shameful *a.* disgraceful, dishonorable, humiliating, embarrassing, mortifying, odious, scandalous, infamous, ignominious, wicked, atrocious, contemptible, despicable, dastardly. ANT. *honorable, noble, good.*

shameless *a.* conscienceless, unprincipled, immodest, wicked, antisocial, abandoned, unblushing, brazen, bold, outrageous, impudent, disgraceful. ANT. *ashamed, modest, principled.*

shanghai *v.* abduct. SEE KIDNAP

Shangri-la *n.* utopia, paradise, heaven on earth, Xanadu, Eden.

shanty *n.* shack, hovel, hut, cabin, hutch.

shantytown *n.* slum, ghetto, skid row.

shape *n.* 1. FORM figure, outline, configuration, profile, contour, conformation, structure, lines, mold, frame, cut, pattern. 2. STATE health, fitness, order, condition, trim, fettle.

shapeless *a.* formless, amorphous, irregular, nebulous, indefinite, ill-defined, asymmetrical, vague, misshapen. ANT. *well-defined, formed, symmetrical.*

shapely *a.* well-proportioned, fit, toned, curvaceous, well-rounded, *wasp-waisted, *hourglass, curvy, *built, *stacked, statuesque, svelte. ANT. *fat, roly-poly, obese, misshapen.*

share *n.* allotment, percent, apportionment, portion, allowance, cut, ration, *piece of the pie, quota, due, parcel, lot.

share *v.* split between one another, *divvy up, divide, allot, allocate, apportion, dole out, ration, mete out, *go Dutch, *give and take. ANT. *monopolize, *hog.*

shark *n.* 1. MARINE ANIMAL fish, predator, *eating machine, man-eater, thresher, great white shark, tiger shark, hammerhead, dogfish, basking shark. 2. SWINDLER cheat, *con man, chiseler, *rip-off artist, crook, *flimflam man. 3. EXPERT *crackerjack, *ace, professional, *hotshot.

sharp *a.* 1. HONED fine-edged, cutting, razor-sharp, knife-edge, acute, keen-edged, piercing, pointed, pronged, barbed, peaked. 2. ABRUPT sudden, quick, rapid, precipitous, extreme. 3. CLEAR clearly defined, distinct, crisp, in focus. 4. SMART quick, acute, perceptive, bright, astute, *on the ball, attentive, keen, discerning, alert, canny, shrewd, clever, sensitive. 5. CRAFTY underhanded, deceitful, cunning, designing, shrewd, wily, conniving. 6. SEVERE intense, acute, violent, fierce, stabbing, piercing, biting. 7. *Sl.* WELL-DRESSED well-groomed, chic, stylish, dapper, debonair, swank, *snappy. ANT. *1. dull, blunted. 2. gradual, slow. 3. hazy, ill-defined. 4. stupid, slow, dense. 5. honest, artless. 6. mild, gentle, subtle. 7. disheveled, frumpy, sloppy.*

sharpen *v.* hone, edge, whet, strop, file, grind, taper. ANT. *blunt, dull, round off.*

sharper *n.* swindler, cheat, *con artist, *rip-off artist, crook.

sharp-tongued *a.* acid-tongued, critical, vitriolic, rapier-tongued, biting, cutting, nasty, negative, mean, blunt, frank. ANT. *diplomatic, nice, mealy-mouthed.*

sharp-witted *a.* saber-witted, rapier-witted, quick-witted, keen, acute, intelligent, astute, *on the ball, bright, smart, alert. ANT. *dull, slow, stupid, bovine.*

shatter *v.* 1. BREAK burst, explode, smash, crack, blast, break into a million pieces, fracture, split, pop, implode. 2. DESTROY wreck, devastate, crush, demolish, ruin, *break one's heart.

shave *v.* cut, scrape, graze, trim, shear, crop, clip, mow.

shawl *n.* wrap, covering, manta.

sheaf *n.* bundle, pile, bale, packet, package, collection.

shear *v.* cut, shave, clip, trim, remove, crop, snip, scissor, mow.

sheath *n.* case, scabbard, covering, receptacle, envelope, holder, casing, wrapper, sleeve, membrane.

shed *n.* shack, shanty, hut, lean-to, outbuilding, shelter, hutch, outhouse, storage building, workshop, hangar.

shed *v.* throw off, cast off, drop, discard, slough off, molt, peel, defoliate, exude, discharge, give off, emit, pour forth, radiate, diffuse.

sheen *n.* shine, brightness, luster, brilliance, gleam, glossiness, gloss, glimmer, dazzle, sparkle, burnish, shimmer.

sheep *n.* ram, ewe, lamb, ruminant, ungulate, Merino, Cheviot, Cotswold, Lincoln.

WORD FIND
caretaker: shepherd
cleaning solution: sheep-dip
cry: bleat, baa, blat
dog: shepherd, collie, shelty
flock: fold
leader: bellwether
meat: mutton
sexual period: rut, heat
wool: fleece, karakul

sheepish *a.* embarrassed, chagrined, ashamed, red-faced, blushing, shamefaced, bashful, mortified. ANT. *proud, bold, puffed up.*

sheer *a.* **1.** THIN diaphanous, see-through, gossamer, transparent, gauzy, airy, delicate, revealing. **2.** STEEP perpendicular, precipitous, vertical, abrupt. **3.** ABSOLUTE utter, complete, outright, out-and-out, pure, unadulterated, unqualified, downright. ANT. *1. opaque, thick, heavy. 2. horizontal. 3. qualified, partial, limited.*

sheet *n.* **1.** COATING, PIECE coat, layer, film, blanket, ply, leaf. **2.** LINEN bed clothing.

shelf *n.* **1.** COUNTER bracket, cupboard, mantle, bookcase. **2.** LEDGE overhang, outcropping, projection, ridge, reef.

shell *n.* **1.** MARINE ANIMAL CASING conch, mollusk, mussel shell, clamshell, periwinkle, triton, oyster, nautilus, baby bonnet, mottled Venus, scallop. **2.** CARAPACE casing, shield, defense. **3.** HULL casing, husk, pod, husk, sheath, jacket, covering. **4.** BOMB projectile, missile, shot, mortar, ball, shrapnel.

shell *v.* **1.** SHUCK husk, peel, open. **2.** BOMBARD bomb, barrage, fire upon, cannonade, strafe.

shellac *n.* varnish, resin.

shellac *v. Sl.* beat, defeat, whip, *whoop, *kick butt.

shellacking *n. Sl.* beating, whipping, flogging.

shelter *n.* protection, safe haven, refuge, asylum, *roof over one's head, sanctuary, retreat, cover, hideout, hole, *port in a storm, harbor.

shelter *v.* protect, shield, provide a roof over one's head, provide safe haven, give refuge, give asylum, give sanctuary, cover, harbor, house, hide.

shelve *v.* put aside, defer, postpone, *put on ice, *put on the back burner, drop, dismiss, scrub.

shenanigans *n.* mischief, nonsense, horseplay, pranks, trickery, *monkey-business, *hanky-panky, sport.

shepherd *v.* herd, tend, lead, care for, look after, guard, protect, watch over, escort, secure.

shield *n.* defense, protection, guard, screen, safeguard, cover, aegis, armor, buffer.

shield *v.* defend, protect, cover, guard, screen, safeguard, arm, shelter, hide.

shift *n.* **1.** MOVE change, turn, switch, variation, reversal, about-face, alteration, modification, veering, conversion. **2.** WORK PERIOD turn, stint, first shift, second shift, third shift, *graveyard shift, watch.

shift *v.* move, change, turn, switch, vary, reverse, *do an about-face, alter, modify, veer, convert.

shiftless *a.* lazy, unmotivated, inefficient, slothful, unambitious, indolent, do-nothing, unenterprising, good-for-nothing. ANT. *industrious, enterprising, *go-getting.*

shifty *a.* deceitful, tricky, dishonest, evasive, devious, treacherous, conniving, artful, slick, slippery, sly, designing. ANT. *honest, trustworthy, virtuous.*

shilly-shally *v.* hesitate, wave, vacillate, hem and haw, fluctuate, *straddle the fence, hedge, be irresolute, seesaw, *blow hot and cold. ANT. *be resolved, decide, take a stand.*

shimmer *v.* **1.** FLASH glimmer, shine, gleam, glow, scintillate, glisten, glint, sparkle, glitter. **2.** WAVER ripple, shudder, sway.

shindig *n.* *wingding, entertainment, dance. SEE PARTY

shine *n.* brightness, radiance, luster, brilliance, glimmer, sheen, gloss, polish, glow. ANT. *dullness, film, patina, tarnish.*

shine *v.* **1.** LIGHT radiate, glare, blaze, gleam, luminesce, glow, glimmer, flash, illuminate, flicker, glint, sparkle, scintillate. **2.** POLISH burnish, finish, rub, buff, brighten. ANT. *2. dull, tarnish.*

shiny *a.* bright, brilliant, gleaming, glinting, glistening, glossy, polished, lustrous, sparkling, scintillating. ANT. *dull, tarnished.*

ship *n.* vessel, craft, watercraft, boat, *tub, *stormslogger, liner, cruise ship, freighter, ferry, transport. "Being in jail with a chance of being drowned."—Samuel Johnson.

WORD FIND
accommodations: first-class, cabin class, tourist class
ammunition compartment: magazine
anchor: bower, kedge, sea anchor, stream anchor
anchor chain winder, unwinder: capstan, windlass
anchoring and securing of vessel: mooring
anchor rope: hawser
bed: berth

boarding platform: gangplank
body: hull
bottom fin or backbone: keel
bottom, rounded portion of: bilges
cabin, small: cuddy
captain: skipper
cargo and debris lost from wrecked ship: flotsam and jetsam
cargo area: hold
cargo conveyance: cargo net
cargo, list of: manifest
chart and navigational instrument room: chart room
compass stand: binnacle
course change: tack
crane, hoisting apparatus: davit, derrick
crew member: hand, mate
crew quarters, structure holding: forecastle
deck: weather deck, poop deck
depth below waterline: draft, draught
drain: scupper
drive: navigate
flag: burgee, jack
floating dock that holds ship for repairs: dry dock
front: bow, prow, fore
hatch: booby hatch, scuttle, companionway
hospital: sick bay
kitchen: galley, caboose, cuddy
knot: 6,080 feet an hour
ladder: jack ladder, ratlines
lean: heel, list
left and right sides (respectively) looking from aft forward: port, starboard
living quarters: cabin
lookout perch: crow's nest
makeshift structure repairs: jury, juryrigging
meal compartment: mess room
merchant ship or fleet of same: argosy
middle: amidships
navigational house: pilot house
numbers of measurements on bow: draft marks
observation platform: bridge
officer: purser, bosun, skipper, captain
officers, upper-class passenger room: state-room
pitch/roll indicator: clinometer
plants and animals living on ship's bottom: foul
porthole cover: deadlight
position finder: Loran
protective shielding made of ropes, tires, etc.: fender, pudding
pulley system: block

pumps, motors, winches, collective term: auxiliaries
pump that removes water: bilge pump
rear: aft, stern, astern
rising and falling fore and aft with waves: pitching
rope-belaying fixture: cleats
rope, collective term: cordage
rope: lanyard
side-to-side motion: roll
steering apparatus: helm; rudder, tiller
steer: navigate, conn
structure above deck: superstructure
supplier: chandler
tarp securer of wood: batten
toilet: head
trailing whitewater: wake
vibrations of bow over waves: panting
waiter: cabin boy
wall, compartment: bulkhead
weight of sand, rocks, concrete or iron, stabilizing: ballast
weight of water, stabilizing: ballast tanks
width: beam
window: porthole
SEE BOAT, NAVY, SAIL, SAILOR

ship *v.* send, transport, mail, convey, forward, dispatch, consign.

shipshape *a.* orderly, trim, tidy. SEE NEAT

shirk *v.* neglect, evade, avoid, get around, dodge, *goldbrick, malinger, slack off, sidestep, *funk. ANT. *be responsible.*

shirker *n.* slacker, malingerer, *goldbricker, *deadbeat, *bum, dodger, truant, evader.

shirt *n.* article of clothing, blouse, pullover, jersey, button-down shirt, dress shirt, formal shirt, shirtwaist, T-shirt.

WORD FIND
African, loose, colorful pullover: dashiki
bare midriff, knotted in front: calypso
false front: dicky
floral print: Hawaiian, aloha shirt
loose-fitting smock: camise
necked, long-sleeved, high-: turtleneck
patch pockets, having large: safari shirt, bush shirt
plaid wool: Pendleton
ruffled: dandy
short-sleeved pullover: polo shirt
sleeveless hot-weather or basketball shirt: tanktop
striped sport pullover: rugby shirt
voluminous: blouson
western: cowboy shirt
SEE SWEATER

shiver n. shudder, trembling, quiver, quaver, quake, chill, goosebumps.

shiver v. shudder, tremble, quiver, shake, tremor, quaver, quake, have one's teeth chatter, catch a chill, *break out in goosebumps.

shoal n. **1.** SHALLOW sandbar, ridge, reef, ledge, bank, navigational hazard. **2.** MASS crowd, group, school, swarm, horde.

shock n. **1.** IMPACT blow, jolt, crash, collision, jounce, jar, concussion, bump, jerk, whiplash, brunt. **2.** SURPRISE trauma, thunderbolt, *bolt from the blue, *bombshell, *kick in the teeth, start, jolt, *eye-opener, stupefaction. **3.** TANGLED MASS bushy mass, mane, mop, tuft, thatch, *rat's nest. SEE HAIR

shock v. surprise, stagger, stupefy, traumatize, jolt, start, electrify, *shake up, *hit like a ton of bricks, *floor, stun, paralyze, *take one's breath away, astound, daze, horrify, *flabbergast.

shocking a. surprising, staggering, stupefying, traumatizing, jolting, startling, electrifying, *hitting like a ton of bricks, unexpected, *flooring, paralyzing, breathtaking, astounding, horrifying, revolting, appalling, disgusting, outrageous. ANT. *expected, anticipated, met with indifference.*

shoddy a. inferior, poor, second-rate, second-class, bad, *crappy, cheap, *tacky, *cheesy, *junky, shabby. ANT. *superior, first-rate, *top-drawer.*

shoe n. footwear, footgear, loafer, pump, sneaker, running shoe.

WORD FIND
backless, woman's: mule
back of shoe: cuff
ballet slipper: toe shoe
boat shoes made of canvas and nonskid soles: deck shoes
bottom of: sole
brown and white oxford: saddle shoe
child's: Mary Jane
Chinese, flat-heeled: Chinese
flap: tongue
fringe-tongued shoe with low heel: kiltie flat
high, ankle-supporting sneakers: *hightops, basketball shoes
high-heeled strapless: pump
high-heeled, strapped: slingback
Indian, leather: moccasin
infant: bootee
instep cover: vamp
lace hole: eyelet
loafer with front slot to hold penny: penny loafer

low-heeled, woman's: flats
low shoe laced over instep: oxford
maker: cordwainer
mender: cobbler
metal tag at end of shoelace: aglet
oxford with holes or perforations for decoration: wing-tip
put on, aid to: shoehorn
raised platform sole, shoe with: platform shoe
removing device: bootjack
rope-soled canvas shoe, sometimes laced up the ankle: espadrille
sandallike with wood or cork sole: clog
sandals: clog, flip-flops, Ganymede, gladiator, thongs
sole, narrow portion of: shank
sport traction shoe: cleats
toeless: open-toed shoe
walking shoe, laced: balmoral
white oxfords: white bucks
work shoe, heavy: brogan, steel-toed shoe
SEE BOOT

shoo interj. scram, scat, get out, go away.

shoot n. sprout, new growth, bud, stem, twig.

shoot v. **1.** FIRE discharge, pull the trigger, *pump full of lead, *blow away, gun down, blast, open fire, barrage, strafe, kill, *smoke. SEE MURDER **2.** THROW hurl, pitch, *chuck, fling, sling, propel, send, launch. **3.** MOVE QUICKLY fly, tear, dart, spring, bound, rocket, bolt, dash, race, whiz, speed, hurtle.

shooting star n. meteor, fireball, bolide, comet, meteorite.

shop n. **1.** STORE market, boutique, retail outlet, five-and-dime, emporium, mart, stall, *Mom and Pop operation. **2.** WORKSHOP studio, atelier.

shop v. buy, purchase, sample the merchandise, look for, market, window-shop, browse.

shopkeeper n. merchant, small businessman/woman, entrepreneur, retailer, trader, dealer, monger, peddler.

shoplift v. steal, pocket, make off with, snatch, filch, pilfer.

shopper n. customer, patron, browser, *shopaholic, bargain hunter.

shopping n. buying, purchasing, sampling the merchandise, marketing, window shopping, browsing.

shore n. beach, seaside, strand, coast, seaboard, waterfront, littoral, verge, brink. SEE BEACH

shore v. support, prop, stabilize, buttress, brace, reinforce, strengthen, hold up, underpin. ANT. *destabilize, weaken, loosen.*

short *a.* **1.** LITTLE of small stature, tiny, *pint-sized, wee, diminutive, *built like a fireplug, runty, dwarfish, *sawed-off, squat, Lilliputian. **2.** BRIEF abbreviated, short-lived, momentary, to the point, fleeting, condensed, compressed, succinct. **3.** LACKING low, wanting, insufficient, tight, short-handed, scant, scarce, sparse, deficient, missing. **4.** CURT abrupt, rude, brief, terse, discourteous, brusque, gruff. ANT. *1. tall, towering, gigantic. 2. long, long-winded, eternal. 3. sufficient, full, well-supplied. 4. polite, courteous, cordial.*

shortage *n.* shortfall, deficit, deficiency, dearth, paucity, lack, scarcity, insufficiency, want, famine. ANT. *glut, surplus, abundance.*

shortchange *v.* *gyp, rook, *pull a fast one. SEE CHEAT

shortcoming *n.* imperfection, fault, drawback, defect, failing, weakness, flaw, peccadillo, inadequacy, liability. ANT. *strength, strong point, virtue.*

short cut *n.* beeline, direct route.

shorten *v.* reduce, lessen, cut, abbreviate, condense, diminish, clip, trim, slash, *boil down, edit, contract, shrink, prune. ANT. *lengthen, stretch, prolong.*

shortfall *n.* deficit, deficiency. SEE SHORTAGE

short-lived *a.* fleeting, momentary, ephemeral, transient, transitory, brief, *over in a heartbeat, *over in the wink of an eye, temporary, quick, passing. ANT. *long-lasting, immortal, permanent, neverending.*

shortly *adv.* soon, momentarily, any minute now, any second now, presently, quickly, directly, before you know it. ANT. *eventually, later.*

shortsighted *a.* **1.** NEARSIGHTED myopic, *blind as a bat, *blind as a mole, *blind as a post, half-blind, *squinty-eyed. **2.** NOT CONSIDERING THE FUTURE unthinking, stupid, myopic, blind, imprudent, rash, reckless, incautious, *unable to see beyond the end of one's nose, having no foresight. ANT. *1. farsighted, eagle-eyed. 2. farsighted, thoughtful.*

short-tempered *a.* short-fused, temperamental, touchy, irritable, grouchy, testy, crabby, cantankerous, waspish, cranky, hot-tempered, fiery. ANT. *long-fused, mild-mannered, easygoing, passive.*

shot *n.* **1.** DISCHARGE firing, blast, detonation, crack. **2.** BULLET buckshot, birdshot, slug, ball, pellet, BB. **3.** MARKSMAN. **4.** THROW toss, pitch. **5.** TRY attempt, turn, effort, chance, go, *crack, *stab, *the old college try. **6.** INJECTION innoculation.

shoulder *v.* carry, pack, bear, push, shove.

shout *n.* yell, holler, bellow, roar, cry, scream, exclamation, howl, whoop, shriek, outcry. ANT. *whisper, murmur, mumble.*

shout *v.* yell, holler, bellow, roar, cry, scream, exclaim, howl, whoop, vociferate, fulminate, thunder, shriek, raise one's voice, cry out. ANT. *whisper, murmur, mumble.*

shove *n.* push, drive, thrust, elbow, jostle, shoulder, press, nudge.

shove *v.* push, drive, thrust, elbow, jostle, *bulldoze, shoulder, strongarm, muscle, *bull, press, propel, move, nudge.

shovel *n.* spade, scoop, implement, *digger, posthole digger, dredge.

shovel *v.* dig, excavate, spade, scoop.

show *n.* **1.** ENTERTAINMENT exhibition, extravaganza, stage production, spectacle, exposition, program, parade, play, theatrical performance, burlesque, musical, revue, movie, drama, comedy, circus. **2.** DEMONSTRATION manifestation, exhibition, display, presentation. **3.** PRETENSE act, facade, front, affectation, pose, semblance, *Oscar performance.

show *v.* **1.** EXHIBIT demonstrate, display, present, reveal, expose, unveil, evince, produce, bare, trot out for inspection. **2.** APPEAR be visible, manifest. **3.** EXPLAIN instruct, demonstrate, simplify, define, *walk through, *run through, clarify. **4.** GUIDE conduct, direct, usher, point out. ANT. *1. hide, conceal. 2. cover up. 3. mystify, confuse.*

show business *n.* Hollywood, theater, entertainment industry, motion picture industry.

showdown *n.* clash, confrontation, climax, face-off, turning point, *moment of truth, duel.

shower *n.* rainfall, downpour, cloudburst, drizzle, sleet, hail, sprinkle, mist, spit, deluge, *gully washer.

shower *v.* **1.** RAIN spray, sprinkle, drizzle, downpour, drizzle, sleet, spit. **2.** LAVISH pour forth, heap.

showoff *n.* *hot dog, braggart, swaggerer, exhibitionist, peacock, *showboat, *grandstander, braggadocio, blowhard.

show off *v.* *hotdog, brag, swagger, strut, peacock, *showboat, *grandstand, flaunt, *strut one's stuff.

showpiece *n.* example, *jewel in the crown, masterpiece, work of art, exceptional piece.

showy *a.* flashy, ostentatious, gaudy, loud, flamboyant, garish, tawdry, cheap. ANT. *understated, dull, plain.*

shred *n.* piece, fragment, strip, scrap, ribbon, sliver, snippet, band, tatter, bit.

shred *v.* rip, cut, tear, fragment, strip, cut to ribbons, snip, tatter, fray.

shrew *n.* nag, *witch, *battle-ax, henpecker, ogress, virago, spitfire, harridan, vixen.

shrewd *a.* **1.** SMART clever, astute, sharp, *savvy, sagacious, wise, keen, intelligent, discerning. **2.** ARTFUL cunning, wily, cagey, sly, crafty, scheming. ANT. *1. stupid, dense, ignorant, naive. 2. artless, innocent, naive.*

shriek *n.* scream, screech, cry, piercing cry, squeal, yell, shout, wail, shrill, howl.

shriek *v.* scream, screech, cry, squeal, yell, shout, wail, howl.

shrill *a.* high-toned, high-pitched, piercing, ear-piercing, ear-shattering, thin, sharp, intense, piping, deafening, blaring. ANT. *low, quiet.* SEE LOUD

shrimp *n.* runt, pipsqueak, midget. SEE DWARF

shrine *n.* tabernacle, altar, reliquary, temple, church, chapel, mausoleum, sanctuary, holy place, monument, memorial.

shrink *v.* **1.** DIMINISH lessen, dwindle, contract, shrivel, compress, deflate, wither, shorten. **2.** DRAW BACK cower, cringe, recoil, wince, flinch, retreat. ANT. *1. grow, inflate, expand. 2. confront, face.*

shrivel *v.* shrink, wither, dry up, dehydrate, desiccate, waste away, wilt, wrinkle, contract, curl up, wizen, mummify, deflate. ANT. *bloom, expand, blow up.*

shriveled *a.* shrunken, withered, dried up, dehydrated, desiccated, wasted away, wilted, wrinkled, wizened, contracted, deflated. ANT. *swollen, plump, ballooning.*

shroud *n.* cover, winding sheet, burial sheet, cloth, wrap, cerements, pall, veil, cloak.

shroud *v.* cover, veil, wrap, cloak, conceal, keep under wraps, shield, screen, hide. ANT. *unveil, expose, reveal.*

shrub/shrubbery *n.* shrubs, bushes, brush, hedges, underbrush, thicket, scrub, copse, boscage.

WORD FIND

aromatic: mint, lavender, rosemary, bergamot

dwarfed: bonsai

ornamental or animal shapes made of: topiary

shrunken *a.* diminished, contracted, shriveled, compressed, deflated, withered, shortened, wasted away, dehydrated. ANT. *enlarged, expanded, puffed up.*

shuck *v.* shell, husk, remove, peel off, slough.

shudder *n.* tremor, trembling, shake, convulsion, quiver, shiver, quaver, quake, spasm, jerking, twitching.

shudder *v.* tremble, shake, convulse, quiver, shiver, quaver, get a chill, quake, have a spasm, jerk, twitch.

shuffle *v.* **1.** MIX jumble, disorder, shift, interchange, disarrange, displace, mess up. **2.** SCUFF THE FEET shamble, drag one's feet, scrape, limp.

shun *v.* avoid, turn away from, *give the cold shoulder to, dodge, evade, reject, snub, steer clear of, shy away from, eschew, forgo. ANT. *embrace, seek out, face.*

shunt *v.* divert, turn off, switch, shift, sidetrack.

shut *v.* close, secure, lock, bolt, fasten, seal, slam, draw closed, block, bar, occlude. ANT. *open, unlock, unfasten.*

shutout *v.* *skunk, *blow out, defeat soundly.

shuttle *n.* orbiter. SEE SPACECRAFT

shuttle *v.* go back and forth, commute, *go on one's run, shuttlecock, transport to and fro.

shy *a.* **1.** BASHFUL self-conscious, backward, reticent, retiring, diffident, reserved, a wallflower, ill-at-ease, nervous, self-effacing, coy, demure, shrinking, introverted, modest, humble, schizoid, quiet. **2.** LACKING short, under, deficient. ANT. *1. loud, overbearing, overconfident, bold, brash. 2. replete, abundant.*

shyness *n.* bashfulness, self-consciousness, reticence, diffidence, nervousness, coyness, introversion, modesty, humbleness, quietness. ANT. *loudness, overconfidence, boldness.*

shyster *n.* *Sl.* pettifogger, unethical lawyer, *ambulance chaser, *fixer.

sic *adv.* thus, as is, as written, so.

sick *a.* **1.** UNHEALTHY ill, unwell, ailing, run down, diseased, *under the weather, *green around the gills, *off one's feed, queasy, nauseated, sickly, infected, feverish, bedridden. **2.** HEARTSICK sick at heart, heartbroken, miserable, stricken. **3.** FED UP *had it up to here with, tired, disgusted, cloyed, sated, satiated. **4.** DERANGED psychotic, *psycho, perverted, strange, sadistic. ANT. *1. healthy, well, *fit as a fiddle. 2. delighted, happy. 3. wanting more, hungry for more. 4. normal, sane.*

sicken *v.* nauseate, make ill, turn one's stomach, disgust, revolt, make one want to throw up, *gross out, repel. ANT. *delight, please, attract.*

sickening a. nauseating, stomach-turning, disgusting, revolting, *gross, foul, vile, distasteful, repugnant, enough to make one vomit. ANT. *delightful, appetizing, attractive.*

sickle n. scythe, *bushwhacker, grass-cutter, cutting implement.

sickly a. ailing, unhealthy, in poor health, unwell, run down, diseased, *under the weather, *green around the gills, *off one's feed, weak, queasy, nauseated, infected, feverish, pale, pallid, ashen, *circling the drain. ANT. *healthy, well, *fit as a fiddle.*

sickness n. illness, ailment, disease, malady, affliction, infection, *bug, virus, weakness, disorder, syndrome, influenza, flu, pneumonia, queasiness, nausea, upset stomach, fever, infirmity. SEE DISEASE, ILLNESS

side n. 1. EDGE border, right, left, brink, margin, flank, front, back, top, bottom, face, aspect, quarter, surface, section. 2. VIEWPOINT aspect, standpoint, angle, facet, position. 3. ONE OF TWO OR MORE OPPOSING VIEWS OR GROUPS party, camp, team, faction, rival, competition, combatant.

side a. secondary, minor, incidental, subordinate, lesser, ancillary, flanking. ANT. *main, central, chief.*

sideburns n. burnsides, *mutton chops, whiskers. SEE BEARD

side by side a. juxtaposing, abreast, cheek by jowl, pari passu.

side effect n. by-product, reaction.

sidekick n. Sl. companion, friend, alter ego, buddy, pal, colleague, confederate, partner, *straight man.

sidelong a. oblique, sideways, lateral. ANT. *direct.*

sidesplitting a. hilarious, hearty, a scream, convulsive. SEE FUNNY

sidestep v. dodge, avoid, evade, elude, sidetrack, bypass, go around, duck, *steer clear, *dance around. ANT. *face, confront, meet head-on.*

sideswipe v. graze, glance off.

sidetrack v. divert, digress, turn off, shunt.

sidewalk n. pavement, walkway, boardwalk.

sideways adv. obliquely, laterally, edgewise, sidelong, askew.

siege n. encirclement, surrounding, investment, blockade, onslaught, offense, assault, campaign.

siege v. besiege, lay siege, encircle, surround, invest, blockade, contain, close off, beset, assault.

sierra n. mountain range, chain.

siesta n. rest, *catnap, snooze. SEE NAP

sieve n. sifter, strainer, filter, screen, mesh, colander.

sift v. strain, sieve, filter, screen, winnow, comb, separate, sort out, scrutinize.

sigh n. exhalation, deep breath, sough, moan, groan, murmur.

sigh v. exhale heavily, breathe out, moan, groan, lament.

sight n. 1. EYESIGHT vision, visual perception, eyes. 2. RANGE OF VISION eyeshot, view, focus. 3. SPECTACLE scene, vision, show, curiosity, picture. 4. MESS fright, horror, monstrosity, spectacle.

sign n. 1. INDICATION mark, clue, hint, intimation, suggestion, trace, *dead giveaway, evidence, earmark, signal, symptom, manifestation, beacon, spoor, trail, herald, omen, harbinger, portent, foreshadowing. 2. POSTED INFORMATION signpost, notice, pointer, marker, guidepost, warning, caution, billboard, placard.

sign v. endorse, write one's name, inscribe, autograph, authorize.

signal n. sign, indication, alert, indicator, cue, *go-ahead, *thumbs-up, gesture, nod, notice, flare, flag, siren, beacon, foghorn, semaphore.

signal v. indicate, alert, cue, *give the go-ahead, *give a thumbs-up, gesture, nod, warn, shoot off a flare, flag, semaphore.

signature n. autograph, name, inscription, *John Hancock, hand, X, endorsement, authorization, OK, identification.

significance n. 1. IMPORTANCE consequence, weight, consideration, matter, meaning, value, gravity, moment, import, interest. 2. MEANING intent, point, sense, implication, idea, drift. ANT. *1. insignificance, frivolity, unimportance.*

significant a. 1. IMPORTANT consequential, weighty, considerable, meaningful, valuable, momentous, major, vital, critical, crucial. 2. MEANINGFUL indicative, suggestive, telling, expressive, symbolic. ANT. *1. insignificant, unimportant, trivial. 2. meaningless.*

signify v. mean, denote, represent, indicate, stand for, suggest, imply, express, communicate, symbolize, connote.

sign language n. signing, fingerspelling, ASL, nonverbal communication.

silence n. 1. STILLNESS quiet, peace, hush, quietude, noiselessness, dead air, calm, tranquility, serenity, blackout. 2. SPEECHLESSNESS muteness, reticence, taciturnity, reservation, uncommunicativeness, secrecy. "The sharper sword."—Robert U. Johnson. "One of the hardest arguments to refute."—Josh Billings. "Unbearable repartee."—Gilbert Keith Chesterson. "The fence around wisdom."—Hebrew proverb. ANT. *1. noise, cacophony, din, uproar. 2. loquaciousness, talk, chatter.*

silence v. quiet, still, shut up, hush, gag, muzzle, inhibit, censor, *squelch, strangle, put down, crush, repress.

silencer n. muffler, mute.

silent a. **1.** QUIET still, peaceful, hushed, noiseless, soundless, calm, tranquil, serene, dead, *deathly silent, *stone silent. **2.** SPEECHLESS mute, uncommunicative, taciturn, *clammed up, reticent, mum, *tongue-tied. ANT. *1. noisy, cacophonous, uproarious, earsplitting. 2. talkative, loquacious, *motor-mouthed.*

silhouette n. outline, profile, contour.

silky a. smooth, satiny, delicate, glossy, sleek. ANT. *rough, coarse.*

silly a. foolish, childish, infantile, juvenile, asinine, goofy, stupid, nonsensical, idiotic, absurd, laughable, wacky, ridiculous, zany, funny, humorous. ANT. *serious, grave, mature.*

silt n. sediment, settlings, alluvium, wash.

silver a. sterling, argent, shiny.

silverware n. silver, cutlery, flatware, eating utensils.

similar a. like, comparable, resembling, much the same, kindred, equivalent, akin, homologous, nearly matching, analogous. ANT. *dissimilar, different, contrasting.*

similarity n. likeness, resemblance, comparison, sameness, equivalence, correspondence, mirror image, semblance, homogeneity, analogy, parity, affinity. ANT. *difference, contrast, opposition.*

simile n. figure of speech, analogy, comparison.

simmer v. bubble, stew, boil, seethe.

simpatico a. **1.** IN AGREEMENT of like mind, compatible, seeing eye to eye. **2.** ATTRACTIVE charming, pleasing.

simper n. smirk. SEE SMILE

simple a. **1.** EASY *child's play, effortless, *cinchy, *a cinch, *a snap , *like falling off a log, *piece of cake, understandable, clear, straightforward, uncomplicated. **2.** MERE bare, sheer, pure, utter. **3.** PLAIN unadorned, unembellished, spare, bare, clean, austere,

modest, humble, Spartan. **4.** INNOCENT artless, unsophisticated, down-to-earth, childlike, natural, naive, ingenuous, honest, real. **5.** STUPID foolish, dense, dull, dumb, moronic, slow, bovine, ignorant, witless, *clueless. ANT. *1. hard, difficult, complicated, complex. 2. qualified. 3. ornate, fancy, embellished. 4. sophisticated, artful, disingenuous. 5. smart, sharp, *on the ball.*

simpleminded a. unsophisticated, stupid, dense, dull, dumb, moronic, slow, bovine, ignorant, witless, *clueless, brainless. ANT. *sophisticated, smart, *savvy.*

simpleton n. fool, idiot, *retard, *dumb-dumb, dunce, moron, imbecile, ignoramus, *dope, dolt, *dimwit, *lunkhead, *bonehead, *airhead. ANT. *genius, savant, *Rhodes scholar.*

simply adv. **1.** PLAINLY easily, naturally. **2.** MERELY only, just.

simulate v. imitate, copy, put on, act, mimic, fake, pretend, assume, pose, feign, affect, counterfeit, sham, replicate.

simulated a. imitation, artificial, synthetic, fake, counterfeit, sham, fabricated, make-believe, mock. ANT. *real, authentic, genuine.*

simulation n. imitation, fake, reproduction, counterfeit, sham, fabrication, copy, mockup, facsimile. ANT. *the real thing, *the real McCoy.*

simulator n. virtual reality apparatus, practice vehicle, mockup, model.

simultaneous a. concurrent, at the same time, synchronous, coincident, concomitant, parallel, coexisting, *in sync. ANT. *differing, divergent.*

sin n. offense, transgression, wrong, wrongdoing, evil, crime, felony, violation, fault, immoral act, misdeed, affront to God, vice, peccadillo, wickedness. "The breaking of one's own integrity."—D.H. Lawrence. "A departure from God."—Martin Luther. ANT. *good deed, virtue, kindness.*

sin v. do an evil deed, do an immoral act, break a commandment, do wrong, transgress, offend God, commit a crime, fall from grace, trespass, stray from the path of righteousness. ANT. *do a good deed, do a kindness.*

sincere a. honest, genuine, real, heartfelt, straightforward, open, ingenuous, up front, *straight-shooting, earnest, forthright, frank, candid, guileless. ANT. *insincere, phony, fake.*

sincerity n. honesty, genuineness, realness, heartfelt emotion, straightforwardness, openness, ingenuousness, *straight shooting, forthrightness, frankness, candidness, guilelessness. "Just what I think, and nothing more or less."—H.W. Longfellow. "Plain dealing."—Ralph Waldo Emerson. ANT. *insincerity, dishonesty, hypocrisy.*

sinewy *a.* tough, strong, muscular, strapping, brawny, burly, athletic, toned, wiry, steely, Herculean. ANT. *fat, flaccid, droopy, flabby.*

sinful *a.* bad, evil, immoral, wicked, wrong, criminal, demonic, corrupt, vile, ungodly, shameful, disgraceful, low. ANT. *virtuous, moral, upright.*

sing *v.* *belt out a song, carry a tune, carol, croon, serenade, warble, hum, trill, pipe, cry out, yodel, bellow, sing in a booming voice.

WORD FIND

singing with a falsely high voice: falsetto
singing without instrumental accompaniment: a cappella; *barbershop quartet
SEE MUSIC, OPERA, SINGER, SONG, VOICE

singe *v.* burn, char, sear, brown, toast, roast, blacken.

singer *n.* vocalist, crooner, songster, caroler, *pop star, soloist, recording artist, minstrel, troubador, nightingale, tenor, baritone, soprano, alto, diva, prima donna. SEE OPERA, SING, SONG, VOICE

single *a.* **1.** ONE individual, sole, lone, singular, separate, distinct, solitary, isolated. **2.** UNMARRIED unwed, unattached, divorced, celibate, available, eligible. ANT. *1. many, several. 2. married, wed.*

single-handed *a.* unaided, unassisted, alone, independent. ANT. *assisted.*

singles bar *n.* bar, lounge, club, *pickup joint, *meat market.

SINGULAR *a.* [SING gyuh lur] unique, one of a kind. *Watching Neil Armstrong take the first moonwalk was a singular experience.* SYN. unique, one of a kind, exceptional, extraordinary, peculiar, unusual, remarkable, rare, odd, strange, different. ANT. *common, usual, ordinary.*

sinister *a.* threatening, ominous, inauspicious, portentous, menacing, black, malignant, malevolent, villainous, bad, evil, wicked, diabolic, satanic. ANT. *good, auspicious, divine.*

sink *n.* basin, washbowl, drain.

sink *v.* **1.** GO DOWN drop, fall, descend, sag, immerse, drown, submerge, dip, settle, slump, plunge. **2.** DECLINE decrease, diminish, fall, drop, subside, deteriorate, regress, wane, ebb. **3.** CAUSE TO SINK swamp, drown, engulf,

overwhelm, scuttle. ANT. *1. rise, ascend. 2. increase, grow.*

sinuous *a.* **1.** WINDING curving, serpentine, wavy, bending, tortuous, meandering, undulating, coiling, twisting, snaking. **2.** DEVIOUS crooked. ANT. *1. straight, unbending. 2. aboveboard.*

sinus *n.* channel, cavity, conduit, hollow, canal.

sip *n.* taste, swallow, drop, sample, lick, *swig, nip, dram, *hit.

sip *v.* taste, *slurp, sample, *take a swig, *take a hit, sup, siphon, suck through a straw.

sir *n.* seignor, monsieur, sahib, my lord.

sire *n.* **1.** YOUR MAJESTY. **2.** FATHER genitor.

sire *v.* beget, father, engender, procreate, spawn, bear, generate, breed, multiply.

siren *n.* **1.** WARNING SIGNAL alarm, klaxon, whistle. **2.** SEDUCTRESS enchantress, temptress, nymph, femme fatale, Lorelei, witch, charmer.

sissy *n.* weakling, *wuss, *wimp, coward, *chicken, effeminate man. ANT. *macho man, *jock, he-man.

sit *v.* **1.** BE SEATED settle, plop oneself down, rest, squat, *take a load off, perch, roost, lounge, recline, straddle, sprawl, deposit oneself. **2.** MEET assemble, gather, convene, deliberate, be in session, come together.

site *n.* location, locale, locality, place, spot, position, plot, point, lot, area, grounds, scene, section, whereabouts.

sit-in *n.* protest, demonstration, strike, rally, shutdown.

sitter *n.* baby-sitter, nanny, attendant, caretaker, wet nurse.

sitting duck *n.* easy target, easy pickings, *dead meat, *toast.

situate *v.* locate, position, place, put, install, set, set up, plant, settle, post, root. ANT. *move, withdraw, leave.*

situated *a.* located, positioned, placed, installed, set, set up, planted, settled, posted, rooted, established. ANT. *rootless, transient.*

situation *n.* **1.** CONDITION predicament, plight, state, state of affairs, circumstances, position, *ball game, fix, *between a rock and a hard place, *deep doo-doo, *sticky wicket. **2.** PLACE locality, locale, location, spot, point, site, position. **3.** JOB employment, position, office, duty, appointment.

sit-up *n.* exercise, crunch.

six-shooter *n.* revolver, pistol. SEE GUN

sixth sense *n.* intuition, *gut feelings, instinct, *feeling in one's bones, *vibes, extrasensory perception, ESP, second sight, telepathy, clairvoyance.

sizable *a.* big, large, considerable, great, hefty, *whopping, respectable, king-size, industrial size, huge. ANT. *small, tiny, piddling.*

size *n.* dimensions, measurements, proportions, scale, extent, area, magnitude, mass, square footage, volume, capacity, amount, stature, breadth, length, height, width, diameter.

size *v.* measure, gauge, graduate, assess, appraise, survey, size up.

sizzle *v.* hiss, fry, splutter, sputter, crackle, fizzle.

skate *v.* slide, glide, glissade, roller-skate, rollerblade, ice skate, figure skate.

WORD FIND

FIGURE SKATING

arena: rink

dance: free dance

figure of three circles: serpentine

figure of two circles: figure eight

flying spin: Arabian

flying spin ending in back camel: flying camel

glide with one skate pointing forward, the other back: spread eagle

jump and splitting apart of legs: split, stag

jump of one and a half revolutions: axel

jump of one revolution: Lutz

jump of three and a half revolutions: triple axel

jump of two and a half revolutions: double axel

jump split and touching of toes: Russian split

jump started off a back inside edge and ended on opposite foot: Salchow

machine that resurfaces ice: Zamboni

moves executed to the sound of music: freestyle, free skating

pair move in which man lifts woman overhead with her legs split: hydrant lift

pair move in which woman is revolved with head held near ice: death spiral

propelling oneself over the ice: stroking

spin in an arabesque position: camel

spin with one leg held high overhead: Bielmann spin

turn forward to back: choctaw

skateboard *n.* board mounted on small wheels and ridden on firm surfaces like concrete.

WORD FIND

axles, front and rear: trucks

back of board: tail

backwards, riding: fakie

curving arc, to skate in a long: carve

fall off and get hurt: slam

front of board: nose

get-together, skateboarding: jam

jump trick made by kicking nose of board: nollie

jump trick made by kicking tail of board: ollie

kicking or flipping the board into the air with toe: kickflip

long skateboard made for cruising as opposed to tricks: longboard

platform of skateboard: deck

pushing with the front foot instead of back: mongo-foot

ramp: bank

ramp park, skateboarding area: skatepark

ramp, U-shaped: half pipe

rotation, half, mid-air: 180

rotation, full, mid-air: 360

rotation while riding fakie (backwards), midair, 360-degree: caballerial

scrape axles on a curb or railing, purposely: grind

sliding along a rail or ledge: boardslide, railslide

stance with right foot forward on board: goofy-foot

skedaddle *v. Sl.* run away, scoot, leave, *beat feet, vamoose, bolt, scat, *make oneself scarce, *blow, decamp, *hightail it. ANT. *loiter, hang around.*

skein *n.* coil, quantity, hank, ball, loop, twist, clump.

skeleton *n.* bones, framework, bony structure, scaffolding.

WORD FIND

breastbone, center: sternum

broken bone: Colles fracture, comminuted fracture, compound fracture, Pott's fracture

broken bone, sound of: crepitation

broken bones, realignment of: traction, countertraction

cheek: malar

collarbone: clavicle

connective tissue: cartilage

disease of bones: osteoarthritis, osteofibrosis, osteoporosis, scoliosis

ear bones: incus (anvil), malleus (hammer), stapes (stirrup)

fingers and toes: phalanges

foot bones: metatarsal

forearm: radius, ulna

funny bone between shoulder and elbow: humerus

hand bones: metacarpal
hipbone: coxae, pelvis, sacrum, coccyx
jawbone, lower: mandible
jawbone, upper: maxilla
kneecap: patella
leg, knee to ankle, outer: fibula
leg, knee to ankle: tibia
shoulder blade: scapula
skull: cranium
spinal column: vertebrae
tailbone: coccyx
thighbone: femur
upper body framework: ribs
vertebrae of neck, first: atlas
wrist bones, collectively: carpal

skeptic n. doubter, cynic, doubting Thomas, nonbeliever, scoffer, naysayer, questioner, freethinker, atheist, agnostic. "Not one who doubts, but one who examines."—Charles Sainte-Beauve. ANT. believer, *sucker.

skeptical a. doubting, questioning, cynical, unbelieving, scoffing, distrusting, mistrusting, dubious, incredulous, leery, unconvinced, agnostic, atheistic. ANT. believing, gullible, trusting.

skepticism n. doubt, questioning, cynicism, disbelief, scoffing, distrust, mistrust, leeriness, suspicion, agnosticism, atheism. "The mark and even the pose of the educated mind."—John Dewey.

sketch n. 1. DRAWING draft, outline, rough outline, diagram, blueprint, skeleton, design, plan, brief, synopsis, apercu, survey. 2. SKIT act, scene, vignette.

sketch v. draw, draft, outline, rough out, diagram, scratch out, block out, design, plot out.

sketchy a. rough, lacking detail, incomplete, unfinished, cursory, brief, crude, preliminary, imperfect, *half-baked. ANT. detailed, thorough, complete.

skew v. twist, distort, pervert, shift, misrepresent, change, falsify, misconstrue, misstate, slant, bias, embellish.

skewer n. pin, spit, brochette.

ski v. schuss, slalom, snowplow, freestyle.

WORD FIND

absorbing impact of bump by flexing knees: swallowing
acrobatic or dance-style skiing: freestyle
acrobatic side revolution like helicopter blade: helicopter
backward somersault with a twist: back mobius
bump or hump of snow: mogul
bumpy or humpy snow field: mogul field
cross-country: langlauf, Nordic skiing, rambling
form left in snow from fallen skier: sitzmark
freestyle dance: ballet
jump made in crouching position: gelendesprung
jump with skis scissored in midair: daffy
lift, covered: gondola
overhang of ice and snow known to cause avalanches: cornice
parallel turn: christie
rifle-shooting and skiing competition: biathlon
ski straight down mountain: schuss
slowing-down or stopping position: snowplow
snow, deep and soft: powder
snow, old granulated: corn
snow with hard surface: crust
turn in which one ski is lifted high in the air: kick turn, royal christie
turns, series of quick: wedelns
uphill diagonal walking method: herringbone
uphill sideways walking method: sidestepping
winding, flagged race: slalom

skid v. slide, slip, sideslip, *burn rubber, swerve, fishtail, glissade.

skill n. 1. ABILITY expertise, talent, proficiency, command, competence, faculty, know-how, gift, mastery, adeptness, knack, aptitude, dexterity, adroitness, prowess, finesse. 2. TRADE art, craft, vocation, profession, forte. ANT. 1. inability, incompetence, inexperience.

skillful a. skilled, expert, proficient, adept, competent, experienced, schooled, adroit, dexterous, masterful, *crack, *crackerjack, practiced, accomplished, talented, gifted. ANT. unskilled, unschooled, incompetent, inept.

skim v. 1. CREAM clear, remove, top. 2. GLANCE AT HASTILY read, scan, *speed read, thumb through, flip through, peruse, spot-check, skip over. 3. GLIDE OVER skip over, bounce over, graze.

skimp v. scrimp, stint, be stingy, be cheap, *be tight, be frugal, *cut corners, *pinch pennies, scrape, conserve. ANT. squander, waste, *blow.

skimpy a. scanty, short, not enough, barely enough, lacking, inadequate, meager, insufficient, slight, spare, *measly. ANT. adequate, sufficient, generous, ample.

skin n. epidermis, dermis, derma, cuticle, hide,

pelt, membrane, *nature's shrinkwrap, coat, membrane, sheath, husk, bark, rind, covering, shell, hull.

skin v. peel, decorticate, excorticate, flay, husk, shell, shuck, shed, slough, strip, pare, scalp, trim.

skin-deep a. superficial, shallow, surface, empty, external. ANT. *deep, profound.*

skin-diving n. scuba diving, snorkeling.

WORD FIND

air flow apparatus: regulator

ascend slowly, stop, ascend: decompress

breathing tube for shallow swimming: snorkel

dangerous narcotic effect of deep water diving: nitrogen narcosis, *rapture of the deep

decompression sickness: bends

diver: frogman, aquanaut, scuba diver, pearl diver

line tied between two divers to keep them together in dark: buddy line

red signal flag with white bar: diver down flag

responsibility for fellow diver: buddy system

rubber suit: wet suit

sharing of air with another diver: buddy breathing

water pressure, lessening of: decompression

weight regulator: buoyancy compensator, weight belt

skin flick n. *Sl.* X-rated movie, blue movie, *porno flick, dirty movie, adult movie.

skinflint n. *cheapskate, miser, *tightwad, niggard, *Scrooge, penny-pincher, curmudgeon, hoarder, money-grubber. ANT. *spendthrift, *big spender, philanthropist.*

skinny a. thin, slender, lean, skeletal, emaciated, bony, scrawny, lank, malnourished, half-starved, raw-boned, gaunt. ANT. *fat, obese, roly-poly.*

skip v. 1. HOP bound, spring, leap, caper, romp, jump, cavort, gambol, prance, frisk, bounce. 2. SKIM bounce, ricochet, skate. 3. OVERLOOK pass over, omit, exclude, leave out, forget about, disregard, nevermind, ignore.

skipper n. captain, master, mariner, pilot, seaman, officer. SEE BOAT, SHIP

skirmish n. fight, flare-up, encounter, battle, engagement, conflict, tussle, brush with the enemy, scrimmage, clash, *run-in, fray, heated exchange.

skirmish v. fight, encounter, battle, engage, conflict, tussle, scrimmage, clash, combat, have a run-in, have a heated exchange.

skirt n. 1. BORDER margin, verge, fringe, edge, rim, periphery, perimeter. 2. ARTICLE OF CLOTHING wrap, mini, midi, maxi.

WORD FIND

ballet dancer's: tutu

broad, nineteenth century: hoop skirt, crinoline

calico with ruffled hem: prairie skirt

grass skirt: hula skirt

Malaysian wrap: sarong

narrow, restrictive skirt of 1910: hobble skirt

narrow, slitted in back: sheath

peasant skirt: dirndl

puffy: bouffant, bubble

rear gathering, nineteenth century: bustle

rustling of silk skirt: froufrou

Scottish, man's: kilt

shorts: culottes

skit n. sketch, vignette, play, playlet, act, parody, takeoff, lampoon.

skittish a. jumpy, nervous, easily frightened, jittery, excitable, anxious, restless, edgy, restive, easily spooked. ANT. *calm, relaxed, tranquil, composed.*

skulduggery n. sneakiness, trickery, craftiness, deception, deceit, artifice, wile, treachery, machination, underhandedness, conspiracy, foul play. ANT. *honesty, innocence.*

skulk v. lurk, slink, sneak, prowl, creep, lie back in the shadows, steal, hide, pussyfoot, move stealthily.

skull n. cranium, head, sconce.

skullcap n. cap, zucchetto, yarmulke, beanie, calotte, pileus, swim cap.

skullduggery n. trickery, deception, fraud, subterfuge.

skunk n. 1. ANIMAL polecat, vermin, *stinker. 2. BAD PERSON *SOB, *bastard, *creep, stinker, scoundrel, *rat, rogue, cad.

sky n. upper atmosphere, firmament, cloudscape, vault, *the wild blue yonder, welkin, biosphere, stratosphere, mesosphere, thermosphere, exosphere, ionosphere, ether. "The roof of the world."—Willa Cather. "That beautiful old parchment in which the sun and the moon keep their diary."—Alfred Kreymborg. "Earth's ethereal armor."—Mark Clarke.

WORD FIND

color: azure, cerulean, celeste

highest point: zenith

referring to: celestial

SEE ASTRONOMY, ATMOSPHERE, CLOUD, SPACE

skydiving n. parachuting, freefalling.

WORD FIND

arms at side position to increase speed of freefall: delta position

automatic deployment line attached inside aircraft: static line

auxiliary chute: reserve chute

cord that deploys parachute: ripcord

descent portion without deployment of parachute: freefall

hazard in which chute fails to unfurl completely: streamer

hazard in which chute is turned inside out after deployment: inversion

horizontal soaring: gliding

joining hands with another diver in midair: docking

landing area: drop zone

positioning the body for horizontal movement: tracking

small chute that helps deploy main chute: pilot chute

spread-eagle falling position with arms upraised: frog position

steering lines: toggle lines

supervisor of jumps: jumpmaster

skyrocket *v.* shoot skyward, soar, take off, shoot up, zoom, catapult, *go through the roof, *blast off to the clouds. ANT. *nosedive, plunge, plummet, spiral earthward.*

skyscraper *n.* high-rise, *cloudscraper, monolith, building, superstructure.

slab *n.* piece, hunk, chunk, plank, slice, block.

slack *n.* excess, play, give, leeway, looseness.

slack/slacken *v.* slacken, loosen, let up, relax, untighten, ease off, lessen, decrease, diminish, soften, moderate. ANT. *tighten, increase.*

slack *a.* **1.** SLOW idle, slow-moving, sluggish, dull, quiet, lethargic, down. **2.** LOOSE relaxed, not taut, sagging, drooping, limp, lax, flaccid. **3.** CARELESS lazy, negligent, remiss, sloppy, slipshod, *asleep on the job, lax, lackadaisical, nonchalant, indifferent, indolent, uncaring. ANT. *1. fast, fast-moving, busy, *hopping. 2. tight, taut. 3. careful, meticulous, exacting.*

slacker *n.* shirker, idler, loafer, malingerer, *goof-off, *goldbricker, *deadbeat, clock watcher, truant.

slake *v.* quench, hydrate, satisfy, sate, satiate, relieve, gratify, allay, extinguish, alleviate, appease, assuage. ANT. *aggravate, increase, exacerbate.*

slam *n.* **1.** LOUD NOISE bang, boom, crash, wham, crack, clap, burst, impact, collision. **2.** CRITICISM *dig, *pan, brickbat, disapproval, bad press, *swipe.

slam *v.* **1.** SHUT bang, close hard, heave, ram, push, crash, smack, dash, clobber, bat, hammer, *bodyslam. **2.** CRITICIZE *dig, *pan, *take a swipe at, shoot down, *blast, attack, *rake over the coals. ANT. *1. open. 2. compliment, praise, laud.*

SLANDER *n.* [SLAN dur] damaging, untrue statements made publicly. *Celebrities have a harder time proving slander because they are public figures.* SYN. lies, untruths, smear, mudslinging, defamation, denigration, misrepresentation, aspersion, false statement, libel, calumny. "The revenge of a coward."—Samuel Johnson. ANT. *praise, commendation, compliment.*

slander *v.* lie, misrepresent, smear, mudsling, defame, denigrate, cast aspersions, make a false statement, libel, malign, *drag one's name through the mud, slur, tarnish one's name. ANT. *praise, commend, honor.*

slang *n.* colloquialism, jargon, argot, lingo, vernacular, vocabulary, *slanguage, pidgin, language of the street, shoptalk, dialect, Americanisms. "Language serving its apprenticeship."—Henry T. Buckle. "Language that takes off its coat, spits on its hands, and goes to work."—Carl Sandburg. ANT. *formal language.*

slant *n.* **1.** INCLINE slope, pitch, lean, tilt, angle, cant, grade, camber, rake. **2.** VIEWPOINT point of view, side, position, angle, opinion, attitude. **3.** DISTORTION bias, prejudice, partiality, leaning.

slant *v.* **1.** INCLINE slope, pitch, lean, tilt, angle, cant, grade, skew. **2.** DISTORT bias, prejudice, color, twist, weight, orient. ANT. *1. straighten, level, flatten.*

slanting *a.* inclined, sloping, tilting, leaning, canting, oblique, diagonal, askew, at an angle. ANT. *straight, level.*

slap *n.* **1.** CUFF blow, smack, hit, hand across the face, *slap upside the head, swat, buffet, clap, swipe, *belt. **2.** INSULT *crack, *shot, *dig, rebuff, offense, *put-down, snub, *cut, affront, slight.

slap *v.* cuff, smack, hit, *slap upside the head, swat, buffet, clap, swipe, *belt, *slap silly, spank.

slapdash *a.* careless, hasty, impetuous, haphazard, sloppy, slipshod, casual, harum-scarum. ANT. *careful, meticulous.*

slaphappy *a.* dazed, punch-drunk, dizzy, lightheaded, *woozy, reeling, giddy, silly. ANT. *sober, clearheaded.*

slash n. stroke, swipe, cut, gash, slit, wound, laceration, incision, score, tear.

slash v. **1.** CUT stroke, swipe, gash, slit, jag, wound, lacerate, incise, slice, score, tear, hack, rip open, mutilate, open. **2.** REDUCE cut, decrease, drop, lower.

slat n. strip, lath, stave, picket, paling.

slate n. ballot, ticket, list, roster.

slaughter n. massacre, bloodbath, murder, mass murder, butchering, carnage, killing, slaying, mass execution, mutilation. SEE MURDER

slaughter v. massacre, murder, butcher, kill, slay, execute, mutilate, savage, decimate, assassinate, annihilate.

slaughterhouse n. abattoir, shambles, butchery, meat-packing house.

slave n. bondman, servant, indentured servant, chattel, drudge, serf, laborer, menial.

slave v. drudge, break one's back, *work one's fingers to the bone, toil, labor, grind, sweat, plod, slog, *bust one's hump.

slavery n. bondage, servitude, forced labor, slave labor, enslavement, captivity, enthrallment, subjugation, serfdom, grind, toil. "A prison for the soul, a public dungeon."—Longinus. "Yoked with the brutes, and fettered to the soil."—Thomas Campbell.

WORD FIND

black woman servant who served as mother to white children: mammy

degrading term for slave in nineteenth-century United States: boy

elimination of: abolition

elimination, one who favored slavery's: abolitionist

field supervisor on plantation: driver, overseer

free from: emancipate, manumit

fugitive slave: maroon

group of slaves tied together: coffle

master's personal slave: body servant

slave owner: master, massa

subservient, deferential slave, degrading term for: Sambo, Uncle Tom

slavish a. servile, submissive, subservient, deferential, subject, obsequious, obeisant, fawning, cowering. ANT. domineering, intractable, arrogant.

slay v. kill, murder, run through, slaughter, assassinate, execute, *do in, massacre, annihilate, destroy. SEE MURDER

sleazebag n. Sl. creep, *slimeball, *scumbag, *sleaze, slob, *pig, *dirtbag, *scuzzo, filthy wretch, *bum, pervert, *scum of the earth.

sleazy a. Sl. cheap, *scuzzy, dirty, foul, *creepy, *raunchy, nasty, sick, gross, *skanky, greasy, oily, disreputable, low, contemptible. ANT. high-class, refined, cleancut, virtuous, wholesome.

sled n. sleigh, toboggan, bobsled, luge, cutter, sledge, pung.

sledge n. sled, sleigh, travois.

sleek a. smooth, shiny, glossy, lustrous, satiny, glistening, groomed, combed, trim. ANT. dull, lackluster.

sleep n. slumber, rest, somnolence, *shut-eye, *Zs, snooze, nap, catnap, dozing, *forty winks, siesta, repose, hibernation, under the spell of Morpheus, land of Nod, unconsciousness, dreaming. "A holiday from reality."—Victor Ratner. "Brother of death."—Thomas Browne. "The death of each day's life."—Shakespeare. ANT. wakefulness, consciousness, alertness.

WORD FIND

bedwetting: enuresis

between wakefulness and sleep: hypnagogic

breathing disorder of: sleep apnea

children's waking nightmare: night terrors

deep sleep: sopor, stupor

dream sleep: REM sleep (rapid eye movement)

drowsy: somnolent

excessive: hypersomnia

expert in: somnologist

god of dreams, Greek: Morpheus

god of sleep, Greek: Hypnos

god of sleep, Roman: Somnus

grogginess caused by sleeping too long: Rip Van Winkle syndrome

hypnotized: trance

inability to: insomnia

inducing sleep: soporific, somniferous, somnolent

internal body clock controlling: circadian rhythm

presleep visions: hypnagogic hallucinations

sex demons of: incubus, succubus

sleeping sickness: narcolepsy, encephalitis

sleepwalk: somnoambulate

sleepwalker: somnoambulist

twitch of body or leg just before sleep: myoclonic jerk, hypnagogic jerk

unconsciousness, prolonged: coma

SEE DREAM

sleep v. slumber, snooze, drowse, *catch some Zs, rest, *hit the sack, *get some rack time, go to bed, *conk out, nod off, turn in, *saw wood, *crash, *hit the hay, take a siesta, fall under the spell of Morpheus, hibernate. ANT. wake, regain consciousness.

sleeper n. *up-and-comer, *late bloomer, *sleeping giant.

sleepless a. insomniac, restless, wakeful, *wired, *saucer-eyed, *tossing and turning. ANT. *sleeping, dreaming, *out like a light.

sleepwalker n. somnambulist. SEE SLEEP

sleepy a. **1.** DROWSY tired, exhausted, weary, *dead-tired, fatigued, slumberous, nodding off, *beat, *dopey, lethargic, asleep, somnolent, falling under the spell of Morpheus. **2.** INACTIVE idle, still, quiet, dull. ANT. 1. *awake, refreshed, alert, invigorated. 2. active, bustline, busy.*

sleet n. frozen rain, precipitation, hail. SEE WEATHER

sleigh n. sled, cutter, pung, *booby hut.

sleight-of-hand n. legerdemain, hand skill, deception, trickery, magic, prestidigitation, palming, feint, hocus-pocus.

slender a. thin, slim, lean, narrow, skinny, willowy, reedy, twiggy, *thin as a broomstick, svelte, lithe, spare, tenuous. ANT. *fat, obese, brawny.*

sleuth n. detective, private detective, P.I., *private eye, *private dick, *bloodhound, investigator, *Sherlock, *gumshoe, shadow, *tail.

slice n. piece, cut, segment, sliver, wedge, slab, hunk, chunk, rasher, shaving, share, portion.

slice v. cut, segment, section, divide, carve, split, sever, pare, shave.

slick a. **1.** SLEEK smooth, glossy, satiny, slippery, oily, greasy. **2.** CLEVER tricky, crafty, smart, sophisticated, ingenious, creative, inventive, sharp. **3.** SUAVE urbane, smooth, worldly. ANT. 1. *rough, coarse, abrasive. 2. moronic, imbecilic, stupid. 3. clumsy, bumbling, unrefined.*

slide n. **1.** CHUTE ramp, trough. **2.** GLIDE slip, coast, glissade, skid.

slide v. glide, slip, coast, glissade, skid, sled, ski, skate, skim, drop, toboggan.

slight n. snub, insult, *cold shoulder, *slap in the face, *cut, rebuff, *put-down, indifference, neglect. ANT. *courtesy, notice, kindness.*

slight v. snub, insult, *give the cold shoulder, *give a slap in the face, *cut, rebuff, put down, neglect, overlook. ANT. *regard, notice, honor.*

slight a. **1.** LIGHT frail, fragile, delicate, spare, slim, gracile, flimsy, attenuated, tenuous, weak. **2.** INSIGNIFICANT small, little, tiny, light, minute, fine, minor, subtle, trivial, negligible. ANT. 1. *heavy, sturdy, rock-solid. 2. huge, gigantic, large, considerable.*

slim a. **1.** SLENDER thin, narrow, lean, skinny, willowy, reedy, twiggy, *thin as a broomstick, svelte, slight, tenuous. **2.** MEAGER slight, scanty, small, *skimpy, inconsiderable, bare, deficient, scarce, remote. ANT. 1. *fat, obese, brawny. 2. large, considerable, great.*

slime n. mucous, mud, ooze, muck, mire, scum, sludge, *gunk, *goo.

slimy a. covered with mucous, viscid, viscous, muddy, mucky, scummy, sludgy, *gunky, *gooey, disgusting, repulsive, foul, vile, *gross.

sling n. slingshot, thong, weapon, stone-thrower.

sling v. throw, fling, hurl, cast, pitch, shoot, heave, catapult, chuck, toss, fire, launch.

slingshot n. SEE SLING

slink v. skulk, sneak, creep, steal, lurk, pussy-foot, prowl, slip quietly, tiptoe, move furtively, move stealthily.

slinky a. **1.** SKULKING sneaky, creeping, stealing, lurking, prowling, slippery, quiet, stealthy, furtive. **2.** Sl. GRACEFUL sinuous, feline, sleek.

slip n. **1.** FALL trip, stumble, misstep, slide, tumble, spill. **2.** ERROR mistake, lapse, slip of the tongue (lapsus linguae), slip of the pen (lapsus calami), *Freudian slip, faux pas, blunder, *boner, *howler, oversight. **3.** WOMAN'S UNDERGARMENT petticoat, chemise, lingerie. **4.** SLIP OF PAPER note, receipt, voucher.

slip v. **1.** FALL trip, stumble, misstep, slide, tumble, take a spill, topple, lose one's balance, take a header, go head over heels, flop. **2.** MAKE A MISTAKE make an error, err, let slip, lapse, blunder, bungle, *goof, *screw up, *blow it.

slippery a. **1.** SLICK icy, oily, greasy, slimy, waxy, smooth, sleek, satiny, glazed, wet. **2.** DECEITFUL deceptive, slick, *like a snake, shady, dishonest, sneaky, devious, shifty, treacherous, elusive, evasive. ANT. 2. *honest, reputable.*

slipshod a. careless, slapdash, slap-bang, sloppy, haphazard, shoddy, messy, slovenly, disheveled, bedraggled, unkempt. ANT. *careful, meticulous, groomed.*

slipup n. error, blunder, *goof. SEE MISTAKE

slit n. slice, tear, slash, gash, rip, rift, incision, rent, hole.

slit v. slice, tear, slash, gash, rip, incise, pierce, sever, split, rend.

slither v. slip, slide, sneak, crawl, *belly along, wriggle, slink, *snake.

sliver *n.* splinter, fragment, shaving, bit, snip, shard, segment.

slobber *v.* drool, slaver, dribble, salivate, drivel.

slob *n.* pig, hog, animal, *grunge, *grub, Neanderthal, *caveman.

slog *v.* plod, toil, laboriously make one's way, labor, grind, trudge, drag, pursue doggedly, put one foot in front of the other, persevere.

slogan *n.* catchphrase, motto, shibboleth, saying, jingle, battle cry, byword.

sloop *n.* vessel, craft. SEE SAILBOAT

slop *n.* slush, mush, snow, mud, swill, puddle.

slop *v.* spill, splash, overflow, slosh, spatter, gush.

slope *n.* incline, inclination, declivity, slant, pitch, grade, gradient, ramp, tilt, cant, lean, tip. ANT. *acclivity.*

slope *v.* incline, slant, pitch, tilt, cant, lean, tip, skew, ascend, descend.

sloppy *a.* messy, dirty, muddy, slushy, soiled, grubby, grimy, *grungy, wet, splattered, unkempt, bedraggled, slovenly, careless, slipshod. ANT. *neat, tidy, orderly, meticulous.*

slosh *v.* splash, slop, spill, overflow, spatter, gush.

slot *n.* **1.** HOLE slit, aperture, groove, channel. **2.** POSITION opening.

sloth *n.* laziness, indolence, idleness, slothfulness, shiftlessness, lack of ambition, sluggishness, lethargy, listlessness, inertia. ANT. *get-up-and-go, ambition, drive.*

slothful *a.* lazy, indolent, idle, shiftless, lacking ambition, unenterprising, sluggish, lethargic, listless. ANT. *energetic, ambitious, *go-getting.*

slouch *n.* *klutz, oaf, lout, *duffer, bumbler, clod, lazybones, idler, loafer, laggard.

slouch *v.* hunch, slump, droop, stoop, bend. ANT. *stand tall.*

slough *n.* swamp, bog, marsh, backwater, muddy hollow, mire. SEE SWAMP

slough *v.* shed, molt, discard, throw off, cast off, get rid of.

slovenly *a.* careless, slipshod, slapdash, sloppy, messy, shabby, bedraggled, unkempt, ungroomed, disheveled, untidy. ANT. *neat, trim, careful, meticulous.*

slow *v.* decelerate, brake, slacken, taper off, let up, restrain, check, restrict, curb, delay, hinder, moderate, *take one's foot off the gas. ANT. *accelerate, speed up, *step on it.*

slow *a.* **1.** NOT FAST leisurely, crawling, dragging, lagging, *slower than a glacier, *slower than the Second Coming, *slower than cold molasses, snaillike, sluggish, slothful, plodding, gradual. **2.** LATE tardy, behind, delayed, overdue, detained, belated. **3.** NOT BUSY inactive, sluggish, quiet, slack, off. **4.** PROLONGED protracted, long, extended, interminable, drawn-out. **5.** STUPID obtuse, dull, dense, *thick, dim, dimwitted, retarded, moronic, bovine, *out to lunch, *dead from the neck up, *dumb as a box of rocks. ANT. *1. fast, swift, fleet, quick. 2. early, punctual. 3. busy, *hopping, *jumping. 4. brief, short, contracted. 5. intelligent, bright, smart, quick.*

slowdown *n.* downturn, slump, decline, fall-off, slackening, recession, depression, *bottoming out, economic cycle. ANT. *boom, upturn, expansion.*

slowpoke *n.* sloth, slug, laggard, snail, dawdler, foot-dragger, procrastinator.

sludge *n.* mud, ooze, mire, sediment, muck, oil, grease, goo, slime, *gunk, *goop, deposit, sewage, waste.

slug *n.* Sl. drink, swig, *hit, *shot.

slug *v.* hit, whack, slam, punch, *clock, pound, wallop, belt, clout, hit, whale, *coldcock, *clean one's clock, haul off on, *roundhouse.

slugfest *n.* fight, donnybrook, brawl, battle royal, *rumble, riot.

sluggish *a.* slothful, slow-moving, lethargic, listless, dull, sleepy, torpid, dragging, inactive, languid, inert, lifeless. ANT. *energetic, fast, lively.*

sluice *n.* channel, passage, waterway, flume, trough, floodgate.

slum *n.* ghetto, inner city, skid row, shanty town, warren.

slumber *n.* rest, *snooze, *shut-eye, land of Nod. SEE SLEEP

slumber *v.* rest, *snooze, *catch some shut-eye. SEE SLEEP

slump *n.* downturn, fall, decline, decrease, drop-off, recession, depression, crash, *falling-off, rut, *hard times. ANT. *boom, good times.*

slump *v.* **1.** DECREASE droop, drop, fall off, recede, crash, *experience hard times, decline, slip, *go downhill. **2.** SLOUCH hunch, droop, sag, bend. ANT. *1. boom, expand. 2. stand tall, straighten.*

slur *n.* smear, *black eye, insult, blot, aspersion, slander, innuendo, insinuation, affront, *dig, stigma. ANT. *compliment, praise, commendation.*

slur *v.* **1.** SLANDER insult, smear, *give a black

eye, cast aspersions, insinuate, affront, *dig, stigmatize, blot, blemish one's name, sully, disparage. **2.** MISPRONOUNCE garble, get tongue-tied. ANT. *1. compliment, praise, commend. 2. enunciate.*

slurp n. Sl. sip, suck, slobber.

sly a. wily, foxy, cunning, crafty, tricky, clever, *cagey, artful, shrewd, sneaky, *weaselly, underhanded, furtive, secretive, stealthy. ANT. *artless, simple, naive.*

smack n. slap, blow, clout, clap, sock, hit, crack, spanking, cuff, whack.

smack v. slap, clout, clap, sock, hit, crack, spank, cuff, whack.

smack adv. directly, squarely, exactly, precisely, point-blank.

small a. **1.** LITTLE tiny, undersized, diminutive, short, wee, teeny, miniature, *pint-sized, *pocket-sized, puny, petite, Lilliputian, dwarf, pygmy, baby, minute, microscopic. **2.** SLIGHT paltry, insufficient, meager, inconsiderable, poor, picayune, modest, trivial. **3.** MINOR insignificant, trivial, light, trifling, unimportant, inconsequential, bush-league, *rinky-dink. **4.** SMALL-MINDED mean, narrow-minded, petty, selfish, cheap, ignoble, vindictive, prejudiced, grudging. ANT. *1. large, huge, gigantic, towering. 2. generous, rich, lavish, considerable. 3. important, major, big, consequential. 4. generous, liberal-minded, noble.*

small-minded a. mean, narrow-minded, petty, selfish, cheap, ignoble, vindictive, prejudice, grudging, ANT. *broad-minded, liberal-minded, noble, generous.*

small talk n. polite chatter, pleasantry, chit-chat, light talk, idle chatter.

small-time a. minor, bush-league, *one-horse, petty, *low-rent, piddling, *tinhorn.

smart v. sting, burn, tingle, throb, hurt, ache, stab.

smart a. **1.** INTELLIGENT bright, brilliant, sharp, knowledgeable, educated, *savvy, astute, *brainy, learned, clever, genius, wise, keen, witty, *on the ball. **2.** NEAT spruce, trim, groomed, stylish, chic, dapper, natty, elegant, dashing. **3.** STINGING harsh, painful, rough, hard, sharp. **4.** BRISK vigorous, lively, energetic. ANT. *1. stupid, dumb, retarded, moronic, slow, dense. 2. sloppy, bedraggled, unfashionable, frumpy. 3. soft, gentle, mild. 4. lethargic, slow.*

smart-aleck n. *wise guy, *wisenheimer, *smart ass, *comedian, *bigmouth, *know-it-all, *wise apple.

smart-alecky a. *wise, *smart-assed, *smart-mouthed, cheeky, flip, sassy, impudent, cocky, nervy.

smash n. **1.** COLLISION crash, wreck, shattering, breakup, burst, smashup, crack, blow, collapse. **2.** SUCCESS winner, hit, sensation, sellout.

smash v. shatter, break, hit, bust, burst, wreck, crack, splinter, pulverize, disintegrate, break into a million pieces, fracture, demolish.

smashing a. great, excellent, extraordinary, outstanding, superb, wonderful, terrific, splendid, exceptional, *spot-on. ANT. *lousy, awful, terrible.*

smashup n. wreck, collision, accident, *fender-bender. SEE CRASH

smattering n. small amount, slight amount, sprinkling, touch, dash, trace.

smear n. **1.** STAIN spot, smudge, blot, mark, splotch, smirch, streak. **2.** SLANDER defamation, mudslinging, denigration, slur, aspersion, character assassination, blot, stain, libel. ANT. *2. honor, praise, compliment.*

smear v. **1.** STAIN spot, smudge, blot, mark, splotch, smirch, streak, dirty, daub, wipe on. **2.** SLANDER defame, mudsling, denigrate, cast aspersions, character assassinate, blot, stain, libel, drag one's name through the mud. ANT. *1. clean, wash, scrub. 2. honor, praise, commend.*

SMEAR CAMPAIGN n. an underhanded campaign to ruin someone's reputation. *The politicians launched smear campaigns against each other.* SYN. mudslinging, character assassination, slander, public denigration, defamation of character, maligning, *dragging one's name through the mud.

smell n. **1.** SENSE OF SMELL olfaction, perception. **2.** ODOR scent, aroma, fragrance, stink, reek, stench, fume, perfume, bouquet, emanation, whiff, essence. SEE ODOR

smell v. sniff, inhale, sample, get a whiff of, snuff, breathe.

smidgen n. bit, tiny amount, iota, trace, speck, sprinkling, pinch, jot, whit, scintilla.

smile n. grin, smirk, simper, beam, happy look, *alligator smile, gap-toothed smile, snaggle-toothed smile, Cheshire cat smile, idiotic grin. ANT. *frown, scowl, black look.*

smile v. grin, smirk, beam, smile ear to ear, smile broadly, smile like a Cheshire cat. ANT. *frown, scowl.*

smirk n. smile, simper, grin, sneer, leer.

smirk v. smile, simper, grin, sneer, leer, make a face.

smite v. strike, hit, *whack, attack, beset, defeat, punish, kill, destroy.

smitten a. taken by, *head over heels, struck, in love, enamored, *swept off one's feet, infatuated, captivated, enthralled, having a crush on, stricken. ANT. *repulsed, turned off.*

smock n. frock, camise, coverall, shirt, garment.

smog n. air pollution, haze, smoke, fog, pall, particulate, gas cloud, soot cloud, carbon monoxide. ANT. *fresh air, *ozone.*

smoke n. fume, gas, soot, vapor, exhaust, smog, carbon, reek, smaze, pollution, carbon monoxide.

smoke v. fume, give off exhaust, pollute.

smoked a. dried, cured. ANT. *hydrated.*

smoke detector n. smoke alarm, fire alarm, fire detector, early warning system.

smokestack n. chimney, flue, funnel, *stack.

smoky a. burning, thick, smoldering, fumy, gassy, sooty, polluted, reeking, choking, hazy, smoggy, foggy.

smolder v. 1. BURN smoke, fume, combust, char. 2. SEETHE stew, fume, suppress one's anger, simmer, fester, steam, boil over.

smooch v. Sl. kiss, smack.

smooth a. 1. NOT ROUGH even, level, leveled, planed, unwrinkled, unruffled, flush, glossy, glassy, slick, sleek, satiny, silky, velvety, polished, glabrous. 2. UNTROUBLED gentle, calm, serene, uneventful, peaceful, undisturbed. 3. SUAVE slick, urbane, graceful, silver-tongued, *having savoir faire, polished, refined, practiced, facile, flattering, oily, unctuous. ANT. *1. rough, bumpy, lumpy. 2. troubled, rough, disturbing. 3. coarse, awkward, simple, bumbling.*

smorgasbord n. spread, banquet, buffet, feast, meal, appetizers.

smother v. 1. SUFFOCATE asphyxiate, cut off one's air supply, stifle, choke, strangle, throttle. 2. SUPPRESS stifle, hide, conceal, put down, squelch, quash, muffle. 3. EXTINGUISH put out, cover, snuff out.

smudge n. smear, blot, stain, mark, blotch, streak, blemish, smirch, smutch, spot.

smudge v. smear, blot, stain, mark, blotch, streak, blemish, smirch, smutch, spot.

smug a. self-satisfied, complacent, proud, *full of oneself, *puffed up, superior, pompous, pleased with oneself, self-righteous, holier-than-thou. ANT. *insecure, self-doubting, sheepish, humble.*

smuggle v. sneak in, bring in, run, *bootleg, import illegally, traffic, deal in contraband.

smuggler n. runner, *bootlegger.

smut n. pornography, *porn, obscenity, dirty talk, X-rated material, *raunch, indecent material.

smutty a. pornographic, obscene, dirty, X-rated, *raunchy, indecent, *blue, prurient, lewd, filthy. ANT. *wholesome, G-rated, clean.*

snack n. bite, nosh, *munchies, light meal, tidbit, nibble, morsel, refreshment.

snack v. have a bite to eat, nosh, nibble, eat, *munch out.

snafu n. Sl. mix-up, *screw-up, mistake, confusion, disorder, mess, disaster, chaos, difficulty.

snag n. catch, obstacle, difficulty, stumbling block, hindrance, road block, impediment, hitch, complication, block.

snake n. serpent, ophidian, viper, python, anaconda, boa constrictor, rattlesnake, coral snake, adder, cobra, garter snake.

snap n. 1. CRACK crackle, pop. 2. *CINCH *child's play, *breeze, no problem, *walk on the beach. 3. FASTENER clip, buckle, catch.

snap v. 1. CRACK crackle, pop, click. 2. COLLAPSE break, crack, fracture, burst, give way. 3. BITE nip, lunge at. 4. LASH OUT yell, bark, roar, shout, scream.

snappish a. irritable, cross, short-tempered, touchy, testy, crabby, grouchy, quick-tempered, waspish, peevish, *short-fused, edgy. ANT. *easygoing, good-humored, mild-mannered.*

snappy a. 1. LIVELY vigorous, quick, swift, instant, brisk. 2. STYLISH fashionable, chic, smart, dapper, sharp, natty. ANT. *1. slow, lifeless. 2. unfashionable, frumpy, dowdy.*

snare n. trap, noose, net, pitfall, *booby trap, decoy, lure, *set-up, *come-on, trick.

snare v. trap, catch, seize, snag, capture, bag, ensnare, land.

snarl n. 1. GROWL rumble, grumble, throaty warning. 2. TANGLE snag, knot, kink, twist. 3. COMPLICATION disorder, confusion, snafu, problem, hitch, catch, difficulty, trouble.

snarl v. 1. GROWL rumble, grumble, threaten, warn, bare the teeth and raise one's hackles. 2. TANGLE knot, snag, kink, twist. 3. COMPLICATE confuse, make trouble, mess up, *throw a wrench in the works.

snatch v. grab, grasp, seize, take, clutch, grapple, *snap up, pluck, snag, *nab, get one's hands on, wrest, swipe, kidnap.

snazzy a. Sl. stylish, sharp, flashy, smart, showy, snappy. ANT. *dowdy, unstylish.*

sneak *n.* weasel, snake, *snake in the grass, thief in the night, dastard, *eel, scoundrel, *backstabber.

sneak *v.* creep, skulk, pussyfoot, stalk, lurk, prowl, slither, move stealthily, slink, steal, *weasel.

sneaker *n.* running shoe, *hightop, sport shoe, tennis shoe, boat shoe. SEE SHOE

sneaky *a.* underhanded, sly, secretive, undercover, backdoor, stealthy, *weasely, feline, furtive, surreptitious, clandestine, devious, treacherous. ANT. *open, honest, aboveboard.*

sneer *v.* smile sarcastically, smile with contempt, mock, scoff, ridicule, make fun of, curl one's lip, taunt.

sneering *a.* scoffing, mocking, disdainful, scornful, derisive, ridiculing, sarcastic. ANT. *respectful, deferential.*

sneeze *n.* reflex, ejection, sternutation.

sneeze at *v.* disregard, take lightly.

snicker *n.* snigger, snort, sniggle, giggle, laugh, chuckle, suppressed laugh. SEE LAUGH

snicker *v.* snigger, snort, sniggle, giggle, laugh, chuckle, titter, suppress a laugh, tee-hee. SEE LAUGH

snide *a.* derisive, sarcastic, malicious, nasty, cutting, insulting, mean, hurtful, low, insinuating, sly. ANT. *nice, friendly, kind.*

sniff *n.* inhalation, sniffle, snuffle, snort, breath.

sniff *v.* inhale, snuff, snuffle, sniffle, snort, breathe.

snigger *v.* SEE SNICKER

snip *n.* cutting, snippet, piece, scrap.

snip *v.* cut, clip, shear, crop, trim, dock, bob, prune, chop, shave.

snipe *v.* ambush, take potshots, shoot, hunt, attack.

sniper *n.* ambusher, gunman, assassin, shooter.

snippet *n.* cutting, snip, piece, scrap, fragment.

snippy *a.* curt, sharp, insolent, short, snappish, abrupt, impertinent, smart-alecky, brusque. ANT. *polite, courteous.*

snit *n.* fit, pique, *tizzy.

snitch *v. Sl.* **1.** STEAL pilfer, lift, pickpocket, shoplift. SEE STEAL **2.** INFORM ON tell on, *rat on, *squeal, tattle, turn in.

snivel *v.* cry, whine, sniffle, snuffle, fret, whimper, blubber, boo-hoo.

snob *n.* elitist, *high-hat, *stuffed shirt, upstart, highbrow, parvenu, name-dropper.

snobbery *n.* snobbishness, elitism, airs, pretension, pretentiousness, haughtiness, conceit, *snootiness, hauteur, superciliousness, pride, *high horse, class conscience, condescension. "The pride of those who are not

sure of their position."—Berton Braley. "Pride in status without pride in function."—Lionel Trilling.

snobbish *a.* snobby, *stuck-up, *uppity, putting on airs, pretentious, haughty, conceited, *snooty, supercilious, proud, *up on one's high horse, class conscious, above it all, arrogant, hoity-toity, high-falutin, high and mighty. ANT. *down-to-earth, humble, modest.*

snoop *n.* busybody, eavesdropper, gossip.

snoop *v.* spy, nose around, pry, stick one's nose in.

snooty *a.* haughty, snotty, *la-di-da, uppity. SEE SNOBBISH

snooze *v.* doze, nap, drowse, *catch some Zs, take a siesta. SEE SLEEP

snore *n.* *sawing wood, stertor, snorting. "That tuneful serenade of that wakeful nightingale, the nose."—George Farquhar.

snort *n.* snuffle, sniff, sniffle, honk. SEE SNICKER

snort *v.* snuffle, sniff, sniffle, honk. SEE SNICKER

snotty *a.* impudent, offensive, insolent, cheeky, flip, sassy, smart-alecky, fresh, snooty, sniffy, arrogant. ANT. *deferential, humble, respectful.* SEE SNOBBISH

snout *n.* nose, muzzle, nozzle, beak, trunk, proboscis, nozzle. SEE NOSE

snow *n.* **1.** PRECIPITATION flurry, flurries, hydrometeors, snowflakes, sleet, hail, blizzard, drift, slush.

WORD FIND

bump or mound of snow on ski trail: mogul
collapse on mountain: avalanche
glacial snow: névé
granules, old, refrozen: corn snow
house of: igloo
old, compacted snow: firn, crust
pellets of: graupel
shelf of snow that collapses and triggers avalanche: cornice
zero visibility due to blizzard: whiteout

2. *Sl.* *coke, *blow, heroin. SEE COCAINE

snow *v.* **1.** PRECIPITATE flurry, blizzard, storm, sleet, hail, blow. **2.** *Sl.* DECEIVE *buffalo, *bamboozle, mislead, *sell a bill of goods, *fast talk, *pull the wool over one's eyes.

snowboard *n.* board ridden to navigate downhill over snow.

WORD FIND

airborne, getting: catching air
backwards, riding: fakie
crash, fall: bail
legs straightened, to ride with one or both: bone
ramp of snow, U-shaped: half pipe

rotation of 180 degrees: alley-oop
rotation of 360 degrees: caballerial
strike a rock or log: bonk
turn, to make a: carve
vibrations at high speed, board: chatter
snowy *a.* niveous, wintry.
snub *n.* slight, affront, *cold shoulder, *slap in the face, rebuff, cut, oversight, neglect, ignoring, insult.
snub *v.* slight, give the cold shoulder, rebuff, cut, overlook, ignore, neglect, insult, shun, *give the brush-off, pass over, offend.
snuff *v.* **1.** PUT OUT smother, pinch out, douse, extinguish. **2.** SNIFF smell, snort.
snuffle *v.* sniff, breathe, snort, snivel.
snug *a.* **1.** PROTECTED sheltered, under cover, secure, warm, cozy, comfortable. **2.** TIGHT close, body-hugging, close-fitting, restrictive.
snuggle *v.* cuddle, nestle, nuzzle, hug, curl up, *spoon together, hold close.
so *adv.* therefore, thus, hence, ergo.
soak *v.* saturate, wet, drench, douse, souse, steep, sop, impregnate, drown, flood, permeate, submerge, immerse. ANT. *dry, dehydrate, desiccate.*
soaked *a.* saturated, wet, drenched, sopping, sodden, soggy, drowned. ANT. *dry, dehydrated.*
soap *n.* detergent, suds, lather, wash powder, cleaning agent, cleanser, solvent, shampoo.
soap opera *n.* melodrama, show, drama, program, play.
soapy *a.* sudsy, lathery, bubbly, foamy, frothy, saponaceous.
soar *v.* fly, rocket, jet, sail, glide, wing, zoom, rise, go skyward, ascend, go aloft, cruise. ANT. *nosedive, drop, plummet.*
soaring *a.* high, towering, lofty, vertiginous, skyscraping. ANT. *plummeting.*
sob *n.* weeping, cry, sniveling, bawling, whimper, wail, blubbering, moan.
sob *v.* weep, cry, snivel, boo-hoo, bawl, whimper, wail, blubber, shed tears, moan, mourn, lament.
sober *v.* sober up, dry out, *go through a detox facility.
sober *a.* **1.** NOT DRUNK temperate, *stone cold sober, rational, lucid, clearheaded, *on the wagon, *detoxed, *dry, in possession of one's faculties, abstemious. **2.** SERIOUS solemn, grave, unsmiling, somber, dignified, sedate, staid, earnest. **3.** PLAIN quiet, understated, mellow, subdued, dull, drab, simple.

ANT. *1. drunk, intoxicated, inebriated, *hammered. 2. silly, giddy, jovial. 3. flashy, loud, ostentatious.*
sobriety *n.* abstinence, soberness, temperance, teetotalism, moderation, self-denial, self-restraint. ANT. *drunkeness, inebriation.*
sobriquet *n.* nickname, pet name, agnomen, moniker, *handle, assumed name, alias.
sob story *n.* tale of woe, heartbreaker, plea.
so-called *a.* professed, alleged, supposed, self-styled, commonly named. ANT. *actual, proven.*
soccer *n.* football, sport.
WORD FIND
curving pass: banana pass, banana kick, curling the ball, bending the ball
dirty player: hacker
goalie's long kick: punt
illegal position: offside
issue a card for a foul: book, card, caution
keep the ball in midair by bouncing off body parts: juggling
kick ball between defender's legs: nutmeg
kick with legs upended high overhead: bicycle kick, scissors kick
officials: linesmen, referee
out-of-bounds sidelines: touch
pass then receive quick return pass: give-and-go
penalty situation in which one team is a man short: power play
positions: back, center back, center halfback, forward, fullback, goalkeeper (goalie), halfback, sweeper, winger
run the ball downfield with one's feet: dribble
soccer field: pitch
steal the ball from opponent: tackle
stop the ball's motion with body part: trap, kill
three goals scored by same player in one game: hat trick
sociable *a.* gregarious, outgoing, extroverted, friendly, amiable, folksy, social, warm, companionable, cordial, approachable, genial. "The art of unlearning to be preoccupied with yourself."—Oscar Blumenthal. ANT. *unfriendly, aloof, cold, reclusive.*
social *a.* **1.** COMMUNAL public, community, group, common, popular, civil, civic, human. **2.** GREGARIOUS outgoing, extroverted, friendly, amiable, folksy. ANT. *1. private. 2. aloof, reclusive.* SEE SOCIABLE
socialism *n.* Marxism, communism. SEE POLITICS
socialize *v.* be friendly, mix, mingle, fraternize,

get together, befriend, associate, entertain, hobnob, *chum with. ANT. *withdraw, be reclusive, shun.

social security n. retirement income, disability insurance, unemployment insurance, old age insurance, entitlement program. SEE GOVERNMENT

society n. **1.** COMMUNITY civilization, public, people, mankind, humankind, humanity, populace, culture, the world, the nation. "The vital articulation of many individuals into a new collective individual."—Thomas Carlyle. **2.** ORGANIZATION alliance, association, club, group, sorority, fraternity, brotherhood, sisterhood, affiliation, institution, league, guild. **3.** UPPER CLASS upper crust, high society, the elite, aristocracy, nobility, gentry, beau monde, haut monde. ANT. *3. lower class, working class, hoi polloi, commoners.*

sociopath n. psychopath, antisocial personality, lunatic, maniac, psychotic, *nut case, deranged person, crazy person, mentally ill person.

sock n. stocking, hose, hosiery, footwear.

sock v. hit, strike, punch, belt, wallop, smack, pound, slap.

socket n. fitting, receiving end, chamber, holder, mortise.

sod n. turf, clod, sward, divot, grass chunk, clump.

soda n. pop, soft drink, carbonated water, soda water, beverage, cola, ginger ale, root beer.

sodden a. soaked, soggy, wet, sopping, saturated, waterlogged, drenched, poachy, dripping, damp, moist, steeped. ANT. *dry, dehydrated, desiccated.*

sodomize v. engage in anal intercourse.

sodomy n. anal intercourse, pederasty.

sofa n. couch, lounge, divan, davenport, chesterfield, love seat, futon, convertible.

soft a. **1.** YIELDING EASILY spongy, squishy, doughy, mushy, fluffy, cushioned, pliable, supple, malleable, flexible, ductile. **2.** SMOOTH fine, silky, satiny, downy, velvety, fine, delicate. **3.** GENTLE mild, light, slight, moderate, delicate, faint, mellow, muted, subdued. **4.** TENDER compassionate, kind, softhearted, merciful, easy, easygoing, humane, lenient, forgiving. **5.** EASY *cushy, simple, plush, *piece of cake, *a snap, *no sweat, unchallenging. **6.** FAT unfit, untoned, fleshy, blubbery, doughy. ANT. *1. hard, rockhard, solid, unyielding. 2. rough, coarse, abrasive. 3. intense, strong, loud. 4. *hard as nails,* merciless, cold, brutal. *5. hard, demanding, challenging, stressful. 6. hard, toned, fit, cut.*

soften a. moderate, mitigate, mellow, temper, diminish, ease, lighten, lessen, assuage, mollify, tone down, slacken. ANT. *harden, intensify, toughen.*

softhearted a. soft, tender, compassionate, sympathetic, merciful, easy, human, lenient, forgiving, *big-hearted, *having a bleeding heart. ANT. *hard, merciless, brutal.*

softly adv. tenderly, lightly, gently, mildly, slightly, moderately, delicately, faintly, easily. ANT. *intensely, strongly, loudly.*

soft-pedal v. play down, tone down, understate.

soft soap n. praise, cajolery, blarney. SEE FLATTERY

soft-spoken a. quiet, low-keyed, gentle. ANT. *loud, boisterous.*

soft touch n. Sl. *softie, *bleeding heart, dupe, *sucker.

software n. program, *shareware, disk, file management system, instructions, command. SEE COMPUTER

soggy a. saturated, soaked, sodden, drenched, waterlogged, sopping, poachy, dripping, moist, damp. ANT. *dry, dehydrated, desiccated.*

soil n. earth, dirt, loam, humus, topsoil, ground, clay, terra firma, turf, loess.

soil v. **1.** DIRTY muddy, begrime, stain, smudge, spot, mess, smear, foul, besmirch. **2.** DISGRACE dishonor, malign, discredit, blot, defame, taint, *drag one's name through the mud. ANT. *1. clean, cleanse. 2. honor, praise.*

soiree n. party, social gathering, get-together.

sojourn n. visit, temporary stay, stopover, layover, vacation, temporary residence.

SOJOURN v. [SO jurn] to visit or stay somewhere temporarily. *She plans to sojourn with her family in California.* SYN. stay temporarily, visit, stop over, tarry, reside, vacation, lodge, linger, *hang out for awhile.

Sol n. Helios, sun god, the sun.

SOLACE n. [SAWL is] a comforting or relief from anguish. *He took solace in the fact that work would be over in one hour.* SYN. comfort, comforting, relief, easing, consolation, succor, condolence, encouragement, cheering, buoyance. ANT. *pain, anguish, exacerbation.*

solace v. comfort, console, relieve, ease, condole, cheer up, encourage, hearten, *buck up, inspirit, buoy. ANT. *pain, anguish, aggravate.*

solarium n. sunroom, sun porch.

solar system n. planetary system. SEE SPACE, SUN

soldier n. 1. WARRIOR fighter, fighting man, GI, infantryman, *leatherneck, *grunt, *dogface, service person, airman, marine, sailor, commando, gunner, bombardier, foot soldier, Green Beret, cadet, mercenary, cannon fodder, *storm trooper, *doughboy, draftee, enlisted man, enlisted woman, guerrilla, paratrooper, POW, MIA. "Food for power."—Shakespeare. "The sinews of war."—Niccolo Machiavelli. SEE ARMY, NAVY, WAR 2. SUPPORTER booster, party member, worker, follower, zealot.

sole a. lone, single, solitary, alone, only, exclusive. ANT. several.

solely adv. only, merely, entirely, singly.

SOLEMN a. [SAWL um] serious, earnest, dignified, formal. The funeral was a solemn affair. SYN. serious, earnest, dignified, formal, somber, sober, funereal, *no-nonsense, staid, grave, unsmiling, ceremonious, reverential, sacred. ANT. jovial, frivolous, lighthearted.

solicit v. 1. ASK FOR plead for, beg, appeal, petition, implore, beseech, supplicate. 2. PROPOSITION tempt, entice, accost, hustle, *drum up business, tout, hawk, peddle.

SOLICITOUS a. [suh LIS uh tus] concerned, worried, showing one's concern. The mayor appeared solicitous about our problems. SYN. concerned, worried, caring, attentive, troubled, apprehensive, disturbed, anxious, heedful. ANT. unconcerned, untroubled, undisturbed.

solicitor n. attorney, counselor. SEE LAWYER

solicitude n. concern, care, worry, regard, uneasiness.

solid a. 1. HARD dense, firm, heavy, thick, rock-solid, compact, concentrated. 2. STRONG sound, sturdy, stable, substantial, massive, hefty. 3. COMPLETE unbroken, continuous, undivided. 4. GENUINE pure, unalloyed, unmixed, 100 percent, complete. 5. UNANIMOUS undivided, of one mind, united, unified. 6. DEPENDABLE firm, rock-solid, reliable, constant, trustworthy. ANT. 1. fluid, porous, gaseous. 2. flimsy, airy, unstable, delicate. 3. incomplete, broken, interrupted. 4. mixed, alloyed, impure. 5. divided. 6. undependable, shaky, unreliable.

solidarity n. unity, unanimity, union, single-mindedness, oneness, harmony, accord, concord, consensus, strength in numbers. ANT. division, dissension.

solidify v. harden, set, stiffen, cake, concrete, gel, jell, thicken, congeal, clot, coagulate, freeze. ANT. liquefy, melt.

SOLILOQUY n. [suh LIL uh kwee] the act of talking to oneself. Also, the dialogue of a stage actor revealing his thoughts to the audience. Shakespeare liked to use the soliloquy as a dramatic tool. SYN. monologue, aside, apostrophe. SEE DRAMA, PLAY

solitary a. lone, alone, lonely, lonesome, single, companionless, friendless, separate, solo, remote, by oneself, isolated, secluded, reclusive, desolate, forlorn, sequestered, hermitical, antisocial, cloistered. ANT. social, gregarious, popular, mixing.

solitude n. aloneness, seclusion, isolation, loneliness, privacy, peace and quiet, withdrawal, retirement, reclusion, remoteness. "The soul's best friend."—Charles Cotton. "Divine retreat."—Edward Young. "Often the best society."—William G. Benham.

solo a. alone, lone, unaccompanied, single-handed, unassisted, unaided. ANT. accompanied, group.

solution n. 1. ANSWER solving, key, explanation, resolution, clarification, uncovering, interpretation. 2. MIXTURE compound, dissolving, blend, combination, emulsion, suspension.

solve v. answer, explain, clear up, figure out, work out, clarify, uncover, crack, fathom, resolve, decode, decipher, *put the pieces together, *put two and two together, unlock, *get to the bottom of, unravel. ANT. mystify, confuse, complicate.

SOLVENT a. [SOL vent] financially stable, able to pay one's bills. The company remained solvent, even throughout the recession. SYN. financially fit, *out of the red, *in the black, on sound financial ground, profitable, able to pay, able to maintain cash flow. ANT. insolvent, bankrupt, *in the red.

somber a. gloomy, dark, depressing, black, bleak, dreary, mournful, melancholy, funereal, gray, solemn, grave. ANT. bright, sunny, cheerful, jovial.

somersault n. flip, tumble, roll, revolution.

somebody n. celebrity, *big shot, *bigwig, *VIP, star, superstar, *name, dignitary, personage, *heavy, *high muck-a-muck, luminary. ANT. nobody, *zero, *second stringer.

someday adv. one day, eventually, sometime, sooner or later, one of these days, in the future.

sometimes adv. occasionally, at times, now and then, every now and again, once in awhile, every so often, periodically, intermittently. ANT. *never.*

somewhat *adv.* rather, to a certain extent, pretty, fairly, partly, to a certain degree, *kind of, a little.

somnambulist. *n.* sleepwalker. SEE SLEEP

somnolent *a.* sleepy, drowsy, dozy, nodding off, half-asleep, *dopey, sleep-inducing. ANT. *wide-awake, alert.*

song *n.* tune, melody, ditty, ballad, serenade, lullaby, hymn, carol, number, *oldie, *golden oldie, *moldy oldie, hit, air, aria, glee, theme song, signature song, *cut, track. "The licensed medium for bawling in public things too silly or sacred to be uttered in ordinary speech."—Oliver Herford.

WORD FIND

advertising: jingle
award: Grammy
busy vocals with arpeggios, trills, runs, etc.: coloratura
catchy part: hook, chorus
collection: anthology
counterpointing vocal: descant
demonstration recording for contract-seeking musicians: demo
evening: evensong, vesper
funeral: dirge, requiem
improvisation: vamp
instrumental accompaniment, sung without: a capella
jazz vocalizations imitating instruments: scat
multiple-voiced: polyphonic
multiple-voiced, singing counterpoint: madrigal
multiple-voiced with same lines begun and sung at different times: canon, round
passage: refrain
popular in more than one genre or market: crossover hit
religious or from Scriptures: anthem, canticle, chorale, psalm, hymn
repetition of theme by two or more vocalists: call and answer
sailor's: shanty, chanty
triumph, of: paean
Venetian gondolier's: barcarole
words: lyrics
SEE MUSIC, OPERA, SING, SINGER

song and dance *n.* *line, *snow job, *jive, *bull, story.

sonorous *a.* resonant, resounding, deep, booming, loud, reverberating, powerful, full, rich, vibrant. ANT. *mute, silent.*

soon *adv.* shortly, coming right up, directly, presently, forthwith, anon, before long, promptly.

soot *n.* carbon, ash, grit, particulate, grime.

soothe *v.* calm, comfort, quiet, ease, salve, mollify, appease, pacify, tranquilize, relax, assuage, allay, soften, settle, lull, cool, relieve, lighten. ANT. *aggravate, exacerbate, intensify.*

soothing *a.* calming, comforting, quieting, easing, mollifying, appeasing, pacifying, tranquilizing, relaxing, softening, settling, palliative, relieving. ANT. *aggravating, exacerbating, intensifying.*

soothsayer *n.* predictor, prophet, seer, fortuneteller, forecaster, augur, oracle, diviner, psychic, Cassandra.

sop *v.* soak, saturate, wet, drench, steep, immerse, dip, dunk.

sophisticated *a.* **1.** WORLDLY worldly-wise, experienced, cultured, refined, urbane, *hip, *hep, *cool, cosmopolitan, *citified, mature, adult, seasoned, *with it, knowing. **2.** COMPLEX complicated, advanced, highly developed, modern, elaborate. ANT. *1. simple, naive, unseasoned. 2. simple, unsophisticated.*

sophistication *n.* worldliness, experience, culture, refinement, urbanity, *hipness, maturity, seasoning, development, advancement, knowledge. ANT. *simplicity, naiveté, inexperience.*

SOPHISTRY *n.* [SAWF is tree] argument or reasoning that is clever but fallacious, deceptive or misleading. *His lawyer was adept at sophistry.* SYN. fallacious argument, deceptive reasoning, subterfuge, misrepresentation, chicanery, idolism, false reasoning. "To reason correctly from a false principle."—Delos Emmons. "The lawyer's chief weapon."—Michael Axt.

SOPHOMORIC *a.* [sawf MOR ik] immature, inexperienced or foolish. *His jokes were painfully sophomoric.* SYN. immature, juvenile, inexperienced, foolish, silly, unsophisticated, naive, green, callow, reckless, childish, shallow. ANT. *mature, experienced, sophisticated, seasoned.*

soporific *a.* sleep-inducing, somnolent, somniferous, sedative, hypnotic, tranquilizing, opiate, narcotic, sleepy, drowsy, tired. ANT. *stimulating, energizing, invigorating.*

sopping *a.* wet, drenched, saturated, dripping, soaked, soggy, sodden, wringing wet. ANT. *dry, dehydrated.*

sorcerer *n.* necromancer, wizard, witch, warlock, magician, shaman, sorceress, sibyl, practicer of black magic, alchemist.

sorcery *n*. black magic, black art, magic, supernatural powers, witchcraft, necromancy, wizardry, mysticism, Satanism, voodoo, spellbinding, diabolism, conjuring, alchemy.

sordid *a*. dirty, filthy, foul, rotten, wretched, bad, mean, ignoble, base, seamy, immoral, corrupt, low, wicked. ANT. *clean, wholesome.*

sore *n*. wound, injury, lesion, cut, laceration, scar, scrape, bruise, abrasion, ulceration, blister, boil, painful area, tender area.

sore *a*. **1.** PAINFUL tender, aching, burning, throbbing, stabbing, hurting, smarting, stinging, sensitive, raw, bruised, irritated. **2.** ANGRY offended, mad, *pissed, irritated, annoyed, peeved, irked, indignant, resentful. ANT. *1. numb, healed. 2. pleased, delighted.*

sorrow *n*. **1.** GRIEF lamentation, sadness, heartache, heartbreak, heavyheartedness, melancholy, despair, depths of despair, misery, woe, mournfulness, desolation, pain, depression. "A rainy corner in your life."—Jean Paul Richter. "The great idealizer."—James Russell Lowell. **2.** LOSS trouble, adversity, hardship, disaster, tribulation, affliction, misfortune, bad luck. ANT. *1. joy, happiness, light-heartedness. 2. fortune, good luck, blessing.*

sorrowful *a*. grieving, grief-stricken, sad, heartbroken, heavyhearted, melancholy, plumbing the depths of despair, miserable, woeful, mournful, desolate, pained, depressed. ANT. *elated, euphoric, happy, joyous.*

sorry *a*. **1.** CONTRITE remorseful, regretful, conscience-stricken, compunctious, guilt-ridden, apologetic, repentant, penitent, ashamed. **2.** SORROWFUL pitying, commiserative, sympathetic, empathetic. **3.** POOR inferior, cheap, bad, *crappy, worthless, pitiful, pathetic, paltry, mean. ANT. *1. proud, delighted, pleased. 2. uncaring, indifferent. 3. superior, excellent.*

sort *n*. **1.** KIND type, order, style, variety, brand, class, set, make, category, genus, race. **2.** NATURE quality, ilk.

sort *v*. classify, class, arrange, order, organize, categorize, group, file, alphabetize, systemize, catalog, grade, rank. ANT. *mix up, jumble.*

sortie *n*. raid, charge, offense, attack, assault, sally, rush, mission.

so-so *a*. okay, fair, fair to middling, not bad, tolerable, passable, mediocre, run-of-the-mill, *nothing to write home about, average. ANT. *superb, first-rate, extraordinary.*

sot *n*. drunkard, drunk, *wino, *rummy, alcoholic, *boozer, drinker, *barfly, *alky, *gin hound, *souse.

soul *n*. **1.** SPIRIT entity, mind, self, ego, psyche, conscience, anima. "A guest in our body, deserving of our kind hospitality."—Hillel. "A portion of the Deity housed in our bodies."—Josephus. "The life whereby we are joined into the body."—Saint Augustine. "A god within each human breast."—Ovid. **2.** WARMTH OF EMOTION spirit, feeling. **3.** ESSENCE heart, vital part, meat, quintessence, pith, center. **4.** PERSON human, being, man, woman, mortal, individual.

soulful *a*. emotional, with feeling, deep, moving, meaningful. ANT. *shallow, trivial.*

soul mate *n*. lover, friend, confidante, companion, alter ego.

soul-searching *n*. introspection, self-examination, self-analysis, reflection.

sound *n*. SEE NOISE

sound *v*. **1.** MAKE A NOISE vibrate, reverberate, echo, resound, ring, resonate, boom, thunder, detonate, thud, slam, rumble, roar, bang, crash, crack, clap, blare, burst, crunch, clang, chime, ding, ping, jangle, tinkle, buzz, hum, drone, whir, purr, creak, rustle, swish, fizz, sizzle, grate, rasp, hiss, rattle, clank, honk, trumpet, squeak, squeal, whisper. **2.** SEEM look, look like, come across, read, give the impression.

sound *a*. **1.** IN GOOD WORKING ORDER healthy, fit, whole, solid, *in good shape, intact, strong, perfect, unimpaired, *running like a Swiss watch, normal. **2.** STABLE secure, safe, firm, reliable, on solid ground, on solid footing, solvent. **3.** ACCURATE valid, sensible, logical, rational, grounded in fact, judicious, true, correct, right-minded, intelligent, commonsensical. **4.** ACCEPTED established, orthodox, recognized, *tried-and-true, traditional, standard. **5.** THOROUGH solid, complete. ANT. *1. unfit, unsound, impaired. 2. unstable, insecure, insolvent. 3. inaccurate, unsound, invalid, nonsensical. 4. new, unaccepted, radical, heterodox. 5. partial, incomplete.*

sound bite *n*. excerpt, snippet, quote, passage.

soundless *a*. still, mute, quiet. SEE SILENT

soundproof *a*. soundproofed, silent, noiseless, insulated. ANT. *noisy.*

soup *n*. broth, bouillon, stock, consommé, bisque, pottage, chowder, stew, gumbo, borscht, minestrone, split pea, gazpacho, bouillabaisse, lentil soup, vichyssoise.

soupçon n. suspicion, trace, suggestion, hint, dash, drop, pinch.

sour v. turn one against, *turn off, disillusion, embitter, disenchant.

sour a. **1.** TART acid, vinegary, sharp, *mouth-puckering, bitter, fermented, bad, rank, spoiled, curdled, rancid, repulsive, unpalatable. **2.** SURLY cross, bad-tempered, irritable, testy, touchy, nasty, crabby, ill-humored, grouchy, morose. ANT. *1. sweet, sugary, saccharine, fresh. 2. sweet, good-natured, nice.*

source n. **1.** SPRING wellspring, fount, fountain, origin, beginning, start, dawn, root, foundation, provenance, derivation. **2.** REFERENCE authority, author, documentation, database, *horse's mouth, informant.

sourpuss n. *Sl.* *crab, grouch, *bellyacher, *picklepuss.

souse v. pickle, steep, soak, saturate, brine, marinate, immerse, dunk, plunge, submerge.

soused a. *Sl.* intoxicated, inebriated. SEE DRUNK

souvenir n. memento, keepsake, relic, reminder, remembrance, memorial, token, trophy.

sovereign n. monarch, ruler, king, queen, crowned head, prince, autocrat, emperor, empress, czar, overlord, dictator.

SOVEREIGN a. [SAWV run] the greatest, supreme, ruling. Also, independent from the rule of others. *We studied the evolution of a sovereign state.* SYN. greatest, supreme, ranking, leading, preeminent, chief, ruling, dominant, kingly, queenly, royal, regal, monarchal, imperial, autonomous, independent, self-governing. ANT. *dependent, powerless, following, subject.*

sovereignty n. supremacy, independent power, authority, domination, dominance, dominion, preeminence, rule, jurisdiction. "Some power or other from which there is no appeal."—Samuel Johnson.

sow v. plant, scatter, seed, broadcast, strew, disperse, spread, imbed, drill.

spa n. resort, health facility, therapeutic facility, health club, bath, tub.

space n. **1.** UNIVERSE outer space, cosmos, infinity, heavens, ether, *eternal horizon, interstellar expanse, *the great beyond, macrocosm, galactic expanse, solar system, galaxy, cooling fires of creation, interstellar regions, void, celestial sphere, vacuum. **2.** AREA room, expanse, range, scope, elbowroom, capacity, volume, territory.

WORD FIND
distant, bright, mysterious object: quasar
galaxy we live in: Milky Way

gas cloud, massive: nebula
measurement, unit of: light year, parsec, astronomical unit
stars, mass grouping of: galaxy
SEE ASTRONOMY, MOON, PLANET, SUN, UNIVERSE

spacecraft n. rocket, rocket ship, spaceship, shuttle, orbiter, capsule, space probe, satellite, Apollo, Gemini, Mariner, flying saucer, UFO.

WORD FIND
activities of astronaut outside of spacecraft: EVA, extravehicular
activity, spacewalk
agency: NASA, National Aeronautics and Space Agency
astronaut's life-support cable used outside craft: umbilical
cancel mission: scrub
cancel mission in progress: abort
cargo: payload
chamber between pressurized and unpressurized compartment: airlock
distant measuring science: telemetry
electronic monitoring systems: avionics
entry into earth's atmosphere: reentry
firing of thrusters or rockets: burn
flight path: trajectory
fuel: hydrazine, hydrogen peroxide, LOX (Liquid Oxygen)
gravity force equal to earth: g
gravity force in earth orbit: microgravity
gravity slingshot method to boost craft further into space: gravity assist
ground station: tracking station
hazardous flying sand grains: micrometeoroids
independent system on board: module, subsystem
launchpad pit: flame pit
loss of orbital altitude due to earth's pull: decay
orbit that matches earth's rotation: geosynchronous orbit
orientation in orbit: attitude
payload, launching into space: deployment
power source: solar cells, photovoltaics SEE FUEL
propellants that ignite on contact with one another: hypergolic propellants
radio signal from earth to spacecraft: uplink
radio signal from spacecraft to earth: downlink
rocket, extra lifting: booster
rocket, slowing or reversing: retro rocket
rolling craft to diffuse external heat: barbecue mode

shuttle's nickname: *flying brick
space probe nerve center: JPL, Jet Propulsion Laboratory
space shuttle nerve center: Mission Control
speed of sound, five times the: hypersonic (above Mach 5)
speed of sound: Mach
speed of sound, twice the: Mach 2
timespan within which craft must be launched: launch window
wall: bulkhead

spacey *a. Sl.* *spaced out, *lost in space, *in a fog, *out to lunch, out of touch with reality, eccentric, weird, *in a zone.

spacious *a.* roomy, commodious, large, vast, capacious, extensive, immense, voluminous, expansive, uncrowded, generous. ANT. *cramped, crowded, confined.*

span *n.* spread, reach, width, length, height, breadth, stretch, distance, period, time.

span *v.* cross, traverse, extend across, stretch across, reach across, bridge, arch over.

spangle *n.* paillette, sequin, glitter, bead.

spank *v.* swat, slap, smack, hit, strike, rap, paddle one's behind, take over one's knee, cuff, lick, wallop, thrash, whip.

spar *n.* pole, beam, mast, sprit, boom, yard, gaff.

spar *v.* box, shadow box, *mix it up, practice, work out, trade punches.

spare *n.* extra, stand-by, backup, auxiliary, substitute, fill-in, surplus, leftover.

spare *v.* **1.** TREAT MERCIFULLY save, free, liberate, go easy on, forgive, excuse, pardon, exempt, release, let go, reprieve. **2.** GIVE UP part with, donate, let go, do without, grant, afford.

spare *a.* **1.** EXTRA stand-by, backup, auxiliary, reserve, substitute, fill-in, superfluous, emergency, odd, surplus, leftover. **2.** LEAN thin, skinny, slim, slender, slight, bony, scrawny, lanky, rawboned. **3.** SCANTY meager, sparse, modest, frugal. ANT. *1. essential. 2. fat, obese, flabby. 3. rich, abundant.*

sparing *a.* **1.** FRUGAL thrifty, economical, *tight, stingy, cheap, saving, parsimonious, miserly, stinting, grudging, niggardly. **2.** SCANTY meager, sparse, modest, spare. ANT. *1. generous, charitable, giving, lavish. 2. rich, abundant.*

spark *n.* **1.** FLASH flicker, scintilla, flare, sparkle, glow, discharge, glint, glimmer, trace, tinge, particle. **2.** STIMULUS spark plug, goad, spur, motivation, impetus, inspiration.

spark *v.* **1.** FLASH flicker, scintillate, flare, sparkle, glow, discharge, glint, glimmer. **2.** STIMULATE ignite, start, activate, goad, spur, motivate, energize, propel, inspire. ANT. *2. extinguish, douse.*

sparkle *v.* **1.** FLASH spark, glitter, shine, flicker, scintillate, glint, glimmer, twinkle, wink, dazzle, shimmer. **2.** BE BRILLIANT be the life of the party, shine, effervesce, dazzle, be animated, be lively, be vivacious.

sparse *a.* scanty, meager, slight, scarce, thin, spare, spotty, scattered, few and far between, skimpy, poor. ANT. *thick, abundant, plentiful.*

Spartan *a.* disciplined, strict, rigorous, demanding, severe, rigid, abstemious, austere, simple, frugal. ANT. *undisciplined, lavish, luxurious,* *cushy.

spasm *n.* contraction, convulsion, jerk, twitch, tic, nervous tic, seizure, fit, throe, cramp, shudder, orgasm, cramp.

spasmodic *a.* convulsive, fitful, spastic, twitching, intermittent, sporadic, periodic, on-and-off, irregular. ANT. *regular, steady, continuous.*

spat *n.* dispute, quarrel, disagreement, argument, fight, tiff, row, squabble, *run-in, falling-out, misunderstanding.

spate *n.* flood, deluge, outpouring, overflow, downpour, freshet, inundation, heavy rain, cloudburst. ANT. *drought.*

spatter *v.* splash, scatter, spray, shower, sprinkle, scatter, dot, speckle, dabble, spot.

spawn *v.* produce young, reproduce, bring forth, generate, engender, bear, give birth to, beget, *hatch, create.

spay *v.* sterilize.

spaz *n. Sl.* *nerd, *geek, oddball, *goofball, *goober.

speak *v.* **1.** UTTER talk, say, state, mouth, voice, vocalize, articulate, verbalize, communicate, express, enunciate, pronounce, babble, blurt, cry, shout, bellow, shriek, rant, rave, exclaim, mutter, mumble, whine, murmur, whisper, stutter, stammer. **2.** MAKE A SPEECH lecture, give a talk, discourse, orate, address, hold forth, preach, pontificate, deliver a sermon. **3.** CONVERSE talk, chat, *shoot the breeze, confabulate. SEE TALK

speaker *n.* talker, lecturer, orator, speechmaker, spokeswoman, spokesman, keynoter, spellbinder.

spear *n.* lance, javelin, dart, bolt, shaft, harpoon, pike, trident, leister.

spear *v.* pierce, stab, stick, run through, impale, lance, puncture, harpoon.

SPEARHEAD *v.* [SPEER hed] to start, pioneer or lead. *He spearheaded the environmental movement.* SYN. start, pioneer, lead, *blaze the trail, *get the ball rolling, launch, originate, initiate.

special *a.* **1.** PARTICULAR specific, specialized, appropriate. **2.** DISTINGUISHED exceptional, extraordinary, distinctive, different, unusual, unique, out-of-the-ordinary, singular, important, *red-letter, momentous, marked, select. ANT. *1. general, standard. 2. usual, ordinary, standard, normal.*

specialist *n.* expert, authority, master, professional, connoisseur, ace, virtuoso, scholar, devotee. ANT. **jack-of-all-trades, master of none, amateur.*

specialize *v.* concentrate on, practice, major in, devote oneself exclusively to.

specialty *n.* line, forte, area of expertise, specialization, métier, major, bailiwick, profession, skill, strength.

species *n.* variety, class, line, type, sort, breed, order, genus, division, stripe, genre.

specific *a.* specified, particular, express, designated, explicit, precise, exact, clear, defined, spelled-out, unequivocal, unambiguous, obvious, concrete. ANT. *vague, indefinite, ambiguous.*

specifically *adv.* particular, expressly, explicitly, precisely, specially, exactly, clearly, definitely, especially.

specification *n.* detail, particular, item, spec, feature, ingredient, stipulation, measurement, size.

specify *v.* be specific, detail, spell out, be precise, name, designate, itemize, define, express, explain.

specimen *n.* sample, sampling, example, instance, exemplar, cross section, model, representative, individual.

SPECIOUS *a.* [SPEE shus] plausible but invalid, having only the appearance of the truth. *Lawyers are adept at putting forth specious arguments.* SYN. plausible, sophistic, seeming, conceivable, possible, misleading, credible, unsound, ostensible, deceptive, fallacious. ANT. *true, valid, unquestionable, genuine.*

speck *n.* bit, spot, fleck, particle, grain, drop, iota, mite, jot, dot, atom, molecule, crumb.

spectacle *n.* sight, curiosity, display, exhibition, show, scene, *eyeful, sensation, marvel, wonder, pageant, exposition, extravaganza, performance, parade.

spectacles *n.* specs, lenses. SEE GLASSES

spectacular *a.* striking, sensational, breathtaking, extraordinary, exceptional, staggering, *eye-popping, stunning, impressive, dazzling, grand, wonderful, magnificent, awesome, marvelous, glorious. ANT. *mediocre, dull, boring, *nothing to write home about.*

spectator *n.* onlooker, watcher, observer, viewer, witness, passerby, bystander, *rubbernecker.

specter *n.* ghost, spirit, apparition, *spook, phantom, phantasm, bogey, poltergeist, wraith, shadow.

spectral *a.* ghostly, phantom, phantasmal, eerie.

speculate *v.* **1.** THINK ABOUT meditate, ponder, reflect, deliberate, contemplate, cogitate, weigh, ruminate, muse, *chew over, deliberate, *turn over in one's mind, mull over. **2.** RISK invest, venture, *toss the dice, buy stocks, sell stocks, gamble, *play the market, trade.

speculation *n.* **1.** THINKING meditation, pondering, reflection, deliberation, contemplation, cogitation, rumination, musing, mulling, weighing. **2.** THEORY guess, guesswork, assumption, conjecture, forecast, presumption, suspicion. **3.** RISK OF CAPITAL investment, venture, *toss of the dice, playing the stock market, gambling, trading.

speculative *a.* theoretical, hypothetical, conjectural, presumptive, questionable, assumed, suppositional, experimental, unproven, iffy, risky, unpredictable. ANT. *certain, sure, guaranteed, unquestionable.*

speculator *n.* guesser, theorist, gambler, stock trader.

speech *n.* **1.** SPEAKING communication, verbalization, vocalization, talk, expression, articulation, utterance, pronunciation, elocution, conversation. "The index and mirror of the soul."—Thomas Robertson. "Speech is power: speech is to persuade, to convert, to compel."—Ralph Waldo Emerson. **2.** LANGUAGE vocabulary, dialect, idiom, tongue, vernacular, parlance, lingo, patois. **3.** LECTURE talk, address, oration, discourse, keynote, sermon, salutation, dissertation, recitation, soliloquy, stem-winder, filibuster, tirade.

WORD FIND

aptness in expression: felicity
art of word usage: rhetoric, oratory
ecstatic: rhapsody
figure of: metaphor, simile, litotes, trope
fluency, expressiveness: eloquence
graduation: valedictory
impairment: dysphasia, speech impediment, dysphonia
incoherent: gibberish, glossolalia
incongruous figure of speech: oxymoron
individual dialect: idiolect

individual dialect quirk: idiologism
informal, conversational: colloquial
insertion of words like "um," "like," "you know," etc.: embolalia
long and tiresome: screed
loss for words, be at a: aporia
loss of: aphasia, muteness
lying, artful: mendaciloquence
modulation, change in tone: inflection
obscuring: obfuscation
pompous: bombast, fustian
pronounce clearly: enunciate
pronunciation, poor or improper: cacology
recall word, inability to: lethologica
showing off one's education through: pedantry
slip of the tongue: lapsus linguae, Freudian slip
speaking easily, fluently: voluble
Ssss or Shh sound in: sibilance
style of: elocution, locution
understatement for ironic effect: meiosis
unexpressive: inarticulate
word and sentence construction: syntax

speechless *a.* tongue-tied, at a loss for words, mute, struck dumb, inarticulate, aphonic, aphasic, voiceless, silent, *choked up. ANT. *loquacious, talkative, *motor-mouthed, voluble.*

speed *n.* swiftness, quickness, velocity, fleetness, rapidity, celerity, hustle, promptness, acceleration, rush, pace. ANT. *slowness, sluggishness.*

speed *v.* rush, hurry, fly, zoom, race, whiz, go like the wind, hustle, dash, tear, sprint, *go like lightning, run, hightail, *go like hell, *floor it, accelerate. ANT. *move in slow motion, crawl, drag.*

speedy *a.* fast, quick, rapid, fleet, *quicker than greased lightning, expeditious, hurried, nimble, prompt. ANT. *slow, sluggish, slothlike.*

spell *n.* **1.** INCANTATION charm, invocation, hex, jinx, voodoo, hoodoo, magic, enchantment, bewitchment, entrancement, sorcery, mesmerism, hypnotism, trance. SEE OCCULT **2.** TIME period, interval, *stretch, course, run, turn, tour, shift, bout, episode, fit.

spell *v.* relieve, give a break, take over, stand in for, cover for, take turns.

spellbind *v.* enchant, entrance, bewitch, mesmerize, hypnotize, charm, fascinate, hold, rivet, enthrall, transfix.

spellbound *a.* enchanted, entranced, bewitched, mesmerized, hypnotized, charmed, fascinated, held, riveted, enthralled, transfixed. ANT. *distracted, bored.*

spelunker *n.* cave explorer. SEE CAVE

spend *v.* exhaust, disburse, squander, pay out, *blow, use up, expend, fritter, consume, dispense, outlay, splurge, *fork over, deplete. ANT. *save, conserve, hoard.*

spendthrift *n.* squanderer, *big spender, *free spender, prodigal, profligate, wastrel, high roller. ANT. *Scrooge, miser, tightwad, *pennypincher.*

spent *a.* exhausted, consumed, burned out, worn out, used up, blown, depleted, expended, drained, prostrate, *beat, *pooped, *fagged out. ANT. *refreshed, energized, invigorated.*

sperm *n.* seed, semen.

spew *v.* gush, flow, issue, spit, eject, vomit, throw up, disgorge, expel.

sphere *n.* **1.** BALL globe, orb, spheroid, globule, moon, planet. **2.** PROVINCE range, domain, realm, scope, territory, field, bailiwick, department, turf.

spherical *a.* globular, spheroid, orbicular, round, oval, elliptical.

sphincter *n.* constrictor.

spice *n.* seasoning, flavoring, flavor, herb, condiment, piquancy, zest, *zing, pungency, sharpness, bite, relish, excitement, allspice, angelica, anise, basil, bay leaf, black pepper, bouquet garni, calamint, capers, caraway seed, celery seed, chervil, chicory, chili pepper, chili powder, chives, cilantro, cinnamon, cloves, coriander, cumin, curry, dill, fennel, flaxseed, garlic, ginger, lemon grass, licorice, mace, marjoram, mint, mustard, nutmeg, oregano, paprika, parsley, pepper, peppermint, poppy seed, rosemary, saffron, sage, sweet basil, tarragon, thyme, turmeric, white pepper.

spice *v.* season, flavor, enliven, enhance.

spick-and-span *a.* neat, clean, trim, fresh. ANT. *untidy.*

spicy *a.* **1.** FLAVORFUL pungent, *zippy, tangy, sharp, hot, zesty, seasoned, savory, lively, piquant, biting, aromatic, fragrant. **2.** RISQUÉ racy, bawdy, suggestive, off-color, *raunchy, obscene, titillating. ANT. *1. bland, blah, dull, tasteless. 2. G-rated, clean, wholesome.*

spider *n.* arachnid, *daddy longlegs, black widow, tarantula, wolf spider, violin spider, trap-door spider.

WORD FIND
web-spinning appendage: spinneret

spiel *n. Sl.* sales pitch, speech, talk, *line, *song and dance, hard sell.

spiffy *a. Sl.* spruce, dapper, smart, neat, trim,

sharp, well-dressed, natty. ANT. *disheveled, bedraggled, frumpy.*

spigot *n.* tap, faucet, valve, cock.

spike *n.* nail, bolt.

spill *n.* tumble, *header. SEE FALL

spill *v.* **1.** SLOP overflow, slosh, dribble, pour, run over, brim over, splatter, splash. **2.** DIVULGE *spill the beans, *let the cat out of the bag, disclose, make known, reveal, confess, *sing.

spin *n.* rotation, twirl, roll, twist, revolution, English.

spin *v.* **1.** ROTATE twirl, roll, revolve, go 'round, whirl, gyrate, wheel, pivot, reel, pirouette. **2.** TELL weave, fabricate, narrate, concoct.

spindle *n.* shaft, rod, pin, axis, axle.

spindly *a.* thin, slim, slender, scrawny, bony, long, tall, lanky, gangling, weak, frail. ANT. *fat, squat, stout.*

spindrift *n.* sea spray, foam, scud.

spine *n.* **1.** BACKBONE vertebrae, spinal column. **2.** NEEDLE thorn, prickle, barb, quill. **3.** WILLPOWER intestinal fortitude, determination, courage, pluck, resolve. ANT. *spinelessness, irresolution.*

spineless *a.* **1.** INVERTEBRATE. **2.** COWARDLY *wimpy, irresolute, *chicken, weak, weak-willed, timid, lily-livered, without backbone, *gutless, fainthearted. ANT. **2.** *tough, determined, courageous, resolute.*

spin-off *n.* by-product, offshoot, outgrowth, offspring, derivative.

spinster *n.* old maid, widow, divorcée, femme sole, single woman.

spiny *a.* barbed, spiked, tined, pronged, bristly, hispid, thorny, prickly. ANT. *smooth, sleek.*

spiral *n.* helix, corkscrew, coil, gyre, curlicue, vortex, whirlpool, eddy, whorl.

spiral *a.* helical, coiled, winding, corkscrew, twisted, whorled, spiroid, turbinate, volute, curled, scrolled, cochleate.

spire *n.* steeple, belfry, tower, bell tower, fleche, campanile, minaret, shaft, peak, pinnacle.

spirit *n.* **1.** SOUL consciousness, anima, life breath, mind, psyche, self, heart, ego. "The life of God within us."—Saint Teresa. "A vital breath of more ethereal air."—H.W. Longfellow. "An inward flame; a lamp the world blows upon but never puts out."—Margot Asquith. **2.** GHOST phantom, phantasm, spook, apparition, specter, poltergeist, shadow, supernatural entity, wraith, presence. **3.** MOOD disposition, frame of mind, attitude, humor, feeling, temper, morale, tone, outlook. **4.** LIVELINESS vigor, vitality,

vivacity, energy, animation, enthusiasm, eagerness, zeal, ardor, courage, bravery. **5.** MEANING intention, intent, sense, aim, purpose.

spirited *a.* lively, energetic, dynamic, animated, vivacious, fiery, *charged, eager, enthusiastic, zealous, effervescent, spunky, perky. ANT. *dead, slothful, lifeless, dispirited.*

spiritless *a.* listless, *out of it, *dead, suffering from malaise, *down in the dumps, depressed, *bummed out, melancholy, indifferent, lifeless, slothful, sluggish, passionless. ANT. *spirited, *charged, lively.*

spiritual *a.* **1.** OF THE SOUL incorporeal, immaterial, extramundane, unearthly, otherworldly, ethereal, metaphysical. **2.** RELIGIOUS sacred, devotional, holy, divine, pious, godly, pure, righteous, heavenly. ANT. *1. of the body, corporeal, of the flesh. 2. secular, worldly.*

spit *n.* **1.** SALIVA spittle, drool, *loogie, sputum, slaver, expectoration. **2.** SKEWER broach, rotisserie, pin.

spit *v.* expectorate, hawk, spray, drool, dribble.

spite *n.* malice, ill will, grudge, hard feelings, resentment, malevolence, maliciousness, vindictiveness, vengeance, hate, meanness. ANT. *goodwill, warmth, affection.*

spite *v.* hurt, injure, offend, get back at, harass, annoy, frustrate, be nasty. ANT. *give a hand, help, be nice to.*

spiteful *a.* malicious, viperous, venomous, vindictive, vengeful, nasty, resentful, mean, catty, hateful, malevolent, vicious, bitter. ANT. *sweet, nice, helpful.*

spitting image *n.* mirror image, twin, likeness.

spittle *n.* SEE SPIT

spittoon *n.* cuspidor.

splash *n.* **1.** SPLATTER squirt, jet, spurt, spray, sprinkle, slosh, slop, plop, *kerplunk. **2.** SMALL AMOUNT drop, touch. **3.** SPECTACLE display, sensation, show.

splash *v.* splatter, squirt, jet, spurt, spray, sprinkle, slosh, slop, plop, *kerplunk.

splatter *v.* splash, spray, sprinkle spatter, streak, stain.

splay *v.* spread, expand, extend.

spleen *n.* malice, spite, hatred, ill will, hard feelings, venom, resentment, malevolence, petulance, waspishness, grouchiness. ANT. *warmth, friendliness, affection, good humor.*

splendid *a.* **1.** LUSTROUS magnificent, shining, brilliant, splendiferous, dazzling, gorgeous, luxurious, sumptuous, elegant, *ritzy, *posh. **2.** EXCELLENT exceptional, great, fabulous, fantastic, wonderful, outstanding, fine, superb, sterling. ANT. 1. *drab, dull, poor.* 2. *poor, inferior, awful, lousy.*

splendor *n.* 1. BRILLIANCE luster, brightness, shine, resplendence, radiance, glitter. 2. MAGNIFICENCE glory, grandeur, pomp, show, spectacle.

splenetic *a.* irritable, grouchy, bad-tempered, nasty, waspish, petulant, crabby, grumpy, peevish, sour. ANT. *good-humored, easygoing.*

splice *v.* join, unite, wed, weave together, bind, connect, twine, braid.

splinter *n.* sliver, fragment, bit, shiver, shard.

splinter *v.* split, break, fragment, crack, separate.

split *n.* 1. BREAK crack, tear, fragmenting, separation, splintering, rip, slash, gash, rupture, rift, cleft. 2. DIVISION OR DIFFERENCE OF OPINION schism, dissension, fragmentation, disunion, breach, rift.

split *v.* 1. BREAK splinter, separate, divide, sever, crack, tear, cleave, fragment, rip, slash, rupture, halve. 2. BE AT ODDS be at opposite ends of the spectrum, polarize, fragment. 3. DIVIDE *divvy up, allocate, apportion, share, mete out, subdivide, distribute. ANT. 1. *join, unite, bind.* 2. *unite.* 3. *collect.*

split up *v.* break up, separate, divorce, go separate ways, part company.

splotch *n.* spot, stain, blob, mark, splash, smudge.

splurge *v.* indulge, *spend like there's no tomorrow, *blow, squander, *go overboard, *go whole hog, be extravagant. ANT. *conserve, *tighten one's belt, *pinch pennies.*

splutter *v.* sputter, spit, hiss, spatter, *spray, stumble, stammer, stutter, *trip over one's words.

spoil *v.* 1. DAMAGE ruin, destroy, injure, impair, wreck, harm, *mess up, *louse up, demolish, mar, blemish. 2. OVERINDULGE pamper, coddle, mollycoddle, cosset, baby, wait on, cater to, *kill with kindness, overprotect, smother, lavish, shelter. 3. DECAY rot, putrefy, go bad, decompose, sour, turn moldy, addle, deteriorate. ANT. 1. *enhance, better, improve.* 2. *harden, be strict with, deprive.*

spoilage *n.* garbage, waste, refuse, damaged goods, rotten food.

spoiled *a.* 1. DAMAGED ruined, destroyed, injured, impaired, wrecked, harmed, *messed up, *loused up, demolished, marred, blemished. 2. OVERINDULGED pampered, coddled, mollycoddled, *bratty, cosseted, babied,

overprotected, smothered. 3. DECAYED rotten, putrid, gone bad, decomposed, sour, moldy, addled, deteriorated, rancid. ANT. 1. *enhanced, improved.* 2. *disciplined, hardened, deprived.* 3. *fresh.*

spoils *n.* plunder, booty, property, pillage, loot, winnings, bounty, prize, reward.

spoilsport *n.* killjoy, *wet blanket, marplot, *party pooper.

spoken *a.* uttered, vocalized, said, articulated, voiced, expressed verbally, declared, pronounced, oral. ANT. *unspoken.*

spokesman *n.* spokeswoman, prolocutor, *mouthpiece, *PR man/woman, voice, speaker, representative, deputy, intermediary, agent.

sponge *n. Sl.* *sponger, *moocher, *bum, *freeloader, beggar, *leech, parasite, *bloodsucker, *deadbeat.

sponge *v.* *mooch, beg, cadge, *bum, *freeload, scrounge.

sponger *n.* SEE SPONGE

spongy *a.* porous, absorbent, elastic, springy, mushy, boggy, marshy, moist, waterlogged.

sponsor *n.* underwriter, endorser, financier, supporter, backer, *angel, patron, guarantor, advertiser, advocate, champion, godfather, godmother.

spontaneous *a.* unrehearsed, off the cuff, extemporaneous, unprepared, spur of the moment, unplanned, impulsive, impromptu, *off the top of one's head, ad-lib, unpremeditated, reflexive, natural, instinctual. ANT. *planned, premeditated, rehearsed, prepared, unnatural.*

spoof *n.* parody, satire, *takeoff, *send-up, caricature, lampoon, burlesque, travesty, joke, comedy.

spoof *v.* satirize, parody, *send up, caricature, lampoon, burlesque, travesty.

spook *n.* ghost, specter, apparition, spirit, poltergeist, phantom, phantasm.

spooky *a.* ghostly, spectral, supernatural, eerie, weird, scary, unnerving, frightening, creepy.

spool *n.* bobbin, reel, cylinder.

spoon *n.* eating utensil, implement, silverware, ladle, scoop.

spoon-feed *v.* pamper, coddle, mollycoddle, baby, indulge, overindulge. SEE SPOIL

spoor *n.* trail, track, footprints, markings, droppings.

sporadic *a.* irregular, on and off, infrequent, intermittent, spotty, random, occasional, periodic, erratic, fitful, scattered. ANT. *regular, steady, constant.*

sport(s) n. **1.** ATHLETICS recreation, pastime, diversion, competitive activity, contest, competition, game, play, amusement, entertainment. "War minus the shooting."—George Orwell. SEE BASEBALL, BASKETBALL, BOWLING, BOXING, BULLFIGHT, FENCING, FOOTBALL, GOLF, MOUNTAINEERING, RACE, SKIN DIVING, SKATING, SKIING, SKYDIVING, SOCCER, TENNIS, VOLLEYBALL, WRESTLING **2.** OBJECT OF TEASING butt, object of ridicule, laughingstock, *easy target, *fair game, *patsy, ridicule. **3.** JOKING AROUND fun, frolic, teasing, jollity, merriment, *jollies, antics, tomfoolery, skylarking, kidding, ridicule.

sporting a. fair, sportsmanlike, even, equitable, *on a level playing field, gentlemanly, honest. ANT. *unfair, dishonest.*

sportive a. playful, fun, romping, merry, joking, frisky, roguish, frolicsome, gamesome, jaunty. ANT. *serious, grave, earnest.*

sportscaster n. *play-by-play man/woman, color commentator, broadcaster.

sportsman n. hunter, fisherman, outdoorsman, adventurist.

sportsmanship n. integrity, honor, honesty, fairness, courtesy. ANT. *dishonesty, cheating.*

sportswear n. casual wear, informal wear.

sporty a. flashy, showy, loud, casual, informal. ANT. *formal, conservative.*

spot n. **1.** STAIN blot, speck, smudge, mark, splotch, discoloration, speckle, dot, patch, daub, smirch. **2.** LOCATION locale, position, point, place, site, area, section, setting, region, space. **3.** DILEMMA bind, *sticky situation, fix, mess, predicament, *pickle, jam.

spot v. **1.** STAIN blot, blemish, smudge, mark, discolor, speckle, daub, dirty, splash, sprinkle, fleck. **2.** SEE detect, recognize, make out, pinpoint, discern, spy, sight, catch sight of, find, identify.

spot-check n. random sampling.

spotless a. **1.** CLEAN immaculate, unstained, unblemished, untainted, laundered, washed, scrubbed, *squeaky clean, pristine, virgin. **2.** IRREPROACHABLE above reproach, pure, innocent, uncorrupted, above suspicion, *having clean hands, faultless, impeccable, virginal, chaste, *squeaky clean. ANT. *1. dirty, filthy, spotty. 2. faulty, defective, tarnished.*

spotlight n. **1.** LAMP klieg light, *spot, floodlight, arc light, search light, pin spot, beam projector, *bon-bon, limelight, *ashcan. **2.** PROMINENCE recognition, notice, public scrutiny, *fishbowl existence, *public microscope, limelight, center stage.

spotlight v. light, illuminate, highlight, cast in the limelight, flood, focus on. ANT. *obscure, conceal, veil.*

spotted a. speckled, flecked, spotty, dotted, dappled, mottled, blotched, piebald, guttate. ANT. *uniform, monochromatic.*

spotty a. irregular, sporadic, inconsistent, intermittent, patchy, uneven, erratic, fitful, on again off again, *running hot and cold, variable. ANT. *consistent, regular, even.*

spouse n. mate, husband, wife, groom, bride, partner, companion, consort, *old man, *old lady, *better half.

spout n. nozzle, spile, spigot, faucet, lip, snout, mouth, tube, outlet, jet, discharge, spurt, geyser, squirt.

spout v. **1.** FLOW shoot, jet, discharge, spurt, squirt, gush, pour, surge, emit, spew, issue. **2.** RANT AND RAVE harangue, *shoot off one's mouth, *go on and on about, orate, gush.

sprain v. wrench, twist, strain, tear ligaments.

sprawl v. spread, stretch out, spread-eagle, loll, slouch, recline, lounge, slump, lie.

spray n. mist, drizzle, sprinkle, spritz, vapor, shower, *mizzle, spindrift, spume, jet, cloud.

spray v. atomize, drizzle, sprinkle, spritz, vaporize, shower, jet, mist, nebulize.

spread n. **1.** EXTENSION expansion, spreading, increase, mushrooming, growth, broadening, contagion, proliferation, diffusion, span, extent, range, scope, expanse. **2.** FEAST banquet, smorgasbord, meal, buffet.

spread v. **1.** UNFOLD open, unfurl, stretch out, stretch, sprawl, splay, uncoil, display. **2.** EXPAND extend, increase, mushroom, grow, broaden, proliferate, cover, disperse, pervade, permeate. **3.** SCATTER strew, distribute, disperse, sprinkle. **4.** DISSEMINATE broadcast, publicize, trumpet, circulate, publish, promulgate, advertise. **5.** APPLY slather, daub, smear, paint, plaster. ANT. *1. close, fold, curl, contract. 2. shrink, contract, recede. 3. gather, amass, pile. 4. censor, keep quiet.*

spreadsheet n. accounting program, bookkeeping program, accounting software. SEE COMPUTER

spree n. frolic, *field day, party, celebration, orgy, carousal, *binge, *tear, *bender, *drunk.

sprig n. twig, spray, nosegay, stem, slip, sprout.

sprightly a. lively, spirited, gay, energetic, brisk, vivacious, animated, playful, jaunty, chipper, blithe, cheerful, spry. ANT. *sluggish, lifeless, glum.*

spring *n.* **1.** LEAP jump, bound, vault, hop, bounce, resilience, elasticity, springiness, recoil. **2.** COIL shock absorber, spiral, helix, compression spring. **3.** WELL upwelling, gush, fountain, waterhole, *drink, pool, spa, baths. **4.** ORIGIN wellspring, source, fountain, fount, beginning, motive, impetus. **5.** SEASON March, April, May, *rebirth, *new beginning, blossoming time, mating season. "A true reconstructionist."—Henry Timrod.

spring *v.* **1.** LEAP jump, bound, vault, hop, hurdle, lunge, skip. **2.** SPRING BACK recoil, rebound. **3.** RISE *pop up, crop up, emerge, grow, emanate, stem, originate.

springy *a.* elastic, resilient, rubbery, spongy, bouncy, flexible. ANT. *stiff, inflexible.*

sprinkle *n.* light rain, mist, drizzle, spit, spray, shower, dash, smattering, pinch, scattering, dusting. ANT. *deluge, flood.*

sprinkle *v.* rain lightly, mist, drizzle, spit, spray, shower, dash, sparge, scatter, dust.

sprint *v.* run, race, *go full out, dash, *run like hell, *beat feet, tear, rush, *hotfoot. SEE RUN

sprite *n.* fairy, elf, pixie, nymph, brownie, gnome, goblin, hobgoblin, leprechaun.

sprout *v.* germinate, grow, shoot, bud, bloom, burgeon, develop, flower. ANT. *die, wither.*

spruce *a.* neat, trim, smart, natty, dapper, chic, well-groomed, sharp, *spiffy, *slick. ANT. *sloppy, bedraggled, frumpy, disheveled.*

spruce up *v.* clean up, neaten up, groom, *fix up, *doll up, *spit and polish, *gussy up, primp.

SPRY *a.* [SPRI] active and nimble, lively. *He was surprisingly spry for a ninety-year-old.* SYN. active, nimble, lively, vigorous, vital, hearty, *peppy, robust, brisk, quick, agile. ANT. *lifeless, lethargic, bedridden.*

spume *n.* foam, froth, fizz, cream, suds, lather, spindrift, scum.

spunk *n.* courage, heart, *guts, spirit, intestinal fortitude, pluck, backbone, mettle, nerve, *moxie, grit, mental toughness. ANT. *timidity, *wimpiness, cowardice.*

spunky *a.* courageous, brave, *gutsy, spirited, game, plucky, gritty, tough, nervy, lionhearted, red-blooded, resolute. ANT. *timid, *wimpy, cowardly.*

spur *n.* goad, impetus, incentive, motivation, *spark, *spark plug, stimulus, trigger, prod, jolt, *swift kick. ANT. *damper, discouragement.*

spur *v.* goad, instigate, provide an incentive, spark, stimulate, trigger, prod, jolt, *give a swift kick, prompt, incite, *goose. ANT. *put a damper on, discourage, slow.*

SPURIOUS *a.* [SPYOOR ee us] false, counterfeit. *The purported Jack the Ripper diary turned out to be spurious.* SYN. fake, ungenuine, bogus, phony, simulated, fraudulent, forged, sham, pseudo, mock, artificial, apocryphal. ANT. *genuine, authentic, real.*

spurn *v.* reject, refuse, decline, scorn, snub, *give the cold shoulder, *turn one's nose up at, *nix, *give a thumbs down, have no part of, rebuff, disdain, sneeze at. ANT. *embrace, accept, welcome.*

spurt *n.* **1.** SQUIRT jet, rush, gush, spray, spate, geyser, surge. **2.** BURST OF ACTIVITY rush, surge, flurry, flare-up, spell.

spurt *v.* squirt, jet, rush, gush, spray, surge, well up, spout, ejaculate.

sputter *v.* **1.** SPLUTTER *spray one's words, spit, stammer, stutter, *gibber-jabber, *trip over one's words, talk excitedly. **2.** SIZZLE spit, crackle, pop, snap.

sputum *n.* spittle, saliva, spit, phlegm, mucus.

spy *n.* intelligence agent, secret agent, undercover agent, double agent, secret service agent, CIA agent, operative, snoop, investigator, *mole, *tail, informer, *private eye, scout. SEE SPYING

spy *v.* **1.** WATCH SURREPTITIOUSLY observe, stake out, keep under surveillance, shadow, *case, *tail, *check out, scout, reconnoiter, eavesdrop, *bug, snoop, investigate, pry, engage in espionage, infiltrate, gather intelligence. SEE SPYING **2.** CATCH SIGHT OF see, perceive, make out, detect, spot, sight, glimpse.

spying *n.* espionage, intelligence gathering, reconnaissance, infiltration, eavesdropping, bugging.

WORD FIND

agent who does not spy but works to confuse enemy: confusion agent

coded communication, science of: cryptology

code form, put information into: encrypt, encipher

concealed microphone: *bug, listening device

decode: decrypt, decipher

decoding encrypted messages: cryptanalysis

expose as a spy: *blow one's cover, *burn

group: cell

infiltrator of enemy intelligence agency: mole, double agent information, secret: classified information, top secret information

International Criminal Police Organization: Interpol

misleading or phony information: disinformation, counterintelligence

penetration into enemy's affairs: infiltration

safe haven or meeting house: safe house

secret code: cipher, password

traitorous work performed for enemy: collaboration

undercover, secret: covert

U.S. government agency: CIA, Central Intelligence Agency

squabble n. quarrel, dispute, argument, fight, tiff, disagreement, difference of opinion, controversy, row, wrangle. ANT. *agreement, harmony, accord.*

squabble v. quarrel, dispute, argue, fight, have a tiff, disagree, have a difference of opinion, *lock horns, wrangle, contend. ANT. *agree, get along.*

squad n. group, team, crew, company, unit, platoon, battalion, band, gang, *outfit.

squadron n. 1. GROUP OF VESSELS convoy, unit, two divisions. 2. FLIGHT FORMATION escadrille.

SQUALID a. [SKWALL id] filthy or run-down due to neglect. *The tenement building was in a squalid section of town.* SYN. filthy, dirty, foul, unclean, grungy, dingy, grimy, rat-infested, stinking, slummy, run-down, dilapidated, wretched, miserable, seedy, sordid. ANT. *clean, immaculate, well-kept.*

squall n. 1. WINDSTORM gale, blow, gust, blast, tempest, downpour, cloudburst, shower, gale, storm, flurry. 2. DISTURBANCE blow-up, furor, tumult, commotion, trouble, fuss. 3. CRY scream, wail, shriek, bawling, yell, yowl, howl, outcry, outburst.

SQUALOR n. [SKWALL ur] filth and poverty, wretchedness. *Many in the inner cities live in squalor.* SYN. filth, poverty, dirtiness, foulness, grunginess, dinginess, slum conditions, seediness, wretchedness, misery, sordidness, *Dickensian poverty. ANT. *luxury, wealth, *bed of roses, *clover.*

SQUANDER v. [SKWAN dur] to waste. *She squandered the last of her inheritance.* SYN. waste, *blow, be extravagant, fritter away, throw away, *spend like there was no tomorrow, lavish, play the profligate, dissipate. ANT. *save, conserve, be frugal.*

square n. 1. QUADRATE quadrangle, rectangle,

cube, box. 2. PLAZA park, common, village green, piazza, quadrangle, quad.

square v. 1. EVEN UP adjust, align, true, plumb, fix, rectify, straighten, fit, settle. 2. SETTLE ONE'S ACCOUNTS pay off, clear, satisfy, discharge, balance, even up. 3. AGREE correspond, match, dovetail, coincide, synchronize, coordinate, harmonize. ANT. *1. misalign, skew. 2. go into debt, be in arrears. 3. disagree, contrast, contradict.*

square a. 1. QUADRANGULAR four-sided, quadrate, boxy, equilateral, rectangular, cube-like. 2. Sl. OLD-FASHIONED *straight, conservative, prudish, conformist, straitlaced, *uptight, prim. 3. EVEN straight, level, true, accurate. 4. HONEST straightforward, just, on the level, *on the up and up, fair, equitable, ethical. ANT. *1. round, circular, triangular. 2. *hip, *cool, *with it, nonconforming. 3. uneven, inaccurate. 4. dishonest, unjust, unethical.*

squash v. 1. SQUISH flatten, compress, press, smash, mash, crush, squeeze, compact, crowd, jam. 2. QUASH bring to an end, stop, bring down, suppress, stifle, crush, squelch, *crack down on, *pull the plug on. ANT. *2. fortify, strengthen, support.*

squat v. crouch, hunker down, sit on one's heels, sit on one's haunches.

squat a. short, *built like a fireplug, stubby, stumpy, stocky, pudgy, dumpy, *fubsy, thickset, tubby. ANT. *tall, gangling, lanky.*

squatter n. settler, claimant, applicant.

squawk n. 1. CRY shriek, screech, call, scream, squeal, crowing, cackle, outcry, howl. 2. Sl. COMPLAINT fuss, protest, objection, gripe, shout, yell.

squawk v. 1. CRY shriek, screech, call, scream, squeal, crow, cackle, outcry. 2. COMPLAIN put up a fuss, protest, object, *cry foul, yell, fume, gripe.

squeak n. cry, peep, cheep, whine, mew, squeal, creak, screech.

squeak v. cry, peep, cheep, whine, mew, squeal, creak, screech.

squeal v. 1. CRY scream, whine, shriek, howl, wail, screech, yelp, squeak. 2. Sl. INFORM *rat on, turn in, *drop a dime on, *snitch, tell, tattle, *sell down the river, *blow whistle on, betray.

squeamish a. oversensitive, dainty, delicate, queasy, qualmish, prudish, prim, easily offended, easily shocked, *having a weak stomach. ANT. *tough, *having a cast-iron stomach, thick-skinned.*

squeeze *n.* embrace, hug, clasp, *clinch, grip, compression.

squeeze *v.* **1.** PRESS compress, squash, squish, crush, contract, tighten, constrict, wring. **2.** HUG embrace, *bear hug, enfold, take in one's arms, clasp, *clinch. **3.** CRAM crowd, jam, pack, wedge, ram. **4.** EXTORT extract, wrest, blackmail.

squelch *v.* squash, suppress, silence, crush, put down, quash, extinguish, kill, smother, shoot down, stifle, defeat. ANT. *help, boost, strengthen.*

squib *n.* firecracker. SEE FIREWORKS

squint *v.* focus intently, peer at with half-closed eyes, look at narrowly, peer, peep, *screw up one's eyes, skew.

squire *n.* gentleman, landowner, proprietor, attendant, armor-bearer, servant, valet, escort, gallant, attendant, date, companion.

squirm *v.* wiggle, wriggle, writhe, twist, turn, twitch, contort, fidget, flounder.

squirt *n.* spritz, jet, spurt, spray, fountain, stream, gush.

squirt *v.* spritz, spray, spurt, shoot, spout, jet, stream, discharge, spew, gush, ejaculate.

squish *v.* compress, flatten. SEE SQUASH

stab *n.* **1.** PRICK, PAIN piercing, puncture, cut, gash, laceration, wound, sharp pain, shooting pain, twinge, pange, searing pain, ache. **2.** TRY shot, crack, attempt, effort, chance, *whirl, *go. SEE STAB IN THE BACK

stab *v.* pierce, prick, stick, slit, gash, puncture, run through, knife, cut, impale, penetrate, lance, plunge, thrust, gore. SEE KILL, MURDER

stability *n.* steadiness, sturdiness, firmness, solidity, equilibrium, balance, strength, soundness, permanence, constancy, dependability, reliability. ANT. *instability, shakiness, unsteadiness.*

stabilize *v.* steady, secure, firm, equalize, balance, strengthen, root, fix, ground, fortify, brace, set, support. ANT. *destabilize, weaken, undermine.*

stab in the back *n.* backstabbing, betrayal, treachery, *doublecross, Judas kiss.

stab in the back *v.* backstab, betray, *doublecross, backbite, sell out, sell down the river, give the Judas kiss, turn traitor.

stable *n.* barn, stall, shelter, pen, paddock.

stable *a.* **1.** STEADY secure, firm, sturdy, equalized, balanced, strong, solid, sound, rooted, fixed, grounded, fortified, braced, set, steadfast, immovable, permanent. **2.** MENTALLY SOUND sane, rational, compos mentis, sensible, of clear mind, composed, self-possessed,

calm. ANT. *1. unstable, shaky, unsteady, unreliable. 2. unstable, crazy, insane, unbalanced.*

stack *n.* **1.** PILE heap, mass, mound, hill, load, assemblage, pack, bundle, sheaf, rick, cord, pyramid. **2.** SMOKESTACK chimney, flue.

stack *v.* pile, heap, amass, mound, load, assemble, stockpile, pyramid.

stacked *a.* *Sl.* built, curvaceous, full-figured, well-endowed.

stadium *n.* arena, bowl, sports complex, athletic field, football field, baseball field, ballpark, astrodome, circus, hippodrome, coliseum, amphitheater. SEE SPORT(S)

staff *n.* **1.** STICK rod, pole, shaft, walking stick, cane, alpenstock, crook, crosier, truncheon, shillelagh, mace, scepter. **2.** ASSISTANTS employees, work force, crew, team, personnel, help, cadre, cast, faculty.

stage *n.* **1.** PLATFORM rostrum, dais, *the boards, podium. **2.** THEATER show business, *show biz, footlights, set, limelight, spotlight, Broadway. SEE THEATER **3.** PERIOD phase, step, point in time, juncture, moment. **4.** LEVEL grade, rung, position, echelon, status.

stage *v.* present, exhibit, put on, perform, produce, arrange, engineer, mount, carry out.

stagecoach *n.* concord, coach, *mud wagon.

WORD FIND

escort who protected against robbers: shotgun rider, outrider

robber: road agent

section of road between relays of animals: stage

section of road comprised of several drives: division

section of road comprised of several stages: drive

trunk: boot

stagehand *n.* grip, callboy. SEE MOVIE

stagger *v.* **1.** TOTTER reel, sway, stumble, wobble, careen, weave, bob, lurch, falter, pitch. **2.** SHOCK bowl over, stun, *hit like a ton of bricks, take one's breath away, astonish, overwhelm, *blow away, jolt, take aback.

staggering *a.* stunning, shocking, awesome, overwhelming, astonishing, mind-blowing, mind-boggling, amazing.

stagnant *a.* unmoving, still, standing, stationary, dormant, inert, dead, foul, stinking, stale, putrid, polluted, dirty. ANT. *fast-moving, flowing, fresh, clean.*

stagnate *v.* stand, idle, stop, be motionless, lie still, go stale, die, rot, decay, putrefy, deteriorate, stink. ANT. *move, flow, freshen.*

STAGNATION n. [stag NA shun] lack of motion or activity, decline, death. *The economy underwent a period of stagnation.* SYN. motionlessness, inactivity, decline, deterioration, death, stillness, quiet, inertia, dormancy. ANT. *activity, movement, growth.*

stagy a. theatrical, melodramatic, affected, *hammy, ostentatious, overdone, showy.

STAID a. [STAYD] sedate, restrained, serious. *He was a staid, bookish character who rarely laughed.* SYN. sedate, restrained, serious, sober, solemn, conservative, subdued, quiet, grave, dignified, proper, formal, decorous, settled. ANT. *wild, abandoned, jovial, frivolous.*

stain n. 1. SPOT discoloration, streak, smudge, mark, blotch, speck, spatter, blemish, smirch. 2. DISHONOR stigma, shame, guilt, taint, disgrace, *black eye, odium, infamy, blot.

stain v. 1. SPOT discolor, streak, smudge, mark, blotch, speck, spatter, blemish, smirch. 2. DISHONOR stigmatize, shame, taint, *drag one's name through the mud, disgrace, *give a black eye, tarnish, discredit.

stairs n. steps, stairway, staircase, flight, perron, spiral staircase, escalator, companionway.

stake n. 1. POST stick, pale, picket, pole, shaft, peg, upright, boundary marker. 2. PRIZE pot, jackpot, purse, pool, winnings, bet, wager, ante.

stake v. 1. MARK OFF demarcate, bound, limit, delineate. 2. BET wager, risk, venture, chance, gamble, pledge.

stale a. 1. FLAT, TASTELESS flavorless, old, bad, musty, dry, hard, unfresh, moldy, bland, vapid, spoiled. 2. UNORIGINAL old, overused, trite, hackneyed, clichéd, tired, threadbare, *old hat, stock, shopworn, dead, banal, vapid, insipid. ANT. *1. fresh, tasty. 2. fresh, original, new, imaginative.*

STALEMATE n. [STAYL mate] a deadlock or draw. *The negotiations ended in a disappointing stalemate.* SYN. deadlock, gridlock, standstill, *Catch 22, impasse, stop, standoff, check, draw, tie.

stalk v. hunt, pursue, sneak up on, follow, tail, trail stealthily, creep up on, shadow, track down, terrorize.

stall n. 1. COMPARTMENT booth, stable, pen, shelter, cubicle, cell, cubby hole, stand, kiosk, enclosure, room, chamber. 2. DELAYING TACTIC evasion, *footdragging, *stonewalling, ruse, subterfuge, ploy.

stall v. 1. DELAY play for time, *drag one's feet,

*stonewall, slow down, postpone, filibuster, dillydally, procrastinate, waste time, hem and haw, put off, temporize. 2. SHUT DOWN conk out, break down, run out of gas, *sputter and die. ANT. *1. rush, hurry, expedite. 2. start, run, perform.*

stallion n. stud, steed. SEE HORSE

stalwart n. supporter, staunch supporter, loyalist, upholder, mainstay.

STALWART a. [STALL wurt] strong, firm, brave, resolute. *The senator was a stalwart member of the Republican party.* SYN. strong, firm, robust, powerful, hearty, vigorous, brave, courageous, tough, fearless, daring, valiant, heroic, resolute, determined, steadfast, staunch, unflinching, unwavering, tenacious. ANT. *weak, fearful, irresolute, halfhearted, spineless.*

stamina n. endurance, *wind, fitness, heart, strength, staying power, energy, vigor, aerobic power, *steam, conditioning, *legs, intestinal fortitude. ANT. *weakness, lack of fitness.*

stammer v. stutter, splutter, hem, trip/stumble over one's words, speak haltingly, falter.

stamp n. 1. IMPRINT mark, seal, impression, symbol, brand, hallmark, emblem. 2. CHARACTER kind, type, variety, sort, class.

stamp v. 1. STOMP tramp, trample, step on, beat, pound. 2. IMPRINT mark, seal, impress, brand, label, engrave, print, emboss. 3. CHARACTERIZE brand, style, tag, distinguish, classify.

stampede n. rush, mad dash, flight, run, race, panic, scattering.

WORD FIND

slow or stop stampede by making cattle circle around: mill

stamping ground n. stomping ground, haunt, hangout.

stamp out v. extinguish, snuff out, crush, put out, squelch, stop, kill.

stance n. position, posture, standpoint, viewpoint, attitude, stand.

stanchion n. support, beam, post, upright, brace.

stand n. 1. RESISTANCE defense, counter, repulsion, opposition. 2. POSITION stance, view, viewpoint, standpoint, attitude, belief, point of view, policy. 3. PLATFORM stage, dais, podium, rostrum, pulpit, lectern, witness box. 4. GRANDSTAND bleachers, seats. 5. KIOSK booth, stall, counter. 6. TABLE holder, rack, shelf, cradle.

stand v. 1. RISE TO ONE'S FEET stay on one's feet,

be erect. **2.** ENDURE take, put up with, withstand, suffer, abide, tolerate, bear, weather, brave. ANT. *1. sit, recline. 2. *cave in, collapse, buckle.*

standard *n.* **1.** CRITERION guideline, norm, measure, model, ideal, rule, gauge, mean, median, specification, yardstick, principle, regulation. **2.** FLAG ensign, banner, pennant, streamer, Old Glory, Stars and Stripes, Union Jack.

standard *a.* regular, conventional, normal, stock, accepted, established, customary, classic, orthodox, usual, traditional, *run-of-the-mill, general, basic, *garden variety. ANT. *unconventional, unusual, out of the ordinary.*

standardize *v.* normalize, regulate, systematize, homogenize, equalize, regulate.

standby *n.* fill-in, substitute, backup, replacement, stand-in, understudy, pinch hitter.

stand for *v.* mean, represent, signify, denote, symbolize, indicate.

standing *n.* **1.** STATUS position, rank, stature, place, class, station, reputation, repute, place in the pecking order, prestige, eminence, importance. **2.** DURATION longevity, time, tenure.

standoff *n.* draw, tie, deadlock, gridlock, stalemate.

standoffish *a.* aloof, cool, cold, reserved, withdrawn, reticent, remote, distant, unsociable, antisocial, unfriendly, unapproachable, snooty, snobby, haughty. ANT. *friendly, warm, sociable.*

standout *n.* *phenom, winner, star, superstar, ace, *crackerjack, talent, *one for the books, *hit, *smash, *whiz kid. ANT. **second-stringer, *benchwarmer, *nothing to write home about, *just another brick in the wall.*

stand pat *v.* resist, resist change, stay put, *stick to one's guns, *stand one's ground, hold out, *die hard.

standpoint *n.* point of view, P.O.V., position, perspective, viewpoint, stance, outlook, belief, opinion, attitude.

standstill *n.* stop, halt, impasse, *dead end, cessation, deadlock, gridlock, *jam-up, *bottleneck, arrest, stalemate, draw. ANT. *progress, movement.*

stanza *n.* stave, quatrain, sextain, triolet, verses. SEE MUSIC

staple *n.* chief commodity, essential product, primary product, necessary product, basic, fundamental, essential, necessity.

staple *a.* principle, leading, main, basic, fundamental, chief, foremost, vital, important, necessary, essential. ANT. *secondary, minor, unnecessary.*

star *n.* **1.** sun, *flaming gasball, celestial body, heavenly body, burning orb, *cooling fires of creation, *candlelight of the gods, *heavenly beacon. "The forget-me-nots of the angels."—H.W. Longfellow.

WORD FIND

brightness measurement: magnitude
brightness, star with variable: variable star
bright star: Sirius, Polaris
chain of galaxies stretching across universe: Great Wall
chart of positions: ephemeris
closest: Proxima Centauri
cloudy, gassy birthplace of: nebula
collapsed star with massive gravity forces: black hole, neutron star, pulsar
concealment by another celestial body: occultation
constellation, group of stars not belonging to any: asterism
cool red star of massive proportions: red giant
double star that may appear as one: binary
effect that reveals whether star is approaching or receding: Doppler effect
erupting, brightening star: nova
exploding star: supernova
galactic-like superobject at ends of universe: quasar
galaxy, nearby: Andromeda
group of stars forming a distinctive configuration: constellation
group of stars in which earth is located: Milky Way galaxy
group of stars or island universe: galaxy, globular cluster
hazy group too distant to be seen with naked eye: stardust
mapping of: uranography
motion unrelated to earth's rotation: proper motion
referring to: stellar, astral
shooting star: SEE METEOR
tiny star with immense mass: white dwarf
twinkling of: scintillation
X-ray emitting: pulsar
SEE ASTRONOMY, COMET, CONSTELLATION, METEOR, MOON, PLANET, SPACE, SUN

2. ASTERISK pentagram, pentacle, hexagram. **3.** CELEBRITY superstar, luminary, *name, *bigshot, *bigwig, *celeb, personage, leading lady, leading man, matinee idol, headliner. ANT. *nobody, unknown.*

star v. headline, be featured, lead.

star a. leading, prominent, outstanding, standout, celebrated, main, famous, renowned, illustrious. ANT. *unknown, secondary.*

starch n. **1.** STIFFNESS formality, rigidity, prudishness, decorum, manners, primness, propriety. **2.** ENERGY vigor, pep, vitality, drive, spirit. ANT. *1. casualness, informality, folksiness. 2. sluggishness, lethargy.*

starchy a. stiff, formal, rigid, prudish, decorous, mannered, prim, a model of propriety, stuffy, strict, conservative, puritanical. ANT. *casual, informal, relaxed.*

star-crossed a. doomed, unfortunate, unlucky, ill-destined, ill-fated, damned, cursed, condemned. ANT. *fortunate, lucky, blessed.*

stardom n. superstardom, notoriety, fame, acclaim, greatness, renown, celebrity status, prominence. ANT. *anonymity, oblivion.*

stare n. gaze, gawking, ogling, eyeballing, glare, withering stare, glower. SEE ANGRY

stare v. watch, gaze, gawk, gape, ogle, eyeball, glare, *rubberneck, peer, fix one's gaze on, *burn holes with one's eyes, *scorch with one's eyes, *regard saucer-eyed, stare down. SEE ANGRY

stargazing n. SEE ASTRONOMY

stark a. **1.** BARE desolate, unadorned, undecorated, plain, simple, Spartan, austere, bald, naked, stripped, barren, bleak, empty, deserted. **2.** UTTER sheer, downright, outright, absolute, complete, unmitigated, out-and-out. ANT. *1. ornate, adorned, decorated. 2. partial, mitigated.*

starry-eyed a. unrealistic, impractical, romantic, optimistic, dreaming. ANT. *pragmatic, down-to-earth, realistic.*

start n. **1.** BEGINNING commencement, opening, outset, onset, *blast-off, conception, inception, birth, origin, genesis, dawn. **2.** SHOCK fright, surprise, jump, startle, flinch, jolt, turn. **3.** HEAD START lead, advantage, *jump, handicap, allowance. ANT. *1. end, termination, finish, death.*

start v. begin, commence, open, *blast off, depart, *get the ball rolling, set off, get going, get underway, *dive in, initiate, conceive, give birth to, give rise to, found, pioneer, institute, create, introduce, invent, spring, arise, emerge. ANT. *end, stop, die, terminate.*

startle v. surprise, alarm, shock, frighten, scare, jolt, *give a turn, stun, unnerve, astonish,

*scare the living daylights out of, *scare the pants off of.

starve v. go hungry, become emaciated, be malnourished, waste away, die of starvation, perish, succumb, be ravenous, be famished, fast, diet. ANT. *stuff oneself, gorge, *pig out.*

starved a. hungry, famished, starving, ravenous, *hungry enough to eat a horse, malnourished, emaciated, wasting away. ANT. *full, *stuffed, gorged.*

state n. **1.** CONDITION status, circumstances, form, shape, situation, mode, position, phase, stage, station, standing, footing, mood, frame of mind. **2.** NATION, STATE republic, union, commonwealth, country, people, land, government, kingdom. "Great engines moving slowly."—Frances Bacon. "A secular deity."—Georg Hegel. "Embodied morality."—Georg Hegel. "That cawing rookery of committees and subcommittees."—V.S. Pritchett.

WORD FIND

STATE NICKNAMES

Alabama: Cotton State, Heart of Dixie

Alaska: Last Frontier

Arizona: Grand Canyon State

Arkansas: Land of Opportunity

California: Golden State

Colorado: Centennial State

Connecticut: Nutmeg State, Constitution State

Delaware: First State, Diamond State

Florida: Sunshine State

Georgia: Peach State, Empire State of the South

Hawaii: Aloha State

Idaho: Gem State

Illinois: Prairie State

Indiana: Hoosier State

Iowa: Hawkeye State

Kansas: Sunflower State

Kentucky: Bluegrass State

Louisiana: Pelican State, Creole State

Maine: Pine Tree State

Maryland: Old Line State

Massachusetts: Bay State

Michigan: Wolverine State

Minnesota: Gopher State, North Star State

Mississippi: Magnolia State

Missouri: Show Me State

Montana: Treasure State

Nebraska: Cornhusker State

Nevada: Sagebrush State, Silver State

New Hampshire: Granite State

New Jersey: Garden State

New Mexico: Land of Enchantment
New York: Empire State
North Carolina: Tar Heel State, Old North State
North Dakota: Flickertail State, Sioux State
Ohio: Buckeye State
Oklahoma: Sooner State
Oregon: Beaver State
Pennsylvania: Keystone State
Rhode Island: Little Rhody
South Carolina: Palmetto State
South Dakota: Coyote State, Sunshine State
Tennessee: Volunteer State
Texas: Lone Star State
Utah: Beehive State
Vermont: Green Mountain State
Virginia: Old Dominion
Washington: Evergreen State
West Virginia: Mountain State
Wisconsin: Badger State
Wyoming: Equality State
SEE GOVERNMENT, POLITICS

state v. say, declare, assert, put forth, utter, voice, express, articulate, deliver, announce, speak, avow.

stately a. dignified, majestic, grand, august, imposing, distinguished, regal, royal, impressive, elegant, formal, palatial, ceremonial. ANT. *undignified, cheap, modest, poor.*

statement n. declaration, assertion, announcement, utterance, pronouncement, comment, remark, profession, proclamation, communication, verbalization, articulation, revelation, testimony, affidavit, deposition.

state-of-the-art a. *cutting edge, *leading edge, *twenty-first century, advanced, new, modern, ultramodern, up-to-the-minute, trendsetting. ANT. *antiquated, old-fashioned, outdated.*

statesman n. politician, diplomat, elder statesman, legislator, solon. "Somebody old enough to know his own mind and keep quiet about it."—Bernard Baruch. SEE POLITICIAN

static n. 1. ELECTRICAL INTERFERENCE *atmospherics, discharges, noise. 2. CRITICISM *flak, *grief.

STATIC a. [STAT ik] unmoving, stationary. *Electric batteries are a static power source.* SYN. unmoving, motionless, stationary, inactive, fixed, still, constant, inert, stagnant. ANT. *dynamic, active, moving.*

station n. 1. DEPOT terminal, terminus, stop, end of the line, transfer station, substation.

2. POST battle station, assigned area, department, position, location. **3.** HEADQUARTERS base, command post, nerve center, office. **4.** SOCIAL STANDING status, class, position, rank, caste, grade, footing.

stationary a. fixed, unmoving, immobile, motionless, static, anchored, rooted, at a standstill, stable, still, inert. ANT. *moving, mobile, on the move.*

stationery n. letterhead, writing papers, envelopes.

statistician n. statist, demographer, pollster, *number cruncher.

statistics n. facts, hard data, *stats, *numbers, percentages, *the book, track record, *dope. "The heart of democracy."—Simeon Strunsky. "Statistics are like a bikini. What they reveal is suggestive, but what they conceal is vital."—Aaron Levenstein.

statue n. statuette, sculpture, figure, figurine, colossus, bust, monument, icon, acrolith, rendering, carving. SEE SCULPTURE

statuesque a. tall, graceful, dignified, well-proportioned, beautiful, handsome, imposing, majestic, stately, *like a Greek god.

statuette n. figurine, *Oscar.

stature n. 1. HEIGHT tallness, size, length, measurement. 2. STANDING status, rank, position, importance, eminence, station, development, growth, prestige.

status n. 1. CONDITION state, shape. 2. RANK position, standing, station, class, *place in the pecking order, *place on the corporate ladder, stature, grade, rating, prestige, distinction, eminence.

STATUS QUO n. the present state of affairs. *They weren't interested in progress but in the preservation of the status quo.* SYN. present state of affairs, current situation, existing condition, state, present reality, norm.

statute n. regulation, law, rule, ordinance, legislation, edict, act, bill. SEE POLITICS, LAW

staunch v. stanch, stop, close off, seal, lessen.

STAUNCH a. [STAWNCH] strong, steadfast, loyal. *Her father was a staunch Republican.* SYN. strong, rock-solid, firm, steadfast, unwavering, resolute, faithful, tried-and-true, unflinching, devoted, stalwart, reliable, constant, red-blooded, dyed-in-the-wool. ANT. *weak, uncommitted, irresolute, unfaithful.*

stave off v. ward off, hold off, fend off, avoid, repel, block.

stay n. 1. STOP stopover, holiday, visit, sojourn.

2. POSTPONEMENT delay, suspension, deferment, reprieve.

stay *v.* **1.** STOP halt, freeze, remain, wait, abide, pause. **2.** VISIT stop over, sojourn, lodge, live, dwell, reside. **3.** CONTINUE endure, last, persist, abide.

staying power *n.* endurance. SEE STAMINA

STEADFAST *a.* [STED fast] constant, fixed, resolute. *He remained steadfast until the end.* SYN. constant, fixed, firm, resolute, resolved, steady, dedicated, devoted, loyal, faithful, settled, firm, persevering, stalwart. ANT. *irresolute, unfaithful, wavering.*

steady *v.* stabilize, secure, firm, balance.

steady *a.* **1.** SOLID fixed, stable, rock-solid, balanced, secure, anchored. **2.** CONSTANT unchanging, unwavering, continuous, incessant, unceasing, unremitting, nonstop, endless, perpetual, regular. **3.** FREQUENT regular, habitual, long-standing, loyal, faithful. **4.** CALM composed, controlled, cool, collected, levelheaded, self-possessed, poised. **5.** RELIABLE dependable, stable. ANT. *1. unstable, insecure, shaky, wobbly. 2. inconstant, irregular, broken. 3. rare, infrequent. 4. nervous, shaky, agitated. 5. unreliable, flighty, unstable.*

steak *n.* cut of beef, sirloin, T-bone, filet mignon, porterhouse.

steal *v.* **1.** TAKE burgle, burglarize, rob, filch, pocket, shoplift, thieve, *rip off, walk off with, swipe, pilfer, *pinch, purloin, misappropriate, lift, embezzle. **2.** SNEAK creep, prowl, skulk, slink, pussyfoot.

stealth *n.* secrecy, sneakiness, surreptitiousness, covertness, slyness, furtiveness, stealthiness.

stealthy *a.* secret, secretive, sneaky, surreptitious, covert, sly, furtive, clandestine, undercover, feline, quiet. ANT. *open, loud, public, conspicuous.*

steam *n.* **1.** VAPOR heat, condensation, moisture, cloud, mist, fog, fume, exhalation, gas. **2.** POWER energy, force, muscle, horsepower, drive, vigor, strength.

steamship *n.* paddlewheeler, sidewheeler, liner, river boat, *floating palace.

steed *n.* charger, stallion. SEE HORSE

steel *v.* harden, toughen, inure, brace, fortify, strengthen.

steely *a.* strong, tough, hard, hardened, severe. ANT. *soft, pliant.*

steep *v.* soak, saturate, imbue, souse, douse, drench, sop, marinate, bathe, immerse, submerge.

steep *a.* **1.** PRECIPITOUS sheer, high, abrupt, vertical, vertiginous, dizzying, *steep enough to scare a mountain goat, sky-high, lofty. **2.** EXPENSIVE high, costly, exorbitant, unreasonable. ANT. *1. gradual, horizontal. 2. cheap, low-priced, reasonable.*

steeple *n.* spire, minaret, belfry. SEE TOWER

steer *v.* guide, direct, navigate, *man the helm, drive, pilot, take the wheel, skipper, captain, point, plot a course, *be in the driver's seat.

stein *n.* SEE MUG

stellar *a.* **1.** OF THE STARS astral, starry, galactic. SEE STAR. **2.** OUTSTANDING excellent, shining, splendid, chief, leading. ANT. *1. terrestrial. 2. mediocre.*

stem *n.* stalk, branch, shoot, petiole, pedicel.

stem *v.* **1.** ARISE rise, originate, issue, spring, emanate, derive. **2.** STOP check, dam, plug, curb, end, arrest, slow down, staunch, block.

stench *n.* smell, odor, stink, reek, fetor, foulness, rankness, rottenness, malodor.

stentorian *a.* loud, booming, thunderous, powerful, resonant, deafening. ANT. *quiet, low.*

step *n.* **1.** FOOTSTEP footfall, stride, gait, pace, tread, walk, hobble, forward movement, footprint. **2.** DOORSTEP stair, tread, riser, rung. **3.** ACT action, maneuver, process, measure, phase, stage. **4.** LEVEL grade, degree, rung.

step *v.* stride, walk, shuffle, carry oneself, pad, tread, saunter, march, ambulate, traipse, trudge, plod, slog, hobble, limp, tiptoe. SEE RUN, WALK

step down *v.* resign, quit, abdicate, retire.

steppe *n.* plain, grassland, savanna, wasteland.

stereo *a.* binaural, stereophonic. ANT. *mono.*

STEREOTYPE *n.* [STER ee oh tipe] a fixed idea, impression or characterization that ignores individuality, a habitual but often inaccurate characterization. *Her misconception was based on a stereotype.* SYN. preconceived notion, type, faulty characterization, classification, convention, mold, average, stock character, cliché. ANT. *individual.*

stereotype *v.* characterize, *paint with a broad brush, *tar with a broad brush, pigeonhole, typecast, generalize, brand, label, prejudge, categorize.

sterile *a.* **1.** UNPRODUCTIVE barren, fruitless, childless, infertile, infecund, impotent, fallow, unprolific. **2.** GERM-FREE antiseptic, disinfected, pure, sanitary, aseptic, clean. **3.** DULL bland, uninteresting, lifeless, unstimulating. ANT. *1. productive, fruitful, fecund. 2. infected, unsanitary. 3. interesting, lively.*

sterilize v. 1. DISINFECT purify, cleanse, decontaminate, sanitize, autoclave, fumigate, kill germs. 2. GELD castrate, emasculate, spay, fix, alter, neuter. ANT. *1. infect, contaminate.*

sterling a. excellent, superb, A-1, first-rate, high-quality, superior, supreme, choice, select, the best, superlative, meritorious. ANT. *poor, inferior, second-rate.*

stern n. aft, rear, back.

stern a. 1. HARD severe, strict, authoritarian, tough, rigid, harsh, frowning, hard-nosed, critical, demanding, dour, ironhanded, sober, grim, austere. 2. FORBIDDING grim, black, dour, grave, cold, icy, frowning, hard, steely, stony. ANT. *1. soft, easygoing, permissive. 2. friendly, warm.*

stevedore n. loader, lumper, longshoreman, dockworker.

stew n. soup, mishmash, goulash, mélange, hodgepodge, ragout, burgoo, chowder, beef stew, salmagundi, *mulligan stew.

stew v. 1. SIMMER bubble, heat, seethe, boil. 2. FRET fume, seethe, fuss over, worry over, brood.

steward n. major domo, seneschal, chamberlain, domestic manager, attendant, maitre d' hotel, butler, manager, administrator.

stewardess n. flight attendant, hostess, host. SEE AIRPLANE

stewed a. inebriated, intoxicated. SEE DRUNK

stick n. branch, twig, limb, stalk, bough, switch, cane, rod, pole staff, stake, stave, bat, club, billy club, truncheon, nightstick, cudgel, shillelagh, baton, wand.

stick v. 1. ADHERE cling, hold, grip, hang on to, stay, cleave, bond, bind, fix, attach, fasten, paste, glue, tape, pin. 2. PRICK stab, poke, jab, puncture, pierce, impale, penetrate, spear. 3. PUT place, lay, set, position, deposit, drop. 4. ENDURE persevere, persist, hold out, *keep on plugging, *stick to one's guns. ANT. *4. give up, quit.*

stick in the mud n. conservative, diehard, *fuddy-duddy.

stickler n. *nitpicker, *fussbudget, perfectionist, disciplinarian.

sticks, the n. *the boonies, boondocks, backwoods, country, *tall timbers.

stick-to-itiveness n. persistence, pertinacity. SEE PERSEVERANCE

stickup n. Sl. holdup, heist, mugging. SEE ROBBERY

sticky a. 1. TACKY adhesive, viscid, viscous, gummy, gluey, gooey, glutinous, *clingy. 2. HUMID muggy, steamy, sultry, close, clammy,

hot. 3. TROUBLESOME difficult, awkward, tricky, delicate, ticklish, thorny, painful. ANT. *1. dry. 2. dry, cool. 3. simple, easy, painless.*

stiff a. 1. RIGID inflexible, unyielding, unbending, hard, firm, rock-solid, inelastic, impliable, tight, taut, *stiff as a board. 2. TIGHT sore, not limber, cold, arthritic. 3. THICK dense, solidified, firm, viscous. 4. STRONG powerful, potent, intense, brisk, vigorous. 5. HARSH severe, punitive, merciless, tough, stringent, extreme, sharp. 6. FORMAL, AWKWARD wooden, forced, unnatural, labored, self-conscious, *uptight, constrained, prim. 7. DIFFICULT formidable, hard, challenging, laborious, heavy, trying, complicated. ANT. *1. soft, flexible, yielding, pliable. 2. loose, limber, warmed-up. 3. thin, loose, watery. 4. gentle, mild. 5. soft, easy, merciful. 6. relaxed, *folksy, spontaneous, warm. 7. easy, simple, unchallenging.*

stiffen v. harden, firm, firm up, tighten, thicken, congeal, set, gel. ANT. *loosen, soften, liquefy.*

stifle v. 1. SUFFOCATE smother, choke, asphyxiate, strangle, throttle. 2. SUPPRESS repress, stop, check, curb, squelch, silence, shut up, still, quash, squash, put an end to, scotch.

STIGMA n. [STIG muh] something that brands one with a negative reputation, mark of disgrace or shame. *He fought hard to escape the stigma of mental illness.* SYN. mark of shame, disgrace, brand, blemish on one's reputation, blot, taint, scar, odium, dishonor, *black eye, reflection.

STIGMATIZE v. [STIG muh tize] to brand with a characterization that detracts from one's reputation. *It's easy to stigmatize the learning-disabled with negative labels.* SYN. brand, characterize, disgrace, ruin one's reputation, defame, *give a black eye, label, mark with shame.

stiletto n. knife, blade. SEE DAGGER

still n. silence, quiet, hush, peace, tranquility, serenity, calm, motionlessness. ANT. *racket, noise, bustle.*

still v. silence, hush, quiet, shut up, muzzle, subdue, calm, becalm, soften, tranquilize, pacify. ANT. *amplify, intensify, agitate.*

still a. 1. SILENT quiet, hushed, noiseless, soundless, peaceful, tranquil, serene, *quiet as a mausoleum, *quiet as the grave, *silent as the vacuum of space, mute, subdued. 2. MOTIONLESS becalmed, lifeless, static, unmoving, inert, dormant, idle, quiescent, dead.

ANT. *1. noisy, uproarious, loud, deafening. 2. bustling, active, busy.*

stillness n. silence, quiet, hush, peace, tranquility, serenity, calm, motionlessness. ANT. *racket, din, noise.*

stilted a. pompous, overly dignified, affected, wooden, pretentious, bombastic, stiff, pedantic, grandiloquent, mannered, formal. ANT. *casual, natural, *folksy.*

stimulant n. excitant, *pick-me-up, energizer, jolt, *upper, bracer, *shot in the arm. ANT. *soporific, depressant, *downer.*

stimulate v. excite, rouse, energize, spark, stir, invigorate, initiate, prompt, *turn on, jolt, revive, incite, instigate, goad, prompt, *light a fire under, *fire up, *fan the flames, galvanize. ANT. *depress, *turn off, tranquilize.*

stimulating a. exciting, rousing, energizing, stirring, invigorating, bracing, exhilarating, heart-quickening, pulse-quickening, *adrenalizing, interesting, fascinating, thought-provoking, titillating, provocative, gripping, enthralling. ANT. *soporific, somnolent, boring.*

stimulus n. incentive, incitement, provocation, impetus, goad, spur, fillip, motive, push, spark, stimulant, impulse, *shot in the arm, *good swift kick, catalyst. ANT. *tranquilizer, soporific, depressant.*

sting n. **1.** INJURY INFLICTED BY INSECT OR ANIMAL bite, wound, venom, poison. **2.** PAIN burning, tingling, smarting, soreness, hurt, irritation, twinge, pang, painful sensation. **3.** POLICE ENTRAPMENT *sting operation, *come-on. **4.** SCAM swindle, *con, *flimflam, *grift, *suckering.

sting v. **1.** PRICK bite, wound, envenom, injure, burn, stick, infect, urticate, nettle. **2.** HURT smart, burn, tingle. **3.** MAKE UNHAPPY distress, hurt, cut to the quick, insult, cut, grieve, offend.

stingy a. **1.** CHEAP tight, tightfisted, miserly, *penny-pinching, niggardly, penurious, parsimonious, grudging, stinting, thrifty, frugal. **2.** SCANTY inadequate, insufficient, sparing, meager, skimpy, paltry, *measly, lean. ANT. *1. generous, charitable, giving. 2. generous, abundant, plentiful.*

stink n. stench, smell, odor, reek, foulness, malodor, fetor, *BO, putridness.

stink v. **1.** SMELL reek, fume, offend, *smell to high heaven. **2.** BE BAD *suck, *bite, *bite the big one, be lousy.

stinking a. smelly, reeking, offensive, malodorous, odiferous, fetid, foul, rank, noisome, spoiled, putrid.

stint n. task, duty, assignment, chore, job.

stint v. limit, restrict, scrimp, conserve.

stipend n. payment, allowance, wage, salary, fee, compensation, remuneration, honorarium, earnings.

STIPULATE v. [STIP yoo late] to specify a requirement, especially in a formal agreement or contract. *He stipulated in the contract that work would begin on the first of the month.* SYN. specify, lay out, require, spell out, detail, fix, set terms, contract, condition, designate.

stipulation n. specification, requirement, agreement, condition, obligation, article, demand, provision, proviso, item.

stir n. commotion, excitement, tumult, uproar, hullabaloo, ado, fuss, furor, pother, turmoil, bustle.

stir v. **1.** MIX mingle, blend, commingle, churn, whip, beat. **2.** MOVE shake, wiggle, shift, budge, jiggle, flutter. **3.** EXCITE move, disturb, stimulate, rouse, electrify, spark, *work up, galvanize, prompt, awaken.

stirring a. rousing, moving, exciting, stimulating, electrifying, exhilarating, inspiring, *mind-blowing, dramatic, soul-stirring. ANT. *boring, soporific.*

stitch v. sew, fasten, thread, suture.

stock n. **1.** MERCHANDISE inventory, products, goods, supply, assortment, variety, array, range, stockpile, reserve, hoard. **2.** FARM ANIMALS livestock, herd, flock, horses, cows, pigs. **3.** ANCESTRY lineage, family, bloodline, pedigree, heritage, extraction. **4.** INVESTMENT shares, security, mutual fund. SEE STOCK MARKET **5.** RAW MATERIAL, MAIN INGREDIENTS makings, *fixings, essence, broth, foundation.

stock v. supply, provision, fill, provide, equip, stockpile, furnish, lay in.

stock a. common, in ready supply, in stock, *off the shelf, *run-of-the-mill, plain, *garden variety, everyday, overused, tired, trite, hackneyed. ANT. *original, fresh, custommade.*

stockade n. enclosure, fort, palisade, pen, prison, jail.

stocking n. sock, hose, nylon.

stock market n. stock exchange, stock brokerage, American Stock Exchange, Wall Street, New York Stock Exchange, NASDAQ.

WORD FIND

agent who buys, sells on behalf of another: broker

Amex: American Stock Exchange

average daily price of thirty blue-chip companies: Dow-Jones Industrial Average

Big Blue: IBM, International Business Machines

Big Board: New York Stock Exchange

blue chip: common stock of a large, high-quality company

broker's frequent trading of client's stocks to generate more commissions: churning

buyer and seller: trader

buying from one market, selling to another at higher price: arbitrage

buying just before price drops, selling just before rise: whipsaw

buying strategy that is opposite from what most others do: contrarian

collapse of market: crash

collecting stock certificates as a hobby: scripophily

company's history, earnings, finances, circular of: prospectus

credit, buying securities on: buying on margin

corporate credit information, company that publishes: Dun and Bradstreet

declining market: bear market

diversified stock investment: mutual fund

dividends paid preferentially over common stock, stock with: preferred stock

dollar, stocks selling under a: penny stocks

earnings distribution: dividend

electronic display of trading activity: ticker

expert: analyst

Fed, the: Federal Reserve System, Federal Reserve Bank

51 percent of company's voting shares, owning: controlling interest

growing or rising market: bull market

high-quality, high-profile company's stock: blue chip

high-risk investing: speculating, taking a flyer

high-risk trader: speculator

holdings, investor's: portfolio

inexperienced investor: lamb

inflated market, downward trend that corrects: correction

investment services, ratings, index, company that offers: Standard and Poor's

load: service or sales charge

membership on an exchange: seat

moving assets to another investment: rollover

optimistic about economy: bullish

order to buy or sell at predetermined price: option, stop order

OTC: over the counter

overlooked stock with great potential: sleeper

pessimistic about economy: bearish

plunge dramatically, day on which stock prices: Black Friday, Black Monday

poorly performing stock: dog, turkey

private company offering shares for the first time: going public

privileged information, one who has access to: insider

privileged information, trading on: insider trading

purchase large volume of stock to control its price: corner, corner the market

reflects market as a whole, individual stock that: barometer, bellwether

skirt lengths, theory that market rises and falls with women's: hemline theory

speculating on a company takeover: arbitrage

stock owner: shareholder

stock's price divided by earnings per share: price-earnings ratio

takeover blackmail: greenmail

takeover of company with borrowed money: leveraged buyout

takeover, one who attempts a company: raider, shark

unstable: volatile

SEE BUSINESS, MONEY

stockpile *n.* supply, reserve, hoard, store, amassment, nest egg, larder, cache, stash.

stockpile *v.* stock, hoard, store, reserve, amass, cache, stash, squirrel away, save, lay in. ANT. *expend, spend, deplete.*

stocky *a.* thickset, short, heavy, stout, sturdy, *built like a fireplug, stubby, pudgy, squat, husky. ANT. *skinny, tall, lean, lanky.*

stodgy *a.* uninteresting, drab, *blah, dull, tedious, *dull as dishwater, boring, wooden, dry, stuffy, formal, staid, old-fashioned. ANT. *exciting, lively, *hip, wild.*

STOIC *a.* [STOH ik] showing indifference toward pain, grief pleasure or any other emotion. *Although he was bleeding profusely, the accident victim remained stoic.* SYN. indifferent, impassive, cool, philosophical, stony, dispassionate, apathetic, uninterested, stolid, detached, resigned. ANT. *emotional, passionate, hysterical.*

stoke *v.* stir, turn the coals, tend, fill, refuel.

STOLID *a.* [STAW lid] showing little emotion, impassive. *The prisoner remained stolid* *throughout his sentencing.* SYN. emotionless, impassive, stoic, stoical, indifferent, apathetic, stony, disinterested, dull, phlegmatic, stupid, bovine. ANT. *hysterical, emotional, wild.*

stomach n. belly, abdomen, gut, midsection, intestinal cavity, digestive organ, bowels, viscera, esophagus, craw, rumen, *breadbasket, *spare tire, *beer belly, paunch. "The greatest of deities."—Euripides.

WORD FIND

backing up of food into esophagus, causing pain: reflux, pyrosis, heartburn

digestive chemical: gastrin, hydrochloric acid, pepsin

infant's stomachache: colic

inflammation: gastritis

lesion caused by too much acid: ulcer

muscular contractions that push food out of: peristalsis

rumbling: borborygmus

soupy mixture made from digested meal: chyme

tube leading to stomach: esophagus

upset: nausea, queasiness, indigestion, dyspepsia

stomp v. stamp, tramp, crush, squash, kill.

stone n. rock, boulder, pebble, granite, cobblestone, gravel, crag, jewel, gemstone, gem, precious stone, semiprecious gem, *ice, birthstone, bijou, diamond, emerald, sapphire, ruby, pearl, topaz, amethyst, tourmaline, onyx, garnet, zircon.

WORD FIND

bits and pieces: rubble, spall, grit

capstone on ancient monument: dolmen

cutter: mason

cutter, polisher, engraver: lapidary

cutting, polishing, engraving, art of: lapidary

excavation pit: quarry

fire-starting: flint

giant: boulder, megalith

globular stone with a crystal-lined center: geode

memorial pile or trailmarker: cairn

piles found on mountain slopes: scree, talus, cairn

polishing: pumice

sharpening: whetstone

stony: petrous, lithoid

transported far from native land by glacier: erratic, glacial erratic

turn to: petrify

SEE ROCK

Stone Age n. Paleolithic, Mesolithic, Neolithic, prehistoric times.

stoned a. Sl. **1.** DRUNK intoxicated, inebriated, *buzzed, *plastered, *bombed, *crocked, *three sheets to the wind, under the influence. **2.** HIGH ON DRUGS *buzzed, *baked, drugged, *blitzed, *doped up, *flying, *fried, *polluted, *spacey, *tripping, *wasted, under the influence. ANT. *sober, *stone-cold sober, clearheaded, lucid.*

stone-deaf a. *deaf as a post, hard of hearing, hearing-impaired.

stonewall v. impede, obstruct, be close-mouthed, *clam up, stall, refuse to cooperate.

stony a. hard, cold, unfeeling, merciless, pitiless, indifferent, heartless, uncaring, callous, tough, harsh, severe, steely. ANT. *soft, warm, sympathetic, compassionate.*

stooge n. foil, dupe, pawn, flunky, victim, dummy, underling.

stool n. **1.** SEAT footstool, ottoman, bar stool. **2.** FECES excrement, dropping, waste, *crap.

stool pigeon n. informer, spy, *narc, decoy.

stoop n. porch, platform, portico, veranda.

stoop v. **1.** BEND OVER bow, crook, crouch, lean forward, tilt, slouch, slump, nod. **2.** LOWER ONESELF degrade oneself, sink, condescend, deign, demean oneself, resort.

stop n. **1.** HALT cessation, termination, suspension, discontinuance, standstill, *freeze, letup, end, intermission, interlude. **2.** STOPOVER destination, sojourn, visit, layover, depot, station, terminal. ANT. *1. start, commencement, progression.*

stop v. **1.** HALT cease, terminate, suspend, discontinue, stand still, *freeze, hold it, let up, end, arrest, turn off, shut down, quit, finish, break, stay. **2.** STAUNCH stanch, plug up, stem the flow, seal, check, block, occlude, choke off. **3.** OBSTRUCT impede, restrain, block. **4.** DEFEAT put down, check, put an end to, crush, quash, silence. ANT. *1. go, proceed, continue. 2. open, unplug. 3. clear the way. 4. strengthen, fortify, help.*

stopgap a. makeshift, temporary, emergency, provisional, improvised, substitute, jury-rigged, impermanent. ANT. *permanent.*

stoppage n. **1.** STOP halt, close, ending, shutdown, layoff. **2.** OBSTRUCTION blockage, impediment, check, hindrance, obstacle.

stopper n. cork, plug, bung, tap, tampion.

storage n. stowage, stockpile, storehouse, storeroom, cache, arsenal, depot, bin, silo, granary, repository.

store n. **1.** SHOP market, mart, retail outlet, *Mom and Pop operation, emporium, *five and dime, supermarket, department store, mall, factory outlet, boutique, convenience store, drugstore, thrift shop, business establishment, canteen, PX. **2.** SUPPLY stock, stockpile, reserve, savings, inventory, provisions, hoard, cache, *nest egg, stash.

store *v.* save, reserve, put away, stow, *squirrel away, stock, stockpile, lay in supplies, hoard, cache, warehouse, stash, provision, load up, *salt away. ANT. *spend, *blow, deplete.*

storekeeper *n.* shopkeeper, grocer, proprietor, merchant.

storeroom *n.* repository, depository, cache, warehouse, depot, arsenal, silo, granary, buttery.

storm *n.* **1.** WEATHER DISTURBANCE cloudburst, thunderstorm, thundershower, *thunderboomer, electrical storm, deluge, downpour, *gullywasher, squall, tempest, gale, windstorm, hurricane, monsoon, tropical storm, typhoon, tornado, whirlwind, cyclone, *twister, snowstorm, northeaster, blizzard, hailstorm, blow, inclement weather.

WORD FIND

fair weather spot in center of storm: eye of the storm

line between clashing air masses: front

raising of shoreline water during storm: storm surge

sandstorm of North Africa, India, Middle East: Haboob

whirlwind over water that sucks up funnel of water: waterspout

SEE CLOUD, RAIN, PRECIPITATION, SNOW, WIND

2. UPROAR controversy, outburst, disturbance, brouhaha, furor, eruption, hubbub, attack, hysteria, outcry, squall.

storm *v.* **1.** RAIN blow, squall, rage, pour, thunder, boom, thunder and lightning, snow. **2.** CHARGE attack, assault, rush, blitz, blitzkrieg, assail, invade, besiege. **3.** RAGE blow up, lose one's temper, rant and rave, fume, *throw a fit, roar, bellow, *go on the rampage, *go ballistic.

stormy *a.* turbulent, wild, tempestuous, violent, rough, windy, squally, blustery, howling, pouring, raining, snowy, inclement. ANT. *calm, becalmed, balmy, mild.*

story *n.* **1.** NARRATIVE account, tale, chronicle, myth, legend, fable, yarn, fairy tale, short story, parable, allegory, folktale, saga, epic, drama, comedy, tragedy, romance, history, novel, novella, novelette, anecdote, plot.

WORD FIND

category of: genre

long, pointless story with anticlimactic ending: shaggy dog story

real-life feeling given to characters, setting: verisimilitude

warning, story given as a: cautionary tale

SEE NOVEL, BOOK

2. LIE fabrication, *tall tale, *fish story, falsehood, excuse, fib, canard, hoax. **3.** REPORT scoop, news, dispatch, rumor.

storyteller *n.* raconteur, author, writer, novelist, narrator, spinner of yarns, historian.

stout *a.* thickset, fat, big, obese, portly, stocky, husky, rugged, sturdy, corpulent, heavy, heavyset, strong, bull-like, brawny, hulking, hefty. ANT. *skinny, anorexic, bony, puny.*

stouthearted *a.* brave, courageous, daring, nervy, lionhearted, valiant, undaunted, fearless, *gutsy, bold. ANT. *cowardly, timid, *wimpy.*

stove *n.* range, oven, microwave, toaster oven, heater, wood stove, furnace.

stow *v.* pack, store away, put away, load, stash, deposit, save, stockpile, cram, wedge, stuff.

straddle *v.* **1.** BESTRIDE sit astride, split. **2.** TAKE BOTH SIDES OF AN ISSUE straddle the fence, hedge, waffle, *talk out of both sides of one's mouth. ANT. *2. be committed.*

strafe *v.* pepper, gun down, spray with bullets, bombard, fire on.

straggle *v.* stray, wander, ramble, meander, deviate, drift, range, rove.

straggler *n.* stray, wanderer, lagger, late arrival.

straight *a.* **1.** UNBENT undeviating, linear, direct, even, vertical, horizontal, in line, plumb, square, aligned. **2.** HONEST straightforward, frank, candid, upfront, forthright, trustworthy, reliable, sincere. **3.** UNDILUTED pure, whole, unmodified, unmixed, *neat. **4.** CONTINUOUS nonstop, unbroken, sustained, uninterrupted, consecutive, constant. **5.** ORDERLY in good order, neat, arranged. **6.** *Sl.* *SQUARE conventional, conformist, conservative. ANT. *1. bent, curving, wavy, deviating. 2. dishonest, unreliable, insincere. 3. diluted, mixed, modified. 4. interrupted, broken. 5. messy, sloppy. 6. *hip, unconventional, *cool, wild.*

straightforward *a.* honest, frank, candid, upfront, forthright, direct, plain, explicit, aboveboard, unambiguous, open. ANT. *dishonest, insincere, ambiguous.*

strain *n.* **1.** STRESS tension, pressure, force, pull, tightness, exertion, effort. **2.** INJURY sprain, muscle pull, wrench, cramp, twist. **3.** ANCES-TRY lineage, extraction, bloodline, stock, pedigree, family, descent, descendants, breed. **4.** TRACE hint, suggestion, streak, shade, touch, suspicion.

strain v. **1.** STRETCH tighten, draw tight, pull, exert, overexert, tax, force, struggle, labor. **2.** INJURE sprain, pull a muscle, wrench, cramp, twist. **3.** DISTORT stretch, exaggerate. **4.** FILTER sieve, screen, sift, refine, percolate.

strained a. labored, forced, unnatural, stiff, studied, affected, uneasy, tense. ANT. *relaxed, natural.*

strait n. narrow, channel, waterway, inlet. SEE STRAITS

straitjacket v. confine, immobilize. SEE RE-STRAIN

straitlaced a. prudish, prim, strict, severe, upright, proper, puritanical, rigid, stiff, stuffy, priggish. ANT. *wild, immoral, *fast.*

straits n. difficulty, plight, emergency, predicament, dilemma, bind, hot water, mess, jam, hole.

strand n. thread, fiber, filament, line, string, cord, hair.

strand v. maroon, run ashore, run aground, beach, wreck, abandon, leave in the lurch.

strange a. **1.** FOREIGN alien, exotic, unfamiliar, otherworldly, new, novel, remote, outlandish. **2.** UNUSUAL weird, peculiar, odd, bizarre, uncommon, unconventional, singular, atypical, queer, outlandish, uncanny, extraordinary, curious, funny, eccentric, *far out. **3.** UNEASY ill, ill at ease, uncomfortable, odd, peculiar, disoriented, out of place, out of sorts. **4.** REMOTE reserved, distant, aloof, reclusive. ANT. *1. familiar, everyday, common, native. 2. usual, typical, conventional. 3. normal. 4. friendly, gregarious, sociable.*

stranger n. unknown, outsider, foreigner, alien, *new kid in town, interloper, *just another face in the crowd. ANT. *friend, acquaintence.*

strangle v. **1.** CHOKE throttle, strangulate, asphyxiate, suffocate, *cut off one's wind, garrote, hang, smother. **2.** SUPPRESS stifle, repress, check, curb, restrict, stop, squelch, silence.

strap n. thong, cord, lash, band, rein, halter, leash, belt, strop.

strap v. tie, tie down, bind, lash, secure, truss, tether, fasten.

strapped a. penniless, *broke, destitute, impoverished, poverty-stricken, needy, *down to one's last dime. ANT. *wealthy, *rolling in dough.*

strapping a. well-built, tall, husky, athletic, brawny, muscular, sinewy, rugged, powerful, fit, healthy, hearty, robust. ANT. *puny, sickly.*

stratagem n. trick, scheme, plan, ploy, subterfuge, maneuver, set-up, machination, artifice, deception, tactic, play.

strategic a. essential, crucial, critical, vital, important, key, decisive, significant, tactical. ANT. *unimportant, inconsequential.*

strategy n. plan, *game plan, design, procedure, blueprint, plot, scheme, approach, machination, tactic.

stratified a. layered, laminated, multileveled.

STRATUM n. [STRAT um] a layer or level, as that of sedimentary rock or a socioeconomic group. *He came from the upper stratum of society.* SYN. **1.** LAYER level, grade, bed, stratification, seam, tier. **2.** CLASS station, standing, position, rank, echelon, *upper crust.

straw in the wind n. indication, indicator, sign, omen, portent, harbinger.

straw vote n. poll, opinion poll, unofficial vote.

stray n. wanderer, rover, waif, orphan, vagabond, lost pet, maverick.

stray v. **1.** WANDER roam, rove, drift, range, get lost, ramble, straggle, meander. **2.** GO WRONG deviate, digress, err, go astray, go off course, be in error.

streak n. **1.** STRIPE mottle, marking, bar, line, dash, smear, slash, stroke, ray, vein. **2.** TRAIT strain, nature, characteristic, idiosyncrasy, touch, trace, tendency, vein.

stream n. **1.** BROOK creek, river, tributary, branch, freshet, creek, rill, runnel, watercourse, waterway, beck.

WORD FIND

sound: murmur, purl, babble, gurgle, white noise

SEE RIVER

2. SERIES succession, steady flow, torrent, outpouring, flood, deluge.

stream v. flow, rush, pour, flood, run, gush, surge, course, spill, overflow.

streamer n. flag, banner, pennant, ribbon, strip.

street n. road, avenue, lane, thoroughfare, boulevard, drive, *main drag, artery, highway, alley, dead end, route, pavement, rue, via.

streetcar n. tram, trolley, rail coach.

street people n. the homeless, transients, street urchins, gamins, vagrants, derelicts, *bag ladies.

street smart a. cunning, shrewd, experienced, seasoned, aware, worldly, savvy, *hip, *streetwise. ANT. *naive, inexperienced, unaware.*

strength *n.* **1.** POWER force, vigor, muscle, brawn, punch, *oomph, horsepower, might, energy, potency, drive. **2.** MENTAL TOUGH-NESS stability, mental health, intestinal fortitude, courage, *guts, *nerve, character, endurance, durability, will, willpower, tenacity, backbone, grit. **3.** SOLIDITY impregnability, durability. **4.** INTENSITY concentration, potency, power, effectiveness, forcefulness. ANT. *1. weakness, impotency. 2. weakness, instability, cowardice, timidity. 3. flimsiness. 4. weakness, impotence.*

strengthen *v.* fortify, prop, beef up, reinforce, bolster, buttress, harden, temper, steel, shore up, intensify, heighten. ANT. *weaken, undermine, sap.*

strenuous *a.* vigorous, hard, arduous, demanding, difficult, laborious, backbreaking, *ball-busting, tough, Herculean, burdensome, taxing. ANT. *easy, simple, effortless.*

stress *n.* **1.** STRAIN tension, pressure, anxiety, nervousness, disquiet, fear, worry, dread, burden, intensity. "Nature's fight or flight mechanism overburdened by modern society's prohibition against fighting and fleeing."—Harmon Maxwell. **2.** EMPHASIS accent, force, importance, weight. ANT. *1. relaxation, peace, tranquility.*

stress *v.* emphasize, accent, underscore, underline, accentuate, highlight, *spotlight, play up.

stress out *v.* fill with tension, tax one's nerves, unnerve, disquiet, agitate, overburden, frighten, worry, make anxious, *adrenalize. ANT. *relax, tranquilize, calm.*

stretch *n.* **1.** EXTENSION expansion, elongation, reach. **2.** EXPANSE area, run, spread, tract, space, distance, sweep, area, extent. **3.** DURATION spell, time, period, span, run, interval, tour of duty, term. **4.** EXAGGERATION. ANT. *1. contraction, retraction.*

stretch *v.* **1.** EXTEND expand, elongate, reach, protract, lengthen, span, traverse, inflate, prolong, drag out. **2.** STRAIN force. **3.** EXAGGERATE. ANT. *1. contract, retract.*

stretcher *n.* litter.

strew *v.* spread, scatter, sprinkle, disperse, broadcast, distribute, diffuse, sow. ANT. *gather, amass.*

stricken *a.* afflicted, affected, beset, struck, hit, wounded, injured, hurt, burdened, plagued.

strict *a.* **1.** EXACT complete, accurate, perfect, precise, faithful, meticulous, unerring, absolute. **2.** STRINGENT punctilious, exacting,

particular, fussy. **3.** AUTHORITARIAN disciplinary, firm, stern, rigid, hard-nosed, tough, dour, demanding, rigorous, puritanical, nononsense. ANT. *1. inexact, loose, broad. 2. loose, easy, permissive.*

stricture *n.* censure, *slam. SEE CRITICISM

stride *n.* step, gait, pace, walk.

stride *v.* step, walk, swagger, strut, tread, trudge, pace, march, traipse. SEE WALK

strides *n.* progress, advancement, headway.

STRIDENT *a.* [STRI dunt] shrill, harsh. *His strident screaming got the governor's attention.* SYN. shrill, harsh, loud, noisy, vociferous, raucous, grating, piercing, stridulous, high-pitched. ANT. *silent, quiet, hushed, soft.*

strife *n.* conflict, discord, dissent, fighting, contention, controversy, struggle, squabbling, war, clash, contest, feud, unrest. ANT. *accord, peace, harmony.*

strike *n.* **1.** MILITARY ASSAULT attack, offensive, bombing, bombardment, air strike, onslaught, raid, invasion. **2.** LABOR DISPUTE walkout, protest, wage dispute, shutdown, lockout, sit-in, hunger strike. "A labor pain."—Leonard Levinson.

strike *v.* **1.** HIT deliver a blow, punch, pound, smack, knock, clobber, box, cuff, whack, pommel, crack, rap, slap, slug, thump, wallop, clout, smite. **2.** ATTACK assault, launch an offensive, bomb, raid, charge, invade, storm. **3.** BUMP crash, smash into, collide with. **4.** DISCOVER find, unearth, uncover, encounter. **5.** PROTEST go on strike, dispute one's labor contract, walk out, shut down, picket, demonstrate. **6.** DAWN ON register, *hit, impress. **7.** REMOVE delete, cross out, erase, cancel.

strikebreaker *n.* *scab, *goon, *fink.

striking *a.* noticeable, outstanding, remarkable, conspicuous, impressive, extraordinary, out of the ordinary, arresting, awesome, prominent, astounding. ANT. *inconspicuous, unnoticeable.*

string *n.* **1.** CORD twine, rope, strand, thread, line, yarn, fiber, filament, gut. **2.** SERIES succession, row, chain, train, file, progression, procession.

STRINGENT *a.* [STRIN junt] strict, rigid, tight. *The bar had stringent rules against rowdy behavior.* SYN. strict, rigid, tight, restrictive, rigorous, exacting, tough, harsh, stiff, severe, demanding. ANT. *loose, relaxed, casual, easy.*

stringy *a.* fibrous, ropy, long, thin, sinewy, wiry.

strip *n.* length, cutting, piece, swath, band, section, segment, ribbon.

strip v. **1.** UNDRESS disrobe, peel off, slip out of, shuck, bare, divest, remove one's clothing, doff, *drop one's drawers. **2.** REMOVE peel, decorticate, excoriate, pare, uncover. **3.** DEPRIVE dispossess, rob, plunder.

stripe n. **1.** BAND streak, line, bar, strip, stroke, slash, striation, mark, chevron. **2.** TYPE kind, sort, ilk, variety, style, breed, race, strain. **3.** WELT wheal, wale.

stripling n. sprig, youth, adolescent, young man, lad.

strive v. try, make an effort, struggle, labor, toil, apply oneself, *bust one's hump, *break one's back, drive oneself, *burn the midnight oil, *work one's fingers to the bone, go after, fight.

stroke n. **1.** BLOW impact, hit, punch, rap, knock, belt, whack, cuff, slap. **2.** CARESS pat, rub, massage. **3.** SEIZURE apoplexy, brain hemorrhage. **4.** ACCOMPLISHMENT feat, coup, coup de grace, blow, move.

stroke v. caress, fondle, pat, pet, rub, massage.

stroll n. walk, constitutional, amble, saunter, excursion, ramble, jaunt.

stroll v. walk leisurely, take one's constitutional, amble, saunter, ramble, meander, take in the scenery.

strong a. **1.** PHYSICALLY POWERFUL mighty, muscular, athletic, rugged, strapping, robust, fit, able-bodied, brawny, stalwart, Herculean, *strong as a bull, *strong as a locomotive, virile, fit, hale, healthy, hearty. **2.** HAVING STRENGTH OF CHARACTER moral, upright, ethical, secure, self-confident, courageous, plucky, tough, *thick-skinned, independent, hardened, resilient. **3.** STRONG-WILLED determined, resolute, staunch, firm, tenacious, strong-minded, *having a mind of one's own. **4.** DURABLE well-constructed, well-built, solid, sturdy, heavy-duty, tough, impregnable. **5.** FORMIDABLE powerful, mighty, challenging, tough, intense, *bigtime, *major league. **6.** INTENSE potent, concentrated, severe, harsh, bright, deep, undiluted, acute, sharp. **7.** EARNEST fervent, zealous, rabid, *gung-ho. ANT. 1. weak, feeble, lame, out of shape, *atrophied. 2. immoral, unethical, insecure, cowardly, thin-skinned, dependent, needy. 3. irresolute, indecisive. 4. flimsy, jerry-built, weak. 5. weak, *lightweight, inconsequential, *bush-league. 6. mild, soft, diluted. 7. half-hearted, apathetic, impassive.

strong-arm v. twist one's arm, intimidate physically, beat, punch, coerce, force, lean on, squeeze.

strongbox n. safe, chest, lockbox, coffer, vault.

stronghold n. fortification, fort, fortress, defensive position, citadel, castle, bastion, bulwark, battlement, rampart. SEE CASTLE

strong-willed a. strong-minded. SEE STRONG

structure n. **1.** BUILDING construction, edifice, erection, skyscraper, high-rise, tower, bridge, dam. **2.** ORGANIZATION arrangement, makeup, framework, shape, form, configuration, construction, infrastructure, composition, fabric.

structure v. construct, arrange, organize, frame, shape, form, compose, plan, put together, assemble.

struggle n. **1.** EFFORT exertion, strain, labor, toil, striving, work, grind, *long haul, *never ending battle, trial. **2.** CONFLICT fight, contention, battle, tug of war, strife, war, tussle, rivalry, combat. ANT. 1. a cakewalk, *a snap, *a breeze.

struggle v. **1.** STRAIN exert, labor, toil, put in great effort, strive, work, *break one's back, *bust one's hump, *work like a dog, sweat, *plug away, *fight an uphill battle. **2.** CONFLICT contend, fight, battle, fight a tug of war, war, combat, vie, grapple, tussle, wrestle, wrangle. ANT. 1. hardly break a sweat, *breeze through, *coast through. 2. harmonize, reach accord, make peace, unite.

strum v. thrum, stroke, pluck, pick.

strumpet n. harlot, whore, hussy, slut, tramp, trollop, *lady of the evening, *call girl, streetwalker. SEE PROSTITUTE

strut n. **1.** COCKY GAIT swagger, promenade, cakewalk, peacock walk, prance. **2.** BRACE support, upright, prop, bolster.

strut v. swagger, sashay, peacock, *strut one's stuff, show off, parade, promenade, cakewalk.

stub n. end, butt, piece, remainder.

stubble n. whiskers, bristles, beard, *five o'clock shadow, growth. SEE BEARD

stubborn a. obstinate, unyielding, inflexible, uncompromising, strong-willed, muleheaded, pigheaded, tenacious, headstrong, dogged, intractable, bullheaded, resolute, unbending, fixed, willful, pertinacious. ANT. yielding, compromising, reasonable, irresolute.

stubby a. short, thickset, stocky, squat, pudgy, *built like a fireplug, heavyset, stout. ANT. tall, gangling, skinny.

stucco n. plaster, cement.

stuck-up a. snobbish, haughty, arrogant, snooty, uppity, conceited, *carrying one's nose in the air, high hat, hoity-toity, snotty.

ANT. *down-to-earth, folksy, modest, humble.*

stud n. stallion, Casanova, Don Juan, *makeout artist, *wolf, *studhammer, *skirtchaser, *tomcat, *buck, playboy, breeder.

student n. pupil, schoolgirl, schoolboy, freshman, sophomore, junior, senior, collegian, cadet, trainee, apprentice, disciple, apostle, follower.

studied a. calculated, practiced, rehearsed, prepared, affected, self-conscious, stiff, unnatural, forced, contrived, labored. ANT. *unstudied, natural, spontaneous.*

studio n. workshop, atelier, room, work room.

studious a. bookish, scholarly, academic, thoughtful, literary, well-read, hard-working, industrious, *hard at it, *plugging away, lettered. ANT. *illiterate, ignorant, unschooled, lazy.*

study n. reading, investigation, review, examination, research, scrutiny, inquiry, survey, analysis, instruction, edification, erudition, memorizing, book learning, schoolwork, academic work, training, course, subject, lesson. "The noblest exercise of the mind within doors, and most befitting a person of quality."—William Ramsey.

study v. read, pore over, *bone up on, *crack the books, learn by rote, *cram, go over, *burn the midnight oil, scrutinize, review, examine, research, inquire, survey, analyze, instruct oneself, memorize, learn, train, weigh, consider, ponder, think about, concentrate on.

stuff n. **1.** MATERIAL raw material, substance, things, contents, *nuts and bolts, elements, makings, debris, *crap, cloth, fabric. **2.** BELONGINGS effects, things, possessions, *junk, gear, paraphernalia, goods, trappings, objects. **3.** ESSENCE substance, character, *the right stuff, heart, core. **4.** FOOLISHNESS rot, idiocy. SEE NONSENSE

stuff v. **1.** LOAD pack, cram, ram, jam-pack, fill, squeeze, wedge, crowd, press. **2.** GORGE gluttonize, glut, gormandize, *pig out, surfeit, sate, *stuff to the gills.

stuffed a. crammed, full, loaded, filled, jam-packed, full, replete. ANT. *empty, deficient.*

stuffing n. fill, wadding, padding, innards.

stuffy a. **1.** STALE close, oppressive, poorly ventilated, stifling, airless, suffocating. **2.** STODGY prim, straitlaced, dull, conservative, staid, old-fogyish, stiff, starched, *square, old-fashioned, *button-down. ANT. *1. fresh, breezy. 2. wild, casual, fun-loving.*

stumble v. **1.** TRIP slip, fall, stagger, lose one's balance, totter, pitch, *take a spill, *take a header, tumble. **2.** TRIP OVER ONE'S WORDS slip, blunder, flub, bungle, trip over one's tongue, *get hung by the tongue. **3.** STUMBLE UPON chance upon, come upon, bump into, meet, hit.

stumbling block n. roadblock, impediment, hindrance, obstacle, barrier, obstruction, drawback, hurdle, bar, snag.

stump n. butt, stub.

stump v. baffle, perplex, puzzle, confound, bewilder, mystify, confuse, muddle.

stun v. daze, stupefy, shock, paralyze, *floor, lay flat, *blow away, *blow one's mind, *drop a bomb on, stagger, overwhelm, *bowl over, *shake up.

stunned a. dazed, stupefied, shocked, paralyzed, nonplussed, dumbfounded, *bowled over, *floored, *blown away, *seeing stars, overwhelmed, astonished. ANT. *composed, unruffled.*

stunning a. **1.** STUPEFYING shocking, paralyzing, staggering, overwhelming, mind-blowing, astonishing, incredible, jolting. **2.** BEAUTIFUL attractive, lovely, dazzling, gorgeous, ravishing, striking. ANT. *1. *ho-hum, *blah, boring. 2. plain, homely.*

stunt n. feat, trick, *daredevilry, act, exploit, performance.

stunt v. check, dwarf, hinder, impede, restrain, shorten, slow, arrest, restrict.

stuntman n. daredevil, double, stunt double, acrobat.

stunted a. dwarf, dwarfed, pygmy, undersized, runty, short, miniature, stubby. ANT. *oversized, giant, towering.*

stupefied a. stunned, dazed, *out of it, staggered, knocked out, struck dumb, *stupid, benumbed, *floored, shocked, paralyzed, *seeing stars, astounded, amazed, astonished. ANT. *placid, composed, *collected.*

stupefy v. stun, daze, stagger, knock out, numb, *floor, shock, paralyze, astound, amaze, astonish.

stupendous a. great, gigantic, huge, prodigious, gargantuan, colossal, vast, titanic, immense, monstrous, massive, overwhelming, astonishing, breathtaking, spectacular, staggering, mind-boggling. ANT. *tiny, puny, modest, trivial, ordinary.*

stupid a. **1.** NOT INTELLIGENT dumb, dull, witless, retarded, intellectually challenged, thick, dense, ignorant, moronic, brainless, mindless, dim-witted, imbecilic, boneheaded, *dense as a post, *chowderheaded, *dead from the neck up, *down a quart, *birdbrained, *pea-brained, *three bricks shy of a load. **2.** IRRATIONAL foolish, silly, brainless, idiotic, nonsensical, senseless, unwise, ridiculous, poorly conceived, *half-baked. ANT. *1.* brilliant, bright, smart, intelligent. *2.* rational, thoughtful, wise.

stupidity *n.* dumbness, witlessness, mental retardation, thickness, denseness, ignorance, brainlessness, mindlessness, dim-wittedness, imbecility, low IQ, idiocy, simple-mindedness. "Unconscious ignorance."—Josh Billings. "Not so much brain as ear-wax."—Shakespeare.

stupor *n.* shock, paralysis, numbness, stupefaction, insensibility, daze, bewilderment, trance, dreaminess, lethargy, torpor, dullness, apathy. ANT. clearheadedness, sharpness, lucidity, alertness.

sturdy *a.* **1.** WELL-CONSTRUCTED strong, solid, rock-solid, well-built, built to last, rugged, tough, sound, stable, stout, muscular. **2.** FIRM resolute, unyielding, uncompromising, steadfast, staunch, determined, fixed, tenacious. **3.** PHYSICALLY STRONG hardy, vigorous, fit, healthy, strapping, robust, hale. ANT. *1.* flimsy, rickety, jerry-built, unstable. *2.* irresolute, indecisive. *3.* weak, unhealthy, unfit.

stutter *v.* stammer, splutter, *trip over one's own words, *get hung by the tongue, falter, hesitate, stumble.

style *n.* **1.** MANNER mode, design, way, type, form, sort, kind, variety, genre, method, cut, expression, execution. **2.** DISTINCTION flair, voice, technique, originality, character. "The dress of thoughts."—Lord Chesterfield. "A man's style is his mind's voice."—Ralph Waldo Emerson. "The creation of one's own language."—Roger Hemings. **3.** STYLISHNESS high fashion, fashion, vogue, rage, fad, craze, trend.

stylish *a.* fashionable, chic, smart, *hip, in vogue, *chichi, *riding the cutting edge, modish, trendy, modern, sharp, dapper. ANT. passé, outmoded, antiquated, obsolete.

STYMIE *v.* [STI mee] to impede or thwart. Travel was stymied by a traffic jam. SYN. impede, thwart, obstruct, stop, block, check, foil, prevent, hinder, frustrate, throw up a stumbling block, get in one's way.

SUAVE *a.* [SWAHV] smooth in social interactions, gracious, tactful and diplomatic. He made everyone feel at ease; he was very suave. SYN. smooth, polished, refined, gracious, urbane, tactful, diplomatic, charming, cultured, worldly, polite, courtly, ingratiating.

ANT. coarse, unrefined, rude, clumsy, impolite.

subconscious *a.* unconscious, unaware. ANT. conscious.

subdue *v.* **1.** CONQUER vanquish, overpower, crush, overthrow, overrun, put down, quell, silence, subjugate, *get the better of, tame. **2.** LESSEN reduce, diminish, soften, mellow, moderate, temper, tone down, allay, mollify, mitigate. ANT. *1.* surrender, give in, *cave in. *2.* increase, intensify.

subject *n.* **1.** TOPIC issue, matter, theme, material, problem, question, point, affair, thesis, lesson, course, study. **2.** CITIZEN national, subordinate, follower.

subject *v.* put through, make vulnerable, expose.

subject *a.* **1.** BOUND BY answerable, governed, controlled, subordinate, owing, under, submissive, dependent, servile. **2.** LIABLE prone to, apt to. ANT. *1.* ruling, dominating, controlling.

SUBJECTIVE *a.* [sub JEK tiv] personal, as felt or seen through the eyes of one individual, not objective. It was a subjective opinion, based only on personal observances. SYN. personal, individual, biased, prejudiced, nonobjective, emotional, idiosyncratic, introspective. ANT. objective, impersonal, impartial.

SUBJUGATE *v.* [SUB juh GATE] to control or bring under one's power. He felt it was a man's responsibility to subjugate women. SYN. conquer, control, dominate, boss, lord over, rule, yoke, subject, keep down, *keep under one's thumb, enslave.

SUBLIMATE *v.* [SUB luh MATE] to refine or put into a socially acceptable form, as channeling one's anger or animal urges into constructive outlets. He sublimated his rage by playing the drums. SYN. channel, redirect, transfer, refine, make acceptable, suppress, repress.

SUBLIME *a.* [suh BLIME] exalted, grand, magnificent, majestic. The ballet presented a sublime performance. SYN. exalted, grand, magnificent, majestic, lofty, ennobled, high, awe-inspiring, superb, overwhelming, breathtaking, glorious, stately. ANT. humdrum, *blah, *ho-hum, pedestrian, ordinary, low.

submarine *n.* sub, U-boat, submersible, *steel shark, *pigboat.

WORD FIND
body of: hull
crew member: submariner
exhaust and air intake: snorkel

hazard: mine, depth charge, shoal
locator: sonar, sonobuoy
miniature: submersible
missile: torpedo
nuclear-powered: Trident
observation tower: conning tower, bridge
propellor sound that gives presence away: cavitation
rudder that helps sub to submerge: hydroplane
safe haven: submarine sanctuary, submarine haven
scope: periscope
stabilizing rudder: sail plane
submarine-like observation vessel: bathyscaphe, submersible
water tanks that control submerging: ballast tanks

submerge v. sink, submerse, plunge, immerse, dip, dunk, descend, go down, dive, swamp, drown.

submersible n. SEE SUBMARINE

submission n. **1.** SURRENDER capitulation, submitting, compliance, giving in, *caving in, yielding, acquiescence, deference, subordination, subjugation, obedience, complaisance. **2.** REMITTANCE mailing in, handing in. ANT. *1. domination, resistance, rebellion.*

submissive a. nonresistant, nonresisting, yielding, docile, meek, tame, *broken, prostrate, compliant, obeisant, deferential, passive, servile, subservient, *bootlicking, *brownnosing. ANT. *dominant, ruling, resistant, rebellious.*

submit v. **1.** SURRENDER capitulate, comply, give in, *cave in, yield, acquiesce, defer, *knuckle under, abide by, relinquish, *say uncle. **2.** PRESENT offer, suggest, propose, put forth, remit, hand in, mail in. ANT. *1. dominate, rule, resist, disobey. 2. rescind, renege.*

subordinate n. inferior, junior, underling, second, attendant, servant, slave, dependent, subaltern, *flunky, *second fiddle, *low man on the totem pole. ANT. *superior, senior, boss.*

subordinate v. subject, dominate, *keep under one's thumb, control, *boss around, order around, *keep down, reduce. ANT. *empower, raise.*

SUBORDINATE a. [suh BORD in et] inferior or secondary to another. *The subordinate members of the group had no power to vote.* SYN. inferior, secondary, below, under, junior, *under one's thumb, minor, lesser, second-class, submissive, subaltern, ancillary. ANT. *superior, first-class, higher, major.*

suborn v. SEE BRIBE

SUBPOENA n. [suh PEE nuh] a written order to appear in court. *The witness was served a subpoena.* SYN. summons, written order, court order, writ, notice, notification, instruction, demand.

subpoena v. summon, serve a court order, serve notice, order to testify, instruct, demand.

subscribe v. support, favor, approve, agree to, consent to, believe in, accept, endorse, go along with, sanction. ANT. *reject, disapprove, oppose.*

subscription n. purchase agreement, sales enrollment.

subsequent a. following, succeeding, later, latter, ensuing, future, resultant, next. ANT. *previous, preceding, prior.*

subsequently adv. later, afterward.

SUBSERVIENT a. [sub SERV ee unt] submissive and compliant, servile, subordinate. *The misogynist divorced his wife because she wasn't subservient enough.* SYN. submissive, compliant, servile, subordinate, obsequious, deferential, fawning, sycophantic, groveling, cringing, *brownnosing, *bootlicking. ANT. *dominant, dominating, ruling, controlling, rebellious, disobedient.*

subside v. sink, fall, lessen, abate, wane, ebb, decline, level off, settle, decrease, recede, die down, ease, diminish, let up, *peter out, fade. ANT. *rise, increase, intensify.*

subsidiary a. secondary, supplementary, auxiliary, subordinate, supportive, in a supporting role, ancillary, accessory, lesser, inferior, minor. ANT. *main, major, primary, chief.*

subsidize v. aid, support, back, finance, fund, underwrite, sponsor, *pick up the tab, *foot the bill, bankroll.

subsidy n. aid, support, grant, subvention, appropriation, money.

subsist v. exist, live, survive, get by, maintain, be sustained, *eke out a living, *make ends meet, persist, endure. ANT. *die, perish, starve to death.*

subsistence n. livelihood, living, support, means of support, means of survival, sustenance, provisions, maintenance, upkeep, sustainment, daily bread, survival, existence, endurance.

substance n. **1.** MATTER material, element, stuff, constituent, ingredient, something. **2.** REALITY solidity, substantiality, concreteness. **3.** ESSENCE meaning, gist, spirit, core, heart, meat, nucleus, thrust, sense, point, *bottom line, *sum total. **4.** WEALTH resources, possessions, affluence, assets, worth, riches, property.

substance abuse n. drug abuse, addiction, alcoholism, drug dependance, *monkey on one's back, *huffing. SEE DRUG

substandard a. inferior, poor, below average, below par, subpar, second-rate, below normal, lousy, shoddy. ANT. *superior, first-rate, above par.*

substantial a. **1.** CONSIDERABLE large, ample, generous, sizable, great, big, healthy, significant, meaningful, goodly, hefty. **2.** STRONG solid, firm, sound. **3.** REAL concrete, actual, physical, material, bodily. **4.** IMPORTANT valuable, fundamental, essential. **5.** WEALTHY rich, affluent, well-to-do, well-off, prosperous. ANT. *1. tiny, paltry, insignificant. 2. weak, flimsy, fragile. 3. imaginary, abstract. 4. unimportant, inessential. 5. poor, impoverished, destitute.*

SUBSTANTIATE v. [sub STAN she ate] to prove to be true by showing evidence. *The detective tried to substantiate her story with circumstantial evidence.* SYN. prove, confirm, authenticate, verify, corroborate, support, validate, demonstrate, attest to, certify. ANT. *disprove, refute, discredit.*

substantive a. actual, solid, real, substantial. ANT. *flimsy, abstract.*

substitute n. alternate, *fill-in, sub, backup, replacement, stand-in, understudy, *temp, double, *pinch hitter, *second-stringer, *bench warmer, surrogate, proxy.

substitute v. alternate, fill in for, sub, replace, switch, stand in, *temp, double, *pinch-hit, *come off the bench, spell, supplant, surrogate.

substitute a. alternate, alternative, backup, temporary, reserve, acting, stopgap. ANT. *primary.*

SUBTERFUGE n. [SUB tur fyooj] a trick or deception, a device used to conceal one's true purpose, actions, etc. *The spy used a clever subterfuge to get by the guard.* SYN. trick, deception, device, ruse, stratagem, artifice, scheme, evasion, maneuver, dodge, machination, Trojan horse, pretense.

subterranean a. underground, below ground, sunken, subsurface, buried, hidden, secret, concealed, under cover. ANT. *above-board, displayed, mainstream.*

subtle a. **1.** NOT OBVIOUS slight, delicate, faint, fine, suggestive, understated, quiet, inconspicuous, implied, inferred, indirect, insinuated, elusive. **2.** THIN tenuous, rare, light,

slight, airy, ethereal, rarefied. **3.** KEEN sharp, acute, astute, discerning, shrewd. **4.** CLEVER sly, skillful, deft, smart, adroit, crafty, sly, cunning. ANT. *1. obvious, conspicuous, heavy, blatant, direct. 2. heavy, dense. 3. dull. 4. stupid, undiscerning.*

subtract v. deduct, take away, detract, lessen, remove, withdraw.

suburb n. residential district, bedroom community, suburbia, *burbs, suburban district, hamlet, outskirt, neighborhood, development, division, subdivision. "The home of the middle class."—Louis Harris. "Where the developer bulldozes out the trees, then names the streets after them."—William Vaughan.

suburbia n. suburbs, *burbs, residential district, bedroom community, environs, city outskirts.

SUBVERSIVE a. [sub VURS iv] contributing to the overthrow or destruction of a government, institution, etc. *He was expelled for his subversive actions.* SYN. destructive, undermining, insurrectionary, seditious, insurgent, treasonous, traitorous, revolutionary. ANT. *helpful, constructive, valuable.*

subvert v. undermine, destroy, weaken, disrupt, ruin, corrupt, poison, upset, damage, overthrow, topple, destroy. ANT. *support, fortify, build.*

subway n. underground railway, *tube, rapid transit system, tunnel, metro.

succeed v. **1.** ACCOMPLISH achieve, make good, win, triumph, *pull off, arrive, fulfill, *make it, prevail, work, score, *nail it, *pan out, *fly, *come through with flying colors, reach one's goals, realize, *make it big, *hit the jackpot, ace, *go over with a bang, *lay them in aisles, *knock 'em dead, *get off the ground, *set the world on fire. **2.** COME AFTER follow, ensue, replace, supplant, take the place of, inherit. ANT. *1. fail, lose, *blow it, flop, *bomb, *lay an egg. 2. precede, antedate.*

succeeding a. successive, following, subsequent, ensuing, next, upcoming. ANT. *preceding, prior, former.*

success n. fulfillment, accomplishment, achievement, attainment, realization, reaching one's goals, arrival, triumph, win, victory, *big time, hit, *smash, *succès d'estime, fame and fortune, winner, sensation, good fortune, prosperity, wealth, riches, *Easy Street, blockbuster. "The reward of toil."—Sophocles. "Not the result of spontaneous combustion. You must set yourself on fire."—Reginald Leach. "The child of audacity."—Benjamin Disraeli. "The bitch-goddess."—William James. ANT. *failure, defeat, *bombing, *washout, nonfulfillment.*

successful *a.* winning, accomplished, triumphant, victorious, favorable, prosperous, well-off, well-to-do, achieving, thriving, booming, fortunate, lucky, *on top, *making it big, *on top of one's game, profitable, lucrative, meeting one's goals, *climbing the corporate ladder. ANT. *failing, losing, unfortunate, unsuccessful.*

succession *n.* 1. SEQUENCE series, procession, progression, train, cycle, course, round. 2. ACCESSION assumption, rise to power, taking over, crowning.

successive *a.* succeeding, consecutive, following, sequential, ensuing, continuous, one after the other. ANT. *inconsecutive, random.*

successor *n.* follower, heir, next in line, replacement, descendant.

SUCCINCT *a.* [suk SINKT] brief and to the point, concise. *The politicians were asked to keep their speeches succinct.* SYN. brief, to the point, concise, pithy, condensed, short, compact, terse, *in a nutshell, *boiled down to its essence, *short and sweet. ANT. *wordy, long-winded, prolix, verbose.*

succor *n.* help, aid, relief, assistance, helping hand.

succor *v.* help, aid, assist, relieve, give relief, give a helping hand.

succulent *a.* juicy, moist, fleshy, dripping, pulpy, mushy. ANT. *dry, dehydrated.*

succumb *v.* 1. DIE perish, expire, pass away, *croak, *bite the dust, *kick the bucket, *cash in one's chips. SEE DIE 2. YIELD submit, give in, give way, surrender, capitulate, *knuckle under, acquiesce, defer to. ANT. 2. *hold out, resist.*

suck *v.* draw, sip, inhale, slurp.

suck *v. Sl.* stink, rot, *blow, *bite, *bite the big one, *stink on ice, *suck eggs.

sucker *n.* 1. DUPE *patsy, *chump, *sitting duck, *pushover, victim, fool, fair game, easy mark. 2. LOLLIPOP.

sudden *a.* abrupt, unexpected, unforeseen, quick, *out of the blue, fast, *in a heartbeat, *in a wink, instantaneous, meteoric, *precipitate, *like a flash. ANT. *gradual, eventual, slow.*

sudden infant death syndrome *n.* SIDS, crib death.

suddenly *adv.* abruptly, unexpectedly, without warning, quickly, *out of the blue, *in a

heartbeat, *in a wink, instantly, meteorically, all of a sudden, all at once, *like a flash. ANT. *gradually, eventually, slowly.*

suds *n.* foam, froth, bubbles, lather, soap.

sue *v.* bring court action, file a lawsuit, prosecute, bring to trial, bring civil action against, litigate against, petition the court.

suffer *v.* 1. EXPERIENCE PAIN hurt, ache, agonize, be racked with pain, writhe in pain, endure, grieve. 2. EXPERIENCE undergo, endure, bear, encounter, live with, *stick it out, *tough it out, tolerate, withstand. 3. ALLOW tolerate, permit, admit, grant.

suffering *n.* pain, misery, agony, torture, torment, ache, distress, grief, depression, heartache, despair, anguish, ordeal, hell, discomfort, burden, *cross to bear. "A cleansing fire that clears away triviality and restlessness."—Louis E. Bisch. "A test of faith."—J. Messner. ANT. *comfort, pleasure, peace.*

suffice *v.* serve, do, satisfy, be enough, be adequate, be sufficient, answer, *fill the bill, *do the trick.

sufficient *a.* adequate, enough, plenty, satisfactory, ample, commensurate, passable, acceptable, tolerable, okay, all right. ANT. *insufficient, inadequate, unsatisfactory, short.*

suffocate *v.* smother, choke, stifle, cut off one's air, strangle, throttle, asphyxiate, burke, garrote, kill, silence.

suffrage *n.* right to vote, the vote, voice, franchise. SEE ELECTION

suffuse *v.* overspread, spread, bathe, infiltrate, permeate, pervade, fill, saturate, imbrue.

sugar *n.* sweetener, sucrose, saccharose, dextrose, fructose, cane sugar, brown sugar, maple sugar, saccharine.

sugarcoat *v.* sweeten, gloss over, make agreeable, make palatable, honey, candy. ANT. *poison.*

sugary *a.* 1. SWEET-TASTING saccharine, candied, honeyed, confectionary. 2. OVERLY NICE OR SENTIMENTAL mawkish, sickeningly sweet, flattering, oversweet, cloying. ANT. 1. *sour, bitter, acid.* 2. *curt, frank, abrupt.*

suggest *v.* 1. PUT FORTH propose, offer, submit, recommend, proffer, advance, *throw out, move, advise. 2. BRING TO MIND imply, insinuate, hint, intimate, allude, evoke, infer.

suggestion *n.* 1. PROPOSAL offering, submission, recommendation, idea, thought, proffer, proposition, presentation, tip, counsel. 2. TRACE hint, intimation, insinuation, suspicion, allusion, inference, telltale, reminder, shade, tinge, touch.

suggestible *a.* impressionable, pliable, easily manipulated, susceptible, easily brainwashed, naive, gullible, malleable, unguarded, *like putty in one's hands. ANT. *defiant, resistant.*

suggestive *a.* **1.** INDECENT improper, risqué, off-color, racy, bawdy, dirty, sexy, erotic, obscene, ribald, titillating, *raunchy. **2.** REMINISCENT signifying, evocative, expressive. ANT. *1. respectable, pure, innocent. 2. meaningless.*

suicidal *a.* **1.** SELF-DESTRUCTIVE *harboring a death wish, reckless, rash, clinically depressed, despondent. **2.** DEADLY lethal, unwise, reckless. ANT. *1. cautious, joyful. 2. careful, safe.*

suicide *n.* self-destruction, self-murder, self-immolation. "The severest form of self-criticism."—Leonard Levinson.

WORD FIND

agreement by two or more: suicide pact

Japanese dive-bombing in World War II: kamikaze

Japanese ritual of disembowelment: hara-kiri, seppuku

one who commits: felo-de-se

suit *n.* **1.** SET group, series, ensemble. **2.** LAWSUIT case, litigation, trial, court action. **3.** SET OF CLOTHES WORN TOGETHER outfit, ensemble, costume, uniform, *threads, *getup, *Sunday go-to-meeting clothes, *Sunday best, *bib and tucker, formal evening wear, dress suit, leisure suit, sack suit, seersucker suit, sport suit, business suit, three-piece suit, tuxedo, zoot suit, jumpsuit. SEE COAT, DRESS, JACKET, PANTS, SHIRT, SKIRT

suit *v.* **1.** BEFIT satisfy, meet one's requirements, meet one's needs, *fill the bill, be appropriate, accommodate, please, conform, fit. **2.** ADAPT fit, adjust, tailor, change, proportion, modify.

suitable *a.* fitting, fit, befitting, appropriate, proper, right, correct, acceptable, apt, meet, becoming, seemly. ANT. *unsuitable, improper, unacceptable.*

suitcase *n.* valise, case, grip, travel case, carry-all, overnight bag.

suite *n.* **1.** SET OF ROOMS penthouse, apartment, flat. **2.** ATTENDANTS servants, retinue, entourage, train, company, cortege, court, escort, following, staff.

suitor *n.* courter, admirer, boyfriend, wooer, *beau, *flame, *steady, swain.

sulk *v.* mope, pout, wallow in self-pity, *have a pity party, brood, fret, be gloomy, be sullen, put on a long face. ANT. *rejoice, jump for joy.*

sulky *a.* sullen, gloomy, down in the mouth, moping, pouting, self-pitying, glum, morose, moody, depressed, withdrawn, resentful, dissatisfied. ANT. *happy, cheerful, elated.*

sullen *a.* withdrawn, morose, resentful, sulky, glum, moody, depressed, glowering, petulant, peevish, brooding. ANT. *happy, cheerful, jovial.*

sully *v.* soil, stain, dirty, blemish, smudge, blacken, taint, disgrace, dishonor, defile, corrupt, *drag through the mud. ANT. *cleanse, shine, honor.*

sultry *a.* **1.** HOT steamy, muggy, humid, sweltering, torrid, baking, tropical, sizzling, *roasting, suffocating, oppressive, fiery. **2.** PASSIONATE hot, inflamed, lustful, amorous, *horny, ardent, torrid, erotic, seductive. ANT. *1. cold, freezing, chilling. 2. turned-off, frigid, cold.*

sum *n.* **1.** AMOUNT money, cash, quantity. **2.** TOTAL aggregate, whole, entirety, lot, *whole shebang, *works, mass. **3.** GIST essence, point, content, crux.

summarize *v.* run down briefly, encapsulate, condense, outline, give main points, *recap, recapitulate, synopsize, review, abridge.

summary *n.* rundown, brief, gist, synopsis, outline, precis, *recap, recapitulation, condensation, compendium, abstract, short version, review, sketch, core.

summary *a.* prompt, expeditious, quick, swift, hasty, peremptory, brief, direct. ANT. *detailed, in-depth.*

summer *n.* summer solstice, *dog days, school vacation, season, *lazy days. "Days dripping away like honey off a spoon."—Wallace Stegner.

summit *n.* top, peak, apex, high point, zenith, crown, height, pinnacle, crest, acme, vertex, head, cap, limit, climax. ANT. *bottom, depth, low.*

summon *v.* **1.** CALL FOR call in, beckon, request one's presence, invite, send for, subpoena, order to appear, page, muster, assemble, convene, rally. **2.** GATHER collect, rouse, call up, invoke, muster up.

summons *n.* subpoena, writ, warrant, call, order, court order, command, evocation, signal, alarm.

sump *n.* pool, cesspool, pit, well, cistern.

sumptuous *a.* lavish, extravagant, rich, costly, expensive, magnificent, luxurious, fancy, posh, deluxe, splendid, *ritzy, opulent. ANT. *cheap, poor, *ratty, plain.*

sum up v. close, finish, summarize, review, *recap, recapitulate.

sun n. *flaming gasball, star, fireball, flaming orb, sphere, luminary, heavenly body, Sol, Helios, Hyperion, Horus, Ra. "The fire that severs day from night."—Shakespeare. "The glorious lamp of heaven."—Dryden.
WORD FIND
dark spots: sunspots
gas: hydrogen, helium
massless particles produced by: neutrinos
mock optical illusion: parhelion, sundog, mock sun
obscuring of by moon: solar eclipse
orbit: ecliptic
outer atmosphere of: chromosphere, corona
plant's movement following: heliotaxis
plant that bends to follow sun: heliotrope
referring to: helio, solar
sunlight therapy: heliotherapy
sunspot cycle of eleven years: solar cycle
sunspot's dark, inner region: umbra
surface: photosphere
tongue of flame and gas, huge: solar flare, solar prominence
variable intensity, sun with: variable star
worship: heliolatry
SEE STAR

sunburned A. burned, red, *red as a cooked lobster, scarlet, crimson, blistering, peeling. ANT. *pale, lily white.*

Sunday n. sabbath, the Lord's day. "The golden clasp that binds together the volume of the week."—H.W. Longfellow.

sunder v. separate, split, part, sever, break apart, cleave, divide, halve, quarter.

sundry A. miscellaneous, assorted, various, divers, diverse, diversified, many, myriad. ANT. *single, uniform.*

sunken A. hollow, depressed, caved-in, fallen-in, concave, indented, submerged, submersed, drowned, inundated. ANT. *raised, swollen, bulging, elevated.*

sunny A. 1. CLEAR bright, radiant, brilliant, cloudless, dazzling, blazing, sunshiny, golden, *honeyed light, clement. 2. HAPPY cheerful, cheery, beaming, smiling, optimistic, blithe, lighthearted, joyous, mirthful, buoyant. ANT. 1. *cloudy, gloomy, dark, overcast. 2. grim, gloomy, miserable, unhappy.*

sunrise n. dawn, daybreak, sunup, daylight, break of day, *the holy light of dawn, crack of dawn, cockcrow, twilight.

WORD FIND
goddess of dawn: Aurora

sunscreen n. sunblock, sun cream, lotion, preparation, skin protection.

sunset n. sundown, dusk, nightfall, evening, gloaming, twilight, eventide. "Like the spreading of a peacock's tail."—John Ashberry.

sunshine n. sunlight, sunbeams, rays, radiance, brilliance, daylight. "Gold embroidery on the grass."—Paul Horgan. "A shower of gold."—Silvia Tennenbaum.

super a. excellent, superb, outstanding, extraordinary, great, terrific, sensational, fine, out of this world, *superhuman, superior. ANT. *terrible, awful, lousy, inferior.*

superabundance n. overabundance, surplus, excess, glut, plethora, flood, overflow, more than enough, surfeit, oversupply. ANT. *shortage, dearth, lack.*

superannuated a. old, worn out, *over the hill, *put out to pasture, past one's prime, antiquated, obsolete, old-fashioned, outdated. ANT. *young, fresh, new, modern, contemporary.*

superb a. excellent, great, superior, superlative, first-class, first-rate, select, choice, magnificent, grand, noble, splendid, super. ANT. *poor, inferior, awful.*

supercharger n. blower, compressor, power booster.

SUPERCILIOUS a. [soo pur SIL ee us] haughtily disdainful, proud, regarding with raised eyebrows. *He found the restaurant critic to be shallow and supercilious.* SYN. haughty, proud, contemptuous, scornful, disdainful, lofty, condescending, imperious, arrogant, high and mighty, superior, snobbish. ANT. *down to earth, humble, modest.*

superficial a. 1. SURFACE exterior, outer, external, outside, outward, peripheral, skin-deep, cosmetic. 2. SHALLOW obvious, apparent, lacking depth, minimal, not profound. 3. QUICK cursory, perfunctory, hasty, slapdash, hurried, slight. 4. FRIVOLOUS shallow, featherbrained, unprofound, silly. ANT. 1. *internal, inner, deep. 2. deep, profound. 3. thorough, careful, complete. 4. serious, deep, profound.*

SUPERFLUOUS a. [suh PUR floo us] unnecessary, more than what is needed. *They lightened their load by getting rid of all superfluous provisions.* SYN. unnecessary, extra, unneeded, excess, surplus, redundant, inessential, nonessential, spare, expendable, more than enough. ANT. *necessary, needed, indispensable, vital.*

superhighway n. freeway, autobahn. SEE HIGHWAY

superhuman a. supernatural, divine, omnipotent, godlike, preternatural, omniscient, otherworldly, extraterrestrial. ANT. *subhuman.*

superintend v. direct, manage, administer. SEE SUPERVISE

superintendent n. **1.** DIRECTOR supervisor, overseer, manager, chief, administrator, boss, head, foreman. **2.** CARETAKER custodian, janitor, super, maintenance man.

superior n. boss, head, senior, chief, leader, *head honcho, *biggest toad in the puddle, master, higher-up, supervisor, CEO, commander in chief, ranking officer, *big cheese. ANT. *inferior, junior, *low man on the totem pole, subordinate.*

superior a. **1.** HIGHER greater, above, better, supreme, superlative, first-class, first-rate, peerless, excellent, outstanding, *a cut above, *tops, unrivaled, predominant, preeminent, incomparable, *A-1, exceptional. **2.** HAUGHTY arrogant, snobbish, high and mighty, proud, supercilious, stuck-up, condescending, patronizing, pretentious. ANT. *1. inferior, lower, second-rate, poor. 2. down to earth, humble, modest.*

superlative a. superior, supreme, highest, greatest, best, first-class, first-rate, peerless, excellent, outstanding, *a cut above, *tops, unrivaled, nonpareil, paramount, preeminent. ANT. *poor, inferior, worst, lowest.*

superman n. superwoman, god, champion, hero, immortal, idol, Renaissance man, Renaissance woman, Olympian, Hercules, ironman, giant, *mover and a shaker.

supernal a. celestial, heavenly, divine, from the sky, ethereal, lofty. ANT. *prosaic, down-to-earth, earthy.*

supernatural a. superhuman, otherworldly, unearthly, not of this world, out of this world, supranatural, metaphysical, transcendental, spiritual, paranormal, occult, psychic, heavenly, divine, breaking the laws of nature, miraculous, ghostly, mysterious, unfathomable, incomprehensible. ANT. *mundane, earthly, natural, normal.*

SUPERSEDE v. [soo pur SEED] take the place of, replace. *The automobile superseded the horse and buggy as a primary means of transportation.* SYN. take the place of, replace,

succeed, displace, supplant, dethrone, oust, outmode.

supersensitive a. ultrasensitive, thin-skinned. SEE SENSITIVE

superstar n. *megastar, idol, celebrity. SEE STAR

superstition n. irrational fear, fallacy, old wives' tale, delusion, false belief. "Religion which has grown incongruous with intelligence."—John Tyndall. "The religion of feeble minds."—Edmund Burke.

superstitious a. fearful, naive, irrational, deluded, apprehensive, obsessed.

supervise v. oversee, manage, direct, superintend, look after, head, administer, run things, *call the shots, *call the plays, quarterback, command, boss, control, guide, regulate.

supervision n. management, control, direction, superintendence, running, administration, guidance, leadership, regulation.

supervisor n. boss, overseer, manager, director, superintendent, head, administrator, quarterback, commander, guide, regulator, *whip, *CEO, chief, foreman.

supine a. **1.** LYING DOWN flat on one's back, prone, recumbent, horizontal, laid out. **2.** SLUGGISH listless, inactive, lifeless, inert, motionless, *brain-dead, vegetative. ANT. *1. standing, upright. 2. lively, active.*

supper n. dinner, repast. SEE MEAL

supplant v. replace, take the place of, supersede, displace, succeed, oust, dethrone, unseat, bump.

supple a. **1.** FLEXIBLE bendable, pliable, pliant, resilient, malleable, elastic, plastic, springy, rubbery. **2.** LIMBER lithe, loose, lissom, agile, nimble, willowy. **3.** COMPLIANT yielding, nonresisting, passive, complaisant, acquiescent, easy. **4.** ADAPTABLE adjustable, flexible, resilient, elastic. ANT. *1. inflexible, hard, rigid, stiff. 2. tight, stiff, out of shape. 3. resistant, rebellious, unyielding. 4. rigid, unchangeable, inflexible.*

supplement n. addition, extension, attachment, amendment, addendum, appendix, augmentation, complement, rider, insert, postscript.

supplement v. add to, augment, complement, enlarge, increase, reinforce.

supplementary a. additional, augmenting, attached, appended, supportive, auxiliary, secondary, ancillary. ANT. *main, primary.*

supplicant n. petitioner, solicitor, applicant, pleader, beggar.

supplicate v. request, pray for, petition, plead,

appeal, beg, entreat, ask for, implore, beseech, adjure.

supplication *n.* request, prayer, petition, pleading, appeal, entreaty, solicitation, application, plea, cry, begging.

supplies *n.* provisions, stores, issues, rations, stock, necessities, essentials, equipment, victuals, food.

supply *n.* reserve, stock, stockpile, store, inventory, amount, quantity, provision, fund, hoard, cache, load, mass.

supply *v.* provide, furnish, stock, fund, provision, equip, outfit, cater, accommodate, contribute, give.

support *n.* **1.** BRACE foundation, buttress, prop, underpinning, substructure, bed, joist, beam, girder, stanchion, stay. **2.** BACKING help, aid, assistance, hand, lift, encouragement, advocacy, approval, promotion, comfort. **3.** SUBSISTENCE living, sustenance, livelihood, upkeep, provisions, necessities, food, money, child support, alimony.

support *v.* **1.** HOLD UP brace, buttress, prop, shoulder, carry, bear, bolster, sustain, shore up. **2.** BACK help, aid, assist, give a hand, give a lift, sustain, comfort, encourage, bolster, foster, advocate, approve, promote, endorse, subscribe. **3.** PROVIDE FOR maintain, pay one's way, finance, bankroll, subsidize, underwrite, *pick up the tab. **4.** CORROBORATE verify, substantiate, confirm, attest, validate, authenticate.

supporter *n.* backer, advocate, champion, defender, stalwart, helper, proponent, abettor, adherent, fan, benefactor, patron.

supportive *a.* bolstering, encouraging, helping, helpful, sympathetic, strengthening. ANT. *criticizing, denigrating.*

support system *n.* family, friends, allies, social network, contacts, support group, *safety net, companions, morale boosters.

suppose *v.* assume, presume, figure, expect, think, guess, imagine, reckon, suspect, theorize, believe, conclude, understand.

supposed *a.* assumed, presumed, figured, expected, thought, guessed, imagined, reckoned, suspected, theorized, believed, understood. ANT. *known, proven.*

supposition *n.* assumption, hypothesis, presumption, thought, guess, suspicion, theory, belief, conjecture, postulate.

suppress *v.* **1.** PUT DOWN stop, crush, quell, squelch, squash, crack down on, subdue, silence, extinguish, kill, put an end to. **2.** CENSOR keep quiet, withhold, stifle, keep in the

dark, silence, shut up, hide, conceal, check, restrain, curb, *put a lid on, muzzle. ANT. *1. throw fuel on the fire, unleash, free up. 2. broadcast, amplify, publish.*

suppression *n.* crushing, quelling, squelching, squashing, silencing, extinguishing, censorship, smothering, stifling, muzzling, restraint.

suppurate *v.* fester, discharge, maturate, ooze.

supremacy *n.* dominance, preeminence, primacy, superiority, transcendence, predominance, rule, authority, mastery, sovereignty.

supreme *a.* greatest, superior, preeminent, dominant, leading, transcendent, highest, ultimate, paramount, crowning, predominant, first, superlative, finest, excellent, utmost, top, ranking, peerless, ruling, chief, sovereign, *eclipsing all others, *overshadowing all others, *standing head and shoulders above all others. ANT. *worst, lowest, poorest.*

surcharge *n.* fee, overcharge, sum, surtax, additional charge, amount over and above.

sure *a.* **1.** CERTAIN definite, assured, doubtless, unquestionable, fixed, set, incontrovertible, positive, conclusive, proven, demonstrated, unmistakable, certified, *beyond a shadow of a doubt. **2.** RELIABLE dependable, trustworthy, tried and true, trusty, faithful, steadfast. **3.** CONVINCED confident, certain, satisfied, positive. **4.** INEVITABLE assured, bound, unavoidable, guaranteed, inescapable, *iced. ANT. *1. uncertain, doubtful, questionable, unproven. 2. unreliable, undependable. 3. unconvinced, uncertain. 4. uncertain.*

surely *adv.* certainly, doubtless, undoubtedly, absolutely, positively, unquestionably, *beyond a shadow of a doubt, definitely, indubitably.

sure thing *n.* safe bet, certainty, *shoo-in, *cinch.

surety *n.* security, guarantee, bond, assurance, pledge.

surf *n.* waves, breakers, rollers, combers, spindrift, seaspray, swells, foam, swash, riptide.
WORD FIND
common wave with convex back: plunger
gray-crested waves: graybeards
hollow between waves: trough
series of waves: train
sound: rote, swash, crash, thunder, lap
SEE BEACH, OCEAN

surf *v.* ride the waves, *hang five, *hang ten, cruise, flip channels, channel surf, explore.

WORD FIND

fall off: wipe out
ride under a breaking wave: *shoot the tube, *shoot the curl
shorts: baggies, jams
show off: *hotdog
surf without a board: body surf

surface n. exterior, outside, top, skin, shell, facade, face, crust, veneer, finish.

surface v. **1.** SMOOTH level, plane, even, pave, finish. **2.** ARISE emerge, break the surface, ascend. **3.** BECOME KNOWN materialize, come up, come to light.

SURFEIT n. [SUR fit] an excessive amount, fullness, overindulgence. *The baker made a surfeit of cookies for the party.* SYN. **1.** EXCESS surplus, overabundance, superabundance, too much, glut, overflow, flood, inundation, overkill, exorbitance, plethora. **2.** SATIETY fullness, satiation, overindulgence, sickness, nausea, disgust, discomfort. ANT. *1. dearth, shortage, lack. 2. hunger, craving, emptiness.*

surfeit v. overindulge, *stuff oneself, overfill, gorge, satiate, glut, *pig out, overdo, cloy, overeat.

surge n. **1.** SWELL wave, billow, flood, torrent, rush, heave, sweep, mass, storm surge, gush, rising tide. **2.** INCREASE escalation, skyrocketing, growth, expansion, explosion, jump, rise. ANT. *2. decline, drop, plunge.*

surge v. **1.** SWELL billow, flood, rush, heave, sweep, roll, amass, rise, gush, wash. **2.** INCREASE escalate, skyrocket, grow, expand, explode, jump, rise.

surgeon n. medical professional, doctor, physician, specialist, *sawbones. "An eagle's eye, a lion's heart, a lady's hand."—John Ray. SEE OPERATION, DOCTOR

surgery n. medical procedure, *the knife, excision, biopsy, bypass, mastectomy, transplant, angioplasty, neoplasty. SEE OPERATION, DISEASE, MEDICINE

surgical a. accurate, precise, exacting, pinpoint, ticklish, delicate. ANT. *rough, approximate, inexact.* SEE OPERATION

surly a. bad-tempered, sour, moody, rude, nasty, cross, sullen, brusque, dour, ugly, hostile, unfriendly, harsh, short, grouchy, grumpy, gruff. ANT. *friendly, cheery, cheerful, warm, good-humored.*

surmise n. guess, conjecture, deduction, assessment, hypothesis, *shot in the dark, assumption, hunch, supposition, idea, speculation, presumption.

surmise v. guess, conjecture, imagine, infer, *put two and two together, *hazard a guess, conclude, deduce, assess, hypothesize, *take a shot in the dark, assume, suppose, speculate, presume, reckon, opine.

surmount v. go over, climb over, mount, clear, prevail over, get the best of, overcome, conquer, vanquish, subdue, triumph over, master, top.

surname n. family name, last name, cognomen. For lists of ethnic surnames and given names SEE NAME

surpass v. excel, beat, exceed, outdo, better, outdistance, eclipse, *leave the competition swirling in one's wake, *leave in the dust, *run circles around, overshadow, trump, put to shame, outperform, outrun, top, transcend, *blow one's doors off.

surplus n. excess, surfeit, glut, overabundance, overstock, overkill, extra, plethora, spate, oversupply, remainder, residue. ANT. *shortage, shortfall, deficiency.*

surplus a. extra, excess, spare, leftover, unused, superfluous, remaining, residual. ANT. *short, deficient.*

surprise n. **1.** SHOCK start, bombshell, thunderbolt, bolt from the blue, eye-opener, stunner, unforeseen turn of events. **2.** AMAZEMENT astonishment, astoundment, wonder, shock, incredulity.

surprise v. **1.** SHOCK give a start, startle, *drop a bombshell on, stun, open one's eyes, astonish, astound, amaze, *take one's breath away, *blow away, *knock for a loop, flabbergast, daze, take aback, floor. **2.** CATCH OFF GUARD catch napping, take unawares, *catch flatfooted, ambush, *catch redhanded.

surprising a. unexpected, unforeseen, shocking, sudden, startling, stunning, eye-opening, astonishing, astounding, amazing, breathtaking, *out of the blue. ANT. *expected, foreseen.*

SURREAL a. [sur RE ul] having the strange or bizarre quality of dreams or the unconscious mind. *Salvador Dali's paintings are known for their surreal quality.* SYN. strange, bizarre, fantastic, grotesque, weird, nightmarish, Kafkaesque, *far out, *reminiscent of the Twilight Zone, odd, queer, peculiar. ANT. *ordinary, everyday, normal.*

surrealistic a. strange, bizarre, fantastic, grotesque, weird, nightmarish, dreamlike, Kafkaesque, *far out, *reminiscent of the Twilight Zone, odd, queer, peculiar. ANT. *ordinary, everyday, normal.*

surrender *n.* yielding, submission, giving up, giving in, *crying Uncle, capitulation, *throwing in the towel, *white flag, relenting, prostration, acquiescence, resignation, relinquishment.

surrender *v.* yield, submit, give up, give in, *cry Uncle, capitulate, *throw in the towel, *raise the white flag, relent, *cave in, prostrate oneself, acquiesce, resign, relinquish, cede. ANT. *defy*, *hang tough*, *dig in*, *fight*.

SURREPTITIOUS *a.* [sur up TISH us] sneaky, secret. *He took a surreptitious glance at her wedding band.* SYN. sneaky, secret, stealthy, clandestine, furtive, covert, hidden, sly, undercover, *on the QT, underhanded, confidential. ANT. *open, public, overt, conspicuous.*

SURROGATE *n.* [SUR uh GIT] a substitute or stand-in. *She served as a surrogate until the boss recuperated.* SYN. substitute, stand-in, representative, *sub, agent, replacement, proxy, deputy, understudy.

surround *v.* envelop, encircle, enclose, encompass, circumscribe, ring, bound, hem in, fence in, confine, blockade.

surroundings *n.* environment, environs, setting, habitat, milieu, background, neighborhood, ambience.

surveillance *n.* observation, watch, spying, *stakeout, vigil, scrutiny, shadowing, *bugging, wiretapping, reconnaissance.

survey *n.* inspection, study, examination, appraisal, exploration, review, overview, scrutiny, inquiry, probe.

survey *v.* **1.** EXAMINE study, inspect, appraise, explore, review, scrutinize, inquire, probe, canvass, assess, measure. **2.** LOOK AT view, regard, scan, study, eyeball, *give a once-over, watch, observe.

survival *n.* living, subsistence, endurance, durability, continuity, lasting, toughing it out.

survival of the fittest *n.* law of the jungle, natural selection, Darwin's law, natural law, social Darwinism.

survive *v.* live, endure, continue, last, tough it out, remain, persist, hold one's ground, carry on, withstand, *weather the storm, *ride out the storm, *stay afloat, outlive, outlast.

susceptible *a.* vulnerable, exposed, sensitive, ultrasensitive, thin-skinned, prone, subject, liable, open. ANT. *invulnerable, hardened, resistant.*

suspect *n.* the accused, defendant, *shady character, supposed perpetrator.

suspect *v.* **1.** DISTRUST mistrust, *trust as far as one can spit, disbelieve, question, doubt, *smell a rat, *harbor suspicions. **2.** GUESS imagine, conjecture, surmise, suppose, think, believe, assume, presume, theorize, hypothesize, infer, gather. ANT. *1. trust, believe.*

suspect *a.* suspicious, *fishy, suspected, unbelievable, questionable, doubted, mistrusted, *shady, dubious. ANT. *believable, reliable, trustworthy.*

suspend *v.* **1.** DEBAR exclude, dismiss, throw out, expel, evict, ban, blackball, shut out. **2.** STOP TEMPORARILY postpone, delay, defer, *put on the back burner, hold off, *put on hold, put off, discontinue. **3.** HANG dangle, sling, swing, pend.

suspenders *n.* garters, braces, galluses.

suspense *n.* tension, anxiety, uncertainty, anticipation, expectation, build-up, *white-knuckle anticipation, *cliffhanger.

suspension *n.* **1.** BARRING exclusion, dismissal, expulsion, eviction, ban, banishment, blackballing. **2.** TEMPORARY STOP postponement, delay, moratorium, stay, deferral, hold, discontinuance. **3.** HANGING dangling, slinging.

suspicion *n.* **1.** MISTRUST distrust, doubt, dubiousness, disbelief, *bad vibes, leeriness, wariness, *funny feeling, *gut feeling, hunch, suspicion, qualm, misgiving. **2.** TRACE touch, hint, suggestion, shadow, tinge, shade, inkling. ANT. *1. trust, belief, confidence.*

suspicious *a.* **1.** SUSPECT questionable, *fishy, *funny, dubious, peculiar, *not kosher, doubtful, *doesn't have the ring of truth, shady. **2.** DISTRUSTING mistrusting, doubting, disbelieving, questioning, wary, leery, incredulous, skeptical, cynical. ANT. *1. aboveboard, *kosher. 2. trusting, believing, confident.*

sustain *v.* **1.** KEEP UP maintain, continue, keep alive, prolong, protract, preserve, keep going. **2.** SUPPORT nourish, nurture, feed, provide for, aid, nurse. **3.** CARRY THE WEIGHT OF support, hold, prop, uphold, shoulder, bear. **4.** ENDURE withstand, tolerate, suffer, brook, stand, live with, abide, undergo.

sustenance *n.* livelihood, support, living, subsistence, upkeep, nourishment, food, daily bread, victuals, rations, provisions, bread and butter, nutriment, groceries, *grub.

suture *n.* sewing, stitching, joining. SEE OPERATION

SVELTE *a.* [SVELT] slender and lithe. *The*

svelte dancers moved as gracefully as cats. SYN. slender, thin, lithe, graceful, lissome, willowy, thin, lanky, slight, trim, lean, slinky. ANT. *fat, obese, roly-poly, awkward.*

SVENGALI n. [sven GAH lee] one who persuades or brainwashes another to do his bidding, often for evil purposes, so named after the hypnotist in the novel *Trilby. He was a Svengali who mesmerized women wherever he went.* SYN. hypnotist, mesmerizer, charmer, persuader, seducer, spellbinder, charismatic person, dominating figure, brainwasher.

swab n. **1.** MOP. **2.** COTTON, CLOTH sponge, wad.

swaddle v. wrap, bind, swathe, bundle up.

swag n. **1.** FESTOON decoration, valance, garland, loop, chain, ornament. **2.** LOOT plunder, stolen money, booty, *haul.

swagger n. strut, parade, bluster, pomp, *the air of one who thinks he's the cock of the walk, peacock walk, braggadocio, bravado, boastfulness, *muscle-flexing.

swagger v. strut, parade, bluster, *act like the cock of the walk, *peacock, brag, boast, *flex one's muscles, show off, flaunt, grandstand, vaunt, *blow one's own horn, stride pompously. ANT. *cringe, skulk.*

swaggerer n. strutter, *cock of the walk, blusterer, *blowhard, peacock, braggart, showoff, *grandstander, pompous ass, swashbuckler.

swain n. lover, suitor, gallant, beau, boyfriend, flame, sweetheart, squire, country boy, rustic.

swallow v. **1.** GULP down, ingest, guzzle, eat, drink, *choke down, gobble, bolt, *wolf down, *chug-a-lug, quaff. **2.** ENGULF absorb, devour, overwhelm, envelop. **3.** PUT UP WITH tolerate, endure, suffer, bear, ignore. **4.** BELIEVE WITHOUT QUESTION *swallow hook, line and sinker, *buy, take on faith, accept, swallow whole, *fall for, be naive. ANT. *1. regurgitate, vomit, throw up. 4. disbelieve, reject, mistrust.*

swami n. lord, master, fakir, teacher, mentor, guru, mystic, yogi.

swamp n. bog, marsh, slough, quagmire, fen, bayou, morass, everglade, swale, mire, wetland, muskeg.

WORD FIND

filling in of a lake by vegetation: eutrophication

floating island of decayed vegetation: battery

gas: methane

luminescence seen at night: foxfire

moss: sphagnum

tree islands: hammocks

SEE LAKE

swamp v. flood, overwhelm, submerge, sink, engulf, inundate, drown, deluge, wash over.

SWAN SONG n. a farewell or final appearance, performance, accomplishment—especially one of distinction—so named after the legendary song sung only once by the swan at its death. *Last night's stage appearance was the crooner's much anticipated swan song.* SYN. farewell, last hurrah, goodbye, final performance, final appearance, parting song, adieu, last gasp, crowning achievement.

swap v. trade, exchange, switch, barter.

sward n. grass, turf, lawn, sod, yard, meadow, field, green.

swank n. style, ostentation, stylishness, showiness, fashion, flashiness, flamboyance.

swanky a. stylish, ostentatious, showy, fashionable, flashy, chic, glamorous, snappy, smart, dapper, classy, *snazzy. ANT. *frumpy, unfashionable, out of style.*

swarm n. hive, cloud, flight, crowd, throng, multitude, mass, horde, shoal, school, assembly.

swarm v. mass together, crowd, throng, cluster, flock, gather together, herd, congregate, concentrate.

swarthy a. dark-complexioned, dark, dusky, black, brown, olive-skinned, coal-black, ebony, chocolate, tawny, nutbrown, obsidian, *dark as the Rio Grande, *dark as the Congo. ANT. *light, white, pale.*

swash v. splash, wash, dash, strike.

swashbuckler n. swaggerer, fighting man, adventurer, fencer, soldier of fortune, pirate, blusterer, daredevil.

swashbuckling a. swaggering, loud, boastful, strutting, adventurous.

swashbuckling n. derring-do, daredevilry, blustering, fighting.

swat n. blow, hit, spank, smack, slap, whack, wallop, belt, slug.

swat v. hit, spank, smack, slap, whack, wallop, belt, slug, clout, smite.

swatch n. sample, piece, bit, scrap, specimen, example.

swath n. clearing, stripe, path, opening, cut, space, strip.

swathe v. wrap, bind, swaddle, bundle up, dress, bandage.

sway *n.* **1.** SWINGING leaning, undulation, fluctuation. **2.** INFLUENCE control, power, command, domination, rule, hand, reign, authority, mastery.

sway *v.* **1.** MOVE FROM SIDE TO SIDE swing, move to and fro, move back and forth, waver, wobble, fluctuate, undulate, oscillate, rock, teeter, vacillate. **2.** INFLUENCE persuade, talk into, divert, control, brainwash, prevail upon, move, convince, impress, win over, lead, guide, *sell on.

swaybacked *a.* sagging, broken-backed, caving in, slumping. ANT. *straightbacked, sturdy.*

swear *v.* **1.** PROMISE vow, pledge, take an oath, give one's word, warrant, avow, attest, declare. **2.** CURSE cuss, use profanity, use dirty language, use four-letter words, *spit barnyard epithets, take the Lord's name in vain, use gutter language.

swear by *v.* have confidence in, recommend, believe in.

swearing *n.* cussing, cursing, foul language, bad language, four-letter words, obscenities, expletives, profanity, dirty words, *barnyard epithet, *cow pasture vulgarism, vulgarity, *henhouse epithet, X-rated language, gutter language. "The garlic in the salad of taste."—Cyril Connolly. ANT. *polite word, euphemism.*

swear off *v.* give up, abjure, renounce, forswear, forego, quit, *turn one's back on.

sweat *n.* **1.** PERSPIRATION sudoresis, excretion, moisture, lather, body odor, *BO. **2.** HARD WORK toil, labor, drudgery, grind, backbreaking work, slavery. **3.** ANXIETY apprehension, stress, tension.

sweat *v.* **1.** PERSPIRE excrete, *glow, *work up a lather, *sweat bullets, swelter, ooze, exude. **2.** GET NERVOUS *stress out, fret, worry, suffer anxiety, suffer distress. **3.** TOIL labor, break one's back, strain, struggle, slave, drudge, work.

sweater *n.* pullover, turtleneck.

WORD FIND
coatlike: cardigan
coat sweater with school letter: letter sweater
deer or geometric pattern on front: jacquard
diamond-designed: argyle, Aran Isle sweater
goat hair: cashmere
Irish, water-repellant: fisherman's sweater
long: fanny sweater
natural-colored, with bands around neck: Icelandic
pullover with rounded neck: crew neck

pullover with wedge-shaped neck: V-neck
sleeveless pullover: shell
white, cable-knit pullover: tennis sweater

sweathouse *n.* sweatlodge, sauna, steam room.

sweatpants *n.* running pants, gym pants.

sweatshirt *n.* pullover, gym shirt.

sweatshop *n.* factory, labor mill, shop, manufacturer, plant, work room, industry, *salt mines.

sweatsuit *n.* exercise suit, running suit, *baggies.

sweep *n.* **1.** RANGE scope, reach, stretch, span, width, breadth, compass, extent. **2.** SWIPE stroke, swing, cut. **3.** COMPLETE VICTORY *skunk, *clean sweep.

sweep *v.* **1.** WHISK take a broom to it, brush, clean up, tidy, clear. **2.** CLEAR destroy, remove, strip, drive out. **3.** RUSH hurry, race, fly, charge, zoom, *zip, glide, tear. **4.** WIN IT ALL *skunk, *pull off a clean sweep.

sweeping *a.* extensive, broad, widespread, far-reaching, all-inclusive, blanket, general, across-the-board, comprehensive, thorough. ANT. *limited, partial.*

sweepstakes *n.* lottery, contest, drawing.

sweet *n.* candy, confection, dessert.

sweet *a.* **1.** SUGARY saccharine, honeyed, nectarous, candied, confectionary, tasty, luscious. **2.** PLEASANT agreeable, enjoyable, delightful. **3.** FRIENDLY kind, gentle, good, nice, charming, angelic, pleasant, agreeable, amiable, helpful. **4.** SWEET-SMELLING fragrant, fresh, perfumed, pure, aromatic. **5.** SWEET-SOUNDING dulcet, melodious, harmonious, euphonic. ANT. *1. sour, bitter, tart, acid. 2. unpleasant, awful, miserable. 3. unfriendly, sour, grouchy. 4. sour, rotten, spoiled. 5. harsh, discordant.*

sweeten *v.* **1.** ADD SUGAR sugarcoat, honey, candy, dulcify, mull. **2.** EASE soften, lighten, mollify, *take the edge off, alleviate, temper, mellow, moderate.

sweetener *n.* saccharine, sugar, *Sweet 'n Low, *Equal.

sweetheart *n.* darling, love, *sweetie, honey, *honeybunch, *honeybun, *honeybunny, dear, *sugar pie, lover, pet, girlfriend, boyfriend, flame, *steady, love of one's life, heartthrob, turtledove, *baby.

sweetmeat *n.* sweet, confection, delicacy, treat, cake, candy, preserve, nougat.

sweet-talk *v.* flatter, *butter up, cajole, softsoap, *lay it on with a trowel.

sweet-talk *n.* *bull, *blarney, flattery.

swell *n.* **1.** BULGE wave, roller, surge, surf, rise, mound, hill, hump, protuberance, prominence, protrusion, distension, expansion, growth. **2.** SMART DRESSER dandy, clothes-horse, Beau Brummel, fop.

swell *v.* **1.** BULGE rise, billow, balloon, inflate, blow up, puff up, bloat, mound, form a hump, protrude, distend, dilate, expand, grow, surge, become turgid. **2.** PUFF UP FROM PRIDE swagger, strut, stick one's chest out, parade, show off, be pleased with oneself. ANT. *1. deflate, shrink, collapse. 2. be crestfallen, cringe, shrink.*

swell *a.* fine, excellent, great, first-rate. ANT. *inferior, substandard.*

swelling *n.* lump, bulge, distension, bump, growth, enlargement, edema, puffiness, inflammation, knob, welt, abcess.

swelter *v.* sweat, perspire, drip, *slow cook under the sun, *burn up under the sun, suffer heatstroke, roast.

sweltering *a.* hot, humid, roasting, scorching, torrid, sultry, stifling, baking, broiling, muggy, close, oppressive. ANT. *cold, frigid, chilling.*

swerve *v.* turn sharply, deviate, veer, diverge, dodge, sheer off, shift, careen.

swift *a.* **1.** FAST quick, rapid, speedy, hasty, fleet, express, *quicker than greased lightning, supersonic, hypersonic, faster than the speed of sound, prompt, brisk, winged, breakneck, meteoric, *on the double. **2.** SHORT-LASTING fleeting, brief, quick, transient, ephemeral, *passing in a heartbeat, *passing in the wink of an eye. **3.** QUICK-ACTING alert, *on one's toes, ready, prompt. ANT. *1. slow, sluggish, *slower than the Second Coming. 2. long-lasting, permanent, eternal. 3. slow, *asleep, *out to lunch.*

swig *n.* mouthful, gulp, slug, *hit, drink, quaff, swill, draft.

swill *n.* garbage, table scraps, slop, hogwash, refuse, waste, remains.

swill *v.* swig, guzzle, gulp, wash down, *take a slug, *take a hit, quaff, *chug-a-lug, *knock off, drain.

swim *v.* **1.** *GO FOR A DIP breaststroke, crawl, backstroke, do the butterfly, dog-paddle, stroke, *skinnydip, tread water, float, bathe, paddle, snorkel, scuba dive, skin dive. **2.** BE SATURATED be soaked, be steeped in, float in. **3.** BE DIZZY be lightheaded, be off balance.

swimming *a.* dizzy, lightheaded, dopey, reeling, whirling, off-balance. ANT. *sober, in control.*

swimmingly *a.* easily, successfully, readily, effortlessly, beautifully, well, smoothly, *without a hitch, perfectly. ANT. *with great effort, with difficulty, unsuccessfully.*

swimsuit *n.* swim shorts, swimming trunks, bathing suit, *jams, bikini, two-piece, T-back, swimwear.

swindle *n.* fraud, cheat, *rip-off, *con, skin game, trickery, scam, shell game, hustle, gyp.

swindle *v.* defraud, cheat, *rip off, *con, trick, *scam, hustle, gyp, dupe, rook, fleece, *chisel, *burn, bamboozle, *take to the cleaners, *screw, bilk, extort, *flimflam, *sell a bill of goods, *take for a ride.

swindler *n.* cheat, *con artist, *con man, fraud, *flimflam man, chiseler, *rip-off artist, crook, *bunco artist, *grifter, *sharper, *hustler, shark.

swine *n.* **1.** PIG hog, porker, piglet, sow, boar. **2.** DESPICABLE PERSON *SOB, creep, pig, animal, rogue, cad, scoundrel, *rat, *jerk.

swing *n.* **1.** OSCILLATION pendulation, sway, swaying, undulation, arc. **2.** PUNCH blow, stroke, uppercut, *roundhouse, left hook. **3.** RHYTHM beat, cadence, meter, pulse, measure.

swing *v.* **1.** OSCILLATE pendulate, sway, rock, teeter, seesaw, waver, wobble, move back and forth. **2.** TURN pivot, come around, spin, wheel, rotate, whirl, swivel, pirouette. **3.** DELIVER A BLOW deliver a roundhouse right, punch. **4.** HAVE AN EXCITING RHYTHM *have a groove, *groove, rock. **5.** BE LIBERAL SEXUALLY swap partners, *bed-hop.

swinish *a.* piggish, *like a hog, beastly, filthy, gross, disgusting, brutish, gluttonous, coarse. ANT. *refined, cultured, delicate.*

swipe *n.* blow, slap, smack, roundhouse, punch, swat, cuff, wallop, clip.

swipe *v.* Sl. steal, pilfer, pocket, take, shoplift, filch, pinch, appropriate, thieve.

swirl *v.* whirl, twirl, twist, eddy, form a whirlpool, revolve, circle, whorl, rotate, gyrate, spin, churn.

swish *v.* hiss, brush, whoosh, rustle.

switch *n.* **1.** CHANGE swap, exchange, reversal, about-face, 360-degree turn, *flip-flop, new tack, change of course. **2.** STICK rod, lash, whip, cane, branch.

swivel *v.* turn, rotate, swing, pivot, revolve, hinge, spin.

swollen *a.* enlarged, distended, bloated, puffy, puffed up, bulging, inflated, edemic, tumid, turgid. ANT. *deflated, contracted, shrunken.*

swoon v. faint, pass out, lose consciousness, collapse, go limp, keel over, feel light-headed, suffer from syncope.

swoop v. **1.** DIVE plunge, plummet, drop down on, pounce on. **2.** SWEEP UP snatch, seize, scoop up.

sword n. weapon, blade, cutlass, saber, broadsword, rapier, samurai sword, scimitar, *cold killing steel.

WORD FIND

belt: baldric

dagger that is notched to catch and break sword: swordbreaker

fencing: foil, épée

handle: haft, hilt, pommel

Indian saber with curved blade: shamshir

legendary, owned by King Arthur: Excalibur

Scottish Highlander's duel-edged broadsword: claymore

shaped like: ensiform, gladiate

sheath: scabbard

short: skean

side projections at hilt: quillons

smaller sword used as a backup: hanger, side-arm

swordplay: fencing, dueling

swordsman: fencer, blade

sworn a. pledged, promised, bound. ANT. available.

SYCOPHANT n. [SIK uh funt] one who flatters and kisses up to others to gain their favor. *The boss had a retinue of sycophants and yes-men.* SYN. toady, flatterer, *brownnose, *bootlicker, yes-man, fawner, groveler, *flunky, *apple-polisher, parasite.

syllabus n. summary, outline, synopsis, abstract, brief, condensation, digest, abridgement, epitome.

sylvan a. woodland, wooded, woody, forested, arboreal. ANT. urban.

SYMBIOTIC a. [sim bee AW tik] referring to a relationship that is mutually beneficial. *Bees and flowers enjoy a symbiotic relationship.* SYN. mutually beneficial, mutually advantageous, give and take, commensalistic. ANT. parasitic, harmful.

symbol n. character, design, letter, emblem, figure, insignia, sign, trademark, representation, badge.

symbolic a. representative, illustrative, metaphorical, indicative, characteristic, symptomatic, emblematic, allegorical. ANT. literal.

symbolize v. represent, stand for, signify, denote, express, epitomize, mean, connote, personify.

symmetrical a. balanced, even, uniform, corresponding, similar, matching, proportionate, harmonious, regular, parallel. ANT. asymmetrical, unbalanced, uneven.

SYMMETRY n. [SIM uh tree] similarity or correspondence in form, uniformity, balance. *They evened out the forms to create a rough symmetry.* SYN. similarity, correspondence, balance, parity, proportion, uniformity, evenness, congruity, harmony, grace. ANT. asymmetry, imbalance, unevenness.

sympathetic a. **1.** COMPASSIONATE concerned, commiserative, caring, feeling, solicitous, understanding, kind, sensitive, tender, pitying, humane, empathetic, charitable, *having a bleeding heart. **2.** CONGENIAL agreeable, like-minded, companionable, simpatico, having a good rapport with, *on the same wavelength, compatible, *en rapport, friendly. ANT. *1.* uncaring, indifferent, cold, stony, unfeeling, insensitive. *2.* disagreeable, clashing, incompatible.

sympathize v. feel for, understand, have compassion for, pity, commiserate, care, empathize, condole, feel sorry for, *have one's heart go out to, *have one's heart bleed for, feel compassion for.

sympathy n. **1.** COMPASSION concern, commiseration, caring, feeling, solicitousness, understanding, kindness, sensitivity, tenderness, pity, humanity, empathy, charity, *bleeding heart. "A fellow-feeling."—Robert Burton. "Two hearts tugging at one load."—Charles Parkhurst. "Dissolved selfishness."—Ludwig Boerne. **2.** AFFINITY OR AGREEMENT BETWEEN TWO PEOPLE harmony, like-mindedness, rapport, compatibility, *same wavelength, accord, congeniality, friendship, unity, mutual attraction. **3.** APPROVAL agreement, assent, consent, *okay, acceptance, acquiescence. ANT. *1.* indifference, coldness, stoniness, insensitivity. *2.* clash, conflict, discord. *3.* disapproval, disagreement.

symphony n. **1.** HARMONY OF SOUNDS euphony, polyphony, multiplicity of sound, chorus. **2.** MUSICAL COMPOSITION opus, piece, concerto, arrangement, suite, score. SEE MUSIC (SYMPHONIC TERMS) **3.** CONCERT performance. **4.** ORCHESTRA philharmonic. **5.** GENERAL HARMONY unity, correspondence, concord, agreement.

symposium n. conference, meeting, gathering, discussion, panel discussion, seminar, forum, round table, debate, assembly, congress.

symptom *n.* indication, sign, warning, warning sign, prodrome, dead giveaway, earmark, manifestation, tip-off, signal, evidence, telltale.

symptomatic *a.* indicative, suggestive, characteristic, peculiar, signaling. ANT. *unusual, abnormal.*

synagogue *n.* place of worship, temple, shul. SEE CHURCH

synapse *n.* connection, junction.

synch *v.* *Sl.* SEE SYNCHRONIZE

synchronize *v.* coordinate, regulate, make simultaneous, *put in sync, harmonize, set.

synchronous *a.* simultaneous, *in sync, concurrent, parallel. ANT. *separated, *out of sync.*

syndicate *n.* association, group, organization, cartel, joint concern, consortium, pool, company, conglomerate, partnership, coalition, trust, Mafia, mob.

syndrome *n.* disease, condition, group of symptoms, disorder, sickness, affliction, malady, spectrum of complaints. SEE DISEASE

synergy *n.* working together, collaboration, cooperative action, coordination, teamwork, joint action, pulling together, *hitching horses, symbiosis.

synod *n.* ecclesiastical council, conclave, meeting of bishops, convocation, assembly, council, session, meeting, tribunal.

SYNONYMOUS *a.* [si NAWN uh mus] having a similar meaning. *Cat is synonymous with feline.* SYN. similar, same, equivalent, parallel, comparable, corresponding, like, alike, interchangeable. ANT. *antonymous, opposite.*

synopsis *n.* summary, abridgement, outline, sketch, brief, epitome, abstract, précis, condensation, digest, rundown.

syntax *n.* word arrangement, sentence structure, word order, phrasing.

synthesis *n.* **1.** ASSEMBLY composition, combination, integration, mixing, blending. **2.** WHOLE FROM MANY PARTS conglomeration, mixture, compound, alloy, blend, amalgam, composite.

synthesize *v.* assemble, combine, integrate, mix, blend, conglomerate, compound, alloy, fuse, meld. ANT. *separate, divide, disassemble.*

synthesizer *n.* electronic keyboard, *sound machine. SEE MUSIC, MUSICAL INSTRUMENT

synthetic *a.* artificial, man-made, manufactured, unnatural, synthesized, imitation, ersatz, sham, fake. ANT. *natural, real, genuine.*

syphilis *n.* venereal disease, sexually transmitted disease (STD), lues, pox. SEE DISEASE

syringe *n.* injector, medical instrument, blood-drawing device. SEE MEDICINE

syrup *n.* treacle, juice, sugar water, molasses.

syrupy *a.* sickeningly sweet, cloyingly sweet, overly sentimental, *dripping with sweetness, mawkish, maudlin, *mushy.

system *n.* arrangement, organization, structure, scheme, set-up, method, plan, operation, procedure, course of action, approach, technique, standard operating procedure, program, way.

systematic *a.* orderly, regular, methodical, arranged, organized, ordered, routine, regulated. ANT. *disorderly, random, unarranged.*

systematize *v.* arrange, order, regulate, organize, methodize, standardize, coordinate, program.

T

tab n. 1. FLAP strip, tongue, tag, projection, loop, ring. 2. BILL check, cost, expenses, tally, account, record, reckoning, score.

tabernacle n. 1. PLACE OF WORSHIP temple, shrine, sanctuary. 2. TENT dwelling.

table n. 1. FURNITURE board, counter, sideboard, stand, dining room table, drop-leaf table, coffee table, end table, parsons table, buffet, writing table, desk. 2. LIST chart, graph, diagram, column, tabulation, index, register.

table v. postpone, delay, shelve, *put on the back burner, put aside, suspend, hold off, sideline, defer, pigeonhole, freeze.

tableau n. picture, scene, view, depiction, spectacle, illustration.

tableland n. karoo, mesa. SEE PLATEAU

tablet n. 1. WRITING PAD pad of paper, notebook, scratch pad. 2. SLAB piece, stone, plaque. 3. PILL capsule, lozenge, troche.

tableware n. flatware, silverware, glassware, dishes.

tabloid n. scandal sheet, *rag, newspaper.

taboo n. prohibition, restriction, *no-no, *don't, *thou-shalt-not, proscription, ban, limitation, forbiddance, reservation.

taboo a. prohibited, restricted, proscribed, *frowned on, forbidden, banned, verboten, unacceptable, out-of-bounds, against social convention, anathema. ANT. accepted, *okay, allowed.

tabulate v. list, put in columns, graph, chart, inventory, index, formulate, figure, arrange, systematize.

TACIT a. [TASS it] implied but unspoken, unexpressed. They had a tacit agreement to stay sober while hunting. SYN. unspoken, unexpressed, silent, implied, implicit, understood, unsaid, unvoiced, inferred. ANT. spoken, expressed, explicit.

TACITURN a. [TAS i TURN] untalkative, uncommunicative, quiet by nature. He was a taciturn old farmer who rarely said anything more than an obligatory "nope"and "yep." SYN. untalkative, uncommunicative, quiet, closemouthed, reticent, reserved, speechless, withdrawn, tight-lipped, mute. ANT. talkative, loquacious, *motor-mouthed, voluble.

tack n. 1. NAIL thumbtack, pushpin, brad, rivet, staple. 2. COURSE heading, direction, way, route, path, approach, line, plan, zigzag.

tack v. nail, pin, attach, fasten, fix, affix, staple.

tackle n. gear, apparatus, equipment, outfit, riggings, paraphernalia, implements, trappings, rope and pulley.

tackle v. 1. THROW DOWN knock down, sack, drop, down, seize, pounce on, grab, intercept, *collar, wrestle to the ground. 2. UNDERTAKE take on, *take a shot at, endeavor, work at, *take a crack at, attack, deal with, try, set about, *give it the old college try.

tacky a. 1. TASTELESS unstylish, cheap, *chintzy, unfashionable, in poor taste, gawdy, garish, *schlocky, loud, shabby, dowdy, frumpy, *grubby, frowzy. 2. STICKY gummy, gluey, adhesive, viscid. ANT. 1. tasteful, stylish, elegant. 2. dry.

tact n. diplomacy, grace, good manners, delicacy, sensitivity, savoir-faire, finesse, discretion, thoughtfulness, consideration, courtesy. "The unsaid part of what you think."— Henry Van Dyke. "Tongue in check."—Susan Dytri. "In the battle of existence, talent is the punch; tact is the clever footwork."— Wilson Mizner. "The art of making a point without making an enemy."—Howard Newton. "The ability to tell a man he's open-minded when he has a hole in his head."—F.G. Kernan. ANT. insensitivity, rudeness, bluntness.

tactful a. diplomatic, gracious, well-mannered, delicate, sensitive, discreet, thoughtful, considerate, courteous, polite, politic, civil. ANT. blunt, rude, insensitive.

tactical a. strategic, cunning, tricky, clever, skillful. ANT. blundering.

tactics n. strategy, *game plan, battle plan, strategics, stratagems, plans, scheme, ploys, moves, maneuvers, machinations, tricks, course of action.

tactile a. touchable, tangible. ANT. intangible, insubstantial.

tactless a. rude, blunt, insensitive, inconsiderate, boorish, indiscreet, thoughtless, rough, undiplomatic, disrespectful, frank, direct, gauche, sharp, offensive. ANT. tactful, diplomatic, gracious, sensitive.

tag n. label, card, ticket, *ID, identification, logo, stub, sticker, tab, slip, marker, trademark, emblem.

tag v. mark, identify, label, name, call, title, style, designate, earmark.

tail n. 1. REAR rump, backside, buttocks, *butt, hind end, posterior, behind, derriere, *tush, *ass. **2.** APPENDAGE extremity, brush, whip, scut, coccyx.

tail *v.* follow, trail, shadow, dog, hound, stalk, tag.

tailing *n.* waste, refuse, leavings, remains.

tailor *n.* garment maker, seamstress, clothier, designer.

tailor *v.* fit, suit, adapt, shape, adjust, modify, alter, cut, style, fine-tune.

tailor-made *a.* made to order, custom-made, custom-fit, tailored. ANT. *ill-fitting, sloppy.*

tailspin *n.* nosedive, dive, stall.

taint *n.* corruption, blot, blemish, disgrace, discredit, stigma, black mark, *black eye, contamination.

taint *v.* infect, corrupt, contaminate, pollute, affect, poison, blemish, blot, disgrace, discredit, stigmatize, *give a black eye, muddy, dirty, defile. ANT. *clean, purify, enhance.*

take *n.* proceeds, profit, yield, *haul, return, gate, net, income, gain.

take *v.* **1.** SEIZE gather up, get, secure, grab, grasp, acquire, snatch, pocket, steal, appropriate, purloin, *nab, *swipe, borrow, help oneself to, pick up, obtain, carry off, pluck, reap. **2.** CHOOSE select, pick, *go with, opt for, single out, settle on, prefer, favor. **3.** CONVEY carry, bring, deliver, transport, haul, tote, lug, *schlep, usher, bear, drive. **4.** ENDURE stand, withstand, put up with, suffer, bear, abide, tolerate, weather, brave, stomach, *hack. **5.** REQUIRE demand, necessitate, call for, need. **6.** CHARM captivate, enchant, win over, bewitch, fascinate, dazzle. **7.** *Sl.* CHEAT trick, *rip off, fleece. ANT. *1. give, leave, let go. 2. reject, pass over.*

take after *v.* emulate, imitate, copy, act like, be like, resemble, look like.

take back *v.* retract, recant, backpedal, disavow, *flip-flop, *eat one's words. ANT. *stand by.*

takeoff *n.* **1.** LAUNCH liftoff, departure, leaving. **2.** SATIRE parody, send-up, spoof, burlesque, caricature, lampoon, mockery, comedy. SEE JOKE

take off *v.* leave, *split, *blow, *book, *beat feet, *scram, depart, skedaddle.

takeover *n.* overthrow, usurpation, coup, coup d'état, vanquishment, conquest, subjugation, rout, dethronement, deposition.

tale *n.* story, narrative, account, fairy tale, fable, myth, legend, yarn, cautionary tale, drama, saga, chronicle.

talent *n.* gift, endowment, natural ability, innate ability, *God-given talent, genius, knack, flair, aptitude, facility, bent, capability, expertise, faculty. "Each man has his vocation. Talent is the call."—Ralph Waldo Emerson. "To do easily what is difficult for others."—Henry Amiel. "Like a grain of pearl sand shifting about in the creative mind. A valued tormentor."—Truman Capote.

talented *a.* gifted, naturally endowed, capable, *having a knack, *having a flair, having innate ability, having an aptitude for, *having the right stuff, proficient. ANT. *deficient, lacking, inept.*

talisman *n.* amulet, charm, good luck charm, fetish, ring, stone.

talk *n.* **1.** SPEECH conversation, verbalization, words, communication, utterance, articulation, expression. **2.** DISCUSSION chat, dialogue, *confab, conference, tête-à-tête, *rap session, *powwow, consultation, argument, *gabfest, interview, *heart-to-heart. **3.** LECTURE address, discourse, oration, speech, sermon, recitation, allocution, tirade. **4.** GOSSIP rumor, scuttlebutt, *buzz, hearsay, word, *grapevine, blabbing, idle talk, *hot air, drivel.

talk *v.* **1.** SPEAK converse, verbalize, frame words, communicate, utter, articulate, express, voice, say, pronounce, enunciate, intone, chatter, babble, prattle, palaver, *shoot the breeze, *yak, *gab, *run off at the mouth, blurt, cry, fume, grumble, huff, rant, rave, shout, snap, sputter, exclaim, grunt, murmur, stammer, whisper. "To open and close the mouth rapidly while the bellows in the throat pumps out the gas in the brain."—Elbert Hubbard. **2.** DISCUSS chat, have a dialogue, confer, consult, *have a powwow, *rap, confabulate, *interface, *touch base, parley. **3.** DELIVER A SPEECH deliver a sermon, address, orate, give a talk. **4.** GOSSIP *fuel the rumor mill, blab. **5.** CONFESS *spill the beans, *let the cat out of the bag, divulge, disclose, *sing, reveal.

talkative *a.* loquacious, garrulous, voluble, *motor-mouthed, *long-winded, chatty, *having the gift of gab, *gabby, rambling, verbose, *bigmouthed. ANT. *taciturn, quiet, reserved, uncommunicative, *clammed up.*

talker *n.* *chatterbox, *motormouth, *windbag, *bigmouth, *magpie, gossip, mouthpiece, spokesman, spokeswoman.

talk show *n.* chat show, program. SEE TELEVISION

tall *a.* **1.** TOWERING high, big, of great stature,

lofty, sky-scraping, sky-high, soaring, elevated. **2.** EXAGGERATED unbelievable, farfetched, hard to believe, outlandish, preposterous. ANT. *1. short, squat, ground-hugging, low. 2. believable, credible.*

tally *n.* total, reckoning, account, score, count, sum, number, amount, *bottom line.

tally *v.* add up, total, reckon, account, score, count, sum up, register, enter, mark, list.

talon *n.* claw, nail. SEE BIRD

tame *a.* **1.** TAMED docile, domesticated, broken, housebroken, trained, gentle, submissive, manageable, tractable, obedient, *busted. **2.** SPIRITLESS lifeless, half-hearted, boring, dull, tedious, uninteresting, *blah, bland, dry. ANT. *1. wild, undomesticated, spirited. 2. spirited, lively, wild.*

tamp *v.* pack, pound down, push down.

tamper *v.* interfere, meddle, mess with, fiddle, fool with, monkey with, *doctor, alter, change, corrupt, bribe.

tan *v.* flog, thrash. SEE WHIP

tan *a.* tawny, brown, golden brown, bronze, copper, fawn, sand, leather, buff, beige.

tang *n.* **1.** SHARP FLAVOR OR SMELL scent, aroma, piquancy, bite, pungency, sharpness, punch, zest, zip. **2.** TOUCH OR TRACE suggestion, hint, tinge, dab.

tangent *a.* touching, contiguous. ANT. *apart, severed.*

tangential *a.* divergent, digressing, off on a tangent, straying, shifting, rambling, peripheral, barely related. ANT. *related, on course, constant.*

TANGIBLE *a.* [TAN juh bul] touchable, palpable, having physical form. *The tire tracks were tangible evidence that a motorbike had torn up the field.* SYN. touchable, palpable, solid, concrete, physical, hard, substantial, real, material, perceivable, tactile, corporeal, visible, actual, definite. ANT. *intangible, immaterial, imperceptible, imaginary.*

tangle *n.* knot, snarl, entanglement, mess, mass of confusion, snag, kink, *ball-up, ravel, web, mat, jumble, labyrinth, *bird's nest, trap, complication, mishmash, mix-up.

tangle *v.* **1.** KNOT snarl, entangle, mess, become a mass of confusion, snag, kink, *ball up, ravel, web, mat, jumble, mix up, enmesh, entwine, trap, catch. **2.** FIGHT wrangle, quarrel, argue, bicker, *lock horns.

tangy *a.* sharp, flavorful, biting, piquant, zesty, tart, spicy, pungent. ANT. *dull, bland, mild.*

tank *n.* **1.** VAT receptacle, tub, container, vessel, cistern, boiler, holding tank, storage tank, reservoir. **2.** ARMORED MILITARY VEHICLE combat vehicle, Abrams M-1, Bradley M-2, Sherman tank, armored personnel carrier.

tankard *n.* cup, mug, stein, pottle.

tantalize *v.* tease, tempt, entice, bait, plague, *make one's mouth water, titillate, *lead on, bewitch, frustrate, *give the Tantalus treatment.

TANTAMOUNT *a.* [TAN tuh mount] equal, equivalent, same. *A prison sentence in some third world countries is tantamount to torture.* SYN. equal, equivalent, much the same, like, as good as, parallel, synonymous, comparable, identical. ANT. *different, opposite, unequal.*

tantrum *n.* rage, outburst, fit, fit of temper, *blowup, rampage, eruption, seizure, storm, temper tantrum, conniption, *hissy fit, *nutty, *freak-out.

tap *n.* faucet, spigot, spout, nozzle, valve, cock, stopper, bung, plug, cork, spile.

tap *v.* **1.** POKE hit, touch, rap, pat, drum, smack, strike. **2.** DRAIN draw, siphon, empty, bleed, milk, pump, broach, pierce. **3.** WIRETAP *bug, eavesdrop.

tap dance *n.* SEE DANCE

tape *n.* strip, band, binding, ribbon, roll, adhesive tape, masking tape, electrician's tape.

tape *v.* **1.** BIND fasten, band together, stick up, mend, close. **2.** RECORD put on tape.

taper *v.* diminish, decrease, dwindle, taper off, lessen, fade, wane, decline, thin out, contract, abate, die out. ANT. *grow, broaden, increase.*

tapestry *n.* wall hanging, decorative cover, dossal, Gobelin.

tar *n.* pitch, asphalt, bitumen.

tardy *a.* late, overdue, past due, delayed, slow, belated, behind, behind schedule, unpunctual, detained, held up, lagging. ANT. *early, on time, punctual.*

target *n.* **1.** OBJECTIVE aim, goal, bull's-eye, destination, mark, point, quarry. **2.** SCAPEGOAT butt, *mark, laughingstock, victim, *patsy, *easy mark.

target *v.* set one's sights on, *draw a bead on, aim for.

tariff *n.* tax, import tax, charge, toll, excise, assessment, fee, levy, duty, bill.

tarnish *n.* dullness, discoloration, oxidation, patina, stain, blemish, wax buildup, cloudiness, haziness, smudge.

tarnish *v.* **1.** DULL discolor, oxidize, fade, dim, smudge, stain, darken, remove luster, blacken. **2.** SULLY ONE'S REPUTATION spoil, ruin, taint, disgrace, dishonor, discredit, defame, degrade, damage, slander. ANT. *1. shine, add luster, polish, brighten. 2. honor, credit, clear one's name.*

tarpaulin *n.* tarp, canvas, cover.

tarry *v.* loiter, stay, linger, remain, wait around, hang around, dilly-dally, lag, dawdle, procrastinate, stall.

tart *n.* **1.** FRUIT PIE pastry, flan, turnover, Danish. **2.** SLUT prostitute, hussy, strumpet, trollop.

tart *a.* sharp, sour, acid, *mouth-puckering, acidulous, acerbic, bitter, biting, piquant, tangy, pungent. ANT. *sweet, honeyed.*

task *n.* job, chore, assignment, duty, charge, work, responsibility, occupation, undertaking, stint, burden, mission, errand.

taskmaster *n.* overseer, *whip, slave driver, boss, commander, supervisor, superintendent, manager, disciplinarian, tyrant.

taste *n.* **1.** FLAVOR flavoring, savor, tang, sensation, bite, *kick, piquancy, zing, zip, aftertaste, saltiness, sweetness, sourness. **2.** SAMPLE spoonful, bite, mouthful, sip, bit, morsel, touch. **3.** PREFERENCE liking, leaning, fancy, predilection, penchant, love, affection, partiality. **4.** GOOD JUDGMENT fashion sense, discrimination, sense of style, discernment, cultivation, refinement, feeling, tastefulness, grace. "A fine judgment in discerning art."—Horace.

taste *v.* sample, savor, relish, discern, try, eat.

tasteful *a.* in good taste, stylish, smart, refined, cultured, restrained, decorous, aesthetically pleasing, elegant, discriminating, correct, fitting. ANT. *tasteless, in poor taste, tacky, ugly, loud, unrefined.*

tasteless *a.* **1.** WITHOUT FLAVOR flavorless, bland, insipid, flat, stale, watery, weak, thin, vapid. **2.** TACKY in poor taste, unrefined, cheap, graceless, vulgar, crude, garish, loud, flashy, gaudy, ostentatious, offensive. ANT. *1. mouth-watering, delicious. 2. tasteful, in good taste, refined.*

tasty *a.* good-tasting, delicious, mouth-watering, *yummy, *scrumptious, toothsome, delectable, savory, appetizing, flavorful, palatable. ANT. *disgusting, gross, nauseating.*

tatter *n.* shred, scrap, piece, torn piece, rip, ribbon.

tattered *a.* shredded, torn to pieces, ripped, ragged, cut to ribbons. ANT. *whole, complete.*

tattle *v.* **1.** TELL ON inform, blab, *squeal on, tattletale, *snitch, *rat on, divulge, reveal,

betray, leak, give away, *spill the beans. **2.** CHATTER talk idly, gossip, *gab, chitchat, *yak, *run off at the mouth, prattle, babble.

tattletale *n.* informer, *squealer, *snitch, *rat, tattler, telltale, blabbermouth, *stool pigeon.

tatoo *n.* drum signal, bugle signal, call, summons.

taunt *n.* mocking, ridicule, jeer, sneer, sarcasm, *swipe, crack, provocation, teasing, jibe, barb, insult.

taunt *v.* jeer at, mock, reproach, ridicule, sneer at, *swipe at, provoke, tease, insult, harass, make fun of, *razz, *rag, ride.

taut *a.* **1.** TIGHT tense, strained, stressed, drawn, stiffened, rigid, firm. **2.** TRIM neat, tidy, efficient, shipshape, spruce, in good order. ANT. *1. relaxed, calm. 2. slack, lazy, sloppy.*

tautology *n.* repetition, redundancy, redundancy, reiteration, verbosity, prolixity, pleonasm.

tavern *n.* bar, saloon, pub, taproom, drinking establishment, ale house, roadhouse, inn, watering hole, cocktail lounge, public house, nightclub.

TAWDRY *a.* [TAW dree] cheap and gaudy, loud, showy. *She spent all her money on tawdry jewelry.* SYN. cheap, gaudy, loud, showy, flashy, sleazy, tacky, garish, meretricious, *chintzy, tasteless, raffish. ANT. *elegant, tasteful.*

tawny *a.* brown, brownish orange, fawn, wheatcolored.

tax *n.* **1.** LEVY toll, tariff, charge, assessment, duty, excise, surcharge, impost, *Uncle's Sam's share, *the Governor's share, *the federal treasury's share, the state treasury's share, custom, percentage, income tax, property tax, sales tax. "The sinews of the state."—Cicero. "Capital punishment."—Jeff Hayes. **2.** BURDEN demand, onus, strain, weight, responsibility, *albatross, *millstone.

tax *v.* **1.** LEVY A CHARGE assess, charge, appraise, exact, demand payment, tithe. "Consists in so plucking the goose as to get the most feathers with the least hissing."—Jean Colbert. **2.** BURDEN weigh down, strain, stress, drain, encumber, saddle, load, push, drive, exhaust. **3.** ACCUSE charge, blame, indict.

taxi *n.* taxicab, cab, hack.

taxing *a.* draining, strenuous, sapping, exhausting, burdensome, wearing, heavy, demanding, backbreaking.

tea *n.* **1.** DRINK beverage, brew, decoction, green

tea, black tea, oolong, pekoe, Lapsang, Darjeeling, herb tea, mint, sassafras, camomile tea. **2.** RECEPTION get-together, party, klatch.

teach *v.* educate, instruct, instill knowledge, school, enlighten, edify, tutor, indoctrinate, *show the ropes, train, drill, *beat into one's head, ground, explain, guide, coach, acquaint with, program. ANT. *learn, be enlightened.*

teacher *n.* educator, instructor, tutor, professor, mentor, trainer, preceptor, schoolmaster, schoolmarm, pedagogue, coach, guide, counselor, guru, don, faculty member. "The child's third parent."—Hyman Berston. "The mediocre teacher tells. The good teacher explains. The superior teacher demonstrates. The great teacher inspires."—William Arthur Ward.

teaching *n.* education, instruction, training, schooling, tutelage, pedagogy, inculcation, grounding, indoctrination, tuition. "To cultivate talent until it ripens for the public to reap its bounty."—Jascha Heifetz.

team *n.* squad, crew, band, company, troupe, corps, duo, trio, quartet, club, gang, string, unit, faction, partners.

teamwork *n.* collaboration, pulling together, tandem work, cooperation, synergy, synergism, concert, interaction, *logrolling.

tear *n.* **1.** TORN PLACE rip, opening, split, slash, slit. **2.** HURRY scramble. SEE RUSH **3.** *Sl.* SPREE *bender, *binge, carousal, *drunk, party, revelry. SEE TEARS

tear *v.* **1.** RIP cut, slash, slit, open, split, shred, fray, tatter, rend, rive, run, come apart at the seams, lacerate, mutilate. **2.** RUSH fly, bolt, run, dart, hurry, speed, shoot, hustle, *zip, *zoom, *go like lightning, *go like the wind.

tear down *v.* raze, level, flatten, bulldoze, demolish, dismantle, destroy, pull down, wreck.

tearful *a.* lachrymose, *weepy, *misty-eyed, teary, dewy-eyed, *brimming with tears, watery-eyed, sobbing, crying, sniveling, blubbering, wailing, sad, mournful, heartbroken, sorrowful. ANT. *remorseless, stoic.*

tears *n.* teardrops, weeping, gushing. "The silent language of grief."—Voltaire. "Holy water."—Shakespeare. "Remorse code."—I. Masai. SEE CRY

tease *v.* **1.** MAKE FUN OF taunt, ridicule, ride, *razz, *josh, *give a hard time, *pick on, kid, *rib, harass, *pull one's leg, *roast, *get a rise out of, pester, mock, bedevil, tantalize. **2.** COMB brush, card, fluff, fluff up.

teat *n.* nipple, *tit, mammilla.

technical *a.* mechanical, technological, *hightech, scientific, professional, specialized, special, methodological. ANT. *simple, *lowtech.*

technicality *n.* minor detail, minor point, specification, formality, *nitpicky rule.

technician *n.* specialist, expert, master, professional, mechanic, authority, journeyman, *pro, *techie.

technique *n.* method, execution, style, approach, artistry, way, procedure, mode, manner, fashion, course, tack, craft, system.

technology *n.* scientific instrumentation, technics, mechanics, mechanization, industrial science, machinery, robotics, scientific know-how, electronics, automation, telecommunications, computers, hardware, software, labor-saving devices.

tedious *a.* boring, tiresome, wearisome, dull, monotonous, uninteresting, *humdrum, prosaic, sleep-inducing, drawn out, longwinded, repetitious, bland, flat, dry. ANT. *stimulating, exciting, electrifying.*

tedium *n.* boredom, monotony, ennui, dullness, sameness, routine, rut, repetitiousness, flatness, deadness. ANT. *excitement, stimulation.*

teem *v.* abound, swarm, be full of, brim, burst, overflow, bristle with, be overrun with.

teeming *a.* abounding, swarming, full, brimming, packed, bursting, thick, overflowing, bristling with, overrun, crawling with, swimming with. ANT. *bare, empty, scanty.*

teenager *n.* adolescent, teen, juvenile, youth, minor, teenybopper, sophomore, *bobby soxer, *punk, high school kid.

teeny *a.* tiny, teentsy, *teensy-weensy, minute, microscopic, wee, Lilliputian, miniature, pint-sized. ANT. *huge, gigantic.*

teepee *n.* wigwam, wickiup, lodge, tent.

tee shirt *n.* pullover, T-shirt.

teeter *v.* seesaw, totter, oscillate, wobble, pivot, balance, rock, waver, vacillate.

teeth *n.* molars, bicuspids, incisors, canines, *grinders, fangs, *pearly whites.
WORD FIND
adolescence, last molars that erupt: wisdom teeth
baby or temporary teeth: deciduous teeth, milk teeth
cavities: caries
cut one's first teeth: teethe
eruption through gums: dentition

gum disease: periodontal disease, periodontitis, pyorrhea

gum inflammation: gingivitis

hard covering: enamel

false: denture

gnashing or grinding: bruxism

large teeth, condition of having: macrodontia

loss of: dedentition

meet, clench or align properly, failure of upper and lower to: malocclusion

pointy part: cusp

small teeth, condition of having: microdontia

sound of clicking: chatter

sticky film that forms on after eating: plaque

tipped over and pushing on adjacent tooth: impacted

yellowish concretion on: tartar

teetotaler *n.* nondrinker, abstainer, *dry.

teetotalism *n.* abstinence. SEE TEMPERANCE

telecast *n.* SEE BROADCAST

telecommunication *n.* telephone transmission, electronic transmission, online data transfer, e-mail, telegraphy.

telecommuting *n.* desktop commuting, remote data entry.

telegram *n.* wire, message, telegraph, cable, *telex, dispatch, transmission.

telegraph *n.* wire, Telex, cable, ticker, news ticker, signaling system.

WORD FIND

code of dots and dashes: Morse code

national service: Western Union

typed wire message and printer itself: teletype

telemarketing *n.* telephone solicitation, telephone advertising, telephone canvassing.

telepathy *n.* extrasensory perception, *ESP, clairvoyance, mindreading, sixth sense, thought transference, psychic power.

telephone *n.* phone, *horn, line, extension phone, car phone, cellular phone, transmitter, receiver, rotary phone, touchtone phone.

WORD FIND

alerting click signaling another call: call waiting

automatic dialing: auto redial, speed dialing

beeper: pager

buzz: dial tone

conference held with speakerphones, closed circuit television: teleconference

connecting phone lines, apparatus for: switchboard

digits of phone number, first three: prefix

eavesdrop electronically on another's phone line: tap

hand instrument: handset

line kept open and accessible without dialing: hot line

long-distance service for companies: WATS (Wide Area Telecommunications Service)

loudspeaker, phone with: speakerphone

message system: voice mail

number identification system: caller I.D.

rest for handset: cradle

room-to-room or interoffice communication device: intercom, PBX (Private Branch Exchange)

science: telephonics, telephony

telescope *n.* optical instrument, scope, spy glass, binoculars, field glass, radio telescope.

telescope *v.* contract, condense, shorten, shrink, truncate, consolidate. ANT. *extend, lengthen.*

telethon *n.* pledge campaign, charity drive, appeal for funding, fundraiser.

televise *v.* broadcast, transmit, show.

television *n.* TV, *tube, *boob tube, video, *telly, *idiot box, console, set, entertainment center, *one-eyed monster. "Chewing gum for the eyes."—Frank Lloyd Wright. "An invention that permits you to be entertained in your living room by people you wouldn't have in your home."—David Frost.

WORD FIND

ABC: American Broadcasting Company

affiliated TV stations, collectively: network

audition for TV show, open: cattle call

award: Emmy

background scene slide: balop

BBC: British Broadcasting Corporation

brief clip of politician's or other newsmaker's remarks: soundbite

broadcast: air, telecast

broadcast on radio and TV at same time: simulcast

"brought to you by" opening of show: opening billboard

camera crane for moving, outdoor shots: cherry picker

camera crane operator: crane grip

camera dolly, one who pushes: dolly grip

camera elevating device: riser

camera shot, moving: crab shot, dolly shot, truck shot

card with performer's lines on it: cue card, idiot card, flip card

CBS: Columbia Broadcasting System
color test strip: color bar, colorburst
commercials, group of: pod
credits at end of show, moving: crawl
directing and engineering room: control room
distribution of TV shows to subscriber stations: syndication
distributor of TV shows: syndicate
8 P.M. to 11 P.M.: prime time
electrician head in studio: gaffer
goofs made by actors or crew edited out of tape: bloopers, outtakes
hand or assistant in studio: grip, hammer, set carpenter
high resolution television: HDTV (High Definition television)
identifying, introductory scenery of television show: signature montage
light, studio: floodlight, klieg light, scoop, basher
local prohibition of program to attract bigger audience at live show: blackout
local station part of national network: affiliate
microphone boom, long: *fishpole
minimum standard fee for performer: scale
monitor console from which director chooses which camera shot will air: preview monitor
moral standards, department that assures program meets society's: standards and practices
narrator's voice heard over program: voice-over
NBC: National Broadcasting System
network performers under contract: stable
optical effect: freeze-frame, superimposition, split screen
optical effect used to create a ghost: Pepper's ghost
optical transition device: wipe, dissolve, fade-in, fade-out, fade to black
performers in a show, collective term for: cast
portable television news camera: minicam
prerecorded laughter: laughtrack
prerecorded material: canned
promo piece of upcoming show: trailer, teaser, preview
rails on which camera may ride in outdoor, moving shot: dolly tracks
ratings company: Arbitron, A.C. Nielson
ratings months: sweeps
read script from front of television camera,

device that allows actor to: prompter, teleprompter
record a program: tape
recorded as it happened with no takeouts: live on tape
record in sound effects, music: dub, foley
red light on camera that lights during recording: tally light
regulating commission: FCC (Federal Communications Commission)
royalty paid to performers for reuse of their work: residual
satellite used for television transmission: *bird
scrambling pay television signals: encryption
show where performer or camera will stand or move: block
situation comedy: sitcom
sound effect: foley
sound effects, one who performs: foley artist
sound effects studio: foley studio, foley stage
studio scaffolding where lights are hung: catwalk
superimposed script read from television camera's lens: prompter script
superimposed text on screen: legend
superimposes bulletins, news, weather on bottom of screen, apparatus that: flashcaster
superimpose text on screen: key
talk show, cancel a guest at the last minute on a: bump
talk show waiting room for guests: green room
tear down a set: strike
time off between show's taping: hiatus
trailer with dressing rooms for shooting on location: honey wagon
transmission of show from network to local station: feed
tryout episode of television show: pilot
union for performers: AFTRA (American Federation of Television and Radio Artists)
videotape cutter, splicer, arranger: editor
"We'll be back after these messages" transitional device: bumper
unscrambling of pay TV signals: decryption
video disk jockey: veejay (VJ)
SEE MOVIE

tell *v.* **1.** COMMUNICATE relate, state, say, declare, make known, speak, divulge, disclose, reveal, impart, voice, announce, utter, *spit it out, inform, mention, report, confess, assert, let slip, *spill the beans, *let the cat

out of the bag, blab, admit, *break the news.
2. TATTLE *blow the whistle on, *squeal,
*rat, betray. **3.** GIVE AN ACCOUNT narrate,
chronicle, recount, relate, detail, describe,
recite. **4.** DISCERN recognize, distinguish, discriminate, make out, detect, ascertain, determine, recognize, identify.

teller *n*. **1.** NARRATOR storyteller, chronicler, reporter, raconteur, recounter. **2.** CASHIER
clerk, bank employee.

telling *a*. **1.** REVEALING indicative, suggestive,
expressive, telltale. **2.** FORCEFUL striking, effective, weighty, important, potent, influential, decisive, consequential, momentous.
ANT. *1. inconclusive, unrevealing. 2. ineffective, inconsequential, insignificant.*

tell off *v*. rebuke, reprimand, upbraid, berate,
admonish, *ream out, *lambaste, *rake over
the coals, *give one a piece of one's mind,
*chew out, *bawl out, *call on the carpet,
*dress down, *give hell, *jump down one's
throat, *let have it with both barrels, *read
the riot act, *rip into. ANT. *commend, give a
pat on the back, praise.*

telltale *a*. revealing, indicative, demonstrative,
giveaway, meaningful, betraying, illuminating, informative. ANT. *meaningless, inconclusive, unrevealing.*

TEMERITY *n*. [tuh MER i tee] foolhardy boldness, recklessness. *I can't believe he had the
temerity to scold the boss.* SYN. rashness, boldness, recklessness, foolhardiness, gall, carelessness, audacity, indiscretion, nerve,
*balls, precipitateness, *chutzpah, impu-
dence. ANT. *timidity, cautiousness, cowardice,
judiciousness.*

temper *n*. **1.** FRAME OF MIND mood, disposition,
temperament, spirits, humor, attitude, outlook, character. **2.** TENDENCY TO BECOME
ANGRY *short fuse, *hairtrigger temper, *low
boiling point, *low critical mass, *hot
blood, *hot head, explosive personality, volatility, impatience, irritability, touchiness,
petulence, *hypersensitivity, *type-A personality, *walking time bomb. **3.** ANGER
rage, tantrum, outburst, fury, wrath, rampage, *blowup, storm. **4.** COMPOSURE calmness, equanimity, good humor, sang-froid,
coolness. ANT. *2. *long fuse, *high boiling
point, easygoing personality, cool head. 3. composure, calmness, tranquility.*

temper *v*. **1.** MODERATE soften, lessen, tone
down, ease, mollify, assuage, dilute, mitigate, relieve, pacify. **2.** TOUGHEN harden,
strengthen, anneal. ANT. *1. intensify, harden,
increase. 2. soften, weaken.*

temperament *n*. nature, frame of mind, disposition, character, makeup, mood, mind-set,
inclination, natural tendencies, humor,
constitution, personality.

temperamental *a*. excitable, *hot-headed,
*hot-blooded, moody, easily upset, volatile,
touchy, irritable, unstable, tempestuous,
high-strung, *thin-skinned, *short-fused.
ANT. *even-tempered, easygoing, stable.*

temperance *n*. moderation, abstemiousness, abstinent, self-restrained, unindulgent, self-
control, sobriety, soberness, forbearance,
teetotalism. "The moderating of one's desires in obedience to reason."—Cicero.
"The golden mean."—Horace. ANT. *indulgence, abandon, immoderation.*

TEMPERATE *a*. [TEM pur it] moderate, mild,
restrained. *Hawaii is known for its temperate
climate.* SYN. moderate, mild, restrained,
agreeable, *middle-of-the-road, fair, clement, unextreme, medium, reasonable, conservative. ANT. *intemperate, extreme, immoderate.*

temperature *n*. hotness, coldness, heat, cold,
degrees, body heat, fever.

tempest *n*. **1.** STORM blow, hurricane, typhoon,
wind storm, squall, tornado, cyclone,
*twister, blizzard. **2.** OUTBURST outbreak, tumult, disturbance, unrest, turmoil, ferment,
eruption, uproar, upheaval, *tempest in a
teapot. ANT. *calm, tranquility, serenity, quiet.*

tempestuous *a*. stormy, wild, violent, turbulent, raging, intense, furious, tumultuous, feverish, impassioned. ANT. *calm, quiet, tranquil.*

template *n*. pattern, guide, outline, prototype,
gauge.

temple *n*. place of worship, house of worship,
church, cathedral, synagogue, holy place,
shrine, sanctuary, pagoda. SEE CHURCH, RELI-
GION

tempo *n*. speed, rate, pace, measure, velocity,
time, meter, cadence, rhythm, pulse, beat.

temporal *a*. **1.** TEMPORARY transitory, fleeting,
ephemeral, short-lived, momentary, passing,
impermanent. **2.** WORLDLY mundane,
earthly, mortal, of this world, terrestrial, material, nonspiritual, secular. ANT. *1. permanent, long-lasting, eternal. 2. spiritual, heavenly, godly.*

temporary *a*. impermanent, transitory, short-
term, passing, transient, fleeting, ephemeral,
brief, pro tempore, stopgap, makeshift,

make-do, provisional, interim. ANT. *perma-nent, lasting, eternal, fixed.*

temporize v. evade, parley, stall, procrastinate, delay, hem and haw, tarry, equivocate, filli-buster.

tempt v. lure, entice, bait, tantalize, seduce, at-tract, court, *suck in, *hold out a carrot, draw, captivate, bewitch. ANT. *repulse, repel, turn off.*

temptation n. lure, enticement, tantalization, seduction, attraction, courting, *carrot, cap-tivation, bait, *come-on, draw, snare.

tempter n. enticer, temptress, tantalizer, se-ducer, seductress, teaser, Satan.

tempting a. alluring, enticing, tantalizing, se-ductive, attractive, magnetic, appetizing, mouth-watering, baiting. ANT. *repulsive, re-pellant, sickening.*

TENABLE a. [TEN uh bul] defensible, can be argued for. *His alibi was entirely tenable.* SYN. defensible, defendable, indisputable, incon-testable, ironclad, solid, maintainable, rea-sonable, credible, viable. ANT. *untenable, in-defensible, unjustifiable.*

TENACIOUS a. [tuh NAY shus] persistent, tough, not giving up readily, holding fast, stubborn. *His tenacious spirit helped him to continue, even in the face of great hardship.* SYN. persistent, tough, stubborn, resolute, dogged, perseverant, strong, steadfast, un-yielding, unwilling to let go, determined, unwavering, staunch. ANT. *irresolute, weak-willed, yielding.*

tenacity n. persistence, toughness, mental toughness, stubbornness, resolve, resolution, backbone, doggedness, perseverance, strength, *stick-to-itiveness, grit, endur-ance. ANT. *weakness, weak will, spinelessness.*

tenant n. renter, leaseholder, lessee, occupant, lodger, roomer, resident.

tend v. **1.** TAKE CARE OF care for, mind, minister to, attend, cater to, look after, wait on, man-age, assist, aid. **2.** INCLINE be apt, be liable, lean, be likely, have a tendency, be disposed.

tendency n. inclination, disposition, leaning, bent, propensity, proclivity, proneness, pen-chant, predisposition, course, drift.

tender n. **1.** OFFER proffer, proposition, presen-tation. **2.** CARETAKER sitter, watcher, main-tenance man.

tender v. offer, proffer, present, proposition, put forth, submit, advance, give.

tender a. **1.** SOFT delicate, fragile, frail, weak, feeble. **2.** GENTLE mild, light, soft, easy. **3.** YOUTHFUL immature, young, unseasoned,

unhardened, soft, raw, vulnerable, *wet be-hind the ears. **4.** TENDERHEARTED loving, kind, compassionate, sympathetic, caring, warm, understanding, supportive, sweet, considerate. **5.** PAINFUL hurting, smarting, sore, raw, sensitive, inflamed. ANT. *1. hard, stony, tough. 2. rough, hard. 3. mature, sea-soned, experienced, hardened. 4. uncaring, cold, indifferent, cruel. 5. calloused, rough.*

tenderfoot n. newcomer, beginner, novice, am-ateur, *greenhorn, *rookie, neophyte, tyro, raw recruit, *new kid on the block.

tenderhearted a. tender, loving, kind, compas-sionate, sympathetic, caring, warm, under-standing, supportive, sweet, considerate. ANT. *coldhearted, brutal, cruel, uncaring.*

tenderness n. tenderheartedness, love and kindness, compassion, sympathy, caring, warmth, understanding, support, sweetness, consideration, humanity, pity, mercy. ANT. *hardheartedness, brutality, cruelty.*

tendon n. sinew, connective tissue, muscle fi-ber, thew.

tenement n. apartment, flat, house, duplex, boarding house, *dump, *rat's nest, slum, rookery.

TENET n. [TEN it] a principle or belief. *She didn't agree with all the tenets of her church.* SYN. principle, belief, doctrine, dogma, con-viction, creed, credo, canon, rule, teaching, maxim.

tennis n. racket sport, lawn tennis, game, sphairistike.

WORD FIND

boundary line marking end of service boxes: service line

championships held in England: Wimble-don

court area between net and service line: forecourt

court on which ball bounces, skids quickly: fast court

court rectangles in which ball must land when served: service court

diagonal shot: crosscourt shot

doubles player's move into partner's court for surprise shot: poaching

drive the ball directly at opponent's body to throw off balance: jam

finesse player: touch player

40-40 tie situation: deuce

four players, game with: doubles

injury or inflammation of elbow tendons: tennis elbow

lines at ends of court: baseline

long back and forth exchange without a miss: rally
officials: baseline judge, linesman, net judge
original name: sphairstike
racket grip: Australian grip, continental grip, eastern, *shake hands grip
racket, middle of: sweet spot
return ball before it hits ground: volley
rotation imparted on ball: topspin, backspin
score of zero: love
scoring unit or point: fifteen
serve in two tries, failure to deliver a legal: double fault
serve on first try, failure to deliver a legal: fault
serve, stepping over baseline while making: foot fault
serve that nicks top of net and must be replayed: let
serve that opponent is unable to return: ace
showoff play to impress spectators: gallery play
spectator area, stands: gallery
stroke: forehand, backhand, lob, smash, drive, slice, chop, chip, dink, volley, punch volley
teams tournament, international: Davis Cup
tie-breaker game: sudden death
tournament open to amateurs as well as pros: open
win a game against the server: break, service break
winning best of three or more sets: match
winning point: game point
winning point in a set: set point
winning point in a set-winning game: game set
win of six games: set
wins a game against the server, point that: break point

tenor n. **1.** ALTO falsetto. SEE MUSIC **2.** MEANING intent, sense, drift, purport, gist, tone.

tense a. **1.** TIGHT taut, stressed, strained, stretched, drawn, stiff. **2.** NERVOUS stressed, *uptight, *bundle of nerves, anxious, edgy, jittery, strained, restless, apprehensive, *having butterflies in stomach, *keyed up, *sweating bullets, *on pins and needles, jumpy. ANT. *1.* loose, slack, relaxed. *2.* calm, composed, relaxed, tranquil.

tense up v. stress out, *choke, *choke under pressure, *swallow the apple.

tension n. **1.** TIGHTNESS tautness, stress, strain, stiffness, rigidity, pressure, pull, stretching.

2. NERVOUSNESS stress, anxiety, edginess, jitters, strain, restlessness, apprehension, *butterflies, *sweat, jumpiness, pressure. ANT. *1.* looseness, slackness, relaxation. *2.* relaxation, calm, tranquility.

tent n. canvas shelter, pup tent, tepee, wigwam, wickiup, yurt, pavilion.

TENTATIVE a. [TEN tuh tiv] indefinite, not firmed up, as one's plans to do something, uncertain, conditional. Also, hesitant or timid. *They made tentative plans to hike the north face of the mountain.* SYN. uncertain, unsure, not firmed up, conditional, possible, proposed, contingent, indefinite, *not carved in stone, subject to change, unconfirmed, hesitant, timid, doubtful, cautious. ANT. *certain, firm, definite, confident.*

TENUOUS a. [TEN yoo us] thin, weak, flimsy, insubstantial, rare. *His excuse for being late was tenuous at best.* SYN. thin, weak, flimsy, insubstantial, rare, fragile, slight, light, negligible, fine, shaky. ANT. *solid, rock-solid, firm, substantial, strong.*

tenure n. **1.** TERM time, occupation, stay, residence, incumbency, reign. **2.** PERMANENCY permanent status, lifetime position, permanent seat, job security.

tepee n. wigwam, wickiup. SEE TENT

tepid a. **1.** LUKEWARM room temperature, barely warm. **2.** UNENTHUSIASTIC halfhearted, cool, apathetic, lukewarm, indifferent, mild, moderate, limp. ANT. *1.* hot, boiling, scalding. *2.* enthusiastic, passionate, fervent, wild.

term n. **1.** PERIOD OF TIME duration, time, span, timespan, cycle, session, semester, quarter, spell, course, interval, stretch. **2.** PHRASE OR WORD description, designation, expression, name, denomination, terminology. **3.** CONCLUSION close, end, finish, completion, limit, limitation. SEE TERMS

term v. name, designate, call, label, title, dub, style.

terminal n. station, depot, junction, end of the line, terminus.

terminal a. ending, concluding, final, closing, last, extreme, fatal. ANT. *beginning, first.*

terminate v. **1.** STOP end, cease, discontinue, conclude, close, finish, cancel, eliminate, halt, desist, fire, dismiss, let go, abort. **2.** BOUND limit, demarcate, circumscribe. ANT. *1.* start, begin, open.

termination n. stoppage, end, cessation, discontinuance, conclusion, close, finish, cancellation, elimination, halt, firing, dismissal, aborting. ANT. *start, beginning, opening.*

terminology n. wording, phraseology, vocabulary, nomenclature, terms, language, *lingo, jargon, cant, argot.

terminus n. end, limit, boundary, extremity, margin, pale.

terms n. conditions, particulars, specifications, provisions, provisos, stipulations, *fine print, qualifications, points, agreement.

terrace n. **1.** PATIO OR VERANDA garden, lawn, gallery, colonnade, balcony, piazza. **2.** STAIR-STEPPING EARTH FORMATION berm, plateaus.

terra firma n. earth, solid ground.

terrain n. ground, topography, lay of the land, tract, landscape, land, turf, country, region, territory.

terrestrial a. earthly, worldly, terrene, tellurian, mundane. ANT. extraterrestrial, spiritual, ethereal.

terrible a. **1.** BAD awful, lousy, inferior, *crappy, horrible, appalling, objectionable, disagreeable, *rotten, revolting, atrocious, dreadful, poor. **2.** FRIGHTFUL terrifying, fearful, dreadful, harrowing, horrifying, horrific, distressing. **3.** EXTREME severe, intense, acute, fierce. ANT. 1. excellent, great, wonderful. 2. reassuring, encouraging, comforting. 3. mild, light, moderate.

terribly adv. very, extremely, awfully, thoroughly, frightfully.

terrific a. **1.** GREAT fabulous, fantastic, excellent, wonderful, first-rate, superb, marvelous, good, sensational, *out of this world, superior, outstanding. **2.** TERRIFYING scary, frightful, fearful, dreadful, appalling, terrible, harrowing, horrifying, distressing. ANT. 1. bad, awful, lousy, terrible. 2. reassuring, comforting, encouraging.

terrify v. frighten, scare, fill with terror, petrify, *curdle one's blood, *paralyze with fear, *put the fear of God into, alarm, *scare stiff, shock, startle, frighten out of one's wits, *make one's hair stand on end, *scare the bejesus out of, *make one's hair curl, panic, trigger one's fight or flight response. ANT. reassure, comfort.

territorial a. proprietary, defensive. ANT. giving.

territory n. **1.** AREA region, district, province, land, country, terrain, locale, zone, vicinity, precinct, neighborhood, tract. **2.** DOMAIN sphere, realm, turf, area, field, bailiwick.

terror n. **1.** FEAR fright, panic, dread, horror, alarm, shock, awe, dismay, heart-pounding terror, paralysis, paroxysm of fear. **2.** UNRULY CHILD hellion, rascal, pest, nuisance, *holy terror, *hell on wheels, imp, troublemaker.

terrorism n. fear campaign, intimidation tactics, arm-twisting, bullying, extortion, coercion, firebombing, hostage-taking, bomb threats.

terrorist n. extortionist, vigilante, bully, arm-twister, radical, revolutionary, rebel, anarchist, subversive.

terrorize v. terrify, frighten, scare, fill with terror, intimidate, threaten, menace, bully, browbeat, arm-twist, strongarm, coerce.

TERSE a. [TURS] concise, to the point, brief. He gave a suprisingly terse speech and left. SYN. concise, succinct, brief, to the point, short, taut, pithy, condensed, trenchant, compact, sparing, laconic. ANT. long-winded, verbose, wordy.

test n. **1.** EXAMINATION exam, quiz, multiple choice, midterm, trial, evaluation, probe, assessment, questionnaire, inspection, inquest. **2.** TRIAL experiment, assay, try, dry run. **3.** STANDARD criterion, *acid test, *litmus test, measure, touchstone, proof.

test v. examine, quiz, try, evaluate, probe, assess, question, inspect, investigate, analyze, conduct a trial run, assay, check, *see which way the wind blows, sound.

TESTAMENT n. [TES tuh munt] that which testifies to the validity or truth of something. That the number of highway fatalities have decreased is a testament to better safety regulations. SYN. testimony, testimonial, affirmation, confirmation, proof, evidence, profession, statement.

tested a. tried, proven. ANT. unproven, unknown.

testicles n. testes, sex glands, gonads.

testify v. **1.** PROVIDE TESTIMONY bear witness, give evidence, attest, affirm, vouch for, corroborate, swear to, declare, verify, uphold, support, substantiate. **2.** BE EVIDENCE OF prove, show, indicate, be a testament to, provide testimony for, demonstrate. ANT. 2. disprove, contradict.

testimonial n. commendation, recommendation, *plug, tribute, compliment, affidavit, endorsement, certificate, letter of recommendation, letter of reference.

testimony n. **1.** DECLARATION profession, affirmation, attestation, proof, evidence, witness, corroboration, statement, sworn statement, affidavit, deposition, documentation, avowal, support. **2.** INDICATION evidence, attestation, confirmation, affirmation, demonstration.

testosterone n. hormone, male hormone, sex hormone, steroid.

testy a. irritable, touchy, grouchy, grumpy, cranky, petulant, *snappy, ornery, thin-skinned, *short-fused, quick-tempered, peevish. ANT. *good humored, easygoing, cheerful.*

tetched a. demented, neurotic, *not right in the head, *a little crazy, touched, *nuts. SEE CRAZY, INSANE, NEUROTIC

tête-à-tête n. heart-to-heart talk, conversation, intimate discussion, talk, discussion, confidential discussion, face-to-face chat.

tether n. rope, leash, chain, halter, restraint, cord, line.

text n. words, wording, main body, body, printed matter, written matter.

textbook n. text, schoolbook, reference book, manual.

textile n. fabric, cloth, woven material, fibrous material, cotton, wool, yarn, dry goods.

texture n. surface quality, feel, character, composition, grade, smoothness, roughness, coarseness, weave, grain, nap, pile, woof, wale.

thank v. acknowledge, show one's appreciation, show one's gratitude, bless.

thankful a. grateful, appreciative, obliged, indebted, beholden. ANT. *unappreciative, thankless.*

thankless a. **1.** UNGRATEFUL unappreciative, rude, inconsiderate. **2.** UNAPPRECIATED unrewarded, unnoticed, unrecognized, unacknowledged. ANT. *1. thankful, grateful. 2. appreciated, rewarded.*

thatch n. mat, straw, rushes, palm leaves, roofing.

thaw v. **1.** MELT liquefy, soften, warm, defrost, dissolve. **2.** LOOSEN UP warm, relax. ANT. *1. freeze, harden, solidify. 2. become stiff and formal, cool.*

theater n. **1.** PLAYHOUSE opera house, auditorium, ampitheater, theater in the round, boards, odeum, dinner theater, hall, arena, movie house, cinema, drive-in. **2.** STAGE PERFORMANCE dramatic arts, drama, show business, the stage. "An escape from reality."— George Nathan. "A tradition of villains and heroes."—George Bernard Shaw. "A window open on the life of our fellow creatures."—Mario Fratti.

WORD FIND

above stage, walk or platform for lights: fly

actor's emergency fill-in: understudy

advertisement at front of theater: marquee

afternoon show: matinee

alcove in center of stage where prompter hides from audience: prompt box

allegorical drama illustrating Christian teaching: morality play

anxiety, performance: stage fright, *flop sweat

award: Tony

background scenery: backdrop, olio, ground row, cyclorama

backstage area: wings

box in front of balcony or mezzanine: loge

Broadway, play not produced on: off-Broadway production

brochure of cast and description: program, playbill

comedy featuring wit: high comedy

comedy of exaggeration: farce

comedy on morbid subject: black comedy

comedy satirizing manners of fashionable society: comedy of manners

comedy, slapstick or physical: low comedy

comedy that spoofs: send-up, parody

company producing several shows with same performers: repertory company

company production of plays in summer: summer stock

cues a song, line of dialogue that: dakota

dim lighting used for effect: pool hall lighting

district of theaters: white light district, Great White Way, Broadway, Rialto

draw attention away from another actor: upstage, steal the show

dress rehearsal before an audience: audience dress

emotions are exaggerated, play in which: melodrama

exaggerated acting or overacting: histrionics

explosion or flash, device that creates: flashpot

falling in love with theater: stagestruck

financier, backer: angel

hit show: boffo

horrifying, macabre or gruesome drama: Grand Guignol

Japanese, all-male: Kabuki

large-scale act or musical number: production number

lights: footlights, limelight, *ace, *ashcan, baby spot, bon-bon, flood, house lights, *keg light, klieg light, pin spot

list of characters: dramatis personae

makeup: grease paint, pancake makeup

mark the stage to direct actors where to stand, move: block

musicals, theater that specializes in: lyric theater

musical with sketches: revue

musician's area: orchestra pit

narrator to audience: raisonneur

object used in show: prop

open audition: *cattle call

outfit a stage with scenery: dress

pack theater by distributing free tickets: paper the house

rehearsal, rough: walk-through

religious play centering around suffering of Christ: passion play

remember lines during show, helps actors: prompter

sad or heartbreaking play: tragedy

segment: act

serious performances as opposed to vaudeville: legitimate theater

set, take down a: strike

set that is real, as opposed to that of facades: practical set

skyline or horizon scenery piece: ground row, cyclorama

sound effects made from offstage: noises off

SRO: standing room only

stage, front of: proscenium, apron

stage props, functioning: practicals

talk with audience, actor's solo: soliloquy

top balcony for lowerclass patrons: peanut gallery

union for actors: Actors Equity Association

unsuccessful play: *flop, *bomb, *turkey, *dog

variety show, old time: vaudeville, burlesque

waiting room, performer's: green room, dressing room

wardrobe assistant: dresser

worker: stagehand

writer of plays: playwright

written music: score

SEE MOVIE, TELEVISION

theatrical a. **1.** SHOW BUSINESS staged, stagy, thespian, operatic, Broadway, off-Broadway. **2.** MELODRAMATIC dramatic, histrionic, *hammy, showy, campy, pretentious, affected, overacted, overwrought, *fake, *put on. ANT. **2.** sincere, natural, real, understated.

theft n. stealing, larceny, grand larceny, petty larceny, thievery, burglary, robbery, purse-snatching, *holdup, mugging, looting, pilferage, shoplifting.

theme n. topic, subject, idea, motif, leitmotif, matter, point, question, keynote, strain, recurrent pattern.

theme song n. signature song.

theologian n. student of religion, religious scholar, divine. SEE RELIGION

theology n. study of religion, divinity, study of God, theosophy, doctrine, dogma, Scripture, the Gospel. "Science of mind applied to God."—Henry Ward Beecher. "The rhetoric of morals."—Ralph Waldo Emerson. SEE RELIGION, GOD

theorem n. assumption, proposition, hypothesis, theory, postulate, principle, law, rule, formula, equation.

theoretical a. hypothetical, speculative, academic, conjectural, abstract, assumed, notional, untried, unproven, presumed, *on paper, untested. ANT. practical, applied, proven.

theorize v. hypothesize, speculate, conjecture, suppose, guess, presume, assume, imagine, formulate, posit, think.

theory n. hypothesis, speculation, conjecture, supposition, guess, presumption, assumption, formulation, idea, thesis, surmise, postulate, hunch. "A hunch with a college education."—J.A. Carter.

therapeutic a. curative, remedial, healthful, healing, corrective, restorative, beneficial, medicinal, sanative, helpful. ANT. harmful, unhealthy, detrimental.

therapist n. counselor, psychologist, psychiatrist, doctor, physician, psychotherapist, *shrink, adviser, analyst, sympathetic ear.

therapy n. treatment, regimen, regime, remedy, healing, curative, homeopathy, rehabilitation, *rehab, physical therapy, speech therapy, group therapy.

thereabouts adv. near, about, around, approximately, roughly.

thereafter adv. afterwards, after, later, subsequently, thenceforth, following.

therefore adv. consequently, thus, so, hence, ergo, for that reason, as a result, accordingly.

thermal a. warm, hot, heated, thermic. ANT. cold, unheated.

thermos n. bottle, flask, insulated container.

thesaurus n. lexicon, word treasury, synonym finder, word book.

thesis n. **1.** PROPOSITION premise, assumption, belief, theory, hypothesis, argument, belief, opinion, idea, theorem, position. **2.** DISSERTATION treatise, research paper, essay, study, investigation, monograph, composition.

thespian n. actor, actress, player, performer, *ham, tragedian. SEE MOVIE, TELEVISION, THEATER

thick *a.* **1.** DEEP extensive, fat, massive, thickset, obese, wide, large, solid, bulky. **2.** DENSE closely packed, concentrated, close, crowded, heavy, condensed, compact, impermeable, luxuriant, viscid, viscous, glutinous, congealed, caked. **3.** HAVING A GREAT NUMBER CLOSELY PACKED crowded, teeming, chock-full, bursting, numerous, great, swarming, replete, overflowing, *jampacked, crammed. **4.** STUPID dense, retarded, dull, bovine, slow, dim-witted, obtuse, dumb, moronic, imbecilic, simple, *chowderheaded, *lamebrained, *dense as a post. ANT. *1. thin, slim, slight. 2. thin, sparse, scant, watery. 3. empty, rare, thin, scarce. 4. brilliant, smart, intelligent, sharp.*

thicken *v.* concentrate, condense, congeal, compact, solidify, harden, clot, coagulate, jell, curdle, set, cake. ANT. *thin, liquefy, dilute.*

thicket *n.* underbrush, shrubs, bushes, brush, scrub, brake, copse, bosket, tangle.

thickset *a.* stocky, stout, beefy, heavyset, big, chunky. ANT. *skinny, slim, slender.* SEE FAT

thick-skinned *a.* hardened, tough, insensitive, callous, hard-boiled, unfeeling, strong, stony. ANT. *thin-skinned, sensitive, ultrasensitive.*

thief *n.* *crook, robber, burglar, shoplifter, mugger, swindler, bandit, criminal, kleptomaniac, *klepto, cheat, *rip-off artist, *con artist, pickpocket, filcher, purse-snatcher, embezzler, larcener, rustler. "One who just has a habit of finding things before people lose them."—Joe E. Lewis.

thieve *v.* steal, rob, burglarize, *rip off, pilfer, filch, shoplift, snatch, *swipe, *walk off with, purloin, appropriate, *heist, embezzle, swindle, cheat.

thievery *n.* theft, robbery, larceny, grand larceny, petty larceny, burglary, stealing, pilfering, shoplifting, kleptomania, embezzlement, swindle.

thin *v.* dilute, cut, reduce, rarefy, water down, decrease, trim, weaken, attenuate, prune. ANT. *thicken, concentrate, condense.*

thin *a.* **1.** SLENDER slight, slim, skinny, lean, emaciated, bony, spare, wispy, *thin as linguine, skin and bones, half-starved, scrawny, gaunt, rawboned, spindly. **2.** SCANTY sparse, rare, few and far between, meager, skimpy, deficient. **3.** WATERY diluted, weak, runny, rarefied. **4.** SHEER transparent, airy, fine, diaphanous, delicate, translucent, wispy, flimsy. ANT. *1. fat, obese, heavy, *broad in*

the beam. *2. full, thick, teeming, swarming. 3. condensed, concentrated, thick. 4. opaque, heavy, dense.*

thing *n.* **1.** ARTICLE object, item, subject, element, substance, matter, entity, it, body, being, creature, organism. **2.** THINGAMAJIG gadget, device, contrivance, *doohickey, *thingamabob, contraption, apparatus, gizmo, widget, mechanism, *whatchamacallit, *dingus, *whatsit. **3.** DEED act, event, happening, action, feat, performance, accomplishment, exploit. **4.** MATTER affair, circumstance, happening, situation. **5.** SEE THINGS

thingamajig *n.* SEE THING, 2.

things *n.* belongings, possessions, stuff, personal effects, paraphernalia, outfit, equipment, trappings, accoutrements, gear.

think *v.* **1.** CONTEMPLATE meditate, cogitate, ponder, concentrate, focus on, study, analyze, intellectualize, turn over in one's mind, evaluate, reflect, deliberate, mull over, ruminate, consider, deduce, reason, conceive, imagine, picture, remember, marshal one's thoughts. **2.** BELIEVE judge, opine, suppose, assume, presume, surmise, gather, guess, imagine, understand, reckon, conclude, estimate.

thinkable *a.* conceivable, imaginable, comprehensible, feasible, possible. ANT. *unthinkable, inconceivable.*

thinker *n.* philosopher, deep thinker, sage, wise man, scholar.

thinking *n.* thought, brain power, contemplation, meditation, cogitation, concentration, study, analysis, evaluation, reflection, deliberation, reasoning, logic, deduction, speculation, *putting two and two together. "The magic of the mind."—Lord Byron. "The talking of the soul with itself."—Plato.

thin-skinned *a.* sensitive, oversensitive, ultrasensitive, hypersensitive, easily hurt, delicate, vulnerable, easily offended, touchy, irritable. ANT. *thick-skinned, hardened, callous, insensitive.*

third world *n.* undeveloped nations, emergent nations.

thirst *n.* craving, desire, want, longing, hunger, hankering, appetite, yen, lust, thirstiness.

thirst *v.* crave, desire, want, long for, hunger for, hanker for, have an appetite for, have a yen for, lust after.

thong *n.* strap, strip, leather, lace, whiplash, leash.

thorn *n.* **1.** PRICKLE needle, barb, spike, point,

spine. **2.** THORN IN ONE'S SIDE irritation, trouble, nuisance, pain, plague, torment, affliction, curse.

thorny *a.* **1.** PRICKLY brambly, barbed, briery, spiny, spiked, bristly. **2.** DIFFICULT complicated, ticklish, delicate, troublesome, challenging, nettlesome, trying, touchy, sticky. ANT. *1. soft, smooth. 2. easy, simple, *child's play.*

thorough *a.* **1.** EXHAUSTIVE complete, total, comprehensive, thoroughgoing, in-depth, *A to Z, all-out, all-inclusive, *whole hog, full, painstaking, *down to the last detail. **2.** ABSOLUTE out-and-out, utter, total, complete, entire, perfect, unmitigated, sheer. **3.** EXACT accurate, painstaking, precise, meticulous, careful, scrupulous. ANT. *1. partial, incomplete, superficial. 2. partial, qualified. 3. sloppy, slipshod, careless.*

thoroughbred *a.* **1.** PURE unmixed, full-blooded, pedigreed. **2.** EXCELLENT first-rate, first-class, trained, educated, cultured, refined, genteel, aristocratic. ANT. *1. half-breed, mongrel, crossbred, mixed breed. 2. second-class, second-rate, unrefined.*

thoroughfare *n.* street, road, passage, highway, avenue, boulevard, thruway, beltway, expressway, turnpike.

thoroughgoing *a.* **1.** THOROUGH exhaustive, painstaking, precise, in-depth, *down to the last detail, precise, exact, meticulous. **2.** COMPLETE utter, absolute, unmitigated, out-and-out, unqualified, sheer. ANT. *1. superficial, partial, careless. 2. partial, incomplete, qualified.*

thoroughly *adv.* completely, utterly, entirely, totally, absolutely, downright, wholly, quite, exhaustively. ANT. *partially, superficially, incompletely.*

thought *n.* **1.** THINKING cogitation, intellection, cerebration, concentration, reflection, consideration, cognition, study, meditation, deliberation, contemplation, rumination, reflection, pondering, speculating, weighing, brown study, reasoning, rationalization, calculation, deduction, introspection. "Dreams till their effects be tried."—Shakespeare. "An electrochemical soup stirred by pleasure, pain and nervous impulses."—Jack E. French. "Feelings gone to seed."—John Burroughs. **2.** INTELLECT imagination, brain power, intelligence, reason, smarts, *gray matter. **3.** IDEA concept, notion, theory, hypothesis, *brainstorm, belief, assumption,

conclusion, opinion, surmise. **4.** ATTENTION consideration, regard, study, notice.

thoughtful *a.* **1.** THINKING meditative, reflective, introspective, pondering, lost in thought, intellectual, meditative, pensive, abstracted. **2.** CONSIDERATE kind, mindful, attentive, solicitous, graceful, diplomatic, sensitive, unselfish, nice, sweet. ANT. *1. mindless, unthinking, brainless. 2. thoughtless, inconsiderate, inattentive.*

thoughtless *a.* inconsiderate, insensitive, unthinking, selfish, inattentive, careless, negligent, heedless, oblivious, rude, impolite, discourteous. ANT. *thoughtful, considerate, attentive.*

thought-provoking *a.* provocative, stimulating, challenging, interesting. ANT. *boring, shallow.*

thrash *v.* **1.** FLOG whip, beat, lash, flail, strap, switch, cane, scourge, flagellate. **2.** DEFEAT SOUNDLY *skunk, *kill, *blow away, rout, drub, *kick butt, *whoop, *whip, trounce, shellac.

thread *n.* **1.** LINE filament, string, yarn, strand, cord, fiber. **2.** THEME motif, subject.

threadbare *a.* **1.** WORN ragged, tattered, motheaten, frayed, holey, raveled, *ratty, shabby. **2.** STALE overused, shopworn, commonplace, clichéd, banal, tired, stock, hackneyed, *old hat, *ho-hum. ANT. *1. new, plush, luxurious. 2. fresh, original, new.*

threat *n.* intimidation, scare, menace, danger, peril, hazard, jeopardy, dark cloud on the horizon, *sword of Damocles, portent, *sleeping giant.

threaten *v.* intimidate, scare, menace, *put the fear of God into, *scare the bejesus out of one, terrorize, frighten, alarm, bully, cow, put on alert, loom.

threatening *a.* intimidating, menacing, terrorizing, frightening, scary, sinister, ominous, impending, looming, foreboding. ANT. *encouraging, bright, reassuring.*

threesome *n.* ménage à trois, trio.

thresh *v.* beat, flail, thrash.

threshold *n.* **1.** DOORSILL entrance. **2.** BEGINNING start, opening, entrance, brink, verge, dawn, starting point, debut, onset. ANT. *2. close, end.*

thrift *n.* thriftiness, frugality, economy, economizing, saving, conservation, parsimony, penny-pinching, scrimping, cheapness. ANT. *waste, improvidence, extravagance.*

thrifty *a.* frugal, economical, economizing,

conserving, saving, parsimonious, *penny-pinching, miserly, stingy, provident. ANT. wasteful, improvident, extravagant.

thrill n. 1. EXCITEMENT *rush, *adrenalin rush, *head rush, kick, *spine-tingling experience, chills, blast, titillation, *charge, *mind-blower, *high, exhilaration, sensation, *heart-pounder, *hair-raiser. 2. TREMOR quiver, fluttering, tingling, vibration.

thrill v. excite, stimulate, electrify, *adrenalize, *give a rush, exhilarate, titillate, *blow one's mind, stir, *turn on, *give a charge. ANT. tranquilize, put to sleep.

thrive v. flourish, prosper, grow, blossom, mushroom, burgeon, luxuriate, succeed, boom, progress, do well, be vigorous. ANT. fail, die, wither, languish.

throat n. neck, gullet, larynx, pharynx, trachea, Adam's apple.

throaty a. hoarse, guttural, husky, gravel-voiced, raspy, whiskey-voiced. ANT. squeaky, high-pitched.

throb n. pulsation, pulse, throbbing, beat, tremor, palpitation, thump.

throb v. pulsate, pulse, beat, palpitate, thump, pound, flutter, vibrate, quiver, drum.

throes n. spasms, pangs, pains, convulsions, seizures, paroxysm.

throne n. seat of power, cathedral.

throng n. crowd, multitude, horde, bunch, congregation, swarm, mass, mob, flock, army, flood, pack, press, host.

throng v. crowd, gather, assemble, congregate, swarm, mass, mob, flock, flood, pack, press, *stand cheek to jowl.

throttle n. accelerator, gas pedal, choke, butterfly valve.

throttle v. 1. CHOKE strangle, garrote, suffocate, smother, stifle, asphyxiate, *cut off one's wind. 2. SUPPRESS censor, shut up, silence, squelch, gag, inhibit.

through a. done, finished, completed, over, ended, concluded, terminated. ANT. underway, beginning.

through prep. 1. IN ONE SIDE AND OUT THE OTHER from one end to the other, from start to finish. 2. BY WAY OF via, inside, in and out of.

throw n. pitch, lob, toss, pass, shot, delivery, hurl, cast, fling, heave, chuck.

throw v. pitch, lob, toss, pass, shoot, hurl, cast, fling, heave, chuck, deliver, propel, catapult, launch, peg, thrust.

throw out v. throw away, dispose of, dump, discard, scrap, cast off, dispense with, junk, jettison.

throw up v. vomit, regurgitate, upchuck, puke, disgorge, *spit up, *barf, *ralph, spew, hurl, *toss one's cookies, *blow lunch, retch, *have the dry heaves.

thrust n. 1. PUSH shove, lunge, drive, advance, propulsion, stab, plunge, poke. 2. ATTACK blitz, blitzkrieg, onslaught, offensive, charge, push, drive, raid, strike. 3. ENERGY power, drive, horsepower, lift, pickup. 4. POINT gist, force, meaning, essence, substance.

thrust v. 1. PUSH shove, lunge, drive, force, advance, power, propel, throw, stab, plunge, poke. 2. IMPOSE ONESELF intrude, force oneself into, inject.

thud n. thump, bump, bang, *whack, *clunk, rap, boom, crash, slam, clump, plunk, blow.

thug n. hoodlum, *hood, brute, gangster, mobster, mafioso, ruffian, hooligan, *roughneck, *goon, gunman, killer, murderer.

thumbnail a. brief, concise, small, minute. ANT. grand, large-scale.

thump n. SEE THUD

thump v. strike, hit, beat, pound, pommel, *slug, slam, drub, cudgel, bludgeon.

thunder n. thunderclap, boom, rumbling, crack, *whiplash, roll, crash, peal, explosion, roar, discharge, report, reverberation.

thunder v. 1. BOOM rumble, crack, roll, crash, peal, explode, discharge, reverberate. 2. FULMINATE roar, boom, shout, bellow, yell, growl, curse, bark, denounce.

thunderbolt n. lightning.

thunderstorm n. thundershower, thunder squall, *thunder-boomer, cloudburst, electrical storm.

WORD FIND

cloud: cumulonimbus, thunderhead

lightning: ball lightning, chain lightning, heat lightning

mythical creature of North American Indians thought to cause: thunderbird

SEE CLOUD, RAIN, STORM

thunderstruck a. shocked, floored, staggered, amazed, astonished, dumbstruck, dumbfounded, flabbergasted, *knocked for a loop, *bowled over. ANT. unmoved, unruffled.

thus adv. therefore, so, hence, ergo.

thwart v. obstruct, hinder, frustrate, slow, stop, roadblock, foil, defeat, check, inhibit, prevent, block, preclude, confound. ANT. facilitate, help, assist, ease.

tiara n. crown, coronet, diadem.

tic n. spasm, contraction, nervous tic, twitch, jerk.

tick n. click, tap, beat, pulse, second.

ticket *n.* **1.** PASS admission, voucher, receipt, stub, token, coupon, *ducat, raincheck, certificate. **2.** LABEL tag, sticker, slip. **3.** BALLOT slate, roster.

WORD FIND

free ticket or pass: *Annie Oakley
resell tickets far above cost: scalp
traffic ticket: summons, citation, fine

tickle *v.* please, delight, thrill, excite, gratify, *tickle to death, *tickle pink, amuse, make one smile, make one laugh.

ticklish *a.* delicate, sensitive, prickly, dicey, touchy, risky, slippery, difficult, thorny, tricky, awkward. ANT. *simple, uncomplicated, straightforward.*

ticky-tacky *a. Sl.* cheap, *tacky, poor quality, dull, shoddy, shabby, *rinky-dink, *chintzy, *cheesy, tawdry.

tidal wave *n.* tsunami, tidal bore, eagre.

tidbit *n.* morsel, bit, mouthful, spoonful, piece, titbit.

tide *n.* flood, wash, ebb, neap, spring tide, rip tide, high tide, low tide. SEE BEACH, OCEAN

tidings *n.* news, information, report, word, communication, *scoop, *lowdown, *scuttlebutt.

tide over *v.* keep one's head above water, keep one going, help, assist, *bridge the gap.

tidy *v.* neaten, clean, order, unclutter, arrange, pick up, spruce up, fix up, straighten up, groom. ANT. *mess, clutter, disorder.*

tidy *a.* **1.** NEAT clean, shipshape, orderly, *spick-and-span, trim, well-ordered, spruce, uncluttered, *in apple pie order, organized. **2.** CONSIDERABLE large, substantial, generous, respectable, healthy, ample. ANT. *1. messy, sloppy, unkempt. 2. small, piddling.*

tie *n.* **1.** FASTENING fastener, connection, knot, link, catch, clip, string, rope, strap, cord, cinch, sash, binding. **2.** NECKTIE ascot, string tie, cravat, bow tie. **3.** RELATIONSHIP association, bond, tie-in, connection, kinship, friendship, liaison, affiliation. **4.** DEADLOCK draw, standoff, *sudden death faceoff.

tie *v.* **1.** FASTEN connect, knot, bind, link, catch, clip, string up, strap, cinch, lash, interlace, moor, secure, tether, leash. **2.** RESTRICT limit, stop, hinder, inhibit, hobble, check, bind, fetter. **3.** MATCH UP be dead even, *be neck and neck. ANT. *1. unfasten, untie, loose, release. 2. facilitate, free, liberate.*

tier *n.* row, line, file, rank, echelon, grade, level, story, floor.

tie-up *n.* snag, gridlock, bottleneck, logjam, traffic jam, *snafu, stoppage.

tiff *n.* quarrel, argument, spat, fight, altercation, squabble, wrangle, run-in, clash, disagreement, *words, *row. ANT. *peace, accord, *meeting of the minds.*

tiger *n.* predator, *big cat, carnivore, hunter, stalker, saber-toothed tiger, jaguar, leopard.

tight *a.* **1.** CLOSE snug, skintight, form-fitting, close-fitting, confined, cramped, taut, drawn. **2.** FIXED secured, secure, set, made fast, immovable, firm, locked. **3.** AIRTIGHT watertight, sealed, plugged, secure, sound, hermetically sealed, impervious, impermeable, nonporous, leakproof. **4.** RIGOROUS strict, stringent, severe, restraining, demanding. **5.** DIFFICULT trying, precarious, delicate, ticklish, tricky, perilous, tough, prickly. **6.** STINGY tightfisted, sparing, frugal, cheap, miserly, penurious, parsimonious, *penny-pinching. ANT. *1. loose, slack, baggy. 2. loose, unsecured, slack. 3. porous, holey. 4. undemanding, mild, easy. 5. easy, simple. 6. generous, charitable, giving.*

tighten *a.* firm up, close up, fix, secure, lock up, tauten, tense, stretch, contract, squeeze, constrict, screw. ANT. *loosen, slacken, unfasten.*

tightfisted *a.* cheap, stingy, miserly, sparing, frugal, *penny-pinching, penurious, parsimonious, niggardly, greedy. ANT. *generous, charitable, giving.*

tight-lipped *a.* silent, mute, taciturn, reserved, reticent, quiet, close-mouthed, secretive, mum. ANT. *loquacious, talkative.*

tightwad *n.* miser, *cheapskate, *Scrooge, *penny-pincher, *pinchpenny. ANT. *philanthropist, giver, free-spender, spendthrift.*

till *n.* cash box, cash drawer, cash tray, cash register.

till *v.* plow, harrow, cultivate, work, turn over, dig, hoe, spade, dress.

tilt *n.* incline, inclination, slant, slope, lean, pitch, grade, gradient, rake.

tilt *v.* tip, incline, slant, slope, lean, turn, upend, list, cant, angle.

timber *n.* **1.** WOOD beam, joist, girder, rafter, pile, board, spar, log, lumber. **2.** TREES forest, woods, woodland, timberland.

timberland *n.* woodland, forest, stumpage.

timbre *n.* tone, pitch, voice.

time *n.* **1.** DURATION span, stretch, spell, period, interval, term, age, epoch, era, juncture, point, second, instant, moment, hour, day, month, year, century, millennium, eon, infinity, continuance, chronology, fourth dimension, *tick of the clock, *water under the bridge, *sand through the hourglass. "A file that wears and makes no noise."—Henry G. Bohn. "A flowing river."—Christopher Morley. "A sandpile we run our fingers in."—Carl Sandburg. "The moving image of eternity."—Plato. "A storm in which we are all lost."—William Carlos Williams. "Time like an ever-rolling stream bears all its sons away."—Isaac Watts. 2. OCCASION opportunity, opening, chance, shot.

time-honored a. classic, vintage, time-tested, venerable, respected, traditional. ANT. newfangled, untested.

timeless a. eternal, neverending, everlasting, ageless, perpetual, immortal, immemorial, infinite, undying. ANT. temporary, passing, ephemeral.

timely a. opportune, well-timed, favorable, auspicious, convenient, fitting, propitious, seasonable. ANT. untimely, unfavorable, inopportune.

timepiece n. clock, watch, sundial, hourglass, horologe.

timetable n. schedule, chronology, timeline, plan.

timid a. afraid, fearful, timorous, mousy, fainthearted, *wimpy, *lily-livered, *chicken, sheepish, cowardly, spineless, shy, bashful, nervous. ANT. courageous, brave, bold, *ballsy, fearless.

timorous a. SEE TIMID

tinderbox n. explosive situation, volatile situation, *hot spot, trouble spot, war zone, powder keg, time bomb, combustible situation.

tinge n. trace, touch, hint, suggestion, smattering, drop, tincture, shade, tint, color, coloring, tone, pigment.

tinge v. shade, color, tint, give a touch of, give a trace of, flavor, season.

tingle n. tickle, electrical sensation, sting, prickle, thrill.

tingle v. tickle, sting, prickle, crawl, creep, quiver.

tinker v. putter, fix, mend, doctor, fuss over, fiddle with, *monkey around with, *mess with, toy with, *diddle, fumble with.

tinkle n. ring, jingle, tingle, tinkling, ding, tintinnabulation, plink, chime.

tinkle v. ring, jingle, tingle, ding, jangle, tintinnabulate, plink, chime.

tinsel a. gaudy, showy, glittery, flashy, garish, ornate, tawdry, cheap. ANT. authentic, quality, valuable.

tint n. hue, tinge, shade, tone, color, cast, tinge, tincture, pigmentation, complexion, touch, trace, hint.

tintinnabulation n. ringing, tinkling, jingling, jangling.

tiny a. small, diminutive, little, wee, puny, miniature, minute, miniscule, Lilliputian, dwarf, pygmy, *pint-sized, *pocket-sized, teeny, *itsy-bitsy, microscopic, infinitesimal. ANT. huge, gigantic, gargantuan, towering, massive.

tip n. 1. INFORMATION *word to the wise, advice, *pointer, *hot tip, suggestion, helpful hint, clue, warning, tip-off, inkling. 2. GRATUITY percentage, compensation, consideration. 3. POINT nib, head, top, peak, pinnacle, apex, summit, crown.

tip v. 1. COMPENSATE *take care of, pay, reward for service. 2. TILT incline, overturn, upend, capsize, upset, topple, slant, lean, turn over, cant.

tipsy a. intoxicated, inebriated, unsteady, *three sheets to the wind, woozy, *pickled, *loaded, *crocked, under the influence. ANT. sober, *stone sober.

TIRADE n. [TYE rade] a long, scolding or condemning speech. Before we knew it, he was launching into another tirade about faulty government policy. SYN. harangue, diatribe, lecture, denunciation, condemnation, *jeremiad, invective, vituperation, censure, *tongue-lashing, outburst.

tire v. 1. EXHAUST wear out, weary, fatigue, drain, *run out of juice, *run one's battery down, enervate, *bush, *poop out, burn out, flag, fail. 2. GET SICK OF lose interest, be bored with, lose patience with, lose fascination with. ANT. 1. energize, invigorate, revive. 2. interest, be fascinated with, stimulate.

tired a. 1. EXHAUSTED worn out, weary, fatigued, drained, *out of juice, out of energy, *run down, enervated, sleepy, drowsy, *bushed, *pooped, burned out, *all in, *beat, spent, flagging, *dog-tired, *dead, *tuckered out. 2. SICK OF bored with, *fed up with. ANT. 1. energized, invigorated, revived, refreshed. 2. fascinated by, stimulated by.

tireless a. untiring, energetic, *high octane, unflagging, hyperactive, *supercharged, indefatigable, determined, persevering, industious, unremitting, slogging, plugging. ANT. tiring, flagging, faltering, failing.

tiresome a. wearisome, tiring, exhausting, fatiguing, arduous, demanding, wearing, strenuous, laborious, boring, dull, tedious, *humdrum, monotonous. ANT. *energizing, invigorating, stimulating.*

tit *n. Sl.* teat, nipple, breast, *boob. SEE BREAST

titan *n.* giant, colossus, deity, Zeus, Prometheus.

titanic *a.* gigantic, colossal, gargantuan, towering, huge, massive, immense, enormous, Herculean, monstrous, Brobdingnagian. ANT. *tiny, microscopic, Lilliputian.*

tithe *v.* levy. SEE TAX

TITILLATE *v.* [TIT ul ate] to stimulate or arouse, excite. *Rock videos are often designed to titillate.* SYN. stimulate, arouse, excite, *turn on, thrill, *stir one's blood, provoke, tantalize, seduce, *tickle one's fancy. ANT. *repulse, annoy.*

title *n.* 1. NAME appellation, epithet, designation, *moniker, nickname, *handle, cognomen, denomination. 2. HEADING caption, legend, name, label, subtitle, inscription. 3. CHAMPIONSHIP crown, claim, right. 4. PROOF OF OWNERSHIP deed.

titter *n.* giggle, laugh, suppressed laugh, snicker, snigger, chuckle, cackle.

titter *v.* giggle, tee-hee, laugh under one's breath, snicker, snigger, chuckle, cackle.

tittle *n.* dot, particle, iota, speck, whit, jot, scintilla, mote, drop.

titular *a.* nominal, by name only, by title only, so-called, honorary, token, self-styled. ANT. *actual, real.*

toady *n.* sycophant, flatterer, *kiss-up, *brownnose, *yes-man, bootlicker, apple polisher, lickspittle, fawner, flunky, lackey, groveler, toadeater.

toady *v.* flatter, *kiss up, *brownnose, fawn, grovel, kowtow, *apple polish, bootlick, curry favor, *suck up to, *fall all over, bow and scrape. ANT. *disrespect, defy, abuse.*

toast *n.* drink, salute, salutation, compliment, honor, *cheers, *to your health, *here's mud in your eye, *skoal, *salut, *salud, *mazel tov, prosit.

toast *v.* 1. SALUTE drink to, honor, compliment, share a sentiment, raise one's glass to, hail. 2. BROWN BREAD heat, warm.

toastmaster *n.* master of ceremonies, emcee, M.C., speaker, host, moderator.

tobacco *n.* weed, leaves, perique, caporal. "Pernicious weed."—William Cowper. "That hell fume in God's clean air."—Carry Nation. "A lone man's companion, a bachelor's friend, a hungry man's food, a sad man's cordial, a wakeful man's sleep, and a chilly man's fire."—Charles Kingsley.

WORD FIND
ash left in pipe after burning: dottle
box: humidor
chew: quid, plug
poor grade: shag
powder inhaled or chewed: snuff
smoke, aversion to the: misocapnia
smoke, one who has an aversion to the: misocapnist
stinky: mundungus

tocsin *n.* alarm, bell, warning.

to-do *n.* fuss, commotion, bother, uproar, *brouhaha, stir, *flap, *hoopla, ado, hubbub, furor, excitement, hurly-burly, *tempest in a teapot.

toddle *v.* falter, totter, be unsteady on one's feet.

toddler *n.* baby, tot, child, preschooler, *rug rat, *holy terror. SEE BABY

toehold *n.* foothold, footing, purchase.

toga *n.* robe, gown, garment, wrap.

WORD FIND
belt formed by the twisted folds of: baltaeus
dark toga for mourning: toga pulla
purple toga with gold embroidery, worn by emperors, consuls: toga picta

together *adv.* 1. AS ONE all at once, all at the same time, in unison, in concert, collectively, simultaneously, en masse, conjointly, concurrently, *in sync, in tandem. 2. IN SUCCESSION consecutively, in a row, successively. ANT. *1. singly, alone, separately. 2. randomly.*

togs *n.* clothes, clothing, *duds, outfit, wear, apparel, *toggery, attire, dress, garb, gear, *threads.

toil *n.* labor, work, grind, drudgery, *sweat of one's brow, exertion, struggle, pains, *elbow grease, slavery. ANT. *ease, leisure, relaxation.*

toil *v.* work, labor, sweat, exert, struggle, slave, *break one's back, *bust one's hump, drudge, strain, *plug away, *knock oneself out, *drive oneself into the grave. ANT. *relax, *take it easy, rest.*

toilet *n.* 1. BATHROOM *john, rest room, wash room, *little boy's room, *little girl's room, head, latrine, *can, *privy, *loo, *throne room, outhouse, *potty, commode, flush, urinal, bidet. 2. GROOMING dressing, toilette, clean-up, bathing.

toilsome *a.* laborious, hard, arduous, difficult, backbreaking, strenuous, fatiguing, exhausting, wearing, demanding. ANT. *easy, simple, effortless.*

toke *n. Sl.* puff, *hit.

token *n.* **1.** INDICATION sign, evidence, mark, expression, manifestation, testimony, testament, symbol. **2.** KEEPSAKE souvenir, memento, reminder.

token *a.* superficial, symbolic, nominal, minimal, perfunctory, for show. ANT. *genuine.*

tolerable *a.* **1.** ENDURABLE sufferable, bearable. **2.** FAIR passable, acceptable, all right, okay, good enough, *so-so, *not bad, mediocre, middling, adequate, sufficient, satisfactory. ANT. *1. intolerable, unbearable. 2. excellent, first-rate, unacceptable, unsatisfactory.*

tolerance *n.* **1.** ACCEPTANCE understanding, open-mindedness, broad-mindedness, grace, sensitivity, liberal-mindedness, magnanimity, goodwill, lack of prejudice, sympathy, receptivity, indulgence. **2.** ENDURANCE strength, mental toughness, stamina, stoicism, sufferance, grit, fortitude. ANT. *1. prejudice, bigotry, intolerance. 2. weakness.*

tolerant *a.* accepting, understanding, open-minded, broad-minded, gracious, sensitive, liberal-minded, magnanimous, sympathetic, receptive, indulgent, unprejudiced. ANT. *rejecting, prejudiced, bigoted, intolerant.*

tolerate *v.* **1.** ACCEPT understand, recognize, respect, be open-minded toward, be broad-minded toward, be sensitive toward, be liberal-minded toward, indulge. **2.** ALLOW permit, put up with, look the other way, let go, condone, bear, stand for, be lenient, indulge. **3.** ENDURE bear, suffer through, stand, put up with, take, *tough out, *stomach, *sit still for. ANT. *1. reject, be intolerant, disapprove. 2. prohibit, forbid, proscribe. 3. collapse, *cave in, *lose it.*

toll *n.* tax, charge, fee, user fee, levy, tariff, assessment, duty, impost, dues. SEE MONEY

toll *v.* ring, sound, strike, clang, chime, peal, knell, announce, summon, signal.

tomb *n.* vault, chamber, grave, crypt, mausoleum, sepulchre, catacomb, ossuary, cenotaph, monument. SEE CEMETERY

tomboy *n.* hoyden, gamine, *one of the boys.

tombstone *n.* gravestone, headstone, monument, stele, grave marker. SEE CEMETERY

tome *n.* book, volume, reference book, opus.

tomfoolery *n.* silliness, foolishness, childish behavior, nonsense, *monkeyshines, *shenanigans, antics, joking, jesting, *horseplay, high jinks. ANT. *seriousness, gravity.*

ton *n.* load, truckload, mass, huge amount, pile, two thousand pounds, short ton, long ton.

tone *n.* **1.** PITCH intonation, sound, note, modulation, voice, frequency, timbre. **2.** ATTITUDE spirit, quality, mood, tenor, air, mode, manner. **3.** SHADE hue, color, tint, tinge, cast.

tone down *v.* quiet down, moderate, temper, soften, mute, dampen.

tongs *n.* pincers, clamp, forceps, *graspers.

tongue *n.* language, dialect, speech, talk, vernacular, idiom, lingo, parlance, native tongue, jargon, slang, argot, articulation. "A wild beast; once let loose it is difficult to chain."—Baltasar Gracian. "The only edged tool that grows keener with constant use."—Washington Irving.

tongue-in-cheek *a.* jokingly, kiddingly, in jest, in fun, ironic, insincere, facetiously. ANT. *sincere, serious.*

tongue-tied *a.* speechless, at a loss for words, dumbstruck, mute, inarticulate, shy, bashful, reticent, reserved, *hung by the tongue. ANT. *loquacious, verbose, long-winded, *motor-mouthed.*

tonic *n.* *pick-me-up, restorative, *shot in the arm, *bracer, stimulant, *upper, drug, medicine, beverage.

tony *a. Sl.* stylish, fashionable, luxurious, chic. ANT. *frumpy, cheap.*

too *adv.* **1.** ALSO as well, additionally, likewise, to boot, furthermore, besides, moreover. **2.** EXCESSIVELY in excess, unduly, beyond, extremely, inordinately.

tool *n.* **1.** IMPLEMENT instrument, utensil, gadget, labor-saving device, apparatus, mechanism, machine, contraption, contrivance, *gizmo, *doohickey, *whatsit.

WORD FIND

SAWS

band, saw comprised of rotating, toothed: band saw

chained blade: chain saw

circular saw, stationary: buzz saw, bench saw

curve-cutting, electrical saw: jigsaw, saber saw

curve-cutting handsaw: compass saw, keyhole saw, coping saw

curving ornamentation, cuts: scroll saw

grain, cuts across: crosscut saw

grain, cuts with: ripsaw

hand-powered saw used with sawbuck: bucksaw

hole-cutting saw: dial saw

Japanese craftsman's hatchetlike saw for cutting dovetails: dozuki

Japanese craftsman's saw with dual-edged blade that cuts on the pull stroke: ryoba

metal-cutting: hacksaw

miter-cutting circular saw: miter saw

miter-cutting guide: miter box
shallow-cutting or veneer-cutting saw: veneer saw
stationary, electrical saw with mobile blade-holding arm: radial arm saw
two-person hand-powered saw for cutting timbers: whipsaw
wire coated with tungsten carbide, used by campers: pocket saw
KNIVES, PIERCERS, CARVERS, CUTTERS
axlike tool for trimming wood: adz
brush or sugar-cane cutter: machete
fabric-cutting shears: pinking shears
glass-cutting device: glass-cutter
grain-cutter with short, curving blade: sickle
grass-cutter with long, curving blade: scythe
hole-piercer, esp. for leather: awl
metal shears: tin snips, hawk's bill snips
pencillike precision knife for cutting light material: precision knife, *Xacto knife
pipe-cutting tool: pipe cutter
pole with hook on end, used by lumberjacks: pickaroon
retractable blade, hollow handle with multiple-uses: utility knife
wedgelike tool that is hammered: chisel
wire-cutting pliers: wire cutter
SHARPENERS, SHAVERS, SMOOTHERS
abrader: file, rasp
gouger: router
planing tool: bullnose plane, chamfering plane, planer, spokeshave
polisher: buffer
sander: belt sander, disk sander
stone for sharpening blades: whetstone
wood-turning machine used to cut, plane and shape: lathe
HAMMERS AND NAIL-PULLERS
automatic, mechanical nail-driver: nail gun
brad driver: brad pusher
clawed, nail-pulling hammer: claw hammer
claws, hammer with straight: rip hammer
hammer with rounded instead of clawed back: ball peen hammer, machinist's hammer
long or short-handled hammer with very heavy metal head: sledgehammer
mallet filled with shot to prevent rebounding: deadblow hammer
nail-pulling steel bar resembling crowbar: cat's paw
sledgehammer, small: engineer's hammer
sledgehammer, sometimes having one ax edge: maul
square or cylindrical head made of wood or rubber, hammer with: mallet

tack driver, magnetized: tack hammer
WRENCHES AND PLIERS
adjustable jaws, pliers with: slip-joint pliers, tongue-and-groove pliers
adjustable jaws, steel wrench with: adjustable wrench, *crescent wrench
clamping pliers: locking pliers, *Vise-Grips
English term for wrench: spanner
L-shaped, hexagonal rod: allen wrench, hex key
lug nut tightener, loosener: lug wrench
needle-nosed pliers for manipulating wire: long-nose pliers
open jaws on one end and closed, toothed ring on the other, wrench with: combination wrench
oversized nuts, large-mouthed wrench used to turn: spud wrench
pipe-turning wrench equipped with power-assisting chain: chain wrench, pipe wrench
plumber's flat bar with varied openings down its length: faucet spanner
plumber's heavy adjustable wrench: monkey wrench, pipe wrench
ratcheting wrench with variable socket fittings: socket wrench
screwdriver-like wrench for turning nuts and bolts in tight spaces: nut driver
toothed rings for tightening or loosening nuts, wrench with: box wrench
wire-manipulating pliers: lineman's pliers, electrician's pliers, long-nose pliers, fence pliers
SCREWDRIVERS
crisscross driving head, screwdriver with: Phillips head screwdriver
powered screwdriver: screw gun
ratcheting screwdriver turned by pushing down on handle: return spiral ratchet screwdriver, impact driver
short screwdriver: *stubby
S-shaped tool that is cranked for use in tight spaces: offset screwdriver, cranked screwdriver
DRILL AND RELATED TOOLS
bit-holder: chuck
borer: auger, trepan, gimlet
drilling part, variable sized: bit
hand-cranked drill: eggbeater
hole enlarger: reamer
stationary power drill: drill press
2. PUPPET instrument, pawn, dupe, *stooge.
toot *n.* honk, whistle, crow, beep, blast.
toot *v.* honk, whistle, crow, beep, blow, blast.

Tooth–Torture

tooth n. **1.** MOUTH GRINDER OR CUTTER molar, incisor, fang, bicuspid, tusk, *chopper. SEE TEETH **2.** TINE OR COG prong, projection, sprocket, snag, spur.

toothed a. notched, indented, serrated, dentate.

toothpaste n. dentrifice.

toothsome a. tasty, palatable, flavorful, good-tasting, delicious, *yummy, scrumptious, mouth-watering, savory, appetizing, *finger-licking good, delectable. ANT. *disgusting, gross, *yucky, nauseating.*

top n. **1.** HIGHEST POINT peak, pinnacle, summit, apex, zenith, height, roof, crown, crest, vertex, cap. **2.** LID cap, cover, stopper, cork. ANT. *1. bottom, low point, foot.*

top v. **1.** SURPASS best, beat, outdistance, outperform, outclass, eclipse, exceed, outshine, outdo, dominate, *leave the competition in one's wake, *blow away, *skunk. **2.** COVER cap, crown, put over. ANT. *1. fail, lose, lag behind, trail.*

top a. highest, uppermost, topmost, leading, chief, dominant, greatest, best, paramount, highest-ranking, capital, most important, supreme, foremost, preeminent. ANT. *bottom, lowest, worst.*

top-drawer a. first-rate, first-class, excellent, the best. ANT. *mediocre, second-rate.*

top hat n. gibus, stovepipe hat.

topic n. subject, subject matter, point of discussion, issue, question, material, theme, problem, text, business, thesis.

topical a. current, contemporary, in the news, up-to-the-minute, up-to-date, popular, local, provincial. ANT. *out-of-date, *yesterday's news.*

top-level a. high-echelon, top-ranking, ranking, chief, leading. ANT. *low-level, minor.*

top-notch a. first-rate, first-class, top-drawer, excellent, the best, supreme, the greatest, A-1, *blue-chip. ANT. *the worst, poor, low.*

topple v. fall, totter, pitch, collapse, tip over, founder, overturn, tumble, knock over, upset, knock down, bring down, overthrow, vanquish, unseat, unhorse.

tops a. SEE TOP-NOTCH

topsy-turvy a. upside-down, upended, wrong side up, inside-out, mixed up, jumbled, confused, backwards, *ass-backwards, helter-skelter, *pell-mell, chaotic. ANT. *right-side up, orderly.*

torch n. light, flambeau, taper, firebrand, beacon.

torment n. suffering, pain, torture, anguish, agony, distress, misery, hell, irritation, trouble, plague, rack, scourge.

torment v. torture, punish, hurt, agonize, abuse, distress, trouble, bother, pain, irritate, bully, hurt, persecute, harass, aggravate, *drive crazy, plague, hector.

torn a. **1.** RIPPED cut, slashed, slit, lacerated, ragged, rent, split. **2.** DIVIDED undecided, of two minds, *on the fence.

tornado n. whirlwind, twister, cyclone, windstorm, tempest.

torpid a. dormant, sluggish, slow, inert, motionless, hibernating, unmoving, lethargic, languid, listless, phlegmatic, lazy, dull, apathetic. ANT. *active, lively, energetic.*

TORPOR n. [TOR pur] a state of inactivity or sluggishness. *The oppressive heat caused widespread torpor.* SYN. inactivity, dormancy, inertia, sluggishness, slothfulness, deadness, lifelessness, languor, listlessness, *the blahs, drowsiness, laziness, apathy. ANT. *liveliness, pep, vigor.*

torrent n. flood, rush, stream, deluge, gush, white water, rapids, waterfall, cataract, cascade, overflow, tsunami, outpouring, downpour, cloudburst, spate.

torrential a. flooding, rushing, streaming, gushing, cascading, overflowing, drowning, swamping, violent. ANT. *gentle, leisurely.*

TORRID a. [TOR id] scorching hot. Also, highly passionate or ardent. *She was having a torrid love affair with her boss.* SYN. *hot, *red hot, *white hot, scorching hot, blazing, blistering, parching, fiery, burning, flaming, sizzling, sweltering, boiling, broiling, passionate, ardent, lustful, amorous, sexually charged, sexual, erotic. ANT. *icy, cold, frigid, wintry.*

torsion n. twisting, turning, torque, stress, strain.

tortuous a. **1.** WINDING twisted, twisting, sinuous, crooked, serpentine, zigzagging, curvy, meandering, labyrinthine, involute, convoluted. **2.** DEVIOUS tricky, deceitful, deceptive, dishonest, misleading, indirect. ANT. *1. straight, direct. 2. straightforward, honest, forthright.*

torture n. agony, torment, suffering, pain, anguish, hell, crucifixion, persecution, excruciation, punishment, abuse, misery, distress, trial, tribulation, rack, third degree. SEE PUNISHMENT

torture v. torment, pain, hurt, put through hell, crucify, persecute, punish, abuse, distress,

600   *Roget's Superthesaurus*

agonize, mistreat, afflict, excruciate, rack, *work over, *make one cry uncle.

toss *n.* throw, pitch, lob, cast, chuck, fling, heave, flip, pass.

toss *v.* throw, pitch, lob, cast, chuck, fling, heave, flip, pass.

tot *n.* child, toddler, preschooler, baby, infant, *rugrat.

total *n.* whole, sum, entirety, totality, bulk, amount, aggregate.

total *v.* add up, tote, number, figure, sum up, count, compute, calculate, reckon.

total *a.* complete, whole, entire, thorough, comprehensive, *A-Z, thoroughgoing, all-inclusive, combined, full, absolute, unconditional, unqualified, unmitigated, all-out. ANT. *partial, limited, incomplete, qualified.*

TOTALITARIAN *a.* [to TAL uh TAIR ee un] authoritarian, autocratic, controlled by only one party or group. *They suffered under a totalitarian regime.* SYN. authoritarian, autocratic, fascist, dictatorial, tyrannical, monolithic, despotic, undemocratic, Nazi. ANT. *democratic.*

totally *adv.* completely, entirely, wholly, comprehensively, fully, utterly, absolutely, thoroughly, unconditionally. ANT. *partially, slightly.*

tote *v.* carry, haul, lug, transfer, convey, *schlep, transport.

totter *v.* falter, rock, stagger, wobble, topple, lurch, shake, stumble, sway, waver, bob, reel.

touch *n.* **1.** CONTACT feel, stroke, pat, kiss, caress, tap, fingering. **2.** SENSE OF TOUCH feel, tactile sense, tactility, sensation. **3.** TEXTURE feel, grain, surface. **4.** SKILL technique, way, sensitivity, finesse, art, flair. **5.** TRACE hint, suggestion, slight amount, tinge. **6.** COMMUNICATION contact.

touch *v.* **1.** FEEL finger, handle, stroke, pat, caress, palpate, fondle, paw, palm, massage. **2.** BRING INTO CONTACT strike, brush, tap, hit, graze, bump into, come up against. **3.** ADJOIN border on, abut, join, meet, converge, impinge upon. **4.** AFFECT move, *pluck at one's heartstrings, *strike a chord, make an impression, influence, arouse, excite, stimulate, stir one's soul, *hit home, *strike a nerve, disturb. **5.** REGARD bear upon, have to do with, involve, deal with, concern, pertain to. **6.** COMPARE WITH equal, rival, *hold a candle to, *be in the same league, match, *be on a par with.

touched *a.* **1.** MOVED affected, stirred, impressed, shaken, disturbed, softened. **2.** DEMENTED unbalanced, unstable, crazy, *nuts, insane, cuckoo, non compos mentis, mentally ill, mad, deranged. ANT. *1. unaffected, stony. 2. sane, competent.*

touching *a.* moving, affecting, heartwarming, soul-stirring, *heavy, disturbing, heartbreaking, heartrending, poignant, tear-jerking, pitiful, pitiable, arousing emotions. ANT. *unemotional.*

TOUCHSTONE *n.* [TUCH stone] any measure or test for worth or genuineness, a standard. *His masterpiece was the touchstone against which all others were judged.* SYN. measure, standard, yardstick, benchmark, gauge, criterion, test, acid test, ideal, model.

touchy *a.* **1.** IRRITABLE oversensitive, ultrasensitive, hypersensitive, easily offended, grouchy, testy, grumpy, cranky, petulant, moody, churlish, thin-skinned, temperamental. **2.** RISKY ticklish, delicate, prickly, precarious, sensitive, tricky, *dicey, touch-and-go. ANT. *1. easygoing, imperturbable, thick-skinned. 2. safe.*

tough *n.* *tough guy, bully, *roughneck, *punk, thug, hoodlum, ruffian, hooligan, *goon.

tough *a.* **1.** STRONG pliable, *tough as shoe leather, unbreakable, *tough as nails, rugged, hardened, durable, enduring, sound, firm, vigorous, solid, conditioned, fit, hardy, brawny, strapping, muscular, Herculean, burly, robust. **2.** CHEWY uncooked, stringy, leathery, gristly, *tough as shoe leather. **3.** STUBBORN obstinate, unyielding, inflexible, *hard-nosed, headstrong, firm, adamant, unbending, resolute, strict, severe, rough, bullheaded. **4.** HARD demanding, difficult, troublesome, vigorous, laborious, toilsome, brutal, harsh, rough, trying, formidable, complicated, complex, violent. ANT. *1. weak, soft, fragile, breakable. 2. softened, tender, tenderized, cooked. 3. yielding, acquiescent, irresolute. 4. easy, undemanding, simple.*

toughen *v.* harden, temper, anneal, season, strengthen, inure, steel, fortify, acclimate. ANT. *weaken, enfeeble.*

tough-minded *a.* realistic, practical, unsentimental, *hard-nosed. ANT. *weak, mawkish.*

toupee *n.* wig, *rug, hairpiece, peruke.

tour *n.* **1.** SHIFT turn, stint, spell, stretch, period, cycle, round. **2.** TRIP sight-seeing expedition, journey, cruise, voyage, excursion, junket, jaunt, expedition, itinerary, grand tour.

tour *v.* visit, sightsee, travel, journey, take a

trip, go on the road, *globetrot, cruise, voyage, take a junket, go on an excursion, explore, *barnstorm.

TOUR DE FORCE n. [toor de FORS] a feat of exceptional skill, talent or strength, a spectacular achievement. *The critics called his latest book a tour de force.* SYN. spectacular achievement, feat of strength, feat of great skill, grand achievement, accomplishment, masterpiece, masterwork, chef d'oeuvre.

tourist n. traveler, visitor, sightseer, *globetrotter, wayfarer, day-tripper, jet-setter, *rubbernecker.

tournament n. contest, tourney, competition, duel, meet, match, sporting event, joust, tilt.

tousled v. mussed, messed up, disordered, disarranged, tangled, entangled, disheveled, rumpled, unkempt, uncombed, ungroomed.

tout v. **1.** RECOMMEND puff, ballyhoo, praise, *talk up, brag about, extol, *hype, idealize, exaggerate, *plug, acclaim, promote. **2.** SOLICIT peddle, *drum up business, hawk, vend, pitch. ANT. *1. condemn, denigrate, *badmouth.*

tout de suite adv. at once, immediately, right away, pronto, without delay, now. ANT. *eventually, in the future.*

tow v. pull, drag, haul, lug, transport, yank, trawl.

toward prep. in the direction of, facing.

towel n. wipe, hand cloth, wash cloth.

tower n. **1.** TALL BUILDING skyscraper, high-rise, spire, monolith, obelisk, belfry, steeple, minaret, belltower. **2.** FORTRESS castle, prison, dungeon, donjon, keep, bastille.

tower v. rise over, soar, overshadow, eclipse, loom, *stand head and shoulders above, ascend.

towering a. **1.** HIGH tall, skyscraping, *cloud-puncturing, *cloud-kissing, sky high, lofty, soaring, airy, titanic, gigantic. **2.** GREAT huge, intense, powerful, extraordinary, massive, extreme, tremendous, stupendous, unrivaled, unmatched, unequaled, *head and shoulders above. ANT. *1. low, short, stubby. 2. insignificant, small, trivial.*

town n. village, settlement, hamlet, community, township, whistlestop, municipality, city, burg. "Where there is no place to go where you shouldn't be."—Alexander Woollcott.

toxic a. poisonous, unhealthy, harmful, noxious, deadly, lethal, fatal, nocuous, venomous, virulent. ANT. *nontoxic, harmless, healthy.*

toxin n. poison, noxious substance, venom, virus, pathogen, contaminant, botulism, hemlock, arsenic, deadly nightshade.

toy n. plaything, game, doll, ball, teddy bear, bauble, trinket.

toy v. play with, entertain oneself with, trifle, dally.

toy a. miniature, dwarf, pygmy, small-scale. ANT. *huge, giant.*

trace n. touch, hint, tinge, suggestion, shade, suspicion, taste, whiff, vestige, evidence, pinch, breath, drop, speck.

trace v. **1.** TRAIL track, follow, search for, shadow. **2.** ASCERTAIN dig up, root out, investigate, discover, unearth. **3.** DRAW OVER duplicate, copy, sketch, delineate.

track n. **1.** PRINT footprint, tread, imprint, trail, spoor, mark. **2.** COURSE race course, roadway, railway, path, walkway, passage.

track record n. history, statistics, *stats, performance history.

tract n. **1.** EXPANSE stretch, acreage, parcel, lot, area, extent, real estate, plot, spread, land. **2.** PAMPHLET booklet, brochure, leaflet, study, sermon, propaganda.

tractable a. obedient, docile, manageable, compliant, controllable, tame, submissive, yielding, meek, pliant, malleable. ANT. *intractable, disobedient, wild, unmanageable.*

traction n. grip, adherence, adhesion, *bite, purchase, hold, pulling, drawing.

tractor-trailer n. truck, *semi, trailer truck, eighteen wheeler.

trade n. **1.** LINE OF WORK occupation, business, profession, vocation, job, metier, craft, skill, employment, calling. **2.** BUYING AND SELLING commerce, marketing, exchange, merchandising, mercantilism, barter, interchange, transaction. **3.** CUSTOMERS clientele, patrons.

trade v. **1.** SWAP exchange, barter, switch, interchange. **2.** DO BUSINESS WITH buy and sell, deal, transact, patronize, shop.

trademark n. symbol, brand, label, logo, logotype, identification, insignia, colophon.

trader n. merchant, monger, buyer and seller, dealer, retailer, trafficker, vendor, hawker, peddler, business person.

trade secret n. proprietary knowledge.

tradition n. custom, practice, convention, habit, unwritten law, institution, observance, ritual, belief, folklore, lore, *generational hand-me-down. "What you resort to when you don't have the time or the money to do it right."—Kurt Adler.

traditional *a.* customary, conventional, habitual, handed down, established, practiced, institutional, accustomed, fixed, classic, orthodox, time-honored, familial, historic. ANT. *new, untried, unconventional.*

traduce *v.* vilify, defame, slander, malign, slur, cast aspersions on, smear, libel, denigrate, *bad-mouth, calumniate, *drag one's name through the mud. ANT. *praise, extol, honor.*

traffic *n.* **1.** VEHICULAR MOVEMENT congestion, *bottleneck, jam, gridlock, *bumper-to-bumper traffic, rush hour, transportation, movement, commuters, travelers. **2.** BUYING AND SELLING trade, commerce, merchandising, marketing, exchange, business, barter, smuggling, black marketing, transactions.

traffic *v.* buy, sell, trade, merchandise, market, exchange, do business in, deal in, peddle, smuggle, sell on the black market, *bootleg.

tragedy *n.* **1.** MISFORTUNE disaster, catastrophe, adversity, calamity, blow, heartbreaker, bad luck, hardship, shock, reversal. "The difference between what is and what might have been."—Alfred North Whitehead. **2.** TRAGIC PLAY drama, melodrama. ANT. *1. blessing, good fortune, boon. 2. comedy.*

tragic *a.* disastrous, unfortunate, catastrophic, calamitous, sad, heartbreaking, unlucky, shocking, unhappy, crushing, dreadful, terrible, grievous, pitiful, wretched, lamentable, horrible. ANT. *blessed, good, wonderful, fortunate.*

trail *n.* **1.** PATH pathway, footpath, track, beaten track, footprints, bridle path, course, rut, trace. **2.** SPOOR scent, markings, telltale.

trail *v.* **1.** DRAG BEHIND haul, tow, pull, train. **2.** FOLLOW track, shadow, hunt down, *dog, stalk, sniff out. **3.** HANG dangle, depend. **4.** LAG BEHIND bring up the rear, fall back, drop behind. ANT. *4. lead, head.*

train *n.* **1.** RAILROAD TRANSPORT *choo-choo, steam train, locomotive, monorail, subway, el, maglev train, express. SEE RAILROAD **2.** PROCESSION caravan, line, cortege, retinue, following, cavalcade, parade, entourage, series, chain.

train *v.* **1.** PREPARE school, drill, educate, teach, coach, qualify, instruct, discipline, practice, condition, work out, get in shape. **2.** AIM draw a bead on, point, level, sight.

trainee *n.* apprentice, student, pupil, novitiate, learner.

trainer *n.* coach, instructor, teacher, mentor, manager, handler.

training *n.* preparation, schooling, drilling, education, teaching, coaching, qualification, instruction, discipline, practice, conditioning, workout, exercise.

traipse *v.* walk, wander, tramp, roam, gad, rove, ramble, meander, walk aimlessly.

trait *n.* characteristic, quality, attribute, distinguishing feature, idiosyncrasy, quirk, property, hallmark, trademark.

traitor *n.* betrayer, *backstabber, turncoat, Judas, renegade, *double-crosser, Benedict Arnold, *snake in the grass, one who commits treason, recreant, deserter, defector. ANT. *loyalist, patriot.*

traitorous *a.* disloyal, treacherous, treasonous, betraying, *backstabbing, *double-crossing, sneaky, untrue, Janus-faced, renegade, turncoat, recreant. ANT. *loyal, faithful, true.*

trajectory *n.* course, path, track, flight, arc, curve, orbit.

tram *n.* rail car, streetcar, trolley.

trammel *n.* restraint, shackle, constraint, impediment, hindrance, fetter, yoke.

trammel *v.* restrain, shackle, restrict, constrain, confine, impede, hinder, obstruct, fetter.

tramp *n.* **1.** HOBO vagrant, transient, *bum, vagabond, derelict, street person, homeless person, panhandler, beggar. **2.** HIKE OR MARCH walk, trek, expedition, traipse.

tramp *v.* stamp, tread, trudge, plod, stump, slog, hike, march, wander, travel, ramble, trek, traipse.

trample *v.* stomp on, crush, walk on, tread on, tramp, flatten, run over, stamp, squash.

trance *n.* hypnotic state, altered state of consciousness, daze, stupor, spell, glaze, transfixed state, dream state, abstraction, reverie.

tranquil *a.* calm, peaceful, serene, quiet, still, relaxed, sedate, motionless, unmoving, halcyon, untroubled, restful. ANT. *wild, noisy, troubled, uproarious.*

tranquility *n.* serenity, calm, peace, peacefulness, quiet, stillness, relaxation, sedation, motionlessness, restfulness. ANT. *wildness, agitation, uproar.*

tranquilize *v.* sedate, calm, quiet, relax, hush, pacify, soothe, put to sleep, *settle one's nerves. ANT. *agitate, stir up, stress out.*

transact *v.* carry out, carry on, perform, make a deal, execute, accomplish, do, discharge, prosecute, take care of, handle.

transaction *n.* deal, agreement, bargaining, contract, buy, sale, business, arrangement, performance, operation, enterprise.

TRANSCEND *v.* [tran SEND] to exceed, surpass or go beyond. *The event transcended expectations.* SYN. exceed, surpass, go beyond, outdo, pass, go above and beyond, excel, eclipse, top, outshine, outdistance, outperform.

TRANSCENDENTAL *a.* [tran sen DENT ul] beyond human experience, supernatural, spiritual. Also, excelling, surpassing. *Deep meditation brings him transcendental experiences.* SYN. **1.** SUPERNATURAL spiritual, otherworldly, mystical, intangible, preternatural, metaphysical, abstract. **2.** EXCELLING surpassing, extraordinary, supreme, unsurpassed, unrivaled, unequalled, incomparable, superior. ANT. *1. worldly, earthly, physical, tangible. 2. common, ordinary.*

transcribe *v.* write out, type out, type up, record, copy, transfer, translate, transliterate, decipher shorthand.

transcriber *n.* stenographer.

transcript *n.* copy, written copy, typed copy, printed copy, translation, transcription, recording, transliteration.

transcription *n.* SEE TRANSCRIPT

transfer *n.* transference, transferal, transposition, repositioning, relocation, move, transplant, displacement, transportation, conveyance.

transfer *v.* **1.** MOVE remove, relocate, convey, reposition, transplant, transpose, transport, send, deliver, forward, transmit. **2.** SIGN OVER deed, convey.

transferal *n.* transference, transfer, move, removal, relocation, conveyance, transportation, transplantation, transposition, displacement.

transfix *v.* **1.** HOLD ONE'S ATTENTION put in a trance, spellbind, hypnotize, mesmerize, fascinate, absorb, enchant, paralyze, rivet, freeze. **2.** IMPALE pierce, nail, spike, skewer, lance, spear.

transform *v.* change, convert, metamorphose, transmute, alter, remodel, *do a chameleon, transmogrify, mutate, switch, *change one's spots, reinvent.

transformation *n.* change, conversion, metamorphosis, transmutation, alteration, remodeling, *a chameleon, transmogrification, mutation, transfiguration, metastasis.

transfuse *v.* transfer, infuse, permeate, instill, imbue.

TRANSGRESS *v.* [trans GRESS] sin, break a law, overstep a limit or boundary. *A recidivist can be counted on to transgress again and again.* SYN. sin, break a law, break a commandment, overstep one's bounds, go beyond the limit, violate, trespass, disobey, infringe.

TRANSGRESSION *n.* [trans GRESH un] sin, a breaking of the law. *The courts will not forgive major transgressions.* SYN. sin, crime, offense, violation, felony, evil, disobedience, trespass, infringement, infraction, misdemeanor, wrong, breach.

transient *n.* drifter, vagrant, vagabond, tramp, hobo, migrant worker, traveler.

TRANSIENT *a.* [TRAN shunt] temporary, passing quickly. *The blue moon is a transient phenomenon.* SYN. temporary, passing, fleeting, impermanent, short-lived, transitory, ephemeral, momentary, short-term, brief, evanescent. ANT. *permanent, long-term, lasting.*

transit *n.* passage, conveyance, transport, progress, transition, change. SEE TRANSITION

transition *n.* change, transformation, switch, shift, conversion, changeover, metamorphosis, passage, transmogrification, transmutation.

transitory *a.* transient, passing, temporary, fleeting, impermanent, short-lived, ephemeral, momentary, short-term, brief, evanescent. ANT. *permanent, long-term, lasting.*

translate *v.* **1.** INTERPRET metaphrase, decipher, transcribe, transliterate, *put in English, render, spell out, clarify, decode, paraphrase, rephrase, reword. **2.** CHANGE convert, transform, alter, transpose, metamorphose, transmogrify, turn.

translation *n.* interpretation, rendition, transcription, metaphrase, paraphrase, rewording, rephrasing, version, rendering, deciphering, decoding, decryption. "Not versions but perversions."—Saint Jerome. "Like viewing a piece of tapestry on the wrong side where though the figures are distinguishable yet there are so many ends and threads that the beauty and exactness of the work is obscured."—Miguel de Cervantes.

translator *n.* interpreter, linguist, polyglot.

translucent *a.* semitransparent, clear, pellucid, gauzy, diaphanous, see-through, transparent. ANT. *opaque.*

transmission *n.* **1.** TRANSMITTING transference, passage, sending, conveyance, carrying. **2.** BROADCAST telecast, relay, airing. **3.** GEARBOX drive train.

transmit *v.* send, transfer, convey, conduct, dispatch, transport, forward, relay, impart, carry, communicate, broadcast, telecast, radio, air. ANT. *receive*.

transmitter *n*. conductor, transceiver, beacon, signal source.

transmogrify *v*. change, metamorphose, mutate, transmute. SEE TRANSFORM

transmute *v*. mutate, change, metamorphose, transmogrify. SEE TRANSFORM

transparent *a*. **1.** CLEAR see-through, glassy, diaphanous, crystalline, sheer, translucent, gauzy, limpid, pellucid, lucid, invisible. **2.** SIMPLE plain, obvious, understandable, apparent, self-explanatory, straightforward, evident, patent. **3.** OPEN frank, honest, candid, forthright, ingenuous, direct, real. ANT. *1. opaque, nebulous, cloudy. 2. complex, unclear, confusing, murky, *clear as mud. 3. dishonest, underhanded, disingenuous*.

transpire *v*. happen, come to pass, occur, come about, take place, materialize, befall, arise, evolve, ensue.

transplant *n*. graft, donor organ.

transplant *v*. **1.** GRAFT transfer, relocate. **2.** REPLANT repot, uproot, transfer, relocate. **3.** MOVE resettle, relocate, transfer, remove.

transport *n*. **1.** TRANSPORTATION transporting, conveyance, movement, carrying, transit, shipment, hauling, trucking, delivery. **2.** JOY rapture, ecstasy, bliss, euphoria, *seventh heaven, exaltation, *high, *rush, *cloud nine, happiness, nirvana. ANT. *2. depression, misery, melancholy*.

transport *v*. **1.** CARRY convey, move, ship, haul, truck, deliver, send, cart, transfer, run, lug, *tote, relay. **2.** ENRAPTURE fill with joy, overjoy, carry away, make ecstatic, entrance, thrill, enthrall, make euphoric, bewitch, charm. ANT. *2. depress, fill with melancholy*.

transportation *n*. transport, conveyance, carrying, carriage, transit, transferal, movement, shipment, hauling, trucking, flight, delivery.

transported *a*. enraptured, overjoyed, filled with joy, carried away, ecstatic, euphoric, blissful, entranced, enthralled, *in seventh heaven, *on cloud nine, experiencing nirvana. ANT. *depressed, melancholic, miserable*.

transpose *v*. interchange, reverse, exchange, switch, change places, swap places, *flip-flop, commute, transfer.

transsexual *n*. epicene, transvestite, cross-dresser.

transverse *a*. crosswise, athwart, crossed, cross, horizontal, diagonal, oblique. ANT. *vertical*.

transvestite *n*. cross-dresser, *drag queen, fetishist, transsexual.

trap *n*. snare, pitfall, deadfall, *booby trap, spring trap, net, ploy, trick, artifice, ambush, bait, lure, hook, deception, machination, stratagem, ruse, decoy, blind.

trap *v*. snare, catch, capture, nab, corner, corral, net, entrap, ambush, trick, take by surprise, hook, bait, lure, *suck in.

trappings *n*. articles, articles of clothing, adornments, outfit, gear, equipment, trimmings, accoutrements, attire, apparel, paraphernalia.

trash *n*. **1.** RUBBISH refuse, waste, garbage, junk, leavings, remains, litter, debris, *crap, scraps, dregs, rubble. **2.** NONSENSE foolishness, drivel, *bilge, *rubbish, *bunk, *crap, *hogwash, *malarkey, balderdash, tripe, *baloney. **3.** CHEAP LITERATURE yellow journalism, tabloid journalism, *crap, sensationalism, kitsch, dime novel. **4.** RIFFRAFF *bum, criminal, *dregs of the earth, scum, *good-for-nothing, scoundrel, rogue.

trash *v*. *Sl*. **1.** CRITICIZE pan, insult, knock, *bad-mouth, *dump on, disparage, put down, slam, *rank out, lambaste. **2.** VANDALIZE destroy, wreck, ruin, demolish, tear apart.

trashy *a*. worthless, junky, *crappy, no good, cheap, useless, *crummy, *cruddy, *tinhorn, *two-bit, *schlocky. ANT. *worthy, meritorious, quality*.

trauma *n*. shock, blow, injury, wound, jolt, bombshell, upset, *emotional minefield, ordeal, stress.

traumatic *a*. shocking, injurious, physically wounding, psychologically wounding, upsetting, disturbing, stressful, horrifying, deeply emotional, scarring, damaging. ANT. *reassuring, comforting*.

traumatize *v*. shock, injure, wound, upset, disturb, *stress out, horrify, *put through hell, *put through an emotional minefield, scar, scar for life, *drop a bomb on, jolt.

travail *n*. **1.** WORK toil, labor, sweat of one's brow, strain, grind, exertion, drudgery, pains, slavery. **2.** PAIN agony, torture, anguish, torment, hurt, suffering, distress. ANT. *1. leisure, relaxation, recreation. 2. pleasure, joy*.

travel *n*. traveling, journeying, touring, transit, voyaging, cruising, globe-trotting, sightseeing, day-tripping, riding, flying, passage, excursion, trek, jaunt. "A fool's paradise."—Ralph Waldo Emerson. "An experience we shall always remember, or an experience, which, alas, we shall never forget."—Julius Gordon.

travel *v*. **1.** JOURNEY take a trip, tour, voyage, cruise, globe-trot, sight-see, day-trip, ride, fly, see the world, go on an excursion, take a junket, *hit the road, go abroad, explore, ramble, roam. **2.** PROGRESS advance, move, go forward, pass. ANT. *1.* *have an armchair adventure, stay put.*

traveler *n*. tourist, journeyer, voyager, sailor, cruiser, globe-trotter, sightseer, day-tripper, rider, flyer, *frequent flyer, explorer, rambler, roamer, wayfarer, vagabond.

traverse *v*. **1.** CROSS pass over, go over, travel over, cut across, span, bridge, intersect, bisect. **2.** OPPOSE thwart, hinder, impede, obstruct, check, foil, frustrate.

TRAVESTY *n*. [TRAV is tee] a farce, an absurd caricature or imitation. *The bungled murder trial was a travesty of justice.* SYN. farce, imitation, poor imitation, caricature, mockery, parody, burlesque, spoof, mimicry, perversion.

travesty *v*. imitate, caricature, mock, parody, burlesque, mimic, lampoon, ridicule, pervert.

trawl *n*. net, dragnet, line.

tray *n*. holder, receptacle, platter, salver, server, serving plate.

treacherous *a*. **1.** DISLOYAL traitorous, backstabbing, untrue, unfaithful, duplicitous, double-dealing, two-faced, Janus-faced, perfidious, treasonous, *like a snake in the grass. **2.** UNRELIABLE untrustworthy, insecure, hazardous, slippery, undependable, precarious, dangerous, unsafe, unstable, shaky. ANT. *1. loyal, true, faithful. 2. safe, secure, reliable.*

treachery *n*. disloyalty, betrayal, traitorous behavior, *stab in the back, backstabbing, perfidy, duplicity, double-dealing, treason, infidelity, *double-cross, *two-timing. ANT. *loyalty, faithfulness, fidelity.*

treacle *n*. syrup, molasses.

tread *v*. **1.** WALK OR WALK ON trod, trample, tramp, march, trudge, step on, plod, hoof, stride, stomp, stump, crush. **2.** OPPRESS subdue, crush, trample, suppress, *jackboot into submission, subjugate.

treason *n*. betrayal, sedition, subversion, disloyalty, treachery, stab in the back, insurrection, insubordination, rebellion, revolt. ANT. *loyalty, patriotism, faithfulness.*

treasonous *a*. betraying, traitorous, seditious, subversive, disloyal, treacherous, *backstabbing, insubordinate, rebellious, mutinous. ANT. *loyal, patriotic, faithful.*

treasure *n*. **1.** WEALTH riches, money and jewels, fortune, hoard, pirate's hoard, miser's hoard, *tidy bundle, treasure-trove, king's ransom. **2.** VALUABLE THING OR PERSON gem, jewel, pearl, rarity, prized possession, prize, *find, *pride and joy.

treasure *v*. cherish, prize, value, appreciate, adore, love, esteem, hold dear, regard highly. ANT. *dislike, hold in contempt, disdain.*

treasure-trove *n*. SEE TREASURE

treasurer *n*. bursar, purser, controller, banker, clerk.

treasury *n*. **1.** BANK vault, coffer, depository, repository, safe, strongbox, safe deposit box, thesaurus. **2.** FUNDS revenue, savings, assets, money, reserve.

treat *n*. rare pleasure, rare delight, special favor or gift to oneself or another, a special joy, a welcome change, goody, tidbit, indulgence, extravagance. ANT. *same old same old, *the usual.*

treat *v*. **1.** ACT OR BEHAVE TOWARD use, deal with, handle, look upon, manage, react toward, relate to. **2.** DOCTOR nurse, tend to, mend, fix, care for, minister, prescribe, remedy, heal, medicate, dress, bandage. **3.** DISCUSS cover, talk about, write about, examine, go over, consider, touch upon, review. **4.** PICK UP THE TAB FOR ANOTHER pay for, cover, *spring for, pick up the check, foot the bill.

treatise *n*. study, article, work, essay, discussion, dissertation, thesis, examination, treatment, composition, paper, book, monograph, tract.

treatment *n*. **1.** HANDLING behavior towards, dealing, usage, processing, management, conduct toward, manner toward. **2.** MEDICAL CARE doctoring, nursing, prescription, remedy, medication, cure, therapy, therapeutics, regimen.

treaty *n*. agreement, contract, pact, entente, covenant, compact, deal, alliance, arrangement, mutual understanding, suspension of hostilities, cease-fire.

treble *a*. high-pitched, shrill, soprano. ANT. *bass.*

tree *n*. hardwood tree, softwood tree, conifer, evergreen, shrub, sapling, timber, acacia, alder, apple, ash, aspen, balsam, banyan, bayberry, beech, birch, breadfruit, butternut, cacao, camphor tree, cashew, cedar, cherry, chestnut, chinaberry, cinnamon, clove, coconut, cottonwood, cypress, date palm, dogwood, ebony, elder, elm, eucalyptus, fig, fir, frankincense, gingko, grapefruit, guava, gum, hawthorn, hazelnut, hemlock, hickory, holly, hornbeam, ironwood, juniper, larch, laurel, lemon, lime, linden, locust, magnolia, mahogany, mango, mangrove, maple, mimosa, mountain ash, mulberry, nutmeg, oak, olive, orange, palm, papaw, papaya, peach, pear, pecan, persimmon, pine, pistachio, plum, pomegranate, poplar, redwood, rosewood, sandalwood, sassafras, satinwood, sequoia, spruce, sycamore, tamarack, tamarind, tangerine, teak, tulip oak, walnut, willow, witch hazel, yew.

WORD FIND
bristles growing out of leaves: beard
center of trunk: heartwood
covering: bark
cultivates, one who: arborculturist
cultivation of: arborculture
dwarfed or stunted, Japanese variety of: bonsai
fantastically shaped, as an animal, by pruning: topiary
flaky bark, such as birch: scurf
fungus sometimes growing out of side: conk
garden of: arboretum
giant: redwood, sequoia
growth rings to determine past climate, study of: dendrochronology
leaf-shedding: deciduous
pertaining to: arboreal
pitch hole: pitch pocket
region, trees of a: sylva
ring marking past location of branch, tough: knot
rings of trunk from which age can be determined: growth rings
root, central: taproot
rope and thread, inner bark used in: bast
rotting leaves and debris collected under a tree: litter
sap or resin, excretes: gland
secretion: resin, sap
shady recess created by boughs: bower
stub: stump
studies trees, one who: dendrologist
study of: dendrology
thicket of shrubby trees: chaparral, copse
thick with branches: ramose
top cut to stimulate growth, tree with: pollard
trunk: bole, stock
tumor in which insect lives: gall
twisted: gnarled

uppermost story of leaves: canopy, crown
walk, tree-bordered: alameda
wartlike protuberance: burl
wind, knocked over by or off by wind: windfall, windthrow
wind, line of trees planted to check: windbreak
wood between bark and heartwood: sapwood
SEE JUNGLE, FOREST

trek n. journey, trip, odyssey, walk, hike, expedition, peregrination, march, migration, exodus, voyage.

trek v. walk, hike, *hoof it, slog, plod, trudge, tramp, *beat feet, hobble along, journey, travel, migrate, roam, rove, range.

trellis n. lattice, latticework, espalier, pergola, grate, grid, arbor, bower.

tremble v. shake, shiver, quiver, shudder, quake, quaver, flutter, shake like a leaf, tremor, oscillate, throb.

tremendous a. **1.** ENORMOUS huge, gigantic, colossal, monumental, massive, titanic, whopping, great, grand, monstrous, gargantuan. **2.** WONDERFUL great, extraordinary, fantastic, fabulous, *super, excellent, marvelous, *out of this world. **3.** TERRIFYING horrifying, dreadful, unnerving, frightening, scary, *bloodcurdling, shocking, horrendous, monstrous. ANT. *1. tiny, miniscule, puny, microscopic, insignificant. 2. terrible, awful, rotten. 3. comforting, reassuring.*

tremor n. shaking, tremble, shiver, shudder, quaking, quaver, fluttering, throb, quiver, ripple, trepidation.

tremulous a. **1.** TREMBLING shaking, shaky, shivering, shuddering, fluttering, throbbing, quivering, quavering, rippling. **2.** FEARFUL scared, timid, timorous, cowardly, flinching, fainthearted, anxious, nervous. ANT. *1. steady, still. 2. fearless, calm, relaxed.*

trench n. ditch, furrow, hole, excavation, channel, gully, fosse, moat, arroyo, gutter, conduit, drain, cut.

TRENCHANT a. [TRENCH unt] sharp, scathing or penetrating. *He gave a trenchant critique of the movie.* SYN. sharp, scathing, cutting, biting, pointed, caustic, acerbic, sarcastic, penetrating, incisive, keen, strong, forceful. ANT. *mild, dull, weak, *watered-down.*

trend n. direction, course, drift, tendency, prevalence, inclination, track, flow, fashion, style, *in thing, rage, craze, fad, vogue.

trend v. run, tend, course, flow, incline, go, lean, drift, gravitate, move.

trendy a. Sl. en vogue, fashionable, *in, stylish, current, *now, *mod, modern, *hip, *up-to-the-minute, *cutting edge, *with it, contemporary. ANT. old-fashioned, outdated, obsolete, passé, *out of it, *out.

TREPIDATION n. [trep uh DA shun] anxiety, fear, trembling. We approached the haunted house with trepidation. SYN. anxiety, fear, apprehension, uneasiness, nervousness, worry, dread, misgiving, cold sweat, fright, panic, terror, *butterflies, *cold feet, consternation. ANT. calm, composure, *nerves of steel.

trespass n. 1. ENCROACHMENT overstepping of bounds, infringement, invasion, intrusion, incursion, *offsides. 2. TRANSGRESSION offense, violation, wrong, sin, misdeed, crime, criminal act, felony.

trespass v. 1. ENCROACH overstep one's bounds, enter unlawfully, invade, infringe, intrude, *gate-crash. 2. VIOLATE offend, commit a wrong, commit a sin, sin, commit a crime, break the law, transgress, misbehave.

tress n. lock of hair, plait, braid, ringlet, hank.

triad n. trinity, trio, threesome.

trial n. 1. TRYOUT test, try, run, dry run, check, experiment, venture, *shot, *crack, *go, examination, essay, trial balloon, road test, lab test, clinical trial, *double blind, qualifying run. 2. HARDSHIP tribulation, test of one's mettle, trial by fire, ordeal, travail, torment, torture, trouble, difficulty, distress, adversity, misfortune, hard times, suffering, grief, *cross to bear. 3. COURT PROCEEDING legal proceeding, hearing, inquisition, jury trial, court case, suit, lawsuit, litigation, action, examination, arraignment, prosecution.

trial a. testing, experimental, tryout, observational, exploratory, probationary, pilot, tentative, provisional, preliminary, *watch and see.

triathlon n. *iron man contest, marathon.

tribe n. clan, family, group, ethnic group, race, kin, stock, *blood brothers, dynasty, community.

tribulation n. misery, distress, suffering, anguish, woe, affliction, misfortune, pain, grief, hardship, trouble, adversity, tragedy, ordeal, burden. ANT. pleasure, good fortune, joy.

tribunal n. court, judiciary, forum, bench, bar.

tributary n. branch, fork, feeder, stream, brook.

tribute n. gift, testimonial, gift of praise, applause, eulogy, accolade, honor, respect, acclaim, recognition, acknowledgement.

trick n. 1. DECEPTION artifice, dodge, ruse, *fast one, machination, device, ploy, subterfuge, hoax, fraud, evasion, feint, fake, cheat, con, decoy. 2. PRANK joke, gag, practical joke, stunt, antic, *monkey business, *funny business, *shenanigan, caper. 3. MAGIC STUNT sleight of hand, presdigitation, *fast shuffle, rabbit out of a hat, *smoke and mirrors, legerdemain, hocus-pocus, illusion, *mind-reading, *mentalism. 4. TECHNIQUE method, skill, secret, art, knack.

trick v. deceive, fool, cheat, take in, *pull a fast one, hoodwink, hoax, delude, *pull the wool over one's eyes, *fake out, *sucker in, *rope in, decoy, defraud, swindle, *play for a fool.

trickery n. deception, deceit, subterfuge, cheating, fraud, hoax, imposture, delusion, artifice, *razzle-dazzle, sleight of hand, *fast shuffle, ledgerdemain, hocus-pocus, *smoke and mirrors, chicanery, *funny business, skulduggery. ANT. honesty, truthfulness, openness.

trickle n. dribble, seepage, weeping, flow, sprinkle, leak, stream, running, percolation, drizzling.

trickle v. dribble, seep, weep, flow, sprinkle, leak, stream, run, percolate, drizzle.

tricky a. 1. DECEPTIVE deceitful, artful, crafty, wily, sly, *clever like a fox, cunning, underhanded, *crooked as a three-dollar bill, slippery, cagey, shrewd. 2. COMPLICATED complex, intricate, delicate, ticklish, sticky, knotty, thorny, touch-and-go. ANT. 1. honest, truthful, open, artless. 2. easy, simple, *a snap.

tried and true a. tried, tested, proven, proved, trustworthy, dependable, reliable, standing the test of time, reputable, *okay.

trifle n. 1. TRIVIAL THING triviality, insignificant matter, nothing, no big thing, *nothing to sweat about, *nothing to get worked up about, *tempest in a teapot, *molehill. 2. SMALL AMOUNT paltry amount, pittance, plug nickel, little, speck, *thimbleful, drop, *tad, smidgen, mite. 3. BAUBLE knickknack, gewgaw, trinket, gimcrack, bagatelle, toy. ANT. 1. *big deal, monumental matter, weighty matter, *mountain. 2. wealth, bonanza, deluge, mass.

trifle v. treat lightly, make light of, play with, toy with, mock, fool with, dally, discount,

shortchange, laugh off, pass over, *play games with, disrespect, *dis. ANT. respect.
trifling *a.* trivial, frivolous, unimportant, insignificant, nominal, inconsequential, petty, minor, worthless, miniscule, piddling, slight, small, negligible, *not worth a hill of beans. ANT. important, weighty, monumental, crucial.
trigger *n.* impulse, spark, impetus, goad, spur.
trigger *v.* set off, initiate, spark, fire, goad, spur, touch off, cause, generate, launch, trip. ANT. dampen, inhibit, stop.
trill *n.* warble, vibrato, tremolo, quaver, chirr, tiralee. SEE BIRD
trill *v.* warble, quaver, pipe, chirr, tiralee.
trim *n.* **1.** CUTTING clipping, pruning, shaping. **2.** CONDITION order, shape, fitness. **3.** DECORATION ornamentation, trimming, adornment, border, edging.
trim *v.* **1.** CUT clip, prune, lop, shear off, snip, shave, crop, bob, pare down, sculpt, reduce, boil down, edit. **2.** DECORATE ornament, adorn, bedeck, embellish, dress, garnish, festoon, *spruce up, edge, border.
trim *a.* **1.** WELL-PROPORTIONED shapely, fit, toned, statuesque, slender, thin, svelte. **2.** NEAT orderly, tidy, shipshape, organized, *in apple-pie order, uncluttered, groomed. ANT. 1. out of shape, fat, roly-poly, obese. 2. messy, sloppy, disarranged.
trimming *n.* overwhelming defeat, loss, beating, thrashing, *skunk.
trimmings *n.* side dishes, extras, fixings, appetizers.
trinity *n.* triad, trio, threesome, unit. SEE TRIO
trinket *n.* bauble, trifle, ornament, toy, gimcrack, gewgaw, knickknack, bagatelle, token, souvenir, keepsake.
trio *n.* group of three, unit of three, triad, trinity, threesome, ménage à trois, trilogy, triangle, triplets, troika, triumvirate.
trip *n.* **1.** JOURNEY voyage, cruise, excursion, trek, expedition, jaunt, junket, outing, hike, flight, run, drive, errand. **2.** STUMBLE misstep, fall, tumble, slip, loss of footing, *header, pratfall, flop, mistake, blunder, faux pas. **3.** Sl. MIND TRIP *rush, hallucination, euphoria, *psychedelic experience, altered state, consciousness raising, *head trip, *high, *buzz.
trip *v.* **1.** STUMBLE misstep, lose one's footing, fall, tumble, slip, *take a header, lose one's balance, go headlong, *fall flat on one's face. **2.** MAKE A MISTAKE blunder, *screw up, slip, err, *blow it, *muff, *flub, commit a faux pas. **3.** Sl. GET HIGH FROM DRUGS *catch

a buzz, *have a psychedelic experience, *fly, experience an altered state, hallucinate.
tripe *n.* Sl. nonsense, *baloney, *BS, *crap, *rot, rubbish, garbage, bilge, drivel, trash.
TRITE *a.* [TRITE] unoriginal, worn out, lacking freshness. His writing is uninspired and trite. SYN. unoriginal, stale, worn out, overused, hackneyed, lacking freshness, cliché, clichéd, stock, threadbare, pedestrian, commonplace, uninspired, stereotyped, tired, shopworn, routine. ANT. original, fresh, imaginative, new.
triumph *n.* **1.** VICTORY success, win, achievement, accomplishment, hit, feat, conquest, score, *home run, *grand slam, *touchdown, *slam-dunk, coup, tour de force. **2.** CELEBRATION elation, rejoicing, happiness, jubilation, exultation, acclamation. ANT. 1. failure, loss, flop, *goose egg. 2. humiliation, shame, dishonor.
triumph *v.* **1.** BE VICTORIOUS win, best, master, defeat, beat, *blow away, conquest, prevail, *leave swirling in one's wake, succeed, achieve, accomplish, score, *hit a home run, *hit a grand slam, *throw a touchdown, *slam-dunk, *skunk. **2.** CELEBRATE rejoice, exult, be elated, bask in the glory, revel, gloat. ANT. 1. lose, *blow it, *choke, flop. 2. mope, fret.
triumphant *a.* **1.** VICTORIOUS winning, successful, masterful, undefeated, unbeaten, conquering, *on top, champion. **2.** REJOICING celebrating, exultant, elated, proud, basking in glory, gloating. ANT. 1. defeated, beaten, *blown away. 2. moping, fretting, humiliated, *taken down a peg, crestfallen.
trivia *n.* **1.** INSIGNIFICANT MATTERS trivialities, trifles, minutiae. **2.** USELESS INFORMATION tidbits, fascinating facts, memorabilia.
trivial *a.* unimportant, insignificant, inconsequential, petty, trifling, slight, picayune, piddling, frivolous, worthless, meaningless, minor, slight, *rinky-dink, *penny-ante, paltry. ANT. important, significant, weighty, monumental.
triviality *n.* trifle, nothing, no big thing, *no big deal, *nothing to sweat about, *nothing to get worked up about, detail.
troglodyte *n.* caveman, cave-dweller, Neanderthal, anthropoid, brute, beast, animal, ape, recluse, hermit.
troika *n.* triumvirate, trinity, group of three. SEE TRIO
troll *n.* mythical beast, giant, goblin, hobgoblin, ogre, monster, imp, gnome, dwarf, troglodyte.

trolley *n*. streetcar, tram, cart.

troop *n*. group, herd, flock, throng, crowd, band, gang, assembly, assemblage, bunch, swarm, host, multitude.

troop *v*. walk, pass, march, parade, file, swarm, tramp, hike.

troops *n*. soldiers, military, men, infantry, G.I.s, armed forces, army, marines, corps, squad, combatants, cannon fodder. SEE ARMY

trophy *n*. prize, award, cup, loving cup, medal, laurel, plaque, blue ribbon, recognition, honor, citation, memorial.

tropical *a*. hot, humid, sweltering, torrid, sultry, *like a steambath, steamy, sticky, damp, muggy, close, oppresive, equatorial. ANT. *frigid, icy, snowy, polar*.

trot *n*. jog, run, lope, gait, canter. SEE HORSE

trot *v*. jog, run, lope, canter, amble, hurry along, move along quickly, *clip-clop.

trot out *v*. show, display, exhibit, parade, show off.

troubador *n*. poet, songwriter, balladeer, lyricist, singer, minstrel.

trouble *n*. **1.** DIFFICULTY distress, problem, predicament, hardship, *hot water, *fix, mess, *scrape, *deep doodoo, spot, dire straits, bind, hole, jam, *pickle, *sticky wicket, adversity, bad news, misfortune, heavy weather, danger, calamity, tribulation, pain, suffering, misery, grief, woe. "The tools by which God fashions us for better things."—Henry Ward Beecher. "What you make it."—Edmund Cooke. **2.** DISTURBANCE agitation, turmoil, disorder, unrest, rebellion, discord, upset, discontent. **3.** BOTHER effort, pains, inconvenience, difficulty, headache, work, labor, stress, strain, exertion, *pain in the neck, *pain in the ass. **4.** TROUBLING PERSON OR THING *pain, *pain in the neck, *pain in the ass, *bad news, troublemaker, nuisance, nag. ANT. *1. ease, pleasure. 2. peace, tranquility, calm*.

trouble *v*. **1.** DISTURB bother, inconvenience, put out, discommode, *bug, impose upon, harass, burden, distress, perturb, pain, worry, upset, stress, agitate, fluster. **2.** MAKE AN EFFORT take pains, exert.

troublemaker *n*. agitator, mischief-maker, imp, devil, hellion, pest, rebel, agent provocateur, *pain in the neck, *pain in the ass, instigator, incendiary, firebrand, malcontent, enfant terrible. ANT. *pacifist, peacemaker, angel*.

troubleshooter *n*. repairman, repair person, maintenance person, technician, serviceman, *Mr. Fixit.

troublesome *a*. difficult, bothersome, distressful, stressful, hard, challenging, demanding, tough, taxing, trying, burdensome, tricky, complex, complicated, thorny, convoluted, vexing, irritating, irksome. ANT. *easy, simple, undemanding, untroubling, *a breeze*.

trough *n*. channel, gutter, hollow, trench, ditch, culvert, drain, sluice, moat.

trounce *v*. beat, thrash, whip, flog, *whoop, *whale on, defeat, *lick, *skunk, *kick butt, rout, drub, best, overwhelm, *walk all over, *kill, *shellac. ANT. *lose, *choke, fail, be beaten soundly*.

troupe *n*. troop, cast, company, band, group, performers, actors, thespians, stock company. SEE THEATER

trousers *n*. pants, slacks, breeches, *britches, pantaloons, jeans, dungarees, overalls, corduroys, *cords. SEE PANTS

trousseau *n*. outfit, clothes, bundle.

truant *n*. absentee, malingerer, shirker, dodger, *goldbricker, idler, *goof-off, layabout, juvenile delinquent.

truant *a*. absent, *playing hooky, *cutting class, *skipping school, absent without leave, AWOL.

truce *n*. armistice, cease-fire, peace treaty, peace agreement, cessation of hostilities, suspension of hostilities, reconciliation, *white flag.

truck *n*. **1.** *BIG RIG eighteen-wheeler, tractor-trailer, trailer truck, *semi, *flatface, flatbed, dump truck, *pickup, van, panel truck, lorry. **2.** DEALINGS relationship, association, business, transactions, commerce, barter, trading, buying and selling.

WORD FIND

cab with sleeping department: sleeper

driver and passenger portion: cab

truck *v*. haul, transport, carry, ship, transfer, convey, run.

truckle *v*. cringe, toady, *kiss up, *brownnose, kowtow, bow before, bow and scrape, grovel, *fall all over, *suck up to, fawn, *bootlick, submit. ANT. *dominate, stand up to, resist*.

truculent *a*. fierce, mean, harsh, pugnacious, nasty, hostile, belligerent, combative, brutal, ferocious, savage, vicious, ruthless, murderous, cruel, rude. ANT. *pleasant, good-natured, good-humored, nice*.

trudge *n*. walk, tramp, slogging, plodding, hike, *schlepp.

trudge *v*. walk, tramp, slog, plod, hike, traipse,

*schlepp, clomp, *drag one's feet, stump, hobble.

true *a.* **1.** FACTUAL real, actual, valid, legitimate, bona fide, accurate, correct, genuine, authentic, veracious, verified, proven, confirmed, straight, literal, beyond question, right. **2.** FAITHFUL loyal, allegiant, devoted, dedicated, trustworthy, steady, reliable, dependable, constant, staunch, pure, dutiful, patriotic, *true-blue. **3.** RIGHTFUL lawful, legitimate, legal. **4.** FITTED aligned, level, plumb. ANT. *1. untrue, false, fictional, imaginary. 2. disloyal, unfaithful, backstabbing. 3. illegal, illegitimate, unlawful. 4. misaligned, skewed.*

true *adv.* truly, truthfully, honestly, accurately, correctly, precisely, exactly. ANT. *falsely, untruthfully.*

true-blue *a.* faithful, loyal, tried and true. SEE TRUE

truffle *n.* fungi, mushroom, delicacy.

truism *n.* platitude, cliché, bromide, saw, commonplace, axiom, fact, maxim, aphorism, truth, universal truth.

truly *adv.* truthfully, honestly, accurately, correctly, genuinely, unquestionably, really, sincerely, actually, literally. ANT. *falsely, questionably, inaccurately.*

trump *v.* surpass, outdo, outsmart, outwit, best, defeat, outperform, excel, beat, outscore, vanquish.

trumped up *a.* false, made up, fraudulent, concocted, invented, fabricated, devised, *cooked up. ANT. *legitimate.*

trumpet *n.* **1.** HORN wind instrument, bugle, flugelhorn. SEE MUSICAL INSTRUMENT **2.** CLARION BLAST toot, trumpeting, fanfare, blare, honk.

trumpet *v.* proclaim, announce, herald, cry out.

truncate *v.* cut off, shorten, lop, clip, trim, prune, pare, dock, curtail, abbreviate.

truncheon *n.* baton, billy club, cudgel, stick, bat, blackjack, mace.

trundle *v.* roll along, wheel.

trunk *n.* chest, box, footlocker, coffer, container, case, *Saratoga trunk.

trunks *n.* shorts, swim shorts, breeches.

truss *n.* framework, bracing, girders, support.

truss *v.* **1.** TIE bind. **2.** SUPPORT hold up, prop, strengthen.

trust *n.* **1.** CONFIDENCE belief, faith, hope, store, reliance, assurance, certainty, conviction, security. **2.** CARE keeping, safekeeping, custody, responsibility, charge, guardianship, protection, watchful eye. **3.** CORPORATION monopoly, cartel, company, conglomeration. ANT. *1. distrust, doubt, reservations.*

trust *v.* **1.** BELIEVE IN have confidence in, have faith in, set store by, rely on, take stock in, depend on, bank on, count on, swear by. **2.** HOPE be optimistic, assume, anticipate. **3.** ENTRUST give for safekeeping, assign. ANT. *1. distrust, disbelieve, have reservations about.*

trustee *n.* warden, custodian, agent, executor, fiduciary.

trusting *a.* trustful, believing, credulous, gullible, unquestioning, unsuspecting, confident, naive, innocent, oblivious. ANT. *suspicious, wary, cynical, skeptical.*

trustworthy *a.* reliable, dependable, honest, honorable, tried and true, upright, ethical, responsible, truthful, loyal, faithful, principled, *okay. ANT. *dishonest, dishonorable, unreliable, irresponsible.*

trusty *a.* SEE TRUSTWORTHY

truth *n.* **1.** REALITY facts, factualness, actuality, veracity, verity, *gospel, *naked truth, *unvarnished truth, plain truth, truthfulness, accuracy. "The heart of morality."— Thomas Henry Huxley. "The strongest argument."—Sophocles. "A jewel which should not be painted over; but it may be set to advantage and shown in a good light."— George Santayana. **2.** FACT principle, rule, universal truth, certainty, truism, axiom, platitude. ANT. *1. fiction, imagination. 2. lie, falsehood.*

truthful *a.* **1.** HONEST straight, candid, plain-spoken, frank, *on the level, *from the heart, sincere, straightforward, forthright, veracious. **2.** ACCURATE precise, exact, literal, true, factual, real. ANT. *1. dishonest, insincere, deceitful. 2. inaccurate, inexact, exaggerated.*

try *n.* attempt, *shot, *crack, *whirl, *go, *stab, effort, trial, turn, essay.

try *v.* **1.** ATTEMPT endeavor, *take a shot at, *take a crack at, *give it a whirl, *give it a go, *make a stab at, make an effort, take a turn, make a bid for, undertake, essay, venture, strive, *knock oneself out, struggle, do one's best, work hard, labor, vie for, *buckle down, *go all out, *give it the old college try. **2.** TEST experiment, try out, evaluate, examine, assay, *put to the test, *check out, appraise, prove, sample, taste. **3.** BRING A CASE TO COURT hear a case, adjudicate, judge, examine, decide. **4.** STRAIN stress, burden, tax, weary, trouble, sap.

trying *a.* stressful, taxing, exasperating, draining, irritating, annoying, irksome, tiresome, wearisome, burdensome, hard, troublesome, aggravating. ANT. *pleasurable, easy, relaxing.*

tryout *n.* audition, test, *cattle call, trial, demonstration, hearing, *shot, opportunity, *opportunity to strut one's stuff. SEE THEATER, SPORT(S)

TRYST *n.* [TRIST] a secret rendezvous made by lovers, an appointment to meet. *The boss and his secretary had a tryst every Friday night after work.* SYN. rendezvous, meeting, appointment, date, engagement, assignation.

T-shirt *n.* tee-shirt, undershirt, pullover, *muscle shirt. SEE SHIRT

tsunami *n.* tidal wave, deluge, flood, tidal bore, eagre, surge, giant sea swell. SEE OCEAN

tub *n.* bathtub, bath, hot tub, washtub, vessel, vat, tank, cask, keg, barrel.

tuba *n.* helicon. SEE MUSICAL INSTRUMENT

tubby *a.* squat, chubby, chunky, fat, pudgy, dumpy. ANT. *lithe, slender.*

tube *n.* cylinder, pipe, conduit, hose, duct, catheter, drain, conductor, line, inlet, outlet, shaft, tunnel, subway.

tubercle *n.* projection, growth, wart, nub, knob, node, nodule, protuberance, tumor.

tubular *a.* cylindrical.

tuck *n.* fold, pleat, crease, gather, pucker.

tuck *v.* **1.** FOLD OR STICK enfold, gather, pleat, insert, stuff, cram. **2.** WRAP enfold, cover, swaddle, swath, enwrap, blanket.

tuckered out *a.* tired, exhausted, worn out, weary, fatigued, *wiped out, spent, drained, *pooped, *dog tired. ANT. *invigorated, energized.*

tuft *n.* clump of hair, cluster, bunch, knot, wisp, thatch, lock, shock, cowlick, topknot, plume, tassel, tussock. SEE HAIR

tug *n.* pull, yank, heave, tow, drag, haul, jerk, wrench.

tug *v.* pull, yank, heave, tow, drag, haul, jerk, wrench, draft, *lug, draw, wrestle, *muscle.

tuition *n.* schooling fee, charge, cost of education.

tumble *n.* **1.** ROLL OR FALL somersault, handspring, stumble, trip, *header, *pratfall, spill, flop, crash, slip, dive. **2.** DISORDER mess, confusion, jumble, disarray, chaos, heap.

tumble *v.* **1.** ROLL OR FALL somersault, handspring, stumble, trip, *take a header, *do a pratfall, spill, flop, crash, slip, dive, drop, pitch, topple, plunge, *lose one's footing, *go flying, collapse, plummet, nosedive.

tumbledown *a.* dilapidated, rickety, unstable, broken-down, shaky, unsteady, ramshackle, *ready to collapse at the word boo, crumbling, rundown, decrepit, condemned. ANT. *rock-solid, secure, stable, sturdy.*

tumescent *a.* swollen, distended, bloated, turgid, puffed up, enlarged, tumid, *ballooned out, bulging. ANT. *limp, flaccid, deflated.*

tummy *n.* abdomen, belly, gut. SEE STOMACH

tumor *n.* growth, mass, tissue mass, neoplasm, lump, carcinoma, sarcoma, cancer, melanoma, malignancy, cyst, polyp. SEE CANCER

tumult *n.* uproar, commotion, disturbance, hubbub, clamor, hullabaloo, pandemonium, upheaval, turmoil, furor, bedlam, ferment, *to-do, ado, riot. ANT. *peace, calm, tranquility.*

TUMULTUOUS *a.* [tuh MUL choo us] uproarious, loud, wild, turbulent. *The meeting turned tumultuous after it was announced that taxes would be raised.* SYN. uproarious, loud, noisy, wild, turbulent, clamorous, riotous, stormy, tempestuous, vociferous, raging, violent, raucous, out of control, rowdy, boisterous. ANT. *peaceful, calm, tranquil.*

tundra *n.* plain, wasteland.

tune *n.* **1.** MELODY song, *ditty, air, number, composition, piece, aria, strain, ballad.

WORD FIND

catchy part: hook, chorus

SEE OPERA, MUSIC, SONG

2. PITCH agreement, harmony, concord, conformity, calibration.

tune *v.* adjust, put in tune, pitch, harmonize, align, calibrate.

tuneful *a.* melodious, melodic, musical, harmonious, lyrical, euphonious, euphonic, symphonic, pleasing to the ear, *catchy. ANT. *cacophonous, discordant, jarring.*

tunic *n.* coat, toga, frock, jupon, gipon, garment, blouse, vestment.

tunnel *n.* subway, subterranean passage, tube, mine, mineshaft, *chunnel, underpass, burrow, hole. SEE CAVE

tunnel *v.* dig, burrow, excavate, cut, mine, blast out.

tunnel vision *n.* narrow outlook, shortsightedness, myopia.

turban *n.* headdress, head covering, hat, scarf, bandanna, tarboosh.

turbid *a.* muddy, cloudy, murky, unclear, dirty, filthy, opaque, thick, soupy, roily, agitated, stirred-up. ANT. *clear, crystal, transparent, limpid.*

turbine *n.* engine, motor, power source, *work horse, generator. SEE MOTOR

turbulence *n.* agitation, violence, swirling, commotion, instability, roughness, disturbance, turmoil, tumult, storminess, wildness, wind shear, gustiness. ANT. *calm, quiet, motionlessness.*

turbulent *a.* agitated, wild, violent, riled up, swirling, full of commotion, unstable, rough, disturbed, tumultuous, stormy, tempestuous, gusty, choppy. ANT. *peaceful, calm, tranquil, still, smooth.*

turf *n.* **1.** SOD earth, clod, clump, divot, sward, grass, patch. **2.** *Sl.* ONE'S TERRITORY neighborhood, ground, home ground, domain, *stomping grounds, backyard.

turgid *a.* **1.** SWOLLEN distended, bloated, puffed up, tumescent, tumid, inflated, *ballooned out. **2.** BOMBASTIC inflated, overblown, grandiose, grandiloquent, florid, pompous, orotund, flatulent. ANT. *1. flaccid, deflated. 2. concise, succinct.*

turkey *n. Sl.* **1.** FAILURE flop, *bomb, *dog, loser, *clunker, *clinker, *dud, *Edsel, *lemon, *washout. **2.** JERK loser, ass, *bozo, clown.

turmoil *n.* turbulence, commotion, tumult, uproar, disturbance, agitation, unrest, wildness, chaos, confusion, disorder, pandemonium, bedlam. ANT. *peace, calm, tranquility.*

turn *n.* **1.** REVOLUTION rotation, gyration, circle, curving, circuit, cycle, gyre, spin, twirl, eddy, whirl, roll, about-face, deviation, pivot, twist, shift, winding, convolution. **2.** CHANGE OF DIRECTION change of course, deviation, swerve, turnabout, reversal, divergence, shift, switch, curve, detour, fork, shunt, deflection. **3.** CURVE bend, hairpin turn, S-curve, zigzag, U-turn, arc, tack, dogleg, oxbow, hook. **4.** OPPORTUNITY *crack, *shot, try, move, time, chance, go, *whack, spell. **5.** SHOCK fright, start, scare. **6.** ACTION act, deed, favor, kindness, service.

turn *v.* **1.** REVOLVE rotate, go round, wheel, gyrate, circle, make a circuit, cycle, spin, twirl, eddy, whirl, roll, pivot, wind, crank, curve, swerve, veer. **2.** CHANGE DIRECTION change course, curve, swerve, veer, deviate, diverge, detour, sidetrack, shunt, *take a fork in the road, diverge, reverse, loop, do an about-face, make a U-turn, follow a serpentine path, zigzag. **3.** REVERSE invert, transpose, flip over, turn upside down, turn inside out. **4.** CHANGE transform, alter, metamorphose, convert, transmute, mutate, transmogrify, reconstruct, remodel. **5.** GO SOUR go bad, spoil, ferment, curdle, putrefy, rot, become

tainted. **6.** SICKEN nauseate, unsettle. **7.** TWIST, AS AN ANKLE sprain, wrench, dislocate, throw out of joint.

turnabout *n.* about-face, reversal, shift, volte-face, turnaround, *switcheroo, *a 180, *flip-flop, backpedaling.

turncoat *n.* traitor, betrayer, renegade, Judas, Benedict Arnold, backstabber, *double-crosser, *two-timer, snake, *squealer, *fink.

turndown *n.* rejection, no, rebuff, *nix, *thumbs-down, refusal, declining, disapproval, *no-go, veto. ANT. *acceptance, approval, okay.*

turn down *v.* reject, say no to, rebuff, *give a thumbs-down, refuse, decline, disapprove, *nix, veto, *shoot down. ANT. *accept, okay, approve.*

turning point *n.* crossroads, pivotal moment, critical moment, crisis point, juncture, *zero hour, Rubicon, point of no return.

turn off *v. Sl.* bore, disinterest, *put to sleep, disgust, *make one sick, nauseate, sicken, *turn one's stomach. ANT. *turn on, excite.*

turn on *v. Sl.* stimulate, excite, titillate, arouse, *get one's motor running, *charge one's battery, impassion, *make hot. ANT. *turn off, disgust, sicken.*

turnout *n.* **1.** GATHERING, NUMBER crowd, multitude, gathering, assemblage, gate, showing, collection, mob, bunch, swarm. **2.** OUTPUT production, productivity, yield, amount.

turn out *v.* make, produce, manufacture, fabricate, build, construct, put out.

turn over *v.* flip, overturn, upset, upend, capsize, tip, *turn turtle.

turnpike *n.* toll highway, toll road, interstate, expressway, superhighway, pike. SEE STREET

TURPITUDE *n.* [TUR pi TOOD] depravity, wickedness. *She divorced him because of his moral turpitude.* SYN. depravity, wickedness, immorality, corruption, vileness, baseness, evil, nastiness, sinfulness, vice, perversion. ANT. *morality, virtue, uprightness, goodness.*

turret *n.* tower, bartizan, watchtower, lookout, cupola, steeple. SEE TOWER

tush *n.* rump, *fanny, rear, gluteus maximus. SEE BUTTOCKS

turtle *n.* terrapin, chelonian, tortoise, snapping turtle, reptile.
WORD FIND
shell: carapace, plastron.

tusk *n.* tooth, fang, ivory.

tussle *n.* struggle, scuffle, fight, wrestling match, boxing match, *scrap, contest, combat, *tug-of-war, battle, conflict, fray, brawl, clash, *locking of horns, melee, donnybrook, *rumble.

tussle *v*. struggle, scuffle, fight, wrestle, box, *scrap, contest, combat, *have a tug-of-war, battle, conflict, brawl, clash, *lock horns, grapple.

tussock *n*. tuft, clump, thicket.

TUTELAGE *n*. [TOOT ul ij] teaching, instruction or care. *Under the tutelage of his current coach, he won three championships.* SYN. teaching, instruction, tutoring, schooling, training, coaching, guidance, direction, care, guardianship, supervision.

tutor *n*. teacher, private teacher, instructor, private instructor, coach, mentor, educator, trainer, guide, guru, master.

tutor *v*. teach, instruct, coach, educate, train, enlighten, cram, *show the ropes, *drum into, drill.

TV *n*. *telly, video, *idiot box. SEE TELEVISION

twaddle *n*. nonsense, foolishness, balderdash, *rot, *rubbish, *crap, claptrap, drivel, prattle, tripe, blather, hogwash, *piffle.

tweak *n*. pinch, twist, turn, squeeze, nip, yank.

tweak *v*. pinch, twist, turn, squeeze, nip, yank.

tweet *n*. chirp, chip, cheep, chirrup, twitter. SEE BIRD

tweezers *n*. nippers, pincers, forceps, tongs.

twiddle *v*. twirl, tweak, twist, spin, finger, fiddle with, toy with, trifle with, fool with.

twig *n*. branch, limb, shoot, bough, stick, stem, sprig, offshoot.

twilight *n*. 1. DUSK gloam, sundown, sunset, eventide, nightfall, evening, moonrise, *shank of the evening, *gauzy light of dawn, *premonition of dawn. 2. DECLINE last days, *last gasp, swan song, ebb, *final curtain, passing, retirement.

twilight zone *n*. hallucinatory state, hypnogogic state, *dream world, nightmare world.

twin *n*. double, match, fellow, duplicate, mirror image, carbon copy, clone, counterpart, *dead ringer, mate, alter ego, brother, sister, identical twin, fraternal twin, Siamese twin.

twin *a*. dual, double, paired, duplicate, matching, same, corresponding, mirroring, identical, fellow. ANT. *different, dissimilar*.

twine *n*. 1. STRING thread, cord, cordage, yarn, rope, hemp, braid, line, cable. 2. TANGLE knot, snarl, twist.

twine *v*. intertwine, interlace, entwine, twist, plait, braid, knit, weave, coil, wreathe.

twinge *n*. 1. PAIN pang, stab, stabbing, stitch, twitch, pinch, cramp, prick, spasm, shooting

pain. 2. REMORSE qualm, regret, pang of conscience, misgiving.

twinkle *n*. scintillation, flicker, flash, sparkle, glint, glimmer, shimmering, gleam, glitter, spark, wink.

twinkle *v*. scintillate, flicker, flash, sparkle, glint, glimmer, shimmer, gleam, glitter, spark, wink.

twinkling *n*. instant, split second, wink, blink of an eye, heartbeat, flash, moment.

twirl *v*. spin, rotate, whirl, wheel, turn, pirouette, revolve, pivot, gyrate, twist.

twist *n*. 1. KNOT turn, winding, twine, twining, braid, kink. 2. ROTATION twirl, spin, revolution, torsion. 3. SPRAIN wrench, turn. 4. TURN IN THE ROAD curve, zigzag, S-curve, hairpin turn, bend, snake. 5. QUIRK eccentricity, idiosyncrasy, peculiarity, oddity, abnormality, aberration. 6. DISTORTION perversion, misrepresentation, misinterpretation, falsification, slant. 7. UNEXPECTED DEVELOPMENT plot twist, surprise, invention.

twist *v*. 1. KNOT turn, wind, twine, braid, kink, entwine, tangle, plait, braid. 2. ROTATE turn, spin, twirl. 3. SPRAIN wrench, turn. 4. TURN IN THE ROAD curve, zigzag, bend, snake, follow a serpentine pattern. 5. DISTORT pervert, misrepresent, misstate, misinterpret, falsify, slant, lie, misconstrue.

twisted *a*. 1. KNOTTED wound up, balled up, entwined, full of kinks, tangled, plaited, braided, convoluted, crooked. 2. DISTORTED wrong, inaccurate, mixed-up. 3. PERVERTED eccentric, weird. ANT. *1. smoothed, untangled. 2. true, accurate. 3. normal, sane.*

twister *n*. cyclone, whirlwind. SEE TORNADO

twit *n*. idiot, jerk. SEE MORON

twit *v*. reproach, tease, taunt, *dig, *razz, gibe, make fun of, kid, *rib, *rag on, disparage.

twitch *n*. jerk, spasm, tic, quiver, shiver, quaver, tremor, shake, throb.

twitch *v*. jerk, go into spasms, quiver, shiver, quaver, tremor, shake, throb, convulse, flutter, vellicate.

twitter *n*. chirping, singing, chirruping, whistling, tweeting, warbling, trilling. SEE BIRD

twitter *v*. chirp, sing, chirrup, vocalize, call, chatter, warble, trill, tweet, whistle. SEE BIRD

two-bit *a*. cheap, inferior, gaudy, *bush, *bushleague, dime-a-dozen, *one-horse, *tinhorn, small-time, piddling, second-rate. ANT. *first-rate, superior, big-league.*

two-faced *a*. deceitful, insincere, double-dealing, treacherous, Janus-faced, hypocritical, disingenuous, dishonest, backstabbing, disloyal. ANT. *loyal, *real, honest, sincere.*

two-time *v. Sl.* betray, cheat, deceive, backstab, stab in the back, be unfaithful, be disloyal.

tycoon *n.* industrialist, mogul, financier, magnate, capitalist, *big shot, bigwig, *big wheel, big-time operator, enterpriser, businessman. SEE BUSINESS

tyke *n.* child, toddler, *little shaver, brat, imp.

type *n.* **1.** KIND sort, class, breed, order, species, variety, persuasion, cast, genre, form, classification, genus, family, stock. **2.** EXAMPLE model, archetype, pattern, standard, epitome, personification, essence, rule. **3.** CHARACTERS typeface, printing, font.

type *v.* **1.** CLASSIFY categorize, sort, stamp, class, grade, order. **2.** TYPEWRITE *hunt and peck, *touchtype, *bang out, key in, word process.

Type A *n.* hostile personality, *high octane personality, *hot reactor, aggressive personality.

typewriter *n.* word processor, office machine, portable.

typhoon *n.* tropical storm, cyclone, hurricane, rain storm, deluge.

typical *a.* normal, standard, average, common, regular, usual, conventional, expected, habitual, stock, par, ordinary, run-of-the-mill. ANT. *atypical, unusual, extraordinary, unexpected.*

typecast *v.* stereotype.

typify *v.* exemplify, represent, personify, epitomize, embody, characterize, stand for, denote, serve as an example.

typist *n.* word processor, secretary, clerk, office worker.

typo *n.* typographical error, spelling error.

tyrannical *a.* despotic, dictatorial, autocratic, ironhanded, authoritarian, high-handed, domineering, oppressive, cruel, harsh, unjust, arbitrary. ANT. *democratic.*

tyrannize *v.* dictate, rule with an iron hand, dominate, oppress, bully, order around, *jackboot into submission, *keep under one's thumb, step on, intimidate, subdue. ANT. *rule democratically.*

tyranny *n.* dictatorship, autocracy, totalitarianism, despotism, oppression, reign of terror, iron hand, *jackboot authority, iron rule, domination, authoritarianism, brutality, cruelty, severity. "Oppression, and swordlaw."—John Milton. "The worst of treasons."—Lord Byron. SEE GOVERNMENT

tyrant *n.* dictator, despot, autocrat, authoritarian, *Hitler, fascist, bully, absolute ruler, oppressor, overlord. "Nothing but a slave turned inside-out."—Herbert Spencer.

tyro *n.* beginner, novice, amateur, *rookie, *greenhorn, neophyte, novitiate, raw recruit, *tenderfoot, trainee. ANT. *expert, master, professional, *old hand.*

U

UBIQUITOUS *a.* [yoo BIK wuh tus] present everywhere at the same time, or seemingly so, omnipresent. *The faithful believe God is ubiquitous.* SYN. everywhere, omnipresent, widespread, all-over, pervasive, universal, worldwide, far and wide, to the four corners of the earth.

U-boat *n.* *steel shark. SEE SUBMARINE

UFO *n.* unidentified flying object, flying saucer, *bogey, extraterrestrial spacecraft.

ugliness *n.* unattractiveness, repulsiveness, homeliness, grotesqueness, unsightliness, plainness, deformity, monstrousness, hideousness, eyesore. ANT. *beauty, attractiveness, loveliness.*

ugly *a.* **1.** UNATTRACTIVE repulsive, homely, hideous, unbecoming, grotesque, unsightly, plain, deformed, monstrous, revolting, *gross, misshapen, unappealing, *toad-faced, *rat-faced, *fish-faced, *not much on looks, *has a great personality, an eyesore. **2.** DISAGREEABLE, BAD offensive, objectionable, unpleasant, disgusting, nasty, repugnant, repellent, obnoxious, sickening, nauseating, vile, distasteful. **3.** THREATENING ominous, menacing, forbidding, portentous, dangerous, black, sinister, malevolent, malignant. **4.** CROSS ill-tempered, *mad, angry, *pissed, quarrelsome, bad-tempered, surly, mean, nasty, cantankerous. ANT. *1. attractive, beautiful, lovely, appealing. 2. agreeable, pleasant, good. 3. auspicious, harmless, promising. 4. good-natured, good-humored, easygoing.*

ulcer *n.* ulceration, sore, peptic ulcer, canker, abscess, festering, lesion.

ulcerous *a.* ulcerated, cankerous, cankered, festering, sore. ANT. *healthy, healing, clean.*

ULTERIOR *a.* [ul TEER ee er] undisclosed, hidden, beyond what is spoken. *John said he wanted to judge the beauty pageant for the money, but we suspected he had an ulterior motive.* SYN. undisclosed, hidden, unspoken, unexpressed, covert, remote, unrevealed, concealed, personal. ANT. *expressed, obvious, evident.*

ultimate *n.* greatest, highest, best, height, top, pinnacle, summit, peak, last word, ne plus ultra, culmination. ANT. *lowest, minimum.*

ultimate *a.* **1.** UTMOST maximum, highest, greatest, uppermost, supreme, paramount,

extreme, best, superlative, preeminent. **2.** FINAL conclusive, last, concluding, ending, completing, finishing, terminal, terminating, closing, furthest, farthest, eventual. ANT. *1. lowest, minimum, worst. 2. beginning, initial, opening.*

ultimately *adv.* in the end, finally, eventually, sooner or later, at last, after all, after all is said and done.

ultimatum *n.* last offer, final proposal, demand, last chance, warning.

ultra *a.* extreme, beyond, excessive, radical, extravagant, inordinate, extraordinary, above and beyond, drastic.

ultramodern *a.* futuristic, advanced, ahead of its time, *cutting edge. ANT. *old-fashioned, archaic, passé*

ululate *v.* howl, wail, lament.

umbrage *n.* offense, resentment, indignation, hurt, displeasure, grudge, pique, anger, huff. ANT. *pleasure.*

umbrella *n.* parasol, shade, sunshade, cover, canopy, bumbershoot. "A portable roof."— Leonard Levinson.

umpire *n.* judge, referee, arbiter, arbitrator, mediator, adjudicator, *ump.

unable *a.* incapable, not up to, helpless, powerless, incompetent, ineffectual, ineffective, impotent, unskilled, unfit, unschooled, unqualified, inoperative, *out of commission. ANT. *able, capable, effective.*

unabridged *a.* uncut, whole, complete, full-length, total, intact, unshortened. ANT. *abridged, cut, condensed.*

unacceptable *a.* unsatisfactory, unsuitable, not acceptable, improper, *not up to snuff, *below par, unfit. ANT. *sufficient, adequate, proper.*

unaccompanied *a.* alone, lone, solo, sole, solitary, unattended, single. ANT. *accompanied, paired, escorted.*

unaccustomed *a.* inexperienced, unseasoned, unused to, *green, raw, ignorant, unacquainted. ANT. *accustomed, experienced.*

unadorned *a.* unembellished, undecorated, bare, bald, stark. SEE PLAIN

UNADULTERATED *a.* [un uh DULT uh rate ed] pure, unpolluted, undiluted, unmixed. *We found the national park still unadulterated and pristine.* SYN. pure, unmixed, undiluted, unpolluted, unalloyed, uncorrupted, untainted, uncontaminated, unspoiled. ANT. *adulterated, contaminated, impure.*

unaffected *a.* **1.** NATURAL real, sincere, down-to-earth, unstudied, *folksy, *down-home, unpretentious, genuine, plain, simple. **2.** NOT AFFECTED unmoved, impassive, cool, hard, callous, *thick-skinned, unimpressed, unconcerned, unchanged. ANT. *affected, phony, pretentious.*

unafraid *a.* fearless, brave, courageous, bold, *having nerves of steel, *having ice water in one's veins, dauntless, unflinching, *gutsy, *ballsy. ANT. *cowardly, fearful, timid.*

unanimous *a.* undivided, universal, united, like-minded, of one mind, concordant, in accord, in concert, as one, solid. ANT. *divided, split, disagreeing.*

unappetizing *a.* unappealing, nauseating, sickening, *stomach-turning, *gross, disgusting, unpalatable, unsavory, distasteful, *yucky. ANT. *appetizing, mouth-watering, appealing.*

unapproachable *a.* **1.** ALOOF cold, distant, remote, standoffish, *snobby, snobbish, inaccesible, forbidding, unfriendly, unsociable. **2.** INCOMPARABLE unbeatable, unrivaled, unequaled, unparalleled, without equal, peerless. ANT. *1. approachable, warm, friendly, open. 2. second-rate, mediocre, poor, average.*

unarmed *a.* defenseless, disarmed, weaponless, unprotected, vulnerable, exposed, weak, open to attack, assailable. ANT. *armed, *bristling with arms, unassailable.*

unassailable *a.* undeniable, incontrovertible, indisputable, beyond argument, sound, certain, firm, rock-solid. ANT. *assailable, open to question, dubious.*

UNASSUMING *a.* [un uh SOO ming] modest and unpretentious. *They were surprised to find the famous actor to be shy and unassuming.* SYN. modest, unpretentious, humble, self-effacing, retiring, down-to-earth, unaffected, natural, quiet, diffident, shy, bashful. ANT. *arrogant, loud, pretentious, conceited.*

unattached *a.* detached, unconnected, disconnected, apart, independent, separate, loose, unaffiliated, autonomous, single, on one's own. ANT. *attached, connected, associated.*

unattractive *a.* repulsive, homely, plain, hideous. SEE UGLY

unauthorized *a.* unsanctioned, uncertified, illegal, unlawful, unapproved, unlicensed, not permitted, illegitimate, illicit, unofficial, criminal. ANT. *authorized, sanctioned, legal.*

unavailing *a.* futile, ineffective, ineffectual, to no avail, vain, unsuccessful, unproductive,

unprofitable, fruitless, worthless. ANT. *fruitful, worthwhile, productive.*

unavoidable *a.* inevitable, inescapable, bound to happen, fated, unpreventable, inexorable, predestined, fixed, certain, *in the stars, required, obligatory, requisite, compulsory. ANT. *avoidable, preventable, optional, elective.*

unaware *a.* unconscious, unknowing, ignorant, oblivious, unsuspecting, unwitting, blind, deaf, asleep, *out to lunch, *off in space. ANT. *aware, conscious, knowing.*

unawares *adv.* unexpectedly, suddenly, by surprise, without warning, unknowingly, unwittingly, off guard, *flat-footed, *out of the blue.

unbalanced *a.* **1.** UNSTABLE OR ASYMMETRICAL off-balance, unsteady, uneven, lopsided, irregular, top-heavy, unequal. **2.** CRAZY *nuts, deranged, insane, mentally ill, psychotic, *psycho, erratic, irrational, eccentric, demented. ANT. *1. balanced, stable, symmetrical, steady, even. 2. sane, rational, stable.*

unbearable *a.* intolerable, insufferable, unendurable, too much, unacceptable, more than one can stand, agonizing. ANT. *bearable, tolerable, endurable.*

unbecoming *a.* unattractive, unappealing, inappropriate, unsuitable, improper, offensive, unseemly, indecent, tasteless, indecorous, ill-fitting, unladylike, ungentlemanly. ANT. *proper, befitting, appropriate, ladylike, gentlemanly.*

unbelievable *a.* beyond belief, incredible, far-fetched, suspect, questionable, outlandish, inconceivable, impossible, implausible, doubtful, dubious, improbable, *fishy. ANT. *believable, credible, conceivable, probable.*

unbeliever *n.* doubter, skeptic, *doubting Thomas, disbeliever, scoffer, nonbeliever, agnostic, atheist, infidel. ANT. *believer, faithful, adherent.*

unbelieving *a.* skeptical, doubting, disbelieving, scoffing, questioning, suspicious, cynical, dubious, incredulous, agnostic, atheist. ANT. *believing, faithful, *buying, *swallowing hook, line and sinker.*

unbending *a.* rigid, firm, stiff, resolute, inflexible, unyielding, uncompromising, *holding one's ground, *sticking to one's guns, determined, hellbent. ANT. *flexible, compromising, yielding.*

unbiased *a.* fair, unprejudiced, impartial, objective, uninvolved, neutral, disinterested, evenhanded, equitable, nondiscriminatory. ANT. *unfair, biased, prejudiced.*

unbidden *a.* uninvited, unasked, unrequested, unprompted, spontaneous. ANT. *urged, coerced, prompted.*

unblemished *a.* perfect, flawless, spotless, unmarred, clean, stainless, immaculate, unmarked, undamaged. ANT. *spotted, stained, flawed.*

unblushing *a.* shameless, with no sense of modesty, bold. ANT. *ashamed, mortified.*

unbounded *a.* boundless, unrestrained, unrestricted, unconfined, uncontrolled, unchecked, wild, free, loose. ANT. *restricted, limited.*

unbridled *a.* unrestrained, wild, loose, unrestricted, uncontrolled, unconstrained, unchecked. ANT. *restrained, restricted.*

unburden *v.* unload, relieve, get rid of, *take a load off, disencumber, lighten one's load, *get off one's chest, confess, disclose, confide, *come clean. ANT. *burden, saddle, weigh down, encumber.*

uncalled-for *a.* unnecessary, needless, unwelcome, inappropriate, unwarranted, gratuitous, uninvited, unjustified, undeserved. ANT. *welcome, invited, wanted, needed.*

uncanny *a.* **1.** STRANGE, MYSTERIOUS weird, bizarre, queer, eerie, unfamiliar, unusual, spooky, creepy, scary, preternatural. **2.** REMARKABLE extraordinary, amazing, incredible, exceptional, astounding, astonishing, fantastic, unbelievable. ANT. *1. normal, usual, commonplace. 2. unexceptional, usual.*

uncaring *a.* indifferent, impassive, remote, uninvolved. SEE APATHETIC

unceasing *a.* incessant, continuous, endless, perpetual, unending, neverending, nonstop, unremitting, undying. ANT. *interrupted, halting.*

uncertain *a.* unsure, indefinite, questionable, hazy, indeterminate, unfixed, undecided, iffy, *up in the air, unpredictable, doubtful, unreliable, changeable, unsettled, unconfirmed, conjectural, vague. ANT. *certain, sure, doubtless, definite.*

uncertainty *n.* doubt, doubtfulness, question, indefiniteness, dubiety, ambiguity, unpredictability, guesswork, guess, speculation, conjecture, unknown. ANT. *certainty, assurance.*

uncharted *a.* unknown, unexplored, unmapped, mysterious. ANT. *known, discovered.*

uncivil *a.* rude, discourteous, coarse, uncivilized, barbarous, nasty, unrefined, boorish, impolite, indelicate, ungentlemanly, unladylike, ill-mannered, unfriendly. ANT. *civil, courteous, gentlemanly, ladylike.*

uncivilized *a.* **1.** BARBAROUS barbarian, barbaric, primitive, uncultured, savage, wild, brutish, crude, coarse, rude, discourteous, vulgar, animal-like. **2.** UNDEVELOPED wild, remote, unsettled, untamed. ANT. *1. civilized, civil, cultured, refined, courteous. 2. developed, civilized, settled.*

unclean *a.* dirty, filthy, soiled, befouled, tainted, grimy, polluted, nasty, impure, contaminated, vile, infected, germ-ridden. ANT. *clean, washed, antiseptic.*

unclear *a.* vague, ambiguous, hazy, fuzzy, blurred, veiled, cloudy, foggy, muddy, indistinct, obscure. ANT. *clear, distinct, obvious.*

uncomfortable *a.* **1.** PAINFUL agonizing, irritating, excruciating, awkward, harsh, cutting, pinching, biting, cramped, troublesome, bothersome. **2.** UNEASY ill-at-ease, self-conscious, nervous, anxious, distressed, on edge, tense, restless, miserable, *on pins and needles, troubled, *sweating bullets. ANT. *1. comfortable, pleasurable, agreeable. 2. relaxed, comfortable, at ease.*

uncommitted *a.* undecided, neutral, not bound, free, unpledged, *sitting on the fence, nonaligned. ANT. *committed, pledged.*

uncommon *a.* **1.** RARE unusual, unique, exceptional, odd, freakish, infrequent, extraordinary, novel, unconventional, different, unheard of, singular, peculiar, queer, one-of-a-kind, scarce, few. **2.** REMARKABLE outstanding, exceptional, extraordinary, incomparable, superior, unique, distinctive, peerless, unequaled. ANT. *1. common, usual, ordinary. 2. average, typical, ordinary, mediocre.*

uncommunicative *a.* closemouthed, *tight-lipped, secretive, silent, mute, reserved, reticent, shy, taciturn, *clammed up, quiet, guarded, speechless, aloof, distant, remote. ANT. *talkative, loquacious, *motor-mouthed.*

uncomplicated *a.* easy, *child's play, *a snap, *a breeze, uninvolved. ANT. *difficult.* SEE SIMPLE

uncompromising *a.* inflexible, rigid, *won't give an inch, stubborn, obstinate, unbending, single-minded, unyielding, set, immovable, hard-line, unrelenting. ANT. *flexible, yielding, open to compromise, conciliatory.*

unconcerned *a.* uncaring, careless, carefree, indifferent, apathetic, dispassionate, uninvolved, detached, cool, uninterested, disinterested, above it all, oblivious, distant, remote. ANT. *concerned, caring, interested, passionate.*

unconditional *a.* unrestricted, unqualified,

complete, total, absolute, categorical, downright, outright, out-and-out, utter, unlimited. ANT. *restricted, qualified, limited.*

unconnected *a.* disconnected, detached, separate, unattached, divided. ANT. *unified.*

unconscionable *a.* **1.** IMMORAL unethical, wicked, criminal, sinful, unscrupulous, antisocial, shameless, perverse, inhuman, beastly, barbaric, Satanic, uncaring. **2.** UNREASONABLE outrageous, extreme, excessive, inordinate, unforgivable, extravagant. ANT. *1. moral, ethical, of good moral conscience. 2. reasonable, fair.*

unconscious *a.* **1.** IN A SLEEPLIKE STATE asleep, comatose, *out cold, *blacked out, *knocked out, insensient, *out like a light, *passed out, *dead to the world, oblivious, stunned, stupefied, anesthetized. **2.** UNAWARE ignorant, unknowing, unwitting. **3.** UNDELIBERATE accidental, inadvertent, involuntary, unintentional, unpremeditated, unwitting, reflex, *gut, instinctual, subconscious. ANT. *1. awake, alert, conscious, aware. 2. aware, knowing. 3. deliberate, conscious, intentional, premeditated.*

unconstitutional *a.* unlawful, against the law. SEE ILLEGAL

uncontrollable *a.* ungovernable, wild, out of control, unmanageable, intractable, out of hand, carried away, unrestrainable, frenzied, beside oneself, rabid, *gone ballistic, riotous. ANT. *governable, manageable, tractable.*

unconventional *a.* unorthodox, unusual, uncommon, irregular, nonconforming, nonconformist, different, weird, unique, odd, out-of-the-ordinary, eccentric, avant-garde, *off the beaten path, experimental. ANT. *conventional, orthodox, conforming, standard.*

unconvincing *a.* open to question, open to doubt, unproven, weak, *full of holes, flimsy, suspect. ANT. *convincing, incontrovertible.*

uncoordinated *a.* clumsy, *klutzy, bumbling, ungraceful, awkward, *can't walk and chew gum at the same time, *graceful as an ox, ungainly, blundering, *like a bull in a china shop, *all thumbs, uncouth, lumbering. ANT. *coordinated, graceful.*

uncouth *a.* boorish, crude, coarse, rude, vulgar, uncivil, uncivilized, ungentlemanly, unladylike, unrefined, uncultured, crass, *tacky, loutish. ANT. *refined, civilized, gentlemanly, ladylike.*

uncover *v.* reveal, expose, remove, lay bare, unwrap, open, unearth, unveil, unmask, disclose, divulge, make known. ANT. *cover, conceal, hide.*

uncovered *a.* exposed, bare, nude, unclothed, unprotected, open. ANT. *shielded, hidden.*

UNCTUOUS *a.* [UNGK choo us] overly slick or suave, insincere, oily. *The unctuous televangelist talked some of his followers into giving up their lifesavings.* SYN. slick, suave, oily, insincere, honey-tongued, smooth, ingratiating, slippery, sycophantic, mealy-mouthed, smug. ANT. *sincere, plainspoken, genuine, frank.*

undaunted *a.* intrepid, bold, *gutsy, fearless, determined, courageous, lionhearted, plucky, *having icewater in one's veins, *having nerves of steel, unshaken, unflinching. ANT. *fearful, frightened, cowed, intimidated.*

undecided *a.* **1.** UNSETTLED undetermined, uncertain, open, unsure, up in the air, unresolved, *a question mark, unknown, pending. **2.** INDECISIVE wavering, unsure, of two minds, ambivalent, vacillating, *torn, *betwixt and between, *on the fence, irresolute, *blowing hot and cold. ANT. *1. decided, determined, known. 2. decisive, resolute, sure.*

undecipherable *a.* illegible, unreadable, indistinct, incomprehensible, unclear. ANT. *legible, readable.*

undeniable *a.* indisputable, incontestable, incontrovertible, beyond argument, unquestionable, certain, beyond a shadow of a doubt, irrefutable, solid, sure, proven, established. ANT. *questionable, debatable, uncertain.*

undependable *a.* unreliable, irresponsible, careless, untrustworthy, *fly-by-night, unpredictable, fickle, capricious, unsafe, unsound, insecure. ANT. *dependable, reliable, responsible, sound.*

under *a.* inferior, lower, subordinate, lesser, junior, subsidiary, ancillary. ANT. *superior, higher.*

under *adv./prep.* beneath, underneath, below, on the bottom, lower, nether. ANT. *over, above.*

underachiever *n.* *late bloomer, slow learner, one with a learning deficit, *sleeper.

underage *a.* minor, juvenile, immature. ANT. *adult.*

underbrush *n.* brush, bushes, shrubs, undergrowth, scrub, thicket.

undercover *a.* covert, secret, clandestine, underground, under wraps, concealed, private, hush-hush, *incognito, stealthy, surreptitious, sneaky, CIA, FBI, KGB. SEE SPY

undercurrent n. feeling, aura, *vibes, atmosphere, suggestion, hint, overtone, sense, latency.

undercut v. weaken, undersell. SEE UNDERMINE

underdog n. *long shot, *dark horse, loser, weakling, *low man on the totem pole, *benchwarmer, unlikely winner.

underdone a. rare, bloody, raw, uncooked. ANT. well done, burnt.

underestimate v. *sell short, *shortchange, *discount, minimize, slight, underrate, *consider a lightweight, scoff at, belittle, *sneeze at. ANT. overestimate, *make a mountain out of a molehill.

undergarment n. slip, chemise. SEE UNDERWEAR

undergo v. experience, go through, endure, suffer, be subjected to, encounter, abide, stand, withstand, sustain, tolerate.

undergraduate n. sophomore, junior, *frosh, *plebe.

underground a. **1.** SUBTERRANEAN nether, buried, below ground, below the surface, underfoot, sunken, subterrestrial. **2.** SECRET covert, undercover, clandestine, under wraps, concealed, private, hush-hush, surreptitious, backdoor. ANT. *1.* aboveground, aerial, surface. *2.* public, open, overt.

underhanded a. deceitful, tricky, sneaky, dishonest, sly, secret, devious, crafty, dirty, crooked, treacherous, two-timing, scheming, cunning, unscrupulous. ANT. aboveboard, open, honest.

underline v. emphasize, stress. SEE UNDERSCORE

underling n. subordinate, inferior, flunky, lackey, *low man on the totem pole, *low man in the pecking order, junior, subaltern, *brownnose, minion. ANT. superior, boss, chief.

underlying a. basic, fundamental, elementary, rudimentary, essential, primary, root.

undermine v. weaken, impair, cripple, undercut, debilitate, sabotage, subvert, disable, erode, wear away. ANT. help, reinforce, strengthen.

underneath adv. beneath, below, under, lower.

underpinning n. foundation, base, footing, support, framework, prop, undercarriage.

underprivileged a. disadvantaged, deprived, impoverished, poor, needy, poverty-stricken, indigent, destitute. ANT. affluent, well-off.

underscore v. underline, stress, emphasize, highlight, accent, play up, bring to the fore.

undersized a. stunted, dwarfed, puny, underdeveloped, tiny, little, pint-sized, midget, underweight, emaciated. ANT. strapping, brawny.

understaffed a. shorthanded, undermanned.

understand v. **1.** COMPREHEND grasp, know, appreciate, figure out, *catch the drift, get it, *get the point, *get through one's head, see, recognize, master. **2.** THINK gather, believe, take it, reckon, perceive, hear, assume, interpret.

understanding n. **1.** COMPREHENSION knowledge, knowing, grasp, appreciation, recognition, mastering, intelligence, intellect, sense, perception, savvy, discernment, awareness. "Hearing in retrospect."—Marcel Proust. **2.** INTERPRETATION inference, estimation, judgment, belief, thinking, reckoning, perception, sense, idea. **3.** MUTUAL AGREEMENT meeting of the minds, covenant, promise, deal, compromise. **4.** EMPATHY sympathy, compassion, commiseration. ANT. *1.* denseness, stupidity, misunderstanding, ignorance, befuddlement.

understated a. restrained, subtle, downplayed, minimized, soft-pedaled, quiet, modest. ANT. loud, blatant.

understudy n. stand-in, substitute, fill-in, double, backup, alternate, apprentice.

undertake v. take on, enter into, assume, tackle, make a commitment, engage in, endeavor, venture, shoulder, promise, pledge, contract. ANT. avoid, shun, reject.

undertaker n. mortician, funeral director, embalmer. SEE FUNERAL

undertaking n. project, endeavor, enterprise, venture, effort, job, commitment, affair, adventure, operation, task.

undertow n. riptide.

underwater a. submarine, submerged, submersed. ANT. grounded, exposed.

underwear n. undershorts, panties, *skivvies, shorts, *undies, briefs, boxers, jockstrap, slip, lingerie, chemise, teddy, *long johns, flannels, underclothes, unmentionables, T-shirt, bra, brassiere, corset, girdle, garter belt.

underweight a. emaciated, undernourished, malnourished, underdeveloped, *skin and bones, boney, skeletal, ANT. overweight, obese.

underworld n. **1.** NETHERWORLD nether regions, Hades, hell, Erebus, Sheol, Orcus. **2.** ORGANIZED CRIME Mafia, Cosa Nostra, the mob, syndicate, criminal element.

underwrite v. pay for, finance, fund, bankroll, sponsor, subsidize, back, support, endow, guarantee, insure, cover.

underwriter n. backer, financier, sponsor, *angel, supporter, insurer, insurance company.

undesirable a. unwanted, unpopular, objectionable, unwelcome, unappealing, unsatisfactory, offensive, unacceptable, unsuitable, disliked, rejected, scorned, disagreeable, nauseating, repellant. ANT. desirable, wanted, appealing.

undeveloped a. immature, unripe, unfinished, underdeveloped, latent. ANT. developed, mature, ripe.

undignified a. unseemly, beneath one's dignity, degrading, childish, juvenile, inelegant, tasteless, crude, rude, indecorous, ungentlemanly, unladylike, *goofy, out of character. ANT. elegant, proper, decorous.

undiluted a. pure, 100 percent, unadulterated, uncut, *unwatered down, umixed. ANT. thinned, watered down, weakened.

undisciplined a. lazy, unregimented, self-indulgent, overindulgent, unrestrained, uncontrolled, inconsistent, unsteady, unreliable, undependable, irresolute, irresponsible. ANT. disciplined, strict, regimented.

undisguised a. unconcealed, open, overt, frank, candid, up front, glaring, blatant, loud, exposed. ANT. disguised, secret, covert.

undisputed a. indisputable, unquestionable, irrefutable, uncontested, clear-cut, accepted, unmistakable, recognized, undeniable, beyond question. ANT. questionable, contested, disputable.

undistinguished a. mediocre, *run of the mill, *same old same old, ordinary, average, typical, common, pedestrian, plain, so-so, *nothing to write home about, unexceptional, *nothing special. ANT. distinguished, exceptional, extraordinary, rare.

undivided a. whole, complete, total, unbroken, uncut, solid, in one piece, intact, in its entirety. ANT. divided, split, fractured.

undo v. 1. UNFASTEN unhitch, unlock, untie, unbuckle, unbutton, loosen, free, detach, disconnect. 2. REVERSE rescind, annul, cancel, nullify, void, make null and void, invalidate, offset, erase. ANT. 1. fasten, tighten, tie, knot, attach. 2. uphold, strengthen.

undoing n. ruin, ruination, destruction, downfall, defeat, collapse, overthrow, fall, bane, disgrace, shame.

undone a. unfinished, uncompleted, incomplete, unperformed, unrealized, unfulfilled, *half-baked, half-done. ANT. completed, concluded, accomplished.

undoubtedly adv. without a doubt, doubtless, *beyond a shadow of a doubt, unquestionably, beyond certainty, surely, assuredly, indubitably, definitely.

undreamed-of a. unexpected, unimagined, inconceivable, unforeseen. ANT. predicted.

undress v. strip, disrobe, remove clothing, doff, peel off, shuck, unclothe, *strip to one's birthday suit, *strip to one's goosebumps, *strip to a growing state of deshabille, *do a striptease. ANT. dress, put on, clothe.

undue a. excessive, immoderate, extreme, extravagant, unnecessary, unwarranted, unjustified, uncalled-for, needless, undeserved. ANT. due, appropriate, reasonable.

undulate v. wave, ripple, swing, move sinuously, roll, billow, flap, sway, swell, heave, oscillate.

undulation n. wave, ripple, roll, billow, flap, sway, swell, heave, oscillation, pulsation, surge.

undying a. immortal, eternal, everlasting, never-ending, perpetual, unceasing, unending, endless, infinite. ANT. mortal, finite, short-lived.

unearned a. undeserved, unmerited, gratis, free. ANT. merited, paid for.

unearth v. dig up, exhume, excavate, dredge up, uncover, bring to light, discover, find, root out, expose, reveal, disclose. ANT. bury, cover, conceal, hide.

unearthly a. otherworldly, extraterrestrial, alien, out of this world, ethereal, heavenly, supernatural, extramundane, spiritual, ghostly, weird, strange, nightmarish, mysterious. ANT. earthly, mundane, terrestrial.

uneasiness n. apprehension, anxiety, fear, insecurity, worry, troubled mind, edginess, restlessness, angst, qualm, misgiving, disquiet, unrest. ANT. tranquility, serenity, relaxation.

uneasy a. apprehensive, anxious, nervous, tense, fearful, insecure, worried, troubled, restive, fidgety, edgy, restless, *on pins and needles, having qualms, having misgivings, fretful. ANT. relaxed, tranquil, serene, calm.

uneducated a. unschooled, untrained, unenlightened, illiterate, ignorant, uncultured, unsophisticated, unrefined, stupid. ANT. educated, schooled, literate, enlightened, scholarly.

unemotional a. dispassionate, unresponsive, indifferent, apathetic, disinterested, remote, cold, *having ice water in one's veins, impassive, deadpan, phlegmatic, unexcitable, laid-back, stony, staid, reserved. ANT. *emotional, passionate, demonstrative, excitable.*

unemployed *a.* out of work, jobless, laid-off, fired, idle, free, off, available for hire, *on the breadline, *on welfare. ANT. *employed, working.*

unending *a.* everlasting, eternal, neverending, ceaseless, incessant, unceasing, immortal, infinite, continuous, perpetual, permanent. ANT. *temporary, finite, ending.*

unenlightened *a.* SEE UNEDUCATED

unequal *a.* **1.** UNEVEN disparate, different, dissimilar, unlike, mismatched, unmatched, diverse. **2.** UNBALANCED asymmetrical, lopsided, disproportionate, uneven, irregular. **3.** UNFAIR unjust, not equitable, one-sided. ANT. *1. equal, same, alike. 2. balanced, symmetrical, regular. 3. fair, just.*

unequaled *a.* unparalleled, peerless, incomparable, unmatched, unrivaled, second to none, unsurpassed, supreme, preeminent. ANT. *rivaled, surpassed, second-rate.*

UNEQUIVOCAL *a.* [un ee KWIV uh kul] clear and unambiguous. *For a change, the politician's answer was unequivocal.* SYN. clear, crystal-clear, unambiguous, plain, explicit, unmistakable, absolute, straight, direct, certain, definite. ANT. *equivocal, ambiguous,* *clear as mud.

unerring *a.* exact, precise, accurate, certain, sure, infallible, perfect, unfailing, flawless, faithful, true. ANT. *inaccurate, imprecise, faulty.*

unessential *a.* inessential, unneeded, needless, unnecessary, unimportant, dispensable, irrelevant, superfluous, extraneous, extra. ANT. *essential, necessary, needed, indispensable.*

unethical *a.* wrong, unfair, immoral, dishonest, dishonorable, illegal, *dirty, *shady, disreputable, underhanded, unprincipled, crooked, unprofessional, corrupt, criminal. ANT. *ethical, honest, upright, moral, reputable.*

uneven *a.* **1.** CROOKED bumpy, slanted, unbalanced, misaligned, not level, broken, rough, jagged, rugged, not smooth. **2.** UNEQUAL lopsided, one-sided, unmatched, different, asymmetrical, unbalanced. ANT. *1. even, smooth, planed, level. 2. equal, matching, symmetrical.*

uneventful *a.* quiet, peaceful, dull, monotonous, routine, *same old same old, boring,

unvaried, tedious, unexciting. ANT. *eventful, exciting, momentous.*

unexceptional *a.* ordinary, mediocre, run-of-the-mill, garden variety, common, commonplace, usual, *same old same old, *nothing to write home about, *dime-a-dozen, undistinguished, *just another brick in the wall. ANT. *exceptional, extraordinary, out of the ordinary, remarkable.*

unexciting *a.* dull, boring, prosaic, humdrum, *blah, *dull as dishwater, *ho-hum, monotonous, uninteresting, dry, routine, tedious, tiresome. ANT. *exciting, thrilling, stimulating.*

unexpected *a.* unforeseen, unanticipated, surprising, shocking, stunning, unpredicted, unprepared for, *out of the blue. ANT. *expected, foreseen, anticipated.*

unexplainable *a.* inexplicable, beyond explanation, mystifying, puzzling, baffling, incomprehensible, unaccountable, bewildering, strange. ANT. *understandable, explicable.*

unexpressive *a.* inexpressive, expressionless, undemonstrative, deadpan, stony, wooden, *poker-faced, unresponsive, vacant, dead, bland. ANT. *expressive, demonstrative, responsive.*

unfailing *a.* never-failing, reliable, dependable, constant, steady, unflagging, inexhaustible, consistent, persistent, faithful. ANT. *unreliable, undependable.*

unfair *a.* unjust, partial, biased, prejudiced, one-sided, bigoted, inequitable, discriminatory, uneven, unethical, *not playing on a level field, unsportsmanlike, unsporting, *dirty, cheating. ANT. *fair, just, equitable, unprejudiced, *on a level playing field.*

unfaithful *a.* **1.** DISLOYAL faithless, untrue, treacherous, adulterous, *two-timing, cheating, backstabbing, false, fickle. **2.** INACCURATE imprecise, inexact, imperfect, incorrect, *off, faulty, erring. ANT. *1. loyal, faithful, true. 2. accurate, precise, true.*

unfamiliar *a.* **1.** UNACQUAINTED ignorant, unconversant, uninitiated, unversed in, inexperienced, unaccustomed, untrained, unschooled. **2.** UNKNOWN strange, alien, foreign, exotic, new, novel, unusual, outlandish, peculiar, rare. ANT. *1. familiar, acquainted, versed. 2. known, familiar, common, everyday.*

unfashionable *a.* unstylish, old-fashioned, outmoded, antiquated, passé, out of style, outdated, obsolete, frumpy, dumpy, *as fashionable as a potato sack, *tacky. ANT. *fashionable, chic, sharp, stylish, in vogue.*

unfasten *v.* unlatch, unbuckle, untie, unclasp, uncouple, undo, loosen, detach, unbutton, unzip, disengage. ANT. *fasten, tie, buckle, clasp.*

unfathomable *a.* incomprehensible, inscrutable, beyond comprehension, impenetrable, unknowable, deep, profound. ANT. *shallow, simple, decipherable.*

unfavorable *a.* adverse, poor, bad, negative, unpromising, contrary, hostile, unhappy, inadvisable, ill-advised, inauspicious, unlucky. ANT. *favorable, lucky, good, auspicious.*

unfeeling *a.* **1.** CALLOUS cold, apathetic, indifferent, unsympathetic, heartless, unemotional, stony, *having veins filled with ice water, cold-blooded, pitiless, merciless, hard. **2.** INSENSATE insensient, numb, paralyzed, unconscious, comatose, dead. ANT. *1. feeling, sympathetic, warmhearted, emotional. 2. sentient.*

unfinished *a.* incomplete, uncompleted, half-done, *half-baked, unperfected, lacking, rough, wanting, crude, deficient, undeveloped. ANT. *finished, perfected, done.*

unfit *a.* **1.** UNSUITABLE inadequate, unacceptable, inappropriate, ill-equipped, useless, out of place, inexpedient, inapplicable. **2.** OUT OF SHAPE unhealthy, unconditioned, sickly, ailing, weak. ANT. *1. suitable, fit, adequate. 2. fit, healthy, conditioned.*

unflagging *a.* unfailing, inexhaustible, tireless, undying, unfaltering, indefatigiable, constant, persistent, unremitting, unceasing. ANT. *failing, tiring, wearing.*

UNFLAPPABLE *a.* [un FLAP uh bul] calm, not excitable. *Even in the midst of the riots, the mayor was unflappable.* SYN. calm, unexcitable, imperturbable, cool, collected, composed, self-contained, unruffled, level-headed, self-possessed, nonchalant. ANT. *excitable, *high-strung, temperamental, *hot-reacting.*

unfledged *a.* undeveloped. SEE IMMATURE

unflinching *a.* unblinking, unfaltering, steadfast, resolute, staunch, firm, unshrinking, unshaken, undaunted, unafraid. ANT. *shrinking, flinching, shaken.*

unfold *v.* **1.** SPREAD OUT unfurl, open, unroll, outstretch, unravel, undo, straighten out, fan out. **2.** MAKE KNOWN disclose, reveal, show, expose, describe, divulge, set forth, expand on. ANT. *1. fold, furl. 2. conceal, cover up.*

unforeseeable *a.* unknowable. SEE UNPREDICTABLE

unforeseen *a.* unexpected, unanticipated, not bargained for, not predicted, unplanned, surprising, *catching by surprise, unprepared for, *out of the blue. ANT. *foreseen, expected, anticipated.*

unforgettable *a.* memorable, *mind-blowing, indelible, meaningful, important, memory-making, powerful, notable, striking, historic. ANT. *forgettable, insignificant, trivial.*

unforgivable *a.* unpardonable, inexcusable, indefensible, unconscionable, shameful, despicable, contemptible, unjustifiable. ANT. *forgivable, pardonable, excusable.*

unfortunate *a.* unlucky, unfavorable, hapless, ill-fated, *jinxed, cursed, *star-crossed, untimely, ill-timed, inopportune, inauspicious, unhappy, sad, bad, deplorable, lamentable, adverse, regrettable, unsuccessful, pitiful, disastrous, tragic, grievous. ANT. *fortunate, lucky, blessed, timely, happy.*

unfounded *a.* baseless, groundless, unproven, unsupported, unsubstantiated, fallacious, false, untrue, tenuous, speculative. ANT. *proven, true, substantiated.*

unfriendly *a.* cold, aloof, hostile, standoffish, distant, remote, unapproachable, snobbish, haughty, unsociable, inhospitable, nasty, mean, surly, not on speaking terms. ANT. *friendly, warm, approachable, nice.*

unfruitful *a.* unprofitable. SEE FRUITLESS

ungainly *a.* awkward, clumsy, oafish, *klutzy, cloddish, bumbling, lumbering, ungraceful, uncoordinated, gawky. ANT. *graceful.*

ungodly *a.* **1.** SINFUL wicked, evil, Satanic, devilish, hellish, criminal, villainous, immoral, impious, not religious, profane. **2.** OUTRAGEOUS dreadful, horrendous, god-awful, frightful, intolerable. ANT. *1. godly, pious, moral. 2. reasonable.*

ungovernable *a.* wild, unmanageable, uncontrollable, out of control, out of hand, unruly, intractable, rebellious, defiant. ANT. *docile, controllable, manageable.*

ungracious *a.* rude, discourteous, impolite, ill-mannered, uncivil, ungentlemanly, unladylike, insulting, boorish, rough. ANT. *gracious, courteous, polite.*

ungrateful *a.* unappreciative, unthankful, *looking a gift horse in the mouth, dissatisfied, *spoiled rotten, *biting the hand that feeds you. ANT. *appreciate, thankful.*

unguarded *a.* **1.** UNPROTECTED exposed, vulnerable, defenseless, unwatched, unpatrolled, assailable. **2.** OPEN honest, sincere, genuine, frank, candid, artless, aboveboard, straightforward, ingenuous. ANT. *1. protected, guarded, defended. 2. guarded, discreet, self-censored.*

unguent n. salve, ointment, balm, lotion, liniment.

unhappy a. **1.** SAD depressed, melancholy, downhearted, miserable, *blue, *down in the mouth, *down in the dumps, low, grief-stricken, mournful, downhearted, heavy-hearted, gloomy, despondent, disconsolate, forlorn, long-faced, disheartened, desolate, cheerless, anguished, glum, *bummed out, wretched, somber, crestfallen. **2.** UNLUCKY unfortunate, inauspicious, hapless, cursed, star-crossed, ill-fated, jinxed, infelicitous. ANT. *1. happy, joyous, glad, beaming, elated, euphoric. 2. lucky, fortunate.*

unharmed a. unhurt, uninjured, unscathed, intact, okay, all right, safe. ANT. *wounded, injured.*

unhealthy a. **1.** SICK sickly, ill, unwell, diseased, in poor health, unfit, weak, run-down, *under the weather, debilitated, bedridden, *in bad shape. **2.** BAD FOR YOU unwholesome, hazardous to one's health, unhealthful, detrimental, deleterious, noxious, toxic, virulent, harmful, malignant. ANT. *1. healthy, fit, in good shape, robust. 2. good for you, wholesome, healthful.*

unheard-of a. unprecedented, unknown, new, novel, outlandish, exceptional, unique, little-known, unusual, unbelievable, outrageous. ANT. *known, usual, ordinary.*

unhinge v. upset, confuse, unnerve, throw into a panic, make crazy, disorient, fluster, agitate, discompose. ANT. *calm, pacify.*

unhitch v. unfasten, detach, release, undo, untie.

unholy a. wicked, evil, sinful, ungodly, immoral, corrupt, sacrilegious, unhallowed, not sacred. ANT. *holy, sacred, godly, hallowed.*

unhorse v. overthrow, upset.

unhurt a. SEE UNHARMED

unhurried a. slow, leisurely, deliberate, snail-like, sluggish, *slower than molasses, nonchalant. ANT. *hurried, rushed, impatient.*

unidentified a. unknown, unrecognized, nameless, unnamed, anonymous, secret, mysterious, incognito, undercover. ANT. *known, recognized.*

unidentified flying object n. UFO, flying saucer, *bogey.

unified a. united, joined, one, together, combined, coupled, consolidated, amalgamated, confederated. ANT. *separated, fractured.*

uniform n. outfit, costume, attire, dress, *getup, suit, livery, habit, vestment, work clothes.

uniform a. **1.** UNCHANGING unvarying, unvariable, the same, undeviating, consistent, even, constant, level, stable. **2.** CONFORMING the same, symmetrical, alike, identical, like, similar, comparable, correspondent, *like two peas in a pod. ANT. *1. changing, varying, uneven, inconsistent. 2. unconforming, different, dissimilar.*

unify v. unite, join, bring together as one, bring together, combine, couple, wed, consolidate, amalgamate, combine, confederate. ANT. *separate, fracture, divorce.*

unilateral a. one-sided. ANT. *multilateral.*

unimaginable a. incomprehensible, beyond comprehension, *beyond one's wildest dreams, inconceivable, unheard-of, undreamed-of, *out of this world, fantastic, *mind-boggling, *mind-blowing, incredible. ANT. *imaginable, conceivable.*

unimaginative a. unoriginal, dull, trite, hackneyed, clichéd, mindless, tired, stock, stale, dry, bland, uninteresting, *same old same old, boring, pedestrian. ANT. *imaginative, original, creative, inventive.*

unimportant a. trivial, trifling, insignificant, petty, minor, *lightweight, frivolous, picayune, inconsequential, worthless, irrelevant, paltry, meaningless, *mickey mouse. ANT. *important, crucial, critical, vital.*

uninformed a. unaware, unenlightened, ignorant, unschooled, *in the dark, uneducated, unacquainted, uninitiated. ANT. *informed, *hip, enlightened.*

uninhibited a. free, open, unreserved, not self-conscious, relaxed, spontaneous, loose, extroverted, outgoing, unrestrained, informal. ANT. *inhibited, reserved, self-conscious.*

uninspired a. lifeless, spiritless, lacking creativity, dull, tired, trite, hackneyed, pedestrian, dull, bland, uninteresting, prosaic. ANT. *inspired, original, imaginative, creative.*

unintelligent a. dumb, moronic, imbecilic. SEE STUPID

unintelligible a. incomprehensible, incoherent, undecipherable, illegible, unreadable, unclear, muddled, meaningless, Greek, jumbled. ANT. *intelligible, legible, clear.*

unintentional a. unintended, inadvertent, unplanned, accidental, undesigned, unconscious, unwitting, unpremeditated, chance, haphazard. ANT. *intended, planned, designed.*

uninterested *a.* disinterested, indifferent, apathetic, uncaring, bored, uninvolved, blasé, incurious, remote, *turned off, cool, *above it all. ANT. *interested, fascinated, passionate, involved, riveted.*

uninteresting *a.* boring, dull, tiresome, monotonous, tedious, prosaic, *ho-hum, *blah, *as interesting as a plain brown wrapper, *dull as dishwater, unexciting, *humdrum, uneventful. ANT. *exciting, fascinating, riveting, heart-stopping.*

uninvited *a.* unwanted, unwelcome, undesired, uncalled for. ANT. *summoned, requested.*

uninviting *a.* unattractive, unappealing, repellent, repulsive, repugnant, stomach-turning, nauseating, sickening, unappetizing. ANT. *appealing, attractive, desirable.*

union *n.* **1.** JOINING combination, unification, consolidation, marriage, merger, amalgamation, unity, fusion, incorporation, coupling, blend. **2.** GROUP WITH COMMON INTEREST alliance, coalition, league, confederation, guild, trade union, labor union, federation, association, partnership, cartel, syndicate. ANT. *1. separation, segregation, breakup.* SEE MARRIAGE

unique *a.* one-of-a-kind, single, sole, unparalleled, lone, only, incomparable, distinctive, unprecedented, extraordinary, special, peculiar, strange, in a class by itself. ANT. *common, commonplace, run-of-the-mill, *common as a brick.*

unison *n.* harmony, agreement, concord, accord, concert, consonance, unity, togetherness. ANT. *disagreement, discord, dissonance.*

unit *n.* part, piece, quantity, member, element, section, segment, constituent, component.

unite *v.* combine, join, bring together, marry, couple, link, merge, connect, unify, blend, consolidate, incorporate, amalgamate, affiliate, confederate, cooperate, band together. ANT. *separate, disband, break up, divide.*

united *a.* combined, joined, brought together, married, coupled, linked, merged, connected, unified, blended, consolidated, incorporated, amalgamated, affiliated. ANT. *separated, disbanded, divided.*

United States *n.* U.S., U.S.A., America, land of opportunity, Uncle Sam, North America, Land of Liberty, Columbia, *the great melting pot. "Half-brother of the world. With something good and bad of every land."— Philip Bailey. "A nation of immigrants."— John F. Kennedy. "The largest shopping center in the world."—Richard Nixon. "A large, friendly dog in a very small room. Every time it wags its tail, it knocks over a chair."—Arnold Toynbee.

unity *n.* oneness, togetherness, wholeness, unification, union, agreement, harmony, accord, concord, solidarity, unanimity. ANT. *separation, division, discord.*

universal *a.* general, generic, common, catholic, all-inclusive, comprehensive, all-over, worldwide, planetary, intercontinental, pandemic, global, widespread, broad, prevalent, unlimited, unrestricted. ANT. *local, exclusive, limited, restricted.*

universe *n.* cosmos, space, outer space, *cooling fires of creation, creation, macrocosm, infinity. "One of God's thoughts."—Friedrich Schiller. "One vast symbol of God."— Thomas Carlyle. SEE SPACE

university *n.* institution of higher learning, graduate school, college. "A place of light, of liberty, and of learning."—Benjamin Disraeli. "A thought-control center."—Joan Tepperman. "Sophistry and affectation."— Francis Bacon. SEE COLLEGE

unjust *a.* unfair, inequitable, wrong, unethical, unjustified, unwarranted, prejudiced, partial, biased, one-sided. ANT. *even-handed, impartial, fair.*

unjustifiable *a.* unwarranted, unpardonable, indefensible, inexcusable, unmerited. ANT. *justifiable, warranted.*

unkempt *a.* disheveled, messy, sloppy, bedraggled, rumpled, tousled, tangled, uncombed, ungroomed, shabby, shaggy, *grungy, grubby. ANT. *neat, groomed, sharp.*

unkind *a.* mean, cruel, brutal, unfeeling, unsympathetic, cold, harsh, unmerciful, heartless, inhumane, inhuman, vicious, coldblooded, insensitive, barbarous, nasty, venomous, insulting, cutting, offensive, rude, callous. ANT. *kind, nice, friendly, compassionate, merciful.*

unknowing *a.* unaware, unenlightened, ignorant, uninformed, unschooled, unwitting, oblivious, *out to lunch, *in the dark. ANT. *aware, enlightened, informed.*

unknown *a.* mysterious, undiscovered, hidden, secret, obscure, unrecognized, undetermined, unidentified, anonymous, unnamed, unexplored, uncharted, unfamiliar, unheard-of, strange, foreign, alien, dark. ANT. *known, famous, celebrated, familiar.*

unlawful *a.* illegal, illicit, prohibited, against the law, forbidden, criminal, illicit, banned, proscribed, felonious. ANT. *legal, lawful, legitimate.*

unleash v. release, let loose, free, untie, let go.

unlike a. different, dissimilar, opposite, unalike, disparate, contrasting, unrelated, *like night and day, *like comparing apples and oranges, clashing. ANT. *alike, similar, matching.*

unlikely a. improbable, implausible, hardly possible, doubtful, inconceivable, dubious, questionable, *as likely as snow in July, remote, *as likely as the sky falling, *as likely as pigs learning to fly, having an outside chance, *a longshot. ANT. *likely, probable, certain.*

unlimited a. limitless, unrestricted, boundless, endless, immeasurable, countless, infinite, vast, complete, total, unqualified, indefinite. ANT. *limited, restricted, bounded.*

unload v. remove, unburden, disburden, lighten one's load, dump, disgorge.

unlock v. open, release, turn the combination, unlatch, unbar.

unlucky a. unfortunate, ill-fated, cursed, jinxed, hapless, star-crossed, *down on one's luck, inauspicious, unhappy, unfavorable. ANT. *lucky, fortunate, happy.*

unmanageable a. ungovernable, intractable, wild, out of control, uncontrollable, indocile, rebellious, defiant, indomitable, stubborn. ANT. *manageable, governable, controllable.*

unmannerly a. rude, discourteous, impolite, uncivil, uncivilized, indelicate, unrefined, uncultivated, ungracious, ungentlemanly, unladylike. ANT. *polite, courteous, gracious.*

unmarried a. single, unwed, unattached, eligible, available, celibate, virgin, maiden. ANT. *married, wed, *spoken for.*

unmask v. reveal, expose, unveil, *blow one's cover, disclose, *come out of the closet, *out. ANT. *disguise, mask, cover.*

unmistakable a. clear, clear-cut, plain, obvious, evident, sure, definite, certain, beyond question, unambiguous, positive, patent, unequivocal, *plain as the nose on one's face, *beyond a shadow of a doubt, glaring, blatant. ANT. *unclear, ambiguous, questionable, hazy, fuzzy.*

UNMITIGATED a. [un MIT uh gate id] not lessened or weakened in any way, absolute, out-and-out. *He had the unmitigated gall to call the mayor a buffoon.* SYN. unlessened, unmoderated, unweakened, unwatered-down,

unqualified, pure, downright, outright, out-and-out, absolute, complete, thoroughgoing, sheer. ANT. *weakened, watered-down, moderated, partial.*

unmotivated a. uninspired, indifferent, apathetic, impassive, lazy, goalless, unambitious, unenterprising. ANT. *motivated, inspired, *sparked.*

unnatural a. **1.** ARTIFICIAL imitation, synthetic, man-made, manufactured, fabricated, processed, ersatz. **2.** AFFECTED contrived, strained, forced, theatrical, put-on, not spontaneous, studied, stiff, labored. **3.** ABNORMAL strange, queer, monstrous, grotesque, freakish. ANT. *1. natural, organic, of the earth. 2. sincere, genuine, spontaneous, unstudied, unaffected. 3. normal, ordinary.*

unnecessary a. unneeded, inessential, needless, unrequired, noncompulsory, uncalled-for, gratuitous, superfluous, extraneous, redundant, surplus, expendable. ANT. *indispensable, essential, needed.*

unnerve v. *shake up, *fill with the fear of God, upset, disconcert, discourage, scare, frighten, daunt, intimidate, spook, demoralize. ANT. *encourage, embolden, fortify.*

unobtrusive a. unnoticed, unnoticeable, inconspicuous, low-key, quiet, *minding one's own business, retiring, unassertive, modest. ANT. *obtrusive, loud, conspicuous, noticeable.*

unoccupied a. empty, vacant, open, free. ANT. *taken.*

unorganized a. disorderly, sloppy, disarranged, unarranged, haphazard, unsystematic, mixed-up, confused, jumbled, cluttered, scrambled, muddled, random. ANT. *organized, arranged.*

UNORTHODOX a. [un ORTH uh doks] unconventional, not standard or accepted. *He was slightly eccentric and had an unorthodox way of painting.* SYN. unconventional, nonstandard, abnormal, out of the norm, out of the ordinary, uncommon, deviant, nonconforming, unaccepted, unofficial, eccentric. ANT. *orthodox, conventional, standard.*

unparalleled a. unmatched, unequaled, incomparable, peerless, without rival, unrivaled, without equal, unprecedented, one-of-a-kind, unique, unheard-of. ANT. *equaled, rivaled, common.*

unperturbed a. calm, unruffled, cool, composed, unflappable, unflustered, tranquil, serene, placid, sedate. ANT. *unnerved, disturbed, flustered.*

unpleasant *a.* disagreeable, nasty, painful, unwelcome, irritating, annoying, aggravating, bothersome, irksome, repellent, repugnant, sickening, nauseating, offensive, bad, objectionable, negative. ANT. *pleasant, agreeable, nice, enjoyable.*

unprecedented *a.* a first, new, novel, unheard-of, unique, singular, original, unexampled, unparalleled, extraordinary, unusual, one-of-a-kind, uncommon. ANT. *precedented, usual, common.*

unpredictable *a.* unforeseeable, *iffy, left to chance, impossible to predict, uncertain, unsure, *up in the air, random, changeable, erratic, *as capricious as the wind, fickle. ANT. *predictable, foreseeable, certain.*

unprejudiced *a.* unbiased, fair, equitable, evenhanded, unbigoted, impartial, nonpartisan, objective, neutral, just. ANT. *prejudiced, biased, bigoted.*

unpremeditated *a.* unplanned, unplotted, unintentional, spontaneous, *spur of the moment, *in the heat of passion, impulsive, impromptu, off the cuff, impetuous. ANT. *premeditated, thought out, planned.*

unprepared *a.* not ready, *caught off guard, *caught napping, *caught flat-footed, caught by surprise, ill-equipped. ANT. *prepared, ready.*

unpretentious *a.* humble, modest, down-to-earth, unassuming, unaffected, *folksy, simple, plain, natural. ANT. *pretentious, affected, arrogant.*

unprincipled *a.* immoral, unethical, unscrupulous, dishonest, dishonorable, corrupt, underhanded, crooked, devious, shady. ANT. *moral, ethical, principled.*

unproductive *a.* fruitless, nonproductive, worthless, unrewarding, unprofitable, vain, barren, useless, counterproductive, unavailing, to no avail, a losing proposition. ANT. *productive, fruitful, successful.*

unprofessional *a.* **1.** AMATEUR amateurish, sloppy, inexperienced, unskillful, inadequate, unschooled, untrained, second-rate, inferior, *bush-league, nonprofessional. **2.** UNETHICAL unprincipled, improper, indecorous, unseemly, unfitting. ANT. *1. professional, skilled, trained, experienced, expert. 2. ethical, principled, proper.*

unprotected *a.* undefended, vulnerable, open, assailable, unsafe, insecure, pregnable, exposed, unarmed. ANT. *protected, defended, armed, guarded.*

unqualified *a.* **1.** NOT MEETING REQUIREMENTS inadequate, unskilled, unschooled, ill-equipped, unequipped, not up to the job, unfit, incompetent. **2.** UNMODIFIED absolute, unmitigated, total, complete, downright, out-and-out, thorough, utter, sheer, categorical. ANT. *1. qualified, fit, competent. 2. modified, qualified, partial.*

unquestionable *a.* without question, without doubt, doubtless, certain, sure, incontrovertible, incontestable, indisputable, irrefutable, indubitable, definite, unmistakable. ANT. *open to question, doubtful, uncertain, dubious.*

unreadable *a.* illegible, undecipherable, incomprehensible. ANT. *clear, plain, legible.*

unreal *a.* imaginary, fanciful, make-believe, visionary, hallucinatory, nonexistent. ANT. *actual, factual, genuine.*

unrealistic *a.* unreasonable, impractical, romantic, starry-eyed, *pie in the sky, *castles in Spain, *castles in the air, fanciful, idealistic, fantastic. ANT. *realistic, reasonable, practical.*

unreasonable *a.* **1.** EXTRAVAGANT outrageous, preposterous, extreme, immoderate, exorbitant, unjustifiable. **2.** IRRATIONAL nonsensical, illogical, senseless, stupid, foolish, unreasoning, unwise, witless, *without rhyme or reason. ANT. *1. reasonable, moderate. 2. rational, logical.*

unrefined *a.* rough, coarse, crude, unfinished, unpolished. ANT. *polished, smooth, finished.*

unrehearsed *a.* extemporaneous, spontaneous, off the cuff, impromptu, spur of the moment, unprepared, unplanned, ad-libbed, improvised, *off the top of one's head. ANT. *rehearsed, prepared, planned.*

unreliable *a.* undependable, irresponsible, untrustworthy, unstable, fickle, changeable, capricious, *blowing hot and cold. ANT. *reliable, dependable, trustworthy, steady.*

unremitting *a.* relentless, unrelenting, incessant, continual, constant, unending, unabating, perpetual, persistent. ANT. *ending, stopping, irregular.*

unreserved *a.* uninhibited, outspoken, bold, forthright, unrestrained, unabashed, blunt, frank, to the point, not shy, loquacious, extroverted, outgoing, *motor-mouthed. ANT. *reserved, reticent, inhibited, shy.*

unresolved *a.* unsettled, *up in the air, undetermined, undecided, pending, debatable, open to debate, unfinished, *hung jury. ANT. *resolved, settled, decided.*

unrest *n.* restlessness, agitation, disturbance,

discontentment, trouble, uneasiness, disquiet, turbulence, rebellion, protest, upset. ANT. *peace, tranquility, serenity.*

unrestrained *a.* uninhibited, unrestricted, free, unhampered, unconfined, abandoned, unreserved, unbridled. ANT. *restrained, restricted, inhibited.*

unrestricted *a.* free, unbounded, unhampered, uninhibited, unlimited, unregulated, *no holds barred, unchecked. ANT. *restricted, limited, regulated.*

unripe *a.* green, immature, premature, unseasoned. ANT. *ripe, mature.*

unrivaled *a.* peerlees, matchless, unmatched, unequaled, unparalleled, supreme, superior, *number one, incomparable, unsurpassed. ANT. *equaled, mediocre, run-of-the-mill, average.*

unruly *a.* unmanageable, uncontrollable, ungovernable, intractable, rebellious, reckless, refractory, riotous, out of control, disorderly, insubordinate. ANT. *manageable, governable, controllable, docile.*

unsafe *a.* dangerous, hazardous, perilous, treacherous, threatening, insecure, unstable, precarious, life-threatening, *on thin ice, menacing, *dicey, *ticklish, *touch and go, *a tinderbox, *a powderkeg, explosive, risky. ANT. *safe, secure, protected, harmless.*

unsanitary *a.* unclean, dirty, unhealthy, unhygienic, filthy, contaminated, foul, polluted, germ-infested, tainted. ANT. *sanitary, clean, sterile, antiseptic.*

unsatisfactory *a.* inadequate, unfulfilling, unacceptable, deficient, insufficient, lacking, wanting, unworthy, *not up to par. ANT. *satisfactory, good enough, adequate.*

unsavory *a.* **1.** TASTELESS OR BAD-TASTING unappetizing, nauseating, sickening, stomach-turning, unpalatable, disagreeable, rotten, *yucky, *gross. **2.** OFFENSIVE, OBNOXIOUS nasty, objectionable, repugnant, repellant, revolting. ANT. *1. tasty, delicious, *yummy. 2. pleasant, good, agreeable.*

UNSCRUPULOUS *a.* [un SCROOP yoo lus] unprincipled, immoral, unethical. *He was unscrupulous enough to steal all of the church's money.* SYN. unprincipled, immoral, unethical, dishonest, dishonorable, without conscience, indifferent to right and wrong, corrupt, underhanded, criminal, antisocial. ANT. *principled, moral, ethical, scrupulous.*

unseat *a.* oust, remove from power, remove from office, unhorse, dislodge, dethrone, depose, overthrow. ANT. *install.*

unseemly *a.* improper, unbecoming, indecorous, in bad taste, undignified, unbefitting, out of place, inappropriate, indelicate, indecent, vulgar, crude. ANT. *seemly, proper, appropriate.*

unselfish *a.* giving, generous, selfless, other-directed, charitable, altruistic, philanthropic, openhanded, magnanimous, kind, bighearted, considerate, compassionate. ANT. *selfish, self-centered, greedy, *a taker, *thinking the world revolves around oneself.*

unsettle *a.* disturb, unnerve, upset, disconcert, trouble, agitate, bother, ruffle, rattle, disquiet, perturb, *shake up, discompose. ANT. *relax, calm, soothe.*

unsettled *a.* SEE UNRESOLVED

unsightly *a.* ugly, unattractive, *an eyesore, repulsive, repellent, *gross, hideous, grotesque, homely, revolting, repugnant. ANT. *attractive, beautiful, pretty.*

unskilled *a.* untrained, unschooled, inexpert, amateurish, inept, incompetent, incapable, unable, inexperienced, bumbling, *all thumbs. ANT. *skilled, proficient, trained, expert.*

unskillful *a.* SEE UNSKILLED

unsociable *a.* unfriendly, aloof, cold, remote, distant, hermitlike, antisocial, withdrawn, introverted, shy, *standoffish, *stuck-up, preferring one's own company. ANT. *extroverted, outgoing, gregarious, friendly.*

unsolicited *a.* unasked, unsought, unrequested, voluntary, spontaneous, free. ANT. *solicited, asked-for, sought.*

unsophisticated *a.* simple, naive, innocent, unworldly, childlike, inexperienced, green, *born yesterday, uncultured, unrefined, unpolished, *down-home, *folksy, *like a hick, *like a hayseed, artless, ingenuous. ANT. *sophisticated, worldly, experienced, *hip.*

unsound *a.* **1.** UNHEALTHY unwell, sickly, ill, ailing, infirm, afflicted, diseased, abnormal, insane, crazy, psychotic, *psycho. **2.** UNSAFE insecure, unstable, flimsy, shaky, unsteady, unreliable, dangerous, perilous, hazardous, rickety. **3.** INACCURATE unreliable, untruthful, erroneous, invalid, irrational, weak, groundless, illogical, fallacious. ANT. *1. healthy, fit, normal. 2. safe, solid, stable, secure. 3. accurate, valid, true, reliable.*

unsparing *a.* liberal, free, lavish, profuse, generous, giving. ANT. *meager, sparse.*

unspeakable a. bad, horrible, terrible, beyond words, beyond description, unimaginable, evil, wicked, vile, horrendous, heinous, monstrous, atrocious. ANT. *good, wonderful.*

unspoiled a. fresh, pristine, untouched, unadulterated, unpolluted, perfect, whole, pure, unblemished, undamaged. ANT. *spoiled, ruined, rotten.*

unspoken a. unsaid, silent, tacit, understood, implicit, assumed. ANT. *spoken, expressed.*

unstable a. **1.** UNFIXED unsteady, unbalanced, variable, wobbling, shaky, rickety, teetering, unanchored. **2.** CHANGEABLE erratic, capricious, fickle, unpredictable, mercurial, vacillating, volatile. ANT. *1. fixed, rock-solid, anchored, secure. 2. constant, steady, unchanging.*

unsteady a. SEE UNSTABLE

unstudied a. natural, unaffected, spontaneous, unconscious, offhand, unlabored, impromptu, *off the cuff, extemporaneous. ANT. *studied, affected, labored.*

unsubstantiated a. uncorroborated, unproven, unconfirmed, open to question, questionable, unauthenticated, uncertified. ANT. *corroborated, proven.*

unsuccessful a. a failure, a loser, *a turkey, *a dog, *a flop, *a bomb, unprofitable, fruitless, futile, vain, useless, abortive, ineffectual, unfortunate, unlucky, unhappy, ill-fated, doomed, disastrous, catastrophic. ANT. *successful, profitable, winning, fortunate.*

unsuitable a. inappropriate, unfit, wrong, improper, inadequate, unacceptable, unsatisfactory, unbefitting, inapt, out of place, ill-fitting. ANT. *appropriate, fit, right, acceptable.*

unsung a. unrecognized, unacclaimed, unapplauded. ANT. *applauded, praised, extolled.*

unsure a. uncertain, doubtful, in doubt, questionable, *iffy, *up in the air, undecided, dubious, skeptical, not confident, insecure. ANT. *sure, certain, confident.*

unsurpassed a. supreme, superior, unrivaled, peerless, unparalleled, the best, incomparable, greatest, leading, preeminent. ANT. *second-rate, average, worst.*

unsuspecting a. trusting, naive, gullible, credulous, unknowing, unaware, innocent, unwary, inexperienced, believing, unsophisticated, oblivious. ANT. *wary, suspicious, questioning.*

unsympathetic a. cold, uncaring, indifferent, apathetic, heartless, lacking compassion, unfeeling, stony, unmoved, callous, mean, hard, *hard as nails, *having ice water in one's veins, insensitive. ANT. *sympathetic, compassionate, caring.*

untamed a. wild, unbroken, ungovernable, uncontrollable, unmanageable, spirited, undomesticated. ANT. *tamed, broken, domesticated.*

untangle v. disentangle, unravel, extricate, straighten out, unsnarl, untie. ANT. *tangle, snarl.*

untarnished a. stainless, spotless, clean, bright, unblemished, uncorrupted, innocent, pure. ANT. *tarnished, corrupted.*

untenable a. indefensible, insupportable, weak, flawed, *full of holes, groundless, unsound. ANT. *tenable, sound, secure.*

unthankful a. ungrateful, unappreciative. ANT. *obliged, grateful*

unthinkable a. inconceivable, unimaginable, incomprehensible, beyond belief, unbelievable, incredible, out of the question. ANT. *possible, feasible.*

untidy a. sloppy, messy, slovenly, disheveled, bedraggled, unkempt, disarranged, disorderly, cluttered, littered. ANT. *tidy, neat, orderly.*

untie v. unfasten, loosen, free, undo, unlace, unbind, loose.

untimely a. ill-timed, inconvenient, inopportune, inexpedient, premature, early, unseasonable, inappropriate, unfavorable, unfortunate, inauspicious. ANT. *timely, opportune, well-timed.*

untold a. innumerable, countless, incalculable, uncountable, myriad, *umpteen, immeasurable, infinite, limitless. ANT. *finite, limited, few.*

untoward a. inappropriate, unseemly, improper, indecorous, in bad taste, unbefitting, out of place, tactless, indelicate, ungentlemanly, unladylike. ANT. *proper, appropriate, seemly.*

untrained a. unschooled, uneducated, inexperienced, green, raw, unskilled, *not knowing the ropes, unqualified, incompetent, inexpert, ignorant. ANT. *trained, schooled, educated.*

untroubled a. unperturbed, unruffled, calm, cool, relaxed, worry-free, *unflappable, dispassionate, tranquil, placid. ANT. *agitated, troubled, worried, anxious.*

untrue a. false, wrong, incorrect, erroneous, inaccurate, not right, in error, fictitious, fallacious, specious, spurious, distorted. ANT. *true, factual, correct.*

untrustworthy *a.* undependable, unreliable, dishonest, deceitful, devious, false, disloyal, unfaithful, treacherous, disreputable. ANT. *trustworthy, dependable, honest, loyal.*

untruthful *a.* lying, dishonest, deceptive, deceitful, mendacious, fraudulent, misleading, insincere. ANT. *truthful, honest.*

unusual *a.* out of the ordinary, odd, rare, atypical, unfamiliar, singular, uncommon, exceptional, unconventional, peculiar, queer, strange, bizarre, weird, extraordinary, unique, unheard-of, unprecedented, unparalleled, different, abnormal, distinguished, refreshing, *far-out, unexpected, unorthodox. ANT. *usual, ordinary, common, run-of-the-mill.*

unvarnished *a.* plain, straightforward, unembellished, unpolished, naked, raw. ANT. *adorned, elaborated.*

unveil *a.* reveal, expose, show, uncover, disclose. ANT. *cloak, hide.*

unwarranted *a.* uncalled-for, unjustified, inexcusable, indefensible, groundless, baseless, gratuitous. ANT. *warranted, justifiable.*

unwary *a.* incautious, heedless, unguarded, unthinking, careless, unsuspecting, rash, reckless, imprudent, unobservant, naive, ignorant. ANT. *wary, cautious, guarded.*

unwavering *a.* steady, firm, consistent, unfaltering, staunch, resolute, determined, single-minded, persistent, steadfast, unswerving. ANT. *wavering, faltering, unsteady.*

unwelcome *a.* unwanted, not wanted, undesirable, rejected, spurned, *shut out, *as welcome as the plague. ANT. *welcome, wanted, desired.*

unwell *a.* unhealthy, sick, sickly, ailing, ill, diseased, bedridden, *out of sorts, *under the weather, *green around the gills, run-down, *off one's feed. ANT. *well, healthy, fit.*

unwholesome *a.* harmful, unhealthy, deleterious, not good for one, unsound, detrimental, hurtful, noxious, pernicious, poisonous, insalubrious. ANT. *wholesome, healthy, good for one.*

unwieldy *a.* hard to handle, awkward, unmanageable, clumsy, cumbersome, bulky, hulking, massive, unhandy, ponderous, heavy. ANT. *handy, pocket-sized, lightweight.*

unwilling *a.* against, disagreeable, loath, opposed, reluctant, not in the mood, disinclined, unobliging, unenthusiastic, averse, unaccommodating, resistant, contrary, balky. ANT. *willing, enthusiastic, eager.*

unwind *v.* relax, take it easy, calm down, relieve one's tension, recreate, *loosen up, *kick back, wind down. ANT. *tense up, *get wound up, *make oneself a nervous wreck, *stress oneself out.*

unwise *a.* imprudent, injudicious, not smart, unintelligent, dumb, stupid, ill-advised, thoughtless, foolish, naive, moronic, brainless, irrational, illogical. ANT. *wise, smart, prudent, intelligent.*

unwitting *a.* unknowing, unaware, unconscious, oblivious, inadvertent, accidental, unplanned, chance, involuntary. ANT. *knowing, aware, planned.*

unwonted *a.* uncommon, unusual, rare, unaccustomed, unfamiliar. ANT. *typical, common.*

unworldly *a.* 1. UNSOPHISTICATED naive, inexperienced, innocent, *born yesterday, *like a babe in the woods, raw, unaffected. 2. SPIRITUAL divine, religious, godly, ethereal, heavenly.

unworthy *a.* undeserving, unmerited, unearned, unqualified, ineligible, worthless, inferior, no good, unacceptable, disgraceful. ANT. *worthy, deserving.*

unyielding *a.* immovable, inflexible, firm, stubborn, obstinate, unbending, uncompromising, headstrong, resolute, determined, hard, stiff. ANT. *flexible, compromising, yielding.*

up *a.* excited, *psyched. ANT. *down, depressed.*

up-and-coming *a.* rising, *climbing the ladder of success, *growing by leaps and bounds, succeeding, growing in status, promising. ANT. *over-the-hill, passé.*

upbeat *a.* positive, optimistic, bright, cheerful, rosy, sunny, happy, heartening, uplifting, encouraging. ANT. *down, negative, dark.*

UPBRAID *v.* [up BRADE] to reproach or scold. *The officer upbraided the motorist for driving drunk.* SYN. reproach, scold, rebuke, reprimand, chastise, *bawl out, *chew out, admonish, berate, reprove, censure, *give a tongue-lashing, *rake over the coals, *take to task. ANT. *commend, praise, approve.*

upbringing *n.* raising, rearing, breeding, grooming, training, nurturing, schooling.

upchuck *v.* vomit, throw up, *puke, spew, *hurl, *ralph, *toss one's cookies, regurgitate, *blow lunch, be sick.

update *v.* bring up to date, modernize, revise, renew, *bring into the twenty-first century, renovate.

upend *v.* invert, turn over, upset, topple.

upgrade *v.* raise, improve, promote, elevate, enhance, better, make better, advance, enrich. ANT. *degrade, downgrade, demote.*

upheaval n. eruption, blowup, explosion, earthquake, cataclysm, destruction, catastrophe, revolution, overthrow, change. ANT. *peace, quiet, tranquility.*

uphill a. laborious, arduous, hard, difficult, taxing, strenuous, grueling, labor intensive, backbreaking, ANT. *downhill, easy, effortless.*

uphold v. support, hold up, maintain, stand by, sustain, carry, back, champion.

upkeep n. maintenance, repair, running, costs, overhead, outlay, expenses, expenditure.

uplift v. raise, elevate, inspire, lift, improve, hearten. ANT. *bring down, depress.*

upper hand n. advantage, control, domination, *driver's seat, whip hand, catbird seat, supremacy, rule, a leg up.

uppermost a. highest, top, loftiest, foremost, greatest, superior, ultimate, chief, maximum, leading. ANT. *lowest.*

uppity a. arrogant, snobbish, haughty, stuck-up, *high-falutin, lofty, proud, uppish, *full of oneself, conceited, presumptuous. ANT. *folksy, down to earth, modest, humble.*

upright a. 1. ERECT standing, vertical, perpendicular, on end, straight up. 2. HONORABLE honest, moral, ethical, decent, good, righteous, upstanding, scrupulous, principled, virtuous, reputable. ANT. *1. prone, lying, horizontal. 2. dishonorable, disreputable, corrupt, dishonest.*

uprising n. rebellion, revolt, revolution, insurrection, insurgence, mutiny, riot, unrest, anarchy, outbreak of violence, overthrow, coup d'état.

uproar n. stir, turmoil, ado, *to-do, clamor, *flap, furor, fuss, noise, riot, brouhaha, *blowup, *hoopla, outburst, *ruckus, disturbance, *big stink, hullabaloo. ANT. *peace, quiet, tranquility.*

uproarious a. 1. NOISY loud, clamorous, tumultuous, boisterous, wild, riotous, deafening, earsplitting. 2. HILARIOUS *a scream, side-splitting, hysterical, *a laugh riot, rollicking. ANT. *1. quiet, peaceful, still. 2. somber, sober, grim.*

uproot v. root up, root out, extirpate, pull out, rip out, move, weed, remove, eradicate, destroy.

ups and downs n. peaks and valleys, highs and lows, feasts and famines, vicissitudes.

upset n. 1. DISTURBANCE unhappiness, agitation, trouble, distress, worry, shake-up, perturbation, illness. 2. DEFEAT overthrow, reversal, surprise loss. 3. TURNOVER flip, tipping, toppling, capsizing.

upset v. 1. DISTURB make unhappy, bother, agitate, trouble, distress, worry, disquiet, hurt, make angry, disconcert, perturb, unsettle, grieve, *stress out, make anxious. 2. OVERTURN upend, turn upside-down, capsize, topple, tip, flip, turn over, knock over. 3. DEFEAT overthrow, triumph over, beat, *get the better of. ANT. *1. make happy, fill with contentment, soothe. 2. turn upright, stand up. 3. lose, be defeated.*

upset a. 1. DISTURBED unhappy, bothered, agitated, troubled, distressed, worried, disquieted, hurt, angry, disconcerted, perturbed, unsettled, grieved. 2. OVERTURNED upended, upside-down, capsized, toppled, flipped. ANT. *1. contented, happy, blissful. 2. upright, standing.*

upshot n. outcome, result, conclusion, end result, end product, effect, payoff, eventuality, culmination, consequence, aftermath, consummation.

upside-down a. inverted, bottom-side up, topside down, reversed, wrong-side up, backward, *bassackwards, topsy-turvy. ANT. *righted, right-side-up.*

upstage v. steal the spotlight, steal the show, draw attention to one's self, outshine.

upstanding a. upright, honorable, honest, reputable, virtuous, moral, ethical, good, principled, uncorrupt, of sterling character. ANT. *corrupt, low, disreputable, immoral.*

upstart n. parvenue, nouveau riche, arriviste, pretender, status seeker, jackanapes, whippersnapper.

upswing n. advancement, expanding market, bull market, upsurge, improvement, rise, progress, recovery, uptick.

uptight a. Sl. nervous, tense, anxious, on edge, edgy, uneasy, troubled, restive, worried. ANT. *relaxed, calm, cool.*

up-to-date a. current, up-to-the-minute, contemporary, *cutting edge, *state of the art, new, modern, in vogue, *all the rage, au courant, fashionable, stylish, trendy, late, *now. ANT. *outdated, out-of-date, old-fashioned, antiquated, passé.*

upturn n. SEE UPSWING

upward adv. skyward, overhead, above, aloft, atop. ANT. *downward, below.*

upward mobility n. social climbing, climbing the corporate ladder, status seeking, *clawing one's way to the top.

urban a. city, citified, metropolitan, cosmopolitan, densely populated, municipal, civic. ANT. *rural, country, deep woods.*

URBANE *a.* [ur BANE] smoothly polite, suave, refined. *The tour guide was charming and urbane.* SYN. smooth, suave, polite, courteous, polished, refined, gracious, debonair, mannerly, elegant, poised, charming. ANT. *rude, coarse, impolite, offensive.*

urchin *n.* kid, boy, youngster, child, imp, *little devil, troublemaker, rogue, rascal, guttersnipe, brat, juvenile delinquent.

urge *n.* drive, yearning, desire, hunger, longing, impulse, craving, compulsion, yen, passion, hankering, stimulus, goad.

urge *v.* **1.** ENCOURAGE press, push for, implore, plead, exhort, beg, beseech, advocate, entreat, ask, solicit. **2.** STIMULATE provoke, incite, push, drive, force, spur, accelerate, speed.

urgency *n.* matter of life or death, emergency, crisis, extremity, exigency.

urgent *a.* a matter of life or death, pressing, crucial, critical, exigent, requiring immediate attention, imperative, first priority, paramount. ANT. *unimportant, insignificant, trivial.*

urinate *v.* micturate, *pee, *piss, relieve oneself.

urn *n.* vase, container, receptacle, jar, vessel, ossuary.

usage *n.* custom, habit, practice, tradition, convention, routine, way.

use *n.* **1.** SERVICE *mileage, usefulness, employment, worth, benefit. **2.** UTILIZATION application, employment, exercise. **3.** FUNCTION service, usefulness.

use *v.* **1.** UTILIZE employ, make use of, work, practice, operate, exercise, manipulate, ply. **2.** ABUSE take advantage of, exploit, *walk on, *play for a sucker, *bleed dry. **3.** EXPEND spend, consume, exhaust, deplete.

used *a.* secondhand, pre-owned, hand-me-down, passed down, recycled, old, castoff. ANT. *new, fresh, brand-new.*

used to *adv.* familiar with, accustomed to, habituated, acclimated.

useful *a.* serviceable, helpful, valuable, practical, utilitarian, beneficial, handy, of use, functional. ANT. *useless, worthless, of no help.*

useless *a.* worthless, of no use, unavailing, unserviceable, ineffectual, ineffective, to no avail, unproductive, unprofitable, futile, vain. ANT. *useful, valuable, helpful.*

usher *n.* usherette, guide, escort, doorkeeper, attendant, page.

usher *v.* **1.** GUIDE escort, lead, conduct, show in, marshal, direct, accompany. **2.** PRECEDE herald, pave the way, introduce, inaugurate.

usual *a.* ordinary, customary, common, everyday, conventional, normal, standard, regular, habitual, routine, accustomed, traditional, stock, run-of-the-mill, average, typical. ANT. *unusual, uncommon, abnormal, irregular.*

USURP *v.* [yoo SURP] to take over a position of power by force, overthrow. *The rebels attempted to usurp the president's office.* SYN. take over, overthrow, depose, dethrone, oust, unseat, unhorse, commandeer, wrest, seize, expropriate.

utensil *n.* implement, tool, instrument, fork, knife, spoon.

UTILITARIAN *a.* [yoo TIL i TAIR ee un] useful, practical. *He chose a car that was utilitarian rather than showy.* SYN. useful, practical, functional, pragmatic, serviceable, efficient, down to earth, sensible. ANT. *impractical, romantic, fanciful.*

utility *n.* usefulness, practicality, service, function, benefit, adaptability.

utilize *v.* use, put to use, employ. SEE USE

utmost *a.* **1.** GREATEST highest, maximum, maximal, most, uppermost, supreme, preeminent, best. **2.** FARTHEST most distant, outermost, extreme, last, remotest. ANT. *1. lowest, smallest, worst. 2. closest, nearest.*

utopia *n.* Shangri-la, paradise, Eden, best of all possible worlds, heaven on earth, perfect society, idealized society, land of milk and honey.

Utopian *a.* idealistic, ideal, visionary, perfect, fanciful, chimerical, grandiose, *pie in the sky, romantic, fictitious, make-believe, impractical, unfeasible. ANT. *realistic, down to earth.*

utter *v.* speak, say, vocalize, emit, articulate, enunciate, voice, state, verbalize, assert, declare, shout, come out with, mouth.

utter *a.* thorough, complete, absolute, outright, out-and-out, total, sheer, pure, perfect, unmitigated. ANT. *partial, rather.*

utterance *n.* vocalization, articulation, expression, speech, statement, verbalization, assertion, declaration, shout, sound, wording, mouthing.

utterly *adv.* completely, totally, entirely, thoroughly, wholly, absolutely, purely, perfectly, fully. ANT. *partially, partly.*

V

vacancy *n.* opening, space, emptiness, gap, room, void, vacuousness, hole, nothing, hollow.

vacant *a.* **1.** EMPTY open, unfilled, unoccupied, clear, bare, deserted, void, devoid, hollow, uninhabited, unused. **2.** MINDLESS stupid, blank, vacuous, oblivious, expressionless, dull, bovine, *bubbleheaded. ANT. *1. full, filled, occupied, used. 2. intelligent, thoughtful, alert.*

vacate *v.* leave, give up, leave behind, quit, desert, withdraw, depart, abandon. ANT. *fill, occupy.*

vacation *n.* holiday, time off, *R&R, rest and relaxation, recess, furlough, sabbatical, respite, hiatus, break, trip, cruise. "A semi-annual reminder that doing nothing is hard work."—Art Hinkle. ANT. *daily grind, hard labor.*

vaccination *n.* inoculation, *shot, immunity.

VACILLATE *v.* [VAS uh LATE] to waver or be indecisive. *He couldn't make up his mind and vacillated between choices all day.* SYN. waver, be indecisive, go back and forth, fluctuate, hesitate, shilly-shally, *blow hot and cold, be irresolute, *sit on the fence, hedge, equivocate, hem and haw.

vacuity *n.* **1.** EMPTINESS nothingness, vacuum, void, blankness. **2.** EMPTY-HEADEDNESS stupidity, ignorance, dullness, denseness, mindlessness, lack of intelligence, *bubbleheadedness, imbecility. ANT. *1. substance, matter, fullness. 2. intelligence, brains, *smarts.*

vacuous *a.* stupid, empty-headed, dumb, dense, unintelligent, ignorant, imbecilic, moronic, *bubbleheaded, blank, bovine. ANT. *intelligent, smart, bright, knowledgeable.*

vacuum *n.* emptiness, nothingness, void, blankness, vacuity.

vagabond *n.* vagrant, drifter, tramp, wanderer, transient, *bum, hobo, nomad, rambler, rover, floater, itinerant.

vagabond *a.* moving, wandering, drifting, traveling, roving, rambling, roaming, wayfaring, itinerant, homeless, shiftless, idle. ANT. *rooted, responsible.*

vagary *n.* caprice, whim, whimsy, impulse, notion, fancy, crotchet, idea, oddity, *flash.

vagina *n.* sex organ, private parts, genitals, genitalia, reproductive organ.

vagrant *n.* wanderer, roamer, vagabond, nomad, rambler, rover, Bohemian, gypsy, tramp, hobo, *bum.

vagrant *a.* wandering, roaming, wayward, vagabond, nomadic, rambling, roving, aimless, Bohemian, gypsy.

vague *a.* indefinite, unclear, uncertain, obscure, fuzzy, hazy, foggy, nebulous, amorphous, indistinct, unspecific, imprecise, ambiguous, equivocal, questionable. ANT. *definite, clear, distinct, explicit.*

vain *a.* **1.** WORTHLESS of no use, useless, empty, hollow, futile, unproductive, fruitless, pointless, unsuccessful, unavailing, idle. **2.** CONCEITED proud, vainglorious, *full of oneself, egotistical, self-important, arrogant, pompous, self-admiring, primping, preening, haughty, dandyish, foppish, swaggering, strutting, *in love with oneself. ANT. *1. productive, effective, worthwhile. 2. modest, humble, self-effacing.*

vainglorious *a.* proud, boasting, vain, singing one's own praises, bragging, *blowing one's own horn, *talking big, swaggering, strutting, arrogant, pompous, basking in one's own glory. ANT. *modest, humble, self-effacing.*

vainglory *n.* pride, boastfulness, vanity, pomp, ostentation, arrogance, bragging, swaggering, strutting, haughtiness. ANT. *modesty, humbleness, shyness.*

valance *n.* drapery, curtain.

vale *n.* dale, dell. SEE VALLEY

valedictory *n.* farewell speech, goodbye speech.

valedictory *a.* farewell, parting, goodbye, departing, last. ANT. *welcoming, greeting.*

valet *n.* dresser, manservant, servant, groom, foot servant, attendant.

valiant *a.* brave, courageous, fearless, bold, heroic, unflinching, lionhearted, unafraid, intrepid, *gutsy, manly, *macho, virile, gallant, chivalrous. ANT. *cowardly, *chicken, timid, craven, *wimpy.*

valid *a.* **1.** LEGAL legitimate, authorized, certified, sanctioned, lawful, warranted, approved, authentic, genuine. **2.** SOUND well-grounded, well-founded, solid, validated, logical, substantiated, correct, accurate, unassailable. ANT. *1. illegal, illegitimate, unauthorized, invalid. 2. flimsy, unsound, unproven.*

validate *v.* **1.** MAKE LEGAL make legitimate, authorize, certify, sanction, warrant, approve. **2.** CONFIRM verify, prove, substantiate, corroborate, back up, support, authenticate, certify. ANT. *1. invalidate, cancel. 2. disprove, invalidate.*

validation n. **1.** LEGALIZATION legitimization, authorization, certification, sanctioning. **2.** CONFIRMATION verification, proof, substantiation, corroboration, support, authentication, certification. ANT. *invalidation.*

validity n. **1.** LEGALITY lawfulness, legitimacy, authority, sanction. **2.** SOUNDNESS solidity, correctness, accuracy, authenticity, genuineness.

valise n. suitcase, bag, travel bag, handbag, carryall, luggage, case, grip.

valley n. dale, dell, vale, canyon, gorge, lowland, basin, gulch, chasm, hollow, glen. ANT. *mountain, highland.*

valor n. courage, bravery, boldness, fearlessness, *guts, nerve, heroism, daring, *derring-do, backbone, *moxie, stoutheartedness, bravado, confidence, manliness, gallantry, chivalry, heart. ANT. *cowardice, fear, *wimpiness, spinelessness.*

valorous a. courageous, brave, bold, fearless, *gutsy, nervy, heroic, daring, stouthearted, confident, manly, gallant, chivalrous, tough. ANT. *cowardly, fearful, *wimpy.*

valuable a. costly, priceless, precious, dear, expensive, high-priced, valued, prized, in demand, worthwhile, invaluable, important, useful, profitable, beneficial, helpful. ANT. *worthless, cheap, *not worth the powder to blow it to hell, unimportant.*

valuation n. appraisal, evaluation, estimate.

value n. **1.** WORTH market price, appraisal, assessment, equivalent, return, face value. **2.** MERIT use, importance, weight, desirability, esteem, respect, benefit, profit, power, utility, marketability. ANT. *insignificance, uselessness, unimportance.*

value v. **1.** APPRAISE assess, evaluate, rate, valuate, estimate, put a price on. **2.** TREASURE prize, cherish, hold dear, respect, esteem, appreciate, consider important, love.

valued a. treasured, prized, cherished, dear, respected, esteemed, appreciated, highly regarded, admired, loved. ANT. *unimportant, underappreciated.*

values n. principles, morals, ideals, standards, ethics, beliefs, mores, what's important.

valve n. stopper, shutoff, cock, gate, flap, plug, lid.

vamoose v. *skedaddle, go, *git. SEE LEAVE

vamp n. seductress, temptress, seducer, flirt, vampire, femme fatale, siren, enchantress.

vamp v. seduce, tempt, flirt, charm, beguile, lure with one's feminine charms.

vampire n. bloodsucker, Dracula, ghoul, bat.

van n. truck, wagon, lorry, trailer.

vandal n. despoiler, wrecker, destroyer, mutilator, graffiti artist, defacer, hoodlum, juvenile delinquent.

vandalism n. destruction, defacing, grafitti, *trashing, wrecking, smashing, breaking, disfigurement, tearing apart, spoiling.

vandalize v. destroy, deface, spray paint, *trash, wreck, smash, break, disfigure, tear apart, ruin, spoil.

VANGUARD n. [VAN gard] the leading or front members of an attacking army. Also, the leading or pioneering members of a movement, project, trend, etc. *He was among the vanguard of the new age artists.* SYN. front, forefront, fore, head, front line, advance guard, cutting edge, leading edge, leaders, trailblazers, pioneers, trendsetters, innovators, avant-garde, forerunners. ANT. *rear, back, followers, stragglers.*

vanish v. disappear, fade, evanesce, dissolve, dematerialize, pass from sight, vanish into thin air, vaporize, evaporate, leave no trace. ANT. *materialize, appear, come into view.*

vanity n. **1.** PRIDE vainglory, self-admiration, conceit, ego, *ego trip, egotism, narcissism, arrogance, boastfulness, self-importance, smugness. "[That which] keeps persons in favor with themselves who are out of favor with all others."—Shakespeare. "The greatest of all flatterers."—La Rochefoucauld. "An itch for the praise of fools."—Robert Browning. **2.** FUTILITY uselessness, worthlessness, emptiness, hollowness. ANT. *1. modesty, humility, humbleness, self-effacement. 2. worth, usefulness.*

vanquish v. conquer, defeat, overcome, beat, best, overpower, overthrow, master, subdue, crush, destroy, trample, prevail over, triumph over. ANT. *lose, be defeated, submit.*

vantage n. advantage, *leg up, leverage, superiority, high ground, edge, *inside track, *jump.

vantage point n. perspective. SEE POSITION

VAPID a. [VAP id] dull, flat, tasteless. *He watched one vapid television show after another and finally fell asleep.* SYN. dull, flat, boring, uninteresting, tiresome, tedious, tasteless, flavorless, colorless, insipid, inane, lifeless, bland, lame, unimaginative, *dull as dishwater, *blah. ANT. *interesting, stimulating, imaginative, exciting.*

vapor *n*. moisture, mist, fog, haze, steam, cloud, spray, breath, exhalation, humidity, condensation, miasma, smog.

vaporize *v*. humidify, mist, steam, fume.

vaporous *a*. humid, misty, steamy, foggy, damp, clammy, muggy, moist, hazy, gaseous, fumy, murky. ANT. *dry*.

variable *a*. changeable, changing, unstable, fluctuating, irregular, inconstant, vacillating, wavering, *like a chameleon, on again off again, *blowing hot and cold, diverse, fickle, capricious, as variable as the wind. ANT. *unchangeable, invariable, fixed, steady, stable*.

variance *n*. **1.** DIFFERENCE discrepancy, divergence, deviation, disparity, departure. **2.** DISPUTE argument, quarrel, disagreement, altercation, division, contention, difference of opinion, conflict. **3.** PERMISSION pass, *okay, pass-through. ANT. **2.** *agreement, harmony, accord*.

variant *n*. different version, variation.

variation *n*. change, difference, alternative, departure, turn, fluctuation, break from the norm, aberration, variant, modification, variety. ANT. *sameness, uniformity*.

varied *a*. various, assorted, diverse, diversified, mixed, miscellaneous, different, motley, sundry, multifarious, heterogeneous, *a mixed bag. ANT. **1.** *the same, uniform, homogeneous*.

variegated *a*. particolored, varicolored, multicolored, polychromatic, streaked, mottled, dappled, spotted, striped, kaleidoscopic, *like a rainbow. ANT. *monochromatic, one-colored, uniform*.

variety *n*. **1.** VARIATION diversity, change, difference, heterogeneity. **2.** ASSORTMENT miscellany, *mixed bag, potpourri, mixture, hodgepodge, collection, melange. **3.** TYPE sort, kind, class, make, category, species, genus. ANT. **1.** *sameness, homogeneity*.

various *a*. **1.** VARIED different, diverse, assorted, sundry, manifold, mixed, motley. **2.** SEVERAL many, countless, numerous, abundant. ANT. **1.** *same, similar*.

varnish *n*. lacquer, shellac, enamel, stain, gloss, veneer, coat, finish, glaze, polish.

vary *v*. differ, alter, change, modify, deviate, diverge, diversify, depart.

varying *a*. variable, changing, alternating, differing, different, fluctuating, deviating, diverging, departing, *blowing hot and cold. ANT. *steady, constant*.

vase *n*. flower holder, pot, jar, vessel, pitcher, jug, amphora, tazza, potiche, urn.

vast *a*. huge, immense, enormous, extensive, boundless, colossal, astronomical, gigantic, titanic, massive, infinite, far-reaching, immeasurable, stupendous. ANT. *tiny, limited, small, microscopic*.

vat *n*. tub, container, tank, cauldron, cistern, cask, tun.

vault *n*. **1.** CHAMBER mausoleum, safe, security room, strongroom. **2.** JUMP leap, hop, bound, spring.

vault *v*. jump, leap, hop, bound, spring, hurdle.

vaunt *v*. boast, brag, crow, *talk big, gloat, swagger, strut, *lay it on thick.

veer *v*. turn, swerve, curve, change direction, change course, wheel, deviate, shift, diverge, tack.

vegetable *n*. **1.** PLANT herb, root, produce, potato, tomato, carrot, cabbage, broccoli, turnip, lettuce, spinach, cucumber, onion, scallion, leek, beet, green bean, asparagus, artichoke, eggplant. **2.** NONFUNCTIONING HUMAN comatose patient, *brain-dead patient, imbecile, idiot, moron, blob.

vegetarian *n*. vegan.

vegetarian *a*. herbivorous, plant-eating. ANT. *carnivorous*.

vegetate *v*. wither and die, languish, stagnate, be brain-dead, be comatose.

vegetation *n*. plants, greenery, plant-life, flora, herbage.

vehemence *n*. intensity, passion, force, violence, fierceness, emotion, zeal, fire, fervor, ardor, fury, enthusiasm, power. ANT. *indifference, apathy, mildness*.

VEHEMENT *a*. [VEE uh munt] intense, passionate, fervent. *She denied her part in the crime vehemently.* SYN. intense, passionate, fervent, ardent, forceful, violent, fierce, emotional, zealous, fiery, furious, enthusiastic, powerful. ANT. *indifferent, apathetic, mild, passive*.

vehemently *a*. intensely, passionately, fervently, ardently, forcefully, violently, fiercely, emotionally, zealously, furiously, enthusiastically, powerfully. ANT. *indifferently, passively, mildly*.

vehicle *n*. **1.** TRANSPORT automobile, car, truck, tractor, van, wagon, *buggy, *heap, jalopy, motorcycle, wheels, *gas hog, *bucket of bolts, *clunker, *crate, *hunk-of-junk, *puddle jumper, boat, bus, train, carriage, coach.

WORD FIND

boxlike coach of 1800s: brougham
bus traveling regular route, small, passenger: jitney
cab, old-time: hackney, hansom cab
carriage, enclosed: coach
carriage, four-wheeled: landau, phaeton, surrey
carriage, two-wheeled: chaise, curricle, gig, sulky
carriage, Western, open, four-wheel: buckboard
funeral: hearse
Oriental cab pulled by one or two persons: ricksha, jinrickisha
parade: float
sledlike conveyance: sleigh, bob-sleigh, carriole, cutter, pung
stagecoach: Concord
streetcar: trolley, cable car
three-wheeled motorcycle for backwoods: ATV, all-terrain vehicle
wagon, covered: Conestoga, prairie schooner
SEE AIRPLANE, AUTOMOBILE, BOAT, MOTORCYCLE, SHIP, TRAIN
2. MEANS medium, instrument, tool, agent, channel, intermediary.

veil *n.* cover, covering, gauze, net, drapery, cloth, caul, shroud, curtain, screen, purdah, mask.

veil *v.* cover, shroud, curtain, screen, mask, disguise, hide, conceal, obscure, darken, cloak, shield.

veiled *a.* disguised, hidden, covered up, concealed, obscured, shrouded, screened, darkened, shielded. ANT. *exposed.*

vein *n.* **1.** BLOOD VESSEL capillary, artery. **2.** TONE quality, feeling, style, manner, mode, strain, mood, way, fashion. **3.** STREAK seam, load, line, layer, stratum.

velocity *n.* speed, rate of speed, pace, quickness, swiftness, fleetness, rapidity, celerity, miles per hour, revolutions per minute, rate.

WORD FIND

measuring device: tachometer

velvet *n.* velveteen, velour, silk.

VENAL *a.* [VEEN ul] easily corrupted or bribed, corrupt. *He was the most venal judge the courts had ever encountered.* SYN. corruptible, easily bribed, unscrupulous, greedy, buyable, unprincipled, immoral, unethical, mercenary. ANT. *scrupulous, principled, ethical, honest, incorruptible.*

vend *v.* sell, peddle, market, retail, hawk.

VENDETTA *n.* [ven DETT uh] a feud or family feud fueled by the need for vengeance. *He launched a personal vendetta against his sister's abuser.* SYN. feud, blood feud, family feud, retaliation, fight, quarrel, bad blood, war, vengeance campaign, vengeance-seeking, revenge.

vendor *n.* seller, salesman, peddler, retailer, hawker, dealer, monger, merchant, trader, merchandiser, huckster.

veneer *n.* **1.** SHOWY LAYER facade, facing, surface, overlay. **2.** FALSE FRONT front, facade, cover-up, show, pretense, guise.

VENERABLE *a.* [VEN ur uh bul] esteemed because of one's age or character. *The venerable judge was retiring after 30 years on the bench.* SYN. respected, revered, esteemed, worthy, venerated, honored, time-honored, august, dignified, old. ANT. *disrespected, dishonorable, undignified.*

VENERATE *v.* [VEN ur ate] revere, look up to, worship. *Everyone venerated the local priest.* SYN. revere, look up to, respect, esteem, honor, worship, adore, idolize, *put on a pedestal, hallow. ANT. *disdain, scorn, regard with contempt, disrespect.*

veneration *n.* respect, reverence, esteem, worship, adoration, awe, idolization, regard, admiration, homage. ANT. *disrespect, disdain, contempt.*

vengeance *n.* revenge, retaliation, retribution, eye for an eye, tooth for a tooth, tit for tat, reprisal, requital, vendetta, settling the score. ANT. *forgiveness, turning the other cheek, letting bygones be bygones.*

vengeful *a.* vindictive, seeking revenge, revengeful, *launching a personal vendetta, retaliatory, avenging, unforgiving, spiteful, bitter, *out to settle the score, punitive. ANT. *forgiving, tolerant.*

venial *a.* forgivable, pardonable, excusable, tolerable, allowable, understandable, minor, *human. ANT. *unforgivable, inexcusable, intolerable, sinful.*

venom *n.* **1.** POISON toxin. **2.** NEGATIVE FEELINGS spite, malice, hatred, animosity, malevolence, malignance, resentment, ill will, bitterness, hostility, acrimony. ANT. *1. antidote, antivenin, antitoxin. 2. love, goodwill, friendliness, warmth.*

venomous *a.* **1.** POISONOUS toxic, lethal, deadly, viperous, stinging. **2.** FULL OF NEGATIVE FEELINGS spiteful, malicious, hating, malevolent, malignant, resentful, bitter, hostile, acrimonious, caustic, antagonistic, vicious. ANT. *1.*

harmless, nontoxic. **2.** *friendly, warm, full of goodwill.*

vent *n.* **1.** HOLE opening, outlet, aperture, orifice, mouth, passage, flue, exhaust duct, ventilating shaft. **2.** EXPRESSION release, voicing.

vent *v.* **1.** DISCHARGE release, let out, expel, give off. **2.** EXPRESS air, spout off, voice, verbalize, let out, tell, unburden oneself. ANT. *1. hold it all in, pent up. 2. remain silent.*

ventilate *v.* **1.** BRING IN OR EXPEL AIR circulate, freshen, renew, air, air out, refresh, fan. **2.** BRING OUT INTO THE OPEN air, voice, discuss, verbalize.

venture *n.* undertaking, enterprise, adventure, business proposition, endeavor, project, investment, risk, gamble, *long shot, stake, speculation, experiment.

venture *v.* **1.** RISK take a chance, gamble, wager, dare, attempt, *take a shot, *lay it all on the line, *go out on a limb, *take a flier, speculate, endeavor, undertake. **2.** DARE SAY express, hazard an opinion.

venturesome *a.* daring, risky, chancy, brave, courageous, bold, *gutsy, *nervy, audacious, intrepid, enterprising, adventurous, speculative. ANT. *safe, cowardly, guaranteed.*

venue *n.* locale, locality, location, place, scene.

Venus *n.* goddess of love, goddess of beauty, Aphrodite.

veracious *a.* truthful, honest, true, factual, accurate, trustworthy, dependable, reliable, faithful, straightforward, *on the up and up, straight. ANT. *false, dishonest, untruthful, inaccurate.*

VERACITY *n.* [vu RAS uh tee] honesty, truthfulness, accuracy. *We never doubted the veracity of her statements.* SYN. honesty, truthfulness, accuracy, dependability, reliability, credibility, authenticity, reality, integrity, faithfulness. ANT. *dishonesty, deception, deceitfulness, inaccuracy.*

veranda *n.* porch, portico, gallery, deck, stoop, balcony.

verbal *a.* in words, oral, spoken, uttered, articulated, expressed, by mouth, voiced, informal, unwritten. ANT. *written, formal.*

verbalize *v.* speak, say, voice, utter, articulate, express, communicate, put forth, put into words, *spit out.

VERBATIM *adv.* [ver BAY tum] word for word. *She quoted passages of the book verbatim.* SYN. word for word, exactly, literally, precisely, as written, faithfully, to the letter, line for line. ANT. *by way of paraphrasing, roughly, inexactly.*

verbiage *n.* wordiness, long-windedness, prolixity, verbosity, logorrhea, repetition, redundancy, loquacity, tautology. ANT. *concision, conciseness, condensation, pithiness.*

verbose *a.* wordy, long-winded, prolix, tautological, loquacious, garrulous, talkative, repetitive, redundant, voluble, *motormouthed. ANT. *concise, succinct, to the point, pithy.*

verbosity *n.* wordiness, long-windedness, prolixity, tautology, loquaciousness. "Shooting without aiming."—William Benham. "Superfluous breath."—Shakespeare.

verdant *a.* green, grassy, leafy, lush. ANT. *arid, sandy.*

verdict *n.* finding, decision, judgment, ruling, conclusion, determination, adjudication, opinion, sentence.

verge *n.* edge, brink, border, margin, limit, threshold, boundary, extremity, fringe, skirt, rim, lip, outer limits.

verge *v.* incline, tend, lean toward, approach, come close, edge, neighbor, touch.

verification *n.* proof, authentication, certification, corroboration, substantiation, confirmation, affirmation, attestation, validation, evidence. ANT. *discredit, invalidation.*

verify *v.* prove, confirm, substantiate, authenticate, certify, corroborate, affirm, attest, validate, testify to, support, demonstrate. ANT. *shoot full of holes, discredit, debunk, invalidate.*

verily *adv.* truly, in truth, certainly.

verisimilitude *n.* realism, appearance of reality, appearance of truth, truth, credibility, believability.

veritable *a.* actual, real, for real, true, bona fide, genuine, authentic. ANT. *false, questionable.*

verity *n.* truth, reality, actuality.

vermin *n.* **1.** PESTS varmints, bugs, flies, lice, fleas, cockroaches, rats. **2.** *CREEP *sleazebag, *scum of the earth, dregs, *scumbag, weasel, snake, riffraff.

VERNACULAR *n.* [vur NAK yoo lur] everyday language or idiom. *Even though he was a highly intellectual author, he always spoke in a relaxed vernacular.* SYN. native tongue, dialect, native language, conversational English, plain English, colloquial speech, slang, idiom, lingo, cant, argot, shoptalk. ANT. *formal English, formal language.*

vernacular *a.* native, regional, local, provincial, common, popular, vulgar, indigenous, informal, conversational. ANT. *formal, elevated, proper, stilted.*

vernal *a*. fresh, young, youthful, *spring-fresh. ANT. *old*.

versatile *a*. multitalented, multifaceted, *Jack-of-all-trades, all-around, multipurpose, resourceful, ingenious, clever, multiskilled, handy, adaptable. ANT. *limited*.

verse *n*. line, stanza, poem, poetry, rhyme, composition, lyrics.

versed *a*. learned, acquainted, experienced, trained, schooled, educated, practiced, familiar with, informed, conversant, skilled, proficient, *up on. ANT. *unschooled, untrained, ignorant*.

version *n*. rendition, rendering, interpretation, reading, depiction, account, story, paraphrase, form, translation.

vertex *n*. apex, summit, highest point, high point, pinnacle, peak, crown, zenith, acme, apogee.

vertical *a*. upright, up and down, perpendicular. ANT. *horizontal*.

vertiginous *a*. causing vertigo, dizzy, dizzying, *making one's head spin, whirling, reeling. ANT. *steady, calm*.

vertigo *n*. dizziness, unsteadyness, whirling, reeling sensation, loss of balance.

verve *n*. energy, spirit, liveliness, vivaciousness, enthusiasm, vitality, animation, vigor, passion, gusto, *pizzazz. ANT. *dullness, sleepiness, weariness*.

very *a*. **1.** COMPLETE absolute, total, entire, out-and-out, downright, unqualified, sheer. **2.** SAME identical, precise, exact, perfect, fitting, suitable, needed. ANT. **1.** *partial*.

very *adv*. **1.** EXTREMELY excessively, exceedingly, profoundly, unusually, highly, *terribly, *awfully, uncommonly, vastly, extraordinarily, deeply, richly, notably. **2.** EXACTLY precisely. ANT. **1.** *slightly, barely, hardly*. **2.** *roughly*.

vespers *n*. evening prayer, canonical hour.

vessel *n*. **1.** BOAT craft, sailboat, trawler, ship, freighter, barge, tugboat, tanker, ocean liner, cruise ship, *tub. SEE BOAT, SHIP **2.** CONTAINER receptacle, holder, utensil, pot, pan, kettle, bottle, vase, jug, tub, vat, cistern, cask, keg, urn.

vest *n*. waistcoat.

vest *v*. place in control, invest, entrust, bestow, authorize, empower, assign, confer, grant.

vested *a*. fixed, absolute, set, inviolable, inalienable, guaranteed by law, protected by law, warranted. ANT. *spurious, unwarranted*.

vestibule *n*. entrance, entranceway, foyer, lobby, reception area, waiting room, antechamber.

vestige *n*. trace, ancestral remnant, relic, memento, surviving evidence, shadow, glimmer, token, remainder, *ancestral hand-me-down.

vestigial *a*. obsolete, ancestral, degenerate, atrophied, nonfunctional, rudimentary, remaining, passed-down. ANT. *functional, advanced*.

vestment *n*. garment, robe, gown, alb, amice, cassock, surplice, tippet, cope.

veteran *n*. professional, pro, seasoned pro, *vet, experienced hand, *old hand, old-timer, past master, senior, authority, expert, trouper, *war horse, ex-soldier. ANT. *amateur, neophyte, beginner*.

veteran *a*. experienced, old, seasoned, professional, senior, practiced, hardened, masterly, battle-scarred, worldly-wise, weathered. ANT. *inexperienced, immature, young, untried, amateur*.

veterinarian *n*. vet, animal doctor. SEE DOCTOR (WORD FIND)

veto *n*. prohibition, no, refusal, rejection, disapproval, *thumbs down, *nix, nay, stoppage, proscription, denial. ANT. *approval, yes, okay, acceptance, ratification*.

veto *v*. prohibit, refuse, reject, disapprove, *give a thumbs down, *give a no vote, *nix, stop, kill, proscribe, deny, bar. ANT. *accept, approve, ratify*.

vex *v*. irritate, annoy, aggravate, trouble, bother, *bug, irk, peeve, ruffle, *rattle one's cage, pester, plague, rile, harass, perturb, *get on one's nerves. ANT. *please, delight, soothe*.

vexation *n*. irritation, annoyance, aggravation, trouble, bother, *pain, *pain in the neck, *headache, *thorn in one's side, disturbance, affliction. ANT. *pleasure, delight, joy*.

vexatious *a*. irritating, annoying, aggravating, troubling, bothersome, irksome, nerve-racking, ruffling, disturbing, perturbing, nagging, nettling. ANT. *pleasing, delightful, joyful*.

via *prep*. by, by way of, through.

VIABLE *a*. [VI uh bul] able to live or survive, workable, doable. *We came up with a number of viable plans to make the company more profitable.* SYN. capable of surviving, workable, doable, practical, feasible, possible, within the realm of possibility. ANT. *likely to perish, impractical, unworkable*.

viaduct *n*. span. SEE BRIDGE

vial *n.* phial, bottle, ampule, vessel, test tube, syringe.

vibrant *a.* **1.** VIBRATING quivering, resonating, resonant, reverberating, reverberant, resounding, ringing, pulsing, throbbing. **2.** LIVELY alive, spirited, vigorous, energetic, animated, throbbing with life, vital, sparkling, radiant. ANT. *1. still. 2. dead, weak, sleepy, dull.*

VICARIOUS *a.* [vye KAIR ee us] experienced indirectly or imagined through the experiences of others. *Although she could not attend it herself, she received vicarious pleasure from watching the concert on television.* SYN. indirect, imagined, fantasized, secondhand, secondary, sympathetic, empathetic, surrogate. ANT. *direct, firsthand, personal.*

vice *n.* sin, evil, wickedness, depravity, wrong, indecency, debauchery, immorality, degeneracy, corruption, prostitution, bad habit, weakness, compulsion, failing, fault, flaw, shortcoming, wrong, crime. "Servility."—Karl Marx. "Instruments to plague."—Shakespeare.

vicinity *n.* proximity, neighborhood, area, *neck of the woods, region, surroundings, environs, vicinage.

vicious *a.* **1.** MEAN, NASTY bad, fierce, cruel, malicious, murderous, brutal, merciless, bloodthirsty, savage, ferocious, hateful, venomous, spiteful **2.** EVIL wicked, sinful, base, corrupt, depraved, immoral, debauched, villainous, degenerate, perverted, shameful, bad. ANT. *1. nice, kind, sweet, good. 2. moral, virtuous, righteous, Christian.*

VICISSITUDES *n.* [vi SIS i TOODS] changes, ups and downs, difficulties. *He learned to accept the vicissitudes of life.* SYN. changes, ups and downs, peaks and valleys, ebb and flow, changes in fortune, reversals, variations, mutability, uncertainty, difficulties.

victim *n.* **1.** SUFFERER fatality, casualty, injured party. **2.** DUPE target, *patsy, *fall guy, *sucker, *sitting duck, *easy mark, quarry, prey.

victimize *v.* prey on, attack, kill, destroy, abuse, torment, molest, sexually abuse, rape, mug, rob, wrong, injure, pick on, take advantage of, single out for abuse, *rip off, trick, *burn, fool, *sucker, con, swindle, *flimflam, defraud, *frame.

victor *n.* winner, champion, *champ, gold medalist, conqueror, vanquisher, *top dog, *number one, master. ANT. *loser, failure.*

Victorian *a.* respectable, prudish, proper, straitlaced, stuffy, puritanical, prim, priggish, antiquated, obsolete. ANT. *free-spirited, loose, fast, liberal.*

victorious *a.* winning, conquering, vanquishing, triumphant, successful, champion, on top, prevailing, dominant, undefeated. ANT. *failing, losing, defeated.*

victory *n.* success, win, triumph, superiority, mastery, sweep, upset, killing, *grand slam, *landslide, *wipe out, the gold medal, the silver medal, the bronze medal, vanquishing, overthrow, subduing. "A matter of staying power."—Elbert Hubbard. "That which must be bought with the lives of young men to retrieve the errors of the old."—Gordon Munnoch. ANT. *loss, failure, defeat, flop, *choke.*

victuals *n.* food, foodstuffs, provisions, groceries, rations, *grub, *eats, *chow, *three squares, sustenance, nourishment, larder.

video *n.* TV, television, tape, videocassette, movie, picture transmission. SEE TELEVISION

videocassette *n.* video, tape, movie, *flick. SEE MOVIE

vie *v.* compete, contend, rival, match up against, struggle, contest, *lock horns, *fight tooth and nail, challenge, *jockey for position, *establish a pecking order.

view *n.* **1.** LOOKING seeing, observation, examination, inspection, scrutiny, scan, look-see, once-over. **2.** SIGHT vision, range. **3.** SCENE scenery, vista, panorama, outlook, prospect, landscape, seascape. **4.** OPINION judgment, perspective, thoughts, feeling, observation, point of view, belief, impression, conviction, attitude.

view *v.* **1.** LOOK AT see, behold, observe, examine, inspect, scrutinize, scan, check out, survey, *get a load of, regard, peep, eyeball. **2.** CONSIDER regard, judge, deem, think, look at.

viewpoint *n.* point of view, opinion, perspective, attitude, way of thinking, position, standpoint, feeling, vantage point, angle, slant.

vigil *n.* watch, standing-by, overnight watch, surveillance, lookout, observation, monitoring.

vigilance *n.* watchfulness, caution, alertness, wariness, attentiveness, circumspection, lookout, carefulness, heed. ANT. *carelessness, disregard, letting down one's guard.*

vigilant *a.* watchful, alert, on the lookout, cautious, wary, attentive, circumspect, careful, *on one's toes, on guard. ANT. *unwary, incautious, off guard, *flat-footed, asleep.*

vigilante *n.* member of a lynch mob, member of a vigilance committee, night rider.

vigilantism *n.* taking the law into one's own hands, mob law, mob rule, lynch law, lynching.

vignette *n.* sketch, scene, cameo, skit, bit, depiction.

vigor *n.* **1.** STRENGTH AND VITALITY energy, zip, power, pep, fire, vim, liveliness, drive, force, potency, might, hardiness, heartiness, health, *get up and go, *punch. **2.** INTENSITY force, spirit, passion, enthusiasm, vehemence, fire, fervor. ANT. *1. weakness, feebleness, failing health. 2. feebleness, halfheartedness, weariness.*

vigorous *a.* strong, vital, energetic, *full of zip, powerful, peppy, *full of fire, lively, forceful, potent, mighty, hardy, hearty, healthy, robust, intense, spirited, passionate, enthusiastic, vehement, fervent. ANT. *weak, feeble, sickly, failing, impotent.*

viking *n.* pirate, sea rover, Norseman.

vile *a.* **1.** BASE immoral, wicked, evil, sinful, debased, bad, degenerate, venal, iniquitous, villainous, depraved, Satanic. **2.** OFFENSIVE disgusting, sickening, nauseating, stomach-turning, rotten, loathsome, despicable, monstrous, atrocious, obnoxious, contemptible. ANT. *1. moral, good, wholesome, virtuous. 2. pleasant, delightful, agreeable.*

VILIFY *v.* [VIL uh FYE] to defame, slander, put down. *He vilified nearly everyone in the organization.* SYN. defame, slander, put down, mudsling, libel, smear, criticize, abuse, denounce, *slam, malign, denigrate, revile, calumniate, vituperate, *bad-mouth, *drag one's name through the mud. ANT. *praise, compliment, commend.*

vilification *n.* defamation, slander, mudslinging, libel, smear, criticism, verbal abuse, denunciation, *slamming, maligning, denigration, calumny, character assassination, *bad-mouthing. ANT. *praising, commendation, acclaim.*

villa *n.* country house, country estate, summer house, *spread, vacation home, hacienda.

village *n.* municipality, hamlet, small town, crossroads, burg, community, settlement, township.

villain *n.* criminal, *bad guy, scoundrel, evildoer, wretch, knave, antihero, *black hat, fiend, rogue, rascal, *weasel, *snake, *rat, *Simon Legree, dastard, cur, *the heavy,

*SOB, cad, *creep, *rotter, *stinker, *bad actor, *bad hombre. ANT. *hero, *good guy, good Samaritan, law-abiding citizen.*

villainous *a.* criminal, evil, wicked, sinful, unlawful, lawbreaking, mean, knavish, black, fiendish, dastardly, ignoble, blackhearted, antisocial, vile, low, felonious, shameful, reprehensible, immoral, diabolic. ANT. *heroic, good, kind, Christian.*

villainy *n.* crime, dirty deed, felony, evil, wickedness, sinfulness, knavery, meanness, delinquency, blackheartedness, antisocial behavior, antisocial act, vileness, immorality, heinous act. ANT. *heroism, goodness, kindness, Christianity.*

vim *n.* vitality, vigor, energy, strength, robustness, liveliness, *pep, *get up and go, *zip, potency, vivacity, spirit. ANT. *feebleness, weariness.*

VINDICATE *v.* [VIN duh KATE] to clear one of blame, charges or suspicion; to absolve. *The new evidence vindicated the accused and he was promptly released with apologies.* SYN. clear, clear one's name, exonerate, prove innocence, absolve, acquit, exculpate, excuse, pardon, uphold one's innocence, defend, support. ANT. *damn, implicate, convict.*

VINDICTIVE *a.* [vin DIK tiv] seeking revenge, seething with the desire for vengeance. *The divorce made both parties mean and vindictive.* SYN. vengeful, revengeful, retaliatory, retributive, spiteful, unforgiving, resentful, hostile, out for revenge, out to even the score, nasty. ANT. *forgiving, *turning the other cheek, accepting.*

vintage *n.* **1.** TIME PERIOD season, year, date, period, model. **2.** CROP harvest, yield. SEE WINE

vintage *a.* **1.** CHOICE the best, select, prize, excellent, superior, good, fine. **2.** HISTORICAL past, period, retro, old-time, old-fashioned, antiquated, antique, outdated. ANT. *1. the worst, poor, inferior. 2. future, modern, contemporary.*

vintner *n.* wine merchant, wine maker. SEE WINE

violate *v.* **1.** BREAK A LAW transgress, breach, disobey, trespass, defy, disregard the law, infringe, commit a felony, commit a crime, commit a misdemeanor. **2.** RAPE molest, sexually abuse, ravish, assault, deflower, take by force. **3.** DESECRATE profane, disrespect, dishonor, defile, blaspheme, degrade, corrupt. **4.** BREAK IN interrupt, invade one's space, invade one's privacy, disturb. ANT. *1. comply, observe, respect. 3. respect, honor, revere.*

violation *n.* **1.** BREAKING OF THE LAW transgression, breach, trespass, defiance, infringement, felony, crime, misdemeanor, nonobservance. **2.** RAPE molestation, sexual abuse, sexual assault, deflowering. **3.** DESECRATION disrespect, defiling, degradation. **4.** INVASION OF PRIVACY invasion of one's space, interruption, disturbance.

violence *n.* **1.** PHYSICAL ANGER AND DESTRUCTION brute force, manhandling, brutality, roughness, terrorism, bloodshed, killing, murder, destructiveness, barbarity, savagery, ferocity, fisticuffs, *rumble, rioting, physical abuse, pummeling, cruelty, torture, *when push comes to shove. "The state calls its own violence law, but that of the individual crime."—Max Stirner. **2.** INTENSE FORCE OF NATURE energy, explosiveness, storminess, ferocity, fury, turbulence, wildness, intensity, fierceness, upheaval, cataclysm, eruption, blowup.

violent *a.* **1.** DESTRUCTIVE brutal, beastly, manhandling, rough, terrorizing, killing, murderous, barbarous, savage, ferocious, riotous, physically abusive, assaultive, cruel, bloodthirsty, homicidal, rabid, maniacal, berserk, rowdy, hurtful, crazed, out of control, vehement, furious. **2.** INTENSE powerful, strong, extreme, severe, acute, rough, explosive, turbulent, stormy, ferocious, wild, fierce, cataclysmic. ANT. *1. nonviolent, pacific, passive, peaceful. 2. mild, gentle, slight.*

violin *n.* string instrument, fiddle, Stradivarius. SEE MUSICAL INSTRUMENT

VIP *n.* very important person, dignitary, *big shot, *big enchilada, *brass hat, *top brass, celebrity, *high muckety-muk, nabob. ANT. *nobody, *lightweight, nobody special.*

viper *n.* *snake, *snake in the grass, scoundrel, rogue, villain, cur, cad, rat, *heel, worm, *rotter. ANT. *nice guy, choirboy, good Samaritan.*

viperous *a.* malicious, vicious, spiteful, nasty, venomous, malignant, mean, vindictive, Satanic, deadly. ANT. *nice, sweet, harmless.*

virago *n.* shrew, nag, scold, witch, *battle-ax, spitfire, fishwife, *biddy, hag.

virgin *n.* maid, maiden, celibate, vestal.

Virgin *n.* Mary, Mother of Jesus, Madonna, the Virgin Mother, Queen of Saints, Blessed Virgin Mary.

virgin *a.* virginal, chaste, celibate, untouched, pure, immaculate, unused, innocent, pristine, unspoiled, inexperienced, without sin,
maidenly, wholesome. ANT. *impure, tried, experienced, defiled.*

virginal *a.* SEE VIRGIN

virginity *n.* chastity, celibacy, purity, maidenhood, innocence, virtue, modesty, continence, abstinence. "A frozen asset."—Clare Boothe Luce. "Peevish, proud, idle, made of self-love, which is the most inhibited sin in the canon."—Shakespeare. ANT. *promiscuity, experience, immodesty.*

virile *a.* manly, masculine, male, *macho, strong, powerful, forceful, vigorous, potent, red-blooded, lusty, two-fisted, strapping, muscular, fearless, *gutsy, bold. ANT. *effeminate, *wimpy, weak, impotent.*

virility *n.* manliness, masculinity, maleness, strength, power, forcefulness, vigor, potency, red-bloodedness, lustiness, muscularity, fearlessness, gutsiness. ANT. *femininity, *wimpiness, weakness, impotency.*

virtual *a.* practical, in effect, just about, tantamount to, essential, equal to, implicit. ANT. *not at all, absent.*

virtually *adv.* practically, for all practical purposes, in effect, just about, tantamount to, equal to, basically, essentially.

virtue *adv.* **1.** MORALITY goodness, righteousness, uprightness, moral excellence, decency, character, integrity, incorruptibility, honor, Christian values, principle, ethic. "The fount whence honor springs."—Christopher Marlowe. "Forebearance."—F. Scott Fitzgerald. "Reason in practice."—Marie de Chenier. "A mean state between two vices, the one of excess and the other of deficiency."—Aristotle. "Blood is an inheritance, virtue an acquisition."—Miguel de Cervantes. "Virtue is insufficient temptation."—George Bernard Shaw. **2.** CHASTITY chasteness, purity, virginity, celibacy, innocence, modesty, abstinence, continence. **3.** EXCELLENCE merit, effectiveness, value. ANT. *1. immorality, evil, wickedness, sin. 2. promiscuity, immodesty, impurity. 3. inferiority, ineffectiveness.*

virtuosity *n.* skill, proficiency, greatness, mastery, expertise, command, artistry, craftsmanship, brilliance. ANT. *inexperience, incompetence, ineptness.*

virtuoso *n.* master, expert, artist, *whiz, craftsman, genius, prodigy, ace, professional, pro, *crackerjack, maestro, mavin. ANT. *amateur, beginner, bumbler, neophyte.*

virtuous *a.* **1.** MORAL AND EXEMPLARY good, righteous, upright, principled, decent, incorruptible, honorable, showing character, having integrity, having Christian values, ethical. **2.** CHASTE virginal, pure, untouched, innocent, celibate, continent, abstinent. ANT. *1. immoral, evil, sinful, wicked. 2. promiscuous, impure, immodest.*

virulence *n.* **1.** TOXICITY noxiousness, harmfulness, deadliness. **2.** ANIMOSITY venom, hostility, malevolence, rancor, malice, acrimony.

virulent *a.* **1.** POISONOUS noxious, toxic, venomous, harmful, unhealthy, lethal, deadly, fatal, malignant, deleterious. **2.** ANTAGONISTIC hostile, venomous, malevolent, rancorous, vicious, malicious, nasty, acrimonious, bitter, spiteful, vindictive. ANT. *1. nontoxic, harmless, benign. 2. friendly, nice, warm.*

virus *n.* *bug, germ, microorganism, microbe, infection, pathogen, prokaryote, cold virus, flu virus.

visa *n.* endorsement, authorization, certification, passport stamp.

visage *n.* face, countenance, expression, appearance, aspect, look, cast, bearing.

vis-a-vis *a.* face to face, opposite.

viscera *n.* internal organs, intestines, guts, bowels, *innards, entrails.

VISCERAL *a.* [VIS ur ul] instinctive, intuitive, felt in one's gut. *The desire to hunt is largely visceral.* SYN. instinctive, intuitive, *gut, internal, natural, unconscious, subconscious, reflexive, emotional. ANT. *intellectual, cerebral.*

viscid *a.* SEE VISCOUS

viscosity *n.* cohesiveness, stickiness, tackiness, adhesion, viscidity, gumminess, pastiness.

viscount *n.* nobleman.

viscous *a.* cohesive, sticky, viscid, tacky, gluey, gummy, adhesive, syrupy, mucilaginous, pasty. ANT. *dry, solid.*

vise *n.* clamp, holder, grip, gripper.

visibility *n.* range of vision, clearness, clarity, cloudiness, cloud ceiling, fogginess, perceptibility.

visible *a.* seeable, perceptible, observable, perceivable, discernible, palpable, apparent, evident, obvious, conspicuous, distinct, clear, plain, manifest. ANT. *invisible, concealed, hidden, imperceptible.*

vision *n.* **1.** EYESIGHT sense of sight, sight, seeing, perception, optical perception. SEE EYE **2.** DREAM hallucination, fantasy, daydream, illusion, mirage, apparition, ghost, specter, phantom, visitation, prophecy, prophetic vision, revelation. **3.** MENTAL PICTURE image, imagining, fantasy, concept, idea. **4.**

FORESIGHT OR IMAGINATION astuteness, farsightedness, understanding, insight, wisdom, perspective, keenness, intuition.

visionary *n.* **1.** DREAMER daydreamer, idealist, romantic, Utopian, castle-builder, Don Quixote. **2.** PROPHET seer, mystic, fortune-teller, psychic.

visionary *a.* imaginary, fantasized, dreamed, fanciful, impractical, unrealistic, idealized, idealistic, starry-eyed, romantic, speculative, ghostly, spectral, prophetic. ANT. *realistic, down-to-earth, practical.*

visit *n.* social call, stopover, stay, sojourn, appointment, talk, chat.

visit *v.* **1.** DROP IN ON call on, stop in, stop over, stop by, see, look up, look in on, pay a call, stay over, sojourn. **2.** AFFLICT inflict, assail, befall, wreak, smite, attack.

visitation *n.* affliction, punishment, plague, curse, blight, disaster, catastrophe, tragedy, calamity, reward, just reward.

visitor *n.* caller, guest, houseguest, company, drop-in company, sojourner, tourist, traveler.

vista *n.* view, outlook, scene, scenery, panorama, sight, prospect.

visual *a.* **1.** OPTICAL optic, ocular. **2.** VISIBLE seeable, observable, perceptible, discernible, perceivable. ANT. *2. invisible, imperceptible, auditory, olfactory.*

visualize *v.* picture, imagine, envision, conceive, fantasize, see in the mind's eye, envisage, conjure up, form a mental image.

vital *a.* **1.** LIVING live, life, animate, life-giving, life-supporting, life-sustaining. **2.** ESSENTIAL necessary, indispensable, critical, crucial, fundamental, basic, important, life or death, key. **3.** VIGOROUS energetic, lively, full of life, spirited, animated, vivacious, vibrant, dynamic, full of zest. ANT. *1. dead, lifeless, inanimate. 2. inessential, unnecessary, dispensable. 3. lifeless, sluggish, sickly, tired.*

vitality *n.* vigor, energy, liveliness, life, spirit, animation, vivacity, zest, vim, robustness, get up and go, power, strength. ANT. *weakness, sluggishness, lethagy, dullness.*

vitriol *n.* bitterness, sarcasm, nastiness, venom, acid, maliciousness, malevolence, hatefulness, contempt, disdain. ANT. *sweetness, kindness, pleasantness.*

VITRIOLIC *a.* [vi tree AWL ik] caustic, bitter or sarcastic. *His vitriolic speech drove many people out of the conference room.* SYN. caustic, bitter, sarcastic, nasty, venomous, acid, malicious, malevolent, hateful, biting, cutting, disdainful. ANT. *sweet, nice, pleasant.*

vittles *n.* victuals, food, edibles, *grub, *chow, eats, nourishment.

vituperate *v.* scold, berate, censure, verbally abuse, revile, reprove, reproach, rebuke, upbraid, chasten, disparage. ANT. *commend, praise, compliment.*

vituperation *n.* scolding, berating, verbal abuse, abusive language, castigation, *dressing down, condemnation, criticism, revilement, denunciation. ANT. *praise, compliments, commendation.*

VIVACIOUS *a.* [vi VAY shus] full of life. *She was bubbly and vivacious.* SYN. lively, bubbly, effervescent, spirited, animated, ebullient, vital, bouncy, cheerful. ANT. *lifeless, dead, dull, sluggish.*

vivacity *n.* life, liveliness, bubbliness, effervescence, spirit, animation, ebullience, vitality, bounciness, cheerfulness. ANT. *deadness, lifelessness, dullness.*

vivid *a.* **1.** BRIGHT brilliant, intense, striking, strong, rich, radiant, resplendent, glowing, brightly colored. **2.** CLEAR crystal-clear, strong, powerful, realistic, graphic, distinct, picturesque, sharp, loud, impressive. ANT. *1. dull, faded, faint, pale. 2. vague, dull, faint.*

vivify *v.* give life to, animate, vitalize, quicken.

vivisection *n.* animal dissection, animal research, medical research.

vixen *n.* shrew, witch, *battle-ax, virago, fishwife, scold, hellcat, spitfire.

vocabulary *n.* lexicon, glossary, word stock, vernacular, language, slang, jargon, lingo, cant, tongue, terminology, phraseology, dictionary, thesaurus.

vocal *a.* **1.** SPOKEN oral, verbal, voiced, vocalized, uttered, articulated, expressed, put into words, sung. **2.** OUTSPOKEN expressive, articulate, vociferous, *not backward about coming forward, loud, noisy, blunt, forthright, making oneself heard. ANT. *1. mute, silent, written. 2. shy, reserved, reticent, quiet.*

vocalist *n.* singer, soloist, crooner, diva, prima donna, *songbird, song stylist, songstress, recording artist, pop star, minstrel. SEE MUSIC, SONG

vocalize *v.* verbalize, voice, put into words, articulate, express, speak, utter, say, communicate, phonate, sing.

vocation *n.* profession, occupation, trade, calling, line of work, career, livelihood, employment, job, line, metier, business, *racket, field, *bag.

vociferate *v.* shout, clamor, holler, bellow, rant, rave, thunder, fume, fuss, *raise a stink, raise one's voice, carry on vehemently. ANT. *whisper, speak softly.*

VOCIFEROUS *a.* [vo SIF ur us] loud, bellowing; making one's point in a noisy manner. *Both sides had become increasingly vociferous over the gun control issue.* SYN. loud, bellowing, shouting, hollering, clamorous, ranting, raving, thunderous, fuming, vehement, vocal, uproarious, loud-mouthed. ANT. *quiet, reserved, silent, shy.*

vogue *n.* mode, fashion, style, *fad, *rage, *craze, trend, latest thing, custom, dernier cri, *last word.

vogue *a.* in vogue, in fashion, fashionable, trendy, *in, current, stylish, *on the cutting edge *hip. ANT. *old-fashioned, outdated, obsolete.*

voice *n.* **1.** SPEECH power of speech, vocal power, vocal cords, tongue. "An arrow for the heart."—Lord Byron. "A second face."—Gerard Bauer.
WORD FIND
descriptive: alto, baritone, bass, bellowing, booming, breathy, cackling, childish, cracking, croaking, cultured, deep, drawling, droning, falsetto, faltering, feeble, flat, fluting, gargling, gravel, guttural, harsh, hoarse, hollow, hushed, husky, inflectionless, lilting, lisping, monotone, nasal twang, powerful, ponderous, purring, quavering, rasping, reedy, resonant, robust, scabrous, sensuous, Shakespearian actor's, sharp, shrill, singsong, soothing, soprano, spluttering, squawking, squeaky, stentorian, strangled, subterranean, sultry, tenor, thick, thin, throaty, thunderous, tremulous, velvety, warbling, wheezing, whining, whiskey-voiced.
loss of: aphonia
loud: megalophonic, megalophonous
organ: larynx, vocal cords, voicebox
pertaining to: phonetic
pitch, variation in: modulation, inflection
quality: timbre
voiceless: mute
SEE SING, SPEECH
2. SAY vote, choice, opinion, *two cents worth, part to play, preference.

voice *v.* express, articulate, say, verbalize, state, announce, air, vocalize, utter, communicate, put into words, sound off, vent.

void *n.* emptiness, vacuum, empty space, vacuity, nothing, nothingness, hole, oblivion, blank.

void *v.* **1.** NULLIFY invalidate, cancel, annul, abolish, repeal, rescind, reverse, revoke, stop. **2.** DISCHARGE evacuate, empty, clear, eliminate, excrete, purge. ANT. *1. validate. 2. fill.*

void *a.* **1.** EMPTY vacant, devoid, vacuous, desolate, barren, unoccupied, bare, hollow, blank. **2.** INVALID null, ineffective, cancelled, ineffectual, not in force, annulled, worthless, meaningless. ANT. *1. full, occupied, filled. 2. valid, in force, binding.*

VOLATILE *a.* [VOL uh tul] unstable, liable to change quickly. Also, likely to explode due to instability. *Tensions between nations created a volatile situation.* SYN. unstable, changeable, rapidly changing, unpredictable, unsettled, erratic, explosive, tense, fickle, capricious, up and down, hot and cold, mercurial. ANT. *stable, steady, predictable.*

volcanic *a.* explosive, violent. SEE VOLCANO

volcano *n.* vent, mountain, crater, Pelée, Vesuvius, Etna, Mt. St. Helens.

WORD FIND

avalanche of hot gas and ash: pyroclastic flow, nuee ardente

blob of lava ejected from: bomb

cavern formed by lava flow: lava tube

cinderlike lava: scoria

crater that eventually fills with water to become lake: caldera

descriptive: devil's throne, hellish forge, festering boil

device that measures bulge in side of mountain: tiltmeter

device that measures vibration: seismograph

ejaculate: clastic, tephra

eruption: cataclysm, upheaval, paroxysm, belching

"fireworks" associated with: pyrotechnics

glass, volcanic: obsidian

god of fire, Roman: Vulcanus

inactive permanently: extinct

lava that hardens and stops up volcano throat: plug

molasses-like lava found in Hawaii: pahoehoe

molten rock after it is expelled: lava

molten rock before it is expelled: magma

mouth: crater

mud or ash flow, heated: lahar

rock, porous: pumice

rock produced by, dark igneous: basalt

reaction of lava when it meets water: base surge

science of: volcanology

scientist: volcanologist, vulcanist

sleeping, inactive: dormant

superheated gas and fire cloud: nuee ardente

vent, secondary: monticule, fumarole, blowhole, cinder cone

truncated cone left after eruption: basal wreck

SEE MOUNTAIN

VOLITION *n.* [vo LISH un] will, a conscious choice. *She went into the dangerous area of her own volition.* SYN. will, free will, willingness, choice, choosing, election, determination, desire. ANT. *coercion, arm-twisting.*

volley *n.* barrage, rain, shower, peppering, burst, salvo, fussilade, enfillade, discharge, wall of fire, bombardment.

volleyball *n.* sport.

WORD FIND

fake spike in which ball is tapped very lightly over net: dink shot, off-speed spike

jump serve that hooks: *candy cane

powerful, driving shot into opponent's court: spike

save near the floor, underhand: dig

sets ball for spiker, one who: setter

soft serve easily returned: *lollipop

spike into opponent's face: *facial

spiking directly into opponent's armpits: *sizzling the pits

spin on the ball: English

touching net illegally: netting

transfer of serve to other team: side out

violation: fault, foul

voluble *a.* talkative, loquacious, garrulous, *motor-mouthed, long-winded, effusive, blabby, *having the gift of gab, fluent, rambling. ANT. *quiet, silent, reticent, taciturn.*

volume *n.* **1.** BOOK work, tome, opus, hardcover, paperback, album. **2.** CUBIC SPACE cubic feet, cubic inches, size, dimensions, capacity, mass, extent. **3.** LOUDNESS amplification, intensity, sound.

voluminous *a.* **1.** HUGE large, sizable, big, great, vast, extensive, bulky, full, expansive, capacious, spacious. **2.** FILLING VOLUMES prolific, comprehensive, profuse, abundant, abounding, plentiful. ANT. *1. small, tiny, slight. 2. brief, succinct.*

voluntarily *adv.* of one's own free will, willingly, of one's own volition, volitionally, electively, freely. ANT. *by force, by coercion, unwillingly, against one's will.*

voluntary *a.* of one's own free will, willing, of one's own volition, volitional, elected, opted, unforced, gratuitous, free, optional, spontaneous. ANT. *forced, compulsory, coerced, against one's will.*

volunteer *v.* offer, sign up, donate one's services, step up, come forward, present, proffer, tender, contribute. ANT. **go kicking and screaming, resist, refuse.*

voluptuary *n.* sensualist, sybarite, hedonist, pleasure seeker.

voluptuous *a.* **1.** SENSUAL sensuous, pleasure-seeking, hedonistic, sybaritic, sexual, erotic, libidinal, erogenous, fleshly, lustful, lascivious, licentious. **2.** SEXUALLY ATTRACTIVE *built, shapely, *stacked, buxom, curvaceous, well-endowed, gorgeous, *hot, *foxy, good-looking. ANT. *1. abstemious, puritanical, ascetic. 2. ugly, repulsive.*

volute *n.* spiral, twist, whorl.

vomit *v.* throw up, upchuck, puke, disgorge, *barf, regurgitate, spew, retch, *hurl, *ralph, *blow lunch, *toss one's cookies, expel.

voodoo *n.* black magic, witchcraft, hoodoo, obeah, sorcery.

WORD FIND

animated corpse or snake deity: zombie
object thought to have magical power: fetish, charm

SEE OCCULT, MAGIC

VORACIOUS *a.* [vo RAY shus] extremely hungry or greedy, insatiable. *He had a voracious appetite and ate every three hours.* SYN. ravenous, gluttonous, edacious, greedy, hungry, starved, devouring, insatiable, unquenchable, wild, rabid, out of control. ANT. *moderate, dainty, satiated.*

vortex *n.* whirlpool, maelstrom, eddy, gyre, whirlwind, tornado, cyclone, *twister.

votary *n.* monk, nun, devotee, worshipper, disciple, follower, adherent, fan.

vote *n.* say, voice, choice, option, right to choose, suffrage, franchise, ballot, poll, referendum, show of hands, *yea, *nay. SEE ELECTION

vote *v.* cast one's ballot, choose, elect, decide on, opt for, *give thumbs up, *give thumbs down, *yea, *nay, go to the polls. SEE ELECTION

vouch *v.* affirm, back up, support, swear to, testify, attest, bear witness, substantiate, corroborate, guarantee, warrant, authenticate, certify.

voucher *n.* receipt, chit, debenture, note, IOU.

vouchsafe *v.* give, grant, confer, bestow, concede, allow, condescend.

vow *n.* promise, pledge, oath, word, solemn word, word of honor, troth, assurance.

vow *v.* promise, pledge, give one's word, give one's solemn word, give one's word of honor, swear to, solemnly swear, assure, *cross one's heart and hope to die, guarantee, warrant.

voyage *n.* cruise, pleasure cruise, ocean-crossing, sail, trip, passage, journey, tour, junket.

voyage *v.* cruise, cross the ocean, sail, take a trip, journey, tour, travel, go abroad.

voyeur *n.* *peeping Tom, pervert, spy, watcher.

vulgar *a.* **1.** COMMON popular, everyday, general, plebeian, folk, of the masses, proletarian, working class, colloquial. **2.** CRUDE coarse, unrefined, *gross, rough, boorish, uncultivated, ill-bred, ill-mannered, uncivilized, loutish, impolite. **3.** INDECENT obscene, tasteless, disgusting, *gross, dirty, offensive, X-rated, blue, ribald, off-color, smutty. ANT. *1. upper class, aristocratic. 2. refined, civilized, well-mannered, well-bred. 3. tasteful, decent, clean, G-rated.*

vulgarity *n.* **1.** CRUDENESS coarseness, lack of refinement, roughness, ill manners, bad manners, rudeness, boorishness, grossness, impoliteness. **2.** OBSCENITY expletive, swear word, four-letter word, profanity, smut, pornography. ANT. *1. refinement, good manners, tact.*

vulnerable *a.* **1.** ASSAILABLE open to attack, defenseless, undefended, weak, helpless, *helpless as a baby, exposed, susceptible, unprotected, pregnable. **2.** SENSITIVE thin-skinned, easily hurt, ultrasensitive. ANT. *1. unassailable, strong, impregnable, invincible. 2. thick-skinned, self-assured, confident.*

vulture *n.* **1.** BIRD OF PREY raptor, condor, scavenger. **2.** RUTHLESS PERSON shark, con man, jackal, bloodsucker, parasite, user, opportunist, *gold digger.

W

wacko n. Sl. *nut, *fruitcake, oddball, *sicko, *psycho, psychotic, deranged person, unstable person, neurotic, *screwball, mentally unbalanced person.

wacky a. crazy, *loony, demented, deranged, *screwy, *psycho, psychotic, eccentric, irrational, *goofy, *buggy, *kooky, *zany, *off the wall. ANT. rational, sensible, reasonable, sober, sane.

wad n. mass, ball, lump, hunk, chunk, gob, clump, plug.

waddle v. toddle, wobble, walk like a duck, sway.

wade v. slog, slosh, plod, ford, bathe.

waders n. hip boots.

wafer n. cracker, cookie, snap, disk, biscuit.

WAFFLE v. [WAU ful] to speak or write vaguely or ambiguously, to equivocate. The senator waffled on the issue and told us to get back to him. SYN. equivocate, dodge, *dance around an issue, sidestep, hem and haw, duck, hedge, speak ambiguously, speak vaguely, tergiversate, evade, *beat around the bush. ANT. be decisive, come to the point, be straightforward, be direct, take a stand.

waft v. float, fly, sail, glide, drift, blow, puff, carry, propel.

wag n. shake, wiggle, wave, waggle, swing, sway, waver, jiggle, bob.

wag v. shake, wiggle, wave, waggle, swing, sway, jiggle, bob.

wage n. pay, wages, salary, income, earnings, stipend, compensation, remuneration, hire, *take-home, net, recompense.

wage v. engage in, carry on, maintain, conduct, undertake, make, prosecute.

wager n. bet, gamble, play, *long shot, *flier, speculation, *toss of the dice, stake, money.

wager v. bet, gamble, put money on, speculate, venture, risk, chance, hazard, stake.

waggish a. merry, playful, funny, comical, jesting, humorous, clowning, teasing, jovial, jolly. ANT. serious, grim, sober.

wagon n. cart, trailer, dray, Conestoga, prairie schooner, truck, carriage, buggy. SEE VEHICLE

waif n. orphan, homeless child, stray, foundling, street child, gamin, ragamuffin.

wail n. cry, outcry, lament, moan, whine, howl, sob, boohoo.

wail v. cry, cry out, cry out in mourning, bewail, weep, moan, whine, howl, sob, boohoo, bawl, whimper, lament, grieve, mourn.

wait n. delay, holdup, stop, halt, suspension, pause, layover.

wait v. hold up, hold, stop, halt, suspend, pause, delay, procrastinate, linger, abide, bide one's time, *sweat it out, dally, *hang back, *hold the phone, *freeze. ANT. go, proceed, start.

waiter n. waitress, server, steward, garçon, carhop, host, hostess, maitre d', servant.

wait on v. serve, attend to, tend to, minister to, be at one's beck and call, *wait on hand and foot, *gopher.

waitress n. SEE WAITER

waive v. 1. GIVE UP relinquish, surrender, forbear, forgo, renounce, dispense with, forsake, abandon. 2. POSTPONE defer, put off, table, *put on hold. ANT. 1. keep, retain, claim.

waiver n. relinquishment, disclaimer.

wake n. 1. WATCH vigil, funeral service, rites. 2. BACKWASH wash, trail, track, path, contrail.

wake v. 1. AWAKEN wake up, awake, get up, rouse, stir, *rise and shine, open one's eyes, *shake the cobwebs out, come around. 2. ACTIVATE animate, come out of dormancy, revive, stir. ANT. 1. sleep, nod off, doze. 2. quiet, deactivate.

wakeful a. awake, alert, wide-eyed, bright-eyed, wide-awake, restless, insomniac. ANT. sleepy, tired, dull.

walk n. 1. STROLL hike, tramp, amble, march, promenade, constitutional, perambulation, traipse, step, stride, gait, saunter, trek. 2. WALKWAY sidewalk, boardwalk, path, pathway, trail, lane, esplanade, promenade, mall, arcade.

walk v. stroll, hike, tramp, amble, pad, march, promenade, *beat feet, *hoof it, tramp, traipse, wend one's way, go on foot, perambulate, shuffle, mosey, step, stride, waddle.

WORD FIND

angry: stalk out, storm out, stamp out, stomp out, catapult into the room

baby: toddle

backward: backpedal, double-back, retrace one's steps

brush, through: blaze, bushwhack, pick one's way, negotiate, weave

casual: walk with elaborate nonchalance, mosey, shuffle, pad, saunter, stroll

complicated path, through or around: pick one's way, negotiate, step nimbly around, thread one's way, edge along, inch forward, take mincing steps

crowd, through a: sidle, jostle, elbow, shoulder, jockey for position, bull one's way through, be borne along by

difficult or laborious: dodder, falter, hobble, limp, lumber, plod, shamble, shuffle, stagger, stumble, totter, trudge, slog, slosh

drunken: stagger, falter, blunder forward, careen, totter

fours, on all: crab

graceful: with feline grace, with the grace of a porteuse, with calculated grace

group: parade, march, file out, tramp, troop, swarm, flood, spill out, be borne along by the crowd

military march: goose-step

show off: swagger, strut, peacock

slide by the soles of one's feet: glissade

sneaky or cautious: creep, edge, inch, slip away, slink, steal, tiptoe, shrink, skulk, prowl, withdraw, lurk, shadow

wet or mud, through: slog, slosh, squelch, splash, wade

wind, against: lean into, battle forward
SEE RUN

walking papers n. dismissal, *pink slip, lay-off, *the door, *the boot, firing, *sack,*heave-ho.

walk on v. walk all over, take advantage of, use, abuse, trample, dominate, exploit.

walk out on v. leave, turn one's back on, abandon, *leave high and dry, leave in the lurch, *dump, reject, jilt, depart, strike.

wall n. partition, divider, screen, bulkhead, load-bearing wall, non-load-bearing wall, panel, barrier, parapet.

wallop v. beat, thrash, pound, pummel, punch, slug, hit, bash, thump, sock, *drub, batter, cuff, *clean one's clock, coldcock, knock senseless, smack, *clobber, belt, bop, defeat, *skunk, *blow away, whip, lick, rout, *bury, *eat for breakfast, massacre.

wallow v. 1. ROLL AROUND lie in, lounge, slosh, splash. 2. INDULGE luxuriate, bask, relish, savor, take pleasure in, revel.

waltz n. valse. SEE DANCE

wan a. 1. PALE colorless, pallid, white, ghostly, pasty, blanched, anemic, ashen, cadaverous. 2. WEAK faint, feeble, sickly, tired, half-hearted, weary, sad, gaunt. ANT. 1. rosy, apple-cheeked, ruddy, flushed. 2. bright, strong, wholehearted.

wand n. stick, rod, staff, baton, scepter, switch.

wander v. 1. ROAM rove, range, wend, wind, go about aimlessly, ramble, drift, meander, trek, straggle, gallivant, gad, idle, stroll, lose one's way, stray, go off the beaten track. 2. DIGRESS get off the subject, deviate, get sidetracked, ramble, go off on a tangent. ANT. 1. make a beeline, go directly. 2. stick to the subject, stay on track.

wanderlust n. urge to travel, urge to explore, urge to wander, restlessness.

wane n. ebb, decline, fading, decrease, drop, recession, falling-off. ANT. increase, growth.

wane v. ebb, recede, decline, fade, decrease, drop, shrink, diminish, dwindle, abate, subside, lessen, fall, lapse, die out. ANT. increase, wax, grow.

wangle v. *finagle, machinate, make happen, *pull off, *pull strings, engineer, *swing, contrive, *wheel and deal.

want n. 1. DESIRE need, longing, wish, yearning, hunger, thirst, craving, appetite, hankering, requirement, demand. 2. LACK absence, need, dearth, shortage, scarcity, deficiency, paucity, privation. 3. POVERTY destitution, indigence, impoverishment.

want v. 1. DESIRE need, long for, wish for, yearn, hunger for, thirst for, crave, have an appetite for, have a hankering for, require, demand, covet. 2. LACK be deficient, be without, require, need.

wanting a. absent, lacking, missing, deficient, insufficient, inadequate, incomplete, bereft, short, substandard, subpar, poor. ANT. sufficient, adequate.

wanton a. 1. UNMANAGEABLE undisciplined, wild, intractable, unruly, wayward, refractory, unrestrained. 2. SEXUALLY UNRESTRAINED loose, libidinous, promiscuous, lustful, licentious, salacious, carnal, lewd, abandoned, fast. 3. UNPROVOKED groundless, uncalled-for, unnecessary, unjustifiable, senseless, needless, gratuitous, malicious, cruel, mean. 4. RECKLESS rash, unrestrained, careless, *devil-may-care. ANT. 1. manageable, disciplined, well-behaved. 2. chaste, celibate, prudish, puritanical. 3. provoked, necessary. 4. judicious, careful.

war n. warfare, hostilities, conflict, clash, strife, contest, struggle, battle, combat, military operation, confrontation, engagement, crusade. "Death's feast."—George Herbert. "A passion play performed by idiots."—William Corum. "A biological necessity of the first order."—Friedrich von Bernhardi. "That attractive rainbow that rises in showers of blood."—Abraham Lincoln. "The most successful of our cultural traditions."—Robert Ardrey. "Only a cowardly escape from the problems of peace."—Thomas Mann. ANT. *peace, friendship, accord, harmony.*

WORD FIND
aircraft, unmanned spy: drone, Global Hawk, Predator
attack, intense, all-out: blitzkrieg, sweep
attack or action: offensive
ceasefire: armistice, truce, peace treaty
chemical and biological agents: anthrax, botulinum, cs (tear gas), cyclosarin (nerve agent), ricin, sarin (nerve agent), sulfur mustard (blister agent), tabun (nerve agent), VX (nerve agent)
games: maneuvers
god of: Mars, Ares
holy: jihad, crusade
nuclear attck to prevent enemy nation's nuclear attack: preemptive strike
operation: campaign
presence of military force in control of another's nation: occupation
pretext for or provocation: casus belli, act of war
referring to: martial
ruining an area before returning it to the enemy: scorched earth policy
science of organization, procurement, deployment, etc.: logistics
surrender: capitulation, white flag
tensions between hostile nations: cold war
threatening another nation with: saber-rattling, gunboat diplomacy
victory won with extremely heavy losses: Pyrrhic victory
winnings: spoils
SEE AIR FORCE, AMMUNITION, ARMY, BOMB, BULLET, GUN, NAVY, NUCLEAR BOMB, SOLDIER, WEAPON
war *v.* conflict, contest, fight, battle, contend, struggle, *lock horns, take up arms, attack, cross swords, skirmish.
warble *v.* sing, trill, quaver, carol, yodel.
ward *n.* 1. WING section, division, room, annex, pavilion. 2. DISTRICT quarter, area, zone, precinct, borough, diocese. 3. CHARGE foster child, dependent, minor, protege, incompetent.
warden *n.* keeper, guard, custodian, caretaker, superintendent, watchman, overseer, prison superintendent.
ward off *v.* fend off, deflect, avert, parry, turn aside, block, defend, *keep at bay, rebuff, check, repulse.
wardrobe *n.* 1. CLOSET clothes closet, cabinet, armoire, locker, bureau, chest. 2. CLOTHES COLLECTION clothes, clothing, apparel, attire, outfits, garments, costumes, garb, togs, duds, *threads.
WORD FIND
bride's outfit: trousseau
ecclesiastical garments: vestments
warhead *n.* bomb, payload, explosive charge, *the business end. SEE MISSILE, NUCLEAR BOMB
warehouse *n.* storage facility, storehouse, stock house, stock room, depot, depository, repository, armory, arsenal, magazine, wholesale store.
wares *n.* merchandise, products, goods, stock, line, articles, stuff, commodities.
warfare *n.* SEE WAR
wariness *n.* caution, circumspection, alertness, guardedness, carefulness, watchfulness, mindfulness. ANT. *carelessness, inattentiveness, devil-may-care attitude.*
warlike *a.* combative, pugnacious, aggressive, militant, bellicose, belligerent, hostile, hawkish, contentious, martial, *bristling with arms. ANT. *peaceful, pacifistic, nonviolent.*
warlock *n.* sorcerer, wizard, magician, conjurer, practicer of black magic, necromancer, shaman, witch doctor, male witch. SEE MAGIC
warlord *n.* tyrant, autocrat. SEE DICTATOR
warm *v.* 1. RAISE TEMPERATURE heat, simmer, toast, cook, thaw. 2. FILL WITH EXCITEMENT excite, stimulate, *turn on, *fire up, stir. 3. GLADDEN make happy, fill with joy, delight, cheer, *melt one's heart, make smile. 4. BECOME FRIENDLY *break the ice, thaw, become intimate, *loosen up. ANT. 1. *lower temperature, cool, chill, freeze.* 2. *bore, tire, *turn off.* 3. *depress, *bum out.* 4. *cool.*
warm *a.* 1. HEATED thermal, lukewarm, body temperature, *toasty, room temperature, comfortable, tepid, sunny, hot, sultry, sweaty, roasting. SEE HOT 2. FERVENT fervid, ardent, enthusiastic, passionate, eager, vehement, *hot, excited, spirited. 3. GENIAL cordial, friendly, affectionate, nice, loving, heartfelt, amiable, warmhearted, hospitable, amorous. ANT. 1. *cold, freezing, cool, chilled, frigid.* 2. *indifferent, apathetic, lukewarm, cool.* 3. *cold, unfriendly, cool, hostile.*
warmhearted *a.* warm, friendly, genial, cordial, affectionate, nice, loving, heartfelt, amiable,

compassionate, sympathetic, understanding, hospitable, tender, amorous. ANT. *cold-hearted, hard-hearted, mean, heartless, *veins filled with ice water.*

warmonger n. hawk, militarist, jingoist.

warmth n. 1. HEAT glow, temperature, *toasti-ness, room temperature, fever. 2. EXCITE-MENT enthusiasm, ardor, zeal, vigor, fervor, passion, intensity, vehemence. 3. WARM-HEARTEDNESS friendliness, geniality, cordial-ity, affection, love, tenderness, compassion, sympathy, understanding, hospitality. ANT. *1. cold, chilliness, frigidity. 2. boredom, indifference, apathy. 3. coolness, coldness, unfriendliness.*

warn v. caution, advise, alert, signal, forewarn, admonish, exhort, apprise, give fair warning, notify, threaten, give a word to the wise, *put the fear of God into.

warning n. caution, advisory, alert, signal, fore-warning, admonition, exhortation, apprisal, notification, threat, *word to the wise, *wake-up call, caveat, portent, sign of things to come, omen.

warp v. 1. BEND OUT OF SHAPE distort, twist, de-form, contort, curve, turn, misshape. 2. PER-VERT twist, bias, prejudice, jaundice.

warrant n. 1. AUTHORIZATION authority, sanc-tion, right, word, *OK, permission, license, permit, mandate, subpoena, summons, writ, order, justification. 2. ASSURANCE guaran-tee, surety, security.

warrant v. 1. AUTHORIZE sanction, give author-ity, give the right, *OK, permit, license, allow, invest, certify, empower. 2. JUSTIFY give grounds for, account for, excuse, de-fend, provide a reason for. 3. ASSURE guaran-tee, back, promise, pledge, vow, swear to, insure, vouch for, underwrite.

warranty n. guarantee, assurance of quality, as-surance, contract, covenant, promise, pledge.

warrior n. fighter, soldier, combatant, com-mando, G.I., service man, infantryman, *grunt, *leatherneck, brave, samurai, gladi-ator. SEE ARMY, SOLDIER

warship n. man o'war, battleship, missile cruiser, destroyer, frigate, aircraft carrier, dreadnought, galleon. SEE NAVY, SHIP

wart n. growth, tumor, papilloma.

wary a. cautious, on one's guard, careful, watchful, circumspect, chary, vigilant, *on one's toes, leery, alert, on the lookout, suspi-cious. ANT. *careless, off guard, unsuspecting.*

wash n. 1. CLEANING rinse, scrubbing, bath,

soak, washing, shower, shampoo, launder-ing, ablution. 2. SURGE rush, sweep, wave, gush, flow, swell, roll.

wash v. 1. CLEAN rinse, scrub, bathe, soak, shower, shampoo, launder, hose down, freshen up. 2. WET drench, moisten, rinse, soak, flood.

washed-out a. faded, pale, bleached-out, blanched, dull, wan, colorless, lackluster. ANT. *bright, vivid.*

washed-up a. finished, through, done, *done for, *shot, *kaput, *over the hill.

washout n. Sl. flop, failure, *bomb, *dud, *clinker, *loser, *turkey, fiasco.

washroom n. lavatory, restroom, bathroom.

washy a. watery, weak, pale. ANT. *strong, potent.*

WASP n. Sl. White Anglo-Saxon Protestant.

waspish a. bad-tempered, hot-tempered, irrita-ble, petulant, testy, venomous, *ornery, touchy, peevish. ANT. *sweet-tempered, agree-able, pleasant.*

wassail n. celebration, carousal, party, *bash, *beer bash, spree, revelry, *shindig, gala, *binge, *bust, bacchanalia, drunk fest, toast, salute.

wassail v. celebrate, party, carouse, drink, get drunk, make merry, *whoop it up, revel, *cut loose, toast, make a toast, salute.

waste n. 1. TRASH rubbish, garbage, refuse, junk, leavings, scrap, debris, rubble, *crap, hazardous waste, discharge. 2. EXCREMENT fe-ces, droppings, *crap, sewage. 3. WASTEFUL-NESS squandering, extravagance, excessive-ness, lavishness, *spending like there's no tomorrow, consumption, conspicuous con-sumption, misuse, dissipation. ANT. *3. con-servation, frugality, economy, saving, thrift.*

waste v. 1. SQUANDER lavish, fritter away, *blow, *piss away, *spend like there's no to-morrow, dissipate, misspend, mismanage, spend extravagantly, splurge, throw away, idle, loiter, fiddle and diddle, loaf, procrasti-nate. 2. LOSE ONE'S HEALTH OR STRENGTH waste away, dwindle, fail, weaken, emaciate, atrophy, *circle the drain, wither, deterio-rate, decay, decline, *go downhill. 3. DE-STROY ruin, devastate, wreck, demolish, lay waste, spoil, strip, ravage. ANT. *1. conserve, save, economize. 2. strengthen, grow, put on weight. 3. build up, repair.*

wasted a. 1. GAUNT emaciated, wizened, atro-phied, deathly, cadaverous, rawboned, with-ered, anorexic, deathly. 2. Sl. *high, *buzzed, intoxicated, *baked, *fried, *loaded, *out of it, *stoned, *tripping. ANT. 1. *healthy, robust.* 2. *sober.*

wasteful *a.* prodigal, extravagant, lavish, spendthrift, improvident, excessive, immoderate, free-spending, overgenerous, penny-wise and pound-foolish. ANT. *thrifty, economical, frugal.*

wasteland *n.* waste, tundra, dust bowl, desert, badlands, *Devil's backyard, *Devil's garden, barrens, wilderness.

wastrel *n.* spendthrift, prodigal, waster, free-spender, good-for-nothing.

watch *n.* **1.** OBSERVATION lookout, surveillance, eye, sharp eye, weather eye, attention, observance, vigil, supervision, inspection, guarding, sentry. **2.** TIMEPIECE wristwatch, chronometer, horologue, *ticker.

watch *v.* **1.** OBSERVE look at, eyeball, eye, pay attention to, inspect, scrutinize, gaze at, view, regard, keep one's eyes on, see, behold, examine. **2.** GUARD watch over, *baby-sit, protect, look after, oversee, keep an eye on, patrol.

watchdog *n.* guard dog, guard, sentry, patrol, sentinel, lookout, guardian.

watchful *a.* observant, alert, wide-eyed, on guard, attentive, vigilant, on the lookout, heedful, wide-awake, cautious, wary, circumspect, *on one's toes. ANT. *inattentive, *asleep at the wheel, *out to lunch, unobservant.*

watchman *n.* guard, security guard, sentry, sentinel, lookout, patrol, policeman, policewoman, police officer, warder.

watchtower *n.* lookout.

watchword *n.* **1.** PASSWORD countersign, shibboleth. **2.** SLOGAN cry, battle cry, catchphrase, rallying cry.

water *n.* H₂O, liquid, fluid, rain, aqua, mineral water, soda water, *Adam's ale. "The noblest of the elements."—Pindar. SEE LAKE, OCEAN, RIVER

water *v.* wet, soak, drench, dampen, irrigate, hose down, saturate, spray, wash, sprinkle.

waterfall *n.* falls, cascade, cataract, chute, whitewater, deluge.

WORD FIND
descriptive: falling like a bridal veil, stair-stepping.
SEE RIVER

waterlogged *a.* saturated, soaked, sopping, sodden, drenched, heavy, swampy. ANT. *dry, arid, parched.*

WATERLOO *n.* [WAW tur loo] defeat. A metaphor coined after Napoleon's defeat in Waterloo, Belgium in 1815. *We were afraid that the match against the crosstown team would prove to be our Waterloo.* SYN. defeat, downfall, ruin, collapse, destruction, upset, rout, conquest, beating, vanquishment, massacre, comeuppance. ANT. *victory, win.*

watershed *n.* turning point, pivotal event, landmark, milestone, crucial event.

watertight *a.* airtight, solid. ANT. *leaky.*

watery *a.* diluted, thin, watered-down, weak, washy, bland, mild, tasteless, flavorless, anemic. ANT. *strong, intense, undiluted, concentrated, condensed.*

wattle *n.* weave, plait, intertwining, twigs, sticks.

wave *n.* **1.** SURGE OR SWELL surf, breaker, comber, plunger, spiller, bore, eagre, whitecap, billow, undulation, ripple, ridge.

WORD FIND
abnormally large wave in a train of smaller ones: rogue wave
concave-backed wave found offshore: spiller
convex-backed wave, common beach: plunger
frothy, gray-crested waves: graybeards
giant, formerly called tidal wave: tsunami
high dangerous wave caused by tidal surge: bore, eagre
high point: crest
hollow between: trough
marine vegetation washed ashore by: wrack
mounds of sand left by waves breaking at right angles: cusps
ripples in sand left by receding waves: swashmarks
roughness at sea: chop
series of: train
shallow sweep up a beach: swash, backwash
sound: lapping, crashing, booming, white noise, hiss
spray: spindrift
structure erected to prevent wave erosion: jetty, groin
tiny: wavelet
towering crests formed by opposing waves colliding: cross seas
upward heaving of ship caused by wave: scend
wind shore receiving smaller waves, low: lee shore
wind travel distance and its relationship to wave size: fetch
SEE BEACH, OCEAN
2. UPSURGE surge, rise, rash, flood, deluge, explosion, groundswell. **3.** CURL curve, roll, twist.

wave v. **1.** UNDULATE swing, sway, oscillate, ripple, flutter, flap, waggle, shake, move to and fro, move back and forth, rise and fall. **2.** SIGNAL gesture, gesticulate, *flag down, acknowledge.

waver v. **1.** VACILLATE go back and forth, blow hot and cold, *waffle, *see-saw, be irresolute, dilly-dally, flip-flop, fluctuate, equivocate, hem and haw, be indecisive. **2.** SWING sway, move to and fro, move back and forth, wobble, wave, shake, oscillate, flutter, flap. ANT. *1. make up one's mind, be resolute, decide one way or another.*

wavy a. rolling, curling, snaking, serpentine, sinuous, undulating, curved, curvilinear, rippling, winding. ANT. *level, flat.*

wax v. grow, enlarge, increase, expand, build, swell, develop, spread, intensify, magnify, strengthen, brighten. ANT. *wane, decrease, diminish.*

way n. **1.** METHOD mode, style, technique, form, practice, usage, approach, course, system, manner, procedure. **2.** DIRECTION route, course, path, tack, bearing, approach, course, passage, track, trail, road, lane, access, entry. **3.** NATURE personality, characteristic manner, behavior, custom, habit. **4.** WILL wish, desire, demand, choice.

wayfarer n. traveler, roamer, rover, hitchhiker, walker, wanderer, nomad, drifter, gadabout.

wayfaring a. hiking, hitchhiking, walking, traveling, roaming, roving, wandering, drifting, nomadic, on the move.

waylay v. ambush, attack, lie in wait, entrap, ensnare, surprise, take by surprise, ambuscade.

wayward a. **1.** DISOBEDIENT headstrong, rebellious, defiant, nonconforming, contrary, willful, delinquent, incorrigible, stubborn, obstinate, bullheaded, unmanageable, ungovernable, refractory. **2.** UNPREDICTABLE erratic, fickle, capricious, changeable, unstable, impulsive, unsteady. ANT. *1. obedient, compliant, deferential. 2. predictable, stable, steady.*

weak a. **1.** FEEBLE powerless, frail, enervated, impotent, limp, faint, flaccid, ineffectual, exhausted, anemic, worn out, spent, sickly, debilitated, unfit, out of shape, infirm, emasculated. **2.** MORALLY OR MENTALLY WEAK cowardly, fainthearted, faint of heart, spineless, mousy, wishy-washy, weak-kneed, irresolute, *wimpy, timid, timorous. **3.** STUPID dim-witted, unintelligent, retarded, moronic, imbecilic, dense, dull. **4.** INSECURE unstable, easily broken, unfortified, vulnerable, delicate, fragile, rickety, flimsy, shaky,

frail. **5.** FAINT soft, dim, mild, gentle, pale, thin, feeble, low, muted, diluted, watered-down. **6.** LACKING deficient, poor, inadequate, wanting, unsatisfactory, shaky, inept. ANT. *1. strong, powerful, fit, robust, effectual, muscle-bound. 2. strong, headstrong, courageous, bold, *gutsy, 3. smart, intelligent, sharp. 4. stable, fortified, rock-solid, unassailable. 5. strong, intense, powerful, undiluted. 6. adequate, satisfactory.*

weaken v. drain, sap, debilitate, cripple, exhaust, flag, impair, tire, enervate, enfeeble, droop, slow, run down, deplete, handicap, diminish, reduce, wane, ebb, fade, *lose one's charge, *run one's battery down, *run out of juice, dilute, water down. ANT. *strengthen, fortify, invigorate, energize.*

weakling n. *wimp, milquetoast, *pansy, pantywaist, sissy, coward, mouse, *lightweight, *pushover, namby-pamby, *mama's boy, *creampuff, crybaby. ANT. *Hercules, scrapper, hero, strongman, *iron man.*

weak-minded a. irresolute, indecisive, mealy-mouthed, wishy-washy, spineless, feeble-minded, dumb, stupid, *weak in the head, retarded, moronic, slow, dense. ANT. *headstrong, resolute, decisive, intelligent, smart, bright.*

weakness n. **1.** LACK OF STRENGTH feebleness, exhaustion, depletion of energy, enervation, anemia, frailty, fragility. **2.** VULNERABILITY imperfection, flaw, weak spot, *Achilles heel, *chink in one's armor, deficiency, failing, soft underbelly, shortcoming. **3.** LIKING fondness, passion, penchant, taste, appreciation, soft spot, sweet tooth, propensity, inclination. ANT. *1. strength, vigor, energy, robustness. 2. strong point, strength. 3. aversion, dislike, hatred.*

weal n. ridge, welt, wale, line.

wealth n. money, riches, resources, plenty, fortune, security, affluence, opulence, prosperity, abundance, luxury, capital, property, assets, means, holdings, stocks and bonds. "The savings of many in the hands of one."—Eugene Debs. "Evidence of greatness."—Thomas Reed. "A contented mind."—Mohammed. ANT. *poverty, destitution, indigence, want, lack.*

wealthy a. rich, affluent, well-off, *rolling in dough, comfortable, prosperous, *well-heeled, *well-to-do, moneyed, opulent, *filthy rich, *on easy street, *loaded, financially secure. ANT. *poor, destitute, penniless.*

weapon n. arm, arms, armament, firearm, gun,

rifle, pistol, knife, sword, defense, offensive weapon, weapon of mass destruction, spear, halberd, lance, pike, poleax, trident, bow and arrow. SEE ARMY, BOMB, BULLET, GUN, MISSILE, NAVY, NUCLEAR BOMB, SWORD

weaponry n. SEE WEAPON

wear n. **1.** CLOTHING clothes, dress, apparel, garb, attire, formal wear, evening wear, sportswear. **2.** DETERIORATION decay, erosion, wear and tear, corrosion, decomposition.

wear v. **1.** DON put on, dress in, be clothed in, fit out, attire, slip on. **2.** DETERIORATE decay, erode, corrode, decompose, abrade, tatter, fall apart, degenerate, rub down, grow threadbare, weather, fray. **3.** DISPLAY show, put on, sport. **4.** TIRE exhaust, fatigue, sap, drain, overwork, tax.

wearing a. tiring, exhausting, fatiguing, taxing, draining, sapping, strenuous, laborious, arduous, wearisome, hard. ANT. *invigorating, energizing.*

wearisome a. tiring, tiresome, exhausting, fatiguing, taxing, draining, sapping, strenuous, laborious, arduous, hard, tedious, boring, monotonous, humdrum, *ho-hum. ANT. *invigorating, energizing, stimulating.*

weary v. tire, get sick of, burn out, exhaust, fatigue, tax, drain, sap, enervate, bore. ANT. *invigorate, energize, stimulate.*

weary a. **1.** TIRED worn out, exhausted, fatigued, taxed, drained, sapped, *wrung out, *trashed out, spent, *pooped, bushed, tuckered out, all in, *beat, *dead, burned out, *shot. **2.** SICK OF *had it, fed up, disgusted, bored, intolerant, jaded, burned out. **3.** TIRESOME tedious, boring, monotonous. ANT. *1. invigorated, refreshed, energized. 2. fascinated, stimulated. 3. stimulating, interesting.*

weasel n. sneak, snake, *snake in the grass, cheater, crook, snitch, *double-crosser, *rat, *squealer.

weasel v. avoid, evade, dodge, equivocate, waffle, hedge, duck, double-talk, *dance around an issue, skirt an issue, get out of, *worm one's way out of, renege.

weather n. climate, clime, atmospheric conditions, temperature, humidity. "A social invention to facilitate small talk."—Anon. SEE CLOUD, FOG, METEOROLOGY, PRECIPITATION, RAIN, SNOW, WIND

weather v. withstand, stand, endure, resist, be exposed to the elements, face, season, harden, survive, *tough out, *ride through. ANT. *die, succumb.*

weatherman n. meteorologist, forecaster, climatologist.

weave v. intertwine, interlace, entwine, intermingle, interweave, braid, plait, combine, mesh, piece together, blend, incorporate, merge, wattle.

web n. webbing, network, net, mesh, skein, lattice, tangle, trap, snare, gossamer.

wed v. **1.** MARRY join together in holy matrimony, *tie the knot, *get hitched, *say "I do," become man and wife, espouse. **2.** UNITE join, marry, merge, fuse, link, combine, ally, connect, unify. ANT. *1. divorce, *split up, separate. 2. separate, split, divide.*

wedding n. **1.** MARRIAGE vows, nuptials, matrimony, espousal, holy wedlock, ceremony. "When the blind lead the blind."—George Farquhar. SEE MARRIAGE **2.** UNIFICATION joining, marriage, merger, fusion, linking, connection. ANT. *1. separation, divorce. 2. division, split, disconnection.*

wedge n. **1.** CHOCK cleat, shim, quoin. **2.** OPENING beginning, start, *foot in the door.

wedge v. split, force apart, force in, squeeze in, cram, open.

wedlock n. matrimony, union. SEE MARRIAGE

wee a. tiny, little, diminutive, pint-sized, pocket-sized, Lilliputian, microscopic, minuscule, miniature, *teeny-weeny. ANT. *giant, huge, Brobdingnagian.*

weed n. "A plant whose virtues have not yet been discovered."—Ralph Waldo Emerson.

weed v. remove, pull, yank, uproot, cull, get rid of, weed out.

weep v. cry, bawl, shed tears, sob, wail, blubber, boohoo, whimper, snivel, *break down, *lose it, lament, bewail, mourn, grieve, bemoan, get misty-eyed.

weepy a. tearful, teary-eyed. SEE SAD

weigh v. **1.** MEASURE WEIGHT put on the scales, tip the scales, heft, gauge. **2.** CONSIDER ponder, deliberate, think about, contemplate, consider the pros and cons, evaluate, mull over, study, examine, reflect on.

weigh down v. saddle, encumber, load. SEE BURDEN

weight n. **1.** HEAVINESS mass, pounds, tons, tonnage, burden, heft, gravity, g force, gs, density, volume. **2.** BURDEN responsibility, load, millstone, cross to bear, albatross, *ball and chain, encumbrance, saddle, handicap, onus, hardship. **3.** IMPORTANCE consequence, significance, seriousness, influence, value, import, clout, power, moment, magnitude.

weight *v.* weigh down, make heavy, load, burden.

weight lifting *n.* power lifting, working out, conditioning, weight training.

weighty *a.* **1.** HEAVY hefty, massive, ponderous, cumbersome, dense, hard to lift. **2.** BURDENSOME hard, difficult, oppressive, demanding, backbreaking, onerous, taxing. **3.** IMPORTANT consequential, significant, serious, influential, valuable, important, powerful, momentous, crucial, critical, life or death. **4.** INFLUENTIAL powerful, forceful, persuasive, having clout. ANT. *1. light, airy, light as a feather. 2. easy, effortless, simple. 3. unimportant, insignificant, inconsequential. 4. powerless, unconvincing.*

weir *n.* dam, milldam, fence, fishtrap.

weird *a.* bizarre, strange, odd, fantastic, unearthly, otherworldly, alien, supernatural, mysterious, outlandish, nightmarish, surrealistic, Kafkaesque, peculiar, queer, grotesque, eerie, uncanny, *freaky, unusual. ANT. *ordinary, conventional, usual, normal.*

weirdo *n. Sl.* oddball, eccentric, character, *space case, *space cadet, *strange bird, *flake, *geek, freak, *kook, *queer duck, *screwball, *sicko, *wacko, nonconformist. ANT. *conformist, *Joe Average, *just another brick in the wall.*

welcome *n.* greeting, reception, salute, salutation, *red carpet treatment, hospitality, acceptance, hail. ANT. *rejection, snub.*

welcome *v.* greet, receive, receive with open arms, receive with a handshake, *roll out the red carpet, hail, salute. ANT. *reject, snub.*

welcome *a.* wanted, accepted warmly, pleasing, pleasant, agreeable, happily received, invited, delightful, esteemed, desirable. ANT. *unwelcome, unwanted, uninvited.*

weld *v.* fuse, unite, bond, join, solder.

welfare *n.* **1.** WELL-BEING health, happiness, good, benefit, profit, prosperity, success, interest, contentment, commonweal. **2.** PUBLIC ASSISTANCE relief, financial assistance, city aid, food stamps, the dole, Social Security.

well *n.* spring, wellspring, reservoir, shaft, chasm, pit, hole, fountain, water hole.

well *a.* **1.** HEALTHY fit, in good shape, strong, fine, hearty, vigorous, sound, in fine fettle, *fit as a fiddle, hale. **2.** GOOD fortunate, happy, lucky, proper, right. ANT. *1. unwell, sickly, in failing health. 2. bad, unlucky, unfortunate.*

well *adv.* **1.** SATISFACTORILY successfully, adequately, happily, nicely, splendidly, famously, capably, ably, in fine fashion. **2.** THOROUGHLY sufficiently, completely, properly, right, correctly, adequately, carefully, conscientiously, competently. ANT. *1. unsatisfactorily, poorly, badly. 2. insufficiently, poorly.*

well up *v.* flow, spring, gush, stream, run, trickle, spout, bubble, boil.

well-advised *a.* wise, smart, intelligent, prudent, judicious. ANT. *imprudent, foolish.*

well-appointed *a.* well-equipped, well-furnished. ANT. *inadequate, lacking.*

well-balanced *a.* sensible, reasonable, rational, prudent, intelligent, sound. ANT. *unreasonable, irrational.*

well-being *n.* welfare, health, happiness, prosperity, profit, good, comfort, contentment, benefit, success.

well-bred *a.* mannerly, cultivated, refined, polite, courteous, civil, gentlemanly, ladylike, polished, groomed, genteel, courtly, gracious, finished, sophisticated. ANT. *ill-bred, unrefined, coarse, vulgar, uncouth, beastly.*

well-defined *a.* clear, distinct, sharp, clearly delineated, graphic, clear-cut, unambiguous. ANT. *vague, hazy, nebulous.*

well-founded *a.* factual, based on hard facts, based on hard data, solid, rock-solid, proven, substantiated, authoritative, well-grounded. ANT. *unfounded, based on speculation, questionable.*

well-informed *a.* schooled, trained, au courant, conversant with, savvy, up to date, aware, versed, *with it, *hip. ANT. *ignorant, *in the dark.*

well-known *a.* famous, famed, prominent, celebrated, illustrious, infamous, notorious, notable, renowned, *on the map. ANT. *obscure, unknown.*

well-off *a.* rich, well-to-do. SEE WEALTHY

well-preserved *a.* youthful. SEE YOUNG

well-read *a.* widely read, bookish, literate, scholarly, educated, au courant, versed. ANT. *illiterate, ignorant.*

wellspring *n.* source, supply, reservoir. SEE WELL

well-to-do *a.* well-off, rich, prosperous. SEE WEALTHY

welsh *v. Sl.* cheat, swindle, *rip off, renege, dodge, *weasel out of.

welt *n.* ridge, wale, weal, mark, swelling.

welter *n.* turmoil, turbulence, confusion, tossing about, commotion, hubbub, disturbance, tumult, uproar, bedlam, *to-do.

wench *n.* girl, young woman, young lady, maiden, lass.

wend *v.* go on one's way, make one's way, go, proceed, journey, travel, progress.

wet *v.* dampen, moisturize, water, drench, soak, sprinkle, wash, rinse, hose down, humidify, irrigate, submerge. ANT. *dry, dehydrate, desiccate.*

wet *a.* moist, damp, watery, liquefied, drenched, soaked, waterlogged, soggy, sodden, dripping, humid, clammy, dank, rainy, foggy. ANT. *dry, *bone-dry, dehydrated.*

wet blanket *n. Sl.* killjoy, spoilsport, poor sport, *drag, *gloomy Gus, *drip, *grinch, *prophet of doom. ANT. *good sport, life of the party.*

wetland *n.* marsh, swamp, everglades, fen, quagmire.

wetness *n.* moisture, dampness, liquid, water, humidity, clamminess, mist, fog, rain. ANT. *dryness, aridity.*

whack *v.* strike, slap, hit, smack, punch, slug, *bop, belt, wallop, bash, rap, cuff, crack.

whale *n.* cetacean, leviathan, aquatic mammal, humpback whale, blue whale, finback, sperm whale, beluga, rorqual, gray whale.

WORD FIND

air hole: blowhole, spiracle

beaching of: stranding

biblical survivor of ingestion: Jonah

bone or tooth carvings: scrimshaw

carcass: kreng

comblike strainer in the mouth of some breeds: baleen

cut blubber off from: flense

diving: sounding

fat: blubber

fatty substance used in candles, ointments: spermaceti

female: cow

fictional hunter: Ahab

fin: dorsal fin

fins, tail: flukes

horned: narwhal

hunter's whale: right whale

killer whale: orca

leaping out of the water: breaching

male: bull

perfumes, waxy substance used in: ambergris

prehistoric: zeuglodon

school: pod, gam

slapping tail down hard on surface: lobtailing

sound location: sonar

study of: cetology

toothed whales, order of: odontoceti

toothless whales that feed on plankton: baleen whale, mysticeti

young: calf

whale *v.* whale on, beat, whip, pound, whack, thrash.

whammy *n. Sl.* jinx, evil eye, curse, spell, hex.

wharf *n.* dock, pier, marina, slip, landing, quay, berth, mooring, jetty.

whatchamacallit *n. Sl.* *thingamajig, *thingamabob, *doohickey, gadget, contraption, *dingus, *doodad, *gidget, *gizmo, *jigger, *whangdoodle, *whatsit, widget.

wheedle *v.* wangle, cajole, persuade, coax, inveigle, influence, flatter, charm, *charm the socks off of.

wheel *n.* tire, caster, roller.

wheel *v.* roll, revolve, rotate, spin, turn, trundle, whirl, twirl, pivot, swivel, gyrate, pirouette, reel.

wheeze *v.* rasp, gasp, whistle, puff, huff and puff, have an asthmatic attack.

whet *v.* **1.** SHARPEN hone, edge, grind, file, rasp, strop. **2.** STIMULATE make keen, arouse, excite, kindle, stir, awaken, *jumpstart, pique. ANT. *1. blunt, dull. 2. dampen, inhibit.*

whiff *n.* **1.** PUFF OF AIR wind, gust, breath, breeze, waft. **2.** SMELL scent, aroma, odor, trace, hint, suspicion.

whim *n.* caprice, impulse, passing fancy, notion, crotchet, idea, *brainstorm.

whimper *v.* cry, sob, whine, snivel, *choke back tears, *have a hitch in one's voice, moan, sniffle.

whimsical *a.* fanciful, odd, out of the ordinary, weird, peculiar, quaint, fantastic, unusual, capricious, amusing, playful.

whimsy *n.* SEE WHIM

whine *n.* pule, whimper, mewl, cry, sob, snivel, moan, complaint.

whine *v.* pule, whimper, mewl, cry, sob, snivel, moan, complain, fret, *bellyache, fuss.

whinny *v.* neigh.

whip *n.* bullwhip, horsewhip, *blacksnake, lash, switch, scourge, rawhide, quirt, thong, crop, cat-o'-nine-tails.

whip *v.* **1.** LASH flog, flagellate, flail, flay, horsewhip, hit, beat, scourge, whale, *take the strap to, *tan one's hide, *whallop, cane, spank, punish. **2.** JERK whip out, yank, pull out, whisk, snatch, grab. **3.** DEFEAT SOUNDLY *lick, beat, *cream, *skunk, *blow away, trounce, clobber, rout, *shellac, overpower, *get the better of, vanquish. **4.** BEAT mix, stir, whisk. **5.** AGITATE stir up, spark, kindle, spur, incite, instigate, foment, prompt.

whippersnapper n. upstart.

whipping n. thrashing, flogging, flagellation, horsewhipping, *whalloping, beating, spanking, pounding, punishment.

whipping boy n. *fall guy. SEE SCAPEGOAT

whip up v. SEE WHIP

whir n. buzz, hum, birr, vibration.

whirl v. spin, twirl, wheel, gyrate, reel, turn, rotate, revolve, swirl, pivot, pirouette.

whirlpool n. maelstrom, vortex, eddy, swirl, whirl.

whirlwind n. tornado, cyclone, twister, hurricane, typhoon, *blow.

whisk v. **1.** BRUSH sweep, flick. **2.** BEAT whip. **3.** MOVE QUICKLY whip, dart, hurry, rush, hasten.

whiskers n. bristles, beard, sideburns, *five o'clock shadow, stubble, hair. SEE BEARD, MUSTACHE

whiskey n. liquor, alcohol, *hard stuff, spirits, *firewater, drink, booze, *moonshine, *rotgut, scotch, rye, bourbon, *sauce, *tarantula juice.

whisper n. **1.** HUSHED VOICE murmur, mutter, undertone, soft voice, mumble, sigh, confidential tone, conspiratorial tone. **2.** SECRET rumor, gossip, confidence, insinuation. **3.** SOFT NOISE sigh, sough, breath. ANT. *1. roar, bellow, shout.*

whisper v. murmur, mutter, speak in an undertone, speak softly, mumble, speak confidentially, speak in a conspiratorial tone, breathe, intimate, confide. ANT. *roar, bellow, shout.*

whistle v. pipe, flute, trill, toot, blow.

whit n. bit, jot, iota, speck, grain, pinch, mite, atom, particle.

white a. **1.** LIGHT-COLORED alabaster, argent, blond, bone, chalk, columbine, dove, eggshell, ivory, milk, oyster, pearl, platinum, snow, snowy, hoary, albino. **2.** PALE blanched, bleached, wan, pallid, sickly, bloodless. **3.** CAUCASIAN light-skinned, fair. ANT. *1. black, dark, ebony. 2. rosy, ruddy, red.*

whiten v. bleach, blanch, fade.

whitewash v. gloss over, cover up, smooth over, conceal, tone down, soft-pedal, palliate.

whittle v. carve, cut, shave, pare, slash, shape, sculpt, reduce, decrease.

whiz n. **1.** WHISTLE buzz, hum, whir, drone, hiss. **2.** Sl. EXPERT wizard, crackerjack, master, prodigy, ace, virtuoso, pro, *whiz kid, genius.

whiz v. buzz, hiss, hum, whir, drone.

whole n. total, sum total, aggregate, all, entirety.

whole a. complete, total, entire, full, undivided, intact, uncut, unbroken, perfect, in one piece. ANT. *partial, incomplete, broken.*

wholehearted a. earnest, all-out, sincere, enthusiastic, eager, complete, emphatic, dedicated, unqualified, fervent, ardent, hearty. ANT. *halfhearted, lukewarm, reserved.*

wholesale a. extensive, sweeping, massive, broad, comprehensive, far-reaching, large-scale, general. ANT. *limited, small-scale.*

wholesome a. healthful, healthy, good for you, beneficial, helpful, hygienic, nutritious, nourishing, virtuous, moral, clean-cut, decent. ANT. *unhealthy, harmful, bad for you.*

wholly adv. totally, completely, entirely, utterly, fully, thoroughly. ANT. *partially.*

whoop n. yell, shout, cry, *holler, scream, shriek, hurrah, cheer, *yahoo, hoot.

whoop v. yell, shout, cry, *holler, scream, shriek, hurrah, cheer, *yahoo, hoot.

whopper n. **1.** GIANT *mother of all, colossus, titan, monster, Goliath, mammoth, behemoth, leviathan, *grandaddy of them all, jumbo. **2.** BIG LIE tall tale, *fish story, stretching of the truth. ANT. *1. midget, dwarf, shrimp.*

whopping a. great, huge, large, gigantic, gargantuan, massive, colossal, extraordinary, enormous, prodigious, immense. ANT. *tiny, insignificant, little.*

whore n. prostitute, lady of the evening, *call girl, *streetwalker, *hooker, *working girl, woman of ill repute, tramp, courtesan, escort. SEE PROSTITUTE

whorl n. spiral, coil, convolution, volution.

wicked a. **1.** EVIL bad, immoral, depraved, sinful, villainous, fiendish, shameless, rotten, nasty, iniquitous, nefarious, blackhearted, unprincipled, low, lawless, criminal. **2.** NAUGHTY mischievous, devilish, rascally, impish, roguish, misbehaving, prankish. **3.** SEVERE bad, awful, nasty, fierce, intense, acute, harsh, horrible. ANT. *1. good, moral, virtuous. 2. well-behaved, well-mannered. 3. mild, gentle, easy, slight.*

wide a. **1.** BROAD roomy, extensive, ample, spread-out, spacious, expansive, capacious, commodious, vast. **2.** SWEEPING broad, comprehensive, all-inclusive, general, large. **3.** OPEN outstretched, extended. **4.** OFF TARGET off, off course, inaccurate. ANT. *1. narrow, cramped, restricted. 2. limited, specific. 3. closed, folded. 4. on target, accurate.*

wide-awake *a.* alert, watchful, sharp, *on one's toes, *on the ball, vigilant, *bright-eyed and bushy-tailed, wary, wide-eyed, *saucer-eyed. ANT. *asleep, sleepy, unobservant.*

wide-eyed *a.* **1.** NAIVE inexperienced, innocent, green, childlike, unschooled, unsophisticated, *born yesterday. **2.** SURPRISED shocked, astonished, saucer-eyed, agog. ANT. *1. jaded, blasé, *ho-hum. 2. bored.*

widen *v.* broaden, expand, extend, spread, enlarge, swell, distend, increase. ANT. *narrow, restrict, taper.*

widespread *a.* all over, far-reaching, far-flung, pervasive, extensive, nationwide, worldwide, universal, rife, rampant, common, prevalent, epidemic, pandemic. ANT. *confined, local, limited, rare.*

widget *n.* gadget, *gizmo, device, contraption, *thingamajig, *doohickey, *whatsit, *thingamabob, *whatchamacallit, *doodad.

widow *n.* widower, surviving spouse, dowager.

width *n.* breadth, wideness, broadness, girth, span, thickness, diameter, spread, extent.

wield *v.* **1.** HANDLE use, ply, manipulate, brandish, swing, hold. **2.** EXERCISE employ, control, command, hold, exert.

wife *n.* spouse, mate, bride, partner, companion, *better half, consort, squaw, soul mate. "A crown to her husband."—Bible. "A former sweetheart."—Henry Louis Mencken.

wig *n.* hairpiece, toupee, *rug, *fall, peruke, periwig.

wiggle *n.* jiggle, wriggle, wag, waggle, squirm, worming, writhing, shake, jerk, twitch, quiver.

wiggle *v.* jiggle, wriggle, wag, waggle, squirm, worm, writhe, shake, jerk, twitch, quiver.

wild *a.* **1.** NATURAL undomesticated, uncultivated, organic, untamed, feral, native, unbroken, uncivilized, primitive, primeval, primordial, untouched, pristine, uninhabited, overgrown, wooded, desert, godforsaken. **2.** SAVAGE barbarous, rough, beastly, brutish, primitive, ignorant, uncivilized. **3.** UNRESTRAINED, UNCONTROLLABLE out of control, unmanageable, intractable, rebellious, unruly, rough, rowdy, crazy, undisciplined, reckless, impulsive, lawless. **4.** MORALLY LOOSE unbridled, unrestrained, dissolute, profligate, wanton, debauched, immoral, orgiastic. **5.** STORMY rough, turbulent, tempestuous, violent, explosive, gusting, windy,

disturbed, wind-whipped. **6.** EXCITED frantic, frenzied, maniacal, hysterical, enthusiastic, eager. **7.** DISORDERED in disarray, confused, tangled, messy, tousled, unkempt. ANT. *1. unnatural, domesticated, tame, man-made, civilized, urbanized. 2. civilized, refined, polished. 3. restrained, polite, well-behaved. 4. moral, prudish, puritanical. 5. calm, mild, gentle, quiet. 6. calm, reserved, low-key. 7. neat, orderly.*

wilderness *n.* wilds, *howling wilderness, woods, forest, jungle, uncultivated area, wasteland, desert, badland, backcountry, outback.

wildlife *n.* animals, fauna, beasts, creatures, game.

wile *n.* artifice, artfulness, trick, trickery, cunning, stratagem, ruse, craftiness, machination, deception, fraud, ploy.

will *n.* **1.** POWER OF CHOICE choice, decision, desire, want, wish, determination, conviction, volition, prerogative, intention, mind, preference, discretion, command, decree. **2.** RESOLVE willpower, determination, singlemindedness, commitment. **3.** DOCUMENT DISPOSING OF WEALTH AFTER DEATH bequest, legacy, testament, last will and testament, dispensation.

will *v.* desire, wish, choose, want, determine, demand, command, direct.

willful *a.* **1.** DELIBERATE intentional, intended, planned, purposeful, volitional, premeditated, willing, conscious. **2.** SELF-WILLED stubborn, obstinate, headstrong, bullheaded, pigheaded, mulish, intractable, uncompromising, inflexible. ANT. *1. involuntary, unintentional, accidental. 2. flexible, compromising, acquiescent.*

willing *a.* agreeable, unreluctant, inclined, enthusiastic, eager, accommodating, obliging, ready, amenable, in favor, consenting, disposed, game. ANT. *unwilling, disinclined, averse.*

willowy *a.* slender, slim, svelte, thin, skinny, twiggy, graceful, lithe, lissome, pliant, supple, limber. ANT. *obese, fat, inflexible.*

willpower *n.* self-control, will, firmness, drive, determination, resolve, strength, backbone, iron will, discipline, grit. ANT. *weakness, lack of control.*

wilt *v.* droop, wither, slump, slouch, sag, sink, shrivel, flag, wane, diminish, ebb, weaken, die.

WILY *a.* [WI lee] sly, crafty. *The wily coyote always manages to survive.* SYN. sly, crafty, cunning, tricky, sharp, designing, shrewd, *cagey, artful, sneaky, foxy, underhanded, astute, slippery, slick. ANT. *stupid, dull, dumb.

win n. victory, triumph, conquest, success, sweep, gold medal, achievement, accomplishment, coup. ANT. *loss, defeat.*

win v. **1.** BE VICTORIOUS defeat, best, beat, triumph, succeed, vanquish, *take home the gold, sweep, clinch, prevail, come in first, *leave competitors swirling in one's wake, carry the day. **2.** ACHIEVE accomplish, gain, obtain, attain, get, earn. ANT. *1. lose, be defeated, fail, *choke. 2. fail.*

wince v. flinch, cringe, blink, recoil, draw back, shrink, cower, grimace, duck, quail, brace oneself.

wind n. **1.** BREEZE gust, draft, breath, waft, zephyr, air current, puff, blast, blow, gale, tempest, whirlwind, cyclone, tornado.
WORD FIND
aircraft hazard: windshear
Asian wind accompanied by heavy rain: monsoon
breeze that ripples water's surface: cat's paw
debris knocked down by: windfall
dry, desert wind of west coast of Africa: harmattan
dry: foehn
force source: Coriolis force
god of: Aeolus
Hawaii, light, consistent wind of: trade wind
high-speed, high-altitude wind: jet stream
hot wind of the Asiatic and African deserts: simoon
indicator, direction: anemoscope
indicator: sock, weather vane
measuring device: anemometer
Mediterranean, cold, northerly: mistral
Mexican, hurricane-borne wind: cordonazo
mountain, warm and dry wind descending leeward side of: chinook
North African: sirocco
pertaining to: eolian
recurring winds over the Mediterranean: etecians
scale: Beaufort
shifting: variable, veering, backing
sound: sough, moan, howl, whistle
squall of North American southwest coast: chubasco
sudden burst, accompanied by rain: squall
windless sea region: doldrums
2. BREATH air, expiration, inhalation, respiration. **3.** INFORMATION scent, smell, news,

inkling, report, rumor. **4.** NONSENSE *hot air, pomposity, idle talk, bluster, empty talk, claptrap, balderdash.

wind v. turn, bend, coil, curl, crook, roll, twine, twist, furl, screw, corkscrew, twirl, reel, crank, meander, snake.

windbag n. *blowhard, *chatterbox, *motormouth, *big-mouth.

windfall n. fortune, stroke of luck, jackpot, godsend, manna from heaven, boon, lucky strike.

window n. opening, glass, portal, casement, dormer, bay window, oriel, skylight, roundel, deadlight.

windy a. blustery, gusting, breezy, tempestuous, stormy, blowing, windswept, wind-whipped, drafty. ANT. *still, calm, becalmed.*

wine n. fermented grape juice, alcohol, red wine, white wine, champagne, vintage, port, muscatel, brandy, Chablis, Chianti, Chardonnay, Zinfandel. "The blood of grapes."—Bible. "Bottled poetry."—Robert Louis Stevenson. "[That which] makes man mistake words for thoughts."—Samuel Johnson.
WORD FIND
addicted to: vinous
aftertaste: finish
American red grape: Catawba
California wine region: Napa Valley
California winery: Gallo, Inglenook
city of, French: Bordeaux
deposit: lees, dregs
distilled from: cognac, brandy
driest of champagnes: brut
flavor, crisp: flinty
flavor, dull: flat
flavor, having delicate: finesse
flavor intensity: body
flavor, lively and acidic: piquant
flavor, multiple: complex
flavor, poor: flabby
flavor, sharp: tart
flavor, soft and full: mellow
flavor, rough: coarse
fragrance: bouquet
French red: Beaujolais, Cabernet Sauvignon, claret
French region: Burgundy
French white: Chablis
German white: Moselle, Rhine
god: Bacchus
inventor of champagne: Dom Perignon
Italian red: Bardolino, Barolo, Chianti, Tuscany

Italian white: Soave
lover: oenophilist
merchant: vintner
new: must
pink: rosé, blush
Portuguese: Madeira, port
pour: decant
pucker factor in red wine: astringency
rice wine: sake
shop: bistro, bodega
Spanish wine and brandy: sherry
steward or waiter: sommelier
storage: cellar
sweeten: mull
sweet, not: dry
vineyard, stone-walled: clos
white wine flavored with herbs: vermouth
year of grape's harvest: vintage

wing n. annex, addition, unit, arm, section, extension, part, flank, branch.

wing v. fly, soar, glide, zoom, hurry, speed.

wing it v. Sl. improvise, ad lib.

wink v. blink, bat an eyelid, nictitate.

winner n. victor, champion, *champ, medalist, gold medalist, *number one, titleholder, *top dog, conqueror, vanquisher. ANT. loser, failure, *also-ran.

winning a. charming, attractive, delightful, pleasing, enchanting, bewitching, captivating, disarming, charismatic, engaging, sweet, winsome. ANT. repulsive, nasty, disgusting.

winnow v. sift, separate, extract, cull, divide the good from the bad, screen, glean, weed out, differentiate, separate the wheat from the chaff.

wino n. Sl. drunk, drunkard, alcoholic.

winsome a. charming, sweet, attractive, nice, engaging, winning, delightful, pleasing, disarming, likable, lovable. ANT. repellent, repulsive, disgusting.

winter n. season, cold season, snow season. "Trees stooping under burdens of snow, windows filligreed with frost, shadows of drifting hummocks turning blue-cold as northerners mummify themselves in coats and scarves."—Henry Clayborne.
WORD FIND
of or like: hiemal, brumal, hibernal
SEE SNOW

wintry a. hiemal, hibernal, brumal, cold, frigid, bone-chilling, raw, biting, bitter, snowy, frost-patterned, filigreed with frost, stark, pristine, frozen, icy. ANT. summery, hot, warm.

wipe v. rub, brush, wash, sponge, clean, dust, towel, dry, remove, swab, polish.

wipeout n. Sl. fall, crash, collapse, spill, dive, tumble, nose-dive.

wipe out v. destroy, eradicate, annihilate, obliterate, exterminate, demolish, get rid of, kill, slaughter, abolish, decimate.

wiry a. lean, strong, tough, sinewy, muscular, strapping, athletic, agile, fit, trim, in shape, hardened. ANT. fat, obese, out of shape, flabby.

wisdom n. knowledge, experience, erudition, good judgment, insight, sagacity, common sense, *horse sense, intelligence, smarts, *brains, discernment, acumen, savvy, enlightenment, foresight. "A special knowledge in excess of all that is known."—Ambrose Bierce. "The soul's natural food."—Jacob Anatoli. "[That which] comes by suffering."—Aeschylus. ANT. ignorance, inexperience, stupidity, foolishness.

wise a. 1. KNOWLEDGEABLE experienced, erudite, prudent, judicious, insightful, sagacious, sage, informed, learned, sensible, intelligent, smart, *brainy, shrewd, astute, discerning, sharp, savvy, enlightened, understanding. 2. Sl. FRESH smart-mouthed, impudent, *smart-alecky, insolent, impertinent, *sassy, disrespectful, flippant, flip. ANT. 1. ignorant, inexperienced, stupid, uninformed, foolish. 2. respectful, polite, deferential.

wiseacre n. *wise guy, *wiseass, *smart-ass, *smartaleck, know-it-all, *wisenheimer.

wisecrack n. joke, dig, gibe, flippant remark, quip, retort.

wise guy n. Sl. SEE WISEACRE

wish n. desire, want, pleasure, aspiration, hope, prayer, will, hunger, thirst, longing, yen.

wish v. desire, want, need, aspire, *set one's heart on, fancy, hope for, pray for, hunger, thirst, crave, hanker, request, ask, order.

wishful a. desirous, longful, hopeful, aspiring, yearning, hankering, wistful, impractical, unrealistic, daydreaming. ANT. practical.

wishy-washy a. indecisive, irresolute, undecided, blowing hot and cold, equivocating, vacillating, feeble, weak, spineless. ANT. resolute, decisive, decided.

wisp n. strand, shred, strip, trace, hint.

wispy a. slight, slender, thin, delicate, frail. ANT. heavy set, stocky.

WISTFUL a. [WIST ful] longing sadly or with a troubled mind. He looked back wistfully at his childhood. SYN. longing, yearning, pining, desirous, wishful, heartsick, pensive, nostalgic, daydreaming, reflective, melancholy, forlorn, introspective.

wit *n.* **1.** INTELLECTUAL POWERS intelligence, reason, *brains, *brain power, intellect, sense, common sense, sagacity, understanding, judgment, acumen, perception, wisdom, comprehension. **2.** CLEVERNESS sense of humor, humor, drollery, satire, irony, repartee, banter, bon mot, jest, wordplay, wisecrack, pun, joke, witticism. "Educated insolence."—Aristotle. "The salt of conversation."—William Hazlitt. **3.** CLEVER HUMORIST comedian, satirist, jokester, comic, *wise guy, wiseacre, quipster, *cutup. ANT. *1.* stupidity, dullness, slowness.

witch *n.* sorceress, enchantress, magician, practitioner of the black arts, *spellcaster, hex, warlock, crone, hag, she-devil, ogress.

witchcraft *n.* sorcery, black magic, black arts, spellcasting, wizardry, magic, enchantment, diabolism, Satanism, necromancy, voodoo. SEE MAGIC

witch doctor *n.* shaman, medicine man.

with *prep.* among, in the company of, alongside of.

withdraw *v.* **1.** TAKE BACK take out, remove, draw, extract. **2.** MOVE BACK retreat, shrink, recede, retire, leave, pull out, quit, evacuate. **3.** RETRACT recall, recant, take back, back down, *do an about-face, backpedal, rescind. **4.** ISOLATE ONESELF *go into one's shell.

withdrawal *n.* **1.** REMOVAL extraction, retreat, shrinking, retirement, leaving, leave, exit, retraction, disavowal. **2.** CRAVING distress, longing, hunger.

withdrawn *a.* introverted, reserved, shy, bashful, reticent, introspective, retiring, aloof, unfriendly, distant, remote, reclusive, solitary. ANT. *extroverted, outgoing, friendly, sociable.*

wither *v.* shrivel, wilt, droop, dry up, decay, waste away, fade, wizen, shrink.

within *prep.* inside.

withhold *v.* **1.** HOLD BACK keep, detain, reserve, deduct, retain, restrain. **2.** REFUSE refrain. **3.** HIDE conceal, deny, cover up, keep from, keep secret.

withstand *v.* take, tolerate, bear, put up with, endure, stand up to, weather, brave, face, cope, *ride out. ANT. *cave in, collapse, give in.*

witless *a.* foolish, nonsensical, stupid, mindless, dumb, imbecilic, moronic, idiotic, brainless, *birdbrained, *dumb as a post. ANT. *intelligent, smart, *brainy.*

witness *n.* **1.** EYEWITNESS observer, onlooker, bystander, spectator, corroborating witness. **2.** ATTESTING testimony, evidence, attestation, proof, corroboration.

witness *v.* **1.** SEE observe, watch, view, notice, behold. **2.** TESTIFY provide testimony, give evidence, attest, prove, corroborate, confirm, certify, verify.

witticism *n.* clever remark, witty remark, bon mot, quip, wisecrack, crack, *one-liner, joke, pun, retort, riposte.

witty *a.* clever, sharp, funny, comical, humorous, *saber-witted, *having a razor wit, droll, quick-witted, amusing, whimsical, entertaining, quick, *wise, sarcastic. ANT. *dull, serious, morbid.*

wizard *n.* **1.** CONJURER magician, sorcerer, witch, warlock, necromancer, Merlin, enchanter, diviner, practitioner of the black arts. **2.** *ACE *crackerjack, genius, prodigy, *whiz, *whiz kid, virtuoso, master.

wizardry *n.* **1.** MAGIC conjuring, sorcery, witchcraft, necromancy, black art, diabolism, Satanism. **2.** CLEVERNESS genius, magic.

wizened *a.* withered, dried up, shriveled, wilted, wrinkled, brown, shrunken, dry, dehydrated, wasted. ANT. *fresh, new.*

wobble *v.* shake, tremble, totter, teeter, seesaw, stagger, waggle, rock, oscillate, sway, reel, move unsteadily.

woe *n.* **1.** SORROW grief, anguish, sadness, misery, suffering, wretchedness, distress, pain, heartache, unhappiness, depression, melancholy. **2.** TROUBLE trial, tribulation, affliction, adversity, blow, burden, hardship, ordeal, misfortune. ANT. *1. happiness, joy, glee. 2. fortune, blessing.*

woebegone *a.* sad, depressed, melancholy, miserable, mournful, grieving, unhappy, woeful, downhearted, heartbroken, wretched, desolate, disconsolate. ANT. *happy, joyful, gleeful.*

woeful *a.* SEE WOEBEGONE

wolfish *a.* predatory, carnivorous, rapacious, beastly, vicious, bloodthirsty, fierce, ferocious. ANT. *benevolent, kind, helpful.*

woman *n.* lady, female, girl, gal, lass, *broad, maid, maiden, *colleen, damsel, matron, miss, Ms., matriarch, mother. "A ministering angel."—Sir Walter Scott. "A creature between man and the angels."—Honore de Balzac. "[One who] has to be twice as good as a man to go half as far."—Fannie Hurst.

womanizer *n.* Don Juan, Casanova, *skirt-chaser, lecher, *wolf, *ladies' man, stud, playboy, *make-out artist, Lothario, heart-breaker.

womanly *a.* womanish, feminine, matronly, ladylike, motherly, sisterly, soft, gentle, tender. ANT. *manly, male.*

wonder *n.* **1.** ASTONISHMENT amazement, wonderment, awe, fascination, enchantment, surprise. "The root of knowledge."—Abraham Heschel. "The seed of our science."—Ralph Waldo Emerson. **2.** MARVEL miracle, phenomenon, spectacle, curiosity, rarity, sight, *mind-blower, *mind-boggler, oddity, freak occurrence, freak of nature.

wonder *v.* **1.** MARVEL be awestruck, be fascinated, gawk, gape, stare saucer-eyed, disbelieve one's eyes, be amazed, be astonished, be stunned. **2.** TO BE CURIOUS question, ponder, think about, speculate, doubt, deliberate, puzzle over, meditate.

wonderful *a.* **1.** MARVELOUS amazing, astonishing, awesome, fascinating, unbelievable, miraculous, spectacular, curious, odd, *freaky. **2.** EXCELLENT great, extraordinary, terrific, fantastic, fabulous, superb, sensational, first-rate, out of the ordinary, *out of this world. ANT. *1.* **ho-hum, common, ordinary. 2. terrible, awful, lousy.*

wonderment *n.* amazement, astonishment, fascination, curiosity, wonder, awe, surprise, spectacle, sensation, sight, rarity, marvel, *mind-blower, *mind-boggler.

woo *v.* court, seek, coax, pursue, persuade, cajole, urge, *curry favor, *butter up.

wood *n.* lumber, timber, board, plank, beam, firewood, kindling, slat.

woodcutter *n.* lumberjack, logger, sawyer.

wooden *a.* stiff, rigid, awkward, graceless, formal, tense, expressionless, blank, stony, dull, lifeless. ANT. *loose, limber, relaxed, informal, expressive.*

woodland *n.* woods, forest, timberland, bush, grove, thicket, wilderness, *howling wilderness. SEE FOREST, JUNGLE, TREE

woods *n.* SEE WOODLAND

woolgathering *n.* absentmindedness, daydreaming, dreaming, reverie, *castle-building, abstraction, preoccupation.

woozy *a. Sl.* dizzy, dazed, muddled, befuddled, unsteady, reeling, unclear, *punch-drunk, *seeing stars. SEE DRUNK

word *n.* **1.** TERM noun, verb, adjective, pronoun, expression, name, lexeme, morpheme. "Words are loaded pistols."—Jean-Paul Sartre. "The soul's ambassadors."—

James Howell. "The dress of thoughts; which should no more be presented in rags, tatters, and dirt, than your person should."—Lord Chesterfield.

WORD FIND
acceptable word used in place of socially unacceptable one: euphemism
antiquated word: archaism
arrangement, construction of words and sentences: syntax
baby words: lallation
backwards, reads the same: palindrome
book: lexicon, dictionary, thesaurus
characterizing: epithet
coiner: neologist
combining words or word parts to form new word: agglutination
confusion, transposition of letters: dyslexia
contradictory juxtaposition of: oxymoron
difficult to pronounce correctly: *jawbreaker
disgust for certain words: logomasia
exact or appropriate word: mot juste
incorrect use of word confused with another: catachresis, malapropism
incorrect word that sounds like another: catchfool
individual word stock: ideolect
informal: colloquial, colloquialism
invention of new word: coinage
figurative: metaphor, simile, trope
foreign word sound English, make: Anglicize
forgotten word, obsession to remember: loganamnosis
humorous transposition of word sounds, such as "Hoobert Heever" for "Herbert Hoover": spoonerism
initials, word constructed of: acronym
local: localism
loss for words, at a: aporia
new: neologism
nonstandard use: barbarism, corruption
opposite in meaning: antonym
origin of: etymology
pronounce clearly: enunciate
pronunciation, poor: cacology
recall word on tip of one's tongue, inability to: lethologica
restate in different words: paraphrase
reversal of standard meaning, such as "bad" meaning "good": melioration
showing off one's knowledge of words: pedantry
similar in meaning: synonym
sounding like the thing it names: onomatopoeia

sounding the same but having different meanings: homonym, homophone
study of meanings: semantics
wrong title, wrong name: misnomer
2. NEWS report, communication, announcement, communique, dispatch, bulletin, intelligence, information. **3.** TALK chat, meeting, consultation, conversation, discussion. **4.** REMARK statement, comment. **5.** PROMISE pledge, solemn word, oath, word of honor, vow, assurance, guarantee.

word *v.* put into words, frame, phrase, rephrase, paraphrase.

wording *n.* phrasing, phraseology, language, syntax, terminology, choice of words, style.

wordy *a.* verbose, long-winded, windy, prolix, redundant, rambling, loquacious, garrulous, voluble, digressive, tautological. ANT. *succinct, concise, to the point, terse.*

work *n.* **1.** LABOR exertion, toil, effort, struggle, drudgery, *daily grind, *elbow grease, muscle, sweat, slavery, pains. **2.** JOB employment, occupation, *daily grind, livelihood, line, trade, profesion, vocation, business, calling. "A remedy against all ills."—Charles Baudelaire. "Paid struggle."—Max Gralnik. "The refuge of people who have nothing better to do."—Oscar Wilde. **3.** CHORE task, duty, assignment, charge, burden, responsibility. ANT. *idleness, sloth, leisure, play, relaxation.*

work *v.* **1.** LABOR exert, toil, put in effort, struggle, drudge, *apply elbow grease, *put muscle into it, sweat, slave, take pains, *break one's back, strain, *plug away, *keep one's nose to the grindstone, *burn the midnight oil, *work one's fingers to the bone, be employed, do business, earn one's living, *moonlight. **2.** OPERATE run, function, perform, tick, go. **3.** SUCCEED be effective, *fly, effect, fulfill, bring about, produce, create. **4.** HANDLE maneuver, run, use, drive. **5.** SHAPE manipulate, knead, mold. ANT. *1. relax, recreate, play, take it easy.*

workable *a.* doable, practical, practicable, feasible, viable, possible. ANT. *unworkable, impractical.*

worker *n.* employee, laborer, blue-collar worker, white-collar worker, hand, workman, wage earner, *working stiff, *nine-to-fiver, slave, *temp. "The wealth of a country."—Theodor Herzl. "Soldiers with different weapons but the same courage."—Winston Churchill.

workmanlike *a.* skilled, well-done, well-crafted, professional, meticulous, expert, competent, thorough. ANT. *incompetent, slack, amateurish.*

workmanship *n.* craftsmanship, skill, artistry, expertise, proficiency, handiwork, technique, style, mastery.

world *n.* **1.** EARTH planet, globe, Gaea, sphere, biosphere, terra, terra firma, orb, ocean world, heavenly body. "A small parenthesis in eternity."—Thomas Browne. "God's epistle to mankind—his thoughts are flashing upon us from every direction."—Plato. "The truth of the existence of God."—William Hocking. **2.** ALL CREATION universe, cosmos, macrocosm, nature. **3.** HUMANKIND humanity, human community, human race, mankind, civilization, society, people, men and women, everybody. "This great stage of fools."—Shakespeare. "A comedy to those who think, a tragedy to those who feel."—Horace Walpole. **4.** REALM domain, sphere, area, province, kingdom, field, group.

worldly *a.* **1.** EARTHLY terrestrial, mundane, material, human, fleshly, physical. **2.** SOPHISTICATED experienced, worldly-wise, knowing, learned, urbane, cosmopolitan, *wise in the ways of the world. ANT. *1. spiritual, heavenly, divine, godly. 2. inexperienced, unsophisticated, naive.*

worldly-wise *a.* SEE WORLDLY

worldwide *a.* global, international, multinational, universal, general, from the four corners of the earth, extensive, pandemic. ANT. *local, localized, limited, domestic.*

worn *a.* **1.** THREADBARE worn out, frayed, ragged, tattered, weathered, deteriorated, abraded, *shot. **2.** EXHAUSTED weary, tired, burned out, haggard, drained, *wrung out, *the worse for wear, drained. ANT. *1. new, fresh. 2. fresh, refreshed.*

worrisome *a.* troublesome, anxiety-provoking, disturbing, distressing, disquieting, unnerving. ANT. *reassuring, calming, relaxing.*

worried *a.* anxious, distressed, troubled, disturbed, apprehensive, uneasy, having misgivings, uncertain, concerned, sick with dread, *on pins and needles. ANT. *at peace, relaxed, reassured.*

worry *n.* anxiety, distress, troubled mind, disturbance, apprehension, uneasiness, misgiving, uncertainty, concern, disquiet, trepidation, care. "Interest paid on trouble before it becomes due."—William Inge. ANT. *peace of mind, reassurance, tranquility.*

worry *v.* distress, trouble, disturb, make apprehensive, make uneasy, concern, disquiet, fill with trepidation, gnaw at, perturb, fill with dread. ANT. *calm, soothe, reassure.*

worsen *v.* deteriorate, degenerate, take a turn for the worse, slip, decay, decline, lapse, *go downhill, *hit the skids, diminish. ANT. *improve, get better.*

worship *n.* homage, reverence, devotion, veneration, honoring, idolization, adoration, love, admiration, glorification, genuflection, exaltation, church service, rite. "Climbing the altar stairs to God."—Dwight Bradley. SEE GOD, RELIGION

worship *v.* pay homage, revere, show devotion, venerate, honor, idolize, adore, love, admire, glorify, look up to, put on a pedestal, exalt, adulate. ANT. *disdain, despise, disparage.*

worth *n.* **1.** VALUE merit, benefit, greatness, worthiness, importance, weight, desirability. **2.** AMOUNT quantity, price, cost, expense, appraisal, valuation, estimation. **3.** WEALTH riches, assets, possessions, holdings.

worthless *a.* valueless, useless, good-for-nothing, unproductive, unprofitable, profitless, vain, futile, impotent, ineffective, empty, *not worth the powder to blow it to hell, *not worth beans. ANT. *valuable, worthwhile, profitable, effective.*

worthwhile *a.* valuable, useful, profitable, lucrative, remunerative, gainful, beneficial, rewarding, worthy, worth the trouble, productive. ANT. *worthless, waste of time, unproductive.*

worthy *a.* meriting, deserving, meritorious, good enough, praiseworthy, creditable, estimable, worthwhile, commendable, exemplary, excellent, virtuous. ANT. *unworthy, worthless, undeserving.*

wound *n.* **1.** INJURY trauma, cut, laceration, lesion, gash, tear, scrape, scratch, abrasion, contusion, bruise, *black-and-blue mark, hurt, sore, tender area, bump. **2.** HURT FEELINGS offense, insult, anguish, pain, grief, heartache, blow to one's self-esteem.

wound *v.* **1.** INJURE cut, lacerate, gash, rip open, scrape, scratch, stick, stab, abrade, bruise, bump, traumatize. **2.** HURT ONE'S FEELINGS offend, insult, grieve, *touch a nerve, *break one's heart, affront, *cut to the quick, traumatize, mortify.

wow *v. Sl.* *bring an audience to their feet, *bowl over, fill with awe, stagger, electrify, make one's jaw drop, impress.

wrangle *n.* quarrel, dispute, argument, fight, altercation, tiff, disagreement, row, squabble, clash, spat.

wrangle *v.* quarrel, dispute, argue, fight, altercate, have a tiff, *lock horns, disagree, have a row, clash, *have words, *cross swords.

wrap *n.* covering, shawl, overcoat, jacket, cloak, cape, mantle.

wrap *v.* cover, envelop, package, bind, pack, bundle, giftwrap, swaddle, swathe, shroud, tuck.

wrath *n.* anger, rage, towering rage, spitting rage, fury, temper, passion, *hot blood, indignation, resentment, venom, virulence. ANT. *good humor, pleasure, cheerfulness.*

wreak *v.* inflict, cause, bring, vent, bring down on, unleash, execute.

wreath *n.* band, garland, decoration, festoon, chaplet, laurel, crown.

wreathe *v.* entwine, encircle, coil, twist, festoon.

wreck *n.* wreckage, destruction, devastation, ruin, debris, smashup, crash, accident, derelict, *heap, *junker, *hulk.

wreck *v.* destroy, ruin, tear apart, smash, devastate, demolish, raze, flatten, *total, sabotage, vandalize, *trash, spoil, shatter, break, gut, blow up, level, bulldoze. ANT. *fix, repair, protect.*

wreckage *n.* debris, flotsam and jetsam, rubble, detritus, bits and pieces, fragments, ruins, smoking remains.

wrench *n.* **1.** TOOL spanner, monkey wrench, pliers. SEE TOOL **2.** TWIST jerk, turn, pull, sprain.

wrench *v.* twist, pull, jerk, turn, wring, sprain, strain.

wrest *v.* twist away from, take, jerk, pull, wrestle, extract, wring, grab.

wrestle *v.* grapple, struggle, fight, combat, muscle, strong-arm, tussle, battle, contend, tangle, *lock horns, *put in a half-nelson, *body slam, *put in a headlock, *put in a hammerlock, *give a bear hug, throw, flip, *turk, *deliver a flying dropkick, clinch, pin.

wretch *n.* **1.** *MISERABLE SOUL *poor soul, martyr, unfortunate, victim, outcast, *loser, *sorry sight. **2.** SCOUNDREL *creep, *jerk, *rat, dog, cur, rogue, criminal, villain.

wretched *a.* **1.** MISERABLE unhappy, depressed, melancholic, sad, brokenhearted, downhearted, forlorn, dejected, disconsolate, *bummed out, pathetic, pitiable. **2.** *LOUSY awful, terrible, miserable, poor, inferior, *rotten, pathetic, bad, inferior, cheap. **3.** CONTEMPTIBLE despicable, *rotten, mean, low, shameless, detestable, beneath contempt. ANT. *1. happy, cheerful, joyous. 2. good, superior, superb, excellent. 3. admirable, commendable, good.*

wriggle v. wiggle, squirm, jiggle, waggle, worm, twist, writhe.

wring v. **1.** TWIST squeeze, press, compress, wrench, choke, throttle, strangle. **2.** EXTORT force, strong-arm, twist one's arm, make, exact, coerce.

wrinkle n. **1.** CRINKLE furrow, ridge, crease, crimp, pucker, line, rumple, fold, pleat, crow's foot, laugh line, frown line. **2.** IDEA trick, device, gimmick.

wrinkle v. crinkle, furrow, crease, crimp, pucker, line, rumple, fold, pleat, corrugate, scrunch up.

writ n. order, legal order, legal document, court order, warrant, injunction, summons, subpoena, command.

write v. pen, compose, print, jot, scrawl, *scratch out, scribble, inscribe, *dash off, set down, draft, type, draw up, record, author, sign, autograph.

writer n. scribe, calligrapher, stenographer, author, wordsmith, poet, reporter, journalist, columnist, novelist, freelancer, hack, man of letters, playwright, screenwriter, ghostwriter. "Apprentices in a craft where no one ever becomes a master."—Hemingway. "A frustrated actor who recites his lines in the hidden auditorium of his skull."—Rod Serling.

writhe v. twist, contort, squirm, thrash, worm, wiggle, recoil in agony, flail.

writing n. **1.** HANDWRITING penmanship, longhand, calligraphy, printing, print. **2.** COMPOSITION work, publication, prose, fiction, novel, short story, poem, poetry, belles-lettres, nonfiction, letters, correspondence, article, editorial. "All writing is a process of elimination."—Martha Albrand. "The art of applying the seat of the pants to the seat of the chair."—Mary Vorse.

wrong n. wrongdoing, sin, crime, offense, misdeed, injustice, evil, insult, wicked act, inequity, infraction, mistake, blunder, oversight.

wrong v. hurt, injure, insult, offend, commit a crime against, sin against, abuse, mistreat, exploit, use, aggrieve, transgress, malign, dishonor, defame, slur.

wrong a. **1.** INCORRECT inaccurate, imprecise, faulty, erroneous, false, mistaken, untrue, off, amiss, erring, unsound, *wide of the mark, *off base, *barking up the wrong tree, *all wet. **2.** IMMORAL bad, improper, unethical, sinful, illegal, criminal, corrupt, dishonest, crooked, wicked, naughty, felonious, dishonorable, reprehensible. **3.** INAPPROPRIATE unsuitable, inapt, improper, unfitting, unseemly, unbecoming, malapropos. **4.** OUT OF ORDER amiss, awry, out of kilter, *out of whack, *haywire. **5.** REVERSE back. ANT. *1. correct, accurate, exact, precise. 2. good, virtuous, righteous, moral. 3. appropriate, apropos, suitable.*

wrongdoer n. sinner, criminal, felon, offender, evildoer, perpetrator, miscreant, malefactor, transgressor, culprit, trespasser, *bad guy.

wrought a. formed, shaped, fashioned, made, built, constructed, crafted. ANT. *natural.*

wry a. **1.** TWISTED distorted, turned to one side, lopsided, crooked, awry, askew. **2.** IRONIC distorted, sarcastic, sardonic, mocking, twisted, perverted. ANT. *1. straight. 2. serious, earnest.*

X

X-rated *a.* adult, obscene, pornographic, hardcore, dirt, blue, carnal, appealing to prurient interests, nasty, raunchy, graphic. ANT. *G-rated, innocent, clean.*

X-ray *n.* roentgenogram, roentgenograph, radiograph, radiogram, fluoroscope.

Y

yacht n. boat, cruiser, cabin cruiser, pleasure craft, vessel. SEE BOAT, SAILING

yahoo n. Sl. brute, *blithering idiot, barbarian, savage, Neanderthal, *redneck, *clod, *clodhopper, *dumb ox, *farmer, *jughead, hick, yokel, lummox, *nitwit, hillbilly.

yak v. talk, chatter, gab, yap, babble, *run on, jabber, prattle, blather, *blah blah blah.

yammer v. whine, complain, whimper, moan, gripe, grumble.

yank n. jerk, pull, tug, plucking, wrenching, extraction, grab.

yank v. jerk, pull, tug, pluck, wrench, extract, grab.

yard n. lawn, property, grounds, lot, plot, court, courtyard, gardens, patio, quad, garth, enclosure, compound.

yardstick n. measuring rod, measure, standard, test, gauge, guide, guideline, touchstone, benchmark, criterion.

yarn n. story, tale, fairy tale, fable, narrative, fiction, *fish story, adventure, myth, legend.

yaw v. swing, pitch, swerve, roll, veer, deviate, wheel, go off course.

yearn v. desire, long for, want, crave, hunger for, thirst for, pine for, hanker for, ache for, wish.

yearning n. desire, longing, want, need, craving, hunger, thirst, hankering, ache, wish, *yen, fancy.

years n. decades, generation, lifetime, centuries, millenium, eon, period, age, epoch.

yell n. shout, *holler, bellow, roar, thundering, howl, scream, shriek, bark, cry, whoop, yelp, hoot, *Stentorian bellow.

yell v. raise one's voice, shout, *holler, bellow, roar, thunder, howl, scream, shriek, bark, cry, whoop, yelp, hoot, cheer. ANT. *whisper, speak softly, murmur.*

yellow a. **1.** GOLDEN flaxen, straw, lemon, saffron, sunny, canary, amber, honey, butter. **2.** COWARDLY spineless, craven, fearful, *mousy, *wimpy, *lily-livered, *chicken, fainthearted, *afraid of one's own shadow. **2.** SENSATIONAL cheap, melodramatic, exaggerated, lurid, *keyhole-peeping. ANT. *2. brave, courageous, *gutsy.*

yelp n. cry, bark, yip, yap, squeal, howl, shout.

yelp v. cry, bark, yip, yap, squeal, howl, shout.

yen n. desire, longing, want, hunger, appetite, thirst, yearning, craving, hankering, urge, itch, passion. ANT. *aversion, revulsion.*

yeoman n. assistant, attendant, servant, subordinate, petty officer.

yes adv. yea, aye, *uh-huh, affirmative, *yeah, *yep, *ayuh, certainly, positively, doubtless, surely, *oui, *sí, *da, *you bet. ANT. *no, nay, negative.*

yes-man n. Sl. sycophant, toady, *brownnose, *kiss-up, *bootlicker, *apple-polisher, fawn, flatterer, underling, groveler, kowtower.

yield n. production, output, proceeds, harvest, crop, profit, return, gain, earnings.

yield v. **1.** PRODUCE furnish, generate, return, pay out, put out, give rise to, bear fruit. **2.** GIVE UP give in, surrender, back down, *cave in, submit, acquiesce, relinquish, accede, capitulate, *knuckle under, grant, concede. ANT. *2. resist, fight.*

yoga n. Hindu discipline, ascetic discipline, meditation, posturing.
WORD FIND
athletic, fast-moving style of: Ashtanga, power yoga, Vinyasa
bliss, state of: samadhi
centers of life energy located between base of spine and head: chakras
chant used during meditation: mantra
chanting and breathing, ancient style featuring: Kundalini
female practicioner: yogini
folded-legs position: lotus position
gentle style featuring thoughtful affirmations: Ananda
hand gestures directing life current: mudras
life energy: prana
meditation or quieting of the mind: dhyana
meditation word repeated over and over: om, aum
one who practices: yogi
path to enlightenment: samadhi
position of arching chest while on back: fish
position of curling upper body up and backward while lying on floor: cobra
position of raising straightened legs off floor while face down: locust
positions: asanas
retreat where yoga is taught or practiced: ashram
scriptures: sutras
teacher or spiritual guide: guru, swami

yoke n. **1.** BOND harness, collar, coupling. **2.** BONDAGE servitude, subjection, enslavement.

yoke *v.* link, couple, bond, join, pair, unite, harness.

yokel *n.* country bumpkin, rustic, farmer, hick, hayseed, clodhopper, *Okie, hillbilly, *sodbuster, yahoo, *one who just fell off the turnip truck.

yonder *a.* yon, faraway, away, beyond, distant, remote, further. ANT. *near, close, here.*

young *n.* children, offspring, litter, babies, progeny.

young *a.* immature, undeveloped, unfinished, growing, youthful, tender, fresh, newborn, infantile, fledgling, childish, juvenile, teenage, adolescent, pubescent, school-age, boyish, girlish, junior, new, untested, unpracticed, unseasoned, unhardened, inexperienced, naive. ANT. *mature, developed, old, experienced, adult, aged.*

youngster *n.* baby, infant, toddler, tot, child, boy, girl, schoolboy, schoolgirl, youth, kid, adolescent, teenager, minor.

youth *n.* **1.** CHILDHOOD infancy, preschool years, school years, young years, teens, adolescence, pubescence, puberty, minority, developing years. "Life's morning march."— Thomas Campbell. "The glad season of life."—Thomas Carlyle. "A feeling of eternity."—William Hazlitt. **2.** CHILD youngster, kid, boy, girl, teen, teenager, adolescent, minor, young man, young lady, juvenile, children, boys and girls, youngsters, teens, adolescents. ANT. **1.** *old age, adulthood, retirement years.*

youthful *a.* young, immature, unseasoned, growing, developing, fresh, new, maturing, juvenile, childish, rosy-cheeked, bright-eyed, full of life, vigorous, callow, naive, inexperienced, carefree. ANT. *old, aged, mature, experienced.*

yummy *a.* delicious, tasty, *scrumptious, mouth-watering, delectable, ambrosial, savory, good, heavenly, out of this world. ANT. *disgusting, nauseating, *gross.*

yuppie *n.* materialistic person, urbanite, status-seeker, young professional.

Z

zaftig *a. Sl.* full-figured, shapely, buxom, rounded, rotund.

zany *a.* foolish, crazy, silly, comical, ludicrous, *loony, hilarious, uproarious, *goofy, *nutty, slapstick, *madcap, funny. ANT. *somber, serious.*

ZEAL *n.* [ZEEL] great passion, enthusiasm. *His zeal for reform was contagious.* SYN. passion, enthusiasm, ardor, fervor, drive, fanaticism, zest, intensity, devotion, gusto, spirit, fire, earnestness. ANT. *indifference, apathy, disinterest.*

zealot *n.* fanatic, enthusiast, devotee, extremist, radical, *nut, champion, disciple, dogmatist, believer, crackpot.

ZEALOUS *a.* [ZEL us] enthusiastic, passionate. *He was a zealous supporter of gun control.* SYN. enthusiastic, passionate, devoted, fervent, fanatical, radical, eager, intense, rabid, impassioned, vehement, earnest, *gung-ho. ANT. *indifferent, apathetic, uncaring.*

Zen *n.* Buddhism, quest for enlightenment, meditation.

zenith *n.* high point, summit, pinnacle, top, peak, height, apex, acme, apogee, maximum, crown, culmination. ANT. *bottom, low point, nadir.*

zephyr *n.* gentle breeze, gentle wind, west wind. SEE WIND

zeppelin *n.* dirigible, blimp.

zero *n.* nothing, naught, *goose egg, *zip, nothingness, *thin air, *zilch, blank, *nobody, nonentity.

zero hour *n.* crisis point, turning point, crossroads, pivotal moment, appointed hour, *D-day, climax, moment of truth, *crunch time.

zest *n.* **1.** FLAVOR relish, zing, piquancy, spice, zip, *pizzazz. **2.** GUSTO enjoyment, pleasure, *kick, spirit, liveliness, elation, excitement, eagerness. ANT. **2.** *boredom, apathy.*

zip *n.* **1.** HISS whiz, whistle, whine, hum. **2.** ENERGY vigor, *get-up-and-go, vitality, life, pep, strength, livelines, drive, zest, spirit. **3.** *Sl.* NOTHING zero, *zilch.

zip *v.* speed, fly, zoom, rush, tear, bolt, dart, dash, hurry, jet.

zippy *a.* energetic, brisk, vigorous, full of life, lively, peppy. ANT. *tired, lethargic.*

zit *n. Sl.* pimple, pustule, papule, blemish.

zombie *n.* the living dead, walking dead, corpse, weirdo, oddball, *dope, dullard.

zone *n.* area, district, sector, section, region, quarter, tract, band, locality, territory, precinct, domain.

zonked *a. Sl.* drunk, intoxicated, inebriated, under the influence, high, *flying, *out of it, exhausted, unconscious.

zoo *n.* menagerie, animal park, animal conservation area, zoological garden, wildlife park.

zoom *v.* **1.** ZIP fly, shoot, rocket, whiz, speed, dive, streak, buzz, hum. **2.** RISE climb, skyrocket, surge.

zydeco *n.* Cajun music, French Caribbean music, Louisiana blues.